M000198590

Roger Ebert's
Movie Yearbook
2005

Other books by Roger Ebert

An Illini Century

A Kiss Is Still a Kiss

Two Weeks in the Midday Sun: A Cannes
Notebook

Behind the Phantom's Mask

Roger Ebert's Little Movie Glossary

Roger Ebert's Movie Home Companion
annually 1986–1993

Roger Ebert's Video Companion
annually 1994–1998

Roger Ebert's Movie Yearbook
annually 1999–

Questions for the Movie Answer Man

Roger Ebert's Book of Film: An Anthology

Ebert's Bigger Little Movie Glossary

I Hated, Hated, Hated This Movie

The Great Movies

The Great Movies II

With Daniel Curley
The Perfect London Walk

With Gene Siskel
The Future of the Movies: Interviews with
Martin Scorsese, Steven Spielberg, and
George Lucas

DVD Commentary Tracks
Beyond the Valley of the Dolls
Citizen Kane
Dark City
Casablanca
Floating Weeds

Roger Ebert's Movie Yearbook 2005

Andrews McMeel Publishing

Kansas City

Roger Ebert's Movie Yearbook 2005
copyright © 1999, 2000, 2001, 2002, 2003, 2004
by Roger Ebert.
All rights reserved.
Printed in the United States of America.
No part of this book may be used or reproduced
in any manner whatsoever except in the case
of reprints in the context of reviews.
For information write
Andrews McMeel Publishing,
an Andrews McMeel Universal company,
4520 Main Street,
Kansas City, Missouri 64111.

ISBN 0-7407-4742-8

All the reviews in this book originally appeared
in the *Chicago Sun-Times*.

This book is dedicated
to Robert Zonka, 1928–1985.
God love ya.

Contents

Introduction

The new material in this year's edition was mostly written between August 2003 and July 2004. During the year I also went through some adventures with illness. I had surgery for salivary cancer in September, and in December spent a month in Seattle for radiation treatments. The surgery was not a big deal but the side effects of radiation were not pleasant, and I didn't really begin to feel restored until May or June.

During that time I didn't miss writing a single review, nor did I neglect the Great Movies series and the Answer Man column. *The Ebert & Roeper* show continued without interruption; thanks to ingenious planning by our staff, we were able to tape several shows in advance to cover December and early January, and then I returned to the tapings. I also attended, as usual, the Conference on World Affairs in Boulder in early April, where we went through Jean Renoir's *The Rules of the Game* a shot at a time during ten hours over five days. And I hosted the sixth annual Overlooked Film Festival in late April, before leaving for Cannes in June.

The radiation made it difficult for me to handle solid food, and I existed on a product named Ensure, which kept everything humming along. Very early on the first morning in Cannes I woke early, as I always do, and wandered, as I always do, down to the all-night café by the port, and ordered, as I always do, a croissant and café au lait. I dunked the croissant into the coffee, as I always do, and ate it, and that was the beginning of real food again.

I supply this information not as a medical bulletin, but as an entry into considering the way movies work for me and perhaps a lot of other people. Even during treatment in Seattle, I was able to attend screenings, catch movies in theaters, and write twenty reviews. One night I went to the local Landmark theater and saw Jean Gabin in *Touchez Pas Au Grisbi* and found it so extraordinary it went into the Great Movies series. Some of my friends and editors said they were impressed that I continued to see movies and file reviews even during the more difficult days of January and February. I tried to explain that it would have been harder not to.

I was not in any great pain, although radiation caused several varieties and degrees of discomfort. My problems were serious but probably not life-threatening. Illness had its greatest effect on my sense of personal immunity. After enjoying extraordinary good health all of my life, I was faced with the dilemma that my body was fallible and my lifespan finite. Radiation causes erratic sleep patterns, and in the middle of the night, in addition to reading every one of the novels of Willa Cather, which were a consolation beyond all measuring, I had time to reflect on my mortality. I may have many years left, but I'd always thought I had forever.

These thoughts did not bother me while I was watching movies. I found myself drawn into them even more deeply than usual, as if giving myself over to them, healing in their glow. In a Seattle theater I saw the new P. J. Hogan version of *Peter Pan*, starring Jason Isaacs, Jeremy Sumpter, and the newcomer Rachel Hurd-Wood, and I was struck by how delightful it really was — how they had tried to make something alive and special, instead of recycling the same familiar material. I had seen Denys Arcand's *The Barbarian Invasions* at Cannes, but now saw it again and was struck personally by its portrait of a difficult but irrepressible man in his 60s surrounded at his deathbed by current and former friends and lovers and presiding over the celebration of his own passing. "Dying is not this cheerful," I wrote, "but we need to think it is."

And in Jacques Becker's *Touchez Pas Au Grisbi,* there's a scene where Max, the Jean Gabin character, a middle-aged gangster tired of risk and danger, is alone in his apartment contemplating how his best friend, Riton, has stupidly allowed himself to be kidnapped. He's less concerned about the loot he will lose, I wrote, than about his pal:

> He has a wonderful soliloquy, an interior monologue which we hear voice-over, as Max paces his apartment. He talks about what a dope Riton is, and what a burden he has been for 20 years: "There's not a tooth in his head that hasn't cost me a bundle." We understand that Max, who is competent above all things, almost values Riton's inability to live without his help. At the end of his soliloquy, instead of growing angry as a conventional gangster might, Max opens a bottle of champagne, plays a forlorn harmonica solo on his juke box, sits in a comfortable chair, and lights a cigarette. He treasures his creature comforts, especially when he might be about to lose them.

I appreciated that moment in Becker's film beyond all reason. I responded to the way it understood that a great movie can involve not plot but life and the daily living of it, and that although movies can amuse and excite us, their greatest consolation comes when they understand us.

A few months later, in June, I saw Julie Bertucelli's *Since Otar Left,* a film set in the Eastern European republic of Georgia. The film stars a ninety-year-old actress named Esther Gorintin, who was eighty-five when she began her acting career. She plays a stubborn old lady who lives with her daughter and granddaughter. Her thoughts are focused on her son, Otar, who has gone to Paris seeking work. We know, but she does not, that Otar has died in Paris. The daughter and granddaughter try to deceive her that he is still alive.

"What is clear," I wrote, "is that this old woman has a life and will of her own. There is a wonderful scene while she is still at home in Georgia. She leaves the house alone, looks up some information in the library, buys two cigarettes, and smokes them while riding on a Ferris wheel. With a lesser actor or character, this would be a day out for a lovable granny. With Esther Gorintin playing Eka, it is the day of a woman who thinks she has it coming to her."

Moments like that glow with a special grace. Writing about them has its consolations, too. I find that when I am actually writing, I enter a zone of concentration too small to admit my troubles. Although I might feel uneasy or unwell when I sit down at the keyboard and feel that way again when I stand up, while I am working I feel — what? There is a kind of focus or concentration, a gathering of thought, language, and instinct, that occupies all the available places and purrs along satisfied with itself. I am known around the office as a "fast writer," but while I'm engaged in the process I don't feel as if I'm writing at all; I'm taking dictation from that place within me that knows what it wants to say.

This has been true all of my life. When I was fifteen and starting out as a sports writer at the *Champaign-Urbana News-Gazette*, I would labor for hours over my lead paragraph. Bill Lyon, who was a year older than I and would later become a famous columnist for the *Philadelphia Inquirer*, advised me, "Get to the end of the piece before you go back to revise the beginning. Until you find out where you're going, how can you know how to get there?" I took his advice and have never looked back. It condenses into a rule most writers discover sooner or later: The Muse visits during the work, not before it.

What I am trying to say is that I love my work. I love movies, I love to see movies, I love to write about movies, I love to talk about movies, I love to go through them a frame at a time in the dark with a room full of people watching them with me and noticing the most extraordinary things. On Monday during the conference in Boulder, we showed *The Rules of the Game* all the way through and several people confessed they found it disappointing. Then we went through it for the rest of the week, a shot or even a frame at a time. By Friday, they embraced it with a true passion. On Monday, we looked at it. By Friday, we had seen it.

Too many moviegoers look at movies and do not see them, but then it has always been that way. Movies are a time-killer or a casual entertainment for most people, who rarely allow themselves to see movies that will jolt them out of that pattern. The jolting itself seems unpleasant to them. I'm not a snob about that; anyone who enjoys a movie is all right in my book. But the movies don't top out; as you evolve, there are always films and directors to lead you higher, until you get above the treetops with Ozu and Murnau, Bresson and Keaton, Renoir and Bergman and Hitchcock and Scorsese. You walk with giants.

* * *

One of our grandchildren told me the other day that he knew why I didn't like *White Chicks*. It was, he said, "because you're not a kid. If you were a kid, you'd know how funny it was."

"Yes," I said, "no doubt you're right. But if you were me, you'd know how bad it was."

"But I'm not you," he said.

"No, but you will be someday," I said. "I started out as a kid, and look how far I've come."

* * *

I finally have my own dedicated website, rogerebert.com, which extends the database of reviews all the way back to 1967 (the previous cutoff was mid-1985). The site's editor is my friend and colleague Jim Emerson, himself a distinguished film critic and one of the editors of the late, lamented Microsoft Cinemania CD-ROM. Jim and I plan to make the site a daily event, with the use of my photos from film festivals, Answer Man exchanges, interviews, and featured selections from the archives. It's a work in progress.

Also on the horizon: *The Great Movies II*, collecting 100 more of my Great Movie essays, will be published in February 2005 by Broadway Books. Because I don't much believe in lists and am not writing these essays in any particular order, this second book is not the "second team" or the "second 100," and indeed includes such towering titles as *Rules of the Game, Breathless, Rashomon, Five Easy Pieces, The Manchurian Candidate, The Searchers* and *Sunrise* — as well as my attempt to deal with how *Birth of a Nation* can be a great film and a racist film, both at once.

Another new book I highly recommend is *Essential Cinema: On the Necessity of Film Canons,* by the great Chicago critic Jonathan Rosenbaum. At a time when many moviegoers seemed as locked in the present as the hero of *Groundhog Day,* Rosenbaum focuses on the key films of the past century.

My friend Kenneth Turan of the *Los Angeles Times* has two new books. *Sundance to Sarajevo: Film Festivals and the World They Made* focuses an insider's eye on twelve major film festivals. And his forthcoming book *Never Coming to a Theater Near You* recommends overlooked films he values.

Another friend, the respected Web-based critic James Berardinelli, has published *Reel Views: The Ultimate Guide to the Best 1,000 Movies on DVD and Video,* and I was happy to contribute the introduction.

For that matter, three other introductions I've recently written have found their way into this *Yearbook:* One introduces the collected film criticism of Carl Sandburg; the second recalls the glory days of science-fiction fandom and perhaps its best fanzine, *Xero;* and the third is a collection of memos of David O. Selznick.

For decades Donald Richie has been an unfailingly literate and perceptive guide to Japanese films. His new *Donald Richie Reader: 50 Years of Writing on Japan* brings together his film and Japanese writings in a book of remarkably original organization and design (compiled by Arturo Silva). It is not for sale everywhere, so use the Internet; the book is like a window into the mind of a wise, perceptive, and amusing man.

* * *

During this unusual year, my wife, Chaz, was constantly at my side with support and encouragement. I wrote in the 2004 *Yearbook:* "Amidst the madness of festivals she is an oasis of sanity, and in times of trouble an unfailing support." Boy, was that ever true this year! To her my love and gratitude.

ROGER EBERT

Acknowledgments

My editor is Dorothy O'Brien, tireless, cheerful, all-noticing. She is assisted by the equally invaluable Julie Roberts. My friend and longtime editor Donna Martin suggested this new approach to the annual volume. The design is by Cameron Poulter, the typographical genius of Hyde Park. My thanks to production editor Christi Clemons-Hoffman, who renders Cameron's design into reality. I have been blessed with the expert and discriminating editing of John Barron, Laura Emerick, Miriam DiNunzio, Jeff Wisser, Darel Jevins, Avis Weathersbee, Jeff Johnson, and Teresa Budasi at the *Chicago Sun-Times*; Sue Roush at Universal Press Syndicate; and Michelle Daniel at Andrews McMeel Publishing. Many thanks are also due to the production staff at *Ebert & Roeper*, and to Marsha Jordan at WLS-TV. My gratitude goes to Carol Iwata, my expert personal assistant, and to Marlene Gelfond, at the *Sun-Times*. And special thanks and love to my wife, Chaz, for whom I can only say: If more film critics had a spouse just like her, the level of cheer in the field would rise dramatically.

Roger Ebert

Key to Symbols

★★★★	A great film
★★★	A good film
★★	Fair
★	Poor

G, PG, PG-13, R, NC-17:
Ratings of the Motion Picture Association of America

G   Indicates that the movie is suitable for general audiences

PG   Suitable for general audiences but parental guidance is suggested

PG-13   Recommended for viewers 13 years or above; may contain material inappropriate for younger children

R   Recommended for viewers 17 or older

NC-17   Intended for adults only

141 m.   Running time

1999   Year of theatrical release

☞   Refers to "Questions for the Movie Answer Man"

Reviews

A

Abandon ★ ★ ½
PG-13, 93 m., 2002

Katie Holmes (Catherine Burke), Benjamin Bratt (Detective Wade Handler), Charlie Hunnam (Embry Larkin), Melanie Lynskey (Mousy Julie), Zooey Deschanel (Samantha), Gabrielle Union (Friend), Joseph Scarimbolo (Sean), John Fallon (Mime). Directed by Stephen Gaghan and produced by Gary Barber, Roger Birnbaum, Lynda Obst, and Edward Zwick. Screenplay by Gaghan.

Abandon is a moody, effective thriller for about 80 percent of the way, and then our hands close on air. If you walk out before the ending, you'll think it's better than it is. Or maybe I'm being unfair: Maybe a rational ending with a reasonable explanation would have seemed boring. Maybe this is the ending the movie needed, but it seems so arbitrary as it materializes out of thin air.

Or maybe I'm still being unfair. Maybe it doesn't come from thin air. Students of *Ebert's Bigger Little Movie Glossary* will be familiar with the Law of Economy of Characters, which states that no movie introduces a character unnecessarily, so that the apparently superfluous character is the one to keep an eye on. That rule doesn't precisely apply here, but it's relevant in a reverse sort of way. Think of "The Purloined Letter."

Enough of this. The movie finally did not satisfy me, and so I cannot recommend it, but there is a lot to praise, beginning with Katie Holmes's performance as Catherine Burke, a smart and articulate student who is on the fast track to a corporate boardroom. She's a student at an unnamed university (McGill in Montreal provided the locations), has just aced an interview with a big firm, studies hard, doesn't date. Her ex-boyfriend Embry Larkin (Charlie Hunnam) vanished mysteriously two years ago, but then he was the kind of weirdo genius who was always pulling stunts like that.

The key question: Did Embry disappear himself, or was he disappeared? Detective Wade Handler (Benjamin Bratt) is on the case, and

although Catherine at first cuts him off, she starts to like the guy. Meanwhile, in what is not as much of a spoiler as it might appear, Embry Larkin reappears on campus, and starts stalking Catherine.

That's all of the plot you'll get from me. I want to talk about casting, dialogue, and the film's general intelligence. This is a movie that convincingly portrays the way students talk, think, get wasted, philosophize, and hang around on a college campus. I emphasize that because when *The Rules of Attraction* opened, I questioned its scenes in which topless lesbians were ignored by male students at campus parties. I have here a letter from Joseph Gallo of Auburn, Alabama, who says such a sight is not uncommon on his campus. Uh-huh.

The students in *Abandon* talk smart. Especially Catherine. Watch the way Katie Holmes handles that interview with the high-powered corporate recruiters. It could be used as a training film. Watch her body language and word choices when she rejects an advance from her counselor. Notice the scene where a friend invites her to attend an "antiglobalization rally." In an ordinary movie, a line like that would be boilerplate, designed to move the plot to its next event. In this movie, Catherine responds. She has an opinion about antiglobalization. Astonishing.

The movie was written and directed by Stephen Gaghan, who won an Oscar for the *Traffic* screenplay and is making his directorial debut. Gaghan has written such convincing characters, including the snotty know-it-all played by Melanie Lynskey and the best friends played by Zooey Deschanel and Gabrielle Union, that it's kind of a shame this is a thriller. A real campus movie, about fears and ambitions, could have been made from this material. Deschanel's drunk scene with the cop is an example of material that is spot-on.

But the movie is a thriller, and so we must watch as the human elements and the intelligence, which have absorbed and entertained us, are ground up in the requirements of the Shocking Climax. Too bad. Here is a movie that never steps wrong until the final scenes, and then, having answered all of our questions up until then, closes with questions even it, I suspect, cannot answer.

About a Boy ★ ★ ★ ½
PG-13, 100 m., 2002

Hugh Grant (Will), Nicholas Hoult (Marcus), Rachel Weisz (Rachel), Toni Collette (Fiona), Victoria Smurfit (Suzie), Sharon Small (Christine). Directed by Paul Weitz and Chris Weitz and produced by Jane Rosenthal, Robert De Niro, Brad Epstein, Tim Bevan, and Eric Fellner. Screenplay by Peter Hedges, Chris Weitz, and Paul Weitz, based on the book by Nick Hornby.

Hugh Grant, who has a good line in charm, has never been more charming than in *About a Boy*. Or perhaps that's not quite what he is. "Charming" in the Grant stylebook refers to something he does as a conscious act, and what is remarkable here is that Grant is—well, likable. Yes, the cad has developed a heart. There are times, toward the end of the film, where he speaks sincerely and we can actually believe him.

In *About a Boy*, he plays Will, a thirty-eight-year-old bachelor who has never had a job, or a relationship that has lasted longer than two months. He is content with this lifestyle. "I was the star of the Will Show," he explains. "It was not an ensemble drama." His purpose in life is to date pretty girls. When they ask him what he does, he smiles that self-deprecating Hugh Grant smile and confesses that, well, he does—nothing. Not a single blessed thing. In 1958, his late father wrote a hit song named "Santa's Super Sleigh," and he lives rather handsomely off the royalties. His London flat looks like a showroom for Toys for Big Boys.

Will is the creation of Nick Hornby, who wrote the original novel. This is the same Hornby who wrote *High Fidelity*, which was made into the wonderful John Cusack movie. He depicts a certain kind of immature but latently sincere man who loves Women as a less-demanding alternative to loving a woman. Will's error, or perhaps it is his salvation, is that he starts dating single mothers, thinking they will be less demanding and easier to dump than single girls.

The strategy is flawed: Single mothers invariably have children, and what Will discovers is that while he would make a lousy husband he might make a wonderful father. Of course, it takes a child to teach an adult how to be a parent, and that is how Marcus (Nicholas Hoult) comes into Will's life. Will is dating a single mom named Suzie, whom he meets at a support group named Single Parents Alone Together (SPAT). He shamelessly claims that his wife abandoned him and their two-year-old son, "Ned."

Suzie has a friend named Fiona (Toni Collette), whose son Marcus comes along one day to the park. We've already met Marcus, who is round-faced and sad-eyed and has the kind of bangs that get him teased in the school playground. His mother suffers from depression, and this has made Marcus mature and solemn beyond his years; when Fiona tries to overdose one day, Will finds himself involved in a trip to the emergency room and other events during which Marcus decides that Will belongs in his life whether Will realizes it or not.

The heart of the movie involves the relationship between Will and Marcus—who begins by shadowing Will, finds out there is no "Ned," and ends by coming over on a regular basis to watch TV. Will has had nothing but trouble with his fictional child, and now finds that a real child is an unwieldy addition to the bachelor life. Nor is Fiona a dating possibility. Marcus tried fixing them up, but they're obviously not intended for each other—not Will with his cool bachelor aura and Fiona with her Goodwill hippie look and her "health bread," which is so inedible that little Marcus barely has the strength to tear a bite from the loaf. (There is an unfortunate incident in the park when Marcus attempts to throw the loaf into a pond to feed the ducks, and kills one.)

Will finds to his horror that authentic emotions are forming. He likes Marcus. He doesn't admit this for a long time, but he's a good enough bloke to buy Marcus a pair of trendy sneakers, and to advise Fiona that since Marcus is already mocked at school, it is a bad idea, by definition, for him to sing "Killing Me Softly" at a school assembly. Meanwhile, Will starts dating Rachel (Rachel Weisz), who turns out to be a much nicer woman than he deserves (she also has a son much nastier than she deserves).

This plot outline, as it stands, could supply

the materials for a film of complacent stupidity—a formula sitcom with one of the Culkin offspring blinking cutely. It is much more than that; it's one of the year's most entertaining films, not only because Grant is so good but because young Nicholas Hoult has a kind of appeal that cannot be faked. He isn't a conventionally cute movie child, seems old beyond his years, can never be caught in an inauthentic moment, and helps us understand why Will likes Marcus—he likes Marcus because Marcus is so clearly in need of being liked, and so deserving of it.

The movie has been directed by the Weitz brothers, Paul and Chris, who directed *American Pie*, which was better than its countless imitators, and now give us a comedy of confidence and grace. They deserve some of the credit for this flowering of Hugh Grant's star appeal. There is a scene where Grant does a double take when he learns that *he* has been dumped (usually it is the other way around). The way he handles it—the way he handles the role in general—shows how hard it is to do light romantic comedy, and how easily it comes to him. We have all the action heroes and Method script-chewers we need right now, but the Cary Grant department is understaffed, and Hugh Grant shows here that he is more than a star, he is a resource.

About Schmidt ★ ★ ★ ½
R, 124 m., 2002

Jack Nicholson (Warren Schmidt), Kathy Bates (Roberta Hertzel), Hope Davis (Jeannie), Dermot Mulroney (Randall Hertzel), Howard Hesseman (Larry), Len Cariou (Ray), June Squibb (Helen Schmidt). Directed by Alexander Payne and produced by Michael Besman and Harry Gittes. Screenplay by Payne and Jim Taylor, based on a novel by Louis Begley.

Warren Schmidt is a man without resources. He has no intellectual curiosity. May never have read a book for pleasure. Lives in a home "decorated" with sets of collector's items accumulated by his wife, each in the display case that came with the items. On his retirement day, he is left with nothing but time on his empty hands. He has spent his entire life working at a job that could have been done by any-

body or, apparently, nobody. He goes to the office to see if he can answer any questions that the new guy might have, but the new guy doesn't. In a lifetime of work, Warren Schmidt has not accumulated even one piece of information that is needed by his replacement.

"The mass of men," Thoreau famously observed, "lead lives of quiet desperation." Schmidt is such a man. Jack Nicholson is not such a man, and is famous for the zest he brings to living. It is an act of self-effacement that Nicholson is able to inhabit Schmidt and give him life and sadness. It is not true to say that Nicholson disappears into the character, because he is always in plain view, the most watchable of actors. His approach is to renounce all of his mannerisms, even the readiness with which he holds himself on-screen, and withdraw into the desperation of Schmidt. Usually we watch Nicholson because of his wicked energy and style; here we are fascinated by their absence.

About Schmidt, directed by Alexander Payne, written by Payne and Jim Taylor, is not about a man who goes on a journey to find himself, because there is no one to find. When Schmidt gets into his thirty-five-foot Winnebago Adventurer, which he and his wife, Helen, thought to use in his retirement, it is not an act of curiosity but of desperation: He has no place else to turn.

The film's opening scenes show him suffering through a meaningless retirement dinner and returning home to ask himself, after forty-two years of marriage, "Who is this old woman who is in my house?" His wife might ask the same question about her old man. They have lived dutiful and obedient lives, he as an actuary for the Woodman of the World Insurance Co. in Omaha, Nebraska, she as a housewife and mother, and now that the corporate world has discarded them they have no other role to assume.

Helen (June Squibb) makes an effort to be cheerful, and surprises him with breakfast in the Adventurer the morning after his retirement dinner, but breakfast is a cheerless meal when it does not begin a day with a purpose. Then Helen drops dead. Warren is astonished and bereft, not at the enormity of his loss, but that he had so little to lose. Here is a man who did not "plan for retirement."

About Schmidt has backed itself into a corner

with its hero, who is so limited it would be torture to watch him for two hours, even played by Nicholson. The film puts Schmidt on the road, in a reversal of Nicholson's youthful journey in *Easy Rider*. He and the film are in search of life, and find it in his daughter's plans to marry a man he (correctly) perceives as a buffoon and a fraud.

The humor in the film comes mostly from the daughter (Hope Davis, fed up with him) and the family she is marrying into. Schmidt's new in-laws include Randall Hertzel (Dermot Mulroney), a waterbed salesman and promoter of pyramid schemes, and his mother, Roberta (Kathy Bates), who embraces the life force with a bone-crushing squeeze. Schmidt, who has hardly had a surprise in forty years, now finds himself wrestling with a water bed, and joined in a hot tub by the topless and terrifyingly available Roberta.

Roberta is intended as a figure of fun, but at least she approaches life hungrily and with good cheer. This is one of Bates's best performances, as a woman of outsize charm and personality, who can turn on a dime to reveal impatience and anger. Her selfishness helps us observe that Schmidt is not a selfish man, mostly because there is nothing he has that he wants and nothing he lacks that he cares about.

Schmidt has one relationship in his life that gives him a place to spill out his fears and discontent. After watching a TV ad for a world children's charity, he "adopts" a six-year-old Tanzanian named Ndugu. Encouraged to write to the boy, he spills out his thoughts in long confessional letters. It is impossible to be sure if he thinks Ndugu can read the letters or understand them, or if he has such a painful need to find a listener that Ndugu will do. Certainly there is no one in America who Schmidt would be able to talk to with such frankness.

About Schmidt is essentially a portrait of a man without qualities, baffled by the emotions and needs of others. That Jack Nicholson makes this man so watchable is a tribute not only to his craft, but to his legend: Jack is so unlike Schmidt that his performance generates a certain awe. Another actor might have made the character too tragic or passive or empty, but Nicholson somehow finds within Schmidt a slowly developing hunger, a desire to start living now that the time is almost gone.

About Schmidt is billed as a comedy. It is funny to the degree that Nicholson is funny playing Schmidt, and funny in terms of some of his adventures, but at bottom it is tragic. In an RV camp, Schmidt is told by a woman who hardly knows him, "I see inside of you a sad man." Most teenagers will probably not be drawn to this movie, but they should attend. Let it be a lesson to them. If they define their lives only in terms of a good job, a good paycheck, and a comfortable suburban existence, they could end up like Schmidt, dead in the water. They should start paying attention to that crazy English teacher.

Adam Sandler's Eight Crazy Nights ★ ★
PG-13, 71 m., 2002

With the voices of: Adam Sandler (Davey/Whitey/Eleanor), Jackie Titone (Jennifer), Austin Stout (Benjamin). Other voices by Kevin Nealon, Rob Schneider, Norm Crosby, Jon Lovitz, and Tyra Banks. Directed by Seth Kearsley and produced by Adam Sandler, Allen Covert, and Jack Giarraputo. Screenplay by Brooks Arthur, Covert, Brad Isaacs, and Sandler.

Heaven help the unsuspecting families that wander into *Adam Sandler's Eight Crazy Nights* expecting a jolly, animated holiday funfest. The holidays aren't very cheerful in Sandlerville, which is why the PG-13 rating mentions "frequent and crude sexual humor." The MPAA doesn't mention it, but there's also a lot of scatological humor in the film, in keeping with Sandler's inexplicable fascination with defecation, flatulence, and bodily fluids.

If this is not a family film, what is it? Well, the audiences for *Jackass* may enjoy a scene where Davey, the hero, slams a sweet little old man into a Porta-Potty and shoves it down a hill. When the geezer emerges at the bottom, he is still alive, but covered from head to toe with excrement. Then Davey sprays him with a garden hose, and he freezes solid. Ho, ho.

Davey (who looks like and is voiced by Sandler) is "a thirty-three-year-old crazy Jewish guy," the film informs us, who is up before the judge on the latest in a long series of brushes with the law, this time for drunkenness. The judge is prepared to send him away for a long time, but kindly little Whitey (voice also by

Sandler) pipes up. Whitey explains that he is the referee of the local youth basketball league, and he could use an assistant. The judge releases Davey to Whitey's custody, not explaining why he thinks this drunk and vandal would be a good role model.

Whitey and his twin sister, Eleanor (also voiced by Sandler), take the lad into their home, but he remains stubbornly ill-mannered, not to mention pathologically violent, until the movie's eventual collapse into obligatory peace and goodwill, etc. If there was ever a movie where the upbeat ending feels like a cop-out, this is the one.

I can understand why Sandler might want to venture into *South Park* territory with a raunchy animated cartoon, but not why he links it to Christmas and Hanukkah. The advertising will inevitably use holiday images, and in the minds of most people those images will not suggest a film this angry and vulgar. There is also an odd disconnect between Sandler's pride in his Jewishness, which is admirable, and his willingness to display the obnoxious behavior of this particular Jewish character to an audience that may not get the point.

That point is, I think, that Davey has lost his way through alcoholism and antisocial neurosis, and is finally redeemed by the elfish saints Whitey and Eleanore, plus the beneficial side effects of working with the basketball team. All well and good, but the movie lingers on the scatological stuff and adds the happy ending as if paying its dues. Did it occur to Sandler that he could touch his bases and make his points in a film that was not quite so offensive? That was, in fact, sweet and cheerful and family-friendly? Considering that his popularity and the movie's holiday packaging will attract large numbers of teenage Middle Americans not necessarily familiar with Jews, does he think this is a good way to get them started?

Yes, I've argued against the requirement that ethnic groups must present "positive" images of themselves in the movies. I've defended Justin Lin's *Better Luck Tomorrow,* with its criminal Chinese-American teenagers, and Chris Eyre's *Skins,* with its portrait of alcoholics and vigilantes on an Indian reservation, and Tim Story's *Barbershop,* with its free-for-all African-American dialogue. But those films are positioned to reach audiences that will understand them—decode them as the directors hoped they would.

Won't *Adam Sandler's Eight Crazy Nights* attract an audience for reasons (holiday images, Sandler's popularity) that have nothing to do with the material? What are people who want to see an Adam Sandler movie going to take home from this one? Sandler's most recent film, the inspired and wonderful *Punch Drunk Love,* was not well received by Sandler fans; I heard from readers appalled by the way his audience responded to the film—before, in some cases, walking out. (How can someone in the dark of a movie theater tell "his audience" from themselves? Easily: The giveaway is inappropriate laughter, especially during serious moments.)

Sandler has painted himself into a corner. His comedies have included generous amounts of antisocial hostility, sudden violence, dodgy material about urination, defecation, and flatulence, and a general air of defiance. A lot of people like that. But they are not the people likely to understand the Hanukkah message in *Eight Crazy Nights.* And those who appreciate the message are likely to be horrified by a lot of the other material in the film. What Sandler has made here is a movie for neither audience.

Adaptation ★ ★ ★

R, 114 m., 2002

Nicolas Cage (Charlie/Donald Kaufman), Meryl Streep (Susan Orlean), Chris Cooper (John Laroche), Tilda Swinton (Valerie), Brian Cox (Robert McKee), Cara Seymour (Amelia), Judy Greer (Alice), Maggie Gyllenhaal (Caroline), John Cusack (Himself), Catherine Keener (Herself). Directed by Spike Jonze and produced by Jonathan Demme, Vincent Landay, and Edward Saxon. Screenplay by Charlie Kaufman and Donald Kaufman, based on the book *The Orchid Thief* by Susan Orlean.

What a bewilderingly brilliant and entertaining movie this is—a confounding story about orchid thieves and screenwriters, elegant New Yorkers and scruffy swamp rats, truth and fiction. *Adaptation* is a movie that leaves you breathless with curiosity, as it teases itself with the directions it might take. To watch the film is to be actively involved in the challenge of its creation.

It begins with a book named *The Orchid Thief*, based on a *New Yorker* article by Susan Orlean (Meryl Streep). She writes about a Florida orchid fancier named John Laroche (Chris Cooper), who is the latest in a long history of men so obsessed by orchids that they would steal and kill for them. Laroche is a con man, and believes he has found a foolproof way to poach orchids from the protected Florida Everglades: Since they were ancestral Indian lands, he will hire Indians, who can pick the orchids with impunity.

Now that story might make a movie, but it's not the story of *Adaptation*. As the film opens, a screenwriter named Charlie Kaufman (Nicolas Cage) has been hired to adapt the book, and is stuck. There is so *much* about orchids in the book, and no obvious dramatic story line. Having penetrated halfway into the book myself, I understood his problem: It's a great story, but is it a movie?

Charlie is distraught. His producer, Valerie (Tilda Swinton), is on his case. Where is the first draft? He hardly has a first page. He relates his agony in voice-over, and anyone who has ever tried to write will understand his system of rewards and punishments: Should he wait until he has written a page to eat the muffin, or . . .

Charlie has a brother named Donald (also played by Cage). Donald lacks Charlie's ethics, his taste, his intelligence. He cheerfully admits that all he wants to do is write a potboiler and get rich. He attends the screenwriting seminars of Robert McKee (Brian Cox), who breaks down movie classics, sucks the marrow from their bones, and urges students to copy the formula. At a moment when Charlie is suicidal with frustration, Donald triumphantly announces he has sold a screenplay for a million dollars.

What is Charlie to do? To complicate matters, he has developed a fixation, even a crush, on Susan Orlean. He journeys to New York, shadows her, is too shy to meet her. She in turn goes to Florida to interview Laroche, who smells and smokes and has missing front teeth, but whose passion makes him . . . interesting.

And now my plot description will end, as I assure you I have not even hinted at the diabolical developments still to come. *Adaptation* is some kind of a filmmaking miracle, a film that is at one and the same time (a) the story of a movie being made, (b) the story of orchid thievery and criminal conspiracies, and (c) a deceptive combination of fiction and real life. The movie has been directed by Spike Jonze, who with Charlie Kaufman as writer made *Being John Malkovich* the best film of 1999. If you saw that film, you will (a) know what to expect this time, and (b) be wrong in countless ways.

There are real people in this film who are really real, like Malkovich, Jonze, John Cusack, and Catherine Keener, playing themselves. People who are real but are played by actors, like Susan Orlean, Robert McKee, John Laroche, and Charlie Kaufman. People who are apparently not real, like Donald Kaufman, despite the fact that he shares the screenplay credit. There are times when we are watching more or less exactly what must (or could) have happened, and then a time when the film seems to jump the rails and head straight for the swamps of McKee's theories.

During all of its dazzling twists and turns, the movie remains consistently fascinating not just because of the direction and writing, but because of the lighthearted darkness of the performances. Chris Cooper plays a con man of extraordinary intelligence, who is attractive to a sophisticated New Yorker because he is so intensely *himself* in a world where few people are anybody. Nicolas Cage, as the twins, gets so deeply inside their opposite characters that we can always tell them apart even though he uses no tricks of makeup or hair. His narration creates the desperate agony of a man so smart he understands his problems intimately, yet so neurotic he is captive to them.

Now as for Meryl Streep, well, it helps to know (since she plays in so many serious films) that in her private life she is one of the merriest of women, because here she is able to begin as a studious New Yorker author and end as, more or less, Katharine Hepburn in *The African Queen*.

I sat up during this movie. I leaned forward. I was completely engaged. It toyed with me, tricked me, played straight with me, then tricked me about that. Its characters are colorful because they care so intensely; they are more interested in their obsessions than they are in the movie, if you see what I mean. And all the time, uncoiling beneath the surface of the film, is the audacious surprise of the last twenty minutes, in which—well, to say the movie's ending works on more than one level is not to imply it works on only two.

Against the Ropes ★ ★ ★
PG-13, 111 m., 2004

Meg Ryan (Jackie Kallen), Omar Epps (Luther Shaw), Charles S. Dutton (Felix Reynolds), Tony Shalhoub (Sam Larocca), Timothy Daly (Gavin Reese), Joseph Cortese (Irving Abel), Kerry Washington (Renee), Skye McCole Bartusiak (Young Jackie Kallen). Directed by Charles S. Dutton and produced by Robert W. Cort and David Madden. Screenplay by Cheryl Edwards.

You know the slow clap scene, where the key character walks into the room and it falls silent? And everybody is alert and tense and waiting to see what will happen? And then one person slowly starts to clap, and then two, three, four, and then suddenly the tension breaks and everyone is clapping, even the sourpuss holdouts? Can we agree that this scene is an ancient cliché? We can. And yet occasionally I am amazed when it works, all the same.

It works near the end of *Against the Ropes,* a biopic about Jackie Kallen, who was (and is) the first female fight promoter in the all-male world of professional boxing. It works, and another cliché works, too: the big fight scene, right out of *Rocky* and every other boxing movie, in which the hero gets pounded silly but then somehow, after becoming inspired between rounds, comes back and is filled with skill and fury.

Against the Ropes meanders until it gets to the final third of its running time, and then it catches fire. Its setup story is flat and lacks authenticity. Meg Ryan is barely adequate as Jackie Kallen, and Omar Epps, as her boxer, Luther Shaw, is convincing but underwritten. The film plays like a quick, shallow, made-for-TV biopic, but then it relies on those ancient conventions, and they pull it through.

When we meet Kallen, she is the assistant to Cleveland's top boxing promoter. She grew up in boxing; her dad ran a gym and when she was a little girl he sometimes had to chase her out of the ring. Now she knows as much about boxing as anyone, but of course as a woman isn't allowed to use that knowledge. Then, observing a fight in a ghetto drug apartment, she sees a (nondrug-related) guy waltz in and cream everyone, and she intuits that he could be a great fighter.

This is Luther Shaw, played by Epps as a man with psychic wounds from childhood that sometimes unleash a terrible fury. Kallen persuades him he can be a fighter, signs him, hires a trainer to prepare him, edges around the Cleveland boycott against her by convincing a Buffalo promoter it's time for him to return the favors he got from her dad. Many of the scenes in this stretch are routine, although the performance by Charles Dutton as a veteran trainer has a persuasive authenticity; he also directs.

Meg Ryan works hard at Jackie Kallen, but this is not a role she was born to play. Ryan is a gifted actress, best at comedy but with lots of *noir* in her; she's good in thrillers, too. But she's not naturally a brassy exhibitionist, and that's what this role calls for. Kallen, who seems to buy her wardrobe from Trashy Lingerie and Victoria's Secret, and who talks like a girl who grew up in a gym, might have better been cast with someone with rougher notes—Gina Gershon. Ryan seems to be pushing it.

There's also a problem with Renee (Kerry Washington), Kallen's best friend, who becomes Luther's girlfriend, I think. I say "I think" because the role is so seriously underwritten that the movie would have been better off just not including it. Although Luther and Kallen are never romantically attracted, theirs is the movie's central relationship. Dutton (working from a screenplay by Cheryl Edwards) doesn't seem much interested in Luther's private emotional life, and so we get inexplicable scenes in which Luther and Renee seem to be best friends, or are hanging out together, or—what? The two of them have hardly any dialogue with each other, and although Renee is cheering during the big fight, there's no scene resolving her feelings for her man; the spotlight is on Kallen, which is all right, but it leaves a loose end.

Epps is always convincing, however, and by the last act of the movie we make our accommodation with Ryan because the character has grown more interesting. Intoxicated by the spotlight of publicity, she starts to think it's about her, not her boxer, and eventually she turns into a media caricature and finds herself forced outside the world she helped to create. Then comes the big fight, and the slow clap, and I'm damned if I wasn't really moved by the payoff.

Agent Cody Banks ★ ★ ½
PG, 110 m., 2003

Frankie Muniz (Cody Banks), Hilary Duff (Natalie Connors), Angie Harmon (Ronica Miles), Keith David (CIA Director), Cynthia Stevenson (Mrs. Banks), Daniel Roebuck (Mr. Banks), Arnold Vosloo (Molay), Ian McShane (Brinkman), Martin Donovan (Dr. Connors). Directed by Harald Zwart and produced by David Glasser, Andreas Klein, David Nicksay, Guy Oseary, and Dylan Sellers. Screenplay by Zack Stentz, Ashley Miller, Scott Alexander, and Larry Karaszewski.

Imagine James Bond as a suburban American fifteen-year-old, and you have *Agent Cody Banks,* a high-speed, high-tech kiddie thriller that's kinda cute but sorta relentless. Frankie Muniz stars as Cody, whose martial arts skills, skateboarding, ceiling-walking, and extreme snowboarding are all the more remarkable when you consider that he goes into action before the CIA has time to give him much more than what in the Bond pictures is the Q routine with the neat gizmos.

Frankie lives with his parents (Cynthia Stevenson and Daniel Roebuck), who mean well but are so inattentive they don't notice their son has become a spy with international missions. His CIA handler (Angie Harmon, low-cut and sexy) wants him to become friends with a classmate named Natalie Connors (Hilary Duff, from *Lizzie McGuire*). Frankie is, alas, so tongue-tied around girls that his grade-school brother boasts, "Cody's almost sixteen and I've had twice as many dates as he has." Cody fights back ("Sitting in a treehouse doesn't count"), but the kid is serene ("It does when you're playing Doctor").

Natalie attends the ultraexclusive William Donovan Prep School, no doubt named for the famous World War II spy "Wild Bill" Donovan, and Frankie transfers there, uses his karate skills to silence hecklers, and ends up on a mission to liberate Natalie's father, Dr. Connors (Martin Donovan), from the clutches of the evil masterminds Brinkman and Molay (Ian McShane and Arnold Vosloo), who want to (we know this part by heart) attain world domination by using the doctor's inventions—microscopic nanorobots that can eat through anything.

The movie imitates its Bond origins with a lot of neat toys. Cody is given a BMW skateboard that has unsuspected versatility, and a jet-powered snowboard, and a sports car, and X-ray glasses (Hello, Angie Harmon!), and a watch that will send electricity through your enemies, although I think (I'm not sure about this) you should not be wearing it yourself at the time.

The set design includes the scientist's laboratory in underground World Domination Headquarters—which includes, as students of *Ebert's Bigger Little Movie Glossary* will not be surprised to learn, commodious and well-lighted overhead air ducts so that Cody can position himself in comfort directly above all important conversations. There also is CIA regional headquarters, with a conference table that looks like it was designed by Captain Nemo in a nightmare. We learn that the CIA runs summer camps to train kids to become junior spies, although why Angie Harmon, who seems to be playing Young Mrs. Robinson, is their handler is hard to explain—maybe she's there for the dads, in the movie and in the audience.

The movie will be compared with the two *Spy Kids* pictures, and it looks more expensive and high-tech, but isn't as much fun. It has a lot of skill and energy, but its wit is more predictable and less delightful. It's a well-made movie, to be sure, and will probably entertain its target audience, but its target audience is probably not reading this review, and you (for whatever reason) are. The difference is, I could look you in the eye and recommend you go see the *Spy Kids* movies, but this one, if you're not a kid, I don't think so.

Agent Cody Banks 2: Destination London ★ ★ ½
PG, 93 m., 2004

Frankie Muniz (Cody Banks), Anthony Anderson (Derek), Hannah Spearritt (Emily),

Daniel Roebuck (Mr. Banks), Keith Allen (Diaz), Keith David (CIA Director), Cynthia Stevenson (Mrs. Banks), Connor Widdows (Alex Banks). Directed by Kevin Allen and produced by David Glasser, Andreas Klein, David Nicksay, Guy Oseary, and Dylan Sellers. Screenplay Don Rhymer.

I've been trying to mind-control myself into the head of a kid the right age to enjoy *Agent Cody Banks 2: Destination London,* but either I was never that age, or I haven't reached it yet. I'm capable of enjoying the *Spy Kids* movies, so I know I'm not totally lacking in range, but the movie seems preassembled, like those kits where it takes more time to open the box than build the airplane.

The movie opens at a secret summer camp where the CIA trains teenagers to become junior James Bonds. The opening scene, in fact, is uncanny in the way it resembles the prologue of David Mamet's *Spartan.* In both movies, characters in combat uniforms with lots of camouflage paint on their faces creep through trees and try to cream one another. For Mamet, that is not the high point of his movie.

Cody Banks (Frankie Muniz) is a smart, resourceful kid who thinks there may be something fishy at the camp, which is run by Diaz (Keith Allen), love child of Patton and Rambo. After a secret plot is revealed, Cody finds himself on assignment in London, where his handler is Derek (Anthony Anderson) and his mission is to prevent the CIA'S bad apples from gaining possession of a mind-control device that fits inside a tooth and turns its wearer into a zombie.

It's a pretty nifty device: At one point, its mad inventor fits it to a dog which then sits upright at a piano and plays a little tune, reminding me inevitably of Dr. Johnson's observation that when a dog walks on its hind legs, "it is not done well, but one is surprised to find it done at all." The dog is impressive but no pianist, and Derek, watching the demonstration on a spy-cam with Cody, decides he won't buy the CD.

The agency, as in the previous film, supplies Cody with various secret weapons, including a pack of Mentos that explode when moistened. Turns out the evil master plan is to subvert a conference of world leaders at Buckingham

Palace; to infiltrate the palace, Cody must join a world-class youth orchestra—not easy, since he doesn't play an instrument, but easier than you might think, since his agency-supplied clarinet plays itself. It seems to know only "Flight of the Bumble Bee," unfortunately.

Hilary Duff, who played Cody's sidekick in the previous movie, is MIA this time, and her place is taken, sort of, by Emily (Hannah Spearritt), a British agent who looks in a certain light as if she might be a teenager, and in another as if she might be, oh, exactly twenty-three. You will recall from the previous film that Cody is too busy being an agent to date much, and his little brother sees more action. (That produced a good exchange: Cody says most of the brother's dating doesn't count because it's limited to a tree house, and the brother replies, "It does if you're playing Doctor.")

The big climax at Buckingham Palace features look-alikes for Tony Blair and the queen, and a scene that is supposed to be funny because the youth orchestra stalls for time by improvising a song with a funky rhythm and the queen boogies with the heads of state. Since I am enough of a realist to believe that a large part of the target audience for this movie doesn't know who the queen is or what she looks like, it's a good thing the action starts up again real soon.

There is a mind-controlled food fight that begins promisingly but is awkwardly handled, and a chase through London that is (sigh) just one more chase through London, and apart from funny supporting work by the inventor of the mind control and the guy in the "Q" role, the movie is pretty routine. I wanted to be able to tell you the names of the actors in those two entertaining roles, but half an hour's research has not discovered them, although the movie's Website has signed me up for junior agent training.

The Agronomist ★ ★ ★ ½
NO MPAA RATING, 90 m., 2004

A documentary directed by Jonathan Demme and produced by Demme, Bevin McNamara, and Peter Saraf.

Jean Dominique was a brave man in a dangerous country, and Jonathan Demme's *The Agronomist* shows him telling the truth as he sees it, day after day, on the radio in Haiti. It is obvious that sooner or later he will be assassinated. Dissent cannot be tolerated in a nation that depends on secrecy to protect its powerful. What is remarkable is how long he survived, and how courageously he owned and operated Radio Haiti-Inter; it became the voice of the powerless in great part because it broadcast in Creole, the language they spoke, instead of in the French of their masters.

Jonathan Demme, who made the documentary, is a man who seems to lead parallel lives. In one, he is the successful director of such films as *The Silence of the Lambs, Philadelphia, Married to the Mob,* and *Melvin and Howard.* In the other, he has made documentaries about Haiti, has visited there countless times, has helped promote Haitian art and music, and has a heart that aches as he sees the country victimized by powerful interests both within and without.

In Jean Dominique and his wife, Michele Montas, Demme finds subjects who reflect the agony of Haiti's struggle. His documentary draws on hundreds of hours of filming and conversations from 1991 until Dominique's death in 2000. It begins at the moment when President Jean-Claude Aristide was overthrown in 1991, follows the Dominiques into exile in New York, watches as they return to Haiti and Aristide is restored to power, and observes how Dominique, originally a supporter of Aristide, became one of his critics.

Dominique is a man who seems to have come to heroism because it was the only choice for a man of his nature. His college education was in agriculture (which explains the movie's title), and he first came up against the ruling clique through his efforts for land reform. He was interested in the arts, started a cinema club in Port-au-Prince, and was shut down by the dictator "Papa Doc" Duvalier after showing Alain Resnais's *Night and Fog.* That was a film about the evil of Nazism; why Papa Doc found it unacceptable is easy to imagine.

At first it seemed that the rebel priest Aristide might force a change in his nation's destiny, but soon he, too, was employing the tactics of those he replaced. There is a sequence in the film where Dominique interviews Aristide and challenges him with pointed questions. The president responds with measured sound bites that repeat the same inanities again and again, as if he is incapable of understanding the actual meaning of the questions he has been asked.

Dominique and Montas are persons of great cheer and energy, leaping into each day with such zeal that they sometimes seem to forget the risks they are taking. Their problem in Haiti is that by honestly speaking to the ordinary people in their own language, they offend not only their obvious enemies but even those they do not know they have made. A nation built on lies cannot tolerate truth even when it agrees with it.

Radio Haiti-Inter comes under siege more than once, and Demme's camera does not overlook the bullet holes in the exterior walls. The station seems to be run informally, as a mixture of music, gossip, local news, and political opinion; at times of crisis, Dominique stays on the air as long as he can, until power outages or the government shut him down.

This is a couple who could have led the good life in Haiti. With the light complexions of the French-speaking Haitian establishment, with education and some wealth, they could have gone along with the ruling elite and earned a nice little fortune with their radio station or other enterprises. What fascinates us is Dominique's inability to do that. He is well enough connected to know what is going wrong, and too principled to ignore it.

Did he know he would be killed? Who can say? His country was in tumult, and the inconsistent policies of the United States did little to help. The country seemed almost to force its rulers into fearful and repressive policies. The wise course for Dominique would have been to return in exile to New York and use a dissenting magazine or Web site to spread his beliefs.

But no. When he could go back, he went back. Demme often followed him. We watch Dominique use humor and cynicism as well as anger, and we understand he is not a zealot but simply a reasonable man saying reasonable things in an unreasonable country. After his murder, Michele Montas goes on the air to insist that Jean Dominique is still alive, because his spirit lives on. But in this film Haiti seems to be a country that can kill the spirit, too.

Aileen: The Life and Death of a Serial Killer ★ ★ ★ ½

NO MPAA RATING, 89 m., 2004

A documentary directed by Nick Broomfield and Joan Churchill and produced by Jo Human.

Aileen Wuornos was trashed by life. That she committed seven murders is beyond dispute and unforgivable, but what can we expect from a child who was beaten by her grandfather, molested by a pedophile, abandoned by her mother, and raped by her brother and other neighborhood boys and men? A child who was selling sex for cigarettes at the age of nine, who had a baby at thirteen and was thrown out of the house, who lived for two years in the woods at the end of the street or, in cold weather, in the backseat of a car, wrapped in a single blanket? Society made Aileen into a weapon and turned her loose.

Aileen: The Life and Death of a Serial Killer is a documentary by Nick Broomfield, the guerrilla filmmaker who works with a crew of one (cinematographer and codirector Joan Churchill) and structures his films into the stories of how he made them. He met Aileen, invariably described as "America's first female serial killer," soon after her original arrest, and made the 1992 documentary *Aileen Wuornos: The Selling of a Serial Killer* about the media zoo and bidding war that surrounded her sudden notoriety. Florida police officers were fired after it was disclosed they were negotiating for a Hollywood deal, and Aileen, meanwhile, was represented by "Dr. Legal," a bearded, pot-smoking ex-hippie who was incompetent and clueless. She saw his ad on late-night TV. She couldn't pay him, but he figured he could cash in, too.

As Wuornos's often-delayed execution date inexorably closed in, Broomfield returned to the story for this film, made in 2002. He had become friendly, if that is the word, with Aileen, and indeed she gave him her last interview. He also interviewed many people instrumental in her life, including childhood friends, former sexual partners, and even her long-lost mother. The portrait he builds of her life is one of cruel suffering and mistreatment. This was a young woman who hitchhiked to Florida when she was thirteen because she was tired of sleeping in the rough, and who became a roadside prostitute because, really, what else was open to her? Social services? Invisible in her case.

Wuornos herself is onscreen for much of the film. Charlize Theron has earned almost unanimous praise for her portrayal of Aileen in the film *Monster,* and her performance stands up to direct comparison with the real woman. There were times, indeed, when I perceived no significant difference between the woman in the documentary and the one in the feature film. Theron has internalized and empathized with Wuornos so successfully that to experience the real woman is only to understand more completely how remarkable her performance is.

Wuornos talks and talks and talks to Broomfield. She confesses and recants. She says at one point that her original defense (she was raped and attacked by her victims, and shot them in self-defense) was a lie—that she was in the "stealing biz" and killed them to cover her tracks. On another day she is likely to return to her original story. We hear her describing a man who tortured her with acid in a Visine bottle, and her vivid details make us feel we were there. Then she tells Broomfield she made it all up. What can we believe? Broomfield's theory is that after more than a decade on Death Row, Wuornos was insane, and that she used her last remaining shreds of reason to hasten the day of her execution. She said whatever she thought would speed her date with death.

Oh, yes, it's clear she was crazy on the day she died. She talks to Broomfield about secret signals and radio waves being beamed into her cell, about how the police knew she was the killer but let her keep on killing because it would make a better story for them to sell, about how she would be beamed up "like on *Star Trek*" to a spaceship waiting for her in Earth orbit.

Remarkably, three psychiatrists "examined" her right before her death and found her sane. No person who sees this film would agree with them. Florida Governor Jeb Bush was scarcely less enthusiastic about the death penalty than his brother George, who supported the notorious execution assembly line in Texas. Aileen died in October of an election year, just in time to send a law-and-order message to the voters. Should she have died? That depends on whether you support the death penalty. She was certainly guilty. The film makes it clear her imprisonment would simply have continued a lifelong sentence that began when she was born. No one should have to endure the life that Aileen Wuornos led, and we leave the movie believing that if someone, somehow, had been able to help that little girl, her seven victims would never have died.

The Alamo ★ ★ ★ ½
PG-13, 137 m., 2004

Dennis Quaid (Sam Houston), Billy Bob Thornton (Davy Crockett), Jason Patric (James Bowie), Patrick Wilson (William Barrett Travis), Emilio Echevarria (Santa Anna), Jordi Molla (Juan Seguin), Laura Clifton (Susanna Dickinson), Leon Rippy (Sergeant William Ward). Directed by John Lee Hancock and produced by Brian Grazer, Ron Howard, and Mark Johnson. Screenplay by Leslie Bohem, Stephen Gaghan, and Hancock.

The advance buzz on *The Alamo* was negative, and now I know why: This is a good movie. Conventional wisdom in Hollywood is that any movie named *The Alamo* must be simplistic and rousing, despite the fact that we already know all the defenders got killed. (If we don't know it, we find out in the first scene.) Here is a movie that captures the loneliness and dread of men waiting for two weeks for what they expect to be certain death, and it somehow succeeds in taking those pop culture brand names like Davy Crockett and James Bowie and giving them human form.

The arc of the Alamo story is a daunting one for any filmmaker: long days and nights of waiting, followed by a massacre. Even though the eventual defeat of Santa Anna by Sam Houston provides an upbeat coda, it's of little consolation to the dead defenders. This movie deals frankly with the long wait and the deadly conclusion by focusing on the characters of the leaders; it's about what they're made of, and how they face a bleak situation.

Davy Crockett, the man in the coonskin hat, surprisingly becomes the most three-dimensional of the Alamo heroes, in one of Billy Bob Thornton's best performances. We see him first in a theater box, attending a play inspired by his exploits. We learn of his legend; even Santa Anna's men whisper that he can leap rivers in a single bound and wrestle grizzly bears to death. And then we watch Crockett with a rueful smile as he patiently explains that he did not do and cannot do any of those things, and that his reputation has a life apart from his reality.

Crockett, who was a U.S. congressman before fate led him to the Alamo, has two scenes in particular that are extraordinary, and Thornton brings a poignant dignity to them. One is his memory of a U.S. Army massacre of Indians. The other occurs when the Mexicans, who have brought along a band, have their drummers put on a show. Crockett knows just what the percussion needs, climbs one of the battlements, takes out his violin and serenades both sides. It is one of those moments, like the Christmas Eve truce in World War I, when fighting men on both sides are reminded of the innocence they have lost. Crockett also has a line that somehow reminded me of the need, in *Jaws*, for a bigger boat: "We're going to need more men."

Leadership of the Alamo is contested between Colonel James Bowie (Jason Patric) and Lieutenant Colonel William Barrett Travis (Patrick Wilson). It involves a show of hands, a contest of wills, a truce, and then the inexorable weakening of Bowie, who is dying of tuberculosis and, it is murmured, other diseases. Travis is a humorless patriot who would rather, he tells us, have moments of glory than a lifetime of drudgery, and he strikes the men as over the top. But he is true to his principles, and at one point, although he has to be informed that the time has come to talk to his men, he delivers a speech filled with fire and resolve, reminding me of Henry V on the night before Agincourt.

Bowie faces the fact that he is a dying man, and it is agonizing to watch him attempt to button up his vest and climb from his deathbed to join in the battle. A revolver is placed in each of his hands, and when the Mexicans burst in, he takes two lives before they claim the few hours of life left in him. Both Travis and Bowie could have been caricatures; Wilson and Patric find their humanity.

The director and cowriter, John Lee Hancock, occupies more than an hour with scenes leading up to the final battle, as the Alamo defenders make their plans and wait for reinforcements that never arrive. As his troops surround them, General Santa Anna (Emilio Echevarria) struts and poses in front of his officers, who are appalled by his ignorance but intimidated by his temper. Ordering the final charge, he's told a twelve-pound cannon will arrive tomorrow that would breach the Alamo's walls without sacrifice of countless Mexican lives, but he disdains to wait, and dismisses the lives with a wave of his hand. (His own life was much more precious to him; he traded it for Texas.)

There are two scenes involving surrender that make an ironic contrast. Surrounded by dead bodies, himself gravely wounded, Davy Crockett is offered surrender terms by Santa Anna and replies by defiantly offering to accept Santa Anna's surrender. This is matched by the scene at the end where Houston (Dennis Quaid) has Santa Anna on his knees, and the general will agree to anything.

Much of the picture takes place at night, illuminated by campfires and candlelight, and Hancock's cinematographer, the gifted Dean Semler, finds color and texture in the shadows that evoke those hours between midnight and dawn that Fitzgerald called the dark night of the soul. Oddly enough, as Santa Anna's troops march up to within one hundred yards of the Alamo, there seem to be no watchmen to see them, and when they attack it is a surprise.

The battle scenes, when they come, are brutal and unforgiving; we reflect that the first Mexicans up the scaling ladders must have known they would certainly die, and yet they climbed them heedlessly. This intimate, hand-to-hand conflict is balanced by awesome long shots, combining the largest sets ever built by modern Hollywood with some special effects shots that are generally convincing.

Although the battle for the Alamo has taken its place as a sacred chapter in American history, the movie deals with the fact that it all came down to one thing: Mexico owned Texas, and ambitious Americans and Texans (or "Texians") wanted it. Many of the fighters had been promised 760 acres of land as a bonus for enlisting. For Bowie, Crockett, and Travis, the challenge was to rehabilitate reputations that had gone astray—to redeem themselves. For Sam Houston, who never sent reinforcements,

it was an opportunity to apply Wellington's strategy in leading Napoleon on a chase until Napoleon's army was splintered and weakened. Houston was too wise to commit his army to the Alamo; that took foolishness, bravery, and a certain poetry of the soul.

Alex & Emma ★ ½
PG-13, 96 m., 2003

Kate Hudson (Emma, Eulva, Elsa, Eldora, and Anna), Luke Wilson (Alex, Adam), Sophie Marceau (Polina), David Paymer (John Shaw), Alexander Wauthier (Andre), Leili Kramer (Michele), Rip Taylor (The General), Gigi Birmingham (Madame Blanche), Jordan Lund (Claude). Directed by Rob Reiner and produced by Todd Black, Alan Greisman, Jeremy Leven, Reiner, and Elie Samaha. Screenplay by Reiner, Leven, Adam Scheinman, and Andrew Scheinman.

Alex & Emma is a movie about a guy who has to write a novel in thirty days in order to collect the money from his publisher to pay two gamblers who will otherwise kill him. So he hires a stenographer to take dictation, and they fall in love. But the thing is, it's a bad novel. Very bad. Every time the author started dictating, I was struck anew by how bad it was—so bad it's not even good romance fiction.

I guess I didn't expect him to write *The Gambler* by Dostoyevsky—although, come to think of it, Dostoyevsky dictated *The Gambler* in thirty days to pay off a gambling debt, and fell in love with his stenographer. I just expected him to write something presentable. You might reasonably ask why we even need to know what he's writing in the first place, since the movie involves the writer and the girl. But, alas, it involves much more: There are cutaways to the story he's writing, and its characters are played by Kate Hudson and Luke Wilson, the same two actors who star in the present-day story.

This other story takes place in 1924 and involves people who dress and act like the characters in *The Great Gatsby*. Not the central characters, but the characters who at*tend* Gatsby's parties and are in those long lists of funny names. It might have been a funny idea for the novelist to actually steal *The Great Gatsby*, confident that neither the gamblers nor his publisher would recognize it, but funny ideas are not easy to come by in *Alex & Emma*.

Alex is played by Luke Wilson. Emma is played by Kate Hudson. He also plays Adam, the young hero of the story within the story, and she plays four different nannies (Swedish, German, Latino, and American) who are employed by a rich French divorcée (Sophie Marceau) who plans to marry a rich guy (David Paymer) for his money, but is tempted by the handsome young Adam, who is a tutor to her children, who remain thoroughly untutored.

So the story is a bore. The act of writing the story is also a bore, because it consists mostly of trying out variations on the 1924 plot and then seeing how they look in the parallel story. Of course chemistry develops between Alex and Emma, who fall in love, and just as well: There is a Hollywood law requiring fictional characters in such a situation to fall in love, and the penalty for violating it is death at the box office. A lot of people don't know that.

Curious, the ease with which Alex is able to dictate his novel. Words flow in an uninterrupted stream, all perfectly punctuated. No false starts, wrong word choices, or despair. Emma writes everything down and then offers helpful suggestions, although she fails to supply the most useful observation of all, which would be to observe that the entire novel is complete crap.

Despite the deadly deadline, which looms ever closer, the young couple find time to get out of the apartment and enjoy a Semi-Obligatory Lyrical Interlude, that old standby where they walk through the park, eat hot dogs, etc., in a montage about a great day together. I do not remember if they literally walk through the park or eat hot dogs, but if they don't, then they engage in parklike and hot dog–like activities.

Now about his apartment. It's at the top of a classic brownstone, with balconies and tall windows, and should cost thousands of dollars a month, but he's flat broke, see, and just to prove it, there's a place where the plaster has fallen off the wall and you can see the bare slats underneath. He has art hanging all over his apartment, except in front of those slats. All Alex has to do is sublet, and his financial worries are over.

The movie has been directed by Rob Reiner and is not as bad as *The Story of Us* (1999), but this is a movie they'll want to hurry past during the AFI tribute. Reiner has made wonderful movies in the past (*Misery*, *The Princess Bride*, *Stand by Me*) and even wonderful romantic comedies (*The Sure Thing*, *When Harry Met Sally*). He will make wonderful movies in the future. He has not, however, made a wonderful movie in the present.

All About Lily Chou-Chou ★ ★
NO MPAA RATING, 146 m., 2001

Hayato Ichihara (Yûichi Hasumi), Shûgo Oshinari (Shusuke Hoshino), Yû Aoi (Shiori Tsuda), Ayumi Ito (Yôko Kuno), Takao Osawa (Tabito Takao), Miwako Ichikawa (Shimabukuro), Izumi Inamori (Izumi Hoshino). Directed by Shunji Iwai and produced by Koko Maeda. Screenplay by Iwai.

All About Lily Chou-Chou is like an ancient text that requires modern commentary. It's not an old film (it's cutting-edge Japanese technoangst), but it's so enigmatic, oblique, and meandering that it's like coded religious texts that require monks to decipher. In this case, the monks are the critics. They won't tell you anything you haven't figured out for yourself, but they will confirm that there's no more to the movie than you thought there was. This movie is maddening. It conveys a simple message in a visual style that is willfully overwrought.

The story: Lily Chou-Chou is a Japanese pop idol who must be real, since she appears in concert, but whom we never see. Ironically, then, one of her songs consists of repetitions of "I see you and you see me." She is idolized by Yûichi (Hayato Ichihara), a student in high school. He has a crush on the real-life Yôko (Ayumi Ito), a gifted pianist. Both Yûichi and Yôko are the targets of cliques of school bullies.

For a while, Yûichi has a friend, Shusuke Hoshino (Shûgo Oshinari), a fellow student who turns into a sadist and forces Yûichi to steal money and give it to him. Shusuke has another sideline: He pimps Shiori (Yû Aoi) to businessmen, and makes her give him most of the money. Shiori has a secret crush on Yûichi, but is under Shusuke's control and pathetically confides on the telephone, "Lately, when I think of men I think of customers."

The elements are in place for a powerful

story of alienated Japanese teenagers, but the writer-director, Shunji Iwai, cannot bring himself to make the story accessible to ordinary audiences. He and his cinematographer, Noboru Shinoda, are in love with their lightweight digital camera and give us jerky, handheld, out-of-focus shots. Some sequences are so incomprehensible they play as complete abstractions. I know, it's a style. It's a style that was interesting for a brief season and is now tiresome and pretentious.

Either you make an experimental film that cuts loose from narrative, characters, and comprehensible cinematography, or you do not. Iwai seems to want to tell the story of his characters, and it could be a compelling one (some of the scenes are poignant or wounding), but he cannot allow himself to make the film in a way that can communicate. That would be, I guess, a compromise. He has made a film that few reasonable ticket-buyers will have the patience to endure. It will be appreciated by a handful of highly evolved film watchers who can generate a simultaneous analysis in their minds, but what is the point, really, in making a film that closes out most moviegoers?

The world that swims murkily to the surface of *All About Lily Chou-Chou* is certainly a frightening one, eclipsing even the anomie of the Columbine killers. These students drift without values or interests, devoting all the passion of their young lives to creatures who may exist only on the Internet. Shiori has sex with strangers for pay, but is too shy to tell Yûichi she likes him. Yûichi's life has been turned into hell by Shusuke, who seems to act not so much out of hatred as boredom. The film's teachers and adults care, but are hopelessly misinformed about what is really going on.

There is a movie here somewhere. Shunji Iwai has gone to a great deal of trouble to obscure it. *Lily Chou-Chou* has been compared by some to Truffaut's *The 400 Blows*, which was also stylistically groundbreaking in its time, but Truffaut broke with traditional styles in order to communicate better, not to avoid communicating at all.

All or Nothing ★ ★ ★

R, 128 m., 2002

Timothy Spall (Phil Bassett), Lesley Manville (Penny Bassett), Alison Garland (Rachel Bassett), James Corden (Rory Bassett), Ruth Sheen (Maureen), Marion Bailey (Carol), Helen Coker (Donna). Directed by Mike Leigh and produced by Simon Channing-Williams. Screenplay by Leigh.

Mike Leigh's *All or Nothing* looks behind three doors in a South London public housing estate and finds loneliness, desperation, and a stubborn streak of spunky humor. His characters try to remember a time when they were lighthearted and had hope. But there is little to cheer them now, except for food and sleep, the telly, the pub on Saturday night, and, for the young, thoughtless sex to hurry them along into raising thankless kids of their own.

Phil Bassett, played by the sad-faced and wounded Timothy Spall, is a minicab driver who stares straight ahead as dramas unfold in his backseat. His common-law wife, Penny (Lesley Manville), is a checkout clerk at the Safeway. They have two fat, unattractive children: Rachel (Alison Garland), who is a cleaner at an old-folks' home and buries herself in romance novels, and Rory (James Corden), who lurches from the table to the sofa, his eyes hypnotically fixed on the television, his voice wavering between anger and martyrdom.

Their flat is on an outside corridor of an anonymous housing project, but it has a wooden door with a knocker—a reminder of when they had hopes for it as a home. Now it's a place where they barely meet. Phil sleeps late, his wife goes to work early, Rachel is in a world of her own, and Rory vibrates with hostility. For Penny, there is at least the companionship of neighbors along the corridor; she hangs out with Carol (Marion Bailey) and Maureen (Ruth Sheen), and they go to karaoke night at the pub. Maureen is a single mom whose daughter Donna (Helen Coker) is abused by a boyfriend. Carol, whose husband, Ron, also drives a minicab, is a drunk sliding off into walking hallucinations.

This sounds grim and is grim, but it is not depressing, because Leigh, who in his earlier films might have found a few laughs at the expense of his characters, clearly loves these people and cares for them. They are, we realize, utterly without resources; they lack the skills to enjoy life and are trapped on an economic treadmill. Phil has the makings of a philosopher, and observes sadly that you work all day and sleep all night and then you die. When a fellow driver complains of a car crash, Phil looks on the bright side: "You might have driven around the corner and killed a little girl."

The film pays attention to the neighbors, but its main attention is on the Bassetts, and one day something unforeseen happens—I will not reveal what it is—and it acts as a catalyst to jolt them out of their depression and lethargy. It is the kind of bad thing that good things come from. Watch carefully how it happens, and who reacts to it and how, and you will see that Leigh has made all of the neighbors into characters whose troubles help to define their response.

There are moments in *All or Nothing* of such acute observation that we nod in understanding. Consider the way Maureen learns that Donna is pregnant and how she deals with the news (at first, and then later), and how she treats the boyfriend. Watch joy and beauty flash briefly in the pub when the women are singing. And observe how Timothy Spall goes through an entire life crisis while scarcely saying a word, and tells us all we need to know with his eyes.

There is a scene that establishes the Bassett family as well as any scene possibly could. Phil needs to put together a sum of money, and he visits his wife and children separately. He searches for a coin under Rory's sofa cushion, but Rory finds it and piggishly snatches it. Rachel lends him money as if money is the least of her worries. Penny tries to find out what he is thinking. He keeps repeating that he will pay her back tomorrow. This is his companion of twenty years, and he treats her loan like one he would get in a pub.

Mike Leigh is now the leading British director— ironic, since after his brilliant *Bleak Moments* (1972) he spent long years making TV films because no one would finance his features. He and his actors improvise their scripts during long periods of living as the characters. His subject is usually working- and middle-class life in Britain, although his jolly *Topsy-Turvy* (2000) entered the backstage world of Gilbert and Sullivan. In *All or Nothing* he returns to more familiar material, in one of his very best films.

The closing scenes of the movie are just about perfect. Rory is the center of attention, and notice when, and how, he suddenly speaks in the middle of a conversation about him. When a director gets a laugh of recognition from the audience, showing that it knows his characters and recognizes typical behavior, he has done his job. These people are real as few movie characters ever are. At the end, it looks as if they will be able to admit a little sunshine into their lives, and talk to each other a little more. We are relieved.

All the Queen's Men ★
NO MPAA RATING, 105 m., 2002

Matt LeBlanc (Steven O'Rourke), Eddie Izzard (Tony Parker), James Cosmo (Archie), Nicolette Krebitz (Romy), Udo Kier (General Lansdorf), David Birkin (Johnno), Oliver Korittke (Franz), Karl Markovics (Liebl), Edward Fox (Colonel Aiken). Directed by Stefan Ruzowitzky and produced by Zachary Feuer, Gabrielle Kelly, and Marco Weber. Screenplay by David Schneider.

All the Queen's Men is a perfectly good idea for a comedy, but it just plain doesn't work. It's dead in the water. I can imagine it working well in a different time, with a different cast, in black and white instead of color—but I can't imagine it working like this.

The movie tells the World War II story of the "Poof Platoon," a group of four Allied soldiers parachuted into Berlin in drag, to infiltrate the all-woman factory where the Enigma machine is being manufactured. This story is said to be based on fact. If it is, I am amazed that such promising material would yield such pitiful results. To impersonate a woman and a German at the same time would have been so difficult and dangerous that it's amazing how the movie turns it into a goofy lark.

The film stars Matt LeBlanc, from *Friends,* who is criminally miscast as Steven O'Rourke, a U.S. officer famous for never quite completing heroic missions. He is teamed with a drag artist named Tony (Eddie Izzard), an ancient major named Archie (James Cosmo), and a scholar named Johnno (David Birkin). After brief lessons in hair, makeup, undergarments, and espionage, they're dropped into Berlin during an air raid, and try to make contact with a resistance leader.

This underground hero turns out to be the lovely and fragrant Romy (Nicolette Krebitz), a librarian who, for the convenience of the plot, lives in a loft under the roof of the library, so that (during one of many unbelievable scenes) the spies are able to lift a skylight window in order to eavesdrop on an interrogation.

The plot requires them to infiltrate the factory, steal an Enigma machine, and return to England with it. Anyone who has seen *Enigma*, *U-571*, or the various TV documentaries about the Enigma machine will be aware that by the time of this movie, the British already had possession of an Enigma machine, but to follow that line of inquiry too far in this movie is not wise. The movie has an answer to it, but it comes so late in the film that although it makes sense technically, the damage has already been done.

The four misfit transvestites totter about Berlin looking like (very bad) Andrews Sisters imitators, and O'Rourke falls in love with the librarian Romy. How it becomes clear that he is not a woman is not nearly as interesting as how anyone could possibly have thought he was a woman in the first place. He plays a woman as if determined, in every scene, to signal to the audience that he's absolutely straight and only kidding. His voice, with its uncanny similarity to Sylvester Stallone's, doesn't help.

The action in the movie would be ludicrous anyway, but is even more peculiar in a cross-dressing comedy. There's a long sequence in which Tony, the Izzard character, does a marked down Marlene Dietrich before a wildly enthusiastic audience of Nazis. Surely they know he is, if not a spy, at least a drag queen? I'm not so sure. I fear the movie makes it appear the Nazis think he is a sexy woman, something that will come as a surprise to anyone who is familiar with Eddie Izzard, including Eddie Izzard.

Watching the movie, it occurred to me that Tony Curtis and Jack Lemmon were not any more convincing as women in *Some Like It Hot*. And yet we bought them in that comedy, and it remains a classic. Why did they work, while the Queen's Men manifestly do not? Apart from the inescapable difference in actual talent, could it have anything to do with the use of color?

B&w is better suited to many kinds of comedy because it underlines the dialogue and movement while diminishing the importance of fashions and eliminating the emotional content of various colors. Billy Wilder fought for b&w on *Some Like It Hot* because he thought his drag queens would never be accepted by the audience in color, and he was right.

The casting is also a problem. Matt LeBlanc does not belong in this movie in any role other than, possibly, that of a Nazi who believes Eddie Izzard is a woman. He is all wrong for the lead, with no lightness, no humor, no sympathy for his fellow spies, and no comic timing. I can imagine this movie as a black-and-white British comedy, circa 1960, with Peter Sellers, Kenneth Williams, et al., but at this time, with this cast, this movie is hopeless.

All the Real Girls ★ ★ ★

R., 108 m., 2003

Paul Schneider (Paul), Zooey Deschanel (Noel), Shea Whigham (Tip), Danny McBride (Bust-Ass), Maurice Compte (Bo), Heather McComb (Mary-Margaret), Benjamin Mouton (Leland), Patricia Clarkson (Elvira). Directed by David Gordon Green and produced by Jean Doumanian and Lisa Muskat. Screenplay by Green.

We like to be in love because it allows us to feel idealistic about ourselves. The other person ennobles, inspires, redeems. Our lover deserves the most wonderful person alive, and that person is ourselves. Paul (Paul Schneider), the hero of *All the Real Girls,* has spent his young manhood having sex with any girl who would have sex with him and some who were still making up their minds, but when he meets Noel he doesn't want to rush things. He wants to wait, because this time is special.

Noel (Zooey Deschanel), who has spent the last several years in a girls' boarding school, is crazy in love with him and is a virgin. She is eighteen, an age when all the hormones in our bodies form ranks and hurl themselves against the ramparts of our inhibitions. That they can discuss these matters with romantic idealism does not entirely work as a substitute.

All the Real Girls, David Gordon Green's second film, is too subtle and perceptive, and knows too much about human nature, to treat their lack of sexual synchronicity as if it supplies a plot. Another kind of movie would be entirely about whether they have sex. But Green, who feels tenderly for his vulnerable characters, cares less about sex than about feelings and wild, youthful idealism. He comes from North Carolina, the state where young Thomas Wolfe once prowled the midnight campus, so in love with life that he uttered wild goat cries at the moon.

Most movies about young love trivialize and cheapen it. Their cynical makers have not felt true love in many years, and mock it, perhaps out of jealousy. They find something funny in a twenty-year-old who still doesn't realize he is doomed to grow up to be as jaded as they are. Green is twenty-seven, old enough to be jaded, but he has the soul of a romantic poet. Wordsworth, after all, was thirty-six when he published:

The rainbow comes and goes,
And lovely is the rose;

How many guys that age would have that kind of nerve today? Green knows there are nights when lovers want simply to wrap their arms around each other and celebrate their glorious destinies.

He centers these feelings on characters who live in the same kind of rusty, overgrown southern mill town he used for his great first film, *George Washington* (2000). His characters grew up together. They look today on the faces of their first contemporaries. Paul's best friend, Tip (Shea Whigham), has been his best friend almost from birth. That he is Noel's brother is a complication, since Tip knows all about Paul's other girls. And more than a complication, because your best friend's sister embodies a history that includes your entire puberty, and may be the first person you noticed had turned into a girl.

Green likes to listen to his characters talk. They don't have much to do. Some of them work at the few remaining mill jobs, and we learn some details about their lives (an hourly sprinkler system washes the fibers out of the air). They stand around and sit around and idly discuss the mysteries of life, which often come down to whether someone did something, or what they were thinking of when they did it, or if they are ever going to do it. I had relatives who lived in towns like these, and I know that when you go to the salad bar it includes butterscotch pudding.

Paul's single mom, Elvira (Patricia Clarkson), works as a clown at parties and in the children's wards of hospitals. Some critics have mocked this occupation, but let me tell you something: A small-town woman with a family to feed can make better money with a Bozo wig and a putty nose than she can working unpaid overtime at Wal-Mart. People will pay you nothing to clean their houses, but they pay the going rate when their kids have birthdays. The fact that Green knows this and a lot of people don't is an indicator of his comfort with his characters.

Green's dialogue has a kind of unaffected, flat naturalism. ("You feel like waffles or French toast?" "No, the places I go are usually not that fancy.") That doesn't mean their speech is not poetic. His characters don't use big words, but they express big ideas. Their words show a familiarity with hard times, disappointment, wistfulness; they are familiar with all the concepts on television, but do not lead lives where they apply.

Two emotional upheavals strike at the narrative. One is inevitable; Tip is enraged to learn that Paul and Noel are dating. The other is not inevitable, and I will not even hint about it. There is a scene where it is discussed in a bowling alley, using only body language, in long shot.

The thing about real love is, if you lose it, you can also lose your ability to believe in it, and that hurts even more. Especially in a town where real love may be the only world-class thing that ever happens.

Almost Salinas ★ ½
PG, 92 m., 2003

John Mahoney (Max Harris), Linda Emond (Nina Ellington), Lindsay Crouse (Allie), Virginia Madsen (Clare), Ian Gomez (Manny), Nathan Davis (Zelder Hill), Tom Groenwald (Leo Quinlan), Ray Wise (Jack Tynan). Directed by

Terry Green and produced by Wade W. Danielson. Screenplay by Green.

Almost Salinas is a sweet and good-hearted portrait of an isolated crossroads and the people who live there, or are drawn into their lives. Shame about the plot. The people are real, but the story devices are clunkers from Fiction 101; the movie generates goodwill in its setup, but in the last act it goes haywire with revelations and secrets and dramatic gestures. The movie takes place in Cholame, the California town where James Dean died in 1955, and maybe the only way to save it would have been to leave out everything involving James Dean.

John Mahoney stars as Max Harris, the proprietor of a diner in a sparsely populated backwater. He's thinking of reopening the old gas station. Virginia Madsen is Clare, his waitress, and other locals include Nathan Davis, as an old-timer who peddles James Dean souvenirs from a roadside table, and Ian Gomez, as the salt-of-the-earth cook.

The town experiences an unusual flurry of activity. A film crew arrives to shoot a movie about the death of James Dean. Max's ex-wife, Allie (Lindsay Crouse), turns up. And a magazine writer named Nina Ellington (Linda Emond) arrives to do a feature about the reopening of the gas station. If this seems like an unlikely subject for a story, reflect that she stays so long she could do the reporting on the reopening of a refinery. She gradually falls in love with Max, while one of the young members of the film crew falls for Clare's young assistant behind the counter.

The place and the people are sound. Mahoney has the gift of bringing quiet believability to a character; his Max seems dependable, kind, and loyal. Virginia Madsen is the spark of the place, not a stereotyped, gum-chewing hashslinger, but a woman who takes an interest in the people who come her way. If Emond is not very convincing as the visiting reporter, perhaps it's because her job is so unlikely. Better, perhaps, to make her a woman with no reason at all to be in Cholame. Let her stay because she has no place better to go, and then let her fall in love.

From the movie's opening moments, there are quick black-and-white shots of Dean's 1955 Porsche Spyder, racing along a rural highway toward its rendezvous with death. The arrival of the film crew, with its own model of the same car, introduces a series of parallels between past and present that it would be unfair to reveal.

Spoiler warning! Without spelling everything out, let us observe, however, that it is unlikely that a character who was locally famous in 1955 could stay in the same area and become anonymous just by changing his name. It is also unlikely that he would be moved, so many years later, to the actions he takes in the film. And cosmically unlikely that they would have the results that they do. Not to mention how pissed off the film company would be.

As the movie's great revelations started to slide into view, I slipped down in my seat, fearful that the simple and engaging story of these nice people would be upstaged by the grinding mechanics of plot contrivance. My fears were well grounded. *Almost Salinas* generates enormous goodwill and then loses it by betraying its characters to the needs of a plot that wants to inspire pathos and sympathy, but inspires instead, alas, groans and the rolling of eyes.

Along Came Polly ★ ★
PG-13, 90 m., 2004

Ben Stiller (Reuben Feffer), Jennifer Aniston (Polly Prince), Philip Seymour Hoffman (Sandy Lyle), Debra Messing (Lisa Kramer), Alec Baldwin (Stan Indursky), Hank Azaria (Claude), Bryan Brown (Leland Van Lew), Jsu Garcia (Javier). Directed by John Hamburg and produced by Danny DeVito, Michael Shamberg, and Stacey Sher. Screenplay by Hamburg.

I will never eat free nuts from the bowl on the bar again, having seen *Along Came Polly*. Not after hearing the expert risk-assessor Reuben Feffer (Ben Stiller) explain who has already handled them, what adventures they have had, and, for all we know, where they might have been. It's his job to know the risks of every situation, which is why his marriage seems like such a sure thing: His new bride, Lisa (Debra Messing), is like a computer printout of an ideal mate for life.

But it doesn't work out that way in *Along Came Polly,* a movie where a lot of things don't work out, including, alas, the movie itself. On the second day of their honeymoon in Saint

Bart's, Lisa cheats on Reuben with a muscular scuba instructor (Hank Azaria), and he returns to New York crushed and betrayed. When he meets Polly (Jennifer Aniston), an old school chum, he doubts they can be happy together (assessing the risks, he sees the two of them as totally incompatible), but to his amazement they are soon involved in a neurotic but not boring relationship.

The problem is that their relationship, and indeed Reuben's entire array of friendships and business associations, are implausible not in a funny way but in a distracting way: We keep doubting that this person would be acting this way in this situation. What kind of a risk assessor is Reuben if he *knows* he has irritable bowel syndrome, and nevertheless goes on a first date with Polly to dinner at a North African spice palace? Yes, his dinner gives the movie the opportunity to launch one of those extended sequences involving spectacular digestive, eliminatory, and regurgitative adventures, but we're aware it's a setup. As Stiller himself classically demonstrated in *There's Something About Mary*, embarrassment is comic when it is thrust upon you by accident or bad luck, not when you go looking for it yourself.

Of the Polly character, it can be said that the risk of her ever falling in love with a man like Reuben is a very long shot. What attracts her? His constipated personality? Low self-esteem? Workaholism? Neurotic inability to engage spontaneously with fun? She's a free spirit who lives in one of those apartments that look like they were inspired by an old Sandy Dennis movie. Her favorite occupation is salsa dancing, which for her approaches virtual sex, especially with her favorite partner, Javier (Jsu Garcia). Reuben, uncoordinated and inhibited, is jealous of Javier until he signs up for salsa lessons, which could have been funny, but are not.

There isn't a lot in the movie that is funny. I did like Philip Seymour Hoffman as Sandy, Reuben's best man; he's a former child star, now reduced to having strangers tell him how amazed they are that he's still alive. How he responds to this in one early scene is a small masterpiece of facial melodrama, but how many times does he have to slip and fall on slick floors before we get tired of it? I grant him this: He knows exactly how a fat man looks in a red cummerbund from a tuxedo rental agency.

Alec Baldwin does a lot of good supporting work (notably in *The Cooler*), and he's Reuben's boss, the head of the agency, a slickster whose toast at the wedding skates artfully at the edge of crudeness and then pirouettes out of danger. He assigns Reuben to somehow make a case for insuring the high-risk Leland Van Lew (Bryan Brown), leading to still more fish-out-of-water material. Reuben's fish is so consistently out of water in this movie, indeed, that after a while we begin to wish it was smoked.

Amandla! ★ ★ ★
PG-13, 105 m., 2003

Featuring Hugh Masekela, Abdullah Ibrahim, Miriam Makeba, and Vusi Mahlasela. A documentary directed by Lee Hirsch and produced by Hirsch and Sherry Simpson.

"We'll catch the early staff boat and get there before the tourists arrive," A. M. Kathrada told my wife and me, in Cape Town in November 2001. We were going the next morning to visit Robben Island, where for twenty-seven years Nelson Mandela and others accused of treason, including Kathrada, were held by the South African apartheid government. We were having dinner with Kathrada, who is of Indian descent, and his friend Barbara Hogan, who won a place in history as the first South African white woman convicted as a traitor.

In those days it was easy to become a traitor. *Amandla!*, a new documentary about the role of music in the overthrow of apartheid, begins with the exhumation of the bones of Vuyisile Mini, who wrote a song named "Beware, Verwoerd! (The Black Man Is Coming!)," aimed at the chief architect of South Africa's racist politics of separation. Mini was executed in 1964 and buried in a pauper's grave.

Robben Island lies some twenty miles offshore from Cape Town, and the view back toward the slopes of Table Mountain is breathtaking. When I was a student at the University of Cape Town in 1965, friends pointed it out, a speck across the sea, and whispered that Mandela was imprisoned there. It would be almost twenty-five years until he was released and asked by F. W. DeKlerk, Verwoerd's last white successor, to run for president. No one in 1965 or for many years later believed there would be a regime change in South Africa without a bloody civil war, but there was, and Cranford's, my favorite used book shop, can now legally be owned by black South Africans; it still has a coffee pot and crooked stairs to the crowded upstairs room.

Kathrada, now in his early seventies, is known by everyone on the staff boat. At the Robben Island Store, where we buy our tickets, he introduces us to the manager—a white man who used to be one of his guards, and who smuggled forbidden letters ("and even the occasional visitor") on and off the island. On the island, we walk under a crude arch that welcomes us in Afrikaans and English, and enter the prison building, which is squat and unlovely, thick with glossy lime paint. The office is not yet open and Kathrada cannot find a key.

"First I am locked in, now I am locked out," he observes cheerfully. Eventually the key is discovered and we arrive at the object of our visit, the cell where Mandela lived. It is about long enough to lie down in. "For the first seven years," Kathrada said, "we didn't have cots. You got used to sleeping on the floor."

White political prisoners like Barbara Hogan were kept in a Pretoria prison. There were not a lot of Indian prisoners, and Kathrada was jailed with Mandela's African group.

"They issued us different uniforms," he observed dryly. "I was an Indian, and was issued with long pants. Mandela and the other Africans were given short pants. They called them 'boys,' and gave them boys' pants."

A crude nutritional chart hung on the wall, indicating that Indians were given a few hundred calories more to eat every day, because South African scientists had somehow determined their minimal caloric requirements were a little greater than those of blacks. Weekdays, all of the men worked in a quarry, hammering rocks into gravel. No work was permitted on Sunday in the devoutly religious Afrikaans society. The prisoners were fed mostly whole grains, a few vegetables, a little fruit, very little animal protein. "As a result of this diet and exercise, plus all of the sunlight in the quarry," Kathrada smiled, "we were in good health and most of us still are. The sun on the white rocks and the quarry dust were bad for our eyes, however."

During the 1970s the apartheid government clamped such a tight lid on opposition that it seemed able to hold on forever. The uplifting film *Amandla!* argues that South Africa's music of protest played a crucial role in apartheid's eventual overthrow. Mandela's African National Congress was nonviolent from its birth until the final years of apartheid, when after an internal struggle one branch began to commit acts of bombing and sabotage (murder and torture had always been weapons of the whites). Music was the ANC's most dangerous weapon, and we see footage of streets lined with tens of thousands of marchers, singing and dancing, expressing an unquenchable spirit.

"We lost the country in the first place, to an extent, because before we fight, we sing," Hugh Masekela, the great South African jazzman, tells the filmmakers. "The Zulus would sing before they went into battle, so the British and Boers knew where they were and when they were coming."

There was a song about Nelson Mandela that was sung at every rally, even though mention of his name was banned, and toward the end of the film there is a rally to welcome him after his release from prison, and he sings along. It is one of those moments where words cannot do justice to the joy.

Amandla! (the Xhosa word means "power") was nine years in the making, directed by Lee Hirsch, produced with Sherry Simpson. It combines archival footage, news footage, reports from political exiles like Masekela and his former wife, Miriam Makeba, visits with famous local singers, an appearance by Archbishop Desmond Tutu, and a lot of music. The sound track CD could become popular like "The Buena Vista Social Club."

After the relatives of Vuyisile Mini disinter his bones, he is reburied in blessed ground under a proper memorial, and then his family holds a party. Among the songs they sing is "Beware, Verwoerd!" It is not a nostalgia piece, not dusty, not yet. They sing it not so much in celebration as in triumph and relief.

American Splendor ★ ★ ★ ★
R, 100 m., 2003

Paul Giamatti (Harvey Pekar), Harvey Pekar (Real Harvey), Hope Davis (Joyce Brabner), Joyce Brabner (Real Joyce), Shari Springer Berman (Interviewer), Earl Billings (Mr. Boats), James Urbaniak (Robert Crumb), Judah Friedlander (Toby Radloff), Robert Pulcini (Bob the Director), Toby Radloff (Real Toby), Madylin Sweeten (Danielle), Danielle Batone (Real Danielle). Directed by Shari Springer Berman and Robert Pulcini and produced by Ted Hope. Screenplay by Berman and Pulcini, based on the comic book series American Splendor by Harvey Pekar and Our Cancer Year by Joyce Brabner.

One of the closing shots of *American Splendor* shows a retirement party for Harvey Pekar, who is ending his career as a file clerk at a V.A. hospital in Cleveland. This is a real party, and it is a real retirement. Harvey Pekar, the star of comic books, the Letterman show, and now this movie, worked all of his life as a file clerk. When I met Harvey and his wife, Joyce Brabner, at Cannes 2003, she told me: "He's grade G-4. Grade G-2 is minimum wage. Isn't that something, after thirty years as a file clerk?"

Yes, but it got them to Cannes. Pekar is one of the heroes of graphic novels, which are comic books with a yearning toward the light. He had the good fortune to meet the legendary comic artist R. Crumb in the 1970s. He observed with his usual sour pessimism that comics were never written about people like him, and as he talked a lightbulb all but appeared above Crumb's head, and the comic book *American Splendor* was born, with Pekar as writer and Crumb as illustrator.

The books chronicle the life of a man very much indeed like Harvey Pekar. He works at a thankless job. He has friends at work, like the "world-class nerd" Toby Radloff, who share his complaints, although not at the Pekarian level of existential misery. The comic book brings him a visit from a fan named Joyce Brabner, who turns out improbably to be able to comprehend his existence while insisting on her own, and eventually they gain a daughter, Danielle Batone, sort of through osmosis (the daughter of a friend, she comes to visit, and de-

cides to stay). The books follow Harvey, Joyce and Danielle as they sail through life, not omitting *Our Cancer Year*, a book retelling his travails after Harvey finds a lump on a testicle.

The comics are true, deep, and funny precisely because they see that we are all superheroes doing daily battle against twisted and perverted villains. We have secret powers others do not suspect. We have secret identities. Our enemies may not be as colorful as the Joker or Dr. Evil, but certainly they are malevolent—who could be more hateful, for example, than an anal-retentive supervisor, an incompetent medical orderly, a greedy landlord? When Harvey fills with rage, only the graphics set him aside from the Hulk.

The peculiarity and genius of *American Splendor* was always that true life and fiction marched hand in hand. There was a real Harvey Pekar, who looked very much like the one in the comic book, and whose own life was being described. Now comes this magnificently audacious movie, in which fact and fiction sometimes coexist in the same frame. We see and hear the real Harvey Pekar, and then his story is played by the actor Paul Giamatti, sometimes with Harvey commenting on "this guy who is playing me." We see the real Joyce Brabner, and we see Hope Davis playing her. We concede that Giamatti and Davis have mastered not only the looks but the feels and even the souls of these two people. And then there is Judah Friedlander to play Toby Radloff, who we might think could not be played by anybody, but there the two Tobys are, and we can see it's a match.

The movie deals not merely with real and fictional characters, but even with levels of presentation. There are documentary scenes, fictional scenes, and then scenes illustrated and developed as comic books, with the drawings sometimes segueing into reality or back again. The filmmakers have taken the challenge of filming a comic book based on a life and turned it into an advantage—the movie is mesmerizing in the way it lures us into the daily hopes and fears of this Cleveland family.

The personality of the real Harvey Pekar is central to the success of everything. Pekar's genius is to see his life from the outside, as a life like all lives, in which eventual tragedy is given a daily reprieve. He is brutally honest. The conversations he has with Joyce are conversations like those we really have. We don't fight over trivial things, because nothing worth fighting over is trivial. As Harvey might say, "Hey, it's important to me!"

The Letterman sequences have the fascination of an approaching train wreck. Pekar really was a regular on the program in the 1980s, where he did not change in the slightest degree from the real Harvey. He gave as good as he got, until his resentments, angers, and grudges led him to question the fundamental realities of the show itself, and then he was bounced. We see real Letterman footage, and then a fictional re-creation of Pekar's final show. Letterman is not a bad guy, but he has a show to do, and Pekar is a good guest following his own agenda up to a point, but then he goes far, far beyond that point. When I talked with Pekar at Cannes, he confided that after Letterman essentially fired him and went to a commercial break, Dave leaned over and whispered into Harvey's ear: "You blew a good thing."

Well, he did. But blowing a good thing is Harvey's fate in life, just as stumbling upon a good thing is his victory. What we get in both cases is the unmistakable sense that Pekar does nothing for effect, that all of his decisions and responses proceed from some limitless well of absolute certitude. What we also discover is that Harvey is not entirely a dyspeptic grump, but has sweetness and hope waving desperately from somewhere deep within his despair.

This film is delightful in the way it finds its own way to tell its own story. There was no model to draw on, but Shari Springer Berman and Robert Pulcini, who wrote and directed it, have made a great film by trusting to Pekar's artistic credo, which amounts to: What you see is what you get. The casting of Giamatti and Davis is perfect, but of course it had to be, or the whole enterprise would have collapsed. Giamatti is not a million miles away from other characters he has played, in movies such as *Storytelling*, *Private Parts*, and *Man on the Moon*, but Davis achieves an uncanny transformation. I saw her in *The Secret Lives of Dentists*, playing a dentist, wife, and mother with no points in common with Joyce Brabner—not in look, not in style, not in identity. Now here she is as Joyce. I've met Joyce Brabner, and she's Joyce Brabner.

Movies like this seem to come out of nowhere, like free-standing miracles. But *American Splendor* does have a source, and its source is Harvey Pekar himself—his life, and what he has made of it. The guy is the real thing. He found Joyce, who is also the real thing, and Danielle found them, and as I talked with her I could see she was the real thing, too. She wants to go into showbiz, she told me, but she doesn't want to be an actress, because then she might be unemployable after forty. She said she wants to work behind the scenes. More longevity that way. Harvey nodded approvingly. Go for the pension.

America's Heart & Soul ★ ★
PG, 84 m., 2004

A documentary directed and produced by Louis Schwartzberg.

America's Heart & Soul may be the first feature-length documentary filmed entirely in the style of a television commercial. It tells the stories of about twenty Americans who are colorful, eccentric, courageous, goofy, or musically talented—sometimes all five—and it uses the shorthand of TV spots, in which the point is that these people are wonderful and so, gosh darn it, are the good folks at (insert name of corporation). In this case, the sponsor is America, a nation where, in this film, poverty is an opportunity, racism doesn't exist, and (most miraculous of all) everyone is self-employed doing a job they love. Nobody grinds away for the minimum wage in this America.

Even though the method of the filmmaker, Louis Schwartzberg, is slick, superficial, and relentlessly upbeat, the people he finds are genuine treasures. I wanted to see a whole film about most of them, which means this film is a series of frustrations. Still, it underlines a point I like to make when students ask me about employment prospects: Figure out what you love and find a way to do it, no matter how badly it pays, because you will enjoy yourself and probably end up happy. Midcareer test: If retirement seems better than the job you're doing, you're doing the wrong job.

The first character we meet in *America's Heart & Soul* is Thomas "Roudy" Roudebush, a cowboy in Telluride, Colorado, whose life has much improved since he got sober, but who still rides his horse into a bar for a drink (water, straight up). Then we meet Marc and Ann Savoy, Cajun musicians, and watch them making gumbo, and visit a black gospel singer named Mosie Burks, and a weaver named Minnie Yancey ("If I've woven ten feet into the rug and it still doesn't say 'yes,' I'll cut it right off and start again"). As she weaves, she looks out the window at her husband, plowing a field on one of the few surviving family farms.

In Vermont, George Woodard, a dairy farmer, milks his cows, plays in a string band, and stars as Dracula in a local production. We say hello to Ben Cohen, of Ben & Jerry's, as he invents a new flavor. We meet a hat maker. A chair maker. A wine maker. Men who fight oil well fires. A New Orleans jazz band. Patty Wagstaff of Florida, who is a champion acrobatic pilot.

Also, people who dance on cliffs at the ends of ropes. A blind mountain climber. Rick Hoyt, a marathon runner with cerebral palsy whose father, Dick, pushes his wheelchair. Paul Stone of Creede, Colorado, who spends his winters blowing up stuff real good (one of his cannon shells is made of ham and cheese). And David Krakauer, a klezmer musician influenced by Jimi Hendrix.

An opera singer. Salsa dancers. Michael Bennett of Chicago, an armed robber who started boxing in the pen, became captain of the U.S. Olympic boxing team, and works to keep kids off the streets. Cecil Williams, the pastor of the progressive Glide Church in San Francisco, which supplies a million meals for the homeless every year. People who decorate their cars as works of art. A Manhattan bike messenger who loves racing through traffic. Dan Klennert, who makes art out of junk. The Indian elder Charles Jimmie Sr., who releases a healed eagle back into the skies.

All of these people are happy, productive, creative, and unconventional, and if there were more of them in our society the news would be a lot more cheerful. They live in a parallel universe where everyone is oddball and fascinating and has a story that can be neatly wrapped up in a few minutes. Surely there is more to all of these people, a lot more, but *America's Heart & Soul* has miles to go before it sleeps.

In the middle of a montage I saw one shot, a few seconds long, that was unmistakably of Howard Armstrong, the legendary African-American string musician who died in August 2003 at the age of ninety-three. At my Overlooked Film Festival, I showed two documentaries made fifteen years apart about this miraculous man, whose art was as distinctive as his music, and whose life was a work in progress. Because I know how much there was to say about him, I can guess how much there is to say about the others in *America's Heart & Soul*. But this movie doesn't pause to find out; it's in such a hurry, it uses "&" because "and" would take too long. Working within the limitations of the star rating system, I give four stars to the subjects of this movie, and two stars to the way they have been boiled down into cute pictures and sound bites.

Analyze That ★ ★

R, 95 m., 2002

Robert De Niro (Paul Vitti), Billy Crystal (Dr. Ben Sobel), Lisa Kudrow (Laura Sobel), Joe Viterelli (Jelly), Cathy Moriarty (Patti LoPresti), Joe D'Onofrio (Gunman), Joseph Bono (Wiseguy), John Finn (Richard Chapin). Directed by Harold Ramis and produced by Jane Rosenthal and Paula Weinstein. Screenplay by Peter Tolan, Peter Steinfeld, and Ramis.

The success of *Analyze This* (1999) made *Analyze That* inevitable, but was it necessary? What seemed like a clever idea the first time feels like a retread the second, as mob boss Paul Vitti (Robert De Niro) goes back into therapy with Dr. Ben Sobel (Billy Crystal). The first film more or less exhausted the possibilities of this idea, as the second one illustrates.

Analyze This was never more than a sitcom, but the casting gave it an aura. De Niro as a neurotic mobster was a funny idea, and Crystal as a shrink was good casting because of his ability to seem smart even during panic attacks. Lisa Kudrow, then the shrink's girlfriend, now his wife, has a nice off-balance disbelieving way with dialogue that plays against Crystal instead of merely outshouting him, and there was also the mammoth presence of Joe Viterelli as Jelly, the boss's loyal chauffeur and sidekick.

All of that worked the first time, and it kind of works, sometimes, in the second film. But the story has the ring of contrivance. If the first film seemed to flow naturally from the premise, this one seems to slink uneasily onto the screen, aware that it feels exactly like a facile, superficial recycling job.

As the film opens, Sobel is attending his father's funeral, but takes a cell call from Sing Sing, right there in the front row at temple. Turns out Vitti has turned goofy and does nothing all day but sing songs from *West Side Story*. Is he crazy, or faking it? Whether he's faking it or not, he knows all the words. He gets no less goofy after he's released into the custody of Sobel and his wife, Laura (Kudrow), and placed under their supervision—in their home. Laura *hates* this idea, but the FBI insists on it: Vitti's good behavior is Sobel's responsibility.

The film then descends into an unconvincing, contrived heist subplot, with Sobel linked with the robbers. And Cathy Moriarty (De Niro's wife in *Raging Bull*) turns up as the head of a rival gang, in a rivalry that never seems anything more than the excuse for some routine mob-war threat routines. Harold Ramis, who directed and cowrote (as he did with the first film), is a gifted filmmaker, the author of many great laughs in the movies, but he should reflect that there is a reason most sequels are not directed by the same men who made the originals: A movie that inspires a sequel, if it is any good, incorporates qualities that cannot be duplicated.

What we get in *Analyze That* are several talented actors delivering their familiar screen personas in the service of an idiotic plot. There is undeniable pleasure to be had in hearing De Niro say, yet once again, "You're good. No! You're good!" to Crystal, and watching De Niro use that beatific smile as if his character is saintly to bestow such praise (a compliment from De Niro is somewhat like being knighted). And Crystal, in this character as in life, is able to suggest that his mind runs so rapidly it spits out the truth before his better judgment can advise him. Lisa Kudrow, sadly underused here, plays not the wife who doesn't understand, but the wife who understands all too well.

There is also the question of Joe Viterelli as Jelly. Writing about his work in the first movie, I saw him playing not just a mobster, but "an older man who is weary after many years in service, but loyal and patient with his weirdo boss." The sad thing about *Analyze That* is that Viterelli is invited back but not made to feel welcome at the party. We miss the sense that De Niro counts on him, that he comes as part of the package. Now De Niro's focus is on Crystal. And if Vitti and Sobel are a double act, the point of the movie is missing.

And Now Ladies and Gentlemen
★ ★ ½
PG-13, 126 m., 2003

Jeremy Irons (Valentin), Patricia Kaas (Jane Lester), Thierry Lhermitte (Thierry), Allesandra Martines (Françoise), Ticky Holgado (Boubou), Yvan Attal (David), Souad Amidou (Police Inspector), Claudia Cardinale (Countess Falconnetti). Directed by Claude Lelouch and produced by Lelouch. Screenplay by Lelouch, Pierre Leroux, and Pierre Uytterhoeven.

And Now Ladies and Gentlemen is a title that stopped me cold. What could it possibly have to do with this movie about jewel thieves, brain tumors, sailing alone around the world, faith healers, adultery, cell-phone trickery, gigolos, police work, Paris, Morocco, and nightclub chantoosies? Suddenly I understood: The title refers not to the plot but to the performance by the director, Claude Lelouch, who pulls a new plot twist or exotic location out of his hat in every reel. The movie is so extravagant and outrageous in its storytelling that it resists criticism: It's self-satirizing.

For such a story you require an actor like Jeremy Irons, someone dour and inward and filled simultaneously with lust and with a conviction that the lust can never be satisfied. You would not want an extroverted actor, or a heroic one; if the story whirls, the actor must remain still, or the audience risks vertigo. For such a story, also, you require an audience in on the joke: The slightest shred of common sense would explode this movie. I fondly recall a conversation I had with Ken Turan of the *Los Angeles Times*, after we had seen *Gerry*, in which two guys get lost in the desert and walk for the rest of the movie. We agreed that the ordinary moviegoer would find it tedious beyond all reason, but that it could be appreciated by experienced and seasoned moviegoers—like ourselves, for example.

And Now Ladies and Gentlemen is not tedious, at least. It errs in the opposite direction. Like a sampler of Claude Lelouch's greatest hits, it has a score by Michel Legrand, and the technique of draining the color from some scenes, which reminds us that Lelouch alternated color and black-and-white in his first great hit, *A Man and a Woman* (1966). Oh, and it begins with a jewel robbery whose technique is inspired by *La Bonne Année* (1973), which itself inspired Peter Falk's astonishing performance in the remake, *Happy New Year* (1987). The theft depends on disguise and deception, and all one can say is that Falk (and Lino Ventura in the original) were a lot more deceptive than Jeremy Irons is this time. His disguise looks like something whipped up for a costume party.

No matter; one thing follows another, and soon Irons (whose character is the ominously named Valentin Valentin) falls in love with Françoise (Allesandra Martines), only to eventually kiss her farewell before setting off to sail single-handedly around the globe. (Thierry Lhermitte, the Other Man du Jour of the French cinema, is poised to step in.) Valentin, alas, gets no further than the middle of the Mediterranean before passing out, and he is eventually found, rescued, and brought to Morocco, where friendly Dr. Lamy (Jean-Marie Bigard) diagnoses a brain tumor.

At this point, one hour into the movie, Valentin meets the other major character. Her name is Jane Lester, she is a nightclub singer played by the German singer Patricia Kaas, and, wouldn't you know, she has a brain tumor too. She knows because she starts blanking on lyrics, although since she sings with a handheld mike while strolling past the tables of oblivious diners, she is the first to notice.

The movie is episodic beyond all reason, as when Valentin Valentin and Jane Lester attend a faith healer, who suggests they go to the grave of a mighty saint who may be able to cure them—and, given the movie's happy ending, who is to say she did not? Meanwhile, in the hotel where Jane is performing, a faded countess (Claudia Cardinale—yes, Claudia Cardinale) loses some priceless jewels while her husband is out of town on business, and the police inspector (Amidou) at first suspects Valentin. This is a neat irony, when you come to think of it, since Valentin is in fact a jewel thief. The inspector is a cop of the world and observes, "I don't check alibis. Only the innocent don't have alibis."

Will the jewels be found, the thief arrested, Valentin cured and healed, Jane Lester healed and loved, Françoise comforted by Thierry, the journey resumed, the lyrics recalled? Oh, and I almost forgot the scam at the auction house. The answers to these questions are handed out at the end to the grateful audience. Did I dislike this movie? Not at all. Was it necessary for me to see it? No, but once it had my attention at least it labored sincerely to keep it. I can't quite recommend the movie, but I confess a certain fugitive affection for it.

Anger Management ★ ★
PG-13, 101 m., 2003

Jack Nicholson (Dr. Buddy Rydell), Adam Sandler (Dave Buznik), Marisa Tomei (Linda), Luis Guzman (Lou), Allen Covert (Andrew), Lynne Thigpen (Judge Daniels), Woody Harrelson (Galaxia), John Turturro (Chuck). Directed by Peter Segal and produced by Barry Bernardi, Derek Dauchy, Todd Garner, Jack Giarraputo, John Jacobs, and Joe Roth. Screenplay by David Dorfman.

The concept is inspired. The execution is lame. *Anger Management*, a film that might have been one of Adam Sandler's best, becomes one of Jack Nicholson's worst. Because Nicholson has a superb track record and a sure nose for trash, it's obvious the movie was a Sandler project with Nicholson as hired talent, not the other way around. The fact that four of the producers were involved in *The Master of Disguise* and *The Animal* indicates that quality control was not an issue.

Everything about the way the movie goes wrong—the dumbing down of plot developments, the fascination with Sandler's whiny one-note character, the celebrity cameos, the cringing sentimentality—indicates a product from the Sandler assembly line. No doubt Sandler's regular fans will love this movie, which is a return to form after the brilliant

Punch-Drunk Love. Nicholson's fans will be appalled.

And yet there might really have been something here. When I heard the premise, I began to smile. Sandler plays a mild-mannered guy named Dave Buznik, who just got a promotion at work and is in love with his fiancée, Linda (Marisa Tomei). Through a series of bizarre misunderstandings on an airplane trip, he is misdiagnosed as a person filled with rage, and is assigned to therapy with the famed anger specialist Dr. Buddy Rydell (Jack Nicholson).

Nicholson's early scenes are his best because he brings an intrinsic interest to every character he plays, and we don't yet know how bad the movie is. He wears a beard making him look like a cross between Stanley Kubrick and Lenin, and works his eyebrows and sardonic grin with the zeal of a man who was denied them during the making of *About Schmidt.* He introduces Dave to a therapy group including the first of many guest stars in the movie, Luis Guzman and John Turturro. Both are clearly nuts—and so is Dr. Rydell, as Dave finds himself trapped in an escalating spiral of trouble, climaxing in a bar fight and a court appearance where he explains, "I was being attacked by someone while stealing a blind man's cane."

The blind man is played by Harry Dean Stanton. Also on display in the movie are Woody Harrelson (as a drag queen), John C. Reilly (as a Buddhist monk who gets a wedgie), Heather Graham, Mayor Rudolph Giuliani, and (ho, ho) the angry Bobby Knight. The use of celebrity walk-ons in a movie is often the sign of desperation, but rarely does one take over the movie and drive it to utter ruin, as Giuliani's role does. The closing scenes in Yankee Stadium, with the hero proposing to his girl over a loudspeaker, passed into the realm of exhausted cliché before Sandler was born.

Most good comedy has an undercurrent of truth. The genius of *Punch-Drunk Love* was that it identified and dealt with the buried rage that does indeed seem to exist in most of Sandler's characters. The falsity of *Anger Management* is based on the premise that Dave Buznik is not angry enough—that he needs to act out more and assert himself. That provides the explanation for the plot's "surprise," which will come as old news to most audiences.

I said that Nicholson brings an intrinsic interest to his characters. Sandler does not. His character is usually a blank slate waiting to be written on by the movie. While Nicholson has infinite variations and notes, Sandler is usually much the same. It's said the difference between character actors and stars is that the star is expected to deliver the same elements in every movie, while the character actor is supposed to change and surprise.

Nicholson, who has been a star character actor since he grinned triumphantly on the back of the motorcycle in *Easy Rider,* was part of a revolution that swept away old-model stars and replaced them with such character-stars as Dustin Hoffman, Robert De Niro, and, recently, Nicolas Cage, William H. Macy, or Steve Buscemi.

Sandler was wonderful in *Punch-Drunk Love* because, for once, he was in a smart movie that understood his screen persona. Paul Thomas Anderson, who wrote and directed that film, studied Sandler, appreciated his quality, and wrote a story for it. Most of Sandler's other movies have been controlled by Sandler himself (he is executive producer this time), and repeat the persona but do not seem willing to see it very clearly. This is particularly true in the cloying romantic endings, in which we see what a very good fellow he is after all.

That there is a market for this I do not deny. But imagine, just imagine, a movie in which Dave Buznik truly was exploding with rage, and Dr. Buddy Rydell really was an anger therapist. This movie should be remade immediately, this time with Jack Nicholson as executive producer, and Adam Sandler as hired gun.

Antwone Fisher ★ ★ ★ ½
PG-13, 113 m., 2002

Derek Luke (Antwone Fisher), Joy Bryant (Cheryl Smolley), Denzel Washington (Jerome Davenport), Salli Richardson (Berta Davenport), Earl Billings (Uncle James), Kevin Connolly (Slim), Viola Davis (Eva), Vernee Watson-Johnson (Antwone's Aunt). Directed by Denzel Washington and produced by Todd Black, Randa Haines, and Washington. Screenplay by Antwone Fisher.

Antwone Fisher is a good sailor, but he has a hair-trigger temper, and it lands him in the office of the base psychiatrist, Dr. Jerome Davenport. He refuses to talk. Davenport says he can wait. Naval regulations require them to have three sessions of therapy, and the first session doesn't start until Antwone talks. So week after week Antwone sits there while the doctor does paperwork, until finally they have a conversation:

"I understand you like to fight."
"That's the only way some people learn."
"But you pay the price for teaching them."

This conversation will continue, in one form or another, until Fisher (Derek Luke) has returned to the origin of his troubles, and Davenport (Denzel Washington) has made some discoveries as well. *Antwone Fisher,* based on the true story of the man who wrote the screenplay, is a film that begins with the everyday lives of naval personnel in San Diego, and ends with scenes so true and heartbreaking that tears welled up in my eyes both times I saw the film.

I do not cry easily at the movies; years can go past without tears. I have noticed that when I am deeply affected emotionally, it is not by sadness so much as by goodness. Antwone Fisher has a confrontation with his past, and a speech to the mother who abandoned him, and a reunion with his family, that create great, heartbreaking, joyous moments.

The story behind the film is extraordinary. Fisher was a security guard at the Sony studio in Hollywood when his screenplay came to the attention of the producers. Denzel Washington was so impressed he chose it for his directorial debut. The newcomer Derek Luke, cast in the crucial central role after dozens of more-experienced actors had been auditioned, turned out to be a friend of Antwone's; he didn't tell that to the filmmakers because he thought it would hurt his chances. The film is based on truth but some characters and events have been dramatized, we are told at the end. That is the case with every "true story."

The film opens with a dream image that will resonate through the film: Antwone, as a child, is welcomed to a dinner table by all the members of his family, past and present. He awakens from his dream to the different reality of life onboard an aircraft carrier. He will eventually tell Davenport that his father was murdered two months before he was born, that his mother was in prison at the time and abandoned him, and that he was raised in a cruel foster home. Another blow came when his closest childhood friend was killed in a robbery. Antwone, who is constitutionally incapable of crime, considers that an abandonment, too.

As Antwone's weekly sessions continue, he meets another young sailor, Cheryl Smolley (Joy Bryant). He is shy around her, asks Davenport for tips on dating, keeps it a secret that he is still a virgin. In a time when movie romances end in bed within a scene or two, their relationship is sweet and innocent. He is troubled, he even gets in another fight, but she sees that he has a good heart and she believes in him.

Davenport argues with the young man that all of his troubles come down to a need to deal with his past. He needs to return to Ohio and see if he can find family members. He needs closure. At first Fisher resists these doctor's orders, but finally, with Cheryl's help, he flies back. And that is where the preparation of the early scenes pays off in confrontations of extraordinary power.

Without detailing what happens, I will mention three striking performances from this part of the movie, by Vernee Watson-Johnson as Antwone's aunt, by Earl Billings as his uncle, and by Viola Davis as his mother. Earlier this year Davis appeared as the maid in *Far from Heaven* and as the space station psychiatrist in *Solaris.* Now this performance. It is hard to believe it is the same actress. She hardly says a word, as Antwone spills out his heart in an emotionally shattering speech.

Antwone's story is counterpointed with the story of Dr. Davenport and his wife, Berta (Salli Richardson). There are issues in their past, too, and in a sense Davenport and Fisher are in therapy together. There is a sense of anticlimax when Davenport has his last heartfelt talk with Antwone, because the film has reached its emotional climax in Ohio and there is nowhere else we want it to take us. But the relationship between the two men is handled by Washington, as the director, with close and caring attention. Hard to believe Derek Luke is a newcomer;

easy to believe why Washington decided he was the right actor to play Antwone Fisher.

Anything but Love ★ ★ ★
PG-13, 99 m., 2003

Andrew McCarthy (Elliot Shepard), Isabel Rose (Billie Golden), Cameron Bancroft (Greg Ellenbogen), Alix Korey (Laney Golden), Ilana Levine (Marcy), Sean Arbuckle (TJ), Victor Argo (Sal), Eartha Kitt (Herself). Directed by Robert Cary and produced by Aimee Schoof and Isen Robbins. Screenplay by Cary and Isabel Rose.

Anything but Love is a new movie like those old musicals you watch on TV late at night. Filmed in the colors of newborn Technicolor, plotted as a tribute to the conventions of Hollywood romance, filled with standard songs, it's by and for people who love those kinds of movies. Others will find it clichéd and predictable, but they won't understand.

Remember the hapless guy Oscar Levant always played? The one who secretly loved the heroine but never won her? The one original element in *Anything but Love* is that Oscar Levant finally gets the girl. She is the flame-haired Billie Golden (Isabel Rose). I'm willing to bet my small change that she was named for Billie Holiday and the Golden Age of MGM musicals. She sings torchy standards in a tacky motel supper club at the "JFK Skytel," where the owner loves her work but has to change formats because business is bad.

That grizzled old Victor Argo plays the owner is almost too good to be true. That he is named Sal is inevitable. That he is the longtime boyfriend of Billie's mother, Laney (Alix Korey), shows that Rose and director Robert Cary have been studying the late show. And, of course, Billie has another job; she's a waitress at a high-class club headlining Eartha Kitt, playing herself. An early shot frames Billie's face in the round window of the door between the kitchen and the showroom, as she yearningly watches Kitt. This shot is obligatory in all movies about waitresses who want to be stars.

Times are hard for Billie and her mother, who hits the bottle. Sal doesn't want to fire her, and suggests a compromise: She might be able to keep working if she accompanies herself on the piano. Her playing is rusty, so she signs up for lessons, only to discover that her new teacher, Elliot (Andrew McCarthy), is the same jerk who sabotaged her at an audition by screwing up the accompaniment. Of course they hate each other. This is essential so that they can love each other later.

There is another possible path Billie could take. Greg Ellenbogen (Cameron Bancroft) has come back into her life. He was the high school hunk she had a crush on, now a thirtyish success story who has lots of money and decides (as a logical exercise, I think) that he should get married. They court, they get engaged, she will be financially secure, and her dream of becoming a chanteuse can be forgotten (Greg suggests) as she raises their children and sings— oh, at parties and benefits and stuff like that.

Is there a person alive who doesn't know whether Billie chooses Greg or Elliot? But, of course, there must be enormous obstacles and pitfalls along the way, not to mention those kinds of overblown fantasy scenes much beloved of old musicals, where everything ratchets up six degrees into dreamy schmaltz before finally ending with a close-up of the heroine's face as she comes back to earth.

The Andrew McCarthy character inhabits a sparsely furnished walk-up studio, is dyspeptic and cynical, doesn't value his talent, and in general is a clone of the Oscar Levant character. He doesn't chain smoke, the cigarette dangling from his lips while he plays, and that's a missed opportunity. When it's announced that he may move to Paris, I thought—of course! He wants to be Gene Kelly's roommate in *An American in Paris*.

The movie is not perfect. It has been shot on a budget close to the minimum wage, and has the usual problem of crowd scenes without a large enough crowd. But it takes joy in its work, and that makes up for a lot. Eartha Kitt has a small but very functional role, singing a song (wonderfully) and offering the kind of advice that absolutely must be supplied in a plot of this kind. Was it Kitt's idea or the filmmakers' that after offering that advice she doesn't get all sentimental but stays tartly in character, reminding Billie that she is the star and Billie is the waitress? I liked that moment.

One obvious flaw: There is a wedding scene (I will not say who with, or even whether it is real or not—and no, don't think that's a hint). The scene bursts into fantasy and imaginings at precisely that moment when it should be played straight in order to exploit the emotions the movie has been building toward. But in general the movie works just as it wants to, and you will either enjoy it for that, or you will be the kind of person for whom the names Kathryn Grayson, Doris Day, Howard Keel, Dennis Morgan, Ann Miller, Jack Carson, Ann Blyth, and Gordon MacRae have no meaning.

Anything Else ★ ★ ★

R, 108 m., 2003

Woody Allen (David Dobel), Jason Biggs (Jerry Falk), Christina Ricci (Amanda), Stockard Channing (Paula), Danny DeVito (Harvey), Jimmy Fallon (Bob Styles). Directed by Woody Allen and produced by Letty Aronson. Screenplay by Allen.

The dialogue in Woody Allen's *Anything Else* is an exercise of neurotic bravery, a defense against fear and insecurity. His characters are doubtful about their prospects in life. Careers aren't going well, and romance works only through self-deception. To hold despair at bay they talk and talk, and because Allen is a master of comic dialogue, it is our pleasure to listen.

The new movie has both a mentor and a narrator, so one character gives insights about life, and the other gives insights about him. The hero is Jerry Falk (Jason Biggs), a would-be comedy writer whose career is going nowhere, and his adviser is David Dobel (Allen), a sixty-ish New Jersey schoolteacher whose career has gone nowhere; he hasn't stopped hoping, but he keeps the day job. They meet in the park for long talks, Dobel doing most of the talking, Jerry grateful at first and then dubious: If Dobel knows so much, how come he's still stuck?

Jerry was once fully and happily in love with Brooke (KaDee Strickland), a woman who presented no difficulties, which was perhaps the problem, since he left her for Amanda (Christina Ricci), a woman who consists of difficulties. Amanda is an actress who seems to keep Jerry around primarily as a foil for intimate improv scenes in which she explains the ways his life must be miserable if he is to continue enjoying her company. He asks if she doesn't love him. "Just because when you touch me I pull away?" she replies. At one point she declares a six-month moratorium on sex. When the ever-optimistic Jerry makes reservations at a fancy restaurant to celebrate their anniversary, she stands him up ("I already ate").

Jerry introduces Amanda to David. David's verdict is instantaneous: "She's cheating on you." He advises Jerry to spy on her, which he does by lurking in stairwells and skulking in doorways for hours at a time, until finally he thinks he has enough proof to confront her, not realizing that in matters of cheating the worst thing you can do is expose the other person—because then they have their excuse to leave. Better to suffer in silence, as the wise Charles Bukowski once advised, until they figure out which one they want.

Anything Else is not simply a comedy about Jerry's romance, Amanda's deceptions, and David's advice, however. There's a darker undercurrent. David has fears, not all of them revealed, and takes his young protégé to a gun shop to buy him a weapon. Everyone needs a gun, he explains, to feel safer, to protect themselves, and so on. Jerry is dubious, Amanda is appalled, and David seems to be revealing only the surface of his fears.

Amanda moves out, moves back in, and then her mother, Paula (Stockard Channing), moves in too, with a personality that overcrowds the apartment. Channing is a great original, an actress with the ability to make absurd statements as if anyone would agree with them. She wants to start over as a torch singer, she says, and has a young boyfriend she met at an AA meeting (apparently not a successful one, since they're soon doing coke together). With a girl who doesn't want to live with him and her mother who does, Jerry's almost ready to listen when David suggests he dump everything so that just the two of them can leave for Los Angeles, where all the jobs are anyway.

But that would mean leaving Harvey (Danny DeVito), Jerry's longtime agent, who charges him 25 percent, which is way above the industry standard, but then again, Jerry is his only client, and never works anyway. DeVito brings electric energy to his scenes, as an intense dynamo who feels so strongly about the agent-client relationship that when Jerry hints it may be ending, he pulls a scene in a restaurant that more or less defines the notion of a public spectacle.

The movie avoids the usual pitfalls of comedies about young romance, and gets jolts from the supporting work by Channing and DeVito. And Allen is inimitable, as the worrywart who backs into every decision, protesting and moaning about the pitfalls and certain disappointment sure to lie ahead. At a time when so many American movies keep dialogue at a minimum so they can play better overseas, what a delight to listen to smart people whose conversation is like a kind of comic music.

Note: Here's a strange thing. The studio, DreamWorks, seems to be trying to conceal Woody Allen's presence in the movie. He is the writer and director, and has top billing in the credits, but he is never seen in the trailer, the commercials, or the TV review clips. The trailer gives full-screen credits to Jason Biggs and Christina Ricci, but only belatedly adds "From Woody Allen," not mentioning that he also stars. It's as if they have the treasure of a Woody Allen movie and they're trying to package it for the American Pie *crowd.*

Ararat ★ ★ ½
R, 116 m., 2002

David Alpay (Raffi), Charles Aznavour (Edward Saroyan), Eric Bogosian (Rouben), Brent Carver (Philip), Marie-Josée Croze (Celia), Bruce Greenwood (Martin/Clarence Ussher), Arsinée Khanjian (Ani), Elias Koteas (Ali/Jevdet Bey), Christopher Plummer (David). Directed by Atom Egoyan and produced by Egoyan and Robert Lantos. Screenplay by Egoyan.

Atom Egoyan has something he wants us to know. In 1915, he tells us in his new film *Ararat*, Turkey committed genocide against its Armenian population, massacring two-thirds of its 1.5 million citizens of Armenian descent. This crime, denied to this day by Turkey, has largely been wiped from the pages of history.

Egoyan is one of Canada's best and most respected directors. He and his wife, the actress Arsinée Khanjian, are Canadians of Armenian descent. When he told his children of the massacre, he has said in interviews, they wanted to know if Turkey had ever apologized. His answer is contained in *Ararat*. Unfortunately, it is couched in such a needlessly confusing film that most people will leave the theater impressed, not by the crime, but by the film's difficulty. Egoyan's work often elegantly considers various levels of reality and uses shifting points of view, but here he has constructed a film so labyrinthine that it defeats his larger purpose.

The story has three central strands: (1) A film is being made about the atrocity; (2) some of the scenes of this film-within-the-film recreate historical incidents for our information; (3) there is a web of connections between the people working on the film and other characters in the story.

We meet an art historian named Ani (Arsinée Khanjian) who lectures on the Armenian artist Arshile Gorky, whose mother was one of the Turkish victims. Ani's husband died in an attempt to assassinate a Turkish official some fifteen years earlier. She has a son named Raffi (David Alpay) from her first marriage, and a stepdaughter named Celia (Marie-Josée Croze) from a second marriage with a man who, Celia believes, was driven to suicide by Ani. When Ani lectures on Gorky, Celia often attends in order to heckle her with questions about her dead father. Further complicating this emotional tangle, Raffi and Celia are sleeping with each other.

There is another sexual-political connection. When Raffi attempts to pass through Canadian customs with several film cans from Europe, he is questioned at length by a customs inspector named David (Christopher Plummer), who is on his last day on the job. Raffi says the cans contain unexposed documentary footage needed for the movie. We know, because of a scene at breakfast that day, that David's son Philip (Brent Carver) is the lover of an actor named Ali (Elias Koteas), who plays the barbaric Turkish general Jevdet Bey in the film. Thus David is in a position to know the film being brought in by Raffi may not be needed for the project.

We meet the director of the film, named Edward (Charles Aznavour), and see him on the set, filming scenes that are often presented as reality before the camera pulls back to reveal another camera. And we meet the screenwriter, Rouben (Eric Bogosian). Both Aznavour and Bogosian, who are of Armenian ancestry, are used to provide more information about the atrocities, as is the character of Clarence Ussher (Bruce Greenwood), a character in Aznavour's film. He was an American physician who was an eyewitness to the massacres and wrote a book about them.

The questioning at the customs station goes on, apparently, for hours, because David, on his last day on the job, is trying to determine through sheer skill whether the cans contain film or heroin. He could open them (in a dark room to avoid spoiling the film), but that would be too simple, and perhaps he thinks that by understanding the young man before him, he can gain a better insight into his own son.

The scenes in the movie-within-a-movie document horrendous acts by the Turks against the Armenians, including one sequence in which women are burned alive. The film also shows Gorky as a young boy, shouldering arms against the Turks. There are flashbacks to show the adult Gorky painting in exile in New York. And discussion of the relative truth of two portraits: one a photo of Gorky with his mother, the other the painting he has based on this portrait. It is the same painting we have heard Ani lecturing about.

You may be feeling some impatience at the complexity of this plot. It is too much, too heavily layered, too needlessly difficult, too opaque. Individual scenes leap out and have a life of their own: Khanjian makes the difficulties of her own character very affecting, the Plummer episode is like a small, perfect character study, and I remember the re-created atrocities as if from another film, which is indeed how they are presented.

Ararat clearly comes from Egoyan's heart, and it conveys a message he urgently wants to be heard: that the world should acknowledge and be shamed that a great crime was committed against his people. The message I receive from the movie, however, is a different one: that it is difficult to know the truth of historical events, and that all reports depend on the point of view of the witness and the state of mind of those who listen to the witness. That second message is conveyed by the film, but I am not sure it presents Eyogan's intention. Perhaps this movie was so close to the director's heart that he was never able to stand back and get a good perspective on it—that he is as conflicted as his characters, and as confused in the face of shifting points of view.

Note: In the film, Hitler is quoted discussing his plans for genocide and asking, "Who remembers the extermination of the Armenians?" The film presents this as fact, although there is enormous controversy over whether Hitler actually ever said it.

Around the World in 80 Days ★ ★ ★
PG, 120 m., 2004

Jackie Chan (Passepartout), Steve Coogan (Phileas Fogg), Cecile De France (Monique La Roche), Jim Broadbent (Lord Kelvin), Kathy Bates (Queen Victoria), Arnold Schwarzenegger (Prince Hapi), John Cleese (Grizzled Sergeant), Owen Wilson (Wilbur Wright), Luke Wilson (Orville Wright), Karen Mok (General Fang). Directed by Frank Coraci and produced by Bill Badalato and Hal Lieberman. Screenplay by David N. Titcher, David Benullo, and David Goldstein, based on the novel by Jules Verne.

Here against all probability is a jolly comedy made from that wheezy high concept, *Around the World in 80 Days*. I grew up with Phileas Fogg and his picaresque journey, plundered the Classics Illustrated comic, read the Jules Verne novel, and attended Michael Todd's 1956 film, but I never thought the story was much of a cliff-hanger. Even in its time, eighty days seemed doable. Verne's *20,000 Leagues Under the Sea* and *From the Earth to the Moon* were more like it.

But here's a film version that does some lateral thinking, that moves Fogg off dead center and makes Jackie Chan's Passepartout the real hero, and lingers for comic effect instead of always looking at its watch. The Todd production was famous for its wall-to-wall cameos ("Look! That piano player! Why, it's Frank Sinatra!"). And here we have Kathy Bates as Queen Victoria, Owen and Luke Wilson as the Wright brothers, John Cleese as a British sergeant, and, funniest of all, Arnold Schwarzenegger as a Turkish prince.

The setup is familiar. Phileas Fogg is much resented by the members of the fogbound Explorers' Club because of his crackpot inventions and fevered schemes. Lord Kelvin (Jim Broadbent), president of the club, is a mainstream scientist who no doubt gave his name to the scientific term "kelvin," which measures how many degrees of separation there are between you and Sir Kelvin Bacon, the inventor of gravity.

Fogg claims the world can be circled in eighty days. Kelvin is outraged by his presumption, and makes him a dare: Either (a) Fogg circles the globe by the deadline and Kelvin resigns from the club, or (b) Fogg resigns and discontinues his confounded experiments. Fogg (Steve Coogan) accepts the bet, and as he's preparing for his journey he hires a new valet, Passepartout (Jackie Chan).

This valet we have already met, making a sudden exit from the Bank of England after having stolen the priceless Jade Buddha, a relic much treasured by his native village in China, but nabbed by the Black Scorpions, hirelings of the evil warlord Fang. Passepartout's hidden motive for joining the journey is to elude the police, sneak out of England, and return the Buddha to China.

So off we go, by horse, train, ship, hot air balloon, and so on. There is a brief stop at an art fair in France, where the beautiful Monique (Cecile De France) insists on joining their expedition and cannot be dissuaded; we think at first she has a nefarious motive, but no, she's probably taken a class in screenplay construction and knows that the film requires a sexy female lead. This is not the first case in cinematic history of a character voluntarily entering a movie because of the objective fact that she is required.

Fogg is the straight man to Passepartout for much of the journey, allowing Chan to steal scenes with shameless mugging, astonished double-takes, and his remarkable physical agility. But all goes more or less as expected until the three arrive in Turkey and are made the guests of Prince Hapi (Arnold Schwarzenegger), whose hospitality is hard to distinguish from captivity. Smitten by the fragrant

Monique, he invites all three to join him in the Turkish equivalent of a hot tub, observing ruefully, "I'm always embarrassing myself in front of visiting dignitaries." It may not be worth the price of admission, but it almost is, to hear Schwarzenegger proudly boast, "Guess who else was in this pool? U.S. president Rutherford B. Hayes!"

The director, Frank Coraci, takes advantage of Verne's structure to avoid the need for any real continuity. When one location runs out of gags, the three move on to the next, including an extended stay in Passepartout's native China, where Fang and the Black Scorpions do all they can to win back the Jade Buddha from the grateful village where it has exerted its benign charm for centuries.

Then across the Pacific and into the American desert, where the travelers encounter a couple of traveling bicycle salesmen, Wilbur and Orville Wright (Owen and Luke Wilson). They generously share their ideas for an airplane, and that comes in handy in the mid-Atlantic, when Fogg's chartered steamer runs out of fuel and the intrepid circumnavigators invent an airplane and fly to London. Oh, and before that there's an extended martial arts scene in the New York warehouse where the head of the Statue of Liberty provides a gigantic prop.

None of this amounts to anything more than goofy fun, but that's what the ads promise, and the movie delivers. It's light as a fly, but springs some genuinely funny moments, especially by Schwarzenegger, the Wilsons, and the irrepressible Chan.

The California governor's scenes were shot before he took office, and arguably represent his last appearance in a fiction film; if so, he leaves the movies as he entered, a man who shares our amusement at his improbability, and has a canny sense of his own image and possibilities. I met him when the documentary *Pumping Iron* was being released, and Mr. Universe was the first of the offices he would hold. I liked him then, I like him now, and I remember that when I introduced the film at the USA Film Festival in Dallas, he greeted the audience and then slipped off to the green room to study his business textbooks. He refused to be dismissed as muscles with an accent, but he got the joke.

Assassination Tango ★ ★ ★

R, 114 m., 2003

Robert Duvall (John J. Anderson), Ruben Blades (Miguel), Kathy Baker (Maggie), Luciana Pedraza (Manuela), Julio Oscar Mechoso (Orlando), James Keane (Whitey), Frank Gio (Frankie), Katherine Micheaux Miller (Jenny). Directed by Robert Duvall and produced by Rob Carliner and Duvall. Screenplay by Duvall.

Robert Duvall's *Assassination Tango* is not entirely about crime or dance, and that will be a problem for some audiences. "More assassination, less tango!" demands the on-line critic Jon Popick. But I have seen countless movies about assassination and not a few about the tango, and while Duvall's movie doesn't entirely succeed, what it attempts is intriguing. It wants to lock itself inside the mind of a man whose obsessions distract him from the wider world.

John J. Anderson (Duvall) talks to himself a lot, carrying on a bemused commentary that may eventually descend into dementia, but not yet. No longer young, he is a professional hit man who plans to retire and devote his life to his woman, Maggie (Kathy Baker), and especially to her ten-year-old daughter, Jenny (Katherine Micheaux Miller). He likes Maggie but loves Jenny with a rather alarming intensity: "She is my soul, my life, my eyes, my everything."

Is he a suppressed child molester? Later in the film a hooker reports, "He wanted me to call him 'daddy.'" But no, I don't believe he represents a threat. He is not an actor-out but a holder-in, a brooder whose emotional weather is stormy but unseen. Most of the people he deals with, including Frankie (Frank Gio), the mobster who employs him, have no idea who he really is or what he really needs.

Sent to Buenos Aires on his final job, assassinating a wealthy general, Anderson meets with local contacts but keeps his own counsel. We realize this is not a conventional crime story; he rejects most of the advice of the local bad guys, drifts off by himself, seems preoccupied or distracted, and happens by chance into a dance club where he is entranced by one of the performers, Manuela (Luciana Pedraza). He returns. He asks her to dance. She has no idea what to make of him. He requests tango lessons. They begin a relationship impossible to define, and it seems for a time that the movie will deny us both of the usual payoffs: no murder, no romance.

Whether or not it delivers on those fronts I will leave for you to discover. Duvall, who wrote as well as directed, never makes them the point. His movie is not about a killer or a lover, but about a man who has been damaged in some unspecified way, and wanders through the world in an unorganized search for something to make him whole again. This could be love for a young girl, mastery of the tango, idealization of a dancer's skill, or exercise of his assassin's craft.

Audiences impatient for plot may miss Duvall's movie altogether. Yes, he spends a lot of time in cafés doing nothing. Yes, his conversation is limited. Yes, not even Manuela knows what he wants. Yes, he meanders toward assassination in maddening digressions. Yes, there are dance scenes that slow the progress—but if, and only if, the progress is the point.

The tango is a dance in which partners join in meticulously rehearsed passion, with such exact timing that no improvisation or error is possible. (You can tell a bad tango dancer by the bruises on the shins.) Why is Anderson so attracted to this dance? Obviously, because it provides a framework for his emotional turmoil—laces it in, gives it structure, allows him to show the world he is disciplined when he is not. For him it is about control, and it supplies rigid rules for how to interact with his partner.

What *Assassination Tango* is about, I think, is John J. Anderson's quiet and inward attempt to slow his descent toward incompetence. He has Maggie but cannot visualize their future. He meets Manuela but does not know whether to offer a future. He has a job but suspects it is a trap. People threaten him but his biggest threat is interior: He is falling to pieces, falling into confusion, losing his sense of himself. The tango is a fragment to shore up against his ruin.

The movie is not quite successful. It is too secretive about its heart. It seems unfocused unless we are quick to get the clues, to look at Anderson in a certain way, to realize it will not be about murder or love but about coping strategies. John J. Anderson has so many secrets from the world that even this movie preserves some of them. Duvall has created it from the inside out, seeing it not through the eyes of the audience but through the mind of Anderson. *Assassination Tango* is all the same a fascinating effort, and I am happy to have seen it. It taught me something about filmmaking strategy.

Austin Powers in Goldmember ★ ★
PG-13, 94 m., 2002

Mike Myers (Austin Powers/Dr. Evil/Fat Bastard/Goldmember), Beyoncé Knowles (Foxxy Cleopatra), Michael York (Basil Exposition), Michael Caine (Nigel Powers), Verne Troyer (Mini Me), Heather Graham (Ms. Felicity Shagwell), Seth Green (Scott Evil), Robert Wagner (Number Two). Directed by Jay Roach and produced by John S. Lyons, Eric McLeod, Demi Moore, Mike Myers, Jennifer Todd, and Suzanne Todd. Screenplay by Myers and Michael McCullers.

Like the James Bond series that provided it with comic inspiration, the Austin Powers series benefits from a certain familiarity. Not every Bond movie is good, but once you get started going to them you would never think of missing one. Same with Austin Powers. The third movie about the shagadelic one, *Austin Powers in Goldmember,* is a step or two down from the first and second, but it has some very funny moments, and maybe that is all we hope for.

The familiar characters are back, including Austin, Dr. Evil, and Fat Bastard (all played by Mike Myers), and Mini Me (Verne Troyer). Is this a good thing? The first time we saw them, they had the impact of novelty, but Dr. Evil is growing a little repetitious, and Fat Bastard, in his attempt to keep our attention, has escalated his adventures with bodily functions into a kind of manic bathroom zeal. There are some things we do not want to know about his bowels, and he informs us of all of them.

Myers adds a new character this time, Goldmember, whose name more or less explains his name. This is a Dutchman with flaking skin, which he likes to peel off and eat. He doesn't really grab the imagination the way Evil and Bastard did, although he provides the inspiration for a large number of Dutch jokes, all of which are supposed to be funny because they're not funny.

One new character I did like was Foxxy Cleopatra (Beyoncé Knowles, from Destiny's Child). With an Afro out to here, she's a 1970s blaxploitation heroine, inspired by the characters played by Pam Grier and Tamara Dobson. Alas, the movie doesn't do much with her except assign her to look extremely good while standing next to Austin. Having journeyed back to her period of 1975 in a time-traveling pimpmobile, it's too bad Austin doesn't do more with the opportunity.

He makes the journey because Dr. Evil has kidnapped Austin's father, Nigel (Michael Caine), and hidden him in 1975. Once found, Nigel has a heart-to-heart with his neglected son, and Caine's comic timing brings a certain zip to the movie. Meanwhile, we learn that Dr. Evil plans to flood Earth with a beam projected from an orbiting satellite that looks like a gigantic brassiere. (He likes things that look like other things; we first saw him in a satellite modeled on Bob's Big Boy, and in this film he cruises in a submarine modeled on himself.)

The funniest parts are self-contained inspirations that pop up from time to time out of the routine. One involves Austin's desperate attempt to stand in for a tinkling statue that has lost its water pressure. Another involves a shadow show when Austin disappears behind a screen to give a urine sample; he's trying to hide Mini Me, but in silhouette the effect suggests he has an extraordinarily versatile anatomy. There is also a lot of fun with subtitles in a Japanese sequence, where white backgrounds obscure some of the words, so that what's left looks obscene. Consider what can be done with "Please eat some shiitake mushrooms."

Those scenes are funny, and so is the title sequence, which introduces the first of a great many cameos involving very big stars, whose names I will not reveal. I also like the whole tone of the Powers enterprise—its wicked joy in Austin's cheerful hedonism. The movie is a little tired; maybe the original inspiration has run its course. It's a small disappointment, but I'm glad I saw it. Sorta.

Auto Focus ★ ★ ★
R, 107 m., 2002

Greg Kinnear (Bob Crane), Willem Dafoe (John Carpenter), Maria Bello (Patricia Crane), Rita Wilson (Anne Crane), Ron Leibman (Lenny). Directed by Paul Schrader and produced by

Scott Alexander, Larry Karaszewski, Todd Rosken, Pat Dollard, and Alicia Allain. Screenplay by Michael Gerbosi, based on the book by Robert Graysmith.

Eddie Cantor once told Bob Crane, "Likability is 90 percent of the battle." It seems to be 100 percent of Bob Crane's battle; there is nothing there except likability—no values, no self-awareness, no judgment, no perspective, not even an instinct for survival. Just likability and the need to be liked in a sexual way every single day. Paul Schrader's *Auto Focus,* based on Crane's life, is a deep portrait of a shallow man, lonely and empty, going through the motions of having a good time.

The broad outlines of Crane's rise and fall are well known. How he was a Los Angeles DJ who became a TV star after being cast in the lead of *Hogan's Heroes,* a comedy set in a Nazi prison camp. How his career tanked after the show left the air. How he toured on the dinner theater circuit, destroyed two marriages, and was so addicted to sex that his life was scandalous even by Hollywood standards. How he was found bludgeoned to death in 1978 in a Scottsdale, Arizona, motel room.

Crane is survived by four children, including sons from his first and second marriages who differ in an almost biblical way, the older appearing in this movie, the younger threatening a lawsuit against it, yet running a Website retailing his father's sex life. So strange was Crane's view of his behavior, so disconnected from reality, that I almost imagine he would have seen nothing wrong with his second son's sales of photos and videotapes of his father having sex. "It's healthy," Crane argues in defense of his promiscuity, although we're not sure if he really thinks that, or really thinks anything.

The movie is a hypnotic portrait of this sad, compulsive life. The director, Paul Schrader, is no stranger to stories about men trapped in sexual miscalculation; he wrote *Taxi Driver* and wrote and directed *American Gigolo.* He sees Crane as an empty vessel, filled first with fame and then with desire. Because he was on TV, he finds that women want to sleep with him, and seems to oblige them almost out of good manners. There is no lust or passion in this film, only mechanical courtship followed by desultory sex. You can catch the women looking at

him and asking themselves if there is anybody at home. Even his wives are puzzled.

Greg Kinnear gives a creepy, brilliant performance as a man lacking in all insight. He has the likability part down pat. There is a scene in a nightclub where Crane asks the bartender to turn the TV to a rerun of *Hogan's Heroes.* When a woman realizes that Hogan himself is in the room, notice how impeccable Kinnear's timing and manner are, as he fakes false modesty and pretends to be flattered by her attention. Crane was not a complex man, but that should not blind us to the subtlety and complexity of Kinnear's performance.

Willem Dafoe is the costar, as John Carpenter, a tech-head in the days when Hollywood was just learning that television could be taped and replayed by devices in the consumer price range. Carpenter hangs around sets, flattering the stars, lending them the newest Sony gadgets, wiring their cars for stereo and their dressing rooms for instant replays. He is the very embodiment of Mephistopheles, offering Crane exactly what he wants to be offered.

The turning point in Crane's life comes on a night when Carpenter invites him to a strip club. Crane is proud of his drumming, and Carpenter suggests that the star could "sit in" with the house band. Soon Crane is sitting in at strip clubs every night of the week, returning late or not at all to his first wife, Anne (Rita Wilson). Sensing something is wrong, he meets a priest one morning for breakfast, but is somehow not interested when the priest suggests he could "sit in" with a parish musical group.

Dafoe plays Carpenter as ingratiating, complimentary, sly, seductive, and enigmatically needy. Despite their denials, is there something homosexual in their relationship? The two men become constant companions, apart from a little tiff when Crane examines a video and notices Carpenter's hand in the wrong place. "It's an orgy!" Carpenter explains, and soon the men are on the prowl again. The video equipment has a curious relevance to their sexual activities; do they have sex for its own sake, or to record it for later editing and viewing? From its earliest days, home video has had an intimate buried relationship with sex. If Tommy Lee and Pamela Anderson ever think to ask themselves why they taped their wedding night, this movie might suggest some answers.

The film is wall-to-wall with sex, but contains no eroticism. The women are never really in focus. They drift in and out of range, as the two men hunt through swinger's magazines, attend swapping parties, haunt strip clubs, and troll themselves like bait through bars. If there is a shadow on their idyll, it is that Crane condescends to Carpenter, and does not understand the other man's desperate need for recognition.

The film is pitch-perfect in its decor, music, clothes, cars, language, and values. It takes place during those heady years between the introduction of the pill and the specter of AIDS, when men shaped as adolescents by *Playboy* in the 1950s now found some of their fantasies within reach. The movie understands how celebrity can make women available—and how, for some men, it is impossible to say no to an available woman. They are hardwired, and judgment has nothing to do with it. We can feel sorry for Bob Crane, but in a strange way, because he is so clueless, it is hard to blame him; we are reminded of the old joke in which God tells Adam he has a brain and a penis, but only enough blood to operate one of them at a time.

The movie's moral counterpoint is provided by Ron Leibman, as Lenny, Crane's manager. He gets him the job on *Hogan's Heroes* and even, improbably, the lead in a Disney film named *Superdad*. But Crane is reckless in the way he allows photographs and tapes of his sexual performances to float out of his control. On the Disney set one day, Lenny visits to warn Crane about his notorious behavior, but Crane can't hear him, can't listen. He drifts toward his doom, unconscious, lost in a sexual fog.

* * *

Postscript: Bob Crane's two sons are on opposite sides in a legal dispute about the biopic *Auto Focus*. Robert David Crane, the son by the first marriage, supports the movie and appears in it as "Bob Crane Jr." Robert Scott Crane, from the second marriage, says it is filled with inaccuracies, and has started a Website to oppose it. The site somewhat undermines its own position by offering for sale photographs and videos taken by Crane of his sexual indiscretions.

"There is no such person as Bob Crane Jr.," says Lee Blackman, the Los Angeles attorney representing the second wife, Patricia, and her son. "Both sons had Robert as a first name, and different middle names. Bob Crane's own middle name was Edward." In life, he told me, the older son is called Bobby, and the younger, his client, is Scotty.

By taking money for his participation in the movie and billing himself Bob Crane Jr., Blackman said, Bobby has compromised himself. (In the movie, the older son has a small role as a Christian TV interviewer.)

But what about his client Scotty's Website, with the Crane sex tapes for sale?

"He is trying to set the record straight. The Website only came into existence because of the film. For example, on Scotty's site you will find the Scottsdale coroner's autopsy on Bob Crane, clearly indicating he never had a penile implant, although the movie claims he did. You will see that his movies were really just homemade comedies: He would edit the sex stuff with cutaways to Jack Benny or Johnny Carson, and a musical sound track."

Other complaints by Blackman and his clients:

"He was reconciled with Patricia, his second wife, at the time of his death. The movie shows her drinking in the middle of the day, but she has an allergic reaction to hard liquor."

"DNA tests have proven Scotty is Bob Crane's son, despite implications in the movie that he is not."

"Bob Crane was not a dark monster. The night he was killed, he was editing *Star Wars* for Scotty, to take out the violence."

"He didn't meet John Carpenter (the Willem Dafoe character) until 1975. The movie has him meeting him in 1965. It implies Bob needed Carpenter to teach him all that technical stuff, but in fact Bob Crane was very knowledgeable about home electronics, and was making home movies even in the 1950s."

"Legally," said Blackman, "you can defame the dead. This movie has massive quantities of defamation. We're trying to work with the distributor, Sony, to tweak the film in a couple of little places to make it more accurate. When it's released, if it still contains actionable material, we'll determine what to do."

B

Baadasssss! ★ ★ ★ ★
R, 108 m., 2004

Mario Van Peebles (Melvin Van Peebles), Joy Bryant (Priscilla), T. K. Carter (Bill Cosby), Terry Crews (Big T), Khleo Thomas (Mario Van Peebles), Ossie Davis (Grandad), David Alan Grier (Clyde Houston), Nia Long (Sandra), Paul Rodriguez (Jose Garcia), Saul Rubinek (Howie), Len Lesser (Manny/Mort Goldberg). Directed by Mario Van Peebles and produced by Bruce Wayne Gillies, Dennis Haggerty, G. Marq Roswell, and Van Peebles. Screenplay by Van Peebles and Haggerty, based on the book by Van Peebles.

I want to show all the faces that Norman Rockwell never painted.
— Melvin Van Peebles

It would be nice if movies were always made the way they are in Truffaut's *Day for Night*, with idealism and romance, or Minnelli's *The Bad and the Beautiful*, with glamour and intrigue. But sometimes they are made the way they are in Mario Van Peebles's *Baadasssss!*, with desperation, deception, and cunning. Here is one of the best movies I've seen about the making of a movie—a fictionalized eyewitness account by Mario of how and why his father, Melvin Van Peebles, made *Sweet Sweetback's Baadasssss Song*, a landmark in the birth of African-American cinema.

The original 1971 movie was scruffy and raw, the story of a man born in a brothel and initiated to sex at the age of twelve, who grows up as an urban survivor, attacks two racist cops, and eludes capture. That Sweetback got away with it electrified the movie's first audiences, who were intrigued by ad lines like "Rated X by an All-White Jury." Although it was not an exploitation film, it was credited by *Variety* with creating "blaxploitation," a genre that gave us Pam Grier, Shaft, Superfly, and a generation of black filmmakers who moved into the mainstream.

That a big-budget action film is unthinkable today without a black costar is a direct consequence of Melvin Van Peebles's $150,000 fly-by-night movie. *Sweet Sweetback* did astonishing business, proving that a viable market existed for movies made by, for, and about blacks. When the movie opened at the Oriental Theater in Chicago, the marquee proclaimed: "The Oriental Is Yo-riental Now!"

Mario Van Peebles was thirteen when the movie was being made, and was pressed into service by his father to play Sweetback as a boy. That involved a scene with a hooker in the brothel that still, today, Mario must feel resentment about, since in *Baadasssss!* he makes a point of showing that some of the crew members and his father's girlfriend, Sandra (Nia Long), objected to it. But Melvin was a force of nature, a cigar-chewing Renaissance man who got his own way. Only sheer willpower forced the production ahead despite cash and personnel emergencies, and *Sweet Sweetback* is like a textbook on guerrilla filmmaking.

Aware that he could not possibly afford to pay union wages (there were days when he could pay no wages at all), Melvin disguises the production as a porn film to elude union rules. The day the union reps visit the set is the day he shoots a sex scene—a little more explicit, of course, than the one he would use in the movie. Determined to have a crew that included at least 50 percent minorities (in an industry where most crews were all white), he trained some of them on the job. At the end of *Baadasssss!*, a white sound man has hired his assistant, a tough black street guy who doubles as security, to be his partner; that detail, like most of the film, is based on fact. Surveying the set, he observes, "No crew has ever looked like this."

Mario plays his own father in the movie, and Khleo Thomas plays Mario. It's clear that (the real) Mario admires his father while at the same time harbors some resentment against his old man's strong-willed, single-minded treatment of people. We see Melvin bouncing checks, telling lies, roughing up a crew member who wants to quit, and even getting a free shot courtesy of the Los Angeles Fire Department when their trucks respond to an alarm for a car fire. The car was blown up for a scene in the movie, and Melvin kept the cameras rolling to get the firemen for free.

As a director, Mario keeps the large cast alive, from Melvin's alluring, exasperated assistant, Priscilla (Joy Bryant), to his long-suffering agent, Howie (Saul Rubinek), his hard-pressed producer, Clyde Houston (David Alan Grier), and Bill Cosby (T. K. Carter), whose $50,000 check bailed out Melvin at a crisis point. There is a double role for Len Lesser as Manny and Mort Goldberg, the dubious Detroit exhibitors who premiere *Sweetback* and are ready to close it after one screening, until they see the lines in front of the theater.

Mario could make another movie about the rest of his father's life, which has included being an officer in the U.S. Air Force, making art films in Paris, working as a trader on Wall Street, composing, painting, winning eleven Tony nominations for Broadway plays, and winning the French Legion of Honor. The last shot in the film is a wink and a cloud of cigar smoke from this living legend, now seventy-one.

What's fascinating is the way Mario, working from his father's autobiography and his own memories, has somehow used his firsthand experience without being cornered by it. He keeps a certain objectivity in considering the character of Melvin, seeing him as brave and gifted and determined, but also as a hustler who gets his movie made, in the words of Malcolm X, "by any means necessary." He steps on toes, hurts feelings, expects sacrifices, doesn't hesitate to use his own son in a scene that no professional child actor would have been allowed to touch.

To one degree or another, all low-budget films are like this one, with cast and crew members bludgeoned into hard work at low pay in the service of the director's ego. Mario Van Peebles captures the elusive sense of family that forms on a movie set, the moments of despair, the times when it seems impossible to continue, the sexual intrigue and (always) the bitching over the food. *Sweet Sweetback's Baadasssss Song* was historically a film of great importance, but in another sense it was just another low-rent, fly-by-night production. *Baadasssss!* manages to get both of those aspects just about right.

Note: This film's original title was How to Get the Man's Foot Outta Your Ass.

Bad Company ★ ★

PG-13, 111 m., 2002

Anthony Hopkins (Gaylord Oakes), Chris Rock (Jake Hayes), Garcelle Beauvais-Nilon (Nicole), Gabriel Macht (Seale), Peter Stormare (Adrik Vas), Kerry Washington (Julie), John Stattery (Roland Yates). Directed by Joel Schumacher and produced by Jerry Bruckheimer and Mike Stenson. Screenplay by Jason Richman, Michael Browning, Gary Goodman, and David Himmelstein.

Hard on the heels of *The Sum of All Fears*, here's Jerry Bruckheimer's *Bad Company*, another movie about an American city threatened by the explosion of a stolen nuclear device. This one is an action comedy. There may come a day when the smiles fade. To be sure, the movie was made before 9/11 (and its original autumn 2001 release was delayed for obvious reasons), but even before 9/11 it was clear that nuclear terrorism was a real possibility. While *The Sum of All Fears* deals in a quasi-serious way with the subject (up until the astonishingly inappropriate ending), *Bad Company* is more lighthearted. Ho, ho.

The nuclear device is really only the Maguffin. It could be anything, as long as bad guys want it and good guys fight to keep them from it. The movie's a collision among three durable genres: Misfit Partners, Fish Out of Water, and Mistaken Identity. After an opening scene in which the Chris Rock character is killed, we learn that he had a twin brother named Jake Hayes; the babies were separated at birth and never knew about each other. The first was adopted by a rich family, went to Ivy League schools, and joined the CIA. Jake is a ticket scalper and chess hustler who's in love with a nursing student (Kerry Washington).

One problem with the movie, directed by Joel Schumacher, is that it jams too many prefabricated story elements into the running time. Consider the training sequence, in which Rock has nine days to perfect the mannerisms and absorb the knowledge of his dead brother. Odd that most of the coaching sessions have him learning to recognize fine vintages of wine and evaluate ancient cognacs; is he going to be dining with the terrorists? Meanwhile, he's apparently expected to learn to speak Czech from a dictionary tossed onto his bunk.

His minder at the CIA is Gaylord Oakes (Anthony Hopkins), a spookily calm veteran oper-ative whose plan is to substitute this twin for the other in a sting operation designed to buy a stolen nuclear device. When another would-be buyer enters the picture, the film descends into a series of chase scenes, which are well enough done, but too many and too long.

Hopkins plays his character right down the middle, hard-edged and serious. Rock has some effective scenes played straight, but at other times he goes into a nonstop comic monologue that is funny, yes, but unlikely; when he's being shot at, how can he think of all those one-liners? The movie's strategy is to make every sequence stand on its own, with no thought to the overall tone of the film, so that we go from the deadly serious to something approaching parody.

Of the plot I can say nothing except that it exists entirely at the whim of the stunts, special effects, chases, and action. The two competing teams of would-be evil bomb buyers function entirely to supply an endless number of guys who fire machine guns a lot but hardly ever hit anything. The motive for blowing up New York is scarcely discussed. And could I believe my eyes? Here in 2002—another Red Digital Readout counting down to zero, just when I thought that was one cliché that had finally outlived its viability.

As for the girls, well, Kerry Washington is sweet and believable as Rock's girlfriend, but a Bruckheimer movie is not the place to look for meaningful female performances. No doubt there was a nice payday, but meanwhile, Washington's fine performance in *Lift*, the shoplifting film from Sundance 2001, goes unheralded. Even more thankless is the role by Garcelle Beauvais-Nilon as a CNN correspondent who was the girlfriend of the first twin, and spots this one because he kisses differently. She disappears entirely from the film after an ironically appropriate slide down a laundry chute. (By the way: During the shoot-out in that hotel, how come not a single guest or employee is ever seen?)

I won't tell you I didn't enjoy parts of *Bad Company*, because I did. But the enjoyment came at moments well separated by autopilot action scenes and stunt sequences that outlived their interest. As for the theme of a nuclear device that might destroy New York, I have a feeling that after this generation of pre-9/11 movies plays out, we won't be seeing it much anymore.

Bad Santa ★ ★ ★ ½
R, 93 m., 2003

Billy Bob Thornton (Willie T. Soke), Tony Cox (Marcus), Bernie Mac (Gin Slagel), Lauren Graham (Sue), John Ritter (Mall Manager), Brett Kelly (The Kid), Cloris Leachman (Grandma). Directed by Terry Zwigoff and produced by Sarah Aubrey, John Cameron, and Bob Weinstein. Screenplay by John Requa and Glenn Ficarra.

The kid gives Santa a carved wooden pickle as a Christmas present.

"How come it's brown?" Santa asks. "Why didn't you paint it green?"

"It isn't painted," the kid says. "That's blood from when I cut my hand while I was making it for you."

Santa is a depressed, alcoholic safecracker. The kid is not one of your cute movie kids, but an intense and needy stalker; think of Thomas the Tank Engine as a member of the Addams Family. Oh, and there's an elf, too, named Marcus. The elf is an angry dwarf who has been working with Santa for eight years, cracking the safe in a different department store every Christmas. The elf is fed up. Santa gets drunk on the job, he's screwing customers in the Plus Sizes dressing room, and whether the children throw up on Santa or he throws up on them is a toss-up, no pun intended.

Bad Santa is a demented, twisted, unreasonably funny work of comic kamikaze, starring Billy Bob Thornton as Santa in a performance that's defiantly uncouth. His character is named Willie T. Soke; W. C. Fields would have liked that. He's a foul-mouthed, unkempt, drunken louse at the beginning of the movie, and sticks to that theme all the way through. You expect a happy ending, but the ending is happy in the same sense that a man's doctors tell him he lost his legs but they were able to save his shoes.

There are certain unwritten parameters governing mainstream American movies, and *Bad Santa* violates all of them. When was the last time you saw a movie Santa kicking a department store reindeer to pieces? Or using the f-word more than Eddie Griffin? Or finding a girlfriend who makes him wear his little red hat in bed because she has a Santa fetish? And for that matter, when was the last movie where a loser Santa meets a little kid and the kid doesn't redeem the loser with his sweetness and simplicity, but attaches himself like those leeches on Bogart in *The African Queen*?

Movie critics have been accused of praising weirdo movies because we are bored by movies that seem the same. There is some justice in that. But I didn't like this movie merely because it was weird and different. I liked it because it makes no compromises and takes no prisoners. And because it is funny.

The director is Terry Zwigoff. He made the great documentary *Crumb,* about R. Crumb, the cartoonist who is a devoted misanthrope. (Crumb drew the *American Splendor* comic books about Harvey Pekar, his equal in misanthropy.) Zwigoff also directed the quirky *Ghost World,* with its unlikely romantic alliance between a teenage girl (Thora Birch) and a sour, fortyish recluse (Steve Buscemi). This is a director who makes a specialty of bitter antisocial oddballs. That he does it in comedy takes more guts than doing it in tragedy.

Zwigoff worked from an original screenplay by John Requa and Glenn Ficarra. And what is their track record, you are wondering? They cowrote *Cats & Dogs* (2001), with its parachuting Ninja cats, and their next movie is *Cats & Dogs 2: Tinkles' Revenge.* Maybe many screenwriters who do sweet, PG-rated movies like *Cats & Dogs* have a script like *Bad Santa* in the bottom desk drawer, perhaps in a lead-lined box.

When Billy Bob Thornton got the script, he must have read it and decided it would be career suicide. Then he put the script to his head and pulled the trigger. For him to play Hamlet would take nerve; for him to play Willie T. Soke took heroism. Wandering through the final stages of alcoholism, he functions only because of the determination of Marcus, who is played by Tony Cox as a crook who considers stealing to be a job, and straps on his elf ears every morning to go to work. Willie and Marcus always use the same MO: They use the Santa gig to get into the store, stay after closing, and crack the safe. Alas, this year the store's security chief (Bernie Mac, also pissed off most of the time) is wise to their plan and wants a cut. Because it's in his interest to keep Bad Santa in the store, he doesn't report little incidents like the reindeer-kicking to the store manager, played by the late John Ritter.

Willie becomes distracted by the arrival in his life of Sue (Lauren Graham), the Santa fetishist, who picks him up at a bar. Then there's the kid (Brett Kelly), who sits on his lap, tells him he isn't Santa Claus, and then doggedly insists on treating him as if he is. The kid is desperately lonely because his parents are away for reasons we understand better than he does, and he's being looked after by his comatose grandmother (Cloris Leachman). I know, I know—I disapproved of the cruel treatment of the comatose baby-sitter, Mrs. Kwan, in *The Cat in the Hat,* and here I am approving of the way they treat the kid's grandmother. The differences are: (1) This film is funny and that film was not, and (2) that one was intended for family audiences, and this one is not.

Is it ever not. I imagine a few unsuspecting families will wander into it despite the "R" rating, and I picture terrified kids running screaming down the aisles. What I can't picture is who *will* attend this movie. Anybody? Movies like this are a test of taste. If you understand why *Kill Bill* is a good movie and *The Texas Chainsaw Massacre* is not, and *Bad Santa* is a good movie and *The Cat in the Hat* is not, then you have freed yourself from the belief that a movie's quality is determined by its subject matter. You instinctively understand that a movie is not about what it is about, but about how it is about it. You qualify for *Bad Santa.*　☞

Ballistic: Ecks vs. Sever ½★
R, 91 m., 2002

Antonio Banderas (Jeremiah Ecks), Lucy Liu (Sever), Gregg Henry (Robert Gant), Talisa Soto (Vinn Gant/Rayne), Ray Park (A. J. Ross), Miguel Sandoval (Julio Martin). Directed by Wych Kaosayananda and produced by Chris Lee, Elie Samaha, and Kaosayananda. Screenplay by Alan B. McElroy.

There is nothing wrong with the title *Ballistic: Ecks vs. Sever* that renaming it *Ballistic* would not have solved. Strange that they would choose such an ungainly title when, in fact, the movie is not about Ecks *versus* Sever but about Ecks *and* Sever working together against a common enemy—although Ecks, Sever, and the audience take a long time to figure that out.

The movie is a chaotic mess, overloaded with special effects and explosions, light on continuity, sanity, and coherence. So short is its memory span that although Sever kills, I dunno, maybe forty Vancouver police officers in an opening battle, by the end, when someone says, "She's a killer," Ecks replies, "She's a mother."

The movie stars Lucy Liu as Sever, a former agent for the Defense Intelligence Agency, which according to www.dia.mil is a branch of the U.S. government. Antonio Banderas is Ecks, a former ace FBI agent who is coaxed back into service. Sever has lost her child in an attack and Ecks believes he has lost his wife, so they have something in common, you see, even though...

But I'll not reveal that plot secret, and will discuss the curious fact that both of these U.S. agencies wage what amounts to warfare in Vancouver, which is actually in a nation named Canada that has agencies and bureaus of its own and takes a dim view of machine guns, rocket launchers, plastic explosives, and the other weapons the American agents and their enemies use to litter the streets of the city with the dead.

Both Sever and Ecks, once they discover this, have the same enemy in common: Gant (Gregg Henry), a DIA agent who is married to Talisa Soto and raising her child, although Sever kidnaps the child, who is in fact . . . but never mind, I want to discuss Gant's secret weapon. He has obtained a miniaturized robot so small it can float in the bloodstream and cause strokes and heart attacks.

At one point in the movie a man who will remain nameless is injected with one of these devices by a dart gun, and it kills him. All very well, but consider for a moment the problem of cost overruns in these times of economic uncertainty. A miniaturized assassination robot small enough to slip through the bloodstream would cost how much? Millions? And it is de-livered by dart? How's this for an idea: Use a poison dart and spend the surplus on school lunches.

Ballistic: Ecks vs. Sever is an ungainly mess, submerged in mayhem, occasionally surfacing for clichés. When the FBI goes looking for Ecks, for example, they find him sitting morosely on a bar stool, drinking and smoking. That is, of course, where sad former agents always are found, but the strange thing is, after years of drinking he is still in great shape, has all his karate moves, and goes directly into violent action without even a tiny tremor of DTs.

The movie ends in a stock movie location I thought had been retired: a steam and flame factory where the combatants stalk each other on catwalks and from behind steel pillars, while the otherwise deserted factory supplies vast quantities of flame and steam. Vancouver itself, for that matter, is mostly deserted, and no wonder, if word has gotten around that two U.S. agencies and a freelance killer are holding war games. *Ballistic: Ecks vs. Sever* was directed by Wych Kaosayananda of Thailand, whose pseudonym, you may not be surprised to learn, is Kaos.

The Banger Sisters ★ ★ ★
R, 97 m., 2002

Susan Sarandon (Lavinia), Goldie Hawn (Suzette), Geoffrey Rush (Harry), Robin Thomas (Raymond), Erika Christensen (Hannah), Eva Amurri (Ginger). Directed by Bob Dolman and produced by Elizabeth Cantillon and Mark Johnson. Screenplay by Dolman.

When you get right down to it, *The Banger Sisters* is pretty thin, but you grin while you're watching it. Later you reflect that it has an obvious story arc and sketchy minor characters, and awkwardly tries to get down and provide uplift at the same time. The screenplay could have used an overhaul before production, but I'm glad I saw it.

I'm glad primarily because of Goldie Hawn. She's infectious and likable in this movie, but not in that ditzy way we remember. Although she plays a legendary groupie who, in her day, "rattled" most of the rock stars ("and road-ies") in the business, she plays a woman who has taken her youthful sense of freedom and combined it with a certain amount of common sense.

Hawn is Suzette. Her costar, Susan Sarandon, is Lavinia. Together, some (cough) years ago, they were such legendary groupies that Frank Zappa named them the Banger Sisters. Hawn has stayed true to her school, and as we meet her she's bartending in a West Hollywood club where she is more beloved by the customers than by the owner, who fires her. (She thinks that's not fair: "See that toilet? Jim Morrison passed out in there one night with me underneath him.") Broke and without plans, she points her pickup to Phoenix for a reunion with Lavinia, whom she hasn't seen in years.

Along the way, in need of gas money, she picks up a lost soul named Harry (Geoffrey Rush), a screenwriter whose dreams have not come true, and who is traveling to Phoenix with one bullet in his gun, to shoot his father. Harry is one of those finicky weirdos who doesn't want anyone upsetting his routine. The very sight of Suzette, with her silicone treasures, is disturbing in more ways than he can bear to think of.

In Phoenix, Lavinia lives with her lawyer husband, Raymond (Robin Thomas), and her two spoiled teenagers, Hannah (Erika Christensen) and Ginger (Eva Amurri). She is so respectable she doesn't even want to think about her former life, which her husband knows nothing about. Are you counting the formulas? And so here we have not one but two fish out of water (Harry and Suzette), plus two examples (Lavinia and Harry) of that other reliable element, the repressed sad sack who needs a taste of freedom.

Give the movie a moment's thought and you see the screenplay's gears turning. This is a movie that could have been a term paper. But Hawn and Sarandon hit the ground running, and are so funny and goofy that they distract and delight us. Lavinia at first resists Suzette's appeal, but then she realizes, "I'm the same color as the Department of Motor Vehicles— and you're like a flower." The girls go out for a wild night on the town, and Suzette brings much-needed reality into the cocooned existence of the two daughters.

The most underwritten character is Lavinia's husband, Raymond. The movie doesn't know what to do with him. They let him be a little surprised, a little shocked, a little too straight, but mostly he just stands there waiting for dialogue that is never supplied. Comic opportunities were lost here. And the Geoffrey Rush character, while more filled in, also seems oddly unnecessary. I can easily imagine the movie without him and with more about the family in Phoenix. He is not and never will be a workable life partner for Suzette, no matter how the movie tries to sentimentalize him.

What Goldie Hawn does is to play Suzette sincerely—as if she really were a groupie who still holds true to her partying past. Her daughter Kate Hudson, of course, played the groupie Penny Lane in *Almost Famous,* and Suzette could be the same character further down the road. The movie's buried joke is that Suzette, the wild girl from West Hollywood, has more commonsense knowledge about life than the movie's conventional types. Listen to how she talks to Harry on the phone. I guess you learn something about human nature after (cough) years as a bartender.

Baran ★ ★ ★ ½
PG, 94 m., 2002

Hossein Abedini (Latif), Zahra Bahrami (Baran), Mohammad Amir Naji (Memar), Hossein Rahimi (Soltan), Gholam Ali Bakhshi (Najaf). Directed by Majid Majidi and produced by Majidi and Fouad Nahas. Screenplay by Majidi.

What are they like, over there in Iran? Are they all glowering fanatics, stewing in resentment of America? What's your mental image? When a land is distant, unknown, and labeled as an enemy, it's easy to think in simple terms. No doubt Iranians are as quick to think evil about us as we are to think evil about them. The intriguing thing about an Iranian movie like *Baran* is that it gives human faces to these strangers. It could be a useful learning tool for those who have not traveled widely, who never see foreign films, who reduce whole nations to labels.

The movie is a romantic fable about a construction worker. His name is Latif, and he labors on a building site not far from the border with Afghanistan. All of the labor here is manual, including hauling fifty-pound bags of cement up a series of ramps. Latif doesn't actually work very hard, since he is Iranian and most of the labor is being done by underpaid refugees from Afghanistan. Latif is the tea boy, bringing hot cups to the workers and drinking more than his own share.

We learn at the beginning of the movie that millions of Afghans have poured into Iran as refugees. Since it is illegal to hire them, they work secretly for low wages, like undocumented Mexicans in America. Many are fleeing the Taliban for the comparatively greater freedom and prosperity of Iran, a distinction that may seem small to us, but not to them. (The title cards carrying this information were already in place when the film debuted at the 2001 Montreal and Toronto festivals, and were not added post-9/11.)

One day there is an accident on the site. A man named Najaf injures his leg, and that is a catastrophe because he has five children to feed in the squatters' camp where his family lives. Najaf sends his son Rahmat to take his place, but the son is small, slight, and young, and staggers under the burden of the concrete sacks. So Memar, the construction boss, who pays low wages but is not unkind, gives Rahmat the job of tea boy and reassigns Latif to real work.

Latif is lazy, immature, resentful. He trashes the kitchen in revenge, and makes things hard for Rahmat. Yet at the same time he finds something intriguing about the new tea boy, and eventually Latif discovers the secret: The boy is a girl. So desperate for money was Rahmat's family that in a society where women are strictly forbidden from mixing with men on a job like this, a deception was planned. In keeping the secret, Latif begins his journey to manhood and tolerance.

The outlines of *Baran*, as they emerge, seem as much like an ancient fable as a modern story. Middle Eastern society, so insistent on the division between men and women, has a literature filled with stories about men and women in disguise, passing through each other's worlds. The vast gulf between Latif and Rahmat is dramatized by the way they essentially fall in love without exchanging a single word.

Meanwhile, watching conditions on the work site and seeing raids by government agents looking for illegal workers, we get an idea of Iran's ground-level economy.

My description perhaps makes the film sound grim and gray, covered with a silt of concrete dust. Not at all. It is the latest work by Majid Majidi, whose *Children of Heaven* (1997) was a heartwarming fable about a brother and sister who lose a pair of sneakers and try to hide this calamity from their parents. The director uses natural colors and painterly compositions to make even the most spartan locations look beautiful, and as Stephanie Zacharek of Salon.com observes: "Majidi uses sunlight, a completely free resource if you can time your filmmaking around it, as a dazzling special effect."

What happens between Rahmat and Latif I will leave you to discover. There are many surprises along the way, one of the best involving a man Latif meets during a long journey—an itinerant shoemaker, who has thoughtful observations about life. *Baran* is the latest in a flowering of good films from Iran, and gives voice to the moderates there. It shows people existing and growing in the cracks of their society's inflexible walls.

The Barbarian Invasions ★ ★ ★ ★
R, 99 m., 2003

Rémy Girard (Rémy), Stéphane Rousseau (Sébastien), Marie-Josée Croze (Nathalie), Dorothée Berryman (Louise), Louise Portal (Diane), Dominique Michel (Dominique), Yves Jacques (Claude), Pierre Curzi (Pierre), Marina Hands (Gaëlle). Directed by Denys Arcand and produced by Daniel Louis and Denise Robert. Screenplay by Arcand.

Dying is not this cheerful, but we need to think it is. *The Barbarian Invasions* is a movie about a man who dies about as pleasantly as it's possible to imagine; the audience sheds happy tears. The man is a professor named Rémy, who has devoted his life to wine, women, and left-wing causes, and now faces death by cancer, certain and soon. His wife divorced him years ago because of his womanizing, his son is a millionaire who dislikes him and everything he stands for, many of his old friends are estranged, and the morphine is no longer controlling the pain. By the end of the story, miraculously, he will have gotten away with everything, and be forgiven and beloved.

The young embrace the fantasy that they will live forever. The old cling to the equally seductive fantasy that they will die a happy death. This is a fantasy for adults. It is also a movie with brains, indignation, irony, and idealism—a film about people who think seriously and express themselves with passion. It comes from Denys Arcand of Quebec, whose *The Decline of the American Empire* (1986) involved many of the same characters during the fullness of their lives. At that time they either worked in the history department of a Montreal university or slept with somebody who did, and my review noted that "everybody talks about sex, but the real subject is wit . . . their real passion comes in the area of verbal competition."

When people are building their careers, they need to prove they're better than their contemporaries. Those who win must then prove—to themselves—that they're as good as they used to be. Whether Rémy was a good history professor is an interesting point (his son has to bribe three students to visit his bedside, but one of them later refuses to take the money). He certainly excelled in his lifestyle, as the lustiest and most Falstaffian of his circle, but every new conquest meant leaving someone behind—and now, at the end, he seems to have left almost everyone behind.

We've all known someone like Rémy. Frequently their children don't love them as much as their friends do. We have a stake in their passions; they live at full tilt so we don't have to, and sometimes even their castaways come to admire the life force that drives them on to new conquests, more wine, later nights. His former wife, Louise (Dorothée Berryman), calls their son Sébastien (Stéphane Rousseau) in London, where he is a rich trader, to tell him his father is near death, and although he hasn't spoken to the old man in a long time, Sébastien flies home with his fiancée, Gaëlle (Marina Hands).

Their first meeting goes badly; it is a replay of Rémy's socialist rejection of Sébastien's values and his "worthless" job. But Sébastien has learned from the financial world how to get

things done, and soon he has bribed a union official to prepare a private room for his father on a floor of the hospital no longer in use. He even wants to fly his father to America for treatment, but Rémy blusters that he fought for socialized medicine and he will stick with it. The movie is an indictment of overcrowded Canadian hospitals and absent-minded caregivers, but it also reveals a certain flexibility, as when the nun caring for Rémy tells his son that morphine no longer kills the pain . . . but heroin would.

How Sébastian responds to that information leads to one of the movie's most delightful sequences, and to the introduction of a drug addict named Nathalie (Marie-Josée Croze), who becomes another of Rémy's caregivers. Nathalie's story and her own problems are so involving that Croze won the best actress award at Cannes 2003.

Sébastian calls up his father's old friends. Some are Rémy's former lovers. Two are gay. One, Rémy's age, has started a new family. They gather at first rather gingerly around the deathbed of this person they had drifted away from, but eventually their reunion becomes a way to remember their younger days, their idealism, their defiant politics. Rémy is sometimes gray and shaking with pain, but the movie sidesteps the horrendous side effects of chemotherapy and uses heroin as the reason why he can play the graceful and even ebullient host at his own passing. There is a scene at a lakeside cottage that is so perfect and moving that only a churl would wonder how wise it is to leave a terminally ill man outside all night during the Quebec autumn, even with blankets wrapped around him.

The Barbarian Invasions, also written by Arcand, is manipulative without apology, and we want it to be. There's no market for a movie about a man dying a miserable death, wracked by the nausea of chemo. Indeed, Rémy is even allowed his taste for good wines and family feasts. And what a marvel the way his wife and his former (and current!) lovers gather around to celebrate what seems to have been the most remarkable case of priapism any of them have ever encountered. They are not so much forgiving him, I think, as envying his ability to live on his own terms and get away with it. His illusions are all he has, and although they were deceived by them, they don't want Rémy to die without them. As a good friend of mine once observed, nobody on his deathbed ever says, "I'm glad I always flew economy class."

Barbershop ★ ★ ★
PG-13, 102 m., 2002

Ice Cube (Calvin), Cedric the Entertainer (Eddie), Leonard Earl Howze (Dinka), Troy Garity (Isaac), Eve (Terri), Sean Patrick Thomas (Jimmy), Michael Ealy (Ricky), Anthony Anderson (J. D.), Lahmard Tate (Billy), Keith David (Lester). Directed by Tim Story and produced by Mark Brown, Robert Teitel, and George Tillman Jr. Screenplay by Brown, Don D. Scott, and Marshall Todd.

I've become embroiled in a controversy recently about whether women engage in audible and detailed discussions of their sexual activities while sitting in beauty salons. Doesn't happen, say some of my correspondents, while a woman from Texas says it happens there all the time—although, being from Michigan, she naturally doesn't join in. I got started on this subject while reviewing a movie named *Never Again,* where there's a scene of sex talk in a salon that's enough to make your hair curl.

My hunch is that most women don't talk that way in most salons. Do I know? No, because I've never been in a beauty salon. But now comes *Barbershop* to argue the question from the male side. The movie takes place during one long day in a barbershop on Chicago's South Side, where seven barbers (six men, one woman; six blacks, one white) man the chairs. Judging by this film, the conversation ranges far beyond sex, but is not above spirited discussions of booty: Who has it, who needs it, who wants it. But sex as a general topic would be far too limiting for this crowd, and the movie plays like a talk show where everyone is the host.

The barbershop is owned by Calvin (Ice Cube), who inherited it from his father. It scrapes by, but doesn't feed his hungers for bigger things—like a recording studio, for example (he dreams of platinum records issuing from his basement). One day, heedlessly, he sells the shop for $20,000 to Lester the loan shark (Keith David), who promises the word

"barbershop" will be permanently on the store, but privately has in mind a gentleman's club by the same name.

The barbers and regular customers are devastated by this news. The shop provides more than employment or service for them; it is community, forum, friendship, camaraderie, continuity. Realizing his error, Calvin tries to buy back the shop, but finds the price is now $40,000. So it appears this will be the last day that the little shop acts as a stage for all the regulars.

The barbers are perhaps too many to be supported by such a shop, but they provide a nice cross section: In addition to Calvin, there's old Eddie (Cedric the Entertainer), who never seems to have a customer but is installed as chief pontificator; Jimmy (Sean Patrick Thomas), a college student who tries to impress everyone with his knowledge (are scallops a mollusk?); Terri (Eve), who knows somebody has been drinking her apple juice from the refrigerator in the back room; Ricky (Michael Ealy), who has two strikes against him and will get life for a third; Dinka (Leonard Earl Howze), from Nigeria, who likes Terri but is too rotund for her tastes; and Isaac (Troy Garity), the token white barber, who explains that, inside, he's blacker than some of the others.

A parallel plot involves J. D. (Anthony Anderson) and Billy (Lahmard Tate), who stage a spectacularly incompetent theft of an ATM machine that has been recently installed in the Indian grocery on the corner. Since they "borrowed" Ricky's van for this job, if they get caught he goes up for life. The unending conversation in the shop is intercut with J. D. and Billy wrestling with the ATM machine, which at one point they even attempt to check in with at a motel.

If nothing significant gets settled in the rambling barbershop conversations, at least many issues are aired, and by the end, in classic sitcom fashion, all problems have been solved. The talk is lively, but goes into overdrive when Eddie is onstage; Cedric the Entertainer has the confidence, the style, and the volume to turn any group into an audience, and he has a rap about Rosa Parks, Rodney King, and O. J. Simpson that brought down the house at the screening I attended.

The film is ungainly in construction but

graceful in delivery. I could have done without both of the subplots—the loan shark and the ATM thieves—and simply sat there in Calvin's barbershop for the entire running time, listening to these guys talk. There is a kind of music to their conversations, now a lullaby, now a march, now a requiem, now hip-hop, and they play with each other like members of an orchestra. The movie's so good to listen to, it would even work as an audio book.

Barbershop 2: Back in Business ★ ★ ½
PG-13, 118 m., 2004

Ice Cube (Calvin Palmer), Cedric the Entertainer (Eddie), Sean Patrick Thomas (Jimmy James), Eve (Terri Jones), Troy Garity (Isaac Rosenberg), Michael Ealy (Ricky Nash), Leonard Earl Howze (Dinka), Harry Lennix (Quentin Leroux), Kenan Thompson (Kenard), Queen Latifah (Gina). Directed by Kevin Rodney Sullivan and produced by Alex Gartner, Robert Teitel, and George Tillman Jr. Screenplay by Don D. Scott.

Calvin's Barbershop is still in business as *Barbershop 2* opens, and the same barbers are at the same chairs, dealing with the usual customers discussing the day's events, and providing free advice on each other's lives. Just like the first movie, the shop is a talk show where everybody is the host. The talk could go on forever, coiling from current events to current romances, but then danger strikes: Nappy Cutz, a slick franchise haircut emporium, is opening across the street, and it may put the little neighborhood shop out of business.

This would be a disaster for Calvin (Ice Cube), whose operation is not single-mindedly devoted to profit. If it were, why would he give a prized chair to Eddie (Cedric the Entertainer), who hardly ever seems to cut any hair? We learn the answer to that mystery in the course of this movie, along with a little of Eddie's background: We see him in a flashback, protecting the shop from rioters and winning the lifelong gratitude of Calvin's father.

Even back then, Eddie was on the conservative side, and again in this movie he delivers his trademark riffs against African-American icons. Although others in the shop cringed when they learned the D.C. sniper was black, for Eddie the contrarian that's something to be proud of: "He's the Jackie Robinson of crime." Alas, Eddie's I-Can't-Believe-He-Said-That act, which worked so well in the original *Barbershop*, seems a little perfunctory and obligatory this time, and it's often hard to understand what Cedric the E is saying; a little work in postproduction could have clarified his dialogue and allowed the zingers to land with more impact.

The plot, just like last time, involves a threat to the beloved neighborhood institution. An entrepreneur named Quentin Leroux (Harry Lennix) has purchased the property across the street and is erecting a huge Nappy Cutz emporium which, it is rumored, will even feature a basketball court. Calvin's could be doomed. And there's a larger issue, because the Chicago City Council, in the pockets of developers, seems bent on tearing down all the little neighborhood stores and moving in giant franchisers.

This could have headed in an interesting direction if the movie wanted to be political, but it doesn't (the talkative crowd in Calvin's never mentions a name like, oh, say, "Daley"). There is an arm's-length recognition of city hall in the character of Jimmy (Sean Patrick Thomas), who used to work in the shop but now has the inside track to a powerful alderman.

Calvin struggles with the idea of new competition, and meanwhile Terri (Eve), the only female barber, tries to decide if there's any future with Ricky (Michael Ealy), and Eddie himself is flummoxed by the arrival of a flame from his torrid past. The only white barber, Isaac (Troy Garity), remains convinced he is the blackest man in the shop, and the African-born barber Dinka (Leonard Earl Howze) has a futile crush on Eve. Jimmy's empty chair is taken over by Calvin's cousin Kenard (Kenan Thompson), who doesn't seem to understand the fundamental purpose of a barbershop, which is to provide a refuge, affirmation, confirmation, entertainment, and occasionally haircuts.

Next door in a beauty salon, stylist Gina (Queen Latifah) stands by for several almost self-contained supporting scenes, including an insult contest with Eddie in which it sounds like Eddie has won, and we would be sure if we could understand him. The Queen has a high-energy presence in the film, and just as well, because she'll star in *Beauty Shop*.

Did I like the film? Yeah, kinda, but not enough to recommend. The first film arrived with freshness and an unexpected zing, but this one seems too content to follow in its footsteps. Maybe *Beauty Shop* is the one to wait for, if they can find half a dozen high-powered foils for the Queen. Prediction: Terri (Eve) will get tired of everyone stealing her apple juice and move next door.

Bartleby ★ ★ ½
PG-13, 82 m., 2002

David Paymer (The Boss), Crispin Glover (Bartleby), Glenne Headly (Vivian), Joe Piscopo (Rocky), Maury Chaykin (Ernie), Seymour Cassel (Frank Waxman), Carrie Snodgress (Book Publisher), Dick Martin (Mayor). Directed and produced by Jonathan Parker. Screenplay by Parker and Catherine DiNapoli, based on the story "Bartleby the Scrivener" by Herman Melville.

The mass of men lead lives of quiet desperation.
—Thoreau

The life work of the employees in the Public Record Office can be easily described: They take enormous quantities of printed documents they have no interest in, and they file them. They are surrounded by the monument to their labor: lots of file cabinets. No wonder they go mad. Vivian distracts herself by flirting. Rocky pretends he has the inside line on everything. For Ernie, changing the toner cartridge in a Xerox machine is an invitation to disaster. Their boss patiently oversees their cheerless existence trying not to contemplate the devastating meaningless of the office.

One day a new employee is hired. His name is Bartleby. The boss asks him to do something. "I would prefer not to," Bartleby says. That becomes his reply to every request. He would prefer not to. He would prefer not to work, not to file, not to obey, not to respond, *not* to. What he prefers to do is stand in the center of the office with his neck cocked at an odd angle, staring at the ceiling.

The boss is checkmated. Bartleby is not doing bad work; he isn't working at all. His refusal to work subverts the entire work ethic of the organization. Everyone in the office—

Vivian, Rocky, Ernie, and the boss himself—would prefer not to work. But that way madness lies. Our civilization is founded on its ability to get people to do things they would prefer not to do.

Bartleby is set in the present day in a vast, monolithic office building that crouches atop a hill like an Acropolis dedicated to bureaucracy. It is based on "Bartleby the Scrivener," a famous story published in 1856 by Herman Melville, who not only wrote *Moby-Dick*, but also labored for many empty years as a clerk in a customs house. Although the story is nearly 150 years old, it is correct to observe, as A. O. Scott does in the *New York Times*, that Melville anticipated Kafka—and Dilbert. This kind of office work exists outside time.

David Paymer plays the boss, a sad-eyed man who has a private office of his own, its prestige undermined by the fact that his window directly overlooks a Dumpster. Glenne Headly is Vivian, who flirts because if a man shows interest in her, that may be evidence that she exists. Joe Piscopo is Rocky, who dresses flamboyantly to imply he is not as colorless as his job. Maury Chaykin is the hopeless nebbish Ernie, who elevates strategic incompetence to an art form.

And Crispin Glover is Bartleby. The teen star of the eighties appears here like a ghost, pale and immobile, arrested by some private grief or fear. When he says, "I would prefer not to," it doesn't sound like insubordination, rebellion, or resistance, but like a flat statement of fact—a fact so overwhelming it brings all possible alternatives to a dead halt.

The film has been directed by Jonathan Parker; he adapted the Melville story with Catherine DiNapoli. It's his first work, and a promising one. I admire it and yet cannot recommend it, because it overstays its natural running time. The Melville short story was short because it needed to be short—to make its point and then stop dead without compromise or consideration. *Bartleby* is short for a feature film, at eighty-two minutes, but might have been more successful at fifty or sixty minutes. Too bad there seems to be an unbreakable rule against features that short, or short subjects that long. In a perfect world, *Bartleby* would establish the office and its workers, introduce Bartleby, develop response to the work, and stop. Side stories, such as Vivian's attraction to the city manager (Seymour Cassel), would not be necessary.

And yet there is a kind of uncompromising, implacable simplicity to *Bartleby* that inspires admiration. In a world where most movies are about exciting people doing thrilling things, here is a film about a job that is living death, and a man who prefers not to do it. My friend McHugh worked his way through college at Acme Pest Control of Bloomington, Indiana. One day while he was crawling under a house with a spray gun, a housewife invited him into the kitchen for a lemonade. As he drank it, while covered in cobwebs and mud, she told her son, "Study your lessons hard, Jimmy, or you'll end up like him." Or like Bartleby.

Basic ★
R, 98 m., 2003

John Travolta (Agent Tom Hardy), Connie Nielsen (Lieutenant Julia Osborne), Samuel L. Jackson (Sergeant Nathan West), Giovanni Ribisi (Levi Kendall), Brian Van Holt (Raymond Dunbar), Taye Diggs (Pike), Timothy Daly (Colonel Bill Styles), Roselyn Sanchez (Nunez), Harry Connick Jr. (Pete Vilmer). Directed by John McTiernan and produced by Mike Medavoy, James Vanderbilt, Arnie Messer, and Michael Tadross. Screenplay by Vanderbilt.

I embarked on *Basic* with optimism and goodwill, confident that a military thriller starring John Travolta and Samuel L. Jackson, and directed by John McTiernan *(Die Hard)*, might be entertaining action and maybe more. As the plot unfolded, and unfolded, and unfolded, and unfolded, I leaned forward earnestly in my seat, trying to remember where we had been and what we had learned.

Reader, I gave it my best shot. But with a sinking heart I realized that my efforts were not going to be enough, because this was not a film that *could* be understood. With style and energy from the actors, with every sign of self-confidence from the director, with pictures that were in focus and dialogue that you could hear, the movie descended into a morass of narrative quicksand. By the end, I wanted to do cruel and vicious things to the screenplay.

There's a genre that we could call the Jerk-

Around Movie, because what it does is jerk you around. It sets up a situation and then does a bait and switch. You never know which walnut the truth is under. You invest your trust and are betrayed.

I don't mind being jerked around if it's done well, as in *Memento*. I felt *The Usual Suspects* was a long ride for a short day at the beach, but at least as I traced back through it, I could see how it held together. But as nearly as I can tell, *Basic* exists with no respect for objective reality. It is all smoke and no mirrors. If I were to see it again and again, I might be able to extract an underlying logic from it, but the problem is, when a movie's not worth seeing twice, it had better get the job done the first time through.

The film is set in a rainy jungle in Panama. I suspect it rains so much as an irritant, to make everything harder to see and hear. Maybe it's intended as atmosphere. Or maybe the sky gods are angry at the film.

We are introduced to the hard-assed Sergeant Nathan West (Jackson), a sadistic perfectionist who is roundly hated by his unit. When various characters are killed during the confusion of the storm, there is the feeling the deaths may not have been accidental, may indeed have involved drug dealing. A former DEA agent named Tom Hardy (Travolta) is hauled back from alcoholism to join the investigation, teaming with Lieutenant Julia Osborne (Connie Nielsen).

The murders and the investigation are both told in untrustworthy flashbacks. We get versions of events from such differing points of view, indeed, that we yearn for a good old-fashioned omnipotent POV to come in and slap everybody around. There are so many different views of the same happenings that, hell, why not throw in a musical version?

Of course, there are moments that are engaging in themselves. With such actors (Giovanni Ribisi, Taye Diggs, Brian Van Holt, Roselyn Sanchez, and even Harry Connick Jr.), how could there not be? We listen and follow and take notes, and think we're getting somewhere, and then the next scene knocks down our theories and makes us start again. Finally we arrive at an ending that gives a final jerk to our chain and we realize we never had a chance.

What is the point of a movie like *Basic*? To make us feel cleverly deceived? To do that, the

49

film would have to convince us of one reality and then give us another, equally valid (classics like *Laura* did that). This movie gives no indication even at the end that we have finally gotten to the bottom of things. There is a feeling that *Basic II* could carry right on, undoing the final shots, bringing a few characters back to life and sending the whole crowd off on another tango of gratuitous deception.

The Battle of Shaker Heights ★ ★
PG-13, 85 m., 2003

Shia LaBeouf (Kelly Ernswiler), Elden Henson (Bart Bowland), Amy Smart (Tabby Bowland), Kathleen Quinlan (Eve Ernswiler), William Sadler (Abe Ernswiler), Shiri Appleby (Sarah), Ray Wise (Harrison Bowland), Anson Mount (Miner Weber). Directed by Efram Potelle and Kyle Rankin and produced by Sean Bailey and Jeff Balis. Screenplay by Erica Beeney.

Gene Siskel liked to ask, "Is this film more interesting than a documentary of the same actors having lunch?" He would have been able to find out with Project Greenlight, the behind-the-scenes cable series. One winning screenplay a year is chosen to be produced by Miramax, and HBO airs a documentary series about the making of the movie, so that we can eavesdrop on the arguments, brainstorms, disagreements, and tantrums of the makers—and on their lunches.

Stolen Summer (2002), the first of the Greenlight movies, passed Siskel's test. It was a lovely coming-of-age story about a friendship between two Chicago kids during the last summer of one of their lives. *The Battle of Shaker Heights,* the second Greenlight movie, fails the test. I have actually had lunch with two of the actors—Elden Henson and Kathleen Quinlan—and that was a lot more interesting than the movie.

It's one of those stories where a formula is juiced up with stuff we don't expect, like the teenage hero's hobby of fighting in reenactments of famous battles. There's also a doomed infatuation with his best friend's college-age sister, which leads to him becoming a part-time honorary member of the friend's family. He finds it exquisitely painful to be in love with the sister, who likes to have him around because he's smart and cute, and doesn't take his puppy love seriously.

The hero is Kelly (Shia LaBeouf, the young lead of *Holes*), and he's the brightest kid in his high school, smart enough to correct his teacher during a class, but not smart enough to know that's a pretty dumb thing to do. His new friend is Bart (Elden Henson), and they meet when Kelly saves Bart's life, sort of, in a virtual kind of way.

Then Kelly meets Bart's sister Tabby (Amy Smart). I hope Tabby is a nickname. If it's a sin to give a pet a saint's name, unimaginable punishments must await anyone giving a daughter a pet's name. Because Kelly is obsessed with the unavailable Tabby, he ignores the hopeful friendliness of Sarah (Shiri Appleby), who shares the graveyard shift with him at a local store, one of those consumer temples where it's not too much of a stretch to imagine Robin Williams behind the photo counter. Sarah likes him, but represents the known, while Tabby is the unknown; for a boy of a certain age, it is a great deal easier (and more relaxing) to imagine sex with someone you don't know than with someone you do.

Bart and Tabby's dad, Harrison (Ray Wise), was once into war memorabilia but now obsesses over nesting dolls. You don't know if the characters in this movie are crazy, or simply the victims of bright ideas by Erica Beeney, the winning screenwriter. More examples of piling on at the story conference: Kelly's dad (William Sadler) is a former drug abuser, and his mom (Kathleen Quinlan) runs a fairly unusual home business involving immigrants who produce art on an assembly line—the kinds of paintings that come free with the bedroom suite.

It is important to note that imagining sex is the only way Kelly experiences it. His bond with Tabby comes through their mutual love of art, about which Kelly knows a surprising amount (this is a bright kid who apparently knows everything known to anyone who worked on the movie). Tabby, who has her own studio, produces paintings a step up from the assembly line at Kelly's house; her work is the kind that wins blue ribbons at fairs. She's heading to Yale in the fall, which means she has periods of ambivalence about her approaching marriage to her sometimes uncomprehending boyfriend Miner (Anson Mount)—which leads, somewhat unconvincingly, to a make-out session between Tabby and Kelly in which the movie focuses on Kelly's emotions, which we can easily imagine, instead of on Tabby's, which exist entirely at the convenience of the screenplay.

Shia LaBeouf makes his character a winning and charming kid, more believable than the movie deserves, and Elden Henson, who I've been monitoring since *The Mighty* (1998), is kind of a junior Vincent D'Onofrio, able to play almost anybody, as you could see when he went from the teenage Shakespearean tragedy *O* to *Dumb and Dumber*.

The Battle of Shaker Heights isn't bad so much as jumbled. One of the problems with Project Greenlight is that everybody tries to cross when the light turns green. You get the sense of too much input, too many bright ideas, too many scenes that don't belong in the same movie. Odd, how overcrowded it seems, for eighty-five minutes. Here's an idea: Next year, Miramax picks the winning screenplay, gives the filmmakers $1 million, and sends them off in total isolation to make a movie with absolutely no input from anybody. The HBO series could be about how the Miramax marketing department sees the result and figures out how to sell it.

Beauty and the Beast ★ ★ ★ ★
G, 94 m., revised 2002

With the voices of: Paige O'Hara (Belle), Robby Benson (Beast), Richard White (Gaston), Jerry Orbach (Lumiere), David Ogden Stiers (Cogsworth), Angela Lansbury (Mrs. Potts), Jesse Corti (LeFou). Directed by Gary Trousdale and Kirk Wise and produced by Don Hahn. Art direction by Brian McEntee. Animation screenplay by Linda Woolverton.

With *The Little Mermaid* (1989) and *Beauty and the Beast* (1991), Disney in two strokes reinvented the animated feature and the movie musical. Both genres were languishing in the 1980s—musicals seemed like a lost art—and these two films brought them to a new kind of life. All the big animated hits since (*The Lion King, Aladdin, Toy Story, Monsters, Inc., Shrek*) descend from that original breakthrough, which blasted animated films out of the kiddie-film category and saw them, as Walt Disney originally saw them, as popular entertainments for all ages.

The Little Mermaid was the film that reminded audiences how entertaining animation could be, and *Beauty and the Beast* was the breakthrough—the first animated film to win an Oscar nomination in the Best Picture category. Disney itself groups the film with *Snow White* and *Pinocchio* as one of its three best. Now *Beauty* is back, in a new version so vibrant it's like experiencing the film anew. For its engagements on giant IMAX screens around the country, the movie has received a frame-by-frame restoration (since even the tiniest blemish isn't tiny on an IMAX screen). The sound track has been prepped for IMAX's seventy-four-speaker surround sound. And there's even new footage.

"Human Again," the added footage, is not a "deleted scene" that has been added to this rerelease in the spirit of countless recent "director's cuts." Although a scene is occasionally dropped from an animated film, the preplanning that goes into them, and the labor-intensive nature of the work, make it rare for scenes to be fully animated and then cut. What Disney started with was an original song by Howard Ashman and Alan Menken, written for the *Beauty and the Beast* score but then dropped from the screenplay. The song was put back in for the Broadway stage version of *Beauty*, was a hit, and belatedly won a place in the movie. It has now been animated for the first time.

The new scene stars three of the Beast's household servants, who fell under the same curse as their master, and were transformed into (hardly inanimate) objects. Lumiere (voice by Jerry Orbach) is a candelabra, Cogsworth (David Ogden Stiers) is the clock, and Mrs. Potts (Angela Lansbury) is the teapot (Chip, of course, is her son, the teacup). Joined by a chorus line of other household utensils, products, and tools, they sing in anticipation of being restored to human form if the Beast makes his deadline and falls in love with Belle before the last petal falls from the enchanted rose.

Sitting in front of the IMAX screen, I was reminded again that the giant format is a major part of the experience. There is a theory that quick cuts in such a large format tend to disorient the audience, and many IMAX films move in a stately manner from one static composition to another, but the quick pace of *Beauty* presented no problems. To be sure, the picture was not originally filmed with IMAX cameras, but this restoration is not a blowup of an existing 35mm print; it's a digital re-creation of it for the bigger screen.

Disney pioneered this form of giant-screen rerelease with its *Fantasia 2000* (1999). Seeing *Beauty and the Beast* again this way, I began to daydream about other classics that could be showcased on IMAX. The year 2001 came and went without a proper national rerelease of *2001: A Space Odyssey,* and although Francis Ford Coppola's *Apocalypse Now Redux* got somewhat more exposure, imagine it on the giant screen. As the average American movie screen grows smaller and smaller, as palaces are phased out for multiplexes, why isn't IMAX the natural home for the great Hollywood epics?

Before Sunset ★ ★ ★ ½
R, 80 m., 2004

Ethan Hawke (Jesse), Julie Delpy (Celine). Directed by Richard Linklater and produced by Linklater and Anne Walker-McBay. Screenplay by Linklater, Julie Delpy, and Ethan Hawke.

Nine years have passed since Jesse and Celine met in Vienna and walked all over the city, talking as if there would be no tomorrow, and then promising to meet again in six months. "Were you there in Vienna, in December?" she asks him. Nine years have passed and they have met again in Paris. Jesse wrote a novel about their long night together, and at a book signing he looks up, and there she is. They begin to talk again, in a rush, before he must leave to catch his flight back to America.

Before Sunset continues the conversation that began in *Before Sunrise* (1995), but at a riskier level. Jesse (Ethan Hawke) and Celine (Julie Delpy) are over thirty now, have made commitments in life, no longer feel as they did in 1995 that everything was possible. One thing they have learned, although they are slow to reveal it, is how rare it is to meet someone you feel an instinctive connection with. They walk out of the bookstore and around the corner and walk, and talk, and director Richard Linklater

films them in long, uninterrupted takes, so that the film feels like it exists in real time.

Before Sunset is a remarkable achievement in several ways, most obviously in its technical skill. It is not easy to shoot a take that is six or seven minutes long, not easy for actors to walk through a real city while dealing with dialogue that has been scripted but must sound natural and spontaneous. Yet we accept, almost at once, that this conversation is really happening. There's no sense of contrivance or technical difficulty.

Hawke and Delpy wrote the screenplay themselves, beginning from the characters and dialogue created the first time around by Linklater and Kim Krizan. They lead up to personal details very delicately; at the beginning they talk politely and in abstractions, edging around the topics we (and they) want answers to: Is either one married? Are they happy? Do they still feel that deep attraction? Were they intended to spend their lives together?

There is the feeling, as they discuss how their adult lives are unfolding, that sometimes the actors may be skirting autobiography. Certainly there is an unmistakable truth when Jesse, trying to describe what marriage is like, says, "I feel like I'm running a small nursery with someone I used to date." But the movie is not a confessional, and the characters don't rush into revelations. There is a patience at work, even a reticence, that reflects who they have become. They have responsibilities. They no longer have a quick instinctive trust. They are wary of revealing too much. They are grown-ups, although at least for this afternoon in Paris they are in touch with the open, spontaneous, hopeful kids they were nine years before.

Before Sunrise was a remarkable celebration of the fascination of good dialogue. But *Before Sunset* is better, perhaps because the characters are older and wiser, perhaps because they have more to lose (or win), and perhaps because Hawke and Delpy wrote the dialogue themselves. The film has the materials for a lifetime project; like the *7-Up* series, this is a conversation that could be returned to every ten years or so, as Celine and Jesse grow older.

Delpy worked often with Krzysztof Kieslowski, the Polish master of coincidence and synchronicity, and perhaps it's from that experience that *Before Sunset* draws its fascination with intersecting time lines. When Celine and Jesse parted, they didn't know each other's last names or addresses; they staked everything on that promise to meet again in six months. We find out what happened in Vienna in December, but we also find out that Celine studied for several years at New York University (just as Delpy did) while Jesse was living there (just as Hawke was). "In the months leading up to my wedding, I was thinking of you," he tells her. He even thought he saw her once, in the deli at 17th and Broadway. She knows the deli. Maybe he did.

What they are really discussing, as they trade these kinds of details, is the possibility that they missed a lifetime they were intended to spend together. Jesse eventually confesses that he wrote his book and came to Paris for a book signing because that was the only way he could think of to find her again. A little later, in a subtle moment of body language, she reaches out to touch him and then pulls back her hand before he sees it.

All this time they are walking and talking. Down streets, through gardens, past shops, into a café, out of the café, toward the courtyard where she has the flat she has lived in for four years. And it is getting later, and the time for his flight is approaching, just as he had to catch the train in Vienna. But what is free will for, if not to defy our plans? "Baby, you are gonna miss that plane," she says.

Behind the Sun ★ ★
PG-13, 94 m., 2002

Jose Dumont (Father), Rodrigo Santoro (Tonio), Rita Assemany (Mother), Ravi Ramos Lacerda (Pacu), Luis Carlos Vasconcelos (Salustiano), Flavia Marco Antonio (Clara), Everaldo De Souza Pontes (Old Blind Man). Directed by Walter Salles and produced by Arthur Cohn. Screenplay by Karim Ainouz and Sergio Machado.

Behind the Sun describes a blood feud elevated to the dignity of tragedy. It takes place in a rural area of Brazil, but it could be set instead in the Middle East, in Bosnia, in India, in Africa, in any of those places where people kill each other because of who their parents were.

Religion, which is often cited as a justifica-tion for these killings, is just a smoke screen for tribalism. The killings spring out of a universal human tendency to dislike anyone who is not like we are.

The movie takes place in 1910. Two families live on either side of a cane field. The Ferreiras are richer, live in a sprawling villa, have an extended family. The Breves are poorer, humble, hardworking. Since time immemorial there has been a feud between these two families, springing from some long-forgotten disagreement over land. Over time a set of ground rules has grown up: First a Ferreira man (or a Breves man) kills a Breves (or a Ferreira) man, and then the tables are turned.

If it amounted only to that, all the Breves and Ferreiras would be dead, or one side would have won. Certain customs somewhat slow the pace of the killing. When someone has been killed, his bloodstained shirt is left out in the sun to dry, and there is a truce until the red has turned yellow. Despite the predictable timetable that would seem to operate, the next victim is somehow always unprepared, as we see when a young Breves stalks his quarry one night after a shirt has turned yellow.

We meet the Kid (Ravi Ramos Lacerda), youngest son of the Breves family, who knows that since his adored older brother Tonio (Rodrigo Santoro) has killed a Ferreira, it is only a matter of time until the blood fades and Tonio is killed. While the ominous waiting period continues, a troupe of itinerant circus performers passes through, and the Kid meets the ringmaster and his sultry fire-eating star. They give him a picture book about the sea, which, wouldn't you know, encourages him to dream about a world different from the one he knows.

The circus itself offers an alternative vision, not that the cheerless sugar cane feud doesn't make anything look preferable. Tonio meets the fire-breather and is thunderstruck by love, and there is the possibility that, yes, he might run away with the circus. More than this I dare not reveal, except to hint that the age-old fate of the two families must play out under the implacable sun.

Behind the Sun is a good-looking movie, directed by Walter Salles, who was much praised for his 1998 Oscar nominee *Central Station*, also about a young boy whose life is scarred by the cruelty of his elders. It has some of the simplicity and starkness of classical tragedy, but what made me impatient was its fascination with the macho blood lust of the two families. Since neither family has evolved to the point where it can see the futility of killing and the pointlessness of their deadly ritual, it was hard for me to keep from feeling they were getting what they deserved. Sure, I hoped Tonio would get the girl and the Kid would see the ocean, but these are limited people and we can care about them only if we buy into their endless cycle of revenge and reprisal. After a certain point no one is right and no one is wrong, both sides have boundless grievances, and it's the audience that wants to run away with the circus.

The Believer ★ ★ ★
R, 98 m., 2002

Ryan Gosling (Danny Balint), Summer Phoenix (Carla Moebius), Theresa Russell (Lina Moebius), Billy Zane (Curtis Zampf), A. D. Miles (Guy Danielson), Joshua Harto (Kyle), Glenn Fitzgerald (Drake), Garret Dillahunt (Billings). Directed by Henry Bean and produced by Susan Hoffman and Christopher Roberts. Screenplay by Bean.

Censors feel *they* are safe with objectionable material, but must protect others who are not as smart or moral. The same impulse tempts the reviewer of *The Believer*. Here is a fiercely controversial film about a Jew who becomes an anti-Semite. When I saw it at Sundance 2000, where it won the Grand Jury Prize, I wrote, "Some feared the film could do more harm than good." I shared those fears. The film's hero is so articulate in his retailing of anti-Semitic beliefs that his words, I thought, might find the wrong ears. I understand the film, I was saying—but are you to be trusted with it?

Certainly the movie has been a hot potato. After a screening at the Simon Weisenthal Center inspired audience members to protest it, no major distributor would pick it up. Showtime scheduled it for a cable showing, which was canceled in the aftermath of 9/11. Then it was finally shown in the spring, and now has theatrical distribution from small Fireworks Pictures. In the meantime, to its Sundance awards it has added Independent Spirit Awards for best

screenplay and best first feature (both to director Henry Bean), best actor (Ryan Gosling), and best supporting actress (Summer Phoenix). Few doubt it is a good film. But do we really need a movie, right now, about a Jewish neo-Nazi?

I am not the person to answer that question for you. You have to answer it for yourself. The film's anti-Semitism is articulate but evil, and the conflict between what the hero says and what he believes (or does not want to believe) is at the very center of the story.

Gosling's character, named Danny Balint, is based on a real person. The *Jerusalem Report* writes: "The film has its roots in a true story. Daniel Burros was a nice Jewish boy from Queens who somehow went from being his rabbi's star pupil to a hotheaded proponent of the long-defunct Third Reich. After a stint in the army, he became involved with the American Nazi Party and the Ku Klux Klan. In 1965, following Burros's arrest at a KKK event in New York City, the *New York Times* disclosed that he was Jewish. Hours after the paper hit the stands, Burros took his own life."

In the film, Danny is seen as a bright young yeshiva student who gets into impassioned arguments with his teachers. Why must Abraham sacrifice his son Isaac? What kind of a God would require such an act? "A conceited bully," Danny decides. As a young man, Danny rejects his Orthodox upbringing, confronts Jews on the street and in subway cars, beats and kicks one, and expresses contempt for a race which, as he sees it, did not fight back during the Holocaust. Eventually he falls into the orbit of a neo-Nazi organization run by Theresa Russell and Billy Zane, who are impressed by his rhetoric but want him to dial down on the subject of Judaism: "It doesn't play anymore."

For Danny, anti-Semitism and the self-hate it implies is the whole point; he is uninterested in the politics of fascism. For Danny, the weakness of Jews is what he sees as their willingness to be victims, and after a court assigns him to an encounter group with Holocaust survivors, he bluntly asks one why he didn't fight back. Israelis, he believes, are not Jews because they own their own land and defend it, and therefore have transcended their Jewishness. You can see this reasoning twisting back into his own unhappy soul; he objects to Abraham taking instructions from God, and he objects to taking instructions from his church. His values involve his muscles, his fighting ability (both physical and rhetorical), his willingness to confront. In some kind of sick way, he attacks Jews, hoping to inspire one to beat him up.

Ryan Gosling (who, incredibly, was a Mouseketeer contemporary of Britney Spears), is at twenty-two a powerful young actor. He recently starred in *Murder by Numbers* as one of two young killers resembling Leopold and Loeb in their desire to demonstrate their superiority by committing a perfect crime. In *The Believer,* he reminds us of Edward Norton in *American History X,* another movie about a bright, twisted kid who is attracted to the transgressive sickness of racism. The movie is not very convincing in its portrayal of the fascist group (Zane and Russell seem less like zealots than hobbyists), but his personal quest is real enough.

When he involves himself in a raid on a temple, there is a revealing paradox: He resents the skinheads who come along with him because they don't understand the traditions they are attacking. What good is it to desecrate the Torah if you don't know what it is? He knows, and we begin to understand that he cares, that he accepts Judaism in the very core of his soul, and that his fight is against himself.

The ending of *The Believer,* if not exactly open, is inconclusive, and this is the kind of movie where you need to budget in time afterward for a cup of coffee and some conversation. The movie is better at portraying Danny's daily reality than at making sense of his rebellion (if sense can be made), but perhaps the movie plus the discussion can add up to a useful experience. Although his film needs more clarity and focus, Henry Bean has obviously taken a big chance because of his own sincere concerns. And if the wrong people get the wrong message—well, there has never been any shortage of wrong messages. Or wrong people.

Below ★ ★ ½
R, 103 m., 2002

Matt Davis (O'Dell), Bruce Greenwood (Brice), Olivia Williams (Claire), Holt McCallany (Loomis), Scott Foley (Coors), Zach Galifianakis (Weird Wally), Jason Flemyng (Stumbo), Dexter Fletcher (Kingsley). Directed by David N. Twohy and produced by Sue Baden-Powell and Michael Zoumas. Screenplay by Twohy, Lucas Sussman, and Darren Aronofsky.

Even before the woman is taken on board, the USS *Tiger Shark* is a submarine in trouble. The captain has been lost overboard, or at least that's the story, and tempers run high in the confined space. Then the sub rescues three drifters in a life raft, one of them a woman, whose presence on board is agreed by everyone to be bad luck on a sub, although her arrival does result in the crew wearing cleaner underwear.

Now dangers increase. The sub is tracked by Germans, who drop depth bombs and later come back to troll for it with giant grappling hooks. There is fearful damage to the periscope and the control tower. An oil leak threatens to betray the sub's position. Oxygen is running low, and hydrogen in the air is a danger to the crew's safety and sanity. And perhaps there is a ghost on board. The creepy sounds from outside the hull—of seaweed, whale songs, and bouncing depth bombs—increase apprehension.

Yes, a ghost. How else to explain why a record of Benny Goodman's "Sing, Sing, Sing" seems to play itself at inopportune times—as when the Germans are listening for the slightest sound from below? And when the late skipper was a Goodman fan? Of course, there could be a saboteur on board, in addition to, or perhaps instead of, the ghost.

Below is a movie where the story, like the sub, sometimes seems to be running blind. In its best moments it can evoke fear, and it does a good job of evoking the claustrophobic terror of a little World War II boat, but the story line is so eager to supply frightening possibilities that sometimes we feel jerked around. Isn't it possible for a submarine to be haunted without turning it into a museum of horror film devices?

Of those devices, the most tiresome is the convention that surprises make sounds. In most horror movies, including many less clever than *Below,* there is a visual strategy in which a character is shown in relative close-up (limiting our ability to see around him) and then startled by the unexpected appearance of another character or other visual surprise. This moment is invariably signaled on the sound track with a loud, alarming musical chord, or perhaps by the sound of a knife being sharpened.

But surprises don't make sounds, and the cliché has become so tiresome that I submit a director might be able to create a *more* frightening sequence by playing the unexpected appearance in total silence.

There are a lot of surprise apparitions in *Below*, and many times we expect them even when they don't arrive. Consider the effective sequence in which four divers have to penetrate the ballast space between the inner and outer hulls to search for the oil leak. Will they find a ghostly body, or what?

The acting skipper of the ship is Brice (Bruce Greenwood). The absence of the former skipper is a secret at first, and the explanations for his disappearance are contradictory; even by the end of the movie, we are not sure we have the correct story. Has he returned to haunt the boat? Oxygen deprivation can encourage hallucinations.

The bad-luck woman on board, Claire (Olivia Williams), turns out to be a nurse from a sunken hospital ship. Who sunk that ship with its big red cross, and why? And what about the two survivors in the boat with her? What are their stories? Although the arrival of a woman on board inspires some heavy-handed scenes in which some men seem to be warming up for an assault, that plot thread is quickly abandoned, and Claire begins to take a surprisingly active role in the onboard discussions. Siding with her is O'Dell (Matt Davis), maybe because he agrees, maybe because he likes her. Brice's command of the ship may include decisions made with a hidden agenda.

The movie is skillfully made by David N. Twohy, whose *The Arrival* (1996) was an uncommonly intelligent science fiction thriller about a hidden alien plot against Earth. But his overpraised *Pitch Black* (2000), which launched Vin Diesel, was weakened by the same faults as *Below*. It had too many obligatory startles, too many unclear possibilities, and not enough definition of the crucial players. But Twohy showed with *The Arrival* that he is a gifted director. *Below* has ambitions to be better than average, but doesn't pull itself together and insist on realizing them.

Bend It Like Beckham ★ ★ ★ ½
PG-13, 112 m., 2003

Parminder K. Nagra (Jesminder ["Jess"]

Bhamra), Keira Knightley (Juliette ["Jules"]), Jonathan Rhys-Meyers (Joe), Anupam Kher (Mr. Bhamra), Shaheen Khan (Mrs. Bhamra), Archie Panjabi (Pinky Bhamra), Juliet Stevenson (Paula). Directed by Gurinder Chadha and produced by Chadha and Deepak Nayar. Screenplay by Chadha, Paul Mayeda Berges, and Guljit Bindra.

I saw more important films at Sundance 2003, but none more purely enjoyable than *Bend It Like Beckham*, which is just about perfect as a teenage coming-of-age comedy. It stars a young actress of luminous appeal, it involves sports, romance, and, of course, her older sister's wedding, and it has two misinformed soccer moms—one who doesn't know a thing about the game and another who doesn't even know her daughter plays it.

The movie, set in London, tells the story of Jesminder Bhamra, known as "Jess," who comes from a traditional Indian family. Her parents are Sikhs who fled from Uganda to England, where her dad works at Heathrow airport. They live in the middle-class suburb of Hounslow, under the flight path of arriving jets, where her mother believes that Jess has two great duties in life: to learn to prepare a complete Indian meal, and to marry a nice Indian boy, in exactly that order.

Jess plays soccer with boys in the park. In her family's living room is a large portrait of a Sikh spiritual leader, but above Jess's bed is her own inspiration—the British soccer superstar David Beckham, better known to some as Posh Spice's husband. To Beckham's portrait she confides her innermost dream, which is to play for England. Of course, a girl cannot hope to be a soccer star, and an Indian girl should not play soccer at all, since in her mother's mind the game consists of "displaying your bare legs to complete strangers."

Jess is seen in the park one day by Juliette (Keira Knightley), who plays for the Hounslow Harriers, a woman's team, and is recruited to join them. The coach is a young Irishman named Joe (Jonathan Rhys-Meyers), and it is love at second or third sight—complicated because Joe cannot date his players, and Juliette has a crush on him, too.

But all of these elements make the film sound routine, and what makes it special is the bubbling energy of the cast and the warm joy with which Gurinder Chadha, the director and cowriter, tells her story. I am the first to admit that Gurinder Chadha is not a name on everybody's lips, but this is her third film and I can promise you she has an unfailing instinct for human comedy that makes you feel good and laugh out loud.

Her previous film was the wonderful *What's Cooking,* about four American ethnic families (African-American, Latino, Jewish, and Vietnamese) all preparing a traditional Thanksgiving dinner, while their younger generations are connected in unsuspected ways. There is an emerging genre of comedies about second- and third-generation young people breaking loose from traditional parents (*My Big Fat Greek Wedding* is the most spectacular example), and I've seen these rite-of-entry comedies by directors with Filipino, Indian, Chinese, Mexican, Iranian, and Korean backgrounds, and even one, *Mississippi Masala,* where Denzel Washington and Sarita Choudhury played two such characters whose stories meet.

Bend It Like Beckham, which adds a British flavor to its London metroland masala, is good not because it is blindingly original but because it is flawless in executing what is, after all, a dependable formula. The parents must be strict and traditional, but also loving and funny, and Mr. and Mrs. Bhamra (Anupam Kher and Shaheen Khan) are classic examples of the type. So is Juliette's mother, Paula (the wry, funny British star Juliet Stevenson), who tries to talk her tomboy daughter into Wonderbras, and spends most of the movie fearing that a girl who doesn't want to wear one must be a lesbian ("There's a reason why Sporty Spice is the only one without a boyfriend"). The editing by Justin Krish gets laughs all on its own with the precision that it uses to cut to reaction shots as the parents absorb one surprise after another.

Jess, played by Parminder K. Nagra, is a physically exuberant girl whose love of soccer crosses over into a love of life. She runs onto the field as if simply at play, she does cartwheels after scoring goals, and although she deceives her parents about her soccer dreams, she loves them and understands their point of view. Her father, who played cricket in Uganda but was discriminated against by the local London club,

still bears deep wounds, but "things are different now," Jess tells him, and there is the obligatory scene where he sneaks into the crowd at a match to see for himself.

Can there be an Indian comedy without a wedding? *Monsoon Wedding* is the great example, and here too we get the loving preparation of food, the exuberant explosion of music, and the backstage drama. All ethnic comedies feature scenes that make you want to leave the theater and immediately start eating, and *Bend It Like Beckham* may inspire some of its fans to make Indian friends simply so they can be invited over for dinner.

The movie's values run deep. It understands that for Jess's generation soccer is not about displaying bare legs (Jess has another reason to be shy about that), but it also understands the hopes and ambitions of parents—and, crucially, so does Jess, who handles the tentative romance with her coach in a way that combines tenderness with common sense. A closing scene at the airport, which in a lesser movie would have simply hammered out a happy ending, shows her tact and love.

Like all good movies, *Bend It Like Beckham* crosses over to wide audiences. It's being promoted in the magazines and on the cable channels that teenage girls follow, but recently we showed it on our Ebert & Roeper Film Festival at Sea to an audience that ranged in age from seven to eighty-one, with a fiftyish median, and it was a huge success. For that matter, the hip Sundance audience, dressed in black and clutching cell phones and cappuccinos, loved it, too. And why not, since its characters and sensibility are so abundantly lovable.

Better Luck Tomorrow ★ ★ ★ ★
R, 98 m., 2003

Parry Shen (Ben), Jason Tobin (Virgil), Sung Kang (Han), Roger Fan (Daric), John Cho (Steve), Karin Anna Cheung (Stephanie). Directed by Justin Lin and produced by Lin, Ernesto M. Foronda, and Julie Asato. Screenplay by Lin, Foronda and Fabian Marquez.

Justin Lin's *Better Luck Tomorrow* has a hero named Benjamin, but depicts a chilling hidden side of suburban affluence that was unseen in *The Graduate.* Its heroes need no career advice;

they're on the fast track to Ivy League schools and well-paying jobs, and their straight-A grades are joined on their résumés by an improbable array of extracurricular credits: Ben lists the basketball team, the academic decathlon team, and the food drive.

What he doesn't mention is the thriving business he and his friends have in selling cheat sheets. Or their drug sideline. Or the box hidden in his bedroom and filled with cash. Ben belongs to a group of overachieving Asian-American students in a wealthy Orange County suburb; they conform to the popular image of smart, well-behaved Asian kids, but although they have ambition they lack values, and step by step they move more deeply into crime. How deep is suggested by the film's opening scene, where Ben (Parry Shen) and his best friend, Virgil (Jason Tobin), are interrupted while sunbathing by the sound of a cell phone ringing on a body they have buried in Virgil's backyard.

Better Luck Tomorrow is a disturbing and skillfully told parable about growing up in today's America. These kids use money as a marker of success, are profoundly amoral, and project a wholesome, civic-minded attitude. They're on the right path to take jobs with the Enrons of tomorrow, in the dominant culture of corporate greed. Lin focuses on an ethnic group that is routinely praised for its industriousness, which deepens the irony, and also perhaps reveals a certain anger at the way white America patronizingly smiles on its successful Asian-American citizens.

Ben, Virgil, and their friends know how to use their ethnic identity to play both sides of the street in high school. "Our straight A's were our passports to freedom," Ben says in his narration. No parents are ever seen in the movie (there are very few adults, mostly played by white actors in roles reserved in most movies for minority groups). The kids get good grades, and their parents assume they are studying while they stay out late and get into very serious trouble.

Better Luck Tomorrow has all the obligatory elements of the conventional high school picture. Ben has a crush on the pretty cheerleader Stephanie Vandergosh (Karin Anna Cheung), but she dates Steve (John Cho), who plays the inevitable older teenager with a motorcycle and an attitude. Virgil is unlucky with girls, but

thinks he once spotted Stephanie in a porno film (unlikely, but gee, it kinda looks like her). Han (Sung Kang) comes up with the scheme to sell homework for cash, and Daric (Roger Fan) is the overachiever who has, no doubt, the longest entry under his photo in the school yearbook.

These students never refer to, or are identified by, specific ethnic origin; they're known as the "Chinese Mafia" at school because of their low-key criminal activities, but that's not a name they give themselves. They may be Chinese, Japanese, Korean, Filipino, but their generation no longer obsesses with the nation before the hyphen; they are Orange County Americans, through and through, and although Stephanie's last name and Caucasian little brother indicate she was adopted, she brushes aside Ben's tentative question about her "real parents" by saying, "These are my real parents."

Better Luck Tomorrow is a coming-of-age film for Asian-Americans in American cinema. Like African-American films that take race for granted and get on with the characters and the story, Lin is making a movie where race is not the point but simply the given. After Ben joins the basketball team, a writer for the high school paper suggests he is the "token Asian" benchwarmer, and when students form a cheering section for him, he quits the team in disgust. He is not a token anything (and privately knows he has beaten the NBA record for free throws).

The story is insidious in the way it moves stealthily into darker waters, while maintaining the surface of a high school comedy. There are jokes and the usual romantic breakthroughs and reversals, and the progress of their criminal career seems unplanned and offhand, until it turns dangerous. I will not reveal the names of the key characters in the climactic scene, but note carefully what happens in terms of the story; perhaps the film is revealing that a bland exterior can hide seething resentment.

Justin Lin, who directed, cowrote, and coproduced, here reveals himself as a skilled and sure director, a rising star. His film looks as glossy and expensive as a mega-million studio production, and the fact that its budget was limited means that his cinematographer Patrice Lucien Cochet, his art director Yoo Jung Han, and the other members of his crew were very able and resourceful. It's one thing to get an expensive look with money, and another thing to get it with talent.

Lin keeps a sure hand on tricky material; he has obvious confidence about where he wants to go and how he wants to get there. His film is uncompromising, and doesn't chicken out with a U-turn ending. His actors expand and breathe as if they're captives just released from lesser roles (the audition reel of one actor, Lin recalls, showed him delivering pizzas in one movie after another). Parry Shen gives a watchful and wary undertone to his all-American boy, and Karin Anna Cheung finds the right note to deal with a boy she likes but finds a little too goody-goody. *Better Luck Tomorrow* is not just a thriller, not just a social commentary, not just a comedy or a romance, but all of those in a clearly seen, brilliantly made film.

Beyond Borders ★ ★

R, 127 m., 2003

Angelina Jolie (Sarah Jordan), Clive Owen (Nick Callahan), Linus Roache (Henry Bauford), Teri Polo (Charlotte), Yorick van Wageningen (Jan Steiger), Noah Emmerich (Elliot Hauser). Directed by Martin Campbell and produced by Dan Halsted and Lloyd Phillips. Screenplay by Caspian Tredwell-Owen.

Beyond Borders has good intentions and wants to call attention to the plight of refugees, but what a clueless vulgarization it makes of its worthy motives. Of course, there's more than one way to send a message, and maybe this movie will affect audiences that wouldn't see or understand a more truthful portrait of refugees, like Michael Winterbottom's *In This World.*

The movie stars Angelina Jolie, who is personally involved in efforts to help refugees and isn't simply dining out on a fashionable cause. She plays Sarah Jordan, a London society woman whose bloodless husband will never understand the passion she feels for social causes—and for Nick Callahan (Clive Owen), the handsome doctor who flies from one trouble spot to another saving lives. Wherever Nick is in need, be it Cambodia, Ethiopia, or Chechnya, Sarah flies in with truckloads of supplies for the sexy, saturnine Nick.

I can understand a beautiful young woman getting a crush on a heroic and dedicated aid worker. Happens all the time in the movies. But could the doctor, just once, look like Giovanni Ribisi or Jack Black instead of like Clive Owen—so that we'd know she loved him for his good heart and didn't just have the hots for a potential James Bond?

Sarah first sees Nick at a charity ball in London, where he strides in carrying a starving Ethiopian boy and accuses the well-upholstered society people of letting kids like this one starve to death because he has the misfortune to be starving in an area controlled by Communist rebels. Good point. Sarah is married to Henry Bauford (Linus Roache), who doesn't understand why she can't just send a check instead of running off to Ethiopia to personally head a caravan of grain trucks. A professional would be better at the job, but wouldn't be so inspired by the need to be near Doctor Nick, in an area of the world where people may indeed be starving but where Sarah and Nick find an adequate supply of romantic vistas, while stirring music wells up behind them. They're serious about the starving masses, but they get *really* serious when they confront their mutual romantic destiny.

Sarah arrives wearing an all-white safari outfit that isn't even a little sweaty and dusty. Did she change right before driving into Nick's camp? She must have spent as much kitting herself out on Regent Street as she did buying the grain. She reminded me of the hero of Evelyn Waugh's *Scoop,* who also goes out to Ethiopia and takes along a trunk jammed with enough supplies to create a camp as cozy as a suite at the Savoy.

But perhaps that's to make a point: The rich woman wants to do well, and doesn't understand inappropriate gestures. Still, what are we to make of a scene where she stops the truck, gathers up a starving baby, and determines to save its life? The baby's mother, near death, reaches out a desperate arm and Sarah reassures her she will take care of the child. Too bad about the mother. Nick says the kid is too far gone to live, but Sarah clutches it to her reassuring bosom and feeds it high-energy fluids a drop at a time.

I know nothing at all about where they found the baby or what condition it was really in. Although it looks like a starving stick figure, I assume it was a healthy child. The point is that it *looks like* a child near death, and the use of the image is offensive in a movie that is essentially a romance. When the suffering of real children is used to enhance the image of movie stars who fall in love against the backdrop of their suffering, a certain decency is lacking. *Beyond Borders* wants it both ways — glamour up front, and human misery in the background to lend it poignancy.

The key shots revealing the movie's priorities are the close-ups right after Sarah meets Nick for the first time in Ethiopia. We've stayed in long and medium shot for most of the way, but then, after a line of dialogue in which it becomes clear Sarah has a romantic as well as a charitable motivation, we get close-ups of the two as they share this realization. Movie grammar suggests that we are being visually informed that their romance is the real subject of the movie. Another approach might show Sarah in long shot, moving through a field of suffering, and then a close-up of a starving child reaching out to her distant figure. You see the difference.

Now consider the climax of the movie. Something tragic happens, and before it does, the movie cuts back and forth between Nick and Sarah in close-ups that reminded me of Bonnie and Clyde in the instant before the shooting started. What is the message being conveyed here? What unspoken words are contained in the looks of these two lovers? It's curiously hard to answer this question; try it yourself if you see the movie. The story has insisted on Sarah's behavior and on the romance to such a degree that by the end no commonsense response is available. The movie has cut loose from real refugees, the real world, and real characters, and committed itself to the foreground romance, and now when implacable reality asserts itself, there is really nothing to be said. ☞

The Big Animal ★ ★ ★

NO MPAA RATING, 72 m., 2004

Jerzy Stuhr (Zygmunt Sawicki), Anna Dymna (Marysia Sawicki), Dominika Bednarczyk (Bank Clerk), Blazej Wojcik (Bank Clerk), Andrzej Franczyk (Bank Manager), Feliks Szajnert (Drunkard), Rublo from Zalewski Circus (Camel). Directed by Jerzy Stuhr and produced by Janusz Morgenstern and Slawomir

Rogowski. Screenplay by Krzysztof Kieslowski, based on a novel by Kazimierz Orlos.

One day a camel appears in a Polish village. It must have been left behind by a circus. Bereft and abandoned, it seeks out the garden of the Sawicki family, Zygmunt and Marysia, and they are happy to give it a home. Not everyone has a camel, and Marysia feels as if there's another guest for dinner when the beast peers through their dining room window during meals.

So begins *The Big Animal,* a fable written by Krzysztof Kieslowski, the Polish poet of serendipity and coincidence, who died in 1996, leaving behind such masterpieces as *The Double Life of Veronique* and the Three Colors Trilogy (*Blue, White,* and *Red*). He wrote this screenplay in 1973, adapted from a novel, six years before *Camera Buff* brought him his first wide attention. Now it has been filmed by his best friend, Jerzy Stuhr, who stars as Zygmunt and appeared in many Kieslowski films, including *White.*

This is not a major Kieslowski work, nor was it intended to be. Kieslowski sometimes liked to work in a minor key, and some of the ten-hour-long films in his masterful *Decalogue* (1988) occupy similar territory: They are small parables about trying to make moral choices in an indifferent universe. He finds unexpected connections between characters, and unexpected meetings, and unintended consequences. Surely, to acquire an orphaned camel is such an event.

At first the village is happy to have a camel in its midst. That may be because the villagers have never seen a camel molting in the spring, when for several weeks it resembles a sofa abandoned to the rain. The camel (played by Rublo the camel) is a docile creature who often seems to be trying to recapture a lost train of thought. Zygmunt takes it for strolls around the village, schoolchildren are delighted by it, and Marysia knits it a shawl that leaves holes for its two humps.

All is well until stirrings of discontent are heard. Even in the most hospitable of communities, there are always malcontents who don't want a camel hanging around. The camel smells, and is unlovely, and it relieves itself in the street. And the Sawickis begin to stand out from the crowd: They are the People Who Have the Camel. In 1973 when Kieslowski wrote his screenplay, perhaps he saw it as a parable about life under the sameness and regimentation of communism. But even in a democracy human nature is intolerant of those who are different, and to own a camel is to be different.

In a capitalist society, this film might not be made because the story is not commercial. In 1973, there were state sources in Poland for production funds, but I have no idea if *The Big Animal* was turned down by the authorities. It is the kind of story that could be seen as a satirical attack on the government, or on the other hand it might simply be the tale of a camel. You never know. It is whimsical, bittersweet, wise in a minor key.

I am reminded of a story Dusan Makavejev told me. When there was a Yugoslavia, it had a censor whose job was to approve film scripts. The censor was a friend of Makavejev's; they had gone to school together. Makavejev submitted a script, and the censor called him into his office. "Dusan, Dusan, Dusan," he said sorrowfully, "you know what this story is about, and I know what this story is about. Now go home and rewrite it so only the audience knows what it is about."

Big Bad Love ★ ★
R, 111 m., 2002

Arliss Howard (Leon Barlow), Debra Winger (Marilyn), Paul Le Mat (Monroe), Rosanna Arquette (Velma), Angie Dickinson (Mrs. Barlow), Michael Parks (Mr. Aaron). Directed by Arliss Howard and produced by Debra Winger. Screenplay by James Howard and Arliss Howard, based on stories by Larry Brown.

It all comes down to whether you can tolerate Leon Barlow. I can't. *Big Bad Love* can, and is filled with characters who love and accept him even though he is a full-time, gold-plated pain in the can. Leon is a college graduate (no doubt of creative writing classes) who has adopted a Good Old Drunk persona that wavers between the tiresome and the obnoxious. The movie has patience with his narcissistic self-pity. My diagnosis: Send Barlow to rehab, haul him to some AA meetings, and find out in a year if he has anything worth saying.

I know there are people in real life who smoke as much as Barlow (Arliss Howard) does, but at today's cigarette prices he is spending $400 a month on cigarettes and almost as much on the manuscripts he ships out to literary magazines. His bar bill is beyond all imagining. The first thing you learn as a poor writer is to cut back on the overhead. Here at H & R Ebert ("Budget Control for Unpublished Drunks"), we could pare $25,000 a year from his costs just by cutting out his bad habits.

Barlow smokes more or less all the time. He becomes a character whose task every morning is to get through sixty to eighty cigarettes that day. Everything else is a parallel activity. He lives in a colorfully rundown house in rural Mississippi—the sort that passes for genteel poverty in the movies and is priced at $300,000 and up, with land, in the real-estate ads. He pounds away on his Royal typewriter as if engaged in a mano-a-mano with Robert E. *(Conan the Barbarian)* Howard in *The Whole Wide World.* Since he is a man without a glimmer of awareness of his own boorishness, one wonders what he writes. Epic fantasy, perhaps?

Like many drunks, he is enabled by his loved ones (or, as is often the case, his former loved ones). His ex-wife, Marilyn, well played by Debra Winger (Arliss Howard's real-life wife), has divorced him but still has a soft spot for the crazy lug. His buddy Monroe (Paul Le Mat) loves him, maybe because you protect your drinking buddy just like you protect your drinking money. Monroe's old lady, Velma (Rosanna Arquette), has a fate that was preordained when she was christened Velma, a name that summons up Raymond Chandler novels and long-suffering girlfriends. Velma sees more than she lets on, but is stuck in her sexpot act.

The movie's basic problem is that it has no distance on Barlow—no way to criticize him. The screenplay, written by Arliss Howard and James Howard, based on stories by the Mississippi writer Larry Brown, lets Barlow get away with murder. We all have a tendency to go easy on ourselves, and *Big Bad Love* is unaware that its hero is a tiresome jerk. Larry Brown writes about "hard-bitten, hard-drinking, hard-living male characters," according to a Website about his work, and is a "bad-boy novelist." One suspects that the movie lacks perspective on Barlow because Brown is, in some respects, Barlow.

Because a movie must be about something

more than smoking, drinking, and talking as if you are the best-read drunk in town, *Big Bad Love* delivers two tragedies, both foreshadowed, right on time. It also involves some visual touches, such as an indoor rainstorm, that may perplex audiences not familiar with the work of Tarkovsky.

Arliss Howard is not a bad actor or a bad director, but in this film he shows himself an unreliable judge of character. Leon Barlow could be saved by an emergency transfusion of irony, or even a film that is cheerfully jaundiced about him. But the martyr act doesn't work. Here is a man who wants us to like him because of his marriage that did not work, his stories that do not sell, and his children that he is not doing a very good job of parenting. Then we are asked to pity him because of all the cigarettes he must smoke and all the booze he has to drink, and because they make him feel so awful in the morning. He's a familiar type, imprisoned by self-monitoring: How am I doing? How do I feel? How long can I continue to abuse myself and those around me? In the movie, he's blessed by people who can see through the facade to the really great guy inside. All I could see was a cry for help.

The Big Bounce ★ ★
PG-13, 89 m., 2004

Owen Wilson (Jack Ryan), Charlie Sheen (Bob Rogers Jr.), Vinnie Jones (Lou Harris), Sara Foster (Nancy Hayes), Morgan Freeman (Walter Crewes), Gary Sinise (Ray Ritchie), Willie Nelson (Joe Lurie), Harry Dean Stanton (Bob Rogers Sr.), Butch Helemano (Hawaiian Priest). Directed by George Armitage and produced by Jorge Saralegui and Steve Bing. Screenplay by Sebastian Gutierrez, based on a novel by Elmore Leonard.

Elmore Leonard is a writer you read with your fingers crossed, amazed at his high-wire act, reading dialogue that always sounds like Leonard even though the characters never quite sound the same. You love the jargon as they explain their criminal specialties. You savor the way he pulls oddballs and misfits out of the shrubbery and sets them to work at strange day jobs and illegal night jobs, and shows them wise to the heartbreaks of the world but vulnerable

to them. Just today I bought Leonard's new novel, because I never miss one. Most of the time they're clear sailing right to the end, and you close the covers with a grin.

Such a distinctive voice translates only rarely to the movies. Although Leonard's plots are ingenious and delightful, they're not the reason we read the books; Agatha Christie, poor soul, has delightful and ingenious plots. It's not the what but the how with Leonard, and the movies (his work has generated thirty of them) are mostly distant echoes of the genius. Of those I've seen, the ones that seem to channel him more or less successfully are John Frankenheimer's *52 Pick-Up*, Barry Sonnenfeld's *Get Shorty*, Quentin Tarantino's *Jackie Brown*, and Steven Soderbergh's *Out of Sight*, although all four cross the Leonard voice with the distinctive voices of their directors.

Now here is *The Big Bounce*, the second screen version of this Leonard novel, which was first filmed in California in 1969 with Ryan O'Neal and Leigh Taylor-Young and has now been transferred to Hawaii. There's a dream cast: Owen Wilson, Charlie Sheen, Vinnie Jones, Sara Foster, Morgan Freeman, Gary Sinise and, I am not kidding you, Willie Nelson and Harry Dean Stanton. And the location is well visualized: not the commercialized Hawaii of so many movies, but a more secluded area with colorful local characters, not least at the resort bungalows managed by Freeman (also the local lawman), where Wilson gets a job halfway between janitor and gigolo.

The area's bad guy is Ray Ritchie (Gary Sinise), a developer who wants to put up high-rise hotels and spoil the flavor of paradise. His foreman, Lou Harris (Vinnie Jones), gets into a televised fight with Jack Ryan (Wilson), a beach bum and sometime athlete. That brings in Ritchie's enforcer, Bob Jr. (Charlie Sheen). And then there's the lithesome Nancy Hayes (Sara Foster), who is Ritchie's mistress but has a jones for criminals and gets really turned on when Jack demonstrates his skills as a burglar.

The destinies of all of these characters intersect in a way it would be unfair to describe, except to say that Leonard has a gift for surprising us with the hidden motives of some of his characters, and their allegiances can shift in an instant. What they want and what they do are not the point, really; that's the excuse for providing them with a stage. The pleasure in the film comes from watching them and listening to them, and Owen Wilson is especially good with his dialogue, which masks hostility with sweet reason.

The movie doesn't work. It meanders and drifts and riffs. There is a part of me that enjoyed its leisurely celebration of its characters. I wanted more focus, and so will you, but on TV late some night you may stumble across it and find yourself bemused for a time by the way they live their lives as if there's nothing more fun than being an Elmore Leonard character. Maybe they're right.

Big Fat Liar ★ ★ ★
PG, 87 m., 2002

Frankie Muniz (Jason Shepherd), Paul Giamatti (Marty Wolf), Amanda Bynes (Kaylee), Amanda Detmer (Monty), Donald Faison (Frank). Directed by Shawn Levy and produced by Brian Robbins and Michael Tollin. Screenplay by Dan Schneider and Robbins.

Big Fat Liar takes the smartest fourteen-year-old fibber in Michigan and pairs him up against the dumbest thirty-something fibber in Hollywood. Jason Shepherd is an eighth-grader who lies about almost everything, so when a movie producer steals his homework and turns it into a movie, naturally Jason's parents and teacher don't believe him. So he enlists his girlfriend Kaylee, and goes to Hollywood to confront the creep and prove he was telling the truth. (Naturally, he lies to cover up his absence from home.)

This premise, which sounds like something a fourteen-year-old might have dreamed up, becomes a surprisingly entertaining movie— one of those good-hearted comedies like *Spy Kids* where reality is put on hold while bright teenagers outsmart the best and worst the adult world has to offer. It's ideal for younger teens, and not painful for their parents.

Jason is played by Frankie Muniz (who was wonderful in *My Dog Skip*), Kaylee is Amanda Bynes, a TV actress making her film debut, and the reprehensible Marty Wolf, Hollywood sleazo supremo, is played by Paul Giamatti with the kind of teeth-gnashing venom the Beagle Boys used against Uncle Scrooge.

Marty, the "Wolfman," has indeed stolen Jason's eighth-grade story, which fell from his backpack into Wolf's limousine, for reasons too complicated to explain. The story, which is autobiographical, involves, of course, an eighth-grader who tells so many lies that no one believes him when he tells the truth. Marty is astonished when confronted in his studio office by the kid, who doesn't want money or even a share of ownership, but just for the guy to call his dad and admit, yes, it's true, I stole your kid's story. Marty laughs incredulously: That'll be the day.

The story is an excuse to take the kids on a tour of Hollywood, starting with the Universal back lot, which, like all back lots in movies, is jammed with countless extras dressed as Romans, aliens, cowboys, biblical figures, and can-can dancers. Jason and Kaylee get onto the lot via the Universal tour, and hide out in the wardrobe and props department, which has everything they need for their skulduggery.

Marty Wolf is such a seven-letter word that Jason quickly wins the sympathy of two key allies: his limo driver, Frank (Donald Faison), and his secretary, Monty (Amanda Detmer). Frank has reason for revenge. He was a hopeful actor until Marty wrote "loser" on his composite and sent it to every casting director in town. Monty does, too: She gets blamed for the Wolfman's every mistake.

A lot of the funniest scenes involve Giamatti, who is the target of so many practical jokes by the two kids that his life becomes miserable. The best: They fill his swimming pool with blue dye, so that on the day of his big meeting with the studio chief, he looks like an understudy for the Blue Man Group. His broad humor here is dramatically different from his needy, imploding documentary producer in Todd Solondz's *Storytelling*.

The movie's charm is that it has confidence in this goofy story, and doesn't push it too hard. Muniz and Bynes have an easy prepubertal relationship (she's a lot taller, of course). It's based on wisecracks and immunity from the problems of the real world, where Hollywood might be a lot more dangerous for fourteen-year-olds. Giamatti's slow burn alternates with his fast burn and his explosive rages, and his comeuppance at the end is entirely appropriate in movie terms. And certain lines have a charm of their own, as when the kids send the Wolf-man (now bright blue) not to the studio head's house as he expects, but to a birthday party, where the little guests joyfully cry, "Hey, it's the clown! Let's hurt him!"

Big Fish ★ ★ ½
PG-13, 125 m., 2003

Ewan McGregor (Young Edward), Albert Finney (Old Edward), Billy Crudup (Will Bloom), Jessica Lange (Sandra Bloom), Helena Bonham Carter (Jenny/The Witch), Alison Lohman (Young Sandra), Robert Guillaume (Dr. Bennett), Marion Cotillard (Josephine), Steve Buscemi (Norther Winslow), Danny DeVito (Amos Calloway), Matthew McGrory (Karl the Giant). Directed by Tim Burton and produced by Bruce Cohen, Dan Jinks, and Richard D. Zanuck. Screenplay by John August, based on the novel by Daniel Wallace.

From his son's point of view, Edward Bloom's timing is off. He spent the years before his son's birth having amazing adventures and meeting unforgettable characters, and the years after the birth telling his stories to his son, over and over and over and over again. Albert Finney, who can be the most concise of actors, can also, when required, play a tireless blowhard, and in *Big Fish* his character repeats the same stories so relentlessly you expect the eyeballs of his listeners to roll up into their foreheads and be replaced by tic-tac-toe diagrams, like in the funnies.

Some, however, find old Edward heroic and charming, and his wife is one of them. Sandra (Jessica Lange) stands watch in the upper bedroom where her husband is leaving life as lugubriously as he lived it. She summons home their son, Will (Billy Crudup). Will, a journalist working in Paris, knows his father's stories by heart and has one final exasperated request: Could his father now finally tell him the truth? Old Edward harrumphs, shifts some phlegm, and starts recycling again.

Tim Burton directed the movie, and we sense his eagerness to plunge into the flashbacks, which show Young Edward (Ewan McGregor) and Young Sandra (Alison Lohman) actually having some of the adventures the old man tirelessly recounts. Those memories involve a witch

(Helena Bonham Carter) whose glass eye reflects the way her visitors will die, and a circus run by Amos Calloway (Danny DeVito), where he makes friends with such as Karl the Giant (Matthew McGrory). One day as Edward walks under the Big Top, he becomes mesmerized by his first glimpse of Sandra, and time crawls into slo-mo as he knows immediately this is the woman he is destined to marry.

There are other adventures, one involving a catfish as big as a shark, but it would be hard to top the time he parachutes onto the stage of a Red Army talent show in China, and meets Ping and Jing, a conjoined vocal duo sharing two legs. Now surely all these stories are fevered fantasies, right? You will have to see the movie to be sure, although, of course, there is also the reliable theory that things are true if you believe them so; if it worked for Tinker Bell, maybe it will work for you.

Because Tim Burton is the director, *Big Fish* of course is a great-looking film, with a fantastical visual style that could be called Felliniesque if Burton had not by now earned the right to the adjective Burtonesque. Yet there is no denying that Will has a point: The old man is a blowhard. There is a point at which his stories stop working as entertainment and segue into sadism. As someone who has been known to tell the same jokes more than once, I find it wise to at least tell them quickly; old Edward, on the other hand, seems to be a member of Bob and Ray's Slow Talkers of America.

There's another movie about a dying blowhard who recycles youthful memories while his loved ones gather around his deathbed. His wife summons home their son from Europe. The son is tired of the old man's stories and just once would like to hear the truth from him. This movie, of course, is *The Barbarian Invasions,* by Denys Arcand, and it is one of the best movies of the year. The two films have the same premise and purpose. They show how, at the end, we depend on the legends of our lives to give us meaning. We have been telling these stories not only to others but to ourselves. There is some truth here.

The difference—apart from the wide variation in tone between Arcand's human comedy and Burton's flamboyant ringmastery—is that Arcand uses the past as a way to get to his character, and Burton uses it as a way to get to his special effects. We have the sensation that Burton values old Edward primarily as an entry point into a series of visual fantasies. He is able to show us a remarkable village named Spectre, which has streets paved with grass and may very well be heaven, and that catfish as big as Jumbo, and magicians and tumblers and clowns and haunted houses and on and on.

In a sense we are also at the bedside of Tim Burton, who, like Old Edward, has been recycling the same skills over and over again and desperately requires someone to walk in and demand that he get to the point. When Burton gives himself the guidance and anchor of a story, he can be remarkable *(Ed Wood, The Nightmare Before Christmas, Sleepy Hollow).* When he doesn't, we admire his visual imagination and technique, but isn't this doodling of a very high order, while he waits for a purpose to reveal itself? 🖙

Biggie & Tupac ★ ★ ★ ½
R, 107 m., 2002

A documentary directed by Nick Broomfield and produced by Michele D'Acosta. Featuring Tupac Shakur, Christopher ("Biggie Smalls," "Notorious B.I.G.") Wallace, and Suge Knight.

Nick Broomfield is the Geraldo Rivera of celebrity documentarians, plunging fearlessly into combat zones, protected only by his pluck, his boom mike, and his apparent cluelessness. Looking something like the guy who sidles up to you in Best Buy and offers advice on bug zappers, Broomfield persuades his subjects to say astonishing things on camera. His *Kurt and Courtney* (1998) more or less blamed Courtney Love for her husband's death; his *Heidi Fleiss: Hollywood Madam* (1996) argued that a Hollywood sleazehead named Ivan Nagy was the real villain and Heidi was the fall girl.

And now here is *Biggie & Tupac,* which claims to solve the murders of rap artists Tupac Shakur and Christopher Wallace (a.k.a Biggie Smalls, a.k.a. the Notorious B.I.G.). According to Broomfield, both killings were ordered and paid for by recording tycoon Suge Knight, and the hit men were off-duty Los Angeles police officers. He produces an eyewitness who names one of Tupac's killers, and a bag man willing to say, on camera, that he delivered the money for the Notorious B.I.G. hit. And in an astonishing sequence, he marches into a California prison and confronts the surprised Suge Knight on camera.

Before moving on to Broomfield's argument, it's worth lingering for a moment or two over that interview with Suge Knight. Knight is the millionaire boss of Death Row Records, has been known to post death threats on his Website, and is a big, intimidating man—so fearsome that Broomfield's photographer, the fellow documentarian Joan Churchill, refused to go into the prison with him, and he had to hire a freelancer for the day. A freelancer so nervous that at one crucial moment the camera was pointed at the clouds overhead.

Broomfield describes all of this in his voice-over track. His movies are, in a sense, about his experiences in making them. Appearing unannounced at the prison, his two-man band is unprepossessing: The sloppy Broomfield with a recorder slung over his shoulder and a boom mike in his hand, and the cameraman trailing nervously behind. A network crew would have required clearances, but maybe Broomfield looks harmless. He says he has an interview scheduled with Suge Knight, and the warden, who takes this at face value, nervously observes that "Mr. Knight" is on the phone.

Broomfield walks fearlessly up to Knight, who carries a mean-looking walking stick and has a couple of apparent bodyguards, and announces he is "here for the interview." What interview? "Your message to the kids," Broomfield brilliantly improvises. Knight, a media creature on autopilot, doesn't miss a beat in delivering his message ("Don't get in trouble because you can't afford high-powered lawyers like artists can"). Then Broomfield segues to Tupac and Biggie, predictably without success.

Tupac Shakur was said to be the leading rap artist of his time, and his work in *Gridlock'd* (1997) showed him as a talented actor. He was shot in Las Vegas in September 1996, while his car was in a motorcade following one containing Suge Knight. In March 1997, his rival Biggie Smalls was shot down outside a Los Angeles party.

Broomfield assembles a case charging that Shakur was ordered killed by Knight because the executive owed the singer unpaid royalties and had heard Shakur planned to jump to another record label. Then he ordered B.I.G.'s death in order to make the two murders seem like part of a fictitious East–West rap rivalry. The film observes that Suge Knight had thirty to forty LAPD officers on his payroll for off-duty bodyguard and other duties. And he produces an LAPD detective whose own investigation into the Shakur murder was stonewalled, leading to his resignation from the force. If nothing else, Broomfield proves that the LAPD bent over backward to avoid questioning the most obvious suspects.

There is another theory about the two murders, developed in a long *Los Angeles Times* investigation by Chuck Phillips, published September 6, 2002. His findings in a nutshell: Shakur was killed by the Crips street gang to avenge Shakur's beating of one of their members, and the gun used was supplied by Notorious B.I.G., who agreed to pay the Crips $1 million. As for B.I.G.'s death: It remains unresolved.

Whether either of these theories is correct is not my purpose to decide. What can be said is that *Biggie & Tupac* is compulsively watchable and endlessly inventive as it transforms Broomfield's limited materials into a compelling argument.

Broomfield himself is the star of the film, complaining about his gas mileage, forcing himself to listen to one of Tupac's tapes, complaining about his incompetent employees, confessing to fear as he walks into dangerous situations. There is something so disarming about the man as he persuades people to say things on camera that, presumably, could land them in trouble. That no trouble has resulted from those things being said seems to support his argument—that the killings were covered up within the LAPD and there is no interest, these days, in being inconvenienced by any additional facts. It goes without saying that the killings only enhanced the aura around rap music, encouraging other artists to adopt the popular gangsta image.

Big Trouble ★ ★ ½
PG-13, 84 m., 2002

Tim Allen (Eliot Arnold), Rene Russo (Anna Herk), Stanley Tucci (Arthur Herk), Tom Sizemore (Snake), Patrick Warburton (Walter), Zooey Deschanel (Jenny Herk), Dennis Farina (Henry Algott), Omar Epps (Seitz), Heavy D (Greer), Jason Lee (Puggy), Janeane Garofalo (Monica Romero), Ben Foster (Matt Arnold). Directed by Barry Sonnenfeld and produced by Tom Jacobson, Barry Josephson, and Sonnenfeld. Screenplay by Robert Ramsey and Matthew Stone, based on the novel by Dave Barry.

Big Trouble is based on a novel by Dave Barry, and I have no trouble believing that. The genius of Dave Barry is that he applies a logical and helpful analysis to a situation that can only be worsened by such intervention. It is impossible, for example, to explain to a policeman why he is wasting his time on your illegal left turn while real criminals go free. Or to the IRS agent that Enron is robbing billions from widows and orphans while he ponders your business-related need to buy lots of CDs. Or to your wife why it is pointless to do the dishes on a daily basis when you can save hot water by letting them accumulate for a week in the dishwasher—which, being airtight, will not stink up the kitchen if you slam it right after adding more dishes.

All of these positions, which make perfect sense, only infuriate the cop, tax man, spouse, etc., by applying logic to a situation they have invested with irrational passion. As a sane voice in a world gone mad, Barry alone sees clearly. The Dave Barry figure in *Big Trouble*, I think, is Puggy (Jason Lee), a man who when he first addresses the camera seems to be Jesus, until he starts munching Fritos between his words of wisdom, observing, "You really can't beat these when they're fresh." Puggy is a homeless man who was living in the rainy north inside a cardboard box, when an article in *Martha Stewart's Living* inspired him to move to sunny southern Florida.

He is the film's omniscient narrator, not because he knows everything in a godlike way, but because he lives outdoors and happens to be ideally positioned during an evening when most of the film's other characters meet at the luxury home of Arthur Herk (Stanley Tucci), who is "one of the few Floridians who actually did vote for Pat Buchanan." (Saddened by the inability of many Republicans to express even token pity about the Jewish senior citizens whose mistaken votes for the Great Foamer tilted the election, I am always happy to have this event recalled.)

Arthur Herk is . . . ah, but if I begin a plot synopsis, we will be here all day, and I have already squandered three paragraphs with fancy writing. There is a plot in *Big Trouble*, quite a logical one actually, with all the threads tied into neat knots at the end, but to explain it would leave you banging your forehead against the newspaper and crying, "Why must I know this?" It might be simpler to describe the characters and let you discover their interactions for yourself.

Herk is a rich man who owes money to the wrong people and wants to buy a bomb. Rene Russo is his wife, Anna, who no longer remembers why she married this jerk. Zooey Deschanel is their daughter Jenny, who is the target of Matt Arnold (Ben Foster), a school classmate who needs to squirt her with a one-gallon water gun. Tim Allen is Eliot Arnold, Matt's father, who was the two-time Pulitzer Prize–winning columnist of the *Miami Herald* until he kicked in the computer screen of an editor who gave him idiotic assignments while refusing to meet his eyes. (It would seem to the casual moviegoer that Eliot Arnold is the Dave Barry figure in the movie, since he closely resembles the author, but no, it's Puggy.)

Then there are Dennis Farina and Jack Kehler as two hit men assigned to kill Arthur Herk. And Janeane Garofalo and Patrick Warburton as two cops who answer a call to the Herk home. And Lars Arenta-Hansen and Daniel London, who have a nuclear bomb they can sell to Arthur Herk. And Omar Epps and Heavy D as FBI agents on the trail of the bomb sellers. And Sofia Vergara as Nina, the Herks's maid, whom Arthur wants to have sex with. She despises Herk, but instantly lusts for Puggy—another clue he is the Dave Barry character. And Tom Sizemore and Johnny Knoxville as Snake and Eddie, who try to stick up the bar where the bomb dealers meet Arthur Herk while the FBI stakes it out. (Sample dialogue: "Snake, let's get the hell out of here. I think I hear one of them silent alarms.") There is also a toad whose spit is hallucinogenic.

The film has been directed by Barry Sonnenfeld, who made *Get Shorty*. It's not in that class—indeed, it seems so crowded that it sometimes feels like the casting call for an eventual picture not yet made—but it has its charms. It's the kind of movie you can't quite recommend because it is all windup and not much of a pitch, yet you can't bring yourself to dislike it. A video or airplane or cable movie. Originally scheduled for an autumn opening, it was pulled from the release schedule after 9/11 because it involves terrorists and a nuclear bomb. But these are terrorists and bombs from a simpler and more innocent time. The movie is a reminder of an age when such plots were obviously not to be taken seriously. It is nice to be reminded of that time.

Biker Boyz ★ ★
PG-13, 111 m., 2003

Laurence Fishburne (Smoke), Derek Luke (Kid), Orlando Jones (Soul Train), Djimon Hounsou (Motherland), Lisa Bonet (Queenie), Brendan Fehr (Stuntman), Larenz Tate (Wood), Kid Rock (Dogg), Vanessa Bell Calloway (Anita), Eriq La Salle (Slick Will). Directed by Reggie Rock Bythewood and produced by Stephanie Allain, Gina Prince-Bythewood, and Erwin Stoff. Screenplay by Bythewood.

Biker Boyz has an idea, but not an approach. The idea comes from an article in the *Los Angeles New Times* about motorcycle clubs that meet for scheduled but illegal road races. The members are affluent enough to maintain expensive bikes (even mechanics are on the payroll) and polite enough that the movie's language slipped in under the ropes at PG-13.

Many but not all of the boys are African American; some are still literally boys but others are men in their forties, and the (unexplored) subtext is that these are successful men who enjoy the excitement of street racing. Not much mention is made of jobs, but you can't buy and maintain these machines without a good one.

We meet Smoke (Laurence Fishburne), longtime undefeated champion of street racing, and his mechanic Slick Will (Eriq La Salle). Slick's son is Kid (Derek Luke). Smoke's longtime fierce competitor is Dogg (Kid Rock).

Races involve money (bets to $5,000) and, even more significant, racing helmets: If you lose, you hand over your helmet to the guy who beat you.

All of this is intriguing material, but the movie doesn't do much with it. There are several races in the film, but they don't generate the kind of pulse-quickening suspense that the races did in *The Fast and the Furious*, a four-wheel street-racing picture. As a general rule the right people win for the right reasons, and during some of the races the spectators inexplicably cluster at the starting line, so there's time for soul-to-soul conversations at the finish line.

Some of those involve a secret revealed halfway through the film; stop reading now unless you want to learn that Kid's mother, Anita (Vanessa Bell Calloway), tells him, after the death of the man he thinks is his father, that Smoke is his real father. This leads to less trauma and more niceness than you might think, in a movie that is gentler and tamer than the ads might suggest. Even insults, when they are traded, seem more written than felt.

This is the third film I've seen Derek Luke in, after *Antwone Fisher* and the Sundance 2003 hit *Pieces of April*. It's his least significant role, and yet confirms his presence: He's a rising star, all right, with a particular way of holding back, as if sizing up a situation to find the best entry point. Like Denzel Washington, who cast him as Antwone, he'll spend most of his career playing nice guys. (Does he have a *Training Day* in him? I can't tell from here.)

Laurence Fishburne is a strong presence in the central role, but the character isn't very interesting; he's good at racing, he's not a bad man, he has few complexities. Vanessa Bell Calloway, a crucial woman in both men's lives, has a kind of sultry power that suggests if she ever got on a bike, she'd have all the helmets.

I think what happened here is that the filmmakers were fascinated by the original article, did some research that hooked them on this world, and then trusted the world would be enough to power the movie. It isn't. We need a stronger conflict, as we had in *The Fast and the Furious*, and better and more special effects (the crashes all seem to happen at a distance). The father–son scenes have an earnestness and

sincerity that would be right in another kind of movie, but seem like sidebars to the main story.

Birthday Girl ★ ★

R, 93 m., 2002

Nicole Kidman (Nadia/Sofia), Ben Chaplin (John Buckingham), Vincent Cassel (Yuri), Mathieu Kassovitz (Alexei), Stephen Mangan (Bank Manager). Directed by Jez Butterworth and produced by Eric Abraham, Steve Butterworth, and Diana Phillips. Screenplay by Jez Butterworth and Tom Butterworth.

Anyone who orders a mail-order bride over the Internet deserves more or less who he gets. The bride may or may not be looking forward to a lifetime as a loving and devoted spouse, but she is certainly looking forward to an air ticket, a visa, and citizenship in a Western democracy. Would-be husbands who do not understand this probably believe that beautiful women gladly offer themselves sight unseen to men merely because they have mastered such skills as logging on, typing, and possessing a credit card.

Yet hope springs eternal. John Buckingham (Ben Chaplin), a bank teller in a small British town, is a lonely guy who clicks forlornly on the photos of Russian mail-order brides and finally orders Nadia, who says she is tall, blonde, speaks English, and is a nonsmoker. When, at the airport, Nadia turns out to look exactly like Nicole Kidman, you would think John might be satisfied. But no: She is tall, all right, but she is a chain-smoker, speaks no English, and throws up out the car window. He tests her language skills in a brief conversation: "Are you a giraffe?" "Yes."

John calls the marriage agency to complain. He wants to return Nadia and get himself a nonsmoking English speaker. Nadia keeps smiling, discovers his secret horde of porn magazines and videos, and cheerfully reenacts some of the scenarios she finds there. Soon John is beginning to reevaluate his consumer complaint.

So goes the setup for *Birthday Girl*, a comedy that starts out lightheartedly and makes some unexpected turns, especially after Nadia's two alleged cousins arrive from Russia. Yuri and Alexei, played by those two hard-edged French actors Vincent Cassel and Mathieu Kassovitz, reminded me of Emil and Oleg, the two Russians who turn up in *15 Minutes,* with the difference that they are not quite as ambitious and sinister; it appears at first they are basically after a free lunch.

There is a curious problem with *Birthday Girl,* hard to put your finger on: The movie is kind of sour. It wants to be funny and a little nasty, it wants to surprise us and then console us, but what it mostly does is make us restless. Strange, how the personalities of characters can refuse to match the work laid out for them by the script. I did not much like anyone in the movie, not even poor John Buckingham, and as for Nadia, she has to go through so many twists and turns that finally we don't know what to believe, nor do we much care.

The movie's downfall is to substitute plot for personality. It doesn't really know or care about the characters, and uses them as markers for a series of preordained events. Since these events take us into darker places than we expect, and then pull us back out again with still more arbitrary plotting, we lose interest; these people do not seem plausible, and we feel toyed with. Even the funny moments feel like nothing more than—well, the filmmakers inventing funny moments.

Black Hawk Down ★ ★ ★ ★
R, 143 m., 2002

Josh Hartnett (Eversmann), Ewan McGregor (Grimes), Tom Sizemore (McKnight), Eric Bana (Hoot), William Fichtner (Sanderson), Ewen Bremner (Nelson), Sam Shepard (Garrison), Gabriel Casseus (Kurth), Kim Coates (Wex). Directed by Ridley Scott and produced by Jerry Bruckheimer and Scott. Screenplay by Ken Nolan and Steve Zaillian, based on the book by Mark Bowden.

Ridley Scott's *Black Hawk Down* tells the story of a U.S. military raid that went disastrously wrong when optimistic plans ran into unexpected resistance. In Mogadishu, Somalia, in October 1993, eighteen Americans lost their lives, seventy more were wounded, and within days President Bill Clinton pulled out troops

that were on a humanitarian mission. By then some 300,000 Somalians had died of starvation, and the U.S. purpose was to help deliver UN food shipments. Somalian warlords were more interested in protecting their turf than feeding their people—an early warning of the kind of zeal that led to September 11.

The movie is single-minded in its purpose. It wants to record as accurately as possible what it was like to be one of the soldiers under fire on that mission. Hour by hour, step by step, it reconstructs the chain of events. The plan was to stage a surprise raid by helicopter-borne troops, joined by ground forces, on a meeting of a warlord's top lieutenants. This was thought to be such a straightforward task that some soldiers left behind their canteens and night vision gear, expecting to be back at the base in a few hours. It didn't work out that way.

What happened is that enemy rockets brought down two of the helicopters. The warlord's troops gathered quickly and surrounded the U.S. positions. Roadblocks and poor communications prevented a support convoy from approaching. And a grim firefight became a war of attrition. The Americans gave better than they got, but from any point of view the U.S. raid was a catastrophe. The movie's implied message was that America on that day lost its resolve to risk American lives in distant and obscure struggles, and that mind-set weakened our stance against terrorism.

The engagement itself seems to have degenerated into bloody chaos. Ridley Scott's achievement is to render it comprehensible to the audience. We understand, more or less, where the Americans are, and why, and what their situation is. We follow several leading characters, but this is not a star-driven project and doesn't depend on dialogue or personalities. It is about the logistics of that day in October, and how training did help those expert fighters (Army Rangers and Delta Force) to defend themselves as well as possible when all the plans went wrong and they were left hanging out to dry.

His longest day begins with a briefing by Major General William F. Garrison (Sam Shepard), who explains how intelligence has discovered the time and location of a meeting by lieutenants of the warlord Mohamed Farah

Aidid. A taxi with a white cross on its roof will park next to the building to guide the airborne troops, who will drop down on ropes, be joined by ground forces, secure the building, and take prisoners. The problem with this plan, as Garrison discovers in steadily more discouraging feedback, is that the opposition is better armed, better positioned, and able to call on quick reinforcements.

We follow several stories. A man falls from a helicopter and is injured when he misses his descent rope. A pilot is taken prisoner. Desperate skirmishes unfold in streets and rubble as darkness falls. The Americans are short on ammo and water, facing enemies not particularly shy about exposing themselves to danger. *Black Hawk Down* doesn't have heroic foreground figures like most war movies. The leading characters are played by stars who will be familiar to frequent moviegoers, but may be hard to tell apart for others. They include Josh Hartnett, much more convincing here than in *Pearl Harbor,* as a staff sergeant in command of one of the raiding teams; Ewan McGregor as a Ranger specialist whose specialties are paperwork and coffee making until he is pressed into service; Tom Sizemore as a veteran who provides steady counsel for younger troops; and William Fichtner as a fighter who seems to have internalized every shred of training, and embodies it instinctively.

The cinematography by Slawomir Idziak avoids the bright colors of upbeat combat movies, and its drab, dusty tones gradually drain of light as night falls. The later scenes of the movie feel chilly and forlorn; the surrounded troops are alone and endangered in the night. The screenplay by Ken Nolan and Steve Zaillian, working from a book by Mark Bowden, understands the material and tells it so clearly and efficiently that we are involved not only in the experience of the day but also in its strategies and unfolding realities.

Films like this are more useful than gung ho capers like *Behind Enemy Lines.* They help audiences understand and sympathize with the actual experiences of combat troops, instead of trivializing them into entertainments. Although the American mission in Somalia was humanitarian, the movie avoids speechmaking and sloganeering, and at one point, dis-cussing why soldiers risk their lives in situations like this, a veteran says, "It's about the men next to you. That's all it is."

Blade II ★ ★ ★ ½
R, 110 m., 2002

Wesley Snipes (Blade), Kris Kristofferson (Whistler), Ron Perlman (Reinhardt), Luke Goss (Nomak), Leonor Varela (Nyssa), Matt Schulze (Chupa), Norman Reedus (Scud). Directed by Guillermo del Toro and produced by Peter Frankfurt and Patrick Palmer. Screenplay by David S. Goyer.

Blade II is a really rather brilliant vomitorium of viscera, a comic book with dreams of becoming a textbook for mad surgeons. There are shots here of the insides of vampires that make your average autopsy look like a slow afternoon at Supercuts. The movie has been directed by Guillermo del Toro, whose work is dominated by two obsessions: war between implacable ancient enemies, and sickening things that bite you and aren't even designed to let go.

The movie is an improvement on *Blade* (1998), which was pretty good. Once again it stars Wesley Snipes as the Marvel Comics hero who is half-man, half-vampire. He was raised from childhood by Whistler (Kris Kristofferson), a vampire hunter who kept Blade's vampirism in check, and trained him to fight the nosferatus. Time has passed, Whistler has been captured by vampires and floats unconscious in a storage tank while his blood is harvested, and Blade prowls the streets in his lonely war.

One night, acrobatic creatures with glowing red eyes invade Blade's space and engage in a violent battle that turns out to be entirely gratuitous, because after they remove their masks to reveal themselves as vampires—a ferocious warrior and a foxy babe—they only want to deliver a message: "You have been our worst enemy. But now there is something else on the streets worse than you!" This reminded me of the night in O'Rourke's when McHugh asked this guy why he carried a gun and the guy said he lived in a dangerous neighborhood and McHugh said it would be safer if he moved.

The Vampire Nation is under attack by a

new breed of vampires named Reapers, who drink the blood of both humans and vampires, and are insatiable. Blade, who is both human and vampire, is like a balanced meal. If the Reapers are not destroyed, both races will die. This news is conveyed by a vampire leader whose brain can be dimly seen through a light blue, translucent plastic shell, more evidence of the design influence of the original iMac.

Blade and Whistler (now rescued from the tank and revived with a "retro-virus injection") join the vampires in this war, which is not without risk, because of course if the Reapers are destroyed, the vampires will turn on them. There is a story line, however quickly sketched, to support the passages of pure action, including computer-aided fight scenes of astonishing pacing and agility. Snipes once again plays Blade not as a confident superhero, but as a once-confused kid who has been raised to be good at his work and uncertain about his identity. He is attracted to the vampire Nyssa (Leonor Varela), but we sense a relationship between a creature of the night and Blade, known as the Daywalker, is sooner or later going to result in arguments over their work schedules.

The Reapers are the masterpieces of this movie. They all have what looks like a scar down the center of their chins. The first time we see one, it belongs to a donor who has turned up at a blood bank in Prague. This is not the kind of blood bank you want to get your next transfusion from. It has a bug zapper hanging from the wall, and an old drunk who says you can even bring in cups of blood from outside and they'll buy them.

The chin scar, it turns out, is not a scar but a cleft. These Reapers are nasty. They have mouths that unfold into tripartite jaws. Remember the claws on the steam shovels in those prize games at the carnival, where you manipulated the wheels and tried to pick up valuable prizes? Now put them on a vampire and make them big and bloody, with fangs and mucous and viscous black saliva. And then imagine a tongue coiled inside with an eating and sucking mechanism on the end of it that looks like the organ evolution forgot— the sort of thing diseased livers have nightmares about. Later they slice open a Reaper's chest cavity and Blade and Whistler look inside.

Blade: The heart is surrounded in bone!
Whistler: Good luck getting a stake through it!

Del Toro's early film *Cronos* (1993) was about an ancient golden beetle that sank its claws into the flesh of its victims and injected an immortality serum. His *Mimic* (1997) was about a designer insect, half-mantis, half-termite, that escapes into the subway system and mutates into a very big bug. Characters would stick their hands into dark places and I would slide down in my seat. His *The Devil's Backbone* (2001), set in an orphanage at the time of the Spanish civil war, is a ghost story, not a horror picture, but does have a body floating in a tank.

Still in his thirties, the Mexican-born director doesn't depend on computers to get him through a movie and impress the kids with fancy fight scenes. He brings his creepy phobias along with him. You can sense the difference between a movie that's a technical exercise (*Resident Evil*) and one steamed in the dread cauldrons of the filmmaker's imagination.

Blood Work ★ ★ ★ ½
R, 111 m., 2002

Clint Eastwood (Terry McCaleb), Wanda De Jesus (Graciella Rivers), Jeff Daniels (Buddy Noone), Anjelica Huston (Dr. Bonnie Fox), Tina Lifford (Detective Jaye Winston), Paul Rodriguez (Detective Arrango), Dylan Walsh (Waller). Directed and produced by Clint Eastwood. Screenplay by Brian Helgeland, based on the novel by Michael Connelly.

Clint Eastwood's *Blood Work* opens with an FBI agent of retirement age chasing a killer and collapsing of a heart attack. Two years later, we meet him living on a boat in a marina, with another person's heart in his chest. A woman asks him to investigate the murder of her sister. He says he is finished with police work. Then she shows him her sister's photograph, and softly adds a personal reason why he might want to help.

Unlike some action stars who want to remain supermen forever, Eastwood has paid attention to his years and found stories to exploit them. *Space Cowboys* (2000) was about proud old astronauts called out of retirement. In *Absolute Power* (1997), accused of climbing a rope to an upper window, he says he'll have to tell that one at his next AARP meeting. In *Blood Work*, he plays Terry McCaleb, a man conscious of his mortality at every moment; all during the movie, other characters tell him how bad he looks.

McCaleb shouldn't be doing police work. His doctor (Anjelica Huston) threatens to stop seeing him if he doesn't slow down. But from the moment he sees the photograph, and meets the dead woman's little boy, and looks in the eyes of her sister, he has no choice.

The movie is not simply a sentimental revenge picture, however, but a police procedural that leads us into an intriguing investigation. Based on a novel by Michael Connelly, the movie is like one of those Ed McBain stories in which the facts add up but make no sense until the key is supplied in a sudden observation.

Before his retirement, McCaleb was on the trail of a man named the Code Killer. Now there seems to be a similar serial killer operating in Los Angeles, one with a particular interest in McCaleb. "Catch me, McCaleb," he writes on a mirror (a nice echo of *Call Northside 777*). The investigation takes McCaleb to distant corners of Los Angeles County, and involves a friendly L.A. cop (Tina Lifford) and her hostile partner (Paul Rodriguez). Because he doesn't want to drive so soon after heart transplant surgery, Eastwood hires a neighbor at the marina (Jeff Daniels) as an assistant. And gradually he grows closer to Graciella (Wanda De Jesus), the dead woman's sister, and to the little boy.

The film establishes a muted, elegiac tone in its early scenes, and sticks to it. There is no false bravado. Terry McCaleb is not a well man, he sometimes touches his chest wonderingly, he develops a fever. But the logic of the chase is a relentless goad, and he pushes on. His health adds an additional dimension to the movie, inspiring a concern in Graciella that eventually, but very slowly, leads to love.

The strength of the picture, directed by Eastwood, is that it has three intersecting story arcs: the investigation, the health issues, and the relationship that builds, step by step.

Almost every scene involves one of these concerns, and the screenplay by Brian Helgeland (*L.A. Confidential*) moves smoothly between them, so that we develop an unusual degree of personal interest in McCaleb; he isn't just the hero of a thriller, but a man with human qualities we grow concerned about.

There is action and violence in *Blood Work*, but not the pumped-up, computer-aided pyrotechnics of so many summer thrillers. Here the action involves people, and the things that people can do. A final confrontation aboard two boats is handled in a way that makes the action seem difficult—but like hard physical labor, not martial arts gymnastics.

And when the movie was all over, what I cared about most was the love between Terry and Graciella. Wanda De Jesus is an actress who has done a lot of television work, but her film work has usually been limited to secondary supporting roles. Here she is crucial to the success of the picture. She avoids all temptations to leap into romance, she plays her scenes not as the hero's sidekick but as a dead woman's sister, and there is such a tenderness in the way she eventually starts to regard Terry that when finally they acknowledge how they feel, it isn't a plot point but an actual emotional transition that feels right and warm.

Clint Eastwood has directed himself in twenty movies, and that may represent the most consistent director-actor relationship in modern movies. He knows himself, he knows his craft; his pride as a director is dominant over his ego as an actor, and the results are films that use a star aura with an uncommon degree of intimacy. Terry McCaleb is one of Eastwood's best characters because, in a way, he's not a new character at all but just the same guy further down the road.

Bloody Sunday ★ ★ ★ ½
R, 107 m., 2002

James Nesbitt (Ivan Cooper), Tim Pigott-Smith (Major General Ford), Nicholas Farrell (Brigadier Maclellan), Gerard McSorley (Chief Superintendant Lagan), Kathy Keira Clarke (Frances), Allan Gildea (Kevin McCorry), Gerard Crossan (Eamonn McCann), Bernadette Devlin

(Mary Moulds). Directed by Paul Greengrass and produced by Arthur Lappin and Mark Redhead. Screenplay by Greengrass, based on the book by Don Mullan.

Both sides agree that on January 30, 1972, a civil rights march in Derry, Northern Ireland, ended with a confrontation between some of the marchers and British Army paratroopers. At the end of the day, thirteen marchers were dead and thirteen in hospital, one of whom later died. No British soldiers were killed. An official inquiry declared that the soldiers had returned the fire of armed marchers. Some of the soldiers involved were later decorated by the Crown.

Beyond this agreement, there is a disagreement so deep and bitter that thirty years later, Bloody Sunday is still an open wound in the long, contested history of the British in Northern Ireland. A new inquiry into the events of the day was opened in 1998, and continued at the time of the film.

Paul Greengrass's film *Bloody Sunday,* which shared the Golden Bear at the Berlin Film Festival this year, is made in the form of a documentary. It covers about twenty-four hours, starting on Saturday evening, and its central character is Ivan Cooper (James Nesbitt), a civil rights leader in Derry. He was a Protestant MP from the nationalist Social Democratic Labour Party. Most of the 10,000 marchers on that Sunday would be Catholic; that a Protestant led them, and stood beside such firebrands as Bernadette Devlin, indicates the division in the north between those who stood in solidarity with their coreligionists, and those of all faiths who simply wanted the British out of Northern Ireland.

Cooper is played by Nesbitt as a thoroughly admirable man, optimistic, tireless, who walks fearlessly through dangerous streets and has a good word for everyone. He knows the day's march has been banned by the British government, but expects no trouble because it will be peaceful and nonviolent. As Cooper hands out leaflets in the streets, Greengrass intercuts preparations by the British Army, which from the top down is determined to make a strong stand against "hooliganism." More than two dozen British soldiers have been killed by the Provisional IRA in recent months, and this is a chance to crack down.

Greengrass also establishes a few other characters, including a young man who kisses his girlfriend good-bye and promises his mother no harm will come to him—always ominous signs in a movie. And we meet the Derry police chief (Gerard McSorley), who is alarmed by the fierce resolve of the soldiers and asks, not unreasonably, if it wouldn't be wiser to simply permit the march, since it is obviously going to proceed anyway.

Greengrass re-creates events with stunning reality. (When he shows a movie marquee advertising *Sunday Bloody Sunday* it's a small glitch, because it seems like a calculated shot in a movie that feels like cinema verité). He is aided by the presence of thousands of extras, who volunteered to be in the movie (some of them marched on Bloody Sunday and are in a way playing themselves). Northern Ireland is still a tinderbox where this film could not possibly be made; streets in a poor area of Dublin were used.

Cooper and the other leaders are on the bed of a truck that leads the column of marchers, and from their vantage point we can see that when the march turns right, away from the army's position, some hot-headed marchers turn left and begin to throw rocks at the soldiers. In the army's HQ, where Major General Ford (Tim Pigott-Smith) is in charge, an order is given to respond firmly. Communications are confused, orders are distorted as they pass down the chain of command, and soon rubber bullets and gas grenades are replaced by the snap of real bullets.

Greengrass shows marchers trying to restrain a few of their fellows who are armed. His film is clear, however, in its belief that the British fired first and in cold blood, and he shows one wounded marcher being executed with a bullet in the back. One of the marchers is apparently inspired by Gerald Donaghey, whose case became famous. After being wounded, he was searched twice, once by doctors, and then taken to an army area where he died. Soldiers then found nail bombs in his pockets that had been "overlooked" in two previous searches. For Greengrass, this is part of a desperate attempt by the army to plant evidence and justify a massacre.

Of course there are two sides to the story of Bloody Sunday, although the score (Army 14,

Marchers o) is significant. The Greengrass view reflects both the theories and the anger of the anti-British factions, and the army's smugness after being cleared in the original investigation was only inflammatory. *Bloody Sunday* is one view of what happened that day, a very effective one. And as an act of filmmaking, it is superb: A sense of immediate and present reality permeates every scene.

Note: The official Website of the inquiry into Bloody Sunday is at www.bloody-sunday-inquiry.org.uk. Thomas Kinsella's famous poem about the day, "Butcher's Dozen," is at www.usm.maine.edu/~mcgrath/poems/butchrs.htm.

Blue Car ★ ★ ★ ½
R, 96 m., 2003

David Strathairn (Auster), Agnes Bruckner (Meg), Margaret Colin (Diane), Regan Arnold (Lily), Frances Fisher (Delia). Directed by Karen Moncrieff and produced by Peer J. Oppenheimer, Amy Sommer, and David Waters. Screenplay by Moncrieff.

Blue Car watches with horror as a vulnerable teenage girl falls into the emotional trap set by her high school English teacher. The teacher watches with horror, too: He knows what he is doing is wrong, but he is weak, and pities himself more than the sad girl he is exploiting. Step by step, they move in a direction only he understands.

The girl is named Meg (Agnes Bruckner). She is beautiful, and her teacher knows that with a desperate urgency. He is Auster (David Strathairn), who poses in the classroom as a stern but inspiring romantic. Meg reads a poem one day about how her father left her family. Auster asks her to stay after class, tells her she can reach deeper, asks her to find more truth. "We need a map of your nerve centers," he says. He thinks maybe the poem is good enough to get her into a poetry competition in Florida.

Meg's home life is in turmoil. Her mother, Diane (Margaret Colin), is distant and overworked, attending night school, complaining that her ex-husband is behind on his payments. Meg is baby-sitter and substitute mother for her kid sister, Lily (Regan Arnold), who is seriously disturbed and sometimes cuts herself.

Auster's approach to Meg is subtle and guarded. He flatters her with his attention. He maintains his authority and seems to keep his distance, but somehow she is sharing his sandwich at the noon hour and getting a ride home in his car. And then, when a family tragedy occurs, Auster comforts her a degree too eagerly.

This teacher is a piece of work. He knows that an open appeal to Meg would be rejected, that she would be creeped out by his lust. But by maintaining a position of power and then overpraising her work, he gets inside her defenses. Her poem is a good poem, but not that good. Sometimes he reads to her from his novel in progress, which sounds like subpar Thomas Wolfe but is as much a fraud as the rest of him. Notice the cruelty in the scene where he gives her a little speech about how we can't all be winners all of the time, and then, after she thinks she has lost the poetry competition, tells her she is a winner.

We see a bright, sad, lonely girl with absent parents, drifting into danger. She thinks she may be able to get a ride to Florida with a friend's family. That falls through. She takes the bus, sleeps on the beach, turns up for the competition, and even finds Auster on the beach, sunning with his wife (Frances Fisher) and son. Fisher has a brief scene, but it is played with acute observation. Watch the way she sizes up Meg and immediately reads her husband's intentions.

Blue Car, written and directed by Karen Moncrieff, is wise in the way it follows the progress of the story. Auster wants to have sex with Meg, but it must be within the twisted terms of his own compromised morality. She must in some sense seem to agree to it. I will leave it to you to witness how this scenario plays out, and to observe the sadness with which he pursues his pathetic goal.

The ending of the film is as calculated and cruel as a verbal assault by a Neil LaBute character. In a few merciless words and an unmistakable implication, Meg fights back. The story has its basis in everyday realism. The teacher is made not a stereotyped monster but a pathetic and weak one. The girl is not a sexpot nor childishly naive, but distracted and deceived. Moncrieff doesn't exploit the situation, but deplores it.

Bruckner, an eighteen-year-old veteran of

soap opera and four smaller feature roles, negotiates this difficult script with complete conviction. Strathairn's role is even trickier, because Moncrieff doesn't want to make him into a stereotyped molester, but wants to show how he is about to manipulate himself into a situation where it seems, because he wants it to seem, that the girl accepts him. He is rotten in an everyday way, not in a horror movie way—and that makes him much more frightening.

Because the movie is an honest and forthright drama about a teenager in danger, of course the MPAA has rated it R. That despite the fact that it contains no nudity, no explicit sex, and only ordinary adolescent language. The theory of the ratings board, apparently, is that all manner of vulgarity and pop violence is suitable for those under seventeen, but any movie that addresses the actual conditions of teenage life must be off-limits. What the MPAA standards amount to is: Let students learn about sexual predators in their lives, not in the movies. *Blue Car* is a valuable cautionary tale.

Blue Collar Comedy Tour: The Movie
★ ★ ★
PG-13, 105 m., 2003

Featuring Jeff Foxworthy, Bill Engvall, Ron White, Larry the Cable Guy, Heidi Klum, and David Allen Grier. A documentary directed by C. B. Harding and produced by Alan C. Blomquist, Casey LaScala, Joseph Williams, Hunt Lowry, and J. P. Williams.

Jeff Foxworthy, the "you know you're a redneck" guy, was ice-fishing in Minnesota once and started thinking of the experience from the point of view of the fish.

"Suppose you get caught and you're thrown back in. What do you tell your buddies? 'Man, I had an out-of-the-body experience. I was just minding my own business, living my life, when suddenly I felt myself under the control of a powerful force. I was drawn up toward the light. I went through a hole in the sky and found myself surrounded by all my dead relatives. And God was wearing a flannel shirt and a Budweiser hat.'"

The humor in that story is typical of all four performers in *Blue Collar Comedy Tour: The*

Movie, a concert film starring Foxworthy, Bill Engvall, Ron White, and Larry the Cable Guy. I am informed that their national tour, just closing after four years, is the most successful in history, although whose history is not specified, and all tours say that. Certainly they're popular, and this film, which is kind of a redneck version of *The Original Kings of Comedy,* is the way to see them without having to find your car in the middle of all the pickups in the parking lot.

White and Cable Guy are the warm-ups, Foxworthy and Engvall are the stars, and then all four come on stage to share stories and listen to Foxworthy's redneck litany. ("If the wedding rehearsal dinner is at Hooter's—you know you're a redneck.") His uncle is such a NASCAR fan, he always gets into his car through the window.

But there I go, stealing his material. How do you review a movie like this without reprinting the jokes? The film consists of four concert segments, larded with "documentary" footage of the four buddies fishing, visiting Victoria's Secret, etc. The concert stuff is consistently funny, good-humored, and surprisingly clean; there's a lot more bathroom humor than sex or profanity, and the PG-13 rating is probably about right.

I do have some doubts about the other stuff. When they go shopping for underwear at Victoria's Secret, the sales clerk is played by supermodel Heidi Klum, which clues us that it's a setup and probably halfway scripted. What's the point? Why not let the boys walk into a real Victoria's Secret and start filming and see what happens? I was also a little puzzled by the role played by David Allen Grier, as the chauffeur and valet. Why have a recognizable star and not make any use of him?

These are minor quibbles. The underlying secret of the four comedians is the way they find humor in daily life, and in their families. In this they're a lot like the Kings of Comedy, and Engvall (the "here's your sign" guy) gets as much mileage out of his family as K of C's Bernie Mac.

Okay, I got a couple more. I liked the whole riff about leaf blowers being banned from airplanes. And I suppose it is thought-provoking that nobody ever has to stop to pee while tubing down a river.

Blue Crush ★ ★ ★
PG-13, 103 m., 2002

Kate Bosworth (Anne Marie), Michelle Rodriguez (Eden), Matthew Davis (Matt Tollman), Sanoe Lake (Lena), Mika Boorem (Penny), Kala Alexander (Kala), Chris Taloa (Drew). Directed by John Stockwell and produced by Brian Grazer and Karen Kehela. Screenplay by Lizzy Weiss and Stockwell.

Blue Crush knows something most surfing movies don't acknowledge—that many non-pro surfers endure blue-collar jobs as a way to support their surfing, which is the only time they feel really alive. Surfers in the movies have traditionally been golden boys and girls who ride the waves to Beach Boys songs—and live, apparently, on air. In *Blue Crush,* we meet three Hawaiian surfers who work as hotel maids, live in a grotty rental, and are raising the kid sister of one of them. Despite this near-poverty, they look great; there is nothing like a tan and a bikini to overcome class distinctions.

The women are Anne Marie (Kate Bosworth), Eden (Michelle Rodriguez), and Lena (Sanoe Lake). Anne Marie was a contender three years earlier in a major surfing competition on Oahu, but nearly drowned. Now she's edging back into competition, encouraged by the others, who seem to take Anne Marie's career more seriously than she does. Life for the women includes surfing at dawn, working hard as a three-maid team at a local luxury resort, and surfing at dusk. Since her mother bailed out, Anne Marie has been raising Penny (Mika Boorem), who attends a local school but is not always delivered quite on time.

The movie, based on Susan Orlean's magazine article named "Surf Girls of Maui," resembles the Nik Cohn journalism that inspired *Saturday Night Fever*. Both stories are about working-class kids escaping into the freedom and glamour of their obsessions. We hear fascination in their voices when they stop at a gas station and see, at another pump, famous professional women surfers who are in Hawaii for a big tournament. While it is true that Anne Marie might be able to make money as a member of a pro surfing team, it is also true, as it was of Tony Manero in *Saturday Night Fever,*

that other things distract her, especially romance. She is not single-mindedly focused on her career.

The movie's surfing scenes are well photographed, and yet we've seen versions of them in many other movies, going all the way back to the lodestone, Bruce Brown's *Endless Summer* (1967). What we haven't seen, what has the delight of life, are the scenes in the hotel, where the three maids deal with the aftermath of a messy party held by pro football players and try on expensive bathing suits in the room of a rich woman.

Anne Marie has a fierce working woman's pride, and at one point gets herself fired by daring to march out onto the beach and demonstrate to a huge football lineman the correct procedure for wrapping a used condom in a Kleenex. She also has a working woman's realism, as when she advises the others not to resign in sympathy because they have rent payments to meet.

The date for the big competition is approaching, and Anne Marie is focused on it when the run-in with the football players (who are not bad guys) changes everything. The quarterback, Matt Tollman (Matthew Davis), asks her out, and although she talks about nonfraternization policies, she accepts, and finds herself falling for him. Here is the crucial question: Is this a vacation romance, or does it really mean something? Matt seems nice, attentive, and genuine, but is it an act? The movie is realistic here too: Anne Marie would not *mind* a vacation romance, but she wants to know if that's what it is—she doesn't want to risk her heart needlessly.

Eden is tougher and more cynical than her friend, and we remember Michelle Rodriguez's performance as an amateur boxer in *Girlfight* (2000). She's alarmed when her friend starts spending too much time with the quarterback and not enough time preparing for the impending competition ("Some guy thinks you look good in a bikini and you forget all about the contest"). And then of course the movie ends with the big showdown, with waves of awesome strength and feats of great surfing, with all the necessary dangers and setbacks. Even here, it doesn't settle for what we thought was the predictable outcome.

Blue Crush was directed by John Stockwell, who made *Crazy/Beautiful* (2001), the movie where Kirsten Dunst plays the wild daughter of a congressman, and her boyfriend is a responsible young Mexican-American. Here again we get the footloose Anglo and the Latino looking out for her, but in an unexpected context. Looking at the posters for *Blue Crush,* which show Bosworth, Rodriguez, and Lake posing with bikinis and surfboards, I expected another mindless surfing movie. *Blue Crush* is anything but.

Boat Trip ½ ★
R, 93 m., 2003

Cuba Gooding Jr. (Jerry), Horatio Sanz (Nick), Vivica A. Fox (Felicia), Roselyn Sanchez (Gabriela), Maurice Godin (Hector), Richard Roundtree (Malcolm), Roger Moore (Lloyd). Directed by Mort Nathan and produced by Frank Hübner, Brad Krevoy, Gerhard Schmidt, and Andrew Sugerman. Screenplay by Nathan and William Bigelow.

Boat Trip arrives preceded by publicity saying many homosexuals have been outraged by the film. Now that it's in theaters, everybody else has a chance to join them. Not that the film is outrageous. That would be asking too much. It is dim-witted, unfunny, too shallow to be offensive, and way too conventional to use all of those people standing around in the background wearing leather and chains and waiting hopefully for their cues. This is a movie made for nobody, about nothing.

The premise: Jerry (Cuba Gooding Jr.) is depressed after being dumped by his girl (Vivica A. Fox). His best buddy Nick (Horatio Sanz) cheers him up: They'll take a cruise together. Nick has heard that the ships are jammed with lonely women. But they offend a travel agent, who books them on a cruise of gay men, ho, ho.

Well, it could be funny. Different characters in a different story with more wit and insight might have done the trick. But *Boat Trip* requires its heroes to be so unobservant that it takes them hours to even figure out it's a gay cruise. And then they go into heterosexual panic mode, until the profoundly conventional screenplay supplies the only possible outcome:

The sidekick discovers that he's gay, and the hero discovers a sexy woman on board and falls in love with her.

Her name is Gabriela (Roselyn Sanchez), and despite the fact that she's the choreographer on a gay cruise, she knows so little about gay men that she falls for Jerry's strategy: He will pretend to be gay, so that he can get close to her and then dramatically unveil his identity, or something. Uh-huh. Even Hector, the cross-dressing queen in the next stateroom, knows a straight when he sees one: "You want to convince people you are gay, and you don't know the words to 'I Will Survive'?"

The gays protesting the movie say it deals in stereotypes. So it does, but then again, so does the annual gay parade, and so do many gay nightclubs, where role-playing is part of the scene. Yes, there are transvestites and leather guys and muscle boys on the cruise, but there are also more conventional types, like Nick's poker-playing buddies. The one ray of wit in the entire film is provided by Roger Moore, as a homosexual man who calmly wanders through the plot dispensing sanity, as when, at the bar, he listens to the music and sighs, "Why do they always play Liza?"

One of the movie's problems is a disconnect between various levels of reality. Some of the scenes play as if they are intended to be realistic. Then Jerry or Nick goes into hysterics of overacting. Then Jerry attempts to signal a helicopter to rescue him, and shoots it down with a flare gun. Then it turns out to be carrying the Swedish suntanning team on its way to the Hawaiian Tropic finals. Then Jerry asks Gabriela to describe her oral sex technique, which she does with the accuracy and detail of a porn film, and then Jerry—but that pathetic moment you will have to witness for yourself. Or maybe you will not.

Note: The credit cookies weren't very funny, either, but at least they kept me in the theater long enough to notice the credits for the film's Greek support team.

Bobby Jones: Stroke of Genius ★ ★ ★
PG, 120 m., 2004

James Caviezel (Bobby Jones), Claire Forlani (Mary Jones), Jeremy Northam (Walter Hagen),

Malcolm McDowell (O. B. Keeler), Connie Ray (Clara Jones), Brett Rice ("Big Bob" Jones), Aidan Quinn (Harry Vardon), Larry Thompson (John Malone). Directed by Rowdy Herrington and produced by Kim Dawson, Kim Moore, and John Shepherd. Screenplay by Herrington and Bill Pryor.

Bobby Jones (1902–1971) was perhaps the greatest golfer who ever lived. Not even Tiger Woods has equaled Jones's triumph in 1930, when he became the only player to win the U.S. Open, the British Open, the U.S. Amateur, and the British Amateur in the same year. Then he retired from competition—still only twenty-eight. Odds are good no golfer will ever equal that record—if only because no golfer good enough to do it will be an amateur. Jones also won seven U.S. titles in a row, an achievement that may be unmatchable.

Jones was not only an amateur, but an amateur who had to earn a living, so that he couldn't play golf every day and mostly played only in championship-level tournaments. This makes him sound like a man who played simply for love of the game, but *Bobby Jones: Stroke of Genius* shows us a man who seems driven to play, a man obsessed; there seems less joy than compulsion in his career, and the movie contrasts him with the era's top professional, Walter Hagen (Jeremy Northam), who seems to enjoy himself a lot more.

Jim Caviezel *(The Passion of the Christ)* plays Jones as an adult, after childhood scenes showing a young boy who becomes fascinated by the game and watches great players while hiding in the rough. He comes from a family dominated by a strict, puritanical grandfather, but Jones's father, "Big Bob" (Brett Rice), is supportive. Not so Jones's wife, Mary (Claire Forlani), who plays a role that has become standard in the biographies of great men—the woman who wishes her man would give up his dream and spend more time at home with her and the children.

Of course, Mary sees a side of Bobby that's invisible to the world. The man is tortured. He feels he must enter tournaments and win them to prove something he can never quite articulate, to show "them" without being sure who they are. And he is often in physical pain. After a sickly childhood, he grows up into a reed-thin man with a tense face, and doctors have only to look at him to prescribe rest. His stomach starts to hurt at about the same time he begins to drink and smoke, and although the movie does not portray him as an alcoholic, we hold that as a hypothesis until we find the pain is caused by syringomyelia, a spinal disease that would cripple him later in life.

Bobby Jones: Stroke of Genius tells this story in a straightforward, calm way that works ideally as the chronicle of a man's life but perhaps less ideally as drama. No doubt we should be grateful that Jones's story isn't churned up into soap opera and hyped with false crises and climaxes; it is the story of a golfer, and it contains a lot of golf. Much of the golf is photographed at the treacherous Old Course in St Andrews, Scotland, where the game began, and where we learn why there are eighteen holes: "A bottle of Scotch has eighteen shots," an old-timer explains, "and they reckoned that when it was empty, the game was over."

A major player in Jones' life is O. B. Keeler (Malcolm McDowell), his friend and "official biographer," and if Jones was an amateur golfer, Keeler seems to be an amateur biographer, with all day free, every day, to follow Jones around, carry his stomach medicine (and his whisky), and chronicle his exploits, sometimes typing while leaning against a stone wall on a course. Little wonder that although Jones retired in 1930, Keeler did not publish his "authorized biography" until 1953.

The director, Rowdy Herrington, has made more excited movies, including *Road House* (1989), legendary for its over-the-top performances by Patrick Swayze, Kelly Lynch, and Ben Gazzara. *Bobby Jones* is more solemn, more the kind of movie you're not surprised was financed by the Bobby Jones Film Co., and authorized by the Jones trustees, who also oversee lines of clothing and the like. It is also not astonishing, I suppose, that although the film mentions that Jones founded the Augusta National Golf Club and started the Masters tournament there, and although a photo over the end credits shows Jones with the course's favorite golfer, Dwight D. Eisenhower, there is no mention of the club's exclusion of blacks and women.

To be fair, the movie isn't really about Jones's entire life; it focuses on his youth and his championship golf. I am not a golfer, although I took the sport in P.E. class in college and have played a few rounds. There are too many movies to see, books to read, cities to explore, and conversations to hold for me to spend great parts of the day following that little ball around and around and around. I do concede that everyone I know who plays golf loves the game, and that most of them seem to derive more cheer from it than Bobby Jones does in this movie.

That Jones should obtain more pleasure than he does is all the more certain because the movie mostly shows him making impossible shots, at one point chipping the ball into the hole from close to the wall of a sand trap higher than his head. Walter Hagen spends a lot of the movie raising his eyebrows and grimacing in reaction shots, after Jones sinks another miracle.

Bon Voyage ★ ★ ★ ½
PG-13, 114 m., 2004

Isabelle Adjani (Viviane Denvers), Gerard Depardieu (Jean-Etienne Beaufort), Virginie Ledoyen (Camille), Yvan Attal (Raoul), Gregori Derangere (Frederic), Peter Coyote (Alex Winckler), Jean-Marc Stehle (Professeur Kopolski). Directed by Jean-Paul Rappeneau and produced by Laurent Petin and Michele Petin. Screenplay by Patrick Modiano, Gilles Marhand, Jean-Paul Rappeneau, Julien Rappeneau, and Jerome Tonnerre.

The Nazi occupation of France may seem like a strange backdrop for an adventure comedy, but consider how *Casablanca* found humor, irony, and courage in a related situation. Not that *Bon Voyage* is *Casablanca*, but it proceeds from the same cynicism, and unites the worlds of politics, science, and the movies. It also provides Isabelle Adjani with one of the best roles of her career, as a movie star who will do anything, say anything, and sleep with anybody, first to further her career and then to save her life.

The movie is a lavish, expensive period production by Jean-Paul Rappeneau, who also made Gérard Depardieu's rabble-rousing *Cyrano de Bergerac* in 1990 and the exhilarating *The Horseman on the Roof* (1995). Depardieu returns in *Bon Voyage*, and he is an unmade bed no longer; he is astonishingly slimmed down, his hair trimmed and slicked back, wearing the tailored suits of a cabinet minister.

The movie opens in Paris, as the Nazis are moving into the city and many prudent citizens with the means or clout are moving to Bordeaux, which they think might be Nazi-free, at least for a while. Adjani plays Viviane Denvers, a great movie star and apparently an even greater lover. To say that she looks much younger than her forty-eight years is not flattery but the simple truth; Adjani was able to play a convincing teenager in *Camille Claudel* (1990). Here her character functions instinctively as a woman who is attracted to men who offer her money and safety. Her fatal flaw is that she is also attracted to men she loves. These tastes become thoroughly confused during the film, as she seeks money, safety, and love simultaneously, which means that no one man is going to be able to fill the bill.

Jean-Etienne Beaufort (Depardieu) is the harassed cabinet minister she's attached to as the movie opens. As some ministers urge collaboration with the Nazis, he commands a car and Viviane joins him on the exodus. But then she is astonished to see a childhood friend named Frederic (Gregori Derangere) on the streets—astonished because she thought he was in jail charged with murder. Such is her power over men that, some days earlier, after she murdered a blackmailer in her apartment, she called him up and because he had always been in love with her, he allowed the police to arrest him. He's free because his jailers helpfully released their prisoners ahead of the Nazi advance.

So now there is a man to care for her, and a man for her to care for. And not to forget Alex Winckler (Peter Coyote), a journalist who seems to have a lot of influence and is mesmerized by her. Can he be trusted? He speaks with an accent, and movie fans will know he has the same last name as one of the Nazi creeps in *The Third Man*. Viviane's strategy is to accept protection from the man of the moment, convince him she loves only him, and jump ship when necessary. How does Adjani create the character? Not by vamping, not by flaunting sexuality, but by creating a kind of vacuum of need that draws men so close they cannot resist the lure of her large, liquid eyes—pools to drown in.

The film introduces a tributary that will eventually join with the mainstream, although at first we can't see how. This involves an emigré Jewish professor named Kopolski (Jean-

Marc Stehle), an intellectual temperamentally unsuited to survive in an evil world. He is in possession of several very large bottles of heavy water, needed for nuclear experiments, and he wants to keep them away from the Nazis and somehow get them to England. (The heavy water bottles here, like the wine bottles filled with heavy earth in Hitchcock's *Notorious*, function essentially as a MacGuffin.) Professor Kopolski's only hope is a young assistant named Camille (Virginie Ledoyen), who rises to the occasion, saving both the professor and the heavy water from Nazi capture; she transports the bottles in the back of a station wagon, where we constantly expect them to break.

There are other characters, a lot of them, including a set of rich aristocrats and tourists who keep turning up in all of the hotels, demanding what cannot be had. But the underlying structure of the movie is farce crossed with action and oiled by romance, and Rappeneau and his four cowriters are virtuosos at keeping all of their balls in the air. The lives and fates of the characters crisscross, their motives are subject to sudden adjustments, and Viviane is like Eliza on the ice floes, leaping from one man to another.

The movie is funny, not in a ho-ho way, but in the way it surprises us with delights and blindsides us with hazards. There's a lot of contrivance involved—it is, after all, improbable that these characters would not only constantly cross paths, but always at moments of crisis. But once we accept the movie's method, it implicates us; the sudden separations and reunions are devices for testing Viviane's powers of romantic invention and Camille's desperate improvisations. There is also the amusement that men, especially powerful men, are powerless in the hands of a woman like Viviane. Their mistake is to love someone who loves only herself; their excuse is that she loves herself so much she loves them, too, or is able to make them believe she does, which comes to the same thing.

I haven't even mentioned the costumes, the sets, the ambience. If Rappeneau's *The Horseman on the Roof* was the most expensive French film to date, *Bon Voyage* must be in the same league. He uses the money not to manufacture a big, clunky entertainment, but to facilitate a world that seems real even into the farthest corners of Paris, Bordeaux, hotels, cabinet meetings, boudoirs, dark roads, and desperate rendezvous. This is a grand, confident entertainment, sure of the power of Adjani, Depardieu, and the others, and sure of itself.

Borstal Boy ★ ★

NO MPAA RATING, 93 m., 2002

Shawn Hatosy (Brendan Behan), Danny Dyer (Charlie), Eva Birthistle (Liz), Michael York (Warden), Robin Laing (Jock), Mark Huberman (Mac). Directed by Peter Sheridan and produced by Arthur Lappin and Pat Moylan. Screenplay by Nye Heron and Sheridan, based on the book by Brendan Behan.

For a dozen years of my life, I gazed into the face of Brendan Behan almost nightly. There was an enormous photograph of him on the wall of O'Rourke's Pub on North Avenue, and it didn't take a lip-reader to guess which word began with his upper teeth posed on his lower lip. Drunk and disheveled, he must have been in a late stage of his brief and noisy progress through life. He wrote that to be drunk in Ireland in his youth was not a disgrace but a sign of status, because it showed you had enough money to pay for the drink. By that measurement, Behan was a millionaire.

Still beloved and read by those who remember him, the boy-o has long since faded from his time of great celebrity, when he enlightened talk shows with his boisterous proletarian philosophy. The recent equivalent of his risky performances as a late-night chat star would be Farrah Fawcett crossed with Andrew Dice Clay. He also wrote some good plays and the classic memoir *Borstal Boy*, and died at forty-one—which was old age, considering how he lived.

That is the Behan I remember. The Behan of *Borstal Boy* (Shawn Hatosy) is another person altogether, an idealistic young lad who naively goes to England on a mission for the IRA, is arrested, sent to juvenile prison ("borstal") and there learns to love those he thinks he hates, including the English (through the warden's daughter) and "queers" (through his prison pal Charlie). After being discharged as a presumably pacified bisexual, he returns to Ireland and the movie ends quickly, before having to deal with the facts that he once again took up arms for the IRA, shot a cop, was sent back to prison, and (despite marriage to the saintly Beatrice) found love most reliably in the arms of the bottle.

Is the Brendan Behan of *Borstal Boy* simply the young man before alcoholism rewrote his script? I haven't read the book in years, but my strongest memory is of Behan's defiance—of his unshakable belief that carrying bombs to Liverpool and shooting cops was not criminal because he was a soldier at war. That has been the policy of the IRA from the beginning, that they are not terrorists but soldiers or prisoners of war. It is the same today with terrorists, with the difference that things were ever so much more innocent in the 1950s, so that the borstal warden (Michael York) could see Brendan as a lad with a good heart who just needed a chance to settle down and think things through.

The story hinges on parallel love affairs, both depending on a permissiveness one is a little startled to find in an English juvenile prison in the 1950s. Young Brendan makes best friends with his fellow prisoner Charlie (Danny Dyer), a young sailor who is "openly gay" (says Stephen Holden of the *New York Times*), although I believe being openly gay in those days, when it was against the law, was more a matter of sending signals to those who knew them and staying prudently in the closet otherwise. Certainly Brendan is slow to catch on, both to Charlie's homosexuality and to the promptings of his own heart. He is more obviously attracted to Liz (Eva Birthistle), the warden's daughter.

My guess is that the likelihood of a borstal boy being allowed to spend quality time with the warden's daughter is approximately the same as his chances of making friends with an "openly gay" prisoner, which is to say less likely than being invited to tea with the queen.

Of course, Liz and Charlie may come directly from the pages of the book and I have simply forgotten them. But my problem with *Borstal Boy* isn't so much with the facts as with the tone. If this is an accurate portrait of Brendan Behan at sixteen, then *Borstal Boy* makes the same mistake *Iris* does—gives us these writers before (and in the case of *Iris*, after) the years in which they were the people they became famous for being. True, Behan's book is *about* that period in his life, but written with a gusto

and rudeness that's lacking in Peter Sheridan's well-mannered film.

Yes, I know I've defended *A Beautiful Mind* against charges that it left out seamy details from the earlier years of John Forbes Nash, but the difference is, *A Beautiful Mind* focused intently on the central story, which is that he was a schizophrenic whose work won the Nobel Prize. Does anyone much think the central story of Brendan Behan is that he was a bisexual sweetheart before he took to drink? The photo on the wall at O'Rourke's shows him forming the first letter of the first word of his response to that theory.

The Bourne Identity ★ ★ ★
PG-13, 118 m., 2002

Matt Damon (Jason Bourne), Franka Potente (Marie Kreutz), Chris Cooper (Ted Conklin), Clive Owen (The Professor), Brian Cox (Ward Abbott), Adewale Akinnuoye-Agbaje (Wombosi). Directed by Doug Liman and produced by Patrick Crowley, Richard N. Gladstein, and Liman. Screenplay by Tone Gilroy and William Blade Herron, based on the novel by Robert Ludlum.

The Bourne Identity is a skillful action movie about a plot that exists only to support a skillful action movie. The entire story is a setup for the martial arts and chases. Because they are done well, because the movie is well crafted and acted, we give it a pass. Too bad it's not about something.

Well, perhaps it is. Perhaps it is about the amoral climate in spy agencies like the CIA. There are no good guys in the movie—certainly not the hero, played by Matt Damon, who is a trained assassin—and no bad guys, either. Even the people who want to kill Damon are only doing their jobs. Just as the guardians of the Navaho windtalkers in another movie are told to kill their charges rather than let them fall into enemy hands, so is Bourne, or whatever his name is, targeted for death after he fails to assassinate an African leader. (There's a good possibility he would also be targeted if he had succeeded.)

As the movie opens, a fisherman on a boat out of Marseilles spots a body floating in what is obviously a studio back-lot tank. Hauled aboard, the body turns out to be alive, to have two bullet wounds, and to have a capsule embedded under the skin that contains the code to a Swiss bank account. The friendly fisherman gives the rescued man (who doesn't remember who he is) money to take the train to Switzerland, and he is welcomed in that nation and withdraws a fortune from a bank despite lacking a name or any form of personal identification.

Indeed, he finds out who he may be by looking inside the red bag from the bank, where he finds several passports, one saying his name is Bourne. Determined to find out his real name and why he was floating in the Mediterranean, Bourne pays $10,000 to a gypsy named Marie (Franka Potente from *Run, Lola, Run*) to drive him to Paris. Meanwhile, the movie cuts to CIA headquarters in Virginia, where we meet Bourne's handler, Conklin (Chris Cooper), and his boss, Abbott (Brian Cox). Bourne was thought to be dead. Now that he is alive, he must be killed, and the assignment goes to several assassins, including the Professor (Clive Owen), who is as highly trained as Bourne.

I forgot to say that Bourne is trained. Is he ever. He speaks several languages, is a formidable martial artist, has highly trained powers of observation and memory, knows all the spy tricks, and is a formidable driver. We see that during a sensational chase scene through the streets of Paris, much of it through narrow alleys, down flights of steps, and against traffic.

There comes a point at which we realize there will be no higher level to the screenplay, no greater purpose than to expend this kinetic energy. The movie's brutally cynical happy ending reveals that it doesn't take itself seriously. And we catch on (sooner than Marie) that the girl stays in the picture only because—well, there has to be a girl to provide false suspense and give the loner hero someone to talk to.

I kind of enjoyed *The Bourne Identity.* I had to put my mind on hold, but I was able to. I am less disturbed by action movies like this, which are frankly about nothing, than by action movies like *Windtalkers,* which pretend to be about something and then cop out. Doug Limon, the director of *Bourne,* directs the traffic well, gets a nice wintry look from his locations, absorbs us with the movie's spycraft, and uses Damon's ability to be focused and sincere. The movie is unnecessary, but not unskilled.

Bowling for Columbine ★ ★ ★ ½
R, 120 m., 2002

Featuring Michael Moore, George W. Bush, Dick Clark, Charlton Heston, Marilyn Manson, John Nichols, and Matt Stone. A documentary directed by Michael Moore and produced by Charles Bishop, Jim Czarnecki, Michael Donovan, Kathleen Glynn, and Moore. Screenplay by Moore.

McHugh and I were sitting in O'Rourke's one day when a guy we knew came in for a drink. The guy pulled back his coat and we could see he had a handgun in his belt. "Why are you carrying a gun?" McHugh asked. "Because I live in a dangerous neighborhood," the guy said. "It would be safer if you moved," said McHugh.

Michael Moore's *Bowling for Columbine,* a documentary that is both hilarious and sorrowful, is like a two-hour version of that anecdote. We live in a nation with millions of handguns, but that isn't really what bothers Moore. What bothers him is that we so frequently shoot them at each other. Canada has a similar ratio of guns to citizens, but a tenth of the shooting deaths. What makes us kill so many times more fellow citizens than is the case in other developed nations?

Moore, the jolly populist rabble-rouser, explains that he's a former sharpshooting instructor and a lifelong member of the National Rifle Association. No doubt this is true, but Moore has moved on from his early fondness for guns. In *Bowling for Columbine,* however, he is not so sure of the answers as in the popular *Roger & Me,* a film in which he knew who the bad guys were, and why. Here he asks questions he can't answer, such as why we as a nation seem so afraid, so in need of the reassurance of guns. Noting that we treasure urban legends designed to make us fearful of strangers, Moore notices how TV news focuses on local violence ("If it bleeds, it leads") and says that while the murder rate is down 20 percent in America, TV coverage of violent crime is up 600 percent.

Despite paranoia that has all but sidetracked the childhood custom of trick-or-treat, Moore points out that in fact no razor blades have ever been found in Halloween apples.

Moore's thoughtfulness doesn't inhibit the sensational set pieces he devises to illustrate his concern. He returns several times to Columbine, at one point showing horrifying security-camera footage of the massacre. And Columbine inspires one of the great confrontations in a career devoted to radical grandstanding. Moore introduces us to two of the students wounded at Columbine, both still with bullets in their bodies. He explains that all of the Columbine bullets were freely sold to the teenage killers by K-Mart, at seventeen cents apiece. And then he takes the two victims to K-Mart headquarters to return the bullets for a refund.

This is brilliant theater, and would seem to be unanswerable for the hapless K-Mart public relations spokespeople, who fidget and evade in front of Moore's merciless camera. But then, on Moore's third visit to headquarters, he is told that K-Mart will agree to completely phase out the sale of ammunition. "We've won," says Moore, not believing it. "This has never happened before." For once, he's at a loss for words.

The movie is a mosaic of Moore confrontations and supplementary footage. One moment that cuts to the core is from a stand-up routine by Chris Rock, who suggests that our problem could be solved by simply increasing the price of bullets — taxing them like cigarettes. Instead of seventeen cents apiece, why not $5,000? "At that price," he speculates, "you'd have a lot fewer innocent bystanders being shot."

Moore buys a map to the stars' homes to find where Charlton Heston lives, rings the bell on his gate, and is invited back for an interview. But Heston clearly knows nothing of Moore's track record, and his answers to Moore's questions are borderline pathetic. Heston recently announced he has symptoms associated with Alzheimer's disease, but there is no indication in this footage that he is senile; it's simply that he cannot explain why he, as a man living behind a gate in a protected neighborhood, with security patrols, who has never felt himself threatened, needs a loaded gun in the house. Heston is equally unhelpful when asked if he thinks it was a good idea for him to speak at an NRA rally in Denver ten days after Columbine. He seems to think it was all a matter of scheduling.

Bowling for Columbine thinks we have way too many guns, don't need them, and are shooting each other at an unreasonable rate. Moore cannot single out a villain to blame for this fact, because it seems to emerge from a national desire to be armed. ("If you're not armed, you're not responsible," a member of the Michigan militia tells him.) At one point he visits a bank that is giving away guns to people who open new accounts. He asks a banker if it isn't a little dangerous to have all these guns in a bank. Not at all. The bank, Moore learns, is a licensed gun dealership.

Note: The movie is rated R, so that the Columbine killers would have been protected from the "violent images," mostly of themselves. The MPAA continues its policy of banning teenagers from those films they most need to see. What utopian world do the flywheels of the ratings board think they are protecting?

The Bread, My Sweet ★ ★ ★
NO MPAA RATING, 105 m., 2002

Scott Baio (Dominic), Kristin Minter (Lucca), Rosemary Prinz (Bella), John Seitz (Massimo), Zachary Mott (Eddie), Shuler Hensley (Pino). Directed by Melissa Martin and produced by Adrienne Wehr and William C. Halley. Screenplay by Martin.

The Bread, My Sweet tells an improbable love story in such a heartfelt way that it's impossible to be cynical in the face of its innocence. Filmed in Pittsburgh, where it has been playing to full houses since January, it now gets a national release thanks to the success of *My Big Fat Greek Wedding*, another unlikely hit about ethnic romance. It's likely to appeal to the same kinds of audiences.

The movie stars Scott Baio as Dominic, who has two careers. He works downtown as a corporate raider whose job is to fire people at the companies he acquires. And he also owns a little pastry shop in an old Italian neighborhood, which provides jobs for his two brothers: Pino (Shuler Hensley), who is retarded, and Eddie (Zachary Mott), who floats through life without direction.

Upstairs over the shop live their landlords, Bella (Rosemary Prinz) and Massimo (John Seitz), who are salt-of-the-earth types, loud, demonstrative, extravagant with affection, always fighting but forever in love. They have a daughter named Lucca (Kristin Minter) who, instead of marrying and providing them with grandchildren, has joined the Peace Corps and disappeared from their lives. Now the boys downstairs are a surrogate family: "Three years ago, I don't know your name," Bella tells Dominic. "Now you are my son."

Like many stories that are too good to be true, this one has some truth in it. I learn from a review by Ron Weiskind of the *Pittsburgh Post-Gazette* that the movie, written and directed by Melissa Martin, "was inspired by a beloved Italian couple who lived above the Strip District bakery Enrico Biscotti, which is run by Martin's husband, Larry Lagatutta." The bakery in the movie is his actual bakery.

The first act establishes these people, their personalities and needs, and shows that Dominic is increasingly unhappy with his corporate job. Having opened the bakery out of love for his brothers, he finds he loves it too—and the old couple who live upstairs. I must explain what happens next to deal with the movie at all, so you might want to file this if you don't want to know that . . .

Bella falls ill. And now her heart is breaking. She doesn't mind dying, but she is filled with grief that she will die with her only child still single and wandering somewhere in the Peace Corps wilderness. Dominic tracks down the daughter and advises her to come home quickly. Lucca materializes, turning out to be a good and loving daughter (perhaps the Peace Corps was a hint), and she and Dominic discuss what is to be done. It quickly becomes obvious to Dominic that only one thing will make a difference: He and Lucca must be married so that the old woman can die in peace.

This development is straight out of romantic comedy, and *The Bread, My Sweet* is rather daring to take it seriously. There is a crucial scene where Dominic explains his thinking to Lucca, and this scene somehow, against all odds, works. Scott Baio and Kristin Minter, who could so easily bog down in soppy truisms, discuss his plan objectively. She is of course astonished by his suggestion, but he keeps talking. "I do deals," he says, and this will be his biggest deal. "We have a very small window of opportunity."

Of course they can get divorced after Bella dies, etc., and need not have sex, etc., but all of these footnotes are brushed aside by the enormity of the deception they are planning, and then—well, two nice young people like that, don't they deserve each other?

The film misses scarcely a chance to tug at our heartstrings. As Bella grows more ill and loses her appetite, Pino bakes smaller and smaller pies for her to eat, until finally in tears he admits that he cannot make a pie any smaller. Martin even adds a touch of magic realism, with a mysterious gypsy woman who dances with a tambourine on the street outside.

What makes the movie special is its utter sincerity. For all of the contrivances in the plot, there is the feeling that the actors love their characters and are trying to play them honestly. Yes, the movie is corny, but no, it's not dumb. It's clever and insightful in the way it gets away with this story, which is almost a fable. The turning point is the key conversation between Dominic and Lucca. Once that works, we can believe almost anything. Now if only Bella will.

Breakin' All the Rules ★ ★ ★
PG-13, 85 m., 2004

Jamie Foxx (Quincy Watson), Gabrielle Union (Nicky Callas), Morris Chestnut (Evan Fields), Peter MacNicol (Philip Gascon), Jennifer Esposito (Rita Monroe), Bianca Lawson (Helen Sharp). Directed by Daniel Taplitz and produced by Lisa Tornell. Screenplay by Taplitz.

Breakin' All the Rules combines a romantic comedy, a little mistaken identity, and some satire about office politics into one of those genial movies where you know everything is going to turn out all right in the end. The movie depends for its success on the likability of Jamie Foxx, Morris Chestnut, and Gabrielle

Union, and because they're funny and pleasant we enjoy the ride even though the destination is preordained.

Foxx plays Quincy Watson, a writer for *Spoils* magazine, one of those men's lifestyle books edited for readers who believe they can become rich, successful, and well groomed by studying a magazine. The magazine has fallen upon hard times, and the editor summons Quincy and gives him a list of people to fire. Quincy recoils; he hates the idea of firing anybody. So does Philip the editor (Peter MacNicol), who explains that one of the spoils of being the boss is that you can get other people to do your dirty work.

Rather than fire anyone, Quincy quits. He's depressed anyway; his fiancée, Helen Sharp (Bianca Lawson), has just broken up with him. He starts writing versions of a wounded, angry letter to her, and somehow the correspondence grows into a book titled *Break Up Handbook*, about how to break up with a girl before she can break up with you (danger signal: she says she "wants to have a talk").

Enter Quincy's cousin, Evan (Morris Chestnut), a moving target who prides himself on breaking up with girls as a preemptive strategy. His girl, Nicky (Gabrielle Union), says she wants to have a talk, and to deny her the opportunity of breaking up with him, Evan sends Quincy to a bar to meet her and tell her the relationship is over. Alas, Nicky has cut her hair and doesn't fit Evan's description; Quincy starts talking with her, and soon they're flirting with love. If the hair trick sounds contrived, recall that Shakespeare was not above mistaken identities even more absurd. Not that I hold it against him.

Gabrielle Union is one of those actresses whose smile is so warm you hope the other characters will say something just to make her happy. As a counterbalance, the movie supplies Rita (Jennifer Esposito), a mercenary mantrap who wants to get her hooks into Philip the editor. Quincy is called in as a consultant on this case, too, but Rita is too crafty to be easily fooled by tricks learned from a book.

There will, of course, be a scene of wounded betrayal, when Evan discovers that Quincy is dating Nicky and decides he loves her after all. And a titanic battle of the wills between Rita and Philip. And jokes about being the author of a best-seller; Quincy's book seems to hit the charts within days after he finishes it, having apparently been printed by magic.

Breakin' All the Rules is not a comic masterpiece, but it's entertaining and efficient and provides a showcase for its stars. It's on the level of a good sitcom. It's unusual in this way: Writer-director Daniel Taplitz has come up with a magazine title that would probably work on the newsstands, and a book idea that would probably sell. Most magazines in movies are completely implausible (in *13 Going on 30*, the heroine redesigned the magazine as a school yearbook). And most best-sellers in the movies sound way too good to ever sell many copies.

Bringing Down the House ★ ★
PG-13, 105 m., 2003

Steve Martin (Peter Sanderson), Queen Latifah (Charlene Morton), Eugene Levy (Howie Rosenthal), Jean Smart (Kate Sanderson), Michael Rosenbaum (Todd Gendler), Betty White (Mrs. Klein), Joan Plowright (Mrs. Arness). Directed by Adam Shankman and produced by Ashok Amritraj and David Hoberman. Screenplay by Jason Filardi.

I confess I expected Steve Martin and Queen Latifah to fall in love in *Bringing Down the House*. That they avoid it violates all the laws of economical screenplay construction, since they are constantly thrown together, they go from hate to affection, and they get drunk together one night and tear up the living room together, which in movies of this kind is usually the closer.

But, no, all they fall into is Newfound Respect, which, in a world of high-performance star vehicles, is the minivan. Eugene Levy is brought off the bench to console the Queen, and Martin ends up back with his divorced wife (Jean Smart), who exists only so that he can go back to her. These two couples had better never double-date, because under the table Queen and Steve are going to have their socks up each other's pants.

Why, I asked myself, is their mutual sexual attraction disguised as roughhousing when they are the stars, and movie convention demands that they get it on? There isn't a shred of chemistry between Latifah and Levy (who likes the Queen's wildness and is infatuated with her cleavage, which is understandable but shallow—his infatuation, not her cleavage). I think it's because the movie, coproduced by Latifah, was making a point, which is that the rich white lawyer had better learn to accept this bitch on her own terms instead of merely caving in to her sex appeal. This may be a point worth making, but not in a comedy.

I use the word "bitch" after some hesitation, to make a point: The movie is all about different ethnic styles of speech. It uses the B-word constantly (along, of course, with lots of "hos"), and I argue that since the MPAA rates the language PG-13, I can use it in a review. You kids under thirteen who are reading this better be getting parental guidance from a POS.

(Emergency definition: POS [n., slang]. Abbreviation used in teenage chat rooms, warning person at other end: "Parent over shoulder!")

Martin plays Peter Sanderson, a high-powered lawyer with a trophy ex-wife who lives in a posh Los Angeles neighborhood and speaks with meticulous precision he elevates to a kind of verbal constipation. Queen Latifah plays Charlene Morton, whom he meets in an Internet chat room, where she is LawyerGirl.

They both misrepresent their appearance—well, all right, she's guiltier than he is—and when they meet he's appalled to find, not a blond legal bimbo, but a trash-talking black ex-con who wants him to handle her case. Charlene *can* talk like a perfect middle-class lady, as she demonstrates, but the movie's point of pride is that she shouldn't have to. Peter can also talk like a black street dude, sort of. Maybe he learned it from his kids' rap records.

The movie's conceit is that Peter keeps throwing Charlene out and she keeps coming back because she's determined to prove her legal innocence. She breaks into his house, throws wild parties, embarrasses him at his club, and so on, until a magic night when she gets him drinking and dancing, plants his hands squarely on what Russ Meyer used to rhapsodically refer to as garbanzos, and breaks down his inhibitions. At this point—what? Wild nuzzling, rapturous caresses, shredded knickers, wild goat cries in the night? Peter takes her case, that's what, while Eugene Levy crawls out of his eyebrows and joins the tag team.

This is all wrong. It violates the immortal Stewart/Reagan principle: Steve Martin for Latifah, Eugene Levy for best friend. A comedy is not allowed to end with the couples incorrectly paired. It goes against the deeply traditional requirements of the audience. Here is a movie that ignores the Model Airplane Rule: First, make sure you have taken all of the pieces out of the box, then line them up in the order in which they will be needed. *Bringing Down the House* is glued together with one of the wings treated like a piece of tail.

Broken Lizard's Club Dread ★ ★ ½
R, 103 m., 2004

Jay Chandrasekhar (Putman), Steve Lemme (Juan), Paul Soter (Dave), Britanny Daniel (Jenny), Erik Stolhanske (Sam), Kevin Heffernan (Lars), M. C. Gainey (Hank), Greg Cipes (Trevor), Bill Paxton (Coconut Pete). Directed by Jay Chandrasekhar and produced by Richard Perello. Screenplay by Broken Lizard.

Broken Lizard's Club Dread is a definitive demonstration, if one is needed, that *The Real Cancun* was way too real. Filmed in Mexico but allegedly set on Coconut Pete's Pleasure Island off the coast of Costa Rica, it's a head-on smashup between spring break weekend and a machete-swinging slasher. Whether it works or not is a little hard to say; like *Super Troopers* (2001), the previous film by the Broken Lizard comedy troupe, it has lovable performances, very big laughs, and then some downtime while everybody (in the cast as well as the audience) waits to see what will happen next.

The leader of the troupe and director of both films is Jay Chandrasekhar, whose character in *Super Troopers* delighted in spreading confusing hints about his ethnic origin. Here he's the dreadlocked Indian (or perhaps British or Caribbean) tennis instructor, whose serve is so powerful that at one point he actually tries to kill the slasher by hitting balls at him.

Pleasure Island is run by Coconut Pete (Bill Paxton), who very briefly, a long time ago, had a record that was a hit for five minutes. It was called "Pina Colada-berg," and who knows what heights it might have reached on the charts had it not been for the treachery of

"Margaritaville." Pete presides over an endless boozy sex-'n'-sand party that looks recycled out of every other movie ever made about beach blanket bingo, and if there is a babe (the film's preferred word) who ever wears anything other than a bikini, my memory fails me.

Alas, this island idyll is marred by the presence of a mad slasher, who stalks about garbed as if he (or she) once saw *I Know What You Did Last Summer* but either forgot how the fisherman dressed, or the costume supply store ran out of Groton's outfits. How a killer can roam a small tropical island dressed like Death in *The Seventh Seal* and never be noticed is one of the many questions this movie answers by keeping the bar open twenty-four hours a day.

The cast includes a cop in charge of enforcing fun, a six-foot-one Swedish masseuse who turns out, to intense disappointment, to be a six-foot-two Swedish masseur, and an aerobics instructor whose best exercises are horizontal. Characters are periodically killed, and at one point a severed head turns up on the deejay's turntable, but the fun goes on because these characters, while admittedly brighter and more articulate than the real people in *The Real Cancun,* realize that the slightest insight would solve the mystery and terminate the movie right then and there, and if we paid for feature length, that's what we deserve.

Do I recommend this movie or not? I am at a loss to say. It is what it is. Criticism is irrelevant. Why are you even reading a review of *Club Dread*? You've seen the TV ads and you already know (a) you won't miss it or (b) not in a million years. There will be better movies playing in the same theater, even if it is a duplex, but on the other hand there is something to be said for goofiness without apology by broken lizards who just wanna have fun. I think I'll give it two and a half stars plus a nudge and a wink, as a signal to those who liked *Super Troopers* and know what they're in for. I gave *Super Troopers* two and a half stars, too, but I'd rather see it again than certain distinguished movies I could mention.

Brother Bear ★ ★ ★

G, 86 m., 2003

With the voices of: Joaquin Phoenix (Kenai), Jeremy Suarez (Koda), Jason Raize (Denahi), Rick Moranis (Rutt), Dave Thomas (Tuke), D. B. Sweeney (Sitka), Joan Copeland (Tanana), Michael Clarke Duncan (Tug), Harold Gould (Old Denahi). Directed by Aaron Blaise and Robert Walker and produced by Chuck Williams. Screenplay by Steve Bencich, Ron J. Friedman, Tab Murphy, Lorne Cameron, and David Hoselton.

Disney's *Brother Bear* is more mystical and New Age than your average animated movie about animals, although it does have a couple of talking moose and a cute cubby bear. It's ambitious in its artistry, incorporating images from prehistoric cave paintings and playing with the screen width. But it doesn't have the zowie factor of *The Lion King* or *Finding Nemo,* and is sweet rather than exciting. Children and their parents are likely to relate on completely different levels, the adults connecting with the transfer of souls from man to beast, while the kids are excited by the adventure stuff.

The story begins in a Native American tribe in the Pacific Northwest, thousands of years ago. We meet three brothers: brave older brother Sitka (D. B. Sweeney), strong-willed middle brother Denahi (Jason Raize), and the troublesome young Kenai (voice by Joaquin Phoenix). Each wears a totem around his neck, representing the animal spirit he is identified with. Sitka wears an eagle, Denahi a wolf, and Kenai—well, Kenai gets a bear, and considers himself shortchanged, especially when he's told that the bear represents the quality of love, which he considers pretty far down, so to speak, on the totem pole.

Kenai doesn't like bears, and picks a fight with one that tries to steal his fishing catch; he recklessly chases the bear, and when Sitka tries to protect him, the older brother is killed and is transformed into an eagle. Kenai is counseled by the tribe's wise man, Tanana (Joan Copeland), to accept this outcome as the will of the universe, but he determines to kill the bear. He succeeds, but the universe proves it has a sense of justice, or perhaps of humor, by transforming Kenai himself into a bear—so that Denahi assumes it was Bear Kenai who killed Kid Brother Kenai. Denahi continues the family tradition of vengeance by tracking down Bear

Kenai, in an irony that is positively Shakespearean, and no wonder, since I learn that this story was originally inspired by *King Lear*, although the notion of three siblings seems to be all that survived.

The opening scenes are in a conventional screen ratio of 1:85 to 1, but after Kenai becomes a bear, the colors deepen and the screen widens to 2:35 to 1, so you'd better hope your projectionist is on his toes. Given Kenai's prejudices about bears, he is extremely unhappy to be one himself, but soon he's getting bear lessons from little Koda (Jeremy Suarez), a cub who shows him the ropes. Kenai discovers from the spirit of Tanana that he must seek Eagle Sitka on a mountain where light touches the Earth, and Koda leads him on the mission—perhaps because he really knows where the mountain is, perhaps for reasons of his own.

Their trek there involves many adventures, including a scary encounter with flowing lava from a volcano. Two Canadian moose named Rutt and Tuke turn up and have conversations that sound amazingly like the MacKenzie Brothers from SCTV, maybe because they are voiced by Rick Moranis and Dave Thomas. The outcome of the story, which I would not dream of revealing, has Kenai making a career choice that is far from practical but certainly shows he has learned to see things from a bear's point of view.

Note: The movie, a product of the same Orlando animation studio that produced Disney's Mulan *and* Lilo & Stitch, *is very good-looking, and sometimes seems to want to burst through the boundaries of conventional animation to present a more visionary portrait of its time and place; a sequence involving cave drawings comes impressively to life. There's also a curious early moment when the animators reproduce the effects of sunlight refracting through a lens, even though animation uses no lens and refracts no light.* Variety *says this will be the last 2-D animated film from Disney for the foreseeable future; the studio is switching to the 3-D style originally popularized by Pixar. Both formats have their strengths; one is not better than the other, simply different.*

Brotherhood of the Wolf ★ ★ ★
R, 146 m., 2002

Samuel Le Bihan (Fronsac), Vincent Cassel (Jean-Francois), Mark Dacascos (Mani), Monica Bellucci (Sylvia), Emilie Dequenne (Marianne), Jeremie Renier (Thomas de'Apcher), Jacques Parrin (Old Thomas). Directed by Christophe Gans and produced by Samuel Hadida and Richard Grandpierre. Screenplay by Stephane Cabel. In French with English subtitles.

Brotherhood of the Wolf plays like an explosion at the genre factory. When the smoke clears, a rough beast lurches forth, its parts cobbled together from a dozen movies. The film involves quasi-werewolves, French aristocrats, secret societies, Iroquois Indians, martial arts, occult ceremonies, sacred mushrooms, swashbuckling, incestuous longings, political subversion, animal spirits, slasher scenes, and bordellos, and although it does not end with the words "based on a true story," it is.

The story involves the Beast of Gevaudan that, in 1764, terrorized a remote district of France, killing more than sixty women and children, and tearing out their hearts and vitals. I borrow these facts from Patrick Meyers of TheUnexplainedSite.com, who reveals that the Beast was finally found to be a wolf. Believe me, this information does not even come close to giving away the ending of the movie.

Directed by Christophe Gans, *Brotherhood of the Wolf* is couched in historical terms. It begins in 1794, at the time of the Revolution, when its narrator (Jacques Parrin), about to be carried away to the guillotine, puts the finishing touches on a journal revealing at last the true story of the Beast. Although a wolf was killed and presented to the court of the king, that was only a cover-up, he says, as we flash back to . . .

Well, actually, the Beast attacks under the opening credits, even before the narrator appears. For the first hour or so we do not see it, but we hear fearsome growls, moans, and roars, and see an unkempt but buxom peasant girl dragged to her doom. Enter Gregoire de Fronsac (Samuel Le Bihan), an intellectual and naturalist, recently returned from exploring the St. Lawrence Seaway. He is accompanied by Mani, an Iroquois who speaks perfect French and perfect tree (he talks to them). Mani is played by Mark Dacascos, a martial arts expert from Hawaii whose skills might seem out of place in eighteenth-century France, but no: Everyone in this movie fights in a style that would make Jackie Chan proud.

Fronsac doubts the existence of a Beast. Science tells us to distrust fables, he explains. At dinner, he passes around a trout with fur, from Canada, which causes one of the guests to observe it must really be cold for the fish there, before Fronsac reveals it is a hoax. The Beast, alas, soon makes him a believer, but he sees a pattern: "The Beast is a weapon used by a man." But what man? Why? How? Charting the Beast's attacks on a map, he cleverly notices that all of the lines connecting them intersect at one point in rural Gevaudan. Fronsac and Mani go looking.

The local gentry include Jean-Francois (Vincent Cassel), who has one arm, but has fashioned a rifle he can brace in the crook of his shoulder. It fires silver bullets (this is also a historical fact). His sister Marianne (Emilie Dequenne) fancies Fronsac, which causes Jean-Francois to hate him, significantly. Also lurking about, usually with leaves in her hair, is the sultry Sylvia (Monica Bellucci), who travels with men who might as well have "Lout" displayed on a sign around their necks, and likes to dance on tabletops while they throw knives that barely miss her.

I would be lying if I did not admit that this is all, in its absurd and overheated way, entertaining. Once you realize that this is basically a high-gloss werewolf movie (but without a werewolf), crossed with a historical romance, a swashbuckler, and a martial arts extravaganza, you can relax. There is, of course, a deeper political message (this movie is nothing if not inclusive), and vague foreshadowings of fascism and survivalist cults, but the movie uses its politics only as a plot convenience.

Brotherhood of the Wolf looks just great. The photography by Dan Laustsen is gloriously atmospheric and creepy; he likes fogs, blasted heaths, boggy marshes, moss, vines, creepers, and the excesses of eighteenth-century interior decorating. He has fun with a completely superfluous scene set in a bordello just because it was time for a little skin. The Beast, when it finally appears, is a most satisfactory Beast indeed, created by Jim Henson's Creature Shop. There are times when its movements resemble the stop-motion animation of a Ray Harryhausen picture, but I like the oddness of that kind of motion; it makes the Beast weirder than if it glided along smoothly.

The one thing you don't want to do is take this movie seriously. Because it's so good-looking, there may be a temptation to think it wants to be high-toned, but no: Its heart is in the horror-monster-sex-fantasy-special-effects tradition. "The Beast has a master," Fronsac says. "I want him." That's the spirit.

Brown Sugar ★ ★ ★
PG-13, 108 m., 2002

Taye Diggs (Dre), Sanaa Lathan (Sidney), Nicole Ari Parker (Reese), Boris Kodjoe (Kelby Dawson), Mos Def (Chris V.), Queen Latifah (Francine). Directed by Rick Famuyiwa and produced by Peter Heller. Screenplay by Michael Elliot and Famuyiwa.

She is the editor of an important music magazine. He produces hip-hop for a major label. They've been best friends since childhood, but never more than that, although they came close a few times. Now, as both approach thirty, Dre (Taye Diggs) feels his career has lost its way. And Sidney (Sanaa Lathan) is working so hard she doesn't have time for romance: "You're turning into a Terry McMillan character," her girlfriend Francine warns her.

Brown Sugar, which charts romantic passages in these lives, is a romantic comedy, yes, but one with characters who think and talk about their goals, and are working on hard decisions. For both Sidney and Dre, hip-hop music symbolizes a kind of perfect adolescent innocence, a purity they're trying to return to as more cynical adults.

The first question Sidney asks an interview subject is always, "How did you fall in love with hip-hop?" For her, it was July 18, 1984, when she discovered for the first time a form that combined music, rhythm, performance, and poetry. Dre, her best buddy even then, grew up to become an important hip-hop producer, working for a label that compromised its standards as it became more successful. Now he's faced with the prospect of producing "Rin and Tin," one white, one black, who bill themselves as "The Hip-Hop Dalmatians."

Dre gets engaged to the beautiful Reese

(Nicole Ari Parker). Sidney can't believe he'll marry her, but can't admit she loves him—although she comes close on the night before their wedding. Francine (Queen Latifah) lectures her to declare her love: "You'll get the buddy and the booty!" When Dre quits his job rather than work with the Dalmatians, he turns instinctively to Sidney for advice, and Reese begins to understand she's sharing his heart.

Sidney, meanwhile, interviews the hunky athlete Kelby Dawson (Boris Kodjoe), and soon they're engaged. Is this the real thing or a rebound? Dre still needs her for encouragement, as he pursues a hip-hop taxi driver named Chris V. (Mos Def), who he believes has potential to return the form to its roots. And Chris, articulate in his music but lacking confidence in his life, doesn't have the nerve to ask out Francine.

Brown Sugar, advertised as a hip-hop comedy, is more like a slice of black professional life (there's not even an entire hip-hop song in the whole movie). Directed and cowritten by Rick Famuyiwa, the movie returns to a world similar to his *The Wood* (1999). But the characters are deeper and more complex.

Consider Reese, the Nicole Ari Parker character. In a less thoughtful movie, she'd be the shallow, bitchy life-wrecker. Here she is blameless and basically reasonable: Mad at Dre for quitting his job without talking it over with her, jealous of Sidney because she (correctly) suspects Sidney and Dre have always been in love, but lied to themselves about it. That feeling comes to a head at the gym where both women work out, during a sparring match that gets a little too sincere.

There's a scene in *Brown Sugar* I never thought I'd see in a movie, where after Reese and Dre have a "final" fight, and in a more conventional film she would disappear forever from the screenplay, she returns to suggest counseling and says they need to work harder at their marriage. How many movie romances are that thoughtful about their characters?

Brown Sugar may be pitching itself to the wrong audience. The ads promise: "The Rhythm . . . the Beat . . . the Love . . . and You Don't Stop!" But it's not a musical, and although it's sometimes a comedy, it's observant about its people. Francine is onto something. They're all Terry McMillan characters.

Bruce Almighty ★ ★ ★
PG-13, 95 m., 2003

Jim Carrey (Bruce Nolan), Jennifer Aniston (Grace), Morgan Freeman (God), Lisa Ann Walter (Debbie), Philip Baker Hall (Jack Keller), Catherine Bell (Susan Ortega), Steven Carell (Evan Baxter), Nora Dunn (Ally Loman), Sally Kirkland (Waitress). Directed by Tom Shadyac and produced by Michael Bostick, James Brubaker, and Shadyac. Screenplay by Steve Oedekerk, Steve Koren, and Mark O'Keefe.

There is about Jim Carrey a desperate urgency that can be very funny, as he plunges with manic intensity after his needs and desires. In *Bruce Almighty,* he plays a man for whom the most important thing on Earth is to become an anchor on the Buffalo TV station. When he fails to achieve this pinnacle, he vents his anger at the very heavens themselves, challenging God to show and explain himself.

One could argue that Bruce Nolan, Carrey's character, is not necessarily qualified to be anchor, on the basis of two remote reports we see him delivering, one from the scene of a chocolate chip cookie of record-breaking size, the other from onboard an anniversary cruise of the *Maid of the Mist,* the famous Niagara Falls tour boat. During the cruise he learns, while on the air live, that he will not be getting the coveted anchor job, and he goes ballistic, even uttering the dread f-word in his dismay.

Now that may argue that he is a loose cannon and not fit to anchor anyway (although he would be replacing a man whose primary skill seems to be smiling). Nevertheless, in anger and grief, and facing the loss of the love of his faithful girlfriend, Grace (Jennifer Aniston), he calls upon God, and God answers.

God is, in this case, a man in a white suit, played by Morgan Freeman with what can only be described as godlike patience with Bruce. Since Bruce is so dissatisfied with the job God is doing, God turns the controls of the universe over to him—or at least, the controls over his immediate neighborhood in Buffalo, although at one point this limited power seems to extend directly above Buffalo to such an extent that Bruce is able to change the distance of the moon, causing tidal waves in Japan.

Bruce Almighty, directed by Tom Shadyac and written by Steve Oedekerk, Steve Koren, and Mark O'Keefe, is a charmer, the kind of movie where Bruce learns that while he may not ever make a very good God, the experience may indeed make him a better television newsman.

The problem with playing God, the movie demonstrates, is that when such powers are entrusted to a human, short-term notions tend to be valued higher than long-term improvement plans. Consider, for example, the way Bruce deals with a dog that pees in the house (the payoff shot, showing the dog learning a new way to use the newspaper, had me laughing so loudly people were looking at me). And consider Bruce's methods for dealing with traffic jams, which work fine for Bruce but not so well for everyone else; when you're God, you can't think only of yourself.

Morgan Freeman plays God with a quality of warm detachment that is just about right, I think. You get the feeling that even while he's giving Bruce the free ride, he has a hand on the wheel, like a driver's training instructor. Jennifer Aniston, as a sweet kindergarten teacher and fiancée, shows again (after *The Good Girl*) that she really will have a movie career, despite the small-minded cavils of those who think she should have stayed on television. She can play comedy, which is not easy, and she can keep up with Carrey while not simply mirroring his zaniness; that's one of those gifts like being able to sing one song while typing the words to another.

Whether *Bruce Almighty* is theologically sound, I will leave to the better qualified. My own suspicion is that if you have God's power, even in a small area like Buffalo, it's likely to set things spinning weirdly everywhere. If a butterfly can flap its wings in Samoa and begin a chain of events leading to a tropical storm in the Caribbean, think what could happen when Bruce goes to work.

Bubba Ho-Tep ★ ★ ★

R, 92 m., 2003

Bruce Campbell (Elvis), Ossie Davis (Jack Kennedy), Ella Joyce (Nurse), Reggie Bannister (Administrator), Bob Ivy (Bubba Ho-Tep), Larry Pennell (Kemosabe), Heidi Marnhout (Callie), Harrison Young (Bull Thomas). Directed by Don Coscarelli and produced by Coscarelli and Jason R. Savage. Screenplay by Coscarelli, based on the short story by Joe R. Lansdale.

Elvis and JFK did not die, and today they're in an east Texas nursing home whose residents are being killed by an ancient Egyptian Soul Sucker named Bubba Ho-Tep. I want to get that on the table right at the get-go, so I can deal with the delightful wackiness of this movie, which is endearing and vulgar in about the right proportion. The movie doesn't exactly work, but sometimes when a car won't start it's still fun to look at the little honey gleaming in the driveway.

The movie's backstory: Elvis (Bruce Campbell) became sick of his lifestyle, his buddies, his groupies, his pills, his songs, his movies, and his Colonel Parker. He struck a deal with an Elvis impersonator to trade places. There's even a contract guaranteeing that Elvis can switch back if he changes his mind, but the contract is burned up in a barbecuing accident, and by then Elvis doesn't mind anyway, because he enjoys the freedom of performing just for the sheer joy, without the sideshow of fame.

The King explains all of this in a thoughtful, introspective voice-over narration that also deals with other matters on his mind, such as the alarming pustule on that part of his anatomy where it is least welcome. He talks about Priscilla and Lisa Marie, about his movies (not a single good one), about his decision to disappear, and about how he broke his hip falling off a stage. This narration is not broad comedy, but wicked, observant, and truthful. *Bubba Ho-Tep* has a lot of affection for Elvis, takes him seriously, and—this is crucial—isn't a camp horror movie but treats this loony situation as if it's really happening.

The man in the room down the hall is John F. Kennedy, played by Ossie Davis. "But, Jack . . . ," Elvis says hesitantly, "you're black." JFK nods in confirmation. When his assassination was faked by Lyndon B. Johnson, "they dyed me." Now the two old men wait for death in their hospital beds, Elvis on a stroller, JFK using a motorized wheelchair for longer trips, talking about what was and wasn't.

The rest home is almost a character in the movie, with its drab institutional corridors, its condescending nurse (Ella Joyce), its supercilious administrator (Reggie Bannister), its worn-out furniture, its flying cockroaches, its sense of being half-deserted. Pleasures here are hard to come by. "Let's get decadent," says JFK, opening his drawer and revealing a horde of Baby Ruth candy bars.

The cockroaches turn out to be giant scarab beetles worshiped by the ancient Egyptians, and that's a clue for JFK, who has been reading up on these matters and realizes that the nursing home is under attack by a Soul Sucker. He explains to Elvis that the soul can be sucked out of any orifice, but souls are small, so you need to suck a lot of them. The two men have a thoughtful conversation about whether a soul, after it is digested, leaves anything to be eliminated through the Soul Sucker's intestinal track. This sounds right: A lot of rest home conversations get around sooner or later to constipation.

The closing scenes of the movie show the two geezers in a fight to the finish with Bubba Ho-Tep (Bob Ivy), who looks like a threadbare version of the Mummy. Here the movie could get laughs by showing the old men with unexpected powers, but no: When Elvis tries out his old karate moves, it's disastrous. Assuming that elderly versions of Elvis and JFK ever really did do battle with an Egyptian Soul Sucker, this, I am forced to conclude, is more or less how it would look.

Of course there are laughs in the movie, which is a comedy, but an odd one. The movie was written and directed by Don Coscarelli, based on a short story by Joe R. Lansdale, the "mojo storyteller" from Nacogdoches, Texas. Coscarelli made the four *Phantasm* pictures, three unseen by me, the fourth unloved. What drew him to this material is not a mystery—the story sounds juicy enough—but what inspired him to tell it in this tone? *Bubba Ho-Tep* wants to be a *good* movie about Elvis, JFK, and the Soul Sucker. It doesn't sneer, it's not about cheap shots, it is perfectly sincere.

You never catch Campbell or Davis winking at the audience or patronizing the material. They approach their characters with all the cu-

riosity and respect they'd deserve in a serious film. Campbell sounds uncannily like Elvis might sound by now, and looks more like Elvis than anyone else I've seen in the role. Davis, of course, looks not at all like JFK, but I don't think we're really supposed to think he is JFK; one of the movie's sweet touches is the way Elvis just takes him at his word and proceeds from there.

I said the movie doesn't work. And so it doesn't. How *could* it work? It doesn't work as a horror movie because a Bubba Ho-Tep monster would make Ed Wood's monsters look slick by comparison. It doesn't work as a cult movie because it challenges the cleverness of the audience instead of congratulating it. It doesn't work as a traditional story arc because the story jumps the rails when Bubba Ho-Tep turns up.

But it does sort of work in one way: It has the damnedest ingratiating way of making us sit there and grin at its harebrained audacity, laugh at its outhouse humor, and be somewhat moved (not deeply, but somewhat) at the poignancy of these two old men and their situation. Elvis asks himself how in the world the King of Rock 'n' Roll ended up in a run-down east Texas nursing home with a boil on the family treasure, and by the end of the movie he has answered this excellent question more amusingly than any reasonable moviegoer could have expected.

Buffalo Soldiers ★ ★ ★
R, 98 m., 2003

Joaquin Phoenix (Ray Elwood), Anna Paquin (Robyn Lee), Ed Harris (Colonel Wallace Berman), Scott Glenn (Sergeant Robert Lee), Dean Stockwell (General Lancaster), Elizabeth McGovern (Mrs. Berman), Gabriel Mann (Knoll). Directed by Gregor Jordan and produced by Rainer Grupe and Ariane Moody. Screenplay by Eric Weiss, Nora MacCoby, and Jordan, based on the book by Robert O'Connor.

Buffalo Soldiers is a black comedy about larceny, theft, drug dealing, adultery, and a cheerful dereliction of duty among U.S. Army troops stationed in Germany in 1989. Although they know how to cook drugs and sell missile launchers on the black market, when the Berlin Wall falls there is a discussion about where Berlin is, and whether they are currently in East or West Germany.

This strain of irreverent Army misbehavior runs in various forms from *Catch-22* to *Apocalypse Now* to *M*A*S*H* to *Beetle Bailey* and in happier times the movie might have opened without controversy. But it premiered three days before 9/11 at the 2001 Toronto Film Festival, and as *Variety*'s critic Todd McCarthy wrote a day or two later, "All of a sudden, this looks like the wrong film at the wrong time."

Is now the right time? Maybe it's time to observe that *Buffalo Soldiers* is not about all soldiers at all times, but about those soldiers at that time—some of them, like company clerk Ray Elwood (Joaquin Phoenix), in uniform because the judge gave them a choice between jail and enlisting. Elwood is a crafty, high-living hustler who steals everything from Mop-n-Glo to missiles, whose men process drugs on the base, who drives a Mercedes, and who has his commander completely buffaloed. In an early scene, Colonel Berman (Ed Harris) and Elwood discuss a letter home to the parents of a soldier whose actual death was not exactly as in-the-line-of-duty as their description of it.

This seems to be the wackiest base in the army. During a session of tank maneuvers, the crew of one tank, zonked out of their minds, steer their tank away from the training field and through a nearby village market before causing a gas station explosion. Elwood and his men, who come upon the scene and find the unlucky drivers of two army trucks burned dead, think quickly and steal the trucks.

Here and elsewhere, Elwood is cold, amoral, and not very likable. We're used to rogues in uniform whom we like because they give the finger to authority, but Phoenix makes Elwood a calculating schemer who isn't a rebel for fun, but for profit. Consider his sex life. He is the secret lover of Colonel Berman's wife (Elizabeth McGovern), and later starts dating Robyn (Anna Paquin), the teenage daughter of the company's new top sergeant, Robert Lee (Scott Glenn).

This sergeant is a piece of work. Lean and

unforgiving as only Glenn can make him, the new top is a Vietnam veteran who quickly figures out Elwood is a thief (the Mercedes is a clue), and methodically sets out to make life miserable for him. Elwood tries to bribe him, but to say that doesn't work is an understatement. And when he starts dating the top's daughter, it's war between the two men—made more complicated because, to his astonishment, Elwood actually starts to like Robyn.

The dark climax of the movie, involving an enormous amount of drugs and money, leads to an ending that is a little too melodramatic—and then to an epilogue that some find too upbeat, although the more you consider it, the more downbeat it becomes. The film is filled with spot-on performances, by Harris, Glenn, and Phoenix, and by Anna Paquin, who has grown up after her debut in *The Piano* to become one of the most gifted actresses of her generation—particularly in tricky, emotion-straddling roles like this one.

To be sure, the movie is not a patriotic hymn to our fighting forces. It illustrates an ancient tradition best summarized in that classic army acronym SNAFU. At a time when the idea of patriotism is sometimes used to stifle dissent, it is important to remember that gripes and disgruntlement and antiauthoritarian gestures are part of our national heritage. I do not approve of Elwood or even much like him, but I think he represents a type, and Gregor Jordan's film is dark enough to suggest that sometimes such types prevail.

Bulletproof Monk ★ ★
PG-13, 103 m., 2003

Chow Yun-Fat (Monk with No Name), Seann William Scott (Kar), Jamie King (Jade/Bad Girl), Karel Roden (Struker), Victoria Smurfit (Nina), Patrick Hagarty (Mr. Funktastic). Directed by Paul Hunter and produced by Terence Chang, Charles Roven, John Woo, and Douglas Segal. Screenplay by Ethan Reiff and Cyrus Voris, based on the comic book by Brett Lewis and RA Jones.

Let us first consider the Scroll of the Ultimate. "Whoever reads it aloud in its entirety," an ancient monk explains to his young acolyte, "will gain the power to control the world." It is Tibet in 1943. The Nazis are there to capture the Scroll of the Ultimate. We recall from *Raiders of the Lost Ark* that the Third Reich was also trying to capture the Ark of the Covenant, perhaps so that Leni Riefenstahl, Hitler's favorite filmmaker, could direct *The Scroll of the Ultimate vs. the Ark of the Covenant,* a title I have just registered with the Writers Guild.

The young acolyte accepts responsibility for the Scroll and renounces his name, becoming the Monk with No Name, a name Clint Eastwood should have registered with the Writers Guild. No sooner does the Monk (Chow Yun-Fat) take possession than the sky churns with sensational visual effects, high winds blow, and the Nazis attack the temple. The Monk escapes by jumping off a high cliff, after first taking a Nazi bullet, which hits him right in the Scroll. He survives the jump, as he later explains, because gravity exists only if you think it does.

Since he walks around on the ground a lot, apparently he thinks it does, most of the time. The knack is to learn how to turn your belief on and off. Sixty years later, which is how long any one monk can guard the Scroll, the Monk is in New York City when he happens upon a pickpocket named Kar (Seann William Scott). Kar is working the subway, and has indeed just picked the Scroll from the Monk's briefcase, when he is forced into the subterranean lair of a gang of young toughs who look as dangerous as the crowd in a leather bar on date night. This gang is led by Mr. Funktastic (Patrick Hagarty), who has his name tattooed across his chest, and also includes the beautiful Bad Girl (Jamie King), who turns out to be a good girl. Kar engages in a violent martial arts struggle with the gang for a long time, after which they stop, because the scene is over, and Mr. Funktastic issues a dire warning should Kar ever stray their way again. Like he wants to hang out down there in the subterranean lair.

The Monk with No Name has secretly observed the fight, perhaps because Mr. Funktastic's men failed to notice the arrival of an unexpected monk, and he becomes friends with Kar, who seems to fit the Three Prophecies made about the one who will be chosen to guard the Scroll for the next sixty years. Of course, Kar is a reckless youth and must learn much about life, and meanwhile the Nazis turn up again and at one point have the Monk with No Name strapped to a torture machine crucifix-style, and are about to screw things into his brain.

Bulletproof Monk is a cross between a traditional Hong Kong martial arts movie and various American genres, incorporating the dubious notion that the wisest and most skilled practitioners of the ancient Asian arts have nothing better to do than tutor young Americans. To be sure, Kar has been studying on his own. "Where do you study fighting?" the Monk asks him. "The Golden Palace," he says. This is the broken-down movie palace where he is the projectionist, and he copies the moves from old karate movies.

The fight scenes in *Bulletproof Monk* are not as inventive as some I've seen (although the opening fight on a rope bridge is so well done that it raises expectations it cannot fulfill). The film demonstrates, *Matrix*-style, that a well-trained fighter can leap into the air and levitate while spinning dozens of times, although why anyone would want to do this is never explained. Chow Yun-Fat and Seann William Scott do as much with the material as they can, although it's always a little awkward trying to shoehorn a romance into a movie like this, especially when you have to clear time for Bad Girl and Nina (Victoria Smurfit), who is a third-generation Nazi and the real bad girl, to have their obligatory hand-to-hand combat.

Bulletproof Monk was written by Ethan Reiff and Cyrus Voris, based on the comic book by Brett Lewis and RA Jones, and will appeal to more or less the same audience as the comic book. The ads and trailer hope we confuse it with *Crouching Tiger, Hidden Dragon,* but this is more like the Young Readers' version.

Bus 174 ★ ★ ★ ½
NO MPAA RATING, 122 m., 2003

A documentary directed by Felipe Lacerda and José Padilha and produced by Padilha and Marcos Prado.

On June 12, 2000, a man named Sandro do Nascimento tried to rob the passengers on a bus in Rio de Janeiro, eventually took them hostage, and initiated a crisis that was televised live and ended in tragedy. *Bus 174* re-creates that crime with TV news footage, interviews with survivors and police, memories of those who knew the young man, and insights into the million or more homeless who live on the streets of Rio.

Sandro do Nascimento is not merely poor, or hungry, or doomed to poverty, but suffers from the agonizing psychic distress of being invisible. Yes, says the movie, literally invisible: Brazilians with homes and jobs go about their lives while unable to see people like Sandro, who exists in a parallel universe. In North America we have similar blindness. One of the blessings of the *Streetwise* paper in Chicago is that it provides not only income for its vendors, but also visibility; by giving them a role, it gives us a way to relate to them—to see them, to nod, to say a word or two, whether or not we buy the paper.

Bus 174 opens with a news bulletin about the attempted robbery on the bus and then, as the bus is surrounded by police and the robber takes hostages, provides details about do Nascimento's early life. He saw his mother shot dead in a robbery. His father was not in the picture. He lived on the streets, and survived an infamous police massacre of homeless who used a downtown square as a sleeping area. He had been in jail. We listen to a social worker who talks of the boy's dreams—of how he wanted to find a job and have a home.

Meanwhile, negotiations continue in the hostage situation. Several of the police who were involved (one hooded and his voice disguised) talk about their decisions and mistakes. After do Nascimento threatened to kill hostages—and after police for a time thought he had killed one—there were many opportunities for a sniper to take him out with one shot. He walked around in plain view, sometimes not close to his hostages, but the police didn't act until the crisis reached a climax in the evening.

By that point in the film we know a lot about the human refuse of Rio's streets. And we have seen one of the most horrifying sequences I've witnessed in a movie. The camera goes inside a crowded jail, where the prisoners press their faces against the bars and shout out their urgent protests against the inhuman conditions they endure. Cells are so crowded that the prisoners must live in shifts, half lying down while the other half stand. The temperature is over 100 degrees. The food is rotten, the water is dirty, disease runs quickly through the cells, and some prisoners are left for months or years without charges being filed; they have been forgotten.

The director, José Padilha, films this scene with a digital camera, using the negative mode that switches black with white. The faces behind the bars cry out to us like souls in hell; nothing in the work of Bosch or the most abysmal horror films prepares us for these images. A nation that could permit these conditions dare not call itself civilized. Since prisoners are the lowest inhabitants of any society, how the society treats them establishes the bottom line of how it regards human beings. That prisons like this exist in Brazil makes it less surprising that the streets are filled with the lost and forgotten.

The conclusion of *Bus 174* is both surprising and inevitable. The bus hijacking captured the public's attention in a way that dramatized the plight of the homeless, and the film, by documenting the conditions of Sandro do Nascimento and countless others, shows that the journey began long before the passengers boarded the bus.

If you have seen the masterful 2002 Brazilian film *City of God* or the 1981 film *Pixote*, both about the culture of Rio's street people, then *Bus 174* plays like a sad and angry real-life sequel. Fernando Ramos Da Silva, the young orphan who played Pixote, died on the streets some years after the film was made, and do Nascimento in a sense stands for him—and for countless others.

The Butterfly Effect ★ ★ ½
R, 113 m., 2004

Ashton Kutcher (Evan Treborn), Amy Smart (Kayleigh Miller), William Lee Scott (Tommy Miller), Elden Henson (Lenny), Eric Stoltz (George Miller), Kevin Schmidt (Lenny at Thirteen), Melora Walters (Andrea Treborn), John Patrick Amedori (Evan at Thirteen), Cameron Bright (Tommy at Eight). Directed by Eric Bress and J. Mackye Gruber and produced by Chris Bender, A. J. Dix, Anthony Rhulen, Lisa

Richardson, and J. C. Spink. Screenplay by Bress and Gruber.

Chaos theory teaches us that small events can have enormous consequences. An opening title informs us that a butterfly flapping its wings in Asia could result in a hurricane halfway around the world. Yes, although given the number of butterflies and the determination with which they flap their little wings, isn't it extraordinary how rarely that happens? *The Butterfly Effect* applies this theory to the lives of four children whose early lives are marred by tragedy. When one of them finds he can go back in time and make changes, he tries to improve the present by altering the past.

The characters as young adults are played by Ashton Kutcher, as Evan, a college psych major; Amy Smart and William Lee Scott as Kayleigh and Tommy, a brother and sister with a pedophile father; and Elden Henson as Lenny, their friend. The story opens in childhood, with little Evan seriously weird. His drawings in kindergarten are sick and twisted (and also, although nobody ever mentions it, improbably good for a child). He has blackouts, grabs kitchen knives, frightens his mother (Melora Walters), becomes a suitable case for treatment.

A shrink suggests that he keep a daily journal. This he does, although apparently neither the shrink nor the mother ever read it, or their attention might have been snagged by entries about how Mr. Miller (Eric Stoltz), father of Kayleigh and Tommy, forced them all to act in kiddie porn movies. Evan hangs onto the journals, and one day while reading an old one at school he's jerked back into the past and experiences a previously buried memory.

One thing he'd always done, after moving from the old neighborhood, was to promise Kayleigh "I'll come back for you." (This promise is made with handwriting as precocious as his drawing skills.) The flashbacks give him a chance to do that, and eventually he figures out that by reading a journal entry, he can return to that page in his life and relive it. The only problem is, he then returns to a present that is different than the one he departed from—

because his actions have changed everything that happened since.

This is a premise not unknown to science

fiction, where one famous story by Ray Bradbury has a time traveler stepping on a butterfly millions of years ago and wiping out humanity. The remarkable thing about the changes in *The Butterfly Effect* is that they're so precisely aimed: They apparently affect only the characters in the movie. From one reality to the next, Kayleigh goes from sorority girl to hooker, Evan zaps from intellectual to frat boy to prisoner, and poor Lenny spends some time as Kayleigh's boyfriend and more time as a hopeless mental patient.

Do their lives have no effect on the wider world? Apparently not. External reality remains the same, apart from minute adjustments to college and prison enrollment statistics. But it's unfair to bring such logic to bear on the story, which doesn't want to *really* study the butterfly effect, but simply to exploit a device to jerk the characters through a series of startling life changes. Strange, that Evan can remember everything that happened in the alternate lifetimes, even though by the theory of the movie, once he changes something, they didn't happen.

Ashton Kutcher has become a target lately; the gossip press can't forgive him for dating Demi Moore, although that is a thing many sensible young men dream of doing. He was allegedly fired from a recent film after the director told him he needed acting lessons. Can he act? He can certainly do everything that's required in *The Butterfly Effect*. He plays a convincing kid in his early twenties, treating each new reality with a straightforward realism when most actors would be tempted to hyperventilate under the circumstances.

The plot provides a showcase for acting talent, since the actors have to play characters who go through wild swings (even Evan's mom has a wild ride between good health and death's door). And there's a certain grim humor in the way the movie illustrates the truth that you can make plans, but you can't make results. Some of the futures Evan returns to are so seriously wrong from his point of view that he's lucky he doesn't just disappear from the picture, having been killed at fifteen, say, because of his meddling.

I enjoyed *The Butterfly Effect*, up to a point. That point was reached too long before the end of the movie. There's so much flashing forward and backward, so many spins of fate, so many chapters in the journals, that after a while I felt that I, as well as time, was being jerked around. Eric Bress and J. Mackye Gruber, the cowriters and directors, also collabo- rated on *Final Destination 2* (2003), another film in which fate works in mysterious ways, its ironies to reveal. I gave that one half a star, so *The Butterfly Effect* is five times better. And outside, the wind is rising ...

C

Cabin Fever ★ ½
R, 94 m., 2003

Rider Strong (Paul), Jordan Ladd (Karen), Joey Kern (Jeff), Cerina Vincent (Marcy), James DeBello (Bert), Arie Verveen (The Hermit), Giuseppe Andrews (Deputy Winston). Directed by Eli Roth and produced by Roth, Lauren Moews, Sam Froelich, and Evan Astrowsky. Screenplay by Randy Pearlstein and Roth.

Unsure of whether it wants to be a horror film, a comedy, an homage, a satire, or a parable, *Cabin Fever* tries to cover every base; it jumps around like kids on those arcade games where the target lights up and you have to stomp on it. It assembles the standard package of horror heroes and heroines (sexy girl, nice girl, stalwart guy, uncertain guy, drunk guy) and takes them off for a postexam holiday in the woods where things get off to a bad start when a man covered with blood comes staggering out of the trees.

What they eventually figure out is that the man has some kind of disease—for which we could, I suppose, read AIDS or SARS—and it may be catching. When the nice girl (Jordan Ladd) comes down with the symptoms, they lock her in a shed, but before long they're all threatened, and there is a scene where the sexy girl (Cerina Vincent) is shaving her legs in the bathtub and finds, eek, that she's shaving a scab.

The film could develop its plague story in a serious way, like a George Romero picture or *28 Days Later,* but it keeps breaking the mood with weird humor involving the locals. Everyone at the corner general store seems seriously demented, and the bearded old coot behind the counter seems like a racist (when at the end we discover that he isn't, the payoff is more offensive than his original offense). There's a deputy sheriff named Winston (Giuseppe Andrews) who is a seriously counterproductive character; the movie grinds to an incredulous halt every time he's onscreen.

The drama mostly involves the characters locking the door against dogs, the locals, and each other; running into the woods in search of escape or help; trying to start the truck (which, like all vehicles in horror films, runs only when the plot requires it to), and having sex, lots of sex. The nature of the disease is inexplicable; it seems to involve enormous quantities of blood appearing on the surface of the skin without visible wounds, and then spreading in wholesale amounts to every nearby surface.

If some of this material had been harnessed and channeled into a disciplined screenplay with a goal in mind, the movie might have worked. But the director and coauthor, Eli Roth, is too clever for his own good, and impatiently switches between genres, tones, and intentions. There are truly horrible scenes (guy finds corpse in reservoir, falls onto it), over-the-top horrible scenes (dogs have eaten skin off good girl's face, but she is still alive), and just plain inexplicable scenes (Dennis, the little boy at the general store, bites people). By the end, we've lost all interest. The movie adds up to a few good ideas and a lot of bad ones, wandering around in search of an organizing principle.

Calendar Girls ★ ★ ★
PG-13, 108 m., 2003

Helen Mirren (Chris Harper), Julie Walters (Annie Clark), John Alderton (John Clark), Linda Bassett (Cora), Annette Crosbie (Jessie), Philip Glenister (Lawrence), Ciaran Hinds (Rod Harper), Celia Imrie (Celia), Geraldine James (Marie), Penelope Wilton (Ruth). Directed by Nigel Cole and produced by Nick Barton and Suzanne Mackie. Screenplay by Tim Firth and Juliette Towhidi.

You may have read about it at the time. A British woman's club, trying to raise money for charity, hit on the idea of having its members pose nude for a pinup calendar. The women were eminently respectable and of a certain age, the photographs were modest if not chaste, and the calendar was an enormous hit, raising something like $1 million for the local hospital.

Calendar Girls retells the story in a very slightly risqué comedy. Every press mention makes the inevitable reference to *The Full Monty,* but this movie is not as bawdy and only about 10 percent as monty. It's the kind of sweet, good-humored comedy that used to star Margaret Rutherford, although Helen Mirren and Julie Walters, its daring top-liners, would have curled Dame Margaret's eyebrows.

People sometimes ask me whether I see the movies in "real theaters" or screening rooms— "or do the studios send them to your home?" (Fat chance of that with the piracy paranoia.) I usually say it doesn't much matter; once the movie starts, if it works, it upstages the venue. But I cannot resist telling you that I saw *Calendar Girls* at the Locarno (Switzerland) film Festival, under the stars in the Piazza Grande, with 12,000 other people, including the presidents of Switzerland and Germany.

A setting like that might have overwhelmed *The Lord of the Rings,* and here was a modest little British comedy. Interesting, how the story was so straightforward and universal that it played perfectly well, got laughs in all the right places, and left maybe 10,000 of us pleased, if not overwhelmed.

The movie begins at a Yorkshire village chapter of the Women's Institute, a community organization widespread in the UK and Canada, where we watch the members nodding through lectures on, if I recall correctly, the private life of the broccoli. Mirren plays Chris Harper, a high-spirited woman who finds a porno magazine in her son's bedroom, sees a girlie calendar on the wall at the local garage, puts two and two together, and gets her big idea.

Some of the women are appalled and others are titillated, but all of them have the first thought any reasonable person over forty would have: How will I look nude? Luckily the W.I.'s long tradition of flower arranging, trellis construction, and greenhouse repair suggests an endless number of foreground items that can obscure the naughty bits, in the tradition of Austin Powers.

Walters plays Chris's best pal Annie, whose husband, John (John Alderton), dies of leukemia early in the film, supplying a cause for the fund-raising. There is, of course, opposition, supplied by reactionary elements in the local and national W.I., and Mirren makes a speech to the national convention that Winston Churchill would have been proud of. (In real life, apparently, everyone thought the calendar was a great idea, but a movie, as Robert McKee teaches us, needs obstacles to overcome.)

After the calendar becomes a best-seller, the calendar girls promote a North American version with a trip to Los Angeles and an appearance on the Jay Leno show; of course fame goes to their heads a little, for a while, but that plot point also suggests the strong hand of McKee. Actually, this is a very simple story: A cute idea caught the fancy of a lot of people, and raised a bundle for charity.

That the movie works, and it does, is mostly because of the charm of Mirren and Walters, who show their characters having so much fun that it becomes infectious. *Calendar Girls* was directed by Nigel Cole, who also made *Saving Grace* (2000), the comedy starring Brenda Blethyn as a new widow who supports herself by growing marijuana in her cottage garden. That one also went for laughs with some naked middle-aged ladies dashing around, but this one is gentler to the ladies, and thank God for the flower arrangements.

Capturing the Friedmans ★ ★ ★ ½
NO MPAA RATING, 107 m., 2003

Featuring Arnold Friedman, David Friedman, Elaine Friedman, and Jesse Friedman. A documentary directed by Andrew Jarecki and produced by Jarecki and Marc Smerling.

After the Sundance screenings of *Capturing the Friedmans,* its director, Andrew Jarecki, was asked point-blank if he thought Arnold Friedman was guilty of child molestation. He said he didn't know. Neither does the viewer of this film. It seems clear that Friedman is guilty in some ways and innocent in others, but the truth may never be known—may not, indeed, be known to Friedman himself, who lives within such a bizarre personality that truth seems to change for him from moment to moment.

The film, which won the Grand Jury Prize at Sundance 2003, is disturbing and haunting, a documentary about a middle-class family in Great Neck, Long Island, that was torn apart on Thanksgiving 1987 when police raided their home and found child pornography belonging to the father. Arnold was a popular high school science teacher who gave computer classes in his basement den, which is where the porn was found—and also where, police alleged, he and his eighteen-year-old son, Jesse, molested dozens of young boys.

Of the porn possession there is no doubt, and in the film Arnold admits to having molested the son of a family friend. But about the multiple molestation charges there is some doubt, and it seems unlikely that Jesse was involved in any crimes.

As Jarecki's film shows the Friedmans and the law authorities who investigated their case, a strange parallel develops: We can't believe either side. Arnold seems incapable of leveling with his family, his lawyers, or the law. And the law seems mesmerized by the specter of child abuse to such an extent that witnesses and victims are coached, led, and cajoled into their testimony; some victims tell us nothing happened, others provide confused and contradictory testimony, and the parents seem sometimes almost too eager to believe their children were abused. By the end of the film there is little we can hang onto, except for our conviction that the Friedmans are a deeply wounded family, that Arnold seems capable of the crimes he is charged with, and that the police seem capable of framing him.

Our confusion about the facts is increased, not relieved, by another extraordinary fact: All during the history of the Friedmans, and even during the period of legal investigations, charges, and court trials, the family was videotaped by another son, David. A third son, Seth, is visible in some of this footage, but does not otherwise participate in the film. At the very time when Arnold is charged with possession of child porn, when the abuse charges make national headlines, when his legal strategy is being mapped and his and Jesse's trials are under way, David is there, filming with the privileged position of a family insider. We even witness the last family council on the night before Arnold goes to prison.

This access should answer most of our questions, but does not. It particularly clouds the issue of Jesse's defense. It would appear—but we cannot be sure—that he was innocent but pled guilty under pressure from the police and his own lawyer, who threaten him with dire consequences and urge him to make a deal. Given the hysteria of the community at the time, it seems possible he was an innocent bystander caught up in the moment.

The dynamics within the family are there to see. The mother, Elaine, who later divorced and remarried, seems in shock at times within a family where perception and reality have only a nodding acquaintance. She withdraws, is passive-aggressive; it's hard to know what she's thinking.

Arnold is so vague about his sexual conduct that sometimes we can't figure out exactly what he's saying. He neither confirms nor denies. Jesse is too young and shell-shocked to be reliable. The witnesses contradict themselves. The lawyers seem incompetent. The police seem more interested in a conviction than in finding the truth. By the end of *Capturing the Friedmans,* we have more information, from both inside and outside the family, than we dreamed would be possible. We have many people telling us exactly what happened. And we have no idea of the truth. None.

The film is an instructive lesson about the elusiveness of facts, especially in a legal context. Sometimes guilt and innocence are discovered in court, but sometimes, we gather, only truths about the law are demonstrated. I am reminded of the documentaries *Paradise Lost* and *Paradise Lost 2: Revelations,* which involve the trials of three teenage boys charged with the murders of three children. Because the boys were outsiders, dressed in black, listened to heavy metal, they were perfect suspects—and were convicted amid hysterical allegations of "satanic rituals," even while the obvious prime suspect appears in both films doing his best to give himself away. Those boys are still behind bars. Their case was much easier to read than the Friedman proceedings, but viewers of the films are forced to the conclusion that the law and the courts failed them.

Carandiru ★ ★ ★
R, 148 m., 2004

Luiz Carlos Vasconcelos (Doctor), Milton Goncalves (Chico), Ivan de Almeida (Ebony), Ailton Graca (Majestade), Maria Luisa Mendonca (Dalva), Aide Leiner (Rosirene), Rodrigo Santoro (Lady Di), Gero Camilo (No Way). Directed by Hector Babenco and produced by Babenco and Oscar Kramer. Screenplay by Babenco, Fernando Bonassi, and Victor Navas, based on the book *Estacao Carandiru* by Dr. Drauzio Varella.

In the Brazilian documentary *Bus 174*, there is a scene that could have been shot in hell. Using the night-vision capability of a digital camera, the film ventures into an unlit Brazilian prison to show desperate souls reaching through the bars. Jammed so closely they have to sit down in shifts, with temperatures above 100 degrees Fahrenheit, with rotten food and dirty water, many jailed without any charges being filed, they cry out for rescue.

Hector Babenco's *Carandiru* is a drama that adds a human dimension to that Dantean vision. Shot on location inside a notorious prison in São Paolo, it shows 8,000 men jammed into space meant for 4,000, and enforcing their own laws in a place their society has abandoned. The film, based on life, climaxes with a 1992 police attack on the prison during which 111 inmates were killed.

How this film came to be made is also a story. Babenco is the gifted director of *Pixote, Kiss of the Spider Woman,* and *At Play in the Fields of the Lord.* An illness put him out of action for several years, and he credits his doctor, Drauzio Varella, with saving his life. As it happens, Varella was for years the physician on duty inside the prison, and his memoir *Carandiru Station* inspired Babenco to make this film, with Varella as his guide.

What we see at first looks like lawless anarchy. But as characters develop and social rules become clear, we see that the prisoners have imposed their own order in the absence of outside authority. The prison is run more or less by the prisoners, with the warden and guards looking on helplessly; stronger or more powerful prisoners decorate their cells like private rooms, while the weak are crammed in head to toe. Respected prisoners act as judges when crimes are committed. A code permits homosexuality but forbids rape. And the prison has such a liberal policy involving conjugal visits that a prisoner with two wives has to deal with both of them on the same day. Some prisoners continue to function as the heads of their families, advising their children, counseling their wives, approving marriages, managing the finances.

Dr. Varella, played in the film by Luiz Carlos Vasconcelos, originally went to Carandiru when AIDS was still a new disease; he lectures on the use of condoms, advises against sharing needles, but is in a society where one of his self-taught assistants sews up wounds without anesthetic or sanitation. The prisoners come to trust the doctor and confide in him, and as some of them tell their stories, the movie flashes back to show what they did to earn their sentences.

In a prison filled with vivid, Dickensian characters, several stand out. There is, for example, the unlikely couple of Lady Di (Rodrigo Santoro), tall and muscular, and No Way (Gero Camilo), a stunted little man. They are the great loves of each other's lives. Their marriage scene is an occasion for celebration in the prison, and later, when the police murder squads arrive, it is No Way, the husband, who fearlessly uses his little body to protect the great hulk of his frightened bride. Their story and several others are memorably told, although the film is a little too episodic and meandering.

Although there are weapons everywhere in the prison, the doctor walks unarmed and without fear, because he is known and valued. The warden is not so trusted, and with good reason. After a prison soccer match ends in a fight that escalates into a protest, he stands in the courtyard, begs for a truce, and asks the inmates to throw down their weapons. In an astonishing scene, hundreds or even thousands of knives rain down from the cell windows. And then, when the prisoners are unarmed, the police attack.

The movie observes laconically that the police were "defending themselves," even though 111 prisoners and no police were killed. The prison was finally closed in 2002, and the film's last shot shows it being leveled by dynamite. Strange, how by then we have grown to respect some of the inmates and at least understand others. *Bus 174* is a reminder that although Carandiru has disappeared, prison conditions in Brazil continue to be inhuman.

Casa de los Babys ★ ★ ★
R, 95 m., 2003

Daryl Hannah (Skipper), Marcia Gay Harden (Nan), Mary Steenburgen (Gayle), Rita Moreno (Señora Muñoz), Lili Taylor (Leslie), Maggie Gyllenhaal (Jennifer), Susan Lynch (Eileen), Vanessa Martinez (Asunción). Directed by John Sayles and produced by Hunt Lowry, Alejandro

Springall, and Lemore Syvan. Screenplay by Sayles.

Casa de los Babys gets its title from a motel in an unnamed South American country where American women wait while the local adoption process slowly matches them with babies. "They're making us pay for our babies with the balance of trade," complains the always-critical Nan (Marcia Gay Harden), as the days and weeks go by. The women shop, sunbathe, go out to lunch, and gossip about each other, and we eavesdrop on conversations that are sometimes cynical, sometimes heartbreaking.

The movie was written and directed by John Sayles, the conscience of American independent filmmaking, who doesn't package it with a neat message because there is nothing easy to be said about the adoption industry. We meet local mothers who have given up their babies for adoption, and local radicals who oppose adoption for ideological reasons, but we also see young children living on the streets.

In one of the movie's most effective passages, two women, one Irish, one Latino, tell the stories of their own longings in monologues. Neither one can understand a word of the other's language, but somehow the emotion comes through. Eileen (Susan Lynch, from Sayles's *The Secret of Roan Inish*) and Asunción (Vanessa Martinez, from his *Lone Star*) speak quietly, inwardly, and we feel the deep pools of emotion they draw from.

Another extraordinary scene is by Daryl Hannah, as Skipper, an athletic woman who is forever running on the beach while the others look on from behind sunglasses and margaritas. One day, as she is giving another woman a massage, she begins to talk about her three miscarriages, and as she names her babies (Cody, Joshua, and Gabriel) we feel how deeply and personally she misses each one.

Nan, the Marcia Gay Harden character, is less sentimental. She won't pay local prices ("bargaining is an accepted part of the culture"), uses pressure to move herself to the head of the line, and steals handfuls of toiletries from the maids' carts. "We don't like her," agree Gayle and Leslie (Mary Steenburgen and Lili Taylor). They even wonder, with her character flaws, if she should be adopting.

Each woman has a story. Gayle isn't a mother because of years of alcoholism. Leslie can't stay with the same man long enough to make parenthood an option. Jennifer (Maggie Gyllenhaal) can't conceive. Señora Muñoz (Rita Moreno), who owns the Casa, has seen hundreds of these women come and go. Her brother is the lawyer who handles the adoptions. Her son thinks of the women as capitalist exploiters, but for that matter, his mother is exploiting them.

John Sayles handles this material with gentle delicacy, as if aware that the issues are too fraught to be approached with simple messages. He shows both sides; the maid Asunción gave up her baby and now imagines her happy life in "el norte," but we feel how much she misses her. The squeegee kids on the corner have been abandoned by their parents and might happily go home with one of these rich Americanos. Sayles sees like a documentarian, showing us the women, listening to their stories, inviting us to share their hopes and fears, and speculate about their motives. There are no answers here, just the experiences of waiting for a few weeks in the Casa de los Babys.

Catch Me If You Can ★ ★ ★
PG-13, 140 m., 2002

Leonardo DiCaprio (Frank Abagnale Jr.), Tom Hanks (Carl Hanratty), Christopher Walken (Frank Abagnale Sr.), Martin Sheen (Roger Strong), Nathalie Baye (Paula Abagnale), Amy Adams (Brenda Strong), Jennifer Garner (Cheryl Ann). Directed by Steven Spielberg and produced by Walter F. Parkes and Spielberg. Screenplay by Jeff Nathanson, based on the book by Frank Abagnale Jr. and Stan Redding.

The trailer for *Catch Me If You Can* is so obvious it could have written itself. It informs us that Frank Abagnale Jr. practiced medicine without attending medical school, practiced law without a law degree, and passed as a pilot without attending flight school—all for the excellent reason that he did all of these things before he was nineteen, and had not even graduated from high school.

That this is a true story probably goes without saying, since it is too preposterous to have been invented by a screenwriter. Abagnale also passed millions of dollars in bogus checks, dazzled women with his wealth and accomplishments, and was, a lot of the time, basically a sad and lonely teenager. At the time the only honest relationships in his life were with his father and with the FBI agent who was chasing him.

In Steven Spielberg's new film, Abagnale is played by Leonardo DiCaprio as a young man who succeeds at his incredible impersonations by the simple device of never seeming to try very hard. While an airline employee might be suspicious of a very young-looking man who insists he is a pilot, what could be more disarming than a man offered a trip in the jump seat who confesses, "It's been a while. Which one is the jump seat?"

DiCaprio, who in recent films like *The Beach* and *Gangs of New York* has played dark and troubled characters, is breezy and charming here, playing a boy who discovers what he is good at, and does it. There is a kind of genius flowing in the scene where he turns up for classes at a new school, walks into the classroom to discover that a substitute teacher is expected and, without missing a beat, writes his name on the blackboard and tells the students to shut up and sit down and tell him what chapter they're on.

It is probably true that most people will take you at face value until they have reason to do otherwise. I had a friend who had risen to a high level in her organization and was terrified her secret would be discovered: She never attended college. My guess, and it proved accurate, was that nobody would ever think to ask her. It is probably an even better guess that no patient in a hospital would ask to see a doctor's medical school diploma.

The movie makes some attempt to explain Abagnale's behavior through adolescent trauma. He is raised by loving parents; his father, Frank Sr. (Christopher Walken), brought his French mother, Paula (Nathalie Baye), back from Europe after military service, and Frank Jr.'s childhood is a happy one until Paula cheats on her husband and walks out. Is that why her son was driven to impersonation and fraud? Maybe. Or maybe he would have anyway. Once he discovers how much he can get away with, there is a certain heady exhilaration in how easily he finds status, respect, and babes.

The movie costars Tom Hanks as Carl Hanratty, an FBI agent whose mission in life evolves into capturing Abagnale. As the only person who really has a comprehensive overview of the scope and versatility of Abagnale's activities, Hanratty develops—well, not an admiration, but a respect for a natural criminal talent. There is a scene where he actually has Abagnale at gunpoint in a motel room, and the kid, a cool customer and quick thinker, tries impersonating a Secret Service agent who is also on the suspect's tail.

Much of the pleasure of the movie comes from its enjoyment of Abagnale's strategies. He doesn't seem to plan his cons very well, but to take advantage of opportunities that fall his way. At one point, in New Orleans, he finds himself engaged to the daughter (Amy Adams) of the local district attorney (Martin Sheen). At a dinner party with his prospective in-laws, he seems to contradict himself by claiming to be both a doctor and a lawyer, when he doesn't look old enough to be either. When the D.A. presses him for an explanation, there is a kind of genius in his guileless reply: "I passed the bar in California and practiced for a year, before saying, 'Why not try out pediatrics?'"

Uh-huh. And then he makes the mistake of saying he graduated from law school at Berkeley. Turns out the Sheen character did, too, and quizzes him about a legendary professor before adding, "Does he still go everywhere with that little dog?" Here is where Abagnale's quickness saves him. Considering the thirty-year age difference between himself and the girl's father, he simply observes, "The dog died." Yes, although the professor may well have died, too, and when the D.A. calls his bluff, he responds by being honest (although that is sort of a lie, too).

This is not a major Spielberg film, although it is an effortlessly watchable one. Spielberg and his writer, Jeff Nathanson, working from the memoir by the real Frank Abagnale Jr. and Stan Redding, don't force matters or plumb for deep significance. The story is a good story, directly told, and such meaning as it has comes from the irony that the only person who completely appreciates Abagnale's accomplishments is the man trying to arrest him. At one point, when the young man calls the FBI agent, Hanratty cuts straight to the point by observing, "You didn't have anyone else to call."

Catch That Kid ★ ★ ★

PG, 92 m., 2004

Kristen Stewart (Maddy Phillips), Corbin Bleu (Austin), Max Thieriot (Gus), Jennifer Beals (Molly), Sam Robards (Tom), Michael Des Barres (Brisbane). Directed by Bart Freundlich and produced by Andrew Lazar and Uwe Schott. Screenplay by Nicolai Arcel, Hans Fabian Wullenweber, Erlend Loe, Michael Brandt, and Derek Haas.

Now here's something you don't see every day: a heist movie involving twelve-year-old kids. *Catch That Kid* respects all of the requirements of the genre, and the heist itself is worthy of *Ocean's Eleven* (either one; take your pick). Kristen Stewart's plucky heroine will win the hearts of the same young audiences who liked *Bend It Like Beckham* and *Whale Rider*.

This is not, to be sure, a movie as good as those two wonderful titles. But it's plenty good, and it has the same buried theme: Anything a guy can do, a girl can do too. It stars Stewart as Maddy Phillips, an athletic young girl whose father, Tom (Sam Robards), once climbed Mount Everest. He had a nasty fall on the way down, which is why he discourages Maddy from climbing, while her mother, Molly (Jennifer Beals), forbids it. But as the movie opens, she's scaling the local water tower.

Maddy has two best friends. Austin (Corbin Bleu) is a computer geek. Gus (Max Thieriot) is a mechanic at the go-kart track operated by her father. They both have crushes on her, although at one point, when she's hanging in danger high in the air during the heist, Gus complains that he never even got a chance to kiss her once.

A crisis comes into her life with all the melodrama of a silent movie. One night while her dad and mom are dancing in the living room, he falls to the floor and says, "I can't feel my legs!" It's paralysis—whether from the neck or waist down, we don't learn, but in any event the condition is incurable, except for an experimental procedure offered in Europe; it costs $250,000 the family doesn't have.

Common sense at this point steps in and suggests that if such an operation really existed, Christopher Reeve would already be on site with a charity to help the Toms of the world, but no: Molly the mother is turned down for a loan at the bank where she has installed the security system. The bank president, named Brisbane (Michael Des Barres), is a teeth-gnashing, scenery-chewing villain whose origins go back even before silent films—back to Horatio Alger, if anybody remembers who that was. Been a while since we've had a banker this evil in the movies.

So the kids take things into their own hands. With Maddy's climbing skills, Austin to hack into the bank's security system, and Gus to devise mechanical devices and the getaway, they'll break into the bank vault and steal the $250,000. This is not so easy, since the vault is suspended in midair, surrounded by motion detectors, protected by savage rottweilers, etc.

The movie is a remake of a Danish film, unseen by me, named *Klatretøsen*, which was hailed at the Berlin Film Festival. This version, directed by Bart Freundlich and sporting five writing credits, is well made, straightforward, and entertaining. It doesn't bog down in a lot of cute kid stuff, but gets on with telling the story, and has some unexpected touches. For example, the getaway scene with the kids in go-karts. Yes, and the police chase them, shouting on loudspeakers: "You kids in the go-karts! Pull over! You're leaving the scene of a crime." Sure, because any cop seeing kids on a city street in go-karts is instinctively going to link them to a bank robbery.

Kristen Stewart is at the center of the movie, stalwart and sure. You may remember her as Jodie Foster's daughter in a more harrowing thriller, *Panic Room* (2002). Corbin Bleu and Max Thieriot, as her two pals, are just plain likable, and the attraction between Bleu and Stewart may be the screen's first example of interracial puppy love. For that matter, Jennifer Beals is cast as a possibly mixed-race mother, and I would not bother to make this point except to observe that all of a sudden racial categories are evaporating in mainstream movies, and for the first time in history actors are being cast because they're right for a role, not because they passed an identity check.

Catch That Kid doesn't have the flash of *Spy Kids*, but it's solid entertainment—better than *Agent Cody Banks*. Faithful readers know that my definition of a good family film is one the parents can enjoy, and you know what? In the middle of the heist scene, we're just about as involved as if the movie starred George Clooney and Julia Roberts. A heist is a heist, and a good one works no matter what.

The Cat's Meow ★ ★ ★
PG-13, 110 m., 2002

Kirsten Dunst (Marion Davies), Cary Elwes (Thomas Ince), Edward Herrmann (William Randolph Hearst), Eddie Izzard (Charlie Chaplin), Joanna Lumley (Elinor Glyn), Jennifer Tilly (Louella Parsons). Directed by Peter Bogdanovich and produced by Kim Bieber and Carol Lewis. Screenplay by Steven Peros.

William Randolph Hearst did, or did not, get away with murder on board his private yacht *Oneida* on November 15, 1924. If he did, there is no question he was powerful enough to cover it up. Hearst was the carnivorous media tycoon of the age, proprietor of newspapers, magazines, radio stations, wire services, movie production companies, a private castle, and his mistress Marion Davies, an actress of great but perhaps not exclusive charms. He was above the law not so much because of clout or bribery but because of awe; the law enforcement officials of the day were so keenly aware of their inferior social status that they lacked the nerve to approach him. The silent movies of the time are filled with scenes in which cops arrest a millionaire, discover who he is, respectfully tip their hats to him, and apologize.

On that day in 1924, the Hollywood producer Thomas Ince possibly died, or was murdered, on board the *Oneida*. Or perhaps not. According to one story, he was shot dead by Hearst through an unfortunate misunderstanding; Hearst mistook him for Charlie Chaplin, and thought Chaplin was having an affair with Davies. Other theories say Hearst accidentally stuck Ince with a hat pin, precipitating a heart attack. Or that Ince drank some bad rotgut. There is even the possibility that Ince died at home. There was no autopsy, so the official cause of death was never determined. No guests on the yacht were ever questioned; indeed, no one can agree about who was on the yacht during its cruise.

In Hollywood at the time, whispers about Ince's death and Hearst's involvement were easily heard, and the story told in Peter Bog-

danovich's *The Cat's Meow* is, the film tells us, "the whisper heard most often." Bogdanovich is not much interested in the scandal as a scandal. He uses it more as a prism through which to view Hollywood in the 1920s, when the new medium had generated such wealth and power that its giants, like Chaplin, were gods in a way no later stars could ever be. Hearst (Edward Herrmann) liked to act the beneficent host, and on the *Oneida* for that cruise were the studio head Ince (Cary Elwes), the stars Davies (Kirsten Dunst) and Chaplin (Eddie Izzard), the British wit Elinor Glyn (Joanna Lumley), and an ambitious young gossip columnist named Louella Parsons (Jennifer Tilly). There were also various stuffed shirts and their wives, and a tame society doctor.

In this company Hearst is an insecure loner, an innocent barely the equal of the life of sin he has chosen for himself. He has the *Oneida* bugged with hidden microphones, and scarcely has time to join his guests because he needs to hurry away and eavesdrop on what they say about him in his absence. Davies knows about the microphones and knows all about Willie; she was a loyal mistress who loved her man and stood by him to the end. Whether she did have an affair with Chaplin is often speculated. According to this scenario, she may have, and Willie finds one of her brooches in Chaplin's stateroom (after tearing it apart in a scene mirroring Kane's famous destruction of Susan's bedroom in the Welles picture).

Bogdanovich has an exact way of conveying the forced and metronomic gaiety on the yacht, where guests are theoretically limited to one drink before dinner, Marion Davies has to order the band to play the Charleston to cover awkward silences, every guest has a personal agenda, and at night, as guests creep from one stateroom to another and deck planks creak, they seem to be living in an English country house mystery—*Gosford Yacht*.

Apart from its theory about the mistaken death of Ince and its cover-up, the movie's most intriguing theory is that Louella Parsons witnessed it, which might explain her lifetime contract with the Hearst papers. In the exquisite wording of a veiled blackmail threat, she tells the tycoon: "We're at the point in our careers where we both need real security."

Since she was making peanuts and he was one of the richest men in the world, one can only admire the nuance of "our careers."

The film is darkly atmospheric, with Edward Herrmann quietly suggesting the sadness and obsession beneath Hearst's forced avuncular chortles. Dunst is as good, in her way, as Dorothy Comingore in *Citizen Kane* in showing a woman who is more loyal and affectionate than her lover deserves. Lumley's zingers as Glyn cut right through the hypocritical grease. Tilly, we suspect, has the right angle on Parsons's chutzpah.

There is a detail easy to miss toward the end of the film that suggests as well as anything what power Hearst had. After the society doctor ascertains that Ince, still alive, has a bullet in his brain, Hearst orders the yacht to moor at San Diego, and then dispatches the dying producer by private ambulance—not to a local hospital, but to his home in Los Angeles! Hearst is on the phone to the future widow, suggesting a cover story, long before the pathetic victim arrives home.

Changing Lanes ★ ★ ★ ★
R, 100 m., 2002

Ben Affleck (Gavin Banek), Samuel L. Jackson (Doyle Gipson), Toni Collette (Michelle), Sydney Pollack (Delano), William Hurt (Doyle's Sponsor), Amanda Peet (Cynthia), Kim Staunton (Valerie Gipson), Dylan Baker (Fixer). Directed by Roger Michell and produced by Scott Rudin. Screenplay by Chap Taylor and Michael Tolkin.

"One wrong turn deserves another," say the ads for *Changing Lanes*. Yes, both of the movie's dueling hotheads are in the wrong—but they are also both in the right. The story involves two flawed men, both prey to anger, who get involved in a fender bender that brings out all of their worst qualities. And their best. This is not a dumb formula film about revenge. It doesn't use rubber-stamp lines like, "It's payback time." It is about adults who have minds as well as emotions, and can express themselves with uncommon clarity. And it's not just about the quarrel between these two men, but about the ways they have been living their lives.

The story begins with two men who need to be in court on time. Gavin Banek (Ben Affleck) needs to file a signed form proving that an elderly millionaire turned over control of his foundation to Banek's law firm. Doyle Gipson (Samuel L. Jackson) needs to show that he has loan approval to buy a house for his family; he hopes that will persuade his fed-up wife to stay in New York and not move with the kids to Oregon. Banek and Gipson get into a fender bender. It's not really anybody's fault.

Of course they are polite when it happens: "You hurt?" Nobody is. Banek, who is rich and has been taught that money is a solution to human needs, doesn't want to take time to exchange insurance cards and file a report. He hands Gipson a signed blank check. Gipson, who wants to handle this the right way, doesn't want a check. Banek gets in his car and drives away, shouting, "Better luck next time!" over his shoulder, and leaving Gipson stranded in the middle of the expressway with a flat tire.

Gipson gets to court twenty minutes late. The case has already been settled. In his absence, he has lost. The judge isn't interested in his story. Banek gets to court in time, but discovers that he is missing the crucial file folder with the old man's signature. Who has it? Gipson.

At this point, in a film less intelligent and ambitious, the vile Banek would pull strings to make life miserable for the blameless Gipson. But *Changing Lanes* doesn't settle for the formula. Gipson responds to Banek's rudeness by faxing a page from the crucial file to Banek with "Better luck next time!" scrawled on it. Banek turns to his sometime mistress (Toni Collette), who knows a guy who "fixes" things. The guy (Dylan Baker) screws with Gipson's credit rating so his home mortgage falls through. Gipson finds an ingenious way to counterattack. And so begins a daylong struggle between two angry men.

Ah, but that's far from all. *Changing Lanes* is a thoughtful film that by its very existence shames studio movies that have been dumbed down into cat-and-mouse cartoons. The screenplay is by Chap Taylor, who has previously worked as a production assistant for Woody Allen, and by Michael Tolkin, who wrote the novel and screenplay *The Player* and wrote and directed two extraordinary films, *The*

Rapture and *The New Age.* The writers, rookie and veteran, want to know who these men are, how they got to this day in their lives, what their values are, what kinds of worlds they live in. A dumb film would be about settling scores after the fender bender. This film, which breathes, which challenges, which is excitingly alive, wants to see these men hit their emotional bottoms. Will they learn anything?

Doyle Gipson is a recovering alcoholic. His AA meetings and his AA sponsor (William Hurt) are depicted in realistic, not stereotyped terms. He's sober, but still at the mercy of his emotions. As he stands in the wreckage of his plans to save his marriage, his wife (Kim Staunton) tells him, "This is the sort of thing that always happens to you—and never happens to me unless I am in your field of gravity." And his sponsor tells him, "Booze isn't really your drug of choice. You're addicted to chaos." At one point, seething with rage, Gipson walks into a bar and orders a shot of bourbon. Then he stares at it. Then he gets into a fight that he deliberately provokes, and we realize that at some level he walked into the bar not for the drink but for the fight.

Gavin Banek leads a rich and privileged life. His boss (Sydney Pollack) has just made him a partner in their Wall Street law firm. It doesn't hurt that Banek married the boss's daughter. It also doesn't hurt that he was willing to obtain the signature of a confused old man who might not have known what he was signing, and that the firm will make millions as a result. His wife (Amanda Peet) sees her husband with blinding clarity. After Banek has second thoughts about the tainted document, Pollack asks his daughter to get him into line, and at lunch she has an extraordinary speech.

"Did you know my father has been cheating on my mother for twenty years?" she asks him. He says no, and then sheepishly adds, "Well, I didn't know it was for twenty years." Her mother knew all along, his wife says, "but she thought it would be unethical to leave a man for cheating on his marriage, after she has enjoyed an expensive lifestyle that depends on a man who makes his money by cheating at work." She looks across the table at her husband. "I could have married an honest man," she tells him. She did not, choosing instead a man who would go right to the edge to make money. You don't

work on Wall Street if you're not prepared to do that, she says.

And what, for that matter, about the poor old millionaire whose foundation is being plundered? "How do you think he got his money?" Pollack asks Affleck. "You think those factories in Malaysia have day-care centers?" He helpfully points out that the foundation was set up in the first place as a tax dodge.

Such speeches are thunderbolts in *Changing Lanes.* They show the movie digging right down into the depths of the souls, of the values of these two men. The director, Roger Michell, has made good movies, including *Persuasion* and *Notting Hill,* but this one seems more like Neil LaBute's *In the Company of Men,* or Tolkin's work. It lays these guys out and X-rays them, and by the end of the day, each man's own anger scares him more than the other guy's. This is one of the best movies of the year.

Charlie's Angels: Full Throttle ★ ★ ½
PG-13, 105 m., 2003

Cameron Diaz (Natalie Cook), Drew Barrymore (Dylan Sanders), Lucy Liu (Alex Munday), Demi Moore (Madison Lee), Bernie Mac (Jimmy Bosley). Directed by McG and produced by Drew Barrymore, Leonard Goldberg, and Nancy Juvonen. Screenplay by John August, Cormac Wibberley, and Marianne Wibberley, based on the television series by Ivan Goff and Ben Roberts.

Sometimes it has more to do with mood than with what's on the screen. *Charlie's Angels: Full Throttle* is more or less the same movie as the original *Charlie's Angels* (2000), and yet I feel more forgiving this time. Wow, did I hate the first one: "a movie without a brain in its three pretty little heads." I awarded it one-half of a star.

But what, really, was so reprehensible about that high-tech bimbo eruption? Imagine a swimsuit issue crossed with an explosion at the special-effects lab, and you've got it. Maybe I was indignant because people were going to spend their money on this instead of going to better movies that were undoubtedly more edifying for them. But if people wanted to be edified every time they went to the movies, Hollywood would be out of business.

Charlie's Angels: Full Throttle is not a funny

movie, despite a few good one-liners, as when Bernie Mac explains that the Black Irish invented the McRib. It is not an exciting movie, because there is no way to genuinely care about what's happening, and it doesn't make much sense, anyway. It is not a sexy movie, even though it stars four sexy women, because you just can't get aroused by the sight of three babes running toward you in slow motion with an explosion in the background. I've tried it.

So what is it? Harmless, brainless, good-natured fun. Leaving *Full Throttle*, I realized I did not hate or despise the movie, and so during a long and thoughtful walk along the Chicago River, I decided that I sort of liked it because of the high spirits of the women involved.

Say what you will, Drew Barrymore, Cameron Diaz, Lucy Liu, and Demi Moore were manifestly having fun while they made this movie. They're given outrageous characters to play, an astonishing wardrobe (especially considering the fact that they go everywhere without suitcases), remarkable superpowers, and lots of close-ups in which they are just gorgeous when they smile.

It's a form of play for them, to be female James Bonds, just as male actors all like to be in Westerns because you get to ride a horse and shoot up saloons. There is a scene where the three angels discuss what Dylan Sanders (Drew Barrymore) was named before she went into the witness protection program. It turns out she was named Helen Zas. Now there's a name to go in the books with Norma Stitz. Natalie (Cameron Diaz) and Alex (Lucy Liu) kid her mercilessly about her name, and as Lucy Liu comes up with wicked puns, you almost get the impression she's thinking them up herself.

The plot . . . but why should I describe the plot? It is an arbitrary and senseless fiction designed to provide a weak excuse for a series of scenes in which the angels almost get killed, in Mongolia and elsewhere, mostly elsewhere, while blowing up stuff, shooting people, being shot at, almost getting killed, and modeling their PG-13-rated outfits.

Two new faces this time: Demi Moore, as Madison Lee, a fallen angel, and Bernie Mac, taking over for Bill Murray in the Bosley role, as Bosley's brother, who I think is also called Bosley. The Angels confront Madison high atop

Los Angeles at the Griffith Observatory, which for mysterious reasons is completely deserted during their showdown and shoot-out.

So. I give the movie 2½ stars, partially in expiation for the half-star I gave the first one. But if you want to see a movie where big stars trade witty one-liners with one another in the midst of high-tech chase scenes and all sorts of explosive special effects, the movie for you is *Hollywood Homicide*. ☞

Charlotte Gray ★ ★

PG-13, 123 m., 2002

Cate Blanchett (Charlotte Gray), Billy Crudup (Julien Lavade), Rupert Perry-Jones (Peter), Michael Gambon (Levarde), Anton Lesser (Benech), Ron Cook (Mirabel). Directed by Gillian Armstrong and produced by Sarah Curtis and Douglas Rae. Screenplay by Jeremy Brock, based on the novel by Sebastian Faulks.

Consider now Cate Blanchett, a wondrous actress. Born in Melbourne in 1969, honored for her stage work in Australia, a survivor of U.S. TV-like *Police Rescue*, she made her first film in 1997 (*Paradise Road*, about female prisoners of war in the Pacific) and then arrived immediately at stardom in the title role of *Elizabeth* (1998), winning an Oscar nomination.

In the four years since then she has played in an astonishing range of roles: as a calculating Londoner in *An Ideal Husband*, as a strong-willed nineteenth-century gambler from the Outback in the wonderful *Oscar and Lucinda*, as an Italian-American housewife from New Jersey in *Pushing Tin*, as a rich society girl in *The Talented Mr. Ripley*, as a gold-digging Parisian showgirl in *The Man Who Cried*, as an Appalachian redneck with psychic powers in *The Gift*, as the woman who convinces both Billy Bob Thornton and Bruce Willis they love her in *Bandits*, as Galadriel in *Lord of the Rings*, as a lanky-haired Poughkeepsie slattern in *The Shipping News*, and now as a British woman who parachutes into France and fights with the Resistance in *Charlotte Gray*. Oh, and also in 2001 she had a baby.

Name me an actress who has played a greater variety of roles in four years, and I'll show you Meryl Streep. Were you counting Blanchett's accents? British, Elizabethan English, Edwardian English, Scots, Australian, French, American southern, midwestern, New England, New Joisey. And she has the kind of perfect profile they used in the "Can You Draw This Girl?" ads. She can bring as much class to a character as Katharine Hepburn, and has a better line in sluts.

While I was watching *Charlotte Gray,* I spent a lot of time thinking about Blanchett's virtues, because she, Billy Crudup, and Michael Gambon were performing life support on a hopeless screenplay. This is a movie that looks great, is well acted, and tells a story that you can't believe for a moment. I have no doubt that brave British women parachuted into France to join the Resistance; indeed, I have seen a much better movie about just such a woman—*Plenty* (1985), starring, wouldn't you know, Meryl Streep. It's just that I don't think such women were motivated primarily by romance. After *Pearl Harbor,* here is another movie where World War II is the backdrop for a love triangle.

Blanchett plays the title character, a Scottish woman in London who speaks perfect French and meets a young airman named Peter (Rupert Perry-Jones) at a publisher's party. They fall instantly in love, they have a one-night stand, he's shot down over France, and (she hears and believes) finds shelter with the Resistance. Charlotte allows herself to be recruited into British Special Operations, goes through training, and is dropped into France—near where Peter is thought to be. She is going to—what? Rescue him? Comfort him in her arms? Get him back to Britain? The movie doesn't spell this out very well.

In France, she comes into contact with a Resistance group led by Julien (Billy Crudup), a Communist, whose father, Levarde (Michael Gambon), disapproves of his son's politics, but keeps quiet because he hates the Nazis. Soon Charlotte is taken along on a raid that underlines the screenplay's basic problem, which is her utterly superfluous presence.

Crudup and his men hide in a ditch, blow up a Nazi train, are chased and nearly killed by Nazi soldiers. The next morning, Charlotte is told: "You did a good job last night." Why? How? What did she accomplish but tag along on a mission she had nothing to do with, watch the men blow up the train, and run for her life? A stranger, not needed, why was she taken along in the first place? This is the Resistance version of the practice of taking a girl along with you on a hunting trip so she can admire you shooting the big bad birds.

Soon Charlotte and Julien are drifting into unacknowledged love, while a subplot involves the fate of two local Jewish children whose parents have been shipped to the camps. Charlotte touches base with a dyspeptic local contact who seems to exist primarily to raise doubts about himself, and . . . but see for yourself, as the plot thickens. One question you might ask: How wise is it for Julien, an important Resistance fighter who wants to remain unnoticed, to shout curses at arriving Nazi troops? Another is: How important is that final letter Charlotte risks her life to type?

Blanchett, Crudup, and Gambon stand above and somehow apart from the absurdities of the screenplay. Their presence in their characters is convincing enough that we care about them and hope they survive—if not the war, at least the screenplay. The movie was directed by Gillian Armstrong, usually so good (*My Brilliant Career,* the overlooked and inspired *Oscar and Lucinda*). This time she excels in everything but her choice of material.

It is Cate Blanchett's fate to be born into a time when intelligence is fleeing from mainstream movies. The script for *Plenty* was based on a great play by David Hare. *Charlotte Gray* is based on a best-selling novel by Sebastian Faulks, unread by me, and on the basis of this movie, not on my reading list. Next Blanchett appears in *Heaven,* based on a screenplay by the late Krzysztof Kieslowski and directed by Tom Tykwer *(Run Lola Run, The Princess and the Warrior).* Good career move.

Charlotte Sometimes ★ ★ ★ ½
NO MPAA RATING, 85 m., 2003

Michael Idemoto (Michael), Jacqueline Kim (Darcy), Eugenia Yuan (Lori), Matt Westmore (Justin), Shizuko Hoshi (Auntie Margie), Kimberly Rose (Annie). Directed by Eric Byler and produced by Marc Ambrose and Byler. Screenplay by Byler.

The man lives alone in his apartment, sometimes reading, sometimes standing quietly in the dark. Through the walls he can hear passionate lovemaking. After a time there is a knock on his door. It is, we know, the young woman who lives next door. She can't sleep, she says. The man and his neighbor sit on his couch to watch television, and in the morning she is still asleep in his arms.

This simply, Eric Byler's *Charlotte Sometimes* draws us into its mysterious, erotic story. The man is named Michael (Michael Idemoto). His neighbor—actually his tenant in a two-unit building—is Lori (Eugenia Yuan). Her lover is Justin (Matt Westmore), and while their sex life is apparently spectacular she seems to have a deep, if platonic, love for Michael. What is their relationship, exactly? Michael is so quiet, so reserved, we cannot know for sure, although it seems clear in his eyes that he does not enjoy what he hears through the wall.

Lori asks Michael if he would like to meet a girl—she knows someone she could introduce him to. Before that can happen, one night in a neighborhood bar, he sees a young woman sitting alone across the room. He looks at her; she looks at him. He leaves, but comes back just as she is leaving—clearly to find her, although he claims he forgot something.

This is Darcy (Jacqueline Kim). She is tall and grave, the opposite of the pretty, cuddly Lori. "Men don't want me," she says. "They only think they want me." She reveals little about herself. As they talk into the night, they develop that kind of strange intimacy two people can have when they know nothing about each other but feel a deep connection. Eventually she offers to have sex with him, but Michael doesn't want that. It's too soon. Sex may be a shortcut to intimacy, but he values something more: perhaps his privacy, perhaps his growing attraction for her, which he doesn't want to reduce to the physical just yet.

Byler's screenplay never says too much, never asks the actors to explain or reveal in words what we sense in their presence and guarded, even coded, conversations. Jacqueline Kim, an experienced classical stage actress (from the Goodman in Chicago and the Guthrie in Minneapolis), brings a quality to Darcy that is intriguing and unsettling at the same time. She leaves and returns unpredictably. There is something she is not saying. Michael feels attracted, and yet warned.

This story, which is almost Gothic in its undertones, is filmed in an ordinary Los Angeles neighborhood. The house is on a winding road on a hillside. Michael owns a garage. "You're a mechanic—and you read," Darcy muses. He took over the family garage, but lives inside his ideas and his loneliness. How does he feel that Lori has sex with Justin but prefers to spend her nights with him? That Darcy is willing to have sex with him but then disappears, and withholds herself and her secrets?

The film has been photographed by Rob Humphreys in dark colors and shadows, sometimes with backlighting that will catch part of a face or an expression and leave the rest hidden. Then there are ordinary daytime scenes, such as a double date when the two couples have lunch. There is subtle verbal fencing; Michael, Darcy, and Lori are Asian, Justin is half-Asian, and when Darcy asks which of his parents taught him to use chopsticks, there is an undercurrent they all feel, and when he says he cannot remember the time when he could not use chopsticks, he is answering more than her question.

The movie has revelations I must not reveal, but let it be said that Byler conceals nothing from us except what is concealed from the characters, and what they learn, we learn. It becomes clear that Darcy came into Michael's life in the wrong way and cannot undo that, and that Lori is deeply disturbed that her platonic friend may become this other woman's lover. Little is actually said about any of this; it is all there in the air between these guarded and wounded characters.

Charlotte Sometimes drew me in from the opening shots. Byler reveals his characters in a way that intrigues and even fascinates us, and he never reduces the situation to simple melodrama, which would release the tension. This is like a psychological thriller, in which the climax has to do with feelings, not actions.

Idemoto brings such a loneliness to his role, such a feeling of the character's long hours of solitary thought, that we care for him right from the start, and feel his pain about this woman who might be the right one for him, but remains elusive and hidden. Kim has a way of being detached and observant in her scenes, as if Darcy is seeing it all happen within a context only she understands. At the end, when we know everything, the movie has not cheated; we sense the deep life currents that have brought these people to this place. There is sadness and tenderness here, and the knowledge that to find true love is not always to possess it.

Chasing Liberty ★ ★
PG-13, 111 m., 2004

Mandy Moore (Anna Foster), Matthew Goode (Ben Calder), Jeremy Piven (Alan Weiss), Annabella Sciorra (Cynthia Morales), Mark Harmon (James Foster), Caroline Goodall (Michelle Foster). Directed by Andy Cadiff and produced by Broderick Johnson, Andrew A. Kosove, and David Parfitt. Screenplay by Derek Guiley and David Schneiderman.

Chasing Liberty is surprisingly good in areas where it doesn't need to be good at all, and pretty awful in areas where it has to succeed. It centers on a couple of engaging performances in impossible roles, and involves a madcap romp through a Europe where 9/11 never happened and *Roman Holiday* was never made. The movie is ideal for audiences who kinda know that we have a president, and he could have a teenage daughter, and she might be protected by the Secret Service, but don't know a whole lot else.

The movie has a view of reality, danger, romance, foreigners, sex, and impulsive behavior that would have made ideal honeymoon viewing for Britney and Jason, had their marriage not tragically ended before the movie could open. It reflects precisely the prudence and forethought of two people who could get married at 5:30 A.M. in a Vegas chapel after seeing *The Texas Chainsaw Massacre* and then file for an annulment after belatedly realizing they hadn't discussed having children, where they want to live, community property, religious affiliation, and whether the toilet paper should roll out or in.

You may protest that I'm hauling Britney and Jason into a review of a movie they have nothing to do with, but you would be wrong. There are going to be people who say that no one could possibly be as glamorous and yet as stupid as the characters in this film, and I give you Jason and Britney, case closed.

The movie stars Mandy Moore, a singer-

actress of precisely Britney's generation, who has undeniable screen presence and inspires instant affection. Britney used to inspire instant affection herself, but now inspires instant alarm and concern. Mandy Moore is just plain likable, a Slurpee blended from scoops of Mary Tyler Moore, Sally Field, and Doris Day.

In *Chasing Liberty* she plays Anna Foster, code-named Liberty, who is the only daughter of U.S. president James Foster (Mark Harmon) and his first lady (Caroline Goodall). Her dating life is impossible. A hapless kid from her class arrives at the White House to take her out on a date, and the Secret Service strips the petals from the sweet little bouquet he brought her, seeking tiny and fragrant weapons of mass destruction.

The president is planning a state visit to Prague, and she wants to go along. What's more, she wants to hook up (in the old-fashioned sense, let us pray) with the daughter of the French ambassador, so they can skip over to Berlin for the annual Love Parade. And she demands freedom from the omnipresent Secret Service.

Her father nixes the Love Parade, promises to assign only two Secret Service agents, and is alarmed when Anna pulls a fast one, slips out of a nightclub, and is able to escape her agents by hitching a ride on the back of a motorcycle driven by Ben Calder (Matthew Goode). Ben is a saturnine Brit of about thirty, very dry and mysterious, and she knows absolutely nothing about him as she entrusts her life to him by embarking on a tour of Berlin, Venice, London, and other popular tourist destinations. Life on the road is easier when, by pure charm, for example, you can find a gondolier in Venice who not only waives his fee but invites you home so his mother can cook dinner for you and you can spend the night. Why does this gondolier remind me of the joke about the housewife who invites the mailman in for breakfast?

Anna doesn't know who Ben is, but she knows who she is, and it's fairly inconsiderate of her to run away and inspire a vast Euro hunt involving the Secret Service, Interpol, countless black helicopters, and millions of the taxpayers' dollars; this is one child who could have been left behind. Ben, however, does know who he is and so do we—he's working for the Secret Service, and has been assigned by the president to keep an eye on Anna while letting her think she's getting away with something.

Mandy Moore and Matthew Goode have a quirky and appealing chemistry, based on her confusion over whether she wants to have sex or not, or maybe over whether she's had sex or not, and his confusion when his private emotions begin to interfere with his job. There's a scene where Anna goes bungee-jumping and you want to explain to Ben that his job is to *prevent* her from bungee-jumping, not to tie himself to her bungee so they can die together. That would be a job for the Last Samurai.

I liked Goode's dry way of sardonically holding his distance, and Moore's unforced charm. It was a useful contrast to the movie's parallel romance between two agents named Weiss and Morales (Jeremy Piven and Annabella Sciorra), who grumble their way into love in dialogue that seems recycled from a shelved sitcom. Harmon is singularly unconvincing as the president, not only because he recklessly endangers his daughter's life and his country's fortune, but also because he reads the newspaper, and there's no telling where that could lead.

Chasing Papi ★ ★ ½
PG, 92 m., 2003

Roselyn Sanchez (Lorena), Sofia Vergara (Cici), Jaci Velasquez (Patricia), Eduardo Verastegui (Papi), Lisa Vidal (Carmen), D. L. Hughley (Rodrigo), Freddy Rodriguez (Victor), Maria Conchita Alonso (Maria), Paul Rodriguez (Costas Delgado). Directed by Linda Mendoza and produced by Tracey Trench and Forest Whitaker. Screenplay by Laura Angelica Simon, Steven Antin, Alison Balian, and Liz Sarnoff.

Chasing Papi is a feature-length jiggle show with Charlie's Angels transformed into Latina bimbos. Well, not entirely bimbos: The movie's three heroines are smart and capable, except when they're in pursuit of the man they love, an occupation that requires them to run through a lot of scenes wearing high heels and squealing with passion or fear or delight, while a stupendous amount of jiggling goes on.

These are great-looking women. Forgive me if I sound like a lecher, but, hey, the entire purpose and rationale of this film is to display Roselyn Sanchez, Sofia Vergara, and Jaci Ve-

lasquez in a way that would make your average *Maxim* reader feel right at home. So high are the movie's standards of beauty that even two supporting roles feature the ravishing Lisa Vidal and the immortal Maria Conchita Alonso.

The three stars are veterans of Spanish-language TV soap operas, a genre that celebrates cleavage with single-minded dedication. In the story, they are the three girlfriends of Thomas Fuentes (Eduardo Verastegui), aka Papi, an advertising executive whose travels require him to visit Lorena (Sanchez) in Chicago, Cici (Vergara) in Miami, and Patricia (Velasquez) in New York. He does not intend to be a three-timer and sincerely loves them all, but asks: "How can you choose between the colors of nature's beautiful flowers?"

All three women happen to be watching the same astrologer on TV, and take the seer's advice to drop everything and race to the side of their man. This leads to an improbable scene when all three burst through doors leading into Papi's bedroom while wearing his gift of identical red lingerie. Papi is not home at the time, supplying an opportunity for the women to discover his betrayal and decide to gang up and have what is described as revenge but looks more like a fashion show by Victoria's Secret.

Meanwhile, let's see, there's a plot about a bag of money, and an FBI agent (Vidal) trails the women to Los Angeles while some tough guys, led by Paul Rodriguez, also are on the trail of the money, and this all leads inevitably to the girls making their onstage dancing debut at a festival headlining Sheila E.

Chasing Papi is as light as a feather, as fresh as spring, and as lubricious as a centerfold. Its three heroines are seen in one way or another as liberated women, especially Lorena, who is said to be a lawyer, but their hearts go a-flutter in the presence of Papi. The movie's purpose is to photograph them as attractively as possible, while covering up the slightness of the plot with wall-to-wall Latin music, infectiously upbeat scenes, and animated sequences that introduce New York, Miami, Chicago, and Los Angeles. (The use of these cartoon intervals is an inspired solution to the problem that the movie was shot entirely in Canada.)

I cannot recommend *Chasing Papi*, but I cannot dislike it. It commits no offense except the puppylike desire to please. It celebrates a vibrant and lively Latino world in which everyone speaks English with a charming accent, switching to Spanish only in moments of intense drama. There is something extroverted and refreshing in the way these women enjoy their beauty and their sexiness. They've got it, and they flaunt it.

The movie could have been smarter and wittier. The plot could have made a slight attempt to be original. There are better ways to pass your time. But it will make you smile, and that is a virtue not to be ignored.

Cheaper by the Dozen ★ ★ ★
PG, 98 m., 2003

Steve Martin (Tom Baker), Bonnie Hunt (Kate Baker), Tom Welling (Charlie Baker), Piper Perabo (Nora Baker), Ashton Kutcher (Hank), Hilary Duff (Lorraine Baker), Forrest Landis (Mark Baker). Directed by Shawn Levy and produced by Michael Barnathan, Ben Myron, and Robert Simonds. Screenplay by Craig Titley, Joel Cohen, Sam Harper, and Alec Sokolow, based on the book by Frank B. Gilbreth Jr. and Ernestine Gilbreth Carey.

Here's my old copy of *Cheaper by the Dozen* right here. The bright orange binding is worn through to the cardboard, there are grape juice stains all through Chapter 3, and a couple of pages are stuck together with what still, incredibly, smells like peanut butter. God, I loved that book. I read it over and over again as pure escapism. I was an only child curled up at the end of the sofa, imagining what it would be like to have eleven brothers and sisters.

Cheaper by the Dozen was a best-seller in the 1940s, and inspired a 1950 movie starring Clifton Webb and Myrna Loy as Frank and Lillian Gilbreth, who raised twelve kids with ingenuity and precision. Now here is the 2003 version, with Steve Martin and Bonnie Hunt. It isn't my purpose to use the old movie to hammer the new one, because they're both sweet and zany, but to notice how much our ideas have changed in fifty-three years; especially our ideas about fathers.

Frank Gilbreth was a real man, and the original book was cowritten by two of his children. He was, they explained, a time-and-motion expert, who broke down every task into its essen-

tial elements and then studied them to see how they could be done more quickly and easily. At work he improved assembly lines. At home he applied his theories to his family, believing that twelve children were as easy to raise as two, if you analyzed the daily family routine and assigned part of it to every kid—even very small parts for very small kids. The unspoken assumption was that the father was the center of authority, he knew best, and his wife was his loyal copilot.

We know now that this model is a case of sexist chauvinism. Gilbreth's view of fathers is long out of date, and American men survive in the movies only as examples of incompetence, unrealistic ambition, and foolish pride. Gene Siskel once started a list of movies with fathers in them, to demonstrate that Hollywood preferred whenever possible to have single mothers and avoid fathers altogether. If there had to be a father, he was (a) in a comedy, the butt of the joke, and (b) in a drama, a child abuser, an alcoholic, an adulterer, an abandoner of families, or preferably all of the above. At some point during a half-century of Hollywood fathering, "father knows best" was replaced by "shut your pie hole."

Tom Baker, the Steve Martin character in *Cheaper by the Dozen*, has a good heart and loves his wife and children, but that leaves him with a few promising character flaws. He is incapable of inspiring discipline, for example, and would sacrifice his family to his ambition. He's a football coach for a cow college in Midland, Illinois, but is offered the head coaching job at Lincoln University in Evanston. We're supposed to think of Northwestern.

Well, of course, fool that Tom is, he takes the job and steps up to national prominence and a big salary, even though this means his kids will have to switch schools and find new boyfriends and girlfriends, and they will have to move out of the overcrowded bungalow where they all lived in each other's pockets, and into a sprawling two-story corner home in a $1 million neighborhood. One of those houses with a circular drive and balconies and garrets and a garden.

Worse, the move is scheduled to coincide with the national tour to promote the new book about the family by Tom's wife, Kate (Bonnie Hunt). This is quite a publishing coup.

113

Her book is submitted, accepted, edited, printed, in the stores, and on the best-seller lists within a week. Forget the coach; make us a movie about the publisher. The book's success means Tom has to run team practices and steer his new team through a couple of big games while Kate is on the road, and although his oldest daughter Nora (Piper Perabo) agrees to come home and baby-sit, she brings along her boyfriend, Hank (Ashton Kutcher), causing a family crisis about where Hank will sleep. This in a family where everybody was sharing two and a half beds until a month ago.

The movie is lighthearted fun, providing little character bits for all of the family members, from young Forrest Landis, whose life centers on his pet frog, all the way up to older sister Hilary Duff, whose romantic adventures involve the usual PG-rated heartbreak. The neighbors complain that they're living next door to Animal House, the alums complain that the small-time coach is not ready for big-time football, the kids complain that they miss home—and of course only evil, stupid, reactionary, ambitious, greedy Dad is standing in the way of a return to Midland, a town so friendly they don't say, "Attention, Shoppers!" at Wal-Mart, but call you by name (only kidding).

Hey, I liked the movie. These actors are skilled at being nice. It's just that the movie settles when it ought to push. Consider the Bonnie Hunt character. Here she's reasonable, exasperated, and loves that lunk of a husband. But compare her work here with what she did in *Stolen Summer* (you remember, that 2002 Operation Greenlight movie I recommended, but you ignored my review and went to see *Sorority Boys* instead). In that one she was the mother of a large Irish Catholic family in Chicago, where she had edge and sass and was not afraid to smack a potty-mouth up alongside the head. *Cheaper by the Dozen* doesn't understand that kind of family; it's based on sitcom families, where the most essential family value is not stepping on anybody's lines.   ☞

Chelsea Walls ★ ★ ★
R, 109 m., 2002

Rosario Dawson (Audrey), Vincent D'Onofrio (Frank), Kris Kristofferson (Bud), Robert Sean Leonard (Terry), Natasha Richardson (Mary),

Uma Thurman (Grace), Steve Zahn (Ross), Tuesday Weld (Geta), Mark Webber (Val), Jimmy Scott (Skinny Bones). Directed by Ethan Hawke and produced by Alexis Alexanian, Pamela Koffler, Christine Vachon, and Gary Winick. Screenplay by Nicole Burdette, based on her play.

A rest stop for rare individuals.
                —Motto of the Chelsea Hotel

Chelsea Walls is the movie for you if you have a beaten-up copy of the Compass paperback edition of Kerouac's *On the Road* and on page 124 you underlined the words, "The one thing that we yearn for in our living days, that makes us sigh and groan and undergo sweet nauseas of all kinds, is the remembrance of some lost bliss that was probably experienced only in the womb and can only be reproduced (though we hate to admit it) in death." If you underlined the next five words ("But who wants to die?"), you are too realistic for this movie.

Lacking the paperback, you qualify for the movie if you have ever made a pilgrimage to the Chelsea Hotel on West 23rd Street in New York, and given a thought to Dylan Thomas, Thomas Wolfe, Arthur C. Clarke, R. Crumb, Brendan Behan, Gregory Corso, Bob Dylan, or Sid and Nancy, who lived (and in some cases died) there. You also qualify if you have ever visited the Beat Bookshop in Boulder, Colorado, if you have ever yearned to point the wheel west and keep driving until you reach the Pacific Coast Highway, or if you have never written the words "somebody named Lawrence Ferlinghetti."

If you are by now thoroughly bewildered by this review, you will be equally bewildered by *Chelsea Walls*, and had better stay away from it. Ethan Hawke's movie evokes the innocent spirit of the Beat Generation fifty years after the fact, and celebrates characters who think it is noble to live in extravagant poverty while creating Art and leading untidy sex lives. These people smoke a lot, drink a lot, abuse many substances, and spend either no time at all or way too much time managing their wardrobes. They live in the Chelsea Hotel because it is cheap, and provides a stage for their psychodramas.

Countless stories have been set in the

Chelsea. Andy Warhol's *Chelsea Girls* (1967) was filmed there. Plays have between written about it, including one by Nicole Burdette that inspired this screenplay. Photographers and painters have recorded its seasons. It is our American Left Bank, located at one convenient address. That Ethan Hawke would have wanted to direct a movie about it is not surprising; he and his wife, Uma Thurman, who could relax with easy-money stardom, have a way of sneaking off for dodgy avant-garde projects. They starred in Richard Linklater's *Tape* (2001), about three people in a motel room, and now here is the epic version of the same idea, portraying colorful denizens of the Chelsea in full bloom.

We meet Bud (Kris Kristofferson), a boozy author who uses a typewriter instead of a computer, perhaps because you can't short it out by spilling a bottle on it. He has a wife named Greta (Tuesday Weld) and a mistress named Mary (Natasha Richardson), and is perhaps able to find room for both of them in his life because neither one can stand to be around him all that long. He tells them both they are his inspiration. When he's not with the Muse he loves, he loves the Muse he's with.

Val (Mark Webber) is so young he looks embryonic. He buys lock, stock, and barrel into the mythology of bohemia, and lives with Audrey (Rosario Dawson). They are both poets. I do not know how good Audrey's poems are because Dawson reads them in close-up—just her face filling the screen—and I could not focus on the words. I have seen a lot of close-ups in my life but never one so simply, guilelessly erotic. Have more beautiful lips ever been photographed?

Frank (Vincent D'Onofrio) is a painter who thinks he can talk Grace (Uma Thurman) into being his lover. She is not sure. She prefers a vague, absent lover, never seen, and seems to know she has made the wrong choice but takes a perverse pride in sticking with it. Ross (Steve Zahn) is a singer whose brain seems alarmingly fried. Little Jimmy Scott is Skinny Bones, a down-and-out jazzman. Robert Sean Leonard is Terry, who wants to be a folk singer. The corridors are also occupied by the lame and the brain-damaged; every elevator trip includes a harangue by the house philosopher.

Has time passed these people by? Very likely.

Greatness resides in ability, not geography, and it is futile to believe that if Thomas Wolfe wrote *Look Homeward, Angel* in Room 831, anyone occupying that room is sure to be equally inspired. What the movie's characters are seeking is not inspiration anyway, but an audience. They stay in the Chelsea because they are surrounded by others who understand the statements they are making with their lives. In a society where the average college freshman has already targeted his entry-level position in the economy, it's a little lonely to embrace unemployment and the aura of genius. To actors with a romantic edge, however, it's very attractive: No wonder Matt Dillon sounds so effortlessly convincing on the audiobook of *On the Road*.

Hawke shot the film for $100,000 on digital video, in the tradition of Warhol's fuzzy 16mm photography. Warhol used a split screen, so that while one of his superstars was doing nothing on the left screen, we could watch another of his superstars doing nothing on the right screen. Hawke, working with Burdette's material, has made a movie that by contrast is action-packed. The characters enjoy playing hooky from life and posing as the inheritors of bohemia. Hawke's cinematographers, Tom Richmond and Richard Rutkowski, and his editor, Adriana Pacheco, weave a mosaic out of the images, avoiding the temptation of a simple realistic look: The film is patterned with color, superimposition, strange exposures, poetic transitions, grainy color palettes.

Movies like this do not grab you by the throat. You have to be receptive. The first time I saw *Chelsea Walls*, in a stuffy room late at night at Cannes 2001, I found it slow and pointless. This time I saw it earlier in the day, fueled by coffee, and I understood that the movie is not about what the characters do, but about what they are. It may be a waste of time to spend your life drinking, fornicating, posing as a genius, and living off your friends, but if you've got the money, honey, take off the time.

Cherish ★ ★ ★
R, 99 m., 2002

Robin Tunney (Zoe), Tim Blake Nelson (Deputy Bill), Brad Hunt (D.J.), Liz Phair (Brynn), Jason

Priestley (Andrew), Nora Dunn (Bell), Lindsay Crouse (Therapist), Ricardo Gil (Max). Directed by Finn Taylor and produced by Mark Burton and Johnny Wow. Screenplay by Taylor.

In most locked-room mysteries, the death takes place inside the room and the hero tries to figure out how it was done. *Cherish* is a variation on the theme: The death takes place outside the room, and then the heroine is locked into it, and has to find the killer without leaving. Throw in a love story, a touch of *Run, Lola, Run,* and a lot of Top 40 songs, and you have *Cherish,* a lightweight charmer with a winning performance by Robin Tunney.

She plays Zoe, the kind of clueless office worker that her coworkers subtly try to avoid (I was reminded of the Shelley Duvall character in Altman's *Three Women*). She has a hopeless crush on coworker Andrew (Jason Priestley), and that leads her one night to a nightclub and to a fateful encounter with a masked man who enters her car, steps on the accelerator, mows down a cop, and then flees on foot.

Zoe is arrested for drunken vehicular homicide and several other things, and given little hope by her attorney, who gets the case continued in hopes that the heat will die down. The court orders her confined to a walk-up San Francisco apartment, with a bracelet on her ankle that will sound alarms if she tries to leave. In charge of the bracelet program: a nerdy technician named Daly (Tim Blake Nelson, from *O Brother, Where Art Thou?*), who tries his best to keep everything on a businesslike footing.

By limiting Zoe to her apartment, the movie creates the opportunity to show her fighting boredom, testing the limits of the bracelet, and making friends with Max (Ricardo Gil), the gay dwarf who lives downstairs. It also allows her, through quite a coincidence to be sure, to get a lead on that masked man who is the real cop-killer. But since absolutely no one believes her story about the masked man in the first place (and since her Breathalyzer test was alarming), it's up to her to gather evidence and nail the perp—all, apparently, without straying from her apartment.

How the movie manages to exploit and sidestep her limitations is a lot of the fun. It's good, too, to see Zoe growing and becoming more real, shedding the persona of office loser. And

although as a general rule I deplore movies that depend on chase scenes for a cheap third act, I concede that in a locked-room plot, a chase scene of any description is a tour de force.

Robin Tunney has a plucky charm that works nicely here; it's quite a shift from her best movie, the overlooked *Niagara, Niagara* (1997), where she played a runaway with Tourette's; and she needed considerable pluck, to be sure, to play the mother of the Antichrist in *End of Days* (1999). Here she brings a quiet goofiness to the role, which is a much better choice than grim heroism or calm competence or some of the other speeds she could have chosen. Tim Blake Nelson is a case study as the kind of man who looks at a woman as if desperately hoping to be handed an instruction manual. And I liked the fire and ingenuity of Ricardo Gil, as the little man downstairs.

Chicago ★ ★ ★ ½
PG-13, 113 m., 2002

Catherine Zeta-Jones (Velma Kelly), Renée Zellweger (Roxie Hart), Richard Gere (Billy Flynn), John C. Reilly (Amos Hart), Queen Latifah (Matron "Mama"), Christine Baranski (Mary Sunshine), Taye Diggs (The Bandleader), Lucy Liu (Go-to-Hell Kitty), Dominic West (Fred Casely). Directed by Rob Marshall and produced by Marty Richards and Harvey Weinstein. Screenplay by Bill Condon, based on the musical by Fred Ebb and Bob Fosse.

Chicago continues the reinvention of the musical that started with *Moulin Rouge.* Although modern audiences don't like to see stories interrupted by songs, apparently they like songs interrupted by stories. The movie is a dazzling song-and-dance extravaganza, with just enough words to support the music and allow everyone to catch their breath between songs. You can watch it like you listen to an album, over and over; the same phenomenon explains why *Moulin Rouge* was a bigger hit on DVD than in theaters.

The movie stars sweet-faced Renée Zellweger as Roxie Hart, who kills her lover and convinces her husband to pay for her defense; and Catherine Zeta-Jones as Velma Kelly, who broke up her vaudeville sister act by murdering her husband and her sister while they were engaged in a sport not licensed for in-laws. Richard Gere is Billy Flynn, the slick, high-priced attorney who boasts he can beat any rap, for a $5,000 fee. "If Jesus Christ had lived in Chicago," he explains, "and if he'd had $5,000, and had come to me—things would have turned out differently."

This story, lightweight but cheerfully lurid, fueled Bob Fosse and Fred Ebb's original stage production of *Chicago*, which opened in 1975 and has been playing somewhere or other ever after—since 1997 again on Broadway. Fosse, who grew up in Chicago in the 1930s and 1940s, lived in a city where the daily papers roared with the kinds of headlines the movie loves. Killers were romanticized or vilified, cops and lawyers and reporters lived in each other's pockets, and newspapers read like pulp fiction. There's an inspired scene of ventriloquism and puppetry at a press conference, with all of the characters dangling from strings. For Fosse, the Chicago of Roxie Hart supplied the perfect peg to hang his famous hat.

The movie doesn't update the musical so much as bring it to a high electric streamlined gloss. The director, Rob Marshall, a stage veteran making his big-screen debut, paces the film with gusto. It's not all breakneck production numbers, but it's never far from one. And the choreography doesn't copy Fosse's inimitable style, but it's not far from it, either; the movie sideswipes imitation on its way to homage.

The decision to use nonsingers and non-dancers is always controversial in musicals, especially in these days when big stars are needed to headline expensive productions. Of Zellweger and Gere, it can be said that they are persuasive in their musical roles and well cast as their characters. Zeta-Jones was, in fact, a professional dancer in London before she decided to leave the chorus line and take her chances with acting, and her dancing in the movie is a reminder of the golden days; the film opens with her "All That Jazz" number, which plays like a promise *Chicago* will have to deliver on. And what a good idea to cast Queen Latifah in the role of Mama, the prison matron; she belts out "When You're Good to Mama" with the superb assurance of a performer who knows what good is and what Mama likes.

The story is inspired by the screaming head-lines of the "Front Page" era and the decade after. We meet Roxie Hart, married early and unwisely to Amos Hart (John C. Reilly), a credulous lunkhead. She has a lover named Fred Casely (Dominic West), who sweet-talks her with promises of stardom. When she finds out he's a two-timing liar, she guns him down, and gets a one-way ticket to Death Row, already inhabited by Velma and overseen by Mama.

Can she get off? Only Billy Flynn (Gere) can pull off a trick like that, although his price is high and he sings a song in praise of his strategy ("Give 'em the old razzle-dazzle"). Velma has already captured the attention of newspaper readers, but after the poor sap Amos pays Billy his fee, a process begins to transform Roxie into a misunderstood heroine. She herself shows a certain genius in the process, as when she dramatically reveals she is pregnant with Amos's child, a claim that works only if nobody in the courtroom can count to nine.

Instead of interrupting the drama with songs, Marshall and screenwriter Bill Condon stage the songs more or less within Roxie's imagination, where everything is a little more supercharged than life, and even lawyers can tap-dance. (To be sure, Gere's own tap dancing is on the level of performers in the Chicago Bar Association's annual revue.) There are a few moments of straight pathos, including Amos Hart's pathetic disbelief that his Roxie could have cheated on him; he sings "Mr. Cellophane" about how people see right through him. But for the most part the film runs on solid-gold cynicism.

Reilly brings a kind of pathetic, sincere naïveté to the role—the same tone, indeed, he brings to a similar husband in *The Hours*, where it is also needed. It's surprising to see the confidence in his singing and dancing, until you find out he was in musicals all through school. Zellweger is not a born hoofer, but then again Roxie Hart isn't supposed to be a star; the whole point is that she isn't, and what Zellweger invaluably contributes to the role is Roxie's dreamy infatuation with herself, and her quickly growing mastery of publicity. Velma *is* supposed to be a singing and dancing star, and Zeta-Jones delivers with glamour, high style, and the delicious confidence the world forces on you when you are one of its most beautiful inhabitants. As for Queen Latifah, she's too young to remember Sophie Tucker, but not to channel her.

Chicago is a musical that might have seemed unfilmable, but that was because it was assumed it had to be transformed into more conventional terms. By filming it in its own spirit, by making it frankly a stagy song-and-dance revue, by kidding the stories instead of lingering over them, the movie is big, brassy fun.

The Chronicles of Riddick ★ ★
PG-13, 118 m., 2004

Vin Diesel (Richard B. Riddick), Colm Feore (Lord Marshal), Alexa Davalos (Kyra), Karl Urban (Vaako), Thandie Newton (Dame Vaako), Judi Dench (Aereon), Keith David (Abu "Imam" al-Walid), Alexis Llewellyn (Ziza). Directed by David Twohy and produced by Vin Diesel and Scott Kroopf. Screenplay by Twohy.

"In normal times, evil should be fought by good, but in times like this, well, it should be fought by another kind of evil."

So says a character named Aereon in the opening moments of *The Chronicles of Riddick*, a futuristic battle between a fascist misfit and a fascist master race. The opening shot shows a gargantuan steel face that looks like Mussolini after a face-lift, and when the evil Necromongers rally to hail their Lord Marshal, it looks like they've been studying *The Triumph of the Will*.

Against this intergalactic tribe stands one man, a man with the somewhat anticlimactic name of Richard B. Riddick. He is one of the few surviving Furions, fierce warriors who have, alas, mostly been captured and turned into Necromongers. Such is his prowess that with merely his flesh and blood he can defeat and capture a Necromonger fighter ship. What a guy. Riddick, played by Vin Diesel, is a character we first encountered in *Pitch Black*, the 2000 film by the same director, David Twohy. Although a few other characters repeat from that film, notably Abu "Imam" al-Walid (Keith David), there's no real connection between them, apart from Riddick's knack of finding himself on absurdly inhospitable planets. Here he fights for life on Crematoria, a planet whose blazing sun rockets over the horizon every fifteeen minutes or so and bakes everything beneath it. That you can shield yourself from it behind rocks is helpful, although it begs the question of why, since the atmosphere is breathable, the air is not superheated.

But never mind. The Necromongers want everybody to be a Necromonger, and they line up behind the Lord Marshal (Colm Feore), who alone among his race has visited the Underverse. Aereon tells us he returned "half alive and half . . . something else." This Aereon, she's awfully well informed, and has a way of materializing out of thin air. She's a member of the race of Elementals, a fact I share with you since I have no idea what an Elemental is, or was, or wants to be.

Her character is one of several who are introduced with great fanfare and then misplaced. There's also a big-eyed, beautiful little girl named Ziza (Alexis Llewellyn), who keeps asking Riddick if he will fight the monsters, and Riddick keeps looking like he may have a heart of stone but this little girl melts it, and we're all set up for a big scene of monster-bashing and little-girl-saving that somehow never comes. (In this movie, a setup is as good as a payoff, since the last shot clearly establishes that there will be a sequel, and we can find out about all the missing stuff then.)

The Chronicles of Riddick is above all an exercise in computer-generated effects, and indeed the project represents the direction action movies are taking, as its human actors (or their digital clones) are inserted into manifestly artificial scenes that look like frames from the darkest of superhero comic books. The jolly reds, yellows, and blues of the classic Superman and Spiderman have been replaced in these grim days with black and gunmetal gray. *Chronicles* doesn't pause for much character development, and is in such a hurry that even the fight scenes are abbreviated chop-chop sessions. There are a lot of violent fights (the movie is made of them, which explains the PG-13 rating), but never do we get a clear idea of the spatial locations of the characters or their complete physical movements. Twohy breaks the fights down into disconnected flashes of extreme action in close-up, just as a comic book would, and maybe this is a style. It's certainly no more boring than most conventional CGI fight scenes.

I think the Lord Marshal wants to conquer all planets colonized by humans and make them Necromongers, but I was never sure that Richard B. Riddick didn't approve of that. Riddick seems more angered that there is a bounty on his head, and when he wreaks vengeance against the Necromongers, it's personal. His travails are intercut with the story of Vaako and Dame Vaako (Karl Urban and Thandie Newton), who want to overthrow the Lord Marshal, although whether they constitute a movement or just a coterie, I cannot say.

Vin Diesel was born to play a character like Riddick, and he growls and scowls impressively. I like Diesel as an actor and trust he was born to play other, better characters, in movies that make sense. None of the other actors do anything we couldn't do if we looked like them. Films like *The Chronicles of Riddick* gather about them cadres of fans who obsess about every smallest detail, but somehow I don't think *Riddick* will make as many converts as *The Matrix*. In fact, I owe an apology to fans of *The Lord of the Rings* trilogy.

When Richard Roeper reviewed the current two-disc DVD of *The Lord of the Rings: The Return of the King* on TV, I noted that a four-disc set of the movie was coming out later. He observed that the complete trilogy will come out on "an accordion-size set that will take up the next six years of your life." I observed that *LOTR* fans should "get a life." I meant this as an affectionate, ironic throwaway, but have received dozens of wounded e-mails from *Ring* devotees who believe *LOTR* has, indeed, given them a life, and after seeing *The Chronicles of Riddick*, I agree. They have a life. The prospect of becoming an expert on *Riddick*, in contrast, is too depressing to contemplate.

Cinemania ★ ★ ★
NO MPAA RATING, 80 m., 2003

Featuring Jack Angstreich, Eric Chadbourne, Harvey Schwartz, Roberta Hill, and Bill Heidbreder. A documentary directed by Angela Christlieb and Stephen Kijak and produced by Gunter Hanfgarn. Screenplay by Christlieb and Kijak.

Cinemania tells the story of five New Yorkers who spend as much of their life as possible going to the movies. They go to a whole lot of movies. It's my job to attend movies, and in a

year I probably see only about 450. If I were one of these cinephiles, I would have seen 700 to 1,000, would know the exact count, and would also have the programs, ticket stubs, press kits, and promotional coffee mugs.

These are not crazy people. Maladjusted and obsessed, yes, but who's to say what normal is? I think it makes more sense to see movies all day than to golf, play video games, or gamble. Not everyone agrees. I know people like these, and I understand their desire to be absorbed in the darkness and fantasy. As a professional moviegoer, my life is even a little nuttier than theirs, because they at least choose which titles to see, and spend a lot of time seeing revivals and classics; I have to monitor whatever is opening every week.

The five cinephiles are Jack Angstreich, Eric Chadbourne, Harvey Schwartz, Roberta Hill, and Bill Heidbreder. They agree that New York ranks with Paris as the best place to see a lot of movies. They have the screening times and subway schedules coordinated to maximize the number of movies they can see in a day, and Jack deliberately eats a constipating diet (no fruits or vegetables) to minimize trips to the rest room. None of them is married (duh), and some talk about their nonexistent sex lives. Bill says he wouldn't want to make love with Rita Hayworth because he couldn't do it in black-and-white, and her dark lips in old b&w movies are crucial to her appeal. Bill was disappointed, too, during a trip to Europe. He loves French movies about people sitting in cafés, but when he went to Paris and sat in a café, he discovered it was—only a café. Not as good as in the movies.

They have their specialties. Bill likes European movies since the French New Wave. Harvey obsesses on running times. Eric will go to see almost anything, including *The Amazing Crab Monster*. Roberta gets in fights with ushers who impede her single-minded determination to see movies. Jack wants to get a cell phone so he can call the booth and complain about the projection without having to walk out to the lobby. For key screenings, they arrive early and save their favorite seats, and they are willing to take direct measures against anyone interfering with their enjoyment of a movie.

They really, really like movies. They cry during them. One stumbled out of *Umbrellas of*

Cherbourg and walked for blocks in the rain, weeping. "A commitment to cinema means one must have a technically deviant lifestyle," Jack acknowledges. That includes being able to avoid the tiresome necessity of earning a living. Jack has inheritance ("If I don't blow it all on hookers, I will never have to work"). Bill is on unemployment. Harvey, Eric, and Roberta are on disability, and at one point discuss the possibility that having to go to the movies should qualify them for disability.

They talk warmly and with enthusiasm about certain titles, but I have the eerie feeling that they must be at a movie whether they enjoy it or not. And only a real movie will do. Except for Eric, who also watches a lot of videos, they insist on movies and hate TV. Sometimes their dreams are movies, they say, perhaps in black-and-white or Cinemascope. But only the nightmares are in video. Or is it that anything on video is a nightmare? To be asleep at all is to lose moviegoing time. "I'm so far behind in the cinema," Jack sighs, "that it's just a hopeless Sisyphean struggle." As the movie ends, Jack and the other four subjects have gathered to watch another movie: This one.

Cinema Paradiso: The New Version
★ ★ ★ ½
R, 170 m., 2002

Salvatore Cascio (Salvatore [Young]), Marco Leonardi (Salvatore [Teenager]), Agnese Nano (Elena [Teenager]), Jacques Perrin (Salvatore [Adult]), Brigitte Fossey (Elena [Adult]), Philippe Noiret (Alfredo), Leopoldo Trieste (Father Adelfio). Directed by Guiseppe Tournatore and produced by Mino Barbera, Franco Cristaldi, and Giovanna Romagnoli. Screenplay by Tournatore.

When *Cinema Paradiso* won the Academy Award as Best Foreign Film in 1990, it was an open secret that the movie the voters loved was not quite the same as the one director Guiseppe Tournatore made. Reports had it that Harvey Weinstein, the boss at Miramax, had trimmed not just a shot here or there, but a full fifty-one minutes from the film. Audiences loved the result, however, and the movie is consistently voted among the 100 best movies of all time at the Internet Movie Database.

Now comes a theatrical release of *Cinema Paradiso: The New Version*, with an ad campaign that promises, "Discover what really happened to the love of a lifetime." Considering that it was Miramax that made it impossible for us to discover this in the 1990 version, the ad is sublime chutzpah. And the movie is now so much longer and covers so much more detail that it almost plays as its own sequel.

Most of the first two hours will be familiar to lovers of the film. Little Salvatore (Salvatore Cascio), known to one and all as Toto, is fascinated by the movies and befriended by the projectionist Alfredo (Philippe Noiret). After a fire blinds Alfredo, Toto becomes the projectionist, and the Cinema Paradiso continues as the center of village life, despite the depredations of Father Adelfio (Leopoldo Trieste), who censors all of the films, ringing a bell at every kissing scene.

The new material of the longer version includes much more about the teenage romance between Salvatore (Marco Leonardi) and Elena (Agnese Nano)—a forbidden love, since her bourgeoisie parents have a better match in mind. And then there is a long passage involving the return of the middle-aged Salvatore (Jacques Perrin) to the village for the first time since he left to go to Rome and make his name as a movie director. He contacts the adult Elena (Brigitte Fossey), and finds out for the first time what really happened to a crucial rendezvous, and how easily his life might have turned out differently. (His discoveries promote the film to an MPAA rating of R, from its original PG.)

Seeing the longer version is a curious experience. It is an item of faith that the director of a film is always right, and that studios who cut films are butchers. Yet I must confess that the shorter version of *Cinema Paradiso* is a better film than the longer. Harvey was right. The 170-minute cut overstays its welcome, and continues after its natural climax.

Still, I'm happy to have seen it—not as an alternate version, but as the ultimate exercise in viewing deleted scenes. Anyone who loves the film will indeed be curious about "what really happened to the love of a lifetime," and it is good to know. I hope, however, that this new version doesn't replace the old one on the video shelves; the ideal solution would be a DVD with the 1990 version on one side and the 2002 version on the other.

City by the Sea ★ ★ ★

R, 108 m., 2002

Robert De Niro (Detective Vincent La Marca), Frances McDormand (Michelle), James Franco (Joey La Marca), Eliza Dushku (Gina), Patti LuPone (Maggie), George Dzundza (Reg Duffy), William Forsythe (Spyder). Directed by Michael Caton-Jones and produced by Matthew Baer, Caton-Jones, Brad Grey, and Elie Samaha. Screenplay by Ken Hixon and Mike McAlary.

City by the Sea tells the sad, fatalistic story of a cop whose father was a baby-killer, and whose son now seems to be a murderer too. Robert De Niro stars as Detective Vincent La Marca, a pro whose years of hard experience have made him into a cop who dismisses sociology and psychology and believes simply that if you did it, you have to pay for it. This code extends to his father and he will apply it if necessary to his son.

La Marca works homicide in a shabby beachfront area; Asbury Park, New Jersey, supplied the locations. He knows so much about police work his autopilot is better than most cops' bright ideas. His partner, Reg (George Dzundza), who has eaten too many doughnuts over the years, soldiers along with him. La Marca walked out on his wife (Patti LuPone) and son fourteen years ago, and now tentatively dates his upstairs neighbor, Michelle (Frances McDormand).

The cop's story is intercut with the life of his son, Joey (James Franco), a strung-out addict who has worked himself into a fearful situation involving debt and need. In a confusing struggle, he knifes a drug dealer and eventually, inevitably, La Marca is working the case and discovers that the killer may have been Joey.

If this story sounds a little too symmetrical and neat, and in a way it does, real life supplies a rebuttal: *City by the Sea* is based on a true story, as described by writer Mike McAlary in a 1997 *Esquire* article. I learn from *Variety,* however, that in fact the murder the son committed was vicious and premeditated, and not, as it is here, more or less an accident.

The plot takes us places we have been before, right down to the scene where La Marca resigns from the force and places his gun and badge on the captain's desk. There is also the possibility in La Marca's mind that his son is innocent—he claims he is—and there is the enormous psychic burden caused by the fact that La Marca's own father was convicted of a heartless murder. The last act of the movie is the sort of cat-and-mouse chase we have seen before, staged with expertise by director Michael Caton-Jones, but the movie's heart isn't in the action but in the character of Vince La Marca.

De Niro has worked so long and so frequently that there is sometimes the tendency to take him for granted. He is familiar. He has a range dictated by his face, voice, and inescapable mannerisms, but he rarely goes on autopilot and he makes an effort to newly invent his characters. Here he is a man with a wounded boy inside. Most of the time the cop routine provides him with a template for behavior: He keeps his head low, he does his job well. But inside is the kid who found out his dad was a killer. That provides the twist when he finds himself on his own son's case. There is hurt here, and De Niro is too good an actor to reduce it to a plot gimmick. He feels it.

Details of the plot I will not reveal, except to observe that the context of the murder and the condition of the son leave enough room for the La Marca character to believe, or want to believe, that his son may be innocent. That leads to the scene where he turns in his badge and gun, accusing his boss of having already made up his mind. And it leaves La Marca free-floating, because without the protection of the job he is now nakedly facing a situation that churns up his own past.

Frances McDormand takes a routine, even obligatory, character and makes her into an important part of the movie. The female confidante is usually dispensable in cop movies, except for a few scenes where she provides an ear for necessary exposition. Not here. McDormand's Michelle likes La Marca, but more important, she worries about him, sees the inner wounds, provides a balm, and knows about tough love.

City by the Sea is not an extraordinary movie. In its workmanship it aspires not to be remarkable but to be well made, dependable, moving us because of the hurt in the hero's eyes. A better movie might have abandoned the crime paraphernalia and focused on the pain between the generations, but then this director,

Michael Caton-Jones, has already made that movie with De Niro. *This Boy's Life* (1993) had De Niro as a harsh adoptive father and Leonardo DiCaprio as his resentful son. A better movie, but *City by the Sea* is a good one.

City of Ghosts ★ ★ ★
R, 116 m., 2003

Matt Dillon (Jimmy Cremming), James Caan (Marvin), Natascha McElhone (Sophie), Gérard Depardieu (Emile), Kem Sereyvuth (Sok), Stellan Skarsgard (Casper), Rose Byrne (Sabrina). Directed by Matt Dillon and produced by Willi Bar, Michael Cerenzie, and Deepak Nayar. Screenplay by Dillon and Barry Gifford.

When a hurricane wipes out large parts of the East Coast, many homeowners are understandably alarmed to learn that their insurer, the Capable Trust Co., is incapable of paying their claims because it has no money in the bank. Jimmy Cremming is also upset, or so he tells the cops. Played by Matt Dillon, he runs the U.S. office of the company, which is owned by a shady figure named Marvin, who when last heard from was in Cambodia. When federal agents start asking difficult questions, Jimmy leaves for Phnom Penh to find Marvin.

This is, you will agree, a preposterous setup for a movie. And the rest of the plot of *City of Ghosts* is no more believable. But believability is not everything, as I have to keep reminding myself in these days of *The Matrix Reloaded*. Character and mood also count for something—and so does location, since Matt Dillon shot his movie mostly on location in Cambodia; it's the first picture primarily filmed there since *Lord Jim* in 1965.

Dillon and his cinematographer, Jim Denault, find locations that don't look like locations; they have the untidiness and random details of real places, as indeed they are, and I particularly liked the hotel and bar run by Gérard Depardieu, who shambles around with a big shirt hanging over his belly and breaks up fights while casually holding a baby in his arms. Although such bars, and such exiles as proprietors, are standard in all *film noir* set in exotic

locations, this one had a funky reality that made me muse about a sequel in which we'd find out more about Depardieu, the baby, and a monkey he seems to have trained as a pickpocket.

In such movies, all visitors to Asia from the West quickly find a local helper who is instantly ready to risk his life to help the foreigner. Mel Gibson's character found Billy Kwan in *The Year of Living Dangerously*, and Dillon's character finds Sok (Kem Sereyvuth), a pedicab driver who serves as chauffeur, spy, and adviser to the outsider. Also hanging around the bar is Casper (Stellan Skarsgard), who says he works with the mysterious Marvin and conveys enigmatic messages. The one character who seems unlikely, although obligatory, is the beautiful woman Sophie (Natascha McElhone), who is an art historian but finds time to get tender with Jimmy. (I wonder if movie Americans who land in Asia are supplied with a list, so they can check off Friendly Bartender, Local Helper, Sinister Insider, Beautiful Girl, Monkey . . .)

Marvin is kept offscreen so long that he begins to take on the psychic heft of Harry Lime in *The Third Man*. Such a concealed character needs to have presence when he is revealed, and James Caan rises to the occasion, as a financial hustler who not only stiffed the policyholders of Capable Trust but now seems to be in bed with the Russian Mafia in a scheme to build a luxury hotel and casino.

When and how Jimmy finds Marvin, and what happens then, are surprises for the plot to reveal. What can be said is that the details of Marvin's scheme, and the plans of his enemies, seem more than a little muddled, and yet Dillon, as director, handles them in a way that makes the moments convincing, even if they don't add up.

City of Ghosts reminded me of *The Quiet American*, which likewise has visiting Westerners, beautiful women, sinister local figures, etc. It lacks a monkey, but has a more sharply told story, one with a message. *The Quiet American* was based on Graham Greene's novel about America's illegal activities, circa 1960, in Vietnam. The screenplay for *City of Ghosts*, by Dillon and sometime David Lynch collaborator Barry Gifford, avoids a rich vein of true Cambodian stories and recycles the kind of generic financial crimes that Hollywood perfected in the 1940s.

Still, sometimes the very texture of the film, and the information that surrounds the characters on the screen, make it worth seeing. I didn't believe in James Caan's cons, but I believed him, and at times like that it's helpful to stop keeping score and live in the moment. Between the Caan and Dillon characters there are atmosphere, desperation, and romance, and, at the end, something approaching true pathos. Enough.

City of God ★ ★ ★ ★
R, 135 m., 2003

Matheus Nachtergaele (Sandro Cenoura), Seu Jorge (Knockout Ned), Alexandre Rodrigues (Rocket), Leandro Firmino da Hora (L'il Zé), Phellipe Haagensen (Bené [Benny]), Jonathan Haagensen (Cabeleira [Shaggy]), Douglas Silva (Dadinho), Roberta Rodriguez Silvia (Berenice), Graziela Moretto (Marina), Renato de Souza (Goose). Directed by Fernando Meirelles and produced by Andrea Barata Ribeiro and Mauricio Andrade Ramos. Screenplay by Bráulio Mantovani, based on the novel by Paulo Lins. In Portuguese with English subtitles.

City of God churns with furious energy as it plunges into the story of the slum gangs of Rio de Janeiro. Breathtaking and terrifying, urgently involved with its characters, it announces a new director of great gifts and passions. Fernando Meirelles. Remember the name. The film has been compared with Martin Scorsese's *Good-Fellas,* and it deserves the comparison. Scorsese's film began with a narrator who said that for as long as he could remember he wanted to be a gangster. The narrator of this film seems to have had no other choice.

The movie takes place in slums constructed by Rio to isolate the poor people from the city center. They have grown into places teeming with life, color, music, and excitement—and also with danger, for the law is absent and violent gangs rule the streets. In the virtuoso sequence opening the picture, a gang is holding a picnic for its members when a chicken escapes.

Among those chasing it is Rocket (Alexandre Rodrigues), the narrator. He suddenly finds himself between two armed lines: the gang on one side, the cops on the other.

As the camera whirls around him, the background changes and Rocket shrinks from a teenager into a small boy, playing soccer in a housing development outside Rio. To understand his story, he says, we have to go back to the beginning, when he and his friends formed the Tender Trio and began their lives of what some would call crime and others would call survival.

The technique of that shot—the whirling camera, the flashback, the change in colors from the dark brightness of the slum to the dusty, sunny browns of the soccer field—alert us to a movie that is visually alive and inventive as few films are. Meirelles began as a director of TV commercials, which gave him a command of technique—and, he says, trained him to work quickly, to size up a shot, and get it and move on. Working with the cinematographer César Charlone, he uses quick-cutting and a mobile, handheld camera to tell his story with the haste and detail it deserves. Sometimes those devices can create a film that is merely busy, but *City of God* feels like sight itself, as we look here and then there, with danger or opportunity everywhere.

The gangs have money and guns because they sell drugs and commit robberies. But they are not very rich because their activities are limited to the City of God, where no one has much money. In an early crime, we see the stickup of a truck carrying cans of propane gas, which the crooks sell to homeowners. Later there is a raid on a bordello, where the customers are deprived of their wallets. (In a flashback, we see that raid a second time, and understand in a chilling moment why there were dead bodies at a site where there was not supposed to be any killing.)

As Rocket narrates the lore of the district he knows so well, we understand that poverty has undermined all social structures in the City of God, including the family. The gangs provide structure and status. Because the gang death rate is so high, even the leaders tend to be surprisingly young, and life has no value except when you are taking it. There is an astonishing sequence when a victorious gang leader is killed in a way he least expects, by the last person he would have expected, and we see that essentially he has been killed not by a person but by the culture of crime.

Yet the film is not all grim and violent. Rocket also captures some of the Dickensian flavor of the City of God, where a riot of life provides ready-made characters with nicknames, personas, and trademarks. Some, like Benny (Phellipe Haagensen), are so charismatic they almost seem to transcend the usual rules. Others, like Knockout Ned and L'il Ze, grow from kids into fearsome leaders, their words enforced by death.

The movie is based on a novel by Paulo Lins, who grew up in the City of God, somehow escaped it, and spent eight years writing his book. A note at the end says it is partly based on the life of Wilson Rodriguez, a Brazilian photographer. We watch as Rocket obtains a (stolen) camera that he treasures, and takes pictures from his privileged position as a kid on the streets. He gets a job as an assistant on a newspaper delivery truck, asks a photographer to develop his film, and is startled to see his portrait of an armed gang leader on the front page of the paper.

"This is my death sentence," he thinks, but no: The gangs are delighted by the publicity, and pose for him with their guns and girls. And during a vicious gang war, he is able to photograph the cops killing a gangster—a murder they plan to pass off as gang-related. That these events throb with immediate truth is indicated by the fact that Luiz Inacio Lula da Silva, the president of Brazil, actually reviewed and praised *City of God* as a needful call for change.

In its actual level of violence, *City of God* is less extreme than Scorsese's *Gangs of New York,* but the two films have certain parallels. In both films, there are really two cities: the city of the employed and secure, who are served by law and municipal services, and the city of the castaways, whose alliances are born of opportunity and desperation. Those who live beneath rarely have their stories told. *City of God* does not exploit or condescend, does not pump up its stories for contrived effect, does not contain silly and reassuring romantic sidebars, but simply looks, with a passionately knowing eye, at what it knows. ☞

The Clearing ★ ★ ★
R, 91 m., 2004

Robert Redford (Wayne Hayes), Helen Mirren (Eileen Hayes), Willem Dafoe (Arnold Mack), Alessandro Nivola (Tim Hayes), Matt Craven (Agent Ray Fuller), Melissa Sagemiller (Jill Hayes), Wendy Crewson (Louise Miller). Directed by Pieter Jan Brugge and produced by Brugge, Jonah Smith, and Palmer West. Screenplay by Justin Haythe and Brugge.

A movie that begins with a pleasant morning in an ordinary marriage is never about mornings or marriages. As *The Clearing* opens, we meet Wayne and Eileen Hayes, long and apparently happily married, in their elegant stone-walled mansion in a woodsy suburb. Wayne (Robert Redford) gets in his car, at the end of his driveway stops for a man who seems to know him, and finds himself kidnapped at gunpoint. Eileen (Helen Mirren) has a cup of coffee at the side of their pool.

We've already met the kidnapper, a man named Arnold Mack (Willem Dafoe). He lives with his perpetually disappointed wife and her father in a row house in a nearby city. We see him paste on a mustache in the mirror, which seems odd, and we follow him as he travels to his work (kidnapping) on a commuter train. Arnold approaches Wayne with such easy familiarity, waving a manila envelope as if it contained important papers, that Wayne automatically stops and puts down the car window for him. Perhaps he even sort of remembers him, or feels that good manners require him to say that he does.

The movie intercuts between two story lines: Wayne, his hands tied, led by Arnold on a long trek at gunpoint through a wooded area; and Eileen, concerned when he doesn't return home and eventually calling in the FBI. These time lines are not parallel, a fact that eventually occurs to us, along with its implications.

We learn a lot about Wayne as he and Arnold talk. Arnold has studied up on him, knows he's a self-made millionaire who bought and sold a car rental company at the right time. Wayne is rich, lives surrounded by luxury, and is expensively dressed, but he has the tough instincts of a negotiator, and tries to talk Arnold out of the kidnapping. Arnold says the men who hired him are waiting in a cottage at the end of their walk, and Wayne asks him why those men should honor their deal with him. Arnold, who is not a professional criminal, listens politely and perhaps agrees with some of what Wayne says.

In the mansion, Eileen deals with an FBI agent (Matt Craven) who is all business, too much business. Her children, Tim and Jill (Alessandro Nivola and Melissa Sagemiller), join the vigil with their mother, and privately share an interesting insight: At first, their mother was afraid Wayne might simply have run away from the marriage. The FBI man finds out about an affair Wayne had, and discusses it in front of the children. That angers Eileen, who knew about it but didn't want them to know. And it sets up one of the most extraordinary scenes in the movie, a meeting between Eileen and Louise Miller (Wendy Crewson), who was her husband's mistress. This scene is written so precisely and acted so well that it sidesteps all the hazards of jealousy and sensation, and becomes simply a discussion of emotional realities.

What happens, of course, I cannot reveal, nor will it be what you expect. Indeed, the events in a late scene are so unexpected and yet so logical that we are nodding with agreement as we react with surprise. And there is another scene, after that, indirectly dealing with psychological truth, with why people do the things they do, although I must say no more.

The Clearing is the first film directed by the successful producer Pieter Jan Brugge *(The Insider, The Pelican Brief, Heat)*. The screenplay is by Brugge and Justin Haythe, a British novelist. They know how to make a conventional thriller, but are not interested in making one. Instead, they use the crime here as the engine to drive their parallel psychological portraits. While Eileen has the reality of her marriage made uncomfortably clear, Wayne and Arnold engage in a little subtle class warfare. Wayne acts as if he was born to lead, and Arnold thinks of himself as a born loser with one last chance to hit a jackpot. Certainly, kidnapping offers enormous penalties and uncertain rewards, and Wayne thinks maybe Arnold doesn't really have the stomach for it.

What finally happens, and how, has a certain inevitable rightness to it, but you can't say you see it coming, especially since *The Clearing* doesn't feel bound by the usual formulas of crime movies. What eventually happens will emerge from the personalities of the characters, not from the requirements of Hollywood endings. Sensing that, we grow absorbed in the story, knowing that what happens along the way will decide what happens at the end.

Clockstoppers ★ ★ ½
PG, 90 m., 2002

Jesse Bradford (Zak Gibbs), French Stewart (Dr. Earl Dopler), Paula Garces (Francesca De La Cruz), Michael Biehn (Henry Gates), Robin Thomas (Dr. George Gibbs), Gariyaki Mutambirwa (Danny Meeker). Directed by Jonathan Frakes and produced by Gale Anne Hurd and Julia Pistor. Screenplay by Rob Hedden, J. David Stem, and David N. Weiss.

In an early scene of *Clockstoppers*, a student in a college physics class is unable to complete the phrase, "Einstein's Theory of . . ." And just as well, too, since any time-manipulation movie has to exist in blissful ignorance of Einstein's theory. Not that it can't be done, at least in the movies. *Clockstoppers* has a new twist: The traveler doesn't travel through time but stays right where he is and lives faster. This is closer to Einstein's Theory of Amphetamines.

Dr. George Gibbs (Robin Thomas) has invented a way for a subject to live much faster than those around him, so that they seem to stand in place while he whizzes around. He is like the mayfly, which lives a lifetime in a day—and that is precisely the trouble. The system works well, but experimenters age so quickly that they return looking worn and wrinkled, like Keir Dullea in *2001*, who checks into that alien bedroom, doesn't check out. Gibbs needs to iron out a few kinks.

Before he can perfect his discovery, intrigue strikes. His teenage son, Zak (Jesse Bradford), is informed by the friendly Dr. Earl Dopler (French Stewart) that Gibbs has been kidnapped into hyperspace by the evil and scheming millionaire Henry Gates (Michael Biehn). Dopler is named after the Effect. I have no idea how they came up with the name of Gates.

Zak has just met the beautiful Francesca De La Cruz (Paula Garces), a pretty student from Venezuela, at his high school, and they find themselves teamed on a mission to venture into hyperspace, rescue his father, outsmart Gates, and return without becoming senior citizens. (That's if hyperspace is the same place as speeded-up-time-space, and frankly the movie lost me there.) To assist in their mission they use a gun that fires marbles filled with liquid nitrogen, which burst on impact and instantly freeze their targets. That this gun is not fatal is a fact the movie wisely makes no attempt to explain.

Clockstoppers has high energy, bright colors, neat sets, and intriguing effects as the speeded-up characters zip around. There is a time when Zak outsmarts characters who are merely speeded-up by speeding up while *in* speed-space, or whatever it's called, so that he whizzes around the whizzers while emitting a kind of pulsing glow.

The movie has been produced by Nickelodeon, and will no doubt satisfy its intended audience enormously. It does not cross over into the post-Nickelodeon universe. Unlike *Spy Kids* or *Big Fat Liar,* it offers few consolations for parents and older brothers and sisters. It is what it is, efficiently and skillfully, and I salute it for hitting a double or maybe a triple. I also like the dialogue of Dr. ("Don't blow your RAM") Dopler. No one can be altogether uninteresting who makes a verb out of "ginzu."

Note: At one point the characters pass a high-security checkpoint and have to submit to a retinal scan. In a subtle bow to the Americans with Disabilities Act, the retinal scan device is at waist level.

Coffee and Cigarettes ★ ★ ★

R, 96 m., 2004

With Roberto Benigni, Steven Wright, Joie Lee, Cinque Lee, Steve Buscemi, Iggy Pop, Tom Waits, Joe Rigano, Vinny Vella, Vinny Vella Jr., Renee French, E. J. Rodriguez, Alex Descas, Isaach De Bankole, Cate Blanchett, Meg White, Jack White, Alfred Molina, Steve Coogan, GZA, RZA, Bill Murray, Bill Rice, and Taylor Mead. Directed by Jim Jarmusch and produced by Joana Vicente and Jason Kliot. Screenplay by Jarmusch.

Jim Jarmusch has been working on *Coffee and Cigarettes* for so long that when he started the project, you could still smoke in a coffee shop. The idea was to gather unexpected combinations of actors and, well, let them talk over coffee and cigarettes. He began with the short film *Coffee and Cigarettes I,* filmed in 1986, before we knew who Roberto Benigni was (unless we'd seen Jarmusch's *Down by Law*). Benigni the verbal hurricane strikes the withdrawn Steven Wright, and is so eager to do him a favor that he eventually goes to the dentist for him.

There's no more to it than that, but how much more do you need? A few minutes, and the skit is over. None of these eleven vignettes overstays its welcome, although a few seem to lose their way. And although Jarmusch has the writing credit, we have the feeling at various moments (as when Bill Murray walks in on a conversation between RZA and GZA of Wu-Tang Clan and exchanges herbal remedies with them) that improvisation plays a part.

My favorite among the segments is one of the longest, starring the actors Alfred Molina and Steve Coogan. Molina has asked for the meeting. Coogan is not sure why, and grows more condescending as Molina, all politeness and charm, explains that his genealogical researchers have discovered that the two men are related through a common Italian ancestor centuries ago. Molina hopes perhaps this connection might lead to them becoming friends and "doing things together." Coogan is distinctly unenthusiastic, until Molina says something that impresses him, and then he becomes ingratiating. In its compact way, this segment contains a lot of human nature.

The structure—smoking and drinking—provides all the explanation we need for the meetings, although sometimes the actors seem to smoke a little too self-consciously, and Murray drinks his coffee straight from the pot. The prize for virtuosity goes to Cate Blanchett, who plays a dual role: herself and her cousin. As herself, she is the movie star Cate Blanchett. As her cousin, she is quietly jealous of Cate's success, and feels patronized when Cate gives her some perfume—a bottle, she correctly guesses, that the star just received as a freebie.

The third of the segments to be filmed, "Somewhere in California," won the award for best short at Cannes and is a little masterpiece of observation about two musicians acutely aware of who they are and who the other one is, while trying to appear unimpressed. Tom Waits and Iggy Pop star, in a subtle bout of one-upmanship. Agreeing that they have given up smoking, they smoke—which is okay, they agree, as long as they've given it up. They're sitting next to a jukebox, which leads to a little understated competition over who does, or doesn't, have songs on the machine.

Sometimes a segment depends largely on the screen persona of an actor. That's the case with a conversation between Cinque and Joie Lee and Steve Buscemi, who confides incredible facts to them in an all-knowing style, so confident they are powerless to penetrate it. Elvis was replaced by his twin brother, Buscemi explains, but it's not the theory that's amusing so much as his determination to force it upon two listeners manifestly not eager to hear it.

Sometimes movies tire us by trying too relentlessly to pound us with their brilliance and energy. Here is a movie pitched at about the energy level of a coffee break. That the people are oddly assorted and sometimes very strange is not so very unusual, considering some of the conversations you overhear in Starbucks.

Cold Creek Manor ★ ½
R, 118 m., 2003

Dennis Quaid (Cooper Tilson), Sharon Stone (Leah Tilson), Stephen Dorff (Dale Massie), Juliette Lewis (Ruby), Kristen Stewart (Kristen Tilson), Ryan Wilson (Jesse Tilson), Dana Eskelson (Sheriff Annie Ferguson), Christopher Plummer (Mr. Massie). Directed by Mike Figgis and produced by Figgis and Annie Stewart. Screenplay by Richard Jefferies.

Cold Creek Manor is another one of those movies where a demented fiend devotes an extraordinary amount of energy to setting up scenes for the camera. Think of the trouble it would be for one man, working alone, to kill a horse and dump it into a swimming pool. The movie is an anthology of clichés, not neglecting both the Talking Killer, who talks when he should be at work, and the reliable climax where both the villain and his victims go to a great deal of inconvenience to climb to a high place so that one of them can fall off.

The movie stars Dennis Quaid and Sharon Stone as Cooper and Leah Tilson, who get fed up with the city and move to the country, purchasing a property that looks like The House of the Seven Gables crossed with The Amityville Horror. This house is going to need a lot of work. In Under the Tuscan Sun, Diane Lane is able to find some cheerful Polish workers to rehab her Tuscan villa, but the Tilsons have the extraordinarily bad judgment to hire the former owner of the house, Dale Massie (Stephen Dorff), an ex-con with a missing family. "Do you know what you're getting yourselves into?" asks a helpful local. No, but everybody in the audience does.

The movie of course issues two small children to the Tilsons, so that their little screams can pipe up on cue, as when the beloved horse is found in the pool. And both Cooper and Leah are tinged with the suggestion of adultery, because in American movies, as we all know, sexual misconduct leads to bad real estate choices.

In all movies involving city people who move to the country, there is an unwritten rule that everybody down at the diner knows all about the history of the new property and the secrets of its former owners. The locals act as a kind of Greek chorus, living permanently at the diner and prepared on a moment's notice to issue portentous warnings or gratuitous insults. The key player this time is Ruby (Juliette Lewis), Dale's battered girlfriend, whose sister is Sheriff Annie Ferguson (Dana Eskelson). Ruby smokes a lot, always an ominous sign, and is ambiguous about Dale—she loves the lug, but gee, does he always have to be pounding on her? The scene where she claims she wasn't hit, she only fell, is the most perfunctory demonstration possible of the battered woman in denial.

No one in this movie has a shred of common sense. The Tilsons are always leaving doors open even though they know terrible dangers lurk outside, and they are agonizingly slow to realize that Dale Massie is not only the wrong person to rehab their house, but the wrong person to be in the same state with.

Various clues, accompanied by portentous music, ominous winds, gathering clouds, etc., lead to the possibility that clues to Dale's crimes can be found at the bottom of an old well, and we are not disappointed in our expectation that Sharon Stone will sooner or later find herself at the bottom of that well. But answer me this: If you were a vicious mad-dog killer and wanted to get rid of the Tilsons and had just pushed Leah down the well, and Cooper was all alone in the woods leaning over the well and trying to pull his wife back to the surface, would you just go ahead and push him in? Or what?

But no. The audience has to undergo an extended scene in which Cooper is not pushed down the well, in order for everyone to hurry back to the house, climb up to the roof, fall off, etc. Dale Massie is not a villain in this movie, but an enabler, a character who doesn't want to kill but exists only to expedite the plot. Everything he does is after a look at the script, so that he appears, disappears, threatens, seems nice, looms, fades, pushes, doesn't push, all so that we in the audience can be frightened or, in my case, amused.

Cold Creek Manor was directed by Mike Figgis, a superb director of drama *(Leaving Las Vegas)*, digital experimentation *(Timecode)*, adaptations of the classics *(Miss Julie)*, and atmospheric *film noir (Stormy Monday)*. But he has made a thriller that thrills us only if we abandon all common sense. Of course, preposterous things happen in all thrillers, but there must be at least a gesture in the direction of plausibility, or we lose patience. When evil Dale Massie just stands there in the woods and doesn't push Cooper Tilson down the well, he stops being a killer and becomes an excuse for the movie to toy with us—and it's always better when a thriller toys with the victims instead of the audience.

Cold Mountain ★ ★ ★

R, 150 m., 2003

Jude Law (Inman), Nicole Kidman (Ada Monroe), Renée Zellweger (Ruby Thewes), Donald Sutherland (Reverend Monroe), Ray Winstone (Teague), Brendan Gleeson (Stobrod Thewes), Philip Seymour Hoffman (Reverend Veasey), Natalie Portman (Sara), Eileen Atkins (Maddy), Giovanni Ribisi (Junior), Kathy Baker (Sally Swanger). Directed by Anthony Minghella and produced by Albert Berger, William Horberg, Sydney Pollack, and Ron Yerxa. Screenplay by Minghella, based on the book by Charles Frazier.

Cold Mountain has the same structural flaw as *The Mexican* (2001), a movie you've forgotten all about. Both stories establish a torrid romantic magnetism between two big stars, and then keep them far apart for almost the entire movie. Filling the gap in both films is a quirky supporting character who makes us unreasonably grateful, because the leads take themselves very seriously indeed, and speak as if being charged by the word. Hardly anybody but me gave *The Mexican* a favorable review, and I'm sort of in favor of *Cold Mountain,* too—not because of the noble and portentous reasons you will read about in the ads, but because it evokes a backwater of the Civil War with beauty, and lights up with an assortment of colorful supporting characters.

The movie stars Nicole Kidman as Ada Monroe, the daughter of a Charleston preacher man (Donald Sutherland) who has moved to the district for his health. The first time she meets Inman (Jude Law), their eyes lock and a deep, unspoken communication takes place. Inman, as shy and awkward as a ploughboy in a ballet, contrives excuses to be standing about slack-jawed when she comes into view, but she has mercy on him, and after he has joined the Confederates and gone off to fight the war, she observes, "I count the number of words that have passed between us, Inman and me—not very many. But I think about it." So few are their meetings, indeed, that later in the story they're able to count off on their fingers every time they have seen each other, and it doesn't take long enough to make us restless.

Ada's father dies, leaving her as a poor city girl to farm the land, something she is ill-equipped to do. A sensible neighbor lady dispatches an energetic young woman named Ruby (Renée Zellweger) to help out, and Ruby sets to work splitting rails, milking cows, wringing turkey necks, and expressing herself of opinions so colorful Garrison Keillor would blush with envy. Ruby and Ada are also prepared to stand in their doorway with a rifle when necessary, and just as well, since the home guard is captained by Teague (Ray Winstone), who figures Inman isn't going to come home, and that Ada will need a man to protect her—against Teague, for that matter.

Inman witnesses one of the most horrible battles of the war, in a set-piece that director Anthony Minghella and production designer Dante Ferratti can be proud of. After Union troops tunnel under Confederate lines and set off powerful explosives, the position caves in— but not with the expected results. The Union men, pushed forward by those behind them, are hurled down into the vast bomb crater, and it's a "turkey shoot" as the Confederates pick them off. That Inman jumps down to save a friend is unwise, that he survives is unlikely, and that he decides to heed the latest letter from Ada and walk away from the war and back to her is unsurprising.

His long trek back to Cold Mountain has been compared with some justice to Homer's *Odyssey*, since he meets fabled characters and seductresses along the way, but in a movie that begins with the two heroes barely meeting each other, this long sequence becomes alarming: Will their reunion take place in old age?

To return to the comparison with *The Mexican*—it too went to extraordinary lengths to tell parallel stories that separated Brad Pitt and Julia Roberts, despite the manifest fact that the audience had purchased tickets in order to see them together. It was only the fortuitous appearance of a colorful crook played by James Gandolfini that saved the film and brought life to Roberts's scenes—just as, this time, Renée Zellweger saves the day.

There is so much to enjoy about *Cold Mountain* that I can praise it for its parts, even though it lacks a whole. I admire the characters played by Kidman and Law, even though each one is an island, entire to himself. I loved Renée Zellweger's gumption, and the way she treats a dress like a dishrag. The battle scenes and the Civil War landscapes (shot in Romania) had beauty and majesty. But Ray Winstone's villain turns up so faithfully when required that he ought to be checking his clock like Captain Hook, and although there is true poignancy in Inman's encounter with the desperate widow Sara (Natalie

Portman), it is poignancy that belongs in another movie. Nothing takes the suspense out of Boy Meets Girl like your knowledge that Boy Has Already Met Star.

By the end of the film you admire the artistry and the care, you know that the actors worked hard and are grateful for their labors, but you wonder who in God's name thought this was a promising scenario for a movie. It's not a story; it's an idea. Consider even the letters that Ada and Inman write each other. You can have a perfectly good love story based on correspondence—but only, I think, if the letters arrive, are read, and are replied to. There are times when we feel less like the audience than like the post office.

Collateral Damage ★ ★ ★
R, 115 m., 2002

Arnold Schwarzenegger (Gordon Brewer), Elias Koteas (CIA Agent Peter Brandt), Francesca Neri (Selena Perrini), Cliff Curtis (Claudio "The Wolf" Perrini), John Leguizamo (Felix Ramirez), John Turturro (Sean Armstrong). Directed by Andrew Davis and produced by David Foster, Peter MacGregor-Scott, and Steven Reuther. Screenplay by David Griffiths and Peter Griffiths.

Collateral Damage is a relic from an earlier (if not kinder and gentler) time, a movie about terrorism made before terrorists became the subject of our national discourse. "You Americans are so naive," says the movie's terrorist villain. "You see a peasant with a gun, you change the channel. But you never ask why a peasant needs a gun." Well, we still don't wonder why the peasant needs the gun (we think we should have the gun), but we're not so naive anymore.

The movie stars Arnold Schwarzenegger as Brewer, a Los Angeles fireman who sees his wife and son killed by a terrorist bomb. Vowing revenge, he flies to Colombia, escapes several murder attempts, survives an improbable trip down a waterfall, penetrates guerrilla territory, kills a lot of people, and blows up a lot of stuff. He is your typical Los Angeles fireman if the fire department sent all of its men through Delta Force training.

To review this movie in the light of 9/11 is not really fair. It was made months earlier, and indeed its release date was postponed in the aftermath of the attack. That has escaped the attention of the Rev. Brian Jordan, a priest who, according to the Associated Press, ministers to workers at Ground Zero. "Making the main character a firefighter who becomes a vigilante is an insult to the firefighters who became heroes after the terrorist attacks," he says. He adds that the film discriminates against Colombians; his fellow protesters said the movie will "cement stereotypes that Colombians are drug traffickers and guerrillas, rather than hardworking, educated people."

Jordan added that he has not seen the film. His criticism is therefore theoretical. He believes making a firefighter a vigilante in a movie made before the attacks is an insult now that the attacks have taken place. Would it have been an insult even if the attacks had not taken place? Why is it an insult? Should a firefighter not feel like avenging the murder of his family? As to the film's view of Colombia, since the guerrillas are shown as drug traffickers and enemies of the government, it seems clear they are not considered the majority of Colombians. The AP, which would not run the review of a critic who had not seen the film, felt Jordan was sufficiently qualified to attack it sight unseen. We await his further insights once he has seen it.

My guess is that the average firefighter, like the average American moviegoer, might sort of enjoy the movie, which is a skillfully made example of your typical Schwarzenegger action film. The Arnold character is uncomplicated, loyal, brave, and resourceful, and does only six or seven things that are impossible in the physical universe. The villains, it is true, give a bad name to Colombian guerrillas and drug traffickers. The only ambiguity comes in the person of a government agent played by Elias Koteas, who first refuses to share information with the FBI, and then appears to be an FBI agent himself. It's the kind of movie where you don't give that a passing thought.

I kept expecting a subtext in which the CIA or other American agencies were involved in skulduggery in Colombia, but no: The plot leads us to believe there may be a double agent on our side, but that's a blind alley. Instead, all leads up to a climax involving the planned de-struction of a Washington skyscraper, which is creepy and disturbing given our feelings about 9/11, but traditional in movies made earlier—when terrorism plots were standard in the movies. You may not want to attend *Collateral Damage* because of 9/11, but it hardly seems fair to attack it for not knowing then what we all know now.

That leaves me with a couple of tactical questions. There is an air attack on a guerrilla base where the fireman is being held captive. How can they be sure their rockets won't kill him? Or do they want to kill him? And there is a neatly timed rendezvous involving a terrorist and a man on a motorcycle that leads us to wonder, thinking back through the plot, how this plan could have been made. There are also some coincidences that are a little too neat, like how a fire ax saves lives in the first scene and then, at the end, becomes the fireman's handy and symbolic tool for creating one of those booby traps where you wonder how in the hell he could have figured that one out.

There will not be any more action stories like this for a long time. We're at the end of the tunnel, the light is out, the genre is closed. *Collateral Damage* may stir unwanted associations for some viewers. Others may attend it with a certain nostalgia, remembering a time when such scenarios fell under the heading of entertainment.

Comedian ★ ★
R, 100 m., 2002

As themselves: Jerry Seinfeld, Orny Adams, Bill Cosby, Robert Klein, Jay Leno, Chris Rock, and Garry Shandling. A documentary directed by Christian Charles and produced by Gary Streiner.

If it takes this much agony to be a stand-up comic, I don't think I could survive a movie about a brain surgeon. *Comedian* follows Jerry Seinfeld and other stand-ups as they appear on stage and then endlessly analyze, discuss, rerun, regret, denounce, forgive, and rewrite their material. To say they sweat blood is to trivialize their suffering.

It looks to the audience as if stand-up comics

walk out on a stage, are funny, walk off, and spend the rest of the time hanging around the bar being envied by wannabes. In fact, we discover, they agonize over "a minute," "five minutes," "ten minutes," on their way to nirvana: "I have an hour." When Chris Rock tells Seinfeld that Bill Cosby does two hours and twenty minutes *without an intermission*, and he does it *twice in the same day*, he becomes very sad and thoughtful, like a karaoke star when Tony Bennett walks in.

Seinfeld can't believe his good fortune. He reached the top with one of the biggest hit TV shows of all time. And yet: "Here I am in Cleveland." After retiring his old nightclub act with an HBO special, he starts from scratch to devise a new act and take it on the road to comedy clubs, half of which are called the Improv. He stands in front of the same brick walls, drinks the same bottled water, handles the same microphones as kids on the way up. Of course, he flies into town on a private jet that costs more than the comedy club, but the movie doesn't rub this in.

Seinfeld is a great star, yet cannot coast. One night he gets stuck in the middle of his act—he loses his train of thought—and stares baffled into space. Blowing a single word can depress him. If it's still a battle for Seinfeld, consider the case of Orny Adams, a rising comedian whom the film uses as counterpoint. Adams shows Seinfeld a room full of boxes, drawers, cabinets, file folders stuffed with jokes. There are piles of material, and yet he confides: "I feel like I sacrificed so much of my life. I'm twenty-nine, and I have no job, no wife, no children." Seinfeld regards him as if wife, children, home will all come in good time, but stand-up, now—stand-up is life.

Orny Adams gets a gig on the David Letterman program, and we see him backstage, vibrating with nervousness. The network guys have been over his material and suggested some changes. Now he practices saying the word "psoriasis." After the show, he makes a phone call to a friend to explain, "I opened my first great network show with a joke I had never used before." Well, not a *completely* new joke. He had to substitute the word "psoriasis" for the word "lupus." But to a comedian who fine-

tunes every syllable, that made it a new joke and a fearsome challenge.

Seinfeld pays tribute to Robert Klein ("he was the guy we all looked up to"). We listen to Klein remember when, after several appearances on *The Tonight Show*, he received the ultimate recognition: He was "called over" by Johnny. Seinfeld recalls that when he was ten he memorized the comedy albums of Bill Cosby. Now he visits Cosby backstage and expresses wonderment that "a human life could last so long that I would be included in your life." Big hug. Cosby is sixty-five, and Seinfeld is forty-eight, a seventeen-year difference that is therefore less amazing than that Shoshanna Lonstein's life could last so long that she could meet Jerry when she was eighteen and he was thirty-nine, but there you go.

Comedian was filmed over the course of a year by director Christian Charles and producer Gary Streiner, who used two "store-bought" video cameras and followed Seinfeld around. If that is all they did for a year, then this was a waste of their time, since the footage, however interesting, is the backstage variety that could easily be obtained in a week. There are no deep revelations, no shocking moments of truth, and many, many conversations in which Seinfeld and other comics discuss their acts with discouragement and despair. The movie was produced by Seinfeld, and protects him. The visuals tend toward the dim, the gray, and the washed-out, and you wish instead of spending a year with their store-boughts, they'd spent a month and used the leftover to hire a cinematographer.

Why, you might wonder, would a man with untold millions in the bank go on a tour of comedy clubs? What's in it for him, if the people in Cleveland laugh? Why, for that matter, does Jay Leno go to comedy clubs every single week, even after having been called over by Johnny for the ultimate reward? Is it because to walk out on the stage, to risk all, to depend on your nerve and skill, and to possibly "die," is an addiction? Gamblers, they say, don't want to win so much as they want to play. They like the action. They tend to keep gambling until they have lost all their money. There may be a connection between the two obsessions, although gamblers at least say they are having fun, and stand-up comics, judging by this film, are miserable, self-tortured beings to whom success only represents a higher place to fall from.

The Company ★ ★ ★ ½
PG-13, 112 m., 2003

Neve Campbell (Ry), Malcolm McDowell (Alberto Antonelli), James Franco (Josh), Barbara E. Robertson (Harriet), William Dick (Edouard), Susie Cusack (Susie). Directed by Robert Altman and produced by Joshua Astrachan and David Levy. Screenplay by Barbara Turner.

"You have to fiddle on the corner where the quarters are."

—Robert Altman

Why did it take me so long to see what was right there in front of my face—that *The Company* is the closest Robert Altman has come to making an autobiographical film? I've known him since 1970, have been on the sets of many of his films, had more than a drink with him in the old days, and know that this movie reflects exactly the way he works—how he assembles cast, story, and location and plunges in up to his elbows, stirring the pot. With Altman, a screenplay is not only a game plan but a diversionary tactic, to distract the actors (and characters) while Altman sees what they've got.

The Company involves a year in the life of the Joffrey Ballet of Chicago, during which some careers are born, others die, romance glows uncertainly, a new project begins as a mess and improbably starts to work, and there is never enough money. The central characters are Ry (Neve Campbell), a promising young dancer; Harriet (Barbara E. Robertson), a veteran who has paid her dues and keeps on paying; Josh (James Franco), a young chef who becomes Ry's lover; and Alberto Antonelli (Malcolm McDowell), the company's artistic director. It is said that "Mr. A" is based on Gerald Arpino, the Joffrey's legendary director and choreographer, and that no doubt is true. But there's another Mr. A standing right there in full view, and his name is Robert Altman.

The Player (1992) was Altman's film about the movie industry, an insider's look at the venality, ambition, romance, and genius of Hollywood. But *The Company* is his film about the creative process itself, and we see that ballet, like the movies, is a collaborative art form in which muddle and magic conspire, and everything depends on that most fragile of instruments, the human body.

There is a moment early in the film when a French-Canadian choreographer named Robert Desrosiers pitches a project named *Blue Snake* to Mr. A and he confesses himself baffled by the work and frightened by the budget. When Altman himself was pitched this screenplay by Neve Campbell and the writer Barbara Turner, he remembers saying: "Barbara, I read your script and I don't get it. I don't understand. I don't know what it is. I'm just the wrong guy for this." But in *The Company* Mr. A finds a glimmer of something in the new ballet, a nugget of authenticity, and begins to play with it. For a long stretch in the middle of the film, we may suspect that *Blue Snake* is a satiric target—a work so absurd that Altman wants it for target practice. The dancers seem to disdain it. Desrosiers can be insufferable. And then somehow, inexplicably, the work falls into place and is actually very good.

The *process* by which both Mr. As transform the material is the subject of the movie. At preview screenings of *The Company,* some Joffrey supporters in the audience were disappointed by the choice of *Blue Snake* and wondered why Altman hadn't closed with one of the pieces for which the company has become famous (several of those works are seen in the movie, including Arpino's *Trinity*). But that would have missed the point. This is a movie, not a dance concert documentary—the record not of a performance but of a process.

Altman is known for the way his camera tries to capture elusive moments as they happen. He uses overlapping dialogue, incomplete thoughts, and unresolved actions, showing us life in development. This time, using the flexibility of a digital camera, he takes what he can use from a fusion of fiction and real life. The love story between Ry and Josh doesn't take the foreground, as it might in a conventional film, but is part of the mix in the exhausting lives of the characters. They like each other and the sex is great, but they're ambitious young professionals with crazy schedules, and there's a scene where Josh cooks an elaborate dinner for Ry but she turns up very late and he has already fallen asleep, and yes, that's about right: He had to cook, she had to be late, because of who they are.

The movie almost offhandedly shows us how hard dancers work. To be a dancer in the Joffrey, one of the most respected companies in the world, is itself back-breaking. But then see how Ry rushes out to her second job, as a waitress in a beer and burger joint. And see the second-floor flat she lives in, with the El trains roaring right outside the window. This is a different reality than the glamorous Monte Carlo existence in a ballet classic like *The Red Shoes*. Altman observes the exhausting lifestyle, and then shows us the older dancer Harriet (Robertson), who is nearing the end of her professional life, and has made such sacrifices for years because—well, because she is one of the very few people in the world who can dance as she dances, and so she must.

There is a moment during rehearsal when a dancer's Achilles' tendon snaps. It is an audible pop, heard all over the stage, and everybody knows exactly what it means. It means she will not ever dance again. Altman handles this moment with cold-blooded realism. Instead of grief and violins and fraught drama, he shows the company almost frightening in its detachment. This could happen to any of them, they know it, there is nothing to be done about it, and the rehearsal must go on.

McDowell's performance as Mr. A is a case study in human management. He has strategies for playing the role of leader, for being inspirational, for being a disciplinarian, for remaining a mystery. He teaches obliquely ("You know how I hate pretty"). He has an assistant named Edouard (William Dick) whose primary duty seems to consist of signaling urgently so Mr. A can escape a situation by being needed elsewhere. Antonelli has a way of praising on the run ("You *are* a genius") and then hurrying out of the room. His style, which is similar to the style of Altman, is to lavish praise while always leaving everyone a little uncertain about whether he really means it.

Neve Campbell trained with the National Ballet of Canada before turning to acting as a career. She has been very good in movies like

Wild Things and *Panic,* and good in a different way in the *Scream* movies, but she had to initiate this project herself, and bring Turner on board as the writer. She plays the role with complete knowledge of Ry (maybe it's as much her autobiography as Altman's), and her dancing is always convincing. The movie comes out at the same time as *Monster,* with its remarkable performance by Charlize Theron; two actresses of about the same age, who have had success in the commercial mainstream, placed bets on themselves that they could do great work, and they were right.

As for Robert Altman, I imagine some of the most heartfelt scenes in the movie for him are the ones involving Mr. A's attempt to create art while always having to think about money. Altman has rarely had big box-office hits (his most popular film was one of his earliest, *M*A*S*H,* and yet he has found a way to work steadily— to be prolific despite almost always choosing projects he wants to work on. How does he do it? *The Company* offers some clues.

Confessions of a Dangerous Mind
★ ★ ★ ½
R, 113 m., 2002

Sam Rockwell (Chuck Barris), Drew Barrymore (Penny), George Clooney (Jim Byrd), Julia Roberts (Patricia Watson), Rutger Hauer (Keeler), Kristen Wilson (Loretta). Directed by George Clooney and produced by Andrew Lazar. Screenplay by Charlie Kaufman, based on the book by Chuck Barris.

I had not read the autobiography of Chuck Barris when I went to see *Confessions of a Dangerous Mind.* Well, how many people have? So I made an understandable error. When the movie claimed that the game show creator had moonlighted as a CIA hit man, I thought I was detecting a nudge from the screenwriter, Charlie Kaufman. He is the man who created the portal into John Malkovich's mind in *Being John Malkovich,* and gave himself a twin brother in *Adaptation.* Now, I thought, the little trickster had juiced up the Barris biopic by making the creator of *The Gong Show* into an assassin. What a card.

I am now better informed. Barris himself claims to have killed thirty-three times for the

CIA. It's in his book. He had the perfect cover: The creator of *The Dating Game* and *The Gong Show* would accompany his lucky winners on trips to romantic spots such as Helsinki in midwinter, and kill for the CIA while the winners regaled each other with reindeer steaks. Who, after all, would ever suspect him?

When I met Barris I asked him, as everyone does, if this story is true. He declined to answer. The book and the movie speak for themselves—or don't speak for themselves, depending on your frame of mind. As for myself, I think he made it all up and never killed anybody. Having been involved in a weekly television show myself, I know for a melancholy fact that there is just not enough time between tapings to fly off to Helsinki and kill for my government.

It matters not whether the story is true or false, because all autobiographies are fictional, made up out of that continuous subconscious rewriting process by which we make ourselves blameless and heroic. Barris has a particular need to be heroic, because he blamed himself for so much. As the movie opens in 1981, he is holed up in a New York hotel (the Chelsea, I think), mired in self-contempt and watching TV as his penance. It is here, he tells us in a confiding voice-over, that he began to record "my wasted life."

That this would be the first project to attract George Clooney as a director is not so surprising if you know that his father directed game shows, and he was often a backstage observer. That Clooney would direct it so well is a little surprising, and is part of that reeducation by which we stop thinking of Clooney as a TV hunk and realize he is smart and curious. His first movie is not only intriguing as a story but great to look at, a marriage of bright pop images from the 1960s and 1970s and dark, cold spyscapes that seem to have wandered in from John le Carré.

Sam Rockwell plays Barris as a man who was given gifts but not the ability to enjoy them. He is depressed not so much because he thinks he could have done better in his life, but because he fears he could not. From his start as an NBC page in 1955, through his backstage work on Dick Clark's *American Bandstand,* to the crushing blow of having ABC choose *Hootenanny* over his *Dating Game* pilot, Barris comes across

as a man who wants to succeed in order to confirm his low opinion of himself. When his shows finally make the air, the TV critics blame him for the destruction of Western civilization, and he doesn't think they're so far off.

The movie has fun with the TV shows. We are reminded once again of the Unknown Comic and Gene-Gene the Dancing Machine, and on an episode of *The Dating Game* we see a contestant choose Bachelor No. 3 when we can see that Bachelors 1 and 2 are Brad Pitt and Matt Damon. Early in his career, Barris is recruited by a CIA man named Jim Byrd (George Clooney), and agrees to become a secret agent, maybe as a way of justifying his existence. "Think of it as a hobby," Clooney says soothingly. "You're an assassination enthusiast."

Two women figure strongly in his life. Patricia Watson (Julia Roberts) is the CIA's Marlene Dietrich, her face sexily shadowed at a rendezvous. She gives him a quote from Nietzsche that could serve as his motto: "The man who despises himself still respects himself as he who despises." And then there's Penny (Drew Barrymore), the hippie chick who comes along at first for the ride, and remains to be his loyal friend, trying to talk him out of that hotel room.

Confessions of a Dangerous Mind makes a companion to Paul Schrader's *Auto-Focus,* the story of the rise and fall of *Hogan's Heroes* star Bob Crane. Both films show men whose secret lives are more exciting than the public lives that win them fame. Barris seems to want to redeem himself for the crimes he committed on television, while Crane uses his fame as a ticket to sex addiction. Both films lift up the cheerful rock of television to find wormy things crawling for cover. The difference is that Crane comes across as shallow and pathetic, while Barris—well, any man who would claim thirty-three killings as a way to rehabilitate his reputation deserves our sympathy and maybe our forgiveness.

Confidence ★ ★
R, 98 m., 2003

Edward Burns (Jake Vig), Rachel Weisz (Lily), Andy Garcia (Gunther Butan), Dustin Hoffman (King), Paul Giamatti (Gordo), Donal Logue (Whitworth), Luis Guzman (Manzano), Frankie G. (Lupus), Brian Van Holt (Miles). Directed by James Foley and produced by Michael Burns,

Marc Butan, Michael Ohoven, and Michael Paseornek. Screenplay by Doug Jung.

Confidence is a flawless exercise about con games, and that is precisely its failing: It is an exercise. It fails to make us care, even a little, about the characters and what happens to them. There is nothing at stake. The screenplay gives away the game by having the entire story narrated in flashback by the hero, who treats it not as an adventure but as a series of devious deceptions that he can patiently explain to the man holding a gun on him—and to us. At the end, we can see how smart he is and how everybody was fooled, but we don't care.

The obvious contrast is with David Mamet's *House of Games*, which also told a story of cons within cons, but which had stakes so high that at the end the victim called the con man's bluff by—well, by shooting him dead, after which he didn't have any twists left. We cared about those characters. *Confidence* lacks that passion and urgency; there are times when the narration sounds like the filmmakers at a pitch meeting, explaining how tricky their plot is and unable to keep the enthusiasm out of their voices.

That's not to say the movie, directed by James Foley, is badly made. It's great-looking, with its *film noir* reds and greens and blues, its neon Bud Ice signs, its shadows and mean streets, its sleazy strip clubs, and its use of wipes and swish-pans (sideways, up, down, sometimes two at a time). You know this is a crime movie, which is nice to be reminded of, except that every reminder also tells us it's only a movie, so that there is no possibility that we can commit to the characters, worry about them, want them to succeed or fail.

The movie stars Edward Burns as Jake Vig, a confidence mastermind, who has a crew of regulars and uses them to stage fake murders in order to scare marks into running away without their money. One day he makes the mistake of stealing $150,000 from the bagman for a nasty crimelord, the King (Dustin Hoffman). He confronts the King in his strip club and tells him he'll get the money back, but first he wants the King to supply an additional $200,000 as seed money for a $5 million scam Jake has in mind.

Jake's last name, Vig, is possibly short for "vigorish," the word gamblers use to describe the money the house takes off the top. If I were looking for someone to play with $200,000 of my money, I don't think I would choose a con man named Vig. But the King is confident that no one would even dream of cheating him, because he has such a fearsome reputation. And to keep an eye on Jake, he sends along his henchman Lupus (Frankie G.) to watch Jake's every move.

Dustin Hoffman's performance as the King is the best thing in the movie—indeed, the only element that comes to life on the screen. The King runs a strip club as a front, launders money for the mob, and suffers from attention deficit disorder—or, as he meticulously specifies, "attention deficit hyperactivity disorder." To control his condition, he takes pills that slow him way down. "Feel my heart," he says to one of the strippers in his club, to prove that it is hardly beating. Hoffman, chewing gum, wearing a beard and glasses, looks like the gnome from hell, and fast-talks his way into a brilliant supporting performance.

So brilliant, I couldn't help wondering how much energy the film would have gained if Hoffman, say, had played the lead instead of Burns. With Hoffman, you look at him and try to figure out what he's thinking. With Burns, you look at him and either you already know, or he doesn't make you care. Burns is the right actor for a lot of roles, especially young men tortured by the pangs of romance, but as a con man he lacks the shadings and edges. Once again, the comparison is with Joe Mantegna in *House of Games*.

Jake Vig's crew includes fellow hoods Gordo (Paul Giamatti) and Miles (Brian Van Holt). He has recently enlisted Lily (Rachel Weisz), who is very pretty and whom he likes—two ominous signs for a con man. And when he needs two guys to turn up and pretend to be L.A. cops, he has two real cops (Donal Logue and Luis Guzman) to play the roles. There is also the enigmatic federal agent Gunther Butan (Andy Garcia), whose name means "butane" in German, and who spends a great deal of time relighting his cigar. Garcia has been on Jake's tail for years, we learn, although he may simply represent a higher level in the game.

Confidence is a jerk-around movie, a film that works by jerking us around. I don't mind being misled and fooled in a clever way, especially when the movie makes me care about the characters before pulling the rug out from under them, or me. But there is no sense of risk here. No real stakes. It's all an entertainment, even for the characters, and at the end of the movie, as one surprise after another is revealed, there is no sense that these amazing revelations are really happening; no, they're simply the screenplay going through its final paces so the audience will appreciate the full extent to which it has been duped. What a shame that such a well-made movie is never able to convince us it is anything more than merely well made.

Connie and Carla ★ ½

PG-13, 98 m., 2004

Nia Vardalos (Connie), Toni Collette (Carla), David Duchovny (Jeff), Stephen Spinella (Robert/Peaches), Alec Mapa (Lee/N'Cream), Chris Logan (Brian/Brianna), Robert Kaiser (Paul), Debbie Reynolds (Herself). Directed by Michael Lembeck and produced by Gary Barber, Roger Birnbaum, Jonathan Glickman, Tom Hanks, and Rita Wilson. Screenplay by Nia Vardalos.

Connie and Carla plays like a genial amateur theatrical, the kind of production where you'd like it more if you were friends with the cast. The plot is creaky, the jokes are laborious, and total implausibility is not considered the slightest problem. Written by and starring Nia Vardalos, it's a disappointment after her hilarious *My Big Fat Greek Wedding*.

This time, in a retread of *Some Like It Hot*, Vardalos and Toni Collette play Connie and Carla, two friends who have been a singing duo since schooldays. Now they're in their thirties, stardom has definitely passed them by, and they perform a medley of musical comedy hits in an airport lounge that resembles no airport lounge in history, but does look a lot like somebody's rec room with some tables and chairs and a cheesy stage.

The guys they date beg them to face facts: They'll never really be any good. But they still dream the dream, and then, in a direct lift from *Some Like It Hot*, they witness a mob murder and have to go on the lam. The way this scene is handled is typical of the film's ham-handed approach: They're hiding in a parking garage when their boss is rubbed out, so what do they

do? Stay hidden? Nope, they both stand up, scream, and wave their hands. They have to: Otherwise, there wouldn't be any movie.

Connie and Carla hit the road, head for Los Angeles, happen into a drag bar, and inspiration strikes: They can pretend to be female impersonators! That way no one will find them, or even know where to look. One of the running gags in *Some Like It Hot* was that Jack Lemmon and Tony Curtis did not make very plausible women, but the movie handled that by surrounding them with dim bulbs like the characters played by Marilyn Monroe and Joe E. Brown. *Connie and Carla* is set in today's Los Angeles gay community, where the other characters are supposed to be real, I guess, and where never in a million years could they pass as boys passing as girls.

Their danger from the mob is put on hold as the movie switches to another reliable formula, the showbiz rags-to-riches epic. Their act, of course, is an immediate hit, they make lots of buddies among the other drag queens, and there are many close calls as they're almost discovered out of drag, or would that be not out of drag? The time scheme of the movie is sufficiently forgiving for them to suggest that their little club remodel itself and double in size; and there is actually a scene where the show goes on while plastic sheeting separates the old club from the new addition. Next scene, the construction work is finished. Forget the drag queens, get the names of those contractors.

Nia Vardalos was of course wonderful in *My Big Fat Greek Wedding*, and Toni Collette has proven she can do about anything—but she can't do this. The movie masks desperation with frenzied slapstick and forced laughs. And when Connie meets a straight guy she likes (David Duchovny), we groan as the plot manufactures Meet Cutes by having them repeatedly run into each other and knock each other down. Uh-huh. I think maybe the point in *Some Like It Hot* was that Joe E. Brown fell in love with Jack Lemmon, not Marilyn Monroe. I'm not saying *Connie and Carla* would have been better if Connie had attracted a gay guy, or maybe a lesbian who saw through the drag, but at least that would have supplied a comic problem, not a romantic one.

My Big Fat Greek Wedding was such a huge success that it gave Vardalos a free ticket for her next movie. Someone should have advised her this wasn't the right screenplay to cash in the pass. Nor does director Michael Lembeck save the day. He's done a lot of TV sitcoms, including many episodes of *Friends,* and his only other feature film, *The Santa Clause 2,* was funny enough, but here he took on an unfilmable premise and goes down with it. By the end, as the gangsters, the midwestern boyfriends, Duchovny, various drag queens, and Debbie Reynolds (herself) all descend on the finale, we're not watching a comedy, we're watching a traffic jam.

Control Room ★ ★ ★
NO MPAA RATING, 84 m., 2004

With Sameer Khader, Lieutenant Josh Rushing, Tom Mintier, Hassan Ibrahim, David Shuster, and Deema Khatib. A documentary directed by Jehane Noujaim and produced by Hani Salama and Rosadel Varela. Screenplay by Noujaim.

The final film I saw at Cannes 2004 came from Egypt and contained a surprise. It was *Alexandrie . . . New York,* by the veteran director Youssef Chahine, and it told the autobiographical story of an Egyptian who comes to America in 1950 to study at the Pasadena Playhouse, and returns again in 1975 and 2000. There is a lot more to it than that, but what struck me was when the student joined his classmates in singing "God Bless America" at the graduation. I hadn't heard that in an American film since *The Deer Hunter* in 1978. The character in 1950, and apparently the seventy-eight-year-old Egyptian who told his story, loved America.

I thought of them as I watched *Control Room,* an enlightening documentary about how the U.S. networks and the Arab satellite news channel Al Jazeera covered the early days of the war in Iraq. If Americans are familiar with Al Jazeera at all, it is because, as Donald Rumsfeld charges in the film, it is a source of anti-American propaganda, "willing to lie to the world to make their case." Yet there is an extraordinary moment in the film when Sameer Khadar, an engaging and articulate producer for Al Jazeera, confides that if he were offered a job with Fox News, he would take it. He wants his children to seek their futures in the United States, he says, and I carefully wrote down his

next words: "to exchange the Arab nightmare for the American dream." These are the words of a man Rumsfeld calls a liar. That many American news organizations, including the *New York Times,* have had to apologize for errors in their coverage of Iraq may indicate that Rumsfeld and his teammates may also have supplied them with . . . inaccuracies.

Khadar is seen in action, interviewing an American "analyst" named Jeffrey Steinberg who attacks U.S. policy. Afterward, Khadar is angry that his network arranged the interview: "He's just a crazy activist. He wasn't an analyst. He was just against America." We also see correspondents from CNN, Fox, and the networks attempting to stay objective, although they collectively lose it when a military spokesman holds up the famous deck of cards with the faces of Iraq's "most wanted" on it, announces the decks will be distributed by the thousands throughout the country, and then refuses to let the journalists see the cards.

The documentary is low-key for the most part, just watching and listening. Many of its scenes take place in and around CentCom, the temporary media center in Qatar where the world's journalists gathered during the run-up to the invasion of Iraq. Here Americans have long conversations with their counterparts at Al Jazeera, which is privately owned and heavily watched in Arab countries because viewers trust it more than their own government channels.

I have not seen Al Jazeera and am in no position to comment on its accuracy. I have seen this film, however, which contains enlightening moments. Remember the TV scene when joyous Iraqis toppled the statue of Saddam Hussein after the capture of Baghdad? TV pictures on the monitors at CentCom clearly see something American audiences were not shown: The square was not filled with cheering citizens, but was completely empty except for the small band of young men who toppled the statue. Al Jazeera producers watch the footage with their U.S. counterparts and observe that those who are interviewed "do not have Baghdad accents." They wonder why one "happened to have the old Iraqi flag in his pocket." The implication: This was a staged event, initiated by the U.S. occupation and bought into by the U.S. media.

The movie listens in on many philosophical

bull sessions between a U.S. marine press spokesman, Lieutenant Josh Rushing, and an Al Jazeera producer named Hassan Ibrahim, who once worked for the BBC. Rushing defends the American line, but is willing to listen to Ibrahim, who deconstructs some of the American claims (his version: "Democratize or we'll shoot you"). Some of Rushing's statements ring a little hollow, as when he says, "The American POWs expect to be treated humanely, just like we are treating our prisoners humanely."

The correspondents are saddened when three journalists are killed in Baghdad by U.S. strikes. We see one of them, working for Al Jazeera, sitting sadly behind sandbags on the roof of a building, looking like a man who has had his last meal. The network carefully informed American authorities of the location of their bureau, it's noted, and American rockets struck that location not long after Rumsfeld and others complained about Al Jazeera's coverage. An accident of war.

Control Room was directed by Jehane Noujaim, an Arab-American documentarian who made *Startup.com,* the absorbing 2001 doc about an ambitious Web site that got caught in the collapse of the Internet bubble. In this film, she seems content to watch and listen as journalists do their jobs and talk about them. She doesn't take sides, but in insisting that there is something to be said for both sides she offends those who want to hear only one side.

What is clear is that the Al Jazeera journalists feel more disappointment than hatred for America. During one of those bull sessions, there's a rhetorical question: "Who's going to stop the United States?" And an Arab replies: "The United States is going to stop the United States. I have absolute confidence in the U.S. Constitution and the U.S. people." The film's buried message is that there is a reservoir of admiration and affection for America, at least among the educated classes in the Arab world, and they do not equate the current administration with America.

Note: Salon.com reported June 6 that Lieutenant Josh Rushing was ordered by the Pentagon not to comment on this film, "and as a result, the fourteen-year career military man, recently promoted to captain, plans to leave the Marines."

The Cooler ★ ★ ★ ½

R, 101 m., 2003

William H. Macy (Bernie Lootz), Alec Baldwin (Shelly Kaplow), Maria Bello (Natalie Belisario), Shawn Hatosy (Mikey), Ron Livingston (Larry Sokolov), Paul Sorvino (Buddy Stafford), Estella Warren (Charlene), Joey Fatone (Johnny Capella). Directed by Wayne Kramer and produced by Sean Furst and Michael A. Pierce. Screenplay by Frank Hannah and Kramer.

Bernie Lootz's sad eyes scan the casino floor, and he shuffles into action. A high roller is having a winning streak at a craps table. Bernie walks near him, maybe just only brushes his sleeve, and the guy's luck sours. For Bernie there is no joy in this, only the confirmation of something he has known for a long time: "People get next to me—their luck turns. It's been like that my whole life." How does he do it? "I do it by being myself."

Bernie, played by William H. Macy as another of his gloomy everymen, is a professional loser: A "cooler," is what his boss Shelly (Alec Baldwin) calls him. He is employed by the Shangri-La casino to wander the floor, bringing an end to winning streaks. But now modern Las Vegas is catching up with Bernie and Shelly. A group of investors have brought in a hotshot from business school to update the Shangri-La, which is the last of the old-style casinos. Shelly hates this idea; taking a dig at Steve Wynn's vision for the new Vegas and saying his place is "not for the stroller crowd" but for old-timers with real money.

Bernie and Shelly go back a long way, to when Shelly had Bernie kneecapped because of a bad debt, then paid to have him patched up, then put him on the payroll, because anyone with his bad luck was worth a lot of money. But now Bernie wants out. He's saved some money and plans to leave town in a week. That's his exit strategy, anyway, until he uses his influence to get a better job for a waitress named Natalie (Maria Bello), and she repays him with the first sex he's had in a long time—and the best sex ever.

The Cooler may sound as if it's a dark sitcom, with broad characters and an easy payoff. But the movie, directed by first-timer Wayne Kramer and written by him with Frank Hannah, has a strange way of being broad and twisted at the same time, so that while we surf the surface of the story, unexpected developments are stirring beneath. There's more to the movie than at first it seems, and what happens to Bernie, Natalie, and Shelly has a rough but poignant justice.

Consider Shelly. This is one of Alec Baldwin's best performances, as a character who contains vast contradictions. He can be kind and brutal simultaneously; affection and cruelty are handmaidens. Look at the way he breaks Bernie's knee and then gives him a job. Or the way he treats Buddy Stafford (Paul Sorvino), the broken-down, smack-addicted lounge singer. Shelly is fiercely loyal to Buddy, and doesn't even want to listen to the new guys with their plans to replace him with a sexy revue. What eventually happens to Buddy has a kind of poetic justice to it, yes, but in a hard, cold way: Shelly is capable of sentimental gestures that make your skin crawl.

Macy and Bello succeed in creating characters who seem to be having a real, actual, physical relationship right there before our eyes. I don't mean anything like hard-core; I mean like the kind of stuff that happens when the bodies involved are made of flesh rather than cinema. One of their sex scenes reminds me of the heedless joy of Jack Nicholson in *Five Easy Pieces,* when he strutted around the room wearing a "Triumph" T-shirt. Macy, who is fifty-three, says he spent thirty years staying in shape in case he was ever asked to be in a sex scene, and he finally got his chance. After a battle with the MPAA we get to see it substantially intact in an R-rated version; it's not porn or anything close, but life—messy, energetic, and sweaty.

Bernie's life at this time seems blessed, except for the detail that Mikey (Shawn Hatosy), his son, turns up unexpectedly with a pregnant wife named Charlene (Estella Warren). Bernie's history with Mikey's mother is complicated, his relationship with his son is fraught, and Mikey is not a nice boy. But because Bernie has always been a loser and is now feeling great about himself, he projects his benevolence onto Mikey, and that turns out to be a mistake. Hatosy is superb in evoking the kind of person who uses lying as a life strategy.

Bernie and Natalie remind us a little of the characters in *Leaving Las Vegas,* although their situation is not as desperate. They fall in love. That turns out to be a problem, because Bernie's luck changes, and he's no longer a cooler, but quite the opposite. Shelly's attempt to deal with this is ingenious—not just for Shelly, but also for the script, which finds drama and tension in a resolution that could have seemed facile, but doesn't. The story's strength is all in the telling; no synopsis will prepare you for the emotional charge that's eventually delivered. And it's unusual to find a screenplay that gives weight to parallel stories; Shelly isn't simply an element in Bernie's life, but is a free-standing character with a dilemma of his own.

The Cooler is old-fashioned in the way the Shangri-La is old-fashioned, and I mean that as a compliment. This is a movie without gimmicks, hooks, or flashy slickness. It gives us characters who are worn and real, who inhabit a world that is seen with unforgiving perception, whose fates have more to do with their personalities than with the requirements of the plot. The acting is on the money, the writing has substance, the direction knows when to evoke *film noir* and when (in a trick shot involving loaded dice) to get fancy.

There is a crucial scene that takes place on the roof of the casino, and while it is happening, I want you to watch the eyes of the two bodyguards who are standing in the background. They're minor characters, and I don't have any idea what the director told them to do, but what their eyes reflect feels like pain and uneasiness, and it seems absolutely real. Not many movies have foregrounds that can inspire backgrounds like that.

The Core ★ ★ ½
PG-13, 135 m., 2003

Aaron Eckhart (Josh Keyes), Hilary Swank (Major Rebecca Childs), Delroy Lindo (Dr. Edward Brazzleton), Stanley Tucci (Dr. Conrad Zimsky), Tchéky Karyo (Serge Leveque), Bruce Greenwood (Colonel Robert Iverson), DJ Qualls (Taz "Rat" Finch), Richard Jenkins (General Thomas Purcell), Alfre Woodard (Talma Stickley). Directed by Jon Amiel and produced by Sean Bailey, David Foster, and Cooper Layne. Screenplay by Layne and John Rogers.

Hot on the heels of *Far from Heaven,* which

looked exactly like a 1957 melodrama, here is *The Core*, which wants to be a 1957 science fiction movie. Its special effects are a little too good for that (not a lot), but the plot is out of something by Roger Corman, and you can't improve on dialogue like this:

"The Earth's core has stopped spinning!"

"How could that happen?"

Yes, the Earth's core has stopped spinning, and in less than a year the Earth will lose its electromagnetic shield and we'll all be toast— fried by solar microwaves. To make that concept clear to a panel of U.S. military men, professor Josh Keyes of the University of Chicago (Aaron Eckhart) borrows a can of room freshener, sets the propellant alight with his Bic, and incinerates a peach.

To watch Josh Keyes and the generals contemplate that burnt peach is to witness a scene that cries out from its very vitals to be cut from the movie and made into ukulele picks. Such goofiness amuses me.

I have such an unreasonable affection for this movie, indeed, that it is only by slapping myself alongside the head and drinking black coffee that I can restrain myself from recommending it. It is only a notch down from *Congo, Anaconda, Lara Croft, Tomb Raider,* and other films that those with too little taste think they have too much taste to enjoy.

To be sure, *The Core* starts out in an unsettling manner, with the crash landing of the space shuttle. Considering that *Phone Booth,* scheduled for release in October 2002, was shelved for six months because it echoed the Beltway Sniper, to put a shuttle crash in a March 2003 movie is pushing the limits of decorum, wouldn't you say?

And yet the scene is a humdinger. Earth's disturbed magnetic field has confused the shuttle's guidance system, causing it to aim for downtown Los Angeles. Pilot Richard Jenkins insists, "It's Mission Control's call," but copilot Hilary Swank has an idea, which she explains *after* the shuttle passes over Dodger Stadium at an altitude of about 800 feet.

If the shuttle glided over Wrigley Field at that altitude, I'm thinking, it would have crashed into the 23d Precinct Police Station by now, or at the very least a Vienna Red Hot stand. But no, there's time for a conversation with Mission Control, and then for the shuttle to change course and make one of those emergency landings where wings get sheared off and everybody holds on real tight.

Other portents show something is wrong with Gaia. Birds go crazy in Trafalgar Square, people with pacemakers drop dead, and then Josh Keyes and fellow scientist Conrad Zimsky (Stanley Tucci) decide that Earth's core has stopped spinning. To bring such an unimaginable mass shuddering to a halt would result, one assumes, in more than confused pigeons, but science is not this film's strong point. Besides, do pigeons need their innate magnetic direction-sensing navigational instincts for such everyday jobs as flying from the top of Nelson's column to the bottom?

Dr. Zimsky leads the emergency team to the Utah salt flats, where eccentric scientist Edward Brazzleton (Delroy Lindo) has devised a laser device that can cut through solid rock. He has also invented a new metal named, I am not making this up, Unobtainium. (So rare is this substance that a Google search reveals only 8,060 sites selling Unobtainium ski gear, jackets, etc.) Combining the metal and the laser device into a snaky craft that looks like a BMW Roto-Rooter, the United States launches a $50 billion probe to Earth's core, in scenes that will have colonoscopy survivors shifting uneasily in their seats.

Their mission: Set off a couple of nuclear explosions that (they hope) will set the core a-spinnin' again. Earth's innards are depicted in special effects resembling a 1960s underground movie seen on acid, and it is marvelous that the crew have a video monitor so they can see out as they drill through dense matter in total darkness. Eventually they reach a depth where the pressure is 800,000 pounds per square inch— and then they put on suits to walk around outside. Their suits are obviously made of something stronger and more flexible than Unobtainium. Probably corduroy.

The music is perfect for this enterprise: ominous horns and soaring strings. The cast includes some beloved oddballs, most notably DJ Qualls *(The New Guy),* who plays Rat, a computer hacker who can talk to the animals, or at least sing to the dolphins. The only wasted cast member is Alfre Woodard, relegated to one of those Mission Control roles where she has to look worried and then relieved.

The Core is not exactly good, but it knows what a movie is. It has energy and daring and isn't afraid to make fun of itself, and it thinks big, as when the Golden Gate Bridge collapses and a scientist tersely reports, "The West Coast is out." If you are at the video store late on Saturday night and they don't have *Anaconda,* this will do.

The Count of Monte Cristo ★ ★ ★
PG-13, 118 m., 2002

Guy Pearce (Fernand Mondego), James Caviezel (Edmond Dantes), Richard Harris (Faria), Dagmara Dominczyk (Mercedes), Luis Guzman (Jacobo), Henry Cavill (Albert Mondego), James Frain (Villefort), Albie Woodington (Danglars). Directed by Kevin Reynolds and produced by Gary Barber, Roger Birnbaum, and Jonathan Glickman. Screenplay by Jay Wolpert, based on the novel by Alexandre Dumas.

The Count of Monte Cristo is a movie that incorporates piracy, Napoleon in exile, betrayal, solitary confinement, secret messages, escape tunnels, swashbuckling, comic relief, a treasure map, Parisian high society, and sweet revenge, and brings it in at under two hours, with performances by good actors who are clearly having fun. This is the kind of adventure picture the studios churned out in the Golden Age— so traditional it almost feels new.

James Caviezel stars, as Edmond Dantes, a low-born adventurer betrayed by his friend Fernand Mondego (Guy Pearce). Condemned to solitary confinement on the remote prison island of Chateau d'If, he spends years slowly growing mad and growing his hair, until one day a remarkable thing happens. A stone in his cell floor moves and lifts, and Faria (Richard Harris) appears. Faria has even more hair than Dantes, but is much more cheerful because he has kept up his hope over the years by digging an escape tunnel. Alas, by digging in the wrong direction, he came up in Dantes's cell instead of outside the walls, but c'est la vie.

"There are 5,119 stones in my walls," Dantes tells Faria. "I have counted them." Faria can think of better ways to pass the time. Enlisting Dantes in a renewed tunneling effort, Faria also tutors him in the physical and mental arts; he's the Mr. Miyagi of swashbuckling. To-gether, the men study the philosophies of Adam Smith and Machiavelli, and the old man tutors the younger one in what looks uncannily like martial arts, including the ability to move with blinding speed.

This middle section of the movie lasts long enough to suggest it may also provide the end, but no: The third act takes place back in society, after Faria supplies Dantes with a treasure map, and the resulting treasure finances his masquerade as the fictitious Count of Monte Cristo. Rich, enigmatic, mysterious, he fascinates the aristocracy and throws lavish parties, all as a snare for Mondego, while renewing his love for the beautiful Mercedes (Dagmara Dominczyk).

The story, of course, is based on the novel by Alexandre Dumas, unread by me, although I was a close student of the *Classics Illustrated* version. Director Kevin Reynolds redeems himself after *Waterworld* by moving the action along at a crisp pace; we can imagine Errol Flynn in this material, although Caviezel and Pearce bring more conviction to it, and Luis Guzman is droll as the count's loyal sidekick, doing what sounds vaguely like eighteenth-century stand-up ("I swear on my dead relatives—and even the ones that are not feeling so good . . .").

The various cliffs, fortresses, prisons, treasure isles, and chateaus all look suitably atmospheric, the fight scenes are well choreographed, and the moment of Mondego's comeuppance is nicely milked for every ounce of sweet revenge. This is the kind of movie that used to be right at home at the Saturday matinee, and it still is.

The Country Bears ★ ★
G, 87 m., 2002

Christopher Walken (Reed Thimple), Stephen Tobolowsky (Mr. Barrington), Meagen Fay (Mrs. Barrington), M. C. Gainey (Roadie), Diedrich Bader (Officer Cheets). And the voices of: Haley Joel Osment (Beary Barrington), Diedrich Bader (Ted Bedderhead), Candy Ford (Trixie St. Claire), James Gammon (Big Al), Brad Garrett (Fred Bedderhead). Directed by Peter Hastings and produced by Jeffrey Chernov and Andrew Gunn. Screenplay by Mark Perez.

The formidable technical skills in *The Country*

Bears must not be allowed to distract from the film's terminal inanity. Here is a story about a young music fan who convinces his favorite band to reunite after ten years for a concert—and the fan and the band members are all bears. Why they are bears, I do not know. Do they know they are bears? Not necessarily. Do any of the humans mention that they are bears? Only in passing. Are there real bears in the woods who would maul and eat their victims, or are all bears benign in this world?

These are not questions one is expected to pose about a movie based on a stage show at Disneyland. We simply have to accept that some of the characters in the movie are people and others are bears, and get on with it. If Stuart Little's family can have a two-inch mouse as a son, then why not musical bears? We must celebrate diversity.

The movie stars Beary Barrington (voice by Haley Joel Osment), whose human parents treat him as one of the family. Then his brother breaks the news that he was adopted after being found by a park ranger, and little Beary runs away from home. His goal: Visit legendary Country Bear Hall, the Grand Ole Opry of singing bears, and pay tribute to the band he idolizes.

Alas, the band has broken up, its members have scattered, and now even Country Bear Hall itself faces the wrecker's ball, thanks to the evil banker Reed Thimple (Christopher Walken). Since the hall is an elegant wooden structure, it is a little hard to understand why Thimple wants to replace it with a vacant lot, but there you have it. Little Beary then begins to meet the members of the Country Bears, and to persuade them, in a series of adventures, to reunite and stage a benefit concert to save the hall.

One of the movie's running gags is that recording stars appear as themselves, talking about the Bears. We see Willie Nelson, Bonnie Raitt, Elton John, Queen Latifah, and others, all talking about the band's influence on them, none mentioning that they are bears. Is the music good enough to influence Willie and the Queen? Don't make me laugh.

It's hard to figure who the movie is intended for. In shape and purpose it's like a G-rated version of *This Is Spinal Tap*, but will its wee target audience understand the joke? Anyone old enough to be interested in the music is unlikely to be interested in the bears—at least, interested in the movie's routine and wheezy plot. True, the movie does a good job of integrating the bears into the action, with animatronics by Jim Henson's Creature Shop and no doubt various CGI effects, not to mention the strong possibility that in some shots we are basically watching actors in bear suits. It's done well, yes, but why?

Cradle 2 the Grave ★ ★
R, 100 m., 2003

Jet Li (Su), DMX (Fait), Anthony Anderson (Tommy), Kelly Hu (Sona), Tom Arnold (Archie), Mark Dacascos (Ling), Gabrielle Union (Daria). Directed by Andrzej Bartkowiak and produced by Joel Silver. Screenplay by John O'Brien and Channing Gibson.

The funniest scene in *Cradle 2 the Grave* comes over the end credits, as supporting actors Tom Arnold and Anthony Anderson debate how the story should be filmed. This scene, which feels ad-libbed, is smart and self-aware in a way the movie never is. The film itself is on autopilot and overdrive at the same time: It does nothing original, but does it very rapidly.

Jet Li and DMX are the stars, both ready for better scripts, playing enemies who become buddies when it turns out they have a common antagonist. DMX plays a character pronounced "fate" but spelled "Fait," which would give you a neat pun you could use in French class, if the spelling of his name were ever seen. Jet Li plays a boy named Su. After Fait and his accomplices break into a Los Angeles diamond vault, their caper is interrupted by Su, who is working for the Taiwanese police.

Bad guys end up with the diamonds and kidnap Fait's beloved little daughter, in a plot that started out as a remake of Fritz Lang's *M* (1931). The journey from *M* to 2 was downhill all the way. The result is a Joel Silver nonstop action thriller, well produced, slickly directed, sure to please slackjaws who are not tired to death of this kind of material recycled again and again and again.

It makes at least a sincere attempt to one-up previous cop-crook-buddy-sex-chase-caper-martial-arts thrillers. Jet Li doesn't merely take on a lot of opponents at the same time, he gets in a fight with all of the competitors in an illegal extreme fighting club. He doesn't merely do stunts, but drops in free-fall from one high-rise balcony to the next. Tom Arnold doesn't merely play a black market arms dealer, he supplies a tank. The black diamonds are not merely black diamonds, but are actually a superweapon that would bring down the cost of weapons of mass destruction into the price range of a nice private jet. There is not merely a hood who has special privileges in jail, but one with a private cell where the prison guards melt butter for his fresh lobster while he waits impatiently. There is not merely a chase, but one involving an all-terrain vehicle, which is driven up the stairs of a store and then jumps from one rooftop to another more or less for the hell of it. And the girl is not merely sexy but Gabrielle Union.

I can see that this movie fills a need. I have stopped feeling the need. The problem with action movies is how quickly state of the art becomes off-the-shelf. We yearn for wit and intelligence, and a movie like *Shanghai Knights* looks sophisticated by comparison.

Cradle 2 the Grave will, however, be a box-office hit, I imagine, and that will be demographically interesting because it demonstrates that a savvy producer like Silver now believes a white star is completely unnecessary in a mega-budget action picture. At one point, there were only white stars. Then they got to have black buddies. Then they got to have Asian buddies. Then *Rush Hour* proved that black and Asian buddies could haul in the mass audience. Long ago a movie like this used a black character for comic relief. Then an Asian character. Now the white character is the comic relief. May the circle be unbroken.

Not only is Gabrielle Union the female lead, but Kelly Hu is the second female lead, slapping the kid around and engaging in a catfight with Union. Lots of mild sex in the movie, although an opening scene assumes a security guard is a very slow study. First Gabrielle Union goes in to flirt with him so he won't look at the TV security monitors. When he turns out to be gay, she sends in the second team, Anthony Anderson, to flirt with him. When two people try to pick you up in ten minutes and you're a security guard on duty, do you suspect anything?

It's a common complaint that the cops are never around during sensational movie chase scenes and shoot-outs. Dozens of squad cars turn up twice in *Cradle 2 the Grave*, however—once when they're told a robbery is in progress, and again at the end, when a battle involving guns, rockets, explosives, and a tank blowing a helicopter out of the sky inspires an alert response after only twenty minutes.

The Crime of Father Amaro ★ ★ ★
R, 120 m., 2002

Gael García Bernal (Padre Amaro), Ana Claudia Talancón (Amelia), Sancho Gracia (Padre Benito), Angélica Aragón (Sanjuanera), Luisa Huertas (Dionisia), Damián Alcázar (Padre Natalio), Ernesto Gómez Cruz (Bishop), Andrés Montiel (Rubén). Directed by Carlos Carrera and produced by Daniel Birman Ripstein and Alfredo Ripstein. Screenplay by Vicente Leñero, based on the novel by Eça de Queirós.

The Crime of Father Amaro arrives surrounded by controversy. One of the most successful Mexican films in history, it has been denounced by William Donohue of the Catholic League for its "vicious" portrait of priests; on the other hand, Father Rafael Gonzalez, speaking for the Council of Mexican Bishops, calls it an "honest movie" and describes it as "a wake-up call for the church to review its procedure for selecting and training priests and being closer to the people."

Both sides treat the film as a statement about the church, when in fact it's more of a melodrama, a film that doesn't say priests are bad but observes that priests are human and some humans are bad. What may really offend its critics is that young Father Amaro's crime is not having sex with a local girl and helping her find an abortion. His crime is that he covers up this episode and denies his responsibility because of his professional ambitions within the Church. Young Father Amaro thinks he has a rosy future ahead of him.

The movie is based on an 1875 Portuguese novel by Eça de Queirós, transplanted to modern Mexico. It gives us Padre Amaro (Gael García Bernal) as a rising star in the Church, a protégé of the bishop (Ernesto Gómez Cruz), who ships him to the provincial capital of Los

Reyes to season a little under an old clerical hand, Padre Benito (Sancho Gracia). Benito has been having a long-running affair with the restaurant owner Sanjuanera (Angélica Aragón), whose attractive daughter Amelia (Ana Claudia Talancón) may possibly be theirs.

There is the implication that the bishop knows about Benito's sex life but doesn't much care, and sends Amaro to Los Reyes for exposure to the Church's realpolitik; that the bishop knows Benito's ambitious program of hospital construction is financed through money he launders for local drug lords. It is likely the bishop approves more of priests like Benito, who raise money and get results, than of another local priest, Padre Natalio (Damián Alcázar), who supports the guerrillas waging war against the drug lords.

Once established in the local basilica, Amaro cannot help but notice the fragrant Amelia. And she develops an instant infatuation with the handsome young priest, whose unavailability makes him irresistible. Amelia has been dating a local newspaperman named Rubén (Andrés Montiel), but drops him the moment Amaro expresses veiled interest. Soon Amaro and Amelia are violating the Church's laws of priestly celibacy, and eventually she is pregnant, and this fate leads them to an illegal abortion clinic on a back road in the jungle.

The film has been attacked for the sacrilege of showing a priest paying for an abortion, but since he related to Amelia as a man, not a priest, there is a certain consistency in his behavior. It is also consistent that he would attempt to hide his crime because, like Benito, he finds it easy to make himself a personal exception to general rules. There is still a little seminary idealism in Amaro, enough to be shocked that Benito is taking drug money to build the hospital, but part of Amaro is already warming to Benito's logic: "We are taking bad money and making it good." This theology is not unique to that time or place, or even to that church; we are reminded of the CIA using drug money to finance its friends.

The film is directed in a straightforward way by Carlos Carrera, who makes it direct and heartfelt, like a soap opera. The presence of Gael García Bernal in the cast is a reminder of his work as one of the two young men in *Y Tu Mamá También* (2002), a film where the ethical

issues were more complex and deeply buried. There are no complexities here, unless they involve Amaro's gradual corruption in the real world of Church politics and money.

Is the film harmful to the Church? I tend to agree with Father Gonzalez, who finds that fresh air is a help, not a harm. Donohue and his league predictably denounce every movie that is unfavorable to the Church, undeterred by the fact that their opposition helps publicize the films and sell tickets (no movie has ever been harmed by being called "controversial").

Predictably, the film's critics are most upset by Amaro's sexual behavior, when in fact the film's real questions run deeper and are political: Has the Church sometimes kept company with unsavory sources of financing? Is the policy of celibacy more observed in the breach than in the observance? Are laws against abortion made by men in the daylight and violated by them in the darkness? Is the Church more comfortable allied with an amoral establishment than with a moral opposition? These questions are lost in the excitement about sex, which is often the way it works: Carnal guilt clouds our minds, distracting us from more important issues.

Crimson Gold ★ ★ ★
NO MPAA RATING, 97 m., 2004

Hussein Emadeddin (Hussein), Kamyar Sheissi (Ali), Azita Rayeji (Bride), Shahram Vaziri (Jeweler), Ehsan Amani (Man in the Tea House), Pourang Nakhayi (Rich Man), Kavey Najmabadi (Seller), Saber Safael (Soldier). Directed by Jafar Panahi and produced by Panahi. Screenplay by Abbas Kiarostami.

The success of *Crimson Gold* depends to an intriguing degree on the performance of its leading actor, a large, phlegmatic man who embodies the rule that an object at rest will stay at rest until some other force sets it into motion. The character, named Hussein and played by Hussein Emadeddin, is a pizza deliveryman in Tehran, heavy-set, tall, undemonstrative. He sits where he sits as if planted there, and when he rides his scooter around the city streets he doesn't lean and dart like most scooter drivers, but seems at one with his machine in implacable motion. When he smokes, he is like an automaton programmed to move the cigarette toward and away from his lips.

He has a friend named Ali (Kamyar Sheissi). We meet Ali for the first time in a teahouse, where he produces a purse he has just found. Its contents are disappointing—a broken gold ring. Another man overhears their conversation, assumes they stole the purse, and delivers a little lecture on the morality of theft. He believes the rewards should suit the crime; you should not put your targets through a great deal of suffering just to relieve them of pocket change.

Hussein, who is engaged to Ali's sister, seems an unlikely candidate for marriage. We learn indirectly that he was wounded in the Iraq-Iran War, and Ali refers to his "medication." Perhaps that accounts for his sphinxlike detachment; he acts as little as it is possible to act and yet, paradoxically, we can't take our eyes off of him.

The film uses Hussein and his life as a lens to look at Tehran today. The director, Jafar Panahi, also made *The Circle* (2000), a film showing the impossibility of being a single woman in modern Iran without having a man to explain your status. *Crimson Gold* was written by Abbas Kiarostami, the best-known Iranian director, and includes his trademark: long, unbroken shots of a character driving somewhere. In this case, it is Hussein on his scooter, sometimes with Ali as a passenger.

Hussein lives a solitary existence in an untidy little flat, venturing out at night to deliver pizzas. One night he delivers a stack of pizzas to the penthouse of an apartment building in a wealthy neighborhood. He is greeted at the door by the occupant (Pourang Nakhayi), who complains that "the women have gone" and he doesn't need the pizza. But he invites Hussein in, asks him to eat the pizza, and talks obsessively about himself: How his parents only lived in the apartment for a month before moving overseas, how he has just returned to Iran and finds it not organized to his liking, how women are crazy and unpredictable.

Hussein eats steadily and regards him. Later, as the man is on the telephone, he walks around the apartment (he has never been so high up in his life), looks at the skyline, visits a bathroom more luxurious than any he could imagine, dives fully clothed into the swimming pool, and is seen later wrapped in towels.

When he leaves the apartment he goes directly to a jewelry store that he and Ali had visited twice before. The first time, they wanted to get a price on the gold ring, and were treated rudely and with suspicion by the store owner and guard. Returning, wearing ties and with Ali's sister along, they said they were shopping for a wedding ring—but were treated rudely again; it is a high-end store and they look like low-end people.

After he leaves the high-rise apartment, Hussein returns to the store. We already know much of what will happen now, because *Crimson Gold* opens with a version of the same scene it closes with. But I will not discuss the opening (and closing) because they proceed with a kind of implacable logic. What seems impulsive and reckless at the beginning of the film takes on a certain logic after we have spent some time in Hussein's company. In his case, still waters run deep and cold. He has been still and implacable for the entire film, but now we understand he was not frozen, but waiting.

Note: In real life, Hussein Emadeddin, a nonactor, is a paranoid schizophrenic. Having learned this information, I felt obliged to share it with you, but the film does not refer to the disease; perhaps Jafar Panahi found that Emadeddin's demeanor, whatever its source, provided the kind of detachment he needed for his character. Hussein (the character) is doubly effective because he does not seem to be an active participant in the story, but an observer carried along by the currents of chance.

The Crocodile Hunter: Collision Course
★ ★ ★
PG, 90 m., 2002

Steve Irwin (Steve Irwin), Terri Irwin (Terri Irwin), Magda Szubanski (Brozzie), Kenneth Ransom (Vaughan Archer), Lachy Hulme (Robert Wheeler), David Wenham (Sam Flynn), Aden Young (Ron Buckwhiler), Kate Beahan (Jo Buckley). Directed by John Stainton and produced by Judy Bailey, Arnold Rifkin, and Stainton. Screenplay by Holly Goldberg Sloan and Stainton.

There are scenes in *The Crocodile Hunter: Collision Course* where Steve Irwin jumps into rivers at night and wrestles crocodiles bare-handed, while his wife, Terri, helps him tie their jaws shut and haul them onto the boat. In another movie you would question the possibility of such scenes.

But there is something about this one that argues they are true: a certain straightforward, matter-of-fact approach that suggests Steve has been wrestling crocodiles all his life. And he has; according to his bio, Steve's dad, Bob, who ran the Queensland Reptile and Fauna Park in Australia, "taught the young Steve everything there was to know about reptiles—even teaching his nine-year-old how to jump in and catch crocodiles in the rivers of North Queensland at night!"

How, I am wondering, *do* you teach a nine-year-old to jump in and catch crocodiles in the rivers of North Queensland at night? Is rehearsal possible, or do you just get a lot of theory and then jump in? Is it child abuse to tell your nine-year-old to wrestle crocodiles, or only tough love? I urgently await a film titled *Young Steve: The Education of a Croc Hunter.*

Studying the bio more closely, I realize that many of its sentences end with an exclamation point. In the movie, nearly every sentence uttered by Irwin does, although supporting players are allowed periods and question marks. Half of his sentences have only one word: "Crikey!" He says this frequently while handling the dangerous creatures of the outback, which he likes to get real close to, so they can snap at him during his lectures.

There is a plot to this movie, which I hardly need to mention, since it's irrelevant to the experience. A secret communications satellite falls to Earth and its black box is gobbled up by a croc, and two rival U.S. intelligence agencies send teams to the outback to retrieve it. Meanwhile, Steve and Terri don't realize it's in the stomach of the croc they plan to move to another river system.

Forget the plot. The movie is really about Steve and Terri taking us on a guided tour of the crocs, snakes, deadly insects, and other stars of the outback fauna. Steve's act is simplicity itself. He holds a deadly cobra, say, by its tail and looks straight at the camera and explains that the cobra has enough venom to kill him one hundred times over. The cobra twists and tries to strike at Steve's bare leg. He jerks it away. Crikey! Steve's monologues about the incredi-

ble danger he's in do sometimes run a bit long, but he has the grace to interrupt them to slap at flies that are biting him.

Later we meet a "bird-eating" spider whose fangs contain venom that would kill Steve, I dunno, a thousand times over, and he pokes it with a stick to make it display its fangs, and it almost bites Steve's thumb. Crikey! Then he shows us the spider's nest, and sticks his finger down it and yanks it back as if he's been bitten. Crikey! But he was only fooling, mate.

The movie is entertaining exactly on the level I have described it. You see a couple of likable people journeying though the outback, encountering dangerous critters and getting too close for comfort, while lecturing us on their habits and dangers and almost being killed by them. The stunts are not faked, and so there is a certain fascination. Steve and Terri are not exactly developed as deeply realized characters, and only on their Website did I discover they were married in 1992 and in 1998 gave birth to little Bindi Sue Irwin, who is now four, and started in as a baby by wrestling tiny gecko lizards. Crikey.

Crossroads ★ ½
PG-13, 90 m., 2002

Britney Spears (Lucy), Zoe Saldana (Kit), Anson Mount (Ben), Taryn Manning (Mimi), Justin Long (Henry), Dan Aykroyd (Lucy's Dad), Kim Cattrall (Lucy's Mom). Directed by Tamra Davis and produced by Ann Carli. Screenplay by Shonda Rhimes.

I went to *Crossroads* expecting a glitzy bimbo fest and got the bimbos but not the fest. Britney Spears's feature debut is curiously low-key and even sad. Yes, it pulls itself together occasionally for a musical number, but even those are so locked into the "reality" of the story that they don't break loose into fun.

The movie opens with three eighth-graders burying a box filled with symbols of their dreams of the future. Four years later, on high school graduation day, the girls are hardly on speaking terms, but they meet to dig up the box, tentatively renew their friendship, and find themselves driving to California in a convertible piloted by a hunk.

Lucy (Spears) hopes to find her long-indifferent mother in Arizona. Kit (Zoe Saldana) wants to find her fiancé in Los Angeles; he has become ominously vague about wedding plans. Mimi (Taryn Manning) is pregnant, but wants to compete in a record company's open audition. Spoiler warning! Stop reading now unless you want to learn the dismal outcome of their trip, as Lucy's mom informs her she was a "mistake," Kit's fiancé turns out to have another woman *and* to be guilty of date rape, and Mimi, who was the rape victim, has a miscarriage.

I'm not kidding. *Crossroads,* which is being promoted with ads showing Britney bouncing on the bed while lip-synching a song, is a downer that would be even more depressing if the plot wasn't such a lame soap opera.

This is the kind of movie where the travelers stop by the roadside to yell "Hello!" and keep on yelling, unaware that there is no echo. Where Britney is a virgin at eighteen and enlists her lab partner to deflower her. Where when that doesn't work out she finds herself attracted to Ben (Anson Mount), the guy who's giving them the ride, even though he is alleged to have killed a man. Where the apparent age difference between Spears and Mount makes it look like he's robbing the cradle. (In real life, he's twenty-nine and she's twenty, but he's an experienced twenty-nine and she's playing a naive eighteen-year-old.)

Of the three girls, Mimi has the most to do. She teaches Kit how to land a punch, tells the others why she doesn't drink, and deals almost casually with her miscarriage. Kit is a slow study who takes forever to figure out her fiancé has dumped her. And Spears, as Lucy, seems to think maybe she's in a serious Winona Ryder role, but with songs.

"What are you writing in that book?" Ben asks her. "Poems," she says. He wants her to read one for him. She does. "Promise not to laugh," she says. He doesn't, but the audience does. It's the lyrics for her song "I'm Not a Girl, Not Yet a Woman." Didn't anyone warn her you can't introduce famous material as if it's new without risking a bad laugh? Later, Ben composes music for the words, and he plays the piano while she riffs endlessly to prove she has never once thought about singing those words before.

The movie cuts away from the payoffs of the big scenes. We get the foreplay for both of Britney's sex scenes, but never see what happens. Her big meeting with her mother lacks the showdown. We can be grateful, I suppose, that after Mimi falls down some stairs after learning that Kit's fiancé is the man who raped her, we are spared the details of her miscarriage and cut to her later in the hospital. Perhaps study of the live childbirth scene in the Spice Girls movie warned the filmmakers away from obstetric adventures in this one.

Like *Coyote Ugly,* a movie it resembles in the wardrobe department, *Crossroads* is rated PG-13 but is going on 17. Caution, kids: It can be more dangerous to get a ride in a convertible with a cute but ominous guy than you might think (see *Kalifornia*).

And you can't always support yourself by tips on Karaoke Night. When the girls sing in a karaoke contest, a three-gallon jug is filled with bills which, after they're piled in stacks on the bar, are enough to pay for car repairs and the rest of the trip. Uh-huh. Curious thing about that karaoke bar: It has a position on the stage with an underlight and one of those poles that strippers twine around. You don't see those much in karaoke clubs.

Crush ★ ★ ★
R, 115 m., 2002

Andie MacDowell (Kate), Imelda Staunton (Janine), Anna Chancellor (Molly), Kenny Doughty (Jed), Bill Paterson (Rev. Gerald Farquar-Marsden). Directed by John McKay and produced by Lee Thomas. Screenplay by McKay.

If I were reviewing *Crush* in England, I would work the name of Joanna Trollope into the first sentence, and my readers would immediately be able to identify the terrain. Trollope, a best-seller who is often quite perceptive and touching, writes at the upper range of the category just below serious fiction. She is a good read for those, like myself, who fantasize about living prosperously in the Cotswolds in an old but comfortably remodeled cottage not far from the village green, the churchyard, the tea shop, the bookstore, and the rail line to London, while growing involved in a web of imprudent adulterous sex. (As a happily married man, you understand, I do not want to *perform* adulterous imprudent sex, only to be involved in a web with such entertaining neighbors.)

This is not England. Few North Americans read Joanna Trollope, and fewer still respond to key words in her vocabulary such as "Aga." An Aga cookstove is so expensive and versatile it does everything but peel the potatoes, and its presence in a kitchen tells you so much about the occupants that in the Brit book review pages, the phrase "Aga romance" perfectly categorizes a novel.

Crush is an Aga romance crossed with modern retro-feminist soft porn, in which liberated women discuss lust as if it were a topic and not a fact. We begin by meeting the three heroines, who are forty-something professionals who meet once a week to (1) drink gin, (2) smoke cigarettes, (3) eat caramels, and (4) discuss their lousy love lives. My advice to these women: stop after (3).

The characters: Kate (Andie MacDowell) is the American headmistress of the local upscale school, Janine (Imelda Staunton) is a physician, and Molly (Anna Chancellor) is the police chief. That these three professional women at their age would all still be smoking can be explained only by a movie that does not give them enough to do with their hands. One day Kate goes to a funeral, is immeasurably moved by the music, and meets the organist. His name is Jed (Kenny Doughty), and he was once a student of hers. She is between fifteen and eighteen years older, but their conversation drifts out of the church and into the churchyard, and soon they are performing the old rumpy-pumpy behind a tombstone while the mourners are still stifling their sobs.

This is, you will agree, an example of lust. In a rabbit, it would be simple lust. In a headmistress, it is reckless lust. (In a twenty-five-year-old organist, it is what comes from pumping the foot pedals for thirty minutes while observing Andie MacDowell.) The movie cannot leave it at lust, however, because then it would be a different movie. So it elevates it into a Love That Was Meant to Be, in which the two lovers overcome differences of age, class, and grooming, and determine to spend their lives together. Because they are attractive people and we like them, of course we identify with their foolishness and feel good when romance triumphs.

A sixth sense tells us, however, that romance has triumphed a little too early in the movie. The only way for *Crush* to get from its romantic triumph to the end of the film is to supply setbacks, and does it ever. I will not reveal what episodes of bad judgment, bad karma, and plain bad luck lead to the ultimate bittersweet denouement, and will distract myself from the temptation by telling you that the pastor of the local church is named the Rev. Gerald Farquar-Marsden, a name to rival Catsmeat Potter-Pirbright.

The movie does its best to work us over, with second helpings of love, romance, tragedy, false dawns, real dawns, comic relief, two separate crises during marriage ceremonies, and the lush scenery of the Cotswolds (or, as the Website refers to the district, "Cotswold"). It's the kind of world where romance begins in tombs among the headstones, or vice versa, and almost immediately requires engraved invitations. Jed is described as being twenty-five years old and Kate is described as being forty "cough," but Andie MacDowell is the definition of a dish, and Jed, just by being a church organist, is mature for his age. Besides, what is an age difference of fifteen or even eighteen years when my old friend Betty Dodson, at seventy-two, is in the third year of a steamy romance with a twenty-five-year-old? You can look it up at Salon.com, under "sex."

D

Daddy Day Care ★
PG, 93 m., 2003

Eddie Murphy (Charlie Hinton), Jeff Garlin (Phil), Anjelica Huston (Miss Harridan), Steve Zahn (Marvin), Khamani Griffin (Ben Hinton), Regina King (Kim Hinton). Directed by Steve Carr and produced by John Davis, Matt Berenson, and Wyck Godfrey. Screenplay by Geoff Rodkey.

Daddy Day Care is a woeful miscalculation, a film so wrongheaded audiences will be more appalled than amused. It imagines Eddie Murphy and sidekick Jeff Garlin in charge of a day-care center that could only terrify parents in the audience, although it may look like fun for their children. The center's philosophy apparently consists of letting kids do whatever they feel like, while the amateur staff delivers one-liners.

I realize that the movie is not intended as a serious work about day-care centers. It is a comedy (in genre, not in effect). But at some point we might expect it to benefit from real life, real experiences, real kids. Not a chance. It's all simply a prop for the Eddie Murphy character. Aggressively simpleminded, it's fueled by the delusion that it has a brilliant premise: Eddie Murphy plus cute kids equals success. But a premise should be the starting point for a screenplay, not its finish line.

In the film, Murphy plays Charlie Hinton, an advertising executive assigned to the account of a breakfast cereal based on vegetables. This leads eventually to desperate scenes involving Murphy dressed in a broccoli suit, maybe on the grounds that once, long ago, he was funny in a Gumby suit. The cereal fails, and he's fired along with his best pal, Phil (Garlin). Charlie's wife, Kim (Regina King), goes to work as a lawyer, leaving her husband at home to take care of their son, Ben (Khamani Griffin). Next thing you know, Charlie has the idea of opening a day-care center.

Enter the villainess, Miss Harridan (Anjelica Huston), whose own day-care center is so expensive that Charlie can no longer afford to send Ben there. Huston plays the role as your standard dominatrix, ruling her school with an iron hand, but you know what? It looks to me like a pretty good school, with the kids speaking foreign languages and discussing advanced science projects. Obviously, in the terms of this movie, any school where the kids have to study is bad, just as a school where the kids can run around and raise hell is good. This bias is disguised as Charlie's insight into child psychology.

The new school is successful almost from the outset, and empty seats begin to turn up in Miss Harridan's school as parents switch their kids to the cheaper alternative. No sane parent would trust a child to Charlie and Phil's chaotic operation, but never mind. Soon the partners hire an assistant, Marvin, played by Steve Zahn as a case of arrested development. Miss Harridan, facing the failure of her school, mounts a counterattack and of course is vanquished. She appears in the movie's final shot in a pathetically unfunny attempt to force humor long after the cause has been lost.

What the movie lacks is any attempt to place Murphy and his costars in a world of real kids and real day care. This entire world looks like it exists only on a studio lot. A few kids are given identifiable attributes (one won't take off his superhero costume), but basically they're just a crowd of rug rats in the background of the desperately forced comedy. Even the movie's poop joke fails, and if you can't make a poop joke work in a movie about kids, you're in trouble.

The movie's miscalculation, I suspect, is the same one that has misled Murphy in such other recent bombs as *I Spy* and *The Adventures of Pluto Nash* (which was unseen by me and most of the rest of the world). That's the delusion that Murphy's presence will somehow lend magic to an undistinguished screenplay. A film should begin with a story and characters, not with a concept and a star package.

The Dancer Upstairs ★ ★ ★
R, 128 m., 2003

Javier Bardem (Augustin Rejas), Laura Morante (Yolanda), Juan Diego Botto (Sucre), Elvira Minguez (Llosa), Alexandra Lencastre (Sylvina), Oliver Cotton (General Merino), Luis Miguel Cintra (Calderon), Abel Folk (Ezequiel/Duran). Directed by John Malkovich and produced by

Malkovich and Andrés Vicente Gómez. Screenplay by Nicholas Shakespeare, based on his novel.

John Malkovich's *The Dancer Upstairs* was filmed before 9/11 and is based on a novel published in 1997, but has an eerie timeliness in its treatment of a terrorist movement that works as much through fear as through violence.

Filmed in Ecuador, it stars Javier Bardem as Augustin, an inward, troubled man who left the practice of law to join the police force because he wanted to be one step closer to justice. Now he has been assigned to track down a shadowy terrorist named Ezequiel, who is everywhere and nowhere, and strikes at random to sow fear in the population. His trademark is to leave dead dogs hanging in public view. In China, a dead dog is symbolic of a tyrant executed by the people, we learn.

The movie's story, based on a novel by Nicholas Shakespeare, is inspired by the Shining Path, a terrorist group in Peru. But this is not a docudrama; it is more concerned with noticing the ways in which terrorism takes its real toll in a nation's self-confidence. Ezequiel commits bold and shocking but small-scale public executions, many of helpless civilians in remote districts, but the central government is paralyzed by fear, martial law is declared, and the army steps into Augustin's investigation. The cure may be more damaging than the crime.

Augustin is a very private man. He seems to be happily married and to dote on his daughter, but he is happy to spend long periods away from home, and doesn't really seem to focus on his wife's obsession with getting herself an improved nose. He never gives a convincing explanation of why he left the law. His approach to the Ezequiel crimes is largely intuitive; faced with an enemy who works through rumor and legend, he looks more for vibes than clues, and at one point revisits the rural district where his family owned a coffee farm, since confiscated. There he will find—well, whatever he will find.

The movie is contemplative for a police procedural; more like Georges Simenon or Nicolas Freeling than like Ed McBain. Bardem, who was so demonstrative as the flamboyant writer in *Before Night Falls,* now turns as subtle and guarded as—well, as John Malkovich. It is typical that when he falls in love with Yolanda (Laura Morante), his daughter's ballet teacher, both he and she are slow to realize what has happened, and reluctant to act on it.

When Ezequiel is finally discovered, it is through a coincidence that I will not reveal here, although his location is made clear to the audience long before Augustin discovers it. I cannot resist, however, quoting one of the film's most cutting lines. We have heard that Ezequiel represents what Marx called "the fourth stage of communism," and when the terrorist is finally dragged into the light of day, Augustin says, "The fourth stage of communism is just a big fat man in a cardigan."

Malkovich has not set out to make a thriller here, so much as a meditation about a man caught in a muddle of his own thinking. By rights, Augustin says at one point, he should be a coffee farmer. The government's confiscation of his family's farm paradoxically did him a favor, by pushing him off the land and into law school, and he is caught between a yearning for the land and a confused desire to make a difference in his society.

As a cop he is trusted by his superiors with great responsibility, but we see him more as a dreamy idealist who doesn't have a firm program for his life and is pushed along by events. He hates the cruelty of Ezequiel, but is baffled, as the whole nation is, by Ezequiel's lack of a program, focus, or identity. His violent acts function as classic anarchism, seeking the downfall of the state with the hope that a new society will somehow arise from the wreckage.

The Dancer Upstairs is elegantly, even languorously, photographed by Jose Luis Alcaine, who doesn't punch into things but regards them, so that we are invited to think about them. That doesn't mean the movie is slow; it moves with a compelling intensity toward its conclusion, which is not a "climax" or a "solution" in the usual police-movie mode, but a small moral victory that Augustin rescues from his general confusion.

When he finally gets to the end of his five-year search for the figure who has distracted and terrorized the country all of that time, his quarry turns out to be a little like the Wizard of Oz. And having pulled aside the curtain, Augustin now has to return to Kansas, or in this case to his wife, who will soon be talking once again about plastic surgery.

Note: The movie, cast with Spanish and South American actors, is entirely in English.

The Dangerous Lives of Altar Boys ★ ★ ½
R, 105 m., 2002

Kieran Culkin (Tim Sullivan), Jena Malone (Margie Flynn), Emile Hirsch (Francis Doyle), Vincent D'Onofrio (Father Casey), Jodie Foster (Sister Assumpta), Jake Richardson (Wade), Tyler Long (Joey Scalisi). Directed by Peter Care and produced by Meg LeFauve, Jay Shapiro, and Jodie Foster. Screenplay by Jeff Stockwell, based on the book by Chris Furhman.

There were times when *The Dangerous Lives of Altar Boys* evoked memories of my own Catholic school days—not to confirm the film, but to question it. There is a way in which the movie accurately paints its young heroes, obsessed with sex, rebellion, and adolescence, and too many other times when it pushes too far, making us aware of a screenplay reaching for effect. The climax is so reckless and absurd that we can't feel any of the emotions that are intended.

Yet this is an honorable film with good intentions. Set in a small town in the 1970s, it tells the story of good friends at St. Agatha's School, who squirm under the thumb of the strict Sister Assumpta (Jodie Foster) and devise elaborate plots as a rebellion against her. At the same time, the kids are growing up, experimenting with smoking and drinking, and learning more about sex than they really want to know.

The heroes are Tim Sullivan (Kieran Culkin) and Francis Doyle (Emile Hirsch). We look mostly through Francis's eyes, as the boys and two friends weave a fantasy world out of a comic book they collaborate on called *The Atomic Trinity,* with characters like Captain Asskicker and easily recognized caricatures of Sister Assumpta and Father Casey (Vincent D'Onofrio), the distracted, chain-smoking pastor and soccer coach who seems too moony to be a priest.

The movie has a daring strategy for representing the adventures of the Trinity: It cuts to animated sequences (directed by Todd McFarlane) that cross the everyday complaints and resentments of the authors with the sort of glorified myth-making and superhero manu-facture typical of Marvel comics of the period. (These sequences are so well animated, with such visual flair and energy, that the jerk back to the reality sequences can be a little disconcerting.) The villainess in the book is Sister Nunzilla, based on Sister Assumpta right down to her artificial leg.

Does the poor sister deserve this treatment? The film argues that she does not, but is unconvincing. Sister Assumpta is very strict, but we are meant to understand that she really likes and cares for her students. This is conveyed in some of Jodie Foster's acting choices, but has no payoff, because the kids apparently don't see the same benevolent expressions we sometimes glimpse. If they are not going to learn anything about Sister Assumpta's gentler side, then why must we?

The kids are supposed to be typical young adolescents, but they're so rebellious, reckless, and creative that we sense the screenplay nudging them. Francis feels the stirrings of lust and (more dangerous) idealistic love inspired by his classmate Margie Flynn (Jena Malone), and they have one of those first kisses that makes you smile. Then she shares a family secret that is, I think, a little too heavy for this film to support, and creates a dark cloud over all that follows.

If the secret is too weighty, so is the ending. The boys have been engaged in an escalating series of pranks, and their final one, involving plans to kidnap a cougar from the zoo and transport it to Sister Assumpta's living quarters, is too dumb and dangerous for anyone, including these kids, to contemplate. Their previous stunt was to steal a huge statue of St. Agatha from a niche high on the facade of the school building, and this seems about as far as they should go. The cougar business is trying too hard, and leads to an ending that doesn't earn its emotional payoff.

Another hint of the overachieving screenplay is the running theme of the boys' fascination with William Blake's books *Songs of Innocence* and *Songs of Experience.* I can believe that boys of this age could admire Blake, but not these boys. And I cannot believe that Sister Assumpta would consider Blake a danger. What we sense here is the writer, Jeff Stockwell, sneaking in material he likes even though it doesn't pay its way. (There's one other cultural reference in the movie, unless I'm seeing it where none was intended: Early in the film, the boys blow up a telephone pole in order to calculate when it will fall, and they stand just inches into the safe zone. I was reminded of Buster Keaton, standing so that when a wall fell on him, he was in the exact outline of an open window.)

The movie has qualities that cannot be denied. Jena Malone *(Donnie Darko, Life as a House)* has a solemnity and self-knowledge that seems almost to stand outside the film. She represents the gathering weather of adulthood. The boys are fresh and enthusiastic, and we remember how kids can share passionate enthusiasms; the animated sequences perfectly capture the energy of their imaginary comic book. Vincent D'Onofrio muses through the film on his own wavelength, making of Father Casey a man who means well but has little idea what meaning well would consist of. If the film had been less extreme in the adventures of its heroes, more willing to settle for plausible forms of rebellion, that might have worked. It tries too hard, and overreaches the logic of its own world.

Note: The movie is rated R, consistent with the policy of the flywheels at the MPAA that any movie involving the intelligent treatment of teenagers must be declared off-limits for them.

Daredevil ★ ★ ★
PG-13, 97 m., 2003

Ben Affleck (Matt Murdock/Daredevil), Jennifer Garner (Elektra Natchios), Michael Clarke Duncan (Kingpin), Colin Farrell (Bullseye), Jon Favreau (Franklin "Foggy" Nelson), Joe Pantoliano (Ben Urich), David Keith (Jack Murdock), Scott Terra (Young Matt Murdock). Directed by Mark Steven Johnson and produced by Avi Arad, Gary Foster, and Arnon Milchan. Screenplay by Johnson, based on the comic by Stan Lee, Bill Everett, and Frank Miller.

The origin is usually similar: A traumatic event in childhood, often involving the loss of parents, leaves the future superhero scarred in some ways but with preternatural powers in others. Daredevil came out of the Marvel Comics stable in the same period as Spider-Man, and both were altered by accidents, which gave Peter Parker his spidey-sense, and blinded Matt Murdock but made his other four senses hypersensitive. They grew up together in Marvel Comics, sometimes sharing the same adventures, but you won't see them fraternizing in the movies because their rights are owned by different studios.

Daredevil stars Ben Affleck as the superhero, wearing one of those molded body suits that defines his six-packs but, unlike Batman's, doesn't give him dime-size nipples. His mask extends over his eyes, which are not needed, since his other senses fan out in a kind of radar, allowing him to visualize his surroundings and "see" things even in darkness.

By day (I love that "by day") he is a lawyer in the Hell's Kitchen area of Manhattan. By night, he tells us, he prowls the alleys and rooftops, seeking out evildoers. Of these there is no shortage, although most of the city's more lucrative crime is controlled by the Kingpin (Michael Clarke Duncan) and his chief minister, Bullseye (Colin Farrell).

There must be a woman, and in *Daredevil* there is one (only one, among all those major male characters), although the fragrant Ellen Pompeo has a slink-on. She is Elektra Natchios (Jennifer Garner), who, like her classical namesake, wants to avenge the death of her father. By day she is, well, pretty much as she is by night. She and Daredevil are powerfully attracted and even share some PG-13 sex, which is a relief, because when superheroes have sex at the R level I am always afraid someone will get hurt. There is a rather beautiful scene where he asks her to stand in the rain because his ears are so sensitive they can create an image of her face from the sound of the raindrops.

Matt Murdock's law partner is Franklin "Foggy" Nelson (Jon Favreau). He has little suspicion of whom he is sharing an office with, although he is a quick study. Another key character is Ben Urich (Joe Pantoliano), who works for the *New York Post,* the newspaper of choice for superheroes.

Daredevil has the ability to dive off tall buildings, swoop thorough the air, bounce off stuff, land lightly, and so forth. There is an explanation for this ability, but I tend to tune out such explanations because, after all, what do they really explain? I don't care what you say, it's Superman's cape that makes him fly. Comic fans, however, study the mythology and methodology with the intensity of academics. It is reassuring, in this world of inexplicabilities, to master a limited subject within a self-contained universe. Understand, truly understand, why Daredevil defies gravity, and the location of the missing matter making up 90 percent of the universe can wait for another day.

But these are just the kinds of idle thoughts I entertain during a movie like *Daredevil*, which may have been what the Vatican had in mind when it issued that statement giving its limited approval of Harry Potter, as long as you don't start believing in him. Daredevil describes himself as a "guardian devil," and that means there are guardian angels, and that means God exists and, by a process of logical deduction, that Matt Murdock is a Catholic. Please address your correspondence to Rome.

The movie is actually pretty good. Affleck and Garner probe for the believable corners of their characters, do not overact, are given semiparticular dialogue, and are in a very goodlooking movie. Most of the tension takes place between the characters, not the props. There is, of course, a fancy formal ball to which everyone is invited (Commissioner Gordon must have been at the rival affair across town).

Affleck is at home in plots of this size, having just recently tried to save Baltimore from nuclear annihilation and the world from *Armageddon,* but Garner, Farrell, and Duncan are relatively newer to action epics, although Garner did see Affleck off at the station when he took the train from Pearl Harbor to New York, and Duncan was Balthazar in *The Scorpion King.* They play their roles more or less as if they were real, which is a novelty in a movie like this, and Duncan in particular has a presence that makes the camera want to take a step back and protect its groin.

The movie is, in short, your money's worth, better than we expect, more fun than we deserve. I am getting a little worn-out describing the origin stories and powers of superheroes, and their relationships to archvillains, gnashing henchmen, and brave, muscular female pals. They weep, they grow, they astonish, they overcome, they remain vulnerable, and their enemies spend inordinate time on wardrobe, grooming, and props, and behaving as if their milk of human kindness has turned to cottage cheese. Some of their movies, like this one, are better than others.

Dark Blue ★ ★ ★
R, 116 m., 2003

Kurt Russell (Eldon Perry Jr.), Scott Speedman (Bobby Keough), Ving Rhames (Arthur Holland), Brendan Gleeson (Jack Van Meter), Michael Michele (Beth Williamson), Lolita Davidovich (Sally Perry). Directed by Ron Shelton and produced by David Blocker, Caldecot Chubb, Sean Daniel, and James Jacks. Screenplay by David Ayer, based on a story by James Ellroy.

Two cops. One a veteran, one a rookie. One corrupt, the other still learning. Two sets of bad guys. One pair guilty of a heartless crime, the other pair guilty, but not of this crime. Two women, one a disillusioned wife, the other a disillusioned girlfriend. Two superior officers, one rotten, the other determined to bring him down. All the action takes place in the final days before the Rodney King verdict was announced in April 1992, and in the immediate aftermath, when the LAPD abandoned some neighborhoods to looters and arsonists.

Dark Blue is a formula picture in its broad outlines, but a very particular film in its characters and details. It doesn't redeem the formula or even tinker with it very much, but in a performance by Kurt Russell and in some location work on the angry streets, it has something to say and an urgent way of saying it.

The movie is based on a story by James Ellroy, a novelist who knows Los Angeles like the back of his hand, just after it has been stepped on. The screenplay for *L.A. Confidential* came from him, and a lot of hard-boiled fiction, punched out in short paragraphs, as if he has to keep ducking. He's been trying to get this story made into a movie for so long it was originally set during the Watts riots. The update works better, because the King verdict fits more neatly with his police department ripe for reform.

Kurt Russell and Scott Speedman star as Perry and Keough, two detectives who prowl the streets like freelance buccaneers; we know this type and even the veteran–rookie relationship from *Training Day, Narc,* and many other movies. The older cop explains you have to play tough to get things done, and the younger one tries to go along, even though he keeps failing the Hemingway test (it's immoral if you feel bad after you do it). They're the street agents, in a sense, of top cop Jack Van Meter (Brendan Gleeson). He has a couple of snitches he's protecting, and after they murder four people in a convenience store robbery, he orders Perry and Keough to frame and kill a couple of sex criminals for the crimes. Now young Keough, having balked at his first chance to execute a perp in the streets, gets a second chance.

The movie surrounds this situation with a lot of other material—too much, so that it sometimes feels hurried. Perry is married to one of those cop wives (Lolita Davidovich) who is stuck with the thankless task of telling him he just doesn't see her anymore ("You care more about the people you hate"). Keough is dating a young black woman (Michael Michele) who insists they not tell each other their last names. A man who sleeps with a woman who will not reveal her last name is marginally to be preferred, I suppose, to a man who will sleep with a woman who tells him her name but he forgets it in the morning.

The good cop, Deputy Chief Arthur Holland, played by Ving Rhames, knows Van Meter is crooked and has to decide whether to stay and prove it, or take an offer to become police chief of Cleveland. Meanwhile, the clock ticks toward an "innocent" verdict for the cops who were videotaped while beating Rodney King. (This does not stop the police academy from scheduling a promotion ceremony at the very same time, so that everyone will be in the same room when they are required for the big scene.)

I'm making the film sound too obvious. It follows well-worn pathways, but it has a literate, colloquial screenplay by David Ayer *(Training Day, The Fast and the Furious)*, whose dialogue sounds as if someone might actually say it, and the direction is by Ron Shelton *(White Men Can't Jump, Bull Durham)*, who marches us right up to clichés and then pulls them out from under us.

Above all, the movie has the Kurt Russell performance going for it. Every time I see Russell or Val Kilmer in a role, I'm reminded of their *Tombstone* (1993), which got lost in the year-end holiday shuffle and never got the recognition it deserved. Russell has reserves he can draw on when he needs them, and he needs them here, as Perry descends into self-disgust

and then, finally, understands the world and the role he has chosen. There is a late shot in which we look over his character's shoulder as Los Angeles burns all the way to the horizon. It takes a lot of setup to get away with a payoff like that, but Shelton and Russell earn it.

Dark Blue is not a great movie, but it has moments that go off the meter and find visceral impact. The characters driving through the riot-torn streets of Los Angeles provide some of them, and the savage, self-hating irony of Russell's late dialogue provides the rest. It is a clanging coincidence that the LAPD would be indicted just at the moment it was being exonerated, but then that's what the movies are for sometimes: to provide the outcomes that history overlooked.

Dark Blue World ★ ★

R, 114 m., 2002

Ondrej Vetchy (Franktisek Slama), Krystof Hadek (Karel Vojtisek), Tara Fitzgerald (Susan), Charles Dance (Colonel Bentley), Oldrich Kaiser (Machaty), Linda Rybova (Hanicka), Lukas Kantor (Tamtam), Hans-Jorg Assmann (Dr. Blaschke). Directed by Jan Sverak and produced by Eric Abraham and Jan Sverak. Screenplay by Zdenek Sverak.

Dark Blue World recycles some of the aerial combat footage shot for *Battle of Britain* (1969), and indeed, some of the same old-fashioned war movie clichés, like the faithful dog pining for its master. Told mostly in English, it's the story of two Czech pilots who escape their Nazi-occupied homeland, go to England, and enlist in the RAF to fight the Germans. Returning to Czechoslovakia after the war, one is rewarded for his pains by being jailed (exposure to British values might cause him to question communism). He finds that former S.S. men are his guards.

The Czech scenes are bookends for the heart of the story, which intercuts aerial dogfights with a love triangle in which both pilots have romances with the same English woman. Susan (Tara Fitzgerald) is minding a houseful of orphans in the countryside, and befriends Karel (Krystof Hadek). They fall in the wartime equivalent of love (her husband is missing in action), and Karel proudly introduces her to his friend Franktisek (Ondrej Vetch). Alas, not long after, he feels embittered and betrayed.

With *Pearl Harbor* fresh in my mind, here is yet another movie in which World War II supplies a backdrop for a love triangle. And not even a convincing, psychologically complex love triangle, but one imposed upon us by the requirements of the screenplay: The participants are attractive and sweet and we like them, but they get shuffled around for pragmatic reasons.

The aerial footage is good. It should be; in many cases, those are real planes, really in the air. Some of the shots come from the 1969 Harry Saltzman production, and well do I remember visiting a British airfield near Newmarket to see the actual Spitfires and other real planes purchased or rented for *Battle of Britain.* I even met Battle of Britain aces Douglas Bader, Ginger Lacey, and Group Captain Peter Townsend, although I inform you at this late date primarily because that old memory is more interesting than this movie.

The director, Jan Sverak, works from a screenplay by his father, Zdenek Sverak. They also made the splendid *Kolya* (1997), in which Zdenek starred as an ideologically untrustworthy cellist who is bounced from the philharmonic, marries a woman to save her from being returned to Russia, and (when she skips town) ends up in an uneasy but eventually heartwarming relationship with her five-year-old son. *Kolya* was as emotionally authentic and original as *Dark Blue World* is derivative and not compelling.

The movie's open and close will be significant in Czechoslovakia, where communism turned out to be preferable only to Nazism, which isn't saying much. As the German doctor observes in the prison hospital: "I'll bet back in England you never thought they'd welcome you back with such a sad song."

Das Experiment ★ ★ ★
NO MPAA RATING, 113 m., 2002

Moritz Bleibtreu (Tarek Fahd, No. 77), Justus von Dohnanyi (Berus), Christian Berkel (Steinhoff, No. 38), Oliver Stokowski (Schutte, No. 82), Wotan Wilke Mohring (Joe, No. 69), Stephan Szasz (No. 53), Polat Dal (No. 40), Danny Richter (No. 21), Ralf Müller (No. 15), Maren Eggert (Dora). Directed by Oliver Hirschbiegel and produced by Marc Conrad, Norbert Preuss, and Friedrich Wildfeuer. Screenplay by Don Bohlinger, Christoph Darnstädt, Mario Giordano, Hirschbiegel, and Wildfeuer, based on the novel *Black Box* by Giordano.

Human behavior is determined to some degree by the uniforms we wear. An army might march more easily in sweatpants, but it wouldn't have the same sense of purpose. School uniforms enlist kids in the "student body." Catholic nuns saw recruitment fall off when they modernized their habits. If you want to figure out what someone thinks of himself, examine the uniform he is wearing. Gene Siskel amused himself by looking at people on the street and thinking: When they left home this morning, they thought they looked good in that.

Das Experiment, a new film from Germany, suggests that uniforms and the roles they assign amplify underlying psychological tendencies. In the experiment, twenty men are recruited to spend two weeks in a prison environment. Eight are made into guards and given quasi-military uniforms. Twelve become prisoners and wear nightshirts with numbers sewn on them. All twenty know they are merely volunteers working for a $1,700 paycheck.

The movie is based on a novel, *Black Box,* by Mario Giordano. The novel was probably inspired by the famous Stanford Prison Experiment of 1971, a classic of role-playing. On that experiment's Website, its director, Philip G. Zimbardo, writes:

> How we went about testing these questions and what we found may astound you. Our planned two-week investigation into the psychology of prison life had to be ended prematurely after only six days because of what the situation was doing to the college students who participated. In only a few days, our guards became sadistic and our prisoners became depressed and showed signs of extreme stress.

So there, I've given away the plot. Some critics of *Das Experiment* question the fact that the guards become cruel so quickly, but the real-life experiment bears that out. What is fascinating is how most of the members of both groups tend to follow charismatic leaders. None of the other guards is as sadistic as Berus (Justus von Dohnanyi) and none of the other prisoners is as rebellious as Tarek Fahd (Moritz Bleibtreu), who remembers, "My father would say 'don't do this,' and I'd do it."

Perhaps uniforms turn us into packs, led by the top dog. There are a few strays. One prisoner seems custom-made to be a victim, but another, a man with military experience, holds back and tries to analyze the situation and provide cool guidance. But he's more or less powerless because—well, the guards are in charge. One of the guards has misgivings about what is happening, but it takes a lot of nerve to defy the pack.

It would make perfect sense for the guards to say, "Look, we're all in this together and we all want the $1,700 at the end of the two weeks. So let's make it easy on ourselves." But at Stanford as in this movie (and in life), that is not human nature. The outcome of the experiment is clear from the setup. We would be astonished if the guards became humane.

What impressed me is how effective the movie was, even though the outcome is a foregone conclusion. That's a tribute to the director, Oliver Hirschbiegel, and the actors, who have been chosen with the same kind of typecasting that perhaps occurs in life. The sadist *looks* mean. The rebel *looks* like a troublemaker. The military guy *looks* competent. The victim *looks* submissive. We see them and read them. Is it the same in life?

By halfway through, I was surprised how involved I was, and I see that I stopped taking notes at about that point—stopped thinking objectively and began to identify. Of course, I identified with the troublemaker. But give me a uniform and who knows what I would have done. The fact that the movie is German inspires thoughts about the Holocaust: The Nazi command structure needed only strong leaders at the top for Hitler to find, as one book called them, willing executioners in the ranks. But is the syndrome limited to Nazi Germany? This movie argues not.

Thinking of World War II, we're reminded not only of the Nazi uniforms, which were fetishistic, but of the genial sloppiness of the average American GI, as unforgettably portrayed by the great Bill Mauldin. His Willie and Joe, unshaven, their helmets askew, cigarettes dangling from their lips, resented authority, but they won the war.

Note: The Stanford Prison Experiment is at www.prisonexp.org.

Dawn of the Dead ★ ★ ★

R, 100 m., 2004

Sarah Polley (Ana), Ving Rhames (Kenneth), Jake Weber (Michael), Mekhi Phifer (Andre), Inna Korobkina (Luda), Michael Kelly (CJ). Directed by Zack Snyder and produced by Marc Abraham, Eric Newman, and Richard P. Rubinstein. Screenplay by James Gunn, based on the original by George A. Romero.

The contrast between this new version of *Dawn of the Dead* and the 1979 George Romero original is instructive in the ways that Hollywood has grown more skillful and less daring over the years. From a technical point of view, the new *Dawn* is slicker and more polished, and the acting is better, too. But it lacks the mordant humor of the Romero version, and although both films are mostly set inside a shopping mall, only Romero uses that as an occasion for satirical jabs at a consumer society. The 1979 film dug deeper in another way, by showing two groups of healthy humans fighting each other; the new version draws a line between the healthy and the zombies and maintains it. Since the zombies cannot be blamed for their behavior, there is no real conflict between good and evil in Zack Snyder's new version; just humans fighting ghouls. The conflict between the two healthy groups in the Romero film does have a pale shadow in the new one; a hard-nosed security guard (Michael Kelly) likes to wave his gun and order people around, and is set up as the bad guy, but his character undergoes an inexplicable change just for the convenience of the plot.

All of which is not to say that the new *Dawn of the Dead* doesn't do an efficient job of delivering the goods. The screenplay, credited to James Gunn (based on Romero's original screenplay), has been coproduced by Richard P. Rubinstein, who produced the original. They use the same premise: An unexplained disease or virus, spread by human bites, kills its victims and then resurrects them as zombies. The creatures then run berserk, attacking healthy humans, infecting them, and so on. The only way to kill them is to shoot them in the head. True to the general speed-up in modern Hollywood, these new-issue zombies run fast, unlike the earlier ones, who lurched along. They also seem smarter and make decisions faster, unlike the 1979 models, who were likely to lurch up the down escalator.

The story begins with Ana (Sarah Polley) greeting a young girl who lives in the neighborhood. As the girl skates away on her in-lines, the shot is held just a little longer than seems natural, informing us that Something Bad Will Happen to Her. And does, as the next morning she attacks Ana's boyfriend, and Ana barely escapes with her life. After zombies roam the streets, newscasters fight hysteria, and neighborhoods burn, Ana eventually finds herself part of a small group in the local shopping mall.

Well, not such a small group. Unlike the tight little group of survivors in *28 Days Later*, this one expands to the point where we don't much care about some of the characters (the blond with the red lipstick, for example). But we do care about Kenneth (Ving Rhames), a gravel-voiced cop with hard-edged authority. We care about Michael (Jake Weber), a decent guy who tries to make the right decisions. And we care about Andre (Mekhi Phifer), whose wife, Luda (Inna Korobkina), is great with child and will give birth at any moment; the way that plot plays out is touching and horrifying. We even work up some feeling for the guy marooned on the roof of the gun shop across the street, who communicates with Kenneth by holding up signs.

For the rest, the movie consists mostly of dialogue and character scenes, alternating with violent attacks by zombies. The movie wisely doesn't give us too many of those scenes where one guy wanders off by himself when we're mentally screaming, "Stick together!" And although there is a cute dog, at least it's made useful in the plot. Of course, the movie makes full use of the shock shot where a zombie suddenly appears in the foreground from out of nowhere.

Of gore and blood there is a sufficiency. When the survivors devise a risky way to escape from the mall (which I will not reveal), a chain saw plays a key role. The survivors take chances that are probably unwise; maybe they should stay in a safe place, since the zombies will presumably sooner or later run out of gas. But taking chances makes for good action scenes, and exploding propane is always useful.

So, yes, *Dawn of the Dead* works, and it delivers just about what you expect when you buy your ticket. My only complaint is that its plot flat-lines compared to the 1979 version, which was trickier, wittier, and smarter. Romero was not above finding parallels between zombies and mall shoppers; in the new version, the mall is just a useful location, although at least there are still a few jokes about the Muzak. ☞

The Day After Tomorrow ★ ★ ★
PG-13, 124 m., 2004

Dennis Quaid (Jack Hall), Jake Gyllenhaal (Sam Hall), Ian Holm (Terry Rapson), Emmy Rossum (Laura Chapman), Sela Ward (Dr. Lucy Hall), Dash Mihok (Jason Evans), Kenneth Welsh (Vice President Becker), Jay O. Sanders (Frank Harris), Austin Nichols (J.D.), Perry King (President), Arjay Smith (Brian Parks). Directed by Roland Emmerich and produced by Emmerich and Mark Gordon. Screenplay by Emmerich and Jeffrey Nachmanoff.

It is such a relief to hear the music swell up at the end of a Roland Emmerich movie, its restorative power giving us new hope. Billions of people may have died, but at least the major characters have survived. Los Angeles was wiped out by flying saucers in Emmerich's *Independence Day*, New York was assaulted in his *Godzilla*, and now, in *The Day After Tomorrow*, Emmerich outdoes himself: Los Angeles is leveled by multiple tornadoes, New York is buried under ice and snow, the United Kingdom is flash-frozen, and lots of the Northern Hemisphere is wiped out for good measure. Thank God that Jack, Sam, Laura, Jason, and Dr. Lucy Hall survive, along with Dr. Hall's little cancer patient.

So, yes, the movie is profoundly silly. What surprised me is that it's also very scary. The special effects are on such an awesome scale that the movie works in spite of its cornball plotting. When tornadoes rip apart Los Angeles (not sparing the Hollywood sign), when a wall of water roars into New York, when a Russian tanker floats down a Manhattan street, when snow buries skyscrapers, when the crew of a space station can see nothing but violent storm systems—well, you pay attention.

No doubt some readers are already angry with me for revealing that Jack, Sam, Laura, Jason, Dr. Lucy Hall, and the little cancer patient survive. Have I given away the plot? This plot gives itself away. When cataclysmic events shred uncounted lives but the movie zeroes in on only a few people, of *course* they survive, although some supporting characters may have to be sacrificed. What's amusing in movies like *The Day After Tomorrow* is the way the screenplay veers from the annihilation of subcontinents to whether Sam should tell Laura he loves her.

The movie stars Dennis Quaid as the paleoclimatologist Jack Hall, whose computer models predict that global warming will lead to a new ice age. He issues a warning at a New Delhi conference, but is sarcastically dismissed by the American vice president (Kenneth Welsh), whom the movie doesn't even try to pretend doesn't look just like Dick Cheney. "Our economy is every bit as fragile as the environment," the vice president says, dismissing Jack's "sensational claims."

Before long, however, it is snowing in India, and hailstones the size of softballs are ripping into Tokyo. Birds, which are always wise in matters of global disaster, fly south double-time. Turbulence tears airplanes from the sky. The president (Perry King) learns the FAA wants to ground all flights, and asks the vice president, "What do you think we should do?"

Meanwhile, young Sam Hall (Jake Gyllenhaal) goes to New York with an academic decathlon team, which includes Laura (Emmy Rossum of *Mystic River*) and Brian (Arjay Smith). They're stranded there. Ominous portents abound and Jack finally gets his message through to the administration ("This time," says a friend within the White House, "it will be different. You've got to brief the president directly.")

Jack draws a slash across a map of the United States and writes off everybody north of it. He issues a warning that supercooled air will kill anybody exposed to it, advises those in its path to stay inside, and then . . . well, then he sets off to walk from Washington to New York to get to his son. Two of his buddies, also veterans of Arctic treks, come along.

We are wondering (a) why walk to New York when his expertise is desperately needed to save millions, (b) won't his son be either dead or alive whether or not he makes the trek? And (c) how quickly *can* you walk from Washington to New York over ice sheets and through a howling blizzard? As nearly as I can calculate, this movie believes it can be done in two nights and most of three days. Oh, I forgot; they drive part of the way, on highways that are gridlocked and buried in snow, except for where they're driving. How they get gas is not discussed in any detail.

As for the answer to (a), anyone familiar with the formula will know it is because he Feels Guilty About Neglecting His Son by spending all that time being a paleoclimatologist. It took him a lot of that time just to spell it. So okay, the human subplots are nonsense—all except for the quiet scenes anchored by Ian Holm, as a sad, wise Scottish meteorologist. Just like Peter O'Toole in *Troy*, Holm proves that a British-trained actor can walk into almost any scene and make it seem like it means something.

Quaid and Gyllenhaal and the small band of New York survivors do what can be done with impossible dialogue in an unlikely situation. And Dr. Lucy Hall (Sela Ward), Jack's wife and Sam's mother, struggles nobly in her subplot, which involves the little cancer patient named Peter. She stays by his side after the hospital is evacuated, calling for an ambulance, which we think is a tad optimistic, since Manhattan has been flooded up to about the eighth floor, the water has frozen, and it's snowing. But does the ambulance arrive? Here's another one for you: Remember those wolves that escaped from the zoo? Think we'll see them again?

Of the science in this movie I have no opinion. I am sure global warming is real, and I regret that the Bush administration rejected the Kyoto treaty, but I doubt that the cataclysm, if it comes, will come like this. It makes for a fun movie, though. Especially the parts where Americans become illegal immigrants in Mexico, and the vice president addresses the world via the Weather Channel. *The Day After Tomorrow* is ridiculous, yes, but sublimely ridiculous—and the special effects are stupendous.

Deadline ★ ★ ★
NO MPAA RATING, 93 m., 2004

A documentary directed by Katy Chevigny and Kirsten Johnson and produced by Dallas Brennan and Chevigny.

If there were one hundred condemned prisoners on death row and one of them was innocent, would it be defensible to kill all one hundred on the grounds that the other ninety-nine deserved to die? Most reasonable people would answer that it would be wrong. Yet evidence has been gathering for years that far more than 1 percent of the inhabitants of death row are innocent. In the Illinois penal system, for example, a study following twenty-five condemned men ended after twelve of them had been executed, and the other thirteen had been exonerated of their crimes after new evidence was produced.

Deadline is a sober, even low-key documentary about how the American death penalty system is broken and probably can't be fixed. It climaxes with the extraordinary January 2003 press conference at which Republican Governor George Ryan commuted the death sentences of all 167 prisoners awaiting execution in Illinois. His action followed a long, anguished, public process scrutinizing the death penalty in Illinois—a penalty here, as throughout the United States, administered overwhelmingly upon defendants who are poor and/or belong to minority groups.

The film opens with Ryan speaking to students at Northwestern University, where students in an investigative journalism class had been successful in proving the innocence of three men on death row. That was a tribute not only to their skills as student journalists but also to the ease with which the evidence against the prisoners could be disproved. Many thoughtful observations in the doc come from Scott Turow, the Chicago lawyer and crime novelist who was appointed by Ryan to a commission to consider clemency for Illinois's condemned. He is not against the death penalty itself, he says, and was completely comfortable with the execution of John Wayne Gacy, killer of thirty-three young men. "But can we construct a system that *only* executes the John Wayne Gacys, without executing the innocent?" Turow doubts it.

Murder cases have high profiles, and the police are under pressure for arrests and charges. They don't precisely frame innocent people, the movie argues, but when they find someone who looks like a plausible perpetrator they tend to zero in with high-pressure tactics, willing their prisoner to be guilty. Confessions were tortured out of some of the Illinois prisoners in *Deadline*, including one who was dangled out of a high window by his handcuffs, and another who signed a confession in English even though he could not speak it.

The death penalty was briefly outlawed by the U.S. Supreme Court in 1972, and then reinstated in 1976 after the justices were persuaded the system's flaws had been repaired. It was during that time, the movie says, that Richard M. Nixon "discovered crime as a national issue." Before then, it had been thought of as a local problem and did not enter into presidential campaigns. After Nixon's law-and-order rhetoric, politicians of both parties followed his lead. "All politicians want to be seen as tough on crime," observes Illinois GOP house leader Tom Cross.

Since 1976 there has been a startling rise in executions in America, one of the few Western countries that still allow the death penalty. The movie cites statistics for American prisoners put to death:

1976–1980: 3 executions.
1981–1990: 140 executions.
1991–2000: 540 executions.

That latest figure was enhanced by just one governor, George W. Bush of Texas; 152 prisoners were executed under his watch between 1995 and 2000, as Texas in five years outstripped the entire nation in the previous decade. In a speech, Bush says he is absolutely certain they were all guilty. For that matter, Bill Clinton must have known one of his Arkansas prisoners was so brain-damaged he asked the warden after his last meal, "Save my dessert so I can have it after the execution." But Clinton was running for president and dared not pardon this man, lest he be seen as soft on crime.

Some of the movie's most dramatic moments take place during hearings before Ryan's clemency commission, which reheard all 167 pending cases. The relatives of many victims say they will not be able to rest until the guilty have been put to death. But then we hear testimony from a group called Murder Victims' Families Against the Death Penalty. Among their witnesses are the father of a woman killed in the Oklahoma City terror attack, and the mother of the Chicago youth Emmett Till, murdered by southern racists fifty years ago. They say they do not want revenge and are opposed to the death penalty.

Deadline is all the more effective because it is calm, factual and unsensational. There are times when we are confused by its chronology and by how its story threads fit together, but it makes an irrefutable argument: Our criminal justice system is so flawed, especially when it deals with the poor and the nonwhite, that we cannot be sure of the guilt of many of those we put to death. George Ryan, not running for re-election, faced that truth and commuted those sentences, and said he could live with his decision. George Bush was absolutely confident he was right to allow 152 prisoners to die. He could live with his decision too.

Death to Smoochy ½★

R, 105 m., 2002

Robin Williams (Rainbow Randolph), Edward Norton (Sheldon Mopes [Smoochy]), Danny DeVito (Burke), Jon Stewart (Stokes), Catherine Keener (Nora), Harvey Fierstein (Merv Green), Vincent Schiavelli (Buggy Ding Dong). Directed by Danny DeVito and produced by Andrew Lazar and Peter MacGregor-Scott. Screenplay by Adam Resnick.

Only enormously talented people could have made *Death to Smoochy*. Those with lesser gifts would have lacked the nerve to make a film so bad, so miscalculated, so lacking any connection with any possible audience. To make a film this awful, you have to have enormous ambition and confidence, and dream big dreams.

The movie, directed by Danny DeVito (!), is about two clowns. That violates a cardinal rule of modern mass entertainment, which is that everyone hates clowns almost as much as they hate mimes. (*Big Fat Liar,* a much better recent

showbiz comedy, got this right. When the clown arrived at a birthday party, the kids joyfully shouted, "Hey, it's the clown! Let's hurt him!") Most clowns are simply tiresome (I exempt Bozo). There are, however, two dread categories of clowns: clowns who are secretly vile and evil, and clowns who are guileless and good. *Death to Smoochy* takes no half-measures, and provides us with one of each.

We begin with Rainbow Randolph, played by Robin Williams, an actor who should never, ever play a clown of any description, because the role writes a license for him to indulge in those very mannerisms he should be striving to purge from his repertoire. Rainbow is a corrupt drunk who takes bribes to put kids on his show. The show itself is what kiddie TV would look like if kids wanted to see an Ann Miller musical starring midgets.

The good clown is Smoochy (Edward Norton), a soul so cheerful, earnest, honest, and uncomplicated you want to slap him and bring him back to his senses. Sample helpful Smoochy song for kids: "My Stepdad's Not Bad, He's Just Adjusting." Both of these clowns wear the kinds of costumes seen at the openings of used-car lots in states that doubt the possibility of evolution. Rainbow is convoluted, but Smoochy is so boring that the film explains why, on a long bus ride, you should always choose to sit next to Mrs. Robinson, for example, rather than Benjamin.

Enter the film's most engaging character, a TV producer named Nora (Catherine Keener), who, like Rachel Griffiths, cannot play dumb and is smart enough never to try. She's taking instructions from the network boss (Jon Stewart, who might have been interesting as one of the clowns). They're trapped in an inane subplot involving two bad guys, Burke (DeVito) and Merv Green (played by the gravel-voiced Harvey Fierstein, who, as he puts on weight, is becoming boulder-voiced). There is also Vincent Schiavelli as a former child star, now a crackhead.

The drama of the two clowns and their battle for the time slot is complicated by Rainbow Randolph's attempts to smear Smoochy by tricking him into appearing at a neo-Nazi rally. One wonders idly: Are there enough neo-Nazis to fill a thundering convention center? Do they usually book clowns? The answer to the second question may be yes.

The movie ends by crossing an ice show with elements of *The Manchurian Candidate*. It involves an odd sexual predilection: Nora has a fetish for kiddie show hosts. It has a lesbian hit-squad leader with a thick Irish brogue. It uses four-letter language as if being paid by the word. In all the annals of the movies, few films have been this odd, inexplicable, and unpleasant.

The Debut ★ ★ ★
NO MPAA RATING, 89 m., 2002

Dante Basco (Ben Mercado), Bernadette Balagtas (Rose Mercado), Tirso Cruz III (Roland Mercado), Gina Alajar (Gina Mercado), Eddie Garcia (Lolo Carlos), Joy Bisco (Annabelle), Darion Basco (Augusto), Dion Basco (Rommel), Fe de Los Reyes (Alice). Directed by Gene Cajayon and produced by Lisa Onodera. Screenplay by Cajayon and John Manal Castro.

There is a moment in *The Debut* where a white man, who has married into a Filipino-American family, solemnly informs a dinner party of Filipinos that they are "not considered Asians, but Malays." He doesn't realize how offensive and condescending it is for an outsider to tell people about themselves, but there is another reason to put the dialogue in this first-ever Filipino-American film: Most Americans don't know that. And now, knowing it, they don't know what a Malay is. And unless they've been in the Philippines, they don't have much idea of the heritage of the islands, where the cultures of the Pacific and Spain intersect with America. And they don't know that Tagalog is the national language, coexisting with English. And that the Philippine film industry is one of the few outside the United States and India to possess more than 50 percent of its own market.

Given the health of the film industry and the availability of English, it's surprising that it took so long for this first Filipino-American feature to be born. It joins a group of films about second-generation immigrants, standing between the traditions of their parents and their own headlong dive into American culture. *Maryam* is about an Iranian-American

teenage girl in conflict with strict Iranian parents. *ABCD* and *American Desi* are about Indian-Americans. *Real Women Have Curves* is about a Mexican-American teenager whose mother opposes her college plans. *Bread and Roses* is about a Mexican-American strike leader whose sister opposes her. *Mi Familia* is a multi-generational story about Mexican-Americans, and *The Joy Luck Club* is a Chinese-American version. For that matter, *Stolen Summer* has an Irish-American dad who wants his son to follow him into the fire department instead of going to college.

The films have elements in common: A bright young person who dreams of personal fulfillment. Parents who worked hard to support their families in a new land, and now want to dictate the choices of their children. A father who is stern, a mother who is a mediator. And with surprising frequency, a stiff, unyielding older man, a grandfather or "sponsor," who is like the ghost at the family feast. The message of all of the movies: The older generation must bend and let the kids follow their dreams. That's not surprising, since the kids make the films, and all of these filmmakers must have had parents who thought they were crazy to dream of becoming movie directors.

The Debut is familiar in its story arc, but fresh in its energy and lucky in its choice of actors. Filmed on a low budget, it looks and plays like an assured professional film, and its young leads are potential stars. The story involves a high school student named Ben Mercado (Dante Basco), who works in a comic-book store and in the opening scene is selling his comics collection to help pay his way into Cal Arts.

He wants to be a graphic artist. His father, Roland (Tirso Cruz III), a postman, has other plans for Ben, who has won a pre-med scholarship to UCLA. The boy will be a doctor, period. Everything comes to a head at the eighteenth birthday party of Ben's sister Rose (Bernadette Balagtas), the "debut" of the title.

Ben has assimilated by always keeping a certain distance between his friends and his family. His best buddies are an Anglo and a Mexican-American, who are curious about Ben's home life, but keep getting shuffled aside. When they mention the inviting cooking aromas, Ben takes that as a criticism of the way his home smells. On the night of Rose's party, Ben has made plans to meet a pretty Anglo girl at a high school party, and is torn between the two events (unlike his friends, who have more fun at Rose's party).

The movie involves some melodrama when Ben meets Rose's pretty Filipino-American friend Annabel (Joy Bisco) and it's love at first sight; Annabel is breaking up with a tough boyfriend who, in the modern equivalent of male possessiveness, wants her to wear a pager. In a scene at a burger joint, there's casual racism in jibes that Filipinos eat dogs, and Ben is called a "Chink." "I'm not Chinese," he murmurs, and we realize one reason for the white man's gauche line about Malays is to get information into the screenplay that Filipinos would hardly tell one another.

The outcome of all of this is not hard to anticipate, but the setting is new, and the birthday party provides an excuse for traditional songs and dances (as well as for a virtuoso performance of hip-hop turntabling, an art where Filipino-Americans often win U.S. contests). In Dante Basco, Bernadette Balagtas, and Joy Bisco the movie has likable, convincing young actors with marquee potential, and all of the major roles are filled with capable pros. There is one surprise. In most movies about artists, the artwork never looks as good as the movie thinks it does. But when Ben shows his father his portfolio, we see he does have the talent to realize his dream of writing graphic novels. Or maybe even go into animation and make some real dough.

Deliver Us from Eva ★ ★

R, 105 m., 2003

Gabrielle Union (Eva), LL Cool J (Ray), Essence Atkins (Kareenah), Mel Jackson (Tim), Meagan Good (Jacqui), Dartanyan Edmonds (Darrell), Robinne Lee (Bethany), Duane Martin (Mike). Directed by Gary Hardwick and produced by Len Amato and Paddy Cullen. Screenplay by Hardwick, James Iver Mattson, and B. E. Brauner.

Deliver Us from Eva is the second movie of the same weekend based on a romantic bet. See my review of *How to Lose a Guy in 10 Days* for my general comments on this unhappy genre. *Eva* has the advantage of being about one bet, not two, preserving at least one of the protagonists as a person we can safely like. But it proceeds so deliberately from one plot point to the next that we want to stand next to the camera, holding up cards upon which we have lettered clues and suggestions.

The movie stars two tall and striking actors, Gabrielle Union and LL Cool J, who have every reason to like each other anyway, even if Union's brothers-in-law were not paying him $5,000 to take her out, make her fall in love, and move with her to a town far, far away. They can't stand the woman. Well, hardly can we.

Union plays Eva, oldest of the four Dandridge sisters. After the untimely death of their parents, Eva took on the task of raising the girls, and has never been able to stop giving the orders—no, not even now that they're grown up. The sisters are Kareenah (Essence Atkins), who won't get pregnant, on Eva's orders; Bethany (Robinne Lee), whom Eva won't let live with her cop boyfriend; and Jacqui (Meagan Good), who is married to a mailman who always feels like there's postage due.

The Dandridge sisters like their local fame and kind of enjoy being under Eva's motherly thumb. The director, Gary Hardwick, often films them cresting a hill, four abreast, hair and skirts flying, arms linked, while straggling after them are their luckless men, left in the rear. Much of the action centers on a beauty parlor, serving, like the title location in *Barbershop*, as the stage upon which daily soap operas are played out to loud acclaim or criticism.

The Dandridge family logjam is broken, as we can easily foresee, when Eva actually begins to fall for that big lug Ray (played by LL Cool J, who says after this movie he is changing his name back to James Todd Smith, a victory for punctuationists everywhere). He wins her over by admiring her spicy beans, which are too hot for the wimps she usually dates. If the way to a man's heart is through his stomach, the way to a woman's heart is through adoring a recipe that only she thinks is edible.

But let's back up. The problem with their love affair, of course, is that although Eva loves Ray and Ray loves Eva, Eva is certain to find out about the bet, causing a scene of heartbreak and betrayal that would be moving if I hadn't also seen it in *How to Lose a Guy in 10 Days* and every other movie in history where lovers begin with secret deception and arrive at the truth.

Any two lovers with the slightest instinct for each other, with the most perfunctory ability to see true romance glowing in the eyes of the beloved, would not have the fight because they would not need the fight. They would know their love was true. I live to see the following scene:

> She: You mean . . . you only went out with me on a bet!?!
>
> He: That's right, baby.
>
> She: Well, you won, you dumb lug. Now haul your lying ass over here and make me forget it.

De-Lovely ★ ★ ★ ½

PG-13, 125 m., 2004

Kevin Kline (Cole Porter), Ashley Judd (Linda Lee Porter), Jonathan Pryce (Gabe), Kevin MacNally (Gerald Murphy), Sandra Nelson (Sara Murphy), Allan Corduner (Monty Woolley), Peter Polycarpou (Louis B. Mayer), Keith Allen (Irving Berlin). Directed by Irwin Winkler and produced by Rob Cowan, Charles Winkler, and Irwin Winkler. Screenplay by Jay Cocks.

I wanted every kind of love that was available, but I could never find them in the same person, or the same sex.

—Cole Porter

Porter floated effortlessly for a time between worlds: gay and straight, Europe and America, Broadway and Hollywood, showbiz and high society. He had a lifelong love affair with his wife, and lifelong love affairs without his wife. He thrived, it seemed, on a lifestyle that would have destroyed other men (and was, in fact, illegal in most of the places that he lived), and all the time he wrote those magical songs. Then a horse fell down and crushed his legs, and he spent twenty-seven years in pain. And *still* he wrote those magical songs.

De-Lovely is a musical and a biography, and brings to both of those genres a worldly sophistication that is rare in the movies. (If you seek to find how rare, compare this film with

Night and Day, the 1946 biopic that stars Cary Grant as a resolutely straight Porter, even sending him off to World War I.) *De-Lovely* not only accepts Porter's complications, but bases the movie on them; his lyrics take on a tantalizing ambiguity once you understand that they are not necessarily written about love with a woman:

> It's the wrong game, with the wrong chips
> Though your lips are tempting, they're
> the wrong lips
> They're not her lips, but they're such
> tempting lips
> That, if some night, you're free
> Then it's all right, yes, it's all right with
> me.

It would appear from *De-Lovely* that on many nights Porter was free, and yet Linda Lee Porter was the love and solace of his life, and she accepted him as he was. One night in Paris they put their cards on the table.

"You know then, that I have other interests," he says.

"Like men."

"Yes, men."

"You like them more than I do. Nothing is cruel if it fulfills your promise."

Dialogue like this requires a certain wistful detachment, and Kevin Kline is ideally cast as Cole Porter: elegant, witty, always onstage, brave in the face of society and his own pain. Kline plays the piano, too, which allows the character to spend a lot of convincing time at the keyboard, writing the sound track of his life. But who might have known Ashley Judd would be so nuanced as Linda Lee? In those early scenes she lets Porter know she wants him and yet allows him his freedom, and she speaks with such tact that she is perfectly understood without really having said anything at all. Yet their relationship was by definition painful for her, because it was really all on his terms. Many of his lyrics are fair enough to reflect that from her point of view:

> Every time we say goodbye, I die a little,
> Every time we say goodbye, I wonder why
> a little,
> Why the gods above me, who must be in
> the know.
> Think so little of me, they allow you to go.

Cole and Linda met in Paris at that time in

the twenties when expatriate Americans were creating a new kind of lifestyle. Scott and Zelda were there, too, and Hemingway, and the movie supplies as the Porters' best friends the famous American exile couple Sara and Gerald Murphy (the originals for Fitzgerald's *Tender Is the Night*). Porter was born with money, made piles more, and spent it fabulously, on parties in Venice and traveling in high style. Linda's sense of style suited his own: They always looked freshly pressed, always seemed at home, always had the last word, even if beneath the surface there was too much drinking and too many compromises. The chain smoking that eventually killed Linda was at first an expression of freedom, at the end perhaps a kind of defense.

The movie, directed by Irwin Winkler *(Life as a House)* and written by Jay Cocks *(The Age of Innocence)*, is told as a series of flashbacks from a ghostly rehearsal for a stage musical based on Porter's life. Porter and a producer (Jonathan Pryce) sit in the theater, watching scenes run past, but the actors cannot see or hear Porter, and the producer may in a sense be a recording angel.

This structure allows the old, tired, widowed, wounded Porter to revisit the days of his joy, and at the same time explains the presence of many musical stars who appear, both on stage and in dramatic flashbacks, to perform Porter's songs. Porter has famously been interpreted by every modern pop singer of significance, most memorably by Ella Fitzgerald in *The Cole Porter Songbook*, but here we get a new generation trying on his lyrics: Elvis Costello, Alanis Morissette, Sheryl Crow, Natalie Cole, Robbie Williams, Diana Krall.

The movie contains more music than most musicals, yet is not a concert film because the songs seem to rise so naturally out of the material and illuminate it. We're reminded how exhilarating the classic American songbook is, and how inarticulate so much modern music sounds by contrast. Kevin Kline plays Porter as a man apparently able to write a perfect song more or less on demand, which would be preposterous if it were not more or less true. One of Porter's friends was Irving Berlin, who labored to bring forth his songs and must have given long thought to how easy it seemed for Porter.

If the film has a weakness, it is that neither Cole nor Linda ever found full, complete, passionate, satisfying romance. They couldn't find it with each other, almost by the terms of their arrangement, but there is no evidence that Porter found it in serial promiscuity, and although Linda Lee did have affairs, they are not made a significant part of this story. They were a good fit not because they were a great love story, but because they were able to provide each other consolation in its absence.

Strange, dear, but true, dear, he began a
  song that confessed:
Even without you,
My arms fold about you,
You know, darling why,
So in love with you am I.

Demonlover ★ ★

NO MPAA RATING, 129 m., 2003

Connie Nielsen (Diane de Monx), Charles Berling (Hervé Le Millinec), Chloë Sevigny (Elise Lipsky), Gina Gershon (Elaine Si Gibril), Jean-Baptiste Malartre (Henri-Pierre Volf), Dominique Reymond (Karen), Edwin Gerard (Edward Gomez). Directed by Olivier Assayas and produced by Xavier Giannoli and Edouard Weil. Screenplay by Assayas.

Demonlover begins in the cutthroat world of big business, and descends as quickly as it can to just plain cutting throats. It's a high-gloss corporate thriller that watches a group of vicious women executives as they battle for control of lucrative new 3-D Internet porn technology. One of the sites in question offers real-time torture and death, leading us to wonder: (1) Can such a dangerously illegal site actually generate the fortune that seems to be involved? and (2) Are any of these women queasy about selling human suffering at retail? The movie's answers are apparently yes, and no.

My description makes the movie sound like a sleazy bottom-feeder, but this is an ambitious production by director Olivier Assayas, whose last film, *Les Destinees* (2000), was about a struggle for control of a family firm that manufactures Limoges china. Yes. Now we have another corporate struggle, but in a corporation with no values, no scruples, and apparently no employees, since all we see are executives.

The movie is set in the chilly world of high-gloss offices, international hotels, and private jets. French, English, and Japanese are spoken interchangeably. The story opens with Henri-Pierre Volf (Jean-Baptise Malartre), Internet millionaire, flying to Tokyo to close a deal with TokyoAnime to buy new 3-D imaging software, which will make online porn unbelievably profitable. Also on board is his ruthless assistant Diane (Connie Nielsen), who slips drugs into the Evian of her rival, Karen (Dominique Reymond). Karen passes out in the airport, her briefcase is stolen, and Diane is promoted to her job.

Until this point the movie has had the look and feel of your average corporate thriller; Michael Douglas could turn up at any moment. Then it takes a sudden drop into some really nasty business. We see demos of cutting-edge Internet porn (not graphic, but close), and we glimpse the first hints that beneath the surface an even more demented level lurks, at which users in real time are able to suggest tortures for the women they see on the screen.

Let's assume we all agree this is depraved and evil. Let's move on to the logic of the story. Would it be cost-effective to torture people online? How would you advertise this site and bill for it? How much would it cost? Who would be reckless enough to pay? An international corporation like Henri-Pierre's would obviously be wiser to sell soft porn instead of this illegal material with a tiny audience.

But never mind. The movie is confused about this and many other things, in a scenario that grows steadily murkier. Back home in Paris, Diane's scheme has paid off in the big job with the big salary, but Elise (Chloë Sevigny), who is loyal to Karen, suspects what she did to get the job, and Elise is a dangerous customer. So is Elaine (Gina Gershon), who works for the American firm Demonlover and is bidding against Magnatronics for the rights owned by Henri-Pierre. Their rivalry is further complicated (or is it made unnecessary?) by the fact that Diane is actually a corporate spy.

If that seems like a secret I should not have revealed, be assured that it is irrelevant to the progress of the movie, which exists largely in content-free visuals of beautiful women, ripped lingerie, luscious suites, sexual jousting, and lots and lots of people coming down all manner of corridors and going into one door after another in order to capture, threaten, ravish, seduce, blackmail, or murder one another.

By the end of the movie, I frankly didn't give a damn. There's an ironic twist, but the movie doesn't pay for it and doesn't deserve it. And I was struck by the complete lack of morality in *Demonlover*. No one seems to question the fact that they all plan to make money by torturing people. It's all just business. As a metaphor for certain tendencies in modern commerce, this may be intended, but somehow I don't think so. I think *Demonlover* is so in love with its visuals and cockeyed plot that it forgets to think about the implications.

Diamond Men ★ ★ ★ ½
NO MPAA RATING, 100 m., 2002

Robert Forster (Eddie Miller), Donnie Wahlberg (Bobby Walker), Bess Armstrong (Katie Harnish), Jasmine Guy (Tina), George Coe (Tip Rountree), Jeff Gendelman (Brad), Douglas Allen Johnson (John Ludwig), Kristin Minter (Cherry). Directed and produced by Daniel M. Cohen. Screenplay by Cohen.

Robert Forster has a note of gentle sadness in some of his roles, revealing a man who has lived according to a code, not always successfully. Whether that is true of his acting career, I cannot say, but it is often true of his characters. Here is an actor who has been bringing special qualities to his work as long as I have been a critic, in early movies like John Huston's *Reflections in a Golden Eye* (1967) and Haskell Wexler's *Medium Cool* (1969), and recent ones like Quentin Tarantino's *Jackie Brown* (1997) and Joe Mantegna's *Lakeboat* (2000). But for the most part he has been relegated to exploitation movies like *Maniac Cop 3* and *Original Gangstas*.

Now here he is in his best performance, in *Diamond Men,* as a man in his fifties who is about to lose the job he loves. Forster plays Eddie Miller, a diamond salesman who has long traveled the mid-sized cities of Pennsylvania, selling to the owners of jewelry stores. He has a heart attack, recovers, and is told that he is no longer "insurable" to drive around with $1 million in stock in his car. His boss introduces him to Bobby Walker (Donnie Wahlberg), a brash kid whose sales experience is limited mostly to pretzels. Eddie is to train Bobby to take over his route.

He takes on the kid because he has no choice. There is a generation gap. Eddie likes jazz; Bobby likes heavy metal. Eddie keeps a low profile: "I stay at out-of-the-way motels, I eat in quiet restaurants, I don't talk about what I do." Bobby is a party animal who has a girl in every town, or hopes to. Eddie winces as Bobby tries to sell diamonds, and fails. "How do you do it?" Bobby asks the older man. "What's the magic word? I never ever saw a diamond until a week ago. I'm afraid of them." Eddie, who has nurtured his clients for years and plays them skillfully, tries to explain: "When they say 'no,' they're looking for a way to say 'yes.'"

Bobby is not a bad kid. He's in over his head, but he wants to learn. And he wants Eddie to have more fun. Eddie's wife, we learn, died of cancer; Forster's reading as he remembers her is an exercise in perfect pitch: "She didn't want to go into a facility because . . . well, you know. And I don't blame her." Bobby takes it as his personal assignment to get Eddie laid, and after various schemes fail because Eddie is too old to attract the barflies Bobby recruits, Bobby takes Eddie to the Altoona Riding Club, which is a discreet rural brothel run by Tina (Jasmine Guy).

Here, too, Eddie strikes out: He doesn't *want* to get laid. He wants to check into that obscure motel and find that quiet restaurant. Finally Tina suggests Katie (Bess Armstrong), who is, she explains, a secretary who lost her job and needs money but doesn't want to go all the way. That's fine with Eddie. Katie treats him politely, calls him "Edward," and administers a gentle massage, and so moved is Eddie that he invites her to dinner. Really, to dinner. A quiet restaurant.

The story, written and directed by Daniel M. Cohen (himself a former diamond salesman), seems to be shaping up as a buddy movie with a good woman at the end of the road. But Cohen has laid the preparations for a series of unexpected developments, which I will not reveal. The movie keeps surprising us. First it's about salesmen, and then it's about

lonely men, and then it's about sex, and then it's about romance, and then it's about crime. It reinvents itself with every act.

Among its gifts is a quick perception of human nature. Eddie is a thoroughly good man, honest and hardworking. Bobby sees work as an unpleasant necessity. Katie is a character study, a woman who has so surrounded her occupation (hooker) with her beliefs (yoga, inner truth, meditation, transcendence) that sex is like a by-product of redemption. As in *Jackie Brown,* where he had a lovely, subtle, almost unstated courtship with the Pam Grier character, Forster plays a man for whom romance sometimes seems like more trouble than it's worth. There is truth in the wary way he regards the women Bobby finds for him.

Diamond Men is the kind of movie the American distribution system is not set up to handle. It does not appeal to teenagers. It doesn't fit into an easy category, but moves from one to another. It has actors who, by playing many different kinds of characters, have never hardened into brand names. It has fun with a crime plot and a twist at the end, but stays true to its underlying direction. It looks and listens to its characters, curious about the unfolding mysteries of the personality. It is a treasure.

The Diaries of Vaslav Nijinsky
★ ★ ★ ½
NO MPAA RATING, 95 m., 2002

Derek Jacobi (Voice of Nijinsky), Delia Silvan (Romola), Chris Haywood (Oscar), Hans Sonneveld (Doctor), Oliver Streeton (Psychiatrist), Jillian Smith (Emilia), Kevin Lucas (Diaghilev). Directed by Paul Cox and produced by Cox and Aanya Whitehead. Screenplay by Cox, from the diaries of Vaslav Nijinsky.

I attended the world premiere of Paul Cox's *The Diaries of Vaslav Nijinsky* in September 2001 at the Toronto Film Festival. It was not a serene event. The film started very late, some audience members found it difficult, and there were walkouts and even audible complaints. Cox took the microphone afterward to castigate those who had left (and could therefore not hear him) and to explain passionately why he had made the film.

His comments came down to: Art defends the final battlements against ignorance and violence. When he read the diaries, he said, "it was the first time I had read something somebody had written not out of his head but out of his heart." And to those who had stayed, in an oblique reference to mainstream commercial cinema: "At least when you walk out of the door you have not become a more disgusting human being."

The screening was held a few days after 9/11, there was borderline hysteria in the air, and the film's own examination of insanity was no doubt more disturbing than it might have been. Nor is it an easy film. I recall a conversation at the Sundance Film Festival with Ken Turan of the *Los Angeles Times*. He asked me about another difficult film.

"Well," I said, "it's the kind of movie it takes an experienced observer to appreciate. Someone who has seen a lot of movies and thought deeply about them."

"Someone like us," Turan said.

"Exactly. The average viewer is going to be incapable of accepting it as only what it is."

Pure snobbery, with our tongues in cheek, and yet not without merit. *The Diaries of Vaslav Nijinsky* is not a biography of the great dancer, or a dramatic reenactment of events in his life, but pure cinema in an experimental form, anchored by the voice of Derek Jacobi reading from the diaries. The images sometimes represent episodes in Nijinsky's life, sometimes symbolize them obliquely, sometimes represent images in his mind, sometimes simply want to evoke his state of mind. The music by Paul Grabowsky, Cox's longtime collaborator, is similarly motivated.

"I made this film in the editing room," Cox said. Out of his heart, not his head, I believe. It took him many months. Although he is a director capable of making films that communicate with anyone (such as his wonderful *Innocence* from 2000), this film will baffle those moviegoers who expect to have everything laid out for them like a buffet supper. If you have never heard of Nijinsky, this film is not going to function like a lecture. It is sensuous, not informational. Those who have seen what we once called underground films will respond, and those familiar with experimental films going back to the silent era. The structure of the film is musical, not dramatic, and attempts a sweep through Nijinsky's psyche during a period in 1919 when he danced for the last time and then was institutionalized. His diaries commenced at just this time.

Any reaction to this film must be intensely personal; it is not a mass-market entertainment but an uncompromising attempt by one artist to think about another. My own subjective feelings are all I can convey. I do not have much knowledge of Nijinsky (I know him mostly through the 1980 Herbert Ross film and countless secondhand references), or much curiosity. I do, however, have a lot of knowledge about the work of Paul Cox, a heroic filmmaker of great gifts and curiosity about everything he does. I was watching not a film about Nijinsky, but a film evoking Cox's need to make it.

What I got then is likely to be different than what a Nijinsky person would understand. I sensed at once in Jacobi's reading and Cox's images the fact of Nijinsky's madness, his identification with God, the oneness between his art and his ego. I sensed his feeling that great currents in the world mirrored and even flowed from his own spirit. I saw how, for him, madness (or whatever it should be called) was the wellspring of creativity. Art can lead (but rarely does) to such ecstasy that it resembles derangement. I think that Cox saw Nijinsky not as a madman but as a man too inspired to be sane.

I sat in the theater in much the same state I might attend a concert of serious music. I do not ask music to have a plot, a story, or characters. It does not make sense in any literal way. It is a collection of feelings, pushed forward through time, expressed by artists who want to flow through the inspiration of the composer. If the technique is good enough not to call attention to itself, it is all emotion.

The Diaries of Vaslav Nijinsky is a film with that musical kind of effect. I have tried to describe it accurately. You will either be in sympathy with it, or not. Much depends on what you bring into the theater. It is possible that those who know the most about Nijinsky will be the most baffled, because this is not a film about knowing, but about feeling.

Dickie Roberts: Former Child Star ★ ★
PG-13, 99 m., 2003

David Spade (Dickie Roberts), Mary McCormack (Grace Finney), Jon Lovitz (Sidney), Craig Bierko (George Finney), Jenna Boyd (Sally Finney), Scott Tessa (Sam Finney), Alyssa Milano (Cyndi), Rob Reiner (Himself). Directed by Sam Weisman and produced by Jack Giarraputo. Screenplay by Fred Wolf and David Spade.

Here is an inspired idea for a comedy, but why have they made it into a dirge? *Dickie Roberts: Former Child Star* has a premise that would be catnip for Steve Martin or Jim Carrey, but David Spade (who, to be fair, came up with the premise) casts a pall of smarmy sincerity over the material. There are laughs, to be sure, and some gleeful supporting performances, but after a promising start the movie sinks in a bog of sentiment.

Spade plays Dickie Roberts, now about thirty-five, who has been struggling ever since the end of his career as a child TV star. As fame and fortune disappeared, so did his mother; a biographical mockumentary about Dickie says he was orphaned after she "moved out of the area." Now he's a car valet and plays poker with other former child stars, including (playing themselves) Danny Bonaduce, Dustin Diamond, Barry Williams, Leif Garrett, and Corey Feldman. His desperate agent Sidney (Jon Lovitz, pitch perfect) can't find him work, and when Dickie hears about the lead in the new Rob Reiner movie, Sidney sighs, "That's out of our league."

But Dickie runs into Brendan Fraser (the movie is like a reality TV version of *Hollywood Squares*), who gets him a meeting with Reiner. And Reiner drops some bad news: "I don't think you can play the part because you're not a real person." Dickie never had a real childhood, he explains, and so he grew up to be—Dickie.

That sets into motion the second, soapy, half of the movie. Dickie advertises for a "real family" where he can spend a month recapturing his lost childhood, and hooks up with the self-promoting ad man George Finney (Craig Bierko) and his nice family: the mother, Grace (Mary McCormack), and the kids, Sally (Jenna Boyd) and Sam (Scott Tessa). And right there a

nice, sharp-edged satire gets traded in for a sappy sitcom.

Spade's comic persona is essentially not sweet and lovable, and his attempt to force Dickie into that mode is never convincing. The best moments in the sitcom half of the movie come when he plays against type, as when he throws a wine cork at a sometime girlfriend, Cyndi (Alyssa Milano), or phones in a false alarm so that Grace can follow the fire trucks to the address she's looking for. Funny, but not so funny are the staged docudramas in which his loving family stages a Christmas in the summertime so he can recapture his lost youth.

The Grace character is played by Mary McCormack with her usual true-blue charm, and for a long time the movie wisely sidesteps any suggestion of romance between Grace and Dickie. When at the end we learn they get married, we give the nuptials about as much of a chance as Liza Minnelli's next matrimony. George, Grace's husband, is an underwritten figure who pops up from time to time in oddly written scenes, and then runs off with Cyndi, so we're told, since by then we haven't seen either one of them for some time.

David Spade has a peculiar but definite screen persona, and in the right role he could be effective. In the old days of the studio system, he could have worked as a supporting player at Warner's, pinch-hitting for Elisha Cook Jr. He is too recessive, narcissistic, and dreamy-voiced to be a star, although he could play the lead in a story that hated his character. As the guy we're supposed to love here, the little lost boy who finally grows up, not a chance.

Note: One of the pleasures of the movie is its population of former child stars. The end credits include a gathering of all those who appeared in the movie and a lot more, singing a song with lyrics that seem to come straight from the heart.

Die Another Day ★ ★ ★
PG-13, 123 m., 2002

Pierce Brosnan (James Bond), Halle Berry (Jinx), Toby Stephens (Gustav Graves), Rosamund Pike (Miranda Frost), Rick Yune (Zao), John Cleese (Q), Judi Dench (M), Michael Madsen (Damian Falco), Samantha Bond (Miss Moneypenny). Directed by Lee Tamahori and produced by

Barbara Broccoli and Michael G. Wilson.
Screenplay by Neal Purvis and Robert Wade.

I realized with a smile, fifteen minutes into the new James Bond movie, that I had unconsciously accepted Pierce Brosnan as Bond without thinking about Sean Connery, Roger Moore, or anyone else. He has become the landlord, not the tenant. Handsome if a little weary, the edges of an Irish accent curling around the edges of the Queen's English, he plays a preposterous character but does not seem preposterous playing him.

Die Another Day is the twentieth Bond film in forty years, not counting *Casino Royale*. Midway through it, Bond's boss, M, tells him, "While you were away, the world changed." She refers to the months he spent imprisoned at the hands of North Korean torturers, but she might also be referring to the world of Bondian thrillers. This movie has the usual impossible stunts, as when Bond surfs down the face of a glacier being melted by a laser beam from space. But it has just as many scenes that are lean and tough enough to fit in any modern action movie.

It also has a heroine who benefits from forty years of progress in the way we view women. When Halle Berry, as Jinx, first appears in the movie there is a deliberate and loving tribute to the first Bond girl, Ursula Andress, in *Dr. No* (1962). In both movies, the woman emerges from the surf wearing a bikini which, in slow motion, seems to be playing catch-up. Even the wide belt is the same. But Jinx is a new kind of Bond girl. She still likes naughty double entendres (Bond says he's an ornithologist, and she replies, "Well, that's a mouthful"). But in *Die Another Day* her character is not simply decoration or reward, but a competent and deadly agent who turns the movie at times into almost a buddy picture.

The film opens with an unusual touch: The villains are not fantastical fictions, but real. The North Koreans have, for the time being, joined the Nazis as reliable villains, and Bond infiltrates in order to—I dunno, deal with some "African Conflict Diamonds," if I heard correctly, but I wasn't listening carefully because the diamonds are only the maguffin. They do, however, decorate the memorable cheekbones of one of the villains, Zao (Rick Yune), who seems to have skidded facedown through a field of them at high impact.

A chase scene involving hover tanks in a minefield is somewhat clumsy, the hover tank not being the most graceful of vehicles, and then Bond is captured and tortured for months. He's freed in a prisoner exchange, only to find that M (Judi Dench) suspects him of having been brainwashed. Is he another "Manchurian candidate"? Eventually he proves himself, and after a visit to Q (John Cleese) for a new supply of gadgets, including an invisible car, he's back into action in the usual series of sensational stunt sequences. For the first time in the Bond series, a computer-generated sequence joins the traditional use of stunt men and trick photography; a disintegrating plane in a closing scene is pretty clearly all made of ones and zeroes, but by then we've seen too many amazing sights to quibble.

The North Koreans are allied with Gustav Graves (Toby Stephens), a standard-issue world-dominating Bond villain, whose orbiting space mirror is not exactly original. What is original is Gustav's decision to house his operation in a vast ice building in Iceland; since his mirror operates to focus heat on Earth, this seems like asking for trouble, and indeed, before long the ice palace is melting down, and Jinx is trapped in a locked room with the water level rising toward the ceiling. (Exactly why the room itself doesn't melt is a question countless readers will no doubt answer for me.)

Other characters include the deadly Miranda Frost (Rosamund Pike), whose name is a hint which side she is on, and Damian Falco (Michael Madsen), whose name unites two villainous movie dynasties and leaves me looking forward to Freddy Lecter. Oh, and Miss Moneypenny (Samantha Bond), who seems to have been overlooked, makes a last-minute appearance and virtually seduces Bond.

The film has been directed by Lee Tamahori (*Once Were Warriors, Mulholland Falls*), from New Zealand, who has tilted the balance away from humor and toward pure action. With *Austin Powers* breathing down the neck of the franchise, he told *Sight & Sound* magazine, it seemed like looking for trouble to broaden the traditional farcical elements. *Die Another Day* is still utterly absurd from one end to the other, of course, but in a slightly more understated way.

And so it goes, Bond after Bond, as the most durable series in movie history heads for the half-century. There is no reason to believe this franchise will ever die. I suppose that is a blessing.

Die, Mommie, Die ★ ★
R, 90 m., 2003

Charles Busch (Angela Arden), Natasha Lyonne (Edith Sussman), Jason Priestley (Tony Parker), Frances Conroy (Bootsie Carp), Philip Baker Hall (Sol Sussman), Stark Sands (Lance Sussman), Victor Raider-Wexler (Sam Fishbein), Nora Dunn (Shatzi Van Allen). Directed by Mark Rucker and produced by Dante Di Loreto, Anthony Edwards, and Bill Kenwright. Screenplay by Charles Busch.

There's a 1950s genre of films that asked to be decoded through a gay lens. They undermined the conventional view of straight, middle-class American life, inviting the irony of outsiders (homosexual or not). Their glamorous, over-wrought heroines were role models for the emerging camp sensibility. Douglas Sirk's melodramas (among them *Imitation of Life, Written on the Wind,* and *All That Heaven Allows*) are at the head of this category, and Todd Haynes's *Far from Heaven* (2002) was a film that moved Sirk's buried themes into the foreground. What made Sirk a great director is that his stories were sappy in a way that was subversive to the restrictive values of the time.

The whole point, though, was that Sirk's movies never copped to what they were doing. They didn't wink or nudge or engage in Wildean double entendres (well, maybe sometimes, as when Rock Hudson is told it's time to get married and says, "I have trouble enough just finding oil"). Sirk was as sincere about his surface story as he was about his subtext, and that's why his movies still function as real melodrama and not as camp. The strength of *Far from Heaven* is its complete earnestness; it isn't a 2002 satire of Sirk, but wants to be the 1957 movie he couldn't make. We can smile at the story's hysteria about homosexual and interracial romance, but those were not laughing

matters in the 1950s, and the movie honors that.

The problem with *Die, Mommie, Die,* a drag send-up of the genre, is that it spoils the fun by making it obvious. While it is true that late in their careers Joan Crawford or Bette Davis sometimes seemed like drag queens, they were not, and would have been offended by the suggestion. The lead in *Die, Mommie, Die* is Charles Busch, a professional drag queen, and the whole point of the movie is precisely that he is a drag queen.

There is a crucial difference between a drag queen and a female impersonator. Impersonators want to be "read" as women, and may sincerely think of themselves as women. That would seem to be the case with Jaye Davidson's character in *The Crying Game.* The drag queen, on the other hand, wants you to know he is a man. Charles Busch is in that category; he looks like a man in drag, and that's the point. The performance consists of a send-up by a gay man of a straight woman, and the story is a lampoon of cherished heterosexual conventions.

It is also, of course, a comedy, and I know I'm getting awfully serious about something that intends to be silly and trashy. But I'm trying to explain to myself why it didn't work, and I think it's because drag queens are no longer funny just because they're drag queens; we've lost the nervousness about gender that once made us need to laugh at a man in drag. The material started out as a play, and probably worked better then because a simpatico audience could make it an event.

The story stars Busch as Angela Arden, a failed singer married to a failing Hollywood producer named Sol Sussman (Philip Baker Hall). He makes bad movies but has lost the touch of making a profit on them. During his latest debacle in Europe, she's had an affair with the young stud Tony Parker (Jason Priestley). Now she wants a divorce from Sol, but nothing doing: "We're a famous couple, Angela, and we're going to stay together." Completing the Sussman household are their maid, Bootsie Carp (Frances Conroy), their slutty daughter, Edith (Natasha Lyonne), and their gay pothead son, Lance (played by an actor whose name may really be Stark Sands, although that sounds like a retro product of the Rock-Troy-Tab name generator).

Angela has a singing engagement in a third-rate resort. Sol cancels it in a fit of rage. Angela strikes back. Sol has been complaining loudly (and, because this is the great Philip Baker Hall, convincingly) about his constipation, and so she poisons his suppository, ho, ho. Many complications ensue, all provoking Angela to run amok through the gamut of emotions.

Some of the dialogue and many of the gags are in fact funny. But the movie's reason for being is Busch's drag performance, and I didn't find anything funny because he was a man in drag. What was funny worked despite that fact. A woman in the role might have been funnier, because then we wouldn't have had to be thinking about two things at once: the gag, and the drag. Imagine a very good actor who is also a very good juggler. You admire his versatility, but during *Hamlet* you'd want him to put down his balls during the soliloquies.

Dinner Rush ★ ★ ★
R, 98 m., 2002

Danny Aiello (Louis Cropa), Edoardo Ballerini (Udo Cropa), Sandra Bernhard (Jennifer), Vivian Wu (Nicole), Mark Margolis (Fitzgerald), Mike McGlone (Carmen), Kirk Acevedo (Duncan), Summer Phoenix (Marti), John Corbett (Ken). Directed by Bob Giraldi and produced by Louis DiGiaimo and Patti Greaney. Screenplay by Rick Shaughnessy and Bryan Kalata.

"Unbelievable. Only in New York can a double murder triple your business."

So it is observed in *Dinner Rush,* a movie set in one of those Italian restaurants that the customers are tickled to believe is mob-connected even though it isn't, because it makes it more thrilling that way. (Rosebud, the Chicago eatery, had billboards saying, "We serve the whole mob.") The story unfolds during one long night at an Italian place in Tribeca that is undergoing an identity crisis. The owner, Louis (Danny Aiello), likes traditional Italian fare. His son Udo (Edoardo Ballerini) is into nouvelle, or nuovo, cuisine, and boasts: "Sausage and peppers is not on my menu."

Louis is in despair. He wants to turn the place over to his son, but not if it means abandoning dishes that make you think of bread sticks and red-and-white checkerboard tablecloths. There are other problems. A man has been murdered, and the identity of his killers may be known to Louis. And two men have come into the restaurant, taken a table, called Louis over, and informed him, "We're not leaving here until we're partners in the business." Louis says they can have the book he runs, but not the restaurant. Never the restaurant. They don't leave.

It's a busy night. The party at one long table is presided over by Fitzgerald (Mark Margolis), a gravel-voiced snob who talks slooow-ly so the cretins of the world can understand him. He runs an art gallery and is treating a visiting Greek artist. The entertainment consists of insulting his waitress (Summer Phoenix) and the maitresse d' (Vivian Wu). At another table, Sandra Bernhard plays a food critic as if she considers the performance personal revenge on every theater and movie critic who has ever said a word against her.

So there's a crisis in management and a crisis in the dining room. A third crisis is unfolding in the kitchen, where Duncan (Kirk Acevedo), the only cook who will still make Louis "salsiccia e peperoni," is deep in debt to a bookmaker. Louis, who takes bets but is a reasonable man, tells Duncan's bookmaker: "Stop taking his action. The kid's a pathological gambler. He needs help, not another bookmaker."

There are enough plots here to challenge a Robert Altman, specialist in interlocking stories, but the director, Bob Giraldi, masters the complexities as if he knows the territory. He does. He owns the restaurant, which in real life is named Giraldi's. His center of gravity is supplied by Danny Aiello, who plays his cards close to his vest—closer than we suspect—and like a man who has been dealing with drunks for a very, very long time, doesn't get worked up over every little thing. He talks to his accountant and the visiting gangsters as if they're in the same business.

Like *Big Night,* a film it resembles, *Dinner Rush* has a keen appreciation for the intricacies of a restaurant. In front, everybody is supposed to have a good time. In the kitchen, the chef is a dictator and the workers are galley slaves. Udo has a scene right at the start where he makes one thing clear: Do it his way or get

171

out. The scenes in the kitchen show the bewildering speed with which hard and exact work is accomplished, and Giraldi is able to break these scenes down into details that edit together into quick little sequences; not surprising, since he has directed hundreds of commercials.

In a plot like this, there isn't a lot of time to establish characters, so the actors have to bring their characters into the film with them. They do. The gangsters walk in menacing. Mark Margolis has a manner that makes Fitzgerald hateful on sight. Bernhard and her long-suffering companion play out nightly private dramas over the work of the city's chefs. And Aiello suggests enormous depths of pride, sympathy, worry, and buried anger.

The last scenes are fully packed, with developments that come one after another, tempting critics to complain it's all a little too neat. Maybe, but then you wouldn't want those story strands left dangling, and to spend any more time on them would be laboring the point: Like a good meal, this movie is about the progression of the main courses and not about the mints at the door.

Dirty Dancing: Havana Nights ★ ★
PG-13, 87 m., 2004

Diego Luna (Javier Suarez), Romola Garai (Katey Miller), Sela Ward (Jeannie Miller), John Slattery (Bert Miller), Jonathan Jackson (James Phelps), January Jones (Eve), Rene Lavan (Carlos Suarez), Mika Boorem (Susie Miller), Mya Harrison (Lola Martinez). Directed by Guy Ferland and produced by Lawrence Bender and Sarah Green. Screenplay by Boaz Yakin and Victoria Arch.

I was not a fan of *Dirty Dancing*, although $150 million in 1987 box-office dollars attempted, unsuccessfully, to convince me I was wrong. I thought Patrick Swayze and Jennifer Grey were terrific dancers, and I thought the plot was a clunker assembled from surplus parts at the Broken Plots Store. The actions of the characters (especially her parents) were so foreordained they played like closing night of a run that had gone on way too long.

Now here is *Dirty Dancing: Havana Nights*. Same characters, new names, same plot, new location. The wealthy Miller family from St. Louis arrives in 1958 Havana with their teenage daughter, Katey (Romola Garai). She is courted by young James Phelps (Jonathan Jackson), son of a wealthier family. Has anybody in the movies named Phelps ever been poor? She meets Javier Suarez (Diego Luna), a nice Cuban waiter about her age, and by her clumsiness gets him fired. But . . .

Well, of course she finds Phelps a bore and Javier a nice and considerate friend, not nearly as sexually vibrant, by the way, as Swayze. Except when he's dancing. She has to choose between the godawful official balls and the excitement at La Rosa Negra, the club where Javier and his friends hang out—a club not a million miles distant in function from the disco in *Saturday Night Fever*.

Can this white-bread American princess learn rhythm? Of course she can, with Javier wading with her into the ocean and teaching her to feel the motion of the waves and allow her body to sway with them, and to listen to the music as if it is the waves, and meanwhile perfecting choreography so complex and demanding that it would have had Rita Moreno, in her heyday, pleading for the Sloan's Liniment.

Is it not clear to all of us that sooner or later Katey and Javier will have to defy social convention and enter the dance contest, and that Mr. and Mrs. Miller will find themselves at the big contest but astonished to discover their own daughter out there on the floor? Of course they will be shocked, but then they will be proud, and Mrs. Miller (Sela Ward), who was a heck of a dancer in her day, will realize that the fruit has not fallen far from the tree, and that Katey must follow her dream, realize her talent, go with the flow, sway with the waves, and bring home the bacon.

Meanwhile, in the hills, Fidel Castro readies his assault on the corrupt Batista regime. All very well, and his revolution could have supplied some good scenes, as we know from *Havana* and the *Godfather* saga. But is Fidel really needed in a retread of *Dirty Dancing*? And do the inevitable scenes of upheaval, people separated from each other, confusion in the streets, etc., create tension, or only tedium? How can we get excited about action that the movie isn't even about? Couldn't Castro at least have crashed the dance contest in disguise, like Douglas Fairbanks would have done?

Why, then, do I give this movie two stars and the original only one? Because I have grown mellow and forgiving? Perhaps, but perhaps too because we go to the movies to look at the pretty pictures on the screen, like infants who like bright toys dangled before us. And *Dirty Dancing: Havana Nights* is a great movie to look at, with its period Havana (actually San Juan, Puerto Rico, with lots of 1950s cars). The dancing is well done, the music will sell a lot of sound tracks, and . . .

Romola Garai and Diego Luna. He you remember from *Y Tu Mama Tambien*, and here again he has that quirky, winning charm. She is a beauty and a gifted comedienne, who played Kate in *Nicholas Nickleby* and was the younger sister, Cassandra, in the wonderful 2003 film *I Capture the Castle*. They must be given credit for their presence and charisma in *Dirty Dancing: Havana Nights*, and together with the film's general ambience they do a lot to make amends for the lockstep plot. But here's an idea. Rent *Y Tu Mama Tambien*, *Nicholas Nickleby*, and *I Capture the Castle*, and eliminate the middleman.

Dirty Pretty Things ★ ★ ★ ½
R, 107 m., 2003

Chiwetel Ejiofor (Okwe), Audrey Tautou (Senay), Sergi López (Sneaky [Juan]), Sophie Okonedo (Juliette), Benedict Wong (Guo Yi), Zlatko Buric (Ivan). Directed by Stephen Frears and produced by Robert Jones and Tracey Seaward. Screenplay by Steve Knight.

The hall porter is sent upstairs to repair a blocked toilet and finds the source of the trouble: a human heart stuck in the pipes. He asks about the recent occupants of the room, but nobody seems to know anything, not even the helpful hooker who acts like an unofficial member of the staff. The porter, a Nigerian named Okwe, takes it up with his boss, Sneaky, and is advised to mind his own business.

This is a splendid opening for a thriller, but *Dirty Pretty Things* is more than a genre picture. It uses the secret and malevolent activities at the hotel as the engine to drive a story about

a London of immigrants, some illegal, who do the city's dirty work. Okwe (Chiwetel Ejiofor) was a doctor in Nigeria, is here as a political exile, has a past that haunts him. He rents couch space in the tiny flat of a chambermaid named Senay (Audrey Tautou, from *Amelie*), who is from Turkey and fled an arranged marriage. His best friend, Guo Yi (Benedict Wong), presides over poker games at the mortuary where he works. His circle also includes the doorman Ivan (Zlatko Buric) and the hooker Juliette (Sophie Okonedo). These characters and the vile night manager Sneaky are the major characters in the story, immigrants all, while white Londoners exist only as customers or immigration officials.

Okwe works hard at two jobs. He drives a minicab during the day, works all night at the hotel, buys illegal herbs at a local café to keep himself more or less awake. He is aware that Senay likes him and would not object if he moved from her couch to her bed, but he must be true to a wife in Nigeria; his faithfulness becomes more poignant the more we learn about the wife ("It is an African story," he says simply).

The heart of the movie, directed by Stephen Frears, is in the lives of these people. How they are always alert to make a little money on the side (as when Okwe and Ivan supply their own cash-only room-service sandwiches after the hotel kitchen closes). How they live in constant fear of immigration officials, who want to deport them even though a modern Western economy could not function without these shadow workers. How there is a network of contact and support in this hidden world, whose residents come from so many places and speak so many languages that they stop keeping score and simply accept each other as citizens of the land of exile.

We get to know these people and something of their lives, as Okwe stubbornly persists in trying to find out where that heart came from. He discovers that Sneaky is the key, and that the hotel is the center of a cruel enterprise that I will not reveal. The movie takes us into dark places in its closing scenes. But this is not a horror movie, not a shocker (although it is shocking). It is a story of desperation, of people who cannot live where they were born and cannot find a safe haven elsewhere.

This is familiar territory for Stephen Frears, an uncommonly intelligent director whose strength comes from his ability to empathize with his characters. They are not markers in a plot, but people he cares about. Two of his early films, *My Beautiful Launderette* (1985) and *Sammy and Rosie Get Laid* (1987), deal with the London of immigrants from India and Pakistan. He's fascinated by people who survive in cracks in the economy, as in two of his American films, *The Grifters* (1990) and *High Fidelity* (2000), one about con artists, the other set in a used-record store.

Crucial to the success of *Dirty Pretty Things* is the performance by Chiwetel Ejiofor—who, I learn, was born in England and copied his Nigerian accent from his parents. A natural actor with leading-man presence, he has the rare ability to seem good without seeming sappy, and his quiet intensity here is deepened by the sense that his character carries great sadness from his past. Audrey Tautou isn't the first actress you'd think of to play the Turkish girl, but her wide-eyed sincerity is right for the role, and Sergi López brings such crafty venality to his night manager that we suspect people must actually work in vile trades such as his.

The strength of the thriller genre is that it provides stories with built-in energy and structure. The weakness is that thrillers often seem to follow foreseeable formulas. Frears and his writer, Steve Knight, use the power of the thriller and avoid the weaknesses in giving us, really, two movies for the price of one.

Distant ★ ★ ★

NO MPAA RATING, 110 m., 2004

Muzaffer Ozdemir (Mahmut), Mehmet Emin Toprak (Yusuf), Zuhal Gencer Erkaya (Nazan), Nazan Kirilmis (Lover), Feridun Koc (Janitor), Fatma Ceylan (Mother), Ebru Ceylan (Young Girl). Directed by Nuri Bilge Ceylan and produced by Ceylan. Screenplay by Ceylan.

How is it that the same movie can seem tedious on first viewing and absorbing on the second? Why doesn't it grow even more tedious? In the case of *Distant*, which I first saw at Cannes in 2003, perhaps it helped that I knew what the story offered and what it did not offer, and was able to see it again without expecting what would not come.

The film takes place in Turkey, but its dynamic could be transplanted anywhere—maybe to our own families. It is about a cousin from the country who comes to the big city searching for work, and asks to stay "for a few days" with his relative, who is a divorced photographer with walls filled with books and an apartment filled with sad memories.

Mahmut (Muzaffer Ozdemir) is the photographer, whose wife has divorced him and is marrying another man; the couple will move to Canada. What went wrong is not hard to guess: Mahmut is a man of habit, silent, introspective, exhausted by life. Yusuf (Mehmet Emin Toprak) comes from a small town where the factory has failed and there are no jobs; he foolishly thinks he can get hired on one of the ships in the port, but there are no jobs, and an old sailor informs him that the wages are so bad he'll never have anything left over to send home.

It is the dead of winter. Yusuf tramps through the snow with no gloves and inadequate shoes, and his job search starts unpromisingly when the first ship he finds is listing and sinking. He haunts the coffee bars of the sailors, who smoke and wait. Mahmut, meanwhile, says good-bye to his wife and then secretly and sadly watches her leaving from the airport. He has a shabby affair with a woman who lives nearby, and who will not make eye contact in a restaurant. He watches art videos (Tarkovsky, I think) to drive Yusuf from the room, and then switches to porno.

For both men, smoking is a consolation, and they spend a lot of time standing alone, doing nothing, maybe thinking nothing, smoking as if it is a task that provides them with purpose. Mahmut has rules (smoking only in the kitchen or on the balcony), but Yusuf sits in his favorite chair and smokes and drinks beer when Mahmut is away, and Mahmut grows gradually furious at the disorder that has come into his life. "Close the door," he says, as Yusuf goes to the guest bedroom, because he wants to shut him away from his privacy.

A photographic expedition to the countryside, with Yusuf hired as his assistant, turns out badly for Mahmut; sharing rented rooms, they invade each other's space. Finally Mahmut has had enough and asks Yusuf, "What are your plans?" But Yusuf has none. He does not even have an opening for plans. He is trapped in unemployment, has no money, no skills, no choices.

The film, directed by Nuri Bilge Ceylan, is shot with a frequently motionless camera that regards the men as they, frequently, regard nothing in particular. It permits silences to grow. Perhaps in the hurry of Cannes, with four or five films a day, I could not slow down to occupy those silences, but seeing the film a second time I understood they were crucial: There is little these men have to say to each other and—more to the point—no one else for them to talk with. Women are a problem for them both. Yusuf shadows attractive women, but is too shy to approach them before they inevitably meet a man and walk off arm-in-arm. A man without funds is in a double bind: He has no way to attract good women, or to hire bad ones. The one sex scene we witness with Mahmut, which is out of focus at the far end of a room, is so joyless that solitude seems preferable.

A movie like this touches everyday life in a way that we can recognize as if Turkey were Peoria. I can imagine a similar film being made in America, although Americans might talk more. What do you say to a relative who is out of work and seems unlikely to ever work again? He is family, and so there is a sense of responsibility embedded in childhood, but there are no jobs and he has no skills, and your own comfort, which seems enviable to him, is little consolation to you. To have joyless work means you have employment but not an occupation. At the end, one of the men is sitting on a bench on a gray, cold day, staring at nothing, and if we could see the other man we could probably see another bench. *Distant* is a good title for this movie.

Note: At Cannes, the movie won the Jury Grand Prize, and Muzaffer Ozdemir and Mehmet Emin Toprak shared the prize as best actors. The previous December, Toprak died in a traffic accident. He was twenty-eight.

Divine Intervention ★ ★ ★
NO MPAA RATING, 89 m., 2003

Elia Suleiman (E. S.), Manal Khader (The Woman), Nayef Fahoum Daher (The Father), Amer Daher (Auni), Jamel Daher (Jamel). Directed by Elia Suleiman and produced by Humbert Balsan. Screenplay by Suleiman.

Divine Intervention is a mordant and bleak comedy, almost without dialogue, about Palestinians under Israeli occupation. Its characters live their daily lives in ways that are fundamentally defined by the divisions between them, and the scene with the most tension simply involves two drivers, one Israeli, one Palestinian, who lock eyes at a traffic light. Neither will look away. In their paralysis, while the light turns green and motorists behind them start to honk, the film sums up the situation in a nutshell.

The movie stars Elia Suleiman, who also wrote and directed it, and who has probably included more political references than an outsider is likely to understand. Most of his ideas are conveyed in scenes that would be right at home in a silent comedy, and on the few occasions when the characters talk, they say nothing more than what could be handled in a title card.

One running gag, for example, involves a household that throws its daily bag of garbage into the neighbor's yard. When the neighbor one day angrily throws it back, the original litterer complains. The neighbor responds: "The garbage we threw in your yard is the same garbage you threw in our garden." Nevertheless, the offender says, it is bad manners to throw it back.

This is the sort of parable that can cut both ways, and I get the sense that, for Suleiman, it doesn't matter at this point which neighbor represents an Israeli and which a Palestinian. The same simmering hostility is reflected in other scenes, as in one where a man takes a sledgehammer to a driveway so that his neighbor's car will get stuck in a hole.

There is a romance in the movie, involving the Suleiman character and a woman played by Manal Khader. Because they live in different districts and cannot easily pass from one to another, they meet in the parking lot of a checkpoint and sit in his car, holding hands and staring with hostility at the Israeli guards. In one stunning shot, she boldly walks across the border and right past the guards, who level their rifles at her but are unwilling to act.

Later, marksmen do shoot at her, in a weird scene involving special effects. After taking target practice at cardboard dummies that resemble her, the riflemen are amazed to see the woman herself materialize before them. She whirls and levitates. They shoot at her, but the bullets pause in midair and form themselves in a crown around her head, an image not impossible to decipher.

The film has been compared to the comedies of Jacques Tati, in which everyday actions build up to an unexpected comic revelation. I was reminded also of the Swedish film *Songs from the Second Floor,* set in a city where all seems normal but the inhabitants are seized with a strange apocalyptic madness. Suleiman's argument seems to be that the situation between Palestinians and Israelis has settled into a hopeless stalemate, in which everyday life incorporates elements of paranoia, resentment, and craziness.

The film was so well received around the world that it seemed likely to get an Oscar nomination but was rejected by the Motion Picture Academy because entries must be nominated by their nation of origin, and Palestine is not a nation. That's the sort of catch-22 that Suleiman might appreciate.

Divine Secrets of the Ya-Ya Sisterhood ★ ½
PG-13, 116 m., 2002

Sandra Bullock (Sidda), Ellen Burstyn (Vivi), Fionnula Flanagan (Teensy), James Garner (Shep Walker), Ashley Judd (Younger Vivi), Shirley Knight (Necie), Maggie Smith (Caro), Angus MacFadyen (Connor). Directed by Callie Khouri and produced by Bonnie Bruckheimer and Hunt Lowry. Screenplay by Khouri and Mark Andrus, based on the novels by Rebecca Walls.

Divine Secrets of the Ya-Ya Sisterhood has a title suggesting that the movie will be cute and about colorful, irrepressible, eccentric originals. Heavens deliver us. The Ya-Ya Sisterhood is rubberstamped from the same mold that has produced an inexhaustible supply of fictional southern belles who drink too much, talk too much, think about themselves too much, try too hard to be the most unforgettable character you've ever met, and are, in general, insufferable. There

must be a reason these stories are never set in Minnesota. Maybe it's because if you have to deal with the winter it makes you too realistic to become such a silly goose.

There is not a character in the movie with a shred of plausibility, not an event that is believable, not a confrontation that is not staged, not a moment that is not false. For their sins the sisterhood should be forced to spend the rest of their lives locked in a Winnebago camper. The only character in the movie who is bearable is the heroine as a young woman, played by Ashley Judd, who suggests that there was a time before the story's main events when this creature was palatable.

The heroine is Vivi, played by Ellen Burstyn in her sixties, Judd in her thirties and, as a child, by a moppet whose name I knoweth not. Yes, this is one of those movies that whisks around in time, as childhood vows echo down through the years before we whiplash back to the revelations of ancient secrets. If life were as simple as this movie, we would all have time to get in shape and learn Chinese.

As the film opens, four little girls gather around a campfire in the woods and create the Ya-Ya Sisterhood, exchanging drops of their blood, no doubt while sheriff's deputies and hounds are searching for them. Flash forward to the present. Vivi's daughter Sidda (Sandra Bullock) is a famous New York playwright, who tells an interviewer from *Time* magazine that she had a difficult childhood, mostly because of her mother. Whisk down to Louisiana, where Vivi reads the article and writes the daughter forever out of her life—less of a banishment than you might think, since they have not seen each other for years and Vivi doesn't even know of the existence of Sidda's Scottish fiancé, Connor (Angus MacFadyen).

Connor seems cut from the same mold as Shep Walker (James Garner), Vivi's husband. Both men stand around sheepishly while portraying superfluous males. No doubt their women notice them occasionally and are reminded that they exist and are a handy supply of sperm. Shep's role for decades has apparently been to beam approvingly as his wife gets drunk, pops pills, and stars in her own mind. Both men are illustrations of the impatience this genre has for men as a gender; they have the presence of souvenirs left on the mantel after a forgotten vacation.

Anyway. We meet the other adult survivors of the Ya-Ya Sisterhood: Teensy (Fionnula Flanagan), Necie (Shirley Knight), and Caro (Maggie Smith). Why do they all have names like pet animals? Perhaps because real names, like Martha, Florence, or Esther would be an unseemly burden for such featherweights. Summoned by Vivi so that she can complain about Sidda, Teensy, Necie, and Caro fly north and kidnap Sidda, bringing her back to Louisiana so that they can show her that if she really knew the secrets of her mother's past, she would forgive her all shortcomings, real and imagined. Since the central great mystery of Vivi's past is how she has evaded rehab for so long, this quest is as pointless as the rest of the film.

Why do gifted actresses appear in such slop? Possibly because good roles for women are rare, for those over sixty precious. Possibly, too, because for all the other shortcomings of the film, no expense has been spared by the hair, makeup, and wardrobe departments, so that all of the women look just terrific all of the time, and when Vivi is distraught and emotional, she looks even more terrific. It's the kind of movie where the actresses must love watching the dailies as long as they don't listen to the dialogue.

The movie is a first-time directing job by Callie Khouri, author of *Thelma and Louise*. She seems uncertain what the film is about, where it is going, and what it hopes to prove apart from the most crashingly obvious clichés of light women's fiction. So inattentive is the screenplay that it goes to the trouble of providing Vivi with two other children in addition to Sidda, only to never mention them again. A fellow critic, Victoria Alexander, speculates that the secret in Vivi's past may have been that she drowned the kids, but that's too much to hope for.

Dodgeball: A True Underdog Story
★ ★ ★
PG-13, 97 m., 2004

Vince Vaughn (Peter La Fleur), Ben Stiller (White Goodman), Christine Taylor (Kate Veatch), Rip Torn (Patches O'Houlihan), Justin Long (Justin), Stephen Root (Gordon), Joel Moore (Owen), Chris Williams (Dwight), Alan Tudyk (Steve the Pirate). Directed by Rawson Marshall Thurber and produced by Stuart Cornfeld and Ben Stiller. Screenplay by Thurber.

Dodgeball: A True Underdog Story is a title that rewards close study. It does not say it is a true story. It says it is about a true underdog. That is true. This is a movie about a spectacularly incompetent health club owner (Vince Vaughn) who tries to save his club from foreclosure by entering a team in the $50,000 world series of dodgeball in Las Vegas. Proof that the team is an underdog: One of the team members believes he is a pirate, and another team member hasn't noticed that.

Vaughn's club, Average Joe's Gym, is rundown and shabby, but has a loyal if nutty clientele. Across the street is a multimillion-dollar muscle emporium known as Globa Gym (there is no "l" in the title because it fell off). Globa is owned by Ben Stiller, overacting to the point of apoplexy as White Goodman; his manic performance is consistently funny, especially when he protects against Small Man Complex by surrounding himself with enormous bodybuilders and building an inflatable crotch into his training pants.

Vaughn, playing the absentminded Peter La Fleur, acts as a steadying influence; he plays it more or less straight, which is wise, since someone has to keep the plot on track. He's visited by the lithesome Kate Veatch (Christine Taylor), who works for the bank and explains that Average Joe's needs $50,000 in thirty days or the bank will foreclose. Standing by to turn Joe's into a parking lot: White Goodman. Among other questionable business practices, La Fleur has neglected to collect membership dues for several months.

Kate hates Globa's White Goodman, not least because at their last meeting he rudely drew attention to his extremely well-inflated crotch. One of the Average Joe staff members comes up with the idea of the dodgeball tournament, and for reasons unnecessary to explain, Kate becomes a member of the team, along with the pirate and four others.

None of them know anything about dodgeball. This may not be a handicap. My own experiences with dodgeball have led me to conclude that it is basically a game of luck; the only skill you need is to pick bigger kids for your side. But I learn that Extreme Dodgeball is actually a real sport, with its own cable TV show.

Dodgeball explains the sport by pausing for a grade-school educational documentary from 1938. It is a very short documentary, because all you need to know about the game are the Five Ds, of which both D No. 1 and D No. 5 are "Dodge!" The film is hosted by dodgeball legend Patches O'Houlihan, who must therefore be in his eighties when he appears at Average Joe's in his motorized wheelchair, and announces that he will coach them to victory. Patches is played by Rip Torn, whose training methods get enormous laughs.

The Las Vegas tournament itself follows the time-honored formulas of all sports movies, but is considerably enhanced by the weird teams in the finals. Weirdest is Globa Gym, captained by White Goodman and including four gigantic musclemen and a very hairy woman from an obscure former Soviet republic. The finals are telecast on ESPN8 ("If it's almost a sport, we have it here!").

I dare not say much more without giving away jokes; in a miraculous gift to the audience, 20th Century Fox does *not* reveal all of the best gags in its trailer. Therefore, let me just gently say that late in the movie a famous man approaches Peter La Fleur at the airport and gets laughs almost as big as the Patches O'Houlihan training technique.

Dogtown and Z-Boys ★ ★
NO MPAA RATING, 120 m., 2003

Maria Hofstatter (Hitchhiker), Christine Jirku (Teacher), Victor Hennemann (Teacher's Lover), Georg Friedrich (Lucky), Alfred Mrva (Alarm Salesman), Erich Finsches (Old Man), Gerti Lehner (Housekeeper), Franziska Weiss (Klaudia). Directed by Ulrich Seidl and produced by Helmut Grasser and Philippe Bober. Screenplay by Seidl and Veronika Franz.

In a suburb of Vienna, during the hottest days of the summer, in a row of cookie-cutter houses facing a river, unhappy people make themselves still more miserable as they indulge in lust, avarice, jealousy, gluttony, anger, and sloth.

Pride is not much of a problem with them. *Dog Days* is an unblinking look at what passes in some minds as everyday life and in others as human misery.

The movie has been made by Ulrich Seidl, known for his documentaries, who shot it over a period of three years in order to be able to work only on the very hottest days. He was able to get his actors to cooperate because most of them were amateurs. Considering that many of them are seen nude and some engage in degrading sexual behavior, it might seem strange that he was able to persuade nonprofessionals to take these roles, but reality television has shown that there are people willing to do almost anything if a camera is recording it. Odd, isn't it? Not too long ago people would do these things only if nobody was watching.

There are nine or ten characters, including a stripper whose boyfriend hangs around the clubs where she performs, beating up anybody who looks at her; a divorced couple who still share the same house and devote themselves to making each other miserable; a fat man who wants his middle-aged housekeeper to do a harem dance in honor of the fiftieth anniversary of his marriage to his long-dead wife; a teacher so desperate for dates that she'll maybe even sleep with the sadistic friend of her latest boyfriend; and so on. Oh, and there's a mentally retarded woman who hitches rides and sits in the backseat asking annoying questions.

The physical action in the movie has been constructed with meticulous care and timing. Sometimes (not often) we almost feel as if we're involved in a sight gag from a Jacques Tati movie—as, for example, when the couple next door won't stop their loud quarrel, and so the fat man simply starts up his power mower and lets it run next to their fence. More often we simply watch sad people degrade each other, as when a man is forced to apologize at gunpoint for his behavior to a woman who is no happier because she is forced to make him do so.

The movie won the Grand Jury Prize at Venice 2001 and arrives festooned with other awards. It is admirable and well made, but unutterably depressing and unredeemed by any glimmer of hope. In that it reminded me a little of the wonderful Swedish film *Songs from the Second Floor,* but that one used style and mordant humor to elevate itself into a kind of joyous dirge. *Dog Days* is a long slog through the slough of despond.

Dogtown and Z-Boys ★ ★ ★
PG-13, 89 m., 2002

Themselves: Jay Adams, Tony Alva, Bob Biniak, Paul Constantineau, Shogo Kubo, Jim Muir, Peggy Oki, Stacy Peralta, Nathan Pratt, Wentzle Ruml, and Allen Sarlo. Directed by Stacy Peralta and produced by Agi Orsi. Screenplay by Peralta and Craig Stecyk.

Dogtown and Z-Boys, a documentary about how the humble skateboard became the launch pad for aerial gymnastics, answers a question I have long been curious about: How and why was the first skateboarder inspired to go aerial, to break contact with any surface and do acrobatics in midair? Consider that the pioneer was doing this for the very first time over a vertical drop of perhaps fifteen feet to a concrete surface. It's not the sort of thing you try out of idle curiosity.

The movie answers this and other questions in its history of a sport that grew out of idle time and boundless energy in the oceanfront neighborhood between Santa Monica and Venice. Today the area contains expensive condos and trendy restaurants, but circa 1975 it was the last remaining "beachfront slum" in the Los Angeles area. Druggies and hippies lived in cheap rentals and supported themselves by working in hot-dog stands, tattoo parlors, head shops, and saloons.

Surfing was the definitive lifestyle, the Beach Boys supplied the sound track, and tough surfer gangs staked out waves as their turf. In the afternoon, after the waves died down, they turned to skateboards, which at first were used as a variation of roller skates. But the members of the Zephyr Team, we learn, devised a new style of skateboarding, defying gravity, adding acrobatics, devising stunts. When a drought struck the area and thousands of swimming pools were drained, they invented vertical skateboarding on the walls of the empty pools. Sometimes they'd glide so close to the edge that only one of the board's four wheels still had a purchase on the lip. One day a Z-boy went airborne, and a new style was born—a style reflected today in Olympic ski acrobatics.

I am not sure whether the members of the Zephyr Team were solely responsible for all significant advances in the sport, or whether they only think they were. *Dogtown and Z-Boys* is directed by Stacy Peralta, an original and gifted team member, still a legend in the sport. Like many of the other Z-boys (and one Z-girl), he marketed himself, his name, his image, his products, and became a successful businessman and filmmaker while still surfing concrete. His film describes the evolution of skateboarding almost entirely in terms of the experience of himself and his friends. It's like the vet who thinks World War II centered around his platoon.

The Southern California lifestyle in general, and surfing and skateboarding in particular, are insular and narcissistic. People who live indoors have ideas. People who live outdoors have style. Here is an entire movie about looking cool while not wiping out. Call it a metaphor for life. There comes a point when sensible viewers will tire of being told how astonishing and unique each and every Z-boy was, while looking at repetitive still photos and home footage of skateboarders, but the film has an infectious enthusiasm, and we're touched by the film's conviction that all life centered on that place, that time, and that sport.

One question goes unanswered. Was anyone ever killed? Maimed? Crippled? There is a brief shot of someone on crutches, and a few shots showing skateboarders falling off their boards, but since aerial gymnastics high over hard surfaces are clearly dangerous and the Z-boys wear little or no protective gear, what's the story?

That most of them survived is made clear by info over the end credits, revealing that although one Zephyr Team member is in prison and another was "last seen in Mexico," the others all seem to have married, produced an average of two children, and found success in business. To the amazement, no doubt, of their parents.

Dogville ★ ★
R, 177 m., 2004

Nicole Kidman (Grace), Paul Bettany (Tom Edison), James Caan (The Big Man), Patricia Clarkson (Vera), Jeremy Davies (Bill Henson), Ben Gazzara (Jack McKay), Philip Baker Hall

(Tom Edison Sr.), John Hurt (Narrator), Chloe Sevigny (Liz Henson), Stellan Skarsgård (Chuck), Lauren Bacall (Ma Ginger), Blair Brown (Mrs. Henson), Bill Raymond (Mr. Henson). Directed by Lars von Trier and produced by Vibeke Windelov. Screenplay by von Trier.

Lars von Trier exhibits the imagination of an artist and the pedantry of a crank in *Dogville,* a film that works as a demonstration of how a good idea can go wrong. There is potential in the concept of the film, but the execution had me tapping my wristwatch to see if it had stopped. Few people will enjoy seeing it once and, take it from one who knows, even fewer will want to see it a second time.

The underlying vision of the production has the audacity we expect from von Trier, a daring and inventive filmmaker. He sets his story in a small Rocky Mountain town during the Great Depression, but doesn't provide a real town (or a real mountain). The first shot looks straight down on the floor of a large sound stage, where the houses of the residents are marked out with chalk outlines, and there are only a few props—some doors, desks, chairs, beds. We will never leave this set and never see beyond it; on all sides in the background there is only blankness.

The idea reminds us of *Our Town,* but von Trier's version could be titled *Our Hell.* In his town, which I fear works as a parable of America, the citizens are xenophobic, vindictive, jealous, suspicious, and capable of rape and murder. His dislike of the United States (which he has never visited, since he is afraid of airplanes) is so palpable that it flies beyond criticism into the realm of derangement. When the film premiered at Cannes 2003, he was accused of not portraying America accurately, but how many movies do? Anything by David Spade come to mind? Von Trier could justifiably make a fantasy about America, even an anti-American fantasy, and produce a good film, but here he approaches the ideological subtlety of a raving prophet on a street corner.

The movie stars Nicole Kidman in a rather brave performance: Like all the actors, she has to act within a narrow range of tone, in an allegory that has no reference to realism. She plays a young woman named Grace who arrives in Dogville being pursued by gangsters (who here,

as in Brecht, I fear, represent native American fascism). She is greeted by Tom Edison (Paul Bettany), an earnest young man, who persuades his neighbors to give her a two-week trial run before deciding whether to allow her to stay in town.

Grace meets the townspeople, played by such a large cast of stars that we suspect the original running time must have been even longer than 177 minutes. Tom's dad is the town doctor (Philip Baker Hall); Stellan Skarsgård grows apples and, crucially, owns a truck; Patricia Clarkson is his wife; Ben Gazzara is the all-seeing blind man; Lauren Bacall runs the general store; Bill Raymond and Blair Brown are the parents of Jeremy Davies and Chloe Sevigny. There are assorted other citizens and various children, and James Caan turns up at the end in a long black limousine. He's the gangster.

What von Trier is determined to show is that Americans are not friendly, we are suspicious of outsiders, we cave in to authority, we are inherently violent, etc. All of these things are true, and all of these things are untrue. It's a big country, and it has a lot of different kinds of people. Without stepping too far out on a limb, however, I doubt that we have any villages where the helpless visitor would eventually be chained to a bed and raped by every man in town.

The actors (or maybe it's the characters) seem to be in a kind of trance much of the time. They talk in monotones, they seem to be reciting truisms rather than speaking spontaneously, they seem to sense the film's inevitable end. To say that the film ends in violence is not to give away the ending so much as to wonder how else it could have ended. In the apocalyptic mind-set of von Trier, no less than general destruction could conclude his fable; life in Dogville clearly cannot continue for a number of reasons, one of them perhaps that the Dogvillians would go mad.

Lars von Trier has made some of the best films of recent years *(Europa, Breaking the Waves, Dancer in the Dark).* He was a guiding force behind the Dogma movement, which has generated much heat and some light. He takes chances, and that's rare in a world where most films seem to have been banged together out of other films. But at some point his fierce determination has to confront the reality that a film does not exist without an audience. *Dogville* can be defended and even praised on pure ideological grounds, but most moviegoers, even those who are sophisticated and have open minds, are going to find it a very dry and unsatisfactory slog through conceits masquerading as ideas.

Note No. 1: Although Lars von Trier has never been to the United States, he does have one thing right: In a small town, the smashing of a collection of Hummel figurines would count as an atrocity.

Note No. 2: I learn from Variety *that* Dogville Confessions, *a making-of documentary, was filmed using a soundproof "confession box" near the soundstage where actors could unburden themselves. In it, Stellan Skarsgård describes von Trier, whom he has worked with many times, as "a hyperintelligent child who is slightly disturbed, playing with dolls in a dollhouse, cutting their heads off with nail clippers." Von Trier himself testifies that the cast is conspiring against him.* Variety *thinks this doc would make a great bell and/or whistle on the eventual DVD.*

Note No. 3: We should not be too quick to condemn von Trier, a Dane, for not filming in the United States when The Prince and Me, *a new Hollywood film about a Wisconsin farm girl who falls in love with the prince of Denmark, was filmed in Toronto and Prague.* ☞

Dopamine ★ ★ ★ ½
R, 79 m., 2003

John Livingston (Rand), Sabrina Lloyd (Sarah), William Windom (Rand's Father), Bruno Campos (Winston), Reuben Grundy (Johnson), Kathleen Antonia (Tammy), Nicole Wilder (Machiko). Directed by Mark Decena and produced by Debbie Brubaker and Ted Fettig. Screenplay by Decena and Timothy Breitbach.

People really do have jobs and they work all day at them and sometimes all night, and have to work so hard at them that their romantic life suffers. Those would be real people. People in the movies have so much free time that their lives are available for the requirements of movie formulas. They get crazy in love. Real people,

on the other hand, look at a potential lover and decide they'd have to be crazy to take a chance on someone like that. Start with two people who think that way and you're describing most of the relationships we really do have. In one way or another, *Dopamine* is about us.

You may not be Rand, trapped in a room with two other guys twenty hours a day, living on coffee and creating a digital pet named Koy Koy. You may not be Sarah, a preschool teacher who sometimes goes to a bar simply because she wants to get laid, and the next morning, when she looks at her prize, she just wants to get out of there and go home. But such details will seem more realistic to you than the romantic comedies of Meg Ryan, which is why Meg Ryan's adventures are so popular: They're about what you're looking for the night before, not what you end up with the morning after.

Dopamine, written and directed by Mark Decena, is about imperfect people who talk a lot, are smart, have big defenses, and have been burned more than once by love. Since Sarah sleeps with a guy on the first date, it may not seem like she has such big defenses, but she does; her defenses are against having the second date. And Rand is so wounded he invests his own emotions in a pathetic little animated bird who is programmed to get to know him. It's all right to be pleased that the bird recognizes you, but sad to feel good because the bird likes you. The bird doesn't really like you. The bird is just some code.

Rand is renting his life to people who want to buy a corrupt version of what he loves to do. He loves artificial intelligence. They want Koy Koy, which they can sell to the children of the world, robbing them of trees and dogs. Rand hates the people but loves the work. The people want to test-market his program in a preschool. What's this? He's spent three years in a room writing this code, and now five-year-olds are going to *criticize* it?

Rand (John Livingston) goes to the classroom and meets the teacher, Sarah (Sabrina Lloyd). Oh, there's no doubt they're meant for each other. They look at each other and each person's empty spaces are the same size as the other person's full spaces. But Rand has issues with women. That's why he's so hung up on programming a girlfriend for Koy Koy: safer to fix up Koy Koy than get fixed up himself. Loneliness is so much less troublesome than this emotional minefield.

Complicating the process is Rand's father (William Windom), who was in perfect love with his wife for fifty years before Alzheimer's replaced her with a space holder. If even a perfect love like his dad's betrays you in the end, what's the sense in beginning? Rand's father is a scientist, and believes love is basically chemical. Endorphins explain it. His father lectures on the scent code, we see visuals of molecules at work, and then there is the most extraordinary shot of Sarah walking near to Rand while he smells her hair.

What's alluring is the way the characters played by John Livingston and Sabrina Lloyd savor each other in between their troubles. Movies are too quick to interrupt romance with sex. Sarah and Rand fascinate us with their dance of dread and desire because they try to discuss their situation in abstractions, and they should let their fingers do the talking.

The movie is one of the Sundance Film Series, movies that were successful at Sundance and are being opened around the country as a package. Perhaps it didn't get picked up for solo distribution because it was too intellectual and talky. You use a word like *endorphin* and you're in trouble in some theaters. *Intolerable Cruelty* is also about two people who are meant to be in love and keep talking themselves out of it. It has big stars and a big budget and it's smart, too, but it lacks the one thing *Dopamine* guards as its treasure: a belief in the possibility of love.

Down with Love ★ ★ ★
PG-13, 94 m., 2003

Renée Zellweger (Barbara Novak), Ewan McGregor (Catcher Block), David Hyde Pierce (Peter MacMannus), Sarah Paulson (Vikki Hiller), Tony Randall (Theodore Banner). Directed by Peyton Reed and produced by Bruce Cohen and Dan Jinks. Screenplay by Eve Ahlert and Dennis Drake.

Down with Love opens with the big CinemaScope logo that once announced 20th Century Fox mass-market entertainments. The titles show animated letters bouncing each other off the screen, and the music is chirpy. The movie's opening scenes confirm these clues: This is a movie set in 1962, and filmed in the style of those Doris Day–Rock Hudson classics about the battle of the sexes. That it adds an unexpected twist is part of the fun.

Maybe the filmmakers believe that movies lost something when they added irony. *Far from Heaven* was in the style of a 1957 Universal melodrama, and now this wide-screen comedy, with bright colors and enormous sets filled with postwar modern furniture, wants to remember a time before the sexual revolution.

Well, just barely before. Its heroine is determined to usher it in. She is Barbara Novak (Renée Zellweger), a New Englander whose new best-seller, *Down with Love*, has just pushed John F. Kennedy's *Profiles in Courage* off the charts (and about time, too, since JFK's book was published in 1956). Novak's book announces a new woman who will not be subservient to men in the workplace, and will call her own shots in the bedroom.

This attracts the attention of Catcher Block (Ewan McGregor), a womanizing male chauvinist pig who works as a magazine writer, specializing in exposés. He bets his boss Peter MacMannus (David Hyde Pierce) that he can seduce Barbara, prove she's an old-fashioned woman at heart, and write a sensational article about it. Meanwhile, Barbara's publisher, Vikki Hiller (Sarah Paulson), announces a publicity coup: She's arranged an interview with . . . well, Catcher Block, of course.

Any movie fan can figure out the 1962 casting of these characters. Barbara and Catcher are Doris Day and Rock Hudson, Vikki is Lauren Bacall, and Peter is Tony Randall; Randall himself, in fact, is in this movie, as chairman of the board. And the plot resembles Doris Day's movies in the sex department: Barbara Novak talks a lot about sex and gets in precarious positions, but never quite compromises her principles.

The movie has a lot of fun with the split-screen techniques of the 1960s, which exploited the extra-wide screen. If you remember the split-screen phone calls in *Pillow Talk*, you'll enjoy the same technique here, in a series of calls where Catcher stands up Barbara on a series of dinner dates. *Down with Love* borrows a technique from the Austin Powers series (itself a throwback to the 1960s) with scenes in which the split screen is used to suggest strenuous sexual activity that is, in fact, quite innocently nonsexual.

I don't believe anyone will equal whatever it was that Doris Day had; she was one of a kind. But Renée Zellweger comes closest, with her wide eyes, naive innocence, and almost aggressive sincerity. She has a speech toward the end of the movie where the camera simply remains still and regards her, as a torrent of words pours out from her character's innermost soul.

Down with Love is no better or worse than the movies that inspired it, but that is a compliment, I think. It recalls a time when society had more rigid rules for the genders, and thus more adventure in transcending them. And it relishes the big scene where a hypocrite gets his comeuppance. The very concept of "comeuppance" is obsolete in these permissive modern times, when few movie characters have a sense of shame and behavior is justified in terms of pure selfishness. Barbara Novak's outrage at sneaky behavior is one of the movie's most refreshing elements from the 1960s—not to say she isn't above a few neat tricks herself.

Dracula: Pages from a Virgin's Diary
★ ★ ★ ½
NO MPAA RATING, 75 m., 2003

Zhang Wei-Qiang (Dracula), Tara Birtwhistle (Lucy Westernra), David Moroni (Dr. Van Helsing), CindyMarie Small (Mina Murray), Johnny Wright (Jonathon Harker), Stephane Leonard (Arthur Holmwood), Matthew Johnson (Jack Seward), Keir Knight (Quincy Morris). Directed by Guy Maddin and produced by Vonnie Von Helmolt. Screenplay by Mark Godden.

The ballet as a silent movie with an orchestra. I'd never thought of it that way before. The dancers embody the characters, express emotion with their bodies and faces, try to translate feeling and speech into physical movement. They are borne up on the wings of the music. *Dracula: Pages from a Virgin's Diary* uses (and improvises on and kids and abuses) the style of silent films to record a production of *Dracula* by the Royal Winnipeg Ballet. The film is poetic and erotic, creepy and melodramatic, overwrought and sometimes mocking, as if

F. W. Murnau's *Nosferatu* (1922) had a long-lost musical version.

The director is Guy Maddin, who lives in Winnipeg and is Canada's poet laureate of cinematic weirdness. His films often look as if the silent era had continued right on into today's ironic stylistic drolleries; he made a 2000 short named *The Heart of the World* that got more applause than most of the films it preceded at the Toronto film festival. Imagine *Metropolis* in hyderdrive.

In *Dracula: Pages from a Virgin's Diary* he begins with the Royal Winnipeg Ballet's stage production of *Dracula,* choreographed and produced by Mark Godden, and takes it through a series of transformations into something that looks a lot like a silent film but feels like avant-garde theater. The music is by Mahler (the first and second symphonies), the visuals include all the favorite devices of the silent period (wipes, iris shots, soft framing, intertitles, tinting), and the effect is—well, surprisingly effective. The emphasis is on the erotic mystery surrounding Dracula, and the film underlines the curious impression we sometimes have in vampire films that the victims experience orgasm as the fangs sink in.

The Dracula story is so easily mocked and satirized that it is good to be reminded of the unsettling erotic horror that it possesses in the hands of a Murnau or Werner Herzog (1979) or now Maddin. Not that Maddin is above poking it in the ribs (sample titles: "Why can't a woman marry two men? Or as many as want her?" and "She's filled with polluted blood!").

It deals primarily with Count Dracula's seduction, if that is the word, of Lucy Westernra (Tara Birtwhistle), whose name in Bram Stoker's novel was Westenra. The "westernization" is no doubt to underline Dracula's own relocation from Transylvania to the mysterious East; he is played here by the ballet's Zhang Wei-Qiang, whose stock melodramatic Asian characteristics are made not much more subtle than D. W. Griffith's Cheng Haun in *Broken Blossoms* (1919).

Jonathon Harker (Johnny Wright), the hapless estate agent, and his fiancée, Mina (Cindy-Marie Small), who both played major roles in the Stoker novel and most of the resulting films, have been somewhat downgraded in importance here, but Van Helsing (David Moroni), the vampire expert and hater, is well employed, and there are the usual crowds of townspeople to exhume coffins and perform other useful tasks. The story is less a narrative than an evocation of the vampire's world. Maddin shoots on sets and locations that resemble silent films in their overwrought and bold imagery, and he combines a number of low-tech filming formats, including 16 mm and Super 8; among the evocative stills on the movie's Website (www.zeitgeistfilms.com) is one in which Maddin is seen photographing with a tiny camera.

For the purposes of this film, the original images are only a starting point. Madden manipulates them with filters, adds grain, softens focus, moves through them with wipes, and takes the silent technique of tinting to a jolly extreme with blood and capes that suddenly flood the screen with red.

Dracula: Pages from a Virgin's Diary is not concerned with the story mechanics of moving from A to B. At times it feels almost like one of those old silent films where scenes have gone missing and there are jumps in the chronology. This is not a problem but an enhancement, creating for us the sensation of glimpsing snatches of a dream. So many films are more or less alike that it's jolting to see a film that deals with a familiar story but looks like no other.

Dreamcatcher ★ ½

R, 134 m., 2003

Morgan Freeman (Colonel Abraham Curtis), Thomas Jane (Dr. Henry Devlin), Jason Lee (Joe "Beaver" Clarendon), Damian Lewis (Gary "Jonesy" Jones), Timothy Olyphant (Pete Moore), Donnie Wahlberg (Douglas "Duddits" Cavell), Tom Sizemore (Captain Owen Underhill). Directed by Lawrence Kasdan and produced by Kasdan and Charles Okun. Screenplay by William Goldman and Kasdan, based on the novel by Stephen King.

Dreamcatcher begins as the intriguing story of friends who share a telepathic gift, and ends as a monster movie of stunning awfulness. What went wrong? How could director Lawrence Kasdan and writer William Goldman be responsible for a film that goes so awesomely cuckoo? How could even Morgan Freeman, an actor all but impervious to bad material, be brought down by the awfulness? Goldman, who has written insightfully about the screenwriter's trade, may get a long, sad book out of this one.

The movie is based on a novel by Stephen King, unread by me, apparently much altered for the screen version, especially in the appalling closing sequences. I have just finished the audiobook of King's *From a Buick 8*, was a fan of his *Hearts in Atlantis*, and like the way his heart tugs him away from horror ingredients and into the human element in his stories.

Here the story begins so promisingly that I hoped, or assumed, it would continue on the same track: Childhood friends, united in a form of telepathy by a mentally retarded kid they protect, grow up to share psychic gifts and to deal with the consequences. The problem of *really* being telepathic is a favorite science-fiction theme. If you could read minds, would you be undone by the despair and anguish being broadcast all around you? This is unfortunately not the problem explored by *Dreamcatcher*.

The movie does have a visualization of the memory process that is brilliant filmmaking; after the character Gary "Jonesy" Jones (Damian Lewis) has his mind occupied by an alien intelligence, he is able to survive hidden within it by concealing his presence inside a vast memory warehouse, visualized by Kasdan as an infinitely unfolding series of rooms containing Jonesy's memories. This idea is like a smaller, personal version of Jorge Luis Borges's *The Library of Babel*, the imaginary library that contains all possible editions of all possible books. I can imagine many scenes set in the warehouse—it's such a good idea it could support an entire movie—but the film proceeds relentlessly to abandon this earlier inspiration in its quest for the barfable.

But let me back up. We meet at the outset childhood friends Henry Devlin, Joe "Beaver" Clarendon, Jonesy Jones, and Pete Moore. They happen upon Douglas "Duddits" Cavell, a retarded boy being bullied by older kids, and they defend him with wit and imagination. He's grateful, and in some way he serves as a nexus for all of them to form a precognitive, psychic network. It isn't high-level or controllable, but it's there.

Then we meet them as adults, played by (in order) Thomas Jane, Jason Lee, Lewis, and Timothy Olyphant (Duddits is now Donnie

Wahlberg). When Jonesy has an accident of startling suddenness, that serves as the catalyst for a trip to the woods, where the hunters turn into the hunted as alien beings attack.

It would be well not to linger on plot details, since if you are going to see the movie, you will want them to be surprises. Let me just say that the aliens, who look like a cross between the creature in *Alien* and the things that crawled out of the drains in that David Cronenberg movie, exhibit the same problem I often have with such beings: How can an alien that consists primarily of teeth and an appetite, that apparently has no limbs, tools, or language, travel to Earth in the first place? Are they little clone creatures for a superior race? Perhaps; an alien nicknamed Mr. Gray turns up, who looks and behaves quite differently, for a while.

For these aliens, space travel is a prologue for trips taking them where few have gone before; they explode from the business end of the intestinal tract, through that orifice we would be least willing to lend them for their activities. The movie, perhaps as a result, has as many farts as the worst teenage comedy—which is to say, too many farts for a movie that keeps insisting, with mounting implausibility, that it is intended to be good. These creatures are given a name by the characters that translates in a family newspaper as Crap Weasels.

When Morgan Freeman turns up belatedly in a movie, that is usually a good sign, because no matter what has gone before, he is likely to import more wit and interest. Not this time. He plays Colonel Abraham Curtis, a hard-line military man dedicated to doing what the military always does in alien movies, which is to blast the aliens to pieces and ask questions later. This is infinitely less interesting than a scene in King's *Buick 8* where a curious state trooper dissects a batlike thing that seems to have popped through a portal from another world. King's description of the autopsy of weird alien organs is scarier than all the gnashings and disembowelments in *Dreamcatcher.*

When the filmmakers are capable of the first half of *Dreamcatcher,* what came over them in the second half? What inspired their descent into the absurd? On the evidence here, we can say what we already knew: Lawrence Kasdan is a wonderful director of personal dramas

(Grand Canyon, The Accidental Tourist, Mumford). When it comes to Crap Weasels, his heart just doesn't seem to be in it.

The Dreamers ★ ★ ★ ★
NC-17, 115 m., 2004

Michael Pitt (Matthew), Eva Green (Isabelle), Louis Garrel (Theo), Robin Renucci (Father), Anna Chancellor (Mother). Directed by Bernardo Bertolucci. and produced by Jeremy Thomas. Screenplay by Gilbert Adair, based on his novel.

In the spring of 1968, three planets—Sex, Politics, and the Cinema—came into alignment and exerted a gravitational pull on the status quo. In Paris, what began as a protest over the ouster of Henri Langlois, the legendary founder of the Cinématheque Français, grew into a popular revolt that threatened to topple the government. There were barricades in the streets, firebombs, clashes with the police, a crisis of confidence. In a way that seems inexplicable today, the director Jean-Luc Godard and his films were at the center of the maelstrom. Other New Wave directors and the cinema in general seemed to act as the agitprop arm of the revolution.

Here are two memories from that time. In the spring of 1968, I was on vacation in Paris. Demonstrators had barricaded one end of the street where my cheap Left Bank hotel was located. Police were massed at the other end. I was in the middle, standing outside my hotel, taking it all in. The police charged, I was pushed out in front of them, and rubber truncheons pounded on my legs. "Tourist!" I shouted, trying to make myself into a neutral. Later I realized they might have thought I was saying "tourista!" which is slang for diarrhea. Unwise.

The second memory is more pleasant. In April 1969, driving past the Three Penny Cinema on Lincoln Avenue in Chicago, I saw a crowd lined up under umbrellas on the sidewalk, waiting in the rain to get into the next screening of Godard's *Weekend.* Today you couldn't pay most Chicago moviegoers to see a film by Godard, but at that moment, the year after the Battle of Grant Park, at the height of opposition to the Vietnam War, it was all part of the same alignment.

Oh, and sex. By the summer of 1969, I was in Hollywood, writing the screenplay for Russ Meyer's *Beyond the Valley of the Dolls*. It would be an X-rated movie from 20th Century-Fox, and although it seems tame today (R-rated, probably), it was part of a moment when sex had entered the mainstream and was part of a whole sense of society in flux.

I indulge in this autobiography because I have just seen Bernardo Bertolucci's *The Dreamers* and am filled with poignant and powerful nostalgia. To be sixteen in 1968 is to be fifty today, and so most younger moviegoers will find this film as historical as *Cold Mountain*. For me, it is yesterday; above all, it evokes a time when the movies—good movies, both classic and new-born—were at the center of youth culture. "The Movie Generation," *Time* magazine called us in a cover story. I got my job at the *Sun-Times* because of it; they looked around the feature department and appointed the longhaired new kid who had written a story about the underground films on Monday nights at Second City.

Bertolucci is two years older than I am, an Italian who made his first important film, *Before the Revolution*, when he was only twenty-four. He would, in 1972, make *Last Tango in Paris*, a film starring Marlon Brando and the unknown Maria Schneider in a tragedy about loss, grief, and sudden sex between two strangers who find it a form of urgent communication. Pauline Kael said, "Bertolucci and Brando have altered the face of an art form." Well, in those days we talked about movies that way.

It is important to have this background in mind when you go to see *The Dreamers* because Bertolucci certainly does. His film, like *Last Tango*, takes place largely in a vast Parisian apartment. It is about transgressive sex. Outside the windows, there are riots in the streets, and indeed, in a moment of obvious symbolism, a stone thrown through a window saves the lives of the characters, the revolution interrupting their introverted triangle.

The three characters are Matthew (Michael Pitt), a young American from San Diego who is in Paris to study for a year, but actually spends all of his time at the Cinématheque, and the twins Isabelle (Eva Green) and Theo (Louis Garrel), children of a famous French poet and his British wife. They also spend all of their time at the movies. Almost the first thing Isabelle tells Matthew is, "You're awfully clean for someone who goes to the cinema so much." He's clean in more ways than one; he's a naive, idealistic American, and the movie treats him to these strange Europeans in the same way Henry James sacrifices his Yankee innocents on the altar of continental decadence.

These are the children of the cinema. Isabelle tells Matthew, "I entered this world on the Champs Élysées in 1959, and my very first words were *New York Herald Tribune!*" Bertolucci cuts to the opening scene in Godard's *Breathless* (1959), one of the founding moments of the New Wave, as Jean Seberg shouts out those words on the boulevard. In other words, the New Wave, not her parents, gave birth to Isabelle. There are many moments when the characters quiz each other about the movies, or reenact scenes they remember; a particularly lovely scene has Isabelle moving around a room, touching surfaces, in a perfect imitation of Garbo in *Queen Christina*. And there's a bitter argument between Matthew and Theo about who is greater—Keaton or Chaplin? Matthew, the American, of course, knows that the answer is Keaton. Only a Frenchman could think it was Chaplin.

But *The Dreamers* is not Bertolucci's version of Trivial Pursuit. Within the apartment, sex becomes the proving ground and then the battleground for the revolutionary ideas in the air. Matthew meets the twins at the Cinématheque during a demonstration in favor of Langlois (Bertolucci intercuts newsreel footage of Jean-Pierre Leaud in 1968 with new footage of Leaud today, and we also get glimpses of Truffaut, Godard, and Nicholas Ray). They invite him back to their parents' apartment. The parents are going to the seaside for a month, and the twins invite him to stay.

At first it is delightful. "I have at last met some real Parisians!" Matthew writes his parents. Enclosed in the claustrophobic world of the apartment, he finds himself absorbed in the sexual obsessions of the twins. He glimpses one night that they sleep together, naked. Isabelle defeats Theo in a movie quiz and orders him to masturbate (on his knees, in front of a photo of Garbo). Theo wins a quiz and orders Matthew to make love to his sister. Matthew is sometimes a little drunk, sometimes high, sometimes driven by lust, but at the bottom he knows this is wrong, and his more conventional values set up the ending of the film, in which sex and the cinema are engines, but politics is the train.

The film is extraordinarily beautiful. Bertolucci is one of the great painters of the screen. He has a voluptuous way here of bathing his characters in scenes from great movies, and referring to others. Sometimes his movie references are subtle, and you should look for a lovely one. Matthew looks out a window as rain falls on the glass, and the light through the window makes it seem that the drops are running down his face. This is a quote from a famous shot by Conrad L. Hall in Richard Brooks's *In Cold Blood* (1967). And although Michael Pitt usually looks a little like Leonardo DiCaprio, in this shot, at that angle, with that lighting, he embodies for a moment the young Marlon Brando. Another quotation: As the three young people run down an outdoor staircase, they are pursued by their own giant shadows, in a nod to *The Third Man*.

The movie is rated NC-17, for adults only, because of the themes and because of some frontal nudity. So discredited is the NC-17 rating that Fox Searchlight at first thought to edit the film for an R, but why bother to distribute a Bertolucci film except in the form he made it? The sexual content evokes that time and place. The movie is like a classic argument for an A rating, between the R and NC-17, which would identify movies intended for adults but not actually pornographic. What has happened in our society to make us embrace violence and shy away from sexuality?

Bertolucci titles his film *The Dreamers*, I think, because his characters are dreaming, until the brick through the window shatters their cocoon and the real world of tear gas and Molotov cocktails enters their lives. It is clear now that Godard and sexual liberation were never going to change the world. It only seemed that way for a time. The people who really run things do not go much to the movies, or perhaps think much about sex. They are driven by money and power. Matthew finds he cannot follow the twins into whatever fantasy the times have inspired in them. He turns away and disappears into the crowd of rioters, walking in the opposite direction. Walking into a fu-

ture in which, perhaps, he will become the director of this movie. ☞

Dr. Seuss' the Cat in the Hat ★ ★
PG, 81 m., 2003

Mike Myers (The Cat), Alec Baldwin (Lawrence Quinn), Kelly Preston (Joan Walden), Dakota Fanning (Sally Walden), Spencer Breslin (Conrad Walden), Sean Hayes (The Fish [voice]), Amy Hill (Mrs. Kwan), Sean Hayes (Mr. Humberfloob). Directed by Bo Welch and produced by Brian Grazer. Screenplay by Alec Berg, David Mandel, and Jeff Schaffer, based on the book by Dr. Seuss.

Dr. Seuss' the Cat in the Hat is a triumph above all of production design. That's partly because the production design is so good, partly because the movie is so disappointing. It's another overwrought clunker like *How the Grinch Stole Christmas*, all effects and stunts and CGI and prosthetics, with no room for lightness and joy. Poor Dr. Seuss, whose fragile wonderments have been crushed under a mountain of technology.

Mike Myers stars as The Cat, in the ritual sacrifice of a big star to a high concept. Like Jim Carrey as The Grinch, he's imprisoned beneath layers of makeup. There is a reason why Myers and Carrey are stars, and that reason is not because they look like cats or grinches. Nor does it much help that The Cat sometimes lapses uncannily into the voice of Linda Richman, Myers's classic *SNL* character. The Cat is a nudge, a scold, a card, an instigator, a tease— oh, lots of things, but one of them isn't lovable. It's been said you should never marry anyone you wouldn't want to take along on a three-day bus trip. I have another insight: Never make a movie about a character you can't stand.

The movie follows the book, sort of, if you can imagine a cute balloon inflated into a zeppelin. The two kids, Conrad and Sally, are played by Spencer Breslin and Dakota Fanning; he's seemingly compelled to mess things up, she's so compulsive that the to do list on her Palm includes: "Make out tomorrow's to do list."

Their mom, Joan (Kelly Preston), is a real estate agent who works for the germophobic Mr. Humberfloob (Sean Hayes); everything depends on her house being spic and span for a big reception, and so, of course, the moment she entrusts the kids into the hands of Mrs. Kwan the baby-sitter (Amy Hill), who should show up but The Cat, and the house is eventually in ruins. What happens then? Is Joan fired? Is the house perhaps magically repaired? I would be happy to tell you, but I had better not give away the ending; there may be unfortunate readers who have not read *The Cat in the Hat,* or had it read to them, or even had it summarized for them by a trusted adviser.

The movie consists of wall-to-wall action, sort of like *The Fast and the Furious* for the third-grade hyperactive set. The Cat's catmobile sprouts three steering wheels, and The Cat leads them on a fantasy tour of the town in search of their runaway dog. The theory is that Mrs. Kwan, apparently a narcoleptic, will never notice their absence since she has fallen asleep immediately after arriving to baby-sit.

But Mrs. Kwan does turn up later, during their visit to an imaginary amusement park, where the dumpy old Chinese lady, still insensate, her body stiff as a board, functions admirably as a raft for the water slide. The cat and the kids mount her and down they go, with a close-up of water splashing over Mrs. Kwan's prow, or brow. To use the unconscious Mrs. Kwan in this way is creepy and offensive. Now I'm not getting P.C. and decrying the movie for making fun of Chinese. I'm glad an Asian-American actress got the job. No, I think it's making fun of old people in general, in a cruel way, and I don't think it's funny.

Other stuff is a little funnier, including the story of what is in the muffins Joan serves at her reception, and how it all got there. And, of course, the movie has the obligatory smart-aleck sidekick, a fish (voice by Sean Hayes) that adds approximately nothing.

Similarly wasted is Alec Baldwin, as the marriage-minded neighbor Lawrence. He wants to marry Joan. The kids rightly suspect him of smarmy nefariousness, and wow, is this the same actor I saw starring on Broadway in *Cat on a Hot Tin Roof*? Baldwin gave an interview recently talking about his fall from stardom and grace, but he is gifted and will make a comeback when the time is right (for advice, he could turn to Joan, played by Mrs. John Travolta). Baldwin is electrifying as a hard-boiled

but old-fashioned casino boss in *The Cooler;* pity about this role.

What went wrong here? Well, the producer is Brian Grazer, who also produced *The Grinch,* and apparently learned little from it, although since it grossed north of $300 million maybe he didn't want to. Grazer is a nice guy and has produced some wonderful movies, often with Ron Howard; this time, he's working with first-timer Bo Welch, a famous and gifted production designer (*Batman Returns, Edward Scissorhands, Beetlejuice, Men in Black*). I should mention this movie's production designer, Alex McDowell, as well as art directors Alec Hammon and Sean Haworth, Anne Kuljian's sets, Rita Ryack's costumes, and all the makeup artists. But this is where we came in.

Drumline ★ ★ ★
PG-13, 134 m., 2002

Nick Cannon (Devon), Zoë Saldana (Laila), Orlando Jones (Dr. James Lee), Leonard Roberts (Sean), GQ (Jayson), Jason Weaver (Ernest), Earl Poitier (Charles), J. Anthony Brown (Mr. Wade). Directed by Charles Stone and produced by Timothy M. Bourne, Wendy Finerman, and Jody Gerson. Screenplay by Tina Gordon Chism and Shawn Schepps.

When the first half is over, the show begins. So *Drumline* advises us, in a story centered on the marching band of a predominantly black university in Atlanta. Devon (Nick Cannon), a drummer so good he was personally recruited by the bandmaster, journeys from Harlem to the middle-class world of Atlanta A&T, where he is the best drummer in the band, and the most troublesome.

He's a cocky hotshot, a showboat who adds a solo to the end of his audition piece and upstages his section leader in front of thousands of fans during a half-time show. The movie shows him gradually drumming himself out of the band, and out of favor with Laila (Zoë Saldana), the dance major he's dating. It also shows him growing up, learning some lessons, and making a friend out of a former enemy.

The film sets Devon's story against the background of the BET Big Southern Classic, a (fictional) annual competition among marching bands that's held in Atlanta. His school's traditional rival is crosstown Morris Brown College, a real school whose band is famed for its half-time shows. MBC's band is flashy and high-stepping, doing anything to please the crowd, while Atlanta A&T's bandmaster, Dr. James Lee (Orlando Jones), has more serious musical tastes and believes the primary job of a band member is to learn.

Drumline, directed by Charles Stone and written by Tina Gordon Chism and Shawn Schepps, is entertaining for what it does, and admirable for what it doesn't do. It gets us involved in band politics and strategy, gives us a lot of entertaining half-time music, and provides a portrait of a gifted young man who slowly learns to discipline himself and think of others. That's what it does.

What it doesn't do is recycle all the tired old clichés in which the Harlem kid is somehow badder and blacker than the others, provoking confrontations. Devon makes the nature of his character clear in a heartbreaking early scene when, after high school graduation, he talks to his father, who abandoned the family, and tells him he doesn't do drugs, doesn't have a lot of little kids running around, and has a full scholarship to a university. This is a movie that celebrates black success instead of romanticizing gangsta defeatism. Nick Cannon plays Devon as a fine balance between a showoff and a kid who wants to earn admiration

The key rivalry in the film is between Devon and Sean (Leonard Roberts), head of the drum section and the band's best drummer—until Devon arrives. They develop a personal animosity that hurts the band, Dr. Lee believes. He disciplines Devon for violations of the band rule book, for provoking a fight with another band member and, most painful, for keeping a secret that Sean makes sure is revealed.

Dr. Lee has a problem, too, with the school president, who likes Devon's showboating and thinks the band needs more pizzazz to please the alums. Orlando Jones makes his character a thoughtful teacher, a little old-fashioned, who believes in values. In creating this character, the writers must have been thinking about real teachers they admired, since they avoid the usual *Mr. Chips/Dead Poets* clichés.

The love story between Devon and Laila is sweet and remarkably innocent, for a contemporary movie. They share one tender kiss, although the eagle-eyed MPAA rates the film PG-13 for "innuendo." Oh, I forgot: The MPAA also singles out "language," although this is one of the cleanest-talking urban movies in history. If this isn't a PG film in today's world, what is?

It is also, in a very sincere way, touching. It pays attention to its characters, gives them weight and reality, doesn't underline the morals but certainly has them. *Drumline* joins titles like *love jones, Soul Food, Barbershop*, and *Antwone Fisher* in the slowly growing list of movies about everyday African-American lives. What a good-hearted film.

Note: The filmmakers filled the Georgia Dome with 50,000 extras for the rousing marching band showdown, which features the actual bands of Morris Brown College and Clark Atlanta University, Bethune-Cookman College in Daytona Beach, and Louisiana's Grambling State. Morris Brown was a good sport to allow its bandmaster to be portrayed as the villain.

Duplex ★ ★
PG-13, 88 m., 2003

Ben Stiller (Alex), Drew Barrymore (Nancy), Eileen Essel (Mrs. Connell), Harvey Fierstein (Realtor), Justin Theroux (Cooper Sinclair), Michelle Krusiec (Dr. Kang), Swoosie Kurtz (Alex's Editor), Wallace Shawn (Nancy's Editor). Directed by Danny DeVito and produced by Drew Barrymore, Stuart Cornfeld, Richard N. Gladstein, Nancy Juvonen, Meryl Poster, and Ben Stiller. Screenplay by Larry Doyle and John Hamburg.

When all the world was agog over the butter scene between Marlon Brando and Maria Schneider in *Last Tango in Paris*, it took Art Buchwald to explain the movie. It was not about sex at all, he said, but about what people are willing to do for a rent-controlled apartment in Paris. *Duplex* is about a yuppie couple who eventually get to the point where they are contemplating murder.

Drew Barrymore and Ben Stiller play Nancy and Alex, young professionals fleeing a Manhattan flat "the size of a small child." In Brooklyn they buy a perfect apartment, with three fireplaces and original stained-glass windows, on a quiet street; there are even shelves for his collection of first editions. Here he'll be able to finish his second novel, while she commutes to her job as a magazine editor. The apartment is even a duplex, but there's a hitch: The upstairs is occupied by a sweet little old rent-controlled lady who pays only $88 a month.

"She hasn't been feeling too well lately," their real estate agent (Harvey Fierstein) optimistically informs them. So it's perfect. They'll move in, the sweet little old lady will die, and then they can take over the upstairs and start their family. The problem is that the sweet little old lady is annoying and obnoxious on a truly alarming scale.

Her name is Mrs. Connell, and she's played by the actress Eileen Essel, who is eighty-one, but skips around the apartment like a cheerleader. Maybe they used doubles for some of the movement, but Essel is filled with energy, aggressively cheerful despite their raids on her sanity, and keeps them guessing: She mentions at one point that her husband died in 1963, after they had been married fifty-eight years. Barrymore's eyes almost cross as she tries to do the math.

Essel's energy and timing are delightful. Stiller and Barrymore are fun, too; few actors have a better slow burn than Stiller, who eventually realizes that he will never finish his novel or have a life as long as Mrs. Connell lives upstairs. But the movie becomes an elaboration on one joke: Mrs. Connell, in her passive-aggressive and sometimes plain aggressive way, makes life miserable for them, and they take it as long as they can, and then snap.

Mrs. Connell, for example, plays her TV at top volume all night long. She wants Alex to run errands for her all day. He helps her go shopping, and she meticulously counts out everything: blueberries, pennies. One day when he is working against the deadline for his novel, she invites some friends over to visit— little old ladies like herself, who turn out to be members of a brass ensemble.

Eventually it becomes possible to contemplate murdering her, and at one point Alex is cruising the subway system hoping to pick up a killer flu bug, so he can sneeze on popcorn and send it upstairs. But murder schemes aimed at Mrs. Connell don't generate the laughter they should, maybe because no matter what she

does, she still seems, irremediably, unredeemably, a sweet little old lady.

The movie was directed by Danny DeVito, who brings some of the same dark comedy he used in his great *The War of the Roses* (1989). But that one was about equals (Michael Douglas and Kathleen Turner) whose hate turns homicidal, and it had psychological depth to justify their extremes. *Duplex* is all about plotting; it tries to impose emotions that we don't really feel. We can't identify with Mrs. Connell, that's for sure, but we can't identify with Alex and Nancy either, because we don't share their frustration—and the reason we don't is because we don't believe it. There's too much contrivance and not enough plausibility, and so finally we're just enjoying the performances and wishing they'd been in a more persuasive movie.

DysFunKtional Family ★ ★ ★
R, 83 m., 2003

A concert documentary by Eddie Griffin. Directed by George Gallo and produced by Griffin, David Permut, and Paul Brooks.

Eddie Griffin uses the N-word 382 times in his new concert film, *DysFunKtional Family*. I know this because David Plummer of the Ebert & Roeper staff counted them. It isn't uncommon for speakers to use placeholders, such as "you know" or "uh" or "like," but in Griffin's case the N-word functions more as a lubricant. It speeds his sentences ahead, provides timing, delays punch words until the right moment. The N-word in his act is so omnipresent that it becomes invisible, like air to a bird or water to a fish. It's his rhythm section.

Much has been written about how African-American musicians, comedians, and writers began to use the N-word in order, they said, to rob it of its poison. When Dick Gregory titled his 1963 autobiography *Nigger*, it was shocking and controversial, but he was making a bold gesture to strip the word of its hurtful power. ("Also," he told his mother, "whenever you hear it, they're advertising my book.")

The N-word is now spoken mostly by those who mean it as a sign of affection and bonding. The rules are: Blacks can say it, but whites should be very sure how, where, when, and why they are using it. (Not all agree. The black scholar Randall Kennedy's new book, *Nigger: The Strange Career of a Troublesome Word,* argues that the word is always wrong.)

I mention this because on a single day recently I received a curiously large number of e-mails criticizing my use of the word "redneck." I've used the word in several reviews over the years, but the occasion this time was a review of *Blue Collar Comedy Tour,* another new comedy concert film. It stars Jeff Foxworthy, who is famous for his litany ending ". . . you may be a redneck." (Example: If the wedding rehearsal dinner is at Hooter's, you may be a redneck.)

Whether these e-mails were all inspired by the same source, I cannot say. Odd that they came in a cluster. They made the same point: "Redneck" is as offensive to white Americans as the N-word is to African Americans. I doubt that this is the case, and suspect some of my correspondents may have even laughed at a Jeff Foxworthy concert.

One correspondent writes: "I notice that as a liberal you are highly sensitive to the rights of minority groups and would never apply a derogatory adjective to an African-American, a Hispanic-American or a Jew. However, when it comes to White Americans, it seems that you apply a different standard."

The implication is that a conservative would not be so "highly sensitive," I guess, although every true conservative would be. The reasoning behind this message derives from David Duke's European-American Unity and Rights Organization, and it's pretty obvious what they're getting at.

Is "redneck" an offensive term? Yes and no. It does not refer to all white people (as the N-word refers to all blacks, or certain terms refer to all Jews or all Mexicans). It is a term for a specific character type. The dictionary says it is "disparaging," but it is often used affectionately, as Foxworthy does. It is in wide usage. A Google search turns up 524,000 sites using "redneck"— amazingly, two and a half times as many as those using the N-word. Among "redneck" sites, Foxworthy's places second and Redneck World is sixth. I doubt that my correspondents have complained to Redneck World.

Of course, "redneck" would be an insult if used against a given person in a particular situation. Most of the time, it is not used in that way. Everything depends on who you are, how you use a word, who you use it to, and in what spirit. Words are not neutral. My use of "redneck" was not intended to offend, but by taking offense at it, my correspondents have made a not very subtle equation of civil rights in general and their own specialized version of white civil rights, which in Duke's case slides smoothly into white supremacy.

Foxworthy's act is genial, not hurtful, and his definitions of "redneck" include so much basic human nature that we often laugh in recognition. Griffin is also not hurtful (the word "genial" does not occur in connection with his sharp-edged material), but his N-word usage creates uncertainty among whites, who are unsure how to respond. It may limit his crossover appeal to general audiences. As he grows and deepens he may find he can live without it, as Bill Cosby, the greatest of all standup comedians, has always been able to.

I haven't said much about Eddie Griffin's film itself, perhaps because it made me think more about the N-word than about his comedy. Griffin is quick, smart, and funny, and presents the critics with the usual challenge in reviewing a comedy concert: What do you write about, apart from quoting his funniest lines? I have a few quibbles about the way he ropes in his actual family members, especially two uncles, one a pimp, the other addicted to porn; although they seem cheerful enough about going along with the joke, is the joke on them? Still, Griffin made me laugh.

As for "redneck," well, as someone who comes from a part of Illinois where the salad bar includes butterscotch pudding, I can use it, but don't you call me that.

E

Eight Legged Freaks ★ ★ ★
PG-13, 99 m., 2002

David Arquette (Chris McCormack), Kari Wuhrer (Sheriff Sam Parker), Scott Terra (Mike Parker), Scarlett Johansson (Ashley Parker), Doug E. Doug (Harlan), Eileen Ryan (Gladys). Directed by Ellory Elkayem and produced by Dean Devlin and Roland Emmerich. Screenplay by Jesse Alexander, Elkayem, and Randy Kornfield.

Eight Legged Freaks may be the movie that people were hoping for when they went to see *Men in Black II.* They no doubt walked into the theater hoping for laughs, thrills, wit, and scary monsters, and they backed their hopes with something like $133 million over twelve days. It is depressing to contemplate that many people spending that much money on a limp retread that runs out of gas long before it's over. Now here is *Eight Legged Freaks,* which has laughs, thrills, wit, and scary monsters, and is one of those goofy movies like *Critters* that kids itself and gets away with it.

The movie is about spiders, but it doesn't make the mistake of *Arachnophobia* (1990), which was about little spiders. Research shows that small insects don't play on the big screen. See also *The Swarm* from 1978, which, despite its Oscar for the beekeeper's uniforms, failed to excite audiences with its clouds of little buzzing dots. No, these spiders are built along the lines of the one Woody Allen encountered in *Annie Hall;* the females are as big as a Buick, and even the jumpers are as big as a dirt bike. I am reminded of the bird-eating spider in *Crocodile Hunter.*

The movie takes place in bankrupt Prosperity, Arizona, which the mayor wants to sell lock, stock, and barrel to a company that will fill its abandoned mines with toxic wastes. Outside of town, an eccentric spider lover (an unbilled Tom Noonan) lives surrounded by glass tanks containing hundreds of exotic species. An ever-reliable fifty-five-gallon drum, that standby of all toxic waste movies, spills into a nearby river and makes the grasshoppers grow so big they're like "spider steroids." Soon a spider escapes and bites the collector, who of course thrashes around in such methodical agony that he overturns every single glass case, releasing all of his spiders, who soon start dining on dirt bikers, etc.

The movie stars David Arquette as a local boy who has returned after ten years and still has a crush on cute Sheriff Sam Parker (Kari Wuhrer). Her son, Mike (Scott Terra), is the owl-eyed little friend of the spider man; her daughter, Ashley (Scarlett Johansson), seems superfluous at first but becomes indispensable in scenes involving a stun gun and, of course, lots of spiders. Little Mike has learned a lot about spiders from his dead friend, and becomes the local expert.

The town is populated mostly by kooks, whose paranoia is led and fed by Harlan (Doug E. Doug); he runs a radio station from his mobile home and warns of alien attacks. The townsfolk are fed up with the mayor, whose get-rich-quick schemes have included a mall and an ostrich farm, but the mall provides a convenient locale for a last-ditch stand (like in *Dawn of the Dead*), and the ostriches disappear gratifyingly when hauled under by giant trap-door spiders.

The movie's director, Ellory Elkayem, has a sure comic touch; he first handled this material in a short subject that played at the Telluride Film Festival and then was hired by Dean Devlin and Roland Emmerich, of *Godzilla* fame, to direct the feature. I like the way he keeps the characters likable and daffy and positions the spiders just this side of satire. The arachnids make strange nonspidery gurgles and chirps, are capable of double takes, and are skilled at wrapping their victims in cocoons to be devoured later.

The movie contains creepy but reliable clichés (sticking your hand into dark places), funny dialogue ("Please! Not the mall!"), and bizarre special effects, as when a spider slams a cat so hard against plasterboarding that its face can be seen on the other side in bas-relief. The chase scene with jumping spiders and dirt bikes adds a much-needed dimension to the boring sport of dirt bike racing. And I liked the way the cute sheriff dismisses her daughter's spider ravings as "media-induced paranoid delusional fantasies." Meanwhile, a love story blossoms, sort of.

I am not quite sure why the basement of the widow Gladys (Eileen Ryan) would lead directly into a mine shaft, or how the exoskeleton of a spider is strong enough to pound through a steel wall, or how, once again, the hero is able to outrun a fireball. But I am not much bothered. *Eight Legged Freaks* is clever and funny, is amused by its special effects, and leaves you feeling like you've seen a movie instead of an endless trailer.

8 Mile ★ ★ ★
R, 118 m., 2002

Eminem (Jimmy Smith Jr.), Kim Basinger (Stephanie Smith), Brittany Murphy (Alex), Mekhi Phifer (David Porter/Future). Directed by Curtis Hanson and produced by Brian Grazer, Hanson, and Jimmy Iovine. Screenplay by Scott Silver.

Pale, depressed, Jimmy Smith Jr. (Eminem), skulks through a life that has been so terribly unkind to him. His girlfriend has gotten pregnant and broken up with him, and although he did the right thing by her—he gave her his old car—he now faces the prospect of moving back into his mother's trailer home with her boyfriend who hates him. Jimmy carries his clothes around in a garbage bag. He has a job as a punch press operator.

We see him, early in *8 Mile*, about to do the only thing he does well and takes joy in doing. He is about to go onstage at the Shelter, a rap club that looks uncannily like a deserted building, and engage in the hip-hop version of a poetry slam. In this world he is known as "Rabbit."

He rehearses in a mirror in the men's room, fiercely scowling at his own reflection and practicing those hand gestures all the rappers use, their outboard fingers pointed down from jerking arms as they jab spastically like Joe Cocker. Then Rabbit throws up. Then he goes onstage, where he has forty-five seconds to outrap his competitor in a showdown. And then he freezes. The seconds creep by in total silence, until Rabbit flees the stage and the Shelter.

We are hardly started in *8 Mile*, and already we see that this movie stands aside from routine debut films by pop stars. It stands aside from Britney Spears and the Spice Girls and the other hit machines who have unwisely tried to transfer musical ability into acting careers. Like Prince's *Purple Rain*, it is the real thing.

Eminem insists on Rabbit's proletarian roots, on his slattern mother, on his lonely progress as a white boy in a black world.

Whether *8 Mile* is close to Eminem's own autobiographical truths, I do not know. It is a faithful reflection of his myth, however, beginning with the title, which refers to the road that separates Detroit from its white suburbs. He lives on the black side of the road, where he has found acceptance and friendship from a posse of homies, and especially from Future (Mekhi Phifer), who emcees the contests at the Shelter. When Rabbit gets into fights with black rivals, and he does, they are motivated not by racism but by more wholesome feelings, like sexual jealousy and professional envy.

The genius of Rabbit is to admit his own weaknesses. This is also the approach of Eminem, who acknowledges in his lyrics that he's a white man playing in a black man's field. In the climactic performance scene in *8 Mile*, he not only skewers his opponent, but preempts any comeback by trashing himself first, before the other guy can. At one point, devastatingly, he even calls another rapper "too generic." They must read rock critics in the inner city.

The movie, directed by Curtis Hanson (*Wonder Boys*) and written by Scott Silver, is a grungy version of a familiar formula, in which the would-be performer first fails at his art, then succeeds, is unhappy in romance but lucky in his friends, and comes from an unfortunate background. He even finds love, sort of, with Alex (Brittany Murphy), who is loyal if not faithful. What the movie is missing, however, is the third act in which the hero becomes a star. We know that Eminem is awesomely successful, but *8 Mile* avoids the rags-to-riches route and shows Rabbit moving from rags to slightly better rags.

There has been criticism of Kim Basinger, who is said to be too attractive and even glamorous to play Rabbit's mother, but this strikes me as economic discrimination: Cannot poor people as well as rich people look like Kim Basinger? Given the numbers of ugly people who live in big houses, why can't there be beautiful people living in trailers? Her performance finds the right note somewhere between love and exasperation; it cannot be easy to live with this sullen malcontent, whose face lights up only when he sees his baby sister, Lily.

As an actor, Eminem is convincing without being electric. Perhaps the Rabbit character doesn't allow for joy; he seems to go through life forever remembering why he shouldn't be happy. As it happens, on the same day that *8 Mile* was screened in Chicago, I also saw *Standing in the Shadows of Motown*, a documentary about the studio musicians who created the Motown sound. The contrast was instructive. On the one hand, a Detroit white boy embracing the emblems of poverty and performing in a musical genre that involves complaint, anger, and alienation. On the other hand, black Detroit musicians making good money, performing joyously, having a good time, and remembering those times with tears in their eyes. What has happened to our hopes, that young audiences now embrace such cheerless material, avoiding melody like the plague? At least in their puritanism they still permit rhymes.

Eminem survives the X-ray truth-telling of the movie camera, which is so good at spotting phonies. He is on the level. Here he plays, if not himself, a version of himself, and we understand why he has been accepted as a star in a genre mostly owned by blacks. Whether he has a future as a movie actor is open to question: At this point in his career, there is no reason for him to play anyone other than himself, and it might even be professionally dangerous for him to try. He can, of course, play versions of Rabbit in other movies, and would probably play them well, but Rabbit, let it be said, is a downer. I would love to see a sequel (maybe *8½ Mile*) in which Rabbit makes millions and becomes world-famous, and we learn at last if it is possible for him to be happy.

8 Women ★ ★ ★
R, 113 m., 2002

Danielle Darrieux (Mamy), Catherine Deneuve (Gaby), Isabelle Huppert (Augustine), Virginie Ledoyen (Suzon), Ludivine Sagnier (Catherine), Fanny Ardant (Pierrette), Emmanuelle Béart (Louise), Firmine Richard (Madame Chanel). Directed by François Ozon and produced by Olivier Delbosc and Marc Missonnier. Screenplay by Ozon and Marina de Van, adapted from the play by Robert Thomas.

Here it is at last, the first Agatha Christie musical. Eight women are isolated in a snowbound cottage, there is a corpse with a knife in his back, and all of the women are potential suspects, plus six song-and-dance numbers. The cast is a roll call of French legends. In alphabetical order: Fanny Ardant, Emmanuelle Béart, Danielle Darrieux, Catherine Deneuve, Isabelle Huppert, Virginie Ledoyen, Firmine Richard, and Ludivine Sagnier.

From the opening shot, the film cheerfully lets us know it's a spoof of overproduced Hollywood musicals. We pan past tree branches impossibly laden with picturesque snow, and find a charming cottage where guests are just arriving. Eight women have gathered to celebrate Christmas with Marcel, who is the husband of Gaby (Deneuve), the son-in-law of Mamy (Darrieux), the brother-in-law of Aunt Augustine (Huppert), the father of Catherine (Sagnier) and Suzon (Ledoyen), the employer of the domestic servants Madame Chanel (Richard) and Louise (Béart), and the brother of the late-arriving Pierrette (Ardant).

"Monsieur died in his bed with a knife in his back," the assembled company is informed. And (significant detail required in all isolated rural murders) "the dogs didn't bark all night." The women absorb this news while dressed in stunning designer fashions (even the maids look chic) and deployed around a large, sunny room that looks like nothing so much as a stage set—even to the detail that all the furniture is behind the actresses most of the time. Only a couple of brief excursions upstairs prevent the movie from taking place entirely on this one bright set, where nothing looks used or lived with.

The artificiality is so jolly that we're not surprised when the first song begins, because *8 Women* is in no sense serious about murder, its plot, or anything else. It's an elaborate excuse to have fun with its cast, and we realize we've been waiting a long time for Catherine Deneuve to come right out and say of Isabelle Huppert: "I'm beautiful and rich. She's ugly and poor." I had also just about given up hope of ever seeing Deneuve and Fanny Ardant rolling around on the floor pulling each other's hair.

In a cast where everybody has fun, Huppert has the most, as Augustine. She and her mother (Darrieux) have been living rent-free in Marcel's cottage with her sister (Deneuve), but that has not inspired Augustine to compromise in her fierce resentment and spinsterish isolation. She stalks around the set like Whistler's mother, frowning from behind her horn-rims and making disapproval into a lifestyle.

The other characters quickly fall into approved Agatha Christie patterns. Young Suzon appoints herself Sherlock Holmes, or perhaps in this case Hercule Poirot, and begins sniffing for clues. The sexy Louise is established as the late Marcel's mistress. Madame Chanel, from French Africa, has been with the family for years and lives out back in the guest cottage, where, as it develops, she often plays cards with Pierrette. And Pierrette herself, who arrives late with the kind of entrance that only the tall, dark, and forcible Ardant could pull off, has secrets that are as amazing as they are inevitable.

I dare not reveal a shred of the plot. And the movie is all plot—that, and stylish behavior, and barbed wit, and those musical numbers. Watching *8 Women*, you have a silly grin half of the time. Astonishing that François Ozon, who directed this, also made *Under the Sand* (2001), that melancholy record of a wife (Charlotte Rampling) whose husband disappears, apparently drowned, and who refuses to deal with the fact that he is dead.

Movies like *8 Women* are essentially made for movie lovers. You have to have seen overdecorated studio musicals, and you have to know who Darrieux and Deneuve and Béart and Huppert and Ardant are, to get the full flavor. It also helps if you have seen Agatha Christie's *The Mousetrap*, now more than fifty years into its London run, with its cast still trapped with the corpse in the isolated cottage. "Do not give away the secret!" the program notes exort. And here too. Not that the secret is anything more than one more twist of the plot's peppermill.

Elephant ★ ★ ★

R, 81 m., 2003

Alex Frost (Alex), Eric Deulen (Eric), John Robinson (John), Elias McConnell (Elias), Jordan Taylor (Jordan), Carrie Finklea (Carrie), Nicole George (Nicole), Brittany Mountain (Brittany). Directed by Gus Van Sant and produced by Dany Wolf. Screenplay by Van Sant.

Gus Van Sant's *Elephant* is a record of a day at a high school like Columbine, on the day of a massacre much like the one that left thirteen dead. It offers no explanation for the tragedy, no insights into the psyches of the killers, no theories about teenagers or society or guns or psychopathic behavior. It simply looks at the day as it unfolds, and that is a brave and radical act; it refuses to supply reasons and assign cures so that we can close the case and move on.

Van Sant seems to believe there are no reasons for Columbine and no remedies to prevent senseless violence from happening again. Many viewers will leave this film as unsatisfied and angry as *Variety*'s Todd McCarthy, who wrote after it won the Golden Palm at Cannes 2003 that it was "pointless at best and irresponsible at worst." I think its responsibility comes precisely in its refusal to provide a point.

Let me tell you a story. The day after Columbine, I was interviewed for the Tom Brokaw news program. The reporter had been assigned a theory and was seeking sound bites to support it.

"Wouldn't you say," she asked, "that killings like this are influenced by violent movies?"

No, I said, I wouldn't say that.

"But what about *The Basketball Diaries*?" she asked. "Doesn't that have a scene of a boy walking into a school with a machine gun?"

The obscure 1995 Leonardo DiCaprio movie did indeed have a brief fantasy scene of that nature, I said, but the movie failed at the box office (it grossed only $2.5 million), and it's unlikely the Columbine killers saw it.

The reporter looked disappointed, so I offered her my theory.

"Events like this," I said, "if they are influenced by anything, are influenced by news programs like your own. When an unbalanced kid walks into a school and starts shooting, it becomes a major media event. Cable news drops ordinary programming and goes around the clock with it. The story is assigned a logo and a theme song; these two kids were packaged as the Trench Coat Mafia.

"The message is clear to other disturbed kids around the country: 'If I shoot up my school, I can be famous. The TV will talk about nothing else but me. Experts will try to figure out what I was thinking. The kids and teachers at school will see they shouldn't have messed with me. I'll go out in a blaze of glory.'"

In short, I said, events like Columbine are influenced far less by violent movies than by *CNN*, the *NBC Nightly News*, and all the other news media who glorify the killers in the guise of "explaining" them. I commended the policy at the *Sun-Times*, where our editor said the paper would no longer feature school killings on Page One.

The reporter thanked me and turned off the camera. Of course, the interview was never used. They found plenty of talking heads to condemn violent movies, and everybody was happy.

Van Sant's *Elephant* is a violent movie in the sense that many innocent people are shot dead. But it isn't violent in the way it presents those deaths. There is no pumped-up style, no lingering, no release, no climax. Just implacable, poker-faced, flat, uninflected death.

Truffaut said it was hard to make an antiwar film because war was exciting even if you were against it. Van Sant has made an antiviolence film by draining violence of energy, purpose, glamour, reward, and social context. It just happens.

I doubt that *Elephant* will ever inspire anyone to copy what they see on the screen. Much more than the insipid message movies shown in social studies classes, it might inspire useful discussion and soul-searching among high school students.

Van Sant simply follows a number of students and teachers as they arrive at the school and go about their daily routines. Some of them intersect with the killers, and many of those die. Others escape for no particular reason.

The movie is told mostly in long tracking shots; by avoiding cuts between close-ups and medium shots, Van Sant also avoids the film grammar that goes along with such cuts, and so his visual strategy doesn't load the dice or try to tell us anything. It simply watches.

At one point he follows a tall, confident African-American student in a very long tracking shot as he walks into the school and down the corridors, and all of our experience as filmgoers leads us to believe this action will have definitive consequences; the kid embodies all those movie heroes who walk into hostage situations and talk the bad guy out of his gun. But

it doesn't happen like that, and Van Sant sidesteps all the conventional modes of movie behavior and simply shows us sad, sudden death without purpose.

"I want the audience to make its own observations and draw its own conclusions," Van Sant told me at Cannes. "Who knows why those boys acted as they did?"

He is honest enough to admit that he does not. Of course a movie about a tragedy that does not explain the tragedy—that provides no personal or social "reasons" and offers no "solutions"—is almost against the law in the American entertainment industry. When it comes to tragedy, Hollywood is in the catharsis business.

Van Sant would have found it difficult to find financing for any version of this story (Columbine isn't "commercial"), but to tell it on a small budget, without stars or a formula screenplay, is unthinkable. He found the freedom to make the film, he said, because of the success of his *Good Will Hunting*, which gave him financial independence: "I came to realize since I had no need to make a lot of money, I should make films I find interesting, regardless of their outcome and audience." ☞

Elf ★ ★ ★
PG, 95 m., 2003

Will Ferrell (Buddy), James Caan (Walter), Zooey Deschanel (Jovie), Mary Steenburgen (Emily), Edward Asner (Santa Claus), Bob Newhart (Papa Elf), Daniel Tay (Michael), Faizon Love (Elf Manager). Directed by Jon Favreau and produced by Jon Berg, Todd Komarnicki, and Shauna Weinberg. Screenplay by David Berenbaum.

If I were to tell you *Elf* stars Will Ferrell as a human named Buddy who thinks he is an elf and Ed Asner as Santa Claus, would you feel an urgent desire to see this film? Neither did I. I thought it would be clunky, stupid, and obvious, like *The Santa Clause* or *How the Grinch Stole Christmas*. It would have grotesque special effects and lumber about in the wreckage of holiday cheer, foisting upon us a chaste romance involving the only girl in America who doesn't know that a man who thinks he is an elf is by definition a pervert.

That's what I thought it would be. It took me

about ten seconds of seeing Will Ferrell in the elf costume to realize how very wrong I was. This is one of those rare Christmas comedies that has a heart, a brain, and a wicked sense of humor, and it charms the socks right off the mantelpiece.

Even the unexpected casting is on the money. James Caan as the elf's biological father. Yes! Bob Newhart as his adoptive elf father. Yes! Mary Steenburgen as Caan's wife, who welcomes an adult son into her family. Yes! Zooey Deschanel as the girl who works in a department store and falls for his elfin charm. Yes! Faizon Love as Santa's elf manager—does it get any better than this? Yes, it does. Peter Dinklage, who played the dwarf in *The Station Agent*, has a brief but sublime scene in which he cuts right to the bottom line of elfhood.

Elf, directed by Jon Favreau and written by David Berenbaum, begins with a tragic misunderstanding on a Christmas long ago. As Santa is making his rounds, a human orphan crawls into his sack and accidentally hitches a ride to the North Pole. Raised as an elf by Papa Elf (Newhart), he knows he's at least four feet taller than most of the other elves, and eventually he decides to go to New York and seek out his birth father.

This is Walter (Caan), a hard-bitten publisher whose heart does not instantly melt at the prospect of a six-foot man in a green tunic and yellow stretch tights who says he is his son. But when Buddy drops the name of Walter's long-lost girlfriend, a faraway look appears in the old man's eyes, and soon Buddy is invited home, where Mary Steenburgen proves she is the only actress in America who could welcome her husband's out-of-wedlock elf into her family and make us believe she means it.

The plot is pretty standard stuff, involving a crisis at the old man's publishing company and a need for a best-selling children's book, but there are sweet subplots involving Buddy's new little brother, Michael (Daniel Tay), and Buddy's awkward but heartfelt little romance with the department store girl (Deschanel). Plus heart-tugging unfinished business at the North Pole.

Of course there's a big scene involving Buddy's confrontation with the department store Santa Claus, who (clever elf that he is) Buddy instantly spots as an imposter. "You sit on a throne of lies!" he tells this Santa. Indeed,

the whole world has grown too cynical, which is why Santa is facing an energy crisis this year. His sleigh is powered by faith, and if enough people don't believe in Santa Claus, it can't fly. That leads to one of those scenes where a flying machine (in this case, oddly enough, the very sleigh we were just discussing) tries to fly and doesn't seem to be able to achieve takeoff velocity, and . . . well, it would be a terrible thing if Santa were to go down in flames, so let's hope Buddy convinces enough people to believe. It should be easy. He convinced me this was a good movie, and that's a miracle on 34th Street right there.

Ella Enchanted ★ ★ ★ ½
PG, 95 m., 2004

Anne Hathaway (Ella), Hugh Dancy (Prince Charmont), Cary Elwes (Prince Regent Edgar), Minnie Driver (Mandy), Vivica A. Fox (Fairy Lucinda), Joanna Lumley (Dame Olga), Patrick Bergin (Sir Peter), Jimi Mistry (Benny the Book), Aiden McArdle (Slannen the Elf), Lucy Punch (Hattie), Jennifer Higham (Olive), Eric Idle (Narrator), Parminder K. Nagra (Areida). Directed by Tommy O'Haver and produced by Jane Startz. Screenplay by Laurie Craig, Karen McCullah Lutz, and Kirsten Smith, based on the novel by Gail Carson Levine.

Ella Enchanted is enchanted, all right. Based on the beloved novel by Gail Carson Levine, it's a high-spirited charmer, a fantasy that sparkles with delights. A lot of the fun is generated because it takes place in a world that is one part *Cinderella,* one part *Shrek,* and one part *The Princess Bride.* It even stars the hero from *The Princess Bride,* Cary Elwes, who has grown up to become evil Prince Regent Edgar, who killed his brother the king and now has his sights on the king's son, who will inherit the throne. So make that one part *Hamlet* crossed with one part *Macbeth.*

Anne Hathaway, that improbably beautiful young woman from *The Princess Diaries,* stars as Ella, who at her birth is burdened with a spell from her fairy godmother, Lucinda (Vivica A. Fox). In this kingdom, everyone gets a fairy spell, but Ella's is a real inconvenience: She is given the spell of obedience, which means she has to do whatever she's told. As she grows older this becomes a real problem, especially after her widowed father, Sir Peter (Patrick Bergin), provides her with an evil stepmother named Dame Olga (Joanna Lumley) and two jealous stepsisters, Hattie and Olive (Lucy Punch and Jennifer Higham).

So we get the Cinderella story, but with a twist, because Ella is sort of a medieval civil rights crusader and thinks it's wrong that Prince Edgar has condemned all the nonhumans in the kingdom to leave the city and live in the forest. That would include the giants, the ogres, and the elves. Ella is in the forest one day when she is captured by ogres, who suspend her above a boiling cauldron and prepare to boil her for lunch. An ogre asks her, "How do you like to be eaten? Baked? Boiled?" I like her answer: "Free range." Ella explains she's on their side, and as she sets out to end discrimination, she takes along a talking book named Benny; the front cover is a hologram showing Benny (Jimi Mistry), whose body was unfortunately lost in a wayward spell. Open the book and he can show you anyone you want to see, although Benny's powers are limited and he can't tell you where to find these people.

She has a Meet Cute (three, actually) with Prince Charmont (Hugh Dancy), and it's love at first, second, and third sight, plunging Ella into the middle of palace intrigue. Edgar plans to murder his nephew and assume the throne, and although Ella discovers this danger, her stepsisters know the secret of the curse and use it to alienate her from Charmont.

The look of the movie is delightful. Special effects create a picture-book kingdom in which the medieval mixes with the suburban (there is a mall). I like the casual way that computer-animated graphics are used with real foregrounds; sure, it doesn't look as convincing as it did (sometimes) in *The Lord of the Rings*, but a certain artifice adds to the style. The cast is appropriately goofy, including the household fairy, Mandy (Minnie Driver), who is not good for much in the spell department; Slannen the Elf (Aiden McArdle), Ella's plucky sidekick; a narrator played by Eric Idle, who sings a few songs; and a slithering snake named Heston, who is Edgar's chief adviser. The role of Ella's best friend, played by Parminder K. Nagra of *Bend It Like Beckham*, seems to have been much abbreviated, alas; we lose track of her for

an hour, until she turns up waving happily at the end.

One of the charms of the movie is its goofiness, which extends to the songs, which verge on sing-along chestnuts; what else would the elves sing, after all, but "Let Us Entertain You"?

And Anne Hathaway is, well, kind of luminous. She has that big smile and open face, and here she's working with a witty and wicked plot, instead of with the wheezy contrivances of *The Princess Diaries*. She looks like she's having fun. So does everyone, even the snake. This is the best family film so far this year.

Elling ★ ★ ★
R, 89 m., 2002

Per Christian Ellefsen (Elling), Sven Nordin (Kjell Bjarne), Marit Pia Jacobsen (Reidun Nordsletten), Jorgen Langhelle (Frank Asli), Per Christensen (Alfons Jorgensen), Hilde Olausson (Gunn), Ola Otnes (Hauger), Eli Anne Linnestad (Johanne), Cecilie A. Mosli (Cecilie Kornes). Directed by Petter Naess and produced by Dag Alveberg. Screenplay by Axel Hellstenius, based on a novel by Ingvar Ambjornsen.

Here are two men, both around forty, with no desire to cope with the world: Elling, who lived all of his life as a mama's boy and had to be hauled by the police out of a cupboard, where he was crouched and trembling, after his mother's death. And Kjell Bjarne, who has been institutionalized so long it is the only world he knows—although he fantasizes endlessly about nubile women in other worlds. Elling is assigned as Kjell's roommate in a care home, and two years later they are moved into an apartment in Oslo and given a shot at independent living.

Elling, the deadpan Norwegian comedy that tells their stories, was nominated for an Oscar in 2002 in the Best Foreign Film category. It's the kind of story that in the wrong hands would be cloying and cornball, but director Petter Naess has the right hands. He gives the movie edge and darkness, is unsentimental about mental illness, makes his heroes into men instead of pets, and still manages to find a happy ending.

Elling (Per Christian Ellefsen) is slight, fastidious, fussy, and extremely reluctant to go outdoors. Kjell Bjarne (Sven Nordin) is burly, unkempt, goes for days without a bath, and knows a certain amount about the world, mostly by hearsay. When their social worker Frank (Jorgen Langhelle) tells them they must leave the apartment to buy food and eat in restaurants, Elling is incredulous: What's the use of putting the Norwegian welfare state to all the expense of renting them a nice flat if they are expected to leave it?

The movie is narrated by Elling, who depends on Kjell Bjarne (always referred to by both names) and is threatened when Reidun, an upstairs neighbor, pregnant and drunk, gets Kjell's attention. Yet Elling is a fiercely honest man who tells both Kjell and Reidun (Marit Pia Jacobsen) that the other is in love. Then he ventures out into the night to poetry readings, having written down some words about Reidun's fall on the stairs and realized, as he puts it, "My God, Elling, all your life you have walked the Earth not knowing you were a poet!"

At a reading he befriends an old man who turns out to be a famous poet and to own a wonderful car, a 1958 Buick Century hardtop. Kjell Bjarne can fix the car, and soon the four of them are heading for the poet's country cottage for a weekend at which matters of love and identity will be settled, not without difficulties, not least when Kjell Bjarne discovers that Reidun is prepared to sleep with him but does not suspect he has been wearing the same underwear for more than a week.

In a subtle, half-visible way, *Elling* follows the movie formula of other movies about mentally impaired characters (the picnic outing is an obligatory scene). But *Elling* has no lessons to teach, no insights into mental illness, no labels, no morals. It is refreshingly undogmatic about its characters, and indeed Elling and Kjell may not be mentally ill at all—simply unused to living in the real world. The humor comes from the contrast between Elling's prim value system, obviously reflecting his mother's, and Kjell Bjarne's shambling, disorganized, goodnatured assault on life. If Felix and Oscar had been Norwegian, they might have looked something like this.

The Embalmer ★ ★ ★
NO MPAA RATING, 101 m., 2003

Ernesto Mahieux (Peppino), Valerio Foglia Manzillo (Valerio), Elisabetta Rocchetti (Deborah), Lina Bernardi (Deborah's Mother), Pietro Biondi (Deborah's Father), Bernardino Terracciano (Boss), Marcella Granito (Manuela). Directed by Matteo Garrone and produced by Domenico Procacci. Screenplay by Ugo Chiti, Garrone, and Massimo Gaudioso.

The little man joins the big man at the zoo, where he is admiring a vulture. The little guy, named Peppino, is a charmer. He's about fifty, balding, under five feet tall. The big guy, named Valerio, is a looker, about twenty, handsome, over six feet tall. As they try to remember where they've met before, the point of view sometimes switches from the humans to the vulture; the image is distorted, the sound is muffled, and we get an inside-out view of the bird blinking its eyes. Valerio says animals are his passion. Funny, says Peppino, they're also his. Peppino is a taxidermist.

Matteo Garrone's *The Embalmer* was originally titled *The Taxidermist,* and while the revised title may be more commercial, it may send the wrong message about this profoundly creepy psychological study from Italy. The movie is an acute study of two personalities, and then a third that acts as a catalyst. Peppino, with a bright personality and a friendly smile, is a predator who likes to court young men with his money and favors. Valerio, who is told he "looks like a god," is not very bright, and likes to be courted. Peppino acts by indirection, taking Valerio to clubs and hiring hookers for parties; the two friends end up in bed with the girls, and Valerio doesn't understand that for Peppino the girls are bait and he is the fish.

This Peppino (Ernesto Mahieux) is a piece of work, with the same electric self-confidence of Danny DeVito, but with undertones that only gradually reveal themselves. He tracks Valerio (Valerio Foglia Manzillo) down to his job as a cook, and offers him a big raise to become a trainee taxidermist. Like a kid displaying his treasures, he shows Valerio some jobs he's proud of: a turtle, a boa constrictor, a tiny shrew. Soon Valerio is learning the right way to sharpen a knife.

Peppino suggests Valerio save rent by moving in with him. Valerio's girlfriend objects, as well she might. This is Manuela (Marcella Granito), who says she's heard the "dwarf" is connected to the Mafia. She walks out, but not long after, in a gas station, Valerio is picked up by the girl behind the counter, who attaches herself to him. This is the sexy, confident brunette Deborah (Elisabetta Rocchetti), who comes from a rich family that is puzzled but hospitable when she turns up with Valerio and . . . Peppino.

The Embalmer is masterful at concealing its true nature and surprising us with the turns of the story. Among the movie's mysteries are: (1) Does Peppino think of himself as a homosexual, or as a swinger who likes good buddies and is open-minded in bed? (2) Does Valerio know Peppino is hot for his bod? (3) Does Valerio prefer Peppino's money and partying to Deborah's considerable sexual prowess? I am tempted to add: (4) Is Valerio completely clueless? Twice he enrages Deborah by standing her up; he keeps falling for Peppino's urging to have "just one more."

Oh, and we should also ask: (5) In that scene where Peppino sends the hookers home and slips in next to Valerio in bed, what goes on? "Something happened between you, didn't it?" screams Deborah at a moment when things are going badly. Is it a weakness or a strength of the film that we don't know what happened? A little of both, as we puzzle over Valerio, an ingenue who, when he's not with the one he loves, loves the one he's with—if he loves anybody.

The movie is set mostly in Italian beach towns, but in a gray season, against cold concrete skies. The sea is distant and cheerless, and Garrone's visuals drain the life out of some scenes. This is not a comedy or a sex romp, but a curious business involving two single-minded hunters (Peppino and Deborah) and their quarry, whose good looks may have made life so easy for him that he never got the knack of living it.

Elisabetta Rocchetti is ideally cast as Deborah, because she has such a palpable, acquisitive sexuality. But the movie's center of energy is Ernesto Mahieux as Peppino. I mentioned Danny DeVito earlier not for the obvious reason that he's short like Mahieux is, but because both men dominate every scene they're in, and convince us they can impose their will on any situation. It may seem unlikely that a balding, middle-aged midget could lure a theoretically straight young male out of the arms of a sexual tigress, but after Deborah sizes up Peppino she knows she has to take him seriously. What the little man wants, he goes after with craft, cunning, and enormous need, and it's fascinating to watch him operate.

And why was that opening scene viewed partly through the vulture's eyes? The vulture is a bird that makes a living by spotting dead meat.

The Emperor's Club ★ ★ ★
PG-13, 109 m., 2002

Kevin Kline (William Hundert), Emile Hirsch (Sedgewick Bell), Embeth Davidtz (Elizabeth), Rob Morrow (James Ellerby), Edward Herrmann (Headmaster Woodbridge), Harris Yulin (Senator Bell), Paul Dano (Martin Blythe). Directed by Michael Hoffman and produced by Andrew Karsch and Marc Abraham. Screenplay by Neil Tolkin, based on the short story "The Palace Thief" by Ethan Canin.

The Emperor's Club tells the story of a teacher who fixes the results of an academic competition and twice allows a well-connected student to get away with cheating. Because he privately tells the cheater he is a heel, the film presents him as a great educator, but he is correct when he tells that student: "I failed you." The chief curiosity of the film is how it seems to present one view of the teacher, but cannot prevent itself from revealing another.

The film will not be generally interpreted in this way, and will be hailed in the latest of a series of sentimental portraits of great teachers, which include *Goodbye, Mr. Chips, The Prime of Miss Jean Brodie, The Dead Poets' Society,* and *Mr. Holland's Opus.* All of those are enjoyable films, except for *Dead Poets,* which is more of a showbiz biopic with students as the audience. None of them have the nerve to venture into the tricky ethical quicksand of *The Emperor's Club.* The movie is too methodical, but it doesn't avoid the hard questions.

Kevin Kline plays William Hundert. who as the film opens has retired after teaching the classics for thirty-four years at St. Benedictus School for Boys, a private East Coast institution that has an invisible conveyor belt leading directly from its door to the Ivy League and the boardrooms of the Establishment. The students are the children of rich men. The purpose of the school is theoretically to mold them into leaders. Hundert tells them, "A man's character is his fate," and asks them, "How will history remember you?" But more truth is contained in the words of a U.S. senator whose son is in trouble at the school: "You, sir, will not mold my son! I will mold him."

The troubled student is Sedgewick Bell (Emile Hirsch), a smart aleck who interrupts in class, disrespects the teacher, and has a valise under his bed that is jammed with men's magazines, booze, condoms, and a pack of Luckies. Despite all of the molding and shaping St. Benedictus has performed on its students, the other boys of course idolize Sedgewick. Strange how, among the young, there is nothing sillier than a man who wants you to think hard and do well, and nothing more attractive than a contemporary who celebrates irony and ignorance.

Mr. Hundert is a bachelor, ferociously dedicated to being a good teacher, and silently in love with the fragrant Elizabeth (Embeth Davidtz), wife of another faculty member. She also loves him, but marriage and rectitude stand between them, and there is an effective scene when she says good-bye—forever, she thinks. Hundert redoubles his teaching efforts, which climax, every school year, with the Mr. Julius Caesar contest, in which the three best students compete in a sort of quiz show.

[Spoilers follow.] After a rocky start, Sedgewick begins to apply himself to his work—not so much because of Hundert as because of dire threats from his father, the no doubt thoroughly corrupt U.S. senator (Harris Yulin). When final exams are written, Sedgewick has so improved that he finishes fourth. But because Hundert wants to reward that improvement, and because even for him a rebel is more attractive than a bookworm, the professor takes another long look as Sedgewick's paper and, after much brow-furrowing, improves his grade and makes him a finalist.

The movie wisely never says if Sedgewick deserves to be upgraded, although we suspect that if he had placed third in the first place, Hundert would not have taken another long look at the fourth-place paper. In any event, Sedgewick competes in the big contest, and cheats, and is seen by Hundert, who finds a silent and tactful way to force him to lose.

Now many years pass. Sedgewick is himself a rich man and wants to run for senator, and will give an enormous endowment to St. Benedictus on the condition that there be a rerun of the original Mr. Julius Caesar contest. Does he at last redeem himself? You will have to see for yourself.

What is interesting about the movie is that Mr. Hundert is fully aware of his ethical shortcomings in the matter of young Sedgewick. He does not let him win, but does not expose him. And the movie does not provide the kind of ending we fear the material is building up to, but finds its own subtle way to see that justice is done. The mechanics of the eventual confrontation between Sedgewick and his own son are ingenious, devastating, and unanswerable.

We are so accustomed to noble teachers that *The Emperor's Club* surprises us by providing one who is dedicated, caring, and skillful, but flawed. As a portrait of the escalator that speeds the sons of the rich upward toward power, it is unusually realistic. Kevin Kline's performance shows a deep understanding of the character, who is, after all, better than most teachers, and most men. We care for him, not because he is perfect, but because he regrets so sincerely that he is not.

The Emperor's New Clothes ★ ★ ★
PG, 105 m., 2002

Ian Holm (Napleon/Eugene Lenormand), Iben Hjejle (Pumpkin), Tim McInnerny (Dr. Lambert), Tom Watson (Gerard), Nigel Terry (Montholon), Hugh Bonneville (Bertrand), Murray Melvin (Antommarchi), Eddie Marsan (Marchand), Clive Russell (Bommel). Directed by Alan Taylor and produced by Uberto Pasolini. Screenplay by Kevin Molony, Taylor, and Herbie Wave, based on the novel *The Death of Napoleon* by Simon Leys.

Napoleon did not die on the island of St. Helena in 1821. That was Eugene Lenormand, who looked a lot like him. *The Emperor's New Clothes*, a surprisingly sweet and gentle comedy, tells how it happened. Lenormand is smuggled onto St. Helena to act as a double for the emperor, who is smuggled off as a cargo hand on a commercial ship ("A position above decks would have been more appropriate"). The theory is, he will arrive in Paris, the impostor will reveal his true identity, and France will rise up to embrace the emperor.

"So many have betrayed me," Napoleon announces grandly at the outset of this adventure. "I place my trust in only two things now: my will, and the love of the people of France." He forgets that he has also placed his trust in Eugene Lenormand—a poor man who grows to enjoy the role of Napoleon, is treated well by his British captors, dines regularly, and refuses to reveal his real identity: "I have no idea what you're talking about."

Both Napoleon and Lenormand are played by Ian Holm (Bilbo Baggins from *The Lord of the Rings*), that invaluable British actor who actually looks so much like Napoleon he has played him twice before, in *Time Bandits* (1981) and on a 1974 TV miniseries. Another actor might have strutted and postured, but Holm finds something melancholy in Bonaparte's fall from grace.

To begin with, the escape ship goes astray, lands at Antwerp instead of a French port, and Napoleon has to use his limited funds for a coach journey with an unscheduled stop at the battlefield of Waterloo—where he can, if he wants, buy souvenirs of himself. Finally in Paris, he goes to see a loyalist named Truchaut, who will engineer the unveiling. Truchaut, alas, has died, and so confidentially has he treated his secret that not even his widow, Pumpkin (Iben Hjejle, from *High Fidelity*), knows the story.

She has no sympathy with this madman who claims to be Napoleon. There is no shortage of those in Paris. But after he injures himself she calls a doctor and grows tender toward this little man, and insightful: "I think you've been in prison." During his convalescence, Napoleon comes to treasure the pleasant young widow, and learns of a guild of melon-sellers who are barely making a living. Planning their retail sales like a military campaign, he dispatches melon carts to the key retail battlefields of Paris, greatly increasing sales.

The story, inspired by Simon Leys's 1992 novel *The Death of Napoleon*, could have gone in several directions; it's not hard to imagine the Monty Python version. But Holm, an immensely likable actor, seems intrigued by the idea of an old autocrat finally discovering the joys of simple life. The director, Alan Taylor, avoids obvious gag lines and nudges Bonaparte gradually into the realization that the best of all worlds may involve selling melons and embracing Pumpkin.

Of course, there must have been countless people in Paris at that time who could have identified Napoleon—but how could he have gotten close enough to them? The government was hostile to him. The British insisted they had the emperor locked up on St. Helena. And at home, Pumpkin wants no more of his foolish talk: "You're not Napoleon! I hate Napoleon! He has filled France with widows and orphans! He took my husband. I won't let him take you."

For Napoleon, this last adventure is a puzzling one: "I have become a stranger to myself." But who knows who we are, anyway? We affix names and identities to ourselves to provide labels for the outside world. When the labels slip, how can we prove they belong to us? Like a modern victim of identity theft, Napoleon has had his name taken away and is left as nothing. Well, not nothing. Pumpkin loves him. And the melon merchants are grateful.

Empire ★ ★ ½
R, 100 m., 2002

John Leguizamo (Victor Rosa), Peter Sarsgaard (Jack), Delilah Cotto (Carmen), Denise Richards (Trish), Vincent Laresca (Jimmy), Isabella Rossellini (La Colombiana), Sonia Braga (Iris), Nestor Serrano (Rafael Menendez), Treach (Chedda), Fat Joe (Tito). Directed by Franc Reyes and produced by Daniel Bigel and Michael Mailer. Screenplay by Reyes.

Empire comes so close to working that you can see there from here. It has the right approach and the right opening premise, but it lacks the zest and goes for a plot twist instead of trusting the material. I recently saw *GoodFellas* again, and this film is similar; they're both about the rise and fall of a gangster, narrated by himself, and complicated by a wife who walks out when she catches him with another woman. And *Em-*

pire has a story hook that could have transformed this story into another classic.

The story is told by Victor Rosa (John Leguizamo), a successful drug distributor of Puerto Rican background who controls a territory in the Bronx. He describes his world in a rich, fact-packed voice-over. He works for La Colombiana (Isabella Rossellini), a rich, ruthless suburban woman with a vicious enforcer. He understands the business inside out; turf wars are not meaningless when "twenty feet of sidewalk means thirty grand a week, easy." He is in love with Carmen (Delilah Cotto), a college student.

Victor is upwardly mobile. He deals with hard street people and is hard himself, a killer, yet we sense an inner goodness trying to be born, a desire to better himself. One day his girlfriend, Carmen, meets Trish (Denise Richards) at school, and they're invited to a party being given by Trish's boyfriend, Jack (Peter Sarsgaard). He's a hotshot young Wall Street wizard who is attracted to Victor's criminal glamour: "We're the same . . ." He offers Victor a chance to invest in a sure thing, an offshore deal that will double his money, and explains to Trish: "He's a businessman. If he were born in the suburbs he'd be running a *Fortune* 500 company."

Investing with Jack fits in with Victor's plans. Carmen is pregnant, and he wants to launder his drug money, leave the business to his top lieutenant, and move to Manhattan with her. When Jack offers him the use of a luxury loft, he grabs at it; he sees himself going legit and becoming an investment wizard like Jack. Carmen isn't so sure. She misses the old neighborhood: "This loft will never be home for me." Especially not after Victor is depressed one day, Jack sends the compliant Trish over to cheer him up, and Carmen walks in on them. Victor is telling the truth when he says, "It's not what it looks like," but tell that to Carmen.

So now we have the setup. I will not reveal the payoff or the twist. For that, you will need to visit the movie's trailer at www.apple.com/trailers, which gives away the surprise with a heedlessness that is astonishing even in these days of trailers that tell too much.

I will couch my objection to the movie cautiously, to preserve its secrets. What disappointed me is that the movie didn't follow through with its original premise and show us a bright, resourceful drug dealer trying to start all over on Wall Street. Is it possible? Is the high-finance club open to outsiders? Does Wall Street play even dirtier than drug dealers, and have more vicious criminal types? The possibility exists in a time when CEOs have led their accountants in the theft of billions from American shareholders.

But no. The movie lacks the ambition or nerve to make the moral critique of American finance that it seems to be heading for. It settles instead for a series of developments that will be familiar to students of similar films. There is poignancy in the situation Victor finds himself in, yes, and real drama in his relationship with Carmen (both Leguizamo and Cotto give full-hearted, convincing performances). And his relationship with the Isabella Rossellini character unfolds with implacable logic, although its final result could have been handled with more imagination.

But *Empire* fails because it lacked the nerve to really be about its people and went for the fancy plot gimmick, which no doubt played better at the pitch meeting. It takes imagination to visualize a movie that sees clearly how finance and morality have diverged (as Oliver Stone's *Wall Street* did), but very little imagination to green-light a mechanical plot device that the audience can see coming long before the characters do. Leaving the theater, still impressed by the reality of Victor, Carmen, and many of the others, I felt a sense of loss. What would La Colombiana have done if Victor really had taken over a *Fortune* 500 company? Now there's a story for you.

The Endurance ★ ★ ★ ½
G, 93 m., 2002

A documentary of Sir Ernest Shackleton's 1914–1916 expedition to Antarctica. Directed by George Butler and produced by Butler, Caroline Alexander, and Louise Rosen. Screenplay by Alexander and Joseph Dorman, based on the book by Alexander.

Footage from a remarkable silent documentary has been combined with new photography, music, and a narration to produce an even more remarkable sound documentary, *The*

Endurance, the story of Ernest Shackleton's doomed 1914 expedition to the South Pole. The expedition failed when its ship, the *Endurance*, became trapped in ice and eventually broke up and sank. It was then that the heroism of Shackleton and his twenty-eight-man crew proved itself, as they survived a long polar winter and a hurricane while eventually finding rescue through an 800-mile journey in a lifeboat.

Shackleton's expedition was not necessarily noble, but its failure created the opportunity for legend. The South Pole had already been reached by the Norwegian Roald Amundsen, who outraced Robert Falcon Scott in 1911–12, in a competition that ended in Scott's death. Shackleton's plan was to cross Antarctica via the pole, and claim it for England; explorers of his generation were inflamed by visions of daring conquests.

What made Shackleton's adventure so immediate to later generations was that he took along a photographer, Frank Hurley, who shot motion picture film and stills (and entered the sinking *Endurance* to rescue it). That film was the basis of *South* (1916), a silent documentary that was restored and rereleased in 2000. It was not a sophisticated film; Hurley employed the point-and-shoot approach to cinematography, but his simple shots spoke for themselves: men with frost on their beards, dogs plowing through snow, the destruction of the *Endurance* in the ice. Above all they underlined the might of nature and the impudence of men; we are surprised by how small the *Endurance* is, and how the crew members seem like dots of life in a frozen world.

That footage has now been used by the documentarian George Butler (*Pumping Iron*) as the basis for *The Endurance*, a new documentary based on Caroline Alexander's book about the expedition. The narration is by Liam Neeson. The old black-and-white footage, retaining all of its power, is intercut with new color footage of the original locations, including Elephant Island, where the *Endurance* crew wintered in the endless night, crouching inside shelters for six months.

Determining that his expedition would have to rescue itself, Shackleton set forth in the lifeboat with six men to try to cross 800 miles of open sea and reach a whaling port at South

Georgia Island. That they survived this journey of seventeen days is extraordinary. Then they had to find the courage to face what they found on the island: "A chaos of peaks and glaciers that had never been crossed." Exhausted, without adequate food or water, they trekked for three more days through this landscape to find the village and bring rescue back to the men who were left behind.

Amazingly, not a single life was lost. When the *Endurance* crew returned to England, it was at the height of World War I; instead of being greeted as heroes, they were suspected of malingering. Some volunteered for the army, and died in the trenches.

The physical toll of polar exploration has taken a psychic price as well from many of its survivors. The best book about Polar ordeals is *The Worst Journey in the World* by Apsley Cherry-Garrard, a member of Scott's expedition, who walked by himself over hundreds of miles of ice to study penguin behavior. In later life he was a broken shell of the confident young man who set out with Scott. *The Endurance* interviews surviving descendants of Shackleton's expedition, including Peter Wordie, the son of James Wordie, who says of his father: "He would never let us read his diaries."

Enigma ★ ★ ★
R, 117 m., 2002

Dougray Scott (Tom Jericho), Kate Winslet (Hester Wallace), Jeremy Northam (Wigram), Saffron Burrows (Claire Romilly), Nikolaj Coster-Waldau ("Puck" Pukowski), Tom Hollander (Logie), Corin Redgrave (Admiral Trowbridge), Matthew MacFadyen (Cave). Directed by Michael Apted and produced by Mick Jagger and Lorne Michaels. Screenplay by Tom Stoppard, based on a book by Robert Harris.

World War II may have been won by our side because of what British code-breakers accomplished at a countryside retreat named Bletchley Park. There they broke, and broke again, the German code named Enigma, which was thought to be unbreakable, and was used by the Nazis to direct their submarine convoys in the North Atlantic. Enigma was decoded with the help of a machine, and the British had captured one, but the machine alone was not enough. My notes, scribbled in the dark, indicate the machine had 4,000 million trillion different positions—a whole lot, anyway—and the mathematicians and cryptologists at Bletchley used educated guesses and primitive early computers to try to penetrate a message to the point where it could be tested on Enigma.

For those who get their history from the movies, *Enigma* will be puzzling, since *U-571* (2000) indicates Americans captured an Enigma machine from a German submarine in 1944. That sub is on display at the Museum of Science and Industry in Chicago, but no Enigma machine was involved. An Enigma machine *was* obtained, not by Americans but by the British ship HMS *Bulldog*, when it captured U-110 on May 9, 1941.

Purists about historical accuracy in films will nevertheless notice that *Enigma* is not blameless; it makes no mention of Alan Turing, the genius of British code-breaking and a key theoretician of computers, who was as responsible as anyone for breaking the Enigma code. Turing was a homosexual, eventually hounded into suicide by British laws, and is replaced here by a fictional and resolutely heterosexual hero named Tom Jericho (Dougray Scott). And just as well, since the hounds of full disclosure who dogged *A Beautiful Mind* would no doubt be asking why *Enigma* contained no details about Turing's sex life.

The movie, directed by the superb Michael Apted, is based on a literate, absorbing thriller by Robert Harris, who portrays Bletchley as a hothouse of intrigue in which Britain's most brilliant mathematicians worked against the clock to break German codes and warn North Atlantic convoys. As the film opens, the Germans have changed their code again, making it even more fiendishly difficult to break (from my notes: "150 million million million ways of doing it," but alas I did not note what "it" was). Tom Jericho, sent home from Bletchley after a nervous breakdown, has been summoned back to the enclave because even if he is a wreck, maybe his brilliance can be of help.

Why did Jericho have a breakdown? Not because of a mathematical stalemate, but because he was overthrown by Claire Romilly (Saffron Burrows), the beautiful Bletchley colleague he loved, who disappeared mysteriously without saying good-bye. Back on the job, he grows chummy with Claire's former roommate, Hester Wallace (Kate Winslet), who may have clues about Claire even though she doesn't realize it. Then, in a subtle, oblique way, Tom and Hester begin to get more than chummy. All the time Wigram (Jeremy Northam), an intelligence operative, is keeping an eye on Tom and Hester, because he thinks they may know more than they admit about Claire—and because Claire may have been passing secrets to the Germans.

Whether any of these speculations are fruitful, I will allow you to discover. What I like about the movie is its combination of suspense and intelligence. If it does not quite explain exactly how decryption works (how could it?), it at least gives us a good idea of how decrypters work, and we understand how crucial Bletchley was—so crucial its existence was kept a secret for thirty years. When the fact that the British had broken Enigma finally became known, histories of the war had to be rewritten; a recent biography of Churchill suggests, for example, that when he strode boldly on the rooftop of the Admiralty in London, it was because secret Enigma messages assured him there would be no air raids that night.

The British have a way of not wanting to seem to care very much. It seasons their thrillers. American heroes are stalwart, forthright, and focused; Brits like understatement and sly digs. The tension between Tom Jericho and Wigram is all the more interesting because both characters seem to be acting in their own little play some of the time, and are as interested in the verbal fencing as in the underlying disagreement. It is a battle of style. You can see similar fencing personalities in the world of Graham Greene, and, of course, it is the key to James Bond.

Kate Winslet is very good here, plucky, wearing sensible shoes, with the wrong haircut—and then, seen in the right light, as a little proletarian sex bomb. She moves between dowdy and sexy so easily it must mystify even her. Claire, when she is seen, is portrayed by Saffron Burrows as the kind of woman any sensible man *knows* cannot be kept in his net—which is why she attracts a masochistic romantic like Tom Jericho, who sets himself up for his own betrayal. If it is true (and it is) that *Pearl Harbor* is the story of how the Japanese staged a sneak attack on an American love triangle, at least *Enigma* is not about how the Nazis devised their code to undermine a British love triangle. That is true not least because the British place puzzle solving at least on a par with sex, and like to conduct their affairs while on (not as a substitute for) duty.

Enough ★ ½
PG-13, 115 m., 2002

Jennifer Lopez (Slim), Billy Campbell (Mitch), Juliette Lewis (Ginny), Russell Milton (Alex), Tessa Allen (Gracie), Dan Futterman (Joe), Chris Maher (Phil), Noah Wyle (Robbie), Fred Ward (Jupiter). Directed by Michael Apted and produced by Rob Cowan and Irwin Winkler. Screenplay by Nicholas Kazan.

Enough is a nasty item masquerading as a feminist revenge picture. It's a step or two above *I Spit on Your Grave*, but uses the same structure, in which a man victimizes a woman for the first half of the film, and then the woman turns the tables in an extended sequence of graphic violence. It's surprising to see a director like Michael Apted and an actress like Jennifer Lopez associated with such tacky material.

It is possible to imagine this story being told in a good film, but that would involve a different screenplay. Nicholas Kazan's script makes the evil husband (Billy Campbell) such an unlikely caricature of hard-breathing, sadistic testosterone that he cannot possibly be a real human being. Of course there are men who beat their wives and torture them with cruel mind games, but do they satirize themselves as the heavy in a B movie? The husband's swings of personality and mood are so sudden, and his motivation makes so little sense, that he has no existence beyond the stereotyped Evil Rich White Male. The fact that he preys on a poor Latino waitress is just one more cynical cliché.

The story: Jennifer Lopez plays Slim, a waitress in a diner where she shares obligatory sisterhood and bonding with Ginny (Juliette Lewis), another waitress. A male customer tries to get her to go on a date, and almost succeeds before another customer named Mitch (Billy Campbell) blows the whistle and reveals the first man was only trying to win a bet. In the movie's headlong rush of events, Slim and Mitch are soon married, buy a big house, have a cute child, and then Slim discovers Mitch is having affairs, and he growls at her: "I am, and always will be, a person who gets what he wants." He starts slapping her around.

Although their child is now three or four, this is a Mitch she has not seen before in their marriage. Where did this Mitch come from? How did he restrain himself from pounding and strangling her during all of the early years? Why did she think herself happy until now? The answer, of course, is that Mitch turns on a dime when the screenplay requires him to. He even starts talking differently.

The plot (spoiler warning) now involves Slim's attempts to hide herself and the child from Mitch. She flees to Michigan and hooks up with a battered-wife group, but Mitch, like the hero of a mad slasher movie, is always able to track her down. Along the way Slim appeals for help to the father (Fred Ward) who has never acknowledged her, and the father's dialogue is so hilariously over the top in its cruelty that the scene abandons all hope of working seriously and simply functions as haywire dramaturgy.

Slim gets discouraging advice from a lawyer ("There is nothing you can do. He will win."). And then she gets training in self-defense from a martial arts instructor. Both of these characters are African-American, following the movie's simplistic moral color-coding. The day when the evil husband is black and the self-defense instructor is white will not arrive in our lifetimes.

The last act of the movie consists of Slim outsmarting her husband with a series of clever ploys in which she stage-manages an escape route, sets a booby trap for his vehicle, and then lures him into a confrontation where she beats the shinola out of him, at length, with much blood, lots of stunt work, breakaway furniture, etc. The movie, in time-honored horror movie tradition, doesn't allow Mitch to really be dead the first time. There is a plot twist showing that Slim can't really kill him—she's the heroine, after all—and then he lurches back into action like the slasher in many an exploitation movie, and is destroyed more or less by accident. During this action scene Slim finds time for plenty of dialogue explaining that any court will find she was acting in self-defense.

All of this would be bad enough without the performance of Tessa Allen as Gracie, the young daughter. She has one of those squeaky, itsy-bitsy piped-up voices that combines with babyish dialogue to make her more or less insufferable; after the ninth or tenth scream of "Mommy! Mommy!" we hope that she will be shipped off to an excellent day-care center for the rest of the story.

Jennifer Lopez is one of my favorite actresses, but not here, where the dialogue requires her to be passionate and overwrought in a way that is simply not believable, maybe because no one could take this cartoon of a story seriously. No doubt she saw *Enough* as an opportunity to play a heavy, dramatic role, but there is nothing more dangerous than a heavy role in a lightweight screenplay, and this material is such a melodramatic soap opera that the slick production values seem like a waste of effort.

Envy ★ ★

PG-13, 99 m., 2004

Ben Stiller (Tim Dingman), Jack Black (Nick Vanderpark), Rachel Weisz (Debbie Dingman), Amy Poehler (Natalie Vanderpark), Christopher Walken (J-Man), Ariel Gade (Lula Dingman), Lily Jackson (Nellie Vanderpark). Directed by Barry Levinson and produced by Levinson and Paula Weinstein. Screenplay by Steve Adams.

Jack Black becomes a zillionaire named Nick Vanderpark in *Envy*, who gets rich by inventing a product named Vapoorize. Yes, with a double O. It makes doggy-do into doggy-didn't. Spray some on your dog's morning gift and it disappears. His best friend, Tim Dingman, played by Ben Stiller, lives across the street. They share the commute every day to the sandpaper factory. When Vanderpark comes up with the idea for Vapoorize, he offers Dingman a 50 percent share, but Dingman turns it down. He can't figure out how it could possibly work. Soon, of course, he is being eaten alive by envy. My memory for some reason dredged up an ancient science fiction story in which a child's toy would zap little metal objects like paper clips into the fourth dimension. Great, until they

started leaking back into our three. When you walk through a speck of paper clip, you can do serious damage. I wondered if maybe the same phenomenon would happen in *Envy*, causing, say, five years of dog poop to reappear all at once. Not a pretty picture.

The plot idea resembles that classic British comedy *The Man in the White Suit*, with Alec Guinness, who invented a fabric that never gets dirty. Of course, Guinness underplayed the comedy, a concept alien to Black and Stiller. Not that we want them to dial down; they're gifted comedians, and it's fun to watch Dingman gnashing while Vanderpark celebrates his untold riches. Vanderpark doesn't lord it over his neighbor; he builds an enormous mansion, yes, but right across the street from his best buddy because he doesn't want to leave the neighborhood. So that every time Dingman looks out the window, he has to witness Vanderpark's latest acquisition: ancient statuary, a proud white stallion, a merry-go-round, whatever.

Because Stiller and Black are in the movie, it contains laughs, and because Christopher Walken is in the movie, it contains more laughs. Walken is becoming Hollywood's version of a relief pitcher who comes on in the seventh and saves the game. You can sense the audience smiling when he appears onscreen.

Here he plays a stumblebum who calls himself J-Man, perhaps in homage to that immortal movie character Z-Man, perhaps not. After Dingman's life melts down, he turns to a saloon for consolation, and finds J-Man standing at the bar ready to provide advice and inspiration. J-Man's dialogue is Walkenized; he says strange things in strange, oracular ways.

So the movie is funny, yes, but not really funny enough. The screenplay, by Steve Adams, reportedly with uncredited input by Larry David, is best at showing a friendship being destroyed by envy, but weak at exploiting the comic potential of the invention itself. It gets sidetracked into the story of how Dingman hits Vanderpark's white horse with a bow and arrow, and we are reminded of the dog set on fire in *There's Something About Mary*. Dingman also hits J-Man with an arrow, although J-Man reacts to this development almost indifferently.

Dingman is married to Debbie (Rachel Weisz) and Vanderpark to Natalie (Amy

207

Poehler), and there is a certain tension when the two families, plus kids, gather for dinner at Vanderpark's palatial mansion. There is also the matter of the fountain that Vanderpark gives to Dingman; it's a nice thought, but it does look a little out of scale with his little suburban home. Meanwhile, there is a certain tension between Dingman and his wife, since Stiller was, after all, *offered* 50 percent of the invention and *refused* it. (That's not the end of it, but I dare not spoil a plot point.)

Toward the end of the film, but not before the final revelations, Dingman has a speech that Stiller delivers with manic comic zeal. Allowing all of his pent-up feelings to explode, he tells Vanderpark what he really thinks about horses and offices and houses and dog poop and having flan for dessert, and his entire being quakes with Stillerian angst. Well done.

But the film, directed by Barry Levinson, doesn't generate heedless glee. Jack Black somehow feels reined in; shaved and barbered, he's lost his anarchic passion and is merely playing a comic role instead of transforming it into a personal mission. Walken, good as he is, isn't used enough by the plot, and Stiller's envy is replaced by plot logistics involving the dead horse, the merry-go-round, and so on, until the characters get mired in the requirements of the screenplay, which lumbers on its way, telling a story that increasingly strays from what was funny to begin with.

Equilibrium ★ ★ ★

R, 106 m., 2002

Christian Bale (Clerick John Preston), Emily Watson (Mary O'Brian), Taye Diggs (Clerick Brandt), Angus MacFadyen (Master Clerick/Father), Sean Bean (Partridge), Oliver Brandl (The Technician), Francesco Cabras (Leader of the Rebels), Daniel Lee Clark (Lead Sweeper), Christian Kahrmann (Special Squad Officer). Directed by Kurt Wimmer and produced by Jan de Bont and Lucas Foster. Screenplay by Wimmer.

Equilibrium would be a mindless action picture, except that it has a mind. It doesn't do a lot of deep thinking, but unlike many futuristic combos of SF and f/x, it does make a statement: Freedom of opinion is a threat to totalitarian systems. Dictatorships of both the left and right are frightened by the idea of their citizens thinking too much, or having too much fun.

The movie deals with this notion in the most effective way, by burying it in the story and almost drowning it with entertainment. In a free society many, maybe most, audience members will hardly notice the message. But there are nations and religions that would find this movie dangerous. You know who you are.

The movie is set in the twenty-first century—hey! that's our century!—at a time after the Third World War. That war was caused, it is believed, because citizens felt too much and too deeply. They got all worked up and started bombing each other. To assure world peace and the survival of the human race, everyone has been put on obligatory doses of Prozium, a drug that dampens the emotions and shuts down our sensual side. (Hint: The working title of this movie was *Librium*.)

In the movie, enforcers known as Clericks have the mandate to murder those who are considered Sense Offenders. This is a rich irony, since True Believers, not Free Thinkers, are the ones eager to go to war over their beliefs. If you believe you have the right to kill someone because of your theology, you are going about God's work in your way, not His.

Christian Bale stars as Clerick John Preston, partnered with Partridge (Sean Bean) as a top-level enforcer. Nobody can look dispassionate in the face of outrageous provocation better than Christian Bale, and he proves it here after his own wife is incinerated for Sense Offenses. "What did you feel?" he is asked. "I didn't feel anything," he replies, and we believe him, although perhaps this provides a clue about his wife's need to Offend.

Preston is a top operative, but is hiding something. We see him pocketing a book that turns out to be the collected poetry of W. B. Yeats, a notorious Sense Offender. He has kept it, he explains, to better understand the enemy (the same reason censors have historically needed to study pornography). His duties bring him into contact with Mary O'Brian (Emily Watson), and he feels — well, it doesn't matter what he feels. To feel at all is the offense. Knowing that, but remembering Mary, he deliberately stops taking his Prozium: He loves being a Clerick, but, oh, you id.

If *Equilibrium* has a plot borrowed from *1984*, *Brave New World*, and other dystopian novels, it has gunfights and martial arts borrowed from the latest advances in special effects. More rounds of ammunition are expended in this film than in any film I can remember, and I remember *The Transporter*.

I learn from Nick Nunziata at www.CHUD.com that the form of battle used in the movie is "Gun-Kata," which is "a martial art completely based around guns." I credit Nunziata because I think he may have invented this term. The fighters transcribe the usual arcs in midair and do impossible acrobatics, but mostly use guns instead of fists and feet. That would seem to be cheating, and involves a lot of extra work (it is much easier to shoot someone without doing a backflip), but since the result is loud and violent it is no doubt worth it.

There is an opening sequence in which Preston and Partridge approach an apartment where Offenders are holed up, and Preston orders the lights to be turned out in the apartment. Then he enters in the dark. As nearly as I could tell, he is in the middle of the floor, surrounded by Offenders with guns. A violent gun battle breaks out, jerkily illuminated by flashes of the guns, and everyone is killed but Preston. There is nothing about this scene that even *attempts* to be plausible, confirming a suspicion I have long held, that the heroes of action movies are protected by secret hexes and *cannot* be killed by bullets.

There are a lot more similar battles, which are pure kinetic energy, made of light, noise, and quick cutting. They seem to have been assembled for viewers with Attention Deficit Disorder, who are a large voting block at the box office these days. The dispassionate observer such as myself, refusing to Sense Offense my way through such scenes, can nevertheless admire them as a technical exercise.

What I like is the sneaky way Kurt Wimmer's movie advances its philosophy in between gun battles. It argues, if I am correct, that it is good to feel passion and lust, to love people and desire them, and to experience voluptuous pleasure through great works of music and art. In an early scene Clerick Preston blowtorches the *Mona Lisa*, the one painting you can be pretty sure most moviegoers will recognize. But in no time he is feeling joy

and love, and because he is the hero, this must be good, even though his replacement partner, Clerick Brandt (Taye Diggs), suspects him, and wants to expose him.

The rebel group in *Equilibrium* preserves art and music (there is a touching scene where Preston listens to a jazz record), and we are reminded of Bradbury and Truffaut's *Fahrenheit 451*, where book lovers committed banned volumes to memory. One is tempted to look benevolently upon *Equilibrium* and assume thought control can't happen here, but of course it can, which is why it is useful to have an action picture in which the Sense Offenders are the good guys.

Eternal Sunshine of the Spotless Mind
★ ★ ★ ½
R, 106 m., 2004

Jim Carrey (Joel Barish), Kate Winslet (Clementine Kruczynski), Kirsten Dunst (Mary), Mark Ruffalo (Stan), Elijah Wood (Patrick), Tom Wilkinson (Dr. Howard Mierzwiak). Directed by Michel Gondry and produced by Anthony Bregman and Steve Golin. Screenplay by Charlie Kaufman.

How happy is the blameless vestal's lot! The world forgetting, by the world forgot. Eternal sunshine of the spotless mind! Each pray'r accepted, and each wish resign'd.
—Alexander Pope, "Eloisa to Abelard"

It's one thing to wash that man right outta your hair, and another to erase him from your mind. *Eternal Sunshine of the Spotless Mind* imagines a scientific procedure that can obliterate whole fields of memory—so that, for example, Clementine can forget that she ever met Joel, let alone fell in love with him. "Is there any danger of brain damage?" the inventor of the process is asked. "Well," he allows, in his most kindly voice, "technically speaking, the procedure *is* brain damage."

The movie is a labyrinth created by the screenwriter Charlie Kaufman, whose *Being John Malkovich* and *Adaptation* were neorealism compared to this. Jim Carrey and Kate Winslet play Joel and Clementine, in a movie that sometimes feels like an endless series of aborted Meet Cutes. That they lose their minds while all about them are keeping theirs is a tribute to their skill; they center their characters so that we can actually care about them even when they're constantly losing track of their own lives. ("My journal . . . ," Joel observes oddly, "is . . . just blank.")

The movie is a radical example of maze cinema, that style in which the story coils back upon itself, redefining everything and then throwing it up in the air and redefining it again. To reconstruct it in chronological order would be cheating, but I will cheat: At some point before the technical beginning of the movie, Joel and Clementine were in love, and their affair ended badly, and Clementine went to Dr. Howard Mierzwiak (Tom Wilkinson) at Lacuna Inc., to have Joel erased from her mind.

Discovering this, Joel in revenge applies to have *his* memories of her erased. But the funny thing about love is, it can survive the circumstances of its ending; we remember good times better than bad ones, and Joel decides in mid-process that maybe he would like to remember Clementine after all. He tries to squirrel away some of his memories in hidden corners of his mind, but the process is implacable.

If you think this makes the movie sound penetrable, you have no idea. As the movie opens, Joel is seized with an inexplicable compulsion to ditch work and take the train to Montauk, and on the train he meets Clementine. For all they know they have never seen each other before, but somehow there's a connection, a distant shadow of déjà vu. During the course of the film, which moves freely, dizzyingly, forward and backward in time, they will each experience fragmentary versions of relationships they had, might have had, or might be having.

Meanwhile, back at the Lacuna head office, there are more complications. Lacuna (www. lacunainc.com) seems to be a prosperous and growing firm (it advertises a Valentine's Day special), but in reality it consists only of the avuncular Dr. Mierzwiak and his team of assistants: Stan (Mark Ruffalo), Patrick (Elijah Wood), and Mary (Kirsten Dunst). There are innumerable complications involving them, which I will not describe because it would not only be unfair to reveal the plot but probably impossible.

Eternal Sunshine has been directed by Michel Gondry, a music video veteran whose first feature, *Human Nature* (2002), also written by Kaufman, had a lunacy that approached genius and then veered away. Tim Robbins starred as an overtrained child who devotes his adult life to teaching table manners to white mice. The scene where the male mouse politely pulls out the chair for the female to sit down is without doubt in a category of its own.

Despite jumping through the deliberately disorienting hoops of its story, *Eternal Sunshine* has an emotional center, and that's what makes it work. Although Joel and Clementine ping-pong through various stages of romance and reality, what remains constant is the human need for love and companionship, and the human compulsion to keep seeking it despite all odds. It may also be true that Joel and Clementine, who seem to be such opposites (he is shy and compulsive; she is extroverted and even wild), might be a good match for each other, and so if they keep on meeting they will keep on falling in love, and Lacuna Inc. may have to be replaced with the Witness Protection Program.

For Jim Carrey, this is another successful attempt, like *The Truman Show* and the underrated *The Majestic*, to extend himself beyond screwball comedy. He has an everyman appeal, and here he dials down his natural energy to give us a man who is so lonely and needy that a fragment of memory is better than none at all. Kate Winslet is the right foil for him, exasperated by Joel's peculiarities while paradoxically fond of them. The shenanigans back at Lacuna belong on a different level of reality, but even there, secrets are revealed that are oddly touching.

Charlie Kaufman's mission seems to be the penetration of the human mind. His characters journeyed into the skull of John Malkovich, and there is a good possibility that two of them were inhabiting the same body in *Adaptation*. But both of those movies were about characters trying to achieve something outside themselves. The insight of *Eternal Sunshine* is that, at the end of the day, our memories are all we really have, and when they're gone, we're gone.

Evelyn ★ ★ ★

PG, 94 m., 2002

Pierce Brosnan (Desmond Doyle), Sophie

Vavasseur (Evelyn Doyle), Julianna Margulies (Bernadette Beattie), Aidan Quinn (Nick Barron), Stephen Rea (Michael Beattie), Alan Bates (Thomas Connolly), John Lynch (Mr. Wolfe), Andrea Irvine (Sister Brigid), Karen Ardiff (Sister Felicity). Directed by Bruce Beresford and produced by Pierce Brosnan, Michael Ohoven, and Beau St. Clair. Screenplay by Paul Pender.

Evelyn is set in 1953, and could have been filmed then. Told with the frank simplicity of a classic, well-made picture, it tells its story, nothing more, nothing less, with no fancy stuff. We relax as if we've found a good movie on cable. Story is everything here. Even though Pierce Brosnan is a movie star, he comes across here as an ordinary bloke, working-class Irish, charming but not all that charming. We hardly need to be told the movie is "based on a true story."

Brosnan plays Desmond Doyle, a drunk and a carpenter, more or less in that order. He has two sons and a daughter. When his wife runs away from the family, the government social workers come around, size up the situation, and advise, "send in the nuns." The children are sent to orphanages on the grounds, then sanctified in Irish law, that a father cannot raise children by himself.

Desmond is devastated. At first that translates into drinking, but eventually he meets an understanding woman (a barmaid, of course, since where else would he meet a woman?). She is Bernadette Beattie (Julianna Margulies), who advises Desmond to get his act together if he ever hopes to have his children back again. With her encouragement, he meets her brother, an attorney named Michael Beattie (Stephen Rea), who holds out little hope of a successful court case. For one thing, Desmond will need the consent of his wife, who is conspicuously unavailable.

Before settling into the rhythms of a courtroom drama, the movie takes a look at the conditions in the orphanage where Evelyn (the fetching Sophie Vavasseur) is being cared for. It apparently contains only two staff members: the fearsome, strict, and cruel Sister Brigid (Andrea Irvine), and the sweet, gentle Sister Felicity (Karen Ardiff). The orphanage itself is one step up from the conditions shown in *The Magdalene Sisters*, another current film, which shows how many Irish women were incarcerated for life for sexual misdeeds, stripped of their identities, and used as cheap labor in church-owned laundries.

In 1953 there was no daylight between the Catholic Church and the Irish government, and Doyle's chances in court are poor. He is trying not merely to regain custody of his children, but to overturn Irish law. The case has great symbolic value, and soon Beattie finds himself joined by an Irish-American lawyer named Nick Barron (Aidan Quinn), and finally by a retired Irish legal legend named Thomas Connolly (Alan Bates).

Courtroom scenes in movies are often somewhat similar, and yet almost always gripping. The format fascinates us. There is great suspense here as Evelyn herself takes the stand to denounce Sister Brigid, and Sophie Vavasseur is a good actress, able to convincingly make us fear she won't choose the right words, before she does.

Evelyn depicts Irish society of fifty years ago with a low-key cheerfulness that shows how humor cut the fog of poverty. The Irish in those days got much of their entertainment in pubs, which often had a lounge bar with a piano and an array of ready singers, and it is a true touch that Desmond Doyle takes a turn with a song (Brosnan does his own singing, no better but no worse than a competent pub singer). The movie also enjoys the Irish humor based on paradox and logic, as when one of Desmond's sons, told Joseph was a carpenter, asks, "Did Joseph ever do a bit of painting and decoration like my dad?"

Evelyn is directed by Bruce Beresford (*Driving Miss Daisy, Crimes of the Heart*), who may have chosen the straightforward, classic style as a deliberate decision: It signals us that the movie will not be tarted up with modern touches, spring any illogical surprises, or ask for other than genuine emotions. Brosnan, at the center, is convincing as a man who sobers up and becomes, not a saint, but at least the dependable person he was meant to be. And Irish law is changed forever.

Everybody Says I'm Fine ★ ★
NO MPAA RATING, 103 m., 2004

Rehaan Engineer (Xen), Koel Purie (Nikita), Rahul Bose (Rage), Pooja Bhatt (Tanya),

Anahita Oberoi (Misha), Boman Irani (Mr. Mittal), Sharokh Bharucha (Bobby), Juneli Aguiar (Tina). Directed by Rahul Bose and produced by Viveck Vaswani. Screenplay by Bose.

The English-language Indian film *Everybody Says I'm Fine* is too cluttered and busy, but as a glimpse into the affluent culture of a country with economic extremes, it's intriguing. Occasionally, it's funny and moving, too. The movie was shot in English not for the export market, but for India's domestic English speakers, who tend to be toward the top of the economic scale and are beginning to tire of endless Bollywood megaproductions. This film, at 103 minutes, almost qualifies in its market as a short subject, although true to Bollywood tradition it does include one completely arbitrary and inexplicable song-and-dance sequence.

Rehaan Engineer stars as Xen, a hairdresser whose parents died tragically when the sound board short-circuited in their recording studio. The trauma has left him with a psychic gift: When he cuts a person's hair, he can read the person's thoughts. He learns of adulteries, deceptions, and hypocrisies, and keeps them all to himself, going upstairs after work to his lonely room, where the shades are never opened and the TV sound is muted.

One day a pretty woman named Nikita (Koel Purie) arrives in his chair, and he picks up nothing. No thoughts. Is her mind a blank? He has acted as a matchmaker for some of his other customers whom he learns are attracted to one another, but now here is a challenge for him.

If the story had stayed more or less focused on Xen and his adventures, it might have been more involving, but it strays outside the salon to tell other stories, including one about a beautiful wife who has been left abandoned and penniless by her faithless husband, and a snoopy friend who has secrets of her own. There is also a flamboyant actor named Rage, played by director Rahul Bose, whose desperate attempts to find work are reflected by his bizarre hairstyles.

Movies like this are intrinsically interesting for the way they regard the culture they are immersed in, one where a Domino's pizza across the street coexists with crowds of desperate beggars. I enjoyed watching it just for the information and attitudes it contained, but as a story, it's too disorganized to really involve us.

The Eye ★ ★ ½
NO MPAA RATING, 99 m., 2003

Lee Sin-Je (Mun), Lawrence Chou (Dr. Wah), Chutcha Rujinanon (Ling), Yut Lai So (Yingying), Candy Lo (Yee), Yin Ping Ko (Mun's Grandmother), Pierre Png (Dr. Eak), Edmund Chen (Dr. Lo). Directed by Oxide Pang Chun and Danny Pang and produced by Lawrence Cheng. Screenplay by Jo Jo Yuet-chun Hui, Pang Chun, and Pang.

The Eye is a thriller about a blind young violinist from Hong Kong whose sight is restored through surgery, but who can then see a little too well, so that she observes the grim reaper leading the doomed in solemn procession to the other side, and shares the anguish of the donor of her eyes. What's more, she's thrown out of the blind orchestra now that she can see.

All I know about restored sight I learned in the books of Oliver Sacks, who writes about a patient whose sight was miraculously restored. The problem turns out to be knowing what you're looking at. Babies do all the hard work in the first months after birth, learning to interpret shapes and colors, dimension and distance. For an adult who relates to the world through the other four senses, the addition of sight is not always a blessing.

The movie touches on that, in a scene where the blind girl, named Mun (Lee Sin-Je) is shown a stapler and asked what it is. She can tell by feeling it. But she's a quick study, and in no time is moving independently through the world and falling in love with Dr. Wah, her handsome young therapist (Lawrence Chou).

Lee has an expressive face, which is crucial to the success of the film, because she has an extraordinary number of reaction shots, and no wonder: The movie is about what Mun sees and how she reacts to it. Unlike the overwrought heroines of most women-in-danger films, Mun is quiet, introspective, reasonable, and persuasive.

Perhaps that's why Dr. Wah believes her. She becomes convinced that she can see the dead leaving this Earth and anticipate tragedies before they happen. She thinks this may be connected in some way with the donor of her new eyes, and Dr. Wah begins to believe her, not least because he falls in love with her. His uncle, Dr. Lo (Edmund Chen), takes a jaundiced view of this development, which violates medical ethics and perhaps common sense, and refuses to divulge the name of the donor.

But Wah and Mun eventually do figure out that the corneas came from a girl in Thailand, and journey there for a conclusion that includes a startling scene of carnage that's all the more unexpected because it comes at the end of a relatively quiet and inward movie.

The Eye is better than it might have been, especially in moments of terror involving Mun's ability to see what no one else can see, and in her relationship with a little girl at the hospital who seems to be dying, and becomes her special friend. But the notion that body parts retain the memories of their owners is an outworn horror cliché, as in *The Beast with Five Fingers* and Oliver Stone's early screenplay, *The Hand.* This is the kind of movie you happen across on TV, and linger to watch out of curiosity, but its inspired moments serve only to point out how routine, and occasionally how slow and wordy, the rest of it is.

Eyes Without a Face ★ ★ ★ ½
NO MPAA RATING, 88 m., 1960 (rereleased 2003)

Pierre Brasseur (Professor Génessier), Alida Valli (Louise), Edith Scob (Christiane Génessier), Juliette Mayniel (Edna Gruberg), François Guérin (Jacques Vernon), Alexandre Rignault (Detective Parot), Béatrice Altariba (Paulette Merodon). Directed by Georges Franju and produced by Jules Borkon. Screenplay by Pierre Boileau, Pierre Gascar, Thomas Narcejac, Jean Redon, and Claude Sautet, based on the novel by Redon.

"I've done so much wrong to perform this miracle."

Professor Génessier has good reason for remorse. He is a Parisian plastic surgeon, respected in the profession, a lecturer on the subject of "heterografting," which involves transferring living tissue from one person to another. The downside to this procedure is that it requires both persons to be alive. Having de-

stroyed the face of his daughter in a reckless car accident, he now wants to repair the damage by transplanting the face of another woman. The "miracle" he refers to involves the face of his lover, nurse, and assistant, Louise. He has restored her face so successfully that she now looks just like Alida Valli, who played Harry Lime's lover in *The Third Man.* Valli's characters have bad luck on dates.

Génessier (Pierre Brasseur) is the mad scientist at the heart of *Eyes without a Face* (1960), Georges Franju's merciless horror classic, now being revived in a new 35-mm print. The professor was presumably at one time a reputable plastic surgeon, but now, in his isolated suburban mansion, he experiments on dogs, birds, and helpless young women who are supplied to him by the faithful Louise. One of the startling elements of the film is how graphic it is about his procedures; we see bloody incisions being made all around a victim's face, and when one transplant is interrupted by a visit with the police, he leaves the skin flaps open and waiting, secured by surgical implements.

The film opens with Louise on a nocturnal mission for the doctor, driving a corpse to the Seine and dumping it in. This is the latest victim of a failed procedure. Since Génessier's great success with Louise, his work has not gone well, and soon he sends her out to kidnap another woman. His daughter, Christiane (Edith Scob), waits sedated in a locked room, her flayed face concealed by a mask so that only her eyes move. Having reported Christiane missing after the accident, Génessier identifies the dead woman in the river as his daughter, and prepares to remove the face of the new victim, Paulette (Béatrice Altariba).

The film is done in a sober, muted style, with stark black-and-whites and the bizarre camera angles much loved by *film noir.* Notice a scene in the cemetery, where the doctor has gone to conceal a body in his own family tomb. At the cemetery gate, a shriek of dead branches against the sky dominates the composition, so that humans seem diminished beneath their stark outline. There is surrealism here, and in the oddly shaped cages that contain his experimental dogs, and the way his mansion seems at once enormous (with limitless corridors) and so small we can hear the dogs from the garage. The matter-of-fact way he presents the outrageous is in the tradition of Buñuel, who felt that the only response to the shocking was to refuse to be shocked by it.

Franju (1912–1987) was a cofounder of the Cinematheque Francaise, worked during the war to hide its treasures from the Nazis, and began making features only in 1949. He worked mostly in the horror genre (*Eyes without a Face* was originally released in North America as *The Horror Chamber of Dr. Faustus,* although it contained no chamber and no Faust). He is concerned with mood, not story, and so this film ends not with a conventional resolution but with an image that could have come from a painting by Dali: The faceless daughter wanders into the wood, surrounded by doves.

One of the tasks faced by serious filmgoers is to distinguish good films in disreputable genres. It is insufferable to claim you "never" see horror movies (or Westerns, musicals, war movies, teenage romances, or slasher pictures). You're presenting ignorance as taste. The trick is to find the good ones. The French auteur critics did a lot of helpful spadework, resurrecting genres and rehabilitating reputations, but they were not always right—and besides, you have to feel it for yourself. If a film holds my attention, it is in one way or another a good one. If it moves or delights me, it may be great. If I am distracted by its conventions, obligatory scenes and carelessness, or lack of ambition, it deserves to be tossed back into the genre.

Eyes without a Face passes my test. It riveted me with its story—or rather, with its lack of one. There is no sense of a conclusion on the way, but more of a sense that the professor may remain forever in his operating theater, slicing off faces while his daughter goes mad. It moved me because the daughter, once she understands what is happening, is more heartbroken over her father's victims than over her own fate. On this foundation Franju constructs an elegant visual work; here is a horror movie in which the shrieks are not by the characters but by the images.

F

Fahrenheit 9/11 ★ ★ ★ ½
R, 110 m., 2004

A documentary directed and produced by
Michael Moore.

Michael Moore's *Fahrenheit 9/11* is less an exposé of George W. Bush than a dramatization
of what Moore sees as a failed and dangerous
presidency. The charges in the film will not
come as news to those who pay attention to
politics, but Moore illustrates them with dramatic images and a relentless commentary
track that essentially concludes Bush is incompetent, dishonest, failing in the war on terrorism, and has bad taste in friends.

Although Moore's narration ranges from
outrage to sarcasm, the most devastating passage in the film speaks for itself. That's when
Bush, who was reading *My Pet Goat* to a classroom of Florida children, is notified of the second attack on the World Trade Center, and yet
lingers with the kids for almost seven minutes
before finally leaving the room. His inexplicable paralysis wasn't underlined in news reports
at the time, and only Moore thought to contact
the teacher in that schoolroom—who, as it
turned out, had made her own video of the
visit. The expression on Bush's face as he sits
there is odd indeed.

Bush, here and elsewhere in the film, is characterized as a man who owes a lot to his friends,
including those who helped bail him out of
business ventures. Moore places particular emphasis on what he sees as a long-term friendship between the Bush family (including both
presidents) and powerful Saudi Arabians. More
than $1.4 billion in Saudi money has flowed
into the coffers of Bush family enterprises, he
says, and after 9/11 the White House helped expedite flights out of the country carrying,
among others, members of the Bin Laden family (which disowns its most famous member).

Moore examines the military records released by Bush to explain his disappearance
from the Texas Air National Guard, and finds
that the name of another pilot has been blacked
out. This pilot, he learns, was Bush's close
friend James R. Bath, who became Texas money
manager for the billionaire Bin Ladens. An-

other indication of the closeness of the Bushes
and the Saudis: The law firm of James Baker, the
secretary of state for Bush's father, was hired by
the Saudis to defend them against a suit by a
group of 9/11 victims and survivors, who
charged that the Saudis had financed al-Qaida.

To Moore, this is more evidence that Bush
has an unhealthy relationship with the Saudis,
and that it may have influenced his decision to
go to war against Iraq at least partially on their
behalf. The war itself Moore considers un-
justified (no WMDs, no Hussein–Bin Laden
link), and he talks with American soldiers, including amputees, who complain bitterly about
Bush's proposed cuts of military salaries at the
same time he was sending them into a war that
they (at least, the ones Moore spoke to) hated.
Moore also shows American military personnel
who are apparently enjoying the war; he has
footage of soldiers who use torture techniques
not in a prison but in the field, where they hood
an Iraqi prisoner, call him "Ali Baba," and pose
for videos while touching his genitals.

Moore brings a fresh impact to familiar material by the way he marshals his images. We are
all familiar with the controversy over the 2000
election, which was settled by the U.S. Supreme
Court. What I hadn't seen before was footage of
the ratification of Bush's election by the U.S.
Congress. An election can be debated at the request of one senator and one representative;
ten representatives rise to challenge it, but not a
single senator. As Moore shows the challengers,
one after another, we cannot help noting that
they are eight black women, one Asian woman,
and one black man. They are all gaveled into silence by the chairman of the joint congressional session—Vice President Al Gore. The
urgency and futility of the scene reawaken old
feelings for those who believe Bush is an illegit-
imate president.

Fahrenheit 9/11 opens on a note not unlike
Moore's earlier films, such as *Roger & Me* and
Bowling for Columbine. Moore, as narrator,
brings humor and sarcasm to his comments,
and occasionally appears onscreen in a gadfly
role. It's vintage Moore, for example, when he
brings along a marine who refused to return to
Iraq; together, they confront congressmen, urging them to have their children enlist in the

service. And he makes good use of candid footage, including eerie video showing Bush practicing facial expressions before going live with his address to the nation about 9/11.

Apparently Bush and other members of his administration don't know what every TV reporter knows—that a satellite image can be live before they get the cue to start talking. That accounts for the quease-inducing footage of Deputy Defense Secretary Paul Wolfowitz wetting his pocket comb in his mouth before slicking back his hair. When that doesn't do it, he spits in his hand and wipes it down. If his mother is alive, I hope for his sake she doesn't see this film.

Such scenes are typical of vintage Moore, catching his subjects off-guard. But his film grows steadily darker, and Moore largely disappears from it, as he focuses on people such as Lila Lipscomb, from Moore's hometown of Flint, Michigan; she reads a letter from her son, written days before he was killed in Iraq. It urges his family to work for Bush's defeat.

Fahrenheit 9/11 is unashamedly partisan: Moore dislikes and distrusts Bush, and wants to motivate his viewers to vote against him. Whether his film will make a big difference is debatable, since it's likely most of the audience members will be in agreement with Moore. We tend to choose films that support our decisions, not those that challenge them. Moore's complaints are familiar to those who share his opinion of Bush; they seem to have had little effect on Bush's supporters. If the film does have an effect on the election, as Moore fervently hopes, it will be because it energizes and motivates those who already plan to vote against the president.

Fahrenheit 9/11 is a compelling and persuasive film, at odds with the White House effort to present Bush as a strong leader. He comes across as a shallow, inarticulate man, simplistic in speech and inauthentic in manner. If the film is not quite as electrifying as Moore's *Bowling for Columbine,* that may be because Moore has toned down his usual exuberance and was sobered by attacks on the factual accuracy of elements of *Columbine;* playing with larger stakes, he is more cautious here, and we get an op-ed piece, not a stand-up routine. But he remains one of the most valuable figures on the political landscape, a populist rabble-rouser,

humorous and effective; the outrage and incredulity in his film are exhilarating responses to Bush's determined repetition of the same stubborn sound bites.   ☞

Far from Heaven ★ ★ ★ ★
PG-13, 107 m., 2002

Julianne Moore (Cathy Whitaker), Dennis Quaid (Frank Whitaker), Dennis Haysbert (Raymond Deagan), Patricia Clarkson (Eleonor Fine), Viola Davis (Sybil), James Rebhorn (Dr. Bowman), Celia Weston (Mona Lauder). Directed by Todd Haynes and produced by Jody Patton and Christine Vachon. Screenplay by Haynes.

Todd Haynes's *Far from Heaven* is like the best and bravest movie of 1957. Its themes, values, and style faithfully reflect the social melodramas of the 1950s, but it's bolder and says out loud what those films only hinted at. It begins with an ideal suburban Connecticut family, a husband and wife "team" so thoroughly absorbed into corporate culture they're known as "Mr. and Mrs. Magnatech." Then it develops that Mr. Magnatech is gay, and Mrs. Magnatech believes that the black gardener is the most beautiful man she has ever seen.

They are the Whitakers, Cathy and Frank (Julianne Moore and Dennis Quaid). They live in a perfect split-level house on a perfect street, where the autumn leaves are turning to gold. Their little son is reprimanded for rude language like "Aw, shucks." Of course she drives a station wagon. Mona Lauder (Celia Weston), the local society editor, is writing a profile about their perfection.

One slight shadow clouds the sun. While being interviewed by Celia, Cathy sees a strange black man in the yard and walks outside to ask, ever so politely, if she can "help" him. He introduces himself: Raymond Deagan (Dennis Haysbert), son of their usual gardener, who has died. Cathy, who has a good heart, instinctively reaches out to touch Raymond on the shoulder in sympathy, and inside the house the gesture is noted by Celia, who adds to her profile that Cathy is a "friend to Negroes."

Frank Whitaker is one of those big, good-looking guys who look like a college athlete gone slightly to seed, or drink. One night Cathy has to pick him up at the police station after an incident involving "one lousy cocktail." In another scene we see him enter a gay bar, where in these days long before Stonewall, the men exchange furtive, embarrassed glances as if surprised to find themselves there. One night Cathy makes the mistake of taking Frank his dinner when he works late, and opens his office door to find him kissing a man.

The movie accurately reflects the values of the 1950s, and you can see that in a scene where Frank says his homosexuality makes him feel "despicable," but he's "going to lick this problem." The key to the power of *Far from Heaven* is that it's never ironic; there is never a wink or a hint that the filmmakers have more enlightened ideas than their characters. This is not a movie that knows more than was known in 1957, but a movie that knows exactly what mainstream values were in 1957—and traps us in them, along with its characters.

Frank and Cathy have no sex life. Cathy is not attracted to Raymond so much sexually, however, as she's in awe of his kindness and beauty, which is so adamantly outside her segregated world. She hardly knows how to talk with him. At one point she says that "Mr. Whitaker and I support equal rights for the Negro." Raymond looks at her level-eyed and says, "I'm happy to hear that." He has a business degree, but has inherited the same gardening business that supported his father; a widower, he dotes on his eleven-year-old daughter.

The plot advances on a public and a private front. Publicly, word starts to get around that Cathy has been "seen" with the black gardener. Only that—"seen." Once when they take a ride in his truck, they enter a black diner, where their reception is as frosty as it would have been in a white place. Neither race approves of mixed couples. Soon people start to "talk," and Frank, the hypocrite, screams at her about all he's done to build up the reputation of the family, only to hear these stories.

Frank's homosexuality, of course, remains deeply buried. A psychiatrist (James Rebhorn) muses about "aversion therapy" but warns that the "majority of cases cannot be cured." Frank drinks heavily and turns ugly, and Cathy's feelings for Raymond grow, but she has no idea how to act on them. Mr. and Mrs. Magnatech need a repairman.

Far from Heaven uses superb craftsmanship to make this film look and feel like a film from the 1950s. Todd Haynes says he had three specific inspirations: Douglas Sirk's *All That Heaven Allows* (1955), which starred Jane Wyman and Rock Hudson in the story of a middle-aged widow and her handsome young gardener; Sirk's *Imitation of Life* (1959), with Lana Turner as a rich woman whose maid's daughter (Susan Kohner) passes for white; and Max Ophuls's *The Reckless Moment* (1949), about blackmail. In Sirk's films you often have the feeling that part of the plot is in code, that one kind of forbidden love stands for another.

The movie benefits enormously from its cinematography by Ed Lachman, who faithfully reproduces the lush 1950s studio style; the opening downward crane shot of autumn leaves is matched by the closing upward crane shot of spring blossoms, and every shot has the studied artifice of 1950s "set decoration," which was not so different, after all, from 1950s "interior decoration." The musical score, by Elmer Bernstein, is true to the time, with its underlining of points and its punching-up of emotions. Haynes said in an interview that "every element" of his film has been "drawn from and filtered through film grammar."

One detail is particularly true to the time: Interracial love and homosexual love are treated as being on different moral planes. The civil rights revolution predated gay liberation by about ten years, and you can see that here: The movie doesn't believe Raymond and Cathy have a plausible future together, but there is bittersweet regret that they do not. When Frank meets a young man and falls in love, however, the affair is not ennobled but treated as a matter of motel rooms and furtive meetings. Haynes is pitch-perfect here in noting that homosexuality, in the 1950s, still dared not speak its name.

Because the film deliberately lacks irony, it has a genuine dramatic impact; it plays like a powerful 1957 drama we've somehow never seen before. The effect is oddly jolting: Contemporary movies take so many subjects for granted that they never really look at them. Haynes, by moving back in time, is able to bring his issues into focus. We care about the characters in the way its period expected us to. (There is one time rupture; Frank uses the f-word to his wife and the fabric of the film breaks, only to be repaired when he apologizes.)

Julianne Moore, Dennis Quaid, and Dennis Haysbert are called on to play characters whose instincts are wholly different from their own. By succeeding, they make their characters real, instead of stereotypes. The tenderness of Cathy and Raymond's unrealized love is filled with regret that is all the more touching because they acknowledge that their society will not accept them as a couple. When Raymond and his daughter leave town, Cathy suggests maybe she could visit them sometime in Baltimore, but Raymond gently replies, "I'm not sure that would be a good idea."

The Fast Runner ★ ★ ★

NO MPAA RATING, 172 m., 2002

Natar Ungalaaq (Atanarjuat), Sylvia Ivalu (Atuat), Peter-Henry Arnatsiaq (Oki), Lucy Tulugarjuk (Puja), Madeline Ivalu (Panikpak), Paul Qulitalik (Qulitalik), Eugene Ipkarnak (Sauri, the Chief), Pakkak Innushuk (Amaqjuaq). Directed by Zacharias Kunuk and produced by Paul Apak Angilirq, Norman Cohn, and Zacharias Kunuk. Screenplay by Paul Apak Angilirq.

We could begin with the facts about *The Fast Runner*. It is the first film shot in Inuktitut, the language of the Inuit peoples who live within the Arctic Circle. It was made with an Inuit cast, and a 90 percent Inuit crew. It is based on a story that is at least 1,000 years old. It records a way of life that still existed within living memory.

Or we could begin with the feelings. The film is about romantic tensions that lead to tragedy within a small, closely knit community of people who depend on one another for survival, surrounded by a landscape of ice and snow. It shows how people either learn to get along under those circumstances, or pay a terrible price.

Or we could begin with the lore. Here you will see humans making a living in a world that looks, to us, like a barren wasteland. We see them fishing, hunting, preparing their kill, scraping skins to make them into clothing, tending the lamps of oil that illuminate their igloos, harvesting the wild crops that grow in the brief summertime, living with the dogs that pull their sleds.

Or we could begin with the story of the film's production. It was shot with a high-definition digital video camera, sidestepping the problems that cinematographers have long experienced while using film in temperatures well below zero. Its script was compiled from versions of an Inuit legend told by eight elders. The film won the Camera d'Or, for best first film, at Cannes, and was introduced at Telluride by the British stage director Peter Sellars; telling the story of its origin, he observed, "In most cultures, a human being is a library."

We could begin in all of those ways, or we could plunge into the film itself, an experience so engrossing it is like being buried in a new environment. Some find the opening scene claustrophobic. It takes place entirely inside an igloo, the low lighting provided only by oil lamps, most of the shots in close-up, and we do not yet know who all the characters are. I thought it was an interesting way to begin: to plunge us into this community and share its warmth as it shelters against the cold, and then to open up and tell its story.

We meet two brothers, Amaqjuaq (Pakkak Innushuk), known as the Strong One, and Atanarjuat (Natar Ungalaaq), known as the Fast Runner. They are part of a small group of Inuit including the unpleasant Oki (Peter-Henry Arnatsiaq), whose father is the leader of the group. There is a romantic problem. Oki has been promised Atuat (Sylvia Ivalu), but she and Atanarjuat are in love. Just like in Shakespeare. In the most astonishing fight scene I can recall, Atanarjuat challenges Oki, and they fight in the way of their people: They stand face to face while one solemnly hits the other, there is a pause, and the hit is returned, one blow after another, until one or the other falls.

Atanarjuat wins, but it is not so simple. He is happy with Atuat, but eventually takes another wife, Puja (Lucy Tulugarjuk), who is pouty and spoiled and put on Earth to cause trouble. During one long night of the midnight sun, she is caught secretly making love to Amaqjuaq, and banished from the family. It is, we gather, difficult to get away with adultery when everybody lives in the same tent.

Later there is a shocking murder. Fleeing for his life, Atanarjuat breaks free, and runs across the tundra—runs and runs, naked. It is one of those movie sequences you know you will never forget.

At the end of the film, over the closing titles, there are credit cookies showing the production of the film, and we realize with a little shock that the film was made now, by living people, with new technology. There is a way in which the intimacy of the production and the 172-minute running time lull us into accepting the film as a documentary of real life. The actors, many of them professional Inuit performers, are without affect or guile: They seem sincere, honest, revealing, as real people might, and although the story involves elements of melodrama and even soap opera, the production seems as real as a frozen fish.

I am not surprised that *The Fast Runner* has been a box-office hit in its opening engagements. It is unlike anything most audiences will ever have seen, and yet it tells a universal story. What's unique is the patience it has with its characters: The willingness to watch and listen as they reveal themselves, instead of pushing them to the front like little puppets and having them dance through the story. *The Fast Runner* is passion, filtered through ritual and memory.

FearDotCom ★ ★
R, 90 m., 2002

Stephen Dorff (Mike Reilly), Natascha McElhone (Terry Huston), Stephen Rea (Alistair Pratt), Udo Kier (Polidori), Amelia Curtis (Denise), Jeffrey Combs (Styles), Nigel Terry (Turnbull), Gesine Cukrowski (Jeannine), Elizabeth McKechnie (Alice Turnbull). Directed by William Malone and produced by Limor Diamant and Moshe Diamant. Screenplay by Josephine Coyle, based on a story by Moshe Diamant.

Strange, how good *FearDotCom* is, and how bad. The screenplay is a mess, and yet the visuals are so creative this is one of the rare bad films you might actually want to see. The plot is a bewildering jumble of half-baked ideas, from which we gather just enough of a glimmer about the story to understand how it is shot through with contradictions and paradoxes. And yet I watched in admiration as a self-contained nightmare formed with the visuals. Not many movies know how to do that.

I'll get to the plot later, or maybe never. Let me talk about what I liked. The film takes place in a city where it always rains and is nearly always night, where even people with good jobs live in apartments that look hammered together after an air raid. Computers and the Internet exist here, and indeed telephones, televisions, and all the other props of the present day, but windows are broken, walls are punctured, lights flicker, streets are deserted, and from time to time a dramatic thunderstorm threatens to sweep everything away. This is like *Dark City* after a hurricane.

It is the kind of city where a man can walk down into a subway and be the only person there, except for a little girl bouncing her ball against the third rail. Or . . . is the man really alone? Is that his fantasy? Whether it is or not, he gets slammed by the next train, and the cops are startled by the expression on his face. It looks, they agree, as if he had just seen something terrifying. Apparently something even worse than the train. And he is bleeding from the eyes.

The film's premise is that a Website exists that channels negative energy into the mind of the beholder, who self-destructs within forty-eight hours, a victim of his or her deepest fear. Our first glimpse of this Website suggests nothing more than a reasonably well-designed horror site, with Shockwave images of dark doorways, screaming lips, rows of knives, and so forth. The movie wisely doesn't attempt to develop the site much more than that, relying on the reactions of the victims to imply what other terrors it contains. And it does something else, fairly subtly: It expands the site to encompass the entire movie, so that by the end all of the characters are essentially inside the fatal Web experience, and we are, too.

The last twenty minutes are, I might as well say it, brilliant. Not in terms of what happens, but in terms of how it happens, and how it looks as it happens. The movie has tended toward the monochromatic all along, but now it abandons all pretense of admitting the color spectrum, and slides into the kind of tinting used in silent films: browns alternate with blues, mostly. The images play like homage to the best Grand Guignol traditions, to *Nosferatu* and some of the James Whale and Jacques Tourneur pictures, and the best moments of the Hammer horror films. Squirming victims are displayed on the Internet by the sadistic killer, who prepares to autopsy them while still alive; subscribers to the site, whose crime is that they want to watch, are addressed by name and are soon paying dearly for their voyeurism.

The movie is extremely violent; it avoided the NC-17 rating and earned an R, I understand, after multiple trims and appeals, and even now it is one of the most graphic horror films I've seen. (The classification is for "violence including grisly images of torture, nudity and language," the MPAA explains, but you'll be disappointed if you hope to see grisly images of language).

Stephen Dorff and Natascha McElhone star, as a cop and a public health inspector, and Stephen Rea, who was so unexpectedly deceived in *The Crying Game,* plays the host of the Website and the torturer. The movie keeps trying to make some kind of connection between Rea and the ghostly little girl, who was his first victim, but if the site is her revenge, why is he running it? And how can what happens to him in the end not have happened before?

Never mind. Disregard the logic of the plot. Don't even go there. Don't think to ask how the Internet can channel thoughts and commands into the minds of its users. Disregard the dialogue (sample: "We will provide a lesson that reducing relationships to an anonymous electronic impulse is a perversion"). This is a movie that cannot be taken seriously on the narrative level. But look at it. Just look at it. Wear some of those Bose sound-defeating earphones into the theater, or turn off the sound when you watch the DVD. If the final twenty minutes had been produced by a German impressionist in the 1920s, we'd be calling it a masterpiece. All credit to director William Malone, cinematographer Christian Sebaldt, production designer Jerome Latour, and art directors Regine Freise and Markus Wollersheim.

Now. Do I recommend the film? Not for the majority of filmgoers, who *will* listen to the dialogue, and *will* expect a plot, and *will* be angered by the film's sins against logic (I do not even mention credibility). But if you have read this far because you are intrigued, because you can understand the kind of paradox I am describing, then you might very well enjoy *FearDotCom.* I give the total movie two stars, but there are some four-star elements that deserve a better movie. You have to know how to look for them, but they're there.

Fellini: I'm a Born Liar ★ ★ ½
NO MPAA RATING, 105 m., 2003

With Roberto Benigni, Italo Calvino, Federico Fellini, Donald Sutherland, Terence Stamp, and Giuseppe Rotunno. A documentary directed by Damian Pettigrew and produced by Olivier Gal. Screenplay by Pettigrew and Gal.

Federico Fellini created a world that was gloriously his own, and there is scarcely a shot—certainly not a scene—in his work that doesn't announce its maker. That's also true of Hitchcock, Ozu, Tati, and a few other filmmakers; their work gives us the impression, somehow, of being in their presence.

Fellini: I'm a Born Liar is a documentary centering on a lengthy interview Fellini gave to the filmmakers in 1993, shortly before his death. As a source of information about his life and work, this interview is almost worthless, but as an insight into his style, it is priceless. Having interviewed the master twice, once on the location of his *Fellini Satyricon,* I was reminded of his gift for spinning fables that pretend to be about his work but are actually fabricated from thin air.

Consider, for example, the way he confides to the camera that he gets on very well with actors, because he loves them and understands them. Then listen to two of the actors he worked with, Donald Sutherland and Terence Stamp, who recall the experience as if their skins are still crawling.

Fellini, we learn, sometimes gave no direction at all, expecting his actors to intuit his desires. At other times (seen in footage of the director at work) he stood next to the camera and verbally instructed his actors on every move and nuance. This was possible because he often didn't record sound, preferring to dub the dialogue later, and some of his actors simply counted, "one, two, three," knowing the words would be supplied. It is clear that Stamp and Sutherland did not enjoy the experience, and so much did Fellini treat them like his puppets that at one point Sutherland says "Fellini" when he means his own character.

The actor he worked with most often and successfully, Marcello Mastroianni, was the most cooperative: "He would turn up tired in the morning, sleep between takes, and do whatever Fellini told him to do without complaining." That this approach created the two best male performances in Fellini's work (in *La Dolce Vita* and *8½*) argues that Mastroianni may have been onto something.

The documentary includes many clips from Fellini's work, none of them identified, although his admirers will recognize them immediately. And we revisit some of the original locations, including a vast field with strange concrete walls (or are they crypts?) where Fellini's hero helped his father climb down into a grave in *8½*.

The movie does not do justice to Fellini's love of sensuous excess, both in his films and in his life, although when he says he "married the right woman . . . for a man like me" he may be telling us something. The film assumes such familiarity with Fellini that although that woman, the actress Giulietta Masina, is seen more than once, she is never identified.

No doubt the existence of the extended Fellini interview is the movie's reason for existing, and yet it is less than helpful. Fellini is maddeningly nonspecific, weaves abstractions into clouds of fancy, rarely talks about specific films, actors, or locations. When he mentions his childhood home of Rimini, it is to observe that the Rimini in his films is more real to him. And so it should be, but why not even a word about his youthful days as a cartoonist, hustling on the Via Veneto for assignments? Why no mention of his apprenticeship in neorealism? Why not a word about the collapse and death of the Rome studio system?

I love Fellini, and so I was happy to see this film, and able to add it to my idea of his charming but elusive personality. But if you know little about Fellini, this is not the place to start. Begin with the films. They are filled with joy, abundance, and creativity. You cannot call yourself a serious filmgoer and not know them.

Femme Fatale ★ ★ ★ ★

R, 110 m., 2002

Rebecca Romijn-Stamos (Laure Ash), Antonio Banderas (Nicolas Bardo), Peter Coyote (Bruce Hewitt Watts), Eriq Ebouaney (Black Tie), Edouard Montoute (Racine), Rie Rasmussen (Veronica), Thierry Frémont (Serra). Directed by Brian De Palma and produced by Tarak Ben Ammar and Marina Gefter. Screenplay by De Palma.

Sly as a snake, Brian De Palma's *Femme Fatale* is a sexy thriller that coils back on itself in seductive deception. This is pure filmmaking, elegant and slippery. I haven't had as much fun second-guessing a movie since *Mulholland Drive*. Consider such clues as the overflowing aquarium, the shirt still stained with blood after many days, the subtitles for dialogue that is not spoken, the story that begins in 2001 and then boldly announces: "Seven years later."

The movie opens with a $10 million diamond theft, with a difference: The diamonds adorn the body of a supermodel attending a premiere at the Cannes Film Festival, and they are stolen with erotic audacity as the model is seduced in a rest room of the Palais du Cinema by the tall, brazen Laure Ash (Rebecca Romijn-Stamos). Her team includes the usual crew of heist-movie types, and we get the usual details, like the guy in the wet suit, the laser cutter, and the TV spycam that attracts the attention of an inquisitive cat. But the movie announces its originality when none of these characters perform as they expect to, and Laure Ash steals the diamonds not only from the model but also from her fellow criminals.

No, I have not given away too much. The fact is, I have given away less than nothing, as you will fully appreciate after seeing the film. The long opening sequence, about forty minutes by my clock, is done almost entirely without dialogue, and as De Palma's camera regards these characters in their devious movements, we begin to get the idea: This is a movie about watching and being watched, about seeing and not knowing what you see.

Romijn-Stamos plays Laure Ash as a supremely self-confident woman with a well-developed sense of life's ironies. Chance plays a huge role in her fate. Consider that not long after the theft, while trying to avoid being spotted in Paris, she is mistaken for a grieving widow, taken home from a funeral, and finds herself in possession of an airplane ticket to New York and a passport with a photo that looks exactly like her. And then . . .

But no. I cannot tell any more. I will, however, describe her relationship with Nicolas Bardo (Antonio Banderas), a paparazzo who photographs her in 2001 on that day she is mistaken for the widow, and photographs her again seven years later (!) when she returns to Paris as the wife of the American ambassador (Peter Coyote). She wants that film: "I have a past here." And then . . .

Well, the movie's story, written by De Palma, is a series of incidents that would not be out of place in an ordinary thriller, but here achieve a kind of transcendence since they are what they seem, and more than they seem, and less than they seem. The movie tricks us, but not unfairly, and for the attentive viewer there are markers along the way to suggest what De Palma is up to.

Above all he is up to an exercise in superb style and craftsmanship. The movie is very light on dialogue, and many of the words that are spoken come across as if the characters are imitating movie actors (the film opens with Laure watching *Double Indemnity*—for pointers in how to be a vixen, no doubt). I've seen the movie twice; it's one of those films like *Memento* that plays differently the second time. Only on the second viewing did I spot the sly moment when the subtitles supply standard thriller dialogue—but the lips of the actors are not moving. This is a movie joke worthy of Buñuel.

Rebecca Romijn-Stamos may or may not be a great actress, but in *Femme Fatale* she is a great Hitchcock heroine—blond, icy, desirable, duplicitous—with a knack for contemptuously manipulating the hero. She is also very sexy, and let it be said that De Palma, at least, has not followed other directors into a sheepish retreat from nudity, seduction, desire, and erotic wordplay. The man who made *Body Double* is still prepared to make a movie about a desirable woman, even in these days of buddy movies for teenage boys. When it comes to sex, the characters in *Femme Fatale* have all been around the block a few times, but it takes this scenario to make them wonder what side of the street they're on.

De Palma deserves more honor as a director.

Consider also these titles: *Sisters, Blow Out, The Fury, Dressed to Kill, Carrie, Scarface, Wise Guys, Casualties of War, Carlito's Way, Mission: Impossible.* Yes, there are a few failures along the way (*Snake Eyes, Mission to Mars, The Bonfire of the Vanities*), but look at the range here, and reflect that these movies contain treasure for those who admire the craft as well as the story, who sense the glee with which De Palma manipulates images and characters for the simple joy of being good at it. It's not just that he sometimes works in the style of Hitchcock, but that he has the nerve to.

50 First Dates ★ ★ ★
PG-13, 96 m., 2004

Adam Sandler (Henry Roth), Drew Barrymore (Lucy Whitmore), Rob Schneider (Ula), Lusia Strus (Assistant Alexa), Blake Clark (Marlin Whitmore), Sean Astin (Doug Whitmore), Dan Aykroyd (Dr. Keats). Directed by Peter Segal and produced by Jack Giarraputo, Steve Golin, Nancy Juvonen, Larry Kennar, and Adam Sandler. Screenplay by George Wing.

50 First Dates is a spin on the *Groundhog Day* notion of a day that keeps repeating itself. This time, though, the recycling takes place entirely inside the mind of Lucy Whitmore (Drew Barrymore), who was in an accident that caused short-term memory loss. Every night while she sleeps, the slate of her memory is wiped clean, and when she wakes up in the morning she remembers everything that happened up to the moment of the accident, but nothing that happened afterward.

Is this possible? I'd like to bring in Oliver Sacks for a second opinion. Seems to me that short-term memory loss doesn't work on a daily timetable, but is more like the affliction of Ten-Second Tom, a character in the movie who reboots every ten seconds. Still, this isn't a psychiatric docudrama but a lighthearted romantic comedy, and the premise works to provide Adam Sandler and Barrymore with a sweet story. They work well together, as they showed in *The Wedding Singer*. They have the same tone of smiling, coy sincerity.

The movie is sort of an experiment for Sandler. He reveals the warm side of his personality, and leaves behind the hostility, anger, and gross-out humor. To be sure, there's projectile vomiting on a vast scale in an opening scene of the movie, but it's performed by a sea lion, not one of the human characters, and the sea lion feels a lot better afterward. This is a kinder and gentler Adam Sandler.

He plays Henry Roth, a marine biologist at a Hawaiian sea world, healing walruses, sea lions, and dolphins, and moonlighting as an expert in one-night stands. He romances babes who are in Hawaii on vacation, and then forgets them when they go home, so imagine his amazement when he meets Lucy and finds that she forgets him every night. Lucy is surrounded by a lot of support (her loving dad and the staff at the local diner), and they're dubious about the motives of this guy who says he's so much in love he's willing to start over with this girl every morning.

You'd think it would be hard to construct an arc for a story that starts fresh every day, but George Wing's screenplay ingeniously uses videotape to solve that problem—so that Lucy gets a briefing every morning on what she has missed, and makes daily notes in a journal about her strange romance with Henry. Eventually this leads her to conclude that it's unfair to Henry to have to endure her daily memory losses, and she says she wants to break up. Of course, the formula requires this, but how the movie solves it is kind of charming.

The movie doesn't have the complexity and depth of *Groundhog Day* (which I recently saw described as "the most spiritual film of our time"), but as entertainment it's ingratiating and lovable. And it suggests that Adam Sandler, whose movies are so often based on hostility, has another speed, another tone, that plays very nicely.

The Fighter ★ ★ ★

NO MPAA RATING, 91 m., 2002

With Arnost Lustig and Jan Wiener. A documentary directed by Amir Bar-Lev and produced by Bar-Lev, Jonathan Crosby, and Alex Mamet.

The Fighter is named after one of its two subjects, Jan Wiener, seventy-seven years old, who describes himself as a "professor, wilderness guide, and old fart," and adds: "But I still can

connect." We see him pounding a punching bag to prove it. His friend is Arnost Lustig, seventy-two. Both of them were born in Czechoslovakia and now live in America. The story of Wiener's escape from the Nazis, how he flew for the RAF against Germany, how he returned to his homeland and was imprisoned by the Communists as a spy, has inspired more than one movie. Lustig has long planned to write a book about it, and the two old men set off on a trip to the places of their youth and their war.

Following them is Amir Bar-Lev, an American documentary filmmaker, born in Israel, who could hardly have anticipated what would happen. *The Fighter* could have been just a travelogue about two old-timers reliving their wartime memories. Even a heroic story can slow in the retelling. But *The Fighter* picks up surprising energy, as old wounds are reopened and the two men express strong opinions that may be unforgivable. What unfolds on-screen is remarkable: The passions and arguments of the past are resurrected in the present.

At first the trip goes smoothly. Both men are fit and quick, not slowed by the ravages of age. Both teach at universities. They retrace Wiener's steps as he recalls the collapse of Czechoslovakia (he and other pilots never dreamed the Nazis would roll in so decisively). In a scene of stunning power, he visits the house where his parents committed suicide rather than be captured by the Nazis. He recalls his father saying: "Tonight I am going to kill myself. That is the only freedom we have left." He remembers how it happened, his father telling him, "I have taken the pills. Hold my hand." And then, says Wiener, sitting in the same chair he sat in all those years ago, "he was asleep."

They visit Terezienstadt, a model concentration camp set up by the Nazis to fool a Swiss Red Cross inspection team (the notorious Nazi documentary *The Fuhrer Gives a City to the Jews* was filmed there). Lustig was a prisoner there, and remembers how the prisoners were terrified to speak to the inspectors, and how food and comforts disappeared along with the Swiss. Together, the two men retrace the route of Wiener's escape, ending in Italy, where a compassionate Italian cop did not betray him to the Nazis. He later became a POW in Italy, later still a pilot for the British.

After the war their lives diverged. Wiener

returned home to Czechoslovakia only to be suspected of spying and sentenced to prison. Lustig became a Communist official until he became disillusioned and left for America. The old friends met again in the United States.

And so the story might end, gripping, fascinating, happily—but then they have a fight. There is a disagreement over why the Italian cop spared Wiener. Another one over why Lustig could have survived Nazism only to become a Communist. Filming shuts down for three days during this impasse, and when it begins again it is clear that the old men are friends no longer. We understand that for them the war is a wound that has not healed, and that it led to decisions that cannot be explained. We stand a little outside: No one who was not there knows for sure what he would have done. Suddenly, we are not in the past but in the present, seeing real emotions, not remembered ones. In this movie the war is not quite over. For those who survived it, maybe it will never be.

Note: The 2002 feature Dark Blue World *also tells a story about a Czech pilot who flies for the British.*

The Fighting Temptations ★ ★ ★
PG-13, 123 m., 2003

Cuba Gooding Jr. (Darrin Hill), Beyonce Knowles (Lilly), Mike Epps (Lucius), Steve Harvey (Miles Smoke), LaTanya Richardson (Paulina Pritchett), T-Bone (Bee-Z Briggs), Mickey Jones (Scooter), Faizon Love (Warden). Directed by Jonathan Lynn and produced by David Gale, Loretha C. Jones, Benny Medina, and Jeff Pollack. Screenplay by Elizabeth Hunter and Saladin K. Patterson.

The Fighting Temptations follows a formula in a kind of easygoing way, and you know it, but it generates so much goodwill and so many laughs that you don't really care. It's sort of a musical and sort of a first cousin of *Barbershop,* and you can feel the audience just plain liking it. Although it represents Beyonce Knowles's first starring role, it's not in awe of her; it uses her in the story instead of just pushing her to the front of every shot, and she comes across as warm and sympathetic.

Cuba Gooding Jr. stars as Darrin, a New York ad executive with roots in the small town of Montecarlo, Georgia. His Aunt Sally dies just as he's fired for falsifying his résumé, and he returns home for a reading of the will, which leaves him $150,000 if he'll direct the church choir and get it into the annual Gospel Explosion contest. With his credit cards maxed out and creditors on his trail, he stays in Georgia—and gets involved in church politics involving Paulina (LaTanya Richardson), the church treasurer. She drove Darrin and his mother out of town twenty years ago by accusing the mother of being immoral because she sang in the local juke joint. Now she's Darrin's enemy, opposed to him leading the choir or perhaps even staying in town.

But he has good reasons to stay. Not just because his creditors are looking for him in New York, but because he's moonstruck by a local singer named Lilly (Beyonce Knowles). She was his childhood sweetheart, and now she may hold the key to the gospel competition—and to his heart.

Darrin has his work cut out for him. The church choir is small and untalented, and his recruiting efforts are not successful. Steve Harvey plays the local disc jockey who reads his recruiting announcements—which start out by specifying that no one need apply who smokes or drinks, and end by saying pretty much anyone, even a heathen, is welcome. There's a funny sequence involving a concert in the nearby prison; when the warden (Faizon Love) says he's got prisoners who can sing better than the choir, Darrin perks up, and before long three prisoners are singing in the choir, wearing their handcuffs and their Sunday best orange convict suits.

Does the choir get into the Gospel Explosion? Do Darrin and Lilly find love and happiness? These are not really questions in a movie like this, which of course supplies the obligatory sequence of temporary defeat before ultimate victory. But the movie doesn't depend on an original story, it simply rides in on one before it starts being funny.

The humor in *The Fighting Temptations,* like the humor in *Barbershop,* isn't based on one-liners or insults, but on human nature. When the characters say something funny, it's usually funny because it's true. A lot of the laughs come when characters who don't like each other say so, out loud, right there in front of everybody.

Although most of the actors in *The Fighting Temptations* are experienced pros, a funny thing happens: In this story, they all seem like real people, maybe because they're playing characters like those they knew, or were, when they were younger. LaTanya Richardson, for example, has been in more than twenty movies (in private life she's Mrs. Samuel L. Jackson), but here, as Paulina, we don't sense a performance, we sense a woman—stubborn, unbending, envious, yet curious to see what happens next. There's lovely body language in the scene where she begins to stalk out of church, and then changes her mind and takes a seat in a back pew.

Another nice, quiet thing about the movie is that white people turn up here and there, without much notion being taken of them. There are some whites in the choir, which is often the case in real life, and when Darrin recruits a new organist named Scooter (Mickey Jones), he's white, bearded, and a mountain man type, but he sure can play.

There's music all through the movie, a lot of it high-energy gospel music, some of it quieter. Beyonce is singing "Fever" the first time we see her, and later does a wonderful job with spirituals. There's no attempt to force her own music into the movie, and that works well, I think; after some supporting work (including the most recent Austin Powers movie), here we get to see her in a lead and sense that she can play dramatic parts and need not always be a version of herself.

I saw the movie, as it happens, at a public preview. A real one, with an audience that bought tickets because they wanted to see this movie, not because they won passes from a radio station. It was a pleasure to be surrounded by so much good feeling. *The Fighting Temptations* is not brilliant and it has some clunky moments where we see the plot wheels grinding, but it has its heart and its grin in the right places.   ☞

Final ★ ★
R, 111 m., 2002

Denis Leary (Bill), Hope Davis (Ann), J. C. MacKenzie (Todd), Jim Gaffigan (Dayton), Jim Hornyak (Orderly), Maureen Anderman (Supervisor), Marin Hinkle (Sherry), Madison Arnold (Bill's Father), Caroline Kava (Bill's Mother). Directed by Campbell Scott and produced by Gary Winik, Alexis Alexanian, Mary Frances Budig, Steve Dunn, and Campbell Scott. Screenplay by Bruce McIntosh.

In a mental hospital in Connecticut, a patient defends his paranoid fantasies against a psychiatrist who gently tries to bring him back to reality. He says it is the year 2399, that he has been cyrogenically frozen for 400 years, and that he has been thawed and awakened so that his organs can be harvested. She says he was in a serious truck accident, was in a coma, and is now being treated to remove his delusions. While they discuss this rather basic disagreement, it becomes clear they are gradually falling in love.

Campbell Scott's *Final* is a movie told mostly through dialogue. It lacks the life and humor of his wonderful *Big Night*, codirected with Stanley Tucci, and burrows into its enigmatic situation with cheerless intensity. Only the innate energy of its actors, Denis Leary and Hope Davis, keep it on its feet. Both are very good—Leary at trying to talk his way out of what looks like a trap he has set for himself, and Davis at remaining professionally responsible even while getting emotionally involved, if that is possible. She cares for him.

Then the plot takes a turn that I will not even begin to reveal, and we have to reevaluate the meaning of their relationship, their characters, their situation. By even mentioning the turn, I know I will get protests from readers who complain that they would have never known there was going to be a turn if I hadn't revealed it, etc., but really, what is a critic to do? Stop writing after the first two paragraphs and completely misrepresent the film? *Final* is "difficult to discuss without giving away the surprise that pops up halfway through," A. O. Scott observes in the first sentence of his *New York Times* review, thereby giving away the surprise that there *is* a surprise. You see what I mean.

So, yes, there is a surprise. I will have nothing to say about it. You will have to deal with it on your own. But if you should see *Final* and start to analyze it, ask yourself these questions: Why is the therapy necessary in the first place? Why are this patient and this psychiatrist even talking? What do they have to accomplish? Unless my logic is flawed (and if it is, other audience members are going to make the same mistake), the entire movie is a red herring.

That doesn't mean it lacks certain virtues. The movie, shot on video by Dan Gillham, creates a convincing space around the characters; the institution seems real enough, if underpopulated, and the claustrophobia it brings on helps define the relationship. Although the screenplay by Bruce McIntosh suffers from that plausibility gap, the characters of course don't know this and establish a rapport so nuanced and subtle it deserves a better story. Maybe one without a surprise.

Final Desination 2 ★ ½

R, 100 m., 2003

Ali Larter (Clear Rivers), A. J. Cook (Kimberly Corman), Michael Landes (Thomas Burke), David Paetkau (Evan Lewis), James Kirk (Tim Carpenter), Lynda Boyd (Nora Carpenter), Keegan Connor Tracy (Kat), Jonathan Cherry (Rory). Directed by David Ellis and produced by Warren Zide and Craig Perry. Screenplay by J. Mackye Gruber and Eric Bress.

"Look, we drove a long way to get here, so if you know how to beat death, we'd like to know."

So say pending victims to a morgue attendant in Final Destination 2, which takes a good idea from the first film and pounds it into the ground, not to mention decapitating, electrocuting, skewering, blowing up, incinerating, drowning, and gassing it. Perhaps movies are like history, and repeat themselves, first as tragedy, then as farce.

The earlier film involved a group of friends who got off an airplane after one of them had a vivid precognition of disaster. The plane crashed on takeoff. But then, one by one, most of the survivors died, as if fate had to balance its books.

That movie depends on all the horror clichés of the Dead Teenager Movie (formula: Teenagers are alive at beginning, dead at end). But it is well made and thoughtful. As I wrote in my review: "The film in its own way is biblical in its dilemma, although the students use the code word 'fate' when what they are really talking about is God. In their own terms, in

their own way, using teenage vernacular, the students have existential discussions."

That was then; this is now. Faithful to its genre, Final Destination 2 allows one of its original characters, Clear Rivers (Ali Larter), to survive, so she can be a link to the earlier film. In the new film, Clear is called upon by Kimberly Corman (A. J. Cook), a twenty-something, who is driving three friends in her SUV when she suddenly has a vision of a horrendous traffic accident. Kimberly blocks the on-ramp, saving the drivers behind her when logs roll off a timber truck, gas tanks explode, etc.

But is it the same old scenario? Are the people she saved all doomed to die? "There is a sort of force—an unseen malevolent presence around us every day," a character muses. "I prefer to call it death."

The malevolent presence doesn't remain unseen for long. Soon bad things are happening to good people, in a series of accidents that Rube Goldberg would have considered implausible. In one ingenious sequence, we see a character who almost trips over a lot of toys while carrying a big Macintosh iMac box. In his house, he starts the microwave and lights a fire under a frying pan, then drops his ring down the garbage disposal, then gets his hand trapped in the disposal while the microwave explodes and the frying pan starts a fire, then gets his hand loose, breaks a window that mysteriously slams shut, climbs down a fire escape, falls to the ground, and finally, when it seems he is safe . . . well, everything that could possibly go wrong does, except that he didn't get a Windows machine.

Other characters die in equally improbable ways. One is ironically killed by an air bag, another almost chokes in a dentist's chair, a third is severed from his respirator, and so on, although strange things do happen in real life. I came home from seeing this movie to read the story about the teenager who was thrown twenty-five feet in the air after a car crash, only to save himself by grabbing some telephone lines. If that had happened in Final Destination 2, his car would have exploded, blowing him off the lines with a flying cow.

There is a kind of dumb level on which a movie like this works, once we understand the premise. People will insist on dying oddly. Remember the story of the woman whose husband left her, so she jumped out the window and landed on him as he was leaving the building?

The thing about *FD2* is that the characters make the mistake of trying to figure things out. Their reasoning? If you were meant to die, then you owe death a life. But a new life can cancel out an old one. So if the woman in the white van can safely deliver her baby, then that means that someone else will be saved, or will have to die, I forget which. This is the kind of bookkeeping that makes you wish Arthur Andersen were still around.

Note: The first Final Destination *(2000) had characters named after famous horror-film figures, including Browning, Horton, Lewton, Weine, Schreck, Hitchcock, and Chaney. The sequel has just two that I can identify: Corman and Carpenter.*

Finding Nemo ★ ★ ★ ★
G, 101 m., 2003

With the voices of: Albert Brooks (Marlin), Ellen DeGeneres (Dory), Alexander Gould (Nemo), Willem Dafoe (Gill), Geoffrey Rush (Nigel), Brad Garrett (Bloat), Barry Humphries (Bruce), Allison Janney (Peach). Directed by Andrew Stanton and produced by Graham Walters. Screenplay by Stanton.

Finding Nemo has all of the usual pleasures of the Pixar animation style—the comedy and wackiness of *Toy Story* or *Monsters Inc.* or *A Bug's Life*. And it adds an unexpected beauty, a use of color and form that makes it one of those rare movies where I wanted to sit in the front row and let the images wash out to the edges of my field of vision. The movie takes place almost entirely under the sea, in the world of colorful tropical fish—the flora and fauna of a shallow warm-water shelf not far from Australia. The use of color, form, and movement make the film a delight even apart from its story.

There is a story, though, one of those Pixar inventions that involves kids on the action level while adults are amused because of the satire and human (or fishy) comedy. The movie involves the adventures of little Nemo, a clownfish born with an undersized fin and an oversized curiosity. His father, Marlin, worries obsessively over him because Nemo is all he has

left: Nemo's mother and all of her other eggs were lost to barracudas. When Nemo goes off on his first day of school, Marlin warns him to stay with the class and avoid the dangers of the drop-off to deep water, but Nemo forgets and ends up as a captive in the saltwater aquarium of a dentist in Sydney. Marlin swims off bravely to find his missing boy, aided by Dory, a bright blue Regal Tang fish with enormous eyes whom he meets along the way.

These characters are voiced by actors whose own personal mannerisms are well known to us; I recognized most of the voices, but even the unidentified ones carried buried associations from movie roles, and so somehow the fish take on qualities of human personalities. Marlin, for example, is played by Albert Brooks as an overprotective, neurotic worrywart, and Dory is played by Ellen DeGeneres as helpful, cheerful, and scatterbrained (she has a problem with short-term memory).

The Pixar computer animators, led by writer-director Andrew Stanton, create an undersea world that is just a shade murky, as it should be; we can't see as far or as sharply in sea water, and so threats materialize more quickly, and everything has a softness of focus. There is something dreamlike about *Finding Nemo's* visuals, something that evokes the reverie of scuba diving.

The picture's great inspiration is to leave the sea by transporting Nemo to that big tank in the dentist's office. In it we meet other captives, including the Moorish Idol fish Gill (voice by Willem Dafoe), who are planning an escape. Now it might seem to us that there is no possible way a fish can escape from an aquarium in an office and get out of the window and across the highway and into the sea, but there is no accounting for the ingenuity of these creatures, especially since they have help from a conspirator on the outside—a pelican with the voice of Geoffrey Rush.

It may occur to you that many pelicans make a living by eating fish, not rescuing them, but some of the characters in this movie have evolved admirably into vegetarians. As Marlin and Dory conduct their odyssey, for example, they encounter three carnivores who have formed a chapter of Fish-Eaters Anonymous and chant slogans to remind themselves that they abstain from fin-based meals.

The first scenes in *Finding Nemo* are a little unsettling, as we realize the movie is going to be about fish, not people (or people-based characters like toys and monsters). But of course animation has long since learned to enlist all other species in the human race, and to care about fish quickly becomes as easy as caring about mice or ducks or Bambi.

When I review a movie like *Finding Nemo*, I am aware that most members of its primary audience do not read reviews. Their parents do, and to them and adults who do not have children as an excuse, I can say that *Finding Nemo* is a pleasure for grown-ups. There are jokes we get that the kids don't, and the complexity of Albert Brooks's neuroses, and that enormous canvas filled with creatures that have some of the same hypnotic beauty as—well, fish in an aquarium. They may appreciate another novelty: This time the dad is the hero of the story, although in most animation it is almost always the mother.

The Flower of Evil ★ ★ ★
NO MPAA RATING, 105 m., 2003

Benoit Magimel (Francois Vasseur), Nathalie Baye (Anne Charpin-Vasseur), Melanie Doutey (Michele Charpin-Vasseur), Suzanne Flon (Aunt Line), Bernard Lecoq (Gerard Vasseur), Thomas Chabrol (Matthieu Lartigue). Directed by Claude Chabrol and produced by Marin Karmitz. Screenplay by Caroline Eliacheff, Louise L. Lambrichs, and Chabrol.

A country house and a corpse. Yes. We are comfortable already. It is a big house, with a sweeping staircase and doorways through which we glimpse life continuing just as if the owner were not dead upstairs. That must be the cook setting the table. But wait. The camera, having climbed the stairs and regarded the dead body, slides on down the corridor and looks through another door, where a young woman sits on the floor, distraught. We have come up these stairs just a few seconds too late to be eyewitnesses to murder.

Claude Chabrol has been climbing these stairs all of his life, and discovering the secrets of the French bourgeois. Many of his murderers have the easy manners of good old families. Before we go back downstairs and join the story of *The Flower of Evil*, which is his fiftieth film, we should pause for a moment to honor this milestone. Chabrol was one of the founders of the French New Wave, so early he did not know it was the New Wave and he was founding it. As a character says in *Citizen Kane*, he was there before the beginning and now here he is, after the end. "He began directing in 1958," Stanley Kauffman writes in the *New Republic*, "and has never committed an ill-made film, has rarely made a dull one, and has occasionally created a gem."

I shared an enormous sea bass once with Chabrol in a New York Chinese restaurant, and on another night we did some drinking and talked about his latest film. That was in 1972, at the New York Film Festival. Five years earlier Andrew Sarris had already been able to write about Chabrol in the past tense: "He quickly became one of the forgotten figures of the nouvelle vague." Now it is 2003 and Chabrol still has his hand in. So does Sarris. "With respect to Mr. Chabrol's *The Flower of Evil*," he writes tactfully in the *New York Observer*, "I would prefer to think of it as a masterly work of the artist's late period rather than as the tired product of his old age."

And so we beat on, boats against the current. I feel such an affection for Chabrol and his work that I probably can't see *The Flower of Evil* as it would be experienced by a first-time viewer. Would that newcomer note the elegance, the confidence, the sheer joy in the way he treasures the banalities of bourgeois life on his way to the bloodshed? And would they understand the truly savage quality that lurks just under the surface—the contempt he feels for these characters who move in such style between their jobs and homes, their political campaigns and love affairs? Here is a movie in which the one romance that nearly everyone approves of is between a brother and a sister.

Their incest requires footnotes: Francois (Benoit Magimel) is the son of Gerard Vasseur (Bernard Lecoq); his mother was killed in an accident, and so his father married Anne Charpin-Vasseur (Nathalie Baye), who brought a daughter into the marriage. This is Michele (Melanie Doutey). So Francois and Michele aren't technically siblings—but they are cousins, because this family has been intermarrying for generations. Francois flew off to Chicago to study law for four years ("The Americans are not as stupid as they like to pretend"), but he couldn't outgrow his infatuation with Michele, and soon after his return they borrow the holiday cottage of old Aunt Line (Suzanne Flon) and consummate what they have so long imagined.

The family is remarkably unruffled. There are other plots afoot. Gerard has made a fortune with his semilegal pharmaceutical factory. His wife is using his money to run for local office, and Gerard has had enough of the way she drags her political adviser Matthieu (Thomas Chabrol) to family gatherings and dinners. Matthieu tries to make his excuses and slip away, but Gerard insists he stay, the better to make him feel uncomfortable.

Someone in the town has sent around an anonymous letter libeling three generations of the family for collaboration with the Nazis, profiteering, corruption, adultery, incest, and not being nice. Most of these charges are true, as old Aunt Line has reason to know, and after Chabrol's elegant establishing scenes and hints of buried shame there is, all of a sudden, a shocking revelation, a dead body, a woman sitting on the floor, and this time the police are coming up the stairs.

Chabrol's buried theme, as frequently, involves the rotten French monied class. He attacks the rich not as a leftist but simply because he is fastidious and cannot stand them. He has also found time for murderers of the middle and lower classes, but his heart quickens when he finds death in corrupt suburban villas. A boxed set of six classic Chabrol DVDs has just been issued, and if you want to see him among the working classes, rent *Le Boucher*, one of his two or three best films, which is about an elegant schoolmistress who falls in love with a charming butcher, only to be faced with the possibility that she is about to be filleted.

The Fog of War ★ ★ ★ ★
PG-13, 106 m., 2004

A documentary directed by Errol Morris and produced by Morris, Michael Williams, and Julie Ahlberg. Screenplay by Morris.

How strange the fate that brought together Robert McNamara and Errol Morris to make *The Fog of War*. McNamara, considered the architect of the Vietnam War, an Establishment figure who came to Washington after heading the Ford Motor Company and left to become the president of the World Bank. And Morris, the brilliant and eccentric documentarian who has chronicled pet cemeteries, Death Row, lion tamers, robots, naked mole rats, a designer of electric chairs, people who cut off their legs for the insurance money, and Stephen Hawking's *A Brief History of Time*.

McNamara agreed to talk with Morris for an hour or so, supposedly for a TV special. He eventually spent twenty hours peering into Morris's "Interrotron," a video device that allows Morris and his subjects to look into each other's eyes while also looking directly into the camera lens. Whether this invention results in better interviews is impossible to say, but it does have the uncanny result that the person on the screen never breaks eye contact with the audience.

McNamara was eighty-five when the interviews were conducted—a fit and alert eighty-five, still skiing the slopes at Aspen. Guided sometimes by Morris, sometimes taking the lead, he talks introspectively about his life, his thoughts about Vietnam, and, taking Morris where he would never have thought to go, his role in planning the firebombing of Japan, including a raid on Tokyo that claimed 100,000 lives. He speaks concisely and forcibly, rarely searching for a word, and he is not reciting boilerplate and old sound bites; there is the uncanny sensation that he is thinking as he speaks.

His thoughts are organized as *Eleven Lessons from the Life of Robert S. McNamara*, as extrapolated by Morris, and one wonders how the planners of the war in Iraq would respond to lesson Nos. 1 and 2 ("Empathize with your enemy" and "Rationality will not save us"), or for that matter, No. 6 ("Get the data"), No. 7 ("Belief and seeing are both often wrong"), and No. 8 ("Be prepared to reexamine your reasoning"). I cannot imagine the circumstances under which Donald Rumsfeld, the current secretary of defense, would not want to see this film about his predecessor, having recycled and even improved upon McNamara's mistakes.

McNamara recalls the days of the Cuban missile crisis, when the world came to the brink of nuclear war (he holds up two fingers, almost touching, to show how close—"this close"). He recalls a meeting, years later, with Fidel Castro, who told him he was prepared to accept the destruction of Cuba if that's what the war would mean. He recalls two telegrams to Kennedy from Khrushchev, one more conciliatory, one perhaps dictated by Kremlin hard-liners, and says that JFK decided to answer the first and ignore the second. (Not quite true, as Fred Kaplan documents in an article at Slate.com.) The movie makes it clear that no one was thinking very clearly, and that the world avoided war as much by luck as by wisdom.

And then he remembers the years of the Vietnam War, inherited from JFK and greatly expanded by Lyndon Johnson. He began to realize the war could never be won, he says, and wrote a memo to the president to that effect. The result was that he resigned as secretary. (He had dinner with Kay Graham, publisher of the *Washington Post*, and told her, "Kay, I don't know if I resigned or was fired." "Oh, Bob," she told him, "of course you were fired.") He didn't resign as a matter of principle, as a British cabinet minister might; it is worth remembering that a few months later Johnson, saying he would not stand for reelection, did effectively resign.

McNamara begins by remembering how, at the age of two, he witnessed a victory parade after World War I, and engages in painful soul-searching about his role in World War II. He was a key aide to General Curtis LeMay, the hard-nosed warrior whose strategy for war was simplicity itself: kill them until they give up. Together, they planned the bombing raids before the atomic bomb ended the war, and Morris supplies a chart showing the American cities equivalent in size to the ones they targeted. After the war, McNamara says, in one of the film's most astonishing moments, LeMay observed to him that if America had lost, they would have been tried as war criminals. Thinking of the 100,000 burned alive in Tokyo, McNamara finds lesson No. 5: "Proportionality should be a guideline in war." In other words, I suppose, kill enough of the enemy but don't go overboard. Lesson No. 9: "In order to do good, you may have to engage in evil."

McNamara is both forthright and elusive. He talks about a Quaker who burned himself to death below the windows of his office in the Pentagon, and finds his sacrifice somehow in the same spirit as his own thinking—but it is true he could have done more to try to end the war and did not, and will not say why he did not, although now he clearly wishes he had. He will also not say he is sorry, even though Morris prompts him; maybe he's too proud, but I get the feeling it's more a case of not wanting to make a useless gesture that could seem hypocritical. His final words in the film make it clear there are some places he is simply not prepared to go.

Although McNamara is photographed through the Interrotron, the movie is far from offering only a talking head. Morris is uncanny in his ability to bring life to the abstract, and here he uses graphics, charts, moving titles, and visual effects in counterpoint to what McNamara is saying. There's also a lot of historical footage, including some shots of Curtis LeMay with his cigar clenched between his teeth—images that describe whatever McNamara neglected to say about him. There are tape recordings of Oval Office discussions involving McNamara, Kennedy, and Johnson. And archival footage of McNamara's years at Ford (he is proud of introducing seat belts). Underneath all of them, uneasily urging the movie along, is the Philip Glass score, which sounds—what? Mournful, urgent, melancholy, driven?

The effect of *The Fog of War* is to impress upon us the frailty and uncertainty of our leaders. They are sometimes so certain of actions that do not deserve such certitude. The farce of the missing weapons of mass destruction is no less complete than the confusion in the Kennedy White House over whether there were really nuclear warheads in Cuba. Some commentators on the film, notably Kaplan in his informative Slate essay, question McNamara's facts. What cannot be questioned is his ability to question them himself. At eighty-five, he knows what he knows, and what he does not know, and what cannot be known. Lesson No. 11: "You can't change human nature."

A Foreign Affair ★ ★ ★

PG-13, 94 m., 2004

David Arquette (Josh), Tim Blake Nelson (Jake), Emily Mortimer (Angela), Larry Pine (Tour

Guide), Lois Smith (Ma), Megan Follows (Lena), Redmond Gleeson (Funeral Director), Allyce Beasley (Librarian). Directed by Helmut Schleppi and produced by David-Jan Bijker, Esli Bijker, Geert Heetebrij, and Schleppi. Screenplay by Heetebrij.

When their mother dies, Josh and Jake are saddened, yes, but they are also frightened, because Ma took care of everything. She cooked, she washed, she darned, she remembered where things were. Now there is no one to perform those tasks, and the boys are helpless. A farm they can manage, but a house is beyond them.

A Foreign Affair shows them taking matters into their own hands. With the help of the friendly town librarian, they find a Web site that features young women from Russia who want to marry Americans and are apparently packed and ready to go. They sign up for the package tour, and find themselves in St. Petersburg, where they never expected to be, and considered very desirable, which they have never been before.

Their task is simpler because they are seeking only one wife. That isn't because they plan to practice reverse polygamy, or because one of them is gay, but because they do not think of this as a true marriage. Jake (Tim Blake Nelson), the serious one, is up-front with the women he interviews: no sex, but you keep house for us for a few years, and you get your citizenship.

His brother, Josh (David Arquette), agreed to this plan back on the farm, but now, attending the nightly parties arranged by the tour group, he finds delightful women throwing themselves at him, and this is a new experience he begins to enjoy. He falls in love more or less nightly, using an ancient formula: When he's not with the one he loves, he loves the one he's with.

The movie, directed by Helmut Schleppi and written by Geert Heetebrij, could have gone several ways. I can imagine it as a sex comedy, as a romance, as a bittersweet exploration of lonely people. Schleppi has a little of all three elements at work here, but it's Tim Blake Nelson's character who keeps the plot from spinning out of control, because he has a natural and unforced respect for these women that yanks his brother's chain and keeps their mission on course.

Watching Josh and Jake as they negotiate this process, Emily Mortimer plays a British documentary-maker named Angela. She's been assigned to make a film about the whole phenomenon of Internet brides, but becomes fascinated by Jake because he is not really looking for a bride in the traditional sense, and is up-front about it. As she shoots his interviews with prospective partners, we see her footage, and we sense that we are close to the line between fiction and reality. Maybe closer than we think: I was talking about the movie with Mortimer at Cannes, and she said the filmmakers and the two actors actually took the real tour to do their research.

Mortimer's character provides a subtle subtext. As she watches Jake, listens to him and films him, she begins to be moved by his honesty and his good heart. He is a simple, forthright man, unlike most of those she meets, and we begin to sense he may find a bride in the last place he's looking. Or maybe that's too easy; maybe there's no way their worlds can meet, and yet she has a way of looking at him . . .

Do marriages like this work? Many Americans find mail-order brides or arranged marriages bizarre, but think how bizarre it is to seek your spouse in a singles bar or on a blind date. There are countless possible partners out there somewhere, but we never meet most of them, and most of those we meet are impossible. Maybe it helps to use a system. If you're interested, the actual Web site is at www.aforeignaffair.com.

Formula 51 ★
R, 92 m, 2002

Samuel L. Jackson (Elmo McElroy), Robert Carlyle (Felix DeSouza), Emily Mortimer (Dakota Phillips), Meat Loaf (The Lizard), Sean Pertwee (Detective Virgil Kane), Ricky Tomlinson (Leopold Durant), Rhys Ifans (Iki). Directed by Ronny Yu and produced by Andras Hamori, Seaton McLean, Malcolm Kohll, David Pupkewitz, and Jonathan Debin. Screenplay by Stel Pavlou.

Pulp Fiction and *Trainspotting* were two of the most influential movies of the past ten years, but unfortunately their greatest influence has been on rip-offs of each other—movies like

Formula 51, which is like a fourth-rate *Pulp Fiction* with accents you can't understand. Here, instead of the descent into the filthiest toilet in Scotland, we get a trip through the most bilious intestinal tract in Liverpool; instead of a debate about Cheese Royales, we get a debate about the semantics of the word "bollocks"; the F-word occupies 50 percent of all sentences, and in the opening scenes Samuel L. Jackson wears another one of those Afro wigs.

Jackson plays Elmo McElroy, a reminder that only eight of the seventy-four movies with characters named Elmo have been any good. In the prologue, he graduates from college with a pharmaceutical degree, is busted for pot, loses his license, and thirty years later is the world's most brilliant inventor of illegal drugs.

Now he has a product named "P.O.S. Formula 51," which he says is fifty-one times stronger than crack, heroin, you name it. Instead of selling it to a drug lord named The Lizard (Meat Loaf), he stages a spectacular surprise for Mr. Lizard and his friends, and flies to Liverpool, trailed by Dakota Phillips (Emily Mortimer), a skilled hit woman hired by The Lizard to kill him, or maybe keep him alive, depending on The Lizard's latest information.

In Liverpool, we meet Felix DeSouza (Robert Carlyle), a reminder that only 6 of the 200 movies with a character named Felix have been any good. (The stats for "Dakota" are also discouraging, but this is a line of inquiry with limited dividends.) Felix has been dispatched by the Liverpudlian drug king Leopold Durant (Ricky Tomlinson), whose hemorrhoids require that a flunky follow him around with an inner tube that makes whoopee-type whistles whenever the screenplay requires.

The movie is not a comedy so much as a farce, grabbing desperately for funny details wherever possible. The Jackson character, for example, wears a kilt for most of the movie. My on-line correspondent Ian Waldron-Mantgani, a critic who lives in Liverpool but doesn't give the home team a break, points out that the movie closes with the words "No one ever found out why he wore a kilt," and then explains why he wore the kilt. "You get the idea how much thought went into this movie," Waldron-Mantgani writes, with admirable restraint.

Many of the jokes involve Felix's fanatic support of the Liverpool football club, and a final confrontation takes place in an executive box of the stadium. Devices like this almost always play as a desperate attempt to inject local color, especially when the movie shows almost nothing of the game, so that Americans will not be baffled by what Brits call football. There are lots of violent shoot-outs and explosions, a kinduva love affair between Felix and Dakota, and an ending that crosses a red herring, a MacGuffin, and a shaggy dog.

40 Days and 40 Nights ★ ★ ★
R, 93 m., 2002

Josh Hartnett (Matt Sullivan), Shannyn Sossamon (Erica), Maggie Gyllenhaal (Samantha), Emmanuelle Vaugier (Susie), Keegan Connor Tracy (Mandy), Vinessa Shaw (Nicole), Paulo Costanzo (Ryan), Adam Trese (John), Monet Mazur (Candy). Directed by Michael Lehmann and produced by Tim Bevan, Eric Fellner, and Michael London. Screenplay by Rob Perez.

Matt is weary of sex. Weary of himself as a sex partner. Weary of the way he behaves around women, weary of the way women make him behave, and weary of his treacherous ex-girl. So weary that he swears off sex for Lent in *40 Days and 40 Nights.* On the scale of single guy sacrifice, this is harder than not drinking but easier than asking for directions.

Matt (Josh Hartnett) is a nice guy who is disgusted by his predatory sexual nature—at the way his libido goes on autopilot when he sees an attractive woman. The breakup with Nicole (Vinessa Shaw) is the final straw. She loved him, dumped him, still excites him, and no wonder; as Bagel Man, who makes morning deliveries to the office, observes, "She's so hot you need one of those cardboard eclipse things just to look at her." Matt gets some support from his brother John (Adam Trese), who is studying to be a priest and offers advice that is more practical than theologically sound, but nobody else in Matt's life believes he can go forty days without sex. Certainly not a co-worker (Monet Mazur), who gives him her phone number on a photocopy of her butt.

Then Matt meets Laundromat Girl. She is sweet, pretty, smart, and something clicks. He tries to keep his distance and end the conversation before his dreaded instincts click in, but a week later he's back in the Laundromat and so is she. Her name is Erica (Shannyn Sossamon), and soon they are engaged in a courtship that proceeds, from her point of view, rather strangely. On their first real date, when the moment comes for their first kiss, they grow closer and quieter and then he gives her a high-five. What's up with this guy?

40 Days and 40 Nights was directed by Michael Lehmann, who has a sympathy for his characters that elevates the story above the level of a sexual sitcom. He uses humor as an instrument to examine human nature, just as he did in the wonderful, underrated *The Truth About Cats and Dogs*. Amazing, what a gulf there is between movies about characters governed by their genitals, and this movie about a character trying to govern his genitals.

The world seems to conspire against him. The movie's single funniest scene involves dinner with his parents, where his father, who has just had a hip replacement, is delighted to show him a checklist of sexual positions still workable even while he is wearing the cast. The second funniest scene involves a roommate who bursts into Matt's flat with an ultraviolet lamp to check for telltale secretions on the sheets.

Then Matt discovers to his horror that his coworkers have not only got up an office pool on how long he can go without sex, but also have put the pool on a Website. Matt looks at the site in disbelief: "You're selling banner ads?" When Erica sees the site, there's hell to pay.

Josh Hartnett shows here a breezy command of his charming, likable character. It is a reminder of his talent and versatility. After an actor stars in a movie that's widely disparaged, as Hartnett did with *Pearl Harbor,* there is an unfair tendency to blame the film on him. The same thing happened to Kevin Costner after *The Postman.* Actors we liked fall out of favor, as if they didn't work just as hard, and hope as much, for their flops as for their hits. Walking into this movie, I heard *Pearl Harbor* jokes ("40 days that will live in infamy"), but during the film the screenplay kicked in and the next stage of Hartnett's career was officially declared open.

40 Days and 40 Nights does observe the plot conventions of a standard comedy, requiring Erica to persist in unreasonably obtuse behavior far beyond its logical time span, but the details are fresh and writer Rob Perez's dialogue about sex has more complexity and nuance than we expect. And a romantic scene involving flower blossoms is unreasonably erotic. The ending, alas, goes astray, for reasons I cannot reveal, except to suggest that Nicole's entire participation is offensive and unnecessary, and that there was a sweeter and funnier way to resolve everything.

Note: Not even under the end titles does the movie use the Muddy Waters classic 40 Days and 40 Nights. In an age when every song title seems to be recycled into a movie, what were they thinking of?

The Four Feathers ★ ★
PG-13, 128 m., 2002

Heath Ledger (Harry Faversham), Wes Bentley (Lieutenant Jack Durrance), Kate Hudson (Ethne Eustace), Djimon Hounsou (Abou Fatma), Michael Sheen (Trench). Directed by Shekhar Kapur and produced by Paul Feldsher, Robert Jaffe, Stanley R. Jaffe, and Marty Katz. Screenplay by Michael Schiffer and Hossein Amini, based on the novel by A.E.W. Mason.

Looking ahead to the Toronto Film Festival, I foolishly wrote that I was looking forward to Shekhar Kapur's *The Four Feathers* because I was "intrigued by the notion that a story of British colonialism has now been retold by an Indian director. We await the revisionist *Gunga Din.* That was foolish because the film is not revisionist at all, but a skilled update of the same imperialist swashbuckler that's been made into six earlier films and a TV movie (the classic is the 1939 version with Ralph Richardson and C. Aubrey Smith). I do not require Kapur to be a revisionist anti-imperialist; it's just that I don't expect a director born in India to be quite so fond of the British Empire. To be sure, his previous film was the wonderful *Elizabeth* (1998), about Elizabeth I, so perhaps he's an Anglophile. So am I. It's permitted.

The Four Feathers tells the story of Harry Faversham (Heath Ledger), a young British soldier, circa 1875, whose father is a general and who finds himself in the army without having much say in the matter. He is engaged to the comely Ethne Eustace (Kate Hudson), and when his regiment is ordered to the Sudan he cannot bear to part from her, and resigns his commission. He acts primarily out of love, but of course his comrades consider the timing, conclude he is a coward, and send him three white feathers—the sign of cowardice. A fourth is added by the patriotic Ethne.

Disowned by his father, renounced by his fiancée, disgraced in society, Harry must regain his good name. He ships out to the Sudan on his own, disguises himself as an Arab, and lives anyhow in the desert, shadowing his former regiment and doing undercover work on their behalf. He is much helped by the noble Abou Fatma (Djimon Hounsou, from *Amistad*), a desert prince who selflessly devotes himself to helping and protecting the Englishman, for reasons I could never quite understand.

The picture is handsomely mounted (the cinematographer is the Oscar winner Robert Richardson). Red British uniforms contrast with the sand of the desert, and Oriental details make many frames look like a painting by David Roberts. Epic battle scenes, including one where the British form a square and gun down waves of horsemen, are well staged and thrilling. And Harry is a dashing hero, if we can distract ourselves from the complete impossibility of his actions; any man naive enough to think he could resign his commission on the eve of battle and not be considered a coward is certainly foolish enough to become a freelance desert commando—a dry run for T. E. Lawrence.

A newly restored print of *Lawrence of Arabia*, as it happens, is opening on the same day as *The Four Feathers* in many cities, and this is bad luck for the new picture. If you want to see drama in the desert, you're best off with the real thing. The problem with *The Four Feathers* is that the characters are so feckless, the coincidences so blatant, and the movie so innocent of any doubts about the White Man's Burden that Kipling could have written it—although if he had, there would have been deeper psychology and better roles for the locals.

Wes Bentley, from *American Beauty,* costars as Harry's best friend, Lieutenant Jack Durrance. He and Hudson are Americans; Ledger is Australian; obviously no British actors existed

who could fill these roles. Non-British actors are often skilled at British accents, but the younger ones usually don't have the right moves or body language. There is an American/Australian manner of informality, casual demeanor, even slouching, that a certain kind of British actor can never be caught committing; British society, it is said, is a stage on which everyone is always playing a role, but Ledger, Hudson, and Bentley seem to be playing dress-up.

I also have problems with the faithful Abou Fatma. Why do the dark-skinned natives always get to be the best buddy, never the hero? Why would a callow, badly trained, unequipped English boy be able to walk into the desert and command the services of a skilled desert warrior as his sidekick? What's in it for Abou? Movies like this are big on those solemn exchanges of significant looks during which deep truths remain unspoken, primarily because there is no way on earth they *can* be spoken without the cast and audience joining in uncontrolled laughter.

But I must not dismiss the qualities of the movie. It looks good, it moves quickly, and it is often a jolly good time. As mindless swashbuckling in a well-designed production, it can't be faulted. The less you know about the British Empire and human nature, the more you will like it, but then that can be said of so many movies.

Frailty ★ ★ ★
R, 100 m., 2002

Bill Paxton (Dad), Matthew McConaughey (Fenton Meiks), Powers Boothe (Agent Wesley Doyle), Matthew O'Leary (Young Fenton Meiks), Jeremy Sumpter (Young Adam Meiks), Luke Askew (Sheriff Smalls), Derk Cheetwood (Agent Griffin Hull), Blake King (Eric). Directed by Bill Paxton and produced by David Blocker, David Kirschner, and Corey Sienega. Screenplay by Brent Hanley.

Heaven protect us from people who believe they can impose their will on us in this world, because of what they think they know about the next. *Frailty* is about such a man, a kind and gentle father who is visited by an angel who assigns him to murder demons in human form. We are reminded that Andrea Yates believed she was possessed by Satan and could save her children by drowning them. *Frailty* is as chilling: The father enlists his two sons, who are about seven and ten, to join him in the murders of victims he brings home.

This is not, you understand, an abusive father. He loves his children. He is only following God's instructions: "This is our job now, son. We've got to do this." When the older son, terrified and convinced his father has gone mad, says he'll report him to the police, his father explains, "If you do that, son, someone will die. The angel was clear on this." The pressure that the children are under is unbearable and tragic, and warps their entire lives.

Frailty is an extraordinary work, concealing in its depths not only unexpected story turns but also implications, hidden at first, that make it even deeper and more sad. It is the first film directed by the actor Bill Paxton, who also plays the father, and succeeds in making "Dad" not a villain but a sincere man lost within his delusions. Matthew McConaughey plays one of his sons as a grown man, and Powers Boothe is the FBI agent who is investigating the "God's Hand" serial murders in Texas when the son comes to him one night, with the body of his brother parked outside in a stolen ambulance.

The movie works in so many different ways that it continues to surprise us right until the end. It begins as a police procedural, seems for a time to be a puzzle like *Usual Suspects,* reveals itself as a domestic terror film, evokes pity as well as horror, and reminded me of *The Rapture,* another film about a parent who is willing to sacrifice a child in order to follow the literal instructions of her faith.

As the film opens, Matthew McConaughey appears in the office of FBI agent Wesley Doyle (Powers Boothe), introduces himself as Fenton Meiks, and says he knows who committed the serial killings that have haunted the area for years. His story becomes the narration of two long flashbacks in which we see Paxton as the elder Meiks, and Matthew O'Leary and Jeremy Sumpter as young Fenton and Adam. Their mother is dead; they live in a frame house near the community rose garden, happy and serene, until the night their father wakes them with the news that he has been visited by an angel.

The film neither shies away from its horrifying events nor dwells on them. There is a series of ax murders, but they occur offscreen; this is not a movie about blood, but about obsession. The truly disturbing material involves the two boys, who are played by O'Leary and Sumpter as ordinary, happy kids whose lives turn into nightmares. Young Adam simply believes everything his father tells him. Fenton is old enough to know it's wrong: "Dad's brainwashed you," he tells Adam. "It's all a big lie. He murders people and you help him."

The construction of the story circles around the angel's "instructions" in several ways. The sons and father are trapped in a household seemingly ruled by fanaticism. There is, however, the intriguing fact that when Dad touches his victims, he has graphic visions of their sins—he can see vividly why they need to be killed. Are these visions accurate? We see them, too, but it's unclear whether through Dad's eyes or the movie's narrator—if that makes a difference. Whether they are objectively true is something I, at least, believe no man can know for sure about another. Not just by touching him, anyway. But the movie contains one shot, sure to be debated, that suggests God's hand really is directing Dad's murders.

Perhaps only a first-time director, an actor who does not depend on directing for his next job, would have had the nerve to make this movie. It is uncompromised. It follows its logic right down into hell. We love movies that play and toy with the supernatural, but are we prepared for one that is an unblinking look at where the logic of the true believer can lead? There was just a glimpse of this mentality on the day after 9/11, when certain TV preachers described it as God's punishment for our sins, before backpedaling when they found such frankness eroded their popularity base.

On the basis of this film, Bill Paxton is a gifted director; he and his collaborators, writer Brent Hanley, cinematographer Bill Butler, and editor Arnold Glassman, have made a complex film that grips us with the intensity of a simple one. We're with it every step of the way, and discover we hardly suspect where it is going.

Note: Watching the film, I was reminded again of the West Memphis Three (www.wm3.org), those three Arkansas teenagers convicted of the brutal murder of three children. One faces death and the other two long sentences. The documentaries Paradise Lost *(1992) and* Paradise Lost 2: Revelations *(2000) make it clear they are probably innocent (a prime suspect all but confesses on-screen), but the three are still in jail because they wore black, listened to heavy metal music, and were railroaded by courts and a community convinced they were Satanists—which must have been evidence enough, since there wasn't much else, and the boys could prove they were elsewhere.*

Freaky Friday ★ ★ ★
PG, 93 m., 2003

Jamie Lee Curtis (Tess Coleman), Lindsay Lohan (Anna Coleman), Mark Harmon (Ryan), Chad Murray (Jake), Ryan Malgarini (Harry), Harold Gould (Grandpa), Lucille Soong (Chinese Grandma). Directed by Mark S. Waters and produced by Andrew Gunn. Screenplay by Heather Hach and Leslie Dixon, based on the novel by Mary Rodgers.

Actors must love to make body-switch movies. Look at the fun Jamie Lee Curtis and Lindsay Lohan have in *Freaky Friday*. Each one gets to imitate the body language and inner nature of the other, while firing salvos across the generation gap. Body-switch plots are a license for adults to act like kids; probably nobody has had more fun at it than Tom Hanks did in *Big*, but Curtis comes close.

The movie is a remake of the 1976 film starring Barbara Harris and Jodie Foster, and also connects with the mid-1980s body-switch craze, when three or four switcheroos were released more or less simultaneously. Curtis plays Tess Coleman, a widowed psychiatrist soon to be remarried, and Lohan is Anna, her fifteen-year-old daughter, who is certainly the most clean-cut garage band guitarist in history. There is a kid brother named Harry (Ryan Malgarini), who, like all kid brothers, thinks his older sister is picking on him.

Anna believes Tess is remarrying with unseemly haste; she's going through what in a Disney movie passes for a rebellious phase, and in real life would be exemplary teenage behavior. Mother and daughter join the future husband, Ryan (Mark Harmon), for dinner in a Chinese restaurant, where they get into a fight. The restaurant family's grandmother (Lucille Soong) zaps them with a fortune-cookie curse, and the next morning when they wake up Tess and Anna are in each other's bodies. (There was an article not long ago about how angels and God always seem to be played by African-Americans in the movies. Another could be written on the usefulness of movie Asian Americans, who can always be counted on to supply magic potions, exotic elixirs, ancient charms, and handy supernatural plot points.)

Anna looks in the mirror and is shocked to see her mother's body: "I look like the crypt-keeper!" Tess oversleeps just like her daughter always does. They go through the obligatory scene of horrified disbelief, although, like all body-switch movie characters, they are not simply paralyzed by astonishment and dread, but quickly decide to lead each other's lives for a while, so that there can be a story.

The movie, directed by Mark S. Waters and written by Heather Hach and Leslie Dixon, delivers scenes we can anticipate, but with more charm and wit than we expect. There is, for example, the case of Anna's flirtation with a slightly older boy named Jake (Chad Murray). He rides a motorcycle, so of course Tess disapproves of him, but now Tess, in Anna's body, is inexplicably cold to the kid, while Anna, in Tess's body, is so delighted to see him that before long she's on the back of the bike and Jake is telling her he feels like they really understand each other and maybe the age gap can be overcome.

Other entertaining scenes: The mother discovers her daughter's body has a pierced navel. The daughter buys her mother's body new clothes and a new haircut and gets her ears pierced. Tess attends a class Anna has been having trouble with, and realizes the teacher has been picking on her daughter because she (the mother) turned him down for a prom date. Everything comes down to a conflict between a rehearsal dinner and the garage band's big chance at the House of Blues, and when Anna, in Tess's body, makes her little speech at the dinner, we hear the daughter's resentments: "It's great we're getting married—even though my husband died. How quickly I've been able to get over it!"

The outlines of body-switch movies almost

write themselves, although I'd like to see what would happen with an R-rated version. The clever writing here helps, but the actors help even more, with Lohan and Curtis taking big physical chances. Curtis, channeling the daughter inside her, has a hilarious scene on a talk show; she's supposed to be a serious psychiatrist discussing her new book, but sits cross-legged in her chair and leads the audience in routines that seem vaguely inspired by summer camp.

Lindsay Lohan, who starred in the recycled *The Parent Trap* (1998), has that Jodie Foster sort of seriousness and intent focus beneath her teenage persona, and Jamie Lee Curtis has always had an undercurrent of playfulness; they're right for these roles not only because of talent, but because of their essential natures. We're always sure who is occupying each body, even if sometimes they seem to forget. Now if only their Chinese enabler doesn't run out of fortune cookies.

Frida ★ ★ ★ ½
R, 120 m., 2002

Salma Hayek (Frida Kahlo), Alfred Molina (Diego Rivera), Antonio Banderas (David Alfaro Siqueiros), Valeria Golino (Lupe Marín), Ashley Judd (Tina Modotti), Mía Maestro (Cristina Kahlo), Edward Norton (Nelson Rockefeller), Geoffrey Rush (Leon Trotsky). Directed by Julie Taymor and produced by Lindsay Flickinger, Sarah Green, Nancy Hardin, Salma Hayek, Jay Polstein, Roberto Sneider, and Lizz Speed. Screenplay by Diane Lake, Clancy Sigal, Gregory Nava, and Anna Thomas, based on the book *Frida: A Biography of Frida Kahlo* by Hayden Herrera.

Early in their marriage, Frida Kahlo tells Diego Rivera she expects him to be "not faithful, but loyal." She holds herself to the same standard. Sexual faithfulness is a bourgeois ideal that they reject as Marxist bohemians who disdain the conventional. But passionate jealousy is not unknown to them, and both have a double standard, permitting themselves freedoms they would deny to the other. During the course of *Frida*, Kahlo has affairs with Leon Trotsky and Josephine Baker (not a shabby dance card), and yet rages at Diego for his infidelities.

Julie Taymor's biopic tells the story of an ex-traordinary life. Frida Kahlo (Salma Hayek), born of a German-Jewish father and a Mexican mother, grew up in Mexico City at a time when it was a hotbed of exile and intrigue. As a student she goes to see the great muralist Diego Rivera at work, boldly calls him "fat," and knows that he is the man for her.

Then she is almost mortally injured in a trolley crash that shatters her back and pierces her body with a steel rod. She was never to be free of pain again in her life, and for long periods had to wear a body cast. Taymor shows a bluebird flying from Frida's hand at the moment of the crash, and later a gold leaf falls on the cast: She uses the materials of magic realism to suggest how Frida was able to overcome pain with art and imagination.

Diego was already a legend when she met him. Played by Alfred Molina in a great bear-like performance of male entitlement, he was equally gifted at art, carnal excess, and self-promotion. The first time Frida sleeps with him, they are discovered by his wife, Lupe (Valeria Golino), who is enraged, of course, but such is Diego's power over women that after Frida and Diego are wed, Lupe brings them breakfast in bed ("This is his favorite. If you are here to *stay*, you'd better learn how to make it").

Frida's paintings often show herself, alone or with Diego, and reflect her pain and her ecstasy. They are on a smaller scale than his famous murals, and her art is overshadowed by his. His fame leads to an infamous incident, when he is hired by Nelson Rockefeller (Edward Norton) to create a mural for Rockefeller Center, and boldly includes Lenin among the figures he paints. Rockefeller commands the mural to be hammered down from the wall, thus making himself the goat in this episode forevermore.

The director, Taymor, became famous for her production of *The Lion King* on Broadway, with its extraordinary merging of actors and the animals they portrayed. Her *Titus* (2000) was a brilliant reimaging of the Shakespeare tragedy, showing a gift for great, daring visual inventions. Here, too, she breaks out of realism to suggest the fanciful colors of Frida's imagination. But real life itself is bizarre in this marriage, where the partners build houses side by side and connect them by a bridge between the top floors.

Artists talk about the "zone," that mental state when the mind, the eye, the hand, and the imagination are all in the same place, and they are able to lose track of time and linear thought. Frida Kahlo seems to have painted in order to seek the zone and escape pain: When she was at work, she didn't so much put the pain onto the canvas as channel it away from conscious thought and into the passion of her work. She *needs* to paint not simply to "express herself," but to live at all, and this is her closest bond with Rivera.

Biopics of artists are always difficult because the connections between life and art always seem too easy and facile. The best ones lead us back to the work itself, and inspire us to sympathize with its maker. *Frida* is jammed with incident and anecdote—this was a life that ended at forty-six and yet made longer lives seem underfurnished. Taymor obviously struggled with the material, as did her many writers; the screenwriters listed range from the veteran Clancy Sigal to the team of Gregory Nava and Anna Thomas, and much of the final draft was reportedly written by the actor Edward Norton. Sometimes we feel as if the film careens from one colorful event to another without respite, but sometimes it must have seemed to Frida Kahlo as if her life did, too.

The film opens in 1953, on the date of Frida's only one-woman show in Mexico. Her doctor tells her she is too sick to attend it, but she has her bed lifted onto a flatbed truck and carried to the gallery. This opening gesture provides Taymor with the setup for the movie's extraordinary closing scenes, in which death itself is seen as another work of art.

Friday After Next ★ ★

R, 85 m., 2002

Ice Cube (Craig Jones), Mike Epps (Day-Day), John Witherspoon (Mr. Jones), Don "D. C." Curry (Uncle Elroy), Anna Maria Horsford (Mrs. Jones), Bebe Drake (Miss Pearly), Terry Crews (Damon), Katt Micah Williams (Money Mike). Directed by Marcus Raboy and produced by Matt Alvarez and Ice Cube. Screenplay by Ice Cube.

Craig and Day-Day are back in the ghetto as *Friday After Next* opens, after a relative's lottery win allowed them to spend the previous film, *Next Friday,* in the lap of luxury. They're behind on the rent, unemployed, and as the picture opens their Christmas presents are being stolen by Santa Claus. That's the ghetto for you—a point the movie makes again and again, with humor that will cause some to laugh and others to cringe. There's already a controversy about the movie's TV spots, which "coincidentally" superimpose Santa's "Ho, ho, ho" over shots of black women.

As it happens, I saw the movie at about the same time as *Adam Sandler's 8 Crazy Nights,* another holiday picture with an ethnic angle. That probably helped me get in a better spirit. Sandler's film is so mean-spirited that *Friday After Next,* for all of its vulgarity (and scatology and obscenity), seems almost benevolent by contrast. At least its characters just wanna have fun and don't seem mad at the world.

The plot involves cousins Craig (Ice Cube) and Day-Day (Mike Epps) as roommates who have made one promise too many to their landlady (Bebe Drake), especially now that her man-mountain son Damon (Terry Crews) is out on parole. Desperate to raise cash, they get jobs as security guards in the neighborhood mall where their fathers, Mr. Jones (John Witherspoon) and Uncle Elroy (Don "D. C." Curry) run Bros. Bar-B-Que. Other stores include Pimp and Ho Fashions and Toys N the Hood, which is a nod to Ice Cube's debut picture *Boys N the Hood* but leaves an opening for *We Be Toys.*

The action mostly centers around attempts to raise the rent money and apprehend the thieving Santa, and there's a rent party that fills the screen with a lot of music and dancing and an improbable number of great-looking women. The landlady complains about the noise until she is rewarded with favors both mind-altering and sexual from upstairs, leading to the usual broad humor when Mrs. Jones (Anna Maria Horsford) finds her husband cheating.

A team of cops, one white, one black, both with ribald names, drift in and out. At one point they find a thriving marijuana bush in the cousins' apartment, and Craig desperately explains that it's for "municipal use." It turns out, once the cops confiscate the plant, that he's right.

Some of the better laughs come from Money Mike (Katt Micah Williams), who is short but, because of his wardrobe, not easy to miss. He plays the neighborhood pimp. Which leads me to wonder: Why, really, does this movie need a pimp? And "hos" that are not part of Santa's dialogue? And as much pot smoking as in a Cheech and Chong movie?

I guess there's an audience for it, and Ice Cube has paid dues in better and more positive movies (*Barbershop* among them). But surely laughs can be found in something other than this worked-over material. The original *Friday* movie, back in 1995, benefited not only from the presence of Chris Tucker but from a sweeter approach more based on human nature. The third picture has reduced the *Friday* series to loud, broad vulgarity, including Mr. Jones's obligatory battle with world-class flatulence. There's an audience for it, but it could have been funnier and more innocent. It's rated R, but when it hits the video stores you somehow know it will be viewed at home as a family movie, and that's kind of sad.

Full Frontal ★ ½
R, 101 m., 2002

Blair Underwood (Nicholas/Calvin), Julia Roberts (Catherine/Francesca), David Hyde Pierce (Carl), Catherine Keener (Lee), Mary McCormack (Linda), Erika Alexander (Lucy), Rainn Wilson (Brian), David Duchovny (Bill/Gus). Directed by Steven Soderbergh and produced by Gregory Jacobs and Scott Kramer. Screenplay by Coleman Hough.

Every once in a while, perhaps as an exercise in humility, Steven Soderbergh makes a truly inexplicable film. There was the Cannes "secret screening" of his *Schizopolis* in 1996, which had audiences filing out with sad, thoughtful faces, and now here is *Full Frontal*, a film so amateurish that only the professionalism of some of the actors makes it watchable.

This is the sort of work we expect from a film school student with his first digital cam-

era, not from the gifted director of *Traffic* and *Out of Sight*. Soderbergh directs at far below his usual level, and his cinematography is also wretched; known as one of the few directors who shoots some of his own films, he is usually a skilled craftsman, but here, using a digital camera and available light, he produces only a demonstration of his inability to handle the style. Many shots consist of indistinct dark blobs in front of blinding backlighting.

The plot involves a film within a film, on top of a documentary about some of the people in the outside film. The idea apparently is to provide a view of a day in the life of the Los Angeles entertainment industry and its satellites. The movie within the movie stars Julia Roberts as a journalist interviewing Blair Underwood; shots that are supposed to be this movie are filmed in lush 35mm, and only serve to make us yearn for the format as we see the other scenes in digital.

The doc is not quite, or entirely, a doc; there are voice-overs describing and analyzing some of the characters, but other scenes play as dramatic fiction, and there's no use trying to unsort it all, because Soderbergh hasn't made it sortable. If this movie is a satire of the sorts of incomprehensible, earnest "personal" films that would-be directors hand out on cassettes at film festivals, then I understand it. It's the kind of film where you need the director telling you what he meant to do and what went wrong and how the actors screwed up and how there was no money for retakes, etc.

The other characters include Catherine Keener and David Hyde Pierce, as an unhappily married couple. She leaves him a good-bye note in the morning, then goes off to work as a personnel director, spending the day in a series of bizarre humiliations of employees (forcing them, for example, to stand on a chair while she throws an inflated world globe at them). In these scenes she is clearly deranged, and yet there is a "serious" lunch with her sister Linda (Mary McCormack), a masseuse who has never met Mr. Right.

Linda does, however, meet Gus (David Duchovny), a producer who is having a birthday party in a big hotel, hires her for a massage, and then offers her $500 to "release his tension." She needs the money because she is flying off the next day to see a guy she met on the Internet. She thinks he's twenty-two, but in fact he's about forty, and is not an artist as he says, but a director whose new play features Hitler as a guy who, he tells Eva Braun, has "so many responsibilities I can't think of a relationship right now."

Meanwhile, Pierce is fired at work ("He said I have confused my personality quirks with standards") and returns home to find his beloved dog has overdosed on hash brownies, after which he has a heart-to-heart with the veterinarian's assistant. All of these scenes feel like improvs that have been imperfectly joined, with no through-line. The scenes that work (notably McCormack's) are perhaps a tribute to the professionalism of the actor, not the director. Among the false alarms are little details like this: A love note that Underwood's character thinks came from Roberts's character is written on the same kind of red stationery as Keener's note to her husband. Is there a connection? Short answer: No.

Just yesterday I saw *Sex and Lucía,* also shot on digital, also involving a story within a story, with double roles for some of the characters. With it, too, I was annoyed by the digital photography (both films have more contrast between shadow and bright sunlight than their equipment seems able to handle). *Sex and Lucía* was even more confusing when it came to who was who (*Full Frontal* is fairly easy to figure out). But at least *Sex and Lucía,* was made by a director who had a good idea of what he wanted to accomplish, and established a tone that gave the material weight and emotional resonance. There is a scene in *Full Frontal* where a character comes to a tragic end while masturbating. That could symbolize the method and fate of this film.

G

Games People Play: New York ★ ★
NO MPAA RATING, 100 m., 2004

As themselves, more or less: Joshua Coleman, Sarah Smith, Scott Ryan, Dani Marco, David Maynard, Elisha Imani Wilson, Dr. Gilda Carle, and Jim Caruso. Directed by James Ronald Whitney and produced by Whitney and Neil Stephens. Screenplay by Whitney.

Games People Play: New York plays most of its games with the audience. It pretends to be a documentary about the filming of a pilot for a TV reality program, but it contains so much full frontal nudity, semi-explicit sex, and general raunchiness that it's impossible to imagine it anywhere on TV except pay-for-view adult cable. As viewers, we intuit that it is more, or less, than it seems: That in some sense the whole project is a scam. Yes, but a scam that involves real actors doing real things while they're really in front of the camera.

The premise: Auditions are held to select six finalists for a game-show pilot. The winner of the contest will be paid $10,000. The actors are asked to be attractive and "completely uninhibited," and so they are. They're awarded points for their success at such events as: (1) asking complete strangers for a urine sample; (2) the men: enacting casting-couch seductions with would-be actresses not in on the gag; (3) the women: seducing delivery men by dropping a towel and standing there naked; (4) persuading strangers to join a man and woman in a "naked trio" in a nearby hotel room, and (5) persuading a stranger in the next toilet stall to join them in the reading of a scene they're rehearsing.

Amazingly (or maybe not, given the times we live in), the movie not only finds actors willing to play these roles, but men and women off the street who volunteer (in the case of the urine and naked trio gags) or are at least good sports (as in the dropped towel routine). After having been tricked into appearing in the film, they actually sign releases allowing their footage to be used.

These episodes are intercut with sessions where a psychologist named Dr. Gilda Carle and a publicist named Jim Caruso interview the finalists. I have no idea if these people are real, but their cross-examinations elicit harrowing confessions: One woman was raped at four and then beaten by her father, another saw her father murdered, a third is bulimic, a man is a male prostitute, and so on. The uncanny thing about the revelations at the end of the movie is that we cannot be absolutely sure if this is all fiction, or only some of it.

The film was made by James Ronald Whitney, whose *Just, Melvin* is one of the most powerful documentaries I've seen, about a man who abused and molested many members of Whitney's extended family and is finally confronted on screen. What's odd about *Games People Play* is that Whitney seems to have set up the film and offered the $10,000 prize in order to manipulate his actors and their victims into abusing themselves.

Although acting is a noble profession, there is little nobility in being an out-of-work actor, and the ambience at a lot of auditions resembles the desperation of a soup line. *Games People Play* proves, if nothing else, that there are actors who will do almost anything to get in a movie. The actors here (Joshua Coleman, Sarah Smith, Scott Ryan, Dani Marco, David Maynard, Elisha Imani Wilson) are all effective in their scenes, sometimes moving, sometimes more convincing than they have a right to be. But we cringe at how the movie uses them.

How do you rate a movie like this? Star ratings seem irrelevant. It is either a brilliant example of an experiment in psychological manipulation (four stars) or a reprehensible exploitation of the ambitions and vulnerabilities of actors and others who did the director no harm (zero stars). Because it evokes a strange and horrible fascination, I suppose the stars must fall in the middle (two), but your reaction will swing all the way to one side or the other. I felt creepy afterward.   ☞

Gangs of New York ★ ★ ★ ½
R, 168 m., 2002

Leonardo DiCaprio (Amsterdam Vallon), Daniel Day-Lewis (Bill the Butcher), Cameron Diaz (Jenny Everdeane), Jim Broadbent (Boss Tweed), John C. Reilly (Happy Jack), Henry Thomas

(Johnny Sirocco), Brendan Gleeson (Monk McGinn), Gary Lewis (McGloin), Liam Neeson (Priest Vallon). Directed by Martin Scorsese and produced by Alberto Grimaldi, Scorsese, and Harvey Weinstein. Screenplay by Jay Cocks, Steven Zaillian, and Kenneth Lonergan.

Martin Scorsese's *Gangs of New York* rips up the postcards of American history and re-assembles them into a violent, blood-soaked story of our bare-knuckled past. The New York it portrays in the years between 1830 and the Civil War is, as a character observes, "the forge of hell," in which groups clear space by killing their rivals. Competing fire brigades and po-lice forces fight in the streets, audiences throw rotten fruit at an actor portraying Abraham Lincoln, blacks and Irish are chased by mobs, and the navy fires on the city as the poor riot against the draft.

The film opens with an extraordinary scene set beneath tenements in catacombs carved out of the Manhattan rock. An Irish-American leader named Priest Vallon (Liam Neeson) pre-pares for battle almost as if preparing for the Mass—indeed, as he puts in a collar to protect his neck, we think for a moment he might be a priest. With his young son Amsterdam trailing behind, he walks through the labyrinth of this torchlit Hades, gathering his forces, the Dead Rabbits, before stalking out into daylight to fight the forces of a rival American-born gang, the Nativists.

Men use knives, swords, bayonets, cleavers, cudgels. The ferocity of their battle is animal-istic. At the end, the field is littered with bod-ies—including that of Vallon, slain by his enemy William Cutting, a.k.a. Bill the Butcher (Daniel Day-Lewis). This was the famous gang fight of Five Points on the Lower East Side of Manhattan, recorded in American history but not underlined. When it is over, Amsterdam disappears into an orphanage, the ominously named Hellgate House of Reform. He emerges in his early twenties (now played by Leonardo DiCaprio) and returns to Five Points, still ruled by Bill, and begins a scheme to revenge his father.

The vivid achievement of Scorsese's film is to visualize this history and people it with char-acters of Dickensian grotesquerie. Bill the Butcher is one of the great characters in mod-ern movies, with his strangely elaborate dic-tion, his choked accent, his odd way of com-bining ruthlessness with philosophy. The canvas is filled with many other colorful char-acters, including a pickpocket named Jenny Everdeane (Cameron Diaz), a hired club named Monk (Brendan Gleeson), the shopkeeper Happy Jack (John C. Reilly), and historical figures such as Boss Tweed (Jim Broadbent), ruler of corrupt Tammany Hall, and P. T. Bar-num (Roger Ashton-Griffiths), whose mu-seum of curiosities scarcely rivals the daily displays on the streets.

Scorsese's hero, Amsterdam, plays much the same role as a Dickens hero like David Cop-perfield or Oliver Twist: He is the eyes through which we see the others, but is not the most colorful person on the canvas. Amsterdam is not as wild, as vicious, or as eccentric as the people around him, and may not be any tougher than his eventual girlfriend Jenny, who, like Nancy Sykes in *Oliver Twist*, is a hell-cat with a fierce loyalty to her man. DiCaprio's character, more focused and centered, is a use-ful contrast to the wild men around him.

Certainly Daniel Day-Lewis is inspired by an intense ferocity, laced with humor and a certain analytical detachment, as Bill the Butcher. He is a fearsome man, fond of using his knife to tap his glass eye, and he uses a pig carcass to show Amsterdam the various ways to kill a man with a knife. Bill is a skilled knife artist, and terrifies Jenny, his target for a knife-throwing act, not only by coming close to killing her but also by his ornate and ominous word choices.

Cameron Diaz plays Jenny as a woman who at first insists on her own independence; as a pickpocket, she ranks high in the criminal hi-erarchy, and even dresses up to prey on the rich people uptown. But when she finally caves in to Amsterdam's love, she proves tender and loyal in one love scene where they compare their scars, and another where she nurses him back to health.

The movie is straightforward in its cynicism about democracy at that time. Tammany Hall buys and sells votes, ethnic groups are deliv-ered by their leaders, and when the wrong man is elected sheriff he does not serve for long. That American democracy emerged from this cauldron is miraculous. We put the Founding

Fathers on our money, but these Founding Crooks for a long time held sway.

Martin Scorsese is probably our greatest active American director (Robert Altman is another candidate), and he has given us so many masterpieces that this film, which from another director would be a triumph, arrives as a more measured accomplishment. It was a difficult film to make, as we know from the reports that drifted back from the vast and expensive sets constructed at Cinecitta in Rome. The budget was enormous, the running time was problematical.

The result is a considerable achievement, a revisionist history linking the birth of American democracy and American crime. It brings us astonishing sights, as in a scene that shows us the inside of a tenement, with families stacked on top of one another in rooms like shelves. Or in the ferocity of the draft riots, which all but destroyed the city. It is instructive to be reminded that modern America was forged not in quiet rooms by great men in wigs, but in the streets, in the clash of immigrant groups, in a bloody Darwinian struggle.

All of this is a triumph for Scorsese, and yet I do not think this film is in the first rank of his masterpieces. It is very good but not great. I wrote recently of *GoodFellas* that "the film has the headlong momentum of a storyteller who knows he has a good one to share." I didn't feel that here. Scorsese's films usually leap joyfully onto the screen, the work of a master in command of his craft. Here there seems more struggle, more weight to overcome, more darkness. It is a story that Scorsese has filmed without entirely internalizing. The gangsters in his earlier films are motivated by greed, ego, and power; they like nice cars, shoes, suits, dinners, women. They murder as a cost of doing business. The characters in *Gangs of New York* kill because they like to and want to. They are bloodthirsty and motivated by hate. I think Scorsese liked the heroes of *GoodFellas, Casino,* and *Mean Streets,* but I'm not sure he likes this crowd.

Gangster No. 1 ★ ★ ★
R, 105 m., 2002

Malcolm McDowell (Gangster 55), David Thewlis (Freddie Mays), Paul Bettany (Young

Gangster), Saffron Burrows (Karen), Kenneth Cranham (Tommy), Jamie Foreman (Lennie Taylor), Eddie Marsan (Eddie Miller), Andrew Lincoln (Maxie King). Directed by Paul McGuigan and produced by Norma Heyman and Jonathan Cavendish. Screenplay by Johnny Ferguson.

If Alex DeLarge of *A Clockwork Orange* had become a London gangster, he might have turned out like the hero of *Gangster No. 1.* The movie encourages that connection by casting Malcolm McDowell, the original Alex, as the character grown old. Paul Bettany, who plays Young Gangster, is often photographed with his eyes glaring up from beneath lowered brows, which was the signature look Stanley Kubrick gave Alex. Another connection: The movie contains a beating of startling brutality, scored by a pop song played at top volume.

The movie is inspired, as all modern London gangster movies are inspired, by the notorious Kray brothers. It isn't based on their lives or deeds, but on the aura of evil they so successfully projected; they often got their way without violence, because they seemed so capable of it. In *Gangster No. 1,* the crime family is led by Freddie Mays (David Thewlis), who in 1968 is a young, sleek, expensively groomed hood who runs a nightclub and surrounds himself with hard men; he's known as the Butcher of Mayfair. One day he summons Young Gangster (Paul Bettany), tosses him a roll of bills, hires him, and seals his own fate.

The movie, directed by Paul McGuigan, begins in 1999, with Young Gangster grown middle-aged and cold-eyed. McDowell plays the character as a man who has lost all joy, retaining only venom. We see him with cronies at a private boxing club; they're laughing uglies, drinking champagne, smoking cigars, recalling the violent days of their youth (significantly, their memories are starting to be unreliable). Then he learns that Freddie is getting out of prison, his eyes narrow, and we go into the flashback.

The 1968 events have been called Shakespearean, which is fair enough, since just about everything is Shakespearean. They also have a touch of Freud. Everything has a touch of Freud. Young Gangster admires Freddie enormously, wants to be like him, and is probably half in love with him. When Freddie falls in love with the nightclub singer Karen (Saffron Burrows), Young Gangster is consumed with jealousy. In one of the movie's strongest scenes, he confronts Karen, who not too subtly offers to help him find a girl, and then spits in his face.

Paul Bettany's reaction shot is a piece of work. His face screws into a rictus of hate, he seems about to hit her, and then, by an act of will, he starts smiling—which is even more frightening. There has been a gangland feud between Freddie and a rival named Lennie Taylor (Jamie Foreman), and when Young Gangster learns of a planned hit on Freddie and Karen, he goes to the location, stays in his car, and watches it like a drama. Then he kills Lennie to frame Freddie for the murder.

The sequence involving this murder is one of the most brutal and, it must be said, successfully filmed acts of violence I have seen. Chilling, how Young Gangster breaks down the door of Lennie's flat, shoots him in the knee, then carefully takes off his coat, shirt, tie, and pants, because he doesn't want them bloodied in the events ahead. Then he unpacks a tool kit, including a hatchet, a hammer, and a chisel. The attack is seen through Lennie's point of view, as he fades in and out of consciousness. Another piece of work.

The movie is exact in its characters and staging, using Freddie's sunken living room conversation pit as a kind of stage; the man in power towers over the others. But I am not sure the ending really concludes anything. We see Freddie and Young (now Old) Gangster in a final exchange of information, revelation, and emotional brinksmanship, but then there's a coda with the older gangster on a rooftop, shouting for all the world like the bitter loser in a 1930s Warner Bros. crime movie. This conclusion is too pat to be satisfying, but the film has a kind of hard, cold effect.

Garage Days ★ ★ ★

R, 105 m., 2003

Kick Gurry (Freddie), Maya Stange (Kate), Pia Miranda (Tanya), Russell Dykstra (Bruno), Brett Stiller (Joe), Chris Sadrinna (Lucy), Andy Anderson (Kevin), Marton Csokas (Shad Kern). Directed by Alex Proyas and produced by

Topher Dow and Proyas. Screenplay by Proyas, Dave Warner, and Michael Udesky.

Garage Days is about an Australian rock band that's a little too old and a little too untalented to make the big time, but kids itself that stardom is on the way—maybe because the alternative is a boring job and no dreams. The movie is set in the Sydney suburb of Newtown, which is a little like Chicago's New Town or Rogers Park, a mixture of clubs, bars, and (relatively) affordable housing. Sleeping in each other's beds and living in each other's pockets, the band members pick up a gig here or there, no thanks to a helpless manager.

Kick Gurry stars as Freddy, the Val Kilmerish lead singer, and the band also includes his girlfriend, Tanya (Pia Miranda), the guitarist, Joe (Brett Stiller), and the usually zonked Lucy (Chris Sadrinna) on drums. Freddy and Joe's girlfriend, Kate (Maya Stange), have a conversation one day that leads to an unexpected kiss, and to all sorts of warfare within the band, leading to a lot of anguished changing of partners.

Meanwhile, the band hangs out in a hotel bar where the owner does everything he can to make them feel unwelcome, and they track down an elusive rock impresario (Marton Csokas) who may or may not give them the big break they may or may not deserve. Always around as an omen of what could happen is Kevin (Andy Anderson), Joe's dad, who was sort of a rock star in the 1970s, and now looks exactly like someone who might have once been sort of a rock star in the 1970s and never got over it.

Garage Days is more about style than plot, and the director, Alex Proyas (*The Crow, Dark City*), hurtles into scenes with gleeful energy, sends words careening into space, uses whammo titles to introduce "Fun with Drugs" segments, and edits some sequences like a music video on fast-forward. We eventually catch on that the purpose of the movie is not to portray these lives, but the scene itself, a bohemian quarter where would-be musicians, well past their sell-by dates, hold onto the lifestyle because, well, it's fun.

The movie has a lot of affection for these scruffy wannabes, and I liked the fact that they were not arrogant, aggressive types, but sort of average, with reasonable values and ambitions.

At the end, when the love of Freddy's life seems to be moving out of town and he desperately pursues her in a taxi, the scene is purely and simply about romance, and Freddy is perfectly prepared to seem uncool.

The movie is not in any sense a musical featuring this band (which, as nearly as I could tell, does not have a name). The sound track has a lot of music, freely selected from pop hits old and new, but the running gag is that the band never gets to play, and so we never get to hear it. When we finally do, at a big annual rock concert, it provides a suitably affectionate ending for this whimsical and kind of lovable story.

Garfield: The Movie ★ ★ ★

PG, 85 m., 2004

Voice of Bill Murray (Garfield), Breckin Meyer (Jon Arbuckle), Jennifer Love Hewitt (Dr. Liz Wilson), Stephen Tobolowsky (Happy Chapman), Eve Brent (Mrs. Baker), Voice of Debra Messing (Arlene), Voice of David Eigenberg (Nermal), Voice of Brad Garrett (Luca), Voice of Alan Cumming (Persnikitty), Voice of Jimmy Kimmel (Spanky). Directed by Peter Hewitt and produced by John Davis. Screenplay by Joel Cohen and Alec Sokolow, based on the comic strip by Jim Davis.

Yep, this is Garfield, all right. *Garfield: The Movie* captures the elusive charm of the most egotistical character on the funny pages, and drops him into a story that allows him to bask in his character flaws. That Garfield is revealed to be brave and conscientious after all will not surprise anyone, although it might embarrass him.

I don't know who had the idea that Bill Murray would be the right actor to do Garfield's voice, but the casting is inspired. Murray's voice-over work finds the right balance for Garfield—between smugness and uncertainty, between affection and detachment, between jealousy and a grudging ability to see the other point of view.

In this case, the other POV belongs to Odie, a dog that is given to Jon (Breckin Meyer), Garfield's owner, by his sexy veterinarian, Dr. Liz (Jennifer Love Hewitt). Garfield is shocked and astonished to have to share pillow space with a dog, not to mention quality time with

Jon ("You're not just my owner—you're my primary caregiver"). Being Garfield, he expresses his displeasure not with a humiliating public display, but by subtle subterfuge. He steers the dog outdoors, and, dogs being dogs, Odie chases a car and then another one, and gets lost, and is picked up by a little old lady who advertises him.

There's a parallel plot involving the talentless Happy Chapman (Stephen Tobolowsky), who hosts a TV show with a pet cat. He thinks maybe using a dog might bring him national exposure, tells the little old lady he is Odie's owner, and as a training strategy gives him electrical shocks from a cruel collar. Whether Garfield is able to break into and out of the pound, save Odie, expose Chapman, and reunite Jon with both the dog and Garfield's own noble presence, I will leave for you to discover.

The movie, based on the comic strip by Jim Davis, has been directed by Peter Hewitt and written by Joel Cohen and Alec Sokolow. The filmmakers obviously understand and love Garfield, and their movie lacks that sense of smarmy slumming you sometimes get when Hollywood brings comic strips to the screen. Although Garfield claims "I don't do chases," the movie does have a big chase scene and other standard plot ingredients, but it understands that Garfield's personality, his behavior, his glorious self-absorption, are what we're really interested in. The Davis strip is not about a story but about an attitude.

If they hadn't gotten Garfield right, nothing else would have mattered. But they did. And they've also solved the perplexing problem of how to integrate a cartoon cat into a world of real humans and animals. Garfield talks all through the movie (this is one of Murray's most talkative roles), but only we can hear him; that's the equivalent of his thought bubbles in the strip. Garfield is animated, the other animals and the humans are real, and the movie does a convincing job of combining the two levels. Garfield looks like neither a cartoon nor a real cat, but like something in between—plump, squinty, and satisfied. Uncanny how when he talks his mouth looks like Murray's.

In a film mostly involved with plot, there are two scenes that are irrelevant but charming. In one of them, Garfield and Odie perform in sort of a music video, and in the other, at the end,

Garfield has a solo, singing "I Feel Good" and dancing along. Oh, and Jon and Dr. Liz fall in love, although Garfield is no doubt confident he will remain the center of their attention.

Gerry ★ ★ ★
R, 103 m., 2003

Casey Affleck (Gerry), Matt Damon (Gerry). Directed by Gus Van Sant and produced by Dany Wolf. Screenplay by Casey Affleck, Matt Damon, and Van Sant.

Not long after Gus Van Sant got the bright idea of doing a shot-by-shot remake of Hitchcock's *Psycho* in color, I ran into him at the Calcutta Film Festival, and asked him why in the hell he'd come up with that bright idea. "So that no one else would have to," he replied serenely. With his new film, *Gerry*, he has removed another project from the future of the cinema and stored it prudently in the past. He is like an adult removing dangerous toys from the reach of reckless kids.

Gerry stars Casey Affleck and Matt Damon as two friends named Gerry who go for a walk in the desert and get lost. There, I've gone and given away the plot. They walk and walk and walk. For a while they talk, and then they walk in silence, and then they stagger, and then they look like those *New Yorker* cartoons of guys lost in the desert who reach out a desperate hand toward a distant mirage of Jiffy-Lube. It would have been too cruel for Van Sant to add Walter Brennan on the sound track, listenin' to the age-old story of the shiftin', whisperin' sands.

A movie like this doesn't come along every day. I am glad I saw it. I saw it at the 2002 Sundance Film Festival, where a fair number of people walked out. I would say half. I was reminded of advice once given me by the veteran Chicago movie exhibitor Oscar Brotman: "Roger, if nothing has happened by the end of the first reel, nothing is going to happen." If I were to advise you to see *Gerry*, you might have a good case on your hands for a class-action suit.

And yet, and yet—the movie is so gloriously bloody-minded, so perverse in its obstinacy, that it rises to a kind of mad purity. The longer the movie ran, the less I liked it and the more I admired it. The Gerrys are stuck out there, and it looks like no plot device is going to come along and save them. The horizon is barren for 360 degrees of flat wasteland. We have lost most of the original eight hours of *Greed* (1925), Erich von Stroheim's film that also ends with its heroes lost in Death Valley, but after seeing *Gerry* I think we can call off the search for the missing footage.

The screenplay for *Gerry*, by Affleck, Damon, and Van Sant, is not without humor. Before they realize the enormity of their predicament, the two Gerrys discuss this dumb contestant they saw on *Jeopardy*, and Affleck expresses frustration about a video game he has been playing (he conquered Thebes, only to discover he needed twelve horses and had but eleven).

One morning one of the characters finds himself standing on top of a tall rock, and is not sure how he got there, or whether he should risk breaking an ankle by jumping down. If I ever get lost in Death Valley, it will be more or less exactly like this.

After seeing the film at Sundance, as I reported at the time, I got in a conversation with three women who said they thought it was "existential."

"Existential?" I asked.

"Like, we have to choose whether to live or die."

"They do not have a choice to make," I said. "They're lost and they can't find their car. They have no water and no food."

"What I think," said one of the women, "is that it's like Samuel Beckett's *Waiting for Godot*, except without the dialogue."

"It has dialogue," her friend said.

"But not serious dialogue."

"The dialogue in *Godot* is not serious," I said. "At least, it is not intended by the speakers to be serious."

"In *Godot*," the woman said, "they wait and wait and Godot never comes. In *Gerry*, they walk and walk and they never get anywhere."

"There you have it," I said.

I arrive at the end of this review having done my duty as a critic. I have described the movie accurately, and you have a good idea what you are in for, if you go to see it. Most of you will not. I cannot argue with you. Some of you will—the brave and the curious. You embody the spirit of the man who first wondered what it would taste like to eat an oyster.

Ghost Ship ★ ★
R, 88 m., 2002

Gabriel Byrne (Murphy), Julianna Margulies (Epps), Ron Eldard (Dodge), Desmond Harrington (Ferriman), Isaiah Washington (Greer), Alex Dimitriades (Santos), Karl Urban (Munder), Emily Browning (Katie). Directed by Steve Beck and produced by Joel Silver, Robert Zemeckis, and Gilbert Adler. Screenplay by Mark Hanlon and John Pogue, based on the story by Hanlon.

Ghost Ship recycles all the usual haunted house material, but because it's about a haunted ocean liner, it very nearly redeems itself. Yes, doors open by themselves to reveal hanging corpses. Yes, there's a glimpse of a character who shouldn't be there. Yes, there's a cigarette burning in an ashtray that hasn't been used in forty years. And yes, there's a struggle between greed and prudence as the dangers pile up.

These are all usual elements in haunted house movies, but here they take place aboard the deserted—or seemingly deserted—hulk of the *Antonia Graza,* an Italian luxury liner that disappeared without a trace during a 1962 cruise to America, and has how been discovered forty years later, floating in the Bering Straits. A salvage crew led by Murphy the skipper (Gabriel Byrne) and Epps the co-owner (Julianna Margulies) sets out to capture this trophy, which could be worth a fortune.

Echoes from long-ago geography classes haunted me as I watched the film, because the Bering Sea, of course, is in the North Pacific, and if the *Antonia Graza* disappeared from the North Atlantic, it must have succeeded in sailing unattended and unnoticed through the Panama Canal. Or perhaps it rounded Cape Horn, or the Cape of Good Hope. Maybe its unlikely position is like a warning that this ship no longer plays by the rules of the physical universe.

The salvage crew is told about the ship by Ferriman (Desmond Harrington), a weather spotter for the Royal Canadian Air Force. He got some photos of it, and tips them off in return for a finder's fee. Onboard the salvage tug are Murphy, Epps, and crew members Greer (Isaiah Washington), Dodge (Ron Eldard), Munder (Karl Urban), and Santos (Alex Dimi-

triades). Under the time-honored code of horror movies, they will disappear in horrible ways in inverse order to their billing—although of course there's also the possibility they'll turn up again.

The most absorbing passages in the film involve their exploration of the deserted liner. The quality of the art direction and photography actually evoke some of the same creepy, haunting majesty of those documentaries about descents to the grave of the *Titanic.* There's more scariness because we know how the original passengers and crew members died (that opening scene has a grisly humor), and because the ship still seems haunted—not only by that sad-eyed little girl, but perhaps by others.

The mystery eventually yields an explanation, if not a solution, and there is the obligatory twist in the last shot, which encourages us to reinterpret everything in diabolical terms, and to think hard about the meanings of certain names. But the appeal of *Ghost Ship* is all in the process, not in the climax. I liked the vast old empty ballroom, the deserted corridors, and the sense of a party that ended long ago (the effect is of a nautical version of Miss Havisham's sealed room). I knew that there would be unexpected shocks, sudden noises, and cadaverous materializations, but I have long grown immune to such mechanical thrills (unless they are done well, of course). I just dug the atmosphere.

Is the film worth seeing? Depends. It breaks no new ground as horror movies go, but it does introduce an intriguing location, and it's well-made technically. It's better than you expect, but not as good as you hope.

Ghosts of the Abyss ★ ★ ★
G, 59 m., 2003

Narrated by Bill Paxton, and featuring Lewis Abernathy, Dr. Lori Johnston, Don Lynch, Ken Marschall, Dr. Charles Pellegrino, and Tava Smiley. A documentary directed and written by James Cameron. Produced by Cameron, Chuck Comisky, and Andrew Wight.

The wreck of *Titanic,* which for decades seemed forever out of reach, has in recent years been visited by documentaries that bring back ghostly images of a party that ended in midsong. These films have an undeniable fascination, and none has penetrated more completely and evocatively than James Cameron's *Ghosts of the Abyss*.

The earliest films about *Titanic* were marvelous just because they existed at all. Cameron mounts a much more ambitious expedition to the bottom of the sea, involving a powerful light "chandelier" that hangs above the wreck and illuminates it, and two remote-controlled cameras named Jake and Elwood that propel themselves into tight corners and explore the inside of the ship.

Guiding them are expedition members in deep-diving exploration subs, including Bill Paxton, who starred in Cameron's *Titanic* and now narrates this documentary and shoots some of it himself. The result is often spellbinding, and to mention some of the sights we see is to praise the film's ambition.

The agile little camera-bots are able, for example, to snake their way into the ship's grand ballroom, and to discover that the Tiffany cut-glass windows are, astonishingly, still intact. Later, Cameron is able to position one of the minisubs outside the ship to shine its light through the windows for the camera inside, and we see the colors brought alive by light for the first time since the ship hit the fatal iceberg.

Other scenes actually discover the brass bed in the suite occupied by the "unsinkable" Molly Brown, who was such a famous survivor she had a Broadway musical named after her, and who always insisted her bed was brass, not wood. We also see a bowler hat, still waiting atop a dresser, and glasses and a carafe, left where they were put down after a final drink.

Cameron, who achieved so much with digital effects in *Titanic,* here uses similar technology to animate his haunted undersea scenes. He shoots the *Titanic* today—its empty corridors, its deserted grand staircase, its abandoned decks—and then populates the ship with a ghostly overlay showing the restored ship with its elegant passengers on their cruise to doom.

The movie is an impressive achievement, but that is not because of its trumpeted selling-point, the fact that it was shot in 3-D. I saw the first 3-D movie *(Bwana Devil)* and I have seen most of them since, as the technology has been improved and perfected, and I have arrived at the conclusion that 3-D will never be ready for prime time: It is an unnecessary and distracting redundancy. It can be done very well (as with the custom-made $200 glasses supplied with some IMAX features) and we can admire its quality and yet doubt its usefulness. Old-fashioned 2-D provides an illusion of reality that has convinced moviegoers for one hundred years. We accept it and do not think about it. The 3-D process is a mistake because it distracts attention away from the content and toward the process.

Ghosts of the Abyss is being shown around the country in 3-D on IMAX screens and also in some regular theaters. Do not feel deprived if your theater does not have 3-D. You won't be missing a thing.

Note: I learn that Cameron's next fiction film, his first since Titanic, *will be a feature shot in 3-D. "People are looking for a new way to be stimulated," industry analyst Paul Dergarabedian said in the announcement story.*

He is correct about people, but wrong that 3-D is a new way to be stimulated. It is an old way that has never lived up to its promise. If Cameron wants to be a pioneer instead of a retro hobbyist, he should obviously use Maxivision 48, which provides a picture of such startling clarity that it appears to be 3-D in the sense that the screen seems to open a transparent window on reality. Ghosts of the Abyss *would have been incomparably more powerful in the process.*

Maxivision 48 would be cheaper than 3-D, would look dramatically better, would not require those silly glasses, would be backward-compatible for standard theaters, and would allow Cameron to introduce the next step forward in movie projection, rather than returning to the obsolete past. Cameron has the clout and the imagination to make this leap forward, not just for his next film but for an industry that needs something dramatic and new and realizes it isn't going to be digital projection. This is his chance to explore the future of cinema as bravely as he ventured to the ocean floor.

Gigli ★★½
R, 124 m., 2003

Ben Affleck (Larry), Jennifer Lopez (Ricki), Justin Bartha (Brian), Christopher Walken (Det.

Jacobellis), Lenny Venito (Louis), Lainie Kazan (Mother). Directed and produced by Martin Brest. Screenplay by Brest.

Jennifer Lopez and Ben Affleck are in love and plan to get married, as you already know unless you are sealed off from all media, in which case you are not reading this review, so put it down. Because they are a famous couple, starring in a movie romance, we expect something conventional and predictable, and that is not what we get from *Gigli*. The movie tries to do something different, thoughtful, and a little daring with their relationship, and although it doesn't quite work, maybe the movie is worth seeing for some scenes that are really very good.

Consider the matching monologues. They've gotten into an argument over the necessity of the penis, which she, as a lesbian, feels is an inferior device for delivering sexual pleasure. He delivers an extended lecture on the use, necessity, and perfect design of the appendage. It is a rather amazing speech, the sort of thing some moviegoers are probably going to want to memorize. Then she responds. She is backlit, dressed in skintight workout clothes, doing yoga, and she continues to stretch and extend and bend and pose as she responds with her speech in praise of the vagina. When she is finished, Reader, the vagina has won, hands down. It is so rare to find dialogue of such originality and wit, so well written, that even though we know the exchange basically involves actors showing off, they do it so well, we let them.

Affleck plays Larry Gigli (rhymes with "Geely") and one wonders, learning that they rejected several earlier titles for the movie, which ones could have been worse than this. He's an errand boy for a tough-talking Los Angeles mobster named Louis (Lenny Venito). Louis wants to do a favor for a New York mob boss, and orders Gigli to kidnap the mentally disabled brother of a federal prosecutor. Gigli does, walking out of a care facility with Brian (Justin Bartha), who has Rain Man's syndrome. He takes him home, there is a knock on the door, and he meets Ricki (Lopez), who is also a mob enforcer. Louis is taking no chances and has assigned both of them to guard the boy.

This is the setup for an obvious plot that the movie, written by director Martin Brest, wisely avoids. Instead of falling in love and psychically adopting Brian, or (alternate cliché) fighting all the time, Gigli and Ricki get to like each other very, very much, even though she makes it perfectly clear that she is a lesbian. So resolute is the movie in its idea of her character that she doesn't even cave in and have a conversion experience, which is what we're expecting, but remains a lesbian—as indeed, as a good lesbian, she should.

Their conversations take on a rather desperate quality, since Gigli feels lust and love, and she feels strong affection. What transpires between them, and whether they ever put their theories about genitalia through a field test, I will not reveal. Meanwhile, Brian behaves like a well-rehearsed Movie Retarded Person, does or doesn't do whatever the script requires, and conveniently disappears into his room when he is not needed.

Lopez and Affleck are sweet and appealing in their performances; the buzz said they didn't have chemistry, but the buzz was wrong. What they don't have is conviction. There is no way these two are killers for the mob. They don't have the disposition for it. And consider this: If you had kidnapped the highly recognizable Rain Man brother of a top federal prosecutor, would you drive him all over Los Angeles in a convertible with the top down, and take him to restaurants and malls? So the crime plot is completely unconvincing. It does, however, open the door for the movie's collection of inspired supporting performances. Christopher Walken, as a cop who knows Gigli, walks into his apartment and does five minutes of Walkenizing and the audience eats up every second. Lainie Kazan, as Gigli's mother, sizes up Ricky instantly, likes her, learns she is a lesbian, chucks her under the chin, and says, "But you've been with guys, right?" Then she talks about her own Highly Experimental youth, while solidifying her position as the ethnic mother of choice in modern American movies. And then toward the end, Starkman, the mob boss from New York, arrives, and is played in a cameo by Al Pacino—who makes the journey from extravagant dopiness to chilling intimidation faster and better than anyone else I can think of.

So the movie doesn't work. The ending especially doesn't work, and what's worse, it doesn't work for a long time, because it fails to work for minute after minute, and includes dialogue that is almost entirely unnecessary. But there is good stuff here. Affleck and Lopez create lovely characters, even if they're not the ones they're allegedly playing, and the supporting performances and a lot of the dialogue is wonderful. It's just that there's too much time between the good scenes. Too much repetitive dialogue. Too many soulful looks. Behavior we can't believe. I wonder what would happen if you sweated 15 minutes out of this movie. Maybe it would work. The materials are there.

The Girl Next Door ½★
R, 110 m., 2004

Emile Hirsch (Matthew Kidman), Elisha Cuthbert (Danielle), Timothy Olyphant (Kelly), James Remar (Hugo Posh), Chris Marquette (Eli), Paul Dano (Klitz). Directed by Luke Greenfield and produced by Harry Gittes, Charles Gordon, and Marc Sternberg. Screenplay by Stuart Blumberg, David Wagner, and Brent Goldberg.

The studio should be ashamed of itself for advertising *The Girl Next Door* as a teenage comedy. It's a nasty piece of business, involving a romance between a teenage porn actress and a high school senior. A good movie could presumably be made from this premise—a good movie can be made from anything, in the right hands and way—but this is a dishonest, quease-inducing "comedy" that had me feeling uneasy and then unclean. Who in the world read this script and thought it was acceptable?

The film stars Emile Hirsch as Matthew Kidman. (Please tell me the "Kidman" is not an oblique reference to Nicole Kidman and therefore to Tom Cruise and therefore to *Risky Business,* the film this one so desperately wants to resemble.) One day he sees a sexy girl moving in next door, and soon he's watching through his bedroom window as she undresses as girls undress only in his dreams. Then she sees him, snaps off the light, and a few minutes later rings the doorbell.

Has she come to complain? No, she says nothing about the incident and introduces herself to Matthew's parents: Her aunt is on vacation, and she is house-sitting. Soon they're in her car together and Danielle is coming on to Matthew: "Did you like what you saw?" He did. She says now it's her turn to see him naked, and makes him strip and stand in the middle of the road while she shines the headlights on him. Then she scoops up his underpants and drives away, leaving him to walk home naked, ho, ho. (It is not easy to reach out of a car and scoop up underpants from the pavement while continuing to drive. Try it sometime.)

Danielle (Elisha Cuthbert) has two personalities: In one, she's a sweet, misunderstood kid who has never been loved, and in the other she's a twisted emotional sadist who amuses herself by toying with the feelings of the naive Matthew. The movie alternates between these personalities at its convenience, making her quite the most unpleasant character I have seen in some time.

They have a romance going before one of Matthew's buddies identifies her, correctly, as a porn star. The movie seems to think, along with Matthew's friends, that this information is in her favor. Matthew goes through the standard formula: first he's angry with her, then she gets through his defenses, then he believes she really loves him and that she wants to leave the life she's been leading. Problem is, her producer is angry because he wants her to keep working. This character, named Kelly, is played by Timothy Olyphant with a skill that would have distinguished a better movie, but it doesn't work here, because the movie never levels with us. When a guy his age (thirty-six, according to IMDB) "used to be the boyfriend" of a girl her age (nineteen, according to the plot description) and she is already, at nineteen, a famous porn star, there is a good chance the creep corrupted her at an early age; think Traci Lords. That he is now her "producer" under an "exclusive contract" is an elevated form of pimping. To act in porn as a teenager is not a decision freely taken by many teenage girls, and not a life to envy.

There's worse. The movie produces a basically nice guy, named Hugo Posh (James Remar), also a porn king, who is Kelly's rival. That a porn king saves the day gives you an idea of the movie's limited moral horizons. Oh, and not to forget Matthew's best friends, named Eli and Klitz (Chris Marquette and Paul Dano). Klitz? "Spelled with a *K*," he explains.

Kelly steals the money that Matthew has raised to bring a foreign exchange student from Cambodia, and to replace the funds, the resourceful Danielle flies in two porn star friends (played by Amanda Swisten and Sung Hi Lee), so that Matthew, Eli, and Klitz can produce a sex film during the senior prom. The nature of their film is yet another bait-and-switch, in a movie that wants to seem dirtier than it is. Like a strip show at a carnival, it lures you in with promises of sleaze, and after you have committed yourself for the filthy-minded punter you are, it professes innocence.

Risky Business (1983), you will recall, starred Tom Cruise as a young man left home alone by his parents, who wrecks the family Porsche and ends up enlisting a call girl (Rebecca De Mornay) to run a brothel out of his house to raise money to replace the car. The movie is the obvious model for *The Girl Next Door,* but it completely misses the tone and wit of the earlier film, which proved you can get away with that plot, but you have to know what you're doing and how to do it, two pieces of knowledge conspicuously absent here.

One necessary element is to distance the heroine from the seamier side of her life. *The Girl Next Door* does the opposite, actually taking Danielle and her "producer" Kelly to an adult film convention in Las Vegas, and even into a dimly lit room where adult stars apparently pleasure the clients. (There is another scene where Kelly, pretending to be Matthew's friend, takes him to a lap dance emporium and treats him.) We can deal with porn stars, lap dances, and whatever else in a movie that declares itself and plays fair, but to insert this material into something with the look and feel of a teen comedy makes it unsettling. The TV ads will attract audiences expecting something like *American Pie;* they'll be shocked by the squalid content of this film. ☞

Girl with a Pearl Earring ★ ★ ★ ★
PG-13, 95 m., 2003

Scarlett Johansson (Griet), Colin Firth (Johannes Vermeer), Tom Wilkinson (Van Ruijven), Judy Parfitt (Maria Thins), Essie Davis (Catharina), Cillian Murphy (Pieter), Joanna Scanlan

(Tanneke), Alakina Mann (Cornelia). Directed by Peter Webber and produced by Andy Paterson and Anand Tucker. Screenplay by Olivia Hetreed, based on the novel by Tracy Chevalier.

Girl with a Pearl Earring is a quiet movie, shaken from time to time by ripples of emotional turbulence far beneath the surface. It is about things not said, opportunities not taken, potentials not realized, lips unkissed. All of these elements are guessed at by the filmmakers as they regard a painting made in about 1665 by Johannes Vermeer. The painting shows a young woman regarding us over her left shoulder. She wears a simple blue headband and a modest smock. Her red lips are slightly parted. Is she smiling? She seems to be glancing back at the moment she was leaving the room. She wears a pearl earring.

Not much is known about Vermeer, who left about thirty-five paintings. Nothing is known about his model. You can hear that it was his daughter, a neighbor, a tradeswoman. You will not hear that she was his lover, because Vermeer's household was under the iron rule of his mother-in-law, who was vigilant as a hawk. The painting has become as intriguing in its modest way as the *Mona Lisa.* The girl's face turned toward us from centuries ago demands that we ask, who was she? What was she thinking? What was the artist thinking about her?

Tracy Chevalier's novel speculating about the painting has now been filmed by Peter Webber, who casts Scarlett Johansson as the girl and Colin Firth as Vermeer. I can think of many ways the film could have gone wrong, but it goes right because it doesn't cook up melodrama and romantic intrigue but tells a story that's content with its simplicity. The painting is contemplative, reflective, subdued, and the film must be too: We don't want lurid revelations breaking into its mood.

Sometimes two people will regard each other over a gulf too wide to ever be bridged and know immediately what could have happened, and that it never will. That is essentially the message of *Girl with a Pearl Earring.* The girl's name is Griet, according to this story. She lives nearby. She is sent by her blind father to work in Vermeer's house, where several small children are about to be joined by a new arrival.

The household is run like a factory with the mother-in-law, Maria Thins (Judy Parfitt), as foreman. She has set her daughter to work producing babies while her son-in-law produces paintings. Both have an output of about one a year, which is good if you are a mother, but not if you are a painter.

Nobody ever says what they think in this house except for Maria, whose thoughts are all too obvious anyway. Catharina (Essie Davis), Vermeer's wife, sometimes seems to be standing where she hopes nobody will see her. It becomes clear that Griet is intelligent in a natural way, but has no idea what to do with her ideas. Of course she attracts Vermeer's attention; she's a hard worker and responds instinctively to the manual labor of painting—to the craft, the technique, the strategy, even the chemistry (did you know that the color named Indian Yellow is distilled from the urine of cows fed on mango leaves?).

In one flawless sequence, Griet is alone in Vermeer's studio and looks at the canvas he is working on, looks at what he is painting, looks back, looks forth, and then moves a chair away from a window. When he returns and sees what she has done, he studies the composition carefully and removes the chair from his painting. Eventually he has her move up to the attic, closer to his studio, where she can mix his paints, which she does very well.

And then of course they start sleeping together? Not in this movie. Vermeer has a rich patron named Van Ruijven (Tom Wilkinson). If Vermeer is too shy to reveal feelings for his maid, Van Ruijven is not. He wants a painting of the girl. This, of course, would be unacceptable to Catharina Vermeer, whose best-developed quality is her insecurity—but it is not unacceptable to her mother, who must keep a rich patron happy. Thus Griet becomes a model.

There is a young man in the town, Pieter (Cillian Murphy), a butcher's apprentice, who is attracted to Griet. He would make her a good husband, in this world where status and opportunity are assigned by caste. Griet likes him. It's not that she likes Vermeer more; indeed, she's so intimidated she barely speaks to the artist. It's that—well, Griet could never be a butcher, but she could be a painter.

Mankind has Shakespeares who were illiterate, Mozarts who never heard a note, Picassos

who never touched a brush. Griet *could* be a painter. Whether a good or bad one, she will never know. Vermeer senses it. The moments of greatest intimacy between the simple peasant girl and the famous artist come when they sit side by side in wordless communication, mixing paints, both doing the same job, both understanding it.

Do not believe those who think this movie is about the "mystery" of the model, or Vermeer's sources of inspiration, or medieval gender roles, or whether the mother-in-law was the man in the family. A movie about those things would have been a bad movie. *Girl with a Pearl Earring* is about how they share a professional understanding that neither one has in any way with anyone else alive. I look at the painting and I realize that Griet is telling Vermeer, without using any words, "Well, if it were *my* painting, I'd have her stand like this."

Gloomy Sunday ★ ★ ★
NO MPAA RATING, 114 m., 2003

Erika Marozsán (Ilona Varnai), Joachim Król (László Szabo), Ben Becker (Hans Wieck), Stefano Dionisi (András Aradi). Directed by Rolf Schübel and produced by Michael André and Richard Schöps. Screenplay by Schübel and Ruth Toma, based on the novel by Nick Barkow.

Odd, how affecting this imperfect film becomes. It's a broad romantic melodrama set in Budapest before and during the Holocaust, and that is not, you will agree, an ideal time to set a love story. And if it is true that the title song drove hundreds to commit suicide, some of them may have merely been very tired of hearing it.

And yet *Gloomy Sunday* held my attention, and there were times when I was surprisingly involved. It's an old-fashioned romantic triangle, told with schmaltzy music on the sound track and a heroine with a smoky singing voice, and then the Nazis turn up and it gets very complicated and heartbreaking.

The movie opened Friday in Chicago. So far as I can tell, this is its first American theatrical booking. But listen to this: In New Zealand, it ran for more than a year and became a local phenomenon.

The story begins in Budapest in the 1930s,

where László Szabo (Joachim Król) runs a restaurant celebrated for its beef rolls. His hostess is the young and fetching Ilona (Erika Marozsán), and he is in love with her. Together they hire a piano player named András (Stefano Dionisi), and András falls in love with Ilona, and she with him, but she still loves László, and since they all like one another, they arrive at a cozy accommodation.

A regular customer in the 1930s is a German named Hans Wieck (Ben Becker), who also falls in love with Ilona, and says if she will marry him, he will build Germany's largest import-export business, just for her. But as she already has her hands full, she turns him down.

András meanwhile composes a song named "Gloomy Sunday" that sweeps the world and which he has to play every night at the restaurant. Soon a legend grows up around the song, that people who hear it commit suicide. Strangely enough, this detail is based on fact; it was written in 1933 by Rezső Seress, became an international hit, was recorded by such as Artie Shaw and Billie Holiday (and later Bjork and Elvis Costello), and was banned by the BBC because of its allegedly depressing effect. On the night that Ilona rejects Hans, indeed, he casts himself into the Danube and is hauled out by László. You see what I mean about melodrama.

The war comes. It is well known what the Nazis are doing to the Jews, but László, who is Jewish, has never given much thought to religion and believes such things will never happen in Hungary. He has more than one chance to escape, but remains, and his restaurant becomes even more popular in wartime. A regular customer is none other than Hans Wieck, now in charge of the Hungarian final solution, and he gives László an exemption; his beef rolls are a contribution to the war effort. Wieck, too, is said to be based on a historical figure, a Nazi named Kurt Becher who held a similar job in Budapest.

The movie, which has been fanciful and romantic, now descends into tragedy and betrayal. The carefree days of romance and denial are over, and the closing scenes of the film have an urgency that blindsides us, given the movie's earlier innocence. Then there is an epilogue, which is gratuitous and overlong; we could have done without it.

But the main story has the strength of its characters, who feel deeply and are brave and foolish in equal measure. András is a basket case who wears his emotions on his sleeve, but Ilona loves him for his vulnerability, and László is one of those good souls who find the calm in every situation, think the best of people, are generous and not jealous, and trusting—too trusting. The actors give the characters a touching presence and reality.

The movie will play for a week or two and disappear from Chicago and, for all I know, from North America. Maybe not. Maybe it will play for eighty weeks, like in Auckland.

Note: My information about the legend of Gloomy Sunday *was obtained at www.phespirit. info/gloomysunday, which includes several sets of lyrics.*

Gods and Generals ★ ½
PG-13, 216 m., 2003

Jeff Daniels (Lieutenant Colonel Joshua Chamberlain), Stephen Lang (General "Stonewall" Jackson), Robert Duvall (General Robert E. Lee), Chris Conner (John Wilkes Booth), C. Thomas Howell (Tom Chamberlain), Kevin Conway (Sergeant "Buster" Kilrain), Patrick Gorman (Brigadier General John Bell Hood), Brian Mallon (Brigadier General Winfield Scott Hancock). Directed and produced by Ronald F. Maxwell. Screenplay by Maxwell, based on the book by Jeff M. Shaara.

Here is a Civil War movie that Trent Lott might enjoy. Less enlightened than *Gone with the Wind,* obsessed with military strategy, impartial between South and North, religiously devout, it waits seventy minutes before introducing the first of its two speaking roles for African-Americans; Stonewall Jackson assures his black cook that the South will free him, and the cook looks cautiously optimistic. If World War II were handled this way, there'd be hell to pay.

The movie is essentially about brave men on both sides who fought and died so that ... well, so that they could fight and die. They are led by generals of blinding brilliance and nobility, although one Northern general makes a stupid error and the movie shows hundreds of his men being slaughtered at great length as the result of it.

The Northerners, one Southerner explains,

are mostly Republican profiteers who can go home to their businesses and families if they're voted out of office after the conflict, while the Southerners are fighting for their homes. Slavery is not the issue, in this view, because it would have withered away anyway, although a liberal professor from Maine (Jeff Daniels) makes a speech explaining it is wrong. So we get that cleared up right there, or for sure at Strom Thurmond's birthday party.

The conflict is handled with solemnity worthy of a memorial service. The music, when it is not funeral, sounds like the band playing during the commencement exercises at a sad university. Countless extras line up, march forward, and shoot at each other. They die like flies. That part is accurate, although the stench, the blood, and the cries of pain are tastefully held to the PG-13 standard. What we know about the war from the photographs of Mathew Brady, the poems of Walt Whitman, and the documentaries of Ken Burns is not duplicated here.

Oh, it is a competently made film. Civil War buffs may love it. Every group of fighting men is identified by subtitles, to such a degree that I wondered, fleetingly, if they were being played by Civil War reenactment hobbyists who would want to nudge their friends when their group appeared on the screen. Much is made of the film's total and obsessive historical accuracy; the costumes, flags, battle plans, and ordnance are all doubtless flawless, although there could have been no Sergeant "Buster" Kilrain in the 20th Maine, for the unavoidable reason that "Buster" was never used as a name until Buster Keaton used it.

The actors do what they can, although you can sense them winding up to deliver pithy quotations. Robert Duvall, playing General Robert E. Lee, learns of Stonewall Jackson's battlefield amputation and reflects sadly, "He has lost his left arm, and I have lost my right." His eyes almost twinkle as he envisions that one ending up in *Bartlett's*. Stephen Lang, playing Jackson, has a deathbed scene so wordy, as he issues commands to imaginary subordinates and then prepares himself to cross over the river, that he seems to be stalling. Except for Lee, a nonbeliever, both sides trust in God, just like at the Super Bowl.

Donzaleigh Abernathy plays the other African-American speaking role, that of a maid

named Martha who attempts to jump the gun on Reconstruction by staying behind when her white employers evacuate, and telling the arriving Union troops it is her own house. Later, when they commandeer it as a hospital, she looks a little resentful. This episode, like many others, is kept so resolutely at the cameo level that we realize material of such scope and breadth can be shoehorned into three and a half hours only by sacrificing depth.

Gods and Generals is the kind of movie beloved by people who never go to the movies, because they are primarily interested in something else—the Civil War, for example—and think historical accuracy is a virtue instead of an attribute. The film plays like a special issue of *American Heritage*. Ted Turner is one of its prime movers, and gives himself an instantly recognizable cameo appearance. Since sneak previews must already have informed him that his sudden appearance draws a laugh, apparently he can live with that.

Note: The same director, Ron Maxwell, made the much superior Gettysburg *(1993) and at the end informs us that the third title in the trilogy will be* The Last Full Measure. *Another line from the same source may serve as a warning: "The world will little note, nor long remember, what we say here."*

Godsend ★ ★

PG-13, 102 m., 2004

Greg Kinnear (Paul Duncan), Rebecca Romijn-Stamos (Jessie Duncan), Robert De Niro (Dr. Richard Wells), Cameron Bright (Adam Duncan). Directed by Nick Hamm and produced by Marc Butan, Sean O'Keefe, and Cathy Schulman. Screenplay by Mark Bomback.

Godsend tells the story of parents whose only son is killed in an accident, and who are offered the opportunity to clone him. If all goes well, the grieving mother will bear a child genetically identical to the dead boy. I would find that unspeakably sad, but the movie isn't interested in really considering the implications; it's a thriller, a bad thriller, completely lacking in psychological or emotional truth.

Greg Kinnear and Rebecca Romijn-Stamos star, as Paul and Jessie Duncan; he's an inner-city high school teacher, and she's a photographer.

Immediately after their son, Adam, is killed, they're approached by Dr. Richard Wells (Robert De Niro), who offers them an illegal opportunity to retrieve one of Adam's cells and implant it in Jessie's womb so that she can bear another Adam. At first they resist, but then they agree, and soon they have another son named Adam. Both boys are played by Cameron Bright.

Dr. Wells, who made millions earlier in his career, operates out of a vast medical laboratory in Vermont, and persuades the Duncans to move up there; they must cut all ties with former friends and family, he explains, because of course the Adam clone will raise difficult questions. To help them settle in, he provides a waterfront house that will have every real-estate agent in the audience thinking in the millions. Adam Two is born (in a particularly unconvincing live childbirth scene) and quickly reaches the same birthday that Adam One celebrated just before he was killed. Until then he has been an ideal child, but now he begins to get weird. "Dad," he tells his father, "I've been thinking. I don't think I like you so much any more." As Kinnear recoils in pain, the kid grins and says he was only kidding. Ho, ho. "There was always the possibility," Dr. Wells intones, "that things could change once he passed the age when he died."

I dare not reveal the secret around which the plot revolves, but I can say that Adam Two has visions and night terrors, and in them sees a little boy whose experiences seem to intersect with his own. At school, Adam Two is not popular, perhaps because he spits on playmates and a teacher, perhaps because he is just plain weird; the movie *Omenizes* him with big close-ups, his face pinched and ominous. At home, he has a habit of hanging around in the woodshed with sharp instruments or invading his mother's darkroom, where a lot of photos of Adam One are kept in a box that really should have been locked.

The movie's premise is fascinating, and has stirred up a lot of interest. Some opponents of cloning reportedly confused its Web site (godsendinstitute.org) for the real thing, although that "confusion" has the aroma of a publicity stunt. No matter; *Godsend* isn't about cloning so much as about shock, horror, evil, deception, and the peculiar appeal that demonic children seem to possess for movie audiences.

The performances are ineffective. I would say they are bad, but I suppose they're as good as the material permits. Kinnear and Romijn-Stamos are required to play a couple whose entire relationship is formed and defined by plot gimmicks, and as for De Niro, there are times when he seems positively embarrassed to be seen as that character, saying those things. His final conversation with Kinnear must be the most absurd scene he has ever been asked to play seriously. The movie is so impossible that even the child actor is left stranded. He seems lovable as Adam One, but as Adam Two he seems to have been programmed, not by genetics, but by sub-"Omen" potboilers.

For a brief time, however, I thought director Nick Hamm was using at least one original strategy. During certain tense scenes, I heard a low, ominous, scraping noise, and I thought it was some kind of audible flash-forward to terrors still to come. Then I realized I was hearing carpenters at work on the floor below the screening room. I recommend they be added to an optional sound track on the DVD.

Note: That's going to be one crowded DVD. My fellow critic Joe Leydon points me to a story at scififx.com reporting that director Hamm shot at least seven alternate endings to the movie, including those in which two different characters are killed two different ways, and little Adam kills everybody. Nothing like covering your bases. ☞

Godzilla ★ ½
NO MPAA RATING, 98 m., 2004

Takashi Shimura (Dr. Kyohei Yamane), Momoko Kochi (Emiko Yamane), Akira Takarada (Hideto Ogata), Akihiko Hirata (Dr. Serizawa), Sachio Sakai (Reporter Hagiwara), Fuyuki Murakami (Dr. Tabata), Toranosuke Ogawa (CEO of Shipping Company), Ren Yamamoto (Masaji). The fiftieth-anniversary release of a film directed by Ishiro Honda and produced by Tomoyuki Tanaka. Screenplay by Takeo Murata and Honda, based on the original story by Shigeru Kayama.

Regaled for fifty years by the stupendous idiocy of the American version of *Godzilla*, audiences can now see the original 1954 Japanese version, which is equally idiotic, but, properly decoded, was the *Fahrenheit 9/11* of its time. Both films come after fearsome attacks on their nations, embody urgent warnings, and even incorporate similar dialogue, such as, "The report is of such dire importance it must not be made public." Is that from 1954 Tokyo or 2004 Washington?

The first *Godzilla* set box-office records in Japan and inspired countless sequels, remakes, and rip-offs. It was made shortly after an American H-bomb test in the Pacific contaminated a large area of ocean and gave radiation sickness to a boatload of Japanese fishermen. It refers repeatedly to Nagasaki, H-bombs, and civilian casualties, and obviously embodies Japanese fears about American nuclear tests.

But that is not the movie you have seen. For one thing, it doesn't star Raymond Burr as Steve Martin, intrepid American journalist, who helpfully explains, "I was headed for an assignment in Cairo when I dropped off for a social call in Tokyo." The American producer Joseph E. Levine bought the Japanese film, cut it by forty minutes, removed all of the political content, and awkwardly inserted Burr into scenes where he clearly did not fit. The hapless actor gives us reaction shots where he's looking in the wrong direction, listens to Japanese actors dubbed into the American idiom (they always call him "Steve Martin" or even "the famous Steve Martin"), and provides a reassuring conclusion in which Godzilla is seen as some kind of public health problem, or maybe just a malcontent.

The Japanese version, now in general U.S. release to mark the film's fiftieth anniversary, is a bad film, but with an undeniable urgency. I learn from helpful notes by Mike Flores of the Psychotronic Film Society that the opening scenes, showing fishing boats disappearing as the sea boils up, would have been read by Japanese audiences as a coded version of U.S. underwater H-bomb tests. Much is made of a scientist named Dr. Serizawa (Akihiko Hirata), who could destroy Godzilla with his secret weapon, the Oxygen Destroyer, but hesitates because he is afraid the weapon might fall into the wrong hands, just as H-bombs might, and have. The film's ending warns that atomic tests may lead to more Godzillas. All cut from the U.S. version.

In these days of flawless special effects, Godzilla and the city he destroys are equally crude. Godzilla at times looks uncannily like a man in a lizard suit, stomping on cardboard sets, as indeed he was, and did. Other scenes show him as a stiff, awkward animatronic model. This was not state-of-the-art even at the time; *King Kong* (1933) was much more convincing.

When Dr. Serizawa demonstrates the Oxygen Destroyer to the fiancée of his son, the superweapon is somewhat anticlimactic. He drops a pill into a tank of tropical fish, the tank lights up, he shouts "Stand back!" The fiancée screams, and the fish go belly-up. Yeah, that'll stop Godzilla in his tracks.

Reporters covering Godzilla's advance are rarely seen in the same shot with the monster. Instead, they look offscreen with horror; a TV reporter, broadcasting for some reason from his station's tower, sees Godzilla looming nearby and signs off, "Sayonara, everyone!" Meanwhile, searchlights sweep the sky, in case Godzilla learns to fly.

The movie's original Japanese dialogue, subtitled, is as harebrained as Burr's dubbed lines. When the Japanese Parliament meets (in what looks like a high school home room), the dialogue is portentous but circular:

"The professor raises an interesting question! We need scientific research!"

"Yes, but at what cost?"

"Yes, that's the question!"

Is there a reason to see the original *Godzilla*? Not because of its artistic stature, but perhaps because of the feeling we can sense in its parable about the monstrous threats unleashed by the atomic age. There are shots of Godzilla's victims in hospitals, and they reminded me of documentaries of Japanese A-bomb victims. The incompetence of scientists, politicians, and the military will ring a bell. This is a bad movie, but it has earned its place in history, and the enduring popularity of Godzilla and other monsters shows that it struck a chord. Can it be a coincidence, in these years of trauma after 9/11, that in a 2005 remake, King Kong will march once again on New York?

Good Boy! ★

PG, 89 m., 2003

Liam Aiken (Owen Baker), Kevin Nealon (Owen's Dad), Molly Shannon (Owen's Mom),

Matthew Broderick (Hubble [voice]), Brittany Moldowan (Connie Flemming [voice]), Hunter Elliott (Franky [voice]), Donald Faison (Wilson [voice]), Brittany Murphy (Nelly [voice]), Carl Reiner (Shep [voice]), Delta Burke (Barbara Ann [voice]). Directed by John Robert Hoffman and produced by Kristine Belson and Lisa Henson. Screenplay by Zeke Richardson and Hoffman.

Millions of Dog Owners Demand to Know: "Who's a Good Boy?"
— headline in the Onion

If a child and a dog love each other, the relationship is one of mutual wonder. Making the dog an alien from outer space is not an improvement. Giving it the ability to speak is a disaster. My dog Blackie used his eyes to say things so eloquent that Churchill would have been stuck for a comeback. Among my favorite movie dogs are Skip, in *My Dog Skip*, who teaches a boy how to be a boy, and Shiloh, in *Shiloh*, who teaches a boy that life is filled with hard choices. Hubble, the dog in *Good Boy!* teaches that dogs will be pulled off Earth and returned to their home planet in a "global recall."

I've told you all you really need to know about the movie's plot. Owen Baker (Liam Aiken), the young hero, adopts a terrier who turns out to have arrived in a flying saucer to investigate why dogs on Earth are our pets, instead of the other way around. This will be a no-brainer for anyone who has watched a dog operating a pooper scooper, nor do dogs look like the master race when they go after your pants leg. But I am willing to accept this premise if anything clever is done with it. Nothing is.

Having seen talking and/or audible dogs in many movies (how the years hurry by!), I have arrived at the conclusion that the best way to present animal speech is by letting us hear their thoughts in voice-over. Sometimes it works to show their lips moving (it certainly did in *Babe*), but in *Good Boy!* the jaw movements are so mechanical it doesn't look like speech, it looks like a film loop. Look at *Babe* again and you'll appreciate the superior way in which the head movements and body language of the animals supplement their speech.

But speech is not the real problem with *Good*

Boy! What they talk about is. The movie asks us to consider a race of superior beings who are built a few feet off the ground, lack opposable thumbs, and walk around nude all the time. Compared to them, the aliens in *Signs* are a model of plausibility. The dogs live within a few blocks of one another in Vancouver, and we meet their owners. I kept hoping maybe Jim Belushi had moved to the neighborhood with Jerry Lee from *K-9*, or that I'd spot Jack Nicholson walking Jill. (Jack and Jill: I just got it.)

But no. The humans are along the lines of Kevin Nealon and Molly Shannon, as Owen's parents. The dogs are voiced by Matthew Broderick (as Hubble), Brittany Moldowan, Brittany Murphy, Donald Faison, Carl Reiner, and Delta Burke. Voicing one of the dogs in this movie is the career move of people who like to keep working no matter what. At least when you do the voice of an *animated* animal, they make it look a little like you, and your character can be the star. But when you voice a real dog, do you have to stand around all day between shots talking to the trainer about what a good dog it is?

Good Bye, Lenin! ★ ★ ★
R, 121 m., 2004

Katrin Sass (Christiane Kerner), Daniel Bruhl (Alex Kerner), Maria Simon (Ariane Kerner), Chulpan Khamatova (Lara), Florian Lukas (Denis). Directed by Wolfgang Becker and produced by Stefan Arndt. Screenplay by Bernd Lichtenberg, Becker, Hendrik Handloegten, and Achim von Borries.

East Berlin, 1989. In the final days before the fall of the Berlin Wall, there are riots against the regime. A loyal Communist named Christiane (Katrin Sass) sees her son Alex (Daniel Bruhl) beaten by the police on television, suffers an attack of some sort, and lapses into a coma. During the months she is unconscious, the Wall falls, Germany is reunified, and the world as she knew it disappears. When she miraculously regains consciousness, the doctors advise, as doctors always do in the movies, "the slightest shock could kill her."

What to do? After her husband abandoned her (for another woman, she told her children), the German Democratic Republic became her life. To learn that it has failed ignominiously would surely kill her, and so Alex decides to create a fictional world for her, in which Erich Honecker is still in office, consumer shortages are still the rule, and the state television still sings the praises of the regime.

Good Bye, Lenin! is a movie that must have resonated loudly in Germany when it was released; it is no doubt filled with references and in-jokes we do not quite understand. But the central idea travels well: Imagine an American Rip Van Winkle who is told that President Gore has led a United Nations coalition in liberating Afghanistan, while cutting taxes for working people, attacking polluters, and forcing the drug companies to cut their bloated profits. Sorry, something came over me for a second.

Change, when it comes to East Germany, arrives in a torrent. Alex is reduced to plundering Dumpsters for discarded cans and boxes that contained GDR consumer products, which were swept away by the arrival of competition. In his day job, he sells satellite systems with his friend Denis (Florian Lukas), and together the two of them produce phony news broadcasts to show his mom—even enlisting a former East German astronaut for plausibility.

This works fine until one day Christiane ventures outside, finds the streets awash with Westerners, and is confused by all the ads for Coke. Improvising desperately, Alex and Denis produce newscasts reporting that the West is in collapse, Westerners are fleeing to the East, and the rights to Coke reverted to the Communist nation after it was revealed that its famous formula was devised, not in Atlanta, but in East Germany.

Good Bye, Lenin! is a comedy, but a peculiar one. Peculiar, because it never quite addresses the self-deception that causes Christiane to support the Communist regime in the first place. Many people backed it through fear, ambition, or prudence, but did anyone actually love it and believe in it? The scenes of joyous East Berliners pouring across the fallen Wall are still fresh in our minds. Toward the end of the movie we get a surprise plot point that suggests Christiane may have replaced her husband with the party in an act of emotional compensation, but that seems to be a stretch.

We all feel nostalgia for the environs of our past, of course, which is why someone like me once treasured a 1957 Studebaker Golden Hawk even though new cars are incomparably better made (they aren't as sexy, though). There are fan clubs in Germany for the Trabant, the singularly ugly and poorly made official auto of the GDR, and great is Christiane's delight when Alex tells her the family now owns one. Our pasts may be flawed, but they are ours, and we are attached to them. What *Good Bye, Lenin!* never quite deals with is the wrongheadedness of its heroine. Imagine a film named *Good Bye, Hitler!* in which a loving son tries to protect his cherished mother from news of the fall of the Third Reich.

Well, maybe that's too harsh. *Good Bye, Lenin!* is not a defense of the GDR, which Alex and his sister Ariane are happy to see gone (she's proud of her new job at Burger King). The underlying poignancy in this comedy is perhaps psychological more than political: How many of us lie to our parents, pretending a world still exists that they believe in but we have long since moved away from? And are those lies based on love or cowardice? Sometimes, despite doctors' warnings, parents have to take their chances with the truth.

The Good Girl ★ ★ ★ ½
R, 93 m., 2002

Jennifer Aniston (Justine Last), Jake Gyllenhaal (Holden Worther), John C. Reilly (Phil Last), Tim Blake Nelson (Bubba), Zooey Deschanel (Cheryl), Mike White (Corny). Directed by Miguel Arteta and produced by Matthew Greenfield. Screenplay by Mike White.

After languishing in a series of overlooked movies that ranged from the entertaining (*Office Space*) to the disposable (*Picture Perfect*), Jennifer Aniston has at last decisively broken with her *Friends* image in an independent film of satiric fire and emotional turmoil. It will no longer be possible to consider her in the same way. In *The Good Girl*, she plays Justine, a desperately bored clerk at Retail Rodeo, a sub-K-Mart where the customers are such sleepwalkers they don't even notice when the "Attention, Shoppers!" announcements are larded with insults and nonsense.

Recent headlines tell of a lawsuit against Wal-Mart for forcing its employees to work unpaid overtime. Retail Rodeo is by contrast relatively benign. Management is particularly flexible with Justine's coworker Cheryl (Zooey Deschanel), who, after getting carried away once too often on the PA system, is reassigned to Women's Makeovers, where she improvises dubious advice. A new makeup style is called "Cirque du Face," she tells one customer. "It's all the rage with the Frenchies."

Justine, who is thirtyish, is married to a house painter named Phil (John C. Reilly), who is attached vertically to the living room sofa and horizontally to his best friend, Bubba (Tim Blake Nelson). Phil and Bubba paint houses during the day and are couch potatoes at night, smoking weed and peering at the television. After a day of drudgery, Justine comes home to stoned indifference. No wonder she's intrigued by Holden (Jake Gyllenhaal), the new checkout kid, who's reading *The Catcher in the Rye* and tells her its hero is a victim of the world's hypocrisy.

Quite a coincidence, that a kid named Holden would be reading a book about a character named Holden. When they become better friends, Holden invites Justine to his house, where his mother calls him "Tom." In the safety of his room, he explains: "Tom is my slave name." Soon Justine and Tom, who is a college dropout with a drinking problem, are having sex everywhere they can: in the car, in his room, in the stockroom at Retail Rodeo, and in a fleabag motel, where, unluckily, Bubba sees them.

For Bubba, this is an ideal opening for emotional blackmail. He has long explained that he is single because he despairs of ever finding a wife as "perfect" as Justine. Now he demands sex with her so his life will be complete. Otherwise, he will tell Phil about her affair. In a decision that Jennifer Aniston would never make but Justine might (this is a crucial distinction), she deals with this demand and with another crisis, when she discovers she is pregnant. She also finds out what she should have suspected, that Bubba would never tell Phil about her secrets, because he adores Phil too much, and, as Phil's wife, she is protected by his immunity.

The Good Girl has been directed by Miguel Arteta and written by Mike White, who plays the Retail Rodeo's security guard. They also collaborated on *Chuck and Buck,* and on the basis of these two strange movies with their skewed perspectives, they are talents with huge promise. They know how much satire and exaggeration is enough but not too much, so that in a subterranean way their movies work on serious levels while seeming to be comedies.

Certainly the last big scene between Aniston and Reilly is an unexpected payoff, delivering an emotional punch while at the same time we can only admire Justine's strategy involving the father of her child. She says it's Phil, and cannot be disproven on the basis of Phil's information; having confessed to cheating, she allows him to suspect someone who could not have a black-haired child; therefore, the father is the dark-haired Phil. Right? Right.

Good Housekeeping ★ ★ ★
R, 90 m., 2002

Bob Jay Mills (Don), Petra Westen (Donatella), Tacey Adams (Marion), Al Schuermann (Joe), Zia (Chuck), Andrew Eichner (Don Jr.), Maeve Kerrigan (Tiffany). Directed by Frank Novak and produced by Mark G. Mathis. Screenplay by Novak.

I watch the guests on *Jerry Springer* with the fascination of an ambulance driver at a demo derby. Where do these people come from? Their dialogue may be "suggested," but their lives are all too evidently real, and they have tumbled right through the safety net of taste and self-respect and gone spiraling down, down into the pit of amoral vulgarity. Now comes *Good Housekeeping,* a film about how the people on *Springer* live when they're not on camera.

No, it's not a documentary. It was written and directed by Frank Novak, otherwise a trendy Los Angeles furniture manufacturer, who regards his white trash characters with deadpan neutrality. How is the audience expected to react? Consider this dialogue:

Don: "Maybe if we cut her in half we could get her in there."

Chuck: "We can't cut her in half!"

Don: "So what are you? Mr. Politically Correct?"

Don and Chuck are brothers. Don (Bob Jay Mills) uneasily shares his house with his wife, Donatella (Petra Westen), while Chuck (credited only as Zia) sleeps with his girlfriend Tiffany (Maeve Kerrigan) in Don's car. Things are not good between Don and Donatella, and he uses two-by-fours and plasterboard to build a wall that cuts the house in two ("She got way more square feet than I got," he tells the cops during one of their frequent visits). Realizing he has forgotten something, Don cuts a crawl hole in the wall so that Don Jr. (Andrew Eichner) can commute between parents. Soon Donatella's new lesbian lover Marion (Tacey Adams) is poking her head through the hole to discuss the "parameters" Don is setting for his son.

Donatella is a forklift operator. Don is self-employed as a trader of action figures, with a specialty in Pinhead and other Hellraiser characters. When Chuck tries to sell him a Sad-Eye Doll, he responds like a pro: "Couldn't you Swap-Meet it? I'm not gonna put that on my table and drag down my other merch." Don Jr. has less respect for action figures, and occasionally saws off their heads.

Terrible things happen to the many cars in this extended family, both by accident and on purpose. One of the funniest sequences shows a big blond family friend, desperately hungover, methodically crunching into every other car in the driveway before she runs over the mailbox. Don lives in fear of Donatella running him down, and at one point discusses his defense with a gun-show trader (Al Schuermann) who scoffs, "You would use a .38 to defend yourself?" He comes back with real protection against vehicular manslaughter: a shoulder-mounted rocket launcher.

Marion, the well-mannered lesbian lover, is the source of many of the film's biggest laughs because of the incongruity of her crush on Donatella. She watches Donatella smoke, eat, talk, and blow her nose all at the same time, and her only reaction is to eat all the more politely, in the hope of setting an example. Marion is an accountant at the factory where Donatella works; she dresses in chic business suits, has smart horn-rimmed glasses and a stylish haircut, and plunges into Springerland with an arsenal of liberal clichés. At one point, after a nasty domestic disturbance, she tries to make peace by inviting Don out to brunch. "There's no way the cops can make you go to brunch," Don's beer-bellied buddies reassure him.

It is perhaps a warning signal of incipient alcoholism when the family car has a Breathalyzer permanently attached to the dashboard. Yet Don is not without standards, and warns his brother against making love in the car because "I drive Mom to church in it." Family life follows a familiar pattern. Most evenings end with a fight in the yard, and Novak and his cinematographer, Alex Vandler, are skilled at getting convincing, spontaneous performances out of their unknown actors; many scenes, including the free-for-alls, play with the authenticity of a documentary.

Just as mainstream filmmakers are fascinated by the rich and famous, so independent filmmakers are drawn to society's hairy underbelly. *Good Housekeeping* plunges far beneath Todd Solondz's territory and enters the suburbs of John Waters's universe in its fascination for people who live without benefit of education, taste, standards, hygiene, and shame. Indeed, all they have enough of are cigarettes, used cars, controlled substances, and four-letter words. The movie is, however, very funny, as you peek at it through the fingers in front of your eyes.

Note: Good Housekeeping has had its ups and downs. It won the grand jury prize at Slamdance 2000, was the only U.S. film chosen for Critic's Week at Cannes that year, and was picked up for distribution by the Shooting Gallery—which alas went out of business, leaving the film orphaned.

The Good Thief ★ ★ ★ ½
R, 109 m., 2003

Nick Nolte (Bob), Tchéky Karyo (Roger), Nutsa Kukhianidze (Anne), Saïd Taghmaoui (Paulo), Gérard Darmon (Raoul), Ralph Fiennes (Tony), Marc Lavoine (Remi). Directed by Neil Jordan and produced by Steven Woolley, John Wells, and Seaton McLean. Screenplay by Jordan, based on the film by Jean-Pierre Melville.

Nick Nolte plays a great shambling wreck of a wounded Hemingway hero in *The Good Thief,* a film that's like a descent into the funkiest dive on the wrong side of the wrong town. He's Bob, the child of an American father and a French mother, so he claims—but he seems to change his story every time he tells it. He lives in Nice, on the French Riviera, moving easily through the lower depths of crime and drugs, and—this is the tricky part—liked by everyone. When it's rumored he is up to a new heist, the policeman Roger (Tchéky Karyo) tells his partner, "Find out before he does it!" He doesn't want to arrest Bob; he wants to save him from himself.

Bob is a thief and a heroin addict. "Heroin is his lady," his friend Raoul observes. "I thought luck was his lady," says another friend. "When one runs out he turns to the other," says Raoul. Bob is intimately familiar with the language of AA, talking about the Twelve Steps and "one day at a time" and even at one point citing the Serenity Prayer. But his only visit to a Narcotics Anonymous meeting involves walking in one door and out the other to elude pursuit ("I'm Bob, and I'm an addict," he says on the way through).

Bob is a good man, a good thief, to the bottom of his soul, a gentleman who rescues a teenage Bosnian hooker (Nutsa Kukhianidze) from a vicious pimp and then becomes her protector, although to be sure he introduces her to bad company. He is headed toward some kind of showdown with his fate. Down to his last 70,000 francs, he goes to the races. "What if you lose?" asks his friend. "I'll have hit rock bottom. I'll have to change my ways."

He hits rock bottom. He changes his ways. "I feel a confinement coming on," he says in that deep gravel voice. He chains himself to a bed, eats ice cream, goes through an agonizing detox, and is ready to consider an ingenious plan to steal the treasures of a Monte Carlo casino. No, not the money. The paintings.

The Good Thief, directed by Neil Jordan *(Mona Lisa, The Crying Game),* is a remake of a famous 1955 French film named *Bob le Flambeur* by Jean-Pierre Melville. *The Good Thief* is drawn to the affectionate study of a character who is admirable in every way except that he cannot bring himself to stop breaking the law. But it is juicier, jazzier, with a more charismatic hero.

Bob le Flambeur was filmed in elegant black and white, with Roger Duchesne playing Bob as a trim, self-contained, sleek operator. Nolte,

on the other hand, has such a bulldog look that even his clothes have jowls. He told a press conference at the Toronto Film Festival that he used "a little heroin" every day while making the movie, just to get in the mood. Not long ago, it is well known, he was arrested while driving under the influence, and his mug shot, widely circulated, showed a man who had made dissipation his life's work. Nolte recently said he was on his way to an AA meeting when something made him turn away and led eventually to his arrest. Maybe he wanted to be arrested, he speculated, so he could get help. *The Good Thief* looks like the direction he took when he turned away.

Whether or not Nolte topped up every day on the set, it is clear that he was born to play Bob. It is one of those performances that flows unhindered from an actor's deepest instincts. Jordan and his cinematographer, Chris Menges, place him in a world of smoke, shadows, and midnight blues, where cops and robbers supply work for each other. Into this world drift occasional outsiders like the kinky art dealer (Ralph Fiennes), who talks like a Batman villain: "If I don't get my money back by Monday, what I do to your faces will definitely be Cubist."

The plot I will not breathe a word about, since it is so elegantly ironic in the way Bob outflanks the cops, his partners, the casino, and ourselves. It leads up to a deeply satisfying conclusion, but along the way what we enjoy is the portrait of this man who is engaged in some kind of lifelong showdown between his goodness and his weakness. This is a struggle Nolte seems to know a great deal about.

Gosford Park ★ ★ ★ ★
R, 137 m., 2002

Eileen Atkins (Mrs. Croft), Bob Balaban (Morris Weissman), Alan Bates (Jennings), Charles Dance (Lord Stockbridge), Stephen Fry (Inspector Thompson), Michael Gambon (Sir William McCordle), Richard E. Grant (George), Derek Jacobi (Probert), Kelly Macdonald (Mary Maceachran), Helen Mirren (Mrs. Wilson), Jeremy Northam (Ivor Novello), Clive Owen (Robert Parks), Ryan Phillippe (Henry Denton), Maggie Smith (Constance, Countess of Trentham), Kristin Scott Thomas (Lady Sylvia McCordle), Emily Watson (Elsie). Directed by

Robert Altman and produced by Altman, Bob Balaban, and David Levy. Screenplay by Julian Fellowes, based on an idea by Altman and Balaban.

Robert Altman's *Gosford Park* is above all a celebration of styles—the distinct behavior produced by the British class system, the personal styles of a rich gallery of actors, and his own style of introducing a lot of characters and letting them weave their way through a labyrinthine plot. At a time when too many movies focus every scene on a $20 million star, an Altman film is like a party with no boring guests. *Gosford Park* is such a joyous and audacious achievement it deserves comparison with his very best movies, such as *M*A*S*H*, *McCabe and Mrs. Miller*, *Nashville*, *The Player*, *Short Cuts*, and *Cookie's Fortune*.

It employs the genre of the classic British murder mystery, as defined by Agatha Christie: Guests and servants crowd a great country house, and one of them is murdered. But *Gosford Park* is a Dame Agatha story in the same sense that *M*A*S*H* is a war movie, *McCabe* is a Western, and *Nashville* is a musical: Altman uses the setting, but surpasses the limitations and redefines the goal. This is no less than a comedy about selfishness, greed, snobbery, eccentricity, and class exploitation, and Altman is right when he hopes people will see it more than once; after you know the destination, the journey is transformed.

The time is November 1932. Sir William McCordle (Michael Gambon) and Lady Sylvia McCordle (Kristin Scott Thomas) have invited a houseful of guests for a shooting party. They include Sir William's sister Constance, the Countess of Trentham (Maggie Smith), who depends on an allowance he is constantly threatening to withdraw. And Lady Sylvia's sister Louisa (Geraldine Somerville), who like Sylvia had to marry for money (they cut cards to decide who would bag Sir William). And Louisa's husband, Commander Anthony Meredith (Tom Hollander). And their sister Lavinia (Natasha Wightman), married to Raymond, Lord Stockbridge (Charles Dance). And the Hollywood star Ivor Novello (Jeremy Northam). And Morris Weissman (Bob Balaban), a gay Hollywood producer who has brought along his "valet," Henry Denton (Ryan Phillippe).

Below stairs we meet the butler Jennings (Alan Bates), the housekeeper Mrs. Wilson (Helen Mirren), the cook Mrs. Croft (Eileen Atkins), the footman George (Richard E. Grant), and assorted other valets, maids, grooms, and servers. When the American Henry comes to take his place at the servants' table and says his name is Denton, Jennings sternly informs him that servants are addressed below stairs by the names of their masters, and he will be "Mr. Weissman" at their table—where, by the way, servants are seated according to the ranks of their employers.

It has been said that the most enjoyable lifestyle in history was British country house life in the years between the wars. That is true for some of the people upstairs in this movie, less true of most of those downstairs. Altman observes exceptions: Some of the aristocrats, like Lady Constance, are threatened with financial ruin, and others, like Novello, have to sing for their supper; while below stairs, a man like Jennings is obviously supremely happy to head the staff of a great house.

The classic country house murder story begins with perfect order, in which everyone up and down the class ladder fits securely into his or her place—until murder disrupts that order and discloses unexpected connections between the classes. That's what happens here, when one of the characters is poisoned and then stabbed, suggesting there are two murderers to be apprehended by Inspector Thompson (Stephen Fry).

Half of those in the house have a motive for the murder, but the investigation isn't the point, and Altman has fun by letting Thompson and his assistant Constable Dexter (Ron Webster) mirror the relative competence of the upper and lower classes in the house. Thompson, like the aristocrats, sets great store by his title and dress (he puffs a pipe that will be recognized by anyone who knows the name Monsieur Hulot). Dexter, like the servants, just gets on with it, doggedly pointing out clues (footprints, fingerprints on a tea cup, a secret door) that Thompson ignores.

The cast of *Gosford Park* is like a reunion of fine and familiar actors (I have not yet even mentioned Derek Jacobi, Kelly Macdonald, Clive Owen, Emily Watson, and James Wilby). This is like an invitation for scene-stealing, and Maggie Smith effortlessly places first, with brittle comments that cut straight to the quick. When Novello entertains after dinner with one song, and then another, and then another, and shows no sign of stopping, Smith crisply asks, "Do you think he'll be as long as he usually is?" and then stage-whispers, "Don't encourage him."

Altman has a keen eye and ear for snobbery. Note the way that when Mr. Weissman introduces himself, Lady Sylvia asks him to repeat his name, and then she repeats it herself. Just that, but she is subtly underlining his ethnicity. And the way Constance puts Novello in his place by mentioning his most recent film and observing, ostensibly with sympathy, "It must be rather disappointing when something flops like that."

The screenplay by Julian Fellowes, based on an idea by Altman and Balaban, is masterful in introducing all of the characters and gradually making it clear who they are, what they've done, and what it means. Like guests at a big party, we are confused when we first arrive: Who are all these people? By the end, we know. No director has ever been better than Altman at providing the audience with bearings to find its way through a large cast. The sense of place is also palpable in this film; the downstairs and attics were entirely constructed on sound stages by production designer Steven Altman, Altman's son, who also supervised the real country house used for the main floors. Andrew Dunn's photography is sumptuous upstairs, while making the downstairs look creamy and institutional. The editor, Tim Squyres, must have been crucial in keeping the characters in play.

Gosford Park is the kind of generous, sardonic, deeply layered movie that Altman has made his own. As a director he has never been willing to settle for plot; he is much more interested in character and situation, and likes to assemble unusual people in peculiar situations and stir the pot. Here he is, like Prospero, serenely the master of his art.

Gothika ★ ★ ★
R, 95 m., 2003

Halle Berry (Miranda Grey), Robert Downey Jr. (Pete Graham), Penelope Cruz (Chloe Sava), Charles S. Dutton (Dr. Douglas Grey), John Carroll Lynch (Sheriff Ryan), Bernard Hill (Phil Parsons), Dorian Harewood (Teddy Howard), Bronwen Mantel (Irene). Directed by Mathieu Kassovitz and produced by L. Levin, Susan Levin, Joel Silver, and Robert Zemeckis. Screenplay by Sebastian Gutierrez.

The sainted Pauline Kael taught us: The movies are so rarely great art that if we cannot appreciate great trash, we might as well stop going. I don't know if she would have defined *Gothika* as great trash, but in trash as in art there is no accounting for taste, and reader, I cherished this movie in all of its lurid glory.

Yes, the plot is preposterous. No, I do not understand for sure how the murder was plotted. True, the function of the ghost is terrifically murky. Yes, the ghost should have communicated more clearly, instead of in cryptic hints like "Not alone." No, I don't know why a man who entertains himself by torturing victims in a hidden video studio would suddenly desire, in middle age, to add a conventional marriage to his mix. Yes, I agree that a prison psychiatrist accused of murder would hardly be locked up in her own prison among her former patients.

But those are all bothersome details of plausibility and logic, and those are the last two qualities you should seek in *Gothika*. This is a psychothriller with the plausibility of a nightmare—which is to say, it doesn't make sense, but it keeps your attention. The movie is by Mathieu Kassovitz, the thirty-five-year-old French director and actor who in *Crimson Rivers* (2001) made one of the most original and stylish of recent thrillers. He's worked with stars before (Jean Reno and Vincent Cassel in that one), but here, with the Oscar winner Halle Berry at the center of the story, he depends on star power to involve us in the classic Hitchcock formula of the innocent character wrongly accused. Hitch explained that if you cast the right star—Jimmy Stewart or Cary Grant, for example—the audience *knew* they didn't do it, and so you moved on from there.

Berry's character is Miranda Grey, a psychiatrist in a prison straight out of Dickens. She works with fellow shrink Pete Graham (Robert Downey Jr.) and is newly wed to her boss, Dr. Douglas Grey (Charles S. Dutton). I'm thinking, hey, this is refreshing: The beautiful woman is married to an overweight guy for a change. But, no, fat equals fate.

On the obligatory dark and stormy night, Miranda takes a detour and swerves to avoid a ghostly, ghastly girl standing in the middle of the road, who bursts into flames. When she wakes up, she's a prisoner in her own institution and Pete breaks the news to her: She's accused of the brutal murder of her husband. How can this be? She tries to remember, but there's a blank. Chloe (Penelope Cruz), a former patient, now a fellow inmate, explains the rules: Now that Miranda is officially insane, it doesn't matter what she says, since it will be dismissed as her illness talking.

The movie introduces several intriguing characters, including Sheriff Ryan (John Carroll Lynch) and Phil Parsons (Bernard Hill), the prison warden. And it teases us with the possibility that any of them—or Pete, of course—could be behind the monstrous misunderstanding. Miranda tries to reason her way free. "Did we have an affair?" she asks Pete. "Did you want to?" Downey and Berry have a lot of fun in a scene where both characters realize they are heading toward a dangerous possibility.

All is finally explained in an appropriately overwrought series of climaxes, which left me wondering how (1) the ghost of the girl triggered Miranda's blackout, (2) whether the murderer(s) of Dr. Grey could have controlled, evoked, or summoned the ghost, (3) how, assuming he/she/they could not have, they could have predicted or triggered Miranda's blackout and timed the murder to match.

But this sort of wondering is not a bad thing, because it keeps you guessing all through the movie and supplies so many possible answers that the heroine seems surrounded by threats. And after the movie ends the questions don't bother you, because *Gothika* is in a genre with the specific duty of involving, scaring, and absorbing us for its precise running time, after which it is over and we can go home. Some plots have to do with life, and must be pondered. Others are engines to cause emotions in the audience, and if they succeed, they have discharged their duty.

The casting of Halle Berry is useful to the movie, because she evokes a vulnerable quality that triggers our concern. Hitchcock might have wanted to work with her. He didn't cast so much for acting ability as for an innate quality. Berry can act, all right (see *Monster's Ball*) but she can also simply evoke, and here, where she's required to fight her way out of a nightmare, that quality is crucial. She carries us along with her, while logic and plausibility (see above) simply become irrelevant.

Any criticism of this movie that says it doesn't make sense is missing the point. Any review that faults it for going over the top into lurid overkill is criticizing its most entertaining quality. Any critic who mocks the line "I'm not deluded, Pete—I'm possessed!" should be honest enough to admit that, in the moment, he liked it. It takes nerve to make a movie like this in the face of the taste police, but Kassovitz and Berry have the right stuff.

The Grey Automobile ★ ★ ★
NO MPAA RATING, 90 m., 1919 (rereleased 2003)

In the film: Juan Manuel Cabrera (Himself), Gang Members (Themselves). On the stage: Irene Akiko Iida (Japanese Benshi), Enrique Arreola (Spanish Dialogue), Thomasi McDonald (English Dialogue), Ernesto Gomez Santana (Pianist). A live performance with a 1919 Mexican silent film. Film originally directed by Enrique Rosas; interpreted, augmented, and staged by Claudio Valdes-Kuri.

A little-known 1919 Mexican silent film . . . and already your attention is drifting, right? You've been meaning to catch up on the Mexican silent cinema, but somehow the time is never right. Now the time has come. *The Grey Automobile* provides the inspiration for an astonishing theatrical experience.

By the Marx Brothers out of Gilbert and Sullivan and incorporating an early Japanese film tradition, the event devised by director Claudio Valdes-Kuri is slapstick, surrealist, charming, and lighthearted, especially considering that an actual automobile gang is literally executed during the course of the film. A Japanese benshi, a Mexican actor, and an English "interpreter" join the film on the stage, as a pianist supplies the score.

To begin with benshis. During the silent film era, Japanese exhibitors supplied a benshi, or interpreting actor, to stand next to the screen and explain films. The benshis might or might not understand the Western stories and characters any more than the audience did, but that didn't matter, because benshis evolved a performance tradition of their own—not only explaining, but praising, criticizing, sympathizing, and applauding, in parallel with the film. Benshis became so popular that their names were billed above the stars, they had theaters of their own, and silent films survived in Japan for almost a decade after the introduction of sound—because audiences could not do without their beloved benshis.

Claudio Valdes-Kuri, an avant-garde theatrical director from Mexico City, discovered the benshi tradition during a visit to Japan, where benshis still flourish, many of them trained in a line going back to the original artists. Back home in Mexico, he decided to adapt the tradition to *The Grey Automobile*, said to be Mexico's finest silent film, which is about the real-life Grey Automobile Gang.

This film, originally a serial, has existed in many forms over the years, but it is safe to say that no one associated with it could have imagined the ninety-minute version now presented by Valdes-Kuri and his Certain Inhabitants Theater. The film stars Juan Manuel Cabrera, the actual detective who apprehended the gang, playing himself. The real gang members also appear, briefly to be sure, in a startling scene where they are (really) executed. Other scenes are fiction.

It is impossible to say, on the basis of this presentation, whether *The Grey Automobile* is a good film or not—my four-star rating refers to the entire theatrical experience. As the performance opens, Irene Akiko Iida, a Japanese-Mexican actress dressed in a traditional kimono, joins the pianist, Ernesto Gomez Santana, by the side of the screen and provides a traditional benshi commentary in Japanese. Then she is joined by Enrique Arreola, who begins a Spanish commentary. Then they are joined by Thomasi McDonald, who supplies commentary and translation in English.

But that sounds straightforward, and the performance quickly jumps the rails into sublime zaniness. Other languages—German, French, and Russian—creep into the commentary. The film seems to have no subtitles, but suddenly generates them, and then the titles

leave the bottom of the screen and begin to emerge from the mouths of the movie actors in a variety of typefaces; the words coil around the screen and take on lives of their own. Then the actors begin to interpret the on-screen dialogue so freely that at times they have the characters barking at one another. At one point the action stops for a little song-and-dance number, and at another Ms. Iida performs a tap dance.

But this description fails to do justice to the technical virtuosity of the verbal performers. For long stretches, they create perfect lip-synch with the actors on-screen while talking at breakneck speed, never missing a cue or a beat; what they do is so difficult, and done so effortlessly, that it suggests a Zenlike identification with the material. I avoid clichés such as "You've never seen anything like this before," but the fact is, you haven't.

The Grey Zone ★ ★ ★ ★
R, 108 m., 2002

David Arquette (Hoffman), Daniel Benzali (Schlermer), Steve Buscemi (Abramowics), David Chandler (Rosenthal), Allan Corduner (Dr. Nyiszli), Harvey Keitel (Muhsfeldt), Natasha Lyonne (Rosa), Mira Sorvino (Dina), Kamelia Grigorova (Girl). Directed by Tim Blake Nelson and produced by Pamela Koffler, Nelson, and Christine Vachon. Screenplay by Nelson, based on the play by Nelson and the book *Auschwitz: A Doctor's Eyewitness Account* by Miklos Nyiszli.

"How can you know what you'd really do to stay alive, until you're asked? I know now that the answer for most of us is—anything."

So says a member of the Sonderkommandos, a group of Jews at the Auschwitz II–Birkenau death camp, who sent their fellow Jews to die in the gas chambers and then disposed of the ashes afterward. For this duty they were given clean sheets, extra food, cigarettes, and an extra four months of life. With the end of the war obviously drawing closer, four months might mean survival. Would you refuse this opportunity? Would I?

Tim Blake Nelson's *The Grey Zone* considers moral choices within a closed system that is wholly evil. If everyone in the death camp is destined to die, is it the good man's duty to die on schedule, or is it his duty to himself to grasp any straw? Since both choices seem certain to end in death, is it more noble to refuse or cooperate? Is hope itself a form of resistance?

These are questions no truthful person can answer without having been there. The film is inspired by the uprising of October 7, 1944, when members of the 12th Sonderkommando succeeded in blowing up two of the four crematoria at the death camp; because the ovens were never replaced, lives were saved. But other lives were lost as the Nazis used physical and mental torture to try to find out how the prisoners got their hands on gunpowder and weapons.

I have seen a lot of films about the Holocaust, but I have never seen one so immediate, unblinking, and painful in its materials. *The Grey Zone* deals with the daily details of the work gangs—who lied to prisoners, led them into gas chambers, killed them, incinerated their bodies, and disposed of the remains. All of the steps in this process are made perfectly clear in a sequence that begins with one victim accusing his Jewish guard of lying to them all, and ends with the desperate sound of hands banging against the inside of the steel doors. "Cargo," the workers called the bodies they dealt with. "We have a lot of cargo today."

The film has been adapted by Nelson from his play, and is based in part on the book *Auschwitz: A Doctor's Eyewitness Account*, by Miklos Nyiszli, a Jewish doctor who cooperated on experiments with the notorious Dr. Josef Mengele, and is portrayed in the film by Allan Corduner.

Is it a fact of human nature that we are hardwired to act for our own survival? That those able to sacrifice themselves for an ethical ideal are extraordinary exceptions to the rule? Consider a scene late in the film when Rosa and Dina (Natasha Lyonne and Mira Sorvino), two women prisoners who worked in a nearby munitions factory, are tortured to reveal the secret of the gunpowder. When ordinary methods fail, they are lined up in front of their fellow prisoners. The interrogator repeats his questions, and every time they do not answer, his arm comes down and another prisoner is shot through the head. What is the right thing to do? Betray the secrets and those who collaborated? Or allow still more prisoners to be murdered? And if all will die eventually anyway, how does that affect the choice? Is it better to die now, with a bullet to the brain, than after more weeks of dread? Or is any life at all worth having?

The film stars David Arquette, Daniel Benzali, Steve Buscemi, and David Chandler as the leaders of the Sonderkommandos, and Harvey Keitel as Muhsfeldt, an alcoholic Nazi officer in command of their unit. Although these faces are familiar, the actors disappear into their roles. The Jewish workforce continues its grim task of exterminating fellow Jews, while working on its secret plans for a revolt.

Then an extraordinary thing happens. In a gas chamber, a young girl (Kamelia Grigorova) is found still alive. Arquette rescues her from a truck before she can be taken to be burned, and now the Jews are faced with a subset of their larger dilemma: Is this one life worth saving if the girl jeopardizes the entire revolt? Perhaps not, but in a world where there seem to be no choices, she presents one, and even Dr. Nyiszli, so beloved by Mengele, helps to save the girl's life. It is as if this single life symbolizes all the others.

In a sense, the murders committed by the Nazis were not as evil as the twisted thought that went into them and the mental anguish they caused for the victims. Death occurs thoughtlessly in nature every day. But death with sadistic forethought, death with a scenario forcing the victims into impossible choices, and into the knowledge that those choices are inescapable, is mercilessly evil. The Arquette character talks of one victim: "I knew him. We were neighbors. In twenty minutes his whole family and all of its future was gone from this Earth." That victim's knowledge of his loss was worse than death.

The Grey Zone is pitiless, bleak, and despairing. There cannot be a happy ending, except that the war eventually ended. That is no consolation for its victims. It is a film about making choices that seem to make no difference, about attempting to act with honor in a closed system where honor lies dead. One can think: If nobody else knows, at least I will know. Yes, but then you will be dead, and then who will know? And what did it get you? On the other hand, to live with the knowledge that you behaved shamefully is another kind of death—

the death of the human need to regard ourselves with favor. *The Grey Zone* refers to a world where everyone is covered with the grey ash of the dead, and it has been like that for so long they do not even notice anymore.

Grind ★ ★
PG-13, 100 m., 2003

Mike Vogel (Eric Rivers), Vince Vieluf (Matt Jensen), Adam Brody (Dustin Knight), Joey Kern (Sweet Lou), Jennifer Morrison (Jamie). Directed by Casey La Scala and produced by La Scala, Bill Gerber, and Hunt Lowry. Screenplay by Ralph Sall.

Grind has a tone like *The Endless Summer,* that dreamy surfing movie in which a bunch of buddies devote their lives to hanging out together and searching for the perfect wave. This time it's skateboards, not surfboards, and the goal is not the perfect wave but sponsorship for their team and a chance to tour with the champion they admire. But the ethic is about the same: Skateboarding is forever, and things like college and girls only ruin an endlessly savored adolescence.

The buddies live in that southern California which is a state of mind, where life centers on the skateboard store and famous skateboarders are mobbed the way rock stars are in another universe. They dream of turning professional, but can't get the pros to look at their demo tapes, and can't win the sponsorship necessary to get into the big tournaments. So they hit the road, stalking the tour of the famous champion Jimmy Wilson, hoping they can get his attention, or somebody's attention; they have T-shirts printed advertising a fake company that they claim is their sponsor.

That's the plot, more or less. The guys are only vaguely differentiated; the lead is Eric (Mike Vogel), but the one who stands out is Sweet Lou (Joey Kern), who fancies himself a ladies' man and sidles up to a potential conquest with a soft-voiced come-on, as if to notice him is to surrender to him. Two women do actually enter their orbit: one who seems too good to be true, and is, and another who likes them and gets them into a tournament.

There is also an interlude with Matt's (Vince Vieluf) parents. They ran away from home to join the circus, and so they should have no complaints about his skateboarding tour. Matt and the guys visit them at a clown college (or Klown Kollege, I suppose), where Matt is embarrassed to find his folks in putty noses, but where the possibility of becoming skateboarding clowns briefly beckons.

That leaves the skateboarding itself. I am no expert on the sport, but I have seen the 2001 documentary *Dogtown and Z-Boys*, which chronicles the birth of skateboarding in Santa Monica, circa 1975. Based on the performances in that movie, the guys in *Grind*, if they were golfers, might shoot par on a few holes, but never for a whole game. The skateboarding footage is underwhelming compared to *Dogtown*. They seem to be repeating the same limited moves over and over again; I was astonished by some of the things I saw in *Dogtown*, but the moves here made me wonder what the crowd was applauding.

The movie is nevertheless sweet, in its meandering way. It has no meanness in it, no cynicism, no desire to be anything other than what it is, an evocation of the fun of living your life as a skateboarder. While there are few things more poignant than an ancient skateboarder (as *Dogtown and Z-Boys* also suggests), these guys are still in their endless summer and don't yet understand that.

Neither this movie nor *Dogtown*, by the way, answers the question I have every time I see high-level skateboarding: In order to learn to fly free, high into the air, and go through body twists, and land again on your board, you presumably must fail a lot of times before you succeed. It looks to me as if that would involve a drop of ten or twenty feet to a hard surface. How many skateboarders are killed? Maimed? Paralyzed? What about that first guy who thought about flying free beyond the lip of his skating surface—how did he think he would get down again?

H

Half Past Dead ½★
PG-13, 99 m., 2002

Steven Seagal (Sascha Petrosevitch), Morris Chestnut (Donny/49er One), Ja Rule (Nick Frazier), Matt Battaglia (49er Three), Richard Bremmer (Sonny Ekvall), Art Camacho (49er Eleven), Steven J. Cannell (Hubbard), Claudia Christian (E. Z. Williams). Directed by Don Michael Paul and produced by Elie Samaha, Steven Seagal, and Andrew Stevens. Screenplay by Paul.

Half Past Dead is like an alarm that goes off while nobody is in the room. It does its job and stops, and nobody cares. It goes through the motions of an action thriller, but there is a deadness at its center, a feeling that no one connected with it loved what they were doing. There are moments, to be sure, when Ja Rule and Morris Chestnut seem to hear the music, but they're dancing by themselves.

The plot is preposterous, but that's acceptable with a thriller. The action is preposterous, too: Various characters leap from high places while firing guns, and the movie doesn't think to show us how, or if, they land. A room is filled with tear gas, but what exactly happens then? The movie takes the form of a buddy movie, but is stopped in its tracks because its hero, played by Steven Seagal, doesn't have a buddy gene in his body. (I know, he takes seven bullets for his partner Nick, but I don't think he planned it: "I'll take seven bullets for Nick!")

Seagal's great contribution to the movie is to look very serious, even menacing, in close-ups carefully framed to hide his double chin. I do not object to the fact that he's put on weight. Look who's talking. I object to the fact that he thinks he can conceal it from us with knee-length coats and tricky camera angles. I would rather see a movie about a pudgy karate fighter than a movie about a guy you never get a good look at.

The film has little dialogue and much action. It places its trust so firmly in action that it opens with a scene where the characters have one of those urban chase scenes where the car barely misses trailer trucks, squeals through 180-degree turns, etc., *and they're not even being chased*. It's kind of a warm-up, like a musician practicing the scales.

Do not read further if you think the plot may have the slightest importance to the movie. Seagal plays an undercover FBI guy who has teamed up with the crook Nick Frazier (Ja Rule), who vouched for him with the master criminal Sonny Ekvall (Richard Bremmer), who runs, if I have this correct, "the biggest crime syndicate between Eastern Europe and the Pacific Rim." He doesn't say whether the syndicate extends easterly or westerly between those demarcations, which would affect the rim he has in mind. Maybe easterly, since Seagal's character is named Sascha Petrosevitch. "You're Russian, right?" he asks Seagal, who agrees. Seagal's answer to this question is the only time in the entire movie he has a Russian accent.

Nick gets thrown into New Alcatraz. Sascha Petrosevitch gets thrown in, too. Later, after his cover is blown, he explains to Nick that the FBI thought if he did time with Nick, it would help him get inside the criminal organization. The sentence is five years. What a guy.

Then, let's see, the prison contains an old man who is about to go to the chair with the secret of $200 million in gold bars. Bad guys want his secret and cooperate with an insider (Morris Chestnut) to break into the prison, taking hostage a female U.S. Supreme Court justice who is on a tour of death row (she's one of those liberals). They want to escape with the old guy and get the gold. Among their demands: a fully fueled jet plane to an "undisclosed location." My advice: At least disclose the location to the pilot.

Nick and Sascha Petrosevitch team up to risk their lives in a nonstop series of shoot-outs, explosions, martial arts fights, and shoulder-launched rocket battles in order to save the Supreme Court justice. We know why Sascha Petrosevitch is doing this. But why is Nick? Apparently he is another example of that mysterious subset of the law of gravitation that attracts the black actor with second billing in an action movie to the side of the hero.

At the end of *Half Past Dead* there is a scene where Nick looks significantly at Sascha Petrosevitch and nods and smiles a little, as if to say, you some kinda white guy. Of course, Sascha Petrosevitch has just promised to spring him from New Alcatraz, which can easily inspire a nod and a little smile.

Meanwhile, I started wondering about that $200 million in gold. At the end of the movie, we see a chest being winched to the surface and some gold bars spilling out. If gold sells at, say, $321 per troy ounce, then $20 million in gold bars would represent 623,052 troy ounces, or 42,720 pounds, and would not fit in that chest. You would expect the FBI guys would know this. Maybe not these FBI guys.

Note: I imagine the flywheels at the MPAA congratulating each other on a good day's work as they rated Half Past Dead *PG-13, after giving the antigun movie* Bowling for Columbine *an R.*

Happy Times ★ ★
PG, 106 m., 2002

Dong Jie (Wu Ying), Zhao Benshan (Zhao), Dong Lihua (Stepmother). Directed by Zhang Yimou and produced by Zhang Weiping , Zhou Ping, and Zhao Yu. Screenplay by Gui Zi.

One of the challenges of foreign movies is to determine how they would play on their native soil. Here, for example, is *Happy Times*, from the sometimes great Chinese director Zhang Yimou. It is about a group of unemployed men who build a fake room in an abandoned factory, move a blind girl into it, tell her it is in a hotel, and become her clients for daily massages, paying her with blank pieces of paper they hope she will mistake for money.

On the basis of that description, you will assume that this movie is cruel and depraved. But turn now to the keywords under "Tones" in the movie's listing at allmovie.com, and you will find: "sweet, reflective, light, humorous, easygoing, compassionate, affectionate." *Happy Times* is a comedy, and has been compared to Chaplin's *City Lights*, which was also about a jobless man trying to help a blind girl.

Consider first how this movie would play if it were a Hollywood production. Imagine a good-hearted everyman (Steve Martin, let's say) with a group of cronies (we'll cast Harvey Keitel, Jeff Daniels, Bill Paxton, Steve Buscemi, and Danny DeVito). They build a fake room and install a young, naive, blind girl (Christina

Ricci), and go for daily massages, etc. Is there any way your imagination can stretch widely enough for this scenario to become a compassionate and affectionate comedy?

I say not. There must be something cultural at work here. When American critics praise the movie (and most of them have), they are making some kind of concession to its Chinese origins. A story that would be unfilmable by Hollywood becomes, in Chinese hands, "often uproariously funny" (*New York* magazine), "subtle and even humorous" (*Film Journal International*), and "wise, gentle and sad" (*New York Times*). The movie's message, according to *FJI*, is that "the underpinning of paternalistic values which once protected the old and ensured a future for the young is now a pretense."

Uh-huh. I can even halfway understand those reviews, because the movie sets up like a comedy, plays like a comedy, and barks like a comedy, so it must be a comedy. It opens with a retired man named Zhao (Zhao Benshan) proposing marriage to a jolly divorcée (Dong Lihua), who meets his high standards for chubbiness. He needs money to bring about the match, however, and so teams up with a buddy to turn an abandoned bus into a "love hotel," which lonely couples can rent by the hour.

He tells his intended he is a hotel owner, but then the bus is hauled away. He meets Wu Ying (Dong Jie), his fiancée's stepdaughter, who is blind and has been abandoned by her father, the divorcée's most recent husband. Acting the big shot, Zhao tells them he will give the girl work in his hotel, and then enlists his buddies in building the fake room, paying the fake money for the massages, etc.

This is all done good-heartedly, you see. The cronies are warm and caring men, who, when they are not receiving massages, sit on the rafters to look down into the roofless room; they nod approvingly at "Little Wu's" happiness, and the movie argues that they practice their deception to make her happy.

That assumes their definition of happiness for a blind young teenage girl is to let her sit in a "hotel room" waiting for one of her newfound friends to come in for a massage. This would not be my definition of happiness, or perhaps yours, although it might fit for the hero of John Fowles's novel *The Collector*. To me it sounds like a cruel deception carried out by men of marginal intelligence, reactionary ideas about women, and a total lack of empathy.

There is a poignant ending that I found particularly inexplicable. Please do not read further unless you are prepared for spoilers. It turns out that Little Wu was aware of the deception all along (we see her using a stick to prove to herself that the room has no ceiling). With the acute hearing and memory of the blind, she also no doubt noticed that the "street noises" outside her "room" were a tape recording, played over and over. She went along with the deception, she tells Zhao, because she was so incredibly touched and moved by the care of her new friends, and the lengths they went to, trying to make her happy. This is all revealed in a tape recording she leaves behind, and then we see her, all by herself, setting out alone on the road of life, while sentimental music plays.

The movie seems to come from a simpler, more innocent culture. There is never a hint of sex in it, for one thing. The massages are completely chaste, the men like them that way, and it never occurs to the girl that it is creepy that she is giving massages to a bunch of anonymous men in a fake hotel room. Apparently the men never, ever, look down into the room while Little Wu undresses. No, the movie is sweet, reflective, light, humorous, easygoing, compassionate, affectionate.

If I did not find it that way, if I found it creepy beyond all reason, that is no doubt because I have been hopelessly corrupted by the decadent society I inhabit. Or, are there moviegoers in China who also find *Happy Times* odd in the extreme? I searched the Chinese Movie Database and the sites of the *People's Daily*, the *South China Morning Post*, and English-language papers from Shanghai and Beijing, without finding any mention of the film at all. The Web is worldwide and perhaps I will hear from a Chinese reader or two. Please slug your message *Happy Times* so it will stand out from all the offers I get for discount Viagra.

The Hard Word ★ ★ ½

R, 102 m., 2003

Guy Pearce (Dale), Rachel Griffiths (Carol), Robert Taylor (Frank), Joel Edgerton (Shane), Damien Richardson (Mal), Rhondda Findleton (Jane), Kate Atkinson (Pamela). Directed by Scott Roberts and produced by Al Clark. Screenplay by Roberts.

The Twentyman brothers—Dale, Shane, and Mal—are stickup men with the motto "Nobody gets hurt." Despite their benevolence, they end up in prison, where Mal practices the butcher's trade and Dale works as a librarian. Then their lawyer, Frank, springs them for one last brilliant job. The job is much complicated by the fact that Dale's wife has become Frank's mistress.

The wife-slash-mistress is Carol, played by Rachel Griffiths with her intriguing ability to combine the qualities of a tomboy and a sex kitten. She's married to Dale Twentyman (Guy Pearce), insists she loves him, yet is having an affair with the crooked lawyer Frank (Robert Taylor). Which one does she really love? Sometimes she seems to be smiling to herself with the evil contentment of a woman whose bread is buttered on both sides.

It is good to hear Pearce (*L.A. Confidential, Memento*) and Griffiths (a star of HBO's *Six Feet Under*) speaking in their native Australian accents in *The Hard Word*, a movie that exists halfway between Tarantinoland and those old black-and-white British crime comedies. The characters seem to have devised themselves as living works of art, as if personal style and being "colorful" is the real point of being a criminal, and the money is only a bothersome technicality.

Consider Shane Twentyman (Joel Edgerton), the brother with a big-time problem with anger. A big guy who looks a little like young Albert Finney, he's assigned a prison counselor named Jane (Rhondda Findleton), and they fall in love with startling speed. Mal Twentyman (Damien Richardson) also has a magnetic attraction for women, which comes as a surprise to him, since he is usually much abashed around them. After the gang steals a getaway car, its owner and driver, Pamela (Kate Atkinson), comes down with a critical case of Stockholm Syndrome and falls in love with Mal.

These scenes have a charm that works all the better considering that they are surrounded by a good deal of startling violence. Frank's big plan involves the brothers stealing the bookies' money after the running of the Melbourne Cup, but an outsider, brought in to keep an eye on them, opens fire and there is blood and carnage as the brothers flee on foot.

The foot chase has a quality missing in a lot of modern action movies, and that is the sensation of physical effort. William Friedken achieved it, too, in the underrated *The Hunted*. The robbers run through malls and down stairs and across pedestrian overpasses and are hauling the money and panting and sweating, and we realize belatedly that one of the things wrong with Spiderman was that he never seemed to go to any effort.

Griffiths is at the center of both of the movie's key relationships, with her husband the crook and her lover the lawyer. Robert Taylor's lawyer is one of those devious creatures from 1940s movies who seem more interested in taking the woman away from a man than in actually having her. If he were a fisherman he would throw her back in. Does Griffiths's character know this? There is the suggestion that she does and is in love with Dale the whole time, but she is so good at looking a guy straight in the eye and telling him she loves him that her actions are eventually going to have to speak louder than her words.

The movie has room for quirky little side trips, as when the loot is hidden in a peculiar place, and for classic *film noir* moments, as when several key characters gather for a showdown that is not quite what some of them had in mind, but they get to engage in a lot of high-style crime dialogue before they find that out.

And then there's more. Too much more. *The Hard Word* feels like it should be more or less over after the Melbourne Cup heist, but it's barely getting started, as writer-director Scott Roberts supplies twists and double crosses and startling developments and surprise revelations and unexpected appearances and disappearances, until finally we give up. This movie could obviously go on fooling us forever, but we are good sports only up to a point, and then our attention drifts. Shame, since there's so much good stuff in it, like how effortlessly Rachel Griffiths keeps two tough guys completely at her mercy.

Harrison's Flowers ★ ★ ½

R, 122 m., 2002

Andie MacDowell (Sarah Lloyd), David Strathairn (Harrison Lloyd), Elias Koteas (Yeager Pollack), Adrien Brody (Kyle Morris), Brendan Gleeson (Marc Stevenson), Alun Armstrong (Samuel Bruceck). Directed by Elie Chouraqui and produced by Chouraqui and Albert J. Cohen. Screenplay by Chouraqui, Michael Katims, Isabel Ellsen, and Didier LePecheur.

I am pleased we have women in our fighting forces, since they are so much better at war than men. *Harrison's Flowers* is about an American wife who journeys to the Balkans to rescue her husband from a hotbed of genocide. In *Charlotte Gray*, a British woman parachuted behind German lines in France to rescue her boyfriend. I can just about believe that Charlotte Gray could deceive the Germans with her perfect French, but that Sarah Lloyd could emerge alive from the Balkans hell is unlikely; much of the movie's fascination is with the way Croatians allow this woman and her new friends to wander through the killing zones intact.

I doubt, for that matter, that a Los Angeles fireman could fly to Colombia in *Collateral Damage* and single-handedly outfight guerrillas and drug empires, but that is an Arnold Schwarzenegger picture and not supposed to be realistic. *Harrison's Flowers* is not based on fact but plays like one of those movies that is, and the scenes of carnage are so well staged and convincing that they make the movie's story even harder to believe. Strong performances also work to win us over, wear us down, and persuade us to accept this movie as plausible. Who we gonna believe, the screenplay or our lyin' eyes?

Andie MacDowell stars, in another reminder of her range and skill, in what is essentially an action role. She plays Sarah Lloyd, mother of two, wife of the celebrated war photographer Harrison (David Strathairn). In an obligatory scene that triggers an uh-oh reflex among experienced filmgoers, he tells his boss he wants to retire and is persuaded to take One Last Job. Off he flies to the early days of the war in the Balkans to investigate "ethnic cleansing," which was I think a term not then quite yet in use. He is reported dead, but Sarah knows he's still alive: "Something would have happened inside if he were dead."

She watches TV obsessively, hoping for a

glimpse of Harrison among POWs, and takes up chain-smoking, which is the movie symbol for grief-stricken obsession and is dropped as soon as it's no longer needed. Because of a hang-up call in the middle of the night and other signs, she decides to fly to the Balkans to find Harrison. A more reasonable spouse might reason that since (a) her husband is reliably reported dead, and (b) she has no combat zone skills, (c) she should stay home with her kids so they will not become orphans, but no.

The war scenes have undeniable power. Violence springs from nowhere during routine moments and kills supporting characters without warning. Ordinary streets are transformed instantly into warscapes. Sarah joins up with three of Harrison's photographer friends who accompany her quest: pill-popping, wisecracking Morris (Adrien Brody), shambling, likable Stevenson (Brendan Gleeson), and bitter, existentialist Yeager Pollack (Elias Koteas). (If any of them are killed, can you predict from the character descriptions which order it will happen in?) They commandeer cars and jeeps, and essentially make a tour of the war zone, while bullets whiz past their ears and unspeakable horrors take place on every side.

They are protected, allegedly, by white flags and large letters proclaiming "TV" on the sides of their cars. But there is a scene where troops are methodically carrying out an ethnic massacre, and the photographers wander in full view at the other end of the street: Does their status as journalists render them invisible? At one point, Sarah wears fatigues, which (I learn from an article by a war correspondent) is the last thing she should do. Civilian clothes mark her as a noncombatant; camouflage marks her as a target even before her gender is determined.

Whether Sarah finds her husband I will leave you to discover. Whether, when she is in a burning building, the flames shoot up everywhere except precisely where she needs to be, you already know. There is a way in which a movie like this works no matter what. Andie MacDowell is a sympathetic actress who finds plausible ways to occupy this implausible role. Brendan Gleeson is a comforting force of nature, and Adrien Brody's work is a tour de force, reminding me of James Woods in *Sal-*

vador in the way he depends on attitude and cockiness to talk his way through touchy situations. Watch the way he walks them all through a roadblock. I don't believe it can be done, but I believe he did it.

As for the war itself, the movie exhibits the usual indifference to the issues involved. Although it was written and directed by Elie Chouraqui, a Frenchman, it is comfortably xenophobic. Most Americans have never understood the differences among Croats, Serbs, and Bosnians, and this film is no help. (I am among the guilty, actually mislabeling the bad guys in my review of *Behind Enemy Lines,* another film set in the region.) All we need to know is: The Americans are tourists in a foreign war involving ruthless partisans with fierce mustaches. Why are those people killing one another? Why is the war being fought? With those crazy foreigners, who knows? The New Jersey housewife wants to return her man to the arms of his family and the peace of his greenhouse. The movie's buried message is that domestic order must be restored. Just like in Shakespeare.

Harry Potter and the Chamber of Secrets ★ ★ ★ ★
PG, 161 m., 2002

Daniel Radcliffe (Harry Potter), (Rupert Grint (Ron Weasley), Emma Watson (Hermione Granger), Jason Isaacs (Lucius Malfoy), Alan Rickman (Professor Snape), Maggie Smith (Professor McGonagall), Robbie Coltrane (Hagrid the Giant), David Bradley (Mr. Argus Filch), Kenneth Branagh (Gilderoy Lockhart), Miriam Margolyes (Professor Sprout), John Cleese (Nearly Headless Nick), Richard Harris (Professor Dumbledore), Tom Felton (Draco Malfoy), Bonnie Wright (Ginny Weasley), Harry Melling (Dudley Dursley). Directed by Chris Columbus and produced by David Heyman. Screenplay by Steve Kloves, based on the novel by J. K. Rowling.

The first movie was the setup, and this one is the payoff. *Harry Potter and the Chamber of Secrets* leaves all of the explanations of wizardry behind and plunges quickly into an adventure that's darker and scarier than anything in the first Harry Potter movie. It's also richer: The second in a planned series of seven Potter films is brimming with invention and new ideas, and its Hogwarts School seems to expand and deepen before our very eyes into a world large enough to conceal unguessable secrets.

What's developing here, it's clear, is one of the most important franchises in movie history, a series of films that consolidate all of the advances in computer-aided animation, linked to the extraordinary creative work of J. K. Rowling, who has created a mythological world as grand as *Star Wars,* but filled with more wit and humanity. Although the young wizard Harry Potter is nominally the hero, the film remembers the golden age of moviemaking, when vivid supporting characters crowded the canvas. The story is about personalities, personal histories, and eccentricity, not about a superstar superman crushing the narrative with his egotistical weight.

In the new movie, Harry (Daniel Radcliffe, a little taller and deeper-voiced) returns with his friends Ron Weasley (Rupert Grint) and Hermione Granger (Emma Watson, in the early stages of babehood). They sometimes seem to stand alone amid the alarming mysteries of Hogwarts, where even the teachers, even the august headmaster Albus Dumbledore (Richard Harris), even the learned professors Snape (Alan Rickman) and McGonagall (Maggie Smith), even the stalwart Hagrid the Giant (Robbie Coltrane) seem mystified and a little frightened by the school's dread secrets.

Is there indeed a Chamber of Secrets hidden somewhere in the vast pile of Hogwarts? Can it only be opened by a descendent of Salazar Slytherin, the more sinister of the school's cofounders? Does it contain a monster? Has the monster already escaped, and is it responsible for paralyzing some of the students, whose petrified bodies are found in the corridors, and whose bodies are carried to the infirmary still frozen in a moment of time? Do the answers to these questions originate in events many years ago, when even the ancient Dumbledore was (marginally) younger? And does a diary by a former student named Tom Marvolo Riddle—a book with nothing written in it, but whose pages answer questions in a ghostly handwriting—provide the clues that

Harry and his friends need? (Answer to all of the above: probably.)

This puzzle could be solved in a drab and routine movie with characters wandering down old stone corridors, but one of the pleasures of Chris Columbus's direction of *Harry Potter and the Chamber of Secrets* is how visually alive it is. This is a movie that answers any objection to computer animation with glorious or creepy sights that blend convincingly with the action. Hogwarts itself seems to have grown since the first movie, from a largish sort of country house into a thing of spires and turrets, vast rooms and endlessly convoluted passageways, lecture halls and science labs, with as much hidden below the ground as is visible above it. Even the Quidditch game is held in a larger stadium (maybe rich alumni were generous?). There are times, indeed, when the scope of Hogwarts seems to approach that of Gormenghast, the limitless edifice in the trilogy by Mervyn Peake that was perhaps one of Rawling's inspirations.

The production designer is Stuart Craig, returning from *Harry Potter and the Chamber of Secrets.* He has created (there is no other way to put it) a world here, a fully realized world with all the details crowded in, so that even the corners of the screen are intriguing. This is one of the rare recent movies you could happily watch with the sound turned off, just for the joy of his sets, the costumes by Judianna Makovsky and Lindy Hemming, and the visual effects (the Quidditch match seems even more three-dimensional, the characters swooping across the vast field, as Harry finds himself seriously threatened by the odious Malfoy).

There are three new characters this time, one delightful, one conceited, one malevolent. Professor Sprout (Miriam Margolyes) is on the biology faculty and teaches a class on the peculiar properties of the mandrake plant, made all the more amusing by students of John Donne who are familiar with the additional symbolism of the mandrake only hinted at in class. The more you know about mandrakes, the funnier Sprout's class is.

She is the delightful addition. The conceited new faculty member, deliciously cast, is Gilderoy Lockhart (Kenneth Branagh), author of the autobiography *Magical Me,* who thinks of himself as a consummate magician but whose spell to heal Harry's broken arm has unfortunate results. And then there is Lucius Malfoy (Jason Isaacs), father of the supercilious Draco, who skulks about as if he should be hated just on general principles.

These characters and plot elements draw together in late action sequences of genuine power, which may be too intense for younger viewers. There is a most alarming confrontation with spiders and a scary late duel with a dragon, and these are handled not as jolly family movie episodes, but with the excitement of a mainstream thriller. While I am usually in despair when a movie abandons its plot for a third act given over entirely to action, I have no problem with the way *Harry Potter and the Chamber of Secrets* ends, because it has been pointing toward this ending, hinting about it, preparing us for it, all the way through. What a glorious movie.

Harry Potter and the Prisoner of Azkaban ★ ★ ★ ½
PG, 136 m., 2004

Daniel Radcliffe (Harry Potter), Rupert Grint (Ron Weasley), Emma Watson (Hermione Granger), Gary Oldman (Sirius Black), David Thewlis (Professor Lupin), Michael Gambon (Albus Dumbledore), Alan Rickman (Professor Severus Snape), Maggie Smith (Professor Minerva McGonagall), Robbie Coltrane (Rubeus Hagrid), Tom Felton (Draco Malfoy), Emma Thompson (Professor Sybil Trelawney), Julie Walters (Mrs. Weasley), Timothy Spall (Peter Pettigrew), Julie Christie (Madame Rosmerta), Richard Griffiths (Uncle Vernon), Pam Ferris (Aunt Marge). Directed by Alfonso Cuaron and produced by Chris Columbus, David Heyman, and Mark Radcliffe. Screenplay by Steven Kloves, based on the novel by J. K. Rowling.

I've just returned from London, where Daniel Radcliffe created a stir by speculating that his famous character, Harry Potter, might have to die at the end of the series. Certainly that seems like more of a possibility in *Harry Potter and the Prisoner of Azkaban*, the third Potter film, than it did in the first two. It's not that Harry, Ron, and Hermione are faced with any really gruesome dangers (there's nothing here on the

order of the spider that wrapped up Frodo for his dinner in the *Ring* trilogy), but that Harry's world has grown a little darker and more menacing.

The film centers on the escape of the sinister Sirius Black (Gary Oldman) from Azkaban Prison; Sirius was convicted in Voldemort's plot to murder Harry's parents, and now it's suspected he must finish the job by killing Harry. As Harry returns for his third year at Hogwarts, grim wraiths named Dementors are stationed at every entrance to the school to ward off Sirius, but the Dementors are hardly reassuring, with their trick of sucking away the soul essence of their victims.

Harry, too, has developed an edge. We first met him as the poor adopted relative of a suburban family who mistreated him mercilessly; this time, Harry is no longer the long-suffering victim but zaps an unpleasant dinner guest with a magical revenge that would be truly cruel if it were not, well, truly funny. Harry is no longer someone you can mess with.

Harry and his friends Ron and Hermione (Radcliffe, Rupert Grint, and Emma Watson) return to a Hogwarts that boasts, as it does every school year, peculiar new faculty members (this school policy promises years of employment for British character actors). New this year are Professor Lupin (David Thewlis), who tutors Harry in a tricky incantation said to provide protection against the dark magic of the Dementors; and Professor Sybil Trelawney (Emma Thompson), whose tea readings don't pull punches—not when she gazes into the bottom of Harry's cup and sees death in the leaves.

To distract Harry from his presumed fate, his friend the gamekeeper Hagrid (Robbie Coltrane) introduces the three friends to a wondrous new beast named Buck Beak, which is a hippogriff, half-bird, half-horse, wholly misunderstood. When a werewolf begins to prowl the grounds, a battle between the two creatures is inevitable. Who could the werewolf be by day? Does no one at Hogwarts find the Latin root of Lupus suggestive?

Among the movie's many special effects, I especially admired the gnarled tree that figures in the third act. The tree is introduced with a wink to the viewer who knows it is CGI: It shakes melting snow from its branches, and some of the snow seems to plop on the camera lens. Beneath this tree is a warren that shelters unimaginable terrors for Ron, when he is dragged into it as part of a longer climactic sequence that plays tricks with time. First the three heroes witness one version of events, and then, after reversing the flow of time, they try to alter them. The ingenuity of the time-tricks worked for me, but may puzzle some of the film's youngest viewers.

Chris Columbus, the director of the first two Potter films, remains as producer but replaces himself as director with Alfonso Cuaron, director of the wonderful *A Little Princess* (1995), as well as the brilliant *Y Tu Mama También.* Cuaron continues the process, already under way in *Harry Potter and the Chamber of Secrets*, of darkening the palate. The world of the first film, with its postal owls and Quidditch matches, seems innocent now, and although there is indeed a Quidditch match in this film, it's played in a storm that seems to have blown in from *The Day After Tomorrow.* I like what Cuaron does with the look of the picture, but found the plotting a little murky; just when we should be focusing on exactly who Sirius Black is and why he killed Harry's parents, there is the sudden appearance of a more interesting, if less important character, Peter Pettigrew (Timothy Spall), a real rat who undergoes a change of purpose.

The actors playing Harry, Ron, and Hermione have outgrown their childhoods in this movie, and by the next film will have to be dealt with as teenagers, or replaced by younger actors. If they continue to grow up, I'm afraid the series may begin to tilt toward less whimsical forms of special-effects violence, but on the other hand I like Radcliffe, Grint, and Watson, and especially the way Watson's Hermione has of shouldering herself into the center of scenes and taking charge. Although the series is named for Harry, he's often an onlooker, and it's Hermione who delivers a long-delayed uppercut to the jaw of Draco Malfoy.

Unlike American movies such as *Spy Kids* where the young actors dominate most of their scenes, the Harry Potter movies weave the three heroes into a rich tapestry of character performances. Here I savored David Thewlis as a teacher too clever by half, Emma Thompson as

the embodiment of daffy enthusiasm, Alan Rickman as the meticulously snippy Snape, Robbie Coltrane as the increasingly lovable Hagrid, and Michael Gambon, stepping into the robes and beard of the late Richard Harris as Dumbledore.

Is *Harry Potter and the Prisoner of Azkaban* as good as the first two films? Not quite. It doesn't have that sense of joyously leaping through a clockwork plot, and it needs to explain more than it should. But the world of Harry Potter remains delightful, amusing, and sophisticated; the challenge in the films ahead will be to protect its fragile innocence and not descend into the world of conventional teen thrillers.　☞

Hart's War ★ ★ ★
R, 125 m., 2002

Bruce Willis (Colonel William McNamara), Colin Farrell (Lieutenant Tommy Hart), Terrence Howard (Lieutenant Lincoln Scott), Vicellous Shannon (Lieutenant Lamar Archer), Cole Hauser (Staff Sergeant Bedford), Marcel Iures (Commandant Visser), Linus Roache (Captain Peter Ross). Directed by Gregory Hoblit and produced by David Foster, Hoblit, David Ladd, and Arnold Rifkin. Screenplay by Billy Ray and Terry George, based on the novel by John Katzenbach.

"Your colonel is throwing you to the wolves," the Nazi commandant of a POW camp tells the young American lieutenant. It looks that way. A white racist American has been murdered, a black officer is charged with the crime, and Lieutenant Tommy Hart (Colin Farrell) has been assigned to defend him in a court-martial. The Nazi has permitted the trial as a gesture (he is a Yale man, not uncivilized, likes jazz). But Colonel William McNamara (Bruce Willis), the senior officer among the American prisoners, doesn't seem much interested in justice.

Because the movie is told mostly from Hart's point of view, we lack crucial pieces of information available to McNamara, and as these are parceled out toward the end of the film, the meaning of the events shifts. But one underlying truth does not change: Racism during World War II in America and in the army was a reality that undercut duty, patriotism, and truth.

As the movie opens, Hart has been captured, interrogated, and sent to Stalag VI in Belgium. He is a senator's son, destined for a desk job. At the POW camp he is cross-examined by Willis, who senses he's lying about the interrogation, and assigns him to a barracks otherwise filled with enlisted men. It's a problem of space, Willis explains, and a few days later the officers' barracks is again too crowded to accommodate two black air corps pilots who have been shot down: Lieutenant Lincoln Scott (Terrence Howard) and Lieutenant Lamar Archer (Vicellous Shannon).

Bunking with black men does not sit well with Vic Bedford (Cole Hauser), a staff sergeant who calls the pilots "flying bellhops." Soon a tent spike, which could be used as a weapon, is found under Archer's mattress, and he's summarily shot by the Nazis without a trial. Since it is pretty clear that Bedford planted the spike, no one is very surprised not long after when the man is found dead with Scott standing over his body.

A clean-cut case of murder, right? Not according to Hart, who believes this is another setup and demands that a trial be held. Colonel McNamara is not enthusiastic about the idea, but the Nazi commandant is, and soon a court-martial is under way with Hart (who has no legal experience) as the defense attorney.

All of this is absorbing, if of course manipulative, but what makes it more intriguing is the sense that something else is going on underneath the action—that McNamara's motives may be more complicated than we know. One hitch is that both the dead man and his alleged killer left the barracks by a secret route at night, a route that cannot be revealed without jeopardizing the other American prisoners. So Hart agrees to a cover story about how his man left the barracks, and then, in a scene built on devastating logic, has to stand mute while the phony cover story is used against his client.

Colin Farrell, the young star of Joel Schumacher's powerful but hardly released *Tigerland* (2000), is a twenty-five-year-old Dublin native obviously destined for stardom. He

does a good job with the conflicted, anguished Lieutenant Hart, and Bruce Willis brings instinctive authority to the colonel. Marcel Iures, a Romanian actor, is sharp-edged and intriguing as the Nazi commandant; when he gets condolences on the death of his son in battle, he muses, "I killed my share of English and French soldiers in the first war. They had fathers too." There is a shade of the Erich von Stroheim character in *Grand Illusion* here, the suggestion of a German whose military ideas do not depend on that little twerp Hitler.

But for all the interest in these performances, *Hart's War* would be just another military courtroom drama if it were not for the work by Terrence Howard as Lincoln Scott, the man on trial. He expects no justice from an American court-martial. He enlisted in the air corps, trained at Tuskegee, wanted to serve his nation, and has seen racism and contempt from whites in uniform. He makes one statement that is chilling because we know it was true: German POWs held in the Deep South were allowed to attend movies and eat in restaurants that were off limits to blacks, even those in uniform. "If I wanted to kill a cracker," Scott says, "I could have stayed at home in Macon."

The movie worked for me right up to the final scene, and then it caved in. Bowing to ancient and outdated convention, director Gregory Hoblit and writers Billy Ray and Terry George put the plot through an awkward U-turn so that Willis can end up as a hero. How and why he does so is ingenious, yes, but the ending gives the impression it is a solution when it is only a remedy. And I would have liked it better if the far-off bugle had been playing under a black character at the end and not a white one. It's as if the movie forgot its own anger.

Harvard Man ★ ★ ★
R, 100 m., 2002

Adrian Grenier (Alan Jensen), Sarah Michelle Gellar (Cindy Bandolini), Joey Lauren Adams (Chesney Cort), Eric Stoltz (Teddy Carter), Rebecca Gayheart (Kelly Morgan), Gianni Russo (Andrew Bandolini), Ray Allen (Marcus Blake),

Michael Aparo (Russell). Directed by James Toback and produced by Daniel Bigel and Mike Mailer. Screenplay by Toback.

James Toback is a gambler and an intellectual—a Harvard graduate who at times in his life has been deeply involved in betting. His first screenplay, for Karel Reisz's masterpiece *The Gambler* (1974), was about a university literature teacher with a compulsion not merely to gamble, but to place himself at risk. "I play in order to lose," his character says. There is a point at which he contemplates the excellent possibility of having his kneecaps shattered. The only reason Toback himself has never been kneecapped, I suspect, is because he likes to talk even more than he likes to gamble.

Harvard Man stars Adrian Grenier as Alan Jensen, a member of the Harvard basketball squad. He is having an affair with his philosophy professor (Joey Lauren Adams), but also has a more conventional girlfriend, Cindy Bandolini (Sarah Michelle Gellar). Her father is widely believed to be a Mafia boss, although Alan brushes aside all such suggestions with the information that he is a "businessman and investor."

Toback is not above using melodrama as a shortcut, and does so here: Alan's parents lose their house in a Kansas tornado, and he needs to raise $100,000, fast, to help them. He turns to Cindy and suggests that perhaps, ah, if the stories about her father are true, he might be in a position to throw the Dartmouth game and make a lot of money for everybody, including his homeless parents. And now it gets interesting, because Cindy, as played by Gellar, is not your standard-issue Mafia princess, but a sharp and shrewd operator who is no pushover and doesn't like unpleasant surprises. What makes the movie work is that the premise, which sounds like a comedy, is treated with the seriousness of life and death. You do not disappoint a Mafia bookmaker and laugh it off.

Some of my favorite scenes involve Joey Lauren Adams, as the professor. You may remember her as the third wheel in *Chasing Amy*. She has a face like your sister's best friend and a voice like Lauren Bacall crossed with an all-night waitress. She would not be your first idea for an actress to play a philosophy professor; you might go with Meryl Streep, say, or someone smart and nervous, like Jennifer Jason Leigh. She seems more like the philosophy professor's secretary. But that's before she starts to talk. She and Alan have several heart-to-hearts about love, gambling, and drugs, and she deals not only in practical advice but in the meaning of it all.

And that's how the whole movie proceeds. "The unexamined life is not worth living," Socrates reminds us, and in a Toback film the characters examine their lives almost more assiduously than they live them. Alan realizes he's in very deep, with possible criminal characters on the one hand and possible Mafia reprisals on the other. It all grows even more complicated when two of the Mafia's gambling advisers (Eric Stoltz and Rebecca Gayheart) turn out to be more, or less, than they seem.

Alan does what any Toback hero might do when boxed into such a corner, and drops acid. This is not a good idea, and the movie's visuals, distorting faces and summoning up scenes that may or may not be happening, create a nightmare for him. How can one man juggle two women, possible expulsion, Mafia baseball bats, and the meaning of life while on acid? This is the kind of question only a Toback film thinks to ask, let alone answer.

The Haunted Mansion ★ ★ ½
PG, 99 m., 2003

Eddie Murphy (Jim Evers), Marsha Thomason (Sara Evers), Nathaniel Parker (Master Gracey), Jennifer Tilly (Madame Leota), Terence Stamp (Ramsley), Wallace Shawn (Ezra), Dina Waters (Emma), Marc John Jefferies (Michael), Aree Davis (Megan). Directed by Rob Minkoff and produced by Andrew Gunn and Don Hahn. Screenplay by David Berenbaum.

The surprising thing about *The Haunted Mansion* isn't that it's based on a Disney theme park ride, but that it has ambition. It wants to be more than a movie version of the ride. I expected an inane series of nonstop action sequences, but what I got was a fairly intriguing story and an actual plot that is actually resolved. That doesn't make the movie good enough to recommend, but it makes it better than the ads suggest.

The movie stars Eddie Murphy as Jim Evers, workaholic real estate agent, who is headed for a weekend vacation with his family when they get sidetracked by the chance to put a vast old mansion on the market. His wife, Sara (Marsha Thomason), is his business partner, but complains, as all movie wives always complain, that her husband is spending too much time at work. Their kids are Michael and Megan (Marc John Jefferies and Aree Davis).

Evers (or more accurately his wife, whose photo appears on their fliers) is invited to visit the Gracey Mansion, isolated behind a forbidding iron gate and surrounded by a jungle of sinister vegetation. It's a triumph of art direction, inspired by the Disney World attraction and by every haunted house ever crept through by Bela Lugosi, Lon Chaney, Christopher Lee, Peter Cushing, Abbott, Costello, et al. Doors bulge, curtains sway, and there's a scenic graveyard behind the house, complete with four marble busts that perform as a barbershop quartet.

The visitors are greeted by the butler, Ramsley (Terence Stamp), gaunt, cadaverous, with a voice that coils up from unimaginable inner caverns. Also on staff are servants Ezra (Wallace Shawn, looking his most homuncular) and Emma (Dina Waters, simpering over). On the premises, but not exactly in residence, is Madame Leota (Jennifer Tilly), whose disembodied head floats in a crystal ball and offers timely if disturbing advice.

The lord of the manor is Master Gracey (Nathaniel Parker), who seems obsessed with Sara Evers. Flashbacks explain why. In antebellum New Orleans, Gracey was in love with a young woman who looked exactly like Sara, and when they could not marry, they both killed themselves. Which means Gracey is a ghost, of course, but leaves unanswered the question of why he could not marry the ghost of his original lover and stop haunting respectable married real estate agents.

The most intriguing element of the movie is the way it does and doesn't deal with the buried racial theme. We learn that the sinister Ramsley sabotaged his master's romance because if he married, the family would be destroyed. Presumably that would be because an interracial

romance was dangerous in old New Orleans, but the movie never says so and indeed never refers to the races of any of its characters. That is either (a) refreshing and admirable, or (b) puzzling, since the whole plot is motivated by race.

The story, in any event, gives the characters a lot to deal with, which means we are not relegated to a movie full of banging doors, swinging chandeliers, and other ghostly effects. There are a lot of those, of course, especially as the kids make their own way around the gloomy pile, but there is a certain poignancy about the central dilemma, and the Gracey character reflects it well, eventually answering one of the questions posed above, although I will not say which one.

The movie doesn't quite work, maybe because the underlying theme is an uneasy fit with the silly surface. Murphy is not given much to do; he's the straight man, in a story involving his wife and ghosts. If anyone steals the movie, it's Stamp, who must have been studying Hammer horror films for years, and puts the ham back into Hammer. *The Haunted Mansion* won't much entertain older family members, but it might be fun for kids, and seems headed for a long run on home video.

Head of State ★ ★ ★
PG-13, 95 m., 2003

Chris Rock (Mays Gilliam), Bernie Mac (Mitch Gilliam), Dylan Baker (Martin Geller), Nick Searcy (Brian Lewis), Lynn Whitfield (Debra Lassiter), Robin Givens (Kim), Tamala Jones (Lisa Clark), James Rebhorn (Senator Bill Arnot), Stephanie March (Nikki). Directed by Chris Rock and produced by Ali LeRoi, Rock, and Michael Rotenberg. Screenplay by Rock and LeRoi.

Head of State is an imperfect movie, but not a boring one, and not lacking in intelligence. What it does wrong is hard to miss, but what it does right is hard to find: It makes an angry and fairly timely comic attack on an electoral system where candidates don't say what they really think, but simply repeat safe centrist banalities.

In *Head of State,* the presidential and vice presidential candidates of an unnamed party, obviously the Democrats, are killed when their campaign planes crash into each other less than two months before the election. Seeking a replacement candidate, the party settles on Mays Gilliam, an obscure Washington, D.C., alderman (Chris Rock), who has saved a woman and her cat from a burning building. He seems to have no chance of victory, but of course party boss Senator Bill Arnot (James Rebhorn) doesn't want him to win—he wants to exploit him as a token black candidate who will lose, but win painless points for the party.

If Mays can't win, then he has nothing to lose, and his strategy is obvious: Instead of trying to please everyone, he should say the unsayable. We've seen this strategy before from movie candidates, notably Kevin Kline in *Dave*, Warren Beatty in *Bulworth*, and Eddie Murphy in *Distinguished Gentleman*, and the notion runs back to Frank Capra. What Chris Rock brings to it is brashness—zingers that hurt. "What kind of a drug policy," he wants to know, "makes crack cheaper than asthma medicine?"

The movie, directed and cowritten by Rock, is wickedly cynical about the American electoral system. It shows Mays being supplied with a prostitute named Nikki (Stephanie March) because, campaign manager Martin Geller (Dylan Baker) explains, "We got tired of getting caught up in sex scandals, so we commissioned our own team of superwhores." And it gives him an opponent, the incumbent vice president (Nick Searcy), whose claim to fame is he's Sharon Stone's cousin, and whose motto has a certain resonance: "God bless America—and no place else."

Mays bumbles through the first weeks of his campaign, following the instructions of his profoundly conventional campaign advisers, Geller and Debra Lassiter (Lynn Whitfield), until his brother, a Chicago bail bondsman named Mitch (Bernie Mac), asks him when he's going to start speaking his mind. When he does, the first thing he says is that he wants Mitch as his running mate.

This is one of the areas that doesn't work. Bernie Mac could be a funny veep candidate, but not as a bondsman whose peculiar personal quirk is to hit people as hard as he can as a sign of friendship. The character should have been redefined, and a scene where Mays and Mitch batter each other should have been edited out; it works only as an awkward puzzlement for the audience.

Another element that doesn't work is the character of Kim (Robin Givens), who begins the movie as Mays's fiancée, is dumped, and then turns into a crazy stalker who follows him everywhere, overacting on a distressingly shrill note until she exits in a particularly nasty way. This character could have been dumped, especially since Mays meets a cute caterer named Lisa (Tamala Jones), who looks like first lady material.

Chris Rock is a smart, fast-talking comedian with an edge; I keep wondering when the Academy will figure out he could host the Oscars. Here he plays his usual persona, more or less, in a movie where some of the edges are rough and others are serrated. We keep getting these movie fantasies where political candidates say what they think, are not afraid to offend, cut through the crap, and take stands. Must be wish fulfillment.

The Heart of Me ★ ★ ★
R, 96 m., 2003

Helena Bonham Carter (Dinah), Olivia Williams (Madeleine), Paul Bettany (Rickie), Eleanor Bron (Mrs. Burkett), Luke Newberry (Anthony), Alison Reid (Bridie), Tom Ward (Jack), Gillian Hanna (Betty), Andrew Havill (Charles). Directed by Thaddeus O'Sullivan and produced by Martin Pope. Screenplay by Lucinda Coxon, based on the novel *The Echoing Grove* by Rosamond Lehmann.

The lovers in *The Heart of Me* have a line of poetry by William Blake as their touchstone: "And throughout all eternity, I forgive you and you forgive me." This implies much to forgive, and the movie involves a decade of suffering, punctuated by occasional bliss, and inspired by their misfortune in falling in love with one another. For theirs is not an ordinary adultery, but one complicated by the inconvenience that he is married to her sister.

The film is a soapy melodrama set from about 1936 to 1946 and done with style—Jerry Springer crossed with *Masterpiece Theater*. Helena Bonham Carter stars as Dinah, a raffish bohemian who is the despair of her sister, Madeleine (Olivia Williams), and their mother (Eleanor Bron). Madeleine at last contrives to get Dinah engaged to a presentable man, but when the intended nuptials are announced at a family dinner, we notice that Madeleine's husband, Rickie, winces. We notice, and so does Dinah, who sends him a barely perceptible shrug. Later that night Rickie (Paul Bettany) opens her bedroom door and announces, "You are not going through with this. Break it off."

She agrees. His statement clarifies what has been vibrating in the air between them, a romantic love of the abandoned, hopeless variety that is most irresistible when surrounded by the codes of a society that places great value on appearances. The family maintains "the smartest house in London," Rickie has one of those jobs in the city that provides a large income for tasks hard to define, and while there is no love between him and his wife, it is simply not done to cheat with your sister-in-law.

The movie is based on a 1953 novel by Rosamond Lehmann, and while it is hard to say it was inspired by her affair with C. Day Lewis, they had an affair, and she wrote a novel about an affair, and there you are. No doubt the facts are different, but the feelings are similar. Helena Bonham Carter does suggest a woman with something of Lehmann's flair for romantic drama; her Dinah is the kind of person it is easy to criticize until you look into her heart and see with what fierce integrity she opposes the strictures of society. It is really Dinah, and not Rickie, who is taking the big chances, because no matter what sins Rickie commits he will always be required to remain on display as Madeleine's husband, while the punishment for Dinah must be exile. "I love you!" Madeleine cries at a crucial moment, and Rickie's reply is dry and exact: "Madeleine, I think if that were true, you would have said it sooner."

Madeleine is not a bad person either, really; she is the aggrieved party, after all, and has good reason to be cross with her sister and her husband. But it never occurs to her to cut loose from Ricky; this man who has betrayed her remains necessary for her to keep up appearances, and she and her mother tell appalling lies to both Dinah and Rickie in trying to force the relationship to an end. The great sadness in the movie is the waste of love, which is a rare commodity and must be consumed in season.

An intriguing supporting character in the movie is Bridie (Alison Reid), who serves as Dinah's confidante and companion in exile, and who, like many privileged insiders, cannot resist sharing what she knows with just those people who least should know it. As Dinah waits sadly in lovers' nests and French hideaways, it is Bridie who harbors resentments.

There are major developments in the story that I will not reveal, but, oh! how sad these people are by the end. And how pathetic. There is a certain nobility in the way Rickie, a wrecked man, displays what is left of himself to Madeleine and bitterly tells her, "This is what you fought so hard to hold onto." If they only had attended to the entire poem by Blake ("My spectre around me night and day") they would not have taken such comfort from its promise of forgiveness.

The movie has won only a mixed reception. Many of the complaints have to do with the fact that the characters are wealthy and upper-class and speak English elegantly. The names of Merchant and Ivory are used like clubs to beat the film. This is the same kind of thinking that led Jack Warner to tell his producers, "Don't give me any more pictures where they write with feathers." The movie is *about* the punishment of being trapped in a system where appearances are more important than reality. After she breaks her engagement at the beginning of the movie, Dinah has lunch with Madeleine, who says, "You've put us all in a very awkward position." Dinah said, "I thought that preferable to marrying a man I didn't love." Madeleine, on the other hand, believes it is better to marry a man you do not love than be put in an awkward position. And just as well, as that turns out to be the story of her marriage.

Heaven ★ ★ ★

R, 96 m., 2002

Cate Blanchett (Philippa), Giovanni Ribisi (Filippo), Remo Girone (The Father), Stefania Rocca (Regina), Alessandro Sperduti (Ariel), Mattia Sbragia (Major Pini), Stefano Santospago (Mr. Vendice). Directed by Tom Tykwer and produced by Stefan Arndt, Frédérique Dumas-Zajdela, William Horberg, and Maria Köpf. Screenplay by Krzysztof Kieslowski and Krzysztof Piesiewicz.

There is a moment early in *Heaven* when the

character played by Cate Blanchett is told something she did not expect to hear. This news piles grief upon unbearable grief, and she cries out in pain. She is a good woman who is prepared to sacrifice her life against evil, but through a great misfortune she has done evil herself.

She plays Philippa, a teacher of English in Turin, Italy. She has seen drugs kill her husband and some of her students. Her complaints to the police have been ignored. She knows the man behind the Turin drug traffic, and one day she plants a bomb in his office. A cleaning lady removes it with the trash, and it explodes in an elevator, killing the cleaner, a man, and his two children. Four innocent dead.

Philippa has lost her husband and her students, and stands ready to lose her freedom. But the deaths of these four crush her. We are reminded of *Running on Empty*, the 1988 Sidney Lumet film about antiwar radicals in America who did not know there would be someone in the building they chose to blow up. As Philippa sits in police headquarters, undergoing a cross-examination, unaware that one of the men in the room is himself connected to the drug trade, she makes a conquest.

His name is Filippo (Giovanni Ribisi). He is a rookie cop, the son of a veteran officer. When Philippa insists on testifying in her native tongue, Filippo offers to act as her translator. This is after she heard the horrifying news, and passed out, and grasped his hand as she came to, and he fell in love with her.

After the ten films of *The Decalogue* and the great trilogy *Blue*, *White*, and *Red*, the Polish director Krzysztof Kieslowski and his writing partner Krzysztof Piesiewicz began writing a new trilogy: *Heaven*, *Purgatory*, and *Hell*. Kieslowski died in 1996 before the project could be filmed. Many good screenplays have died with their authors, but occasionally a director will step forward to rescue a colleague's work, as Steven Spielberg did with Kubrick's *A.I.* and now as Tom Tykwer has done with *Heaven*.

This is, and isn't, the sort of project Twyker is identified with. It is more thoughtful, proceeds more deliberately, than the mercurial haste of *Run Lola Run* and *The Princess and the Warrior*. At the same time, it has a belief in fateful meetings that occur as a side effect of violence or chance, as both of those films do.

And it contains the same sort of defiant romanticism, in which a courageous woman tries to alter her fate by sheer willpower.

Philippa and Filippo have almost identical names for a reason, and later when they shave their heads and dress alike, it is because they share a common lifeline. It is not a case of merger so much as of Filippo being assumed into Philippa. She is older, stronger, braver, and he invests the capital of his life in her account. He betrays his uniform to do whatever he can to help her escape.

After she agrees to his brilliant plan, she tells him: "Do you know why I said I agree? I don't want to escape punishment. I want to kill him." Him—the man behind the drugs. Whether she gets her wish is not the point. What she focuses on is her original plan; if she can finally carry it out, she will have made amends, however inadequately, for the innocents who died.

Kieslowski was fascinated by moral paradoxes, by good leading to evil and back again. In *The Decalogue*, a child's brilliance at the computer leads to a drowning. A woman wants to know if her husband will die, because if he will not, she will have her lover's baby aborted. A wife breaks it off with her lover—but her husband tarnishes her decision by spying on them. To do good is sometimes to cause evil. We can make plans, but we can't count on the consequences.

The ending of *Heaven* is disappointing. It becomes just what it should not be, the story of an escape. I wonder if Kieslowski and Piesiewicz ended their version this way, in a fable of innocence regained. The tough ending would have had Philippa and Filippo paying for their crimes. It would not have been an unhappy ending for them; they are fully prepared to take the consequences, and that is what's most admirable about them.

Still, many lesser films—almost all commercial films these days, in fact—contrive happy endings. This one is poetic in its sadness, and the Cate Blanchett performance confirms her power once again. She never goes for an effect here, never protects herself, just plays the character straight ahead as a woman forced by grief and rage into a rash action, and then living with the consequences. We require theology to get to the bottom of the story: It is wrong to commit an immoral act in order to bring about a good outcome. No matter how beneficial the result, it is still a sin. This is a good movie that could have been great if it had ended in a form of penance.

Hellboy ★ ★ ★ ½
PG-13, 132 m., 2004

Ron Perlman (Hellboy) John Hurt (Professor Bruttenholm), Selma Blair (Liz Sherman), Jeffrey Tambor (Tom Manning), Karel Roden (Grigori Rasputin), Rupert Evans (John Myers), Corey Johnson (Agent Clay), Doug Jones (Abe Sapien), Bridget Hodson (Ilsa), Ladislav Beran (Kroenen). Directed by Guillermo del Toro and produced by Lawrence Gordon, Lloyd Levin, and Mike Richardson. Screenplay by Guillermo del Toro, based on the comic by Mike Mignola.

Hellboy is one of those rare movies that's not only based on a comic book, but feels like a comic book. It's vibrating with energy, and you can sense the zeal and joy in its making. Of course it's constructed of nonstop special effects, bizarre makeup, and a preposterous story line, but it carries that baggage lightly; unlike some CGI movies that lumber from one set piece to another, this one skips lightheartedly through the action. And in Ron Perlman it has found an actor who is not just playing a superhero, but enjoying it; although he no doubt had to endure hours in makeup every day, he chomps his cigar, twitches his tail, and battles his demons with something approaching glee. You can see an actor in the process of making an impossible character really work.

The movie, based on comics by Mike Mignola and directed by the Mexican-born horror master Guillermo del Toro (*Cronos, Blade II*), opens with a scene involving Nazis, those most durable of comic book villains. In a desperate scheme late in World War II, they open a portal to the dark side and summon forth the Seven Gods of Chaos—or almost do, before they are thwarted by U.S. soldiers and Professor Bruttenholm (John Hurt), who is President Roosevelt's personal psychic adviser. Nothing slips through the portal but a little red baby with horns and a tail; he spits and hisses at the professor, who calms him with a Baby Ruth bar, cradles him in his arms, and raises him to

become mankind's chief warrior against the forces of hell.

Meanwhile, the psychic practitioner Grigori Rasputin (Karel Roden), who is working for the Nazis, is sucked through a portal and disappears. Yes, he's *that* Rasputin. We flash-forward to the present. The professor, now in his eighties, is told he will die soon. Two of his old enemies have inexplicably not grown older, however: a Nazi named Ilsa (Bridget Hodson) and a weirdo named Kroenen (Ladislav Beran), who is addicted to surgical modifications on his body. In an icy pass in Mondavia they perform ceremonies to bring Rasputin back from the other side, and they're ready to rumble.

Cut to a secret FBI headquarters where Hellboy lives with the professor and an aquatic creature named Abe Sapien (Doug Jones)—a fishboy who got his name because he was born the day Abraham Lincoln was assassinated. The professor is showing the ropes to young FBI agent Myers (Rupert Evans) when the Nazis attack a museum and liberate a creature imprisoned inside an ancient statue. This creature, a writhing, repellant, oozing mass of tentacles and teeth, reproduces by dividing, and will soon conquer the Earth, unless Hellboy can come to the rescue.

Which he does, of course, in action sequences that seem storyboarded straight off the pages of a comic book. Hellboy gets banged up a lot, but is somehow able to pick himself up off the mat and repair himself with a little self-applied chiropractic; a crunch of his spine, a pop of his shoulders, and he's back in action. Abe the fishboy, who wears a breathing apparatus out of the water, is more of a dreamer than a fighter, with a personality that makes him a distant relative of Jar Jar Binks.

Hellboy's life is a lonely one. When you are seven feet tall and bright red, with a tail, you don't exactly fit in, even though HB tries to make himself look more normal by sawing his horns down to stumps, which he sands every morning. He is in love with another paranormal: Liz Sherman (Selma Blair), a pyrokineticist who feels guilty because she starts fires when she gets excited. There is a terrific scene where Hellboy kisses her and she bursts into flames, and we realize they were made for each other, because Hellboy, of course, is fireproof.

The FBI, which is occasionally accused of not sharing its information with other agencies, keeps Hellboy as its own deep secret; that droll actor Jeffrey Tambor plays the FBI chief, a bureaucrat who is just not cut out for battling the hounds of hell. He has some funny setup scenes, and indeed the movie is best when it's establishing all of these characters and before it descends to its apocalyptic battles.

Hellboy battles the monsters in subway tunnels and subterranean caverns, as Liz, Myers, and Abe the fishboy tag along. I know, of course, that one must accept the action in a movie like this on faith, but there was one transition I was utterly unable to follow. Liz has saved them all from the monsters by filling a cave with fire, which shrivels them and their eggs into crispy s'mores, and then—well, the movie cuts directly to another cave in which they are held captive by the evil Nazis, and Hellboy is immobilized in gigantic custom-made stocks that have an extra-large hole for his oversized left hand. How did that happen?

Never mind. Doesn't matter. Despite his sheltered upbringing, Hellboy has somehow obtained the tough-talking personality of a Brooklyn stevedore, but he has a tender side, not only for Liz but for cats and kittens. He has one scene with the FBI director that reminded me of the moment when Frankenstein enjoys a cigar with the blind man. He always lights his stogies with a lighter, and Tambor explains that cigars must always be ignited with a wooden match. Good to know when Liz isn't around.   ☞

Herod's Law ★ ★
R, 120 m., 2003

Damián Alcázar (Juan Vargas), Leticia Huijara (Gloria), Pedro Armendáriz Jr. (López), Delia Casanova (Rosa), Juan Carlos Colombo (Ramírez), Alex Cox (Gringo), Guillermo Gil (Padre), Eduardo López Rojas (Doctor), Salvador Sánchez (Pek), Isele Vega (Doña Lupe). Directed and produced by Luis Estrada. Screenplay by Estrada, Jaime Sampietro, Fernando León, and Vicente Leñero.

Juan Vargas is a simple man with unswerving loyalty to the party, and that is why he is chosen to be the mayor of San Pedro. There is an election coming up, three mayors have been killed in the last five years, and López, the regional party leader, hopes Vargas can keep the lid on and not cause much trouble. As Juan (Damián Alcázar) and his wife, Gloria (Leticia Huijara), drive to San Pedro in the dusty Packard supplied by the party, they dream of his assignment to bring "Modernity, Peace, and Progress" to the little town, little suspecting how little it is.

"Where is San Pedro?" Juan asks a man. "This is it," the man replies. "I am Pek, your secretary." Vargas and his wife look around in dismay at the pathetic hamlet he is to lead. Pek (Salvador Sánchez) will be invaluable, because he speaks the Indian language, and few of the residents speak Spanish. Vargas quickly meets other important local figures, including the doctor (Eduardo López Rojas), the priest (Guillermo Gil), and Doña Lupe (Isele Vega), the madam of the local brothel.

All of the trouble in San Pedro comes from the brothel, the doctor bitterly tells Vargas. It is responsible for disease, corruption, murder. The padre is more forgiving: "San Pedro lacks many things, and Doña Lupe performs an important social function." The priest advises Vargas to accept Doña Lupe's bribes so that village life will continue as before. This is a mercenary padre: In the confessional, he charges one peso per sin and pointedly informs Vargas he would like a car: "A Ford ... or perhaps a Packard, like yours."

Herod's Law uses Vargas and his backwater town to form a parable about political corruption in Mexico in 1949—and before and since, we have no doubt. It is a savage attack on the Institutional Revolutionary Party (PRI), which ruled Mexico from the days of revolution until the recent rise of President Vicente Fox and his National Action Party. In the figure of Juan Vargas, it sees a humble working-class man with high ideals, who caves in to the temptations of high office, even in so low a town, and is soon demanding bribes, making himself mayor for life, and paying free visits to Doña Lupe's girls. He justifies his actions with a motto learned from his party leader, who quotes Herod's Law, which is (somewhat reworded), "Either you screw them or you get screwed."

His wife, who is not blind to Juan's visits to the brothel, finds consolation from a visiting

American (Alex Cox). The gringo's function in the parable is not difficult to decipher: He repairs Juan's car, demands an exorbitant payment, moves into Juan's house, and has sex with his wife. I think (I am pretty sure, actually) this is intended to suggest the helpful role of American advisers in Mexico.

The film is bold and passionate, but not subtle, and that is its downfall. Luis Estrada, the writer and director, uses his characters so clearly as symbols that he neglects to give them the complexity of human beings. Juan Vargas begins as a simple and honest idealist and then converts to corruption so instantly at the sight of money that we have little idea of who he really was before or after. His escalation into a madman and murderer is laying it on a little thick; the recent Mexican film *The Crime of Father Amaro* made a similar critique of Mexican society and the church without such heavy-handed, almost comic, melodrama.

There are a couple of scenes that suggest a more moderate approach Estrada might have taken. One involves a dinner in the midst of all the chaos, at which the principal characters sit down to discuss their nation. The American is asked his opinion, and refers to Mexico as a "dictatorship," which makes the others, except the doctor, laugh. The doctor observes, "In Mexico if there were true democracy, the president would be a priest."

Note: Isele Vega, who plays Doña Lupe, starred as a prostitute in Sam Peckinpah's Bring Me the Head of Alfredo Garcia. *It must be a nod to that movie that this one has a character named Alfredo Garcia.*

Hidalgo ★ ★ ★
PG-13, 135 m., 2004

Viggo Mortensen (Frank Hopkins), Omar Sharif (Sheikh Riyadh), Zuleikha Robinson (Jazira), Adam Alexi-Malle (Aziz), Louise Lombard (Lady Anne Davenport), Said Taghmaoui (Prince Bin al Reeh). Directed by Joe Johnston and produced by Casey Silver. Screenplay by John Fusco.

Hidalgo is the kind of movie Hollywood has almost become too jaundiced to make anymore. Bold, exuberant, and swashbuckling, it has the purity and simplicity of something Douglas Fairbanks or Errol Flynn might have bounded

through. Modern movies that attempt the adventure genre usually feel they have to tart it up, so in *Pirates of the Caribbean*, which once would have been played straight, we get animated cadavers and Johnny Depp channeling Keith Richards. Well, okay, *Pirates* was fun, but *Hidalgo* is a throwback to a more innocent time when heroes and their horses risked everything just because life was so damned boring in the slow lane.

The movie is a completely fictionalized version of the life of a real cowboy named Frank Hopkins; a moment's research on the Web will suggest that an accurate portrait of his life would have been much briefer and very depressing. But never mind. Let us assume, as the movie does, that Hopkins was a half-Indian cowboy who bonded with an uncommonly talented mustang pony named Hidalgo. And that after he grew drunk and morose while laboring in Buffalo Bill's Wild West Show, he risked everything to travel to the Saudi Desert and enter the Ocean of Fire, a legendary race across the sands with a $10,000 prize.

Hopkins is played by Viggo Mortensen, fresh from *The Lord of the Rings,* as a bronzed, lean loner who (if I guess right) enters the race as much for the sake of his horse as for the prize. He respects and loves Hidalgo, especially after the scornful Arab riders scoff at the notion that a mixed-breed mustang could challenge their desert stallions with their ancient lineages. Of course, Hopkins is a half-breed, too, and so we're dealing with issues here.

The race is so grueling that many men and horses die, and some are murdered by their rivals. Hopkins functions in this world like a duck in a shooting gallery. When he is discovered in the tent of the beautiful princess Jazira (Zuleikha Robinson), he is brought before her father, powerful Sheikh Riyadh (Omar Sharif), and threatened with the loss of that possession he would least like to part with, even more than his horse. But then, in the kind of development that sophisticates will deplore but true children of the movies will treasure, his manhood is spared when the sheikh discovers that Hopkins knew—actually worked with, and spoke with, and could tell stories about!—that greatest of all men, that paragon of the sheikh's favorite pulp magazines, Buffalo Bill!

Hopkins is quite a babe magnet for an ex-drunk cowpoke who bunks with his horse. Not only does the lovely Jazira hope he will rescue her from capture by her father's lustful rival, but there's a rich woman named Lady Anne Davenport (Louise Lombard), who throws herself at him in an attempt to influence the outcome of the race, or maybe just because her husband is fifty years older. Hopkins passes up so many of these opportunities that we're forced to speculate that his life might have gone on much as before if the sheikh had carried out his plans for the cowboy's netherlands.

This is a movie that has concealed pits in the sand with sharpened stakes at the bottom; exotic sprawling villas made with corridors and staircases and balconies and rooftops where countless swordsmen can leap forward to their doom; sandstorms that can be outrun by a horse like Hidalgo; tents as large and elaborately furnished as a Malcolm Forbes birthday party; blazing close-ups of the pitiless sun; poisoned oases; tantalizing mirages; parched lips; six-shooters, whips, daggers, and . . . no, I don't think there were any asps. Some will complain that Hidalgo magically arrives on the scene whenever Hopkins whistles, but Hidalgo knows that if he could whistle, Hopkins would be right there for him, too.

I have done my duty. Not a moviegoer alive will be able to attend *Hidalgo* and claim that I have not painted an accurate portrait of the film. Whether you like movies like this, only you can say. But if you do not have some secret place in your soul that still responds even a little to brave cowboys, beautiful princesses, and noble horses, then you are way too grown up and need to cut back on cable news.

High Crimes ★ ★ ★
PG-13, 115 m., 2002

Ashley Judd (Claire Kubik), Morgan Freeman (Charles Grimes), James Caviezel (Tom Kubik), Adam Scott (Lieutenant Terrence Embry), Amanda Peet (Jackie Grimaldi), Michael Gaston (Major Waldron), Tom Bower (FBI Agent Mullins), Jesse Beaton (Ramona Phillips). Directed by Carl Franklin and produced by Arnon Milchan, Janet Yang, and Jesse B'Franklin. Screenplay by Yuri Zeltser and Cary Bickley, based on the novel by Joseph Finder.

Although I believe Ashley Judd could thrive in more challenging roles, and offer *Normal Life* (1996) as an example, her career seems to tilt toward thrillers, with the occasional comedy. She often plays a strong, smart woman who is in more danger than she realizes. Although her characters are eventually screaming as they flee brutal killers in the long tradition of Women in Danger movies, the setups show her as competent, resourceful, independent.

High Crimes is a movie like that. Judd plays Claire Kubik, a high-profile defense attorney for a big firm. When her ex-soldier husband (Jim Caviezel) is arrested by the FBI, charged with murder, and arraigned before a military tribunal, she defiantly says she will defend him herself. And because she doesn't know her way around military justice, she enlists a lawyer named Grimes (Morgan Freeman) as co-counsel. Grimes is that dependable character, a drunk who is on the wagon but may (i.e., will) fall off under stress.

This is the second movie Judd and Freeman have made together (after *Kiss the Girls* in 1997). They're both good at projecting a kind of southern intelligence that knows its way around the frailties of human nature. Although Freeman refers to himself as the "wild card" in the movie, actually that role belongs to Caviezel, whose very identity is called into question by the military charges. "Is your name Tom Kubik?" Claire asks her husband at one point. She no longer knows the answer.

The plot involves a massacre in a Latin American village and a subsequent cover-up. Did Claire's husband gun down innocent civilians, or was he framed by a scary marine vet and his straight-arrow superior? Does the military want justice or a cover-up? We are not given much reason to trust military tribunals—evidence the screenplay was written before 9/11—and the Freeman character intones the familiar refrain, "Military justice is to justice as military music is to music."

And yet . . . well, maybe there's more to the story. I wouldn't dream of revealing crucial details. I do like the way director Carl Franklin and writers Yuri Zeltser and Cary Bickley, working from Joseph Finder's novel, play both ends against the middle, so that the audience has abundant evidence to believe two completely conflicting theories of what actually happened.

In the very season of the DVD release of *Rashomon*, which is the template for stories with more than one convincing explanation, here's another example of how Kurosawa's masterpiece continues to inspire movie plots.

High Crimes works to keep us involved and make us care. Although Freeman's character may indeed start drinking again, it won't be for reasons we can anticipate (of course, like all heroic movie drunks, he retains the exquisite timing to sober up on demand). The unfolding of various versions of the long-ago massacre is handled by Franklin in flashbacks that show how one camera angle can refute what another angle seems to prove. And if we feel, toward the end, a little whiplashed by the plot manipulations, well, that's what the movie promises and that's what the movie delivers.

As for Miss Judd. From the first time I saw her, in *Ruby in Paradise* (1993), I thought she had a unique sympathy with the camera, an ability that cannot be learned but only exercised. In the years since then, she has often been better than her material—or do her advisers choose mainstream commercial roles for her as the safest course? When she strays out of genre, as she did in *Smoke, Heat, Normal Life*, and *Simon Birch*, she shows how good she is. Of course, she's good in *High Crimes*, too, and involves us more than the material really deserves. But this is the kind of movie any studio executive would green light without a moment's hesitation—always an ominous sign.

Holes ★ ★ ★ ½
PG, 111 m., 2003

Sigourney Weaver (The Warden), Jon Voight (Mr. Sir), Patricia Arquette (Kissin' Kate), Tim Blake Nelson (Mr. Pendanski), Dule Hill (Sam), Shia LaBeouf (Stanley IV), Henry Winkler (Stanley III),Nathan Davis (Stanley II), Khleo Thomas (Hector Zero), Eartha Kitt (Madame Zeroni). Directed by Andrew Davis and produced by Davis, Lowell D. Blank, Mike Medavoy, and Teresa Tucker-Davies. Screenplay by Louis Sachar, based on his novel.

"You take a bad boy, make him dig holes all day long in the hot sun, it makes him a good boy. That's our philosophy here at Camp Green Lake."

So says Mr. Sir, the overseer of a bizarre juvenile correction center that sits in the middle of the desert, surrounded by countless holes, each one five feet deep and five feet wide. It is the fate of the boys sentenced there to dig one hole a day, day after day; like Sisyphus, who was condemned to forever roll a rock to the top of a hill so that it could roll back down again, they are caught in a tragic loop.

Holes, which tells their story, is a movie so strange that it escapes entirely from the family genre and moves into fantasy. Like *Willy Wonka and the Chocolate Factory*, it has fearsome depths and secrets. Based on the much-honored young adult's novel by Louis Sachar, it has been given the top-shelf treatment: The director is Andrew Davis *(The Fugitive)* and the cast includes not only talented young stars but also weirdness from such adults as Jon Voight, Sigourney Weaver, Tim Blake Nelson, and Patricia Arquette.

In a time when mainstream action is rigidly contained within formulas, maybe there's more freedom to be found in a young people's adventure. *Holes* jumps the rails, leaves all expectations behind, and tells a story that's not funny ha-ha but funny peculiar. I found it original and intriguing. It'll be a change after dumbed-down, one-level family stories, but a lot of kids in the upper grades will have read the book, and no doubt their younger brothers and sisters have had it explained to them. (If you doubt the novel's Harry Potter–like penetration into the youth culture, ask a seventh-grader who Armpit is.)

The story involves Stanley Yelnats IV (Shia LaBeouf), a good kid who gets charged with a crime through no fault of his own, and is shipped off to Camp Green Lake, which is little more than a desert bunkhouse surrounded by holes. There he meets his fellow prisoners and the ominous supervisory staff: Mr. Sir (Jon Voight) and Mr. Pendanski (Tim Blake Nelson) report to the Warden (Sigourney Weaver), and both men are thoroughly intimidated by her. All three adult actors take their work seriously;

they don't relax because this is a family movie, but create characters of dark comic menace. Voight's work is especially detailed; watch him spit in his hand to slick back his hair.

Holes involves no less than two flashback stories. We learn that young Stanley comes from a long line of Yelnatses (all named Stanley, because it is the last name spelled backward). From his father (Henry Winkler) and grandfather (Nathan Davis) he learns of an ancient family curse, traced back many generations to an angry fortune-teller (Eartha Kitt; yes, Eartha Kitt). The other flashback explains the real reason the Warden wants the boys to dig holes; it involves the buried treasure of a legendary bandit queen named Kissin' Kate Barlow (Arquette).

There is a link between these two back stories, supplied by Zero (Khleo Thomas), who becomes Stanley's best friend and shares a harrowing adventure with him. Zero runs away despite Mr. Sir's warning that there is no water for miles around, and when Stanley joins him they stumble upon ancient clues and modern astonishments.

Shia LaBeouf and Khleo Thomas are both new to me, although LaBeouf is the star of a cable series, *Even Stevens*. They carry the movie with an unforced conviction, and successfully avoid playing cute. As they wander in the desert and discover the keys to their past and present destinies, they develop a partnership which, despite the fantastical material, seems like the real thing.

The whole movie generates a surprising conviction. No wonder young viewers have embraced it so eagerly: It doesn't condescend, and it founds its story on recognizable human nature. There are all sorts of undercurrents, such as the edgy tension between the Warden and Mr. Sir that add depth and intrigue; Voight and Weaver don't simply play caricatures.

Davis has always been a director with a strong visual sense, and the look of *Holes* has a noble, dusty loneliness. We feel we are actually in a limitless desert. The cinematographer, Stephen St. John, thinks big, and frames his shots for an epic feel that adds weight to the story. I walked in expecting a movie for thirteen-somethings, and walked out feeling challenged and satisfied. Curious, how much more grown-up and sophisticated *Holes* is than *Anger Management*.

Hollywood Ending ★ ★ ½
PG-13, 114 m., 2002

Woody Allen (Val Waxman), Tea Leoni (Ellie), George Hamilton (Ed), Debra Messing (Lori), Mark Rydell (Al Hack), Tiffani Thiessen (Sharon Bates), Treat Williams (Hal), Barney Cheng (Translator). Directed by Woody Allen and produced by Letty Aronson. Screenplay by Allen.

Val Waxman is a movie director going through a slow period in his career. Maybe it's more like a slow decade. He left his last movie project, explaining, "I quit over a big thing." What was that? "They fired me." Then he gets a big break: Galaxie Studios has just green-lighted *While the City Sleeps,* and his ex-wife has convinced the studio head that Val, despite his laundry list of psychosomatic anxieties and neurotic tics, is the right guy to direct it.

Woody Allen's new comedy, *Hollywood Ending,* quickly adds a complication to this setup: Waxman goes blind. It may all be in his mind, but he can't see a thing. For his ever-smiling agent, Al Hack (Mark Rydell), this is insufficient cause to leave the project. Al says he will glide through the picture at Waxman's elbow, and no one will ever notice. When the studio demurs at the agent being on the set, Al and Val recruit another seeing-eye man: the business student (Barney Cheng) who has been hired as the translator for the Chinese cinematographer. The translator says he'll blend right in: "I will practice casual banter."

Further complications: Waxman's ex-wife, Ellie (Tea Leoni), is now engaged to Hal (Treat Williams), the head of Galaxie Studios. Waxman casts his current squeeze, Lori (Debra Messing), to star in the movie, but while Lori is away at a spa getting in shape, costar Sharon (Tiffani Thiessen) moves on Waxman. In his dressing room, she removes her robe while explaining that she is eager to perform sexual favors for all of her directors (Waxman, who cannot see her abundant cleavage, helpfully suggests she advertise this willingness in the *Directors Guild* magazine).

What is Val Waxman's movie about? We have no idea. Neither does Waxman, who agrees with every suggestion so he won't have to make any decisions. He's not only blind but apparently has ears that don't work in stereo, since he can't tell where people are standing by the sound of their voices, and spends much of his time gazing into space. No one notices this, maybe because directors are such gods on movies that they can get away with anything.

The situation is funny, and Allen of course populates it with zingy one-liners, orchestrated with much waving of the hands (he's a virtuoso of body language). But somehow the movie doesn't get over the top. It uses the blindness gimmick in fairly obvious ways, and doesn't bring it to another level—to build on the blindness instead of just depending on it. When Waxman confesses his handicap to the wrong woman—a celebrity journalist—because he thinks he's sitting next to someone he can trust, that's very funny. But too often he's just seen with a vacant stare, trying to bluff his way through conversations.

Why not use the realities of a movie set to suggest predicaments for the secretly blind? Would Val always need to take his translator into the honey wagon with him? Could there be tragic misunderstandings in the catering line? Would he wander unknowingly into a shot? How about the cinematographer offering him a choice of lenses, and he chooses the lens cap? David Mamet's *State and Main* does a better job of twisting the realities of a movie into the materials of comedy.

Because Allen is a great verbal wit and because he's effortlessly ingratiating, I had a good time at the movie even while not really buying it. I enjoyed Tea Leoni's sunny disposition, although she spends too much time being the peacemaker between the two men in her life and not enough time playing a character who is funny in herself. George Hamilton, as a tanned studio flunky, suggests a familiar Hollywood type, the guy who is drawing a big salary for being on the set without anybody being quite sure what he's there for (he carries a golf club to give himself an identity—the guy who carries the golf club). And Mark Rydell smiles and smiles and smiles, as an agent who reasons that anything he has 10 percent of must be an unqualified good thing. As Waxman's seeing eyes, Barney Cheng adds a nice element: Not only is Waxman blind, but he is being given an inexact description of the world

through the translator's English, which is always slightly off-track.

I liked the movie without loving it. It's not great Woody Allen, like *Sweet and Lowdown* or *Bullets Over Broadway,* but it's smart and sly, and the blindness is an audacious idea. It also has moments when you can hear Allen editorializing in the dialogue. My favorite is this exchange:

"He has made some very financially successful American films."

"That should tell you everything you need to know about him."

Hollywood Homicide ★ ★ ★
PG-13, 111 m., 2003

Harrison Ford (Joe Gavilan), Josh Hartnett (K. C. Calden), Lena Olin (Ruby), Lolita Davidovich (Cleo), Bruce Greenwood (Bennie Macko), Keith David (Lieutenant Fuqua). Directed by Ron Shelton and produced by Lou Pitt and Shelton. Screenplay by Robert Souza and Shelton.

The most popular occupations in movies about Hollywood are cops, crooks, hookers, psychics, and actors, and to this list we must add the people they are all terrified of, real estate brokers.

Hollywood Homicide covers these bases with a murderer, a cop who is a realtor, a cop who wants to be an actor, and a psychic who can visualize that the murderer will be in an SUV on Rodeo Drive in half an hour. There are also two hookers, although one scarcely counts, being an undercover cop in drag. Still, in Hollywood, maybe that does count.

The movie stars Harrison Ford and Josh Hartnett as the two cops, named Joe Gavilan and K. C. Calden, who are detectives assigned to Hollywood. Gavilan is so preoccupied with his real estate business that he tries to sell a house to the owner of a club where four rappers have just been killed, and later negotiates the purchase price during a police chase. Calden has decided he wants to be an actor, and makes Gavilan run lines for him from *A Streetcar Named Desire.* Gavilan is not impressed: "Who wrote this stuff?"

The movie was directed by Ron Shelton, who cowrote with Robert Souza. Shelton also made *Bull Durham* and *White Men Can't Jump* and specializes in funny dialogue for guy characters who would rather talk than do just about anything else. One of the pleasures of *Hollywood Homicide* is that it's more interested in its two goofy cops than in the murder plot; their dialogue redeems otherwise standard scenes. It's kind of a double act, between a man who has seen everything and a man who's seen too much.

Consider a scene where K. C. commandeers a vehicle containing a mother and her two small children. He needs it to chase a bad guy. "We're gonna die!" whines one of the kids. "Yes," agrees K. C., who moonlights as a yoga instructor, "we *are* all going to die someday, but . . ." His philosophical observations are cut short by a crash.

The movie opens with a hit on a rap group in a music club. Four people are dead when Joe and K.C. turn up to investigate. Joe immediately sends out for food. K.C. tells the club owner he is an actor. Their investigation is hampered by an inconvenient development: They are under investigation by Bennie Macko (Bruce Greenwood), the Internal Affairs guy who hates Joe, and who reminds us once again that movie villains usually have a hard C or K in their names.

Joe is suspected of "mingling funds," which is to say, he confuses his personal debts and the debts of his real estate business. He has been seen with Cleo (Lolita Davidovich), who is a known hooker. No wonder; you do not get to be an unknown hooker by being chauffeured around town in your own stretch limousine. Internal Affairs thinks he is fooling around with Cleo, but he isn't; he's fooling around with Ruby the psychic (Lena Olin). She's yet another in the baffling legion of Los Angeles women who believe it is fun to make love on a blanket on the hardwood floor of an empty house while surrounded by a lot of candles.

At Harrison Ford's age, this qualifies as a dangerous stunt. But Ford just gets better, more distilled, more laconic, and more gruffly likable year after year. It is hard to catch him doing anything at all while he's acting, and yet whatever it is he isn't doing, it works. You don't feel he's going for laughs when he tries to sell the club owner a house while the two of them are standing in fresh pools of blood, metaphorically speaking; you feel he desperately needs to unload the house.

Hartnett makes an able partner for Ford,

trading deadpan dialogue and telling everyone he's really an actor. He's given one of Shelton's nicest little scenes, when he goes to the morgue and looks at the dead bodies of the murder victims (he hates looking at dead bodies), and then notices some other dead bodies that have just arrived at the morgue, checks their shoe sizes, and says, "Hey . . . those guys shot these guys."

There is a chase and a half near the end of the movie, a lot of it near the Kodak Theatre at Hollywood and Highland. That gives the movie a chance to interrupt Robert Wagner as he's leaving his handprints in front of Graumann's Chinese Theater, and indeed the movie is filled with cameos and walk-bys, including Frank Sinatra Jr. as a showbiz lawyer, Martin Landau very funny as a fading producer who needs to unload his mansion, Lou Diamond Phillips as Wanda the cop in drag, Gladys Knight, Dwight Yoakam, Isaiah Washington, Master P, Kurupt, Eric Idle, Dr. Dre, and just plain Dre.

Much of the closing excitement depends on the Fallacy of the Climbing Killer, that dependable chase cliché in which the killer climbs to a high place, from which he cannot escape unless he can fly. *Hollywood Homicide* uses this as an excuse to show police helicopters and TV news helicopters crowding each other out of the skies. It's a skillful chase, well done, but the dialogue is the reason to see the movie. This may be the most exciting film ever made about real estate.

Home Movie ★ ★ ★

NO MPAA RATING, 65 m., 2002

As themselves: Linda Beech, Francis Mooney, Diana Peden, Ed Peden, Darlene Satrinano, Ben Skora, Bill Tregle, Bob Walker. A documentary film directed by Chris Smith and produced by Barbara Laffey and Susane Preissler.

The five homes in Chris Smith's *Home Movie* are no doubt strange and eccentric. Not everyone would choose to live on a houseboat in alligator country, or in a missile silo, or in a tree house, or in a house modified for the comfort of dozens of cats, or in a house that looks like Rube Goldberg running berserk.

But what is a normal house, anyway? In *The Fast Runner*, we see a civilization that lives in igloos. In *Taiga*, we visit the yurt dwellers of Outer Mongolia. Their homes are at least functional, economical, and organic to the surrounding landscape. It's possible that the most bizarre homestyles on Earth are those proposed by Martha Stewart, which cater to the neuroses of women with paralyzing insecurity. What woman with a healthy self-image could possibly dream of making those table decorations?

The five subjects of *Home Movie* at least know exactly why they live where they do and as they do, and they do not require our permission or approval. There is Bill Tregle, whose Louisiana houseboat is handy for his occupation of trapping, selling, and exhibiting alligators. He catches his dinner from a line tossed from the deck, has electric lights, a microwave and a TV powered by generator, pays no taxes, moves on when he feels like it, and has decorated his interior with the treasures of a lifetime.

Or consider the Pedens, Ed and Diana, who live in a converted missile silo. The concrete walls are so thick that they can have "tornado parties," and there's an easy commute down a buried tunnel from the living space to the work space. True, they had to build a greenhouse on the surface to get some sun or watch the rain, because otherwise, Diana observes, it's too easy to stay underground for days or weeks at a time. Their living room is the silo's former launch center: interesting karma.

Linda Beech speaks little Japanese, yet once starred on a Japanese soap opera. Now she lives in the Hawaiian rain forest, in a tree house equipped with all the comforts of home. To be sure, family photos tend to mildew, but think of the compensations, such as her own waterfall, which provides hydroelectric power for electricity, and also provides her favorite meditation spot, on a carefully positioned "water-watching rock." She can't imagine anyone trying to live without their own waterfall.

Bob Walker and Francis Mooney have dozens of cats. They've renovated the inside of their house with perches, walkways, and tunnels, some of them linking rooms, others ending in hidey-holes. They speculate about how much less their house is worth today than when they purchased it, but they're serene: They seem to live in a mutual daze of cat-loving. The cats seem happy too.

Ben Skora lives in a suburb of Chicago. His house is an inventor's hallucination. Everything is automatic: the doors, which open like pin-

wheels, the toilets, the lights, the furniture. The hardest task, living in his house, must be to remember where all the switches are and what they govern. He also has a remote-controlled robot that is a hit at shopping malls. The robot will bring him a can of pop, which is nice, although the viewer may reflect that it is easier to get a can out of the refrigerator than build a robot to do it for you. Skora's great masterwork is a ski jump that swoops down from his roof.

Are these people nuts? Who are we to say? I know people whose lives are lived in basement rec rooms. Upstairs they have a living room with the lamps and sofas still protected with the plastic covers from the furniture store. What is the purpose of this room? To be a Living Room Museum? What event will be earth-shaking enough to require the removal of the covers? Do they hope their furniture will appreciate in value?

There is no philosophy, so far as I can tell, behind Chris Smith's film. He simply celebrates the universal desire to fashion our homes for our needs and desires. Smith's previous doc was the great *American Movie*, about the Wisconsin man who wanted to make horror movies, and did, despite all obstacles. Perhaps the message is the same: If it makes you happy and allows you to express your yearnings and dreams, who are we to enforce the rules of middle-class conformity?

Home on the Range ★ ★ ½
PG, 76 m., 2004

With the voices of: Roseanne Barr (Maggie), Judi Dench (Mrs. Caloway), Jennifer Tilly (Grace), Cuba Gooding Jr. (Buck), Randy Quaid (Alameda Slim), Richard Riehle (Sheriff Brown), Charles Dennis (Rico), Steve Buscemi (Wesley), Charles Haid (Lucky Jack), Estelle Harris (Audrey). Directed by Will Finn and John Sanford and produced by Alice Dewey Goldstone. Screenplay by Finn and Sanford.

Home on the Range, Disney's new animated feature, has the genial friendliness of a 1940s singing cowboy movie, and the plot could have been borrowed from Hopalong Cassidy or Roy Rogers, apart from the slight detail that they aren't cows. The new songs by Alan Menken ("The Little Mermaid," "Beauty and the Beast") are in the tradition of western swing; I can easily imagine

Gene Autry performing any of them, including the yodeling number, and wasn't too surprised to find that the Sons of the Pioneers starred in a 1946 movie with the same name.

The pace is up-to-date, though. Gene Autry and Roy Rogers always had time to relax next to a campfire and sing a tune, but *Home on the Range* jumps with the energy of a cartoon short subject. The movie is said to be Disney's last release in the traditional 2-D animation style; its feature cartoons in the future will have the rounded 3-D look of *Finding Nemo*. Whether that is a loss or not depends on how you relate to animation; there are audiences even for those dreadful Saturday morning cartoon adventures that are so stingy on animation they're more like 1.5-D.

The story takes place on the Patch of Heaven ranch, which faces foreclosure because of the depredations of the vile cattle rustler Alameda Slim (voice by Randy Quaid). Pearl, the owner, could raise money by selling her cows—but they're family, you see, and so presumably they'll all be homeless soon. But then the cows get a bright idea: Why not track down Slim, collect the $750 reward, pay off the bank, and save the ranch?

Each of the cows has unique qualities to contribute to this effort. Mrs. Caloway (Judi Dench) is the voice of prudence. Grace (Jennifer Tilly) is the New Age cow, who makes observations like, "This is an organic problem and needs a holistic solution." Their catalyst is a newcomer to the farm, Maggie (Roseanne Barr), who quickly becomes the aggressive, in-your-face leader. Rounding out the team is Buck (Cuba Gooding Jr.), the stallion, who is a master of the martial arts.

The voices are all quickly recognizable, especially Barr's; the idea of using the voices of familiar stars instead of anonymous dubbing artists has added an intriguing dimension to recent animated features. Listen, for example, to Randy Quaid as the dastardly Slim. It's traditional in Disney animation to fill the edges of the screen with hyperactive little supporting characters, and we get Lucky Jack the jackrabbit (Charles Haid) and Audrey the chicken, who is chicken (Estelle Harris). There are also three very busy little pigs, and Steve Buscemi almost seems to be playing himself as a critter named Wesley.

Buck, by the way, has delusions of grandeur; he thinks maybe he can capture Slim and collect the reward, especially after he becomes the horse of the famed bounty hunter Rico (Charles Dennis), which leads to a fierce competition with the cows. The plot makes pit stops at all the obligatory Western sights: saloons, mine shafts, main streets, deserts with Monument Valley landscapes, and trains. All of these locations become the backdrops of chases in a movie that seldom stands still.

The songs are performed by k.d. lang, Bonnie Raitt, Tim McGraw, and the Bleu Sisters. None of the songs is likely to be requested by fans at future concerts. They sound generic and don't have the zest of Menken's earlier work.

A movie like this is fun for kids: bright, quick-paced, with broad, outrageous characters. But *Home on the Range* doesn't have the crossover quality of the great Disney films like *Beauty and the Beast* and *The Lion King*. And it doesn't have the freshness and originality of a more traditional movie like *Lilo & Stitch*. Its real future, I suspect, lies in home video. It's only seventy-six minutes long, but although kids will like it, their parents will be sneaking looks at their watches.

Honey ★ ★ ½
PG-13, 89 m., 2003

Jessica Alba (Honey Daniels), Mekhi Phifer (Chaz), Lil' Romeo (Benny), Joy Bryant (Gina), David Moscow (Michael Ellis), Lonette McKee (Darlene Daniels), Zachary Isaiah Williams (Raymond). Directed by Bille Woodruff and produced by Marc Platt and Andre Harrell. Screenplay by Alonzo Brown and Kim Watson.

"Hey, kids! Let's rent the old barn and put on a show!"

These words are so familiar that surely I must have actually heard them in a movie at one time or another, but I confess I cannot remember when. They summarize one of the most persistent of all movie formulas, pioneered in the days of Mickey Rooney and Judy Garland, reborn in the era of Frankie Avalon and Annette Funicello, and now finding new life with Jessica Alba and Lil' Romeo.

If I were to tell you (a) that Jessica Alba works

as a dance instructor in a neighborhood center, (b) that she discovers Lil' Romeo and his friends break-dancing in the streets, (c) that city inspectors shut down the center because of leaks and unsafe construction, and (d) that there is an empty church nearby that could be borrowed for an evening, what would you say the chances are that Alba will hit on the notion of using the old church to put on a show with the kids, to raise money for the community center?

It's amazing that this formula still survives, but it does, right down to the crucial moment when the doors open and her parents (who disapprove of her hip-hop dance style) join the audience, are moved by the performance, and have maybe a few tears in their eyes, having seen the light and understood their daughter's dream at last. *Honey* crosses this formula with another: the talented girl from the neighborhood who is discovered by a big producer, who lures her away from her old friends. Will she be dazzled by the bright lights and the big city? Will the slickster's limousine and champagne lifestyle make her forget the honest and dependable neighborhood barber who truly loves her? Will she let the kids down?

There is not a lot of suspense behind these questions, because Jessica Alba doesn't have the face and smile of the kind of creep who would sell out to a crass big-shot producer and dump the dear hearts and gentle people back in the neighborhood. She plays Honey Daniels, who teaches a dance class at the center run by her mother (Lonette McKee). She hangs out with her best friend, Gina (Joy Bryant), and dreams of someday surviving an audition and being selected to dance in a music video. Meanwhile, Honey and Gina dance at clubs on weekends, and a scout supplies a video of her style to Michael (David Moscow), a famous video producer. He bypasses the auditions, gives her a role in his new video, hires her to choreograph three more, and takes her to fancy parties and opening nights. It takes her just a little too long to figure out what's perfectly obvious to us: He wants to be her lover.

Honey has been inspired by the free dance styles of Benny (Lil' Romeo) and his buddies, borrows some of them for her choreography, and convinces Michael to let her use the kids in a new video starring Ginuwine. Meanwhile, Chaz (Mekhi Phifer), the faithful barber, won-

ders if Honey is lost to him—even though she likes him a lot and likes Michael less and less.

A movie like *Honey* is aimed at younger teenagers, who may not precisely be students of Mickey and Judy; scenes that have unfolded in a thousand other movies can seem new if you're seeing them for the first time. I wasn't seeing them for the first or even the fiftieth time, but the warmth of Jessica Alba and likability of Mekhi Phifer were real enough—a consolation even when their characters were repeating all the old moves. *Honey* doesn't have a shred of originality (except for the high-energy choreography), but there's something fundamentally reassuring about a movie that respects ancient formulas; it's like a landmark preservation program.

Horns and Halos ★ ★ ★
NO MPAA RATING, 79 m., 2003

A documentary featuring Sander Hicks, J. H. Hatfield, Peter Slover, and Mark Crispin Miller. Directed by Suki Hawley and Michael Galinsky and produced by Hawley, Galinsky, and David Beilinson.

It is forgotten now that a book published in 1999 charged, among other things, that George W. Bush was arrested for cocaine possession in the early 1970s, and the bust was covered up through the influence of his father. The charge was made in *Fortunate Son*, which briefly made the best-seller lists and sparked a flurry of press interest before lawyers for Bush threatened a lawsuit, and it was revealed that the book's author, James Howard Hatfield, had served five years in prison after being convicted of attempted murder.

Bush never precisely denied the charge, nor did he need to: "Obviously," he said, "if he's a convicted felon, his credibility's nothing." A discredited author amounted to a discredited story, and Hatfield's actual past trumped Bush's alleged past. St. Martin's Press, which published the book, withdrew its edition and destroyed all copies. Then a fly-by-night publisher named Soft Skull reprinted *Fortunate Son*, and Hatfield, who had refused to reveal the source of his information about the alleged cocaine arrest, now dropped a bombshell: His source, he said, was Karl Rove, Bush's closest political adviser.

All sensational stuff, very questionable, and there was even a *60 Minutes* segment on the would-be scandal, but Hatfield was a loose cannon, and his personal life was coming apart at the seams. Eventually he was found dead in a motel room after an overdose of prescription pills, in what appeared to be a genuine suicide. In a sense, his book was a service to the Bush campaign, because the cocaine story and its author, generally seen to be discredited, drew attention away from the roughly simultaneous charges that the future commander in chief had been AWOL for a year from the Air National Guard.

Horns and Halos, a documentary that resurrects this political footnote, begins with Hatfield and his book, but the attention keeps getting stolen by a mercurial eccentric named Sander Hicks, the owner, operator, and sole employee of the Soft Skull Press. He works from his home, and his home is a tiny apartment in a New York apartment building where he is the janitor. Hicks is a splendid argument for diversity in media ownership, since with almost no capital he was able to print and distribute the book.

The filmmakers, Suki Hawley and Michael Galinsky, focus on Hicks's passion for the book, which easily outstrips Hatfield's. "Not a day goes by that I don't regret writing this book," Hatfield says at one point, and there are signs toward the end that, despite his joy over the birth of a baby daughter, he is coming unhinged.

The movie suggests that the Dallas story identifying Hatfield as a convicted felon was planted by the Bush campaign, and indeed there is a dubious conspiracy theory that Rove *did* give Hatfield information, because he knew of Hatfield's past and thought it was best that the scandal come to light through an easily discredited source. Hatfield hardly needed outside help to undermine his book; his introduction to the Soft Skull edition included comments about his conviction that inspired a lawsuit by a former associate.

Although Hicks shepherds Hatfield to Book Expo and other book shows, the book, once dismissed, is no longer news. And after Hatfield's death the entire episode disappears from our collective memory. *Horns and Halos* is effective in presenting its portraits of these two men, Hatfield so depressed, Hicks so optimistic, but it's not successful at getting to the bottom of the cocaine charges. It commits the same mistake it charges the mainstream press with: It allows Hatfield's story to upstage his allegations. The adventures of Hicks in taking on the media establishment from his janitor's quarters make a great human-interest story, but it too has nothing to do with the underlying charges.

All that can be said at this late date is that the cocaine use, if any, is a dead issue, and Bush covered himself during the campaign by saying he had not used drugs since 1974. (He did not say if he had used drugs before 1974, and his campaign quickly called his original words a misstatement.) In today's political climate, this movie and its people all seem to come from a very long time ago.

The Hot Chick ★ ½
PG-13, 101 m., 2002

Rob Schneider (Clive), Anna Faris (April), Matthew Lawrence (Billy), Rachel McAdams (Jessica Spencer). Directed by Tom Brady and produced by Carr D'Angelo and John Schneider. Screenplay by Tom Brady and Rob Schneider.

The Hot Chick is about a woman who is magically transported into a man's body, and takes several days to learn how to urinate correctly with her new equipment. This despite getting a how-to lecture from a helpful washroom attendant. Luckily, she finds that passing gas is a skill that ports easily between the genders. Meanwhile, the former occupant of her male body has been magically transported into her former female body, and immediately becomes a hooker and a stripper.

How is this switch possible? It happens because of a pair of magic earrings. Their history is shown in an introductory scene helpfully subtitled, "Abyssinia, 50 B.C." The scene is clearly inspired by *The Arabian Nights;* the screenplay is by the director, Tom Brady, and the star, Rob Schneider, who have confused Africa with the Middle East, but the prologue is over before we can grow depressed by its geographical and ethnographic ignorance.

In modern times, we are introduced to a cadre of hot chicks who all go to the same high school. The Rob Schneider character, named

Clive, no doubt after Clive of India, who would have been a much more interesting character, mugs one of the hot chicks and gets one of her earrings. When Clive and the chick put on the earrings, they are wondrously transported into each other's bodies. Jessica (Rachel McAdams) occupies Clive.

Clive also occupies Jessica, but only gets a couple of scenes, in which he quickly masters feminine skills, starting with buying tampons and progressing quickly to stripping. The movie's conviction that we would rather see the outside of Rob Schneider's body than the outside of Rachel McAdams's body is not the least of its miscalculations. Rob Schneider's outside has most of its scenes with Jessica's best friend, played by Anna Faris, whose resemblance to Britney Spears in the hair and makeup departments is a complete coincidence.

The way the movie handles the switch is that Rob Schneider, visually appearing as himself, has Jessica trapped inside. He/she convinces his/her best girlfriends of this transformation. This is one of the most astonishing events in the history of mankind, incredible and miraculous, and so what inflames the curiosity of the three girlfriends? His penis.

That they are stupid goes without saying. That the filmmakers could think of nothing more creative to do with their premise is a cause for despair. Body-switch movies had a brief vogue in the 1980s, when there were some cute ones (*Big, Vice Versa*), but Hollywood has so downgraded its respect for the audience that *The Hot Chick* is now considered acceptable.

The movie resolutely avoids all the comic possibilities of its situation, and becomes one more dumb high school comedy about sex gags and prom dates. Jessica, as Clive, becomes the best boy/girl friend a girl could want, during a week in which the female Jessica's parents absentmindedly observe that she has been missing for days. (That a girl looking exactly like the most popular girl in high school is stripping and hooking escapes the attention of the local slackwits.)

Lessons are learned, Jessica sees things from a different point of view, sweetness triumphs, and the movie ends with one of those "deleted" scenes over the final credits. This particular credit cookie is notable for being even more boring and pointless than the movie. Through superhuman effort of the will, I did not walk out of *The Hot Chick*, but reader, I confess I could not sit through the credits.

Note: The MPAA rates this PG-13. It is too vulgar for anyone under thirteen, and too dumb for anyone over thirteen.

Hotel ★ ★ ★
NO MPAA RATING, 119 m., 2003

Rhys Ifans (Trent Stoken), David Schwimmer (Jonathan Danderfine), Salma Hayek (Charlee Boux), Andrea Di Stefano (Assassin), John Malkovich (Omar Jonnson), Valeria Golino (Italian Actress), Saffron Burrows (Duchess of Malfi), Lucy Liu (Kawika), Chiara Mastroianni (Nurse), Julian Sands (Tour Guide), Danny Huston (Hotel Manager). Directed by Mike Figgis and produced by Andrea Calderwood, Figgis, Annie Stewart, Lesley Stewart, and Ernst Etchie Stroh. Screenplay by Figgis and John Webster.

Here's a strange case. *Hotel* is a movie that works in no conventional sense, and succeeds in several unconventional ones. Most audiences will find it baffling and unsatisfactory. Those who are open to its flywheel peculiarities may find it bold, funny, peculiar, and delightful.

The movie is told like three stories running in a circle, snapping at one anothers' tails. One story involves a self-important movie director named Trent Stoken (Rhys Ifans), who is in Venice shooting a version of John Webster's *The Duchess of Malfi* in the Dogma style. The second involves a documentary crew led by Charlee Boux (Salma Hayek) that is making one of those "making of" films about the production. The third involves the workings of the hotel itself, which is run by and for cannibal vampires. All of this is much in the spirit of Webster, Shakespeare's contemporary, whose plays dripped with violence, melodrama, conspiracy, and sexual intrigue.

Figgis is a bold experimenter whose films often leave conventional pathways to achieve their effect. His *Leaving Las Vegas* (1995) was shot on Super 16-mm so that the cast and crew could work quickly on locations without clearances or permits. His *Timecode* (2000) was shot on digital video that used a four-way split screen to tell the story with four simultaneous and unbroken shots (*Russian Ark* had only one ninety-minute take). In *Hotel* he shows the film-within-a-film on digital video, goes outside it with conventional celluloid, and sometimes presents the same scene with messy location sound and then polished postproduction sound.

Now imagine all this stylistic freedom with an all-star cast of actors invited to play broadly, wryly, erotically. There is a feud between the Ifans character and his producer (David Schwimmer), and a stunning moment when the director is shot, only to linger in a long, eyes-open coma that inspires an extraordinary erotic monologue by his nurse (Chiara Mastroianni). Saffron Burrows plays the Duchess of Malfi and is involved first with Ifans, then with Schwimmer.

Familiar faces are everywhere: Lucy Liu as an instinctive enemy of Hayek; Danny Huston as the helpful, sinister hotel manager; Julian Sands as the tour guide, whose explanations of Venice and the Webster play provide a road map, Valeria Golina as another of the actresses, and Burt Reynolds, who convincingly occupies what seems to be a completely superfluous role. Used most oddly of all is John Malkovich, in an opening sequence where he is taken down into the catacombs of the hotel and participates in a formal feast where, it becomes clear, the main dish is human flesh. Malkovich's seat at the table, ominously, is behind bars separating it from the others.

The movie does a fair job of satirizing the conceits of the Dogma movement—showing the hapless Burrows trying to perform period costume scenes in the middle of a Piazza San Marco filled with rubbernecking tourists. It shows the competition for power, money, and sex that can take place when gigantic egos are assembled. It has more than one unusually erotic scene, including a monologue as evocative as the one in Bergman's *Persona*. Salma Hayek finds more than a documentarian could hope for when she wanders into hidden passages and discovers dismembered body parts. The treatment of the comatose director is cruel, funny, sad, and creepy. The fact that all of these characters are being preyed on by vampires may

be a metaphor for the megacorporations that own the movie industry. Or maybe not.

Many critics have agreed that *Hotel* is not successful, but I would ask: Not successful at what? Before you conclude that a movie doesn't work, you have to determine what it intends to do. This is not a horror movie, a behind-the-scenes movie, a sexual intrigue, or a travelogue, but all four at once, elbowing each other for screen time. It reminds me above all of a competitive series of jazz improvisations, in which the musicians quote from many sources and the joy comes in the way they're able to keep their many styles alive in the same song. Figgis is a musician (he composed for the film, in addition to cowriting, cophotographing, and coproducing). Maybe that occurred to him. There is a heady freedom in his riffs here that might appeal to you, if you don't doggedly insist that everything reduce itself to the mundane. The movie has to be pointless in order to make any sense.

The Hours ★ ★ ★ ½
PG-13, 114 m., 2002

Meryl Streep (Clarissa Vaughn), Julianne Moore (Laura Brown), Nicole Kidman (Virginia Woolf), Stephen Dillane (Leonard Woolf), Ed Harris (Richard), John C. Reilly (Dan Brown), Claire Danes (Julia), Allison Janney (Sally). Directed by Stephen Daldry and produced by Robert Fox and Scott Rudin. Screenplay by David Hare, based on the novel by Michael Cunningham.

Three women, three times, three places. Three suicide attempts, two successful. All linked in a way by a novel. In Sussex in 1941, the novelist Virginia Woolf fills the pockets of her coat with rocks and walks into a river to drown. In Los Angeles in 1951, Laura Brown fills her purse with pills and checks into a hotel to kill herself. In New York in 2001, Clarissa Vaughn watches as a friend she loves decides whether to let himself fall out of a window, or not.

The novel is *Mrs. Dalloway*, written by Woolf in 1925. It takes place in a day during which a woman has breakfast, buys flowers, and prepares to throw a party. The first story in *The Hours* shows Virginia writing about the woman, the second shows Laura reading the book, the third shows Clarissa buying flowers after having said one of the famous lines of the book. All three stories in *The Hours* begin with breakfast, involve preparations for parties, end in sadness. Two of the characters in the second story appear again in the third, but the stories do not flow one from another. Instead, they all revolve around the fictional character of Mrs. Dalloway, who presents a brave face to the world but is alone, utterly alone within herself, and locked away from the romance she desires.

The Hours, directed by Stephen Daldry and based on the Pulitzer Prize–winning novel by Michael Cunningham, doesn't try to force these three stories to parallel one another. It's more like a meditation on separate episodes linked by a certain sensibility—Woolf's, a great novelist who wrote a little book named *A Room of One's Own,* which in some ways initiated modern feminism. Her observation was that throughout history women did not have a room of their own, but were on call throughout a house occupied by their husbands and families. Jane Austen wrote her novels, Woolf observed, in a corner of a room where all the other family activities were also taking place.

In *The Hours,* Woolf (Nicole Kidman) has a room of her own, and the understanding of her husband, Leonard (Stephen Dillane), a publisher. Laura (Julianne Moore), whom we meet in the 1950s, is a typical suburban housewife with a loving and dependable husband (John C. Reilly) she does not love, and a son who might as well be from outer space. A surprising kiss midway through her story suggests she might have been happier living as a lesbian. Clarissa (Meryl Streep), whom we meet in the present, is living as a lesbian; she and her partner (Allison Janney) are raising a daughter (Claire Danes) and caring for their friend (Ed Harris), now dying of AIDS. (We may know, although the movie doesn't make a point of it, that Virginia Woolf was bisexual.)

If this progression of the three stories shows anything, it demonstrates that personal freedom expanded greatly during the decades involved, but human responsibilities and guilts remained the governing facts of life. It also shows that suicides come in different ways for different reasons. Woolf's suicide comes during a time of clarity and sanity in her struggle

with mental illness; she leaves a note for Leonard saying that she feels the madness coming on again, and wants to spare him that, out of her love for him. Laura attempts suicide out of despair; she cannot abide her life and sees no way out of it, and the love and gratitude of her husband is simply a goad. Richard, the Ed Harris character, is in the last painful stages of dying, and so his suicide takes on still another coloration.

And yet—well, the movie isn't about three approaches to sexuality, or three approaches to suicide. It may be about three versions of Mrs. Dalloway, who in the Woolf novel is outwardly a perfect hostess, the wife of a politician, but who contains other selves within, and earlier may have had lovers of both sexes. It would be possible to find parallels between *Mrs. Dalloway* and *The Hours*—the Ed Harris character might be a victim in the same sense as the shell-shocked veteran in the novel—but that kind of list-making belongs in term papers. For a movie audience, *The Hours* doesn't connect in a neat way, but introduces characters who illuminate mysteries of sex, duty, and love.

I mentioned that two of the characters in the second story appear again in the third. I will not reveal how that happens, but the fact that it happens creates an emotional vortex at the end of the film, in which we see that lives without love are devastated. Virginia and Leonard Woolf loved each other, and Clarissa treasures both of her lovers. But for the two in the movie who do not or cannot love, the price is devastating.

The Housekeeper ★ ★ ★
NO MPAA RATING, 90 m., 2003

Jean-Pierre Bacri (Jacques), Émilie Dequenne (Laura), Brigitte Catillon (Claire), Jacques Frantz (Ralph), Axelle Abbadie (Helene), Catherine Breillat (Constance). Directed by Claude Berri and produced by Berri. Screenplay by Berri, based on the novel by Christian Oster.

Claude Berri's *The Housekeeper* opens with a leisurely survey of a Paris apartment. The place is a mess. Dirty laundry, unmade beds, clothes thrown anywhere, the man sleeping on a couch and then stumbling to his bed in the middle of the night. His wife has walked out and he needs a housekeeper. He finds a notice in a store, calls the number on the little tag of paper, and finds himself in a café having coffee with a young woman who says she will be happy to take the job.

She is young, sexy in a certain light, says she has not worked as a housekeeper before, but needs the job and will work hard. He hires her. We might cynically assume he has erotic thoughts in the back of his mind, but apparently not: He scarcely seems to notice her, and at first arranges for her to work during hours when he is not at home.

He is Jacques (Jean-Pierre Bacri), a serious man in his fifties, balding, good-looking, masculine, preoccupied, busy. She is Laura (Émilie Dequenne), has two-tone hair, the roots growing out, and seems a little sloppy, but she does a capable job of cleaning the apartment and very slowly, with instinctive craft, she expands her role in his life, insinuating herself, being useful in unexpected ways, doing some of the domestic things a wife might do—and eventually, all of the things a wife might do. That he sleeps with her is more a result of his capitulation than his lust. Soon he hears the momentous words "I love you," and the crucial question, "Do you love me?" and the camera is looking directly at his face as he agrees, not with enthusiasm, that he does.

He doesn't love her, of course; his emotions are a mixture of pity, gratitude, fondness, and lust, but men have ineffective defenses against tears and sex. With the same application she brings to the housework, she elevates herself from housekeeper to that undefined sort of female companion that his friends think they understand, even though they do not.

There is a vacation trip to visit an old friend of his. She comes along. She is soon wearing a ring, and there is a story behind the ring, which I will not reveal, but which helps to define the gulf between his adult life and this accidental liaison that is almost certainly going to be more trouble than it's worth. A confrontation with his friend reveals how much more important his wife is, even absent and despite his resentment, than the girl who shares his bed. (We get a few glimpses of the wife, played by Catherine Breillat, the director of such more harrowing examinations of sex as *Fat Girl* and *Romance*.) Many movies celebrate romances between older men and younger women. That is because most movie directors are older men, and they find such stories congenial and plausible. In their eyes older men are more attractive, irresistible, fascinating than the callow boys the same age as their young partners. What these movies often fail to observe is that their young lovers are callow, too. When you are forty or fifty or sixty, to sleep with a girl of twenty might indeed be delightful, but to live with her day in and day out might be an ordeal beyond all imagining.

There is, first of all, the business of dancing. Young girls want to stay out very late and dance endlessly to barbaric music. Mature men are amused to spend a little time on the dance floor—but not hours and hours and hours, surrounded by inexhaustible youth, the music so loud they can make no use of their treasured conversational abilities. They do not understand, or have forgotten, that the whole point of loud music is to make it possible to date without talking. There are other problems. Girls want to swim when the water is too cold. They want to sunbathe far beyond any reasonable period that a person with an active mind can abide remaining prone on the sand. They have limited interest in spending hours listening to the older man and his old friends remembering times and people they will never, ever know for themselves.

The Housekeeper is wise and subtle in the way it presents its older man. A less interesting movie would make him lustful and self-deceiving, a man who believes his is the secret of eternal youth and virility. In the case of Jacques, however, he goes along, up to a point, indulges his weakness and his curiosity, up to a point, and then he finds that point—or, more poignantly, has it pointed out for him. The closing shots of the movie, which use Jean-Pierre Bacri's face as their primary canvas, say all that needs to be said about what he has learned, and with what wry acceptance he has received the message.

House of Fools ★ ★ ★

R, 104 m., 2003

Julia Vysotsky (Janna), Sultan Islamov (Akhmed), Bryan Adams (Himself), Vladas Bagdonas (Doctor), Stanislav Varkki (Ali). Directed by Andrei Konchalovsky and produced by Konchalovsky and Felix Kleiman. Screenplay by Sergei Kozlov.

Why are madhouses seen as such useful microcosms of human society? Why are their inhabitants invariably seen, in the movies anyway, as saner than the rest of us? The inmates are invariably choreographed as a group, acting like a Greek chorus. These groups I like to describe as the Baked Potato People, a name suggested by my old friend Billy ("Silver Dollar") Baxter, who once found a flag stuck into his baked potato, which read: "I've been tubbed, I've been rubbed, I've been scrubbed! I'm lovable, hugable, and eatable!"

Andrei Konchalovsky's *House of Fools* begins with ominous signs that it will be yet another recycling of simple fools, angelic heroines, and Baked Potatoes, with the familiar moral that it's the outside world that's crazy. It doesn't help that the movie is "based on a true story." But Konchalovsky was not born yesterday, has no doubt seen *King of Hearts, One Flew Over the Cuckoo's Nest,* and all the others, and shows courage in pressing ahead into this fraught territory. To my amazement, he salvages a good film from the genre—a film that succeeds not by arguing that the world is crazier than the asylum, but by arriving at the melancholy possibility that both are equally insane.

His true story: In 1996, during the Chechen war, the staff of a mental institution abandoned their posts as Russian and Chechen troops approached, and the inmates ran the place by themselves. Konchalovsky, a Russian who has worked for Hollywood (and made two admirable pictures there, *Shy People* and *Runaway Train*), not only shot in a real mental asylum, but used its actual inmates, who are blended with actors in the leads. This lends an authenticity and a certain unpredictability to the story.

We meet Janna (Julia Vysotsky), blonde and cheerful, in her twenties, an inmate who cheers the others with her accordion; so effective is her music that the image, usually a gray-green-blue, brightens up and admits yellow tones when she plays. In charge is the doctor (Vladas Bagdonas), who goes in search of a bus to evacuate his charges, and Ali (Stanislav Varkki), a poet who never goes anywhere without his knapsack, and even sleeps with it.

For the inmates, the daily high point comes right before bedtime, when they cluster around a window to watch a train roll past. Improbably bedecked with glittering lights like a Christmas tree, it still more improbably has an engineer who not only looks like the Canadian singer Bryan Adams but *is* the Canadian singer Bryan Adams, who sings "Have You Ever Really Loved a Woman?" while he guides the train.

A later shot of a passing train shows that it carries Russian tanks, and there is a good possibility, I think, that so does the Bryan Adams train. But Janna believes Adams is her fiancé and will come to marry her, and has a giant poster of him over her bed, like the poster of David Beckham in *Bend It Like Beckham*. She is all primed for love, and so when Chechen troops arrive it is only a matter of time until she transfers her affections to an Adamesque blond soldier named Akhmed (Sultan Islamov), who goes along with the joke and agrees to be engaged to her.

The early scenes in the asylum are conventionally in Baked Potato land, but the arrival of the troops nudges the film into new and riskier territory, and there are frightening moments when the inmates wander oblivious in the face of danger. One shot shows Janna completely unaware that a helicopter has crashed and exploded behind her. Intriguingly, the soldiers are shown, not as violent outsiders, but as essentially confused and alarmed creatures who are as surprised to find themselves in this situation as the inmates are. One adroit bit of plotting even allows a soldier to enlist in the ranks of the mad.

House of Fools doesn't take sides in the Chechen conflict but offers us two groups of soldiers equally uncomfortable with the situation. The masterstroke is the use of Bryan Adams, who seems like a joke when he first appears (the movie knows this), but is used by Konchalovsky in such a way that eventually he becomes the embodiment of the ability to imagine and dream—an ability, the movie implies, that's the only thing keeping these crazy people sane.

House of Sand and Fog ★ ★ ★ ★
R, 126 m., 2003

Jennifer Connelly (Kathy Nicolo), Ben Kingsley (Massoud Amir Behrani), Ron Eldard (Lester Burdon), Shohreh Aghdashloo (Nadi Behrani), Jonathan Ahdout (Esmail Behrani), Frances Fisher (Connie Walsh). Directed by Vadim Perelman and produced by Michael London and Perelman. Screenplay by Perelman and Shawn Lawrence Otto, based on the novel by Andre Dubus III.

It's so rare to find a movie that doesn't take sides. Conflict is said to be the basis of popular fiction, and yet here is a film that seizes us with its first scene and never lets go, and we feel sympathy all the way through for everyone in it. To be sure, they sometimes do bad things, but the movie *understands* them and their flaws. Like great fiction, *House of Sand and Fog* sees into the hearts of its characters, and loves and pities them. It is based on a novel by Andre Dubus III, and there must have been pressure to cheapen and simplify it into a formula of good and evil. But no. It stands with integrity, and breaks our hearts.

The story is simply told. Kathy Nicolo (Jennifer Connelly), a recovering alcoholic, has been living alone since her husband walked out eight months ago. She has fallen behind on the taxes for her modest split-level home that has a view, however distant, of the California shore. She neglects warnings from the county, the house is put up for auction, and it is purchased by Massoud Amir Behrani (Ben Kingsley), an Iranian immigrant who was a colonel in the Shah's air force but now works two jobs to support his family, and dreams that this house is the first step in rebuilding the lives of his wife and son.

The director and cowriter, Vadim Perelman, doesn't lay out the plot like bricks on a wall, but allows it to reveal itself. We see Massoud working on a highway construction gang, washing himself in a rest room, getting into a Mercedes, and driving to his other job, as an all-night clerk in a roadside convenience store. When the wealthy have a fall, the luxury car is often the last treasure to go; better an expensive old car than a cheap new one. And they are a reminder. Yes, Massoud has memories of the good life they led and their shore cottage in Iran.

Kathy has memories, too. The house was left to her and her brother when their father died. The brother lives in the East, sometimes loans her money, is not sure he believes she is clean and sober. She hasn't had a drink in three years, but is depressed by the departure of her husband, has started smoking again, has needed this shock to blast her out of her lethargy. After she is evicted, she drives past her house in disbelief, seeing this foreigner with his family and his furniture, and one night she sleeps in her car, right outside the gate.

Both of these people desperately need this house. Both have a moral claim to it. Neither can afford to let go of it. Yes, Kathy should have opened her mail and paid her taxes. Yes, perhaps, Massoud should agree with Kathy's public defender (Frances Fisher) and sell the house back for what he paid. But we know, from looking into his books (where every Snickers bar is accounted for), that he is almost broke. This is his last chance to keep up appearances for his wife and son, and to look substantial in the eyes of his daughter's new Iranian husband and her in-laws.

Into the lives of these two blameless parties comes a third, Lester Burdon (Ron Eldard), the deputy sheriff who evicts Kathy but is touched by her grief, then stirred by her beauty. If we are keeping a moral accounting, then his is the blame for what eventually happens. It is fair enough to fight for your home and family, but not fair to misuse your uniform—not even if your excuse is love, or what is spoken of as love. Lester says he will leave his wife and family for Kathy, and although maybe he will, he certainly shouldn't. There is a moment when they start sharing an empty cottage in the woods, and as he leaves she asks if he'll come back, and then quickly adds, "I'll understand if you don't." But he holds himself to a bargain he should not have made and cannot fulfill, and because he is not a moral man he brings unimaginable suffering into the lives of Kathy and the Behrani family, who in all of their dealings after all acted only as good people would from strong motives.

There is much more that the movie will unfold to you, but although I will not reveal it, it isn't in the nature of a surprise plot development. At every step, we feel we are seeing what could and would naturally happen next—not because of coincidence or contrivance, but because of the natures of the people involved.

Not much is said about Massoud Amir Behrani's background in Iran; he has nightmares, he lived in a bad time, but now has pulled back to the simplest things: to find a house for his wife and a wife for his son. Kingsley is such an unbending actor when he needs to be, has such reserves of dignity, that when the deputy attempts to intimidate him with the uniform and the badge, Massoud stands his ground and says, "I don't know who you think you're talking to," and we see at once that he is the man and the deputy is the boy.

As for Kathy, misfortune and injury follow her. Even new love is bad luck. There are scenes involving her being taken back into her old house. And a crisis when the Behranis, whose family is threatened by this woman, simplify everything with one simple sentence: "We have a guest in the house." And a subtle subtext in the way Nadi Behrani (Shohreh Aghdashloo), Massoud's wife, treats the sad girl as a mother would, while hardly understanding a word she says.

I have not read the novel by Andre Dubus III, and no doubt changes have been made in the adaptation—they always are. But I sense that the essential integrity has been defended. *House of Sand and Fog* relates not a plot with its contrived ups and downs, but a story. A plot is about things that happen. A story is about people who behave. To admire a story you must be willing to listen to the people and observe them, and at the end of *House of Sand and Fog* we have seen good people with good intentions who have their lives destroyed because they had the bad luck to come across a weak person with shabby desires. And finally there is a kind of love and loyalty, however strange to us, that reveals itself in the marriage of Massoud and Nadi, and must be respected. ☞

How I Killed My Father ★ ★ ★ ½
NO MPAA RATING, 100 m., 2002

Michel Bouquet (Maurice), Charles Berling (Jean-Luc), Natacha Régnier (Isa), Stéphane Guillon (Patrick), Amira Casar (Myriem), Hubert Koundé (Jean-Toussaint), Karole Rocher (Laetitia). Directed by Anne Fontaine and produced by Philippe Carcassonne. Screenplay by Jacques Fieschi and Fontaine. In French with English subtitles.

One day a letter comes from Africa, regretting to inform him that his father has died and was not able to return to France "as he had planned." That night, during a party in his honor, Jean-Luc sees his father standing among the other guests in the garden, beaming, nodding, his eyes twinkling: *Yes, it's really me*. Is this the father returned from the dead, or was the letter mistaken? The end of the film presents a third possibility.

How I Killed My Father is not about murder in the literal sense, although that seems a possibility. It is about a man who would like to kill his father, and who may have been killed spiritually by his father. Because his father abandoned him and embraced freedom on a continent far away, the son has turned in the opposite direction and jammed himself into a corner, denying himself love, freedom, even children. This is a harrowing movie about how parents know where all the buttons are, and how to push them. Unlike most such stories, however, it doesn't blame the father for pushing the buttons, but the son for having them. We choose to be unhappy.

The background is easily told. Thirty years ago, when Jean-Luc (Charles Berling) was about ten, his father, Maurice (Michel Bouquet), walked out and never returned. Jean-Luc's younger brother Patrick (Stéphane Guillon) doesn't remember the old man, isn't as wounded, but is a feckless failure whom Jean-Luc has hired as a driver and assistant. It's almost as if this relationship forces Jean-Luc to take over the father's responsibility for Patrick.

Jean-Luc is a wealthy doctor in Versailles, running a clinic that promises to combat the process of aging. A woman client asks about botox. A man complains he will be elderly when his two-year-old is grown. At home, Jean-Luc lives with his wife, Isa (Natacha Régnier), a "perfect" wife, hostess, and adornment. He has determined it would be dangerous for her to have children.

And then old Maurice materializes in the garden. Michel Bouquet, whose thin lips and twinkling eyes have added a knowing mystery to so many films by Chabrol and others, has returned unexplained. He would like money to reopen his clinic in Africa, but that doesn't seem to be his real motive. Perhaps he has returned simply because he is curious. He and Jean-Luc have that sort of infuriating relationship where the father does not have to say anything at all in order to be critical. His very silences are a reproach. His pleasantries carry an edge of irony. Like many parents, he is more beloved by strangers than by his children. Isa, for example, is drawn to him. And Patrick, who has no history with him, likes him. Only hard, cold Jean-Luc, who has founded his life on resentment, who takes no chances so he can never be hurt, hates him.

The film, cowritten and directed by Anne Fontaine, plays like a thriller that is toying with us by delaying its explosion of violence. But the violence in the film doesn't involve guns or blood. It involves quiet little statements, some of them pleasantries, by which the father literally devastates his son's system of defenses. By the end, hardly having raised his voice, Maurice has returned to the son he hurt so much and finished the job.

Fontaine tells the story with many scenes of unexpected insight. Curious, how Jean-Luc wants to buy an expensive apartment for his mistress (Amira Casar), who doesn't want one. Odd how he dotes on her child. One night a hooker takes him home, and Fontaine shows him looking through a door that is ajar, so he can see the hooker's parents at their evening meal. What are these scenes for? To show him always yearningly on the outside of a family? Who put him there? Is his wife really not capable of child-bearing?

How I Killed My Father is about cold people and their victims. It is the misfortune of the brother and the wife to have Jean-Luc to deal with. He treats them both with financial generosity, but they can never heal his wound, and he lets them know that. So imagine Jean-Luc's pain when a young African appears in Versailles to visit old Maurice. This visitor is a doctor, too: "Your father was my mentor." One night Jean-Luc glimpses them laughing together in a way he has never laughed with his father.

Sometimes in life we trade parents. Others are closer to our parents than we are. We are closer to the parents of others than they are. Maybe it is so hard to be successful as a parent and a child that this is what we're forced to do. Jean-Luc's tragedy is not that he lost a father, but that he never found another. He refused to look for one. And the father he never found is the one he killed.

How to Lose a Guy in 10 Days ★ ½
PG-13, 116 m., 2003

Kate Hudson (Andie), Matthew McConaughey (Ben), Adam Goldberg (Tony), Michael Michele (Spears), Shalom Harlow (Green), Bebe Neuwirth (Lana), Robert Klein (Phillip). Directed by Donald Petrie and produced by Christine Forsyth-Peters, Lynda Obst, and Robert Evans. Screenplay by Kristen Buckley, Brian Regan, and Burr Steers, based on the book by Michele Alexander and Jeannie Long.

I am just about ready to write off movies in which people make bets about whether they will, or will not, fall in love. The premise is fundamentally unsound, since it subverts every love scene with a lying subtext. Characters are nice when they want to be mean, or mean when they want to be nice. The easiest thing at the movies is to sympathize with two people who are falling in love. The hardest thing is to sympathize with two people who are denying their feelings, misleading each other, and causing pain to a trusting heart. This is comedy only by dictionary definition. In life, it is unpleasant and makes the audience sad.

Unless, of course, the characters are thoroughgoing rotters in the first place, as in *Dirty Rotten Scoundrels* (1988), in which Steve Martin and Michael Caine make a $50,000 bet on who will be the first to con the rich American Glenne Headly. They deserve their comeuppance, and we enjoy it. *How to Lose a Guy in 10 Days* is not, alas, pitched at that modest level of sophistication, and provides us with two young people who are like pawns in a sex game for the developmentally shortchanged.

He works at an ad agency. She works for a magazine that is *Cosmopolitan*, spelled a different way. She pitches her editor on an article about how to seduce a guy and then drive him away in ten days. He pitches his boss on an idea that involves him being able to get a woman to fall in love with him in ten days. They don't even Meet Cute, but are shuffled together by a treacherous conspirator.

Now, of course, they will fall in love. That goes without saying. They will fall in love even though she deliberately creates scenes no man could abide, such as nicknaming his penis Princess Sophia. She allows her disgusting miniature dog to pee on his pool table. She even puts a plate of sandwiches down on top of the pot in their poker game, something Nancy would be too sophisticated to do to Sluggo.

He puts up with this mistreatment because he has his own bet to win, and also because, doggone it, he has fallen in love with this vaporous fluffball of narcissistic cluelessness. That leaves only one big scene for us to anticipate, or dread: the inevitable moment when they both find out the other made a bet. At a moment like that, a reasonably intelligent couple would take a beat, start laughing, and head for the nearest hot-sheets haven. But no. These characters descend from the moribund fictional ideas of earlier decades and must react in horror, run away in grief, prepare to leave town, etc., while we in the audience make our own bets about their IQs.

Matthew McConaughey and Kate Hudson star. I neglected to mention that, maybe because I was trying to place them in this review's version of the Witness Protection Program. If I were taken off the movie beat and assigned to cover the interior design of bowling alleys, I would have some idea of how they must have felt as they made this film.

Hukkle ★ ★ ★

NO MPAA RATING, 75 m., 2003

Ferenc Bandi (Uncle Cseklik), Józsefné Rácz (Midwife), József Forkas (Police Officer), Ferenc Nagy (Beekeeper), Ferencné Virag (Beekeeper's wife), Jánosné Nagy (Boske), Milhalyne Kiraly (Grandmother), Mihaly Kiraly (Grandfather). Directed by György Pálfi and produced by Csaba Bereczki and András Bohm. Screenplay by Pálfi.

An old man hiccups. He shuffles slowly about his morning ritual and then takes his place on a bench outside his cottage beside the road, still hiccupping. A goose goes about its business. flies buzz. A cat earns its living. A runaway cart causes a stir in the village. The old man hiccups.

These opening shots announce György Pálfi's *Hukkle* as a film that will proceed in its own way to its own destination, without regard to convention. The title, a Hungarian word that sounds like a hiccup, is not much help. The film is told almost entirely without dialogue, but is alive to sound; we spend observant, introspective time in a Hungarian hamlet where nothing much seems to happen—oh, except that there's a suspicious death.

The murder enters the film like another chapter in *Hukkle*'s natural history. We have already seen the violence of nature: a frog, to its astonishment, suddenly eaten whole; a bee crushed; a cat dead; bees shaken from their hives; the very firmament shaken by what seems to be an earthquake but is only a low-flying jet. These omens are portents of trouble, in a film that finds a new tone: ominous pastoral.

The film is photographed with loving care, and seems at first to be merely a slice of life from a village day; in its attention to the smallest details of life (animal, vegetable, insect) it has been compared to *Microcosmos*. But there is a macro level, too, almost too large in scale to be seen, and the ingenuity of the film is in suggesting a larger reality—a forest it almost cannot see because it clings so closely to the trees.

This reality involves the dead body, pale and cold at the bottom of a stream, and the investigation of a local policeman, who takes photos of the riverbank where the victim was fishing before his—accident? Murder? Later, in a scene that's a quiet nudge to *Blowup*, the policeman studies the photos and notices a missing bottle. Still later, in another wordless scene, a woman who is brewing illegal spirits in a cave looks up from her still and sees the policeman standing in the cave opening, regarding her.

Can this murder mystery be extracted from *Hukkle* and explained with the clarity of a newspaper account? I doubt it. I think the murder is part of the whole warp and woof of the movie, which studies the events in this village with the attention and yet the random choices of an alien observer who is very interested but doesn't know quite what to look for.

Given its odd choices of perspective and subject, the movie's point of view is almost a character. *Hukkle* doesn't suggest, but I will, as a possible approach to the film, that the opening shot of the old man could be the first glimpse of Earth life by this objective observer, which pokes here and there in the village, so that we—who know what to look for and pick up on the clues—know a murder has been committed, but to the observer all the images are equal. We have the knowledge to find meaning in a pattern that the observer doesn't perceive. Since the hypothetical observer doesn't speak a human language, of course the movie doesn't much notice such sounds.

That may, of course, simply be my fancy. On another level, *Hukkle* is a lovingly photographed natural history of a day of village life. Some audience members will find it maddening. It requires patience and attention. It is not soothing, like a nature study, but disturbing, seeing life as an arena for deadly struggles in which most creatures earn a living by eating each other. To my imaginary alien, perhaps the fisherman was not murdered at all, but simply drowned while attempting to asphyxiate a fish. Maybe, like hunters who shoot themselves, he found a certain justice.

And still the old man hiccups.

Hulk ★ ★ ★
PG-13, 138 m., 2003

Eric Bana (Bruce Banner), Jennifer Connelly (Betty Ross), Sam Elliott (Ross), Josh Lucas (Talbot), Nick Nolte (Father), Paul Kersey (Young David Banner), Cara Buono (Edith Banner), Todd Tesen (Young Ross). Directed by Ang Lee and produced by Avi Arad, Larry J. Franco, Gale Anne Hurd, and James Schamus. Screenplay by John Turman, Michael France, Schamus, Jack Kirby, and Stan Lee, based on the story by Schamus.

The Hulk is rare among Marvel superheroes in that his powers are a curse, not an advantage. When rage overcomes Dr. Bruce Banner and he turns into a green monster many times his original size, it is not to fight evil or defend the American way, but simply to lash out at his tormentors. Like the Frankenstein stories that are its predecessors, *Hulk* is a warning about the folly of those who would toy with the secrets of

life. It is about the anguish of having powers you did not seek and do not desire. "What scares me the most," Banner tells his only friend, Betty Ross, "is that when it happens, when it comes over me, when I totally lose control, I like it."

Ang Lee's *Hulk* (the movie's title drops "the") is the most talkative and thoughtful recent comic book adaptation. It is not so much about a green monster as about two wounded adult children of egomaniacs. Banner (Eric Bana) was fathered by a scientist (Nick Nolte) who has experimented on his own DNA code and passed along genes that are transformed by a lab accident into his son's hulkhood. Betty Ross (Jennifer Connelly) is his research partner; they were almost lovers, but it didn't work out, and she speaks wryly of "my inexplicable fascination with emotionally distant men." Her cold father is General Ross (Sam Elliott), filled with military bluster and determined to destroy the Hulk.

These two dueling Oedipal conflicts are at the heart of *Hulk,* and it's touching how in many scenes we are essentially looking at damaged children. When the Hulk's amazing powers become known, the military of course tries to kill him (that's the routine solution in most movies about aliens and monsters), but there's another villain who has a more devious scheme. That's Talbot (Josh Lucas), a venal entrepreneur who wants to use Banner's secret to manufacture a race of self-repairing soldiers. Lots of money there.

The movie brings up issues about genetic experimentation, the misuse of scientific research, and our instinctive dislike of misfits, and actually talks about them. Remember that Ang Lee is the director of such films as *The Ice Storm* and *Sense and Sensibility,* as well as *Crouching Tiger, Hidden Dragon;* he is trying here to actually deal with the issues in the story of the Hulk, instead of simply cutting to brainless special effects.

Just as well, too, because the Hulk himself is the least successful element in the film. He's convincing in close-up but sort of jerky in long shot—oddly, just like his spiritual cousin, King Kong. There are times when his movements subtly resemble the stop-frame animation used to create Kong, and I wonder if that's deliberate; there was a kind of eerie oddness about Kong's movement that was creepier than the slick smoothness of modern computer-generated creatures.

King Kong is of course one of Lee's inspirations, in a movie with an unusual number of references to film classics. *Bride of Frankenstein* is another, as in a scene where Hulk sees his reflection in a pond. No prizes for identifying *Dr. Jekyll and Mr. Hyde* as the source of the original comics. Other references include *Citizen Kane* (the Hulk tears apart a laboratory) and *The Right Stuff* (a jet airplane flies so high the stars are visible). There is also a shade of General Jack D. Ripper in General Ross, who is played by Sam Elliott in a masterful demonstration of controlled and focused almost-overacting.

The film has its share of large-scale action sequences, as rockets are fired at the Hulk and he responds by bringing down helicopters. And there are the obligatory famous landmarks, real and unreal, we expect in a superhero movie: the Golden Gate Bridge, Monument Valley, and of course an elaborate secret laboratory where Hulk can be trapped in an immersion chamber while his DNA is extracted.

But these scenes are secondary in interest to the movie's central dramas, which involve the two sets of fathers and children. Banner has a repressed memory of a traumatic childhood event, and it is finally jarred loose after he meets his father again after many years. Nolte, looking like a man in desperate need of a barber and flea powder, plays Banner's dad as a man who works in the same laboratory, as a janitor. He uses DNA testing to be sure this is indeed his son, and in one clandestine conversation tells him, "You're going to have to watch that temper of yours."

Connelly's character also has big issues with her father—she trusts him when she shouldn't— and it's amusing how much the dilemma of this character resembles the situation of the woman she played in *A Beautiful Mind*. Both times she's in love with a brilliant scientist who's a sweetheart until he goes haywire, and who thinks he's being pursued by the government.

The movie has an elegant visual strategy; after countless directors have failed, Ang Lee figures out how split-screen techniques can be made to work. Usually they're an annoying gimmick, but here he uses moving frame-lines and pictures within pictures to suggest the dynamic storytelling techniques of comic books. Some shots are astonishing, as foreground and background interact and reveal one another. There is another technique, more subtle, that reminds me of comics: He often cuts between different angles in the same close-up—not cutting away, but cutting from one view of a face to another, as graphic artists do when they need another frame to deal with extended dialogue.

Whether *Hulk* will appeal to its primary audience—teenage science fiction fans—is hard to say. No doubt it will set the usual box office records over the weekend, but will it reach audiences who will respond to its dramatic ambition? Ang Lee has boldly taken the broad outlines of a comic book story and transformed them to his own purposes; this is a comic book movie for people who wouldn't be caught dead at a comic book movie.

Human Nature ★ ★ ★
R, 96 m., 2002

Tim Robbins (Nathan Bronfman), Patricia Arquette (Lila Jute), Rhys Ifans (Puff), Miranda Otto (Gabrielle), Robert Forster (Nathan's Father), Mary Kay Place (Nathan's Mother), Rosie Perez (Louise). Directed by Michel Gondry and produced by Anthony Bregman, Ted Hope, Spike Jonze, and Charlie Kaufman. Screenplay by Kaufman.

Is human life entirely based on sex, or is that only what it seems like on cable television? *Human Nature*, a comedy written and produced by the writer and director who made us the great gift of *Being John Malkovich*, is a study of three characters at war against their sexual natures.

Lila (Patricia Arquette) fled to the woods at the age of twenty, after hair entirely covered her body. She becomes a famous reclusive nature writer, a very hairy Annie Dillard, but finally returns to civilization because she's so horny. Puff (Rhys Ifans) is a man who was raised as an ape, thinks he's an ape, and is cheerfully eager on all occasions to act out an ape's sexual desires. And Nathan (Tim Robbins) was a boy raised by parents so strict that his entire sexual drive was sublimated into the desire to train others as mercilessly as he was trained.

With these three characters as subjects for investigation, *Human Nature* asks if there is a happy medium between natural impulses and the inhibitions of civilization—or if it is true, as Nathan instructs Puff, "When in doubt, don't ever do what you really want to do." The movie involves these three in a ménage à trois that is (as you can imagine) very complicated, and just in order to be comprehensive in its study of human sexual behavior, throws in a cute French lab assistant (Miranda Otto).

None of which gives you the slightest idea of the movie's screwball charm. The writer, Charlie Kaufman, must be one madcap kinda guy. I imagine him seeming to wear a funny hat even when he's not. His inventions here lead us down strange comic byways, including Disneyesque song-and-dance numbers in which the hairy Arquette dances nude with the cute little animals of the forest. (Her hair, like Salome's veil, prevents us from seeing quite what we think we're seeing, but the MPAA's eyeballs must have been popping out with the strain.)

Early scenes show poor Nathan as a boy, at the dinner table with his parents (Robert Forster and Mary Kay Place), where every meal involves as much cutlery as a diplomatic feast, and using the wrong fork gets the child sent to his room without eating. As an adult, Nathan dedicates his life to training white mice to eat with the right silver, after the male mouse politely pulls out the female mouse's chair for her.

Then he gets a really big challenge, when the ape-man (Ifans) comes into his clutches. Nicknaming him Puff, Nathan keeps him in a Plexiglas cage in his lab, and fits Puff with an electrified collar that jolts him with enough juice to send him leaping spasmodically into the air every time he engages in sexual behavior, which is constantly. Lila, the hairy girl, meanwhile has turned herself over to a sympathetic electrologist (Rosie Perez), who fixes her up with Nathan—who does not know she is covered with hair and, if he did, would be sure it was bad manners.

The movie has nowhere much to go and nothing much to prove, except that Stephen King is correct and if you can devise the right characters and the right situation, the plot will

take care of itself—or not, as the case may be. Ifans is so dogged in the determination of his sex drive, despite the electrical shocks, that when the professor sets his final examination at a Hooters-type place, we're grinning before he gets inside the door.

The movie is the feature debut of Michel Gondry, who directed a lot of Bjork's videos and therefore in a sense has worked with characters like these before. His movie is slight without being negligible. If it tried to do anything more, it would fail and perhaps explode, but at this level of manic whimsy, it is just about right. You had better go alone, because in any crowd of four there will be three who find it over their heads, or under their radar. They would really be better off attending *National Lampoon's Van Wilder*, unless you want to go to the trouble of having them fitted with electric collars.

The Human Stain ★ ★ ★ ½
R, 106 m., 2003

Anthony Hopkins (Coleman Silk), Nicole Kidman (Faunia Farley), Ed Harris (Lester Farley), Gary Sinise (Nathan Zuckerman), Wentworth Miller (Young Coleman Silk), Jacinda Barrett (Steena Paulsson), Phyliss Newman (Iris Silk), Ann Deavere Smith (Mrs. Silk). Directed by Robert Benton and produced by Gary Lucchesi, Tom Rosenberg, and Scott Steindorff. Screenplay by Nicholas Meyer, based on the novel by Philip Roth.

The Human Stain contains a significant secret about one of the characters. This review discusses it. "There's no way we can contain the secret, and we're not even trying to," the producer, Tom Rosenberg, told me at the Toronto Film Festival. "It's out there already with the Philip Roth novel. And this isn't a movie like *The Crying Game*, which is really about its secret."

That's because the secret belongs to the character, not the movie. It is one he has lived with all of his adult life. Coleman Silk is a professor of classics at a university whose stature he has enhanced. One day he notes that two students have not attended class. "What are they, spooks?" he asks his students. Because they are

African-Americans, his wisecrack is interpreted as a racist remark, and he is called before a faculty tribunal. Rather than defend himself, he resigns in a rage. His rage is fueled by his secret: He is an African-American himself.

The world thinks Coleman Silk (Anthony Hopkins) is Jewish. His family knows otherwise. In flashbacks, we see a bright young man, light-skinned enough to pass, who sees two career paths ahead of him, one as a white, the other as a black. He decides the choice is clear, enlists in the navy as a white man, and severs his links with his past. There are heartbreaking scenes involving his mother (Anna Deavere Smith), whom he treats with cool disregard. Early in the film, dating a white girl, he takes her home to meet his mother having not made it clear he is black; his revelation is made through the fact of her appearance, which seems cowardly and cruel.

Passing for white is not as uncommon as some of the reviewers of *The Human Stain* seem to think. Many black family trees have branches that drifted over the color line. One problem with *The Human Stain,* however, is that Anthony Hopkins doesn't look anything at all like Wentworth Miller, who plays him as a young man. We simply have to accept the mismatch as a given, and move on. (Does Hopkins look as if he "could" have been black? How can you answer that question about a man who successfully passes for white? The racist white man on the train who berates the porter is played by Allison Davis, a Chicago attorney who is black.)

Hopkins makes our acceptance easier because he is a fine actor and involves us so directly in the character's life that we forget about the technical details. After his resignation, unexpectedly, in middle age, he begins a passionate affair with Faunia Farley (Nicole Kidman), an unlettered school janitor half his age. Whether Kidman convinces us she is a working-class woman with a wife-beating ex-husband (Ed Harris) is another hurdle the movie sets for itself. I think she clears it. Harris is frighteningly effective as the ex-husband; hard to believe this is the same man who plays the kind football coach in *Radio.*

The movie's narrator is Nathan Zuckerman (Gary Sinise), a recurring character in Roth's later novels. Silk must have someone to confide in, and Zuckerman provides a listener. Eventually there is Faunia, but his talks with her are more confessional; with Zuckerman, he expresses his rage at the P.C. extremism that cost him his job because of an innocent verbal slip, and asks him to write about it. (It's tempting to say the response to his slip is exaggerated, but every campus has a story or two about P.C. fascism; what's harder to believe is the self-abasing apology delivered late in the movie by one of Silk's tormentors.)

The story involves two different kinds of passing: crossing the race line, and the class line. Which is more difficult? Consider that Coleman and Faunia must deal with each other despite their lack of common references, education, background, assumptions, manners of speech, tastes, and instincts. To cross the race line involves deep psychological anguish, as you betray yourself and your past, but in the routine of daily existence it is perhaps easier than crossing the class line. You can talk and think just the way you do now. It was different 50 or 100 years ago, but today most of us find it more difficult to deal in depth with someone of another class than with someone of another race. (I am not forgetting that to cross from white to black would be much more difficult, because you'd take on the impact of racism.)

What makes *The Human Stain* ambitious and fascinating is how it considers both of these journeys. Once he decides to pass, Coleman Silk finds it relatively easy to exist as a white navy officer, college student, and professor; he must have had problems, but we don't see them. I wish the movie had told us more about how he handled his new Jewish identity (by claiming to be completely secularized, I imagine). But when he becomes the lover of a night-shift janitor who is younger and semiliterate, who has an ex-husband from the world of *Deliverance,* who looks to strangers as if she is too pretty and tall for this balding sixtyish guy, he has his work cut out for him.

They do, of course, communicate through sex, the universal language, although we may have some doubt about how well Coleman speaks it. And this is crucial: They can communicate through revelation, confession, and empathy. Anyone who works a twelve-step program knows how strangers from different backgrounds become friends because they identify with similar experiences. Coleman and Faunia have been cruelly devalued by life, and find in each other a spark of identification that can cross any barrier. And there's the lifeboat factor; since they're both under extreme pressure, they're not looking for a "match" but need bailing out—they respond to each other as rescuers.

The Human Stain has been directed by Robert Benton with a sure feel for the human values involved. Yes, we have to suspend disbelief over the casting, but that's easier since we can believe the stories of these people. Not many movies probe into matters of identity or adaptation. Most movie characters are like Greek gods and comic-book heroes: We learn their roles and powers at the beginning of the story, and they never change. Here are complex, troubled, flawed people, brave enough to breathe deeply and take one more risk with their lives.

The Hunted ★ ★ ★ ½
R, 94 m., 2003

Tommy Lee Jones (L. T. Bonham), Benicio Del Toro (Aaron Hallam), Connie Nielsen (Abby Durrell), Jenna Boyd (Loretta Kravitz), Leslie Stefanson (Irene Kravitz), Robert Blanche (Crumley), Aaron Brounstein (Stokes), Ron Canada (Van Zandt). Directed by William Friedkin and produced by James Jacks and Ricardo Mestres. Screenplay by David Griffiths, Peter Griffiths, and Art Monterastelli.

The Hunted is a pure and rather inspired example of the one-on-one chase movie. Like *The Fugitive,* which also starred Tommy Lee Jones, it's about one man pursuing another more or less nonstop for the entire film. Walking in, I thought I knew what to expect, but I didn't anticipate how William Friedkin would jolt me with the immediate urgency of the action. This is not an arm's-length chase picture, but a close, physical duel between its two main characters.

Jones plays L.T. Bonham, a civilian employee of the U.S. Army who trains elite forces to stalk, track, hunt, and kill. His men learn how to make weapons out of shards of rock, and forge knives from scrap metal. In a sequence proving we haven't seen everything yet, they learn how to kill an enemy by the numbers—leg artery, heart, neck, lung. That Jones can make this training seem real goes without saying; he has an understated, minimalist acting style that implies he's been teaching the class for a long time.

One of his students is Aaron Hallam (Benicio Del Toro), who fought in Kosovo in 1999 and had experiences there that warped him ("his battle stress has gone so deep it is part of his personality"). Back home in Oregon, offended by hunters using telescopic sights, he claims four victims—"those hunters were filleted like deer." Bonham recognizes the style and goes into the woods after him ("If I'm not back in two days that will mean I'm dead").

Hallam's stress syndrome has made him into a radical defender of animal rights; he talks about chickens on assembly lines, and asks one cop how he'd feel if a higher life form were harvesting mankind. Of course, in killing the hunters, he has promoted himself to that superior life form, but this is not a movie about debate points. It is a chase.

No modern director is more identified with chases than Friedkin, whose *The French Connection* and *To Live and Die in L.A.* set the standard. Here the whole movie is a chase, sometimes at a crawl, as when Hallam drives a stolen car directly into a traffic jam. What makes the movie fresh is that it doesn't stand back and regard its pursuit as an exercise, but stays very close to the characters and focuses on the actual physical reality of their experience.

Consider an early hand-to-hand combat between Bonham and Hallam. We've seen so many fancy, high-tech, computer-assisted fight scenes in recent movies that we assume the fighters can fly. They live in a world of gravity-free speedup. Not Friedkin's characters. Their fight is gravity-based. Their arms and legs are heavy. Their blows land solidly, with pain on both sides. They gasp and grunt with effort. They can be awkward and desperate. They both know the techniques of hand-to-hand combat, but in real life it isn't scripted, and you know what? It isn't so easy. We are involved in the immediate, exhausting, draining physical work of fighting.

The chase sequences—through Oregon forests and city streets, on highways and bridges—are also reality-oriented. The cinematography, by the great Caleb Deschanel (*The*

Right Stuff), buries itself in the reality of the locations. The forests are wet and green, muddy and detailed. The leaves are not scenery but right in front of our faces, to be brushed aside. Running, hiding, stalking, the two men get dirty and tired and gasp for breath. We feel their physical effort; this isn't one of those movies where shirts are dry again in the next scene and the hero has the breath for long speeches.

The Hunted requires its skilled actors. Ordinary action stars would not do. The screenplay, by David Griffiths, Peter Griffiths, and Art Monterastelli, has a kind of minimalist clarity, in which nobody talks too much and everything depends on tone. Notice scenes where Del Toro is interrogated by other law officials. He doesn't give us the usual hostile, aggressive clichés, but seems to be trying to explain himself from a place so deep he can't make it real to outsiders. This man doesn't kill out of rage but out of sorrow.

There are moments when Friedkin lays it on a little thick. The early how-to sequence, where Bonham's trainees learn how to make weapons from scratch, implies there will be a later sequence where they need to. Fair enough. But would Hallam, in the heat of a chase, have the time to build a fire from shavings, heat an iron rod and hammer it into a knife? Even if Bonham cooperates by meanwhile pausing to chip his own flint weapon? Maybe not, or maybe the two hunters are ritualistically agreeing to face each other using only these tools of their trade. The resulting knife fight, which benefits from the earlier knife training sequence, is physical action of a high order.

There are other characters in the movie, other relationships. A woman with a child, whom Hallam visits (she likes him but is a little afraid). A woman who is an FBI field officer. Various cops. They add background and atmosphere, but *The Hunted* is about two hardworking men who are good at their jobs, although only one can be the best.

I

I Am Sam ★ ★
PG-13, 133 m., 2002

Sean Penn (Sam Dawson), Michelle Pfeiffer (Rita), Dakota Fanning (Lucy Dawson), Dianne Wiest (Annie), Doug Hutchison (Ifty), Stanley DeSantis (Robert), Brad Silverman (Brad), Joseph Rosenberg (Joe), Richard Schiff (Turner), Laura Dern (Randy). Directed by Jessie Nelson and produced by Marshall Herskovitz, Nelson, Richard Solomon, and Edward Zwick. Screenplay by Kristine Johnson and Nelson.

"Daddy, did God mean for you to be like this, or was it an accident?"

That's little Lucy Dawson, asking her father why he isn't quite like other people. She's a bright kid and figures out the answer herself, and when a classmate at grade school asks, "Why does your father act like a retard?" she explains, "He is."

I Am Sam stars Sean Penn as Lucy's dad, Sam, who has the IQ of a seven-year-old but is trying to raise the daughter he fathered with a homeless woman. The mother disappeared right after giving birth (her farewell words: "All I wanted was a place to sleep"), and now Sam is doing his best to cope, although sometimes Lucy has to help him with her homework. Eventually Lucy decides to stop learning so she won't get ahead of her dad. "I don't want to read if you can't," she tells him.

Sam loves the Beatles (his favorite is George). He named his daughter after "Lucy in the Sky With Diamonds," and has learned most of life's lessons from Beatles songs. The lesson *I Am Sam* wants to teach us is, "All you need is love." This is not quite strictly true. Sam loves his daughter more than anyone else, and she loves him, but it will take more than love for him to see her through grade school and adolescence and out into the world. Since the movie does not believe this, it has a serious disagreement with most of the audience.

Sean Penn does as well as can be expected with Sam, but it is painful to see an actor of his fire and reach locked into a narrow range of emotional and intellectual responses. Not long ago a veteran moviegoer told me that when he sees an actor playing a mentally retarded person, he is reminded of a performer playing "Lady of Spain" on an accordion: The fingers fly, but are the song or the instrument worthy of the effort? The kind of performance Sean Penn delivers in *I Am Sam*, which may look hard, is easy compared, say, to his amazing work in Woody Allen's *Sweet and Lowdown*. As Robert Kohner observes in his *Variety* review: "In a way, Edward Norton's turn in *The Score*, in which his thief used a mental handicap as a disguise, gave the trade secret away when it comes to this sort of performance."

The movie sets up the Department of Children and Family Services and its attorney as the villains when they take Lucy away from Sam and try to place her with a foster family. The heroine is a high-velocity Beverly Hills lawyer named Rita (Michelle Pfeiffer), who takes Sam's case on a pro bono basis to prove to the other people in her office that she's not a selfish bitch. This character and performance would be perfect in an edgy comedy, but they exist in a parallel universe to the world of this film.

Sam has the kinds of problems that come up in story conferences more than in life. For example, he's sitting in a diner when an attractive young woman smiles at him. He smiles back. She comes over and asks him if he would like to have a good time. He says he sure would. Then a cop pounces and arrests him for frequenting a prostitute. Back at the station, the cop admits, "This is the first time in nineteen years I actually believe a guy who says he didn't know she was a hooker." Hey, it's the first time in history that a man has been arrested on sex charges for talking to a woman in a diner before any clothes have come off, money has changed hands, or services have been discussed.

The movie climaxes in a series of courtroom scenes, which follow the time-honored formulas for such scenes, with the intriguing difference that this time the evil prosecutor (Richard Schiff) seems to be making good sense. At one point he turns scornfully to the Pfeiffer character and says, "This is an anecdote for you at some luncheon, but I'm here every day. You're out the door, but you know who I see come back? The child." Well, he's right, isn't he?

The would-be adoptive mother, played by Laura Dern, further complicates the issue by not being a cruel child-beater who wants the monthly state payments, but a loving, sensitive mother who would probably be great for Lucy. Sam more or less understands this, but does the adoptive mother? As the film ends, the issue is in doubt.

I Am Sam is aimed at audiences who will relate to the heart-tugging relationship between Sam and Lucy (and young Dakota Fanning does a convincing job as the bright daughter). Every device of the movie's art is designed to convince us Lucy must stay with Sam, but common sense makes it impossible to go the distance with the premise. You can't have heroes and villains when the wrong side is making the best sense.

I Capture the Castle ★ ★ ★ ½
R, 113 m., 2003

Romola Garai (Cassandra Mortmain), Rose Byrne (Rose Mortmain), Henry Thomas (Simon Cotton), Marc Blucas (Neil Cotton), Bill Nighy (James Mortmain), Tara Fitzgerald (Topaz Mortmain), Sinead Cusack (Mrs. Cotton), Henry Cavill (Stephen). Directed by Tim Fywell and produced by David Parfitt, Anant Singh, and David M. Thompson. Screenplay by Heidi Thomas, based on the novel by Dodie Smith.

I Capture the Castle is the kind of novel dreamy adolescents curl up with on rainy Saturdays, imagining themselves as members of a poor but brilliantly eccentric family living in a decrepit English castle. It's that kind of movie, too, about a sublimely impractical family given to sudden dramatic outbursts. It's a romance ever so much more inspiring for teenage girls than the materialist propaganda they get from Hollywood, teaching them to value genius above accessories. And there's a serious undercurrent; this story was close to the heart of the author Dodie Smith, whose other novel, *101 Dalmatians,* was more lighthearted and aimed at younger readers.

As the movie opens, the Mortmain family on a country outing finds a castle—small and rundown, it is true, but undeniably a castle—and the father, James, stands on the battlements and declares, "I will write masterpieces here!" He is given to such pronouncements, often followed by a sideways glance to see if anyone believes him. He did write one well-regarded book, it is true, but now he descends into a long barren period, and in 1936, when the story takes place, the Mortmains are behind on the rent, short on food money, and increasingly desperate.

The Mortmains are: James (Bill Nighy), the father, who seems to be going around the bend; his wife, Topaz (Tara Fitzgerald), a long-tressed artist; younger sister Cassandra (Romola Garai), who is the narrator; and the official family beauty, Rose (Rose Byrne), who is so impatient with poverty that at one point she runs out into the rain and announces she plans to sell herself on the streets and will borrow the train fare to the city from the vicar.

The girls' mother died some years earlier, and Topaz does her best with two ungrateful girls and a husband who seems on the edge of madness. Then one day all changes when two young Americans arrive in the district. They are Simon and Neil Cotton (Henry Thomas and Marc Blucas), the sons and heirs of the owner of the property, and rather than collect the back-due rent they proceed to fall in love with Rose—Simon obviously, Neil quietly. Their British mother (Sinead Cusack) is both appalled and amused by the family, and invites them over to dinner, an event that has to be seen to be believed.

"Why are you all dressed in green?" the brothers ask on their first meeting with this family. It has to do with a surfeit of dye and too much time on their hands. The family is educated, literate, creative, but alarmingly unworldly; what the brothers take for artful naïveté is artless lack of sophistication. Rose, however, knows that she will marry anyone to get out of the leaky, drafty castle, and that leads to a complicated romantic melodrama that also involves Cassandra's and Neil's secret feelings, not necessarily for each other.

The film is shot with that green British palette that makes everything look damp and makes us imagine the sheets will be clammy. The countryside is unspeakably picturesque, and the girls flourish here; it is sad to see the wild-haired Rose in town, after her engagement and after the hairdressers have styled her into a copy of everyone else. The father meanwhile sinks into despond, and the family finds a way to treat his writer's block that is heartless but effective.

The first-time director, Tim Fywell, handles his material with an excusable fondness for the eccentricities of his characters, but generates touching emotion through the plight of Cassandra, who is honest and true, and finds her way almost blindly through the labyrinth of love, trusting to her best instincts. Romola Garai, who was Kate in *Nicholas Nickleby*, is heart-winning in the role.

We like these people, which is important, and we are amused by them, which is helpful, but most of all we envy them, because they negotiate their romantic perplexities with such dash and style. It would be fun to be a member of the Mortmain family—maybe the younger brother, who shows every sign of growing up to be Harry Potter.

Note: The R rating ("for brief nudity") is another attempt by the MPAA to steer teenagers away from useful and sophisticated entertainments, and toward vulgarity and violence. If this movie is R and Charlie's Angels: Full Throttle *is PG-13, then the rating board has no shame. Better the Angels as strippers than an innocent nipple during a swim in the castle moat.*

Ice Age ★ ★ ★
PG, 88 m., 2002

Denis Leary (Diego the Saber-Toothed Tiger), John Leguizamo (Sid the Sloth), Ray Romano (Manfred the Mammoth), Goran Visnjic (Soto the Saber-Toothed Tiger), Jack Black (Zeke), Tara Strong (Roshan), Cedric the Entertainer (Rhino). Directed by Chris Wedge and produced by Lori Forte. Screenplay by Peter Ackerman, Michael Berg, and Michael Wilson.

Ice Age is a pleasure to look at and scarcely less fun as a story. I came to scoff and stayed to smile. I confess the premise did not inspire me: A woolly mammoth, a saber-toothed tiger, and a sloth team up to rescue a human baby and return it to its parents. Uh-huh. But the screenplay is sly and literate, and director Chris Wedge's visual style so distinctive and appealing that the movie seduced me.

The film takes place during a southward migration of species during a great ice age. Such migrations took place over millennia

and were not the pre-Cambrian equivalent of going to Florida for the winter months, but no matter: As the ice packs advance, the animals retreat. There is no time to lose. Baby mammoths, playing in a tar pit, are told by their parents to hurry up: "You can play Extinction later."

We meet Manfred the Mammoth (voice by Ray Romano) and Sid the Sloth (John Leguizamo). Of course they can speak. (It is the humans, they believe, who have not yet mastered language.) When Sid and Manfred come upon a small, helpless human child, they decide to protect it and return it to its parents—even though those same parents, they know, have developed weapons for killing them. Along the trail they are joined by Diego the Saber-Toothed Tiger (Denis Leary), who has a hidden agenda. They are potentially each other's dinners, and yet through Sid's insouciance and Manfred's bravery in saving Diego from certain death, they bond and become friends.

It is true that altruism is a positive evolutionary trait; a species with individuals willing to die for the survival of the race is a species that will get somewhere in the Darwinian sweepstakes. But listen closely. When Diego the Saber-Toothed Tiger asks Manfred the Mammoth why he saved him, Manfred replies, "That's what you do as a herd." Yes, absolutely. But herds are by definition made up of members of the same species (and tigers are not herd animals anyway). If Manfred's philosophy were to get around in the animal kingdom, evolution would break down, overpopulation would result, there would be starvation among the nonvegetarians, and it would be an ugly picture. Much of the serenity and order of nature depends on eating the neighbors.

Ice Age does not preach Darwinian orthodoxy, however, but a kinder, gentler worldview: Ice Age meets New Age. And the philosophy scarcely matters anyway, since this is an animated comedy. Enormous advances have been made in animation technology in recent years, as computers have taken over the detail work and freed artists to realize their visions. But few movies have been as painterly as *Ice Age*, which begins with good choices of faces for the characters (note the tiger's underslung jaw and the sloth's outrigger eyes). The landscape is convincing without being realistic, the color palate is harmonious, the character movements include little twists, jiggles, hesitations, and hops that create personality. And the animals blossom as personalities.

That's because of the artwork, the dialogue, and the voice-over work by the actors; the filmmakers have all worked together to really see and love these characters, who are not "cartoon animals" but as quirky and individual as human actors, and more engaging than most.

I would suggest the story sneaks up and eventually wins us over, except it starts the winning process in its very first shots, showing a twitchy squirrel desperately trying to bury an acorn in an icy wilderness. We follow the progress of this squirrel all through the picture, as a counterpoint to the main action, and he is such a distinctive, amusing personality I predict he'll emerge as the hero of a film of his own.

Identity ★ ★ ★
R, 90 m., 2003

John Cusack (Ed), Ray Liotta (Rhodes), Amanda Peet (Paris), Alfred Molina (Doctor), Clea DuVall (Ginny), Rebecca De Mornay (Caroline), John C. McGinley (George York), John Hawkes (Larry), William Lee Scott (Lou), Jake Busey (Robert Maine), Pruitt Taylor Vince (Man), Leila Kenzle (Alice York), Bret Loehr (Timothy York). Directed by James Mangold and produced by Cathy Konrad. Screenplay by Michael Cooney.

It is a dark and stormy night. A violent thunderstorm howls down on a lonely Nevada road. A family of three is stopped by a blowout. While the father tries to change the tire, his wife is struck by a passing limousine. Despite the protests of the limo's passenger, a spoiled movie star, the driver takes them all to a nearby motel. The roads are washed out in both directions. The phone lines are down. Others seek shelter in the motel, which is run by a weirdo clerk.

Altogether, there are ten guests. One by one, they die. Agatha Christie fans will assume that one of them is the murderer—or maybe it's the clerk. Meanwhile, the story intercuts an eleventh-hour hearing for a man (Pruitt Taylor Vince) convicted of several savage murders. A grumpy judge has been awakened for this appeal, and unless he overturns his own ruling,

the man will die. His psychiatrist (Alfred Molina) comes to his defense.

We don't know yet how these two stories will intersect, although they eventually must, but meanwhile events at the motel take our attention. We know the formula is familiar, and yet the treatment owes more to horror movies than to the classic whodunit. The group gathered at the motel includes the limousine driver (John Cusack), who says he is a former cop and seems kind of competent. There's another cop (Ray Liotta), who is transporting a killer (Jake Busey) in leg irons. The driver with the blowout (John C. McGinley) tenderly cares for his gravely injured wife (Leila Kenzle) while his solemn little son (Bret Loehr) looks on.

Also at the rain-swept rendezvous are the movie star (Rebecca De Mornay) that Cusack was driving, a hooker (Amanda Peet) on her way out of Nevada, and a young couple (William Lee Scott and Clea DuVall) who recently got married, for reasons still in dispute. The motel manager (John Hawkes) finds them all rooms—numbered from 1 to 10, of course.

While lightning rips through the sky and the electricity flickers, gruesome events start to occur. I will not describe them in detail, of course, since you will want to be horrified on your own. Although many in the group fear a mad killer is in their midst, and the Busey character is a prime suspect, some of the deaths are so peculiar it is hard to explain them—or to know whether they are murders, or a case of being in the wrong place at the wrong time.

That there is an explanation goes without saying. That I must not hint at it also goes without saying. I think it is possible that some audience members, employing the Law of Economy of Characters, so usefully described in my *Bigger Little Movie Glossary,* might be able to arrive at the solution slightly before the movie does, but this isn't the kind of movie where all is revealed in a sensational final moment. The director, James Mangold, and the writer, Michael Cooney, play fair, sort of, and once you understand their thinking you can trace back through the movie and see that they never cheated, exactly, although they were happy enough to point to the wrong conclusions.

A movie like this is an acid test for actors. Can they keep their self-respect while jammed in a room while grisly murders take place, everybody is screaming and blaming one another, heads turn up without bodies, bodies disappear—and, of course, it is a dark and stormy night?

John Cusack does the best job of surviving. His character is a competent and responsible person, while all about him are losing their heads (sometimes literally) and blaming it on him. I also liked Amanda Peet's hooker, who suggests she's seen so much trouble that all of this is simply more of the same. And there is something to be said for the performance of John Hawkes as the motel manager, although I can't say what it is without revealing a secret (no, it's not the secret you think).

I've seen a lot of movies that are intriguing for the first two acts and then go on autopilot with a formula ending. *Identity* is a rarity, a movie that seems to be on autopilot for the first two acts and then reveals that it was not, with a third act that causes us to rethink everything that has gone before. Ingenious, how simple and yet how devious the solution is.

Igby Goes Down ★ ★ ★ ½
R, 97 m., 2002

Kieran Culkin (Jason "Igby" Slocumb Jr.), Susan Sarandon (Mimi Slocumb), Jeff Goldblum (D. H. Baines), Claire Danes (Sookie Sapperstein), Ryan Phillippe (Oliver Slocumb), Bill Pullman (Jason Slocumb), Amanda Peet (Rachel). Directed by Burr Steers and produced by Lisa Tornell and Marco Weber. Screenplay by Steers.

Holden Caulfield formed the mold, and Jason "Igby" Slocumb Jr. fits it perfectly in *Igby Goes Down*, an inspired example of the story in which the adolescent hero discovers that the world sucks, people are phonies, and sex is a consolation. Because the genre is well established, what makes the movie fresh is smart writing, skewed characters, and the title performance by Kieran Culkin, who captures just the right note as an advantaged rich boy who has been raised in discontent.

Igby is the child of a malevolently malfunctioning family. His mother, Mimi (Susan Sarandon), is a tart, critical, perfectionist mandarin ("I call her Mimi because Heinous One is a bit cumbersome"). His father, Jason (Bill Pull-

man), went through meltdown and is in a mental hospital, staring into space. His godfather, D. H. (Jeff Goldblum), is a slick operator, who converts both lofts and the young girls he installs in them. His brother, Oliver (Ryan Phillippe), is a supercilious Columbia student who regards Igby as a species of bug. Igby, like Citizen Kane before him, has been thrown out of all the best schools, and early in the movie he escapes from a military school and hides out in New York City.

Of course a boy with his advantages is fortunate even in hideouts. He has an understanding meeting with his godfather, finds shelter in one of his lofts, and soon is on very good terms with Rachel (Amanda Peet), his godfather's mistress, who is an artist in every respect except producing anything that can be considered art. Through Rachel he meets Sookie Sapperstein (Claire Danes), a Bennington student who likes him because he makes her laugh. Among the lessons every young man should learn is this one: All women who like you because you make them laugh sooner or later stop laughing, and then why do they like you?

The movie has a fairly convoluted plot, involving who is sleeping with whom, and why, and who finds out about it, and what happens then. There is also the problem of the older brother, who does not make women laugh, which may be his strong point. The Goldblum character is especially intriguing, as a charmer with unlimited personal style and a hidden vicious streak.

Movies like this depend above all on the texture of the performances, and it is easy to imagine *Igby Goes Down* as a sitcom in which the characters don't quite seem to understand the witty things they're saying. All of the actors here have flair and presence, and get the joke, and because they all affect a kind of neo-Wildean irony toward everything, they belong in the same world. It is refreshing to hear Igby refer to his "Razor's Edge" experience without the movie feeling it is necessary to have him explain what he is talking about.

The Culkins are approaching brand-name status, but the thing is, the kids can act. Kieran emerges here as an accomplished, secure comic actor with poise and timing, and there is still another younger brother, Rory, who appears as a younger Igby. Kieran's role is not an easy one.

He is not simply a rebellious, misfit teenager with a con man's verbal skills, but also a wounded survivor of a family that has left him emotionally scarred. One of the movie's touching scenes has him visiting his father in the mental hospital, where his father's total incomprehension suggests a scary message: I don't understand my family or anything else, and I've given up thinking about it.

Sarandon, as Mimi the Heinous One, treats her boys as if they're straight men in the ongoing sitcom of her life. That there are tragic secrets involved, which I will not reveal, makes her all the more frightening: Is nothing entirely sincere with this woman? Goldblum's sense of possession is the scariest thing about him, since Igby finds out it's bad to be considered his property and worse not to be. And Ryan Phillipe is pitch-perfect as the affected college student, whose elevated style and mannered speech seem designed to hide the same wounds that Igby bears.

There is a lot of sex in the movie, but it is sane sex, which is to say, sex performed by people who seem to have heard of sex and even experienced it before the present moment. Sex is seen here as part of the process of life, rather than as cinematic mountain-climbing. Everyone except Igby is fairly casual about it, which is kind of sad, and among the things Igby has been deprived of in life, one is an early romance with a sincere girl of about the same age who takes him seriously. Perhaps the sad inherited family trait among the Slocumbs is premature sophistication.

The movie was written and directed by Burr Steers (who acted in *Pulp Fiction* and *The Last Days of Disco*, among others). It is an astonishing filmmaking debut, balancing so many different notes and story elements. What Steers has not lost sight of, in all the emotional chaos, is heart. The film opens and closes on different kinds of pain, and by the end Igby has discovered truths that Holden Caulfield, we feel, could not have handled.

I'm Going Home ★ ★ ★

NO MPAA RATING, 90 m., 2002

Michel Piccoli (Gilbert Valence), Antoine Chappey (George), Leonor Baldaque (Sylvia), Catherine Deneuve (Marguerite), John Malkovich (John Crawford). Directed by Manoel de Oliveira and produced by Paulo Branco. Screenplay by de Oliveira.

There are a few movies where you can palpably sense the presence of the director behind the camera, and *I'm Going Home* is one of them. The movie is about an old actor who has lost many of those he loves, but continues to work. The actor is played by France's great Michel Piccoli, who at seventy-seven has appeared in 200 movies since 1945. And the director, whose breathing we can almost hear in our ear, is Manoel de Oliveira of Portugal, who is ninety-four and directed his first film in 1931.

When we first see the actor, named Gilbert Valence, he is onstage in a production of Ionesco's *Exit the King*, and the film lingers on speeches in which the old man rails against his mortality and defines the unending memorials that he fancies will keep his name alive. After the play, he learns of a tragic accident that has robbed him of his wife, daughter, and son-in-law. "Some time later," we see him living with his young grandson and the nanny.

Gilbert's offstage life is one of routine, and it is here, in a touch both subtle and glancing, that de Oliveira makes his most poignant observation about how we die but life heedlessly goes on without us. Gilbert takes his coffee every morning in the same Paris café, sitting in the same chair at the same table and always reading the same morning paper, *Liberation*. As he gets up to go, another man enters, sits at the same table, and unfolds his copy of *Le Figaro*. This happens day after day.

One morning, the other man arrives early and takes another table. But when Gilbert frees his regular table, the man gets up with alacrity to claim it—only to be headed off by a stranger who sits down first. These little scenes had a surprising impact on me. I often think of myself as a ghost at places I have visited: There is "my" café, and "my" table, and when I return to a city there is a satisfaction in occupying them again, because it proves my own continuity. Of course those cafés also "belong" to others I will never know, and someday I will never return to them, and someday neither will the others, and someday the café will not be there. Yet daily ritual encourages us to believe that because things have been the same for a long time, they will always be the same.

The old actor sees a handsome pair of shoes in a store window, and buys them. For a man past a certain age, to buy new shoes is an act of faith. (One is reminded of the Irish story about the shoe clerk who assured an old man, "These will see you out.") We see the shoes in close-up as Gilbert talks with his agent, a venal man who hints that a young actress might like to meet him. After all, the agent says, when Pablo Casals was in his eighties, he married a teenage student. "But I am nowhere near my eighties," Gilbert snaps. "And I am not Casals."

What eventually happens to these shoes is a reminder that we can make plans, but we cannot count on them. There are tender little scenes in which the old man and his grandson play with battery-powered trucks and enjoy each other's company, and fraught scenes in which the agent tries to get the actor to take a tawdry TV show. And a scene from a production of *The Tempest*, in which Gilbert gives Prospero's speech beginning, "Our revels now are ended . . ."

How the film plays out you will have to see for yourself. Few films seem so wise and knowing about the fact of age and the approach of the end. And at his great age, de Oliveira dispenses with the silliness of plot mechanics and tells his story in a simple, unadorned fashion, as episodes and observations, trusting us to understand.

In the very final scene, as Gilbert leaves a café without drinking the wine he has ordered, the camera lingers to watch another man walk in and order a beer. Life goes on. You might think that *I'm Going Home,* about an artist at the end of his career, is de Oliveria's own farewell, but no: He made a new film in 2002, named *The Uncertainty Principle,* and it played at Cannes in May. Some directors burn out early, others flower late. Luis Buñuel began a remarkable series of twelve great films when he was sixty-one. De Oliveira has made thirteen films since 1990. There is a time when going to the café is a habit, but if you go long enough it becomes a triumph.

I'm Not Scared ★ ★ ★ ½
R, 108 m., 2004

Guiseppe Cristiano (Michele), Aitana Sanchez-Gijon (Anna), Dino Abbrescia (Pino), Diego Abatantuono (Sergio), Giorgio Careccia (Felice), Mattia Di Pierro (Filippo). Directed by Gabriele Salvatores and produced by Marco Chimenz, Giovanni Stabilini, Maurizio Totti, and Riccardo Tozzi. Screenplay by Niccolo Ammaniti (based on his novel) and Francesca Marciano.

Michele is a ten-year-old boy whose summer is unfolding as one perfect day after another. He lives in a rural district in southern Italy, and spends his days exploring the countryside with his friends. One day they go poking about an old abandoned house, and later he returns alone to look for his sister's lost glasses. In the yard he finds a slab of sheet metal, and when he lifts it up he sees, at the bottom of a pit, a leg sticking out from under a blanket.

Michele (Guiseppe Cristiano) lets the covering slam down and races for home. He doesn't tell anyone what he has seen. Returning again, he discovers that the pit holds a small boy named Filippo (Mattia Di Pierro), who is chained. On the television news Michele will learn that Filippo has been kidnapped.

I'm Not Scared tells its story mostly through Michele's eyes. He is just at that age when he has glimmers of understanding about adult life, but still lives within the strange logic of childhood. A year or two older, and he might have known to call the police. But no. Filippo becomes his secret, and he visits him frequently, bringing him bread to eat. It is almost as if he takes pride of possession.

We learn that Michele's father, Pino (Dino Abbrescia), is involved in the kidnapping, along with a friend named Sergio (Diego Abatantuono). Sergio has recently returned from Brazil, is clearly a criminal, is capable of violence. But Michele comes to understand this only gradually. His father is a figure of awe to him, a truck driver whose visits home are great occasions for Michele, his sister, and his mother, Anna (Aitana Sanchez-Gijon). The father is tall and strong and enveloped in a cloud of cigarette smoke, and his conversations with Sergio contain hints of menace.

This story unfolds surrounded by an almost improbable pastoral beauty. The children race their bicycles down country lanes, explore caves and ravines, roll down hillsides through boundless fields of golden wheat. Life at the farmhouse centers around dinners and much conversation, and later, when the children are asleep, the drinking and the talk continue. Michele pieces the clues together and understands that Filippo has been kidnapped by his father and Sergio, and when a police helicopter is seen in the neighborhood, he understands enough to realize that Filippo could be murdered—unless he saves him.

The film has been directed by Gabriele Salvatores, whose *Mediterraneo* won an Oscar for Best Foreign Film in 1992. The screenplay is by Niccolo Ammaniti and Francesca Marciano, based on Ammaniti's novel. The plot is essentially a thriller, but the film surrounds those elements with details of everyday life, with ambiguities and mysteries seen through a child's eyes, and a puzzle about the nature of the agreement between Pino and Sergio. Certainly the family is poor, and at one crucial moment, his mother asks Michele to promise, when he grows up, to "get away from here." The ransom money represents a hope for a new beginning.

Salvatores is not in a hurry to get to the climax. He allows summer days to follow one upon another, as Michele's secret grows in the boy's mind. There are details that enrich the portrait, as when he longs for a blue toy truck that belongs to a friend, and strikes a bargain to get it. We are acutely conscious of Filippo, chained in the hole, but for Michele, there are other things to think about, and the urgency of the situation only gradually grows upon him.

The film reminds us that, in childhood, days and weeks seemed to last forever. Summer was not a season but a lifetime. Parents represented a law that stood above our own best thinking, because they had demonstrated time and again that they knew best, that we were only children. The coming-of-age experience, which *I'm Not Scared* incorporates, involves that moment or season when we realize that we can see outside the box of childhood, that it is time to trust our own decisions.

Hollywood movies give us children who are miniature adults, secret agents like Cody Banks and the Spy Kids, who control technology and save the world. *I'm Not Scared* is a reminder of true childhood, of its fears and speculations, of the way a conversation can be overheard but

not understood, of the way that the shape of the adult world forms slowly through the mist.

The Importance of Being Ernest
★ ★ ★
PG, 100 m., 2002

Rupert Everett (Algernon Moncrieff), Colin Firth (Jack Worthing), Reese Witherspoon (Cecily Cardew), Judi Dench (Lady Bracknell), Frances O'Connor (Gwendolen Fairfax), Tom Wilkinson (Dr. Chasuble), Anna Massey (Miss Prism), Edward Fox (Lane). Directed by Oliver Parker and produced by Uri Fruchtmann and Barnaby Thompson. Screenplay by Parker, based on the play by Oscar Wilde.

Be careful what you ask for; you might get it. Recently I deplored the lack of wit in *Star Wars: Episode II—Attack of the Clones*, which has not one line of quotable dialogue. Now here is *The Importance of Being Earnest*, so thick with wit it plays like a reading from *Bartlett's Familiar Quotations*. I will demonstrate. I have here the complete text of the Oscar Wilde play, which I have downloaded from the Web. I will hit "page down" twenty times and quote the first complete line from the top of the screen:

"All women become like their mothers. That is their tragedy. No man does. That's his."

Now the question is, does this sort of thing appeal to you? Try these:

"Really, if the lower orders don't set us a good example, what on earth is the use of them?"

"To lose one parent, Mr. Worthing, may be regarded as a misfortune. To lose both looks like carelessness."

It appeals to me. I yearn for a world in which every drawing room is a stage, and we but players on it. But does anyone these days know what a drawing room is? The Universal Studios theme park has decided to abolish its characters dressed like the Marx Brothers and Laurel and Hardy because "a majority of people no longer recognize them." I despair. How can people recognize wit who begin with only a half-measure of it?

Oscar Wilde's *The Importance of Being Earnest* is a comedy constructed out of thin air. It is not really about anything. There are two romances at the center, but no one much cares whether the lovers find happiness together. Their purpose is to make elegant farce out of mistaken identities, the class system, mannerisms, egos, rivalries, sexual warfare, and verbal playfulness.

Oliver Parker's film begins with music that is a little too modern for the period, circa 1895, following the current fashion in anachronistic movie scores. It waltzes us into the story of two men who are neither one named Ernest and who both at various times claim to be. Jack Worthing (Colin Firth) calls himself Jack in the country and Ernest in town. In the country, he is the guardian of the charming Miss Cecily Cardew (Reese Witherspoon), who is the granddaughter of the elderly millionaire who adopted Jack after finding him as an infant in a handbag he was handed in error at the cloakroom in Victoria Station. When Jack grows bored with the country, he cites an imaginary younger brother named Ernest who lives in London and must be rescued from scrapes with the law.

This imaginary person makes perfect sense to Jack's friend Algernon Moncrieff (Rupert Everett), who lives in town but has a fictitious friend named Bunbury who lives in the country and whose ill health provides Algernon an excuse to get out of town. I have gone into such detail about these names and alternate identities because the entire play is constructed out of such silliness, and to explain all of it would require—well, the play.

In town Jack is much besotted by Gwendolen Fairfax (Frances O'Connor), daughter of the formidable Lady Bracknell (Judi Dench), Algernon's aunt, who is willing to consider Jack as a suitor for the girl but nonplussed to learn that he has no people—none at all—and was indeed left in a bag at the station. Thus her remark about his carelessness in losing both parents.

Algernon in the meantime insinuates himself into the country estate where young Cecily is being educated under the watchful eye of Miss Prism (Anna Massey), the governess; eventually all of the characters gather at the manor house, Woolton, where there's some confusion since Algernon has taken the name Ernest for his visit and proposed to Cecily, so that when Cecily meets Gwendolen, they both believe they are engaged to Ernest, although

Cecily, of course, doesn't know that in town Gwendolen knows Jack as Ernest.

But now I have been lured into the plot again. The important thing about *The Importance* is that all depends on the style of the actors, and Oliver Parker's film is well cast. Reese Witherspoon, using an English accent that sounds convincing to me, is charming as Jack's tender ward, who of course falls for Algernon. She is a silly, flighty girl, just right for Algernon, for whom romance seems valuable primarily as a topic of conversation. Frances O'Connor is older and more sensuous as Gwendolen, and gently encourages the shy Jack to argue his case ("Mr. Worthing, what have you got to say to me?"). Judi Dench keeps a stern eye on the would-be lovers and a strong hand on the tiller.

The Importance of Being Earnest is above all an exercise in wit. There is nothing to be learned from it, no moral, no message. It adopts what one suspects was Wilde's approach to sex—more fun to talk about than to do. As Algernon observes, romance dies when a proposal is accepted: "The very essence of romance is uncertainty." Wilde takes this as his guide. When the play's uncertainties have all been exhausted, the play ends. The last line ("I've now realized for the first time in my life the vital importance of being earnest") takes on an interesting spin if we know that "earnest" was a vernacular term for "gay" in 1895. Thus the closing line may subvert the entire play, although not to the surprise of anyone who has been paying attention.

In America ★ ★ ★ ★
PG-13, 103 m., 2003

Paddy Considine (Johnny), Samantha Morton (Sarah), Sarah Bolger (Christy), Emma Bolger (Ariel), Djimon Hounsou (Mateo). Directed by Jim Sheridan and produced by Arthur Lappin and Jim Sheridan. Screenplay by Jim Sheridan, Naomi Sheridan, and Kirsten Sheridan.

In America has a moment when everything shifts, when two characters face each other in anger and there is an unexpected insight into the nature of their relationship. It is a moment sudden and true; we realize how sluggish many movies are in making their points, and how quickly life can blindside us.

The moment takes place between Johnny (Paddy Considine), the father of an Irish immigrant family recently arrived in New York, and Mateo (Djimon Hounsou), the angry Nigerian painter who lives below them in a shabby tenement. Mateo is known as "the man who screams" because his anguish sometimes echoes up the stairs. But when Johnny's young daughters knock on his door for trick-or-treating, he is unexpectedly gentle with them. Johnny's wife, Sarah (Samantha Morton), invites Mateo to dinner, he becomes friendly with the family during a time when Paddy is feeling hard-pressed and inadequate, and slowly Paddy begins to suspect that romantic feelings are developing between his wife and the man downstairs.

All of that grows slowly in the movie, in the midst of other events, some funny, some sad, all rich with life. It is a suspicion rustling beneath the surface, in Paddy's mind and ours. Finally Paddy confronts Mateo: "Do you want to be in my place?"

"I might," says Mateo.

"Do you love my wife?"

"I love your wife. And I love you. And I love your children," Mateo says, barking the words ferociously.

There is a silence, during which Paddy's understanding of the situation changes entirely. I will not reveal what he believes he has discovered (it may not be what you are thinking). The rest of the film will be guided by that moment, and what impressed me was the way the dialogue uses the techniques of short fiction to trigger the emotional shift. This is not a "surprise" in the sense of a plot twist, but a different way of seeing—it's the kind of shift you find in the sudden insight of the young husband at the end of Joyce's *The Dead*. It's not about plot at all. It's about how you look at someone and realize you have never really known them.

The screenplay is by Jim Sheridan, the director, and his daughters Naomi and Kirsten. It is dedicated "to Frankie," and in the movie the family has two young daughters, and there was a son named Frankie who died of a brain tumor after a fall down the stairs. *In America* is not literally autobiographical (the real Frankie was Sheridan's brother, who died at ten), but it is intensely personal. It's not the typical story of turn-of-the-century immigrants facing prejudice and struggle, but a modern story, set in the 1980s and involving new sets of problems, such as racism and drug addiction in the building and the neighborhood.

It is also about the way poverty humiliates those who have always prided themselves on being able to cope. It is a very hot summer in New York, the apartment is sweltering, and there is a sequence involving the purchase of a cheap air conditioner that is handled perfectly: We see a father trying to provide for his family and finding shame, in his own eyes, because he does not do as well as he wants to.

The film is also about the stupid things we do because we are human and flawed. Consider the scene at the street carnival, where Johnny gets involved in a "game of skill"—throwing balls at a target, hoping to win a prize for his daughters. The film knows exactly how we try to dig ourselves out, and only dig ourselves deeper.

The mother is played by Samantha Morton, who in film after film (as the mute in *Sweet and Lowdown* and one of the psychics in *Minority Report*) reveals the power of her silences, her quiet, her presence. The two young girls are played by real sisters, Sarah and Emma Bolger, who are sounding boards and unforgiving judges as the family's troubles grow. "Don't 'little girl' me," Sarah says. "I've been carrying this family on my back for over a year."

Paddy Considine is new to me; I saw him in *24 Hour Party People*, I guess, but here he makes an impression: He plays Johnny as determined, insecure, easily wounded, a man who wants to be an actor but fears his spirit has been broken by the death of his son. Djimon Hounsou, given his first big role by Steven Spielberg in *Amistad*, often plays strong and uncomplicated types (as in *Gladiator*). Here, as an artist despairing for his art and his future, he reveals true and deep gifts.

From Ireland and Nigeria, from China, the Philippines, Poland, India, Mexico, and Vietnam, we get the best and the brightest. I am astonished by the will and faith of the recent immigrants I meet. Think what it takes to leave home, family, and even language, to try for a better life in another country. *In America* is not unsentimental about its new arrivals (the movie has a warm heart and frankly wants to move us), but it is perceptive about the countless ways in which it is hard to be poor and a stranger in a new land.   ☞

The In-Laws ★ ★
PG-13, 98 m., 2003

Michael Douglas (Steve Tobias), Albert Brooks (Jerry Peyser), Robin Tunney (Angela Harris), Ryan Reynolds (Mark Tobias), Candice Bergen (Judy), David Suchet (Jean-Pierre Thibodoux), Lindsay Sloane (Melissa Peyser), Maria Ricossa (Katherine Peyser). Directed by Andrew Fleming and produced by Bill Gerber, Elie Samaha, Joel Simon, and Bill Todman Jr. Screenplay by Nat Mauldin and Ed Solomon, based on a screenplay by Andrew Bergman.

The In-Laws is an accomplished but not inspired remake of a 1979 comedy that was inspired and so did not need to be accomplished. The earlier movie was slapdash and at times seemed to be making itself up as it went along, but it had big laughs and a kind of lunacy. The remake knows the moves but lacks the recklessness.

Both movies begin with the preparations for a wedding. The father of the bride is a dentist in 1979, a podiatrist this time. The father of the groom is a secret agent, deeply involved in dubious international schemes. The spy takes the doctor along on a dangerous mission, and they encounter a loony foreign leader who cheerfully proposes to kill them.

Now consider the casting: Peter Falk and Alan Arkin in the earlier film, versus Michael Douglas and Albert Brooks this time. Splendid choices, you would agree, and yet the chemistry is better in the earlier film. Falk goes into his deadpan lecturer mode, slowly and patiently explaining things that sound like utter nonsense. Arkin develops good reasons for suspecting he is in the hands of a madman.

Michael Douglas makes his character more reassuring and insouciant, as if he's inviting his new in-law along on a lark, and that's not as funny because he seems to be trying to make it fun, instead of trying to conceal the truth of a deadly situation. Albert Brooks is portrayed as neurotic and fearful by nature, and so his reactions are not so much inspired by the pickle he's in as by the way he always reacts to everything.

These are small adjustments in the natures of the two characters, but crucial to the success of the films. Comedy works better when the characters seem utterly unaware that they are being funny. And something else is missing, too: the unexpected craziness of the foreign leader, who in the 1979 film brought the movie almost to a halt (I wrote that I laughed so hard, I laughed at myself laughing). The new film plows much more familiar comic terrain.

Richard Libertini was the South American dictator in the earlier film, a sublime nutcase who had an intimate relationship with a sock puppet he addresses as Señor Wences. His two North American visitors desperately try to play along with the gag, without being sure whether the guy really believes the sock puppet is alive or is only testing them.

In the new version, the foreign madman is an international arms dealer named Thibodoux. He's played by David Suchet with sublime comic timing, and is very funny in a scene where he explains that he was once ruthless, but after studying under Depak Chopra has become more gentle, and now allows his victims a running start before shooting at them. All very well, but where is the sock puppet? Why remake a movie and leave out its funniest element—a sequence so funny, it's all a lot of people can remember about the movie? My guess is that David Suchet could have risen to the occasion with a masterful sock puppet performance.

There are moments when the movie seems perverse in the way it avoids laughs. Consider a scene where Douglas is at the controls of a private jet and Brooks is terrified not simply because he hates flying, but also because they are flying so low—"to come in under the radar," Douglas explains. Why, oh why, isn't there an exterior shot showing the jet ten feet above the ground?

Another missed opportunity: Since the arms dealer develops a crush on the podiatrist, why no sex scenes involving toes? Or not toes necessarily, but anything involving the bad guy discovering a new kind of bliss while the podiatrist improvises desperately with nail clippers and corn removal techniques? True, the podiatrist defends himself by pressing on the dealer's painful foot nerve. But that's level one. The sock puppet was level three.

I'm suggesting such notions not because I want to rewrite the screenplay, but because I miss a certain kind of zany invention. *The In-Laws* seems conventional in its ideas about where it can go and what it can accomplish. You don't get the idea anyone laughed out loud while writing the screenplay. It lacks a strange light in its eyes. It is too easily satisfied. The one moment when it suggests the lunacy of the earlier film is when the Brooks character refuses to get into the water because, he explains, he was born with an unusual condition; his skin is not waterproof.

Now consider the character of Douglas's ex-wife, played by Candice Bergen, who has a lot of fun with it. She hates the guy, but confides that at least the sex was great. "Great, great, great." This is the setup for a scene of potential comic genius, but the movie uses it only for a weak curtain line. The notion of Michael Douglas and Candice Bergen having great sex while she continues to hate him is, I submit, a scene this movie should not be lacking. Think how mad you'd be at someone who could arouse you as no one else before or since, but who is such a complete jerk you can't stand to have him around. Bergen could have an orgasm while screaming passionate vituperations. Now that's a scene I'd like to see.

In Praise of Love ★

NO MPAA RATING, 98 m., 2002

Bruno Putzulu (Edgar), Cecile Camp (Elle), Jean Davy (Grandfather), Françoise Verny (Grandmother), Audrey Klebaner (Eglantine), Jérémy Lippmann (Perceval), Claude Baignères (Mr. Rosenthal). Directed by Jean-Luc Godard and produced by Alain Sarde and Ruth Waldburger. Screenplay by Godard.

What strange confusion besets Jean-Luc Godard? He stumbles through the wreckage of this film like a baffled Lear, seeking to exercise power that is no longer his. *In Praise of Love* plays like an attempt to reconstruct an ideal film that might once have existed in his mind, but is there no more.

Yes, I praised the film in an article from the 2001 Cannes Film Festival, but have now seen it again, and no longer agree with those words.

Seeing Godard's usual trademarks and preoccupations, I called it "a bittersweet summation of one of the key careers in modern cinema," and so it is, but I no longer think it is a successful one.

Godard was the colossus of the French New Wave. His films helped invent modern cinema. They were bold, unconventional, convincing. To see *Breathless, My Life to Live,* or *Weekend* is to be struck by a powerful and original mind. In the late 1960s he entered his Maoist period, making a group of films *(Wind from the East, Vladimir and Rosa, Pravda)* that were ideologically silly but still stylistically intriguing; those films (I learn from Milos Stehlik of Facets, who has tried to find them) have apparently been suppressed by their maker.

Then, after a near-fatal traffic accident, came the Godard who turned away from the theatrical cinema and made impenetrable videos. In recent years have come films both successful *(Hail Mary)* and not, and now a film like *In Praise of Love,* which in style and tone looks like he is trying to return to his early films but has lost the way.

Perhaps at Cannes I was responding to memories of Godard's greatness. He has always been fascinated with typography, with naming the sections of his films and treating words like objects (he once had his Maoist heroes barricade themselves behind a wall of Little Red Books). Here he repeatedly uses intertitles, and while as a device it is good to see again, the actual words, reflected on, have little connection to the scenes they separate.

He wants to remind us that *In Praise of Love* is self-consciously a movie: He uses not only the section titles, but offscreen interrogators, polemical statements, narrative confusion, a split between the b&w of the first half and the saturated video color of the second. What he lacks is a port of entry for the viewer. Defenses of the film are tortured rhetorical exercises in which critics assemble Godard's materials and try to paraphrase them to make sense. Few ordinary audience members, however experienced, can hope to emerge from this film with a coherent view of what Godard was attempting.

If you agree with Noam Chomsky, you will have the feeling that you would agree with this film if only you could understand it. Godard's anti-Americanism is familiar by now, but has spun off into flywheel territory. What are we to make of the long dialogue attempting to prove that the United States of America is a country without a name? Yes, he is right that there are both North and South Americas. Yes, Brazil has united states. Yes, Mexico has states and is in North America. Therefore, we have no name. This is the kind of tiresome language game schoolchildren play.

It is also painful to see him attack Hollywood as worthless and without history, when (as Charles Taylor points out on Salon.com), Godard was one of those who taught us about our film history; with his fellow New Wavers, he resurrected film noir, named it, celebrated it, even gave its directors bit parts in his films. Now that history (his as well as ours) has disappeared from his mind.

His attacks on Spielberg are painful and unfair. Some of the fragments of his film involve a Spielberg company trying to buy the memories of Holocaust survivors for a Hollywood film (it will star, we learn, Juliette Binoche, who appeared in *Hail Mary* but has now apparently gone over to the dark side). Elsewhere in the film he accuses Spielberg of having made millions from *Schindler's List* while Mrs. Schindler lives in Argentina in poverty. One muses: (1) Has Godard, having also used her, sent her any money? (2) Has Godard or any other director living or dead done more than Spielberg, with his Holocaust Project, to honor and preserve the memories of the survivors? (3) Has Godard so lost the ability to go to the movies that, having once loved the works of Samuel Fuller and Nicholas Ray, he cannot view a Spielberg film except through a prism of anger?

Critics are often asked if they ever change their minds about a movie. I hope we can grow and learn. I do not "review" films seen at festivals, but "report" on them—because in the hothouse atmosphere of three to five films a day, most of them important, one cannot always step back and catch a breath. At Cannes I saw the surface of *In Praise of Love,* remembered Godard's early work, and was cheered by the film. After a second viewing, looking beneath the surface, I see so little there: It is all

rote work, used to conceal old tricks, facile name-calling, the loss of hope, and emptiness.

Insomnia ★ ★ ★ ½
R, 118 m., 2002

Al Pacino (Will Dormer), Robin Williams (Walter Finch), Hilary Swank (Ellie Burr), Martin Donovan (Hap Eckhart), Maura Tierney (Rachel), Jonathan Jackson (Randy Stetz). Directed by Christopher Nolan and produced by Broderick Johnson, Paul Junger Witt, Andrew A. Kosove, and Edward McDonnell. Screenplay by Hillary Seitz, Nikolaj Frobenius, and Erik Skjoldbjaerg.

He looks exhausted when he gets off the plane. Troubles are preying on him. An investigation by Internal Affairs in Los Angeles may end his police career. And now here he is in—where the hell is this?—Nightmute, Alaska, land of the midnight sun, investigating a brutal murder. The fuels driving Detective Will Dormer are fear and exhaustion. They get worse.

Al Pacino plays the veteran cop, looking like a man who has lost all hope. His partner, Hap Eckhart (Martin Donovan), is younger, more resilient, and may be prepared to tell the Internal Affairs investigators what they want to know—information that would bring the older man down. They have been sent up north to help with a local investigation, flying into Nightmute in a two-engine prop plane that skims low over jagged ice ridges. They'll be assisting a local cop named Ellie Burr (Hilary Swank), who is still fresh with the newness of her job.

Insomnia, the first film directed by Christopher Nolan since his famous *Memento* (2001), is a remake of a Norwegian film of the same name, made in 1998 by Erik Skjoldbjaerg. That was a strong, atmospheric, dread-heavy film, and so is this one. Unlike most remakes, the Nolan *Insomnia* is not a pale retread, but a re-examination of the material, like a new production of a good play. Stellan Skarsgard, who starred in the earlier film, took an existential approach to the character; he seemed weighed down by the moral morass he was trapped in. Pacino takes a more physical approach: How much longer can he carry this burden?

The story involves an unexpected development a third of the way through, and then the introduction of a character we do not really expect to meet, not like this. The development is the same in both movies; the character is much more important in this new version, adding a dimension I found fascinating. Spoilers will occur in the next paragraph, so be warned.

The pivotal event in both films, filmed much alike, is a shoot-out in a thick fog during a stakeout. The Pacino character sets a trap for the killer, but the suspect slips away in the fog, and then Pacino, seeing an indistinct figure loom before him, shoots and kills Hap—his partner from L.A. It is easy enough to pin the murder on the escaping killer, except that one person knows for sure who did it: the escaping killer himself.

In the Norwegian film, the local female detective begins to develop a circumstantial case against the veteran cop. In a nice development in the rewrite (credited to original authors Nikolaj Frobenius and Erik Skjoldbjaerg, working with Hillary Seitz), the killer introduces himself into the case as sort of Pacino's self-appointed silent partner.

The face of the killer, the first time we see it, comes as a shock, because by now we may have forgotten Robin Williams was even in the film. He plays Walter Finch, who does not really consider himself a murderer, although his killing was cruel and brutal. These things happen. Everyone should be forgiven one lapse. Right, detective? Pacino, sleepless in a land where the sun mercilessly never sets, is trapped: If he arrests Finch, he exposes himself and his own cover-up. And the local detective seems to suspect something.

Unusual for a thriller to hinge on issues of morality and guilt, and Nolan's remake does not avoid the obligatory Hollywood requirement that all thrillers must end in a shoot-out. There is also a scene involving a chase across floating logs, and a scene where a character is trapped underwater. These are thrown in as—what? Sops for the cinematically impaired, I suppose. Only a studio executive could explain why we need perfunctory action, just for action's sake, in a film where the psychological suspense is so high.

Pacino and Williams are very good together.

Their scenes work because Pacino's character, in regarding Williams, is forced to look at a mirror of his own self-deception. The two faces are a study in contrasts. Pacino's is lined, weary, dark circles under his eyes, his jaw slack with fatigue. Williams has the smooth, open face of a true believer, a man convinced of his own case. In this film and *One Hour Photo*, which played at Sundance 2002, Williams reminds us that he is a considerable dramatic talent—and that, while over the years he has chosen to appear in some comedic turkeys (*Death to Smoochy* leaps to mind), his serious films are almost always good ones.

Why Christopher Nolan took on this remake is easy to understand. *Memento* was one of a kind; the thought of another film based on a similar enigma is exhausting. *Insomnia* is a film with a lot of room for the director, who establishes a distinctive far-north location, a world where the complexities of the big city are smoothed out into clear choices. The fact that it is always daylight is important: The dilemma of this cop is that he feels people are always looking at him, and he has nowhere to hide, not even in his nightmares.

Intacto ★ ★ ½
R, 108 m., 2003

Leonardo Sbaraglia (Tomás), Eusebio Poncela (Federico), Max von Sydow (Sam), Mónica López (Sara), Antonio Dechent (Alejandro). Directed by Juan Carlos Fresnadillo and produced by Sebastián Álvarez. Screenplay by Fresnadillo and Andrés M. Koppel.

The Spanish film *Intacto*, like the recent Sundance entry *The Cooler*, believes that luck is a commodity that can be given and received, won or lost, or traded away. Most people have ordinary luck, some have unusually good or bad luck, and then there is a character like Tomás, who is the only survivor of an airplane crash, beating the odds of 237 million to 1. (I am not the statistician here, only the reporter.)

The movie involves a man named Sam (Max von Sydow), who survived the Holocaust and now operates a remote casino at which rich people bet against his luck, usually unsuccessfully. So unshakable is his confidence that he will remove one bullet from a gun holding six and then bet that he will not die. That he is alive to be a character in the movie speaks for itself.

Von Sydow, who in *The Seventh Seal* played a game of chess with Death, believes that he will lose his luck if the wrong person looks on his face at the wrong time, or takes his photograph. To guard himself, he must often sit in a closed room with a hood over his face. We wonder, but he does not tell us, if he thinks this is a high price to pay for good fortune. He has a young man named Federico (Eusebio Poncela) as his confederate; Federico also has good luck, and searches for others who have his gift. When Sam steals his luck from him, he goes searching for a protégé of his own, and finds Tomás.

The single-mindedness of these men assumes that winning at gambling is the most important thing in the world. Certainly there are gamblers who think so. Another of the Sundance entries, *Owning Mahowny*, starred Philip Seymour Hoffman as a Toronto bank clerk who steals millions in order to fund his weekend getaways to Atlantic City and Las Vegas. He has a winning streak at roulette that in its intensity of focus has a kind of awesome power. In *The Cooler*, William H. Macy plays a man whose luck is so bad that he is employed by a casino to merely rub up against someone in a winning streak; then his luck changes.

The two North American films are pretty straightforward in telling their stories. *The Cooler* involves an element of fantasy, but it involves the story, not the visual approach. *Intacto*, directed by the talented young Juan Carlos Fresnadillo, is wilder visually, using the fractured narrative and attention-deficit camera style that can be effective or not, but often betrays a lack of confidence on the simple story level.

The story involves another more human element, centered on Sara (Mónica López), a cop who is chasing Tomás while grieving a tragic loss of her own. Will his luck protect him? What happens when it's luck versus luck?

I admired *Intacto* more than I liked it, for its ingenious construction and the way it keeps a certain chilly distance between its story and the dangers of popular entertainment. It's a Hollywood premise, rotated into the world of the art film through mannerism and oblique storytelling. The same ideas could be remade into a straightforward entertainment, and perhaps they already have been.

There's a fashion right now among new writers and directors to create stories of labyrinthine complexity, so that watching them is like solving a puzzle. I still haven't seen Alejandro Amenabar's *Open Your Eyes*, which a lot of people admire, but when I saw Cameron Crowe's American remake, *Vanilla Sky*, I knew as I walked out of the theater that I would need to see it again. I did, and got a different kind of overview, and liked the film. I liked it the first time, too, but through instinct, not understanding.

When you solve a film like this, have you learned anything you wouldn't have learned in a straight narrative, or have you simply had to pay some dues to arrive at the same place? Depends. *Pulp Fiction*, which jump-started the trend, depends crucially on its structure for its effect. *Intacto*, which is not as complex as the other films I've mentioned, may be adding the layer of style just for fun. That is permitted, but somewhere within that style there may be a hell of a thriller winking at us.

Intermission ★ ★ ★ ½
R, 105 m., 2004

Cillian Murphy (John), Kelly Macdonald (Deirdre), Colin Farrell (Lehiff), Colm Meaney (Detective Jerry Lynch), David Wilmot (Oscar), Brian F. O'Byrne (Mick), Shirley Henderson (Sally), Michael McElhatton (Sam), Deirdre O'Kane (Noeleen). Directed by John Crowley and produced by Neil Jordan, Alan Moloney, and Stephen Woolley. Screenplay by Mark O'Rowe.

Here is a movie where the characters discover that brown steak sauce tastes great in coffee, where a TV producer wants "more reality" after filming a rabbit race, where a cop's car is stolen while he's carrying out a drug bust, where . . . but *Intermission* goes on and on, in a tireless series of inventions, like a plot-generating machine in overdrive. That it succeeds is some kind of miracle; there's enough material here for three bad films, and somehow it becomes one good one.

The movie is a dark comedy—no, make that a dark, dark, *dark* comedy—set in Dublin and starring more or less everyone in town. That its cast includes Colin Farrell, now a big movie star, is less remarkable than the fact that the cast is so large and colorful that we sometimes lose track of him. Here is yet more evidence that *Pulp Fiction* was the most influential movie of recent years, as eccentric characters with distinctive verbal styles coil around a plot involving romance, betrayal, kidnapping, bank robbery, and a lot of brown sauce. Whether the sauce is Daddy's or HP, the two favorite brands in Ireland, is impossible to say, perhaps because both sauce manufacturers preferred to keep their labels out of this movie.

Like *Pulp Fiction,* the movie begins with sweet talk that suddenly turns violent, as Lehiff (Farrell) betrays a hard side. We meet his mates, including John (Cillian Murphy), who hates his job in a supermarket, and Oscar (David Wilmot), who despairs of finding a girlfriend and is advised to target older ladies who will be grateful for his attention. Meanwhile, John breaks up with his girlfriend, Deirdre (Kelly Macdonald), who begins dating a married bank manager, Sam (Michael McElhatton), while Sam's abandoned wife, Noeleen (Deirdre O'Kane, not to be confused with the character Deirdre), goes to a lonely-hearts dance and meets, of course, Oscar.

But to summarize the plot is insanity. There are a dozen major characters whose lives intersect in romance, crime, and farce; the screenplay by Mark O'Rowe is so ingenious and energetic that we almost don't feel like we're being jerked around. The other character who must be introduced is Jerry Lynch (Colm Meaney), who has watched too many cop reality shows and thinks he should star in one himself. Oh, and I should mention Sally (Shirley Henderson), who after a tragic disappointment in love has become a recluse and doesn't seem to realize she has enough of a mustache to be referred to occasionally as Burt Reynolds. Her character brings a new dimension to the classic movie scene in which a plain girl is told she would be beautiful if she got rid of the glasses/braces/bangs, etc.

Director John Crowley, a first-timer with enormous promise, seems to know his way through this maze even if we don't, and eventually with a sigh and a smile we give up and let him take us where he will. That will include a kidnapping that combines the motives of bank robbery and cuckold's revenge, and a bus crash caused by a particularly vile little boy in a red coat, who has no connection with the other characters except that he occasionally turns up and causes horrible things to happen to them.

The movie is astonishing in the way it shifts gears, again like Tarantino. There are scenes of sudden, brutal violence. Scenes of broad comedy (especially involving the detective's attempts to be *C.S.I.* when he was born to be *Starsky and Hutch*). Moments of raw truth, as when an older woman at a pickup bar tells a younger man exactly how she feels. Moments of poignancy, as when John tries to win back Deirdre by saying all the things he should have told her in the first place. And moments of exquisitely bad timing, as when the bank manager unzips his pants in the living room just as Deirdre's mother walks in.

It's interesting how the stars fit right into the ensemble. Not only Farrell but Colm Meaney have famous faces for American audiences, and devoted moviegoers will recognize Kelly Macdonald from *Trainspotting* and Shirley Henderson from the wonderful *Wilbur Wants to Kill Himself.* What all of these actors do is fit seamlessly into the large cast, returning in some cases to the accents and body language of their preacting days. *Intermission* is a virtuoso act from beginning to end, juggling violence and farce, coincidence and luck, characters with good hearts and others evil to the core. In a movie filled with incredulities, the only detail I was absolutely unable to accept is that brown sauce tastes good in coffee. ☞

In the Cut ★ ★ ½
R, 113 m., 2003

Meg Ryan (Frannie Avery), Mark Ruffalo (Detective James Malloy), Jennifer Jason Leigh (Pauline), Kevin Bacon (John Graham), Nick Damici (Detective Richard Rodriguez), Sharrieff Pugh (Cornelius), Nancy La Scala (Tabu). Directed by Jane Campion and produced by Nicole Kidman and Laurie Parker. Screenplay by Campion and Susanna Moore, based on the novel by Moore.

Jane Campion's *In the Cut* has ornaments of a thriller about sexually bold women, but ticking away underneath is the familiar slasher genre in which women are the victims. What makes it stranger, and a little scarier than it might have been, is the way its heroine willfully sleepwalks into danger, dreaming of orgasm.

Frannie Avery (Meg Ryan, reshaping her image with a bad-girl role) is a high school English teacher who likes sex and wishes she got more of it, but not from the guys she's been getting it from, who tend to be obsessed weirdos. Her half-sister Pauline (Jennifer Jason Leigh) is also sex-deprived; at one point, as they're discussing a man that Frannie has every reason to be wary of, Pauline advises her sister to sleep with the guy "if only for the exercise."

This man is James Malloy (Mark Ruffalo), a homicide detective, who meets Frannie while investigating the murder and "de-articulation" of a woman whose severed limb was found beneath Frannie's window. James is the kind of man who talks about sex in a way that would be offensive if he didn't deliver so skillfully what he describes so crudely. "How did you make me feel like that?" Frannie asks him after their first encounter. He must have made her feel really good, because later, even after she begins to suspect he is the de-articulator, she goes on another date. This is a new variety of high-risk sex: Get as much action as you can before being de-articulated.

James wanders in a musky daze, too, in a movie where the sex is so good they both keep getting distracted by their duties as potential victim and possible killer. Campion's screenplay, cowritten with Susanna Moore and based on Moore's novel, locates these characters close to street level in a hard-bitten New York neighborhood where people act on their needs without apology. The story has fun playing against certain conventions of the slasher genre, and the dialogue has a nice way of sidestepping clichés. Listen to the words and watch the body language as James responds when Frannie asks him, "Did you kill her?" Without for a moment revealing if he did or didn't, I can promise you that Ruffalo's choices here are true to this character and do not come from the pool of slasher clichés.

The movie is leisurely, as thrillers go, but I liked that, especially in the intimate conversations of the two sisters, who sound and behave like two women who have understood each other very well for a long time. Ryan and Leigh have a verbal and emotional shorthand that

creates a kind of conspiracy against the mechanics of the plot: Sometimes, even when you're in danger you can still feel horny. And James's introductory pitch to Frannie, when he tells her who he can be and what he can do, shows that he knows who he is and who she is; that's why she lets him talk that way—even though she walks out when his partner (Nick Damici) tries for the same crude note.

So all of this is well done, and yet the movie is kind of a shambles. The key supporting characters are awkwardly used, as if the movie thinks it ought to have them but doesn't know why. Sharrieff Pugh plays Cornelius, a muscular African-American who is Frannie's student; she meets him for tutoring in a pool hall with sex in the shadows, and the movie keeps trying to suggest something about them but never knows what it is. Kevin Bacon turns up as John Graham, an intern who works eighteen hours a day, needs someone to walk his dog, and takes it very badly when Frannie breaks up with him—but in such an odd way that when Bacon went home that night he must have told someone that Campion didn't know what the hell to do with him. And Damici, as James Malloy's partner, is so obviously the deus ex machina that you can almost hear the gears grinding as he's lowered into play.

The most intriguing element in the movie is the way Frannie is made so heedless of danger. She's drunk sometimes, but she acts like she's on other stuff too, like maybe hog tranquilizers. She's smart enough to make sure James is really a cop before letting him into her apartment, but why does she get into various cars, go to various meetings, trust various situations, and arrive at obvious conclusions, but then act as if she's forgotten them?

And what kind of eyesight does she have that she can see a three of spades tattooed on the hand of a man whose face she looks right at but isn't sure about? For that matter, what kind of coincidence is involved in that whole scene in the basement of the bar? Incredible that she would just happen to see the de-articulator and the de-articulatee together—and, no, I'm not giving something away.

In the Cut reminds me a little of the Coen brothers' film *Intolerable Cruelty*. Here are two genre movies, a slasher thriller and a screwball comedy, made by assuredly great directors, but both movies are too hip for the room. It is possible to transcend genres, but I think you have to go through them, not around them. Both films are concerned with being good (and are good) in ways that are irrelevant to whether they arrive at their goals. In the case of *In the Cut*, Meg Ryan does such an effective job of evoking her sexually hungry lonely girl that it might have been better to just follow that line and not distract her and the audience with a crime plot that becomes transparent the moment you recall the Rule of Economy of Characters ("no unnecessary character is unnecessary").

And what the *hell* was the point of those ice-skating flashbacks?

In This World ★ ★ ★
R, 88 m., 2003

Jamal Udin Torabi (Himself), Enayatullah (Himself), Imran Paracha (Travel Agent), Hiddayatullah (Enayat's Brother), Jamau (Enayat's Father), Mirwais Torabi (Jamal's Older Brother). Directed by Michael Winterbottom and produced by Andrew Eaton and Anita Overland. Screenplay by Tony Grisoni.

In This World tells the story of a sixteen-year-old Afghan boy who journeys by land and sea to London from a refugee camp in Pakistan. What makes the film astonishing is that it follows a real boy on a real journey, and the boy is in England at this moment. What's real and what's fiction in the film is hard to say, but we trust that the images are informed by truth, and there is a scene at night in the mountains of Turkey where it looks as if real gunfire is being aimed at the travelers.

The film's hero is Jamal Udin Torabi, playing himself. He lives with his family in a refugee camp in Pakistan. His uncle, Wakeel, wants to send his son Enayat to London; Jamal speaks English and is allowed to go along as a translator and companion. The two make a deal with a professional smuggler of humans, who starts them off on a long journey through Iran, Turkey, Italy, and France.

The film is not a documentary, although many scenes might as well be. Director Michael Winterbottom and his cinematographer, Marcel Zyskind, shot with a small digital camera, and many shots were apparently taken

without the knowledge of the people in them. I learn that the film's producer, Anita Overland, worked as an advance scout, staying a day or two ahead of Winterbottom and his actors and arranging scenes—up to a point, we gather. Most of the dialogue is improvised, based on a script by Tony Grisoni, who interviewed others who had made the journey.

We read all the time of ships, trucks, and containers filled with human beings desperate to live in another land. Sometimes this illegal cargo arrives dead, and there is an agonizing scene in *In This World* where Jamal, his cousin, and many others are locked inside a shipping container where the air is running out and their desperate cries and bangings cannot be heard. Jamal survives this and other harrowing experiences with a resilience, adaptability, and defiant wit that is impossible to fake: The real Jamal, like the Jamal he plays in the movie, must be both a heroic survivor and quite a character.

The film's politics are muddled. Winterbottom wants us to identify with Jamal because of the risks he has taken and the excruciating experiences he has survived during the long months of his journey. The movie ends with the information that the real Jamal, who actually made this journey, was ordered by a court to leave England by the day before his eighteenth birthday. We are, I guess, supposed to find this heartless, and of course we sympathize with Jamal and his ordeal. But immigrants are not allowed into countries on the basis of the trouble they endured to get there, and Jamal doesn't qualify as a political rufugee.

The movie strikes a curious note right at the beginning, as it shows us the Shamshatoo refugee camp in Pakistan. Here live more than 50,000 Afghans, we're told, who fled from the 1979 Soviet invasion of their land, and again because of the "U.S. bombing" in 2001. But surely many of these people fled the Taliban in the years in between, and although it is true that the United States bombed Afghanistan, it is also true that there was a reason for that.

Winterbottom surely does not expect his audiences to be so simple-minded that these observations do not occur to them, so why does he allow that alienating glitch right at the outset? The unspoken subtext of his movie is that his characters, and millions more, are willing to undergo unimaginable danger and hardship in order to live in the West instead of where they are.

But the movie never brings that notion to the surface, and indeed is not an overtly political film anyway. It is more the story of these people—or, more exactly, of their journey, for which we can read the journeys of exiles all over the world. The dilemma is that the planet has more undesirable societies to live in than desirable ones. The answer is perhaps not for the discontented and visionaries to leave, but for them to stay and try to bring about change. Yet I instinctively identify with Jamal's desire, and suspect that in his shoes I would want to do what he has done. The next time I read about desperate immigrants trying to sneak into another land, the images in this film will inform me.

Intolerable Cruelty ★ ★ ½

PG-13, 100 m., 2003

George Clooney (Miles Massey), Catherine Zeta-Jones (Marylin Rexroth), Geoffrey Rush (Donovan Donaly), Cedric the Entertainer (Gus Petch), Edward Herrmann (Rex Rexroth), Paul Adelstein (Wrigley), Richard Jenkins (Freddy Bender), Billy Bob Thornton (Howard D. Doyle). Directed by Joel Coen and Ethan Coen and produced by Ethan Coen and Brian Grazer. Screenplay by Robert Ramsey, Matthew Stone, Ethan Coen, and Joel Coen.

The camera just stands there and gawks at Catherine Zeta-Jones, and so does George Clooney, and so do we. She goes on the list with Ava Gardner and Deborah Kerr. It's not a long list. She has the kind of beauty that could melt a divorce lawyer's heart and soften his brain, which is what happens in *Intolerable Cruelty*, a comedy by the Coen brothers.

Clooney plays Miles Massey, the millionaire author of the Massey Pre-Nup, a prenuptial agreement so tightly written that it has, we learn, never been cracked. "They spend an entire semester on it at Harvard Law." We meet him in divorce court, representing an outraged husband (Geoffrey Rush) who discovered his wife with the pool man and found that odd, since they didn't have a pool.

Massey is hired by Rex Rexroth (Edward Herrmann), who has been briefly married to Marylin (Zeta-Jones). She has a video, taken by her detective Gus (Cedric the Entertainer) exposing Rex as a cheater, and wants to win his millions in the settlement. Miles wins the case, so it's curious that Marylin wants to hire him to draft a Massey Pre-Nup for her next marriage, which will be to a gulping, blushing Texas oil billionaire named Howard (Billy Bob Thornton in full display). Miles, who is already gobsmacked with Marylin's bewitching sex appeal, can't understand why she wants to marry a yahoo like Howard. Or, actually, he can: She wants Howard's money. In that case, why does she want the Massey Pre-Nup? To prove she really loves him, she says. Since she really doesn't, Miles can only look on in wonderment and admiration. He's fascinated by the brilliance with which she violates conventional morality.

The Coens start with nothing but ducks in this movie, and for a long time it looks like they're all in a row. Clooney and Zeta-Jones are both great-looking people, both smart, both able to play comedy, both able to handle the kind of dialogue fondly described in our nation's literate past as witty repartee. Both characters are sharks, but both are human, too, and their mutual sexual attraction is so palpable you could cook with it. Miles is moved with the profound admiration only one slickster can have for another; when Marylin actually inspires Howard to eat the uncrackable Massey Pre-Nup (with barbecue sauce), Miles realizes he is witnessing not just beauty and genius, but a will to challenge his own.

Plots like this have fueled lovely screwball comedies, and *Intolerable Cruelty* is in the genre, but somehow not of it. The Coens sometimes have a way of standing to one side of their work: It's the puppet and they're the ventriloquists. The puppet is sincere, but the puppet master is wagging his eyebrows at the audience and asking, can you believe this stuff? Joel and Ethan are bounteously gifted filmmakers, but sometimes you just want them to lay off the irony and climb down here with the groundlings. Their *Fargo* was a movie that loved its characters, and it's one of the best movies I've ever seen.

It is hard to show the Coens' distancing process at work without revealing the movie's secrets, but let me try. The film is told from Massey's point of view. There is something that he wants: Marylin. He desires her so badly that in order to get her, he would balance the Massey Pre-Nup on his own head and crack it himself, with a hammer. We sympathize with this desire, because we share it. We *want* him to win her. The question is, does she want him? Of course she wants his money; that goes with the territory. But does she want to marry a millionaire, or simply become one herself?

I was reminded of Ernst Lubitsch's great *Trouble in Paradise,* which is about a con man, a con woman who loves him but can't afford him, and a rich widow who thinks she can buy him but would be happy enough to rent him for the season. By the end of that movie, everyone knows all about each other, and they accept the situation; if we cannot have what we want, they agree, let us at least be able to admire the way we behaved.

Miles and Marylin acknowledge their mutual chicanery. Neither one is very nice. But, aw, come on, when she walks across the room and his heart leaps up, or when she looks at him in a close-up that undresses itself, what makes the Coens pull back from this emotion? Why won't they give us the payoff their setup demands? We enjoy many turns of the screw in this movie, but there comes a time when the screw is seated and they keep turning until they strip the groove. We poor saps, who invested our emotions in the movie, are hung out to dry. The materials are available in *Intolerable Cruelty* to create a movie with an irresistible comic payload, so why must they skew it into a warning against itself?

That said: The movie has scenes of delicious comedy, Clooney and Zeta-Jones play their characters perfectly in an imperfect screenplay, and the man with the asthma puffer gets the biggest single laugh since the hair gel in *There's Something About Mary.*

Invincible ★ ★ ★ ★
PG-13, 133 m., 2002

Tim Roth (Erik-Jan Hanussen), Jouko Ahola (Zishe Breitbart), Anna Gourari (Marta Farra), Max Raabe (Master of Ceremonies), Jacob Wein (Benjamin), Gustav-Peter Wöhler (Landwehr). Directed by Werner Herzog and produced by Gary Bart and Herzog. Screenplay by E. Max Frye and Herzog.

Werner Herzog's *Invincible* tells the astonishing story of a Jewish strongman in Nazi Germany, a man who in his simple goodness believes he can be the "new Samson" and protect his people. He is a blacksmith in Poland in 1932 when discovered by a talent scout, and soon becomes the headliner in the Palace of the Occult in Berlin, which is run by the sinister Hanussen (Tim Roth), a man who dreams of becoming minister of the occult in a Nazi government.

The strongman, named Zishe Breitbart, is played by a Finnish athlete named Jouko Ahola, twice winner of the title World's Strongest Man. Much of the movie's uncanny appeal comes from the contrast between Ahola's performance, which is entirely without guile, and Roth's performance, which drips with mannered malevolence. Standing between them is the young woman Marta (Anna Gourari), who is under Hanussen's psychological power, and whom the strongman loves.

Invincible is based, Herzog says, on the true story of Breitbart, whose great strength contradicted the Nazi myth of Aryan superiority. I can imagine a dozen ways in which this story could be told badly, but Herzog has fashioned it into a film of uncommon fascination, in which we often have no idea at all what could possibly happen next. There are countless movies about preludes to the Holocaust, but I can't think of one this innocent, direct, and unblinking. In the face of gathering evil, Zishe trusts in human nature, is proud of his heritage, and believes strength and goodness (which he confuses) will triumph.

The movie has the power of a great silent film, unafraid of grand gestures and moral absolutes. Its casting of the major characters is crucial, and instinctively correct. Tim Roth is a sinister charlatan, posing as a man with real psychic powers, using trickery and showmanship as he jockeys for position within the emerging Nazi majority. There is a scene where he hypnotizes Marta, and as he stares boldly into the camera I wondered, for a moment, if it was possible to hypnotize a movie audience that way. Late in the film there is a scene where his secrets are revealed, and he makes a speech of chilling, absolute cynicism. Another actor in another movie might have simply gnashed his teeth, but Roth and Herzog take the revelations as an opportunity to show us the self-hatred beneath the deception.

As for Jouko Ahola, this untrained actor, who seems by nature to be good-hearted and uncomplicated, may never act again, but he has found the one perfect role, as Maria Falconetti did in *The Passion of Joan of Arc*. He embodies the simple strongman. The camera can look as closely as it wants and never find anything false. As a naive man from a backward town, not especially devout, he gets into a fight when Polish customers in a restaurant insult him and his little brother as Jews. A little later, entering a circus contest, he watches as the strongman lifts a boulder—and then puts an end to the contest by lifting the strongman *and* the boulder.

The talent scout takes him to see his first movie. Soon he is in Berlin, where Hanussen sizes him up and says, "We will Aryanize you. A Jew should never be as strong as you." Zishe is outfitted with a blond wig and a Nordic helmet, and presented as "Siegfried." He becomes a great favorite of Nazi brownshirts in the audience, as Hanussen prattles about "the strength of the body against the dark powers of the occult." But Zishe's mind works away at the situation until finally he has his solution, tears off the helmet and wig, and identifies himself as a Jew.

Here as throughout the film Herzog avoids the obvious next scene. Is Hanussen outraged? To a degree. But then he reports: "There's a line three blocks long outside! It's the Jews. They all want to see the new Samson." And then, at a time when Hitler was on the rise but the full measure of Jewish persecution was not yet in view, the Palace of the Occult turns into a dangerous pit where audience members are potentially at one another's throats.

This is the first feature in ten years from Werner Herzog, one of the great visionaries among directors. He strains to break the bonds of film structure in order to surprise us in unexpected ways. His best films unashamedly yearn to lift us into the mythical and the mysti-

cal. "Our civilization is starving for new images," he once told me, and in *Invincible* there is an image of a bleak, rocky seashore where the sharp stones are littered with thousands or millions of bright red crabs, all mindlessly scrabbling away on their crabby missions. I think this scene may represent the emerging Nazi hordes, but of course there can be no literal translation: Perhaps Herzog wants to illustrate the implacable Darwinian struggle from which man can rise with good heart and purpose.

The strongman in *Invincible* is lovable and so deeply moving precisely because he is not a cog in a plot, has no plan, is involved in no machinations, but is simply proud of his parents, proud to be a Jew, in love with the girl, and convinced that God has made him strong for a reason. He may be wrong in his optimism, but his greatest strength is that he will never understand that. The Roth character is equally single-minded, but without hope or purpose—a conniver and manipulator.

Watching *Invincible* was a singular experience for me, because it reminded me of the fundamental power that the cinema had for us when we were children. The film exercises the power that fable has for the believing. Herzog has gotten outside the constraints and conventions of ordinary narrative, and addresses us where our credulity keeps its secrets.

Iris ★ ★

R, 90 m., 2002

Judi Dench (Iris Murdoch), Jim Broadbent (John Bayley), Kate Winslet (Young Iris Murdoch), Hugh Bonneville (Young John Bayley). Directed by Richard Eyre and produced by Robert Fox and Scott Rudin. Screenplay by Eyre and Charles Wood.

I must look into myself and ask why I disliked *Iris* so intensely. Was it entirely a complaint against the film, or was it also a protest against the fate that befell the great novelist? There is no modern writer whose work I admire more than Iris Murdoch's, and for that mind to disappear in Alzheimer's is so sad that perhaps I simply refused to accept a film about it. Perhaps. Or perhaps it is true that the movie fails to do her justice—simplifies the life of one whose work was open to such human complexities.

Iris Murdoch (1919–1999) was one of the most important and prolific British novelists of her century, and wrote and taught philosophy as well. She wrote twenty-eight novels (between books, she said, she "took off for about half an hour"). Her novels involved "the unique strangeness of human beings," played against philosophical ideas. There were also touchstones that her readers looked forward to: a lonely child, a magus, an architectural oddity, an old friendship sorely tested, adulteries and unexpected couplings, intimations of the supernatural, theoretical conversations, ancient feuds. Her novel *The Sea, The Sea* won the Booker Prize and is a good place to start.

For years I looked forward to the annual Murdoch. Then her final novel arrived, shorter than usual, and at about the same time the dread news that she had Alzheimer's. "I feel as if I'm sailing into darkness," she said, a line used in the movie. After her death, her husband, John Bayley, wrote two books about her, dealing frankly and compassionately with her disease.

The film *Iris*, directed by the London stage director Richard Eyre and written by Eyre and the playwright Charles Wood, is literate, fair, and well acted, but is this particular film necessary? It moves between the young and old Iris, painting her enduring relationship with Bayley while at the same time suggesting her openness to affairs and sexual adventures. As a young woman she is played by Kate Winslet, as an older woman by Judi Dench (Bayley is played by Hugh Bonneville and Jim Broadbent). We see her high spirits and fierce intelligence at the beginning, and the sadness at the end. What is missing is the middle.

What Iris Murdoch basically did is to write books. It is notoriously difficult to portray a writer, because what can you show? The writer writing? It isn't the writing that makes a writer interesting—it's the having written. In Murdoch's case, that would suggest that instead of making a film of her life, it might be a good idea to make a film of one of her books. Only one Murdoch novel has ever been made into a film (the undistinguished *A Severed Head*, 1971). Her stories are rich in characters, conflict, and

sexual intrigue, and I'm surprised more haven't been filmed.

Instead of honoring the work, *Iris* mourns the life. It's like a biopic of Shakespeare that cuts back and forth between his apprentice days and his retirement in Stratford. Alzheimer's is especially tragic because it takes away the person while the presence remains. The character of Bayley, meanwhile, is presented as a befuddled and ineffectual man who contends with the baffling Murdoch, young and old, accepting her infidelity at the beginning and giving her love and support at the end. Yes, but there is much more to Bayley. He is one of the most brilliant of literary critics, whose essays grace the *New York Review of Books* and the *Times Literary Supplement*, but on the basis of this film you would think of him, frankly, as a fond old fool.

Because the film is well acted and written with intelligence, it might be worth seeing despite my objections. I suspect my own feelings. Perhaps this is so clearly the film I did not want to see about Iris Murdoch that I cannot see the film others might want to see. Stanley Kauffmann's case in praise of the film in *The New Republic* is persuasive, but no: I cannot accept this Iris. The one in my mind is too alive, too vital, too inspiring.

Irreversible ★ ★ ★

NO MPAA RATING, 99 m., 2003

Monica Bellucci (Alex), Vincent Cassel (Marcus), Albert Dupontel (Pierre), Philippe Nahon (Philippe), Jo Prestia (Le Tenia), Stéphane Drouot (Stéphane), Mourad Khima (Mourad). Directed by Gaspar Noé and produced by Christophe Rossignon and Richard Grandpierre. Screenplay by Noé.

Irreversible is a movie so violent and cruel that most people will find it unwatchable. The camera looks on unflinchingly as a woman is raped and beaten for several long, unrelenting minutes, and as a man has his face pounded in with a fire extinguisher, in an attack that continues until after he is apparently dead. That the movie has a serious purpose is to its credit, but makes it no more bearable. Some of the critics at the screening walked out, but I stayed, sometimes closing my eyes, and now I will try to tell you why I think the writer and director, Gaspar Noé, made the film in this way.

First, above all, and crucially, the story is told backward. Two other films have famously used that chronology: Harold Pinter's *Betrayal* (1983), the story of a love affair that ends (begins) in treachery, and Christopher Nolan's *Memento* (2001), which begins with the solution to a murder and tracks backward to its origin. Of *Betrayal*, I wrote that a sad love story would be even more tragic if you could see into the future, so that even this joyous moment, this kiss, was in the shadow of eventual despair.

Now consider *Irreversible*. If it were told in chronological order, we would meet a couple very much in love: Alex (Monica Bellucci) and Marcus (Vincent Cassel). In a movie that is frank and free about nudity and sex, we see them relaxed and playful in bed, having sex and sharing time. Bellucci and Cassel were lovers at the time the film was made, and are at ease with each other.

Then we would see them at a party, Alex wearing a dress that makes little mystery of her perfect breasts. We would see a man hitting on her. We would hear it asked how a man could let his lover go out in public dressed like that: Does he like to watch as men grow interested? We would meet Marcus's best friend, Pierre (Albert Dupontel), who himself was once a lover of Alex.

Then we would follow Alex as she walks alone into a subway tunnel, on a quick errand that turns tragic when she is accosted by Le Tenia (Jo Prestia), a pimp who brutally and mercilessly rapes and beats her for what seems like an eternity, in a stationary-camera shot that goes on and on and never cuts away.

And then we would follow Marcus and Pierre in a search for Le Tenia, which leads to an S&M club named the Rectum, where a man mistaken for Le Tenia is finally discovered and beaten brutally, again in a shot that continues mercilessly, this time with a handheld camera that seems to participate in the beating.

As I said, for most people, unwatchable. Now consider what happens if you reverse the chronology, so that the film begins with shots of the body being removed from the nightclub and tracks back through time to the warm and playful romance of the bedroom scenes. There

are several ways in which this technique produces a fundamentally different film:

1. The film doesn't build up to violence and sex as its payoff, as pornography would. It begins with its two violent scenes, showing us the very worst immediately, and then tracking back into lives that are about to be forever altered.

2. It creates a different kind of interest in those earlier scenes, which are foreshadowed for us but not for the characters. When Alex and Marcus caress and talk, we realize what a slender thread all happiness depends from. To know the future would not be a blessing but a curse. Life would be unlivable without the innocence of our ignorance.

3. Revenge precedes violation. The rapist is savagely punished before he commits his crime. At the same time, and this is significant, Marcus is the violent monster of the opening scenes, and Le Tenia is a victim whose crime has not yet been seen (although we already know Alex has been assaulted).

4. The party scenes, and the revealing dress, are seen in hindsight as a risk that should not have been taken. Instead of making Alex look sexy and attractive, they make her look vulnerable and in danger. While it is true that a woman should be able to dress as she pleases, it is not always wise.

5. We know by the time we see Alex at the party, and earlier in bed, that she is not simply a sex object or a romantic partner, but a fierce woman who fights the rapist for every second of the rape. Who uses every tactic at her command to stop him. Who loses, but does not surrender. It makes her sweetness and warmth much richer when we realize what darker weathers she harbors. This woman is not simply a sensuous being, as women so often simply are in the movies, but a fighter with a fierce survival instinct.

The fact is, the reverse chronology makes *Irreversible* a film that structurally argues against rape and violence, while ordinary chronology would lead us down a seductive narrative path toward a shocking, exploitative payoff. By placing the ugliness at the beginning, Gaspar Noé forces us to think seriously about the sexual violence involved. The movie does not end with rape as its climax and send us out of the theater as if something had been communicated. It starts with it, and asks us to sit there for another hour and process our thoughts. It is therefore moral at a structural level.

As I said twice and will repeat again, most people will not want to see the film at all. It is so violent, it shows such cruelty, that it is a test most people will not want to endure. But it is unflinchingly honest about the crime of rape. It does not exploit. It does not pander. It has been said that no matter what it pretends, pornography argues for what it shows. *Irreversible* is not pornography.

The Isle ★ ★ ★

NO MPAA RATING, 89 m., 2003

Suh Jung (Hee-Jin), Yoosuk Kim (Hyun-Shik), Sung-hee Park (Eun-A), Jae-Hyun Cho (Mang-Chee), Hang-Seon Jang (Middle-aged Man). Directed by Ki-duk Kim, and produced by Eun Lee. Screenplay by Kim.

The audiences at Sundance are hardened and sophisticated, but when the South Korean film *The Isle* played there in 2001, there were gasps and walkouts. People covered their eyes, peeked out, and slammed their palms back again. I report that because I want you to know: This is the most gruesome and queasiness-inducing film you are likely to have seen. You may not even want to read the descriptions in this review. Yet it is also beautiful, angry, and sad, with a curious sick poetry, as if the Marquis de Sade had gone in for pastel landscapes.

The film involves a lake where fishermen rent tiny cottages, each on its own raft, and bob with the waves as they catch and cook their dinners. It is the ultimate getaway. Once they have been delivered to their rafts by Hee-Jin, a woman who lives in a shack on the bank and operates a motorboat, they depend on her for all of their supplies and for the return to shore. She also sometimes brings them prostitutes, or services them herself.

Hee-Jin (Suh Jung) does not speak throughout the film, and is thought to be a mute, until she utters one piercing scream. She is like the heroine of *Woman of the Dunes*, ruling a domain in which men, once lured, can be kept captive. Most of the time she simply operates her business, ferrying the fishermen back and forth to their floating retreats. The men treat Hee-Jin and the prostitutes with brutality and

contempt, even making them dive into the water to get their payments; that these women are willing to work in this way is a measure of their desperation.

Hee-Jin is indifferent to most of the men, but becomes interested in Hyun-Shik (Yoosuk Kim). Because we share his nightmares, we know that he was a policeman, killed his girlfriend, and has come to the floating hut to hide and perhaps to die. Watching him one day, she sees that he is about to commit suicide and interrupts his chain of thought with sudden violence, swimming under his raft and stabbing him through the slats of the floor. They develop what on this lake passes for a relationship, but then he tries suicide again (you might want to stop reading now) by swallowing a line knotted with fishhooks and pulling it up again. This leads to a sex scene I will not describe here, and later to an equally painful sequence involving Hee-Jin's use of fishhooks.

It is not uncommon for South Korean films to involve sadomasochism, as indeed do many films from Japan, where bondage is a common subject of popular adult comic books. The material doesn't reflect common behavior in those countries, but is intended to evoke extremes of violent emotion. It also dramatizes hostility toward women, although in *The Isle* the tables are turned. Between these two people who have nothing in common, one of them mute, sex is a form of communication—and pain, this movie argues, is even more sincere and complete.

Why would you want to see this film? Most people would not. I was recently at a health resort where a movie was shown every night, and one of the selections was Pedro Almodóvar's *All About My Mother*, which involves transgendered characters. "Why," a woman asked me, "would they show a movie with things I do not want to see?" She is not unusual. Most people choose movies that provide exactly what they expect, and tell them things they already know. Others are more curious. We are put on this planet only once, and to limit ourselves to the familiar is a crime against our minds.

The way I read *The Isle*, it is not about fishhooks and sex at all. It is a cry of pain. The man on the raft, as we have seen in flashbacks, is violent and cruel, and he killed his girlfriend because he was jealous. Of course, jealousy is the face of low self-esteem. The woman sells her body and dives into the water for her payment. Her power is that she can leave these hateful men stranded on their rafts. I believe that Hee-Jin comes to "like" Hyun-Shik, although that is the wrong word. Maybe she feels possessive because she saved his life. His second attempt, with the fishhooks, reveals the depth of his sad self-loathing. When she employs the fishhooks on herself, what is she saying? That she understands? That she feels the same way too? That even in agony we need someone to witness and share?

The film, as I said, is beautiful to look at. The little huts are each a different color. The mist over the water diffuses the light. What a lovely postcard this scene would make, if we did not know the economy it reflects, and the suffering it conceals. Now there's a subject for meditation.

I Spy ★ ★

PG-13, 96 m., 2002

Eddie Murphy (Kelly Robinson), Owen Wilson (Alexander Scott), Famke Janssen (Rachel), Malcolm McDowell (Gundars), Gary Cole (Carlos). Directed by Betty Thomas and produced by Mario Kassar, Thomas, Jenno Topping, and Andrew G. Vajna. Screenplay by Marianne Wibberley, Cormac Wibberley, David Ronn, and Jay Scherick.

The thing about old TV shows is they have established brand names. People have heard of them and maybe enjoyed them once. So when Hollywood recycles them into movies, they have instant name recognition, and if the casting is plausible, audiences are intrigued. Some shows, like *Mission: Impossible*, get the A-list treatment, but *I Spy* is more of a throwaway, an attempt, as *Variety* might put it, to rake in quick coin during a hasty playoff.

Having written that, I turned to the *Variety* review to see if my hunch was correct. I was close. *Variety* writes: "Snoops should sneak out of the B.O. with a nifty opening sum, but expect steep dropoffs in the ensuing weeks. . . ." Yes. But it's a shame that Eddie Murphy and Owen Wilson should be wasted on a ho-hum project like this. Why not either (1) save them for something worth doing, or (2) have the nerve to remake *I Spy* into an offbeat, contemporary project that slices and dices the old clichés?

Not a chance. This is a remake by the numbers, linking a half-witted plot to a series of stand-up routines in which Wilson and Murphy show how funny they could have been in a more ambitious movie. When they riff with each other, there's an energy that makes us smile. When they slog through the plot, we despair. Does *anyone* other than a Hollywood producer believe that in an Eddie Murphy movie the audience cares about special effects, action sequences, and desperate struggles to save the world? That kind of material is played out; it can be brought briefly back to life in a James Bond movie or an all-out thriller, but in a comedy, what we want to do is, we want to laugh.

Murphy and Wilson play Kelly Robinson and Alexander Scott. Students of the 1960s TV series will note that the roles have switched their races; Murphy is playing the Robert Culp character, and Wilson is in the Bill Cosby role. This makes not the slightest difference, since nothing in this movie refers to the TV series in a way that matters. There is a little color-coding going on, I think, in the decision to change the Culp occupation (tennis player) into a prizefighter for Eddie Murphy to play, the filmmakers apparently not having heard that there are black tennis stars.

The plot: Kelly Robinson (who always refers to himself as "Kelly Robinson") is recruited by spy Alexander Scott. Robinson is about to fight a title bout in Budapest, and an evildoer named Gundars (Malcolm McDowell) will be there. Robinson will provide entrée for Scott, who is trying to get back an invisible spy plane named the *Switchblade*, which Gundars has stolen and plans to use for, I dunno, world domination or something.

Murphy and Wilson are very funny men, and occasionally one of their lines swims up from out of the murk of the screenplay and winks at us. I like Wilson looking at his new spy gear and observing, "My stuff looks like you could get it from Radio Shack in 1972." And later, in a briefing, they learn that the *Switchblade* is, "in the hands of the evildoers, a delivery system for weapons of mass destruction." One of the signs that the White House announced its anti-Saddam policy prematurely is when key catchphrases are recycled in movie comedies and the invasion is still in the talking stage. That's too much lead time.

The spy plane shimmers in and out of sight thanks to special effects, while the loyalties of a beautiful spy named Rachel (Famke Janssen) also shimmer in and out of sight, as does the Hispanic accent of the enigmatic spy Carlos (Gary Cole). The movie comes to life when Murphy and Wilson are trading one-liners, and then puts itself on hold for spy and action sequences of stunning banality. Don't moviemakers know that action scenes without context have got to be really, really good or our eyes glaze over? We've seen it all. We don't need one more boring fight on a rooftop with the future of the world hanging in the balance. If the characters are interesting, the story is involving, or the effects are really special, that's another story. *I Spy*, alas, is the same old story.

Italian for Beginners ★ ★ ★

R, 112 m., 2002

Anders W. Berthelsen (Andreas), Ann Eleonora Jorgensen (Karen), Anette Stovelbaek (Olympia), Peter Gantzler (Jorgen Mortensen), Lars Kaalund (Hal-Finn), Sara Indrio Jensen (Giulia), Elsebeth Steentoft (Kirketjener), Rikke Wolck (Sygeplejerske). Directed by Lone Scherfig and produced by Ib Tardini. Screenplay by Scherfig.

What a masterstroke it was for Lars von Trier to invent the Dogma movement! Every review of a Dogma film must begin with the announcement that it is a Dogma film, and then put it to the Dogma test to see if it conforms. Von Trier's name is often mentioned more prominently than the name of the film's actual director. He exacts a tax on our attention to the film. Since most people reading reviews don't know what Dogma is and don't care, this discussion puts them off the movie. Wise Dogma directors should no more trumpet their affiliation than should a movie begin with an announcement of the film stock it was shot on.

I say this because *Italian for Beginners* is a charming Danish comedy, and the fact that it's a Dogma film has little to do with its appeal. Yes, like all Dogma films, it's shot on video, on location, with only music found at the source—but so what? You see how Dogma changes the subject. What is appealing about it, the fresh-

ness and quirkiness of its characters and their interlinked stories, has nothing to do with Dogma—although, of course, lower costs may have helped it get made.

The movie takes place near Copenhagen, mostly in a small complex that includes a sports facility, a restaurant, a hair salon, and a nearby church. New to the church is Pastor Andreas (Anders W. Berthelsen), taking the place of a former pastor who took his ideas about services a little too seriously (he pushed the organist off the balcony). Short tempers seem to run in this little community; we meet Hal-Finn (Lars Kaalund), manager of the restaurant, who treats his job like a military command and is hilariously rude to customers who have bad manners.

Ordered to get a haircut, he meets the hairdresser Karen (Ann Eleonora Jorgensen). Everyone seems to cross paths in Karen's salon, including Pastor Andreas, who stops in for a haircut and has to dispense emergency spiritual advice to Olympia (Anette Stovelbaek), a bakery employee who gets a crush on Andreas.

Giulia (Sara Indrio Jensen) is an Italian waitress in the restaurant. It is not beside the point that she is Italian. Jorgen (Peter Gantzler), the manager of the complex, likes her so much he signs up for Italian classes. The Italian teacher suddenly drops dead, and Hal-Finn, who finds himself with some free time, decides to take over the class, which he teaches as if he is instructing Cub Scouts on fire-building techniques.

The movie gradually reveals certain unsuspected connections between some of the characters, and allows romances to bloom or fade among others, and all comes to a head during a class trip to Venice, which they all take more or less in desperation. The film has been written and directed by Lone Scherfig, who has a real affection for her characters, and likes to watch them discovering if happiness can be found in the absence of crucial social skills.

Because it comes attached to the Dogma label, I suppose we assume going into it that *Italian for Beginners* will test our taste or our patience. The film only wants to amuse. It's a reminder that Dogma films need not involve pathetic characters tormented by the misuse of their genitalia, but can simply want to have a little fun. This is the sort of story American independent filmmakers also like to tell, right down to the setting in a restaurant—which, like a bar or an apartment in a sitcom, is convenient because all the characters can drop in without explanation. I was surprised how much I enjoyed *Italian for Beginners*, and made a mental note not to get all hung up on the Dogma movement in my review.

The Italian Job ★ ★ ★
PG-13, 105 m., 2003

Mark Wahlberg (Charlie Croker), Charlize Theron (Stella Bridger), Edward Norton (Steve Frezelli), Seth Green (Lyle), Jason Statham (Handsome Rob), Mos Def (Left-Ear), Donald Sutherland (John Bridger). Directed by F. Gary Gray and produced by Donald De Line. Screenplay by Donna Powers and Wayne Powers.

I saw *The Italian Job* in a Chicago screening room, in the midst of a rush of new summer releases. I recollect it now from the Cannes Film Festival, which has assembled one unendurable film after another for its worst year in memory. That doesn't make *The Italian Job* a better film, but it provides a reminder that we do, after all, sometimes go to the movies just to have a good time, and not to be mired in a slough of existential despond. Don't get me wrong. I like a good mire in despond now and again; it's just that the despond at Cannes has been so unadmirable.

F. Gary Gray's *The Italian Job*, on the other hand, is nothing more, or less, than a slick caper movie with stupendous chase scenes and a truly ingenious way to steal $35 million in gold bars from a safe in a Venetian palazzo.

The safe is stolen by a gang led by Donald Sutherland, who must be relieved to note that Venice has no dwarfs in red raincoats this season. His confederates include Charlie (Mark Wahlberg), a strategic mastermind; second-in-command Steve (Edward Norton); the computer whiz Lyle (Seth Green); the getaway driver Handsome Rob (Jason Statham); and Left-Ear (Mos Def), who can blow up stuff real good.

After a chase through the canals of Venice, which in real life would have led to the loss of six tourist gondolas and the drowning of an accordion player, the confederates go to an extraordinary amount of trouble to meet, with the gold, in a high Alpine pass apparently undisturbed since Hannibal. I have no idea how hard it is to move $35 million in gold from Venice to the Alps with Interpol looking for you, or for that matter how hard it would be to move it back down again, but golly, it's a pretty location.

After betrayal and murder, the action shifts to Los Angeles. Think of the overweight baggage charges. Wahlberg and company, who have lost the gold, are determined to get it back again, and enlist Sutherland's daughter, Stella (Charlize Theron), who is a safecracker. A legal one, until they enlist her.

Stella drives a bright red Mini Cooper, which is terrifically important to the plot. Eventually there is a fleet of three. That the crooks in the original *Italian Job* (1968) also drove Mini Coopers is one of the few points of similarity between the two movies. Good job that the Mini Cooper was reintroduced in time for product placement in this movie.

Actually, that's unfair; they need Mini Coopers because their size allows them to drive through very narrow spaces, although they have no idea how handy the little cars will become when they drive down the stairs and onto the tracks of the Los Angeles subway system. They're also handy in traffic jams, and there are nice sequences in which traffic lights are manipulated by the Seth Green character, who hilariously insists he is the real inventor of Napster, which was stolen by his roommate while he was taking a nap, thus the name.

There are a couple of nice dialogue touches; Edward Norton is not the first actor to say, "I liked him right up until the moment I shot him," but he is certainly the latest. The ending is suitably ironic. This is just the movie for two hours of mindless escapism on a relatively skilled, professional level. If I had seen it instead of the Cannes entry *The Brown Bunny*, I would have wept with gratitude.

It Runs in the Family ★ ★ ½
PG-13, 101 m., 2003

Michael Douglas (Alex Gromberg), Kirk Douglas (Mitchell Gromberg), Cameron Douglas (Asher Gromberg), Diana Douglas (Evelyn Gromberg), Bernadette Peters (Rebecca Gromberg), Rory Culkin (Eli Gromberg), Sarita Choudhury (Peg Maloney), Irene Gorovaia

(Abigail Staley). Directed by Fred Schepisi and produced by Michael Douglas. Screenplay by Jesse Wigutow.

I have no idea how accurately the story of *It Runs in the Family* parallels the actual story of the Douglas family, whose members play four of the characters. My guess is that most of the facts are different and a lot of the emotions are the same. Like *On Golden Pond,* which dealt obliquely with the real-life tensions between Jane Fonda and her father Henry, this new film seems like a way for the Douglases to test and resolve assorted family issues—to reach closure, that most elusive of psychobabble goals.

The film is certainly courageous in the way it deals with Kirk Douglas's stroke, Michael Douglas's infidelity, and the drug problems of a son played by Cameron Douglas. Even if the movie doesn't reflect real life, any attentive reader of the supermarket sleaze sheets will guess that it comes close. In a way, just by making the film, the Douglases have opened themselves up to that.

My wish is that they'd opened up a little more. The movie deals with these touchy subjects, and others, but in a plot so jammed with events, disputes, tragedies, and revelations that the most serious matters don't seem to receive enough attention. The film seems too much in a hurry.

It introduces us to the Grombergs. Alex (Michael Douglas) is a prosperous attorney whose father, Mitchell (Kirk Douglas), was a founder of the firm. Not a bad man, Alex volunteers in a soup kitchen, where a sexy fellow volunteer (Sarita Choudhury) finds him so attractive that she all but forces them to have sex, which they do—almost. Their scenes are stunningly unconvincing, except as a convenience to the plot.

At home, Alex is married to Rebecca (Bernadette Peters) and his father is married to Evelyn (Diana Douglas, who was, in an intriguing casting choice, Kirk's real-life first wife). Alex and Rebecca have two sons, the college student Asher (Cameron Douglas, Michael's son by his first marriage) and the eleven-year-old Eli (Rory Culkin, whose family could also inspire a movie). Mitchell also has a brother who is senile and lives in a care facility.

During the course of the movie, there will be two deaths, Alex's marriage will almost break up because of suspected infidelity, Asher will get in trouble with the law, Eli will go on a walk on the wild side with a nose-ringed eleven-year-old girlfriend, and Alex and Mitchell will seem incapable of having a conversation that doesn't descend into criticism and resentment. Only the old folks, Mitchell and Evelyn, seem to have found happiness, perhaps out of sheer exhaustion with the alternatives.

The film, directed by Fred Schepisi, has moments I fear are intended to be more serious than they play. One involves a midnight mission by Alex and Mitchell to set a rowboat adrift with an illegal cargo. I did not for a moment believe this scene, at least not in an ostensibly serious movie. Would two high-powered lawyers collaborate on such an act? When it is clear they can be traced? Really?

The scenes between Michael and Kirk Douglas, which are intended as the heart of the movie, seem inadequately realized in Jesse Wigutow's screenplay. They fret, fence, and feud, but without the sense of risk and hurt we felt between the two Fondas. Even less satisfying are the marital arguments between Alex and Rebecca, who has found a pair of panties in her husband's pocket. How they got there and what they mean, or don't mean, could be easily explained by the defensive husband—but he can never quite get the words out, and his dialogue remains infuriatingly inconclusive. As a result, all of the tension between them feels like a plot contrivance.

There are some good moments. I liked Kirk Douglas's fierce force of personality, and I liked moments, almost asides, in which Michael Douglas finds simple humanity amid the emotional chaos. There is a lovely scene involving Rory Culkin and his first date (Irene Gorovaia), in which their dialogue feels just about right for those two in that time and place. Their first kiss is a reminder that few first kisses are exactly wonderful. And a scene where Kirk and Diana Douglas dance has a simple warmth and truth.

But the movie is simply not clear about where it wants to go and what it wants to do. It is heavy on episode and light on insight, and although it takes courage to bring up touchy topics it would have taken more to treat them frankly.

What about a movie in which a great actor,

now somewhat slowed by a stroke, collaborates with his successful son in a movie that will involve other family members and even the great actor's first wife? What does the great actor's second wife (who has been married to him for almost fifty years) think of that? What about a movie in which the son divorces his first wife to marry a famous beauty, who then wins an Oscar? These musings may seem unfair, but *It Runs in the Family* makes them inevitable. The Douglas family would have to make one hell of a movie to do justice to their real lives.

Ivans xtc. ★ ★ ★ ★

NO MPAA RATING, 94 m., 2002

Danny Huston (Ivan Beckman), Peter Weller (Don West), Lisa Enos (Charlotte White), Adam Krentzman (Barry Oaks), Alex Butler (Brad East), Morgan Vukovic (Lucy Lawrence), Tiffani-Amber Thiessen (Marie Stein), James Merendino (Danny McTeague), Caroleen Feeney (Rosemary). Directed by Bernard Rose and produced by Lisa Enos. Screenplay by Rose and Enos, based on *The Death of Ivan Ilyich* by Leo Tolstoy.

There is much sadness but little mourning at the funeral of Ivan Beckman. All agree he brought about his own death. He had few close friends. It is said he died from cancer. Insiders whisper, "The cancer is a cover story." You know you have lived your life carelessly when cancer is your cover story.

Ivans xtc., a remarkable film by Bernard Rose, stars Danny Huston, the rich-voiced, genial, tall son of John Huston, as a powerful Hollywood agent whose untidy personal life becomes a legend. Cocaine was the solution to his problems, which were caused by cocaine. He is headed for a shipwreck anyway when the diagnosis of lung cancer comes, but instead of looking for medical help he bulldozes ahead with cocaine, denial, and call girls.

The film opens with his funeral. There is a fight between a writer fired from a new movie and the star (Peter Weller) who fired him. Their disagreement cannot wait upon death. In voice-over, we hear the voice of the dead agent, who says that at the end, "the pain was so bad I took every pill in the house." And he tried, he says, "to find one simple image to get me through it."

Then we flash back through his life, as Ivan appears on-screen, one of those charming but unknowable men who have perfect courtesy, who lean forward with the appearance of great attention, and whose minds seem to be otherwise involved. As it happens, that is precisely the impression I had of John Huston on the three or four occasions when I met him: He was a shade too courteous, too agreeable, too accommodating, leaning forward too attentively from his great height, and I felt that he was playing a nice man while thinking about other things.

Danny Huston plays Ivan Beckman as the sort of man who believes he cannot be touched. Who has been given a pass. To whom all things come because they must, and for whom addictions like cocaine do not bring the usual ravages. I am told that if you have enough money for enough cocaine you can hold out like that for quite a while, which is not good, because you are building up a deficit in your mind and body that eventually cannot be repaid.

When Ivan doesn't return phone calls, when he doesn't appear at the office, when clients can't find him, he doesn't get in the same kind of trouble that a less legendary agent might experience, because—well, that's Ivan. When his girlfriend Charlotte (Lisa Enos) can't find him, and then discovers he was partying with hookers—well, who did she think he was when she started going out with him? Surely she heard the stories? Surely this doesn't come as news? When his bosses grow restless at his irresponsibility—hey, he has the big client list. If the clients like him, then the agency must.

The diagnosis of cancer comes like a telegram that should have been delivered next door. It is the final, irrefutable reply to his feeling of immunity. There are two painful scenes where he tries, in one way or another, to deal with this news. One comes in a meeting with his father, whose ideas have made him a stranger. One comes during a party with two call girls, who are happy with the money, happy with the cocaine, happy to be with Ivan Beckman, and then increasingly unhappy and confused as their services are needed, not to pretend, but to be real. You cannot hire someone to really care about you.

The movie is allegedly inspired by *The Death of Ivan Ilyich* by Leo Tolstoy. I say "allegedly," because Bernard Rose has charged that the powerful Creative Artists Agency tried to prevent the film, seeing it as a transparent version of the life of Jay Moloney, an agent who at one time (I learn from a news story) represented Leonardo DiCaprio, Steven Spielberg, Bill Murray, Uma Thurman, Tim Burton—and Rose himself. Fired from CAA in 1996 because of cocaine, the story says, he moved to the Caribbean and killed himself in 1999.

Well, the story could be based on a lot of lives. The parabola of serious addiction often looks a lot the same. If the victim has more money, the settings are prettier. The tragedy of Ivan Beckman is that he doesn't know how to call for help, and has no one to call if he did. It is important to recognize that he is not a bad man. He can be charming, does not wish to cause harm, is grateful for company, and, as such people like to say, "If I'm hurting anybody, I'm only hurting myself." It is not until too late that he discovers how much it hurts.

Note: The story of the making of Ivans xtc. *is the story of how a lot of movies can now be made, according to Bernard Rose, its director.*

Because of its controversial subject matter and because the Hollywood establishment has no wish to fund the thinly veiled story of the death of one of its own, the movie could not find conventional financing.

"So we went ahead and filmed it anyway," Rose told me after the film's screening at Cannes 2001. *"We got a 24-fps digital video camera, and we shot it in our own homes, and the crew was the cast and the cast was the crew and we took care of catering by calling for carryout."*

Rose, forty-two, is the British-born director of a number of commercial hits, notably Candyman *(1992) and* Immortal Beloved *(1995), and he is known for the power of his visual imagery. In* Paperhouse *(1988), he created a real landscape based on a child's imaginary drawings. In* Immortal Beloved, *a boy runs through the woods at night and plunges into a lake, floating on his back as the camera pulls back to show him surrounded by the reflections of countless stars.*

Ivans xtc., *made on a $500,000 budget, did not support or require such images. Produced by Lisa Enos, who also stars in it, it was directed by Rose on high-def video, which looks—appropriate, I think, is the word. Some shots are beautiful, others are functional, and there are no shots that do not work.*

"We finished the movie, we took it to Artisan Entertainment, and we made a deal," he said. *"A 50-50 split of all the proceeds from dollar one. It was made so cheaply that we'll make out and so will they."*

Does he wish he'd had film? "It's no use saying you'd rather have film, because this project on film could not have existed."

J

Japanese Story ★ ★ ★ ½
R, 110 m., 2004

Toni Collette (Sandy Edwards), Gotaro
Tsunashima (Tachibana Hiromitsu), Matthew
Dyktynski (Bill Baird), Lynette Curran (Mum),
Yumiko Tanaka (Yukiko Hiromitsu), Kate
Atkinson (Jackie), John Howard (Richards), Bill
Young (Jimmy Smithers). Directed by Sue
Brooks and produced by Sue Maslin. Screenplay
by Alison Tilson.

Toni Collette can have an angular presence on
the screen; she can look hard and tough, and is
well cast in *Japanese Story* as an unmarried geologist whose idea of dinner is a can of baked
beans poured over two slices of toast. But then
there comes another side that is tender and
dreamy. Her body becomes sensuous instead of
distant, and her eyes are seeing from a different
part of her soul.

Both of those identities are used in Sue
Brooks's *Japanese Story*, a film in which her
character journeys into the Australian desert
with a Japanese businessman she begins by hating, and then begins to ... not love, but cherish.
She plays Sandy, an expert on the mining of
minerals. She's assigned to baby-sit Tachibana
(Gotaro Tsunashima), who has flown in from
Kyoto and whose father owns 9 percent of the
company.

Sandy flies with him to a dorp town in the
interior, rents a Jeep, and shows him the mine:
a massive hole in the ground whose terraces remind him of a Mayan temple. Then he wants to
drive on, farther, into the vastness. She protests.
There's only a one-track dirt road, and "People
die in this desert. Frequently." Their Jeep gets
mired in the fine powder of the red earth, they
can't drive it out or dig it out, they spend a cold
night around a campfire, and she is very, very
angry, because Tachibana got them into this
mess, and it looks as if they may die, and he refuses to use his cell phone because of shame:
Having caused their trouble, he refuses to
admit it to his colleagues.

This sounds like some sort of survival adventure, but even in the moments of despair in
the desert, *Japanese Story* is about characters,
not plot. The Japanese man is not fluent in

English, but he knows a great many more
words than he first reveals. He doesn't know
she's a geologist, and treats her like his driver
(he lets her wrestle his heavy suitcase into the
Jeep). But during the long, cold night (at one
point she shifts to put her back against his, for
warmth), something rotates in his consciousness, and the next day there are scenes in which
each looks at the other for a long time, thinking, sensing, beginning to like. That night in a
motel, they make love; undressing, she puts on
his pants before walking over to the bed.

And now you must put the review aside, if
you plan to see the movie. There is something I
want you to experience for yourself.

What future do they have? None, really, even
before she sees the photograph of his wife and
family in his billfold. They're strangers with a
thousand words between them, in the middle
of a limitless empty place. What they have is
not merely sex, yet not love; it is more like a
means of communication to show relief and
acceptance. Then, in a moment of heedless fun,
he has an absurd accident and dies. Snap, the
movie breaks in two. She must wrestle his body
into the Jeep, take it to a small town, find
Smithers the undertaker ("We'll put it in the
cold room so it doesn't go off"), and deal with
the police, the report, her colleagues ... and the
widow, who is flying in from Japan.

It's here that the movie demonstrates what
it's been trying to say all along. Alison Tilson's
screenplay follows its logic into deep feelings.
What does another person mean to us, really, if
they are not available to share our lives, and we
cannot really know them—but we cherish
them for the transient joy they have shared
with us? Who was he, really? She had to ask
which was his first and which his family name.
Did he ever know her surname? After surviving
death in the desert, after saving each other's
lives, after making love and looking at the belit-
tling landscape and becoming a team of two in
an ocean of emptiness, they have come to this:
his corpse, its head lolling from side to side, as
she cleans off the sand and mud with a cloth.

Japanese Story never steps wrong in its crucial closing passages, especially in the precise
and exact way that Sandy and the widow have a
limited but bottomless communication. The

mundane details of the undertaker, the coroner, the police, and the funeral are like a series of events that are—wrong. Wrong, all wrong, because Tachibana should not be dead. There is no sense in it. He lost his life in a senseless instant, and brought a horrible finality to a relationship not real enough to support it; it should have ended with a kiss and some tears and a rueful smile at an airport. It imposed enormous significance on their time together, which did not deserve and cannot support such significance. What she feels at the end, I think, is not love for him or sorrow, but a great pity that his whole life should have been wiped away and lost for no reason at all, just like that, carelessly, thoughtlessly, in the middle of things.

The movie wants to record how such things happen, and how they present the survivor with an insoluble challenge: What does Sandy think, how does she behave, what should she feel, what should she do now? Patiently, observantly, it takes her through all of these question's and shows her clumsy but honest attempt to answer them. And gradually the full arc of Toni Collette's performance reveals itself, and we see that the end was there even in the beginning. This is that rare sort of film that is not about what happens, but about what happens then.

Jason X ½★
R, 93 m., 2002

Kane Hodder (Jason Voorhees), Lexa Doig (Rowan), Lisa Ryder (Kay-Em 14), Chuck Campbell (Tsunaron), Jonathan Potts (Professor Lowe), Peter Mensah (Sergeant Brodski), Melyssa Ade (Janessa), Todd Farmer (Dallas), Melody Johnson (Kinsa). Directed by James Isaac and produced by Noel Cunningham and Isaac. Screenplay by Victor Miller and Todd Farmer.

"This sucks on so many levels."
—Dialogue from *Jason X*

Rare for a movie to so frankly describe itself. *Jason X* sucks on the levels of storytelling, character development, suspense, special effects, originality, punctuation, neatness, and aptness of thought. Only its title works. And I

wouldn't be surprised to discover that the name *Jason X* is copyrighted © 2002, World Wrestling Federation, and that Jason's real name is Dwayne Johnson. No, wait, that was last week's movie.

Jason X is technically *Friday the 13th, Part 10*. It takes place centuries in the future, when Earth is a wasteland and a spaceship from Earth II has returned to the Camp Crystal Lake Research Facility and discovered two cryogenically frozen bodies, one of them holding a machete and wearing a hockey mask.

The other body belongs to Rowan (Lexa Doig), a researcher who is thawed out and told it is now the year 2455: "That's 455 years in the future!" Assuming that the opening scenes take place now, you've done the math and come up with 453 years in the future. The missing two years are easily explained: I learn from the Classic Horror Website that the movie was originally scheduled to be released on Halloween 2000, and was then bumped to March 2001, summer 2001, and Halloween 2001 before finally opening on the sixteenth anniversary of Chernobyl, another famous meltdown.

The movie is a low-rent retread of the *Alien* pictures, with a monster attacking a spaceship crew; one of the characters, Dallas, is even named in homage to the earlier series. The movie's premise: Jason, who has a "unique ability to regenerate lost and damaged tissue," comes back to life and goes on a rampage, killing the ship's plentiful supply of sex-crazed students and staff members. Once you know that the ship contains many dark corners and that the crew members wander off alone as stupidly as the campers at Camp Crystal Lake did summer after summer, you know as much about the plot as the writers do.

With *Star Wars Episode II: Attack of the Clones* opening, there's been a lot of talk lately about how good computer-generated special effects have become. On the basis of the effects in *Jason X* and the (much more entertaining) *Scorpion King*, we could also chat about how bad they are getting. Perhaps audiences do not require realistic illusions, but simply the illusion of realistic illusions. Shabby special effects can have their own charm.

Consider a scene where the spaceship is about to dock with *Solaris*, a gigantic mother ship, or a city in space, or whatever. Various controls go haywire because Jason has thrown people through them, and the ship fails to find its landing slot and instead crashes into *Solaris*, slicing off the top of a geodesic dome and crunching the sides of skyscrapers (why *Solaris* has a city-style skyline in outer space I do not presume to ask).

This sequence is hilariously unconvincing. But never mind. Consider this optimistic dialogue by Professor Lowe (Jonathan Potts), the greedy top scientist who wants to cash in on Jason: "Everyone OK? We just overshot it. We'll turn around." Uh-huh. We're waiting for the reaction from *Solaris* Air Traffic Control when a dull thud echoes through the ship and the characters realize *Solaris* has just exploded. Fine, but how could they hear it? Students of *Alien* will know that in space, no one can hear you blow up.

The characters follow the usual rules from Camp Crystal Lake, which require the crew members to split up, go down dark corridors by themselves, and call out each other's names with the sickening certainty that they will get no reply. Characters are skewered on giant screws, cut in half, punctured by swords, get their heads torn off, and worse. A veteran pilot remains calm: "You weren't alive during the Microsoft conflict. We were beating each other with our own severed limbs."

There is one good effects shot, in which a scientist's face is held in supercooled liquid until it freezes, and then smashed into smithereens against a wall. There is also an interesting transformation, as the onboard regenerator restores Jason and even supplies him with superhero armor and a new face to replace his hockey mask and ratty army surplus duds. I left the movie knowing one thing for sure: There will be a *Jason XI*—or, given the IQ level of the series, *Jason X, Part 2*.

Jeepers Creepers 2 ★

R, 103 m., 2003

Ray Wise (Jack Taggart), Jonathan Breck (The Creeper), Travis Schiffner (Izzy Bohen), Eric Nenninger (Scott Braddock), Al Santos (Dante Belasco), Nicki Lynn Aycox (Minxie Hayes).

Directed by Victor Salva and produced by Tom Luse. Screenplay by Salva.

Every 23rd spring, for 23 days, it gets to eat.
—opening title of Jeepers Creepers 2

The next shot is ominously subtitled: *Day 22.* A young boy is installing scarecrows in a field when he notices that one of them looks—not right. He approaches, sees the claws, and then becomes the first of many characters in this movie to fortify the Creeper for his next twenty-three-year hibernation. Cut to a school bus filled with a team returning from an out-of-town game along a highway where there is not one single other vehicle. The team and cheerleaders are singing a song, which is more or less required, I think, on buses where the passengers will soon be faced with unspeakable horrors.

Victor Salva's *Jeepers Creepers 2* supplies us with a first-class creature, a fourth-rate story, and dialogue possibly created by feeding the screenplay into a pasta maker. The movie basically consists of a half-man, half-bat that whooshes down out of the sky and snatches its prey. Sometimes it rips the tops off of old Rambler station wagons, and it opens up a pretty good hole in the top of the school bus. Meanwhile local farmer Jack Taggart (Ray Wise) tears himself away from his post-hole puncher, narrows his eyes, and stares intently at the edge of the screen while remembering that this all happened twenty-three years ago (maybe) or that the creature has eaten his youngest son (certainly).

The most notable character on the bus is Scott Braddock (Eric Nenninger), a virulent homophobe who doth, I think, protest too much as he accuses fellow team members of being gay. Later he tries to clear the bus of everyone the Creeper looked at, because then the ones who aren't his targets will be safe. This sidesteps the fact that the Creeper looked at Scott. One of the pom-pom girls has a hallucination or vision or something, and is able to explain that the creature chooses his victims according to body parts he requires, both as nutrition and as replacements. (Think through the lyrics of the song "Jeepers Creepers," and you'll get the idea.)

To call the characters on the bus paper thin

would be a kindness. Too bad, then, that we spend so much time on the bus, listening to their wretched dialogue and watching as they race from one window to another to see what foul deeds are occurring outside. Speaking of outside, Scott is the obligatory obstreperous jerk who is forever speculating that the creature has gone and won't return; he keeps suggesting they leave the bus to trek to a hypothetical nearby farmhouse. He's a direct throwback to the standard character in Dead Teenager Movies who's always saying, "Hmmm . . . all of the other campers have been found dead and eviscerated, Mimsy, so this would be an ideal time to walk out into the dark woods and go skinny-dipping in the pond where dozens of kids have died in the previous movies in this series."

Despite Scott's homophobia, the movie has a healthy interest in the male physique, and it's amazing how many of the guys walk around bare-chested. The critic John Fallon writes, "At a certain point, I thought I was watching soft gay erotica," and observes that when four of the guys go outside to pee, they line up shoulder to shoulder, which strikes him as unlikely since they are in a very large field. True in another movie, but in a film where the Creeper is likely to swoop down at any second and carry someone away, I would pick the tallest guy and stand next to him, on the theory that lightning will strike the tree and not you.

It is futile to bring logic to a film like this, but here goes: At one point, we hear local newscasters discussing the shocking discovery of 300 corpses knit together into a tapestry in the basement of an old church—all of them with one body part missing. So obviously the Creeper has been operating in the area for years. Would anyone notice 300 disappearances in a county so small that the main road has no traffic? Maybe that's what Jack Taggart is thinking about as he studies the side of the screen: "Hmmm . . . wonder if the disappearance of my son is connected to the carnage that occurs every twenty-three years hereabouts?"

The movie wants to work at the level of scaring us every so often with unexpected sudden attacks of the Creeper, although in this genre you expect sudden unexpected attacks, so you end up evaluating the craftsmanship instead of being scared. On that level, praise for the makeup and costume departments, including Richard Redlefsen, credited for "Creeper makeup and lead suit." Why the creature is called the Creeper when he leaps and flies, I am not sure. Why Francis Ford Coppola decided to produce this movie, I am also not sure.

Jersey Girl ★ ★ ★ ½
PG-13, 103 m., 2004

Ben Affleck (Ollie Trinke), Liv Tyler (Maya Harding), George Carlin (Bart Trinke), Raquel Castro (Gertie Trinke), Jason Biggs (Arthur Brickman), Jennifer Lopez (Gertrude). Directed by Kevin Smith and produced by Scott Mosier. Screenplay by Smith.

Jersey Girl is a romantic comedy written and directed by a kinder, gentler Kevin Smith. It's the kind of movie Hugh Grant might make, except for the way Smith has with his dialogue, which is truer and more direct than we expect. There are a couple of scenes here where a video store clerk cuts directly to the bottom line, and it feels like all sorts of romantic rules and regulations are being rewritten.

The movie stars Ben Affleck as Ollie Trinke, a hotshot Manhattan publicist whose beloved wife, Gertrude (Jennifer Lopez), is great with child. I would hesitate to reveal that she dies in childbirth if I had not already read and heard this information, oh, like 500 times, so obsessed is the nation with Ben and J-Lo. Lopez is luminous in her few scenes, helping to explain why Ollie remains so true to her memory that he remains celibate for many years.

His career meanwhile goes to pieces. Under pressure to hold a job while raising a daughter, he loses it one day, fatally offending his employers by causing a scene at the opening of a Hard Rock Café; he fails to understand why he should take Will Smith seriously ("Yeah, like the Fresh Prince of Bel Air is ever gonna have a movie career"). By the time the story resumes, he has moved back to New Jersey and is living in the same house with his father, Bart (George Carlin), and his beloved daughter, Gertie (Raquel Castro), who is now about seven. He's not in public relations anymore; he works with his dad in the public works department.

Because Ben Affleck is a movie star and looks like one, you might expect him to start dating eventually, but no. You might expect that he could find another high-paying PR job, but no. He doesn't because *then there wouldn't be a movie*. When a movie isn't working, we get all logical about things like this, but when it works, we relax.

Several times a week, Ollie and Gertie go to the local video store, where she plunders the kiddie section while he makes a quick dash through the bamboo curtain to grab a porno. One night he's confronted by Maya (Liv Tyler), the clerk, who claims she's taking a survey about pornography usage and asks Ollie how many times a week he masturbates. She is seriously disturbed by his reply, alarmed to learn he has had no sex in seven years, and informs him, "We're gonna have some sex."

And it's in a scene like this that Kevin Smith shows why he's such a good comedy writer. There is a bedrock of truth in the scene, which is based on embarrassment and shyness and Maya's disconcerting ability to say exactly what she's thinking, and when Ollie tries to explain why he has remained celibate (except for his relationship with countless porno titles), she patiently explains about sex: "It's the same thing only you're saving the $2 rental fee."

Inarguable logic, but he demurs, finally breaking down and agreeing to a lunch date. And thus does love reenter Ollie's life. For Maya may be bold about sex, but she is serious about love, and soon Gertie is saying, "Hey, you're the lady from the video store" at a moment when it would be much, much better had she not walked into the room.

Liv Tyler is a very particular talent who has sometimes been misused by directors more in love with her beauty than with her appropriateness for their story. Here she is perfectly cast as the naive and sincere Maya, whose boldness is *not* a seduction technique but an act of generosity, almost of mercy. It takes a special tone for a woman to convince us she wants to sleep with a man out of the goodness of her heart, but Tyler finds it, and it brings a sweetness to the relationship.

Kevin Smith, I believe, has spent almost as much time in video stores as Quentin Tarantino, and his study of ancient clichés is put to

good use in the closing act of his movie, which depends on not one but three off-the-shelf formulas: (1) the choice between the big city and staying with your family in a small town; (2) the parent who arrives at a school play just at the moment when the child onstage is in despair because that parent seems to be missing; and (3) the slow clap syndrome. Smith is a gifted writer and I believe he knew exactly what he was doing by assembling these old reliables. I'm not sure he couldn't have done better, but by then we like the characters so much that we give the school play a pass.

Besides—without the school play, we wouldn't get a chance to see the set constructed for little Gertie by two of the guys who work with Bart and Ollie in the public works department. Let it be said that the Lyric Opera's set for *Madame Butterfly* was only slightly more elaborate.

Jet Lag ★ ★
R, 85 m., 2003

Jean Reno (Felix), Juliette Binoche (Rose), Sergi Lopez (Sergio), Scali Delpeyrat (Doctor), Karine Belly (Air France Hostess), Raoul Billerey (Felix's father). Directed by Daniele Thompson and produced by Alain Sarde. Screenplay by Christopher Thompson and Daniele Thompson.

Jet Lag is sort of a grown-up version of *Before Sunrise*. In both films two travelers Meet Cute by chance and spend a long night in a strange city, talking and eating and flirting and concealing and revealing. The difference between the two films is sort of depressing.

In *Before Sunrise* (1995), Ethan Hawke and Julie Delpy were young students, and they wandered all over Vienna, encountering fortune-tellers, street poets, and friendly bartenders. In *Jet Lag*, Jean Reno and Juliette Binoche are meant to be twenty years older, and although they are in Paris they do not wander the streets or meet fascinating people, but huddle in airport lounges, hotel rooms, and tourist restaurants. The younger people talk about reincarnation, dreams, death, etc. The older people talk about abusive boyfriends, parental alienation, and cuisine.

That's the whole story, right there: The

young people have their lives ahead of them and are filled with hope. The older ones are stuck with responsibilities, relationships, careers, and fears. Although *Jet Lag* has a certain morose appeal, we cannot help thinking that this night they've spent together is the most interesting time either character has had in years, and if they get married, they will look back on it as if they were out of their minds.

There are, however, moments of intrigue. Some of them involve Juliette Binoche's makeup. If you know her from her many movies (she won the Oscar for *The English Patient*), you know she has a fresh, natural complexion. As we first see her in *Jet Lag*, she is wearing too much makeup of the wrong kind, and it doesn't flatter her. Makeup is her business, in a vague way. At one point she wipes it all off, and looks younger and more beautiful. Because the director, Daniele Thompson, devotes a lot of the movie to the close-up scrutiny of her actors, this transformation has a fascination entirely apart from the character Binoche plays.

Jean Reno is a rough-hewn French star, always with what looks like a two-week-old beard, often seen in action movies (*La Femme Nikita*). Here he shows gentleness and humor, and we believe him as a celebrity chef who was once great but is now merely rich. When the Binoche character mixes a vinaigrette for him and he likes it, their fate seems possibly sealed.

The plot is based on contrivance. They meet because she needs to borrow his cell phone. When their flights are canceled, he offers to let her stay in his hotel room, the last one available at the airport. We meet her current, former, and perhaps future boyfriend, a jealous creep. We hear about how the Reno character walked out of the life of his father, also a famous chef. They keep getting calls on the wrong phone.

But somehow none of this really matters. The movie is set up as if it should matter—as if much depends on whether they fall in love. The beauty of *Before Sunrise* was that nothing was supposed to matter. They talked, they walked, and the movie (directed by Richard Linklater) was content to let them do that, without forcing false obstacles and goals upon them.

I don't know if the distance between the two films is because of the difference in filmmakers

or the difference in ages. It may be that we have a heedlessness around twenty that we have lost, perhaps prudently, around forty. One thing I know for sure: When you're twenty you know that one night could change your life forever, and when you're forty, not only do you doubt that, but you're sort of relieved.

Johnny English ★ ½
PG, 87 m., 2003

Rowan Atkinson (Johnny English), John Malkovich (Pascal Sauvage), Natalie Imbruglia (Lorna Campbell), Ben Miller (Bough), Douglas McFerran (Klaus Vendetta), Tim Pigott-Smith (Pegasus), Kevin McNally (Prime Minister). Directed by Peter Howitt. and produced by Tim Bevan, Eric Fellner, and Mark Huffam. Screenplay by Neal Purvis, Robert Wade, and William Davies.

Can we all pretty much agree that the spy genre has been spoofed to death? The James Bond movies have supplied the target for more than forty years, and generations of Bond parodies have come and gone, from Dean Martin's Matt Helm to Mike Myers's Austin Powers. If *Austin Powers* is the funniest of the Bondian parodies, *Johnny English* is the least necessary, a mild-mannered ramble down familiar paths.

The movie stars Rowan Atkinson, best known in America as Mr. Bean, star of *Bean* (1997), and as the star of the PBS reruns of *The Black Adder*, where he played countless medieval schemers and bumblers in "the most gripping sitcom since 1380." He's the master of looking thoughtful after having committed a grievous breach of manners, logic, the law, personal hygiene, or common sense.

In *Johnny English*, he plays a character who became famous in Britain as the star of a long-running series of credit-card commercials. Johnny English is a low-level functionary in the British Secret Service pressed into active duty when a bomb destroys all of the other agents. His assignment: Foil a plot to steal the crown jewels.

The evil mastermind is Pascal Sauvage (John Malkovich), a French billionaire who believes his family was robbed of the crown two centuries ago. Now the head of a mega-billion-dollar international chain of prisons, he poses as a benefactor who pays to protect the jewels in new theft-proof quarters in the Tower of London—but actually plans to steal them and co-opt the archbishop of Canterbury to crown him king. And how does Queen Elizabeth II feel about this? The film's funniest moment has her signing an abdication form after a gun is pointed at the head of one of her beloved corgis.

The movie is a series of scenes demonstrating how dangerously incompetent Johnny English is, as when he lectures on how the thieves got into the tower without noticing he is standing on the edge of a tunnel opening. He can't even be trusted to drive during a chase scene, and spends most of one in a car suspended from a moving wrecker's crane. Meanwhile the beautiful Lorna Campbell (Natalie Imbruglia) turns up coincidentally wherever he goes, performing a variety of functions, of which the only explicable one is to be the beautiful Lorna Campbell.

John Malkovich does what can be done with Pascal Sauvage, I suppose, including the French accent we assume is deliberately bad, since Malkovich lives in France and no doubt has a better one. The character is such a stick and a stooge, however, that all Malkovich can do is stand there and be mugged by the script. Funnier work is done by Ben Miller, as Johnny's sidekick Bough (pronounced "Boff"). After Johnny breaks up the wrong funeral, Bough saves the day by passing him off as an escaped lunatic.

And so on. Rowan Atkinson is terrifically popular in Britain, less so here, because as a nation we do not find understatement hilarious. *Johnny English* plays like a tired exercise, a spy spoof with no burning desire to be that, or anything else. The thing you have to credit Mike Myers for is that he loves to play Austin Powers and is willing to try anything for a laugh. Atkinson seems to have had Johnny English imposed upon him. And thus upon us.

John Q. ★ ½
PG-13, 118 m., 2002

Denzel Washington (John Q.), Robert Duvall (Grimes), James Woods (Dr. Turner), Anne Heche (Rebecca Payne), Ray Liotta (Monroe), Shawn Hatosy (Mitch), Kimberly Elise (Denise), Keram Malicki-Sanchez (Freddy), Daniel E. Smith (Mike). Directed by Nick Cassavetes and produced by Mark Burg and Oren Koules. Screenplay by James Kearns.

John Q. is the kind of movie *Mad* magazine prays for. It is so earnest, so overwrought, and so wildly implausible that it begs to be parodied. I agree with its message—that the richest nation in history should be able to afford national health insurance—but the message is pounded in with such fevered melodrama, it's as slanted and manipulative as your average political commercial.

The film stars Denzel Washington as John Q. Archibald, a Chicago factory worker whose apparently healthy son collapses during a Little League game. John Q. and his wife, Denise (Kimberly Elise), race the kid to an emergency room, where his signs are stabilized, and then a cardiologist (James Woods) explains that young Mike's heart is three times normal size.

There are two options: a heart transplant, or optimizing Mike's "quality of life" during the "months . . . weeks . . . days" left to him. Joining the doctor is appropriately named hospital administrator Rebecca Payne (Anne Heche), who already knows the Archibalds have no money and argues for the "quality of life" choice.

John Q. thinks he's covered by insurance, but no: His company switched to a new HMO that has a $20,000 ceiling, and since John has been downsized to twenty hours a week, he's lucky to have that much coverage. Payne demands a $75,000 down payment on the $250,000 operation, and explains the harsh realities of life for "cash patients." John Q. considers taking the kid to County Hospital, but is urged by a friendly hospital employee to stay right there at the ominously named Crisis of Hope Memorial Hospital.

The TV ads helpfully reveal that John Q. exhausts all his options and eventually pulls a gun and takes hostages, demanding that his son be put at the top of the list of eligible recipients. (He wouldn't be jumping the queue because the Heche character explains Mike is so sick he would automatically be the first recipient—if the money were available.)

The hostages are your usual cross section of supporting roles: a gunshot victim, a battered woman and her violent boyfriend, a pregnant mother who has "started to dilate!" and so on. Plus Dr. Turner. The cops surround the building, and veteran negotiator Grimes (Robert Duvall) tries to build a relationship with John Q., while hotshot police chief Monroe (Ray Liotta) grandstands for the TV cameras—displaying sixteen stars on his uniform, four each on both collars and both lapels. Any more and he'd be Tinker Bell.

The underlying situation here is exactly the same as in *Dog Day Afternoon* (1975), an infinitely smarter hostage picture. What *John Q.* lacks is the confidence to allow its characters to act intelligently. Chief Monroe is almost hilariously stupid. Consider this. A local TV station somehow manages to tap the police feed from the hospital's security cameras, and broadcasts live video and sound of John Q. inside the hospital. Monroe smuggles a sniper into the hospital who has John Q. in his sights. John Q. is in the act of having an emotional and heartbreaking telephone conversation with his little boy when Monroe, who is (a) unaware of the TV feed, or (b) too dumb to live, orders the marksman to fire.

Does John Q. die? That's a question you find yourself asking a lot during this film. To avoid spoilers, I won't go into detail, but there is a moment when the movie just plain cheats on the question of John Q.'s status, and I felt conned.

There are passages where the actors transcend the material. John Q.'s farewell to his son is one. Kimberly Elise's relationship with her husband is well handled. But in a sense special honors should go to James Woods and Robert Duvall for achieving what they can with roles so awkwardly written that their behavior whipsaws between good, evil, and hilarious. Anne Heche is deep sixed by her role, which makes her a penny-pinching shrew and then gives her a cigarette to smoke just in case we missed that she's the villain. The Grim Reaper would flee from this woman.

Johnson Family Vacation ★ ★
PG-13, 95 m., 2004

Cedric the Entertainer (Nate Johnson), Vanessa L. Williams (Dorothy Johnson), Bow Wow (DJ Johnson), Solange Knowles (Nikki Johnson), Shannon Elizabeth (Chrishelle), Gabby Soleil (Destiny), Steve Harvey (Max Johnson), Shari Headley (Jackie Johnson), Tanjareen Martin (Tangerine), Lorna Scott (Gladys), Aloma Wright (Glorietta). Directed by Christopher Erskin and produced by Cedric the Entertainer, Paul Hall, Wendy Park, and Eric Rhone. Screenplay by Todd R. Jones and Earl Richey Jones.

Cedric the Entertainer can be a break-out comic force if given the least opportunity, but *Johnson Family Vacation* tames him in a routine cross-country comedy that feels exactly like a series of adventures recycled out of every other cross-country comedy. There's even a semi that tries to run them off the road.

The movie begins in a California suburb, where the Johnson family is on thin ice. Nate (Cedric) lives in the family house with his son, DJ (Bow Wow), while his wife, Dorothy (Vanessa L. Williams), teenage daughter, Nikki (Solange Knowles), and preschooler Destiny (Gabby Soleil) have moved into a second house nearby. Dorothy agrees to go along on the trip in a last-gasp attempt to save the marriage. So off they go in Nate's new Lincoln Navigator, which has been pimped out by the overeager car dealer (hard to explain, however, the Burberry pattern on the head rests). It will be a running gag that Nate has to return the car unscratched in order to get a replacement, which of course means the car will be scratched, dented, crashed, and covered in concrete before the trip is over. To repair the car, Cedric turns up in a dual role as Uncle Earl, a wizard mechanic.

Many of their adventures along the way involve Nate's decision to pick up a sexy but obviously flaky hitchhiker named Chrishelle (Shannon Elizabeth), who for fairly obscure reasons sneaks a Gila monster into their hotel room, but this subplot just doesn't work; better to stick with family dynamics than have Nate pick up a hitchhiker his wife obviously wants nothing to do with. Dorothy's idea of revenge—luring her husband into a hot tub and stealing his clothes, so that he has to tip-toe through the "Four Seasonings" hotel in the nude—is meant to be funny, but is cringe-inducing. Nothing about Dorothy's character makes us believe she would do that.

The family reunion, when they finally arrive, is all too brief, considering its comic possibilities. We meet Nate's older brother and lifetime rival, Max (Steve Harvey), who always wins the reunion trophy, and his mother, Glorietta (Aloma Wright), whose comic possibilities aren't developed. The rest of the family consists mostly of extras, and the Johnsons seem to be on their way home again after only a few hours.

The success of a movie like this depends on comic invention. The general outline is already clear: During the trip, the Johnsons will endure many misadventures, but the broken marriage will be mended. Whether we laugh or not depends on what happens to them along the way. Cedric, whose character is channeling Chevy Chase from *National Lampoon's Summer Vacation,* is a gifted comedian who could have brought the movie to life, but the screenplay by Todd R. Jones and Earl Richey Jones is paint-by-numbers, and onetime music video director Christopher Erskin films in a style without zing.

There's one funny scene where Nate bans his son from playing rap music by "anyone who got shot"—like Tupac or Biggie. He throws those CDs out the window. Then the son goes to work on his dad's CD collection, also with singers who got shot, like Marvin Gaye. This is such a neat turnaround that you wonder why the movie doesn't have more inspirations like that. It deals with specifics, but the movie itself is genial and unfocused and tired.

The Jungle Book 2 ★ ½
G, 72 m., 2003

With the voices of: Haley Joel Osment (Mowgli), John Goodman (Baloo), Mae Whitman (Shanti), Connor Funk (Ranjan), Tony Jay (Shere Khan), Bob Joles (Bagheera), Jim Cummings (Kaa/Colonel Hathi), Phil Collins (Lucky). An animated film directed by Steve Trenbirth and produced by Christopher Chase and Mary Thorne. Screenplay by Karl Geurs.

The Jungle Book 2 is so thin and unsatisfying it seems like a made-for-DVD version, not a theatrical release. Clocking in at seventy-two minutes and repeating the recycled song "The Bare Necessities" three if not four times, it offers a bare-bones plot in which Mowgli wanders off into the jungle, is threatened by a tiger and a snake, is protected by a bear, takes care of his little girlfriend, and sings and dances with Baloo.

There's none of the complexity here, in story or style, we expect in this new golden age of animation. It's a throwback in which cute animals of no depth or nuance play with the hero or threaten him in not very scary ways.

As the film opens, Mowgli (who once, long ago and at another level of literacy, was the hero of stories by Rudyard Kipling) lives in a village and is forbidden to cross the river. But "you can take boy out of the jungle, but you can't take the jungle out of boy," we learn. Whoever wrote that dialogue must have gone home weary after a hard day's work.

Mowgli (voice by Haley Joel Osment) and his little village playmate Shanti (voice by Mae Whitman) do, however, venture into the forest, where Mowgli's old friend Baloo the Bear (John Goodman) is delighted to see him, although a little jealous of all the attention he is paying to Shanti. Maybe Baloo should discuss this problem with a counselor. They dance and sing and peel mangos, and then Mowgli and/or Shanti wander off alone to be threatened by the tiger and the snake (whose coils are cleverly animated), and to be rescued by Baloo, with a reprise or two of "The Bare Necessities."

In a time that has given us Miyazaki's great animated film *Spirited Away* (also a Disney release), parents have some kind of duty to take a close look at the films offered. I got in an argument at Sundance with a Salt Lake City man who sells software that automatically censors DVDs in order to remove offending scenes and language. (Theoretically, there could be a version of *Fight Club* suitable for grade-schoolers, although it would be very short.) By this yardstick, *The Jungle Book 2* is inoffensive and harmless.

But it is not nutritious. A new book argues that the average American child spends twice as much time watching television than interacting with his parents, and movies like *The Jungle Book 2* are dim-witted baby-sitters, not growth experiences. If kids grow up on the movie equivalent of fast food, they will form an addiction to that instant action high and will never develop the attention span they need to love worthwhile fiction.

Disney can do better, will do better, usually does better. To release this film theatrically is a compromise of its traditions and standards. If you have children in the target age range, keep them at home, rent an animated classic or Miyazaki's great *My Neighbor Totoro*, and do them a favor.

Just a Kiss ★

R, 89 m., 2002

Ron Eldard (Dag), Kyra Sedgwick (Halley), Patrick Breen (Peter), Marisa Tomei (Paula), Marley Shelton (Rebecca), Taye Diggs (Andre), Sarita Choudhury (Colleen), Bruno Amato (Joe), Zoe Caldwell (Jessica). Directed by Fisher Stevens and produced by Matthew H. Rowland. Screenplay by Patrick Breen.

If only it were clever, *Just a Kiss* would be too clever by half. Here is a movie that was apparently made by working its way through a list of styles, so that we have poignancy jostling against farce, thoughtful dialogue elbowed aside by one-liners, and a visual style that incorporates rotoscope animation for no apparent reason except, maybe, that it looks neat.

Just a Kiss, directed by the actor Fisher Stevens, begins with a kiss between two people who should not be kissing, and ends after those people, and their significant others and assorted insignificant others, undergo sexual and emotional misunderstandings, survive plane crashes, end up in hospital or comatose, etc., while occasionally appearing to be animated like the characters in *Waking Life*.

Now *Waking Life* was an accomplished movie, in which Richard Linklater took live-action footage of his characters and passed it through a software program that kept their basic appearances and movements while allowing artists to overlay an animated layer. It worked. It does not work in *Just a Kiss*, and I'm about to explain why.

In *Waking Life*, all of the characters are animated. That is what they are and how we accept them, and whatever reality they have is conveyed visually through the animation. But in *Just a Kiss*, the characters are photographed realistically, so that when they suddenly undergo "rotomation," their reality is violently displaced and our attention is jerked up to the surface of the movie. They exist now, not as characters, but as animated displays who used to be characters and may be characters again.

I can imagine a way in which this could work, in a *Roger Rabbit*–type movie that moves in and out of the cartoon dimension. But it doesn't work here, because it is manifestly and distractingly only a stunt. And the whole movie, in various ways, has the same problem: It's all surface, without an entry point into whatever lurks beneath. The characters, dialogue, personal styles, and adventures are all mannerisms. The actors are merely carriers of the director's contrivances.

Consider, for example, a sequence in which one character on an airplane uses his cell phone to tell another that he loves her. His phone emits lethal transmissions that cause the plane to crash. Everyone in first class lives; everyone in tourist class dies. I smile as I write the words. This would be a good scene in *Airplane!* What is it doing here, in a movie where we are possibly expected to care about the characters' romances and infidelities? To admit farce into a drama is to admit that the drama is farce.

But is it a drama? I haven't a clue. The movie seems to reinvent itself from moment to moment, darting between styles like a squirrel with too many nuts. There is one performance that works, sort of, and it is by Marisa Tomei, as a bartender whose psychic gifts allow her to find meaning in the rings left by cold beers. She is a crazy, homicidal maniac, but, hey, at least that means that nothing she does is out of character.

As for the other actors, they know Stevens from the indie films they've made together and were good sports to volunteer for this project.

Ron Eldard, Kyra Sedgwick, Patrick Breen (who wrote the screenplay), Marley Shelton, Taye Diggs, Sarita Choudhury, and Bruno Amato do what they can with characters who are reinvented from minute to minute. And Zoe Caldwell, as a choreographer who is the mother of the Shelton character, has moments of stunningly effective acting that are so isolated from the rest of the movie that they appear like the result of channel-surfing.

Just Married ★ ½
PG-13, 94 m., 2003

Ashton Kutcher (Tom Leezak), Brittany Murphy (Sarah McNerney), Christian Kane (Peter Prentis), Monet Mazur (Lauren McNerney), David Moscow (Kyle), Valeria (Wendy), David Rasche (Mr. McNerney), Veronica Cartwright (Mrs. McNerney), Raymond Barry (Mr. Leezak). Directed by Shawn Levy and produced by Robert Simonds. Screenplay by Sam Harper.

Just Married is an ungainly and witless comedy, made more poignant because its star, Brittany Murphy, made such a strong impression as Eminem's sometime girlfriend in *8 Mile*. With her fraught eyes and husky voice, she has a rare and particular quality (I think of Jennifer Jason Leigh), and yet here she's stuck in a dumb sitcom.

She and Ashton Kutcher play newlyweds in a plot that proves that opposites repel. She's a rich kid named Sarah, expensively raised and educated. He's Tom, an example of the emerging subspecies Sports Bar Man. They have a perfect relationship, spoiled by marriage (I think that may even be one of the lines in the movie). They're too tired for sex on their wedding night, but make up for it on their honeymoon flight to Europe with a quickie in the toilet of the airplane. There is perhaps the potential for a glimmer of comedy there, but not in Sam Harper's overwritten and Shawn Levy's overdirected movie, which underlines and emphasizes like a Power Point presentation for half-wits.

Consider. It may be possible to find humor in a scene involving sex in an airplane rest room, but not by pushing the situation so far that Tom's foot gets caught in the toilet and the bitchy flight attendant suffers a broken nose. Later, in their honeymoon hotel in Venice, it

may be possible that energetic sex could break a bed frame—but can it actually destroy the wall to the adjoining room? And it may be possible for an improper electrical device to cause a short in a hotel's electrical system, but need the offending device be a vibrator? And for that matter, isn't it an alarming sign of incipient pessimism to take a vibrator along on your honeymoon?

Europe was not the right choice for this honeymoon. He should have gone to Vegas, and she should have stayed single. Sarah wants to visit every church and museum, but Tom abandons her in the middle of Venice when he finds a bar that's showing an American baseball game. This is as likely as a sports bar in Brooklyn televising *boules* in French.

Sarah and Tom have nothing to talk about. They are a pathetic, stupid couple and deserve each other. What they do not deserve, perhaps, is a screenplay that alternates between motivation and slapstick. Either it's character-driven or it isn't. If it is, then you can't take your plausible characters and dump them into Laurel and Hardy. Their rental car, for example, gets a cheap laugh, but makes them seem silly in the wrong way. And earlier in the film, Tom is responsible for the death of Sarah's dog in a scenario recycled directly from an urban legend everyone has heard.

Would it have been that much more difficult to make a movie in which Tom and Sarah were plausible, reasonably articulate newlyweds with the humor on their honeymoon growing out of situations we could believe? Apparently.

Juwanna Mann ★ ★
PG-13, 91 m., 2002

Miguel A. Nunez Jr. (Jamal/Juwanna Mann), Vivica A. Fox (Michelle Langford), Tommy Davidson (Puff Smokey Smoke), Kevin Pollak (Lorne Daniels), Ginuwine (Romeo), Kim Wayans (Latisha Jansen), Kimberly "Lil' Kim" Jones (Tina Parker). Directed by Jesse Vaughan and produced by Bill Gerber, James G. Robinson, and Steve Oedekerk. Screenplay by Bradley Allenstein.

Let us now consider predictability. Most of the time, I consider it an insult to the audience. We can sense when a movie is on autopilot, and we wonder, not unreasonably, why the filmmakers couldn't be bothered to try a little harder. Then a movie like *Juwanna Mann* comes along and is predictable to its very core, and in a funny way the predictability is part of the fun. The movie is in on the joke of its own recycling.

How predictable is it? It begins with a pro basketball star who is thrown out of the league (he gets so angry at a referee's call that he takes off all of his clothes and flashes the audience). He's faced with foreclosure, bankruptcy, and the loss of all his commercial endorsements, is fired by his manager, and has no skills except the ability to play basketball. In desperation, he dresses in drag and passes himself off as Juwanna Mann, a female player, and is soon a star of the women's pro basketball league.

With that information in mind, there are scenes we can all predict: (1) A date with an obnoxious man who doesn't know Juwanna is male. (2) Weird times in the shower. (3) A crush on a beautiful teammate who likes Juwanna as a friend but, of course, doesn't realize she's a man. (4) Unruly erections. (5) Ill-disciplined falsies. We can also predict that Juwanna will lead her team into the finals, become a big star, learn useful lessons about human nature, be faced with a crisis and exposure, and emerge as a better person, all of her problems solved, while the team wins the big game.

These predictable scenes are, I submit, inevitable. There is no way to make this movie without them—not as a comedy, anyway. So the pleasure, if any, must come from the performances, not the material. Up to a point, it does. Although *Juwanna Mann* is not a good movie, it isn't a painful experience, and Miguel A. Nunez Jr. is plausible as Juwanna, not because he is able to look like a woman, but because he is able to play a character who thinks he can look like a woman.

Vivica A. Fox plays Michelle, the teammate Juwanna falls in love with, and it is a challenging assignment, because almost all her dialogue needs to be taken two ways. Screenplay gimmicks like this are hard for actors, because if they are too sincere they look like chumps, and if they seem to be grinning sideways at the audience, they spoil the illusion. Fox finds the right tone and sticks to it; there is skilled professionalism at work, even in a rent-a-plot like this.

Since the entire movie is, of course, completely implausible, it seems unkind to single out specific examples of implausibility. But there's a difference between the implausibility of the basic gimmick (man passing as a woman) and the implausibility of plot details *within* the gimmick. The most obvious comes at the end, when Juwanna is exposed as a man. The movie deals with that exposure, but ignores another fact that almost every audience member will pick up on: If Juwanna's team played the season with an ineligible player, doesn't it have to forfeit all of its games?

We aren't supposed to ask questions like that, I suppose, but there's another glitch that stands out because the movie insists on it. Early in the film, Juwanna is informed that dunking is illegal in the women's league. Late in the film, she wins a game with a last-second dunk. Say what? Has everyone in the league forgotten the rules?

Such glitches would matter more, I suppose, if the movie were serious. In a comedy, they're distractions, suggesting the filmmakers either weren't paying attention or didn't care. I can't recommend *Juwanna Mann,* and yet I admire the pluck of the actors, especially Nunez, Fox, and Tommy Davidson, as a spectacularly ineligible lothario, and I liked the way Kevin Pollak soldiers away as the manager who must be perpetually offended, astonished, or frustrated. *Juwanna Mann* is unnecessary, but not painful.

K

Kandahar ★ ★ ★ ½
NO MPAA RATING, 85 m., 2002

Nelofer Pazira (Nafas), Hassan Tantai (Tabib Sahid), Sadou Teymouri (Khak). Directed and produced by Mohsen Makhmalbaf. Screenplay by Makhmalbaf.

When she was a child, Nafas was taken to Canada, while her sister stayed behind in Afghanistan. Now Nafas has received a letter from her sister, who lost both legs after stepping on a land mine, and plans to kill herself during the final eclipse of the twentieth century. Nafas sets off on a desperate journey to smuggle herself from Iran into Afghanistan, to convince her sister to live. *Kandahar* follows that journey in a way that sheds an unforgiving light on the last days of the Taliban.

I saw the movie, by Iran's Mohsen Makhmalbaf, at Cannes 2001, where it was admired but seemed to have slim chances of a North American release. Of course, 9/11 changed that, and Kandahar became a familiar place name. The movie is especially accessible because most of it is in English—the language of the heroine, who keeps a record of her journey on a tape recorder, and also the language of one of the other major characters.

Nafas (Nelofer Pazira) is unable to get into Afghanistan by conventional means, perhaps because her family fled for political reasons. In Iran, she pays an itinerant trader, who travels between the two countries, to bring her in as one of his wives; she wears a burka, which covers her from head to toe, making the deception more possible. And as she sets out, we begin to realize that the journey, not the sister's fate, is the point of the film: Nafas is traveling back into the world where she was born.

Makhmalbaf and his cinematographer, Ebraham Ghafouri, show this desert land as beautiful but remote and forbidding. Roads are tracks from one flat horizon to another. Nafas bounces along in the back of a truck with other women, the burka amputating her personality. There are roadblocks, close calls, confusions, and eventually the merchant turns back, leaving her in the company of a boy of ten or twelve named Khak (Sadou Teymouri).

With that terrible wisdom that children gain in times of trouble, he knows his way around the dangers and takes $50 to lead her to Kandahar. At one point they trek through a wilderness of sand dunes, and when he finds a ring on the finger of a skeleton he wants to sell it to her.

Nafas grows ill, and Khak takes her to a doctor. She stands on one side of a blanket, the doctor on the other, and he talks to her through a hole in the fabric. The Taliban forbids any more intimate contact between unmarried men and women; he can ask her to say "ah," and that's about it. But this doctor (Hassan Tantai) has a secret—a secret he reveals when he hears her English with its North American accent. Khak hangs around, hungry for any information he can sell, until the doctor bribes him with peanuts and sends him away.

Kandahar does not provide deeply drawn characters, memorable dialogue, or an exciting climax. Its traffic is in images. Who will ever forget the scene of a Red Cross helicopter flying over a refugee camp and dropping artificial legs by parachute, as one-legged men hobble on their crutches to try to catch them? The movie makes us wonder how any belief system could convince itself it was right to make so many people miserable, to deny the simple human pleasures of life. And yet the last century has been the record of such denial.

Khak, the boy, has been expelled from school. We see one of the Taliban schools. All of the students are boys, of course—women are not permitted to study. That may be no great loss. The boys rock back and forth while chanting the Koran. Not studying or discussing it, simply repeating it. Then they are drilled on the parts of a rifle. "Weapons are the only modern thing in Afghanistan," the doctor tells Nafas.

The Kid Stays in the Picture ★ ★ ★ ½
R, 93 m., 2002

A documentary film about Robert Evans, directed by Brett Morgen and Nanette Burstein and produced by Graydon Carter, Morgen, and Burstein. Screenplay by Morgen, based on the book *The Kid Stays in the Picture* by Robert Evans.

"If you could change one thing about your life," someone in the audience asked Robert Evans, "what would it be?"

"The second half," he said.

Everyone in the Sundance Film Festival audience knew what he meant. We had just seen *The Kid Stays in the Picture*, a new documentary about the life of this producer who put together one of the most remarkable winning streaks in Hollywood history, and followed it with a losing streak that almost destroyed him. It's one of the most honest films ever made about Hollywood; maybe a documentary was needed, since fiction somehow always simplifies things.

Evans made the kinds of movies that would never have played at Sundance; it's poetic justice that he finally got into the festival with a documentary. As the boy-wonder head of production at Paramount, he took the studio from last to first in annual ticket sales, dominating the late 1960s and 1970s with *The Godfather, Chinatown, Love Story, Rosemary's Baby, The Odd Couple, Black Sunday, Popeye,* and *Urban Cowboy.* And he married Ali MacGraw, his star in *Love Story.*

Then everything that had gone right started to go wrong. MacGraw left him for Steve McQueen. He had exited the studio job with a lucrative personal production deal when disaster struck. He was involved in a cocaine-purchasing sting set up by the DEA, rehabilitated himself with a series of public-service broadcasts, tried a comeback by producing a high-visibility flop (*The Cotton Club*), and then was linked by innuendo and gossip with the murder of a man obscurely involved in the film's financing.

Evans was never charged with anything. But to this day people vaguely remember the drug and murder stories, and at one point in the 1980s he was so depressed he committed himself to a mental hospital, afraid he would kill himself.

The Kid Stays in the Picture is narrated by Evans himself, in a gravely, seen-it-all, told-it-all tone of voice. The film edits out some details, such as his other marriages, but only for purposes of time, we feel. Certainly nothing is papered over; Evans sounds like a man describing an accident he barely survived. Based on his autobiography, the doc is a collage of film and TV clips, countless photographs, news headlines, and magazine covers assembled by Brett Morgen and Nanette Burstein, whose documentary *On the Ropes* was an Oscar nominee two years ago. Remarkable, how they animate the photos with graphics, animation, and juxtapositioning so that instead of looking like a collection of stills it feels like, well, moving pictures.

In the beginning, Evans was a man who seemed blessed with luck. A child actor, he had joined his brother in manufacturing women's clothes when he was spotted poolside at the Beverly Hills Hotel by Norma Shearer, and asked to play her husband, the producer Irving Thalberg, in the Jimmy Cagney picture *The Man With 1,000 Faces.* Then came the prize role of a bullfighter in *The Sun Also Rises.* Author Ernest Hemingway and actors Tyrone Power, Ava Gardner, and Eddie Albert sent studio head Darryl F. Zanuck a telegram saying the film would be a disaster with Evans. Zanuck flew to the Mexican location, took a look, and said, "The kid stays in the picture."

Evans's next film, *The Fiend Who Walked the West,* ended his acting career. But after being tapped to run Paramount by Charles Bludhorn, whose conglomerate Gulf and Western had inhaled the studio, he had more than a decade of success, and then a decade of disaster. Early on, he purchased the legendary home of Shearer and Thalberg. He sold it in the 1980s, then realized he could not live without it. His loyal pal Jack Nicholson flew to Monte Carlo and "got down on his knees" (perhaps Evans exaggerates slightly) to convince its new owner, a French millionaire, to sell it back.

Evans stood on the stage at Sundance, still trim and handsome at seventy-two, and answered the questions of filmmakers half or a third his age. Here was a room full of young people who dream of the kind of success he had. Did they find his life an object lesson? Probably not. At Sundance, they're still trying to change the first halves of their lives.

Kill Bill: Volume 1 ★ ★ ★ ★
R, 93 m., 2003

Uma Thurman (The Bride), Lucy Liu (O-Ren Ishii), Daryl Hannah (Elle Driver), Vivica A. Fox (Vernita Green), Michael Parks (Sheriff), Sonny Chiba (Hattori Hanzo), Chiaki Kuriyama (Go Go

Yubari), Julie Dreyfus (Sofie Fatale), David Carradine (Bill), Michael Madsen (Budd). Directed by Quentin Tarantino and produced by Lawrence Bender and Tarantino. Screenplay by Tarantino.

Kill Bill: Volume 1 shows Quentin Tarantino so effortlessly and brilliantly in command of his technique that he reminds me of a virtuoso violinist racing through "Flight of the Bumble Bee"—or maybe an accordion prodigy setting a speed record for "Lady of Spain." I mean that as a sincere compliment. The movie is not about anything at all except the skill and humor of its making. It's kind of brilliant.

His story is a distillation of the universe of martial arts movies, elevated to a trancelike mastery of the material. Tarantino is in the Zone. His story engine is revenge. In the opening scene, Bill kills all of the other members of a bridal party, and leaves The Bride (Uma Thurman) for dead. She survives for years in a coma, and is awakened by a mosquito's buzz. (Is QT thinking of Emily Dickinson, who heard a fly buzz when she died? I am reminded of Manny Farber's definition of the auteur theory: "A bunch of guys standing around trying to catch someone shoving art up into the crevices of dreck.")

The Bride is no Emily Dickinson. She reverses the paralysis in her legs by "focusing." Then she vows vengeance on the Deadly Viper Assassination Squad, and as *Volume 1* concludes she is about half-finished. She has wiped out Vernita Green (Vivica A. Fox) and O-Ren Ishii (Lucy Liu), and in *Volume 2* will presumably kill Elle Driver (Daryl Hannah), Budd (Michael Madsen), and, of course, Bill (David Carradine). If you think I have given away plot details, you think there can be doubt about whether the heroine survives the first half of a two-part action movie, and should seek help.

The movie is all storytelling and no story. The motivations have no psychological depth or resonance, but are simply plot markers. The characters consist of their characteristics. Lurking beneath everything, as it did with *Pulp Fiction,* is the suggestion of a parallel universe in which all of this makes sense in the same way that a superhero's origin story makes sense. There is a sequence here (well, it's more like a third of the movie) where The Bride single-handedly wipes out O-Ren Ishii and her entire team, including the Crazy 88 Fighters, and we are reminded of Neo fighting the clones of Agent Smith in *The Matrix Reloaded,* except the Crazy 88 Fighters are individual human beings, I think. Do they get their name from the Crazy 88 blackjack games on the Web, or from Episode 88 of the action anime *Tokyo Crazy Paradise,* or should I seek help?

The Bride defeats the eighty-eight superb fighters (plus various bodyguards and specialists) despite her weakened state and recently paralyzed legs because she is a better fighter than all of the others put together. Is that because of the level of her skill, the power of her focus, or the depth of her need for vengeance? Skill, focus, and need have nothing to do with it: She wins because she kills everybody without getting killed herself. You can sense Tarantino grinning a little as each fresh victim, filled with foolish bravado, steps forward to be slaughtered. Someone has to win in a fight to the finish, and as far as the martial arts genre is concerned, it might as well be the heroine. (All of the major characters except Bill are women, the men having been emasculated right out of the picture.)

Kill Bill: Volume 1 is not the kind of movie that inspires discussion of the acting, but what Thurman, Fox, and Liu accomplish here is arguably more difficult than playing the nuanced heroine of a Sundance thumb-sucker. There must be presence, physical grace, strength, personality, and the ability to look serious while doing ridiculous things. The tone is set in an opening scene, where The Bride lies near death and a hand rubs at the blood on her cheek, which will not come off because it is clearly congealed makeup. This scene further benefits from being shot in black and white; for QT, all shots in a sense are references to other shots—not particular shots from other movies, but archetypal shots in our collective moviegoing memories.

There's b&w in the movie, and slo-mo, and a name that's bleeped entirely for effect, and even an extended sequence in anime. The animated sequence, which gets us to Tokyo and supplies the backstory of O-Ren Ishii, is sneaky in the way it allows Tarantino to deal with material that might, in live action, seem too real for his stylized universe. It deals with a Mafia kingpin's pedophilia. The scene works in animated long shot; in live action close-up it would get the movie an NC-17.

Before she arrives in Tokyo, The Bride stops off to obtain a sword from Hattori Hanzo ("special guest star" Sonny Chiba). He has been retired for years, and is done with killing. But she persuades him, and he manufactures a sword that does not inspire his modesty: "This my finest sword. If in your journey you should encounter God, God will be cut." Later the sword must face the skill of Go Go Yubari (Chi-aki Kuriyama), O-Ren's teenage bodyguard and perhaps a major in medieval studies, since her weapon of choice is the mace and chain. This is in the comic-book tradition by which characters are defined by their weapons. To see The Bride's God-slicer and Go Go's mace clashing in a field of dead and dying men is to understand how women have taken over from men in action movies. Strange, since women are not nearly as good at killing as men are. Maybe they're cast because the liberal media wants to see them succeed. The movie's women warriors remind me of Ruby Rich's defense of Russ Meyer as a feminist filmmaker (his women initiate all the sex and do all the killing).

There is a sequence in which O-Ren Ishii takes command of the Japanese Mafia and beheads a guy for criticizing her as half-Chinese, female, and American. O-Ren talks Japanese through a translator, but when the guy's head rolls on the table everyone seems to understand her. Soon comes the deadly battle with The Bride, on a two-level set representing a Japanese restaurant. Tarantino has the wit to pace this battle with exterior shots of snowfall in an exquisite formal garden. Why must the garden be in the movie? Because gardens with snow are iconic Japanese images, and Tarantino is acting as the instrument of his received influences.

By the same token, Thurman wears a costume identical to one Bruce Lee wore in his last film. Is this intended as coincidence, homage, impersonation? Not at all. It can be explained by quantum physics: The suit can be in two movies at the same time. And when the Daryl Hannah character whistles the theme from *Twisted Nerve* (1968), it's not meant to suggest she is a Hayley Mills fan but that leakage can occur between parallel universes in the movies.

Will *Volume 2* reveal that Mr. Bill used to be known as Mr. Blond? ☞

Kill Bill: Vol. 2 ★ ★ ★ ★
R, 137 m., 2004

Uma Thurman (The Bride), David Carradine (Bill), Daryl Hannah (Elle Driver), Michael Madsen (Budd), Gordon Liu (Pei Mei). Directed by Quentin Tarantino and produced by Lawrence Bender and Tarantino. Screenplay by Tarantino and Uma Thurman.

Quentin Tarantino's *Kill Bill: Vol. 2* is an exuberant celebration of moviemaking, coasting with heedless joy from one audacious chapter to another, working as irony, working as satire, working as drama, working as pure action. I liked it even more than *Kill Bill* (2003). It's not a sequel but a continuation and completion, filmed at the same time; now that we know the whole story, the first part takes on another dimension. *Vol. 2* stands on its own, although it has deeper resonance if you've seen *Kill Bill*.

The movie is a distillation of the countless grind house kung-fu movies Tarantino has absorbed, and which he loves beyond all reason. Web sites have already enumerated his inspirations—how a sunset came from this movie, and a sword from that. He isn't copying, but transcending; there's a kind of urgency in the film, as if he's turning up the heat under his memories.

The movie opens with a long close-up of the Bride (Uma Thurman) behind the wheel of a car, explaining her mission, which is to kill Bill. There is a lot of explaining in the film; Tarantino writes dialogue with quirky details that suggest the obsessions of his people. That's one of the ways he gives his movies a mythical quality; the characters don't talk in mundane, everyday dialogue, but in a kind of elevated geekspeak that lovingly burnishes the details of their legends, methods, beliefs, and arcane lore.

Flashbacks remind us that the pregnant Bride and her entire wedding party were targeted by the Deadly Viper Assassination Squad in a massacre at the Two Pines Wedding Chapel. Bill was responsible—Bill, whom she confronts on the porch of the chapel for a conversation that suggests the depth and weirdness of their association. He's played by David Carradine in a performance that somehow, improbably, suggests that Bill and the Bride had a real relationship despite the preposterous details surrounding it. (Bill is deeply offended that she plans to marry a used record store owner and lead a normal life.)

The Bride, of course, improbably survived the massacre, awakened after a long coma, and in the first film set to avenge herself against the Deadly Vipers and Bill. That involved extended action sequences as she battled Vernita Green (Vivica A. Fox) and O-Ren Ishii (Lucy Liu), not to mention O-Ren's teenage bodyguard Go Go Yubari (Chiaki Kuriyama) and the martial arts team known as the Crazy 88.

Much of her success came because she was able to persuade the legendary sword maker Hattori Hanzo (Sonny Chiba) to come out of retirement and make her a weapon. He presented it without modesty: "This my finest sword. If in your journey you should encounter God, God will be cut."

In *Vol. 2*, she meets another Asian legend, the warrior master Pei Mei, played by Gordon Liu. Pei Mei, who lives on the top of a high, lonely hill reached by climbing many stairs, was Bill's master, and in a flashback, Bill delivers his protégé for training. Pei Mei is a harsh and uncompromising teacher, and the Bride sheds blood during their unrelenting sessions.

Pei Mei, whose hair and beard are long and white and flowing, like a character from the pages of a comic book, is another example of Tarantino's method, which is to create lovingly structured episodes that play on their own while contributing to the legend. Like a distillation of all wise, ancient, and deadly martial arts masters in countless earlier movies, Pei Mei waits patiently for eons on his hilltop until he is needed for a movie.

The training with Pei Mei, we learn, prepared the Bride to begin her career with Bill ("jetting around the world making vast sums of money and killing for hire"), and is inserted in this movie at a time and place that makes it function like a classic cliff-hanger. In setting up this scene, Tarantino once again pauses for colorful dialogue; the Bride is informed by Bill that Pei Mei hates women, whites, and Americans, and much of his legend is described. Such

speeches function in Tarantino not as long-winded detours, but as a way of setting up characters and situations with dimensions it would be difficult to establish dramatically.

In the action that takes place "now," the Bride has to fight her way past formidable opponents, including Elle Driver (Daryl Hannah), the one-eyed master of martial arts, and Budd (Michael Madsen), Bill's beer-swilling brother, who works as a bouncer in a strip joint and lives in a mobile home surrounded by desolation. Neither one is a pushover for the Bride— Elle because of her skills (also learned from Pei Mei), Budd because of his canny instincts.

The showdown with Budd involves a sequence where it seems the Bride must surely die after being buried alive. (That she does not is a given, considering the movie is not over and Bill is not dead, but she sure looks doomed.) Tarantino, who began the film in black and white before switching to color, plays with formats here, too; to suggest the claustrophobia of being buried, he shows the Bride inside her wooden casket, and as clods of earth rain down on the lid, he switches from wide-screen to the classic 4x3-screen ratio.

The fight with Elle Driver is a virtuoso celebration of fight choreography; although we are aware that all is not as it seems in movie action sequences, Thurman and Hannah must have trained long and hard to even seem to do what they do. Their battle takes place inside Bill's trailer home, which is pretty much demolished in the process, and provides a contrast to the elegant nightclub setting of the fight with O-Ren Ishii; it ends in a squishy way that would be unsettling in another kind of movie, but here all the action is so ironically heightened that we may cringe and laugh at the same time.

These sequences involve their own Tarantinian dialogue of explanation and scene-setting. Budd has an extended monologue in which he offers the Bride the choice of Mace or a flashlight, and the details of his speech allow us to visualize horrors worse than any we could possibly see. Later, Elle Driver produces a black mamba, and in a sublime touch reads from a Web page that describes the snake's deadly powers.

Of the original *Kill Bill*, I wrote: "The movie is all storytelling and no story. The motivations have no psychological depth or resonance, but are simply plot markers. The characters consist of their characteristics." True, but one of the achievements of *Vol. 2* is that the story is filled in, the characters are developed, and they do begin to resonate, especially during the extraordinary final meeting between the Bride and Bill—which consists not of nonstop action but of more hypnotic dialogue, and ends in an event that is like a quiet, deadly punch line.

Put the two parts together, and Tarantino has made a masterful saga that celebrates the martial arts genre while kidding it, loving it, and transcending it. I confess I feared that *Vol. 2* would be like those sequels that lack the intensity of the original. But this is all one film, and now that we see it whole, it's greater than its two parts; Tarantino remains the most brilliantly oddball filmmaker of his generation, and this is one of the best films of the year.   ☞

King Arthur ★ ★ ★
PG-13, 130 m., 2004

Clive Owen (Arthur), Keira Knightley (Guinevere), Stellan Skarsgard (Cerdic), Stephen Dillane (Merlin), Ray Winstone (Bors), Hugh Dancy (Galahad), Til Schweiger (Cynric), Ioan Gruffudd (Lancelot), Joel Edgerton (Gawain). Directed by Antoine Fuqua and produced by Jerry Bruckheimer. Screenplay by David Franzoni.

For centuries, countless tales have been told of the legend of King Arthur. But the only story you've never heard . . . is the true story that inspired the legend.

—trailer for *King Arthur*

Uh, huh. And in the true story, Arthur traveled to Rome, became a Christian and a soldier, and was assigned to lead a group of yurt-dwelling warriors from Sarmatia on a fifteen-year tour of duty in England, where Guinevere is a fierce woman warrior of the Woads. His knights team up with the Woads to battle the Saxons. In this version, Guinevere and Lancelot are not lovers, although they exchange significant glances; Arthur is Guinevere's lover. So much for all those legends we learned from Thomas Malory's immortal *Le Morte d'Arthur*

(1470), and the less immortal *Knights of the Round Table* (1953).

This new *King Arthur* tells a story with uncanny parallels to current events in Iraq. The imperialists from Rome enter England intent on overthrowing the tyrannical Saxons, and find allies in the brave Woads. "You—all of you—were free from your first breath!" Arthur informs his charges and future subjects, anticipating by a millennium or so the notion that all men are born free and overlooking the detail that his knights have been pressed into involuntary servitude.

The movie is darker and the weather chillier than in the usual Arthurian movie. There is a round table, but the knights scarcely find time to sit down at it. Guinevere is not a damsel in potential distress, but seems to have been cloned from Brigitte Nielsen in *Red Sonja*. And everybody speaks idiomatic English—even the knights, who as natives of Sarmatia might be expected to converse in an early version of Uzbek, and the Woads, whose accents get a free pass because not even the Oxford English Dictionary has heard of a Woad. To the line "Last night was a mistake" in *Troy*, we can now add, in our anthology of unlikely statements in history, Arthur's line to Guinevere as his seven warriors prepare to do battle on a frozen lake with hundreds if not thousands of Saxons: "There are a lot of lonely men over there."

Despite these objections, *King Arthur* is not a bad movie, although it could have been better. It isn't flat-out silly like *Troy*, its actors look at home as their characters, and director Antoine Fuqua curtails the use of CGI in the battle scenes, which involve mostly real people. There is a sense of place here, and although the costumes bespeak a thriving trade in tailoring somewhere beyond the mead, the film's locations look rough, ready, and green, (it was filmed in Ireland).

Clive Owen, who has been on the edge of stardom for a decade, makes an Arthur who seems more like a drill instructor, less like a fairy-tale prince, than most of the Arthurs we've seen. Lean, dark, and angular, he takes the character to the edge of antihero status. Keira Knightley, who was the best friend in *Bend It Like Beckham*, here looks simultaneously sexy and muddy, which is a necessity in this movie, and fits right into the current appetite for women action heroes who are essentially honorary men, all except for the squishy parts. The cast is filled with dependable actors with great faces, such as Ray Winstone as a tough-as-nails knight who inexplicably but perhaps appropriately anticipates the Cockney accent, and Stephen Dillane as Merlin, leader of the Woads and more of a psychic and sorcerer than a magician who does David Copperfield material.

The plot involves Rome's desire to defend its English colony against the invading Saxons, and its decision to back the local Woads in their long struggle against the barbarians. But Rome, declining and falling right on schedule, is losing its territorial ambitions and beginning to withdraw from the far corners of its empire. That leaves Arthur risking his neck without much support from the folks at home, and perhaps he will cast his lot with England. In the traditional legends he became king at fifteen, and went on to conquer Scotland, Ireland, Iceland—and Orkney, which was flattered to find itself in such company.

The movie ends with a pitched battle that's heavy on swords and maces and stabbings and skewerings, and in which countless enemies fall while nobody we know ever dies except for those whose deaths are prefigured by prescient dialogue or the requirements of fate. I have at this point seen about enough swashbuckling, I think, although producer Jerry Bruckheimer hasn't, since this project follows right on the heels of his *Pirates of the Caribbean*. I would have liked to see deeper characterizations and more complex dialogue, as in movies like *Braveheart* or *Rob Roy,* but today's multiplex audience, once it has digested a word like *Sarmatia,* feels its day's work is done.

That the movie works is because of the considerable production qualities and the charisma of the actors, who bring more interest to the characters than they deserve. There is a kind of direct, unadorned conviction to the acting of Clive Owen and the others; raised on Shakespeare, trained for swordfights, with an idea of Arthurian legend in their heads since childhood, they don't seem out of time and place like the cast of *Troy.* They get on with it.

Kissing Jessica Stein ★ ★ ★
R, 94 m., 2002

Jennifer Westfeldt (Jessica Stein), Heather Juergensen (Helen Cooper), Scott Cohen (Josh Meyers), Tovah Feldshuh (Judy Stein), Jackie Hoffman (Joan), Michael Mastro (Martin), Carson Elrod (Sebastian), David Aaron Baker (Dan Stein). Directed by Charles Herman-Wurmfeld and produced by Eden Wurmfeld and Brad Zions. Screenplay by Heather Juergensen and Jennifer Westfeldt.

Same-sex romance, a controversial topic in movies millions now alive can still remember, is a lifestyle choice in *Kissing Jessica Stein.* Yes, a "choice"—although that word is non-PC in gay circles—since one of the two women in the movie is nominally straight, and the other so bisexual she pops into her art gallery office during an opening for a quickie with her boy toy. Helen (Heather Juergensen), the gallery manager, is a lesbian in about the same way she would be a vegetarian who has steak once in a while. Jessica (Jennifer Westfeldt), disillusioned after a series of blind dates with hopeless men, answers Helen's personals ad not because she is a woman but because she quotes the poet Rilke.

Jessica is above all a hopeless perfectionist. This places her in contrast with her mother (Tovah Feldshuh), whose idea of an eligible mate for her daughter is any single Jewish male between the ages of twenty and forty-five in good enough shape to accept a dinner invitation. Like many perfectionists, Jessica works as a copy editor and fact checker, finding writers' mistakes with the same zeal she applies to the imperfections of would-be husbands. In a funny montage, she goes through a series of disastrous dates, including one with a man whose word choices would make him a copy editor's nightmare (he uses the phrase "self-defecating").

Helen is more flexible, knowing, and wise. She seeks not perfection in a partner, but the mysteries of an intriguing personality. She finds it challenging that Jessica has never had a lesbian experience, and indeed approaches sex with the enthusiasm of a homeowner consid-

357

ering the intricacies of a grease trap. Jessica arrives at their first real date with an armload of how-to manuals, and makes such slow progress that Helen is driven all but mad by weeks of interrupted foreplay.

The movie makes of this situation not a sex comedy but more of an upscale sitcom in which the romantic partners happen both to be women. Jessica is fluttery and flighty, breathy and skittish; Helen is cool, grounded, and amused. Adding spice is Jessica's panic that anyone will find out about her new dating partner. Anyone like Josh (Scott Cohen), her boss at work and former boyfriend. Or Joan (Jackie Hoffman), her pregnant coworker. Or especially her mother, who brings single IBM executives to dinner as if they are the Missing Link.

There are a couple of serious episodes to give the story weight. One involves Jessica's reluctance to invite Helen to her brother's wedding, thus revealing to the family the sex of the mysterious "person" she has been dating. The other is a heart-to-heart talk between Jessica and her mother, during which Feldshuh takes an ordinary scene and makes it extraordinary by the way she delivers the simple, heartfelt dialogue.

What makes the movie a comedy is the way it avoids the more serious emotions involved. I reviewed a movie about a man who gives up sex for Lent, and received a reader's letter asking, hey, aren't Catholics supposed to give up extramarital sex all of the time? A theologically excellent question; I am reminded of the priest in *You Can Count on Me*, asked about adultery and reluctantly intoning "That . . . would . . . be . . . wrong."

The would-be lovers in *Kissing Jessica Stein* are not having sex, exactly, because of Jessica's skittish approach to the subject, but if they did, it would be a leisure activity like going to the movies. If it really meant anything to either one of them—if it meant as much as it does to the mother—the comedy would be more difficult, or in a different key. We can laugh because nothing really counts for anything. That's all right. But if Jessica Stein ever really gets kissed, it'll be another story. Right now she's like the grade-school girl at the spin-the-bottle party who changes the rules when the bottle points at her.

K-19: The Widowmaker ★ ★ ★
PG-13, 138 m., 2002

Harrison Ford (Captain Alexi Vostrikov), Liam Neeson (Captain Mikhail Polenin), Peter Sarsgaard (Vadim Radtchenko), Christian Camargo (Pavel Loktev), George Anton (Konstantin Poliansky), Shaun Benson (Leonid Pashinski), Dmitry Chepovetsky (Sergei Maximov). Directed by Kathryn Bigelow and produced by Bigelow, Edward S. Feldman, Chris Whitaker, and Joni Sighvatsson. Screenplay by Christopher Kyle.

Movies involving submarines have the logic of chess: The longer the game goes, the fewer the possible remaining moves. *K-19: The Widowmaker* joins a tradition that includes *Das Boot* and *The Hunt for Red October* and goes all the way back to *Run Silent, Run Deep*. The variables are always oxygen, water pressure, and the enemy. Can the men breathe, will the sub implode, will depth charges destroy it? The submarine *K-19* is not technically at war, so there are no depth charges, but the story involves a deadlier threat: Will the onboard reactor melt down, causing a nuclear explosion and possibly triggering a world war?

The movie is set in 1961, at the height of the cold war, and is loosely based on a real incident. A new Soviet nuclear sub is commissioned before it is shipshape, and sails on its first mission as a bucketful of problems waiting to happen. Many of the problems are known to its original captain, Mikhail Polenin (Liam Neeson). But when he insists after a test run that the submarine is not capable, he is joined on board by Captain Alexi Vostrikov (Harrison Ford), who outranks him and is married to the niece of a member of the Politboro.

Both men are competent naval officers, and Polenin does his best to work with Vostrikov; his men consider Polenin their captain but are persuaded to go along with the senior man, even after Vostrikov orders a dive that tests the ultimate limits of the sub's capabilities. (Such scenes, with rivets popping and the hull creaking, are obligatory in submarine movies.) Most of the big scenes take place in close quarters on the command desk, where dramatic lighting illuminates the faces and eyes of men who are waiting for the sub's shell to crack. By casting the two leading roles with authoritative actors, *K-19* adds another level of tension; if one were dominant and the other uncertain, there would be a clear dramatic path ahead, but since both Vostrikov and Polenin are inflexible, self-confident, and determined, their rivalry approaches a standoff.

The sub's mission is to demonstrate the Soviet Union's new nuclear submarine power to the spy planes of the Kennedy administration. The sub's voyage is shadowed by a U.S. destroyer, which is not unwelcome, since the purpose of this mission is to be seen. When there is an accident involving one of the onboard nuclear reactors, however, the game changes: If the reactor explodes and destroys the U.S. ship, will that event be read, in the resulting confusion, as an act of war? *K-19* could surface and put its men in lifeboats, but for Vostrikov the thought of the United States capturing the new technology is unthinkable. Therefore, the options are to repair the reactor or dive the boat to its destruction.

More problems. The *K-19*'s original reactor officer, an experienced man, has been fired for alcoholism and replaced with a recent naval academy graduate. This man, Vadim (Peter Sarsgaard), is not only inexperienced but scared to death, and he freezes when the accident occurs. As the reactor core overheats, the crew comes up with a jury-rigged quick fix— diverting the onboard water supply—but that involves men entering the sealed reactor compartment to weld pipes and make repairs. They should wear protective radiation suits, but alas, the captains are told, "the warehouse was out. They sent us chemical suits instead." Neeson: "We might as well wear raincoats."

The scenes involving the repair of the reactor are excruciating, and director Kathryn Bigelow creates a taut counterpoint between the men who take ten-minute shifts in the high-radiation zone, and the growing tension between the two captains. Footage involving radiation sickness is harrowing. A mutiny is not unthinkable. And meanwhile, in Moscow, *K-19*'s sudden radio silence inspires dark suspicions that the sub has been captured or given away by traitors.

The physical limitations of a submarine create technical difficulties for filmmakers—who can, after all, only move their cameras back and forth within the narrow tube. That claustrophobia also heightens the tension, and we get a sense of a small group of men working desperately together under the pressure of death. *K-19* draws out the suspense about as far as possible, and Bigelow, whose credits include *Point Break* and *Strange Days,* is an expert technician who never steps wrong and is skilled at exploiting the personal qualities of Ford and Neeson to add another level of uncertainty.

It is rare for a big-budget Hollywood production to be seen entirely through the eyes of foreigners, and rarer still for actors like Neeson and Ford to spend an entire role with Russian accents. There isn't even a token role for an American character, and the movie treats the Soviets not as enemies but as characters we are expected to identify with; the same approach allowed us to care about the German U-boat crew in *Das Boot.*

Are Harrison Ford and Liam Neeson, both so recognizable, convincing as Russians? Convincing enough; we accept the accents after a few minutes, and get on with the story. The fact that both men seem unyielding is crucial, and the fact that Vostrikov may be putting political considerations above the lives of his men adds an additional dimension. There is one surprise in the movie, a decision having nothing to do with the reactor, that depends entirely on the ability of the characters to act convincingly under enormous pressure; casting stars of roughly equal weight helps it to work.

Knockaround Guys ★ ★ ★
R, 93 m., 2002

Barry Pepper (Matty Demaret), Vin Diesel (Taylor Reese), Seth Green (Johnny Marbles), Andrew Davoli (Chris Scarpa), Dennis Hopper (Benny Chains), John Malkovich (Teddy Deserve), Tom Noonan (Sheriff). Directed by Brian Koppelman and David Levien and produced by Lawrence Bender, Koppelman, and Levien. Screenplay by Koppelman and Levien.

When Matty Demaret is twelve, he fails a test. His uncle gives him a gun and asks him to shoot a squealer. Matty just can't do it. "That's all right," his uncle says. "You're just not cut out for it." Matt grows into a young man determined to make a place for himself in the mob, and hangs around with other young heirs to a shrinking empire. Their fathers sat around counting money, but they're expected to work the noon and evening shifts at the family restaurant.

Matty (Barry Pepper) wants a chance to prove himself. He begs his dad, Benny Chains (Dennis Hopper) for a job, and finally gets one—picking up some money in Spokane. His friend Johnny Marbles (Seth Green) owns a private plane, and Matty asks him to fly the money back east. In the small town of Wibaux, Montana, Johnny Marbles gets rattled by cops in the airport, drops the bag in a luggage zone, and loses it. This is not good.

Knockaround Guys is inspired by the same impulse as *The Sopranos*. It considers gangsters in the modern age, beset by progress, unsure of their roles, undermined by psychobabble. "Used to be there was a way to do things and things got done," Matty's Uncle Teddy (John Malkovich) complains. "Now everybody's *feelings* are involved."

The heart of the movie takes place in Wibaux, a town ruled by a tall, taciturn, ominous sheriff, played by that unmistakable actor Tom Noonan. Matty flies out to Montana with backup: his friends Taylor (Vin Diesel) and Chris (Andrew Davoli). They stick out like sore thumbs in the little town. "Looks like they're multiplying," the sheriff observes to his deputy. He assumes they're involved with drugs, doesn't much care "as long as they move on through," but is very interested in the possibility of money.

The movie crosses two formulas, Fish Out of Water and Coming of Age, fairly effectively. Because it isn't wall-to-wall action but actually bothers to develop its characters and take an interest in them, it was not at first considered commercial by its distributor, New Line, and languished on the shelf for two years until the growing stardom of Vin Diesel (*XXX*) and Barry Pepper (*We Were Soldiers*) made it marketable. It's more than that—it's interesting in the way it shows these guys stuck between generations. And it makes good use of Diesel, who as he develops into an action superstar may not get roles this juicy for a while. He's a tough

guy, yes, a street fighter, but conflicted and with a kind of wise sadness about human nature.

The movie's basic question, I suppose, is whether the rising generation of mobsters is so self-conscious it will never gain the confidence of its ancestors. If it's true that the mob in the 1930s learned how to talk by studying Warner Bros. crime pictures, it's equally true that *The Sopranos* and all the other post-Scorsese *GoodFellas* stories bring in an element of psychological complexity that only confuses an occupation that used to have a brutal simplicity. *Knockaround Guys* opens with Matty being turned down for a job because of his infamous last name. It ends with him not living up to it. "To the regular people we're nothing but goombas," Matty complains. "But to our fathers, we're nothing but errand boys."

Kwik Stop ★ ★ ★ ½
NO MPAA RATING, 110 m., 2002

Michael Gilio (Mike), Lara Phillips (Didi), Rich Komenich (Emil), Karin Anglin (Ruthie). Directed by Michael Gilio and produced by Rachel Tenner. Screenplay by Gilio.

Kwik Stop starts out with a shoplifter and a teenager who sees him stealing. She threatens to turn him over to the cops, but actually all she wants is to escape from her life in a Chicago suburb. He explains he's going to Los Angeles to become a movie actor. "Take me with you," she says. "Can I kiss you?" he says.

At this point, maybe ten minutes into the story, we think we know more or less where the movie is going: It'll be a road picture. We are dead wrong. *Kwik Stop*, which never quite gets out of town, blindsides us with unexpected humor and sadness, and is one of the unsung treasures of recent independent filmmaking.

The movie is the work of Michael Gilio, who wrote it, directed it, and stars in it as Mike, the guy who thinks he could be a movie star. Gilio, in fact, is already an established actor; he played opposite Sidney Poitier in the TV movie *To Sir with Love 2*, and has appeared in four other films, but this movie proves he's not only an actor but has a genuine filmmaking talent.

In the way it is developed, and seen, and especially in the way it ends, *Kwik Stop* shows an imagination that flies far beyond the conventions it seems to begin with.

Mike is a complicated guy. He dreams of going to Los Angeles and breaking into the movies, yes—but perhaps the dream is more important than actually doing it. He's like a lot of people who are stuck in the planning stage and like it there. Didi (Lara Phillips) has no plans but she has urgent desires and is prepared to act on them. We learn all we need to know about her home life in a shot taken from the curb that watches her go inside to get some stuff and come back out again, unconcerned that she is leaving town, she thinks, forever.

Neither one is dumb. They talk about Henry Miller and Harvey Keitel, two names that suggest you have advanced beyond life's training wheels. Gilio finds a motel room for them with its own disco ball hanging from the ceiling, and as its twinkle disguises the shabbiness, they make and pledge love, and then the next morning Mike is gone. If this couple is going to make it through the entire film, we realize, they are going to have to do it without using the usual clichés.

They meet again. Never mind how. Mike takes Didi to a diner for a meal, where a waitress named Ruthie (Karin Anglin) greets them with a strangely skewed attitude. Watch the way Gilio introduces mystery into the scene and then resolves it, getting humor out of both the mystery and the solution. The diner scene suggests strangeness deep in Mike's character: He doesn't need to go to Los Angeles since he stars in his own drama, and doubles back to be sure he hasn't lost his audience.

Mike and Didi try to burgle a house. Didi is whammed by a homeowner's baseball bat, and ends up imprisoned in the Midwest School for Girls. Mike has a plan to spring her, which involves Ruthie making what is, under the circumstances, a truly selfless gesture (she explains she doesn't want to "waste the time I put into you").

Just as Mike never gets out of town, just as the plot doubles back to pick up first Didi and then Ruthie, so Emil (Rich Komenich), the homeowner with the baseball bat, is also not abandoned. *Kwik Stop* is the opposite of the picaresque journey in which colorful characters are encountered and then left behind. It gathers them all up and takes them along.

The movie contains genuine surprises, some delightful (like the plan to spring Didi from the home) and others involving loneliness, loss, and desperation. I cannot say much more without revealing developments that are unexpected and yet deeply satisfying. Poignancy comes into the movie from an unexpected source. Depths are revealed where we did not think to find them. The ending is like the last paragraph of a short story, redefining everything that went before.

Kwik Stop, made on a low budget, has all the money it needs to accomplish everything it wants to do. It has the freedom of serious fiction, which is not chained to a story arc but follows its characters where they insist on going. Gilio, Phillips, Komenich, and Anglin create that kind of bemused realism we discover in films that are not about plot but about what these dreamy people are going to do next.

L

The Lady and the Duke ★ ★ ★
PG-13, 129 m., 2002

Lucy Russell (The Lady, Grace Elliott), Jean-Claude Dreyfus (Duke of Orleans), Francois Marthouret (Dumouriez), Leonard Cobiant (Champcenetz), Caroline Morin (Nanon), Alain Libolt (Duc de Biron), Helena Dubiel (Madame Meyler). Directed by Eric Rohmer and produced by Francoise Etchegaray. Screenplay by Eric Rohmer, based on the memoir *Journal of My Life During the French Revolution* by Grace Elliott.

In the Paris of the mob, during the French Revolution, a patrician British lady supports the monarchy and defies the citizens' committees that rule the streets. She does this not in the kind of lamebrained action story we might fear, but with her intelligence and personality—outwitting the louts who come to search her bedroom, even as a wanted man cowers between her mattresses.

Eric Rohmer's *The Lady and the Duke* is an elegant story about an elegant woman, told in an elegant visual style. It moves too slowly for those with impaired attention spans, but is fascinating in its style and mannerisms. Like all of the films in the long career of Rohmer, it centers on men and women talking about differences of moral opinion.

At eighty-one, Rohmer has lost none of his zest and enthusiasm. The director, who runs up five flights of stairs to his office every morning, has devised a daring visual style in which the actors and foreground action are seen against artificial tableaux of Paris circa 1792. These are not "painted backdrops," but meticulously constructed perspective drawings that are digitally combined with the action in a way that is both artificial and intriguing.

His story is about a real woman, Grace Elliott (Lucy Russell), who told her story in a forgotten autobiography Rohmer found ten years ago. She was a woman uninhibited in her behavior and conservative in her politics, at one time the lover of the prince of Wales (later King George IV), then of Phillipe, the duke of Orleans (father of the future king Louis Phillipe). Leaving England for France and living in a Paris town house paid for by the duke (who remains her close friend even after their ardor has cooled), she refuses to leave France as the storm clouds of revolution gather, and survives those dangerous days even while making little secret of her monarchist loyalties.

She is stubbornly a woman of principle. She dislikes the man she hides between her mattresses, but faces down an unruly citizens' search committee after every single member crowds into her bedroom to gawk at a fine lady in her nightgown. After she gets away with it, her exhilaration is clear: She likes living on the edge, and later falsely obtains a pass allowing her to take another endangered aristocrat out of the city to her country house.

Her conversations with the duke of Orleans (attentive, courtly Jean-Claude Dreyfus) suggest why he and other men found her fascinating. She defends his cousin the king even while the duke is mealymouthed in explaining why it might benefit the nation for a few aristocrats to die; by siding with the mob, he hopes to save himself, and she is devastated when he breaks his promise to her and votes in favor of the king's execution.

Now consider the scene where Grace Elliott and a maid stand on a hillside outside Paris and use a spyglass to observe the execution of the king and his family, while distant cheering floats toward them on the wind. Everything they survey is a painted perspective drawing—the roads, streams, hills, trees, and the distant city. It doesn't look real, but it has a kind of heightened presence, and Rohmer's method allows the shot to exist at all. Other kinds of special effects could not compress so much information into seeable form.

Rohmer's movies are always about moral choices. His characters debate them, try to bargain with them, look for loopholes. But there is always clearly a correct way. Rohmer, one of the fathers of the New Wave, is Catholic in religion and conservative in politics, and here his heroine believes strongly in the divine right of kings and the need to risk your life, if necessary, for what you believe in. Lucy Russell, a British actress speaking proper French we imagine her character learned as a child, plays Grace Elliott as a woman of great confidence and verve. As a woman she must sit at home and wait for news; events are decided by men and reported to women. We sense her imagination placing her in the middle of the action, and we are struck by how much more clearly she sees the real issues than does the muddled duke.

The Lady and the Duke is the kind of movie one imagines could have been made in 1792. It centers its action in personal, everyday experience—an observant woman watches from the center of the maelstrom—and has time and attention for the conversational styles of an age when evenings were not spent stultified in front of the television. Watching it, we wonder if people did not live more keenly then. Certainly Grace Elliott was seldom bored.

The Ladykillers ★ ★ ½
R, 104 m., 2004

Tom Hanks (Professor G. H. Dorr), Marlon Wayans (Gawain MacSam), J. K. Simmons (Garth Pancake), Tzi Ma (The General), Ryan Hurst (Lump Hudson), Irma P. Hall (Marva Munson). Directed by Joel Coen and Ethan Coen and produced by Ethan Coen, Joel Coen, Tom Jacobson, Barry Sonnenfeld, and Barry Josephson. Screenplay by Joel Coen and Ethan Coen, based on *The Ladykillers*, written by William Rose.

The genius of Alec Guinness was in his anonymity. He could play a character so ingratiating that he ingratiated himself right into invisibility, and that was the secret of his work in *The Ladykillers*, a droll 1955 British comedy that also starred Peter Sellers and Herbert Lom. Now comes a Coen brothers remake with Tom Hanks in the Guinness role, and although Hanks would be the right actor to play a low-key deceiver, the Coens have made his character so bizarre that we get distracted just by looking at him.

Hanks plays Goldthwait Higginson Dorr, who claims to be a professor of Latin and Greek, who dresses like Colonel Sanders, and who seems to be channeling Tennessee Williams, Edgar Allen Poe, and Vincent Price. As in the original, he rents a room from a sweet little old lady, and plans to use her home as a base for a criminal scheme. In this case, he and four associates will tunnel from her root cellar into the cash room of a nearby casino named the Bandit Queen. The professor explains to the little old lady that the five of them are a classical music ensemble who need a quiet place to practice; they play music on a boom box to cover the sounds of their tunneling.

The other crooks represent the extremes of available casting choices; all of them, like the professor, are over the top in a way rarely seen outside Looney Tunes. Gawain MacSam (Marlon Wayans) is a trash-talking hip-hop janitor at the casino; Garth Pancake (J. K. Simmons) is a mustachioed explosives expert who asphyxiates a dog in an unfortunate gas mask experiment; the General (Tzi Ma) is a chain-smoker who once apparently specialized in tunnels for the Viet Cong; and Lump (Ryan Hurst) is a dim-witted muscle man who will do the hard labor.

The little old lady is named Marva Munson, and she is played by Irma P. Hall in the one completely successful comic performance in the movie. Yes, she's a caricature, too: a churchgoing widow who doesn't allow smoking in the house, has regular conversations with the portrait of her dead husband, and is not shy about complaining to the sheriff. But her character is exaggerated from a recognizable human base, while the others are comic-strip oddities.

Even Marva is sometimes betrayed by the Coens, who give her speeches that betray themselves as too clever by half (protesting a neighbor's loud "hippity-hop" music, she complains that the songs use the n-word "2,000 years after Jesus! Thirty years after Martin Luther King! In the Age of Montel!" If she'd said "Oprah," it might have been her talking, but when she says "Montel" you can feel the Coens' elbow digging in your side. There's also a subplot involving Mrs. Munson's generous donations to Bob Jones University; she is apparently unaware of its antediluvian attitudes about race. There are too many moments where dialogue seems so unmatched to the characters that they seem to be victims of a drive-by ventriloquist.

Now let me say that although the movie never jells, its oddness keeps it from being boring. Tom Hanks provides such an eccentric performance that it's fun just to watch him behaving—to listen to speeches that coil through endless, florid ornamentation. That the purpose of a criminal in such a situation would be to become invisible—as Guinness, despite the bad teeth, tried to do in the 1955 film—escapes the Coens. But I am importing unwanted logic into a narrative that manifestly is uninterested in such fineries of specification, as the professor might declare. There are some big laughs in the movie, some of them involving body disposal and another one as Garth Pancake demonstrates the safe handling of explosives. When Mrs. Munson invites the church ladies over for tea and invites the nice gentlemen in the basement to play something, Hanks offers a poem by Poe as a consolation prize, and rises to a peak of mannered sublimity. As the church ladies gaze in speechless astonishment at his performance, I was reminded of a day in the 1960s I was in a working-class pub in a poor neighborhood of Sligo, in the west of Ireland. The TV set over the bar was tuned to *The Galloping Gourmet.* The regulars stared at him speechlessly, until finally one said: "Will you *look* at that fellow!" That's how they feel about Professor G. H. Dorr.

There's a lot of high-spirited gospel music in the movie, which brings the plot to a halt for a concert in Mrs. Munson's church. It's wonderful as music, but not really connected to the movie, unlike the music in the Coens' *O Brother, Where Art Thou?* For that matter, the four- and twelve-letter dialogue of the Wayans character fits awkwardly into a story where no one else talks that way; his potty mouth also wins the film an otherwise completely unnecessary "R" rating.

What the movie finally lacks, I think, is modesty. The original *Ladykillers* was one of a group of small, inspired comedies made at the low-rent Ealing Studios near London, where Alec Guinness was the resident genius; his other titles from the period include *Kind Hearts and Coronets* (1949), *The Lavender Hill Mob* (1950), and *The Man in the White Suit* (1951). These were self-effacing films; much of their humor grew out of the contrast between nefarious schemes and low-key, almost apologetic behavior.

The Coens' *Ladykillers,* on the other hand, is always wildly signaling for us to notice it. Not content to be funny, it wants to be *funny!* Have you ever noticed that the more a comedian wears funny hats, the less funny he is? The old

and new *Ladykillers* play like a contest between Buster Keaton and Soupy Sales.

Lagaan: Once Upon a Time in India
★ ★ ★ ½
PG, 225 m., 2002

Aamir Khan (Bhuvan), Gracy Singh (Gauri), Rachel Shelley (Elizabeth Russell), Paul Blackthorne (Captain Andrew Russell), Suhasini Mulay (Yashodamai), Kulbhushan Kharbanda (Rajah Puran Singh), Raghuvir Yadav (Bhura), Rajendra Gupta (Mukhiya), Yashpal Sharma (Lakha), Rajesh Vivek (Guran), Pradeep Rawat (Deva). Directed by Ashutosh Gowariker and produced by Aamir Khan. Screenplay by Kumar Dave, Sanjay Dayma, Gowariker, and K. P. Saxena.

Lagaan is an enormously entertaining movie, like nothing we've ever seen before, and yet completely familiar. Set in India in 1893, it combines sports with political intrigue, romance with evil scheming, musical numbers with low comedy and high drama, and is therefore soundly in the tradition of the entertainments produced by the Bombay film industry, "Bollywood," which is the world's largest.

I have seen only five or six Bollywood movies, one of them in Hyderabad, India, in 1999, where I climbed to the highest balcony and shivered in arctic air conditioning while watching a movie that was well over three hours long and included something for everyone. The most charming aspect of most Bollywood movies is their cheerful willingness to break into song and dance at the slightest pretext; the film I saw was about a romance between a rich boy and a poor girl, whose poverty did not prevent her from producing backup dancers whenever she needed them.

Lagaan is said to be the most ambitious, expensive, and successful Bollywood film ever made, and has been a box-office hit all over the world. Starring Aamir Khan, who is one of the top Indian heartthrobs, it was made with an eye to overseas audiences: If *Crouching Tiger, Hidden Dragon* could break out of the martial arts ghetto and gross $150 million, then why not a Bollywood movie for non-Indians? It has succeeded in jumping its genre; it won an Academy Award nomination in 2002 as Best Foreign Film, and has been rolling up amazing per-screen averages in North American theaters.

All of which evades the possibility that most readers of this review have never seen a Bollywood movie and don't want to start now. That will be their loss. This film is like nothing they've seen before, with its startling landscapes, architecture, and locations, its exuberant colors, its sudden and joyous musical numbers right in the middle of dramatic scenes, and its melodramatic acting (teeth gnash, tears well, lips tremble, bosoms heave, fists clench). At the same time, it's a memory of the films we all grew up on, with clearly defined villains and heroes, a romantic triangle, and even a comic character who saves the day. *Lagaan* is a well-crafted, hugely entertaining epic that has the spice of a foreign culture.

The story takes place at the height of the Raj, England's government of occupation in India. In a remote province, the local British commander is Captain Russell (Paul Blackthorne), a lip-curling rotter with a racist streak, who insults the local maharajah to his face and thinks nothing of whipping a Hindu upstart. Even his fellow officers think he's over the top. He administers "lagaan," which is the annual tax the farmers must pay to their maharajah, and he to the British. It is a time of drought and hunger, and the farmers cannot pay.

Enter Bhuvan (Aamir Khan), a leader among his people, who confronts Russell and finds his weak point: The captain is obsessed by cricket, and believes it's a game that can never be mastered by Indians. Bhuvan says it is much like an ancient Indian game, and that Indians could excel at it. Russell makes Bhuvan a bet: The Brits and a village team will play a cricket match. If the Indians win, there will be no lagaan for three years. If the Brits win, lagaan will be tripled. The villagers think Bhuvan is insane, since a triple tax would destroy them, but he points out that since they cannot pay the current tax, they have nothing to lose.

Bhuvan assembles and starts to coach a local team. Elizabeth Russell (Rachel Shelley), the evil captain's sister, believes her brother's deal is unfair, and secretly sneaks out to the village to provide pointers on cricket. Her closeness to Bhuvan disturbs Gauri (Gracy Singh), a local

woman who has believed since childhood that she and Bhuvan are fated to marry. There's another coil of the plot with the two-faced Lakha (Yashpal Sharma), who wants Gauri for himself, and acts as a spy for Russell because he feels that if Bhuvan loses face, he'll have a better chance with her.

We meet the members of the village team, an oddly assorted group that includes a low-caste fortune-teller named Guran (Rajesh Vivek), whose crippled arm allows him to throw a wicked curve ball. There is also Deva (Pradeep Rawat), whose service in the British army has fueled his contempt for his former masters. As training proceeds in the village and the British sneer from their regimental headquarters, the action is punctuated by much music.

The British hold dances, at which single young women who have come out from home hope to find an eligible young officer. (Elizabeth, dreaming about Bhuvan, is not much interested in the candidate selected for her.) And in the village music wells up spontaneously, most memorably when storm clouds promise an end to the long drought. In keeping with Bollywood tradition, the singing voices in these sequences are always dubbed (the voice-over artists are stars in their own right), as the camera plunges into joyous choreography with dancers, singers, and swirls of beautifully colored saris. Such dance sequences would be too contrived and illogical for sensible modern Hollywood, but we feel like we're getting away with something as we enjoy them.

Lagaan somehow succeeds in being suspenseful at the same time it's frivolous and obvious. The final cricket match (which we can follow even if we don't understand the game) is in the time-honored tradition of all sports movies, and yet the underlying issues are serious. And there is the intriguing question of whether the hero will end up with his childhood sweetheart, or cross color lines with the Victorian woman (this is hard to predict, since both women are seen in entirely positive terms).

As a backdrop to the action, there is India itself. It is a long time since I praised a movie for its landscapes; I recall *Dr. Zhivago* or *Lawrence of Arabia,* and indeed, like David Lean, director Ashutosh Gowariker is not shy about lingering on ancient forts and palaces, vast plains, and the birthday-cake architecture of the British Raj, so out of place and yet so serenely confident. Watching the film, we feel familiarity with the characters and the showdown, but the setting and the production style are fresh and exciting. Bollywood has always struck a bargain with its audience members, many of them poor: You get your money's worth. Leaving the film, I did not feel unsatisfied or vaguely shortchanged, as after many Hollywood films, but satisfied: I had seen a *movie*.

Lana's Rain ★ ★ ★

R, 107 m., 2004

Oksana Orlenko (Lana), Nickolai Stoilov (Darko Lucev), Luoyong Wang (Julian), Stephanie Childers (Katrina), Stacey Slowid (Vermonica), David Darlow (General Donoffrio). Directed by Michael S. Ojeda and produced by Joel Goodman. Screenplay by Ojeda.

Lana's Rain tells the dark, hard-edged story of a brother and sister who escape from the war-torn Balkans, conceal themselves in a shipping container to travel to America, and try to survive on Chicago streets that have never seemed meaner. The picture is even bleaker than that: The brother is a war criminal who forces his sister into prostitution, and by the end of the film he's a low-life Scarface, with a stable of hookers, a big cigar, and a bottle and gun under his coat.

The story is seen through the eyes of the sister, Lana (Oksana Orlenko), who grew up apart from her brother and meets him again after many years on the eve of his escape from the Balkans. In a grisly prelude, the brother is having facial reconstruction to disguise himself, and is interrupted in the middle of the surgery; he wears an eye patch through the movie, while his enemies and Interpol search for him.

Lana speaks no English, is naive, is dominated by her brother, and despises the life of prostitution. She is savagely beaten by one client. Darko (Nickolai Stoilov), her brother, keeps all her earnings, scornfully tossing her $10 for "spending money." She speaks so little English that she tries to learn the language

from a Dr. Seuss book she finds in a Dumpster. Her only friend is an Asian-American sculptor named Julian (Luoyong Wang), who befriends her, likes her, offers her shelter, but cannot get her away from the insidious domination of her brother.

The film, written and directed by Michael S. Ojeda, shows a sure sense of *noir* style and a toughness that lasts right up to the very final scene, which feels contrived and tacked-on. It lives through the performance of Oksana Orlenko, who won the best actress award at Milan. On the basis of his work as the brother, Nickolai Stoilov has a future as a Bond villain. They are both never less than convincing, and Ojeda makes no effort to glamorize their lifestyle; even after Darko is running three or four call girls (advertising "Eastern European Beauties"), he lives in a shabby trailer in a neighborhood that looks more like Siberia than Chicago.

The movie has a lot of plot, including a revenge twist so ingenious I will not even hint of it. It also has too many endings; there is a time when it seems that Darko must certainly be dead, but with the resilience of a zombie he reappears. In a late confrontation where they are both drenched with gasoline, Lana's decision is drawn out for too long, and then the situation is settled with a shameless *deus ex machina*. And as for the nice Asian man, is it really that nice of him to make love to her in the night and reveal in the morning that he is committed to another woman? Well, given her need and desperation, maybe he did the right thing, but the subplot disappears just when we think it might amount to something interesting.

So *Lana's Rain* is not a perfect picture, but it has the flaws of ambition, not compromise. It doesn't soften the character of the brother, who is unremittingly evil from beginning to end, and it doesn't sentimentalize the sister's ordeal. Her stamina and endurance, during a harsh Chicago winter, give some hint of the harsh world she was raised in, and her struggle is all the more moving because it comes from courage, not cleverness. Even as I noted a glitch here and there in the plot, I was aware that the movie itself, and especially the character of Lana, had enlisted my sympathy.

Lantana ★ ★ ★ ½
R, 121 m., 2002

Anthony LaPaglia (Leon Zat), Geoffrey Rush (John Sommers), Barbara Hershey (Dr. Valerie Sommers), Kerry Armstrong (Sonja Zat), Rachael Blake (Jane), Vince Colosimo (Nik), Daniella Farinacci (Paula), Peter Phelps (Patrick). Directed by Ray Lawrence and produced by Jan Chapman. Screenplay by Andrew Bovell, based on the play *Speaking in Tongues*.

Lantana opens with a camera tracking through dense Australian shrubbery to discover the limbs of a dead woman. We are reminded of the opening of *Blue Velvet*, which pushed into lawn grass to suggest dark places hidden just out of view. Much of the movie will concern the identity of the dead woman, and how she died, but when the mystery is solved it turns out to be less an answer than a catalyst—the event that caused several lives to interlock.

Ray Lawrence's film is like Robert Altman's *Short Cuts* or Paul Thomas Anderson's *Magnolia* in the way it shows the lives of strangers joined by unsuspected connections. It discovers a web of emotional hope and betrayal. At its center is a cop named Leon Zat (Anthony LaPaglia) in the process of meltdown; he is cheating on his wife, he has chest pains, he beats a suspect beyond any need or reason, he is ferocious with his son, he collides with a man while jogging and explodes in anger.

Zat's wife, Sonja (Kerry Armstrong), worried about him, is seeing a psychiatrist named Valerie Sommers (Barbara Hershey). Valerie is married to John (Geoffrey Rush). A few years ago their daughter was killed. Valerie wrote a book as a way of dealing with the experience. John hides behind a stolid front. One of her clients (Peter Phelps) is a gay man who wants to talk about his married lover, and Valerie comes to suspect that the lover is, in fact, her own husband.

Other characters. Jane (Rachel Blake) is the separated housewife who is cheating with Leon. Her neighbors are the happily married Nik and Paula (Vince Colosimo and Daniella Farinacci). When Valerie's car is found abandoned

and she is missing, murder is feared, and Leon is assigned to the case. He suspects her husband, John, and there is another suspect—Nik, the father of three, seen throwing a woman's shoe into the underbrush by Jane. When Leon arrives to question Jane it is significant, of course, that they were lovers.

This description no doubt makes the film seem like some kind of gimmicky puzzle. What's surprising is how easy it is to follow the plot, and how the coincidences don't get in the way. Lawrence's film, based on a play by Andrew Bovell, only seems to be a murder mystery. As it plays out, we're drawn into the everyday lives of these characters—their worries, their sorrows, the way they're locked into solitary sadness. Nik and Paula are the only happy couple, blessed with kids, happiness, and uncomplicated lives. When the evidence seems overwhelming against Nik, we can hardly believe it. Certainly Valerie's husband, or even an ominous dance instructor, might make better suspects.

Anthony LaPaglia makes his cop into a focus of pain: He cheats, takes no joy in cheating, is violent, takes no joy in violence, is shut inside himself. LaPaglia is so identified with American roles that *Lantana* comes as a little surprise, reminding us that he has an Australian background. The other actors, especially Hershey, Rush, and the two unhappy women in the cop's life (played by Armstrong and Blake) are so attentive to the nuances of their characters, so tender with their hurts, that maybe we shouldn't be surprised when the crime plot turns out to be a form of misdirection.

One particularly effective scene involves a conversation between LaPaglia and Rush. It comes at a point when LaPaglia clearly thinks the other man has murdered his wife, and the Rush character almost willfully says things that will not help his case. In another kind of movie, his dialogue could be cheating—deliberately misleading the audience. Here we sense it grows out of a disgust he feels that he is not a better man.

Lawrence and Bovell ground their stories in a lot of domestic details, involving children: the daughter Valerie and John lost; the sons Leon is alienated from; Nik and Paula's kids, who need baby-sitting and get earaches. After Jane reports her suspicions about the neighbors, she ends up minding the kids, and there is a wonderfully observed moment when the little one gets sick and the slightly older one knows just what medication is necessary.

Lantana is, we learn, the name of a South American plant that, transplanted to Sydney, prospered and became a nuisance. What is its connection to the film? Perhaps suspicion can also grow out of control, when people get out of the habit of assuming that others are good and mean well.

The Last Kiss ★ ★
R, 114 m., 2002

Stefano Accorsi (Carlo), Giovanna Mezzogiorno (Giulia), Stefania Sandrelli (Anna), Giorgio Pasotti (Adriano), Claudio Santamaria (Paolo), Marco Cocci (Alberto), Martina Stella (Francesca), Pierfrancesco Favino (Marco). Directed by Gabriele Muccino and produced by Domenico Procacci. Screenplay by Muccino.

The Last Kiss is a comedy, I guess, about male panic at the specter of adult responsibility. If you're a guy and want to figure out what side of the question you're on, take this test. You're a young, single man. Your girlfriend announces at a family dinner that she is pregnant. You (a) accept the joys and responsibilities of fatherhood; (b) climb up into a treehouse at a wedding to begin a passionate affair with an eighteen-year-old; (c) join three buddies in discussing their plan to buy a van and trek across Africa.

Carlo (Stefano Accorsi), the hero of the film, is torn between (b) and (c). Marriage looms like a trap to him, and he complains to Francesca (Martina Stella), the eighteen-year-old, that he fears "the passion is going" from his life. When his girlfriend, Giulia (Giovanna Mezzogiorno), takes him along to look at a house they could buy, he complains that buying a house seems so "final." Not encouraging words for a pregnant fiancée to hear. "If I catch him cheating, I'll kill him," she says, in the ancient tradition of Italian movie comedy.

But the movie isn't all comedy, and has fugitive ambitions, I fear, to say something significant about romance and even life. Consider some of Carlo's friends. Paolo (Claudio Santamaria) is expected to take over his father's clothing store, has no interest in retail, but is wracked with guilt because his father is dying and this is his last wish. Marco (Pierfrancesco Favino) is a serial lover. Adriano (Giorgio Pasotti) is depressed because his girlfriend has lost all interest in sex after giving birth. Their thirties and indeed their forties are breathing hot on the necks of these friends, who cling to golden memories of adolescence.

There is also the case of Anna (Stefania Sandrelli), Carlo's mother, who is married to a detached and indifferent psychiatrist, and seeks out a former lover with hopes of, who knows, maybe now taking the path not chosen. The lover is delighted to see her for a chat over lunch, but reveals that he has recently married and is the proud father of a one-year-old. How cruelly age discriminates against women (at least those prepared to consider it discrimination and not freedom).

The Last Kiss specializes in dramatic exits and entrances. Anna bursts into her husband's office when he is deep in consultation with a patient, who seems alarmed that his own house is so clearly not in order. Carlo awakens with dread after a night spent imprudently, and flees. Giulia makes a dramatic appearance at a deathbed after discovering Carlo lied to her. And so on.

The problem is that the movie has no idea whether it is serious or not. It combines heartfelt self-analysis with scenes like the one where Carlo is taken by his teenage squeeze to her friend's birthday, and tries to party with the kids. This is either funny or sad, not both, but the movie doesn't know which.

The message behind all of this is difficult to nail down. Mars and Venus? Adults who haven't grown up? The last-fling syndrome? Doing what you want instead of doing what you must? I have just finished *Without Stopping*, the autobiography of the novelist and composer Paul Bowles, who as nearly as I can tell always did exactly what he wanted, and was married to Jane Bowles, who did the same. The answer, obviously, is not to choose between marriage and the van trip through Africa, but to dump the buddies and find a wife who wants to come along.

Last Orders ★ ★ ★ ½
R, 109 m., 2002

Michael Caine (Jack), Tom Courtenay (Vic), David Hemmings (Lenny), Bob Hoskins (Ray), Helen Mirren (Amy), Ray Winstone (Vince), Laura Morelli (June). Directed by Fred Schepisi and produced by Elisabeth Robinson, Schepisi, and Gary Smith. Screenplay by Schepisi, based on the novel by Graham Swift.

Too many films about the dead involve mourning, and too few involve laughter. Yet at lucky funerals there is a desire to remember the good times. The most charismatic man I ever knew was Bob Zonka, an editor at the *Chicago Sun-Times,* and even five years after his death his friends gathered just to tell stories and laugh about them. Yes, he was infuriating in the way he treasured his bad habits, but it was all part of the package. There is the impulse to try to analyze the departed, figure out their motives, ask the questions they never answered, wonder what they were really thinking.

Last Orders, Fred Schepisi's new film, based on the Booker Prize–winning novel by Graham Swift, knows all about those stages in the process of grieving and celebration. It is about four old friends in London who, at one level, simply drank together for years at a pub called the Coach and Horses, and at another level came as close as people can to sharing each others' lives. Now one has died—the most enigmatic and problematical of the four—and the three survivors and the dead man's son gather in the pub with his ashes and set off on a journey to Margate, where he thought to retire. His wife does not make the journey but chooses to spend the day with their retarded daughter.

The three friends and the widow all have faces that evoke decades of memories for moviegoers. In a certain way, we have lived our lives with them, so it feels right to find them on this mission at the end.

Tom Courtenay electrified me in *Loneliness of the Long Distance Runner* when I was still in college. I had lunch with him in 1967 in London, and in a sense have just gotten up from that meal. David Hemmings was the photographer in *Blow-Up,* the movie everybody was talking about when I became a film critic. Michael Caine was one of the first stars I ever interviewed (about *Hurry, Sundown,* a film he had a hard time keeping a straight face about). Bob Hoskins joined the crowd later, with *The Long Good Friday,* walking onto the screen with the authority of a lifelong leaseholder. Helen Mirren I became aware of when I saw *Cal* at the 1984 Cannes festival. Ever since, she has been brave in her film choices, going her own way, so that her character's behavior here mirrors her career.

Because I share history and memories with these actors, it is easy to stand at the bar with their characters as they regard the urn of ashes. "So that's Jack, is it?" they say, looking at the container as if it might explode. Have you noticed that although people feel odd around a corpse, they sometimes have a little smile when looking at ashes, because the ashes so clearly are *not* the departed—who has left for other pastures, leaving behind this souvenir. Having scattered a few ashes myself, I find it more cheerful than putting someone into the ground. It's a way the dead have of telling the living to go outdoors to some nice place and remember them.

The fact that Jack wants his ashes to be scattered into the sea at Margate has a lot to do with his widow Amy's decision not to go along. It was there they met, as kids from London, gathering hops as a summer job. It was there that their daughter was conceived. And when June (Laura Morelli) was born retarded, Jack refused to deal with her—refused even to acknowledge her existence. All these years Amy (Mirren) has visited the daughter in an asylum once a week. The girl has never given the slightest sign of recognizing her mother, and so Amy is trapped between two great gulfs of disregard. That Jack would think Amy would want to retire to a place associated with these memories is—well, typical of the deep misunderstandings a marriage can engender and somehow accommodate.

Jack, we might as well say, is the character played by Michael Caine. It is no secret after the first scene of the film. We get to know him well, because Schepisi's flashback structure shows Jack as a young man at war, as a second-generation butcher, as a young man courting

Amy, and as a jolly regular in the pub. The other friends include benign Vic (Courtenay), an undertaker; Ray (Hoskins), who likes to play the ponies; and Lenny (Hemmings), once a boxer, now a portly greengrocer. The actors have logged time in pubs and know the form. Notice how Caine captures the look of a drinker late at night, with the saggy lower eyelids and the slight loosening of tension in the lips.

They all live and work in the same south London neighborhood, and are joined at the pub by Vince (Ray Winstone), who is Jack and Amy's son. It was Jack's wish that Vince join him in the family butcher business, but Vince instead became a car dealer, and turns up in a Mercedes to drive the pals and the ashes to Margate. Many old secrets are revealed in the course of the journey, but they are not really what the movie is about. The details are not as important as the act of memory itself.

A death in the family is a sudden interruption of the unconscious assumption that things will go on forever. There can be a certain exhilaration at this close contact with eternal truths; we were not aware at our births, so death is the only conscious contact we have with this mysterious journey. The final shot of Schepisi's movie finds a visual way to suggest the great silence that surrounds us. Another scene near the end puts it in human terms. On the day the friends go to scatter Jack's ashes, Amy pays her usual visit to June—to the daughter who was denied the gift of awareness; as Amy tells Ray, "Not once in fifty years did she ever give me a sign—not even a flicker—that she knew me." As we consider June's uncomprehending eyes and fixed smile, we think, death is not so bad. Not knowing we live, not knowing we die, that would be bad. Ashes are scattered in more ways than one in the film's closing scenes.

Note: Some reviews have complained about the Cockney accents. All of these actors can speak the Queen's English if they choose to. The Cockney is their gift to us in creating the world of their characters. You may miss a word or two, but you hear the music.

The Last Samurai ★ ★ ★ ½

R, 150 m., 2003

Tom Cruise (Nathan Algren), Timothy Spall (Simon Graham), Ken Watanabe (Katsumoto), Billy Connolly (Zebulon Gant), Tony Goldwyn (Colonel Bagley), Hiroyuki Sanada (Ujio), Koyuki (Taka), Shichinosuke Nakamura (Emperor). Directed by Edward Zwick and produced by Tom Cruise, Tom Engelman, Marshall Herskovitz, Scott Kroopf, Paula Wagner, and Zwick. Screenplay by John Logan, Herskovitz, and Zwick.

Edward Zwick's *The Last Samurai* is about two warriors whose cultures make them aliens, but whose values make them comrades. The battle scenes are stirring and elegantly mounted, but they are less about who wins than about what can be proven by dying. Beautifully designed, intelligently written, acted with conviction, it's an uncommonly thoughtful epic. Its power is compromised only by an ending that sheepishly backs away from what the film is really about.

Tom Cruise and Ken Watanabe costar, as a shabby Civil War veteran and a proud samurai warrior. Cruise plays Nathan Algren, a war hero who now drifts and drinks too much, with no purpose in life. He's hired by Americans who are supplying mercenaries to train an army for the Japanese emperor, who wants to move his country into the modern world and is faced with a samurai rebellion.

The role of the samurai leader Katsumoto (Watanabe) is complex; he is fighting against the emperor's men, but out of loyalty to the tradition the emperor represents; he would sacrifice his life in an instant, he says, if the emperor requested it. But Japan has been seized with a fever to shake off its medieval ways and copy the West, and the West sees money to be made in the transition: Representatives from the Remington arms company are filling big contracts for weapons, and the U.S. Embassy is a clearinghouse for lucrative trade arrangements.

Into this cauldron Algren descends as a cynic. He is told the samurai are "savages with bows and arrows," but sees that the American advisers have done a poor job of training the modernized Japanese army to fight them. Leading his untried troops into battle, he is captured and faces death—but is spared by a word from Katsumoto, who returns him as a prisoner to the village of his son.

It's at this point that *The Last Samurai* begins to reveal itself as more than an action picture. Katsumoto, who conveniently speaks English, explains he has kept Algren alive because he wants to know his enemy. Algren at first refuses to speak, but gradually, during a long, rainy winter of captivity, he begins to have philosophical conversations with the other man about the ethics of war and warriors. Some of these talks sound like Socratic exchanges:

Katsumoto: Do you believe a man can change his destiny?

Algren: I believe a man does what he can until his destiny is revealed.

For Algren, the traditional village life is a soothing tonic. Haunted by nightmares from his wartime experiences, he confesses, "Here I have known my first untroubled sleep in many years." He has been lodged in the house of Taka (Koyuki), the widow of a man he killed in battle, and although she complains bitterly to Katsumoto, she maintains a smiling facade in Algren's presence.

Algren: I killed her husband!

Katsumoto: It was a good death.

Katsumoto has pledged his life to defending the dying code of the samurai. Algren finds himself gradually shifting allegiances, away from the mercenaries and toward the samurai, but his shift is visceral, not ideological. He bonds with Katsumoto, respects him, wants to find respect in his eyes. The movie illustrates the universal military truth that men in battle are motivated not by their cause but by loyalty to their comrades.

The Last Samurai breaks with the convention that the Western hero is always superior to the local culture he immerses in. It has been compared to *Lawrence of Arabia* and *Dances with Wolves,* films in which Westerners learn to respect Arabs and Indians, but this film goes a step further, clearly believing that Katsumoto's traditional society is superior to the modernism being unloaded by the Americans. Katsumoto is the teacher and Algren is the student, and the film wonderfully re-creates the patterns and textures of the Japanese past; its production design, sets, and costumes are astonishing.

Watanabe is a deep, powerful presence; he has the potential to become the first world star from Japan since Toshiro Mifune. Cruise is already a star, and will be targeted by those predisposed to see him and not his character, but here I think his stardom works for the film, because he takes with him into battle both the cocksure pilot of *Top Gun* and the war-weary veteran of *Born on the Fourth of July.* The casting helps the film with its buried message, which is about the reeducation of a conventional American soldier.

The supporting cast is splendid: Koyuki quietly stirs as the widow who feels sexual attraction but suppresses it; Tony Goldwyn blusters and threatens as the hard American mercenary; Timothy Spall is the British translator who knows the words but not the music. Shichinosuke Nakamura plays the emperor as a tormented, shy man who admires Katsumoto's values even while agreeing with his advisers that the rebellion must be put down. "I am a living god—as long as I do what they say is right," he muses at one point, in words I somehow doubt any Japanese emperor would ever have employed.

The director is Edward Zwick, whose other war films (*Glory, Legends of the Fall, Courage Under Fire*) have also dealt with men whose personal loyalties have figured more importantly than political ideology. Here he gives Algren a speech attacking Custer, whose last stand was fresh in everyone's mind. ("He was a murderer who fell in love with his own legend, and his troops died for it.") Yes, but how would Algren describe this film's final battle scene, in which Katsumoto leads his men into what appears to be certain death? To be sure, his men share his values, but is there an element of seeking "a good death"? Is there a line between dying *for* what you believe in, and dying *because* of what you believe in?

That the film raises this question shows how thoughtful it is. If *The Last Samurai* had ended in a way that was consistent with its tone and direction, it would have been true to its real feelings. But the ending caves in to Hollywood requirements, and we feel the air going out of the picture. An art film can trust its audience to follow along to the necessary conclusion. A Hollywood ending assumes that the audience caves in at the end, turns dim-witted and sentimental, and must be fed its lollypop. *The Last Samurai* has greatness in it, but sidesteps the ending that would have given it real impact. If there's going to be an alternative ending on the DVD, I know what it would have to show—and so, I suspect, does Edward Zwick.

Note: Which character is the "last samurai"—Katsumoto or Algren? A case can be made for either answer, which suggests the nature of their relationship.

The Last Waltz ★ ★ ★
PG, 117 m., 2002

Featuring The Band, Eric Clapton, Neil Diamond, Bob Dylan, Emmylou Harris, Joni Mitchell, Van Morrison, Robbie Robertson, The Staples, Muddy Waters, Ronnie Wood, Neil Young, and Martin Scorsese. A concert documentary directed by Martin Scorcese and produced by Robbie Robertson.

I wonder if the sadness comes across on the CD. The music probably sounds happy. But the performers, seen on-screen, seem curiously morose, exhausted, played out. Recently I was at a memorial concert for the late tenor sax man Spike Robinson, and the musicians—jazz and big-band veterans—were cheerful, filled with joy, happy to be there. Most of the musicians in *The Last Waltz* are, on average, twenty-five years younger than Spike's friends, but they drag themselves onstage like exhausted veterans of wrong wars.

The rock documentary was filmed by Martin Scorsese at a farewell concert given on Thanksgiving Day 1976 by The Band, which had been performing since 1960, in recent years as the backup band for Bob Dylan. "Sixteen years on the road is long enough," says Robbie Robertson, the group's leader. "Twenty years is unthinkable." There is a weight and gravity in his words that suggests he seriously doubts if he could survive four more years.

Drugs are possibly involved. Memoirs recalling the filming report that cocaine was everywhere backstage. The overall tenor of the documentary suggests survivors at the ends of their ropes. They dress in dark, cheerless clothes, hide behind beards, hats, and shades, pound out rote performances of old hits, don't seem to smile much at their music or each other. There is the whole pointless road war-

rior mystique, of hard-living men whose daily duty it is to play music and get wasted. They look tired of it.

Not all of them. The women (Joni Mitchell, Emmylou Harris) seem immune, although what Mitchell's song is about I have no clue, and Harris is filmed in another time and place. Visitors like the Staples Singers are open-faced and happy. Eric Clapton is in the right place and time. Muddy Waters is on sublime autopilot. Lawrence Ferlinghetti reads a bad poem, badly, but seems pleased to be reading it. Neil Diamond seems puzzled to find himself in this company, grateful to be invited.

But then look at the faces of Neil Young or Van Morrison. Study Robertson, whose face is kind and whose smile comes easily, but who does not project a feeling of celebration for the past or anticipation of the future. These are not musicians at the top of their art, but laborers on the last day of the job. Look in their eyes. Read their body language.

The Last Waltz has inexplicably been called the greatest rock documentary of all time. Certainly that would be *Woodstock*, which heralds the beginning of the era that The Band gathered to bury. Among 1970s contemporaries of The Band, one senses joy in the various Rolling Stones documentaries, in Chuck Berry's *Hail! Hail! Rock and Roll*, and in concert films by the Temptations or Rod Stewart. Not here.

In *The Last Waltz*, we have musicians who seem to have bad memories. Who are hanging on. Scorsese's direction is mostly limited to close-ups and medium shots of performances; he ignores the audience. The movie was made at the end of a difficult period in his own life, and at a particularly hard time (the filming coincided with his work on *New York, New York*). This is not a record of serene men, filled with nostalgia, happy to be among friends.

At the end, Bob Dylan himself comes on. One senses little connection between Dylan and The Band. One also wonders what he was thinking as he chose that oversize white pimp hat, a hat so absurd that during his entire performance I could scarcely think of anything else. It is the haberdashery equivalent of an uplifted middle finger.

The music probably sounds fine on a CD.

Certainly it is well rehearsed. But the overall sense of the film is of good riddance to a bad time. Even references to groupies inspire creases of pain on the faces of the rememberers: The sex must have been as bad as anything else. Watching this film, the viewer with mercy will be content to allow the musicians to embrace closure, and will not demand an encore. Yet I give it three stars? Yes, because the film is such a revealing document of a time.

Late Marriage ★ ★ ★
NO MPAA RATING, 100 m., 2002

Lior Louie Ashkenazi (Zaza), Ronit Elkabetz (Judith), Moni Moshonov (Yasha [Father]), Lili Kosashvili (Lily [Mother]), Sapir Kugman (Madona), Aya Steinovits Laor (Ilana). Directed by Dover Kosashvili and produced by Marek Rozenbaum and Edgard Tenembaum. Screenplay by Kosashvili.

When children are grown they must be set free to lead their own lives. Otherwise it's no longer a parent guiding a child, but one adult insisting on authority over another. Wise parents step back before they cross this line. Wise children rebel against parents who do not. *Late Marriage* is about parents who insist on running the life of their thirty-two-year-old son, and a son who lets them. The characters deserve their misery.

The film is set in Israel, within a community of Jewish immigrants from the former Soviet republic of Georgia. Zaza at thirty-one has still not filled his obligation to marry and produce children. His parents have marched a parade of potential wives past him, without success. His secret is that he's in love with Judith, a divorcée from Morocco, four years older, with a daughter. His parents would never approve of Zaza marrying such a woman.

As the movie opens, Zaza and his family descend on the home of Ilana, a sulky seventeen-year-old who has been proposed as a prospective bride. There may be a difference in age and education, but at least she is single, childless, and arguably a virgin. In a scene of excruciating social comedy, the two families arrange themselves in the living room and discuss Zaza and Ilana as if they were this week's Tupperware specials. Then Ilana is produced and the would-be couple dispatched to her bedroom "to get to know one another."

"Is that a dress or a nightgown?" Zaza (Lior Louie Ashkenazi) asks her when they are alone. "What do you think?" asks Ilana (Aya Steinovits Laor). She shows him her portfolio and confides her desire to be a dress designer. She seems to be designing for the hostesses in an Havana hooker bar, circa 1959. "I want a rich man," she tells him. Obviously he will not do, but they fall on her bed and neck for a while until summoned back to the family council.

Zaza's parents find out about Judith (Ronit Elkabetz), the divorcée. They stake out her house and eventually break in upon the romantic couple, calling Judith a whore and demanding that the relationship end. Does Zaza stand up to his mother, Lily (Lili Kosashvili—the director's own mother)? No, he doesn't, and Judith sees this, and wisely drops him because there is no future for her.

The contest between arranged marriages and romantic love is being waged in novels and movies all over those parts of the world where parents select the spouses of their children. Art is on the side of romance, tradition on the side of the parents. Sometimes, as in Mira Nair's wonderful *Monsoon Wedding,* set in Delhi, there is a happy medium when the arranged couple falls in love. But look at Rohinton Mistry's new novel, *Family Matters,* about a man who spends a lifetime of misery after having a widow foisted on him by a family that disapproves of the Christian woman from Goa he truly loves.

The most important sequence in *Late Marriage* is a refreshingly frank sex scene involving Zaza and Judith. We don't often see sex like this on the screen. The scene is not about passion, performance, or technique, but about (listen carefully) familiarity and affection. They know each other's bodies. They have a long history of lovemaking, and you can see how little movements and gestures are part of a shared physical history. Watching this scene, we realize that most sex scenes in the movies play like auditions.

Late Marriage is not a one-level film, and

one of its most revealing moments shows the strong-minded mother expressing respect for the equally iron-willed Judith. These women understand each other, and the mother even realistically discusses the chances that her Zaza will defy her and choose the divorcée. The mother would, if forced to, actually accept that—but Zaza is too frightened of her to intuit that there is a crack in his mother's heart of stone.

I know couples whose marriage were arranged, and who are blissful. I know couples who married for love, and are miserable. I am not saying one way is right and another wrong. The message of *Late Marriage*, I think, is that when a marriage is decided by the parents crushing the will of the child, it is wrong for the child and unfair to the new spouse. I have more thoughts on this subject, but have just remembered this is not the advice column, so I will close with the best all-purpose advice I have heard on this subject: Never marry anyone you could not sit next to during a three-day bus trip.

Latter Days ★ ★ ½
NO MPAA RATING, 108 m., 2004

Steve Sandvoss (Davis), Wes Ramsey (Christian), Rebekah Jordan (Julie), Amber Benson (Traci), Khary Payton (Andrew), Jacqueline Bisset (Lila), Joseph Gordon-Levitt (Ryder), Rob McElhenney (Harmon). Directed by C. Jay Cox and produced by Kirkland Tibbels and Jennifer Schafer. Screenplay by Cox.

A movie should present its characters with a problem and then watch them solve it, not without difficulty. So says an old and reliable screenplay formula. Countless movies have been made about a boy and a girl who have a problem (they haven't slept with each other) and after difficulties (family, war, economic, health, rival lover, stupid misunderstanding) they solve it, by sleeping with each other. Now we have a movie about two homosexuals that follows the same reliable convention.

Although much will be made of the fact that one of the characters in *Latter Days* is a Mormon missionary and the other is a gay poster boy, those are simply titillating details. Consider the subgenre of pornography in which nuns get involved in sex. We know they're not really nuns, but the costuming is supposed to add a little spice. By the same token, Davis (Steve Sandvoss) is a Mormon only because that makes his journey from hetero- to homosexual more fraught and daring. He could have been a Presbyterian or an atheist vegan and the underlying story would have been the same: A character who considers himself straight is seduced by an attractive gay man, and discovers he has been homosexual all along.

Since it is obvious to us from the opening shots that these two characters are destined for each other, the plot functions primarily to add melodrama to the inevitable. And there's change in both men. Christian (Wes Ramsey), who at the beginning is a shameless slut, bets a friend $50 he can seduce his new neighbor, but by the end of the film he truly loves him, and has been so transformed by this experience that he volunteers for an AIDS charity and in general is transformed into a nice guy. It's as if the Mormon missionary achieved his goal and converted him, in slightly different terms than he expected.

The $50 bet is a cliché as old as the movies, and of course it always results in the bettor *really* falling in love, while the quarry finds out about the bet and is crushed. One of the sly pleasures of *Latter Days* is the sight of this gay-themed movie recycling so many conventions from straight romantic cinema, as if it's time to catch up.

The film is made with a certain conviction, and the actors deliver more than their roles require; there are times when they seem about to veer off into true and accurate drama (as when Christian encounters a bitter dying man), but by the end, when Davis is back in Pocatello, Idaho, and his homophobic mother (Mary Kay Place) is sending him for shock treatment, we realize the movie could have been (a) a gay love story, or (b) an attack on the Mormon church, but is an awkward fit by trying to be (c) both at the same time.

I also question the character of one of Davis's fellow missionaries, who is outspokenly antigay in a particularly ugly way. Is this character modeled on life, or he is a version of the mustache-twirling villain? And then there's Christian's best friend, Julie (Rebekah Jordan), who of course is a hip and sympathetic African-American woman. You get to the point where you realize everyone in this movie has been ordered off the shelf from the Stock Characters Store, and none of them wandered in from real life.

Is there a way in which the movie works? Yes, it works by delivering on its formula. We sense immediately that Davis and Christian are destined to be lovers, and so we watch patiently as the screenplay fabricates obstacles to their destiny. We identify to some degree with them because—well, because we always tend to identify with likable characters in love stories. Maybe the fact that they're gay will help some homophobic audience members to understand homosexuality a little better, although whether they will attend the movie in the first place is a good question.

What I'm waiting for is a movie in which the characters are gay and that's a given, and they get on with a story involving their lives. Or maybe for a satire in which two heterosexuals move in next to each other and battle their inner natures until finally love tears down the barriers and they kiss, even though one is a boy and the other a girl. That would obviously be silly, and the day will come when a movie like this seems silly, too.

L'Auberge Espagnole ★ ★ ★
R, 122 m., 2003

Romain Duris (Xavier), Cécile De France (Isabelle), Judith Godrèche (Anne-Sophie), Audrey Tautou (Martine), Kelly Reilly (Wendy), Kevin Bishop (William), Federico D'Anna (Alessandro), Christian Pagh (Lars), Cristina Brondo (Soledad), Barnaby Metschurat (Tobias). Directed by Cédric Klapisch and produced by Bruno Levy. Screenplay by Klapisch.

Xavier, a French student worried about his career choices, is advised by a family friend that learning Spanish will be his ticket to success. He signs up for the Erasmus program of the European Community, which arranges student exchanges as a way for the young people of the New Europe to get to know one another by living and studying together for a year.

L'Auberge Espagnole is the story of Xavier's adventures during a year in Barcelona with, if I have this straight, fellow students from Spain, England, Belgium, Germany, Italy, and Denmark. An American wanders through, but makes no impression. Although all of their languages make cameo appearances, English is the common language of choice.

That makes the title all the more puzzling. I saw this movie for the first time at the 2002 Karlovy Vary Film Festival in the Czech Republic, where it won the audience award under the title *Europudding*. It opened in England as *Pot Luck,* in Spain as *Una Casa de Locos,* was announced for North America as *The Spanish Hotel,* and now arrives with the Spanish version of that title. This is not a good omen for the movie's message about the harmony of national cultures.

The movie has Xavier (Romain Duris) say good-bye for a year to his French girlfriend (Audrey Tautou, of *Amelie*) and fly to Spain on an odyssey which he narrates, not very helpfully (much dialogue along the lines of, "My story starts here . . . no, not here, but . . . "). In Barcelona he shares an apartment with six other students plus a revolving roster of lovers, most straight, one gay. Imagine the American students in *The Real Cancun* as if they were literate, cosmopolitan, and not substance abusers, and you've got it.

The subplots edge up to screwball comedy without ever quite reaching it, except in a sequence where a girl is in bed with the wrong boy and her current boyfriend arrives unexpectedly at the apartment. Writer-director Cédric Klapisch uses a three-way split screen to show the roommates racing to head off the boyfriend and provide an alibi, and what they come up with provides the movie's biggest laugh.

The romantic adventures of all of the students provide, not surprisingly, most of the movie's plot. I don't remember a whole lot of discussion about the euro as a currency. Unlike *The Real Cancun,* which was dripping with sex but was subtly homophobic, *L'Auberge Espagnole* is refreshingly frank about its lesbian, the Belgian girl named Isabelle (Cécile De France, who won the César Award as most promising newcomer). Although Xavier fancied himself an adequate lover when he arrived in Spain, he benefits greatly from Isabelle's expert lecture-demonstration about what really turns a woman on.

The movie is as light and frothy as a French comedy, which is what it is, a reminder that Cédric Klapisch also directed *When the Cat's Away* (1996), the lighthearted story of a woman who involves an entire neighborhood in the search for her cat. Klapisch likes a casual tone in which human eccentricity is folded into the story and taken for granted.

For Xavier, the year in the Erasmus program leads to a fundamental change in his career goals; he can't face a lifetime of French bureaucracy after the anarchy of his year of Europudding. Travel broadens the mind, they say, and certainly living for a year or so outside your native land helps you view it as part of the larger world. Depressing to contrast these young people with the cast of *The Real Cancun*, who hardly realize they're in Mexico.

Laurel Canyon ★ ★

R, 103 m., 2003

Frances McDormand (Jane), Christian Bale (Sam), Kate Beckinsale (Alex), Natascha McElhone (Sara), Alessandro Nivola (Ian). Directed by Lisa Cholodenko and produced by Susan A. Stover and Jeffrey Levy-Hinte. Screenplay by Cholodenko.

Frances McDormand's first film was *Blood Simple* (1984), but I really noticed her for the first time in *Mississippi Burning* (1988), standing in that doorway, talking to Gene Hackman, playing a battered redneck wife who had the courage to do the right thing. From that day to this I have been fascinated by whatever it is she does on the screen to create such sympathy with the audience.

Her Marge Gunderson in *Fargo* is one of the most likable characters in movie history. In almost all of her roles, McDormand embodies an immediate, present, physical, functioning, living, breathing person as well as any actor ever has, and she plays radically different roles as easily as she walks.

Laurel Canyon is not a successful movie—it's too stilted and preprogrammed to come alive—but in the center of it McDormand occupies a place for her character and makes that place into a brilliant movie of its own. There is nothing wrong with who she is and what she does, although all around her actors are cracking up in strangely written roles.

She plays Jane, a woman in her forties who has been a successful record producer for a long time—long enough to make enough money to own one house in the hills of Laurel Canyon and another one at the beach, which in terms of Los Angeles real estate prices means that when she goes to the Grammys a lot of people talk to her. A sexual free spirit from her early days, she is currently producing an album with a British rock singer named Ian (Alessandro Nivola), who is twenty years younger and her lover.

Jane has a son about Ian's age named Sam (Christian Bale), who is the product of an early and fleeting liaison. Sam is the opposite of his mother, fleeing hedonism for the rigors of Harvard Medical School, where he has found a fiancée named Alex (Kate Beckinsale). He studies psychiatry, she studies fruit flies, and true to their professions he will grow neurotic while she will buzz around seeing who lands on her.

Sam and Alex drive west; he'll do his residency, she'll continue her studies, and they'll live in the Laurel Canyon house while Jane moves to the beach. Alas, Laurel Canyon is occupied by Jane—and Ian and various members of the band—when they arrive because Jane has given the beach place to an ex-husband who needed a place to live.

Significant close-ups and furtive once-overs within the first few scenes make the rest of the movie fairly inevitable. Ian and Jane, whose relationship is so open you could drive a relationship through it, telepathically agree to include Alex in their embraces. Alex is intrigued by a freedom that she never experienced, shall we say, at Harvard Medical School, while Sam meanwhile meets the sensuous Sara (Natascha McElhone), a colleague at the psychiatric hospital, and soon they are in one of those situations where he gives her a ride home and they get to talking so much that he has to turn the engine off. (That act—turning the key in the ignition—is the often-overlooked first step in most adulteries.)

Sam and Alex are therefore on separate trajectories, and *Laurel Canyon* makes that so clear with intercutting that we uneasily begin to sense the presence of the screenplay. The movie doesn't have the headlong inevitability of *High Art* (1998), by the same writer-director, Lisa Cholodenko. The earlier movie starred Radha Mitchell in a role similar to Alex, as a woman lured away from a safe relationship by the dark temptations of new friends. But *High Art* seemed to *happen,* and *Laurel Canyon* seems to unfold from an obligatory scenario.

Still, there is Frances McDormand, whose character happens and does not unfold, and who is effortlessly convincing as a sexually alluring woman of a certain age. In fact, she's a babe. Of the three principal female characters in the movie—played by McDormand, Beckinsale, and McElhone—it's McDormand whom many wise males (and females) would choose. She promises playful carnal amusement while the others threaten long, sad conversations about their needs.

How McDormand creates her characters I do not understand. This one is the opposite of the mother who worries about her rock-writer son in *Almost Famous*. She begins with a given—her physical presence—but even that seems to transmute through some actor's sorcery. In this movie she's a babe, a seductive, experienced woman who trained in the 1970s and is still a hippie at heart. Now go to the Internet Movie Database and look at the photo that goes with her entry. Who does she look like? A high school teacher chaperoning at the prom. How she does it is a mystery, but she does, reinventing herself, role after role. *Laurel Canyon* is not a success, but McDormand is ascendant.

Lawless Heart ★ ★ ★

R, 102 m., 2003

Bill Nighy (Dan), Tom Hollander (Nick), Douglas Henshall (Tim), Clementine Celarie (Corrine), Stuart Laing (David), Josephine Butler (Leah), Ellie Haddington (Judy), Sukie Smith (Charlie), Dominic Hall (Darren), David Coffey (Stuart). Directed by Tom Hunsinger and Neil Hunter and produced by Martin Pope. Screenplay by Hunsinger and Hunter.

Lawless Heart begins with a funeral, which, like all funerals, assembles people who may not often see one another but have personal connections—old, new, hidden, and potential. The dead man, named Stuart, ran a restaurant on the Isle of Man, off the British coast. To his funeral come Nick, who was his lover; Dan, who was his brother-in-law; and Tim, a childhood friend who has been long absent from the village.

The film opens with the reception after the funeral. We meet the characters and get to know them a little, we think, and we hear the kinds of profundities and resolutions that people utter when reminded of the possibility of their own deaths. The conversation is bright and quick, the people are likable, and at the end of the afternoon they go their various ways.

It's then that the film, written and directed by Tom Hunsinger and Neil Hunter, reveals its own hidden connections. It follows the three men, one after another, in sequences that take place at the same time but change their meaning depending on the point of view, so that the sight of a man crouching out of sight behind a car makes perfect sense, or no sense at all, depending on what you know about why he is doing it.

Nick (Tom Hollander) helped Stuart run the restaurant, and if Stuart had left a will, we learn, he would have left the business to his lover. But he left no will. Stuart's sister Judy therefore inherits the business, but discusses with her husband, Dan (Bill Nighy), the possibility of giving it to Nick anyway.

Nick, meanwhile, discovers that the long-lost friend Tim (Douglas Henshall) is broke and homeless, and lets him stay in the house he shared with Stuart. Tim moves in, drinks too much, and throws a party. The next morning Nick finds a girl named Charlie (Sukie Smith) in his bed, and she wants to know if they had sex. She had sex, all right, but not with the gay Nick—who throws out Tim but begins a friendship with Charlie that leads, to his own amazement, to them having sex after all. Judy discovers this heterosexual excursion by her brother's lover, and takes it as a reason (or an excuse) to keep the restaurant for herself.

Meanwhile, her husband, Dan, follows up on an intriguing conversation he had at the funeral with Corrine (Clementine Celarie), a

Frenchwoman who lives in the town, thinks he is single, and boldly invites him to dinner. Will he accept? The way that he handles himself on the crucial night is true, funny, and ultimately ironic.

These intrigues and others are all interconnected, as we gradually understand. *Lawless Heart* is an exercise in interlocking narratives, in which the same scene means first one thing and then another, the more we know about it. But it isn't simply an exercise; the characters are full-bodied and authentic, capable of surprising themselves, and their dialogue is written with a good ear for how smart people try to be truthful and secretive at the same time.

We discover, for example, that the reason Tim threw his apparently senseless party at Nick's was to create a place to which he could invite Leah (Josephine Butler), whom he met at the funeral. What Tim doesn't know is that his brother David had an unhappy affair with Leah. Tim is in love with Leah himself, or thinks he is, and the outcome of this liaison is one that none of the three could have anticipated.

My description of the plot no doubt makes it sound like a jigsaw puzzle, and yet it's surprising how clear all these relationships become when we're actually seeing and hearing the characters. They're so well drawn, so clear in their needs and fears, that we get drawn into the plot just as we might get drawn into the intrigues of a real village; the movie watches its characters like a nosy neighbor, changing its view as more information surfaces.

The purpose of the movie is perhaps to show us, in a quietly amusing way, that while we travel down our own lifelines, seeing everything from our own points of view, we hardly suspect the secrets of the lives we intersect with. We tend to think people exist when we are with them, but stay on hold the rest of the time. Our lives go forward—but so, *Lawless Heart* reminds us, do theirs.

Laws of Attraction ★ ★

PG-13, 90 m., 2004

Pierce Brosnan (Daniel Rafferty), Julianne Moore (Audrey Woods), Parker Posey (Serena), Michael Sheen (Thorne Jamison), Nora Dunn (Judge Abramovitz), Frances Fisher (Sara Miller). Directed by Peter Howitt and produced by Julie Durk, David T. Friendly, Beau St. Clair, and Marc Turtletaub. Screenplay by Aline Brosh McKenna and Robert Harling.

Opposites attract, it's true, but the problem with the two divorce lawyers in *Laws of Attraction* is that they're not opposites. They're perfectly well suited to each other, recognize that almost immediately, and tumble into bed at least half an hour, maybe an hour, before that's permitted by the movie's formula. Then they annoy us by trying to deny the attraction while the plot spins its wheels, pretending to be about something.

The two attractive people are Daniel Rafferty (Pierce Brosnan) and Audrey Woods (Julianne Moore). Neither one has ever lost a case. Both are, somewhat oddly, still single despite being awesomely attractive. Maybe it's because of all the divorces they see. Audrey blames it on being the plain daughter of a raving beauty (Frances Fisher), but, I don't know about you, I can't picture Julianne Moore as plain. As for Pierce Brosnan, anyone who thinks he needs to be replaced as James Bond is starkers.

As we all know, the formula for this kind of movie requires the two protagonists to hate each other at first sight. Only gradually do they discover they're in love. I recommend *Two Weeks Notice* (2002), with Sandra Bullock and Hugh Grant, as a superior example of the formula. But in *Laws of Attraction,* Brosnan is always more or less in love with Moore, usually more, and so the movie has to resort to wheezy devices to be about anything at all.

It gives him offices, for example, above a grocery in Chinatown. Why? Because Chinatown is a colorful location, although an undefeated divorce lawyer could afford uptown rents. I am reminded of *What a Girl Wants* (2003), in which Amanda Bynes and her mother, Kelly Preston, live in an apartment in Chinatown, again without a single Chinese person saying one word in the movie, simply because you get the colorful location for free.

One colorful location is not enough. Brosnan and Moore find themselves on opposite sides of a divorce case involving a rock star (Michael Sheen) and a dress designer (Parker Posey), who both want possession of a castle in Ireland, which of course requires Brosnan and Moore to jet to Ireland, visit the castle, attend a local fete, participate in Irish jigs, get drunk, and get married. Come to think of it, they were drunk when they went to bed for the first time too. Maybe Brosnan was drunk when he rented the apartment in Chinatown.

Now these two actors are perfectly lovable people, and so we are happy for them, and enjoy watching them and listening to them, but this is a movie, not an audition, and they really deserved more from the director, Peter Howitt, and cowriters Aline Brosh McKenna and Robert Harling, who between them come up with less than one serviceable screenplay.

One of the consequences of a reedy story like this is that you start looking in the corners. I remember that during *What Women Want* (2000), a much better movie starring Mel Gibson, I was gobsmacked by the office for his ad agency, which was the neatest office I had ever seen in a movie. In *Laws of Attraction,* I liked Brosnan's apartment, which is not in Chinatown and so we don't need to know where it is. It looks like a showroom for the Arts and Crafts Movement, with dark wood everywhere. It was a little shadowy, to be sure, but I wonder if even things like the sink and the sofa were made out of wood. Possibly even the sheets. This apartment looks so odd that one of the movie's most implausible moments comes when Moore sees it and says nothing about it. Oh, she was drunk.

The League of Extraordinary Gentlemen ★

PG-13, 110 m., 2003

Sean Connery (Allan Quatermain), Shane West (Tom Sawyer), Stuart Townsend (Dorian Gray), Peta Wilson (Mina Harker), Jason Flemyng (Jekyll and Hyde), Naseeruddin Shah (Captain Nemo), Tony Curran (Rodney Skinner), Richard Roxburgh (M). Directed by Stephen Norrington and produced by Trevor Albert and Don Murphy. Screenplay by James Robinson, based on comic books by Alan Moore and Kevin O'Neill.

The League of Extraordinary Gentlemen assembles a splendid team of heroes to battle a plan for world domination, and then, just when it seems about to become a real corker of an adventure movie, plunges into incomprehensible action, idiotic dialogue, inexplicable motiva-

tions, causes without effects, effects without causes, and general lunacy. What a mess.

And yet it all starts so swimmingly. An emissary from Britain arrives at a private club in Kenya, circa 1899, to invite the legendary adventurer Allan Quatermain (Sean Connery) to assist Her Majesty's Government in averting a world war. Villains have used a tank to break into the Bank of England and have caused great destruction in Germany, and each country is blaming the other. Quatermain at first refuses to help, but becomes annoyed when armored men with automatic rifles invade the club and try to kill everybody. Quatermain and friends are able to dispatch them with some head butting, a few rights to the jaw, and a skewering on an animal horn, and then he goes to London to attend a meeting called by a spy master named—well, he's named M, of course.

Also assembled by M are such fabled figures as Captain Nemo (Naseeruddin Shah), who has retired from piracy; Mina Harker (Peta Wilson), who was involved in that messy Dracula business; Rodney Skinner (Tony Curran), who is the Invisible Man; Dorian Gray (Stuart Townsend), who, Quatermain observes, seems to be missing a picture; Tom Sawyer (Shane West), who works as an agent for the U.S. government; and Dr. Henry Jekyll (Jason Flemyng), whose alter ego is Mr. Hyde.

These team members have skills undreamed of by the authors who created them. We are not too surprised to discover that Mina Harker is an immortal vampire, since she had those puncture wounds in her throat the last time we saw her, but I wonder if Oscar Wilde knew that Dorian Gray was also immortal and cannot die (or be killed!) as long as he doesn't see his portrait; at one point, an enemy operative perforates him with bullets, and he comes up smiling. Robert Louis Stevenson's Mr. Hyde was about the same size as Dr. Jekyll, but here Hyde expands into a creature scarcely smaller than the Hulk and gets his pants from the same tailor, since they expand right along with him while his shirt is torn to shreds. Hyde looks uncannily like the WWF version of Fat Bastard.

Now listen carefully. M informs them that the leaders of Europe are going to meet in Venice, and that the mysterious villains will blow up the city to start a world war. The league must stop them. When is the meeting?

In three days, M says. Impossible to get there in time, Quatermain says, apparently in ignorance of railroads. Nemo volunteers his submarine, the *Nautilus*, which is about ten stories high and as long as an aircraft carrier, and which we soon see cruising the canals of Venice.

It's hard enough for gondolas to negotiate the inner canals of Venice, let alone a sub the size of an ocean liner, but no problem; *The League of Extraordinary Gentlemen* either knows absolutely nothing about Venice, or (more likely) trusts that its audience does not. At one point, the towering *Nautilus* sails under the tiny Bridge of Sighs and only scrapes it a little. In no time at all there is an action scene involving Nemo's newfangled automobile, which races meaninglessly down streets that do not exist, because there are no streets in Venice and you can't go much more than a block before running into a bridge or a canal. Maybe the filmmakers did their research at the Venetian Hotel in Las Vegas, where Sean Connery arrived by gondola for the movie's premiere.

Bombs begin to explode Venice. It is Carnival time, and Piazza San Marco is jammed with merrymakers as the basilica explodes and topples into ruin. Later there is a scene of this same crowd engaged in lighthearted chatter, as if they have not noticed that half of Venice is missing. Dozens of other buildings sink into the lagoon, which does not prevent Quatermain from exalting, "Venice still stands!"

Now back to that speeding car. Its driver, Tom Sawyer, has been sent off on an urgent mission. When he finds something—an underwater bomb, I think, although that would be hard to spot from a speeding car—he's supposed to fire off a flare, after which I don't know what's supposed to happen. As the car hurtles down the nonexistent streets of Venice, enemy operatives stand shoulder-to-shoulder on the rooftops and fire at it with machine guns, leading us to hypothesize an enemy meeting at which the leader says, "Just in case they should arrive by submarine with a fast car, which hasn't been invented yet, I want thousands of men to line the rooftops and fire at it, without hitting anything, of course."

But never mind. The action now moves to the frozen lakes of Mongolia, where the enemy leader (whose identity I would not dream of revealing) has constructed a gigantic factory palace to manufacture robot soldiers, apparently an early model of the clones they were manufacturing in *Attack* of the same. This palace was presumably constructed recently at great expense (it's a bitch getting construction materials through those frozen lakes). And yet it includes vast, neglected, and forgotten rooms.

I don't really mind the movie's lack of believability. Well, I mind a little; to assume audiences will believe cars racing through Venice is as insulting as giving them a gondola chase down the White House lawn. What I do mind is that the movie plays like a big wind came along and blew away the script and they ran down the street after it and grabbed a few pages and shot those. Since Oscar Wilde contributed Dorian Gray to the movie, it may be appropriate to end with his dying words: "Either that wallpaper goes, or I do."

Le Cercle Rouge ★ ★ ★ ★
NO MPAA RATING, 140 m., 2003

Alain Delon (Corey), Gian Maria Volonté (Vogel), Yves Montand (Jansen), André Bourvil (Captain Mattei), François Périer (Santi), Paul Crauchet (The Fence), Pierre Collet (Prison Guard), André Ekyan (Rico). Directed by Jean-Pierre Melville and produced by Robert Dorfmann. Screenplay by Melville.

Gliding almost without speech down the dawn streets of a wet Paris winter, these men in trench coats and fedoras perform a ballet of crime, hoping to win and fearing to die. Some are cops and some are robbers. To smoke for them is as natural as breathing. They use guns, lies, clout, greed, and nerve with the skill of a magician who no longer even thinks about the cards. They share a code of honor that is not about what side of the law they are on, but about how a man must behave to win the respect of those few others who understand the code.

Jean-Pierre Melville watches them with the eye of a concerned god in his 1970 film *Le Cercle Rouge*. His movie involves an escaped prisoner, a diamond heist, a police manhunt, and mob vengeance, but it treats these elements as the magician treats his cards; the cards are insignificant, except as the medium through which he demonstrates his skills.

Melville is a director whose films are little known in America; he began before the French New Wave, died in 1973, worked in genres but had a stylistic elegance that kept his films from being marketed to the traditional genre audiences. His *Bob le Flambeur,* now available on a Criterion DVD, has been remade as *The Good Thief* and inspired elements of the two *Ocean's Eleven* films, but all they borrowed was the plot, and that was the least essential thing about it.

Melville grew up living and breathing movies, and his films show more experience of the screen than of life. No real crooks or cops are this attentive to the details of their style and behavior. Little wonder that his great 1967 film about a professional hit man is named *Le Samourai;* his characters, like the samurai, place greater importance on correct behavior than upon success. (Jim Jarmusch's *Ghost Dog* owes something to this value system.)

Le Cercle Rouge, or *The Red Circle* (restored for 2003 release by his admirer John Woo), refers to a saying of the Buddha that men who are destined to meet will eventually meet, no matter what. Melville made up this saying, but no matter; his characters operate according to theories of behavior, so that a government minister believes all men, without exception, are bad; and a crooked nightclub owner refuses to be a police informer because it is simply not in his nature to inform.

The movie stars two of the top French stars of the time, Alain Delon and Yves Montand, as well as Gian Maria Volonté, looking younger here than in the spaghetti Westerns, and with hair. But it is not a star vehicle—or, wait, it is a star vehicle, but the stars ride in it instead of the movie riding on them. All of the actors seem directed to be cool and dispassionate, to guard their feelings, to keep their words to themselves, to realize that among men of experience almost everything can go without saying.

As the film opens, we meet Corey (Delon) as he is released from prison. He has learned of a way to hold up one of the jewelry stores of Place Vendôme. Then we meet Vogel (Volonté),

who is a handcuffed prisoner on a train, but he picks the locks of the cuffs, breaks a window, leaps from the moving train, and escapes from the veteran cop Mattei (André Bourvil).

Fate brings Vogel and Corey together. On the run in the countryside, Vogel hides in the trunk of Corey's car. Corey sees him do this, but we don't know he does. He drives into a muddy field, gets out of his car, stands away from it, and tells the man in the trunk he can get out. The man does, holding a gun that Corey must have known he would find in the trunk. They regard each other, face to face in the muddy field. Vogel wants a smoke. Corey throws him a pack and a lighter.

Notice how little they actually say before Corey says, "Paris is your best chance," and Vogel gets back in the trunk. And then notice the precision and economy of what happens next. Corey's car is being tailed by gunmen for a mob boss he relieved of a lot of money. It was probably due him, but still, that is no way to treat a mob boss. Corey pulls over. The gunsels tell him to walk toward the woods. He does. Then we hear Vogel tell them to drop their guns and raise their hands. Vogel picks up each man's gun with a handkerchief and uses it to shoot the other man—so the fingerprints will indicate they shot each other. Corey risked his life on the expectation that Vogel would know what to do and do it, and Corey was right.

There is one cool, understated scene after another. Note the way the police commissioner talks to the nightclub owner after he knows that the owner's son, picked up in an attempt to pressure the owner, has killed himself. Note what he says and what he doesn't say, and how he looks. And note, too, how Jansen, the Yves Montand character, comes into the plot, and think for a moment about why he doesn't want his share of the loot.

The heist itself is performed with the exactness we expect of a movie heist. We are a little startled to realize it is not the point of the film. In most heist movies, the screenplay cannot think beyond the heist, and is satisfied merely to deliver it. *Le Cercle Rouge* assumes that the crooks will be skillful at the heist because they are good workmen. The movie is not about their jobs but about their natures.

Melville fought for the French Resistance during the war. Manohla Dargis of the *Los Angeles Times,* in a review of uncanny and poetic perception, writes: "It may sound far-fetched, but I wonder if his obsessive return to the same themes didn't have something to do with a desire to restore France's own lost honor." The heroes of his films may win or lose, may be crooks or cops, but they are not rats.

Le Divorce ★ ★ ★
PG-13, 115 m., 2003

Kate Hudson (Isabel Walker), Naomi Watts (Roxeanne de Persand), Leslie Caron (Suzanne de Persand), Stockard Channing (Margeeve Walker), Glenn Close (Olivia Pace), Sam Waterston (Chester Walker), Bebe Neuwirth (Julia Manchevering), Matthew Modine (Tellman), Thierry Lhermitte (Edgar Cosset), Stephen Fry (Piers Janely), Melvil Poupaud (Charles-Henri de Persand). Directed by James Ivory and produced by Ismail Merchant and Michael Schiffer. Screenplay by Ruth Prawer Jhabvala and Ivory, based on the novel by Diane Johnson.

Le Divorce, which is about contrary French and American standards for marriage, adultery, divorce, and affairs, finds that the two nations are simply incompatible. While there are too many characters in too much story for the movie to really involve us, it's amusing as a series of sketches about how the French they are a funny race (or the Americans, take your choice). I am reminded of the British writer Peter Noble, who said everything he knew about France could be summed up in this story: "An English guy walks into a café in Cannes and asks if they have a men's room. The waiter replies: 'Monsieur! I have only two hands!' "

The movie stars Naomi Watts as Roxeanne, a pregnant American whose faithless French husband, Charles-Henri de Persand (Melvil Poupaud), has walked out on her because of his obsession with a married Russian woman named Magda. Roxeanne's sister Isabel (Kate Hudson) flies to Paris to support her sister, and soon promotes an affair for herself with Edgar (Thierry Lhermitte), the brother of Roxeanne's mother-in-law. Meanwhile, Magda's American husband (Matthew Modine) becomes a stalker, threatening Roxeanne. Doesn't he understand that it was her *husband* who stole away his wife?

Roxeanne's husband begs for a divorce. "She must understand," her husband patiently explains to Isabel, "that I have met the love of my life." He sees himself as the wronged party. Meanwhile, Edgar moves swiftly on his first lunch date with Isabel, explaining that the only question before them is whether she will become his mistress. What … ah … what exactly would that involve, Isabel asks, in a moment that reminds us that Kate Hudson is Goldie Hawn's daughter and has that same eyelid-batting trick of seeming naive and insinuating at the same time. Edgar explains that they would amuse each other: "I find you entertaining, and I hope you find me entertaining." Isabel says she wouldn't want their families to know. "Frankly," he says, "it would never occur to me to tell them."

The movie is based on a best-selling novel by Diane Johnson, and has been directed by James Ivory and produced by Ismail Merchant, working with their usual screenwriter, Ruth Prawer Jhabvala. The Merchant-Ivory firm are masters of movies about manners, and have fun with the rules by which Edgar conducts his affairs. A new conquest is immediately given a Kelly bag; that's a $6,000-and-up purse from Hermés, of the sort Grace Kelly always carried. Glenn Close, who plays an expatriate American writer in Paris, was a lover of Edgar's years ago, we learn, and observes that his affairs always begin with the bag and end with the gift of a scarf.

What is remarkable is that Suzanne de Persand (Leslie Caron), Edgar's sister, immediately finds out about the affair, and soon so does his wife. Caron makes a bracing analysis of the situation: It is bad enough that her son has behaved foolishly by allowing such a troublesome emotion as love to cause disrepair to his marriage, but for Isabel to fall for Edgar's tired routine is unforgivable, especially at a time like this. The Americans, she observes, have no idea how to conduct affairs, and do not realize they are intended to be temporary. When one ends, they get all serious and tragic. Even Edgar has his doubts, telling Isabel, "If you are keeping a diary, I hope your style will meet the expectations of the French public." And then, fearing the feckless American will not understand the Gallic sense of humor: "You're not, are you?"

The movie is so heavy on story that no character fully engages our sympathy—although some don't take long to make us dislike them. There's a subplot involving a painting that belongs to Isabel and Roxeanne's family, and which the faithless husband, incredibly, believes is half his. That leads to an amusing excursion into art values, with an expert from the Louvre pronouncing the painting inferior, and an expert from Christie's insisting it is by the master Georges de la Tour. The Christie's man is played by Stephen Fry, tall, cheery, and plummy, who explains why museums undervalue paintings and auction houses overvalue them. It's entertaining, but is it on topic?

I could have done without Matthew Modine's jealous husband, a dizzy basket case who generates a contrived and unnecessary scene atop the Eiffel Tower. But Stockard Channing is wonderful as the mother of the American girls. As sophisticated in her American way as the Leslie Caron character, she takes the wind out of French sails with her no-B.S. California style. I admire those who speak French whether or not they can, as when she orders in a restaurant: "Could I just get like a steak poivre and a salad vert, trés well?"

Le Divorce doesn't work on its intended level because we don't care enough about the interactions of the enormous cast. But it works in another way, as a sophisticated and knowledgeable portrait of values in collision. If you are familiar with France and have a love-hate affair with that most cryptic of nations, you are likely to enjoy the movie from moment to moment, whether or not it adds up for you.

Legally Blonde 2: Red, White and Blonde ★ ★

PG-13, 105 m., 2003

Reese Witherspoon (Elle Woods), Sally Field (Representative Victoria Rudd), Bob Newhart (Sidney Post), Luke Wilson (Emmett Richmond), Jennifer Coolidge (Paulette Bonafonte), Regina King (Grace Stoteraux), Jessica Cauffiel (Margot), Alanna Ubach (Serena McGuire), Bruce McGill (Stanford Marks). Directed by Charles Herman-Wurmfeld and produced by David Nicksay and Marc Platt. Screenplay by Kate Kondell.

Legally Blonde 2: Red, White and Blonde evokes a fairy-tale America in which a congresswoman's ditzy blonde junior staff member, pretty in pink, is asked to address a joint session of Congress and sways them with her appeal for animal rights. Not in this world. It might happen, though, in the world of the movie—but even then, her big speech is so truly idiotic she'd be laughed out of town. That the movie considers this speech a triumph shows how little it cares about its "ideas." The model for the movie is obviously *Mr. Smith Goes to Washington*, but in that one James Stewart's big speech was actually sort of about something.

The movie chronicles the continuing adventures of Elle Woods, the Reese Witherspoon character introduced in the winning *Legally Blonde* (2001). Elle, for whom pink is not a favorite color but a lifestyle choice, is like a walking, talking beauty and cosmetics magazine, whose obsession with superficial girly things causes people, understandably, to dismiss her at first sight. Ah, but beneath the Jackie Kennedy pillbox hat there lurks a first-class brain; Elle is a Harvard Law graduate who, as the sequel opens, has a job in a top legal firm.

It's impossible to determine if Elle knows what she's doing—if it's all a strategy—or whether she truly is *über*-ditzy. Always smiling, never discouraged, deaf to insults, blind to sneers, dressed in outfits that come from a fashion universe of their own, she sails through life like the good ship *Undefeatable*. How she stumbles upon the cause of animal rights is instructive. It begins with her search for the biological birth parent of Bruiser, her beloved Chihuahua. When she finds the mother captive in an animal testing laboratory ("We test makeup on animals so you don't have to"), she becomes an animal rights advocate, is fired from her law firm, and finds herself on the staff of Representative Victoria Rudd (Sally Field), who is sponsoring an animal-rights bill.

The movie's vision of Congress is hopelessly simplistic and idealistic. Characters have the same kinds of instant conversions that are standard on sitcoms, where the unenlightened oppose something, have a sudden epiphany, and then see the light. Consider the character of Stan, a self-described Southern conservative who discovers, along with Elle, that both their dogs are gay and have fallen in love with each other. This softens him up on the pending legislation because he loves his gay dog, you see.

The movie has its share of funny lines ("This is just like C-SPAN except it's not boring") and moments (congressional interns form a pompom squad), but the plot developments in Congresswoman Rudd's office are heavy-handed. Rudd's top aide (Regina King) is cold and antagonistic to Elle when the plot needs her to be and then turns on a dime. Rudd herself admits to dropping her bill in return for big campaign contributions. And Elle's top adviser is a hotel doorman (Bob Newhart) who knows how Washington works because of what he overhears. Uh-huh. Meanwhile, back home in Boston, Elle's fiancé (Luke Wilson) is incredibly understanding when his marriage is put on hold during Elle's legislative campaign. There could be a whole comedy just about being engaged or married to the creature in pink.

Ramping up for this review, I came across a curious column by Arianna Huffington, who attended a preview screening and wrote, "Sitting between my teenage daughters while watching Elle take on the U.S. Congress, I was struck by the palpable effect it had on them: They left the theater inspired, empowered, and talking about the things they wanted to change and the ways they might be able to change them." She quotes approvingly from Elle's big speech: "So speak up, America. Speak up for the home of the brave. Speak up for the land of the free gift with purchase. Speak up, America!"

Amazing, that the usually tough-minded Huffington fell for the movie. Amazing, too, that two teenage girls who have their own mother as a role model were inspired and empowered by the insipid Elle. I have a movie for them to see together: *Whale Rider*. Now there's a great movie about female empowerment, and the heroine doesn't even wear makeup.

America will no doubt speak up, alas, by spending millions of dollars on *Legally Blonde 2* in obedience to the movie's advertising blitz (buses in several cities have been painted entirely pink). And so the myth of a populist Congress will live on, entirely apart from the real world of lobbyists, logrolling, punishment to the disloyal, and favors for friends. In the real world, Elle Woods would be chewed up faster than one of little Bruiser's Milk-Bones.

Les Destinées ★ ★ ★ ½
NO MPAA RATING, 180 m., 2002

Emmanuelle Béart (Pauline), Charles Berling (Jean Barnery), Isabelle Huppert (Nathalie), Mathieu Genet (Max Barnery), Rémi Martin (Dahlias). Directed by Oliver Assayas and produced by Bruno Pésery. Screenplay by Jacques Fieschi and Assayas, based on the novel by Jacques Chardonne. In French with English subtitles.

Les Destinées is a long, attentive epic about the span of a life and the seasons of a love. It will not appeal to the impatient, but those who like long books and movies will admire the way it accumulates power and depth. It is about youthful idealism, headstrong love, and fierce ambition, and is pessimistic about all of them. At the end, its hero, who has accomplished a great deal and always tried to do his duty, can only say, "Everything I've done is worthless. I was always wrong."

He's wrong about that, too. The film follows Jean Barnery (Charles Berling), born into a porcelain-manufacturing family in the Limoges region of France. The ruling families here make china and cognac, laying down their stocks, treasuring their vintages, transferring power in an orderly way from one generation to the next.

Jean steps outside the mold. He leaves the family business and becomes a Protestant minister, filled with conviction. When he learns that his wife, Nathalie (Isabelle Huppert), may have had affection for another, he divorces her. She is probably innocent (certainly of any physical adultery), but he has read a compromising letter and there is no room in his heart for forgiveness. So concerned is he to appear just in the eyes of the world, however, that he signs over the bulk of his fortune to Nathalie and their daughter, Aline.

In the congregation one day is Pauline (Emmanuelle Béart), just returned from study in England. She loves this stiff and proper man with an inexplicable passion, and soon they have married. He leaves the church. He grows ill, and they move to a chalet in Switzerland for his health, and there they are happy, living a simple life, alone with each other.

Then Jean's father dies, and he is summoned home to take over the firm from his brother, who is incapable of running it. Jean gets the necessary takeover votes from—Nathalie, who continues to think of herself as his wife. Pauline is against the move back to the factory: "This is the end of our love." Not really, but the end of the sweet and uncomplicated part of it, because now their love must survive in the real world.

The film by Oliver Assayas, written by Jacques Fieschi from a novel by Jacques Chardonne, assumes a French audience as familiar with the traditions and politics of fine porcelain and cognac as we are with the Detroit auto dynasties. At three hours, the film is long enough to show us how the factory works, and how the laborers, underpaid, are skilled craftsmen alert to the slightest nuance of tone and texture. Jean becomes an artist, driven by his search for colors he likens to the face of the moon, or to seawater, and he is unable to compromise quality even as he pushes for a modern factory.

The film covers more than thirty years, enough to show us how people change and marriages must change to accommodate them. One of the most startling scenes comes when Jean volunteers for the First World War, and Pauline, visiting him near the front, finds him a crude, rough man, shoveling food into his mouth, made gross by the hard life of the trenches. Later he returns, slowly, to civilization, and even to tenderness, symbolized by a sunny afternoon in their orchard that both remember as a blessed moment.

Social currents thrust into the complacency of the Barnery family. It faces strikes, Marxist organizers, competition from cheap German goods. The film is remarkable in the way it gains epic sweep without ever descending into the merely picturesque. These are always people living in a real world—except for one scene, toward the beginning, where Pauline stars at a formal dance, her head turning left and then right as she sweeps through the room. Emmanuelle Béart, always beautiful, has never looked more radiant, and Jean Barnery agrees.

As long as the film is, there are loose ends. In the dance scene, for example, Pauline is approached by Dahlias (Rémi Martin), an ugly-handsome man who inspires much gossip. He is attracted to her, stands too close, speaks with too much familiarity, violates her space, creates a threat, excites our interest. And then disappears from the movie. There is also the sense of something missing in the transition of the daughter, Aline, from an adolescent who is scandalously "seen everywhere" to a young woman who takes the vows of a deaconess and walls herself from the world.

But nothing is missing in the central relationship. Jean lives according to his driven inner codes, and Pauline, who loves him, cannot make him happier. But she is able to bring him a perfect example of his new design of china and spread it on the counterpane of his deathbed. Their marriage is not perfect, but it endures and stands for something. This is not a movie about episodes but about the remorseless bookkeeping of life, which sends such large payments so early, and collects so much interest at the end.

Levity ★ ½
R, 100 m., 2003

Billy Bob Thornton (Manuel Jordan), Morgan Freeman (Miles Evans), Holly Hunter (Adele Easley), Kirsten Dunst (Sofia Mellinger), Manuel Aranguiz (Señor Aguilar), Geoffrey Wigdor (Abner Easley), Luke Robertson (Young Abner Easley), Dorian Harewood (Mackie Whittaker). Directed by Ed Solomon and produced by Richard N. Gladstein, Adam Merims, and Solomon. Screenplay by Solomon.

Levity is an earnest but hopeless attempt to tell a parable about a man's search for redemption. By the end of his journey, we don't care if he finds redemption, if only he finds wakefulness. He's a whiny slug who talks like a victim of overmedication. I was reminded of the Bob and Ray routine about the Slow Talkers of America.

That this unfortunate creature is played by Billy Bob Thornton is evidence, I think, that we have to look beyond the actors in placing blame. His costars are Morgan Freeman, Holly Hunter, and Kirsten Dunst. For a director to assemble such a cast and then maroon them in such a witless enterprise gives him more to redeem than his hero. The hero has merely killed a fictional character. Ed Solomon, who wrote and directed, has stolen two hours from the lives of everyone who sees the film, and weeks from the careers of these valuable actors.

The movie stars Thornton as Manuel Jordan, a man recently released from custody after serving twenty-two years of a sentence for murder. That his first name reminds us of Emmanuel and his surname echoes the Jordan River is not, I fear, an accident; he is a Christ figure, and Thornton has gotten into the spirit with long hair that looks copied from a bad holy card. The only twist is that instead of dying for our sins, the hero shot a young convenience store clerk—who died, I guess, for Manuel's sins.

Now Manuel returns to the same district where the killing took place. This is one of those movie neighborhoods where all the characters live close to one another and meet whenever necessary. Manual soon encounters Adele Easley (Holly Hunter), the sister of the boy he killed. They become friendly and the possibility of romance looms, although he hesitates to confess his crime. She has a teenage son (Geoffrey Wigdor), named Abner after her late brother.

In this district a preacher named Miles Evans (Freeman) runs a storefront youth center, portrayed so unconvincingly that we suspect Solomon has never seen a store, a front, a youth, or a center. In this room, which looks ever so much like a stage set, an ill-assorted assembly of disadvantaged youths are arrayed about the room in such studied "casual" attitudes that we are reminded of extras told to keep their places. Preacher Evans intermittently harangues them with apocalyptic rantings, which they attend patiently. Into the center walks Sofia Mellinger (Dunst), a lost girl who is tempted by drugs and late-night raves, who wanders this neighborhood with curious impunity.

We know that sooner or later Manuel will have to inform Adele that he murdered her brother. But meanwhile the current Abner has fallen in with bad companions, and a silly grudge threatens to escalate into murder. This generates a scene of amazing coincidence, during which in a lonely alley late at night, all of the

necessary characters coincidentally appear as they are needed, right on cue, for fraught action and dialogue that the actors must have studied for sad, painful hours, while keeping their thoughts to themselves.

Whether Manuel finds forgiveness, whether Sofia finds herself, whether Abner is saved, whether the preacher has a secret, whether Adele can forgive, whether Manuel finds a new mission in life, and whether the youths ever tire of sermons, I will leave to your speculation. All I can observe is that there is not a moment of authentic observation in the film; the director has assembled his characters out of stock melodrama. A bad Victorian novelist would find nothing to surprise him here, and a good one nothing to interest him. When this film premiered to thunderous silence at Sundance 2003, Solomon said he had been working on the screenplay for twenty years. Not long enough.

The Life of David Gale no stars
R, 130 m., 2003

Kevin Spacey (Dr. David Gale), Kate Winslet (Elizabeth [Bitsey] Bloom), Laura Linney (Constance Harraway), Gabriel Mann (Zack), Matt Craven (Dusty), Rhona Mitra (Berlin), Leon Rippy (Braxton Belyeu). Directed by Alan Parker and produced by Nicolas Cage and Parker. Screenplay by Charles Randolph.

The Life of David Gale tells the story of a famous opponent of capital punishment, who, in what he must find an absurdly ironic development, finds himself on Death Row in Texas, charged with the murder of a woman who was also opposed to capital punishment. This is a plot, if ever there was one, to illustrate King Lear's complaint, "As flies to wanton boys, are we to the gods; They kill us for their sport." I am aware this is the second time in two weeks I have been compelled to quote Lear, but there are times when Eminem simply will not do.

David Gale is an understandably bitter man, played by Kevin Spacey, who protests his innocence to a reporter named Bitsey Bloom (Kate Winslet), whom he has summoned to Texas for that purpose. He claims to have been framed by right-wing supporters of capital punishment, because his death would provide such poetic irony in support of the noose, the gas, or the chair. Far from killing Constance Harraway (Laura Linney), he says, he had every reason not to, and he explains that to Bitsey in flashbacks that make up about half of the story.

Bitsey becomes convinced of David's innocence. She is joined in her investigation by the eager and sexy intern Zack (Gabriel Mann), and they become aware that they are being followed everywhere in a pickup truck by a gaunt-faced fellow in a cowboy hat, who is either a right-wing death penalty supporter who really killed the dead woman, or somebody else. If he is somebody else, then he is obviously following them around with the MacGuffin, in this case a videotape suggesting disturbing aspects of the death of Constance.

The man in the cowboy hat illustrates my recently renamed Principle of the Unassigned Character, formerly known less elegantly as the Law of Economy of Character Development. This principle teaches us that any prominent character who seems to be extraneous to the action will probably hold the key to it. The cowboy lives in one of those tumbledown shacks filled with flies and peanut butter, with old calendars on the walls. The yard has more bedsprings than the house has beds.

The acting in *The Life of David Gale* is splendidly done, but serves a meretricious cause. The direction is by the British director Alan Parker, who at one point had never made a movie I wholly disapproved of. Now has he ever. The secrets of the plot must remain unrevealed by me, so that you can be offended by them yourself, but let it be said this movie is about as corrupt, intellectually bankrupt, and morally dishonest as it could possibly be without David Gale actually hiring himself out as a joker at the court of Saddam Hussein.

I am sure the filmmakers believe their film is against the death penalty. I believe it supports it and hopes to discredit the opponents of the penalty as unprincipled fraudsters. What I do not understand is the final revelation on the videotape. Surely David Gale knows that Bitsey Bloom cannot keep it private without violating the ethics of journalism and sacrificing the biggest story of her career. So it serves no functional purpose except to give a cheap thrill to the audience slackjaws. It is shameful.

One of the things that annoys me is that the story is set in Texas and not just in any old state—a state like Arkansas, for example, where the 1996 documentary *Paradise Lost: The Child Murders at Robin Hood Hills* convincingly explains why three innocent kids are in prison because they wore black and listened to heavy metal, while the likely killer keeps pushing himself on-screen and wildly signaling his guilt. Nor is it set in my own state of Illinois, where Death Row was run so shabbily that Governor George Ryan finally threw up his hands and declared the whole system rotten.

No, the movie is set in Texas, which in a good year all by itself carries out half the executions in America. Death Row in Texas is like the Roach Motel: Roach checks in, doesn't check out. When George W. Bush was Texas governor, he claimed to carefully consider each and every execution, although a study of his office calendar shows he budgeted fifteen minutes per condemned man (we cannot guess how many of these minutes were devoted to pouring himself a cup of coffee before settling down to the job). Still, when you're killing someone every other week and there's an average of 400 more waiting their turn, you have to move right along.

Spacey and Parker are honorable men. Why did they go to Texas and make this silly movie? The last shot made me want to throw something at the screen—maybe Spacey and Parker.

You can make movies that support capital punishment *(The Executioner's Song)* or oppose it *(Dead Man Walking)* or are conflicted *(In Cold Blood)*. But while Texas continues to warehouse condemned men with a system involving lawyers who are drunk, asleep, or absent; confessions that are beaten out of the helpless; and juries who overwhelmingly prefer to execute black defendants instead of white ones, you can't make this movie. Not in Texas.

Life or Something Like It ★
PG-13, 104 m., 2002

Angelina Jolie (Lanie Kerigan), Stockard Channing (Deborah Connors), Edward Burns (Pete), Melissa Errico (Andrea), Tony Shalhoub (Prophet Jack), Christian Kane (Cal Cooper), Gregory Itzin (Dennis), Lisa Thornhill (Gwen).

Directed by Stephen Herek and produced by Kenneth Atchity, John Davis, Toby Jaffe, Arnon Milchan, and Chi-Li Wong. Screenplay by John Scott Shepherd and Dana Stevens.

Someone once said, live every day as if it will be your last.

Not just someone once said that. Everyone once said it, over and over again, although *Life or Something Like It* thinks it's a fresh insight. This is an ungainly movie, ill-fitting, with its elbows sticking out where the knees should be. To quote another ancient proverb, "A camel is a horse designed by a committee." *Life or Something Like It* is the movie designed by the camel.

The movie stars Angelina Jolie as Lanie Kerigan, a bubbly blond Seattle TV reporter whose ignorance of TV is equaled only by the movie's. I don't know how the filmmakers got their start, but they obviously didn't come up through television. Even a *viewer* knows more than this.

Example. Sexy Pete the cameraman (Edward Burns) wants to play a trick on Lanie, so he fiddles with her microphone during a stand-up report from the street, and her voice comes out like Mickey Mouse's squeak—like when you talk with helium in your mouth. Everybody laughs at her. Except, see, your voice comes out of your *body,* and when it goes through the air it sounds like your voice to the people standing around. When it goes into the microphone, it kind of *stays* inside there, and is recorded on videotape, which is not simultaneously played back live to a street crowd.

Lanie dreams of going to New York to work on *AM USA,* the network show. She gets her big invitation after attracting "national attention" by covering a strike and leading the workers in singing "Can't Get No Satisfaction" while she dances in front of them, during a tiny lapse in journalistic objectivity. Meanwhile, she is afraid she will die, because a mad street person named Prophet Jack has predicted the Seattle Mariners will win, there will be a hailstorm tomorrow morning, and Lanie will die next Thursday. They win, it hails, Lanie believes she will die.

This leads to a romantic crisis. She is engaged to Cal Cooper (Christian Kane), a pitcher with the Mariners. He's on the mound, he looks lovingly at her, she smiles encourag-

ingly, he throws a pitch, the batter hits a home run, and she jumps up and applauds. If he sees that, she may not last until Thursday. Meanwhile, she apparently hates Pete the sexy cameraman, although when Cal is out of town and she thinks she's going to die, they make love, and *then* we find out, belatedly, they've made love before. The screenplay keeps doubling back to add overlooked info.

Cal comes back to town and she wants a heart-to-heart, but instead he takes her to the ballpark, where the friendly groundskeeper (who hangs around all night in every baseball movie for just such an opportunity) turns on the lights so Cal can throw her a few pitches. Is she moved by this loving gesture? Nope: "Your cure for my emotional crisis is batting practice?" This is the only turning-on-the-lights-in-the-empty-ballpark scene in history that ends unhappily.

Lanie and Pete the sexy cameraman become lovers, until Pete whipsaws overnight into an insulted, wounded man who is hurt because she wants to go to New York instead of stay in Seattle with him and his young son. This about-face exists *only* so they can break up so they can get back together again later. It also inspires a scene in the station's equipment room, where Jolie tests the theoretical limits of hysterical overacting.

Lanie's *AM USA* debut involves interviewing the network's biggest star, a Barbara Walters type (Stockard Channing), on the star's twenty-fifth anniversary. So earthshaking is this interview, the *AM USA* anchor breathlessly announces, "We welcome our viewers on the West Coast for this special live edition!" It's 7 A.M. in New York. That makes it 4 A.M. on the West Coast. If you lived in Seattle, would you set your alarm to 4 A.M. to see Barbara Walters plugging her network special?

Lanie begins the interview, pauses, and is silent for thirty seconds while deeply thinking. She finally asks, "Was it worth everything?" What? "Giving up marriage and children for a career?" Tears roll down Channing's cheeks. Pandemonium. Great interview. Network president wants to hire Lanie on the spot. Has never before heard anyone ask, "Was it worth it?" The question of whether a woman can have both a career and a family is controversial in *Life or Something Like It*—even when posed by Ms. Jolie, who successfully combines tomb-raiding with Billy Bob Thornton.

I want to close with the mystery of Lanie's father, who is always found stationed in an easy chair in his living room, where he receives visits from his daughters, who feel guilty because since Mom died they have not been able to communicate with Dad, who, apparently as a result, just sits there waiting for his daughters to come back and feel guilty some more. Eventually there's an uptick in his mood, and he admits he has always been proud of Lanie and will "call in sick" so he can watch Lanie on *AM USA*. Until then I thought he *was* sick. Maybe he's just tired because he's on the night shift, which is why he would be at work at 4 A.M.

Like Mike ★ ★ ★
PG, 100 m., 2002

Lil' Bow Wow (Calvin Cambridge), Morris Chestnut (Tracey Reynolds), Jonathan Lipnicki (Murph), Jesse Plemons (Ox), Robert Forster (Coach Wagner), Crispin Glover (Stan Bittleman), Anne Meara (Sister Theresa), Eugene Levy (Frank Bernard). Directed by John Schultz and produced by Peter Heller and Barry Josephson. Screenplay by Michael Elliot and Jordan Moffet.

Kids can't be Michael Jordan, but they can wear his basketball shoes, and in their fantasies the shoes give them the power to be like Mike. Sports shoes are one of the most powerful totems in kid society, in part because of M. J.'s TV ads, and *Like Mike* is not merely a good idea for a movie, but an inevitable one.

Lil' Bow Wow (whose name should properly be spelled Li'l' Bow Wow, but never mind) stars as Calvin Cambridge, an orphan who comes into possession of a pair of faded Nikes with the initials "MJ" written inside the tongue. We might doubt that Michael Jordan writes his initials in his shoes (and if he does, he probably has someone to do it for him), but Calvin has no doubts, not even when the shoes are a perfect fit, which seems unlikely.

He lives in an orphanage that seems to be running as a profitable scam. His best buddy is Murph (Jonathan Lipnicki) and his worst enemy is Ox (Jesse Plemons). Ox throws the shoes so they hang by their laces from a power line, Calvin climbs up a tree in a storm to re-trieve them, lightning strikes, and somehow the shoes and the lightning magically combine to make him like Mike.

Really like Mike. The kind coach of the local NBA team (Robert Forster) gives him some tickets to a game, he ends up in a half-time shooting contest with an NBA star, and, wearing the shoes, outshoots the star so dramatically that the team owner signs him up—as a gimmick, of course, although Calvin is soon in the starting lineup and leading his team to the finals. Wearing the magic shoes, he makes Air Jordan look like a puddle-jumper.

Lil' Bow Wow is responsible for a lot of the movie's success. He is confident and relaxed on the screen, engaging, and has good moves on the basketball court. In a role that could have been deadly with the wrong kind of kid actor, he's the right kind, a no-nonsense professional who wisely plays the fantasy as if it were real.

A lot of the surrounding plot is recycled from other movies, of course, including the playground bully, the tried-and-true orphanage situations (the kids are like puppies hoping for new owners), and the last-minute cliffhanging plays of the big games. But the movie overcomes its lack of originality in the setup by making good use of its central idea, that a pair of shoes could make a kid into an NBA star. This is a message a lot of kids have been waiting to hear.

Lilo & Stitch ★ ★ ★ ½
PG, 85 m., 2002

With the voices of: Daveigh Chase (Lilo), Chris Sanders (Stitch) Jason Scott Lee (David Kawena), Tia Carrere (Nani), Kevin McDonald (Pleakley), Ving Rhames (Cobra Bubbles), David Ogden Stiers (Jumba). Directed by Chris Sanders and Dean Deblois and produced by Clark Spencer. Screenplay by Sanders and Deblois.

Only a week ago I deplored the wretched *Scooby-Doo* as a blight on the nation's theaters. My fellow critics agreed. Checking the Websites that monitor reviews, I find that at RottenTomatoes.com the movie scored a 26, at Metacritic.com a 27. Passing grade is 60. The American public effortlessly shrugged off this warning cry and raced to the box office to throw away $57 million.

Now here comes a truly inspired animated feature named *Lilo & Stitch*. How will it do? It's one of the most charming feature-length cartoons of recent years, funny, sassy, startling, original, and with six songs by Elvis. It doesn't get sickeningly sweet at the end, it has as much stuff in it for grown-ups as for kids, and it has a bright offbeat look to it.

If *Scooby-Doo* grossed $57 million in its first weekend, then if there is justice in the world, *Lilo & Stitch* will gross $200 million. But there is not justice. There is a herd instinct. On Monday a man on an elevator asked me what I thought about *Scooby-Doo*. I said it was a very bad movie. "My kids want to see it," he said. Yes, I said, because they've heard of nothing else all week. But, I said, there is a *much better* animated family film opening this weekend, named *Lilo & Stitch*, that your kids are sure to like much more than *Scooby-Doo*, and you will enjoy it too. Take my word, I said; I do this for a living. Take the kids to *Lilo & Stitch*.

I could see from the man's eyes that he was rejecting my advice. How could I possibly be right when $57 million said I was wrong? How could human taste be a better barometer of movie quality than the success of a marketing campaign? Prediction: This weekend, more parents and their children will dutifully file into the idiotic wasteland of *Scooby-Doo* than will see the inspired delights of *Lilo & Stitch*.

That will be a shame. *Lilo & Stitch*, produced by the same Disney team that made *Mulan*, is a toothy fantasy about an alien monster that accidentally finds itself adopted as the pet of a little girl in Hawaii. The creature, named Stitch (voice by Chris Sanders), was produced by an illegal genetic mutation, and is so horrifyingly hostile that it's been locked up by its inventors. It escapes to Earth, is mistaken for a very strange dog, and adopted by Lilo (voice by Daveigh Chase), who essentially uses her innocence and the aloha spirit to confuse and even civilize the creature.

This all takes place against a cheerful background of pop-culture references, including scenes spoofing *Men in Black, Jaws,* and *Godzilla* (with Stitch first building a model of San Francisco, then destroying it). And the film firmly positions itself in Hawaii—both the Hawaii of tourist kitsch, and the Hawaii of the aloha spirit. The plot revolves around concepts of "ohana,"

or family, since Lilo is being raised by her big sister Nani (voice by Tia Carrere), who is disorganized and not always a perfect substitute mom, and is up against a disapproving social worker named Cobra Bubbles (voice by Ving Rhames).

Nani works as a waitress in one of those "traditional" Hawaiian musical revues, where her boyfriend, David Kawena (Jason Scott Lee), is a fire dancer. Lilo takes Stitch to the show, and Stitch is much confused, especially after David sets the stage on fire, but even more confusing episodes are ahead, as the little girl teaches her alien pal how to be an Elvis imitator.

Lilo and Stitch, of course, have trouble communicating, since Lilo is very young and Stitch speaks no English, but the alien, who is a quick study, picks up some words and, more important, some concepts that challenge its existence as a destructive being. Lilo and Nani are learning, too, how to be a family and take care of each other, but the movie doesn't get all soppy at the end and is surprisingly unsentimental for a Disney animated feature. It keeps its edge and its comic zest all the way through, and although it arrives relatively unheralded, it's a jewel.

Note: I was far off in my prediction; Lilo & Stitch *opened like gangbusters and was a huge box-office success.*

Lilya 4-Ever ★ ★ ★

R, 109 m., 2003

Oksana Akinshina (Lilya), Artyom Bogucharsky (Volodya), Lyubov Agapova (Lilya's mother), Liliya Shinkaryova (Aunt Anna), Elina Benenson (Natasha), Pavel Ponomaryov (Andrei), Tomas Neumann (Witek). Directed by Lukas Moodysson and produced by Lars Jonsson. Screenplay by Moodysson.

Lilya 4-Ever provides a human face for a story that has become familiar in the newspapers. It follows a sixteen-year-old girl from the former Soviet Union as she is abandoned by her mother, places her faith in the wrong stranger, and is sold into prostitution. She is naive and innocent, and what looks like danger to us looks like deliverance to her. That there are countless such stories makes this one even more heartbreaking.

Lilya (Oksana Akinshina) lives in a barren

urban wasteland of shabby high-rises and wind-swept vacant lots. Her best friend Volodya (Artyom Bogucharsky) plays basketball by throwing a tin can through a rusty hoop. Her mother announces that she is engaged to marry a Russian who now lives in the United States. Lilya is joyous, and brags to Volodya that she is going to America. But her mother has other plans, and explains Lilya must stay behind, to be "sent for" later.

The mother is heartless, but then this is a society crushed by poverty and despair. There must be better neighborhoods somewhere, but we do not see them and Lilya does not find them. Within a day of her mother's departure, she is ordered by an embittered aunt to clear out of her mother's apartment and move into the squalor of a tenement room. Here she hosts glue-sniffing parties for her friends, and Volodya comes to live after his father throws him out. Volodya is young—perhaps eleven or twelve—and although he talks hopefully about sex, he is a child and she treats him like a little brother.

Lilya's descent into prostitution does not surprise us. There is no money for food, no one cares for her, she is pretty, she is desperate, and when she finds her first client in a disco, the movie focuses closely on her blank, indifferent face, turned away from the panting man above her. Later there is a montage of clients, seen from her point of view (although she is not seen), and it says all that can be said about her disgust with them.

The money at least allows her to buy junk food and cigarettes, and give a basketball to Volodya, whose father is enraged by the gift. Then friendship seems to come in the form of a young man named Andrei (Pavel Ponomaryov), who does not want sex, offers her a ride home, takes her on a date (bumper cars, that reliable movie cliché), and says he works in Sweden and can get her a job there. We see through him, and even Volodya does, but she is blinded by the prospect he describes: "You'll make more money there in a week than a doctor here makes in a month." Perhaps, but not for herself.

The movie, written and directed by Lukas Moodysson, has the directness and clarity of a documentary, but allows itself touches of tenderness and grief. It is so sad to see this girl, even after weeks of prostitution, saying the

Lord's Prayer in front of a framed drawing of a guardian angel. And there are two fantasy sequences toward the end that provide her with an escape, however illusory.

The movie should inspire outrage, but I read of thousands of women from Eastern Europe who are lured into virtual slavery. I hope some of their clients will attend this movie, even if for the wrong reasons, and see what they are responsible for.

Little Secrets ★ ★ ★
PG, 107 m., 2002

Evan Rachel Wood (Emily), Michael Angarano (Philip), David Gallagher (David), Vivica A. Fox (Pauline). Directed by Blair Treu and produced by Don Schain, Treu, and Jessica Barondes. Screenplay by Barondes.

The biggest surprise in *Little Secrets* is that Ozzie and Harriet don't live next door. The movie takes place in an improbably perfect suburban neighborhood where all the kids wear cute sportswear and have the kinds of harmless problems that seem to exist only so that they can be harmless problems. Then, of course, there are some Big Problems, which are rendered harmless, too. This is a very reassuring film.

The heroine of the movie, Emily (Evan Rachel Wood), is a budding young violinist who as a sideline runs a Little Secrets stand in her backyard, where kids can tell her their secrets at fifty cents apiece. The secrets are then written on scraps of paper and locked in a chest.

The theological and psychological origins of her practice would be fascinating to research. The neighborhood kids sure take it seriously. When she's a few minutes late in opening her stand, there's an impatient line of kids clamoring to unburden themselves. The fifty-cent price tag doesn't discourage them; these are not kids who remember the days when a quarter used to buy something.

But what kinds of kids are they, exactly? Consider Philip and David. Philip tells David: "Her name is Emily. Like Emily..." "...Dickinson?" says David. "And Emily Brontë," says Philip. Heartened as I am to know that the grade-school kids in this movie are on first-name terms with these authors, I am nevertheless doubtful that Dickinson and Brontë will ring many bells in the audience.

Vivica A. Fox is the only widely known star in the film, playing a violin teacher who is wise and philosophical. Much suspense centers around Emily's audition for the local symphony orchestra (every suburb should have one). The problems of the kids range from a girl who hides kittens in her room to a boy who is digging a hole to China. Larger issues, including adoption, are eventually introduced.

I am rating this movie at three stars because it contains absolutely nothing to object to. That in itself may be objectionable, but you will have to decide for yourself. The film is upbeat, wholesome, chirpy, positive, sunny, cheerful, optimistic, and squeaky-clean. It bears so little resemblance to the more complicated worlds of many members of its target audience (girls four to eleven) that it may work as pure escapism. That it has been rated not G but PG (for "thematic elements") is another of the arcane mysteries created by the flywheels of the MPAA. There is not a parent on Earth who would believe this film requires "parental guidance."

Looney Tunes: Back in Action ★ ★ ★
PG, 91 m., 2003

Brendan Fraser (D. J. Drake/Himself), Jenna Elfman (Kate Houghton), Steve Martin (Mr. Chairman), Timothy Dalton (Damien Drake), Joan Cusack (Mother), Heather Locklear (Dusty Tails). With the voices of: Joe Alaskey: Bugs Bunny, Daffy Duck, Beaky Buzzard, Sylvester, Mama Bear; Jeff Glenn Bennett: Yosemite Sam, Foghorn Leghorn, Nasty Canasta; Billy West: Elmer Fudd, Peter Lorre; Eric Goldberg: Tweety Bird, Marvin the Martian, Speedy Gonzales. Directed by Joe Dante and produced by Paula Weinstein and Bernie Goldmann. Screenplay by Larry Doyle.

As *Looney Tunes: Back in Action* opens, Daffy Duck is in a heated salary dispute with Warner Bros. For years Bugs Bunny has been pulling down the big bucks, and now, as they prepare to costar in another movie, Daffy is fed up. He wants equal pay for equal work. But Kate (Jenna Elfman), the studio VP in charge of animated characters, won't budge. She cites demographic studies that indicate Daffy's fan base

"is limited to angry fat guys in basements." Daffy throws a tantrum, and Kate orders a security guard (Brendan Fraser) to throw him off the lot.

I don't mind telling you my sympathies were entirely with Daffy in this scene. Let me tell you a personal story involving Daffy Duck, which also takes place on the Warner lot. I quote from an interview I did with Albert Brooks in 1991, when his movie *Defending Your Life* was about to be released.

As I was getting up to leave his office, Brooks said, "Look at these funny coffee mugs the studio sent over."

He had four or five of them on a shelf, cups shaped like the Warner cartoon heroes.

"Here," he said. "Have one. I want you to have one."

He pressed Elmer Fudd into my hands.

"No, that's okay," I said.

"Take one. What is this, a bribe? They're worth ten cents apiece. Twenty-five cents, tops."

"You know," I said, looking at the shelf, "I've never really been a fan of Elmer Fudd. My hero has always been Daffy Duck."

Brooks took the Daffy Duck mug from the shelf.

"Here, take it," he said. "I want you to have it. Really."

I could tell from the subtle intonation in his voice exactly what had happened. He had given me Elmer Fudd because he didn't like Elmer Fudd, either. He liked Daffy Duck. I had taken his favorite mug.

"No, you keep Daffy," I said. "I'll bet it's your favorite."

"Come on, come on," he said. "Take Daffy Duck. Take the one you want."

I tried to put Daffy back on the shelf. He pressed Daffy into my hands. I left with Daffy, but I would have bet a hundred bucks that the moment I was out of his office, Brooks had his secretary call Warner to see if they could send another Daffy Duck over.

And so now we are back in the present, and my eyes lift up from this review and regard the very same Daffy Duck coffee mug, which has pride of place in my office. And I reflect that while things always came easily for Bugs, Daffy had to fight every inch of the way. Bugs was insouciant. Daffy was outraged. Bugs was always a step ahead. Daffy was always a step behind.

In *Looney Tunes: Back in Action*, Daffy walks out of the meeting, and it doesn't take Kate and Bugs long to realize that without a foil the bunny is just spinning his paws. The security guard, whose name is D. J. Drake, and who is the twin brother of the egotistical Brendan Fraser, joins them in following Daffy to Vegas, where they get into trouble with the Acme megacorporation run by Steve Martin, discover Drake's dad is a secret agent (Timothy Dalton), and encounter the new Q (Joan Cusack) and a lot of amazing new inventions.

With the same kind of anarchic temporal and spatial logic that always inspired the Warner cartoons, the animals are soon in Paris and jumping into paintings in the Louvre. You can imagine the characters in a painting by Dali, and maybe even in Serrault's pointillist style, but in Munch's *The Scream*? You have to see that for yourself. This segment is possibly a tribute to the late, beloved Chuck Jones, who liked to plunge his cartoon characters into high art.

A whole gallery of cartoon stars eventually gets involved, including Sylvester, Yosemite Sam, Foghorn Leghorn, Elmer Fudd, Tweety Bird, and Speedy Gonzales, who may be seen in some circles as politically incorrect, but seems quite correct to himself, thank you. How the action ends up in Earth orbit I will leave you to discover.

The director is Joe Dante, whose segment of *Twilight Zone* (1983) involved a traveler who unwisely entered a house where the reality was warped by a kid's obsession with cartoon characters. Again this time, he combines live action with animation, in a film not as inspired as *Who Framed Roger Rabbit* but in the same spirit. It's goofy fun. Or maybe we should make that daffy fun.

The Lord of the Rings: The Return of the King ★ ★ ★ ½

PG-13, 200 m., 2003

Elijah Wood (Frodo), Ian McKellen (Gandalf), Liv Tyler (Arwen), Viggo Mortensen (Aragorn), Sean Astin (Sam), Cate Blanchett (Galadriel), John Rhys Davies (Gimli), Bernard Hill (Theoden), Billy Boyd (Pippin), Dominic Monaghan (Merry), Orlando Bloom (Legolas), Hugo Weaving (Elrond), Miranda Otto (Eowyn), David Wenham (Faramir), Karl Urban (Eomer), John Noble (Denethor), Andy Serkis (Gollum/Smeagol). Directed by Peter Jackson and produced by Jackson, Barrie M. Osborne, and Fran Walsh. Screenplay by Walsh, Philippa Boyens, Jackson, and Steven Sinclair, based on the novel by J. R. R. Tolkien.

At last the full arc is visible, and the *Lord of the Rings* trilogy comes into final focus. I admire it more as a whole than in its parts. The second film was inconclusive, and lost its way in the midst of spectacle. But *The Return of the King* dispatches its characters to their destinies with a grand and eloquent confidence. This is the best of the three, redeems the earlier meandering, and certifies the *Ring* trilogy as a work of bold ambition at a time of cinematic timidity.

That it falls a little shy of greatness is perhaps inevitable. The story is just a little too silly to carry the emotional weight of a masterpiece. It is a melancholy fact that while the visionaries of a generation ago, like Francis Ford Coppola with *Apocalypse Now*, tried frankly to make films of great consequence, an equally ambitious director like Peter Jackson is aiming more for popular success. The epic fantasy has displaced real contemporary concerns, and audiences are much more interested in Middle Earth than in the world they inhabit.

Still, Jackson's achievement cannot be denied. *The Return of the King* is such a crowning achievement, such a visionary use of all the tools of special effects, such a pure spectacle, that it can be enjoyed even by those who have not seen the first two films. Yes, they will be adrift during the early passages of the film's 200 minutes, but to be adrift occasionally during this nine-hour saga comes with the territory; Tolkien's story is so sweeping and Jackson includes so much of it that only devoted students of the *Ring* can be sure they understand every character, relationship, and plot point.

The third film gathers all of the plot strands and guides them toward the great battle at Minas Tirith; it is "before these walls that the doom of our time will be decided." The city is a spectacular achievement by the special effects artisans, who show it as part fortress, part Emerald City, topping a mountain, with a buttress reaching out over the plain below where the battle will be joined. In a scene where Gandalf rides his horse across the drawbridge and up the ramped streets of the city, it's remarkable how seamlessly Jackson is able to integrate computer-generated shots with actual full-scale shots, so they all seem of a piece.

I complained that the second film, *The Two Towers*, seemed to shuffle the hobbits to the sidelines—as humans, wizards, elves, and orcs saw most of the action. The hobbits are back in a big way this time, as the heroic little Frodo (Elijah Wood) and his loyal friend Sam (Sean Astin) undertake a harrowing journey to return the Ring to Mount Doom—where, if he can cast it into the volcano's lava, Middle Earth will be saved and the power of the enemy extinguished. They are joined on their journey by the magnificently eerie, fish-fleshed, bug-eyed creature Smeagol, who is voiced and modeled by Andy Serkis in collaboration with CGI artists, and introduced this time around with a brilliant device to illustrate his dual nature: He talks to his reflection in a pool, and the reflection talks back. Smeagol loves Frodo but loves the Ring more, and indeed it is the Ring's strange power to enthrall its possessors (first seen through its effect on Bilbo Baggins in *The Fellowship of the Ring*) that makes it so tricky to dispose of.

Although the movie contains epic action sequences of awe-inspiring scope (including the massing of troops for the final battle), the two most inimitable special-effects creations are Smeagol, who seems as real as anyone else on the screen, and a monstrous spider named Shelob. This spider traps Frodo as he traverses a labyrinthine passage on his journey, defeats him, and wraps him in webbing to keep him fresh for supper. Sam is very nearly not there to save the day (Smeagol has been treacherous), but as he battles the spider we're reminded of all the other movie battles between men and giant insects, and we concede that, yes, this time they got it right.

The final battle is kind of magnificent. I found myself thinking of the visionaries of the silent era, like Fritz Lang (*Metropolis*) and F. W. Murnau (*Faust*), with their desire to depict fantastic events of unimaginable size and power, and with their own cheerful reliance on visual trickery. Had they been able to see this scene, they would have been exhilarated. We see men and even an army of the dead join battle against orcs, flying dragons, and vast lumbering elephantine creatures that serve as moving platforms for machines of war. As a flaming battering ram challenges the gates of the city, we feel the size and weight and convincing shudder of impacts that exist only in the imagination. Enormous bestial trolls pull back the springs for catapults to hurl boulders against the walls and towers of Minas Tirith, which fall in cascades of rubble (only to seem miraculously restored in time for a final celebration).

And there is even time for a smaller-scale personal tragedy; Denethor (John Noble), steward of the city, mourns the death of his older and favored son, and a younger son named Faramir (David Wenham), determined to gain his father's respect, rides out to certain death. The outcome is a tragic sequence in which the deranged Denethor attempts to cremate Faramir on a funeral pyre, even though he is not quite dead.

The series has never known what to do with its female characters. J. R. R. Tolkien was not much interested in them, certainly not at a psychological level, and although the half-elf Arwen (Liv Tyler) here makes a crucial decision to renounce her elven immortality in order to marry Aragorn (Viggo Mortensen), there is none of the weight or significance in her decision that we feel, for example, when an angel decides to become human in *Wings of Desire*.

There is little enough psychological depth anywhere in the films, actually, and they exist mostly as surface, gesture, archetype, and spectacle. They do that magnificently well, but one feels at the end that nothing actual and human has been at stake; cartoon characters in a fantasy world have been brought along about as far as it is possible for them to come, and while we applaud the achievement, the trilogy is more a work for adolescents (of all ages) than for those hungering for truthful emotion thoughtfully paid for. Of all the heroes and villains in the trilogy, and all the thousands or hundreds of thousands of deaths, I felt such emotion only twice, with the ends of Faramir and Smeagol. They did what they did because of their natures and their free will, which were explained to us and known to them. Well, yes, and I felt something for Frodo, who has matured and grown on his long journey, although as we last see him it is hard to be sure he will remember what he has learned. Life is so pleasant in Middle Earth, in peacetime. ☞

The Lord of the Rings: The Two Towers
★ ★ ★
PG-13, 179 m., 2002

Elijah Wood (Frodo Baggins), Ian McKellen (Gandalf the White), Viggo Mortensen (Aragorn), Sean Astin ("Sam" Gamgee), Billy Boyd ("Pippin" Took), Liv Tyler (Arwen Undomiel), John Rhys-Davies (Gimli/voice of Treebeard), Dominic Monaghan ("Merry" Brandybuck), Christopher Lee (Saruman), Miranda Otto (Éowyn), Brad Dourif (Grima Wormtongue), Orlando Bloom (Legolas), Cate Blanchett (Galadriel), Karl Urban (Éomér), Bernard Hill (Théoden). Directed by Peter Jackson and produced by Barrie M. Osborne, Frances Walsh, and Jackson. Screenplay by Walsh, Philippa Boyens, Stephen Sinclair, and Jackson, based on the novel by J. R. R. Tolkien.

With *The Lord of the Rings: The Two Towers* it's clear that director Peter Jackson has tilted the balance decisively against the hobbits and in favor of the traditional action heroes of the Tolkien trilogy. The star is now clearly Aragorn (Viggo Mortensen), and the hobbits spend much of the movie away from the action. The last third of the movie is dominated by an epic battle scene that would no doubt startle the gentle medievalist Tolkien.

The task of the critic is to decide whether this shift damages the movie. It does not. *The Two Towers* is one of the most spectacular swashbucklers ever made, and, given current audience tastes in violence, may well be more popular than the first installment, *The Fellowship of the Ring*. It is not faithful to the spirit of Tolkien and misplaces much of the charm and whimsy of the books, but it stands on its own as a visionary thriller. I complained in my review of the first film that the hobbits had been short-changed, but with this second film I must accept that as a given, and go on from there.

This is a rousing adventure, a skillful marriage of special effects and computer animation, and it contains sequences of breathtaking beauty. It also gives us, in a character named Gollum, one of the most engaging and convincing computer-generated creatures I've seen. Gollum was long in possession of the Ring, now entrusted to Frodo, and misses it ("my precious") most painfully; but he has a split personality and (in between spells when his dark side takes over) serves as a guide and companion for Frodo (Elijah Wood) and Sam (Sean Astin). His body language is a choreography of ingratiation and distortion,

Another CGI character this time is Treebeard, a member of the most ancient race in Middle Earth, a tree that walks and talks and takes a very long time to make up its mind, explaining to Merry and Pippin that slowness is a virtue. I would have guessed that a walking, talking tree would look silly and break the spell of the movie, but no, there is a certain majesty in this mossy old creature.

The film opens with a brief reprise of the great battle between Gandalf the Gray (Ian McKellen) and Balrog, the monster made of fire and smoke, and is faithful to the ancient tradition of movie serials by showing us that victory is snatched from certain death, as Gandalf extinguishes the creature and becomes in the process Gandalf the White.

To compress the labyrinthine story into a sentence or two, the enemy is Saruman (Christopher Lee), who commands a vast army of Uruk-Hai warriors in the battle of Helm's Deep, assaulting the fortress of Théoden (Bernard Hill). Aragorn, with Legolas (Orlando Bloom) and Gimli the Dwarf (John Rhys-Davies), joins bravely in the fray, but the real heroes are the computer effects, which create the castle, landscape, armies, and most of the action.

There are long stretches of *The Two Towers* in which we are looking at mostly animation on the screen. When Aragorn and his comrades launch an attack down a narrow fortress bridge, we know that the figures toppling to their doom are computer-generated, along with everything else on the screen, and yet the impact of the action is undeniable. Peter Jackson, like some of the great silent directors, is unafraid to use his entire screen, to present images of wide scope and great complexity. He paints in the corners.

What one misses in the thrills of these epic splendors is much depth in the characters. All of the major figures are sketched with an attribute or two, and then defined by their actions. Frodo, the nominal hero, spends much of his time peering over and around things, watching others decide his fate, and occasionally gazing significantly upon the Ring. Sam is his loyal sidekick on the sidelines. Merry and Pippin spend a climactic stretch of the movie riding in Treebeard's branches and looking goggle-eyed at everything, like children carried on their father's shoulders. The Fellowship of the first movie has been divided into three during this one, and most of the action centers on Aragorn, who operates within the tradition of Viking swordsmen and medieval knights.

The details of the story—who is who, and why, and what their histories and attributes are—still remain somewhat murky to me. I know the general outlines and I boned up by rewatching the first film on DVD the night before seeing the second, and yet I am in awe of the true students of the Ring. For the amateur viewer, which is to say for most of us, the appeal of the movies is in the visuals. Here there be vast caverns and mighty towers, dwarves and elves and Orcs and the aforementioned Uruk-Hai (who look like distant cousins of the aliens in *Battlefield Earth*). And all are set within Jackson's ambitious canvas, and backdropped by spectacular New Zealand scenery.

The Two Towers will possibly be more popular than the first film, more of an audience-pleaser, but hasn't Jackson lost the original purpose of the story somewhere along the way? He has taken an enchanting and unique work of literature and retold it in the terms of the modern action picture. If Tolkien had wanted to write about a race of supermen, he would have written a Middle Earth version of *Conan the Barbarian*. But no. He told a tale in which modest little hobbits were the heroes. And now Jackson has steered the story into the action mainstream. To do what he has done in this film must have been awesomely difficult, and he deserves applause, but to remain true to Tolkien would have been more difficult, and braver.

Lost in La Mancha ★ ★ ★
R, 93 m., 2003

Featuring Terry Gilliam, Phil Patterson, Toni Grisoni, Nicola Pecorini, René Cleitman, Bernard Bouix, Johnny Depp, and Jean Rochefort. Narrated by Jeff Bridges. A documentary directed by Keith Fulton and Louis Pepe and produced by Lucy Darwin. Screenplay by Fulton and Pepe.

Blow, winds, and crack your cheeks! rage! blow!
You cataracts and hurricanoes, spout
Till you have drench'd our steeples . . .

History does not record whether these words of King Lear passed through Terry Gilliam's mind as his beloved film about Don Quixote turned to ashes. It is hard to believe they did not. *Lost in La Mancha*, which started life as one of those documentaries you get free on the DVD, ended as the record of swift and devastating disaster.

Gilliam, the director of such films as *Brazil*, *12 Monkeys*, and *The Fisher King*, arrived in Spain in August 2000 to begin filming a project he had been preparing for ten years. *The Man Who Killed Don Quixote* would star Johnny Depp as a modern-day hero who is transported back in time, and finds himself acting as Sancho Panza to old Don Quixote, who tilts at windmills and remains the most bravely romantic figure in Western literature.

The film was budgeted at $32 million, making it the most expensive production ever financed only with European money, although, as Gilliam observes, that's "far below what a film like this would usually cost."

In the title role he had cast Jean Rochefort, the tall, angular French star of more than 100 films, including *The Tall Blond Man with One Black Shoe* and *The Hairdresser's Husband*. Rochefort arrives on the set looking suitably gaunt and romantic, and showing off the English he has learned during seven months of lessons.

The first day of the shoot begins ominously. Someone has forgotten to rehearse the extras who are yoked to Depp in a chain gang. F-16 fighter planes roar overhead, spoiling shot after shot. Gilliam's optimism remains unchecked, and we get a notion of the film from his sketches and storyboards and his conferences with members of the production team. There's an amusing episode when he casts three men as giants.

Day two involves a change of location and an adjustment in the shooting schedule. The actors have arrived late in Spain, but are on hand, and as Gilliam and his first assistant director, Philip Patterson, juggle the schedule, the location becomes too windy and dusty. And then all hell breaks loose.

Thunderheads form overhead and rain begins to fall. Then hail. Winds blow over sets, tents, props. A flash flood crashes down the mountain and turns the area into a muddy quagmire. The damned jets continue to fly. Gilliam and his team regroup and are able to cobble together a shot involving Don Quixote on his horse. But: "Did you see Jean Rochefort's face as he was riding on the horse? He was in pain."

So much pain, as it develops, that although the actor is an experienced horseman, he cannot mount the horse alone, and needs two men and an hour of struggle to get himself down from it. Rochefort flies off to Paris to see his doctors, and the company shuts down, except for a day when they go through some motions to impress a busload of doomed visiting investors.

Rochefort will be gone three days, a week, ten days, indefinitely. His problem is described as two herniated discs. Or perhaps prostate trouble. Like vultures, the insurance agents begin to gather, followed by the completion bond guarantors, who step in when a film goes over budget. There are discussions, not with the optimism of Don Quixote, about what constitutes an act of God.

Midway through the second week of the shooting schedule, with brutal swiftness, *The Man Who Killed Don Quixote* is shut down. Some films end with a whimper; this one banged into a stone wall. The camera often rests on Gilliam's face, as the enormity of the disaster sinks in. "The movie already exists in here," he says, tapping his head. "I have visualized it so many times." But that is the only place it will ever exist.

Many films play dice with nature. I once stood in a barren field outside Durango, Colorado, as workers placed thousands of melons on the ground because the melon crop had failed, and the movie was about a melon farmer. I watched on the Amazon as an expensive light and all of its rigging slowly leaned over and fell forever beneath the waters. Once in the Ukraine, I waited for days with 20,000 extras, all members of the Red Army, who were dressed as Napoleon's Old Guard—and who could not be filmed without a lens that was being held up in customs.

There are many sad sights in *Lost in La Mancha*. One comes when the producers try to evoke the oldest rule in the book: "Fire the first assistant director." Gilliam stands firm behind his longtime assistant Patterson. It is not his fault. Day by day, it becomes increasingly clear that the film will never be made. Finally comes the shot of props being loaded into cardboard shipping boxes and sealed with tape. Maybe they are destined for eBay.

Other men have tilted at Quixote's windmill. Orson Welles famously spent years trying to piece together a film of the material, even after some of his actors had died. Peter O'Toole starred in *Man of La Mancha* (1972), not a good movie. Of that production I wrote: "I've always thought there was a flaw in the logic of *Man of La Mancha*. What good does it do to dream the impossible dream when all you're doing anyway is killing time until the Inquisition chops your block off?"

Lost in Translation ★ ★ ★
R, 105 m., 2003

Bill Murray (Bob Harris), Scarlett Johansson (Charlotte), Giovanni Ribisi (John), Anna Faris (Kelly). Directed by Sofia Coppola and produced by Coppola and Ross Katz. Screenplay by Coppola.

The Japanese phrase *mono no aware* is a bittersweet reference to the transience of life. It came to mind as I was watching *Lost in Translation*, which is sweet and sad at the same time it is sardonic and funny. Bill Murray and Scarlett Johansson play two lost souls rattling around a Tokyo hotel in the middle of the night, who fall into conversation about their marriages, their happiness, and the meaning of it all.

Such conversations can really be held only with strangers. We all need to talk about metaphysics, but those who know us well want details and specifics; strangers allow us to operate more vaguely on a cosmic scale. When the talk occurs between two people who could plausibly have sex together, it gathers a special charge: You can only say, "I feel like I've known you for years" to someone you have not known for years. Funny, how your spouse doesn't understand the bittersweet transience of life as well as a stranger encountered in a hotel bar. Especially if drinking is involved.

Murray plays Bob Harris, an American movie star in Japan to make commercials for whiskey. "Do I need to worry about you, Bob?" his wife asks over the phone. "Only if you want to," he says. She sends him urgent faxes about fabric samples. Johansson plays Charlotte, whose husband, John, is a photographer on assignment in Tokyo. She visits a shrine and then calls a friend in America to say, "I didn't feel anything." Then she blurts out: "I don't know who I married."

She's in her early twenties; Bob's in his fifties. This is the classic setup for a May-November romance, since in the mathematics of celebrity intergenerational dating you can take five years off the man's age for every million dollars of income. But *Lost in Translation* is too smart and thoughtful to be the kind of movie where they go to bed and we're supposed to accept that as the answer. Sofia Coppola, who wrote and directed, doesn't let them off the hook that easily. They share something as personal as their feelings rather than something as generic as their genitals.

These are two wonderful performances. Bill Murray has never been better. He doesn't play "Bill Murray" or any other conventional idea of a movie star, but invents Bob Harris from the inside out, as a man both happy and sad with his life—stuck, but resigned to being stuck. Marriage is not easy for him, and his wife's voice over the phone is on autopilot. But he loves his children. They are miracles, he confesses to Charlotte. Not his children specifically, but—children.

He is very tired, he is doing the commercials for money and hates himself for it, he has a sense of humor and can be funny, but it's a bother. She has been married only a couple of years, but it's clear her husband thinks she's in the way. Filled with his own importance, flattered that a starlet knows his name, he leaves her behind in the hotel room because—how does it go?—he'll be working, and she won't have a good time if she comes along with him.

Ingmar Bergman's *Scenes from a Marriage* was about a couple who met years after their divorce and found themselves "in the middle of the night in a dark house somewhere in the world." That's how Bob and Charlotte seem to me. Most of the time nobody knows where they are, or cares, and their togetherness is all that keeps them both from being lost and alone. They go to karaoke bars and drug parties, pachinko parlors and, again and again, the hotel bar. They wander Tokyo, an alien metropolis to which they lack the key. They don't talk in the long, literate sentences of the characters in *Before Sunrise,* but in the weary understatements of those who don't have the answers.

Now from all I've said you wouldn't guess the movie is also a comedy, but it is. Basically, it's a comedy of manners—Japan's, and ours. Bob Harris goes everywhere surrounded by a cloud of white-gloved women who bow and thank him for—allowing himself to be thanked, I guess. Then there's the director of the whiskey commercial, whose movements for some reason reminded me of Cab Calloway performing *Minnie the Moocher.* And the hooker sent up to Bob's room, whose approach is melodramatic and archaic; she has obviously not studied the admirable Japanese achievements in porno. And the B-movie starlet (Anna Faris), intoxicated with her own wonderfulness.

In these scenes there are opportunities for Murray to turn up the heat under his comic persona. He doesn't. He always stays in character. He is always Bob Harris, who *could* be funny, who *could* be the life of the party, who *could* do impressions in the karaoke bar and play games with the director of the TV commercial, but doesn't—because being funny is what he does for a living, and right now he is too tired and sad to do it for free. Except . . . a little. That's where you see the fine-tuning of Murray's performance. In a subdued, fond way, he gives us wry, faint comic gestures, as if to show what he could do, if he wanted to.

Well, I loved this movie. I loved the way Coppola and her actors negotiated the hazards of romance and comedy, taking what little they needed and depending for the rest on the truth of the characters. I loved the way Bob and Charlotte didn't solve their problems, but felt a little better anyway. I loved the moment near the end when Bob runs after Charlotte and says something in her ear, and we're not allowed to hear it. We shouldn't be allowed to hear it. It's between them, and by this point in the movie they've become real enough to deserve their privacy. Maybe he gave her his phone number. Or said he loved her. Or said she was a good person. Or thanked her. Or whispered, "Had we but world enough, and time ..." and left her to look up the rest of it.   ☞

The Lost Skeleton of Cadavra ★ ½
PG, 90 m., 2004

Larry Blamire (Dr. Paul Armstrong), Fay Masterson (Betty Armstrong), Jennifer Blaire (Animala), Brian Howe (Dr. Roger Fleming), Susan McConnell (Lattis), Andrew Parks (Krobar), Dan Conroy (Ranger Brad), Robert Deveau (The Farmer). Directed by Larry Blamire and produced by F. Miguel Valenti. Screenplay by Blamire.

"It is a curious attribute of camp that it can only be found, not made." So observes Dave Kehr, in his *New York Times* review of *The Lost Skeleton of Cadavra*. I did not read the rest of the review, because (1) I had to write my own, and (2), well, his first sentence says it all, doesn't it? True camp sincerely wants to be itself. In this category I include the works of Ed Wood and the infinitely more talented Russ Meyer. False camp keeps digging you in the ribs with a bony elbow. In this category falls *The Lost Skeleton of Cadavra*. Movies like the *Austin Powers* series are in a different category altogether, using the framework of satire for the purpose of comedy.

The Lost Skeleton of Cadavra, which is a loving tribute to the worst science fiction movies ever made, is about a three-way struggle for possession of the rare element atmosphereum. The contestants include an American scientist and his wife, a married (I think) couple from outer space, and a mad scientist and his sidekick, which is, of course, the lost skeleton of Cadavra. There is also a creature that seems to have been created by an explosion at a sofa factory, and a sexy girl named Animala, whose role is to appear in the movie and be a sexy girl. More about her later.

The photography, the dialogue, the acting, the script, the special effects, and especially the props (such as a space ship that looks like it would get a D in shop class) are all deliberately bad in the way that such films were bad when they were *really* being made. The locations remind me of the old *Captain Video* TV series, in which the same fake rocks were always being moved around to indicate we were in a new place on the alien planet. The writer and director, Larry Blamire, who also plays the saner of the scientists, has the look so well mastered that if the movie had only been made in total ignorance fifty years ago, it might be recalled today as a classic. A minor, perhaps even minuscule, classic.

A funny thing happened while I was watching it. I began to flash back to *Trog* (1970). This is an example of camp that was made, not found. That it was directed by the great cinematographer Freddie Francis I have absolutely no explanation for. That it starred Joan Crawford, in almost her final movie role, I think I understand. Even though she was already enshrined as a Hollywood goddess, she was totally unable to stop accepting roles, and took this one against all reason.

The plot of *Trog*, which I will abbreviate, involves a hairy monster. When it goes on a killing spree and is captured, Joan Crawford, an anthropologist, realizes it is a priceless scientific find: the Missing Link between ape and man. Then Trog kidnaps a small girl and crawls into a cave, and reader, although many years have passed since I saw the movie, I have never forgotten the sight of Joan Crawford in her designer pants suit and all the makeup crawling on her hands and knees into the cave and calling out, "Trog! Trog!" As if Trog knew the abbreviation of its scientific name.

But never mind; you see the point. *Trog* is perfect camp because Freddie Francis and Joan Crawford would never have allied themselves with a movie that was deliberately bad. (I am not so sure about Joe Cornelius, who played Trog.) It is bad all on its own. *The Lost Skeleton of Cadavra* has been made by people who are trying to be bad, which by definition reveals that they are playing beneath their ability. Poor Ed Wood, on the other hand, always and sincerely made the very best film he possibly could. How rare is a director like Russ Meyer, whose work satirizes material that doesn't even exist except in his satire of it, and who is also very funny; no coincidence that the *Austin Powers* movies are always careful to quote him.

But what have I neglected to tell you about *The Lost Skeleton of Cadavra*? Reading my notes, I find that "there is enough atmosphereum in one teaspoon to go to the moon and back six times," which is not quite the statement it seems to be. Oh, and the sexy girl named Animala is described as: "part human, part four different forest animals, and she can dance! Oh, how she can dance! Like I've never seen a woman dance before!" A possible mate for Trog?

Love Actually ★ ★ ★ ½
R, 129 m., 2003

Hugh Grant (Prime Minister), Liam Neeson (Daniel), Colin Firth (Jamie), Laura Linney (Sarah), Emma Thompson (Karen), Alan Rickman (Harry), Keira Knightley (Juliet), Martine McCutcheon (Natalie), Bill Nighy (Billy Mack), Rowan Atkinson (Rufus), Billy Bob Thornton (The U.S. President), Rodrigo Santoro (Karl), Thomas Sangster (Sam), Lucia Moniz (Aurelia). Directed by Richard Curtis and produced by Tim Bevan, Eric Fellner, and Duncan Kenworthy. Screenplay by Curtis.

Love Actually is a belly flop into the sea of romantic comedy. It contains about a dozen couples who are in love; that's an approximate figure because some of them fall out of love and others double up or change partners. There's also one hopeful soloist who believes that if he flies to Milwaukee and walks into a bar he'll find a friendly Wisconsin girl who thinks his British accent is so cute she'll want to sleep with him. This turns out to be true.

The movie is written and directed by Richard Curtis, the same man who wrote three landmarks in recent romantic comedy: *Four Weddings and a Funeral, Notting Hill,* and *Bridget Jones's Diary.* His screenplay for *Love Actually* is bursting with enough material for the next three. The movie's only flaw is also a virtue: It's jammed with characters, stories, warmth, and laughs, until at times Curtis seems to be working from a checklist of obligatory movie love situations and doesn't want to leave anything out. At 129 minutes it feels a little like a gourmet meal that turns into a hot dog–eating contest.

I could attempt to summarize the dozen (or so) love stories, but that way madness lies. Maybe I can back into the movie by observing the all-star gallery of dependable romantic comedy stars, led by Hugh Grant, and you know what? Little by little, a movie at a time, Hugh Grant has flowered into an absolutely splendid romantic comedian. He's getting to be one of those actors like Christopher Walken or William Macy who make you smile when you see them on the screen. He has that Cary Grantish ability to seem bemused by his own charm, and has so much self-confidence that he plays the British prime minister as if he took the role to be a good sport.

Emma Thompson plays his sister, with that wry way she has with normality, and Alan Rickman plays her potentially cheating husband with the air of a lawyer who hates to point out the escape clause he's just discovered. Laura Linney plays his assistant, who is shy to admit she loves her coworker Karl (Rodrigo Santoro), who is also shy to admit he loves her, and so you see how the stories go round and round.

Oh, and the prime minister walks into 10 Downing Street his first day on the job and Natalie the tea girl (Martine McCutcheon) brings him his tea and biscuits, and the nation's most prominent bachelor realizes with a sinking heart that he has fallen head over teapot in love. "Oh, no, that is *so* inconvenient," he says to himself, with the despair of a man who wants to be ruled by his head but knows that his netherlands have the votes.

Wandering past these lovable couples is the film's ancient mariner, a broken-down rock star named Billy Mack, who is played by Bill Nighy as if Keith Richards had never recorded anything but crap, and knew it. By the time he is fifty, George Orwell said, a man has the face he deserves, and Nighy looks as if he spent those years turning his face into a warning for young people: look what can happen to you if you insist on being a naughty boy.

Billy Mack is involved in recording a cynical Christmas version of one of his old hits. The hit was crappy, the Christmas version is crap squared, and he is only too happy to admit it. Billy Mack is long past pretending to be nice just because he's on a talk show. At one point he describes his song with a versatile torrent of insults of which the only printable word is "turd." And on another show, when he's told he should spend Christmas with someone he loves, he replies, "When I was young I was greedy and foolish, and now I'm left with no one. Wrinkled and alone." That this is true merely adds to his charm, and Nighy steals the movie, especially in the surprising late scene where he confesses genuine affection for (we suspect) the first time in his life.

Look who else is in the movie. Billy Bob Thornton turns up as the president of the United States, combining the lechery of Clinton with the moral complacency of Bush. After the president makes a speech informing the British that America is better than they are, America is stronger than they are, America will do what is right and the Brits had better get used to it, Hugh Grant's PM steps up to the podium, and what he says is a little more pointed than he intended it to be because his heart is breaking: He has just glimpsed the president flirting with the delectable tea girl.

The movie has such inevitable situations as a school holiday concert, an office party, a family dinner, a teenage boy who has a crush on a girl who doesn't know he exists, and all sorts of accidental meetings, both fortunate and not. Richard Curtis always involves a little sadness in his comedies (like the funeral in *Four Weddings*), and there's genuine poignancy in the relationship of a recently widowed man (Liam Neeson) and his wife's young son by a former marriage (Thomas Sangster). Their conversations together have some of the same richness as *About a Boy*.

The movie has to hop around to keep all these stories alive, and there are a couple I could do without. I'm not sure we need the wordless romance between Colin Firth, as a British writer, and Lucia Moniz, as the Portuguese maid who works in his cottage in France. Let's face it: The scene where his manuscript blows into the lake and she jumps in after it isn't up to the standard of the rest of the movie.

I once had ballpoints printed up with the message, "No good movie is too long. No bad movie is short enough." *Love Actually* is too long. But don't let that stop you.   ☞

Love Don't Cost a Thing ★ ★ ★
PG-13, 100 m., 2003

Nick Cannon (Alvin Johnson), Christina Milian

(Paris Morgan), Steve Harvey (Clarence Johnson), Al Thompson (Big Ted), Kal Penn (Kenneth Warman), Kenan Thompson (Walter Colley), Vanessa Bell Calloway (Vivian Johnson), Melissa Schuman (Zoe Parks). Directed by Troy Beyer and produced by Mark Burg, Reuben Cannon, Broderick Johnson, and Andrew A. Kosove. Screenplay by Michael Swerdlick and Beyer.

Love Don't Cost a Thing is a remake of *Can't Buy Me Love* (1987), a movie I despised, and yet this version is sweet and kind of touching, and I liked it. The difference, I think, is that the new one is lower on cynicism and higher on wisdom, and might actually contain some truth about the agonies of high school insecurity.

Both films have the same premise: A nerd in his senior year is getting good grades, but doesn't have a clue about dating. In desperation he bribes the most popular girl in school to date him long enough to change his image. She agrees. The 1987 movie painted its characters (played by Patrick Dempsey and Amanda Peterson) in fairly mercenary terms, but the characters in the remake are softened and made more likable.

Alvin Johnson (Nick Cannon) sees his chance when Paris Morgan (Christina Milian) turns up at the auto shop where he works, seeking emergency repairs to the front end of her mother's Cadillac SUV. The shop can't meet her deadline, but Alvin offers to help her out—in return for two weeks of dating. What she doesn't know is that he'll have to take the money he was saving for a science fair in order to pay for a replacement part.

Their high school is portrayed as a series of cruel no-go zones; an unpopular student would never venture into the corridor where the popular kids have their lockers, and so the first time Alvin (with Paris) ventures into that forbidden territory, it's a giddy victory. And it goes to his head; intoxicated by his newfound popularity, which has indeed rubbed off from Paris, he drops his old buddies from science class and starts acting out like a demented Chris Rock.

The movie's buried message is that Alvin really is a nice guy, if only he could learn to trust himself. Paris begins to realize that, values their long talks, and at one crucial point really would like to be kissed by Alvin—but he can't see that, or admit it. At home, he mystifies his parents (Steve Harvey and Vanessa Bell Calloway) with an overnight transformation, complete with the new wardrobe Paris has dressed him in. His old friends come to visit, but are turned away, forlorn.

Alvin's act is all bravado; Paris is so high-powered she intimidates him. "Chicks like Paris don't date outside the NBA," one of Alvin's friends observes early in the film, and indeed her alleged boyfriend is in his first year in the pros. But when he disses her on ESPN by claiming that, romantically, he's a "free agent," Paris is wounded—and more available than Alvin realizes.

The movie, directed by the actress Troy Beyer and written by her and Michael Swerdlick, makes a low-key attempt to teach some lessons. Steve Harvey's acting may go over the top in a scene where he lectures his son on the theory and use of condoms, but it's useful information and more realistic than the blissful sexual ignorance of most high school movies. And Paris shares some wisdom, too, explaining, "Popularity is a job, Alvin."

Nick Cannon is in his second starring role (he was infectiously likable as the kid from Harlem who's recruited by a southern university in *Drumline*), and he shows again an easy screen presence; maybe he, too, goes a little over the top in showing Alvin in full egotistical explosion, but in this script it comes with the territory. Christina Milian has had a lot of smaller roles, but this is her first lead, and she fills it with confidence and charm; if she's the most popular girl in school, she convinces us she deserves the title and wasn't simply assigned it by the screenplay.

Movies like this are lightweight and forgettable; only this sequel reminded me of *Can't Buy Me Love*, which had otherwise faded from memory. But for its running time *Love Don't Cost a Thing* does its job, and a little more. It has better values than the original, a little more poignancy, some sweetness. And Cannon and Milian have a natural appeal that liberates their characters, a little, from the limitations of the plot.

Love Liza ★ ★ ★
R, 90 m., 2003

Philip Seymour Hoffman (Wilson Joel), Kathy Bates (Mary Ann Bankhead), Jack Kehler (Denny), Sarah Koskoff (Maura Haas), Stephen Tobolowsky (Tom Bailey), Erika Alexander (Brenda). Directed by Todd Louiso and produced by Ruth Charny, Corky O'Hara, Chris Hanley, Jeffrey Roda, and Fernando Sulichin. Screenplay by Gordy Hoffman.

Diane Lane, who worked on Philip Seymour Hoffman's second movie, remembers that the cast almost tiptoed around him, he seemed so fragile. He's a bulky man, substantial, and yet in many of his roles he seems ready to deflate with a last exhausted sigh. It is a little startling to meet him in person and discover he is outgoing, confident, humorous. On the other hand, who knows him better than his brother Gordy, whose screenplay for *Love Liza* creates a Hoffman role teetering on the brink of implosion.

Hoffman plays Wilson Joel, a tech-head whose wife has recently committed suicide, although it takes us a while to figure that out. He presents a facade of conviviality in the office, sometimes punctuated by outbursts of laughter that go on too long, like choked grief. His home seems frozen in a state of mid-unpacking, and he sleeps on the floor. Eventually he stops going in to work altogether.

What he feels for his late wife is never usefully articulated. She left a letter for him, but he has not opened it; her mother, played by Kathy Bates, would like to know what it says, but what can she do to influence this man whose psyche is in meltdown? Wilson gives the sense of never having really grown up. One day he begins sniffing gasoline, a dangerous way to surround himself with a blurred world. He doesn't even have grown-up vices like drinks or drugs, but reverts to something he may have tried as a teenager.

The movie proceeds with a hypnotic relentlessness that hesitates between horror and black comedy. Searching to explain all the gas he's buying, he blurts out that he needs it for his model airplanes (this would have been a teenager's alibi). A friendly coworker thinks maybe this is an opening to lure him back into life, and sends over a relative who is an enthusiast of remote-controlled planes and boats. This sends Wilson careening into a series of cover-ups; he has to buy a model airplane, he finds himself attending remote control gatherings in which he has not the slightest interest, and finally, after a series of events that Jim Carrey could have performed in another kind of movie, he finds himself inexplicably swimming in a lake while angry little remote-controlled boats buzz like hornets around him.

Love Liza, directed by Todd Louiso, is not about a plot but about a condition. The condition is familiar to students of some of Hoffman's other characters, and comes to full flower in *Happiness* (1998), where he plays a man who lives in solitary confinement with his desperate and antisocial sexual fantasies. Sex hardly seems the issue with Wilson Joel, but he seems incapable of any kind of normal socializing, other than a kind of fake office camaraderie he might have copied from others. The mystery is not why Liza killed herself, but why she married him.

The purpose of a movie like this is to inspire thoughts about human nature. Most movies do not contain real people; they contain puppets who conform to popular stereotypes and do entertaining things. In the recent and relatively respectable thriller *The Recruit,* for example, Colin Farrell doesn't play a three-dimensional human, nor is he required to. He is a place-holder for a role that has been played before and will be endlessly played again—the kid who chooses a mentor in a dangerous spy game. He is pleasant, sexy, wary, angry, baffled, ambitious, and relieved, all on cue, but these emotions do not proceed from his personality. They are generated by the requirements of the plot. Leaving the movie, we may have learned something about CIA spycraft (and a lot more about the manufacture of thrillers), but there is not one single thing we will have learned about being alive.

Al Pacino is the costar of that movie, defined and motivated as narrowly as Farrell is. In a new movie named *People I Know,* he plays a breathing, thinking human being, a New York press agent driven by drugs, drink, duty, and a persistent loyalty to his own political idealism. We learn something about life from that performance. Pacino teaches us, as he is always capable of doing in the right role.

Philip Seymour Hoffman is a teacher, too. You should see *Love Liza* in anticipation of his new movie, *Owning Mahowny,* which I saw at

Sundance this year (*Love Liza* was at the 2002 festival, where it won the prize for best screenplay). The Mahowny character is at right angles to Wilson, but seems similarly blocked at an early stage of development. Observing how Mahowny, an addicted gambler, relates to his long-suffering fiancée (Minnie Driver), we can guess at the ordeal Wilson put Liza through. He's not cruel or angry or mean; he's simply not . . . there. His eyes seek other horizons.

In an age when depression and Prozac are not unknown, when the popularity of New Age goofiness reflects an urgent need for reassurance, Hoffman may be playing characters much closer to the American norm than an action hero like Colin Farrell. We cannot all outsmart the CIA and win the girl, but many of us know what it feels like to be stuck in doubt and confusion, and cornered by our own evasions.

There is a kind of attentive concern that Hoffman brings to his characters, as if he has been giving them private lessons, and now it is time for their first public recital. Whether or not they are ready, it can be put off no longer, and so here they are, trembling and blinking, wondering why everyone else seems to know the music.

Lovely and Amazing ★ ★ ★ ★
R, 89 m., 2002

Catherine Keener (Michelle Marks), Brenda Blethyn (Jane Marks), Emily Mortimer (Elizabeth Marks), Raven Goodwin (Annie Marks), Aunjanue Ellis (Lorraine), Clark Gregg (Bill), Jake Gyllenhaal (Jordan), James LeGros (Paul), Dermot Mulroney (Kevin McCabe), Michael Nouri (Dr. Crane). Directed by Nicole Holofcener and produced by Anthony Bregman, Eric d'Arbeloff, and Ted Hope. Screenplay by Holofcener.

The four women in *Lovely and Amazing* have been described as a dysfunctional family, but they function better than some, and at least they're out there looking. Here is a movie that knows its women, listens to them, doesn't give them a pass, allows them to be real: It's a rebuke to the shallow *Ya-Ya Sisterhood.*

Jane Marks (Brenda Blethyn), the mother, fiftyish, had two daughters at the usual season of her life, and now has adopted a third, eight-year-old Annie (Raven Goodwin), who is African-American. Her grown daughters are Michelle (Catherine Keener), who tries to escape from a pointless marriage through her pointless art, and Elizabeth (Emily Mortimer), who is an actress who cares more about dogs than acting.

All of these women are smart, which is important in a story like this. The mistakes they make come through trying too hard and feeling too insecure. They're not based on dumb plot points. They're the kinds of things real people do. And thank God they have a sense of humor about their lives, and a certain zest: They aren't victims but participants. They're even mean sometimes.

Men are a problem. Michelle's husband, Bill (Clark Gregg), is tired of paying all the bills while she sits at home making twee little chairs out of twigs. She accuses him of stepping on one of the chairs deliberately. He informs her that her "art" is worthless. Indeed her chairs are the sorts of collectibles made by the clueless for the clueless. But there is a deeper impulse at work: Her art allows her a zone free of her husband, a zone that insists she is creative and important.

Elizabeth, the actress, is like most actresses, filled with paralyzing doubt about her looks, her body, her talent. Annie, the adopted child, understandably wonders why she is black when everyone else in the family is white, and asks blunt questions about skin and hair. She also eats too much, and is already learning denial: "I'm not gonna eat *all* this," she tells Michelle, who finds her at McDonald's after she has disappeared from home. "I just couldn't make up my mind."

Where did she learn that reasoning? Perhaps from her mother. As the film opens, Jane has gone into the hospital to have liposuction, and there is a complicated dynamic going on because in some sense she dreams that her handsome surgeon (Michael Nouri) will first improve her, then seduce her.

All of these women are obsessed by body image. There is a scene of uncomfortable truth when Elizabeth sleeps with Kevin, a fellow actor (an indifferent, narcissistic hunk played by Dermot Mulroney), and then stands before him naked, demanding that he subject her body to a minute commentary and critique.

When he misses her flabby underarms, she points them out.

When I saw the movie for the first time at Telluride, I noticed a curious thing about the audience. During most nude scenes involving women, men are silent and intent. During this scene, which was not focused on sexuality but on an actual female body, attractive but imperfect, it was the women who leaned forward in rapt attention. Nicole Holofcener, who wrote and directed *Lovely and Amazing,* is onto something: Her movie knows how these women relate to men, to each other, to their bodies, and to their prospects of happiness.

Consider Elizabeth again. She picks up stray dogs—even dogs not much hoping to be adopted. One of them bites her. We have already seen how obsessed she is with her body, and yet she never even mentions the scarring that will result; it's as if the dog bite releases her from a duty to be perfect. Little Annie is certainly obsessed by being plump—she got that from Jane, probably along with the overeating—but she finds another unexpected image problem. An adult black woman, who volunteers to be her big sister, is disappointed: "When I signed up, I thought I was going to get somebody who was poor."

Michelle's husband is manifestly no longer interested in her. When he insists she get a job, she goes to work at a one-hour photo stand, where a fellow employee, a teenage boy (Jake Gyllenhaal), gets a crazy crush on her. She is not impervious to being adored. She likes this kid. She even winds up in his bedroom. And here Holofcener does something almost no other movie ever does: holds an adult woman to the same standard as an adult man. Michelle knows the age difference makes them wrong as a couple. The kid's mother calls the cops and accuses Michelle of statutory rape. There is some doubt about what exactly has taken place, but at least *Lovely and Amazing* doesn't repeat the hypocrisy that it's all right for adult women to seduce boys, but wrong for adult men to seduce girls.

Scene after scene in this movie has the fascination of lives lived by those willing to break loose, to try something new. *Lovely and Amazing* is not about the plight of its women but about their opportunities, and how in their disorganized, slightly goofy way they persist in seeking the good and the true. I hope I haven't made the film sound like a docudrama or a message picture: It has no message, other than to celebrate the lives of these imperfect women, and the joy of their imperfections.

Love Me If You Dare ★ ★
R, 99 m., 2004

Guillaume Canet (Julien), Marion Cotillard (Sophie), Thibault Verhaeghe (Julien at Eight), Josephine Lebas-Joly (Sophie at Eight), Gerard Watkins (Julien's Father), Emmanuelle Gronvold (Julien's Mother), Laetizia Venezia (Christelle). Directed by Yann Samuell and produced by Christophe Rossignon. Screenplay by Jacky Cukier and Samuell.

Do I dislike this film, or only its characters? There can be good films about bad people. Remember Travis Bickle. For that matter, do I dislike it because the characters are bad, or simply because they make me feel uneasy? Perhaps they're simply insane, and trapped in their mutual obsession. Perhaps because the film makes me feel so crawly, it is actually good. Yet still I cannot like it.

Love Me If You Dare tells the story of Julien and Sophie, who meet in grade school and make a pact that binds them together for a lifetime. Their treaty revolves around a little tin box, a toy painted to look like a merry-go-round. When one hands the other the box, along with it comes a dare. The other *must* do what they've been dared to do. This begins as a childhood game and continues into adulthood, where it gathers dangerous and dark undertones.

The movie will appeal to lovers of *Amelie*, according to the ads. Not if they loved *Amelie* for its good cheer. This is *Amelie* through the looking-glass. Yes, it has some of the same visual invention and delight, and director Yann Samuell's camera swoops and circles and flies through windows and into dreams. Yes, there's a bright color palate. Yes, the movie riffs through techniques, including animated sequences. Yes, Marion Cotillard has sweetness and appeal as Sophie, and yes, she and Julien (Guillaume Canet) seem destined to spend their lives together. But like this?

When they meet, they're eight years old and Sophie is being picked on at school because she's a foreigner. Julien defends her. They become friends for life. Even their first childish dares are risky, as when Sophie dares Julien to release the parking brake on the school bus; as it rolls downhill, do they get a fix of excitement that hooks them for life? Before long Julien is in the principal's office, peeing his pants—not because he's scared, but because Sophie dared him to.

The dares get riskier and more embarrassing as they grow older. Julien dares Sophie to take an oral exam at university while wearing her panties and bra outside her clothes. Sophie dares Julien to say "no" at the altar on his wedding day. Of course he won't be marrying her; that would be too easy, because she'd be in on the joke.

For that matter, what *is* their relationship? Are they in love, or simply trapped in a hypnotic mutual fascination? There's a flash-forward in the movie from a scene where Sophie sleeps over at Julien's house when they're eight, to the two of them as adults, still in the same position in bed. But have they had sex in the meantime? Does it matter? Their bond is deeper than sex and love; it's the bond of shared madness.

At one point in the movie, they dare each other to stay completely out of contact for ten years. Will they get their pact out of their system? Not at all. Every moment of those ten years, they're acutely aware of the passage of time and the fulfillment of their dare, and when they meet again at the end it's to escalate the dare to a new and disturbing level.

The movie's first shot tells us something we don't understand at the time. The last scene explains it, and is profoundly creepy. There is, I suppose, a tradition of lovers' pacts, but are they lovers, and what are they proving with the way they end their own pact? I know these are questions not intended for answers. I realize that the movie establishes a premise and follows it relentlessly. I understand that the playful camera strategies are supposed to take the edge off, and that scenes are played like comedy so that we won't grow completely depressed by the strange fate of Sophie and Julien.

But at the end, I didn't like them. In fact, reader, I loathed them. Did I loathe them as people, or as characters? Are their characters intended as real people, or as a fictional device? I'm not sure. What I do know is that the movie is strangely frustrating, because Julien and Sophie choose misery and obsession as a lifestyle, and push far beyond reason. Perhaps I should applaud the movie for its conviction? Perhaps the snakier it made me feel, the better it was? Perhaps, but I can't say so if I don't think so. I can say this: If despite everything my description has intrigued you, go ahead and take a chance. You won't be bored, he said with a little smile.

Love Object ★ ★
R, 88 m., 2004

Desmond Harrington (Kenneth), Melissa Sagemiller (Lisa), Rip Torn (Novak), Brad Henke (Dotson), Udo Kier (Radley), John Cassini (Jason), Lyle Kanouse (Stan). Directed by Robert Parigi and produced by Kathleen Haase and Lawrence Levy. Screenplay by Parigi.

Robert Parigi's *Love Object* tells the story of a painfully shy writer of software manuals, a man inhibited to the point of paralysis, who discovers a Web site that sells realistic, life-size love dolls. Kenneth (Desmond Harrington) is already a user of porn, frequenting a cryptlike adult shop that looks like the horror chamber at Madame Tussaud's and seems to have the Elephant Man behind the cash register. Now he maxes out his line of credit to order Nikki, a custom-crafted mannequin made to his specifications: hair color, eyes, etc.

While this drama is unfolding in his private life, Kenneth is under pressure from his boss. That would be Mr. Novak (Rip Torn), who seems to have modeled his performance on Samuel Ramey as Mephistopheles. Gravel-voiced and goateed, he alternates threat and praise as he assigns Kenneth to produce a three-volume instruction manual in a month. To assist him, Novak supplies a temp who can do the typing. This is Lisa (Melissa Sagemiller), an attractive young blond.

Kenneth doesn't want help. He prefers to work alone. But then an eerie thing occurs; Lisa, as it happens, looks a little like the love doll, Nikki. Kenneth starts buying things for the doll: dresses, wigs, lipstick, fingernail pol-

ish. He rigs up a harness so he can dance with the doll. And meantime, Lisa makes no secret of her attraction to him, which is odd, since Kenneth is so odd he might as well have "Weirdo Freak" tattooed on his forehead.

The establishing scenes of *Love Object* are voyeuristic in a creepy way; there's a strange fascination in stories about sexual fetishes, and as Kenneth works to make Nikki look more like Lisa, and then to make Lisa look more like Nikki, the music by Nicholas Pike subtly reminds us of the *Vertigo* theme. The *Vertigo* connection seems deliberate: There's even a scene in a dress store, where Kenneth takes Lisa to buy the same dress he earlier bought for Nikki, and the sales clerk looks at him in that same complicit way the clerk regarded James Stewart in the Hitchcock film. Kenneth wants Lisa and Nikki to look alike, just as Stewart coached Kim Novak to resemble the woman of his dreams.

Both times there was a trap for the man: In Hitchcock, because Novak secretly really was the woman Stewart was obsessed by, and in Parigi, because Kenneth begins to confuse the woman and the doll. We can't be sure exactly what defines the level of his madness, but certainly he believes Nikki has the upper hand—she orders him around, calls him at work, handcuffs him in his sleep, and so on. Sooner or later Lisa is going to find out about this, and then . . .

Well, up to that point Parigi had me fairly well involved. I was reminded of Michael Powell's *Peeping Tom* (1960), about a voyeuristic photographer who kills with his camera, and *Kissed* (1996), the Canadian film about a woman's strangely sympathetic necrophilia. It wasn't as good as those films, but it had the same attention to the sad, inward obsession of the character. If Parigi had continued in the way he began, he might have produced a successful film.

But he lacks confidence in Kenneth and his inward life, and so the movie reaches with increasing desperation toward humor and grisly sadism, and the mood is broken. There is a workable subplot involving Kenneth's strange building manager (Udo Keir), who listens in amazement through the walls, but another neighbor, a Los Angeles detective named Dotson (Brad Henke), is a goofball who does everything wrong that he possibly can, just to wring cheap laughs out of a situation that by then is desperately unfunny.

And the film's violent conclusion is too gruesome to be earned by what has gone before. Instead of somehow finding a psychological climax for his hero's dilemma, as Hitchcock and Powell did, Parigi goes for horror film developments that he pushes far beyond any possible interest we have in seeing them. The movie turns cruel and ugly, and hasn't paid the dues to earn its last scenes. Parigi had me there for a while, but when he lost me, it was big time.

Love the Hard Way ★ ★ ★
NO MPAA RATING, 104 m., 2003

Adrien Brody (Jack), Charlotte Ayanna (Claire), Jon Seda (Charlie), August Diehl (Jeff), Pam Grier (Linda Fox). Directed by Peter Sehr and produced by Wolfram Tichy. Screenplay by Marie Noelle and Sehr.

The Pianist was not only a fine movie but also served the purpose of bringing Adrien Brody into focus for moviegoers who might otherwise have missed this lean, smart, tricky actor. Odd, that his Oscar-winning role displayed him as passive and quiet, when Brody fits more comfortably into roles like Jack in Love the Hard Way—a street hustler and con artist, playing the angles, getting into danger "to feel the juice." He teams up with his partner, Charlie (Jon Seda), and a couple of young actresses to play a risky game of street theater: The actresses pretend to be hookers, and then Jack and Charlie, dressed as cops, bust them in hotel rooms—and can be bribed by the johns, of course, to drop the charges.

There is another side to Jack, in this movie made in 2001 but released now on the strength of The Pianist. He drops certain names in conversation—Pound, Kerouac, Melville—that lead us to suspect he is not your average street guy, and in the opening scene of the movie we glimpse his secret life. He rents a cubicle in a storage facility, and inside he jams a cramped office where he keeps a journal and works on a novel. He's not exactly a con artist only to get material, however; it's more like one of his personalities is criminal and the other personality

is a shy intellectual watching to see what the first guy will do next.

One day he goes to the movies at a Lower Manhattan art theater (I guess this is the shy guy) and meets Claire (Charlotte Ayanna), a Columbia student. He uses the usual pickup lines, which should turn off your average college woman, but Claire is intrigued, and agrees to meet him again, and the better half of him falls in love with all of her.

This story, written by director Peter Sehr and Marie Noelle, is a little like David Mamet's House of Games, in which an academic woman falls for the dangerous appeal of a con man. The difference is Mamet's heroine took revenge on the guy who deceived her, and Claire, in a way, wants to be deceived and degraded. When she takes revenge, it is against herself.

One day a con goes wrong. Jack and Charlie are not arrested, but to stay in business they're going to need new bait. "Maybe we should give Claire a try," Charlie muses. "She's not built for it," Jack says, and indeed he tries his best to break up with her, maybe because he senses how dangerous he is to a woman like her.

But Claire will not be rejected, keeps coming back, wants to know the secret of Jack's other life, and eventually turns a trick—after which, in a pitiful and lonely scene, she sits alone with her sadness in a photo booth. Jack did not intend this, tries again to alienate her, and then is repaid in full for his deceptions when Claire drops out of school to become a hooker full-time, as if proving something.

This is the kind of psychological self-punishment we might expect in a French film, not in an American film where plot is usually more important than insight. But Love the Hard Way is curious about the twisted characters it has set into motion and follows them through several more twists and turns—perhaps a few more than necessary. The film approaches several possible endings as if flirting with them.

Charlotte Ayanna is very good as Claire—we realize, as the film goes on and the character deepens, how challenging the role really is. Brody brings a kind of slick complexity to his role; he's so conflicted about what he's doing and why that he may be the real target of all his own cons.

It is not unknown for authors to embrace the

experiences they want to write about (of Jack's heroes, Melville went to sea, Kerouac went on the road, and Pound journeyed into madness), but we sense that Jack is on the edge of schizophrenia; his criminal persona scares him, despite all his bravado, and he wants to push Claire away to save her. The secret Jack, huddled in the container, writing in his journal, is an attempt to diagnose and understand himself.

Love the Hard Way is not perfect; a vice cop played by Pam Grier is oddly conceived and unlikely in action, and the movie doesn't seem to know how to end. But as character studies of Jack and Claire, it is daring and inventive and worthy of comparison with the films of a French master of criminal psychology like Jean-Pierre Melville. The success of *The Pianist* made Adrien Brody visible, probably won this film a theatrical release, and promises him many more intriguing roles. Surely Brody was born to play Bobby Fischer.

Lucía, Lucía ★ ★ ½
R, 113 m., 2003

Cecilia Roth (Lucía), Carlos Álvarez-Novoa (Félix), Kuno Becker (Adrián), Javier Díaz Dueñas (Inspector Garcia), Margarita Isabel (Lucía's Mom), Max Kerlow (Old Wehner), Mario Iván Martínez (Mr. Wehner), Jose Elias Moreno (Ramon), Héctor Ortega (The Cannibal). Directed by Antonio Serrano and produced by Matthias Ehrenberg, Christian Valdelievre, and Epigmenio Ibarrar. Screenplay by Serrano.

Perhaps because they have grown bored beyond all imagining with the formula plots in most crime stories, a lot of young directors play tricks with the facts. Audiences, who also know the basic plots by heart, think they're seeing another one and are willingly fooled. *Swimming Pool* is an example of the technique when it works; *Lucía, Lucía* illustrates the technique grown a little tiresome.

If the trickery is tiresome, the movie at least has life, especially in the lead performance by Cecilia Roth, from Pedro Almodóvar's *All About My Mother*. She plays a happily married woman who is stunned when her husband disappears at the Mexico City airport, just as they're leaving for a holiday in Brazil. The police seem incompetent to find him, but an elderly neighbor named Félix (Carlos Álvarez-Novoa) volunteers to help, and so does a handsome kid named Adrián (Kuno Becker) whom they literally run into on the stairs.

There's a ransom call. The husband is being held by a revolutionary group. He tells his wife where she can find millions of pesos in a safe-deposit box. That is only the beginning of the story. And in a way, not even that, because Lucía, who narrates, reveals that she has made things up. She doesn't look like the woman we've been seeing. She doesn't live in the apartment we've been shown. And so on. Her inventions are the stuff of fiction (she writes children's books), but her husband's deceptions are part of a tangled web of political corruption and intrigue that unravels and unravels and unravels and unravels, until we want to get out the knitting needles.

The movie is within the recent tradition of colorful, fast-paced, Mexican films that play with narrative; remember *Amores Perros* and *Y Tu Mama También*. But director Antonio Serrano also wants to really tell a story, and to make a political statement with his depiction of a corrupt political system; in that it resembles *Herod's Law*. The date of the story is a little obscure, but since Félix fought in the Spanish civil war and says he is now seventy, it perhaps takes place in the 1970s or 1980s. That means the ruling party, not named, is the Institutional Revolutionary Party (PRI).

Serrano is a dues-paying member of the New Mexican Cinema, if that is what we should be calling it; his first film, *Sex, Shame and Tears*, was one of Mexico's biggest box-office winners. Fox Searchlight has prudently released this one as *Lucía, Lucía* instead of under its original title, "Daughter of the Cannibal," no doubt figuring that English-speaking audiences would not know the title referred to a political, not a dietetic, cannibal.

This Félix is quite a guy. A lifelong leftist whose résumé includes all the best Latin American revolutionary causes, he's still quick on his feet and fast to draw, if not to fire, a gun. He loves Lucía for her spirit. Adrián, on the other hand, lusts after her, although she protests she is too old for him; if the characters are the same age as the actors playing them, he is twenty-five and she is forty-seven—a young forty-seven, who begins to glow with excitement as the plot thickens and the risks begin to mount. Roth has a wonderful way of keeping the kid at arm's length with her don't-tempt-me smile.

There are some sweet interludes in the film, including one when the three partners take a long road trip through vast canyons to visit an old friend of Félix's. And a nice sequence the first time they try to deliver the ransom. But the ransom refuses to be delivered, and the millions of pesos hang around so long we grow impatient with them, and with the plot twists that revolve around them. The fancy stuff and foolery impedes the story and its emotions. The underlying story was strong enough that maybe a traditional narrative would have been best, after all. Heresy, but there you are.

Lucky Break ★ ★ ★
PG-13, 107 m., 2002

James Nesbitt (Jimmy), Olivia Williams (Annabel), Timothy Spall (Cliff), Bill Nighy (Roger), Lennie James (Rudy), Christopher Plummer (Graham Mortimer). Directed by Peter Cattaneo and produced by Barnaby Thompson. Screenplay by Ronan Bennett.

Lucky Break is the new film by Peter Cattaneo, whose *The Full Monty* is the little British comedy that added a useful expression to the language. This movie is set in prison but uses much the same formula: A group of guys without much hope decide to band together and put on a show. This time they stage a musical comedy written by the prison warden, which means that instead of stripping they perform in costume. I am not sure if this is the half-monty, or no monty at all.

British prisons are no doubt depressing and violent places in real life, but in *Lucky Break*, the recent *Borstal Boy*, and the summer 2001 movie *Greenfingers*, they are not only benign places with benevolent governors, but also provide remarkable access to attractive young women. Jimmy (James Nesbitt), the hero of *Lucky Break*, finds abundant time to fall in love with Annabel, the prison anger-management

counselor (Olivia Williams). Brendan Behan, the hero of the biopic *Borstal Boy*, has a youthful romance with Liz, the warden's daughter. And in *Greenfingers*, which is about a prize-winning team of prison gardeners, one of the green-thumbsmen falls in love with the daughter of a famous TV garden lady. Only in these movies is prison a great place for a wayward lad to go in order to meet the right girl.

Lucky Break stars James Nesbitt and Lennie James as Jimmy and Rudy, partners in an ill-conceived bank robbery that lands them both in prison. The prison governor (Christopher Plummer) is an amateur playwright who has written a musical based on the life of Admiral Nelson, whose statue provides a congenial resting place for pigeons in Trafalgar Square. The lads agree to join in a prison production of the musical after learning that the play will be staged in the old prison chapel—which they consider the ideal place from which to launch a prison break.

Much of the humor of the film comes from the production of *Nelson, the Musical*, with book and lyrics by the invaluable actor and comic writer Stephen Fry; we hear a lot of the songs, see enough of the scenes to get an idea of the awfulness, and hardly notice as the prison break segues into a movie about opening night and backstage romance.

I am not sure that the average prisoner has unlimited opportunities to spend time alone with beautiful young anger-management counselors, wardens' daughters, or assistant TV gardeners, but in *Lucky Break*, so generous is the private time that Jimmy and Annabel even share a candlelight dinner. To be sure, a can of sardines is all that's served, but it's the thought that counts.

The key supporting role is by Timothy Spall, sort of a plump British Steve Buscemi—a sad sack with a mournful face and the air of always trying to cheer himself up. What keeps him going is his love for his young son; this whole subplot is more serious and touching than the rest of the film, although it leads to a scene perhaps more depressing than a comedy should be asked to sustain.

The climax of the film, as in *The Full Monty*, is the long-awaited stage performance, which goes on as various subplots solve themselves, or not, backstage. There is not much here that comes as a blinding plot revelation, but the movie has a raffish charm and good-hearted characters, and like *The Full Monty* it makes good use of the desperation beneath the comedy.

Luther ★ ★

PG-13, 112 m., 2003

Joseph Fiennes (Martin Luther), Alfred Molina (Johann Tetzel), Jonathan Firth (Girolamo Aleandro), Claire Cox (Katharina von Bora), Peter Ustinov (Frederick), Bruno Ganz (Johann von Staupitz), Uwe Ochsenknecht (Pope Leo XII), Mathieu Carriere (Cardinal Cajetan), Marco Hofschneider (Ulrick). Directed by Eric Till and produced by Brigitte Rochow, Christian P. Stehr, and Alexander Thies. Screenplay by Bart Gavigan and Camille Thomasson, based on the play by John Osborne.

Martin Luther was the moral force of the Reformation, the priest who defied Rome, nailed his 95 theses to the castle door, and essentially founded the Protestant movement. He must have been quite a man. I doubt if he was much like the uncertain, tremulous figure in *Luther*, who confesses, "Most days, I'm so depressed I can't even get out of bed." It is unlikely audiences will attend this film for an objective historical portrait; its primary audience is probably among believers who seek inspiration. What they will find is the Ralph Nader of his time, a scold who has all his facts lined up to prove the Church is unsafe at any speed.

Who was Joseph Fiennes channeling when he chose this muddled tone? Obviously, he was reluctant to give a broad, inspirational performance of the kind you find in deliberately religious films. Jesus comes across in some Christian films as a Rotarian in a robe, a tall, blue-eyed athlete who showers every morning. I remember defending *The Last Temptation of Christ* against a critic who complained that all of the characters were dirty. At a time when most people owned only one garment and walked everywhere in the desert heat, it's unlikely Jesus looked much like the Anglo hunks on the holy cards.

Martin Luther's world is likewise sanitized, converted into a picturesque movie setting where everyone is a type. The movie follows the movie hat rule: The more corrupt the character, the more absurd his hat. Of course Luther has the monk's shaven tonsure. He's one of those wise guys you find in every class who knows more than the teacher. When one hapless cleric is preaching "There is no salvation outside the church," Luther asks, "What of the Greek Christians?" and the professor is stumped.

The film follows the highlights of Luther's life, from his early days as a law student, through his conversion during a lightning storm, to his days as a bright young Augustinian monk who catches the eye of his admiring superior, Johann von Staupitz (Bruno Ganz). He is sent to Rome, where he's repelled by the open selling of indulgences (Alfred Molina plays a church retailer with slogans like Burma-Shave: "When a coin in the coffer rings, a soul from Purgatory springs"). He's also not inspired by the sight of the proud Pope Leo XII (Uwe Ochsenknecht) galloping off to the hunt, and when he returns to Germany it is with a troubled conscience that eventually leads to his revolt.

One thing the movie leaves obscure is the political climate that made it expedient for powerful German princes to support the rebel monk against their own emperor and the power of Rome. In scenes involving Frederick the Wise (Peter Ustinov), we see him using Luther as a way to define his own power, and we see bloody battles fought between Luther's supporters and forces loyal to the church. But Luther stands aside from these uprisings, is appalled by the violence, and, we suspect, if he had it all to do over again, would think twice.

That's the peculiar thing about Fiennes's performance: He never gives us the sense of a Martin Luther filled with zeal and conviction. Luther seems weak, neurotic, filled with self-doubt, unwilling to embrace the implications of his protest. When he leaves the priesthood and marries the nun Katharina von Bora (Claire Cox), where is the passion that should fill him? Their romance is treated like an obligatory stop on the biographical treadmill, and although I am sure Katharina told Martin many tender things, I doubt one of them was "We'll make joyous music together." This Martin Luther is simply not a joyous music kind of guy.

The most fun comes from the performance of grand old Sir Peter, who treasures his collection of sacred relics but sweeps them all aside after Luther casts doubt on their worth and authenticity (Luther has a funny speech pointing out that many saints left behind more body parts than they started out with). Ustinov here reminded me a little of his great Nero in *Quo Vadis,* collecting his tears in tiny crystal goblets—a big boy, playing with the toys of power.

Another major role is the papal adviser Girolamo Aleandro (Jonathan Firth), who correctly sees the threat posed by Luther and demands his excommunication and punishment, but for a political insider, misjudges the climate among the princes of Germany. The movie makes it clear to us, as it should to him, that for the power brokers in Germany, Luther's rebellion has as much secular as spiritual significance: He provides the moral rationale for a break they already desired to make.

I don't know what kind of movie I was expecting *Luther* to be, or what I wanted from it, but I suppose I anticipated that Luther himself would be an inspiring figure, filled with the power of his convictions. What we get is an apologetic outsider with low self-esteem, who reasons himself into a role he has little taste for.　☞

M

Madame Sata ★ ★
NO MPAA RATING, 105 m., 2003

Lázaro Ramos (Madame Satã/João Francisco), Marcelia Cartaxo (Laurita), Flavio Bauraqui (Taboo), Felipe Marques (Renatinho), Emiliano Queiroz (Amador), Renata Sorrah (Vítoria dos Anjos), Giovana Barbosa (Firmina), Ricardo Blat (José), Guilherme Piva (Alvaro). Directed by Karim Ainouz and produced by Marc Beauchamps, Isabel Diegues, Vincent Maraval, Mauricio Andrade Ramos, Donald Ranvaud, Juliette Renaud, and Walter Salles. Screenplay by Ainouz.

Madame Sata is a portrait of João Francisco dos Santos, a flamboyant, fiercely proud drag queen with a hair-trigger temper, who became a legend in the clubs and slums and prisons of Brazil. Born about 1900, dead in 1976, he spent nearly thirty of those years in prison, ten of them for murder. "There's something eating me up inside," he tells a friend. Performing his drag act provides a release, but requires a lifestyle that attracts trouble.

The character is never called Madame Sata during the film; we learn from the closing credits that he took the name, inspired by the De Mille film *Madame Satan*, later in life, when he began to win drag contests. The film opens not in victory but defeat: There is a long close-up of the hero, played by Lázaro Ramos, as his police record is read. It's quite a reading.

The movie has the same familiarity with the slums of Rio as the great film *City of God*, but provides less insight into the characters. João Francisco remains a puzzle to the end of the film, a person who fascinates us but doesn't share his secrets. The writer-director, Karim Ainouz, understands the milieu, and Ramos provides an electrifying, sometimes scary, performance, but it is always a performance, just as João is always, in a sense, onstage. Whatever is eating him up remains inside.

Homosexuality was an invitation to violence in the milieu of the film, but João is more than able to defend himself, and indeed makes a point of telling one of his attackers that being a queen makes him no less of a man. His domestic life is a parody of the nuclear family; he lives with a female prostitute named Laurita (Marcelia Cartaxo) and her child, not by him. They share a servant named Taboo (Flavio Bauraqui), who is more effeminate than his two employers put together. At home, João rules with the short temper and iron hand of the stereotypical dominant male, and is in many ways the most masculine character I've seen in any recent movie—certainly more macho than, say, Ben Affleck in *Gigli*.

The story occupies the dives, cabarets, brothels, and jail cells of the Rio underworld, where João starts as a backstage assistant to an European singer; in an effective early scene, he mimics the onstage performance from his position just offstage, and when a friendly bartender gives him a gig, at first he simply imitates the European woman's act, while cranking up the voltage. He quickly becomes the object of curiosity and lust for the half-hidden but numerous gay population, and has a passionate, violent affair with a lover named Renatinho (Felippe Marques), who is a thief and sees no reason why being João's lover and stealing João's money should not be compatible.

If we never really understand João, there is another problem with the character, and that is: He isn't very nice. I refer not to his crimes, but to the way he treats those who care for him. He clouts the faithful Taboo, insults his admirers, is not imperious so much as just simply hostile. That would not be an objection if the film dealt with it, but the film seems as uneasy about João as we are. He serves as our guide to the world of 1930s sex and crime in Rio, but there comes a point when we want to leave the tour and continue on our own, because this man's demons are not only eating him, but devouring everyone around him.

The Magdalene Sisters ★ ★ ★ ½
R, 119 m., 2003

Geraldine McEwan (Sister Bridget), Anne-Marie Duff (Margaret), Nora-Jane Noone (Bernadette), Dorothy Duffy (Rose/Patricia), Eileen Walsh (Crispina), Mary Murray (Una), Britta Smith (Katy), Frances Healy (Sister Jude), Eithne McGuinness (Sister Clementine).

Directed by Peter Mullan and produced by Frances Higson. Screenplay by Mullan.

I was an unmarried girl
I'd just turned twenty-seven
When they sent me to the sisters
For the way men looked at me.
— *Joni Mitchell,* The Magdalene Laundries

Here is a movie about barbaric practices against women, who were locked up without trial and sentenced to forced, unpaid labor for such crimes as flirting with boys, becoming pregnant out of wedlock, or being raped. These inhuman punishments did not take place in Afghanistan under the Taliban, but in Ireland under the Sisters of Mercy. And they are not ancient history. The Magdalene Laundries flourished through the 1970s and processed some 30,000 victims; the last were closed in 1996.

The Magdalene Sisters is a harrowing look at institutional cruelty, perpetrated by the Catholic Church in Ireland and justified by a perverted hysteria about sex. "I've never been with any lads ever," one girl says, protesting her sentence, "and that's the god's honest truth." A nun replies: "But you'd like to, wouldn't you?" And because she might want to, because she flirted with boys outside the walls of her orphanage, she gets what could amount to a life sentence at slave labor.

This film has been attacked by the Catholic League, but its facts stand up; a series of *Irish Times* articles on the Internet talks of cash settlements totaling millions of pounds to women who were caught in the Magdalene net. What is inexplicable is that this practice could have existed in our own time, in a western European nation. The laundries were justified because they saved the souls of their inmates—but what about the souls of those who ran them?

Raised in the Catholic Church in America at about the same time, I had nothing but positive experiences. The Dominican sisters who taught us were dedicated, kind, and brilliant teachers, and when I see a film like this I wonder what went wrong in Ireland—or right at St. Mary's Grade School in Champaign-Urbana.

The Magdalene Sisters focuses on the true stories of three girls who fell into the net. As the film opens, we see Margaret (Anne-Marie Duff) lured aside by a relative at a family wedding and raped. When she tells a friend what has happened, the word quickly spreads, and within days it is she, not the rapist, who is punished. Her sentence, like most of the Magdalene sentences, is indefinite, and as she goes to breakfast on her first morning she passes a line of older women who have been held here all their lives.

Two others: Bernadette (Nora-Jane Noone) is the girl who flirted with boys outside her orphanage, and Rose (Dorothy Duffy) is pregnant out of wedlock. She bears her child because abortion would be a sin, only to have it taken from her by the parish priest, who ships her off to a Magdalene institution.

Other inmates include Crispina (Eileen Walsh), whose crime is that she is mentally handicapped and might fall victim to men if not institutionalized. And there is an older prisoner who acts as a snitch to gain favor with the sisters. The nun in charge of this institution is a figure of pure evil named Sister Bridget (Geraldine McEwan), a sadist with a cruel streak of humor, who in one scene presides as new girls are forced to strip so their bodies and the size of their breasts can be compared. This is not fiction; the screenplay, by director Peter Mullan, is based on testimony by Magdalene inmates. Geraldine McEwan's powerful, scary performance evokes scarcely repressed sadomasochism.

The drama in *The Magdalene Sisters* is not equal to its anger. The film turns, as I suppose it must, into a story of escape attempts. A previously inexperienced girl finds herself making direct carnal offers to a young truck driver, if he will slip her a key to the gate. A priest who violates Crispina is paid back with poison ivy in his laundry. There is an escape attempt at the end that belongs more in an action film than in this protest against injustice.

But the closing credits remind us once again that the Magdalene Laundries existed and did their evil work in God's name. The church in Ireland has changed almost beyond recognition in recent years, and is now, like the American church, making amends for the behavior of some clergy. And the *Irish Times* articles report that some Protestant denominations had (and have) similar punishments for sexuality, real or suspected. The movie is not so much an attack on the Catholic Church as on the universal mind-set that allows transgressions be-

413

yond all decency, if they are justified by religious hysteria. Even today there are women walled up in solitary confinement in closed rooms in their own homes in the Middle East, punished for crimes no more serious, or trivial, than those of the Magdalene laundresses.

Maid in Manhattan ★ ★ ★
PG-13, 105 m., 2002

Jennifer Lopez (Marisa Ventura), Ralph Fiennes (Christopher Marshall), Tyler Garcia Posey (Ty Ventura), Natasha Richardson (Caroline), Marissa Matrone (Stephanie Kehoe), Bob Hoskins (Lionel Bloch), Stanley Tucci (Jerry Siegel). Directed by Wayne Wang and produced by Elaine Goldsmith-Thomas, Paul Schiff, and Deborah Schindler. Screenplay by Kevin Wade.

Maid in Manhattan is a skillful, glossy formula picture, given life by the appeal of its stars. It has a Meet Cute of stunning audacity, it has a classic Fish Out of Water, it works the Idiot Plot Syndrome overtime to avoid solving a simple misunderstanding, and there won't be a person in the audience who can't guess exactly how it will turn out. Yet it goes through its paces with such skill and charm that, yes, I enjoyed it.

We go to the movies for many reasons, and one of them is to see attractive people fall in love. This is not shameful. It is all right to go to a romantic comedy and not demand it be a searing portrait of the way we live now. What we ask is that it not be dumb, or at least no dumber than necessary, and that it involve people who embody star quality.

Maid in Manhattan is not dumb; the Kevin Wade screenplay deals with several story lines and makes them all interesting. And Jennifer Lopez and Ralph Fiennes make an intriguing couple because their characters have ways of passing the time *other* than falling in love. (I grow impatient when movie characters are so limited they can think of nothing better to do than follow the plot.)

Lopez plays Marisa Ventura, a maid in a posh Manhattan hotel. She has a bright grade-schooler named Ty (Tyler Garcia Posey) who for reasons of his own has become an expert

on Richard M. Nixon. Marisa hopes to be promoted to management one day, but despite the nudging of fellow maid and best friend Stephanie (Marissa Matrone) is hesitant about applying.

Fiennes plays Christopher Marshall, a Republican candidate for U.S. senator. Camera crews and herds of paparazzi follow him everywhere, perhaps under the impression that he is Rudolph Giuliani. He has a personal assistant named Jerry (Stanley Tucci) whose job is to advise him not to do almost everything that he thinks of doing.

The movie uses the device of a hotel staff briefing to fill us in on various VIP guests, including an exhibitionist, two sticky-fingered French ladies, and especially Caroline (Natasha Richardson), a flighty airhead from Sotheby's who has checked into an expensive suite. Future senator Marshall has checked into another one.

And then, in a dazzling display of time-honored movie developments, writer Wade and director Wayne Wang arrange for Marisa to be trying on one of Caroline's expensive dresses just as her son meets Marshall and talks them all into walking the senatorial dog in Central Park. Marshall understandably thinks this impostor is the inhabitant of the other suite. Prince Charming, of course, falls instantly in love with Cinderella, who must race back to the hotel and resume her life of scrubbing and bed-making. Marshall meanwhile invites the inhabitant of the expensive suite to lunch, only to find that it is the real Caroline, not the mistaken one.

And so on. One word by Marisa at any moment could have cleared up the confusion, but perhaps she fears a Republican candidate would not want to date a Puerto Rican maid, except under false pretenses. It is the duty of the screenplay to keep them separated through various misunderstandings and devices, but the movie makes this process surprisingly interesting by dealing with Marisa's application to become an assistant manager. A kind veteran butler (Bob Hoskins, self-effacing but lovable) teaches her the ropes, even when the two of them are called upon to serve Marshall and the real Caroline at the luncheon from hell.

Other issues arise. Marisa's mother, of course, does not think she deserves to be anything more than a maid (hasn't she learned from the mother in *Real Women Have Curves?*). Young Ty, of course, sees clearly that his mom belongs in the arms of this Republican. And the press turns a series of meetings into a front-page romance.

There's a little spunk in the movie. Marisa tells Marshall what's wrong with his ideas about housing and poverty. He's teachable. Marisa attends a charity benefit, looking gorgeous in a dress borrowed from the hotel boutique and wearing Harry Winston diamonds supplied, no doubt, in return for the plug. And when she runs away from the ball and he follows her, well, it worked in *Cinderella* and it works here, too.

Malibu's Most Wanted ★ ★ ½
PG-13, 86 m., 2003

Jamie Kennedy (Brad Gluckman), Taye Diggs (Sean), Anthony Anderson (P. J.), Blair Underwood (Tom Gibbons), Damien Dante Wayans (Tec), Regina Hall (Shondra), Ryan O'Neal (Bill Gluckman), Snoop Dogg (Ronnie Rizat), Bo Derek (Bess Gluckman). Directed by John Whitesell and produced by Fax Bahr, Mike Karz, and Adam Small. Screenplay by Bahr, Nick Swardson, Small, and Jamie Kennedy.

"This is my ghetto—the mall," Brad Gluckman explains at the beginning of *Malibu's Most Wanted*. He's the son of a millionaire who is running for governor of California under the slogan "California is my family," but the candidate has had little time for his own son, who has morphed into a gangsta rapper. Since he's rich and white and lives in Malibu, he's warned against "posing," but explains, "I ams who I say I ams."

Brad is played by Jamie Kennedy, star of the Fox show *JKX: The Jamie Kennedy Experiment*. The movie has a good satirical idea and does some nice things with it, but not enough. Flashes of inspiration illuminate stretches of routine sitcom material; it's the kind of movie where the audience laughs loudly and then falls silent for the next five minutes.

Brad's parents (Ryan O'Neal and Bo Derek) have not been around much to raise him; in a flashback to his childhood, they're seen communicating with him via satellite video from Tokyo and Paris. Although Brad has "never been east of Beverly Hills," he identifies with "his" homies in the inner city and talks about the hardships of his youth, for example when "the public be up on your private beach." He and his mall-rat friends like to pose as gangstas, but one ferocious and intimidating visit to a convenience store turns out to be about getting parking validation, and picking up some aromatherapy candles.

Brad's image is awkward for his father, especially when the kid unfurls a new political slogan on live TV: "Bill Gluckman is down with the bitches and hos." Gluckman's black campaign manager (Blair Underwood) advises a desperation move: Have the boy kidnapped by actors posing as gangstas and let them take him on a tour of the hood, so that he'll understand his own act is a fake.

Taye Diggs and Anthony Anderson play Sean and P. J., the two actors hired for the roles. They know exactly nothing about the hood. "I studied at Julliard," Sean explains. "I was at the Pasadena Playhouse," says P. J. Still, the campaign manager's money talks, and they enlist the help of the only hood dweller they know, P. J.'s cousin Shondra (Regina Hall). Before long the kidnappers and their victim are kidnapped by real gangstas, led by Tec (Damien Dante Wayans), and there's a gun battle that's supposed to be funny because Brad thinks it's all an act and the bullets aren't real.

The movie has one comic insight: The gangsta lifestyle is not authentic to any place or race, but is a media-driven behavioral fantasy. Why should it be surprising that Eminem is the most successful rapper in America when most rap music is purchased by white suburban teenagers? Many of those who actually live in the ghetto have seen too much violence first-hand to be amused by gangsta rap.

Jamie Kennedy is a success on TV, where this same character, nicknamed B-Rad, originated. He's fresh and aggressive, a natural clown, and has a lot of funny lines, as when he's asked where he learned to handle an automatic rifle and he replies, "Grand Theft Auto 3." This inspires a detailed conversation with a real gangster about competing game platforms.

The elements here might have added up to a

movie with real bite, but *Malibu's Most Wanted* plays it safe. It doesn't help that Eminem's *8 Mile* provided a recent and convincing treatment of what it might be like for a white rapper in the inner city. The subject is touchy, of course—race often is—but the solution might have been to push harder, not to fall back on reliable formulas.

Mambo Italiano ★ ★
R, 99 m., 2003

Luke Kirby (Angelo Barberini), Ginette Reno (Maria Barberini), Paul Sorvino (Gino Barberini), Claudia Ferri (Anna Barberini), Peter Miller (Nino Paventi), Sophie Lorain (Pina Lunetti), Mary Walsh (Lina Paventi), Tara Nicodemo (Aunt Yolanda). Directed by Émile Gaudreault and produced by Daniel Louis and Denise Robert. Screenplay by Gaudreault, based on a play by Steve Galluccio.

In *Mambo Italiano,* which we can refer to for convenience as *My Big Fat Gay Wedding,* the hero's Italian-Canadian parents grade sex for their son as follows: (1) No sex at all is best—just stay here at home with us; (2) if you must have sex, have it with a nice Italian girl; (3) if you get engaged to a non-Italian we'll kill you; but (4) if you become a homosexual we will first die of mortification and *then* kill you, and (5) no points for having gay sex with an Italian boy, because no Italian boy has ever been gay except for you, and you're not really gay anyway, you just haven't met the right girl, and look, here she is.

The movie takes place in a colorfully romanticized version of the Petite Italie neighborhood in Montreal, where the neighbors line up beside their garden allotments like the chorus members in an opera, and anyone is likely to break into song. Of their Italian accents, let it be said that none clash with Dean Martin's version of the title song. And, of course, there is one family member who pretends she knows nothing about homosexuality just so she can drop big clanging questions in the middle of tense family situations.

The movie stars Luke Kirby, looking here like a skinny John Belushi, as Angelo Barberini, teased since his childhood for being a sissy. Now he is grown and still living at home, which is fine with his parents, Maria (Ginette Reno) and Gino (Paul Sorvino). They nod approvingly at a neighbor's porch, where an elderly mother is still whacking her middle-aged son alongside the head. Angelo is growing increasingly desperate, and finally moves out, breaking the hearts of his parents, which are easily and frequently broken.

Love arrives unexpectedly. Nino Paventi (Peter Miller), one of the kids who picked on Angelo in school, has grown up to be a cop and a closeted gay man. They move in together, each one trying to keep his sexuality a secret, and then their families start churning, as families will, with matchmaking and awkward questions. Angelo has an ally in his sister Anna (Claudia Ferri), who is also quietly growing mad under the thumb of their parents. If they're told Angelo is gay, she says, "This is going to kill them." She pauses, and adds: "Tell them."

Meanwhile, there's a concerted push by Nino's parents to fix him up with an eligible woman, Pina Lunetti (Sophie Lorain). The plot unfolds in basic sitcom style, with surprise revelations, sudden reversals, and very, very broad characterizations (Sorvino, an amateur opera singer, doesn't distinguish himself with underacting). There are laughs in the movie, and a lot of good feeling, but it seems more interested in its Italian stereotypes than its gay insights, and it must be said there is absolutely no feeling that Angelo and Nino are really lovers. I don't know anything about the personal sexuality of these actors, but let it be said that in this movie they're straight.

Note: For a better movie dealing with homosexuality and ethnic stereotypes, there's What's Cooking? *with its fraught yet hilarious scenes involving Kyra Sedgwick, her lover, Julianna Margulies, and her parents, Lainie Kazan and Maury Chaykin.*

A Man Apart ★ ★
R, 114 m., 2003

Vin Diesel (Sean Vetter), Larenz Tate (Demetrius Hicks), Timothy Olyphant (Hollywood Jack Slayton), Geno Silva ("Memo" Lucero), George Sharperson (Big Sexy), Jacqueline Obradors (Stacy Vetter), Mateo Santos (Juan Fernandez). Directed by F. Gary Gray and produced by Robert John Degus,

Vincent Newman, Joey Nittolo, and Tucker Tooley. Screenplay by Christian Gudegast and Paul Scheuring.

A Man Apart sets chunks of nonsense floating down a river of action. The elements are all here—the growling macho dialogue, the gunplay, the drugs, the cops, the revenge—but what do they add up to? Some sequences make no sense at all, except as kinetic energy.

The movie stars Vin Diesel and Larenz Tate as drug cops named Vetter and Hicks. They're partners in the DEA, attempting to slam shut the Colombia-Mexico-California cocaine corridor. When they capture a cartel kingpin named Memo Lucero (Geno Silva), the cartel has its revenge by attacking Vetter's home and killing his beloved wife, Stacy (Jacqueline Obradors).

I have not given anything away by revealing her death; the movie's trailer shows her dying. Besides, she has to die. That's why she's in the movie. My colleague Richard Roeper has a new book named *Ten Sure Signs a Movie Character Is Doomed.* One of the surest signs is when a wife or girlfriend appears in a cop-buddy action picture, in gentle scenes showing them dining by candlelight, backlit by the sunset on the beach, dancing in the dawn, etc. Action movies are not about dialogue or relationships, and women characters are a major dialogue and relationship hazard. The function of the woman is therefore inevitably to die, inspiring revenge. This time, as they say, it's personal.

Vin Diesel inhabits *A Man Apart* easily, and continues to establish himself as a big action star. Tate gets good mileage from the thankless sidekick role. Geno Silva, as the drug kingpin, gives us glimpses of a character who was probably more fully developed in the earlier drafts: There is very little of Memo, but what there is suggests much more.

The plot is routine. Cops capture kingpin. Kingpin is replaced by shadowy successor named El Diablo. Successor sends hit men to shoot at Vetter and wife. Vetter loses his cool during a drug bust when a guy disses dead wife. As a result, three cops are killed. The chief takes away Vetter's badge. Then the rogue ex-cop goes on a personal mission of revenge against El Diablo, with ex-partner obligingly helping. We have seen this plot before. But Vin Diesel

has an undeniable screen charisma. And the movie is good-looking, thanks to cinematographer Jack N. Green, who gives scenes a texture the writing lacks. So everything is in place, and then we find ourselves confused about the basic purpose of whole sequences.

Example. Early in the movie, the DEA raids a club where Memo is partying. "You expect us to go into a building full of drunken cartel gunmen unarmed?" asks Vetter, who conceals a gun. So does everyone else, I guess, since the subsequent gun battle is loud and long and includes automatic weapons. While I was trying to find the logic of the "unarmed" comment, Memo flees from the club through an underground tunnel and emerges on the street to grab a getaway cab.

Okay. Later in the film, Vetter and Hicks return to the same club, enter through the getaway hatch, wade through waist-high water in the tunnels, emerge in the original room, and find a man sitting all by himself, who they think is El Diablo. "You think . . . I am El Diablo?" the man asks, all but cackling. As an action sequence unfolds and the guys retrace their steps through the flooded tunnel, etc., I'm asking what the purpose of this scene was. To provide mindless action, obviously. But was it also a strategy to use the same set twice, as an economy move?

The closing scene is even more illogical. I will give away no details except to say that, from the moment you see Vetter in the funny sun hat, smoking the cigarette and walking in the dusty village street, the entire scene depends on backward choreography: The omnipotent filmmakers know what is going to happen at the end of the scene and rewind it to the beginning. (Even so, the specific logistics of the payoff shot are muddled.)

Faithful readers will know I am often willing to forgive enormous gaps of logic in a movie that otherwise amuses me. But here the Vin Diesel character often seems involved in actions that are entirely without logical purpose. The movie's director is F. Gary Gray, whose *Set It Off* (1996) and *The Negotiator* (1998) were notable for strong characters and stories. This time the screenplay tries to paper over too many story elements that needed a lot more thought. This movie has been filmed and released, but it has not been finished.

The Man from Elysian Fields ★ ★ ★ ★
R, 106 m., 2002

Andy Garcia (Byron Tiller), Mick Jagger (Luther Fox), Julianna Margulies (Dena Tiller), Olivia Williams (Andrea Allcott), James Coburn (Tobias Allcott), Anjelica Huston (Jennifer Adler), Michael Des Barres (Greg). Directed by George Hickenlooper and produced by Andy Garcia, David Kronemeyer, Andrew Pfeffer, and Donald Zuckerman. Screenplay by Phillip Jayson Lasker.

"Elysian Fields is an escort service. We tend to the wounds of lonely women in need of emotional as well as spiritual solace."
"Only women?"
"Call me old-fashioned."

It's not just the reply, it's the way Mick Jagger delivers it. The way only Mick Jagger could deliver it. There is a brave insouciance to it, and George Hickenlooper's *The Man from Elysian Fields* finds that tone and holds it. This is a rare comedy of manners, witty, wicked, and worldly, and one of the best movies of the year. It has seven principal characters, and every one of them is seen sharply as an individual with faults, quirks, and feelings.

With the craftsmanship of a sophisticated film from Hollywood's golden age, with the care for dialogue and the attention to supporting characters that have been misplaced by the star system, the movie is about what people want and need, which are not always the same thing. It contains moments of tender romance, but is not deceived that love can solve anything.

Byron Tiller (Andy Garcia), the hero, is the author of a good first novel and now has written a bad second one. He is afraid to tell his wife, Dena (Julianna Margulies), that his new novel has been rejected, and that they desperately need money. In a bar, he meets a man with the obscurely satanic name Luther Fox (Mick Jagger). Fox runs Elysian Fields, an escort service for wealthy women. Byron agrees to take an assignment, and finds himself with the lovely Andrea Allcott (Olivia Williams). Why would she need to pay for companionship? It is a form of loyalty to her husband, who is old and diabetic, and whom she loves. It would be cheating to go out with an available man.

Her husband is Tobias Allcott (James Coburn), who has won Pulitzer prizes for his novels. He knows about his wife's arrangement, treats Byron in a dry, civilized manner, and enlists the younger writer's help with his current novel. Soon Byron is providing solace, of different kinds to be sure, to both of the Allcotts. He's a little dazzled by their qualities. And then there are two other characters, who add depth to the peculiar emotional complexity of the escort business: Jennifer Adler (Anjelica Huston), who pays for Luther Fox's services but doesn't want them for free; and Greg (rock star Michael Des Barres), a successful escort who gives Byron helpful tips on the clients.

The literate, sophisticated screenplay by Phillip Jayson Lasker understands that what happens to one character affects how another one feels; there's an emotional domino effect. By working for Elysian Fields, Byron supports his family, but it loses his attention. By risking everything in telling Jennifer that he loves her, Luther discovers his own self-deception. By accepting Byron's help with his novel, Tobias loses stature in his own eyes. Andrea fiercely tells Byron of the old man: "The only thing he has left is his reputation, and when he dies I want him holding onto it." Yes, but she saves it in public by destroying it in private. She isn't very sensitive that way.

This is a grown-up movie, in its humor and in its wisdom about life. You need to have lived a little to understand the complexities of Tobias Allcott, who is played by James Coburn with a pitch-perfect balance between sadness and sardonic wit. Listen to his timing and his word choices in the scene where he opens his wife's bedroom door and finds Byron, not without his permission, in his wife's bed. You can believe he is a great novelist. The scene is an example of the dialogue's grace and irony. Another example: "This business you're in," Byron asks Luther. "Does it ever make you ashamed?" Luther replies: "No. Poverty does that."

Julianna Margulies, as Byron's wife, has what could have been the standard role of the wronged woman, but the screenplay doesn't dismiss her with pathos and sympathy. Dena stands up and fights, holds her ground, is correctly unforgiving. Olivia Williams, as Andrea, has a hint of selfishness: Her concern for Tobias's reputation is connected to the way it reflects on her. There is a scene between Luther and Byron on the beach, where the older man shares a lesson he has just learned; it makes exactly the point it needs to make, and stops. The movie is confident enough it doesn't need to underline everything. It makes its point about the Michael Des Barres character even more economically; for him, the song "Just a Gigolo" is sad or jolly, depending on his mood.

Andy Garcia's performance took some courage because his Byron is not a very strong man. Not strong enough to tell his wife the novel didn't sell. Not strong enough to resist the temptations of Elysian Fields, or the flattery of Tobias's attention. By the time the ending comes around, we observe that it is happy, but we also observe that the movie has earned it: Most movies are too eager to wrap things up by providing forgiveness before it has been deserved. Not this one.

Manic ★ ★
R, 100 m., 2003

Don Cheadle (David), Joseph Gordon-Levitt (Lyle), Michael Bacall (Chad), Zooey Deschanel (Tracey), Cody Lightning (Kenny), Elden Henson (Michael), Sara Rivas (Sara). Directed by Jordan Melamed and produced by Trudi Callon and Kirk Hassig. Screenplay by Michael Bacall and Blayne Weaver.

I haven't seen *Manic* before, but it feels like I have. The opening scenes place us in a familiar setting and more or less reveal what we can expect. In an institution for troubled teenagers, an encounter group is overseen by a therapist who tries his best to steer his clients toward healing. But the unruly young egos have wills of their own, and there will be crisis and tragedy before the eventual closure.

The plot is a serviceable device to introduce characters who need have no relationship to one another, and to guarantee conflict and drama. We are all indoctrinated in the wisdom of psychobabble, and know that by the end of the film some of the characters will have learned to deal with the anger, others will have stopped playing old tapes, and with any luck at all there will even be a romance.

The screenplay by Michael Bacall and Blayne Weaver finds no new approaches to the material, but it does a skillful job of assembling the characters and watching them struggle for position within the group dynamic. Don Cheadle, who plays the counselor, has a thankless task, since the heroes and heroines will all eventually heal themselves, but Cheadle is a fine actor and finds calm and power in the way he tries to reason with them: "You don't think you chose the actions that caused you to be in this room with me?"

Joseph Gordon-Levitt, from *Third Rock from the Sun*, shows the dark side of his funny TV personality, as Lyle, a newcomer to the group, who was institutionalized for outbursts of angry violence in school, one leading to the serious injury of a classmate. His challenge now is to somehow learn to control his rage despite the provocations of the aggressive fellow inmate Michael (Elden Henson), who learns how to push his buttons. He shows promise as a serious actor.

With admirable economy, the screenplay provides Lyle not only with an antagonist, but also with a close friend, his Native American roommate, Kenny (Cody Lightning), and a romance (with Tracey, played by Zooey Deschanel). In stories of this sort, a minority group member who is the best friend of the hero has a disquieting way of dying when the movie requires a setback. Just as the romance must seem to have ended just before it finds a new beginning.

If the movie is not original, at least it's a showcase for the actors and writers. It does not speak as well, alas, for director Jordan Melamed and his cinematographer, Nick Hay. The movie was shot on video, which is an appropriate choice, giving the story an immediate, pseudo-documentary quality, but Melamed and Hay made an unfortunate decision to use the handheld style that specializes in gratuitous camera movement, just to remind us it's all happening right now. There are swish-pans from one character to another, an aggressive POV style, and so much camera movement that we're forced to the conclusion that it's a deliberate choice. A little subtle handheld movement creates a feeling of actuality; too much is an affectation.

There are moments of truth and close observation in *Manic*, and a scene where the Cheadle character does what we're always waiting for a long-suffering group leader to do, and completely loses it. Deschanel and Gordon-Levitt succeed in keeping their problems in the foreground of their romance, so those scenes don't simply descend into courtship. But at the end of *Manic* I'd seen nothing really new, and the camera style made me work hard to see it at all.

Manito ★ ★ ★ ½

NO MPAA RATING, 77 m., 2003

Franky G. (Junior Moreno), Leo Minaya (Manny Moreno), Manuel Cabral (Oscar Moreno), Julissa Lopez (Miriam), Jessica Morales (Marisol), Héctor González (Abuelo). Directed by Eric Eason and produced by Allen Bain and Jesse Scolaro. Screenplay by Eason.

Manito sees an everyday tragedy with sadness and tenderness, and doesn't force it into the shape of a plot. At the end, the screen goes dark in the same way a short story might end; there isn't one of those final acts where we learn the meaning of it all. Sometimes in life, bad things happen, and they just happen. There's nothing you could have done, and no way to fix them, and you are never going to get over the pain.

The movie, a heartfelt debut by writer-director Eric Eason, takes place in Washington Heights, a Latino neighborhood of New York City, where we meet the Moreno family. Junior (Franky G.) runs a plastering and painting crew, and his kid brother, Manny (Leo Minaya), is an honor student who is graduating today from high school, and headed to Syracuse on a scholarship.

In an unforced, natural way, we meet the characters. Junior spent time in prison, and is determined to stay straight. Manny, known as Manito, is not tough like his brother. Junior is a ladies' man; there's a well-observed scene with his wife, Miriam (Julissa Lopez), who won't even listen to his excuses when he sends her home without him. Manito is more shy, but gets up the nerve to ask Marisol (Jessica Morales), his classmate, to the graduation party in his honor.

This party is a big deal. The family is proud of Manito and his scholarship, and has rented a hall and hired a band—paid for by Junior, and also by Abuelo (Héctor González), who in a scene of sly comedy visits a local bordello and

brings out his line of trashy lingerie. Humor pops up unexpectedly, as when Junior needs to hire day laborers and discovers that all of the prospects are wearing white shirts and ties. Why? A restaurant closed, and they lost their jobs.

There is a man on the fringes of the story, seen drinking alone, and that is Oscar (Manuel Cabral), the father. We learn later that he was responsible for Junior going to jail; he let his son take the rap for him. Now he wants to send one of those six-foot sub sandwiches to the party, but Junior furiously takes it right back.

Will this man, drinking heavily, do something violent to spoil the big day? It's a possibility. But the movie isn't about overplotted angst between family members. It's about how the city is a dangerous place to live, and has people in it who are not nice, and how it can break your heart and change your destiny in the blink of an eye. One thing leads to another and the result is tragedy. But *Manito* pushes further, to what happens then, and can never be fixed, and helps nothing, and leads to a place where all you can do is sob helplessly.

The film has been compared to *Mean Streets*, and has the same driving energy as the 1973 picture. But some of Scorsese's characters wanted to be criminals—you could see that again in *GoodFellas*. The Morales family has had all the crime it wants, thanks to the father, and wants only to pay the bills, have a party, and see Manito succeed.

Where do the actors come from, who can walk into their first picture and act with such effortless effect? Franky G. has had three roles since he finished *Manito*, in big pictures like *The Italian Job*, and we'll hear more of him. Leo Minaya and Jessica Morales have not worked before or since, but what freshness and truth they bring to their performances.

The film's flaw, not a crucial one, is in the handheld camera style. There are times when the camera is too close for comfort, too jerky, too involved. Just because you can hold a digital camera in your hand doesn't mean you have to; the danger is that a shot will not be about what is seen, but about the act of seeing it. *Manito* settles down a little after the opening scenes, too absorbed in its story to insist on its style.

Man on Fire ★ ★ ½
R, 146 m., 2004

Denzel Washington (Creasy), Dakota Fanning (Pita), Marc Anthony (Samuel), Radha Mitchell (Lisa), Christopher Walken (Rayburn), Giancarlo Giannini (Manzano), Rachel Ticotin (Mariana), Jesus Ochoa (Fuentes), Mickey Rourke (Jordan). Directed by Tony Scott and produced by Lucas Foster, Arnon Milchan, and Scott. Screenplay by Brian Helgeland, based on a novel by A. J. Quinnell.

Tony Scott's *Man on Fire* employs superb craftsmanship and a powerful Denzel Washington performance in an attempt to elevate genre material above its natural level, but it fails. The underlying story isn't worth the effort. At first we're seduced by the jagged photography and editing, which reminds us a little of *City of God* and *21 Grams*. We're absorbed by Washington's character, an alcoholic with a past he cannot forgive himself for. And we believe the relationship he slowly develops with the young Mexico City girl he's hired to protect. But then the strong opening levels out into a long series of action scenes, and the double-reverse ending works more like a gimmick than a resolution.

The screenplay is by Brian Helgeland, whose work on *Mystic River* dealt with revenge in deep, painful, personal terms. But this time, action formulas take over. The hero outshoots and outsmarts half the bad guys in Mexico City. He seems to be homeless, yet has frequent changes of wardrobe and weaponry, even producing a shoulder-mounted missile launcher when necessary. And as he plows his way through the labyrinth of those responsible for kidnapping the girl, the body count becomes a little ridiculous, and Washington's character, who seemed very human, begins uncomfortably to resemble an invulnerable superhero. Sure, he gets shot now and again, but can you walk around Mexico City as an accused cop-killer and outgun professional killers indefinitely? When it seems that everyone who could possibly be killed is dead and the movie must surely be over, there's another whole chapter. We count those still alive, and ask ourselves if the Law of Economy of Characters applies: That's the one that says a movie contains no unnecessary characters, and so the otherwise unexplained presence of a star

in a seemingly insignificant role will be richly explained by the end.

All of this is true, and yet the movie has real qualities. Denzel Washington creates a believable, sympathetic character here—a character complex enough to deserve more than fancy action scenes. Even the last scene involving his character is a disappointment; there's a moment when one thing and one thing only should happen to him, and it doesn't, and the movie lets him, and us, down gently.

Washington plays Creasy, whose résumé includes antiterrorism. He's fallen on hard times, drinks too much, and travels to Mexico for a reunion with his old military buddy Rayburn (Christopher Walken). "Do you think God will forgive us for what we've done?" Creasy asks Rayburn. "No," says Rayburn. "Me either," says Creasy.

Rayburn has a job for him: acting as a bodyguard for Mexico City industrialist Samuel Ramos (Marc Anthony), his American wife, Lisa (Radha Mitchell), and their daughter, Pita (Dakota Fanning). At the job interview, Creasy is frank about himself: "I drink." Ramos is able to live with this information, but advises Creasy to tell nobody, especially Mrs. Ramos. As we think back over the film, this conversation will take on added importance.

Creasy keeps his distance on the job. Pita wants to be his friend; he explains he was hired as a bodyguard, not a friend. But eventually he bottoms out in his despair, begins to love the little girl, and becomes her swimming coach, Marine-style. These scenes have a real resonance. After she is kidnapped, the movie goes through the standard routine (police called in, telephones tapped, ransom drop arranged), but with additional local color, since off-duty Mexico City police were apparently involved in the snatch, and Creasy feels surrounded by vipers. Rayburn may be the only person he can trust.

At the Ramos home, Samuel negotiates with the kidnappers, gets advice from his family lawyer (Mickey Rourke), and consults with the head of the Anti-Kidnap Squad, who is a busy man if the movie is correct in its claim that someone is kidnapped in Mexico every ninety minutes. Creasy, meanwhile, depends on a plucky journalist named Mariana (Rachel Ticotin), and she depends on an ex-Interpol expert named Manzano (Giancarlo Giannini). As the net and the cast widen, we begin to wonder if anyone in Mexico City is not involved in the kidnapping in one way or another, or related to someone who was.

Man on Fire has a production too ambitious for the foundation supplied by the screenplay. It plays as if Scott knows the plot is threadbare and wants to patch it with an excess of style. He might have gotten away with that in a movie of more modest length, but *Man on Fire* clocks in at close to two and a half hours, and needs more depth to justify the length.

Too bad, because the performances deserve more. Denzel Washington projects the bleak despair he's revealed before, and his character arc involves us. Christopher Walken supplies another of his patented little speeches: "Creasy's art is death. He's about to paint his masterpiece." Dakota Fanning *(Uptown Girls)* is a pro at only ten years old, and creates a heart-winning character. Ticotin and Giannini supply what is needed, when it's needed. There are scenes that work with real conviction. The movie has the skill and the texture to approach greatness, but Scott and Helgeland are content with putting a high gloss on formula action.

The Man on the Train ★ ★ ★ ★
R, 90 m., 2003

Jean Rochefort (Manesquier), Johnny Hallyday (Milan), Charlie Nelson (Max), Pascal Parmentier (Sadko), Jean-François Stévenin (Luigi), Isabelle Petit-Jacques (Viviane). Directed by Patrice Leconte and produced by Philippe Carcassonne. Screenplay by Claude Klotz.

Two men meet late in life. One is a retired literature teacher. The other is a bank robber. Both are approaching a rendezvous with destiny. By chance, they spend some time together. Each begins to wish he could have lived the other's life.

From this simple premise, Patrice Leconte has made one of his most elegant films. It proceeds as if completely by accident and yet foreordained, and the two men—who come from such different worlds—get along well because both have the instinctive reticence and tact of born gentlemen. When the robber asks the teacher if he can borrow a pair of slippers, we get a glimpse of the gulf that separates them: He

wants them, not because he needs them, but because, well, he has never worn a pair of slippers.

The teacher is played by Jean Rochefort, seventy-three, tall, slender, courtly. It tells you all you need to know that he was once cast to play Don Quixote. The robber is played by Johnny Hallyday, fifty-nine, a French rock legend, who wears a fringed black leather jacket and travels with three handguns in his valise. This casting would have a divine incongruity for a French audience. In American terms, think of James Stewart and Johnny Cash.

Leconte is a director who makes very specific films, usually with an undertone of comedy, about characters who are one of a kind. His *The Hairdresser's Husband,* which also starred Rochefort, was about a man who loved to watch women cut hair. His *The Girl on the Bridge* was about a sideshow knife-thrower. His *The Widow of Saint Pierre* was about a nineteenth-century community on a French-Canadian fishing island that comes to love a man condemned to death. His *Ridicule* was about an eighteenth-century provincial who has an ecological scheme, and is told that the king favors those who can make him laugh. His *Monsieur Hire* was about a meek little man who spies on a woman, who sees him spying, and boldly challenges him to make his move.

These films have nothing in common except the humor of paradox, and Leconte's love for his characters. He allows them to talk with wit and irony. "Were you a good teacher?" the robber asks the teacher, who replies: "Not one pupil molested in thirty years on the job." "Not bad," the robber says dryly.

I have seen *The Man on the Train* twice, will see it again, cannot find a flaw. The man gets off the train in a drear November in a French provincial town, and falls into conversation with the teacher, who is quietly receptive. The teacher's elegant old house is unlocked ("I lost the key"). The village hotel is closed for the winter. "I know," the teacher says when the man returns. "I'll show you to your room."

Over a period of a few days, they talk, eat together, drink, smoke, gaze at the stars. There is no reason for them to be together, and so they simply accept that they are. There is a coincidence: At 10:00 A.M. on Saturday, the teacher is scheduled for a triple heart bypass, and the man from the train is scheduled to stick up a bank. The teacher offers the man money if he will abandon the plan, but the man cannot, because he has given his word to his confederates.

Early in the film, the teacher goes into the man's room, tries on his leather jacket, and imitates Wyatt Earp in the mirror. A little later, he gets a new haircut, telling the barber he wants a style "halfway between fresh out of jail, and world-class soccer player." One day when the teacher is away, one of his young tutorial pupils appears, and the robber says, "I'll be your teacher today," and leads him through a lesson on Balzac while successfully concealing that he has never read the novel, or perhaps much of anything else.

It is so rare to find a film that is about male friendship, uncomplicated by sex, romance, or any of the other engines that drive a plot. These men become friends, I think, because each recognizes the character of the other. Yes, the bank robber is a criminal, but not a bad man; the teacher tells him, quite sincerely, that he wishes he could help with the holdup. They talk about sex (the teacher points out the 200-year-old oil painting he masturbated before when he was young). They agree "women are not what they once were." The robber observes that, after a point, they're simply not worth the trouble. When the teacher's longtime friend Viviane (Isabelle Petit-Jacques) chatters away during dinner, the robber snaps, "He wants tenderness and sex, not news of your brat."

At the end of the film, the two men do exchange places, in a beautiful and mysterious way. Leconte brings his film to transcendent closure without relying on stale plot devices or the clanking of the plot. He resorts to a kind of poetry. After the film is over, you want to sigh with joy, that in this rude world such civilization is still possible.

The Man Without a Past ★ ★ ★ ½
PG-13, 97 m., 2003

Markku Peltola (Man), Kati Outinen (Irma), Juhani Niemela (Nieminen), Kaija Pakarinen (Kaisa Nieminen), Sakari Kuosmanen (Anttila), Annikki Tahti (Flea Market Manageress), Anneli Sauli (Bar Owner), Elina Salo (Shipyard Clerk). Directed and produced by Aki Kaurismäki. Screenplay by Kaurismäki.

We sense that the parcel the man clutches contains everything he owns, or has managed to hang onto. He gets off the train as if it doesn't much matter what city it is. He settles down on a park bench, falls asleep, and is beaten by muggers to within an inch of his life. He flatlines in the hospital, then suddenly awakens and walks out onto the street with no idea who he is. He finds a community of people who live in shipping containers. There is a kind of landlord, who agrees to rent him one.

"If you don't pay up," the landlord says, "I'll send my savage dog to bite your nose off."

"It only gets in the way," the man says.

"You wouldn't be able to smoke in the shower," the landlord points out.

The dog regards all of this, curious and friendly. He never barks once during the entire film.

Aki Kaurismäki's *The Man Without a Past,* from Finland, was a 2003 Oscar nominee for best foreign film. It follows the adventures of its nameless hero in a series of episodes that are dry, deadpan, and either funny or sad, maybe both. The man has no job, no name, no memory, and yet his face reflects such a hard and sorrowful past that we suspect he has never been happier.

The man (Markku Peltola) gets to know his neighbors. A security guard and his wife help him settle in; their generosity is casual, not dramatic. He goes to the Salvation Army for help, work, anything, and meets an Army officer named Irma (Kati Outinen). I remember her from Kaurismäki's *Drifting Clouds* (1996), where she and her husband both lost their jobs and faced destitution with quiet resolve. She has a face, too; one of those faces that tells us there are sometimes small joys in the midst of the general devastation.

To describe the plot is sort of pointless, because it doesn't unfold so much as just plain happen. Without a name, a plan, or (despite the evidence of his callused hands) even an occupation, the man depends on luck and the kindness of strangers—and the love of the Salvation Army woman, who sees him as a soul only marginally more bereft than herself. The only thing keeping her going is rock 'n' roll.

Eventually, through a happy or perhaps unhappy chance, he is identified and journeys to meet the woman who says she was his wife.

"You were my first love," she tells him. "That was beautifully said," he says. "Yes," she says. She tells him a little about the past he has forgotten: "You gambled. You lost all your LPs playing blackjack." The former wife is living with a man now, and the two men step outside because they think they probably ought to fight, but that turns out to be unnecessary.

Kaurismäki is an acquired taste—hard to acquire, because most of his films have never played here. You may have come across *Leningrad Cowboys Go America* (1989), about a group of Finnish rock 'n' rollers who hope to make the big time in this country. His characters tend to plant their feet and deliver their dialogue as if eternal truths are being spoken, and the camera tends to plant itself and regard them without a lot of fancy work. His characters don't smile much; they nod sadly a lot, they smoke and think and expect the worst.

And yet there is a joy in them, a deep humor that's all the richer because it springs from human nature and the absurdity of existence, instead of depending on one-liners and gags. If there is something funny about a container having a landlord with a savage watchdog, we have to figure that out for ourselves, because the movie is not going to nudge us in the ribs and laugh for us.

At the end of *The Man Without a Past*, I felt a deep but indefinable contentment. I'd seen a comedy that found its humor in the paradoxes of existence, in the way that things may work out strangely, but they do work out. I felt a real affection for the man, and for the Salvation Army officer, and for the former wife who is not too happy to see her onetime husband again, and even for the poor sap who thinks he has to fight to preserve appearances.

Martin Lawrence Live: Runteldat
★ ★ ★

R, 100 m., 2002

A live performance by Martin Lawrence, directed by David Raynr and produced by Michael Hubbard, David Gale, Beth Hubbard, Loretha C. Jones, Lawrence, and Van Toffler. Screenplay by Lawrence.

There is no bodily fluid, secretion, emission, odor, ejaculate, orifice, protuberance, function, or malfunction that Martin Lawrence overlooks in *Martin Lawrence Live: Runteldat*. The word "runteldat" is short for "run and tell that," but Lawrence doesn't abbreviate much else, spelling out his insights into the human physiognomy in detail that would impress a gynecologist. If it proves nothing else, this movie establishes that it is impossible for a film to get the NC-17 rating from the MPAA for language alone. This takes the trophy for dirty talk, and I've seen the docs by Richard Pryor, Eddie Murphy, and Andrew Dice Clay.

Pryor and Murphy are genteel humanists in comparison to Lawrence. Clay is a contender. He doesn't rise to quite the same standard of medical detail, but he has the same rage, and the same tendency to reduce the female gender to its orifices and functions. When Lawrence reveals that he was married but is now divorced because "it didn't work out," we think, "No kidding!" His attitude toward women is that of a man who has purchased a cooperative household device that works perfectly until the day it astonishes him by giving birth.

The film is nevertheless funny, if you can get beyond the language or somehow learn to relate to it as the rhythm and not the lyrics. (If you can't, don't go. This movie is as verbally offensive as Lawrence can make it, and he gives it his best shot.) It is funny because Lawrence is a gifted performer with superb timing and an ability to mimic many characters and suggest attitudes and postures with lightning-quick invention. There's something almost musical in the way his riffs build, turn back on themselves, improvise detours, find the way again, and deliver.

Curious, but the humor is almost *all* generated by the style. Buddy Hackett once demonstrated to me how you can do Catskills-style humor with irrelevant words and it's still funny because the timing and delivery instruct the audience to laugh. Lawrence elevates that technique to an art form. If you read the script of this concert film, I doubt if you'd laugh much, because the content itself is not intrinsically funny. There are no jokes here that you can take home and use on your friends. You have to be there. It's all in the energy and timing of the delivery, in the way Lawrence projects astonishment, resentment, anger, relief, incredulity, and delight.

The film opens with a montage devoted to his well-publicized troubles, including an arrest for disturbing the peace and a collapse from heat exhaustion that put him into a coma. There are segments from news programs reporting on these difficulties—not real programs, curiously, but footage shot for this movie. Then he launches into a tired attack on "the media," as if somehow it created his problems by reporting them. He also discusses those problems, not in the confessional style of Richard Pryor, but almost as if he was a bystander. He moves on to berate critics, which is unwise, because the average audience correctly decodes attacks on critics as meaning the performer got bad reviews. (No performer has ever attacked a critic for a good review.)

This opening segment is shaky, as Lawrence finds his footing and gets a feel for the audience. Then he's off and running, for nearly ninety minutes, in what can only be described as a triumph of performance over the intrinsic nature of the material. His description of childbirth, for example, makes it sound simultaneously like a wonderful miracle, and like a depraved secret that women hide from men. His descriptions of sexual activities, in all imaginable variations, depend heavily on what can go wrong in terms of timing, cleanliness, technique, equipment, and unforeseen developments. Sex for Lawrence seems like the kind of adventure for which you should wear protective gear.

You wonder how long Lawrence can keep this up, and at the end you conclude he could keep it up forever. I would summarize more of it, except that a lot of his riffs are about events and activities that cannot tactfully be described in print. I urge you to stay for the closing credits, not because there are hilarious outtakes, but because there is one of the most astonishing credits I can imagine: a thanks to the Daughters of the American Revolution for the use of their Constitution Hall in Washington, D.C. This is the same hall once denied because of racism to Marian Anderson, who then sang instead, at the invitation of Eleanor Roosevelt, from the steps of the Lincoln Memorial. Now Martin Lawrence records a concert film there. RuntelDAT!

Maryam ★ ★ ★ ½
NO MPAA RATING, 90 m., 2002

Mariam Parris (Mary/Maryam Armin), David Ackert (Ali Armin), Shaun Toub (Darius Armin), Shohreh Aghdashloo (Homa Armin), Maziyar Jobrani (Reza), Sabine Singh (Jill), Victor Jory (Jamie), Michael Blieden (Pete). Directed by Ramin Serry and produced by Shauna Lyon. Screenplay by Serry.

Girls just want to have fun, says Cyndi Lauper, and Maryam, a high school senior, is one of them. Yes, she's an honor student and anchors the news on the in-school TV program, but she also likes to hang out at the roller rink with her slacker boyfriend, and pot and booze are not unknown to her. In New Jersey in 1979, she is a typical teenage girl—until the Iran hostage crisis slaps her with an ethnic label that makes her an outsider at school and a rebel in her own home.

Maryam (Mariam Parris) is Iranian-American—or Persian, her father would say. Her parents immigrated from Iran before the fall of the shah, and settled comfortably into suburbia; her father is a doctor, her mother a warm, chatty neighbor, and Maryam (or "Mary," as she calls herself at school) doesn't think much about her Iranian or Muslim heritage. Then two things happen to force her to confront her history. The hostage crisis inspires knee-jerk hostility from her classmates (whose families also come from somewhere else), and her radical cousin Ali arrives from Tehran.

Ramin Serry's *Maryam,* a film that cares too deeply for its characters to simplify them, doesn't indulge in tired clichés about the generation gap. Maryam's home life is strict but not unreasonable. Her father doesn't want her to date, places great emphasis on her grades, doesn't know about her boyfriend. He is not a cruel or domineering man, and Maryam, to her credit, knows her parents love her. She's caught between trying to be a good daughter and a typical teenager, and has found a workable middle ground before Ali arrives.

With Ali comes a history of family tension she knows nothing about. Ali is an orphan, the son of Mary's uncle, and so he must be taken in. It is more complicated than that. Her father, we learn, turned his brother in to the shah's secret police; he felt he had no choice, but is consumed by guilt. The bloodstained backgammon board Ali brings as a "gift" is an ominous reminder of times past.

Ali is such an observant Muslim that he cannot touch his cousin Maryam, even to shake her hand. Pressed into service as a chaperone, he finds himself plunged into teenage culture that offends and attracts him. He calls Maryam a "whore" to her mother, but subtly flirts with her. More disturbing is his alliance with a campus radical, and his obsession with the deposed shah, who has just entered a New York hospital for cancer treatment. (Maryam's take on this: "He calls the U.S. the Great Satan. I mean, the guy could lighten up a little.")

Maryam was made before 9/11, and indeed I first saw it at the 2000 Hawaii Film Festival and invited it to my own Overlooked Film Festival in April 2001. It is, I learned, the somewhat autobiographical story of writer-director Ramin Serry, who grew up in Chicago and was made sharply aware of his Iranian heritage during the 1979 hostage crisis.

In the film, Maryam's neighbors put a yellow ribbon around the tree in their front yard, and discontinue their friendly chats and visits. Maryam's boyfriend drops her like a hot potato. She is deposed from her TV show (she suggests her newly arrived cousin might make a good interview; the other students prefer to cover a homecoming controversy). A brick comes through the front window. A public demonstration turns into shouts of "Iranians go home." Through all of this, the gifted actress Mariam Parris (British, but seamlessly playing American) finds the right notes: wounded, sad, angry, but more balanced than distraught.

Whatever hostility Serry felt in 1979 is no doubt much worse today for Arab-Americans, who have, like most immigrants since the Pilgrims, left a native land to seek the American dream. Strange how many Americans, themselves members of groups that were hated a few generations ago, now turn against newcomers. (I could hear the pain in my German-American father's voice as he recalled being yanked out of Lutheran school during World War I and forbidden by his immigrant parents ever to speak German again.) *Maryam* is more timely now than ever.

Masked and Anonymous ½★

PG-13, 107 m., 2003

Jeff Bridges (Tom Friend), Penelope Cruz (Pagan Lace), Bob Dylan (Jack Fate), John Goodman (Uncle Sweetheart), Jessica Lange (Nina Veronica), Luke Wilson (Bob Cupid). Directed by Larry Charles and produced by Nigel Sinclair and Jeff Rosen. Screenplay by Rene Fontaine and Sergei Petrov.

Bob Dylan idolatry is one of the enduring secular religions of our day. Those who worship him are inexhaustible in their fervor, and every enigmatic syllable of the great poet is cherished and analyzed as if somehow he conceals profound truths in his lyrics, and if we could only decrypt them, they would be the solution to—I dunno, maybe everything.

In *Masked and Anonymous,* where he plays a legendary troubadour named (I fear) Jack Fate, a religious fanatic played by Penelope Cruz says: "I love his songs because they are not precise—they are completely open to interpretation." She makes this statement to characters dressed as Gandhi and the pope, but lacks the courtesy to add, "But hey, guys, what do *you* think?"

I have always felt it ungenerous to have the answer but wrap it in enigmas. When Woody Guthrie, the great man's inspiration, sings a song, you know what it is about. Perhaps Dylan's genius was to take simple ideas and make them impenetrable. Since he cannot really sing, there is the assumption that he cannot be performing to entertain us, and that therefore, there must be a deeper purpose. The instructive documentary *The Ballad of Ramblin' Jack* suggests that it was Ramblin' Jack Elliott who was the true follower of Woody, and that after he introduced Dylan to Guthrie he was dropped from the picture as Dylan studiously repackaged the Guthrie genius in 1960s trappings.

That Dylan still exerts a mystical appeal there can be no doubt. When *Masked and Anonymous* premiered at Sundance 2003, there was a standing ovation when Dylan entered the room. People continued to stand during the film, in order to leave, and the auditorium was half-empty when the closing credits played to thoughtful silence. One of the more poignant moments in

Sundance history then followed, as director Larry Charles stood on the stage with various cast members, asking for questions and then asking, "Aren't there any questions?"

The movie's cast is a tribute to Dylan's charisma. Here are the credits which, after Dylan, proceed alphabetically: Bob Dylan, Jeff Bridges, Penelope Cruz, John Goodman, Jessica Lange, Luke Wilson. Also Angela Bassett, Steven Bauer, Paul Michael Chan, Bruce Dern, Ed Harris, Val Kilmer, Cheech Marin, Chris Penn, Giovanni Ribisi, Mickey Rourke, Richard Sarafian, Christian Slater, Fred Ward, Robert Wisdom. In a film where salaries must have been laughable, these people must have thought it would be cool to be in a Dylan movie. Some of them exude the aw-shucks gratitude of a visiting singer beckoned onstage at the Grand Ole Opry. Ironically, the credits do not name the one performer in the movie whose performance actually was applauded; that was a young black girl named Tinashe Kachingwe, who sang "The Times They Are a-Changin'" with such sweetness and conviction that she was like a master class.

The plot involves a nation in the throes of postrevolutionary chaos. This is "a ravaged Latin American country" (Variety) or perhaps "a sideways allegory about an alternative America" (Salon). It was filmed in run-down areas of Los Angeles, nudge, nudge. A venal rock promoter named Uncle Sweetheart (John Goodman) and his brassy partner Nina Veronica (Jessica Lange) decide to spring Jack Fate from prison to give a benefit concert to raise funds for poverty relief (maybe) and Uncle and Nina (certainly). That provides the pretense for Dylan to sing several songs, although the one I liked best, "Dixie," seemed a strange choice for a concert in a republic that, wherever it is, looks in little sympathy with the land of cotton.

The enormous cast wanders bewildered through shapeless scenes. Some seem to be improvising, and Goodman and Jeff Bridges (as a rock journalist) at least have high energy and make a game try. Others look like people who were asked to choose their clothing earlier in the day at the costume department; the happenings of the 1960s come to mind.

Dylan occupies this scenario wearing a couple of costumes borrowed from the Tinhorn Dictator rack. Alarmingly thin, he sprawls in chairs in postures that a merciful cinematographer would have talked him out of. While all about him are acting their heads off, he never speaks more than one sentence at a time, and his remarks uncannily evoke the language and philosophy of Chinese fortune cookies.

Masked and Anonymous is a vanity production beyond all reason. I am not sure, however, that the vanity is Dylan's. I don't have any idea what to think about him. He has so long since disappeared into his persona that there is little received sense of the person there. The vanity belongs perhaps to those who flattered their own by working with him, by assuming (in the face of all they had learned during hard days of honest labor on a multitude of pictures) that his genius would somehow redeem a screenplay that could never have seemed other than what it was—incoherent, raving, juvenile meanderings. If I had been asked to serve as consultant on this picture, my advice would have amounted to three words: more Tinashe Kachingwe.

Master and Commander: The Far Side of the World ★ ★ ★ ★
PG-13, 139 m., 2003

Russell Crowe (Captain Jack Aubrey), Paul Bettany (Dr. Stephen Maturin), Billy Boyd (Barrett Bonden), James D'Arcy (Lieutenant Thom Pullings), Lee Ingleby (Hollom), George Innes (Joe Plaice), Mark Lewis Jones (Mr. Hogg), Chris Larkin (Marine Captain Howard), Richard McCabe (Mr. Higgins), Robert Pugh (Mr. Allen), David Threlfall (Killick), Max Pirkis (Lord Blakeney), Edward Woodall (2nd Lieutenant William Mowett), Ian Mercer (Mr. Hollar), Max Benitz (Peter Calamy). Directed by Peter Weir and produced by Samuel Goldwyn Jr., Duncan Henderson, John Bard Manulis, and Weir. Screenplay by Weir and John Collee, based on the novels by Patrick O'Brian.

Peter Weir's *Master and Commander* is an exuberant sea adventure told with uncommon intelligence; we're reminded of well-crafted classics before the soulless age of computerized action. Based on the beloved novels of Patrick O'Brian, it re-creates the world of the British Navy circa 1805 with such detail and intensity that the sea battles become stages for personality and character. They're not simply swash-buckling—although they're that, too, with brutal and intimate violence.

The film centers on the spirits of two men, Captain Jack Aubrey and ship's surgeon Stephen Maturin. Readers of O'Brian's twenty novels know them as friends and opposites—Aubrey, the realist, the man of action; Maturin, more intellectual and pensive. Each shares some of the other's qualities, and their lifelong debate represents two sides of human nature. There's a moment in *Master and Commander* when Maturin's hopes of collecting rare biological specimens are dashed by Aubrey's determination to chase a French warship, and the tension between them at that moment defines their differences.

Aubrey, captain of HMS *Surprise,* is played by Russell Crowe as a strong but fair leader of men, a brilliant strategist who is also a student, but not a coddler, of his men. He doesn't go by the books; his ability to think outside the envelope saves the *Surprise* at one crucial moment and wins a battle at another. Maturin is played by Paul Bettany, whom you may recall as Crowe's imaginary roommate in *A Beautiful Mind.* He's so cool under pressure that he performs open-skull surgery on the deck of the *Surprise* (plugging the hole with a coin), and directs the removal of a bullet from his own chest by looking in a mirror. But his passion is biology, and he is onboard primarily because the navy will take him to places where there are beetles and birds unknown to science.

The story takes place almost entirely onboard the *Surprise,* a smaller vessel outgunned by its quarry, the French warship *Acheron.* Using an actual ship at sea and sets in the vast tank in Baja California where scenes from *Titanic* were shot, Weir creates a place so palpable we think we could find our own way around. It is a very small ship for such a large ocean, living conditions are grim, some of the men have been shanghaied on board, and one of the junior officers is thirteen years old. For risking their lives, the men are rewarded with an extra tot of grog, and feel well paid. There are scenes at sea, including the rounding of Cape Horn, which are as good or better as any sea journey ever filmed, and the battle scenes are harrowing in their closeness and ferocity; the object is to get close enough in the face of withering cannon fire to board the enemy vessel and hack its crew to death.

There are only two major battle scenes in the movie (unless you count the storms of the Cape as a battle with nature). This is not a movie that depends on body counts for its impact, but on the nature of life on board such a ship. Maturin and Aubrey sometimes relax by playing classical duets, the captain on violin, the doctor on cello, and this is not an affectation but a reflection of their well-rounded backgrounds; their arguments are as likely to involve philosophy as strategy. The reason O'Brian's readers are so faithful (I am one) is because this friendship provides him with a way to voice and consider the unnatural life of a man at sea: By talking with each other, the two men talk to us about the contest between man's need to dominate and his desire to reflect.

There is time to get to know several members of the crew. Chief among them is young Lord Blakeney (Max Pirkis), the teenager who is actually put in command of the deck during one battle. Boys this young were often at sea, learning in action (Aubrey was not much older when he served under Nelson), and both older men try to shape him in their images. With Maturin he shares a passion for biology, and begins a journal filled with sketches of birds and beetles they encounter. Under Aubrey he learns to lead men, to think clearly in battle. Both men reveal their characters in teaching the boy, and that is how we best grow to know them.

There is a sense here of the long months at sea between the dangers, of loneliness and privation on "this little wooden world." One subplot involves an officer who comes to be considered bad luck—a Jonah—by the men. Another involves the accidental shooting of the surgeon. There is a visit to the far Galapagos, where Darwin would glimpse the underlying engines of life on earth. These passages are punctuation between the battles, which depend more on strategy than firepower—as they must, if the *Surprise* is to stand against the dangerous French ship. Aubrey's charge is to prevent the French from controlling the waters off Brazil, and although the two-ship contest in *Master and Commander* is much scaled down from the fleets at battle in O'Brian's original novel, *The Far Side of the World,* that simply brings the skills of individual men more into focus.

Master and Commander is grand and glorious, and touching in its attention to its characters. Like the work of David Lean, it achieves the epic without losing sight of the human, and to see it is to be reminded of the way great action movies can rouse and exhilarate us, can affirm life instead of simply dramatizing its destruction.

The Master of Disguise ★
PG, 80 m., 2002

Dana Carvey (Pistachio), Jennifer Esposito (Jennifer), Harold Gould (Grandfather), James Brolin (Fabbrizio), Brent Spiner (Bowman), Edie McClurg (Mama), Maria Canals (Sophia), Austin Wolff (Barney). Directed by Perry Andelin Blake and produced by Sid Ganis, Alex Siskin, Todd Garner, and Barry Bernardi. Screenplay by Dana Carvey and Harris Goldberg.

The Master of Disguise pants and wheezes and hurls itself exhausted across the finish line after barely sixty-five minutes of movie, and then follows it with fifteen minutes of end credits in an attempt to clock in as a feature film. We get outtakes, deleted scenes, flubbed lines, and all the other versions of the "credit cookie," which was once a cute idea but is getting to be a bore.

The credits go on and on and on. The movie is like a party guest who thinks he is funny and is wrong. The end credits are like the same guest taking too long to leave. At one point they at last mercifully seemed to be over, and the projectionist even closed the curtains, but no: There was Dana Carvey, still visible against the red velvet, asking us what we were still doing in the theater. That is a dangerous question to ask after a movie like *The Master of Disguise*.

The movie is a desperate miscalculation. It gives poor Dana Carvey nothing to do that is really funny, and then expects us to laugh because he acts so goofy all the time. But *acting* funny is not funny. Acting in a situation that's funny—that's funny.

The plot: Carvey plays an Italian waiter named Pistachio Disguisey, who is unfamiliar with the First Law of Funny Names, which is that funny names in movies are rarely funny. Pistachio comes from a long line of masters of disguise. His father Fabbrizio (James Brolin),

having capped his career by successfully impersonating Bo Derek, retires and opens a New York restaurant. He doesn't tell his son about the family trade, but then, when he's kidnapped by his old enemy Bowman (Brent Spiner), Pistachio is told the family secret by his grandfather (Harold Gould).

Grandfather also gives him a crash course in disguise craft, after locating Fabbrizio's hidden workshop in the attic (a Disguisey's workshop, we learn, is known as a nest). There is now a scene representative of much of the movie, in which Pistachio puts on an inflatable suit, and it suddenly balloons so that he flies around the room and knocks over granddad. That scene may seem funny to kids. Real, real little, little kids.

Carvey, of course, is himself a skilled impersonator, and during the film we see him as a human turtle, Al Pacino from *Scarface*, Robert Shaw from *Jaws*, a man in a cherry suit, a man with a cow pie for a face, George W. Bush, and many other guises. In some cases the disguises are handled by using a double and then employing digital technology to make it appear as if the double's face is a latex mask that can be removed. In other cases, such as Bush, Carvey simply impersonates him.

The plot helpfully supplies Pistachio with a girl named Jennifer (Jennifer Esposito) who becomes his sidekick in the search for Fabbrizio, and they visit a great many colorful locations. One of them is a secret headquarters where Bowman keeps his priceless trove of treasures, including the lunar landing module, which is used for one of those fight scenes where the hero dangles by one hand. The movie's director, Perry Andelin Blake, has been a production designer on fourteen movies, including most of Adam Sandler's, and, to be sure, *The Master of Disguise* has an excellent production design. It is less successful at disguising itself as a comedy.

Matchstick Men ★ ★ ★ ★
PG-13, 120 m., 2003

Nicolas Cage (Roy), Sam Rockwell (Frank Mercer), Alison Lohman (Angela), Bruce McGill (Frechette), Bruce Altman (Dr. Klein). Directed by Ridley Scott and produced by Sean Bailey, Ted Griffin, Jack Rapke, Scott, and Steve

Starkey. Screenplay by Nicholas Griffin and Ted Griffin, based on the book by Eric Garcia.

Ridley Scott's *Matchstick Men* tells three stories, each one intriguing enough to supply a movie. It is: (1) the story of a crisis in the life of a man crippled by neurotic obsessions; (2) the story of two con men who happen onto a big score; and (3) the story of a man who meets the teenage daughter he never knew he had, and finds himself trying to care for her. The hero of all three stories is Roy (Nicolas Cage), who suffers from obsessive-compulsive disorder, agoraphobia, panic attacks, you name it. His con-man partner is Frank (Sam Rockwell). His daughter is Angela (Alison Lohman), and Roy is so fearful that when he decides to contact her, he persuades his shrink to make the phone call.

I wish that you had seen the movie so we could discuss what a sublime job it does of doing full justice to all three of these stories, which add up to more, or perhaps less, than the sum of their parts. The screenplay for *Matchstick Men* is an achievement of Oscar caliber— so absorbing that whenever it cuts away from "the plot," there is another, better plot to cut to. Brothers Ted and Nicholas Griffin adapted it from the novel by Eric Garcia. Cage bought the movie rights before it was published, and no wonder, because the character of Roy is one of the great roles of recent years; he's a nut case, a clever crook, and a father who learns to love, all in one. Cage effortlessly plays these three sides to his character, which by their nature would seem to be in conflict.

As the movie opens, Roy and Frank are playing a sophisticated form of the Pigeon Drop, in which victims are convinced they have a tax refund coming, and are then visited by Frank and Roy themselves, posing as federal agents who want cooperation in catching the tax frauds. Elegant. Frank keeps wondering when Roy will be ready to pull a really big job, but it's all Roy can do to get out of bed in the morning.

An open door can cause a panic attack. He goes into spasms of compulsive behavior, and only the pills prescribed by Dr. Klein (Bruce Altman) seem to hold him together at all. When he spills his pills down the drain and Klein's office is closed, Cage has a scene in a pharmacy that is the equal of his opening moments in *Leaving Las Vegas* as an illustration of

a man desperately trying to get what he needs before he implodes.

Enter the mark: Frechette (Bruce McGill), a man who might want to turn a profit laundering large sums of British money that Roy and Frank happen to have on hand. The way they bait this trap, spring it, and then move Frechette up to a really large sum has the fascination of any good con. The secret, Roy explains, is that he doesn't take people's money: "They give it to me." The victims always think it's their own idea. And since they're breaking the law, who can they complain to?

Meanwhile, Dr. Klein learns more about Roy's early, unhappy marriage, which produced a daughter after Roy left. Would it help to meet this girl, who would now be about fifteen? It might. After Klein makes the first advance, Roy approaches Angela after school, his tics and jerks and twitches all in demo mode. Angela comes for a "trial weekend," stays for a while, and eventually becomes a steadying influence for her father. At first Roy is reluctant to tell her about himself, but when he finally does admit he's not very proud of what he does, that's the first moment in the movie when he seems calm and even relaxed.

Nicolas Cage is accused of showboating, but I prefer to think he swings for the fences. Sometimes he strikes out *(Gone in 60 Seconds)*, but more often he connects (he took enormous risks in *Leaving Las Vegas, Bringing Out the Dead,* and *Adaptation*). He has a kind of raging zeal that possesses his characters; what in another actor would be overacting is, with Cage, a kind of fearsome intensity.

Rockwell, Lohman, McGill, and Altman are all perfectly cast, which is essential, since they must convince us without the movie making any effort to insist. Lohman in particular is effective; I learn to my astonishment that she's twenty-four, but here she plays a fifteen-year-old with all the tentative love and sudden vulnerability that the role requires when your dad is a whacko confidence man.

Because this is a movie about con men and a con game, there are elements I must not reveal. But let's talk about the very last scene— the one that begins "One Year Later." This is a scene that could have gone terribly wrong, spoiled by being too obvious, sentimental, angry, or tricky. Ridley Scott and his players know just how to handle it; they depend on who these characters really are. If you consider what the characters have gone through and mean to one another, then this scene has a kind of transcendence to it. It doesn't trash the story or add one more twist just for fun, but looks with dispassionate honesty at what, after all, people must believe who do this sort of thing for a living.   ☞

The Matrix Reloaded ★ ★ ★ ½
R, 138 m., 2003

Keanu Reeves (Neo), Laurence Fishburne (Morpheus), Carrie-Anne Moss (Trinity), Hugo Weaving (Agent Smith), Jada Pinkett Smith (Niobe), Gloria Foster (Oracle), Monica Bellucci (Persephone), Collin Chou (Seraph), Nona Gaye (Zee), Randall Duk Kim (Keymaker), Harry Lennix (Commander Lock), Harold Perrineau (Link), Neil and Adrian Rayment (Twins), Lambert Wilson (Merovingian), Helmut Bakaltis (Architect). Directed by Andy Wachowski and Larry Wachowski and produced by Joel Silver. Screenplay by Wachowski and Wachowski.

Commander Lock: *"Not everyone believes what you believe."*
Morpheus: *"My beliefs do not require that they do."*

Characters are always talking like this in *The Matrix Reloaded,* which plays like a collaboration involving a geek, a comic book, and the smartest kid in Philosophy 101. Morpheus in particular unreels extended speeches that remind me of Laurence Olivier's remarks when he won his honorary Oscar—the speech that had Jon Voight going "God!" on TV, but in print turned out to be quasi-Shakespearean doublespeak. The speeches provide, not meaning, but the effect of meaning: It sure sounds like those guys are saying some profound things.

That will not prevent fanboys from analyzing the philosophy of *The Matrix Reloaded* in endless Web postings. Part of the fun is becoming an expert in the deep meaning of shallow pop mythology; there is something refreshingly ironic about becoming an authority on the transient extrusions of mass culture, and

Morpheus (Laurence Fishburne) now joins Obi Wan Kenobi as the Plato of our age.

I say this not in disapproval, but in amusement. *The Matrix* (1999), written and directed by the brothers Andy and Larry Wachowski, inspired so much inflamed pseudophilosophy that it's all *The Matrix Reloaded* can do to stay ahead of its followers. It is an immensely skillful sci-fi adventure, combining the usual elements: heroes and villains, special effects and stunts, chases and explosions, romance and oratory. It develops its world with more detail than the first movie was able to afford, gives us our first glimpse of the underground human city of Zion, burrows closer to the heart of the secret of the Matrix, and promotes its hero, Neo, from confused draftee to a Christ figure in training.

As this film opens, we learn that the Machines need human bodies, millions and millions of them, for their ability to generate electricity. In an astonishing sequence, we see countless bodies locked in pods around central cores that extend out of sight above and below. The Matrix is the virtual reality that provides the minds of these sleepers with the illusion that they are active and productive. Questions arise, such as, is there no more efficient way to generate power? And, why give the humans dreams when they would generate just as much energy if comatose? And, why create such a complex virtual world for each and every one of them when they could all be given the same illusion and be none the wiser? Why is each dreamer himself or herself occupying the same body in virtual reality as the one asleep in the pod?

But never mind. We are grateful that 250,000 humans have escaped from the grid of the Matrix and gathered to build Zion, which is "near the Earth's core—where there is more heat." And as the movie opens we are alarmed to learn that the Machines are drilling toward Zion so quickly that they will arrive in thirty-six hours. We may also wonder if Zion and its free citizens really exist, or if the humans only think so, but that leads to a logical loop ending in madness.

Neo (Keanu Reeves) has been required to fly, to master martial arts, and to learn that his faith and belief can make things happen. His fights all take place within virtual reality spaces, while he reclines in a chair and is linked to the cyberworld, but he can really be killed, because if the mind thinks it is dead, "the body is controlled by the mind." All of the fight sequences, therefore, are logically contests not between physical bodies, but between video-game players, and the Neo in the big fight scenes is actually his avatar.

The visionary Morpheus, inspired by the prophecies of the Oracle, instructs Neo—who gained the confidence to leap great distances, to fly, and in *Reloaded* destroys dozens of clones of Agent Smith (Hugo Weaving) in martial combat. That fight scene is made with the wonders of digital effects and the choreography of the Hong Kong action director Yuen Wo Ping, who also did the fights in *Crouching Tiger, Hidden Dragon*. It provides one of the three great set pieces in the movie.

The second comes when Morpheus returns to Zion and addresses the assembled multitude—an audience that looks like a mosh pit crossed with the underground slaves in *Metropolis*. After his speech, the citizens dance in a percussion-driven frenzy, which is intercut with Neo and Trinity (Carrie-Anne Moss) having sex. I think their real bodies are having the sex, although you can never be sure.

The third sensational sequence is a chase involving cars, motorcycles, and trailer trucks, with gloriously choreographed moves including leaps into the air as a truck continues to move underneath. That this scene logically takes place in cyberspace does not diminish its thrilling fourteen-minute fun ride, although we might wonder—when deadly enemies meet in one of these virtual spaces, who programmed it? (I am sure I will get untold thousands of e-mails explaining it all to me.)

I became aware, during the film, that a majority of the major characters were played by African Americans. Neo and Trinity are white, and so is Agent Smith, but consider Morpheus; his superior, Commander Lock (Harry Lennix); the beautiful and deadly Niobe (Jada Pinkett Smith), who once loved Morpheus and now is with Lock, although she explains enigmatically that some things never change; the programmer Link (Harold Perrineau); Link's wife, Zee (Nona Gaye), who has the obligatory scene where she complains he's away from home too much; and the Oracle (the late Gloria Foster, very portentous). From what we can see of the extras, the population of Zion is largely black.

It has become commonplace for science fiction epics to feature one or two African-American stars, but we've come a long way since Billy Dee Williams in *Return of the Jedi*. The Wachowski brothers use so many African Americans, I suspect, not for their box-office appeal, because the Matrix is the star of the movie, and not because they are good actors (which they are), but because to the white teenagers who are the primary audience for this movie, African Americans embody a cool, a cachet, an authenticity. Morpheus is the power center of the movie, and Neo's role is essentially to study under him and absorb his mojo.

The film ends with "To Be Concluded," a reminder that the third film in the trilogy arrives on November 5, 2003. Toward the end there are scenes involving characters who seem pregnant with possibilities for part three. One is the Architect (Helmut Bakaltis), who says he designed the Matrix, and revises everything Neo thinks he knows about it. Is the Architect a human, or an avatar of the Machines? The thing is, you can never know for sure. He seems to hint that when you strip away one level of false virtual reality, you find another level beneath. Maybe everything so far is several levels up?

Stephen Hawking's *A Brief History of Time* tells the story of a cosmologist whose speech is interrupted by a little old lady who informs him that the universe rests on the back of a turtle. "Ah, yes, madame," the scientist replies, "but what does the turtle rest on?" The old lady shoots back: "You can't trick me, young man. It's nothing but turtles, turtles, turtles, all the way down." 🖝

The Matrix Revolutions ★ ★ ★
R, 130 m., 2003

Keanu Reeves (Neo), Laurence Fishburne (Morpheus), Carrie-Anne Moss (Trinity), Hugo Weaving (Agent Smith), Jada Pinkett Smith (Niobe), Mary Alice (The Oracle). Directed by Andy Wachowski and Larry Wachowski and produced by Grant Hill and Joel Silver. Screenplay by Andy Wachowski and Larry Wachowski.

My admiration for *The Matrix Revolutions* is limited only by the awkward fact that I don't much give a damn what happens to any of the characters. If I cared more about Neo, Morpheus, Niobe, and the others, there'd be more fire in my heart. But my regard is more for the technical triumph of the movie, less for the emotions it evokes. Neo is no more intended to have deep psychological realism than Indiana Jones, but the thing is, I *liked* Indy and hoped he got out in one piece—while my concern about Neo has been jerked around by so many layers of whether he's real or not, and whether he's really doing what he seems to be doing, that finally I measure my concern for him not in affection but more like the score in a video game.

Consider, too, the apocalyptic battle scene of the movie, as the vast, mechanical, all-too-symbolic screw of the Machines penetrates the dome of Zion and unleashes the Sentinels, nasty whiplashing octopi. The humans fight back by climbing into fearsome robotic fighting machines, so their muscles control more powerful muscles made of steel and cybernetics. Each of their surrogate arms ends in a mighty machine gun that sprays limitless streams of ammo at the enemy. All well done in a technical way (the computer-generated special effects are awesome), but I'm thinking: (a) The Machines use machines, so shouldn't the humans be fighting back in a more human manner? And then (b) but it's silly of me to think in this way, because neither the humans nor Machines are really there, and what we're seeing are avatars in a computer program. Who wins the battle wins the world, but the world is not what we see; what we see is a projection of the cyber-reality of the Matrix.

Or is it? See, that's where I get confused. Do humans have a separate physical reality and did they really construct Zion, that city buried deep within the Earth, and is it really there, made of molecules and elements? Because if they do and if they did, then why don't the Machines just nuke them? Why all the slithering mechanical octopi? And why, in a society that is unimaginably advanced over our own, do they still use machine guns anyway? So it would seem that the battle is a virtual battle, not a real one, and that impression is reinforced by the way the laws of physics seem to be on hold; as Niobe and Morpheus race to the rescue in their speeding ship, for example, it bounces off the walls and sheds so many vital parts that if it were a real ship it would have crashed.

I am sure my information is flawed. No doubt I will get countless e-mails demonstrating my ignorance in tiresome detail. But the thing is: A movie should not depend on the answers to questions like this for its effect. The first *Matrix* was the best because it really did toy with the conflict between illusion and reality—between the world we think we inhabit and its underlying nature. The problem of *The Matrix Reloaded* and *The Matrix Revolutions* is that they are action pictures that are forced to exist in a world that undercuts the reality of the action.

There is, to be sure, the movie's underlying philosophy, but this grows more underwhelming as the series continues. When Neo finally sits down with the Oracle (Mary Alice) and demands the 411, what he gets is about what you'd pay fifty bucks for from a storefront Tarot reader. When the dust has settled and we all look back on the trilogy from a hype-free zone, we'll realize that the first movie inspired its fans to imagine that astonishing philosophical revelations would be made, and the series hasn't been able to live up to those anticipations. Maybe that would have been impossible. No matter how luridly the barker describes the wonders inside his tent, it's always just another sideshow.

Still, in a basic and undeniable sense, this is a good movie, and fans who have earned their credit hours with the first two will want to see this one and graduate. To the degree that I was able to put aside my questions, forget logic, disregard continuity problems, and immerse myself in the moment, *The Matrix Revolutions* is a terrific action achievement. Andy and Larry Wachowski have concluded their trilogy with all barrels blazing. Their final apocalypse in the bowels of the Earth plays like *Metropolis* on steroids. There are sights here to stir the sense of wonder, and a marriage between live action and special effects that is about as good as these things get in the movies. It's a rich irony that the story is about humans occupying a world generated by computers, and the movie consists of actors occupying a world also created by computers. Neo may or may not exist in a universe created by computers, but Keanu Reeves certainly does.

Note: The Matrix Reloaded *was notable for the number of key characters who were black; this time, what we notice is how many strong women there are. Two women operate a bazooka team, Niobe flies the ship, the women have muscles, they kick ass, and this isn't your grandmother's* Second Sex *anymore.*

Max ★ ★ ★ ½
R, 106 m., 2002

John Cusack (Max Rothman), Noah Taylor (Adolf Hitler), Leelee Sobieski (Liselore Von Peltz), Molly Parker (Nina Rothman), Ulrich Thomsen (Captain Mayr). Directed by Menno Meyjes and produced by Andras Hamori. Screenplay by Meyjes.

Und . . . der Fuhrer vas a better artist than Churchill!
　　　　　　　　　—The Producers

The central mystery of Hitler, William Boyd writes in a recent *Times Literary Supplement,* is: "How on earth could a dysfunctional, deranged, down-and-out homeless person in pre–First World War Vienna become, twenty years later, chancellor of Germany?" A peculiar and intriguing film named *Max* argues that he succeeded because he had such a burning need to be recognized—and also, of course, because of luck, good for him, bad for us. If Hitler had won fame as an artist, the century's history might have been different. Pity about his art.

Max imagines a fictional scenario in which the young Adolf Hitler (Noah Taylor) is befriended by a one-armed Jewish art dealer named Max Rothman (John Cusack) in Munich in the years following World War I. Both served in the German army and fought in the same battle, where Rothman lost his arm. The dealer opens an avant-garde art gallery in a vast abandoned factory, showcasing artists like George Grosz and attracting important collectors—and Hitler, clutching his portfolio of kitsch. Rothman takes pity on this man and is friendly to him, moved by the pathos beneath his bluster.

The film, written and directed by Menno

Meyjes, who scripted *The Color Purple,* has been attacked because it attempts to "humanize" a monster. But of course, Hitler was human, and we must understand that before we can understand anything else about him. To dehumanize him is to fall under the spell that elevated him into the führer, a mythical being who transfixed Germans and obscured the silly little man with the mustache. To ponder Hitler's early years with the knowledge of his later ones is to understand how life can play cosmic tricks with tragic results.

Max suggests that Hitler's real work of art was himself and the Nazi state he first envisioned in fantasy terms; even as a young man we see him doodling with swastikas and designing comic-book uniforms. Clothes make the man, and to some extent Hitler's skill as a fashion designer made men into Nazis. "I am the new avant-garde and politics is the new art," he tells Rothman, not inaccurately.

If Hitler is a mystery, what are we to make of Max Rothman? John Cusack plays him as a man of empathy, who endures the tantrums of his artists, and feels pity for this bedraggled Hitler whom he first meets as a liquor deliveryman. Rothman himself wanted to be an artist but has put that on hold after losing his arm. He has returned to a comfortable bourgeois life in Munich, with his doctor father-in-law, his secure wife, Nina (Molly Parker), and his stimulating mistress, Liselore (Leelee Sobieski). When he's quizzed about his friendship with the pathetic Hitler, his answers are simple: "He came back from the war to nothing. He doesn't have any friends."

Yes, Hitler is anti-Semitic and makes no secret of it. But in Germany in those days anti-Semitism was like the weather; you couldn't do anything about it, and you had to go out in it. Rothman takes Hitler's rantings with weariness and sadness, and at one point tells Liselore, "I told him his insane f——— ideas are holding him back as an artist."

There is never, even for a moment, a glimmer of evidence to suggest that Hitler could have been a successful artist. His drawings look like the kind of cartoon caricatures that bored boys create in their notebooks in the back row of geometry class, playing with their protractors and dreaming of supermen. Hitler instinctively fails to see the point of abstract

act; at one point he suggests that Rothman frame his diarrhea. We are reminded that, in power, both the Nazis and the Soviets banned and burned abstract art. Curious, that art which claimed to represent nothing nevertheless represented so much to them. Perhaps art is a threat to totalitarianism when it does not have a clear, censurable subject, and is left to the musings of the citizen.

As the title suggests, *Max* centers more on Rothman than on Hitler. Max is a kind, dreamy, hopeful man, who we presume saw his share of the horrors of that particularly nasty war, and trusts that art is taking him in the right direction. He is also smooth and sophisticated, a master of one-armed cigarette technique, who moves seamlessly between his bourgeois home and the cafés and dives of bohemian Munich. He is worldly in a way that Hitler is not, and their differences are suggested when he says in exasperation to the fierce failed artist, "Listen— do you want to meet some girls?"

Hitler's other patron is an army propagandist named Mayr (Ulrich Thomsen), like Hitler an outcast in the German economic ruin. He is attached to a small splinter party and thinks Hitler might make a good spokesman. What Mayr sees in this hapless nonentity is hard to say, but he is quite right, and soon Hitler is fascinating crowds in beer halls with his emerging Nazi vision. (Mayr, I learn, is an actual historical figure, who later, for his pains, was beheaded by Hitler.)

But what, we may ask, parroting Soviet realism, is the *purpose* of this movie? What is its *message*? It is not abstract but presents us with two central characters whose races have a rendezvous with destiny. I think the key is in Max, who is a kind, liberal humanist, who cares for the unfortunate, who lives a life of the mind that blinds him to the ominous rising tide of Nazism. Can a man like this, with values like this, survive against a man like Hitler, who has no value except the will for power? It is the duty of the enlightened state to assure that he can. Dissent protects the body politic from the virus of totalitarianism.

May ★ ★ ★ ★
R, 95 m., 2003

Angela Bettis (May Canady), Jeremy Sisto (Adam Stubbs), Anna Faris (Polly), James Duval (Blank), Nichole Hiltz (Ambrosia), Kevin Gage (Papa), Merle Kennedy (Mama), Chandler Hect (Young May). Directed by Lucky McKee and produced by Marius Balchunas and Scott Sturgeon. Screenplay by McKee.

May is a horror film and something more and deeper, something disturbing and oddly moving. It begins as the story of a strange young woman, it goes for laughs and gets them, it functions as a black comedy, but then it glides past the comedy and slides slowly down into a portrait of madness and sadness. The title performance by Angela Bettis is crucial to the film's success. She plays a twisted character who might easily go over the top into parody, and makes her believable, sympathetic, and terrifying.

The movie will inevitably be compared with *Carrie*, not least because Bettis starred in the 2002 TV version of that story. Like *Carrie*, it is about a woman who has been wounded by society and finds a deadly revenge. But *May* is not a supernatural film. It follows the traditional outlines of a horror or slasher film, up to a point—and then it fearlessly follows its character into full madness. We expect some kind of a U-turn or cop-out, but no; the writer and director, Lucky McKee, never turns back from his story's implacable logic. This is his solo directing debut, and it's kind of amazing. You get the feeling he's the real thing.

Bettis plays May Canady, who as a girl had a "lazy eye" that made her an outcast at school. After a brief prologue, we meet her in her twenties, as an assistant in a veterinary clinic. She is shy, quirky, askew, but in a curiously sexy way, so that when she meets the good-looking Adam Stubbs (Jeremy Sisto), he is intrigued. "I'm weird," she tells him. "I like weird," he says. "I like weird a lot."

Uh-huh. His idea of weird is attending the revival of a Dario Argento horror film. He shows May his own student film, which begins with a young couple kissing and caressing and then moves on inexorably into mutual cannibalism. May likes it. She snuggles closer to him on the sofa. Afterward, she gives him her review: "I don't think that she could have gotten his whole finger in one bite, though. That part was kind of far-fetched."

Bettis makes May peculiar but fully human. There are scenes here of such close observation, of such control of body language, voice, and behavior, evoking such ferocity and obsession, that we are reminded of Lady Macbeth. It is as hard to be excellent in a horror film as in Shakespeare. Harder, maybe, because the audience isn't expecting it. Sisto's performance as Adam is carefully calibrated to show an intelligent guy who is intrigued, up to a point, and then smart enough to prudently back away. He's not one of those horror movie dumbos who makes stupid mistakes. Notice the look in his eye after he asks her to describe some of the weird stuff that goes on at the animal hospital, and she does, more graphically than he requires.

May's colleague at the clinic is Polly (Anna Faris), a lesbian, always open to new experiences. One day when May cuts herself with a scalpel, Polly is fascinated. Then May unexpectedly cuts her. Polly recoils, screams, considers, and says, "I kind of liked it. Do me again." Like Adam, she is erotically stirred by May's oddness—up to a point. There is an erotic sequence involving May and Polly, not explicit but very evocative, and it's not just a "sex scene," but a way to show that for Polly sex is entertainment and for May it is of fundamental importance.

McKee uses various fetishes in an understated way. May is not a smoker, but she treasures a pack of cigarettes that Adam gave her, and the precious cigarettes are measured out one by one as accomplices to her actions. She has a doll from childhood that gazes from its glass cabinet; in a lesser movie, it would come alive, but in this one it does all the necessary living within May's mind. When May volunteers to work with blind kids, we fear some kind of exploitation, but the scenes are handled to engender suspense, not disrespect.

The movie subtly darkens its tone until, when the horrifying ending arrives, we can see how we got there. There is a final shot that would get laughs in another kind of film, but *May* earns the right to it, and it works, and we understand it.

There are so many bad horror movies. A good one is incredibly hard to make. It has to feel a fundamental sympathy for its monster, as movies as different as *Frankenstein, Carrie,* and *The Silence of the Lambs* did. It has to see that they suffer, too. The crimes of too many horror monsters seem to be for their own entertainment, or ours. In the best horror movies, the crimes are inescapable, and the monsters are driven toward them by the merciless urgency of their natures.

Mayor of the Sunset Strip ★ ★ ★
R, 94 m., 2004

As themselves: Rodney Bingenheimer, David Bowie, Deborah Harry, Courtney Love, Cher, Nancy Sinatra, Mick Jagger. A documentary directed by George Hickenlooper and produced by Chris Carter, Greg Little, and Tommy Perna. Screenplay by Hickenlooper.

Mayor of the Sunset Strip tells the story of Rodney Bingenheimer, a man who loved music and musicians so much that he willed himself from obscurity into a position of power as the most influential hit-maker on the most important rock radio station in Los Angeles, and then faded from view as his moment passed. Now he is like a ghost, haunting the scenes of his former triumphs, clinging to a last gig from midnight to 3 A.M. every Sunday night on the station he once ruled. "They're afraid to fire him," another employee speculates, "because he's the soul of KROQ."

The Rodney Bingenheimer of today seems always to be smiling through a deep sadness. He is a small man who still has the youthful cuteness that must have won him friends in his early days. His hair is still combed in the same tousled, mid-1970s, rock star style, and his T-shirts are the real thing, not retro. He lives now in an inexpensive apartment jammed with records, tapes, discs, and countless autographed photos of his friends the stars. And, yes, they are still his friends; they have not forgotten him, and David Bowie, Cher, Deborah Harry, Courtney Love, Nancy Sinatra, and Mick Jagger all appear in this film and seem genuinely fond of Rodney.

Well they might. He introduced some of them—Bowie in particular—to American radio. He was known for finding new music and playing it first: the Ramones, the Sex Pistols, the Clash, Nirvana. Stations all over the country stole their playlists from Rodney. "Sonny and Cher were kinda like my mom and my dad," he says wistfully at one point. He ran a little club for a while, featuring British glam rock, and the stars remember with a grin that it was so small the "VIP Area" consisted simply of a velvet rope separating a few chairs from the dance floor.

The story of how Bingenheimer entered into this world is apparently true, unlikely as it sounds. As a kid, he was obsessed with stars, devoured the fan magazines, collected autographs. One day when he was a teenager, his mother dropped him off in front of Connie Stevens's house and told him he was on his own. He didn't see his mother for another five or six years. Connie wasn't home.

He migrated to Sunset Strip, but instead of dying there or disappearing into drugs or crime, he simply ingratiated himself. People liked him. He hustled himself into a job as a gofer for Davy Jones of the Monkees (they looked a little alike), and then became a backstage caterer; a survivor of a Doors tour remembers a Toronto concert where Rodney had enormous platters of fresh shrimp backstage. But the Beatles were backstage visitors, and Rodney gave them the shrimp, so there were only a few left for the Doors, who had paid for them. Challenged by the Doors, Rodney shrugged and said, "Well, they're the Beatles."

Wherever Bingenheimer went in the music and club scene, his face was his passport. Robert Plant says, "Rodney got more girls than I did." We hear a little of his radio show from the old days, and what comes across is not a vibrating personality or a great radio voice—it's kind of tentative, really—but an almost painful sincerity. He loves the music he plays, and he introduces it to you like a lover he thinks is right for you.

The road downhill was gradual, apparently. We get glimpses of Rodney today, repairing his mom's old Nova with a pair of pliers, shuffling forlornly through souvenirs of his glory days. He seems very even, calm, sad but resigned, except for one moment the documentary camera is not supposed to witness, when he finds that another deejay, a person he sponsored and gave breaks to, is starting a show of new music—stealing Rodney's gig. He explodes in anger.

We're glad he does. He has a lot to feel angry about.

The film was directed by George Hickenlooper, who made the classic doc *Hearts of Darkness* (1991) about the nightmare of Francis Ford Coppola's *Apocalypse Now*, and the wonderful fiction film *The Man from Elysian Fields* (2001). Why did he make this film (apart from the possibility that someone named Hickenlooper might feel an affinity for someone named Bingenheimer)? Hickenlooper has been around fame from an early age. He was twenty-six when he released the doc about the Coppola meltdown. He cast Mick Jagger and James Coburn in *Elysian Fields*. He was aware of Rodney Bingenheimer when the name opened doors. His film evokes what the Japanese call "mono no aware," which refers to the impermanence of life and the bittersweet transience of things. There is a little Rodney Bingenheimer in everyone, but you know what? Most people aren't as lucky as Rodney.

Mean Girls ★ ★ ★
PG-13, 93 m., 2004

Lindsay Lohan (Cady Heron), Rachel McAdams (Regina George), Lizzy Caplan (Janis), Daniel Franzese (Damian), Jonathan Bennett (Aaron), Lacey Chabert (Gretchen), Tina Fey (Ms. Norbury), Tim Meadows (Mr. Duvall), Amanda Seyfried (Karen). Directed by Mark S. Waters and produced by Lorne Michaels. Screenplay by Tina Fey, based on the book *Queen Bees and Wannabes* by Rosalind Wiseman.

In a wasteland of dumb movies about teenagers, *Mean Girls* is a smart and funny one. It even contains some wisdom, although I hesitate to mention that, lest I scare off its target audience. The TV ads, which show Lindsay Lohan landing ass over teakettle in a garbage can, are probably right on the money; since that scene is nothing at all like the rest of the movie, was it filmed specifically to use in the commercials?

Lindsay Lohan stars as Cady Heron, a high school junior who was home-schooled in Africa while her parents worked there as anthropologists. She is therefore the smartest girl in school when her dad is hired by Northwestern and she enrolls in Evanston Township High

School—which, like all American high schools in the movies, is physically located in Toronto. What she's not smart about are the ways cliques work in high school, and how you're categorized and stereotyped by who you hang with and how you dress.

Cady makes two friends right away: Janis (Lizzy Caplan), a semi-Goth whose own anthropology includes an analysis of who sits where in the cafeteria, and why; and Damian (Daniel Franzese), Janis's best friend, described as "too gay to function." They clue her in: The three most popular girls in the junior class are the Plastics, so-called because they bear an uncanny resemblance to Barbie. They're led by Regina George (Rachel McAdams), a skilled manipulator whose mother's boob job has defined her values in life. Her sidekicks are Gretchen (Lacey Chabert) and Karen (Amanda Seyfried).

Janis and Damian warn Cady against the girls from hell. But when Regina invites Cady to join their table, Janis urges her to: She can be a spy and get inside information for their campaign to destroy Regina. And she can recommend an obscure brand of Swedish "diet bar" actually used by athletes to gain weight, so that slim Regina with her flawless complexion can find out how it feels to be chubby and spotty.

Mean Girls dissects high school society with a lot of observant detail that seems surprisingly well informed. The screenplay by *Saturday Night Live*'s Tina Fey is both a comic and a sociological achievement, and no wonder; it's inspired not by a novel but by a nonfiction book by Rosalind Wiseman. Its full title more or less summarizes the movie: *Queen Bees and Wannabes: Helping Your Daughter Survive Cliques, Gossip, Boyfriends, and Other Realities of Adolescence.* The mothers in the movie are not much help, however, and Fey's screenplay wisely uses comedy as a learning tool.

Fey also plays a math teacher named Ms. Norbury, who is more plausible and likable than most high school teachers in the movies, and also kind of lovable, especially in the vicinity of the school principal, Mr. Duvall (Tim Meadows, a former *SNL* star). Although many of producer Lorne Michaels's movies with *SNL* cast members have been broad, dumb, and obvious, this one has a light and infectious touch, and it's a revelation to see how Meadows gets

real laughs not with big gestures but with small ones: Notice particularly his body language and tone of voice during the new prom queen's speech.

The movie was directed by Mark S. Waters, who also made *Freaky Friday* (2003), a superior remake, and emerged from Sundance 1997 with *The House of Yes,* an uneven but intriguing dark comedy with Parker Posey convinced she was Jackie Onassis. Here he avoids amazing numbers of clichés that most teenage comedies cannot do without. When Cady throws a party while her parents are out of town, for example, a lot of uninvited guests do crash, yes, but amazingly they do *not* trash the house. Although Principal Duvall lectures the student body about a pushing-and-shoving spree, he does *not* cancel the prom ("We've already hired the deejay"). When Cady gets a crush on Aaron (Jonathan Bennett), who sits in front of her in math class, she deals with it in a reasonable way that does *not* involve heartbreak. When there are misunderstandings, they're understandable, and *not* awkward contrivances manufactured for the convenience of the plot.

In the middle of all this, Lindsay Lohan, who was seventeen when the movie was filmed, provides a center by being centered. She has a quiet self-confidence that prevents her from getting shrill and hyper like so many teenage stars; we believe her when she says that because of her years in Africa, "I had never lived in a world where adults didn't trust me." She never allows the character to tilt into caricature, and for that matter, even the Plastics seem real, within their definitions of themselves, and not like the witch-harridans of some teenage movies.

Will teenage audiences walk out of *Mean Girls* determined to break with the culture of cliques, gossip, and rules for popularity? Not a chance. That's built into high school, I think. But they may find it interesting that the geeks are more fun than the queen bees, that teachers have feelings, and that you'll be happier as yourself than as anybody else. I guess the message is, you have to live every day as if you might suddenly be hit by a school bus.

Mean Machine ★ ★ ★

R, 98 m., 2002

Vinnie Jones (Danny Meehan), Jason Statham

(Monk), David Kelly (Doc), David Hemmings (Prison Governor), Vas Blackwood (Massive), Jason Flemyng (Bob), Danny Dyer (Billy the Limpet), Robbie Gee (Trojan). Directed by Barry Skolnick and produced by Guy Ritchie. Screenplay by Tracy Keenan Wynn, Charlie Fletcher, Chris Baker, and Andrew Day.

The formula is familiar but enjoyable. A group of British tough guys are assembled for an enterprise that combines violence with humor, while cherishing their peculiar personalities and even finding goodness where none should grow. We've had prisoners winning a gardening competition, pot dealers helping little old ladies, and crooks leaving crime for life as real-estate agents. Now here is *Mean Machine*, about a corrupt British soccer champion, jailed for rigging an important match and ordered by the prison governor to coach the inmates' team. The big match will be against the guards' team.

If this premise rings a faint, far-off bell, you may be remembering Robert Aldrich's *The Longest Yard* (1974), with one of Burt Reynolds's best performances, that told the same story, more or less, in terms of American football. Barry Skolnick's *Mean Machine* is more than inspired by *The Longest Yard*; it's based on the same Tracy Keenan Wynn screenplay, and indeed *The Mean Machine* was even the original title of *The Longest Yard*.

The movie stars Vinnie Jones, a real-life footballer so tough he didn't even play for England; he played for Wales. According to the BBC Website, he was known for dirty football, just like Danny Meehan, his character in the film. You may recognize Jones's Fearless Fosdick features from *Lock, Stock and Two Smoking Barrels*, directed by Guy Ritchie, who produced this film. And he has appeared as a fearsome background presence in *Snatch, Gone in 60 Seconds,* and *Swordfish.* In his first lead role, he handles the dialogue like meat and potatoes, one line at a time, chewed carefully.

The deal: The prison governor (David Hemmings) has a gambling problem and is crazy about football. He orders his new celebrity prisoner to coach the team. This does not sit well with the head guard, who coaches the guards' team, but what can he say? Danny doesn't much want to enter the coaching profession, but the governor makes him a threat he can't ignore.

The most enjoyable passages are some of the most predictable, recycled out of countless other movies where a leader has to pick his men. Danny finds himself with the prison contraband retailer, Massive (Vas Blackwood), as his right-hand man, and a violent, feared con named Monk (Jason Statham) as his star player. He gets a lot of valuable prison lore and advice from the ancient convict Doc (David Kelly, whom you will remember from his naked scooter ride in *Waking Ned Devine*). Kelly has had a whole late flowering playing twinkly geezers, clouded only by the distressing tendency of his characters to end up in sentimental death scenes.

All leads up to the big match, which of course involves hard play and dirty tricks, and dovetails neatly with the governor's gambling problem. *Mean Machine* lacks the social satire of *The Longest Yard*, which was a true early 1970s film and therefore antiestablishment. It's interested only in the characters and the game. Guy Ritchie, who started out as such an innovator in *Lock, Stock, etc.,* seems to have headed directly for reliable generic conventions as a producer. But they *are* reliable, and have become conventions for a reason: They work. *Mean Machine* is what it is, and very nicely too.

The Medallion ★ ★ ★
PG-13, 90 m., 2003

Jackie Chan (Eddie Yang), Lee Evans (Arthur Watson), Claire Forlani (Nicole), Christy Chung (Charlotte Watson), Julian Sands (Snakehead), John Rhys-Davies (Hammerstock-Smythe), Anthony Wong Chau-Sang (Lester). Directed by Gordon Chan and produced by Alfred Cheung. Screenplay by Bey Logan and Chan.

The child who was born in the fourth month of the Year of the Snake and is destined to meld the two halves of the sacred medallion is always surrounded by candles. Well, of course he is. He sits in the lotus position and gazes into infinity and there are hundreds, maybe thousands of candles surrounding him, and I am left with questions:

1. Who obtains the candles? Is there a wholesale source?

2. Is the child's meditation disturbed when it takes hours to light all of those candles, with some burning down before others have even been lighted? Do the candle-lighters work in shifts?

3. What kind of a kid can sit still for that long? When we went on vacation with our grandsons, Taylor and Emil, we made the mistake of buying them pedometers, and they clocked 4,000 steps before they even got out of bed.

These questions are of course utterly beside the point, but to ask them is one of the pleasures with a movie like *The Medallion*. I realize I am not stern enough with such movies, permitting myself to be entertained when I should be appalled, but just when I am trying to adjust my frown, in walks John Rhys-Davies and introduces himself as "Commander Hammerstock-Smythe," and there I go again.

The movie stars Jackie Chan, who has never to my knowledge been described as handsome, and who pokes fun at his own nose in this movie. His command of the English language should more properly be called a duel, and most of his movies are sensationally derivative of most of his other movies. Yet he is so likeable that if you let him, he'll grow on you. And every once in a while he'll pull something like the stunt in this movie, where he approaches a locked gate and gracefully climbs right up the wall next to it and jumps over it—and then, in that endearing touch he often uses after a feat like that, he shakes his head and grins as if to suggest even he can't believe how good he is.

The plot of *The Medallion* involves the two halves of an ancient medallion, which the above-mentioned child can join, after which it can grant eternal life, but first you have to die. There are some other complications, so study the instructions before attempting this at home. The evil Snakehead (Julian Sands) wants to get his hands on the child and the medallion, and Jackie Chan is a Hong Kong cop who tries to prevent him. His allies include an Interpol operative named Arthur Watson (Lee Evans), and another Interpol cop named Nicole (Claire Forlani), who used to have something going with Jackie, as we can tell because she slaps him a lot and then smiles at him.

The plot we will sidestep. The effects we can talk about. Jackie Chan does a lot of his own stunts, and then there's a sensational climactic scene in which Chan and Snakehead have a duel in midair, which I think is fairly pointless since by then they are both immortal—or sort of immortal, which is the loophole. Earlier, there's a nice scene where Jackie is locked into a shipping container with the boy (but without the candles) and then the container is dumped into the ocean, which would seem to be the wrong strategy if you want to grab the kid. How or if they get out of that, I'm not telling.

The Medallion is what it is, disposable entertainment, redeemed by silliness, exaggeration, and Jackie Chan's skill and charm. I would not want to see it twice, but I liked seeing it once. If you are the kind of person who doubts you will ever see a Jackie Chan movie, this is not the one to start with. If you are an admirer of Chan, you will find this a big step above *The Tuxedo* but not up to *Shanghai Knights*.

Men in Black II ★ ½

PG-13, 88 m., 2002

Tommy Lee Jones (Kay), Will Smith (Jay), Rip Torn (Zed), Lara Flynn Boyle (Serleena), Johnny Knoxville (Scrad/Charlie), Rosario Dawson (Laura Vasquez), Tony Shalhoub (Jeebs), Patrick Warburton (Tee), (voice of) Tim Blaney (Frank). Directed by Barry Sonnenfeld and produced by Walter F. Parkes and Laurie MacDonald. Screenplay by Robert Gordon and Barry Fanaro, based on the Malibu Comic by Lowell Cunningham.

Some sequels continue a story. Others repeat it. *Men in Black II* creates a new threat for the MIB, but recycles the same premise, which is that mankind can defeat an alien invasion by assigning agents in Ray-Bans to shoot them into goo. This is a movie that fans of the original might enjoy in a diluted sort of way, but there is no need for it—except, of course, to take another haul at the box office, where the 1997 movie grossed nearly $600 million worldwide.

The astonishing success of the original *MIB* was partly because it was fun, partly because it was unexpected. We'd never seen anything like it, while with *MIB II* we've seen something exactly like it. In the original, Tommy Lee Jones played a no-nonsense veteran agent, Will Smith was his trainee, Rip Torn was their gruff boss, and makeup artist Rick Baker and a team of f/x wizards created a series of fanciful, grotesque aliens. Although the aliens had the technology for interplanetary travel, they were no match for the big guns of the *MIB*.

In *MIB II*, the guns are even bigger and the aliens are even slimier, although they do take sexy human form when one of them, Serleena, morphs into Lara Flynn Boyle. Another one, named Scrad (Johnny Knoxville), turns into a human who has a second neck with a smaller version of the same head, although that is not as amusing as you might hope.

The plot: The aliens are here to capture something, I'm not sure what, that will allow them to destroy Earth. The top MIB agent is now Jay (Smith), who needs the help of Kay (Jones), but Kay's memory has been erased by a "deneuralizer" and must be restored so that he can protect whatever it is the aliens want. Kay is currently working at the post office, which might have inspired more jokes than it does.

Smith and Jones fit comfortably in their roles and do what they can, but the movie doesn't give them much to work with. The biggest contribution is a dog named Frank (voice by Tim Blaney), whose role is much expanded from the first movie. Frank is human in everything but form, a tough-talking streetwise canine who keeps up a running commentary as the reunited MIB chase aliens through New York. One of the eyewitnesses they question is a pizza waitress named Laura, played by the beautiful Rosario Dawson, who Jay likes so much he forgets to deneuralize.

The special effects are good, but often pointless. As the movie throws strange aliens at us, we aren't much moved—more like mildly interested. There's a subway worm at the outset that eats most of a train without being anything more than an obvious special effect (we're looking at the technique, not the worm), and later there are other aliens who look more like doodles at a concept session than anything we can get much worked up about. There is, however, a very odd scene set in a train-station locker, which is occupied by a chanting mob of little creatures who worship the keyholder, and I would have liked to see more of them: What possible worldview do they have? If *Men in Black III* opens with the occupants of the locker, I will at least have hope for it.

Merci Pour le Chocolat ★ ★ ★

NO MPAA RATING, 99 m., 2002

Isabelle Huppert (Mika Muller-Polonski), Jacques Dutronc (André Polonski), Anna Mouglalis (Jeanne Pollet), Rodolphe Pauly (Guillaume Polonski), Brigitte Catillon (Louise Pollet), Michel Robin (Dufreigne), Mathieu Simonet (Axel). Directed by Claude Chabrol and produced by Marin Karmitz. Screenplay by Caroline Eliacheff and Chabrol, based on the Charlotte Armstrong novel, *The Chocolate Cobweb*.

Isabelle Huppert has the best poker face since Buster Keaton. She faces the camera with detached regard, inviting us to imagine what she is thinking. Since so often the thoughts of her characters run toward crime, revenge, betrayal, lust, and sadism, it is just as well she can seem so passive; an actress who tried to *portray* these inner emotions would inevitably go hurtling over the top and into the next movie.

Consider *Merci Pour le Chocolate*, her new film, directed by her longtime admirer Claude Chabrol. There is hardly any suspense about what she's up to. The title, and the fact that it is a thriller, inspire us to regard the movie's frequent cups of hot chocolate with as much suspicion as the arsenic-laced coffee in Hitchcock's *Notorious*. Even if an early scene hadn't warned us that the chocolate contains a date-rape drug, we'd be wary just because of the dispassionate way Huppert serves it. She doesn't seem like a hostess so much as a clinician.

Huppert plays Mika Muller-Polonski, the first and third wife of the famous pianist André Polonski (tired-eyed Jacques Dutronc). They were married "for a few minutes" many years ago. After their divorce, he remarried, had a son named Guillaume, and then lost his wife in a car crash. She apparently dozed off while they were all visiting . . . Mika.

The movie opens with the remarriage of Mika and André, eighteen years after their first ceremony. The spectators look less than ecstatic. The new family moves into Mika's vast, gloomy Gothic mansion in Lausanne, paid for with the profits from her family's chocolate company. One of the rituals is hot chocolate at bedtime, personally prepared by Mika ("In this house, I serve the chocolate").

An unexpected development. An attractive young piano student, Jeanne Pollet (Anna Mouglalis), finds a clipping in her mother's papers reporting that on the day of her birth, she was briefly switched with Guillaume. Using this as a pretext, she calls on the Polonski family, not because she thinks she is André's daughter, but because she wants, she says, piano lessons. Her arrival causes Guillaume to recede into more of a funk than usual, Mika to greet her with the outward show of friendliness, and André to devote himself with unseemly enthusiasm to her piano lessons.

Curious, isn't it, that Jeanne is a piano virtuoso, and Guillaume has a tin ear? Thought-provoking, too, that Guillaume is not Mika's son, but the son of her husband's second wife, who died so tragically during that visit to ... Mika's. And interesting that André has taken such an interest in Jeanne. And Mika keeps serving the hot chocolate.

There is no mystery about what Mika is doing with the hot chocolate. The mysteries are: to whom, and why. The motives may differ. She may, indeed, simply be amusing herself. Huppert's bland expression masks her motives to such a degree that even when she *does* smile or frown, we suspect the honesty of the expression: What is she really thinking?

Claude Chabrol is a master of domestic suspense, and he has used Huppert before as a cold-blooded killer, notably in *Violette Noziere* (1978). What is fascinating is how little Huppert has seemed to change in the intervening years. She has worked ceaselessly, usually in good pictures, often with good directors. Filmmakers seem drawn to her because of her mysterious detachment; while many actors seek out the secrets of their characters, Huppert keeps such secrets as she may have discovered, and invites us to figure them out for ourselves.

The appeal of *Merci Pour le Chocolate* is not in the somewhat creaky old poisoning plot, not in the hints of suppressed family secrets, not in the suspense about what will happen next—but in the enigma within which Huppert conceals her character. While all those around her plot, scheme, hope, and fear, she simply looks on and pours the chocolate. What is she thinking? What does she want? Who is she? Her appeal in film after film is maddening, perverse, and seductive.

Metropolis ★ ★ ★ ★
PG-13, 107 m., 2002

With the voices of: Jamieson Price (Duke Red), Yuka Imoto (Tima), Kei Kobayashi (Kenichi), Kouki Okada (Rock), Toshio Furukawa (General), Dave Mallow (Pero), Scott Weinger (Atlas). Directed by Taro Rin and produced by Yutaka Maseba and Haruyo Kanesaku. Screenplay by Osamu Tezuka and Katsuhiro Otomo, based on Tezuka's comic book. Dubbed into English.

There's something about vast futuristic cities that stirs me. Perhaps they awaken memories of my twelfth year, when I sat in the basement on hot summer days and read through the lower reaches of science-fiction magazines: *Imagination, Other Worlds, Amazing.* On the covers, towering cities were linked by sky-bridges, and buses were cigar-shaped rockets. In the foreground a bug-eyed monster was attacking a screaming heroine in an aluminum brassiere. Even now, the image of a dirigible tethered to the top of the Empire State Building is more thrilling to me than the space shuttle, which is merely real.

Those visions are goofy and yet at the same time exhilarating. What I like about Tokyo is that it looks like a 1940s notion of a future city. I placed *Dark City* first on my list of the best films of 1998, loved *Blade Runner*'s visuals more than its story, liked the taxicabs in the sky in *The Fifth Element.* Now here is *Metropolis,* one of the best animated films I have ever seen, and the city in this movie is not simply a backdrop or a location, but one of those movie places that colonize our memory.

The Japanese anime is named after the 1926 Fritz Lang silent classic, and is based on a 1949 *manga* (comic book) by the late Osamu Tezuka, which incorporated Lang's images. The movie was directed by Taro Rin and written by the anime legend Katsuhiro Otomo, who directed *Akira* and wrote *Roujin Z.* It uses the Lang film as a springboard into a surprisingly thoughtful, ceaselessly exciting sci-fi story about a plot to use humanoids to take over the city. In the romance between Tima, the half-human heroine, and Kenichi, the detective's nephew who falls in love with her, the movie asks whether a machine can love. The answer is an interesting spin on *A.I.* and *Blade Runner,* because the debate goes on within Tima herself, between her human and robotic natures.

The film opens with astonishing visuals of the great city, which, like Lang's Metropolis, exists on several levels above- and belowground. We see the skyscraping Ziggurat, a complex of towers linked by bridges and braces. The building seems to be a symbol of progress, but actually masks a scheme by the evil Duke Red to wrest control of the city from elected officials. Deep inside Ziggurat is a throne suspended in a hall filled with giant computer chips; it is intended for Tima, a humanoid in the image of Duke Red's dead daughter, built for him by the insane Dr. Lawton. Tima's role will be to merge the power of computers and the imagination of the human brain into a force that will possess the city.

Rock, the adopted son of Duke Red, hates this plan and wants to destroy Tima. He is jealous that his father prefers this artificial girl to his son, and believes Duke Red himself should sit on the throne. Other characters include an elderly detective who arrives in the city to explore the mystery of Ziggurat; his nephew Kenichi becomes the hero.

The story is told with enormous energy; animation is more versatile than live action in making cataclysmic events comprehensible. Mob scenes at the beginning and explosions and destruction throughout have a clarity and force that live action would necessarily dissipate. The animation owes less to mainstream American animation than to the comic book or *manga* tradition of Japan, where both comics and animation are considered art forms worthy of adult attention.

In the figures of Tima and Kenichi, the movie follows the anime tradition of heroes who are childlike, have enormous eyes, seem innocent and threatened. The other characters have more realistic faces and proportions, and indeed resemble Marvel superheroes (the contrast between these characters' looks is unusual: Imagine Nancy visiting Spider-Man). The backgrounds and action sequences look like the anime version of big-budget Hollywood f/x thrillers.

The music, too, is Western. The introduction to the city is scored with Dixieland, Joe Primrose sings "St. James Infirmary" at one point,

and the climactic scene is accompanied by Ray Charles singing "I Can't Stop Loving You" (the effect is a little like "We'll Meet Again" at the end of *Dr. Strangelove*).

The movie is so visually rich I want to see it again to look in the corners and appreciate the details. Like all the best Japanese anime, it pays attention to little things. There is a scene where an old man consults a book of occult lore. He opens it and starts to read. A page flips over. He flips it back in place. Considering that every action in an animated film requires thousands of drawings, a moment like the page flip might seem unnecessary, but all through the movie we get little touches like that. The filmmakers are not content with ordinary locations. Consider the Hotel Coconut, which seems to be a lobby with a desk clerk who checks guests into ancient luxury railway carriages.

Metropolis is not a simpleminded animated cartoon, but a surprisingly thoughtful and challenging adventure that looks into the nature of life and love, the role of workers, the rights (if any) of machines, the pain of a father's rejection, and the fascist zeal that lies behind Ziggurat. This is not a remake of the 1926 classic, but a wild elaboration. If you have never seen a Japanese anime, start here. If you love them, *Metropolis* proves you are right.

Me Without You ★ ★ ★ ½
R, 107 m., 2002

Anna Friel (Marina), Michelle Williams (Holly), Oliver Milburn (Nat), Kyle MacLachlan (Daniel), Trudie Styler (Linda). Directed by Sandra Goldbacher and produced by Finola Dwyer. Screenplay by Goldbacher and Laurence Coriat.

Marina and Holly's childhood friendship evolves into a toxic relationship when they grow up, but they still remain close because even when they're hurting each other, there's no one else they'd rather hurt. Ever had a friend like that? Although Marina is more neurotic and Holly is more the victim, maybe it's because they like it that way. If Holly knew the whole story of how Marina betrays her, she'd be devastated — but then, of course, she doesn't.

Me Without You has a bracing truth that's refreshing after the phoniness of female-bonding pictures like *Divine Secrets of the Ya-Ya Sisterhood*. It doesn't mindlessly celebrate female friendship, but looks at it with a level gaze. If Holly and Marina remain friends despite everything—well, maybe it would be a shame to throw away all that history.

Sandra Goldbacher's film begins in London in 1974 and continues for another twenty years, paying close attention to changing fashions in clothing, music, and makeup, while not making too big a point of it. We meet Holly (Michelle Williams, from *Dawson's Creek*) and Marina (Anna Friel) as adolescents who seal their friendship by placing treasures in a box and hiding it (there is a law requiring all female friends to perform this ritual in the movies). We meet their parents. Marina has a mother who fancies herself a sexpot and is a little drunk all day long, and a father who is, understandably, distant. Holly comes from a Jewish family that is warm but not especially supportive; she learns from her mother that she is more clever than pretty, and is not clever enough to figure out that she's pretty too.

Marina has a brother named Nat (Oliver Milburn) whom Holly has always been in love with. He is a decent sort, and likes her too, and one night during their hippie party phase he makes love to her, but this is not on Marina's agenda, and she destroys a crucial letter that could have changed everything.

Another rivalry over a male takes place at college, when both women fall for a handsome dweeb American lecturer named Daniel (Kyle MacLachlan). And here the movie does something that few female bonding pictures have the nerve to do, and introduces a fully formed, fascinating male. In a superbly modulated performance by MacLachlan, Daniel comes across as a man who can easily be tempted but not easily secured. He's willing to be seduced but frightened of commitment; his posture is always that of the male prepared to back away and apologize at the slightest offense. He has a highly developed line in chitchat, quoting all the best poets, and Holly is deceived by him while the more cynical Marina strip-mines him and moves on.

What's fascinating about the Daniel character is that he illustrates how men are not always the villains in unfaithful relationships, but sometimes simply the pawns of female agendas. Daniel gives both women what they want, and they want it more than he wants to give it. So although he appears to be a two-timer, he's more of a two-time loser. Rare, to see a character portrayed in this depth instead of simply being used as a plot ploy.

Michelle Williams is the surprise. I am not a student of *Dawson's Creek*, but I know she uses an American accent on it, and here, like Renée Zellweger in *Bridget Jones's Diary*, she crosses the Atlantic, produces a perfectly convincing British accent, and is cuddly and smart both at once. Anna Friel, as Marina, has a tricky role because she is only ostensibly the sexy, worldwise woman, and in fact is closer to her insecure mother. What eats at her is that in the long run Holly is more appealing to men, and it has nothing to do with hair or necklines.

The movie isn't entirely free of clichés (the secret treasure box, dredged up from a pond after decades, of course is still intact). But the screenplay, by Sandra Goldbacher and Laurence Coriat, plays as if the authors have based it on their observations of life, not of movies. There is ultimately a species of happy ending, although you realize it represents maturity and weariness more than victory. The struggles of the teens and twenties are so fraught, so passionate, so seemingly desperate, that when you grow older and learn balance and perspective, there's a bittersweet sense of loss. In years to come Marina and Holly may reflect that they were never happier than when they were making each other miserable.

A Mighty Wind ★ ★ ½
PG-13, 92 m., 2003

Christopher Guest (Alan Barrows), Michael McKean (Jerry Palter), Fred Willard (Mike LaFontaine), Catherine O'Hara (Mickey), Eugene Levy (Mitch), Bob Balaban (Jonathan Steinbloom), Parker Posey (Sissy Knox), Ed Begley Jr. (Lars), Harry Shearer (Mark Shubb), David Blasucci (Tony Pollono), Laura Harris (Miss Klapper), Michael Hitchcock (Lawrence Turpin), Jane Lynch (Laurie Bohner). Directed by Christopher Guest and produced by Karen Murphy. Screenplay by Guest and Eugene Levy.

If your idea of the ultimate circle of hell is singing along with Burl Ives on "I Know an Old Lady Who Swallowed a Fly"—if even as a child you refused to go "hee haw, hee haw"—then *A Mighty Wind* will awaken old memories. Christopher Guest's new mockumentary is about a reunion of three groups from the 1960s folk boom, and in the film's final concert the audience is indeed required to imitate chickens and horses.

The premise: The beloved folk promoter Irving Steinbloom has passed away, and his son Jonathan (Bob Balaban) wants to stage a concert in his honor at Town Hall, legendary site of so many folk performances. He assembles the relentlessly upbeat New Main Street Singers, the Folksmen (Christopher Guest, Harry Shearer, Michael McKean) and—the stars of the show—the long-estranged Mitch and Mickey (Eugene Levy and Catherine O'Hara).

These acts are all uncannily close to types we vaguely remember from *Hootenanny* and other shows, if we are over forty, and *A Mighty Wind* does for aging folkies what Rob Reiner's *This Is Spinal Tap* did for aging heavy-metal fans. If you ever actually spent money on an album by the Brothers Four, you may feel you vaguely remember some of the songs.

Guest follows the general outlines of the real (and wonderful) documentary *The Weavers: Wasn't That a Time!*, joining his characters in their current lives and then leading them through apprehensions and rehearsals to their big concert. The Folksmen are the most analytical about their comeback ("It wasn't retro then, but it's retro now"), the New Main Street Singers the most inanely cheerful (most of the members weren't born when the original group was formed), and Mitch and Mickey the most fraught with painful old memories and (in Mitch's case) new emotional traumas.

Mitch and Mickey dominate the film, providing a dramatic story that takes on a life of its own. Mitch is played by Levy as a deeply neurotic man who doubts he can still sing or even remember lyrics, and who still has a broken heart because a famous onstage kiss with Mickey did not lead to lasting offstage romance. When he disappears from backstage shortly before show time, we may be reminded of Ringo's solo walk in *A Hard Day's Night*.

Guest surrounds his talent with the usual clueless types he likes to skewer in his films. Fred Willard, hilarious as the color commentator in *Best in Show*, is back playing a promoter and onetime TV star who was famous for five minutes for the catchphrase "Wha' happened?" He laughs at his own jokes to demonstrate to his silent listeners that they are funny. Ed Begley Jr. plays an obtuse public television executive named Lars, whose speech is punctuated by an impenetrable thicket of Yiddish. Bob Balaban, as the dutiful son and impresario, frets over every detail of the performance, and is the singularly ill-at-ease emcee.

A lot of the movie consists of music, much of it written by Guest and other collaborators in the cast, and that is an enjoyment and a problem. The songs actually do capture the quality of the lesser groups of the time. They are performed in uncanny imitations of early TV musical staging. The movie demolishes any number of novelty songs with the Folksmen's version of "Eat at Joe's," based on a faulty neon sign that reads, "E . . . A . . . O."

But there comes a point when the movie becomes . . . well, performances and not comedy. The final act of the movie mostly takes place during the televised concert, and almost against its will takes on the dynamic of a real concert and not a satirical one.

There is another difficulty: Christopher Guest is rather fond of his characters. He didn't hate his targets in *Best in Show* or *Spinal Tap*, but he skewered them mercilessly, while the key characters in *A Mighty Wind*, especially Levy and O'Hara, take on a certain weight of complexity and realism that edges away from comedy and toward sincere soap opera.

There were many times when I laughed during *A Mighty Wind* (not least at lines like, "the kind of infectious that it's good to spread around"). But the edge is missing from Guest's usual style. Maybe it's because his targets are, after all, so harmless. The deluded *Spinal Tap* and the ferocious dog owners in *Best in Show* want to succeed and prevail. The singers in *A Mighty Wind* are grateful to be remembered, and as we watch them, we cut them the kind of slack we often do for aging comeback acts. Hey, the Beach Boys may be old, fat, and neurotic, but we don't want to spoil the fun by taking their T-Bird away.

Minority Report ★ ★ ★ ★
PG-13, 145 m., 2002

Tom Cruise (John Anderton), Samantha Morton (Agatha [Precog]), Max von Sydow (Lamarr Burgess), Colin Farrell (Danny Witwer), Tim Blake Nelson (Gideon), Steve Harris (Jad), Neal McDonough (Officer Fletcher). Directed by Steven Spielberg and produced by Jan de Bont, Bonnie Curtis, Gerald R. Molen, and Walter F. Parkes. Screenplay by Scott Frank and Jon Cohen, based on a short story by Philip K. Dick.

At a time when movies think they have to choose between action and ideas, Steven Spielberg's *Minority Report* is a triumph—a film that works on our minds and our emotions. It is a thriller and a human story, a movie of ideas that's also a whodunit. Here is a master filmmaker at the top of his form, working with a star, Tom Cruise, who generates complex human feelings even while playing an action hero.

I complained earlier this summer of awkward joins between live action and CGI; I felt the action sequences in *Spider-Man* looked too cartoonish, and that *Star Wars: Episode II,* by using computer effects to separate the human actors from the sets and CGI characters, felt disconnected and sterile. Now here is Spielberg using every trick in the book and matching them without seams, so that no matter how he's achieving his effects, the focus is always on the story and the characters.

The movie turns out to be eerily prescient, using the term "precrime" to describe stopping crimes before they happen; how could Spielberg have known the government would be using the same term in the summer of 2002? In his film, inspired by, but much expanded from, a short story by Philip K. Dick, Tom Cruise is John Anderton, chief of the Department of Precrime in the District of Columbia, where there has not been a murder in six years. Soon, it appears, there will be a murder—committed by Anderton himself.

The year is 2054. Futuristic skyscrapers coexist with the famous Washington monuments and houses from the nineteenth century. Anderton presides over an operation controlling three "precogs," precognitive humans who drift in a flotation tank, their brain waves tapped by computers. They're able to pick up thoughts of premeditated murders and warn the cops, who swoop down and arrest the would-be perpetrators before the killings can take place.

Because this is Washington, any government operation that is high-profile and successful inspires jealousy. Anderton's superior, bureau director Burgess (Max von Sydow), takes pride in him, and shields him from bureaucrats like Danny Witwer (Colin Farrell) from the Justice Department. As the precrime strategy prepares to go national, Witwer seems to have doubts about its wisdom—or he is only jealous of its success?

Spielberg establishes these characters in a dazzling future world, created by art director Alex McDowell, that is so filled with details large and small that we stop trying to figure out everything and surrender with a sigh. Some of the details: a computer interface that floats in midair, manipulated by Cruise with the gestures of a symphony conductor; advertisements that crawl up the sides of walls and address you personally; cars that whisk around town on magnetic cushions; robotic "spiders" that can search a building in minutes by performing a retinal scan on everyone in it. *Blade Runner,* also inspired by a Dick story, shows a future world in decay; *Minority Report* offers a more optimistic preview.

The plot centers on a rare glitch in the visions of the precogs. Although "the precogs are never wrong," we're told, "sometimes . . . they disagree." The dissenting precog is said to have filed a minority report, and in the case of Anderton the report is crucial, because otherwise he seems a certain candidate for arrest as a precriminal. Of course, if you could outsmart the precog system, you would have committed the perfect crime.

Finding himself the hunted instead of the hunter, Anderton teams up with Agatha (Samantha Morton), one of the precogs, who seemed to be trying to warn him of his danger. Because she floats in a fluid tank, Agatha's muscles are weakened (have precogs any rights of their own?), and Anderton has to half-drag her as they flee from the precrime police. One virtuoso sequence shows her foreseeing the immediate future and advising Anderton about what to do to elude what the cops are going to do next. The choreography, timing, and wit of this sequence make it, all by itself, worth the price of admission.

But there are other stunning sequences. Consider a scene where the "spiders" search a rooming house, and Anderton tries to elude capture by immersing himself in a tub of ice water. This sequence begins with an overhead cross section of the apartment building and several of its inhabitants, and you would swear it has to be done with a computer, but no: This is an actual, physical set, and the elegant camera moves were elaborately choreographed. It's typical of Spielberg that, having devised this astonishing sequence, he propels it for dramatic purposes and doesn't simply exploit it to show off his cleverness. And watch the exquisite timing as one of the spiders, on its way out, senses something and pauses in midstep.

Tom Cruise's Anderton is an example of how a star's power can be used to add more dimension to a character than the screenplay might supply. He compels us to worry about him, and even in implausible action sequences (like falls from dizzying heights) he distracts us by making us care about the logic of the chase, not the possibility of the stunt.

Samantha Morton's character ("Agatha" is a nod to Miss Christie) has few words and seems exhausted and frightened most of the time, providing an eerie counterpoint for Anderton's man of action. There is poignance in her helplessness, and Spielberg shows it in a virtuoso two-shot, as she hangs over Anderton's shoulder while their eyes search desperately in opposite directions. This shot has genuine mystery. It has to do with the composition and lighting and timing and breathing, and like the entire movie, it furthers the cold, frightening hostility of the world Anderton finds himself in. The cinematographer, Janusz Kaminski, who has worked with Spielberg before (not least on *Schindler's List*), is able to get an effect that's powerful and yet bafflingly simple.

The plot I will avoid discussing in detail. It is as ingenious as any *film noir* screenplay, and plays far better than some. It's told with such clarity that we're always sure what Spielberg wants us to think, suspect, and know. And although there is a surprise at the end, there is no cheating: The crime story holds water.

American movies are in the midst of a transition period. Some directors place their trust in technology. Spielberg, who is a master of technology, trusts only story and character, and then uses everything else as a workman uses his tools. He makes *Minority Report* with the new technology; other directors seem to be trying to make their movies *from* it. This film is such a virtuoso high-wire act, daring so much, achieving it with such grace and skill. *Minority Report* reminds us why we go to the movies in the first place.

Miracle ★ ★ ★
PG, 135 m., 2004

Kurt Russell (Herb Brooks), Patricia Clarkson (Patti Brooks), Noah Emmerich (Craig Patrick), Michael Mantenuto (Jack O'Callahan), Eddie Cahill (Jim Craig), Patrick O'Brien Dempsey (Mike Eruzione), Nathan West (Rob McClanahan). Directed by Gavin O'Connor and produced by Mark Ciardi and Gordon Gray. Screenplay by Eric Guggenheim.

Miracle is a sports movie that's more about the coach than about the team, and that's a miracle too. At a time when movies are shamelessly aimed at the young male demographic, here's a film with a whole team of hockey players in their teens and early twenties, and the screenplay hardly bothers to tell one from another. Instead, the focus is on Herb Brooks (Kurt Russell), a veteran hockey coach from Minnesota who is assigned the thankless task of assembling a team to represent America in the 1980 Winter Olympics. The United States hasn't won since 1960, and the professionals on the Soviet team—not to mention the Swedes, the Finns, and the Canadians—rule the sport.

This is a Kurt Russell you might not recognize. He's beefed up into a jowly, steady middle-aged man who still wears his square high school haircut. Patricia Clarkson, playing his wife, has the thankless role of playing yet another movie spouse whose only function in life is to complain that his job is taking too much time away from his family. This role, complete with the obligatory shots of the wife appearing in his study door as the husband burns the midnight oil, is so standard, so ritualistic, so boring, that I propose all future movies about workaholics just make them bachelors, to spare us the dead air. At the very least, she could occasionally ask her husband if he thinks he looks good in those plaid sport coats and slacks.

Herb Brooks was a real man (he died just after the film was finished), and the movie presents him in all his complexity. It's fascinated by the quirks of his personality and style; we can see he's a good coach, but, like his players, we're not always sure if we like him. That's what's good about the film: the way it frankly focuses on what a coach does, and how, and why. Brooks knows hockey and disappointment: He was cut from the 1960 American hockey team only a week before the first game, and so in this film, when he has to cut one more player at the last moment, we know how he feels—and he knows how the player feels.

Brooks's strategy is to weave an air of mystery about himself. He assigns his assistant coach, Craig Patrick (Noah Emmerich), to become a friend to the players—because Brooks deliberately does not become a friend, stays aloof, wants to be a little feared and a little resented. At one point, after chewing out his team in the locker room, he stalks out and, passing Patrick, says in a quiet aside, "That oughta wake 'em up."

After Brooks is selected for the job, his first task is to select his team. He immediately breaks with tradition. Amateur sports are overrun with adults who are essentially groupies, loving to get close to a team, treasuring their blazers with the badges on the breast pockets. These guys think they will join Brooks in choosing the American finalists after a week of tryouts, but Brooks announces his final cut on the first day of practice; he already knows who he wants, and doesn't require any advice. He's looking for kids who are hungry and passionate and *need* to win.

Most of the time, the team is seen as a unit. We begin to recognize their faces, but not much is done to develop them as individuals. The exception is the goaltender, Jim Craig (Eddie

Cahill). He refuses to take a psychological exam that Brooks hands out, and Brooks tells him that, by not taking it, "you just took it." Later, when Craig seems to falter, he benches him, and says, "I'm looking for the guy who refused to take the test."

We know all the clichés of the modern sports movie, but *Miracle* sidesteps a lot of them. Eric Guggenheim's screenplay, directed by Gavin O'Connor, is not about how some of the players have little quirks that they cure, or about their girl, or about villains that have to be overcome. It's about practicing hard and winning games. It doesn't even bother to demonize the opponents. When the team finally faces the Soviets, they're depicted as—well, simply as the other team. Their coach has a dark, forbidding manner and doesn't smile much, but he's not a Machiavellian schemer, and the Soviets don't play any dirtier than most teams do in hockey.

Oddly enough, the movie this one reminds me of is Robert Altman's *The Company,* about the Joffrey Ballet. Altman was fascinated by the leadership style of the company's artistic director, and how he deliberately uses strategy and underlings to create an aura of mysterious authority. And he dealt dispassionately with injuries, which are a fact of life and end a career in a second. *Miracle* has a similar orientation.

In keeping with its analytical style, the movie doesn't use a lot of trick photography in the hockey games. Unlike the fancy shots in a movie like *The Mighty Ducks,* this one films the hockey matches more or less the way they might look in a good documentary, or a superior TV broadcast. We're in the middle of the confusion on the ice, feeling the energy rather than focusing on plot points.

That leaves Kurt Russell and his character Herb Brooks as the center and reason for the film. Although playing a hockey coach might seem like a slap shot for an actor, Russell does real acting here. He has thought about Brooks and internalized him; the real Brooks was available as a consultant to the film. And Russell and O'Connor create a study of a personality, of a man who is leading young men through a process that led him to disappointment twenty years earlier. He has ideas about hockey and ideas about coaching, and like the Zen master Phil Jackson, begins with philosophy, not strategy. The film doesn't even end with the outcome of the Big Game. It ends by focusing on the coach, after it is all over.

The Missing ★ ★
R, 135 m., 2003

Tommy Lee Jones (Samuel Jones), Cate Blanchett (Maggie Gilkeson), Evan Rachel Wood (Lily), Jenna Boyd (Dot Gilkeson), Aaron Eckhart (Brake Baldwin), Eric Schweig (Chidin). Directed by Ron Howard and produced by Brian Grazer and Daniel Ostroff. Screenplay by Ken Kaufman, based on the novel by Thomas Eidson.

New York magazine ran a cover story years ago calling John Ford's *The Searchers* the most influential movie in American history. Movies like *Taxi Driver, Hard Core,* and *Paris, Texas* consider the theme of an abducted girl and the father or husband or cab driver who tries to rescue her from sexual despoliation at the hands of people he despises. The beat goes on with Ron Howard's *The Missing,* a clunky Western that tries so hard to be politically correct that although young women are kidnapped by Indians to be sold into prostitution in Mexico, they are never molested by their captors.

In the tradition of Robert De Niro *(Taxi Driver)*, George C. Scott *(Hard Core)*, and Harry Dean Stanton *(Paris, Texas)*, the movie has Tommy Lee Jones as a craggy loner who turns up when needed for the rescue. But in its update of the story, *The Missing* supplies a strong woman as the heroine. This is Maggie Gilkeson (Cate Blanchett), as a frontier rancher who lives with two daughters and has a hired man (Aaron Eckhart) who provides sex but isn't allowed to spend the night because she doesn't want to give anyone the wrong idea. She has some doctoring skills, and as the film opens is pulling an old woman's tooth—her last one, ho, ho.

Jones plays Maggie's father, Samuel, who abandoned the family years ago and has been living with Indians, learning their customs and sharing their firewater. He turns up desperate, but she sends him away. Then her daughter Lily (Evan Rachel Wood) is captured by Indians, and she needs his expertise in the ways of the Indian; she asks him to join her in the search.

Also coming along is her younger daughter, Dot (Jenna Boyd).

So okay. An old drunk, a woman, and a kid are chasing a resourceful band of Indians and half-breeds, led by a psychic male witch named Chidin (Eric Schweig). What are their chances? Excellent, I'd say, although of course there will have to be several close calls, assorted escapes and recaptures, and gunfights so prolonged that our attention drifts.

Sorry, but I couldn't believe any part of this movie. It's such a preposterous setup that I was always aware of the plot chugging away, and the logistics of the chase defy all common sense. The underlying assumption (that an old white coot and his daughter can out-Injun the Injuns) would be offensive if it did not border on the comedic, and why else, really, did they bring the ten-year-old along except to provide a young girl who'd be handy for scenes in which she is in danger?

When you see good actors in a story like this, you suspect they know how bad it is, but work to keep their self-respect. Tommy Lee Jones has sad eyes in the film, and underplays his role to avoid its obvious opportunities for parody; Cate Blanchett is strong and determined, and the only flaw in her performance is that it's in the wrong movie.

At 135 minutes, *The Missing* is way too long. This is basically a B Western jumped up out of its category. As a lean little oater, this story could have held down half of a double bill back when Westerns were popular, but these days audiences need a reason to see a Western. Kevin Costner gives them one in *Open Range*, but Ron Howard, who often makes wonderful movies, has taken a day off.

Mona Lisa Smile ★ ★ ★
PG-13, 117 m., 2003

Julia Roberts (Katherine Watson), Kirsten Dunst (Betty Warren), Julia Stiles (Joan Brandwyn), Maggie Gyllenhaal (Giselle Levy), Ginnifer Goodwin (Constance Baker), Dominic West (Bill Dunbar), Juliet Stevenson (Amanda Armstrong), John Slattery (Paul Moore), Marcia Gay Harden (Nancy Abbey), Marian Seldes (Jocelyn Carr). Directed by Mike Newell and produced by Elaine Goldsmith-Thomas, Paul

Schiff, and Deborah Schindler. Screenplay by Lawrence Konner and Mark Rosenthal.

I find it hard to believe that Wellesley College was as reactionary in the autumn of 1953 as *Mona Lisa Smile* says it was—but then I wasn't there. Neither were the screenwriters, who reportedly based their screenplay on Hillary Clinton's experience at Wellesley in the early 1960s. The film shows a school that teaches, above all, that a woman's duty is to stand by her man, and if Clinton learned that, she also learned a good deal more. No doubt she had a teacher as inspiring as Katherine Watson (Julia Roberts), who trades in the bohemian freedom of Berkeley for a crack at Wellesley's future corporate wives.

This is the kind of school that actually offers classes in deportment, grooming, and table-setting, and the teacher of those classes, Nancy Abbey (Marcia Gay Harden), takes them so seriously that we begin to understand the system that produced Cathy Whitaker, Julianne Moore's showpiece wife in *Far from Heaven*. Watson finds her students scornful of her California background (every student makes it a point to be able to identify every slide of every painting in her first lecture), but she counterattacks with a blast of modern art, and there is a scene where she takes them to watch the uncrating of a new work by Jackson Pollock.

Of course, the board of trustees is suspicious of Katherine Watson, modern art, and everything else that is potentially "subversive," and resistance among the undergraduates is led by Betty (Kirsten Dunst), whose mother is a trustee, whose plans include marrying an upward-bound but morally shifty Harvard man, and whose editorials in the school paper suggest Watson is leading her girls in the direction of communism and, worse, promiscuity. (A school nurse who gives advice on contraception has to leave her job.)

We are pretty sure what the story parabola of *Mona Lisa Smile* will be (the inspiring teacher will overcome adversity to enlighten and guide), but the movie is more observant and thoughtful than we expect. It doesn't just grind out the formula, but seems more like the record of an actual school year than about the needs of the plot. In the delicate dance of audience identification, we get to be both the teacher and her students—to imagine ourselves as a free spirit in a closed system, and as a student whose life is forever changed by her. But, you're wondering, how can I identify with a thirtyish teacher and her twentyish female students? Don't you find yourself identifying with just about anybody on the screen, if the movie is really working? Katherine Watson is smart and brave and stands by her beliefs, and so of course she reminds us of ourselves.

Julia Roberts is above all an actress with a winning way; we like her, feel protective toward her, want her to prevail. In *Mona Lisa Smile* she is the conduit for the plot, which flows through her character. The major supporting roles are played by luminaries of the first post-Julia generation, including not only Dunst, but Julia Stiles as Joan Brandwyn, a girl smart enough to be accepted by Yale Law but perhaps not smart enough to choose it over marriage; Maggie Gyllenhaal as Giselle Levy, who is sexually advanced and has even, it is said, slept with the studly young Italian professor; and Ginnifer Goodwin as Constance Baker, who is too concerned about her looks.

"A few years from now," the Wellesley students are solemnly informed, "your sole responsibility will be taking care of your husband and children." This is not a priority Watson can agree to. She tells the competent but conservative school president (Marian Seldes), "I thought I was headed to a place that would turn out tomorrow's leaders—not their wives." Unlike the typical heroes of movies about inspiring teachers, however, she doesn't think the answer lies in exuberance, freedom, and letting it all hang out, but in actually studying and doing the work, and she despairs when competent students throw away their futures (as she sees it) for marriage to men who have already started to cheat before their wedding days.

Watson herself has a fairly lively love life, with a boyfriend in California (John Slattery) and now a warmth for the above-mentioned studly Italian teacher (Dominic West), although it is probably not true, as a student rumor has it, that she had to come east because of a torrid affair with William Holden. The movie is not really about her romances at all, but about her function as a teacher and her determination to install feminism on the campus before that noun was widely in use. The movie, directed by Mike Newell, may be a little too aware of its sexual politics and might have been more absorbing if Katherine and her students were fighting their way together out of the chains of gender slavery. But the characters involve us, we sympathize with their dreams and despair of their matrimonial tunnel vision, and at the end we are relieved that we listened to Miss Watson and became the wonderful people that we are today.

Mondays in the Sun ★ ★ ½
R, 115 m., 2003

Javier Bardem (Carlos "Santa" Santamaria), Luis Tosar (José Suarez), José Ángel Egido (Paulino "Lino" Ribas Casado), Nieve de Medina (Ana), Enrique Villén (Reina), Celso Bugallo (Amador), Joaquin Climent (Rico), Laura Domínguez (Ángela). Directed by Fernando León de Aranoa and produced by Elías Querejeta and Jaume Roures. Screenplay by de Aranoa and Ignacio del Moral.

Mondays in the Sun chronicles the lives of men who were shipbuilders in Spain until the yards closed, and now measure out their lives in drinking and despair. One still goes to apply for jobs, but is too old, and considers hair dye to make himself look younger. Others buy lottery tickets, hoping for good luck, and benefit from the free cheese samples at the supermarket. They all feel unmanned by the inability to support themselves and their families, and free time is like a swamp they have to wade through every day.

The film stars Javier Bardem, whose range as an actor is demonstrated here by the way he seems to have aged, put on weight, lost his athletic poise, and become a bar stool jockey. He plays "Santa," the unelected leader of a small group of friends who meet most days in a bar opened by Rico (Joaquin Climent) when he was laid off at the shipyards. Among the regulars: Amador (Celso Bugallo), who has developed into a pitiful alcoholic and won't go home even when he has clearly had too much to drink; Reina (Enrique Villén), who found a job as a security guard and whose employment is

like a silent rebuke to them all; and José (Luis Tosar), whose wife, Ana (Nieve de Medina), has a job at the cannery and drowns herself in deodorants to get rid of the fishy smell.

In one of the movie's most sharply focused scenes, José and Ana go to the bank to apply for a loan, and the questions of the loan officer, on top of José's bitterness that his wife works and he does not, lead to an angry outburst. But outburst or no, there was no way they were going to get the loan. All of these characters are at a dead end.

There are moments of sad insight, as when they take Amador home to his apartment and find it an emptied-out mess; the wife he keeps talking about has abandoned him. And when Santa meets a friendly woman named Ángela (Laura Domínguez), there's no way he feels able to pursue a relationship because he has nothing to offer her, not even self-esteem. Better to stay in Rico's bar and drink, and go through a pretend flirtation with Rico's teenage daughter.

You can see here fairly clearly the way in which a neighborhood bar can become a surrogate family for men with nowhere to go, nothing to do, and a tendency to drink too much. The bartender is the authority figure, and day after day, week after week, his customers appear in his court for their daily sentence. Sometimes Santa and a friend sit outside in the sun, talking aimlessly about nothing much, because even with the tabs that Rico runs for them they lack the funds to be as drunk as they would like.

The movie, directed by Fernando León de Aranoa, was the most honored film in Spain in 2002, chosen by the Spanish as their Oscar contender over Pedro Almodóvar's *Talk to Her*. Bardem won the Goya, Spain's Oscar, as best actor, and the picture picked up four other Goyas, including one for best film. It is intensely involving at the outset, but it faces an insoluble problem: The story, like the characters, has no place to go. If they get jobs or win the lottery, the movie would be dishonest, and if they do not, then day will follow day with increasing gloom. For the viewer, it seems as if *Mondays in the Sun* is simply repeating the same dilemma over and over. For its characters, of course, it feels that way, too.

Monsieur Ibrahim ★ ★ ★
R, 95 m., 2004

Omar Sharif (Monsieur Ibrahim), Pierre Boulanger (Momo), Gilbert Melki (Momo's Father), Isabelle Renauld (Momo's Mother), Lola Naynmark (Myriam), Anne Suarez (Sylvie), Mata Gabin (Fatou), Celine Samie (Eva), Isabelle Adjani (Brigitte Bardot). Directed by François Dupeyron and produced by Michele Petin and Laurent Petin, based on the book and play by Eric-Emmanuel Schmitt.

On the rue Bleue in a working-class Jewish neighborhood in Paris, people know each other and each other's business, and live and let live. That includes the streetwalkers who are a source of fascination to young Momo, who studies them from the window of his flat before preparing supper for his father. Momo's mother is dead, an older brother has left the scene, and his father is distant and cold with the young teenager. But his life is not lonely; there is Monsieur Ibrahim, who runs the shop across the street. And there is Sylvie, who provides Momo with his sexual initiation after the lad breaks open his piggy bank.

Although Brigitte Bardot (played by Isabelle Adjani) pays a visit to the street one day to shoot a scene in a movie, there was another movie character I almost expected to see wandering past: Antoine Doinel, the hero of *The 400 Blows* and four other films by François Truffaut. Not only are both films set within about five years of each other (circa 1958 and 1963), but they share a similar theme: the lonely, smart kid who is left alone by distant parents and seeks inspiration in the streets.

Antoine found it at the movies and in the words of his hero, Balzac. Momo (Pierre Boulanger), whose life is sunnier and his luck better, finds it from Monsieur Ibrahim (Omar Sharif). Although Ibrahim is Turkish, his store is known in Parisian argot as "the Arab's store," because only Arabs will keep their stores open at night and on weekends. Ibrahim establishes himself like a wise old sage behind his counter, knows everyone who comes in, and everything they do, so of course he knows that Momo is a shoplifter. This he does not mind so much: "Better you should steal here, than somewhere you could get into real trouble."

The old man sees that the young one needs a friend and guidance, and he provides both, often quoting from his beloved Koran. He knows things about Momo's family that Momo does not know, and is discreet about Momo's friendship with the hookers. What Ibrahim dreams about is to return someday to the villages and mountains of his native land, to the bazaars and dervishes and the familiar smells of the food he grew up with. What Momo desires is a break with a home life that is barren and crushes his spirit.

The movie was directed by François Dupeyron, based on a book and play by Eric-Emmanuel Schmitt. Its best scenes come as the characters are established and get to know one another. Omar Sharif at seventy-one still has the fire in his eyes that we remember from *Lawrence of Arabia,* and is still a handsome presence, but he settles comfortably into Monsieur Ibrahim's shabby life, and doesn't bore us with his philosophy. And young Boulanger, like Jean-Pierre Leaud all those years ago, has a quick, open face that lets us read his heart.

The last third of the film is more like a fantasy. Momo and Ibrahim both want to escape. Ibrahim buys a fancy red sports car (like the one Bardot was driving), and they drive off to Turkey. What happens there, you will have to discover on your own, but while *The 400 Blows* ended on a note of bleak realism, *Monsieur Ibrahim* settles for melodrama and sentiment. Well, why not? Momo is not as star-crossed as Antoine Doniel, and Ibrahim achieves a destiny he accepts.

But isn't it sort of sad that a movie has to be set forty years ago for us to accept an elderly storekeeper buying a sports car and driving away with a teenager, without ever for an instant suspecting the purity of his motives? The innocence that Antoine and Momo lose in their stories is nothing compared to the world teenagers live in today.

Monsoon Wedding ★ ★ ★ ½
R, 114 m., 2002

Naseeruddin Shah (Lalit Verma), Lillete Dubey (Pimmi Verma), Shefali Shetty (Ria Verma), Vasundhara Das (Aditi Verma), Parvin Dabas (Hemant Rai), Vijay Raaz (P. K. Dubey), Tilotama Shome (Alice), Rajat Kapoor (Tej Puri), Neha

Dubey (Ayesha), Randeep Hooda (Rahul).
Directed by Mira Nair and produced by Caroline
Baron and Nair. Screenplay by Sabrina Dhawan.

Mira Nair's *Monsoon Wedding* is one of those
joyous films that leaps over national boundaries and celebrates universal human nature.
It could be the first Indian film to win big at
the North American box office; like *Tampopo*,
the Japanese noodle-shop romance, or *Crouching Tiger, Hidden Dragon*, which escaped the
subtitled martial arts ghetto, it's the kind of
film people tell their friends they ought to see.

The movie follows the events in the large
Verma family of New Delhi, as their daughter
Aditi prepares to marry Hemant, a computer
programmer from Houston. He is an "NRI"
(nonresident Indian), who has returned to
meet the bride selected by his parents for an
arranged marriage. Such marriages are an
ancient tradition, but these are modern young
people, and in the opening scene we see Aditi
in a hurried exchange with her married lover,
a TV host. She has agreed to the arranged
marriage partly out of impatience with her
lover's vague talk about someday divorcing his
wife.

As in an Altman film, we plunge into the
middle of an event and gradually figure out
who everyone is—just as the members of the
two families must. The key players are the parents of the bride, Lalit (Naseeruddin Shah)
and Pimmi (Lillete Dubey). He worries about
the weather, the happiness of his family, his
duties as a host, and especially about the cost
of everything. In charge of the festivities and
apparently overcharging him is the wedding
planner, P. K. Dubey (Vijay Raaz), who does
not reassure Lalit with his use of such invaluable Indian English expressions as "exactly and
approximately."

All of the characters speak English. Also
Hindi and, in some cases, Punjabi, sometimes
in the same sentence. The effect is delightful.
We have the pleasure of seeing a foreign film
and the convenience of understanding almost
everything that's said. The spontaneous movement between languages, typical of modern
middle-class Indians, reflects the mixture of
characters: Some are returning from America
or Australia and work with computers or on
television, while others occupy ancient life

patterns. One young family member wants to
study creative writing in America, and a relative, no doubt aware of the current boom in
English-language best-sellers about India, tells
her, "Lots of money in writing."

The wedding creates a certain suspense:
What if the bride and groom do not like each
other? They sneak off for quiet talks and find
that they do like each other—at least, each
other's looks and as much as they can learn in
a few hours. Meanwhile, subterranean romances surround them. Aditi's pretty cousin
Ayesha (Neha Dubey) makes no mystery of
her attraction to Rahul (Randeep Hooda), the
visitor from Australia; P. K. Dubey is thunderstruck by the beauty of the Verma's family
maid, Alice (Tilotama Shome). And there is
intrigue of a darker sort as Aditi's cousin observes a family friend who once assaulted her
and now may have his eye on a young relative.

I have not even started on the groom's family. You will meet them at the wedding. What
strikes you immediately about *Monsoon
Wedding* is the quickness of the comedy, the
deft way Nair moves between story lines, the
brilliant colors of Declan Quinn's cinematography, and the way music is easily woven into
the narrative. Nair, whose films include
Salaam Bombay! and *Mississippi Masala*, says
she wanted to make a Bollywood movie in her
own way, and she has. "Bollywood" is the term
for the Bombay film industry, the world's
largest, which produces broad popular entertainments in which the characters are likely to
start singing and dancing at any moment, in
any context. There is a lot of singing and
dancing in *Monsoon Wedding*, but all of it
emerges in a logical way from the action, as it
might in a Hollywood musical.

There are moments of truth in the romance
between Aditi and Hemant, especially when
they level with each other about their pasts.
But the real heart-tugging moment, the moment audiences will love, is when P. K. Dubey
falls to his knees before a heart made of mari-
golds, in a hopeless gesture of adoration before Alice. A harsher moment of truth comes
when Aditi's father, who places loyalty to family above everything, breaks with tradition to
do the right thing in a painful situation, no
matter what.

The hope for *Monsoon Wedding* is that those

who like it will drag their friends into the theater. There's such an unreasonable prejudice in this country against any film that is not exactly like every other film. People cheerfully attend assembly-line junk but are wary of movies that might give them new experiences or take them new places. *Monsoon Wedding*, which won the Golden Lion as the best film at Venice 2001, is the kind of film where you meet characters you have never been within 10,000 miles of, and feel like you know them at once.

Monster ★ ★ ★ ★
R, 109 m., 2004

Charlize Theron (Aileen Wuornos), Christina Ricci (Selby Wall), Bruce Dern (Thomas), Scott Wilson (Horton Rohrback), Lee Tergesen (Vincent Corey), Pruitt Taylor Vince (Gene), Annie Corley (Donna Tentler), Marco St. John (Evan). Directed by Patty Jenkins and produced by Mark Damon, Donald Kushner, Clark Peterson, Charlize Theron, and Brad Wyman. Screenplay by Jenkins.

What Charlize Theron achieves in Patty Jenkins's *Monster* isn't a performance but an embodiment. With courage, art, and charity, she empathizes with Aileen Wuornos, a damaged woman who committed seven murders. She does not excuse the murders. She simply asks that we witness the woman's final desperate attempt to be a better person than her fate intended.

Wuornos received a lot of publicity during her arrest, trial, conviction, and 2002 execution for the Florida murders of seven men who picked her up as a prostitute (although one wanted to help her, not use her). The headlines, true as always to our compulsion to treat everything as a sporting event or an entry for the *Guinness Book*, called her "America's first female serial killer." Her image on the news and in documentaries presented a large, beaten-down woman who did seem to be monstrous. Evidence against her was given by Selby Wall (Christina Ricci), an eighteen-year-old who became the older woman's naive lesbian lover and inspired Aileen's dream of earning enough money to set them up in a "normal" lifestyle. Robbing her clients led to murder, and each

new murder seemed necessary to cover the tracks leading from the previous one.

I confess that I walked into the screening not knowing who the star was, and that I did not recognize Charlize Theron until I read her name in the closing credits. Not many others will have that surprise; she won the Academy Award for Best Actress. I didn't recognize her—but more to the point, I hardly tried, because the performance is so focused and intense that it becomes a fact of life. Observe the way Theron controls her eyes in the film; there is not a flicker of inattention, as she urgently communicates what she is feeling and thinking. There's the uncanny sensation that Theron has forgotten the camera and the script and is directly channeling her ideas about Aileen Wuornos. She has made herself the instrument of this character.

I have already learned more than I wanted to about the techniques of disguise used by makeup artist Toni G. to transform an attractive twenty-eight-year-old into an ungainly street prostitute, snapping her cigarette butt into the shadows before stepping forward to talk with a faceless man who has found her in the shadows of a barren Florida highway. Watching the film, I had no sense of makeup technique; I was simply watching one of the most real people I had ever seen on the screen. Jenkins, the writer-director, has made the best film of the year. Movies like this are perfect when they get made, before they're ground down by analysis. There is a certain tone in the voices of some critics that I detest—that superior way of explaining technique in order to destroy it. They imply that because they can explain how Theron did it, she didn't do it. But she does it.

The movie opens with Wuornos informing God that she is down to her last $5, and that if God doesn't guide her to spend it wisely she will end her life. She walks into what happens to be a lesbian bar and meets the eighteen-year-old Selby, who has been sent to live with Florida relatives and be "cured" of lesbianism. Aileen is adamant that she's had no lesbian experience, and indeed her sordid life as a bottom-rung sex worker has left her with no taste for sex at all. Selby's own sexuality functions essentially as a way to shock her parents and gratify her need to be desired. There is a stunning scene when the two women connect with raw sexual energy, but soon enough sex is unimportant compared to daydreaming, watching television, and enacting their private soap opera in cheap roadside motels.

Aileen is the protector and provider, proudly bringing home the bacon—and the keys to cars that Selby doesn't ask too many questions about. Does she know that Aileen has started to murder her clients? She does and doesn't. Aileen's murder spree becomes big news long before Selby focuses on it. The crimes themselves are triggered by Aileen's loathing for prostitution—by a lifetime's hatred for the way men have treated her since she was a child. She has only one male friend, a shattered Vietnam veteran and fellow drunk (Bruce Dern). Although she kills for the first time in self-defense, she is also lashing out against her past. Her experience of love with Selby brings revulsion uncoiling from her memories; men treat her in a cruel way and pay for their sins and those of all who went before them. The most heartbreaking scene is the death of a good man (Scott Wilson) who actually wants to help her, but has arrived so late in her life that the only way he can help is to be eliminated as a witness.

Aileen's body language is frightening and fascinating. She doesn't know how to occupy her body. Watch Theron as she goes through a repertory of little arm straightenings and body adjustments and head tosses and hair touchings, as she nervously tries to shake out her nervousness and look at ease. Observe her smoking technique; she handles her cigarettes with the self-conscious bravado of a thirteen-year-old trying to impress a kid. And note that there is only one moment in the movie where she seems relaxed and at peace with herself; you will know the scene, and it will explain itself. This is one of the greatest performances in the history of the cinema.

Christina Ricci finds the correct note for Selby Wall—so correct some critics have mistaken it for bad acting, when in fact it is sublime acting in its portrayal of a bad actor. She plays Selby as clueless, dim, in over her head, picking up cues from moment to moment, cobbling her behavior out of notions borrowed from bad movies, old songs, and barroom romances.

Selby must have walked into a gay bar for the first time only a few weeks ago, and studied desperately to figure out how to present herself. Selby and Aileen are often trying to improvise the next line they think the other wants to hear.

We are told to hate the sin but not the sinner, and as I watched *Monster* I began to see it as an exercise in the theological virtue of charity. It refuses to objectify Wuornos and her crimes and refuses to exploit her story in the cynical manner of true crime sensationalism—insisting instead on seeing her as one of God's creatures worthy of our attention. She has been so cruelly twisted by life that she seems incapable of goodness, and yet when she feels love for the first time she is inspired to try to be a better person.

She is unequipped for this struggle, and lacks the gifts of intelligence and common sense. She is devoid of conventional moral standards. She is impulsive, reckless, angry, and violent, and she devastates her victims, their families, and herself. There are no excuses for what she does, but there are reasons, and the purpose of the movie is to make them visible. If life had given her anything at all to work with, we would feel no sympathy. But life has beaten her beyond redemption. ☞

Monster's Ball ★ ★ ★ ★
R, 111 m., 2002

Billy Bob Thornton (Hank Grotowski), Halle Berry (Leticia Musgrove), Heath Ledger (Sonny Grotowski), Peter Boyle (Buck Grotowski), Sean "Puffy" Combs (Lawrence Musgrove), Coronji Calhoun (Tyrell Musgrove). Directed by Marc Forster and produced by Lee Daniels. Screenplay by Milo Addica and Will Rokos.

Monster's Ball is about a black woman and a white man who find, for a time anyway, solace in each other for their pain. But their pain remains separate and so do they; this is not a message movie about interracial relationships, but the specific story of two desperate people whose lives are shaken by violent deaths, and how in the days right after that they turn to each other because there is no place else to turn. The movie has the complexity of great fiction, and requires our empathy as we interpret the decisions that are made—especially at the end, when the movie avoids an obligatory scene that would have been conventional and forces us to cut straight to the point.

Billy Bob Thornton and Halle Berry star as Hank and Leticia, in two performances that are so powerful because they observe the specific natures of these two characters and avoid the pitfalls of racial clichés. What a shock to find these two characters freed from the conventions of political correctness and allowed to be who they are: weak, flawed, needful, with good hearts tested by lifetimes of compromise. They live in a small Georgia town, circa 1990. She works the night shift in a diner, has a fat little son, and an ex-husband on Death Row. He works as a guard on Death Row, has a mean, racist father and a browbeaten son, and will be involved in her husband's execution. ("Monster's Ball" is an old English term for a condemned man's last night on Earth.)

At first Hank and Leticia do not realize the connection they have through the condemned man. For another movie that would be enough plot. We can imagine the scenes of discovery and revelation. How this movie handles that disclosure is one of its great strengths: how both characters deal with it (or don't deal with it) internally, so that the movie blessedly proceeds according to exactly who they are, what they need, what they must do, and the choices open to them.

The screenplay by Milo Addica and Will Rokos is subtle and observant; one is reminded of short fiction by Andre Dubus, William Trevor, Eudora Welty, Raymond Carver. It specifically does not tell "their" story, but focuses on two separate lives. The characters are given equal weight and have individual story arcs, which do not intersect but simply, inevitably, meet. There is an overlay of racism in the story; Hank's father, Buck (Peter Boyle), is a hateful racist, and Hank mirrors his attitudes. But the movie is not about redemption, not about how Hank overcomes his attitudes, but about how they fall away from him like a dead skin because his other feelings are so much more urgent. The movie, then, is not about overcoming prejudice, but sidestepping it because it comes to seem monstrously irrelevant.

Hank is an abused son and an abusive father. His old man, Buck, confined to a wheelchair and a stroller, still exercises an iron will over the family. All three generations live under his roof, and when Hank's son, Sonny (Heath Ledger), opts out of the family sickness, Buck's judgment is cruel: "He was weak." We do not learn much about Leticia's parents, but she is a bad mother, alternately smothering her son, Tyrell (Coronji Calhoun), with love, and screaming at him that he's a "fat little piggy." She drinks too much, has been served with an eviction notice, sees herself as a loser. She has no affection at all for Tyrell's father, Lawrence (Puffy Combs), on Death Row, and makes it clear during a visitation that she is there strictly for her son. There is no side story to paint Lawrence as a victim; "I'm a bad man," he tells Tyrell. "You're the best of me."

Leticia is all messed up. She sustains a loss that derails her, and it happens by coincidence that Hank is there when he can perform a service. This makes them visible to each other. It is safe to say that no one else in the community is visible, in terms of human need, to either one. Hank's shy, slow courtship is so tentative it's like he's sleepwalking toward her. Her response is dictated by the fact that she has nowhere else to turn. They have a key conversation in which the bodies of both characters are tilted away from each other, as if fearful of being any closer. And notice another conversation, when she's been drinking, and she waves her hands and one hand keeps falling on Hank's lap; she doesn't seem to notice and, here is the point, he doesn't seem willing to.

Their intimate scenes are ordinary and simple, a contrast to Hank's cold, mercenary arrangement with a local hooker. The film's only flaw is the way Marc Forster allows his camera to linger on Halle Berry's half-clothed beauty; this story is not about sex appeal, and if the camera sees her that way we are pretty sure that Hank doesn't. What he sees, what she sees, is defined not by desire but by need.

Students of screenwriting should study the way the film handles the crucial passages at the end, when she discovers some drawings and understands their meaning. Here is where a lesser movie would have supplied an obligatory confrontation. Leticia never mentions the drawings to Hank. Why not? Because it is time to move on? Because she understands why he withheld information? Because she has no alternative? Because she senses that the drawings would not exist if the artist hated his subject? Because she is too tired and this is just one more nail on the cross? Because she forgives? What?

The movie cannot say. The characters have disappeared into the mysteries of the heart. *Monster's Ball* demonstrates that to explain all its mysteries, a movie would have to limit itself to mysteries that can be explained. As for myself, as Leticia rejoined Hank in the last shot of the movie, I was thinking about her as deeply and urgently as about any movie character I can remember.

Monty Python's Life of Brian ★ ★ ★
R, 94 m., 2004

Multiple roles by Monty Python's Flying Circus: Graham Chapman, John Cleese, Terry Gilliam, Eric Idle, Terry Jones, and Michael Palin. Directed by Terry Jones and produced by John Goldstone. Screenplay by the Monty Python Troupe.

Monty Python's Life of Brian has been re-released, I suspect, because of the enormous box office of *The Passion of the Christ*. This is a classic bait-and-switch, because Brian, of course, is not Christ, but was born in the next stable. In cinema as in life, poor Brian never did the big numbers. When the film was released in 1979 it was attacked as blasphemous by many religious groups. Consulting my original review, I find I quoted Stanley Kauffmann in the *New Republic*, who speculated that Jesus might have enjoyed it; he had a sense of humor, proven by his occasional puns. That opens up another line of controversy: Are puns funny? Certainly *Monty Python's Life of Brian* is funny, in that peculiar British way where jokes are told sideways, with the obvious point and then the delayed zinger.

The tragedy of Brian (Graham Chapman) is that he has everything it takes be a success, except divinity. Not that he has any desire to found a religion. He attracts followers who convince themselves he is the savior, is the object of cult veneration, and unsuccessfully tries to convince his (small) multitudes that he is not who they think he is. No, that's the other guy. His followers seize upon the smallest hints and misunderstood fragments of his speech to create an orthodoxy they claim to have received from him.

We see the real Jesus twice, once in the next manger (unlike Brian, he has a halo) and again when he delivers the Sermon on the Mount. Most biblical movies show the sermon from a point of view close to Jesus, or looking over his shoulder. *Life of Brian* has the cheap seats, way in the back at the bottom of the mount, where it's hard to hear: "What did he say? Blessed are the cheesemakers?"

Unlike Brian, Monty Python's Flying Circus gang had a distinguished family line. It was in direct descent from the *The Goon Show* on BBC radio (Spike Milligan, Peter Sellers) and the satirical revue *Beyond the Fringe* (Peter Cook, Dudley Moore, Jonathan Miller, Alan Bennett), which was inspired by Second City. Cook and Moore also had a TV show named "Not Only . . . But Also," which along with Second City more or less invented *Saturday Night Live*. Then came the Pythons, who adapted best to movies *(Monty Python and the Holy Grail, Monty Python's The Meaning of Life)*.

The success of *Life of Brian* is based first of all on Brian's desperation at being a redeemer without portfolio. He's like one of those guys you meet in a bar who explains how he would have been Elvis if Elvis hadn't been so much better at it. Brian is, in fact, not a religious leader at all but the member of an underground political organization seeking to overthrow Pontius Pilate and kick the Romans out of the Holy Land. There are uncomfortable parallels with the real-life situation in the Middle East, and a jab at the second-class status of women in the scene where men stone a blasphemer. The joke is that the "men" are women pretending to be men, because as women they never get to have fun attending stonings and suchlike. Monty Python rotates the joke into another dimension, since all of the women in the movie are men in drag (some of them risking discovery, you would think, by wearing beards).

The movie benefits by looking vaguely historically accurate (it used the sets built by Lord Lew Grade for Franco Zeffirelli's *Jesus of Nazareth*). It incorporates familiar figures such as Pontius Pilate (Michael Palin), but observes that he speaks with a lisp (his centurions helplessly crack up behind his back). At crucial moments it breaks into song, and there is a particular irony, considering how it is used in the movie, that "The Bright Side of Life" has taken on a long life in exactly the opposite context.

If the film has a message, and it may, it's that much of what passes in religion for truth is the result of centuries of opinion and speculation. Its version of the Brian legend is like a comic parallel to the theories of Christian history in *The Da Vinci Code*—itself a ripe target for Pythonizing. The difficulty with a literal interpretation of the Bible is that it is a translation of a translation of a translation of documents that were chosen by the early church from among a much larger cache of potential manuscripts. "You've all got to think for yourselves!" Brian exhorts his followers, who obediently repeat after him: "We've all got to think for ourselves!"

Moonlight Mile ★ ★ ★

PG-13, 112 m., 2002

Jake Gyllenhaal (Joe Nast), Dustin Hoffman (Ben Floss), Susan Sarandon (JoJo Floss), Holly Hunter (Mona Camp), Ellen Pompeo (Bertie Knox), Dabney Coleman (Mike Mulcahey). Directed by Brad Silberling and produced by Mark Johnson and Silberling. Screenplay by Silberling.

After the funeral is over, and the mourners have come back to the house for coffee and cake and have all gone home, the parents and the boyfriend of Diana, the dead girl, sit by themselves. Her mother criticizes how one friend expressed her sympathy. And the father asks, what *could* she say? "Put yourself in their shoes."

That little scene provides a key to Brad Silberling's *Moonlight Mile*. What do you say when someone dies—someone you cared for? What are the right words? And what's the right thing to do? Death is the ultimate rebuke to good manners. The movie, which makes an unusually intense effort to deal with the process of grief and renewal, is inspired by a loss in Silberling's own life. The TV actress Rebecca Schaeffer, his girlfriend at the time, was killed in 1989 by a fan. Silberling has grown very close to her parents in the years since then, he told me,

and more than a decade later he has tried to use the experience as the starting point for a film.

Moonlight Mile, which takes place in 1973, opens in an elliptical way. At first only quiet clues in the dialogue allow us to understand that someone has died. We meet Joe Nast (Jake Gyllenhaal), the fiancé of the dead girl, and her parents, Ben and JoJo Floss (Dustin Hoffman and Susan Sarandon). They talk not in a sentimental way, but in that strange, detached tone we use when grief is too painful to express and yet something must be said.

After the funeral and the home visitation, the film follows what in a lesser film would be called the "healing process." *Moonlight Mile* is too quirky and observant to be described in psychobabble. Joe stays stuck in the Floss house, living in an upstairs bedroom, his plans on hold. Ben, who has lost a daughter, now in a confused way hopes to gain a son, and encourages Joe to join him in his business as a real estate developer. JoJo, protected by intelligence and wit, looks closely and suspects a secret Joe is keeping, which leaves him stranded between the past and future.

Gyllenhaal, who in person is a jokester, in the movies almost always plays characters who are withdrawn and morose. Remember him in *Donnie Darko, The Good Girl,* and *Lovely and Amazing*. Here, too, he is a young man with troubled thoughts. At the post office, and again at a bar where she has a night job, he meets Bertie Knox (Ellen Pompeo), who sees inside when others only look at the surface. They begin to talk. She has a loss too: Her boyfriend has been missing in action in Vietnam for three years. While it is possible that they will mend each other's hearts by falling in love, the movie doesn't simplemindedly pursue that plot path, but meanders among the thoughts of the living.

Silberling's screenplay pays full attention to all of the characters. Ben and JoJo are not simply a backdrop to a romance involving Joe and Bertie. The movie provides key scenes for all of the characters, in conversation and in monologue, so that it is not only about Joe's grieving process but about all four, who have lost different things in different ways.

Anyone regarding the Hoffman character will note that his name is Benjamin and remember Hoffman's most famous character, in *The Graduate*. But Joe is the Benjamin of this film, and Hoffman's older man has more in common with another of his famous roles: Willy Loman, the hero of *Death of a Salesman*. Ben occupies a low-rent storefront office on Main Street in Cape Anne, Massachusetts, but dreams of putting together a group of properties and bringing in a superstore like K-Mart. This will be his big killing, the deal that caps his career, even though we can see in the eyes of the local rich man (Dabney Coleman) that Ben is too small to land this fish. Ben's desire to share his dream with his surrogate son Joe also has echoes from the Arthur Miller tragedy.

Sarandon's JoJo is tart, with a verbal wit to protect her and a jaundiced view of her husband's prospects. The deepest conversation JoJo has with Joe ("Isn't it funny, that we have the same name?") is about as well done as such a scene can be. She intuits that Joe is dealing not only with the loss of Diana's life, but with the loss of something else.

Ellen Pompeo, a newcomer, plays Bertie with a kind of scary charisma that cannot be written, only felt. She knows she is attractive to Joe. She knows she likes him. She knows she is faithful to her old boyfriend. She is frightened by her own power to attract, especially since she wants to attract even while she tells herself she doesn't. She is so vulnerable in this movie, so sweet, as she senses Joe's pain and wants to help him.

Holly Hunter is the fifth major player, as the lawyer who is handling the case against Diana's killer. She embodies the wisdom of the law, which knows, as laymen do not, that it moves with its own logic regardless of the feelings of those in the courtroom. She offers practical advice, and then you can see in her eyes that she wishes she could offer emotional advice instead.

Moonlight Mile gives itself the freedom to feel contradictory things. It is sentimental but feels free to offend, is analytical and then surrenders to the illogic of its characters, is about grief and yet permits laughter. Everyone who has grieved for a loved one will recognize the moment, some days after the death, when an irreverent remark will release the surprise of laughter. Sometimes we laugh that we may not cry. Not many movies know that truth. *Moonlight Mile* is based on it.

Morvern Callar ★ ★ ★ ½
NO MPAA RATING, 97 m., 2002

Samantha Morton (Morvern Callar), Kathleen McDermott (Lanna), Raife Patrick Burchell (Boy in Room 1022), Dan Cadan (Dazzer), Carolyn Calder (Sheila Tequila), Jim Wilson (Tom Boddington), Dolly Wells (Susan), Ruby Milton (Couris Jean). Directed by Lynne Ramsay and produced by George Faber, Charles Pattinson, and Robyn Slovo. Screenplay by Liana Dognini and Ramsay, based on the novel by Alan Warner.

In the opening scene of *Morvern Callar*, a young woman awakens next to the body of her boyfriend, who has committed suicide during the night. Lights blink on their Christmas tree. His blood is all over the floor. His presents for her are still wrapped and under the tree. On his computer he has left a suicide note ("It just seemed like the right thing to do"), instructions on how to withdraw money from his account, and the manuscript of a novel that he wants her to submit to a list of publishers.

Morvern reads the note, opens the presents (she likes the leather jacket), and walks out into the winter gloom of Glasgow. She stands for a long time on a train platform until a pay phone rings. She listens to the stranger on the other end of the line and finally says, "I'm sure he'll be all right." That night, she dresses sexy and meets her best friend, Lanna, for a night at the pub that ends with drunken, confused sex with strangers. The boyfriend's body remains on the floor.

Morvern is played by Samantha Morton, who, like Isabelle Huppert, has a face that can convey enormous emotions without visibly changing. Because she reveals so little, we are drawn into her, fascinated, trying to read her thoughts. You may remember Morton as the musician's deaf-mute girlfriend in Woody Allen's *Sweet and Lowdown*, or as the pale, limp "pre-cog" in Spielberg's *Minority Report*. Here she is a working-class girl, prisoner of a thankless job in a supermarket, whose boyfriend is better educated and more successful.

One of the mysteries of the early stages of *Morvern Callar* is Morvern's behavior after finding the body. She cries, inwardly and privately, but such is her aura that we don't know if she's crying for him or for herself. He left money for a funeral, but after several days, when she can ignore the body no longer, she cuts it up and throws it away. There is a close-up of the computer screen as she deletes his name on the title page of the novel and types in her own. Is she heartless, crazy, or what?

I think the answer is right there in the film, but less visible to American viewers because we are less class-conscious than the filmmakers (the director, Lynne Ramsay, is the daughter of a bartender; Samantha Morton is a survivor of foster homes).

Consider. Morvern lives in her boyfriend's fairly expensive and comfortable Glasgow flat, but still works at the supermarket. If they were truly a couple with a future and had been together for some time, isn't it reasonable to expect that she would no longer be holding onto that job? My guess is that their relationship began fairly recently, based on sex between incompatibles and fueled by a lot of drinking, and that by killing himself he has, from her point of view, shown how unimportant she was to him and how lightly he took their relationship and his life. (When a young person who is not dying or in unbearable crisis commits suicide, it is often an act of selfish, unforgivable egotism.)

By signing her name to his novel, Morvern is sending a message beyond the grave: "I will not clean up this mess and finish your life for you." She will begin to live her own. Unfortunately, she has few resources. She lacks even her friend Lanna's gift for silly, aimless hedonism. After she actually sells the novel, she uses the publisher's check to buy them both a package holiday in Spain, where Lanna is skilled at drinking, partying, and getting laid, but Morvern is a ghost at the feast, a silent, inward person who looks not so much sad as disengaged.

Her style is passive-aggressive. She withholds herself, is not quite present. She sits at times alone and silent, and we feel she is not alone with her thoughts, but only with her feelings. There is the sense that she broods

about hurt. We have little idea what her early life was like, but when we learn that Samantha Morton never talks about her own foster childhood, we are bold enough to wonder if the sense-memories she draws upon for the performance have converted her early years into Morvern's.

The movie doesn't have a plot in the conventional sense, and could not support one. People like Morvern Callar do not lead lives that lend themselves to beginnings, middles, and ends. She is on hold. Somehow, in some way, she's stuck in neutral. The gray-brown tones of her life in Glasgow reflect her emotional habitat, and the bright colors of Spain cause her to wince in pain. She can only handle so much incoming experience at a time. "Sorry, Morvern," her boyfriend wrote in that note. "Don't try to understand." What a bloody condescending jerk. Yet she is not drifting because of his death. She drifts anyway, and always has. What great wrong has made her so damaged? We watch Samantha Morton so closely, with such fascination, because she is able to embody a universe of wounded privacy.

This is Lynne Ramsay's second film, after *Ratcatcher* (1999). That one was about a small boy living with the guilt of a terrible act. Her short films include one in which two small girls, half-sisters, try to understand the wreckage of the marriages that created them. She has been signed to direct the film of Alice Sebold's best-seller *The Lovely Bones,* narrated by the ghostly voice of a young girl who has been raped and murdered. These stories all seem to explore similar dread lifescapes. Why she knows it so well we cannot guess, but she does.

The Mother ★ ★ ★ ½
R, 112 m., 2004

Anne Reid (May), Peter Vaughan (Toots), Cathryn Bradshaw (Paula), Steven Mackintosh (Bobby), Daniel Craig (Darren), Oliver Ford Davies (Bruce), Anna Wilson-Jones (Helen). Directed by Roger Michell and produced by Kevin Loader. Screenplay by Hanif Kureishi.

The Mother peers so fearlessly into the dark needs of human nature that you almost wish it would look away. It's very disturbing. It begins as one of those conventional family dramas with a little love, a little sadness, and a few easy truths, but it's anything but conventional. By the end we've seen lives that aren't working and probably can't be fixed, and we've seen sex used so many different ways it seems more a weapon than a comfort.

The film opens in the reassuring environs of British domesticity. A long-married couple travel into London to visit their children. May (Anne Reid) still has her health and the remains of her beauty, but Toots (Peter Vaughan) seems always out of breath. They arrive at the expensive new home of their son, Bobby (Steven Mackintosh), go for dinner at the flat of their daughter, Paula (Cathryn Bradshaw), and then Toots dies of a heart attack.

It's clear that Bobby and Paula do not much love their mother, although Paula goes through the motions; Bobby is always darting away for urgent conversations on his cell phone. May understands this, and yet when she returns home she finds she simply cannot stay there: "I'll be like all the other old girls around here, and then I'll go into a home. I'd rather kill myself." She returns to London, is greeted coolly by Bobby and his wife, but finds a role with Paula, who needs a baby-sitter.

At Bobby's expensive house, work is under way: His best friend, Darren (Daniel Craig), is building a new solarium. One night May hears Paula having sex in her living room, peers into the room, and discovers that Darren is Paula's lover. This discovery causes something to shift within May, who becomes friendly with Darren, brings him breakfast and lunch on a tray, and asks him, "Would you come to the spare room with me?"

She is in her sixties; he is in his thirties (and married, with an autistic child). She is a sweet-faced matron; he is bearded and muscular. I was reminded of Fassbinder's *Ali: Fear Eats the Soul* (1974), with its tall Moroccan immigrant and its doughy German widow, and indeed Anne Reid looks a little like Brigitte Mira, Fassbinder's star. But Fassbinder's couple had nothing in common but need; May and Darren find that they talk easily, laugh at the same things, are comfortable together. We follow them to lunch along the Thames and to the churchyard where Hogarth is buried; they are probably the only two people in the story who know who Hogarth was.

We think we know where the film stands: It will be about love transcending age. Not at all. That reassuring subject would leave Paula out of the picture, and she desperately pursues Darren and expects him to leave his wife. As sex gives May an inner glow and inspires her to improve her hair and wardrobe, desperation eats away at Paula until she looks almost as old as her mother, and more haggard and needy. She drinks, which doesn't help. After she and her brother guess the truth about May and Darren, Paula pushes to the center of the story with cold, unforgiving fury.

The Mother was written by Hanif Kureishi, whose screenplays include *My Beautiful Laundrette* and *My Son the Fanatic*. It has been directed by Roger Michell, who, hard to believe, is also the director of the comedy *Notting Hill*. Kureishi is relentless in peeling away the defenses of his characters, exposing their naked needs and fears. Familiar with the conventions of fiction, we expect to like someone in this movie. In the middle stretch we like May and Darren, even while we're aware of something not right in their relationship (it isn't the age gap, it's something trickier). But by the end there is nobody to like; we're faced with the possibility that to truly know someone is to wish you knew them less.

There is courage everywhere you look in *The Mother*. In Anne Reid, who follows May with unflinching honesty into the truth of her life. In Cathryn Bradshaw, whose Paula has never felt loved or valued by anyone. In Daniel Craig, who seems to understand why Darren wants to have sex with May, and helps us understand it, and then, when we think we do, shows us we don't. By the end, *The Mother* has told us all we need to know about the characters, except how to feel about them. It shows how people play a role and grow comfortable with it, and how that role is confused with the real person inside. And then it shows the person inside, frightened and pitiful and fighting for survival. I have a lot of questions about what happens in this movie. I am intended to.

The Mothman Prophecies ★ ★
PG-13, 119 m., 2002

Richard Gere (John Klein), Laura Linney (Sergeant Connie Parker), Will Patton (Gordon),

Debra Messing (Mary Klein), Shane Callahan (Nat Griffin), Alan Bates (Alexander Leek), Nesbitt Blaisdell (Chief Josh Jarrett). Directed by Mark Pellington and produced by Gary W. Goldstein, Gary Lucchesi, and Tom Rosenberg. Screenplay by Richard Hatem, based on the novel by John A. Keel.

The Mothman Prophecies claims to be based on a true story, which sent me racing to the Web for a little research. And, yes, there is a belief among the folks in Point Pleasant, West Virginia, that a mothlike creature with red eyes can occasionally be glimpsed in the area. Some say he is a spirit evoked by a long-dead Indian chief. Others blame him for a deadly bridge collapse.

John A. Keel has written a book about Mothman, and now here is this movie. The "true story" part involves the possible existence of Mothman; the human characters are, I believe, based not on facts but on an ancient tradition in horror movies, in which attractive people have unspeakable experiences.

Richard Gere stars as a *Washington Post* reporter named John Klein, who is so happily married (to Debra Messing) that when they agree to buy a new house, they decide to test the floor of a closet for lovemaking purposes, to the surprise of the real-estate agent who walks in on them. If there's one thing you demand in a real-estate agent, it's the good judgment to leave a closet door closed when he hears the unmistakable sounds of coitus coming from behind it. Furthermore: Richard Gere is fifty-three. He's in great shape, but to make love at fifty-three on the floor of a closet with a real-estate agent lurking about is, I submit, not based on a true story.

Then Klein and his wife are in a crash. "You didn't see it, did you?" she asks, and before she dies she draws a picture of a mothlike creature she saw flattened against the windshield. Unlike most windshield bugs, this creature has many forms and lives, as Klein discovers when his life takes a turn into the twilight zone. Driving, as he thinks, to Virginia, he ends up hundreds of miles away in West Virginia, and when he knocks on a door for help the frightened householder accuses Klein of having harassed him for three nights in a row.

Laura Linney plays Connie Parker, a local cop. She trusts Klein, and together they get involved in a strange series of events that culminate in a bridge collapse and a dramatic rescue of the sort that is always particularly annoying to me, because it displaces the focus of the movie. Is this a movie about the Mothman, or about a daring rescue after a bridge collapse? And since the Mothman presumably still exists, how does the happy end after the bridge collapse really settle the story? It's lazy for a movie to avoid solving one problem by trying to distract us with the solution to another.

The director is Mark Pellington *(Arlington Road)*, whose command of camera, pacing, and the overall effect is so good it deserves a better screenplay. The Mothman is singularly ineffective as a threat because it is only vaguely glimpsed, has no nature we can understand, doesn't operate under rules that the story can focus on, and seems to be involved in space-time shifts far beyond its presumed focus. There is also the problem that insects make unsatisfactory villains unless they are very big.

Richard Gere and Laura Linney have some nice scenes together. I like the way he takes a beat of indecision before propelling himself into an action. This is Linney's first movie since *You Can Count on Me*, which won her an Oscar nomination. I saw it again recently and was astonished by her performance. The melancholy lesson seems to be, if you make a small independent movie for very little money and are wonderful in it, you can look forward to being paid a lot of money to appear in a big-budget production in which the talent that got you there is scarcely required.

Mr. Deeds ★ ½
PG-13, 96 m., 2002

Adam Sandler (Longfellow Deeds), Winona Ryder (Babe Bennett), John Turturro (Emilio), Steve Buscemi (Crazy Eyes), Jared Harris (Mac), Peter Gallagher (Chuck Cedar), Allen Covert (Marty), Conchata Ferrell (Jan), Roark Critchlow (William). Directed by Steven Brill and produced by Sidney Ganis and Jack Giarraputo. Screenplay by Tim Herlihy.

At one point during the long ordeal of *Mr. Deeds*, it is said of the Adam Sandler character, "He doesn't share our sense of ironic detachment." Is this a private joke by the writer? If there's one thing Sandler's Mr. Deeds has, it's ironic detachment. Like so many Sandler characters, he seems fundamentally insincere, to be aiming for the laugh even at serious moments. Since the 1936 Frank Capra film *Mr. Deeds Goes to Town* was above all sincere, we wonder how this project was chosen; did Adam Sandler look at Gary Cooper and see a role for himself?

He plays Longfellow Deeds, pizzeria owner in the hamlet of Mandrake Falls, New Hampshire. The pizzeria is one of those establishments required in all comedies about small towns, where every single character in town gathers every single day to provide an audience for the hero, crossed with a Greek chorus. Nobody does anything in Mandrake Falls except sit in the pizzeria and talk about Deeds. When he leaves town, they watch him on the TV.

Turns out Deeds is the distant relative of an elderly zillionaire who freezes to death in the very act of conquering Everest. Control of his media empire and a $40 billion fortune goes to Deeds, who is obviously too good-hearted and simpleminded to deserve it, so a corporate executive named Cedar (Peter Gallagher) conspires to push him aside. Meanwhile, when Deeds hits New York, a trash TV show makes him its favorite target, and producer Babe Bennett (Winona Ryder) goes undercover, convinces Deeds she loves him, and sets him up for humiliation. Then she discovers she loves him, too late.

Frank Capra played this story straight. But the 2002 film doesn't really believe in it, and breaks the mood with absurdly inappropriate "comedy" scenes. Consider a scene where Deeds meets his new butler Emilio (John Turturro). Emilio has a foot fetish. Deeds doubts Emilio will like his right foot, which is pitch black after a childhood bout of frostbite. The foot has no feeling, Deeds says, inviting Emilio to pound it with a fireplace poker. When Deeds doesn't flinch, Turturro actually punctures the foot with the point of the poker, at which point I listened attentively for sounds of laughter in the theater and heard none.

There's no chemistry between Deeds and Babe, but then how could there be, considering that their characters have no existence except as the puppets in scenes of plot manipulation.

After Deeds grows disillusioned with her, there is a reconciliation inspired after she falls through the ice on a pond and he breaks through to save her using the black foot. In story conferences, do they discuss scenes like this and nod approvingly? Tell me, for I want to know.

The moral center of the story is curious. The media empire, we learn, controls enormous resources and employs 50,000 people. The evil Cedar wants to break it up. The good-hearted Deeds fights to keep it together so those 50,000 people won't be out of work. This is essentially a movie that wants to win our hearts with a populist hero who risks his entire fortune in order to ensure the survival of Time-AOL-Warner-Disney-Murdoch. What would Frank Capra have thought about the little guy bravely standing up for the monolith?

Of the many notes I took during the film, one deserves to be shared with you. There is a scene in the movie where Deeds, the fire chief in Mandrake Falls, becomes a hero during a Manhattan fire. He scales the side of a building and rescues a woman's cats, since she refuses to be rescued before them. One after another, the cats are thrown onto a fireman's net. Finally there is a cat that is on fire. The blazing feline is tossed from the window and bounces into a bucket of water, emerging wet but intact, ho, ho, and then Deeds and the heavy-set cat lady jump together and crash through the net, but Deeds's fall is cushioned by the fat lady, who is also not harmed, ho, ho, giving us a heartrending happy ending.

That is not what I wrote in my notes. It is only the setup. What I noted was that in the woman's kitchen, nothing is seen to be on fire except for a box of Special K cereal. This is a species of product placement previously unthinkable. In product placement conferences, do they discuss scenes like this and nod approvingly? Tell me, for oh, how I want to know.

The Mudge Boy ★ ★ ★
R, 94 m., 2004

Emile Hirsch (Duncan Mudge), Tom Guiry (Perry Foley), Richard Jenkins (Edgar Mudge), Pablo Schreiber (Brent), Zachary Knighton (Travis), Ryan Donowho (Scotty), Meredith Handerhan (Tonya), Beckie King (April). Directed by Michael Burke and produced by Beth

Alexander, Alison Benson, and Randy Ostrow. Screenplay by Burke.

The Mudge Boy tells the story of a strange and quiet mama's boy whose mother dies in the film's first scene, leaving him defenseless in the hard world of men—men like his stern and distant father, and the beer-swilling local kids who haunt the back roads in their red pickup truck. They're in basic training for a lifetime of alcoholism and wife-beating.

Duncan Mudge (Emile Hirsch) doesn't fit into this rural world. He is so direct we think at first he might be retarded; but no, he's simply clueless about how to relate to the louts who circle him. The great love of his life is a chicken, named Chicken, who follows him around and rides in the basket of his bicycle. Chicken is called "she" by just about everybody, but looks like a rooster to me; this may be a reference to the sexual uncertainty that uncoils during the film.

Duncan, who is fifteen or sixteen, has no friends as the story opens, but makes one: Perry (Tom Guiry), a neighbor, who is friendlier to him than the other local boys. One day at the swimming hole Duncan reaches out to feel the muscles in Perry's arm, and Perry recoils as if stung. But the touch sets something into motion between them. We think at first it may be Duncan's discovery that he is gay, but we're getting ahead of the plot, and Duncan may not be gay at all. Perry, the macho tough kid with the swagger, is another story.

Watching the movie, I wondered if *The Mudge Boy* is supposed to take place in the real world, and decided it is not quite. Duncan and his father, Edgar (Richard Jenkins), live not in a farmhouse but in a Farmhouse, an archetypal place filled not with furniture but with props— a dresser, a chair, a couch, a kitchen table. The district seems less like working farmland than like offstage in a psychological problem play. The local boys arrive in their pickup like messengers of fate, and Duncan passively allows himself to be swept up in their ignorance. He buys his way in by paying for their beer; when they come by looking for him, Edgar stares at them long and hard, suspecting their motives.

Edgar is not a cruel father. He is simply unable to talk with his son, except for a few rigid rules no doubt handed down by his own father. After he catches Duncan in an embarrassing situation, his response is to make him dig a hole, wide and deep, to learn what work is like. "You can't even get into trouble like a normal boy," he complains.

Some scenes work with cruel precision. Others seem uncertain—like the scene in church, with Duncan singing "The Old Rugged Cross" way off-key. The movie doesn't seem to know the point of this scene. Certainly it understands Perry, the neighbor boy, whose behavior toward Duncan is directly related to the fact that his father beats him. Duncan has at least been freed by his upbringing to be the person that he is; Perry is trapped in a maze of macho acting-out and baffled by his own behavior.

The film was written and directed by Michael Burke, who seems to be tapping deep, fearful feelings. The movie wants to be dark and truthful, but the spell is sometimes broken by scenes that edge too close to silly, such as the chicken cemetery, and others that seem just plain weird: Did you know you can "becalm" a chicken by putting its head in your mouth? Dr. Johnson said it was a brave man who ate the first oyster, but that was nothing compared to the discovery of chicken becalming.

At the end there is a scene of sudden emotional truth that explains nothing but feels like it does. Duncan will go out into life and probably find a way, in a big city, to be himself. We should seek Perry's future adventures on the shelves of true crime books. *The Mudge Boy* is odd and intense, very well acted, and impossible to dismiss. I think the key is to understand that Duncan is not the one with the problems, but the kind of person who, by being completely and mysteriously on his own wavelength, causes the uncertain people around him to insist loudly and with growing unease on how certain they are of themselves.

Murder by Numbers ★ ★ ★
R, 119 m., 2002

Sandra Bullock (Cassie Mayweather), Ryan Gosling (Richard Haywood), Michael Pitt (Justin Pendleton), Ben Chaplin (Sam Kennedy), Agnes Bruckner (Lisa), Chris Penn (Ray), R. D. Call

(Rod), Tom Verica (Al Swanson). Directed by Barbet Schroeder and produced by Richard Crystal and Susan Hoffman. Screenplay by Tony Gayton.

Richard and Justin, the high school killers in *Murder by Numbers,* may not have heard of Leopold and Loeb, or seen Hitchcock's *Rope,* or studied any of the other fictional versions *(Compulsion, Swoon)* of the infamous murder pact between two brainy and amoral young men. But they're channeling it. *Murder by Numbers* crosses Leopold/Loeb with a police procedural, and adds an interesting touch: Instead of toying with the audience, it toys with the characters. We have information they desperately desire, and we watch them dueling in misdirection.

The movie stars Sandra Bullock as Cassie Mayweather, a veteran detective, experienced enough to trust her hunches and resist the obvious answers. Ben Chaplin is Sam Kennedy, her by-the-books partner, the kind of cop who gets an A for every step of his investigation, but ends up with the wrong conclusion. Paired against them are Richard Haywood and Justin Pendleton (Ryan Gosling, from *The Believer,* and Michael Pitt, from *Hedwig and the Angry Inch).* These are two brainy high school kids, fascinated, as Leopold and Loeb were, by the possibility of proving their superiority by committing the perfect murder.

Their plan: Pick a victim completely at random, so that there is no link between corpse and killers, and leave behind no clues. The film opens with the suggestion of a suicide pact between the two teenagers, who face each other, holding revolvers to their heads, in a crumbling Gothic building so improbably close to the edge of a seaside cliff that we intuit someone is going to be dangling over it by the end of the film.

Bullock's Cassie is the central character, a good cop but a damaged human being, whose past holds some kind of fearsome grip on her present. Cassie and Sam are assigned to a creepy case; the body of a middle-aged female has been found in a wooded area, and close analysis of clues (hair, strands from a rug) seem to lead back to a suspect. Sam is happy to follow the clues to their logical conclusion. Cassie isn't so sure, and a chance meeting with one of the young sociopaths leads to a suspicion: "Something's not right with that kid."

We learn a lot about police work in *Murder by Numbers,* and there's a kind of fascination in seeing the jigsaw puzzle fall into place, especially since the audience holds some (not all) of the key pieces. Many of the best scenes involve an intellectual and emotional duel between the two young men, who seem to have paused on the brink of becoming lovers and decided to sublimate that passion into an arrogant crime. Richard and Justin are smart—Justin smarter in an intellectual way, Richard better at manipulating others. The movie wisely reserves details of who did what in the killing, and why.

These are affluent kids with absent parents, who are their own worst enemies because their arrogance leads them to play games with the cops to show how smart they are. They'd be better off posing as vacant-headed slackers. It is Cassie's intuition that the boys are inviting her attention, are turned on by the nearness of capture. Meanwhile, of course, her partner and the brass at the station are eager for a quick solution. A janitor is the obvious suspect? Arrest the janitor.

The movie has been directed by the versatile Barbet Schroeder, who alternates between powerful personal films *(Our Lady of the Assassins)* and skillful thrillers *(Single White Female).* When the two strands cross you get one-of-a-kind films like *Reversal of Fortune* and *Barfly.* After the semidocumentary freedom and scary Colombian locations of *Our Lady of the Assassins,* here's a movie that he directs as an exercise in craft—only occasionally letting his mordant humor peer through, as in an inexplicable scene where Cassie is bitten by a monkey.

Sandra Bullock does a good job here of working against her natural likeability, creating a character you'd like to like, and could like, if she weren't so sad, strange, and turned in upon herself. She throws herself into police work not so much because she's dedicated as because she needs the distraction, needs to keep busy and be good to assure herself of her worth. As she draws the net closer, and runs into more danger and more official opposition, the movie more or less helplessly starts thinking to itself about that cliff above the sea, but at least the climax shows us that Bullock can stay in character no matter what.

My Architect: A Son's Journey ★ ★ ★ ½

NO MPAA RATING, 116 m., 2004

A documentary directed by Nathaniel Kahn and produced by Susan Rose Behr and Kahn. Screenplay by Kahn.

What a sad film this, and how filled with the mystery of human life. When Nathaniel Kahn read the obituary of his father, the great American architect Louis I. Kahn, he expected, somehow, to see his own name listed among the survivors. But in death as in life his father kept his secrets. Louis Kahn had an "official" family including his wife, Esther, and daughter Sue Ann. He had two other secret families: With fellow architect Anne Tyng he had a daughter, Alexandra, and with his colleague Harriet Pattison he had Nathaniel.

That Kahn was a great architect is clear from the loving photography of his work by his son. His masterpiece, the capitol of Bangladesh in Dhaka, is a building that invites the spirit to soar. His other works included the Kimball Art Museum in Fort Worth, the Yale Art Gallery, the Salk Institute in California, and, most surprising, a "music boat" he designed almost like a vessel from a cartoon. The boat sails into a harbor, folds up into a proscenium stage, and presents a concert for the listeners on shore.

Against these achievements the movie sets a lifetime of struggle, secrecy, stubbornness, deception, and frequent failure. He was "short, scarred, and ugly, and had a funny voice," a colleague states flatly. His face badly burned by a fire when he was an infant, Louis moved with his family from Estonia to Philadelphia when he was six. Called "Scarface" in school, he buried himself in his studies, won a college scholarship, had grand ideas about architecture, but was supported for twenty years by his first wife and didn't open his own office until he was almost fifty.

He would die at seventy-three, and only in the last ten years of his life did he achieve the stature for which he is remembered. But what a death. Returning from Bangladesh—a hard journey for a man his age—he collapsed and died in a rest room of Penn Station, and his body went unclaimed for two days because he had scratched out his address on his passport, and the police did not recognize his name. To this day, Nathaniel's mother remains convinced he blotted out the address because he planned to make good on a promise to come and live with them. Nathaniel is not so sure.

The movie begins as the story of a son searching for his father, and ends as the story of the father searching for himself. Kahn would visit Nathaniel and Harriet unexpectedly, always leaving before morning. He told the boy stories about his life, drew him a book of funny boats (at the time he was designing the music ship), but "left no physical evidence he had ever been in our home—not even a bow tie hanging in the closet."

Nathaniel interviews both his mother and Anne; Esther, who died in 1996, is seen in an old video. He talks to many of his father's colleagues, from contemporaries like Philip Johnson and I. M. Pei to Frank Gehry, who once worked in Kahn's shop. Their memories mix affection and respect with exasperation. He was a difficult man. When his plan to redesign downtown Philadelphia was rejected, there was a hint that anti-Semitism might have been involved, but when Nathaniel tracks down Ed Bacon, the czar in charge of the project, he gets a sharp verdict: "Totally irresponsible. Totally impractical." Kahn wanted Philadelphians to park their cars in a ring around the city and walk to work, a utopian idea not likely to win tax dollars.

There are moments of sudden poignance. A colleague remembers that Kahn always spent Christmas with them, and Nathaniel repeats "Christmas?" and we realize he never spent a Christmas with his father. And Robert Boudreau, the man who commissioned the music ship, realizes he is talking to Louis's son, and tears well in his eyes. "I saw you when you were six years old," he says. "At the wake." Kahn's wife had sent orders for Anne and Harriet to stay away from the funeral, but they came anyway, and were ignored.

A portrait emerges of Louis I. Kahn as a man constantly in motion, an elusive target who lived more at his office than in any home, who worked his employees beyond the endurance of some of them, who would appear for two or three days and then fly off in search of a commission or to supervise a job. It was his great disappointment that his plans for a synagogue in Jerusalem were never taken up; ironic, that his greatest work was built by a Muslim country.

When he died, Nathaniel says, his father was $500,000 in debt. He narrates a catalog of projects that were canceled or never commissioned. At the end of the film, meeting with his two half-sisters, he wonders if they are a family, and they decide they are because they choose to be—not because of who their father was. That was the only choice Louis left them.

My Big Fat Greek Wedding ★ ★ ★
PG, 95 m., 2002

Nia Vardalos (Toula Portokalos), John Corbett (Ian Miller), Lainie Kazan (Maria), Michael Constantine (Gus), Gia Carides (Nikki), Louis Mandylor (Nick), Joey Fatone (Angelo), Bruce Gray (Rodney Miller). Directed by Joel Zwick and produced by Gary Goetzman, Tom Hanks, and Rita Wilson. Screenplay by Nia Vardalos.

All the people in this movie look like they could be real people. The romance involves not impossibly attractive people, but a thirty-year-old woman who looks okay when she pulls herself out of her Frump Phase, and a vegetarian high school teacher who urgently needs the services of SuperCuts. Five minutes into the film, I relaxed, knowing it was set in the real world, and not in the Hollywood alternative universe where Julia Roberts can't get a date.

My Big Fat Greek Wedding is narrated by Toula Portokalos (Nia Vardalos), who, like all Greek women, she says, was put upon this Earth for three purposes: to marry a Greek man, to have Greek children, and to feed everyone until the day she dies. Toula is still single and works in the family restaurant (Dancing Zorbas), where, as she explains, she is *not* a waitress, but a "seating hostess." One day a guy with the spectacularly non-Greek name of Ian Miller (John Corbett) walks in, and she knows instinctively that marriage is thinkable.

The movie is warmhearted in the way a movie can be when it knows its people inside out. Watching it, I was reminded of Mira Nair's *Monsoon Wedding*, about an Indian wedding. Both cultures place great emphasis on enormous extended families, enormous extended weddings, and enormous extended wedding feasts. Nia Vardalos, who not only stars but based the screenplay on her own one-woman play, obviously has great affection for her big Greek family, and a little exasperation, too—as who wouldn't, with a father who walks around with a spray jar of Windex because he is convinced it will cure anything? Or a mother who explains, "When I was your age, we didn't *have* food."

Vardalos was an actress at Chicago's Second City when she wrote the play. The way the story goes, it was seen by Rita Wilson, a Greek-American herself, and she convinced her husband, Tom Hanks, that they had to produce it. So they did, making a small treasure of human comedy. The movie is set in Chicago but was filmed in Toronto—too bad, because the dating couple therefore doesn't have a chizbooger at Billy Goat's.

As the film opens, Toula the heroine is single at thirty and therefore a failure. Ian Miller causes her heart to leap up in love and desire, and Ian likes her too. Really likes her. This isn't one of those formula pictures where it looks like he's going to dump her. There's enough to worry about when the families meet. "No one in our family has ever gone out with a non-Greek," Toula warns him uneasily, and indeed her parents (Lainie Kazan and Michael Constantine) regard Ian like a lesser life form.

The movie is pretty straightforward: Ian and Toula meet, they date, they bashfully discover they like each other, the families uneasily coexist, the wedding becomes inevitable, and it takes place (when Ian's mother brings a bundt cake to the wedding, no one has the slightest idea what it is). One key shot shows the church with the bride's side jammed, and the groom's handful of WASP relatives making a pathetic show in their first four rows. Toula explains to Ian that she has twenty-seven first cousins, and at a prenuptial party, her dad even introduces some of them: "Nick, Nick, Nick, Nick, Nick, Nick, Nicky—and Gus."

The underlying story of *My Big Fat Greek Wedding* has been played out countless times as America's immigrants have intermarried. If the lovers have understanding (or at least reluctantly flexible) parents, love wins the day and the melting pot bubbles. This is nicely illustrated by Toula's father, Gus. He specializes in finding the Greek root for *any* word (even "kimono"), and delivers a toast in which he explains that "Miller" goes back to the Greek word for apple, and "Portokalos" is based on the Greek word for oranges, and so, he concludes triumphantly, "in the end, we're all fruits."

My Life Without Me ★ ★ ½

R, 106 m., 2003

Sarah Polley (Ann), Amanda Plummer (Laurie), Scott Speedman (Don), Leonor Watling (Neighbor Ann), Deborah Harry (Ann's Mother), Mark Ruffalo (Lee), Alfred Molina (Ann's Father), Julian Richings (Dr. Thompson). Directed by Isabel Coixet and produced by Esther Garcia and Gordon McLennan. Screenplay by Coixet.

It's not probable that I will die before attending Sofia Coppola's Lifetime Achievement Award, but I can't deny that death has been on my mind these days. Having surgery for cancer concentrates the mind wonderfully. I have some notions of what I would do if I had little time to live, and things I would not do. I would not, for example, do any of the things that are done by Ann, the heroine of *My Life Without Me*, who would be a cruel egocentric if she weren't so obviously just a fictional pawn.

I would let everyone know what was what. I would expect them to be open with me. I would try to remember the dying woman in Ingmar Bergman's *Cries and Whispers*, who writes in her journal: "This is happiness. I cannot wish for anything better. I feel profoundly grateful to my life, which gives me so much." I would remember my dying Aunt Marjorie, who told me with total contentment, "I've enjoyed my life, Rog, and you know this day comes for all of us sooner or later." And I would start reading a long novel. We both knew Margie had maybe a month to live. She was a great reader. I asked her what she was reading. "I've just started Tom Clancy's new novel," she said, and her smile finished the sentence.

The heroine of *My Life Without Me*, on the other hand, engineers her death as a soap opera that would be mushy if it were about her, but is shameless because it is by her. Told she has inoperable ovarian cancer, she keeps it a secret from everyone in her life, lies to cover up her growing weakness, and on good days works through a checklist of "Ten Things to Do Before I Die." Number eleven should maybe be, rent the video of *Things to Do in Denver When You're Dead*.

One of the items on her list is, "Find out what it would be like to make love with another man." She was married at seventeen, to the only boy she ever slept with, and now she is twenty-three and lives with Don and their daughters in a house trailer in her mother's backyard. They have the happiest marriage I have ever seen in the movies, maybe because strict plot economy allows no time to provide them with problems. Nevertheless when she meets a guy named Lee at the Laundromat, she allows them to drift into a relationship that quickly leads to love.

I don't understand her need to do this. I understand that a twenty-three-year-old woman might be curious about sleeping with a second man, but would she act on mere curiosity if she loved her husband, they were happy, and had great sex? Okay, maybe, although I think she'd be wrong. But to do it when she's dying is so unfair to the other guy, who doesn't understand part of her appeal is the urgent, bittersweet quality that dying has given her. And it's not enough for her to have sex. She wants to make someone fall in love with her. It's not enough to spring a mournful surprise on one man who loves her. She wants two heartbreaks. Maybe she stops at only two because of time pressure. At her funeral they should play, "Don't Cry for Me, Argentina."

Her egocentric decision puts enormous pressure on the kind doctor who gives her the bad news and is forbidden to treat her. And on her kids, who know something is very wrong, because kids always do, and who have to believe her lies about being tired. And on her husband, her mother, her best friend at work, and even the woman (also named Ann) who has moved in next door. After testing her baby-sitting skills, she has chosen this Ann as Don's next wife, and arranges a dinner they don't realize is their first date. It's bad enough for a second wife to feel like she's sharing her husband with the ghost of his first wife, but how does it feel during sex when the ghost is cheering, "You go, girl!"

Now of course all of this is handled with exquisite taste. Actors do not often get roles this challenging, and they find honesty in the moments even while the movie as a whole grows into a manipulation. Ann is played by Sarah Polley, from *The Sweet Hereafter,* and she accepts the character's decisions and invests them, wrong as they are, with simplicity and glowing conviction. Lee, the second lover, is played by Mark Ruffalo, who amazes me in one movie after another with the intensity of his presence and his gentle response to other actors. Scott Speedman is Ann's husband, Deborah Harry is her mother, Alfred Molina is her father, currently in prison; Amanda Plummer is the best friend, and Leonor Watling is the other Ann, who tells a story about dying Siamese twins that starts out sad and then becomes increasingly inconceivable.

And an actor named Julian Richings is Dr. Thompson, the man who tells her she has ovarian cancer. He sits next to her in a row of chairs while telling her this, and admits he has never been able to look a patient in the eye when telling them they're about to die. This character, and this scene, point to a better way the movie could have gone. The doctor has the empathy for other humans that Ann lacks. What he does may be professionally questionable, but it comes from his heart.

That the performances are so good, that they find truth in scenes to which we have fundamental objections, makes this a tricky movie to review. I think the screenplay, written by director Isabel Coixet, is shameless in its weepy sentiment. But there is truth here, too, and a convincing portrait of working-class lives. These people don't stagger under some kind of grim proletarian burden, but are smart and resourceful, and I suspect Ann—had she lived—might have someday turned into a pretty good writer.

On the other hand, there are several scenes of Ann making tape recordings intended to be played by her daughters on their birthdays until they're eighteen. If I were one of those daughters and had grown old enough to have a vote on the matter, I would burn the goddamn tapes and weep and pound the pillow and ask my dead mother why she was so wrapped up in her stupid, selfish fantasies that she never gave me the chance to say good-bye.   ☞

The Mystic Masseur ★ ★ ★
PG, 117 m., 2002

Aasif Mandvi (Ganesh), Om Puri (Ramlogan), James Fox (Mr. Stewart), Sanjeev Bhaskar (Beharry), Ayesha Dharker (Leela), Jimi Mistry (Partap), Zohra Segal (Auntie), Sakina Jaffrey (Suruj Mooma). Directed by Ismail Merchant and produced by Nayeem Hafizka and Richard Hawley. Screenplay by Caryl Phillips, based on the novel by V. S. Naipaul.

The West Indies were a footnote to the British Empire, and the Indian community of Trinidad was a footnote to the footnote. After slavery was abolished and the Caribbean still needed cheap labor, thousands of Indians were brought from one corner of the empire to another to supply it. They formed an insular community, treasuring traditional Hindu customs, importing their dress styles and recipes, re-creating India far from home on an island where it seemed irrelevant to white colonial rulers and the black majority.

The great man produced by these exiles was V. S. Naipaul, the 2001 Nobel laureate for literature, whose father was a newspaperman with a great respect for books and ideas. *A House for Mr. Biswas* (1961) is Naipaul's novel about his father and his own childhood, and one of the best books of the century. But Naipaul's career began in 1957 with *The Mystic Masseur,* a novel casting a fond but dubious light on the Indian community of Trinidad. It is now the first of Naipaul's novels to be filmed, directed by Ismail Merchant, himself an Indian, usually the producing partner for director James Ivory.

The Mystic Masseur is a wry, affectionate delight, a human comedy about a man who thinks he has had greatness thrust upon him when in fact he has merely thrust himself in the general direction of greatness. It tells the story of Ganesh, a schoolteacher with an exaggerated awe for books, who is inspired by a dotty Englishman to write some of his own. Abandoning the city for a rural backwater, he begins to compose short philosophical tomes which, published by the local printer on a foot-powered flatbed press, give him a not-quite-deserved reputation for profundity.

If Ganesh allowed his success to go to his head, he would be insufferable. Instead, he is played by Aasif Mandvi as a man so sincere he really does believe in his mission. Does he have the power to cure with his touch and advise troubled people on their lives? Many think he does, and soon he has become married to the pretty daughter of a canny businessman, who runs taxis from the city to bring believers to Ganesh's rural retreat.

There is rich humor in the love-hate relationship many Indians have with their customs, which they leaven with a decided streak of practicality. In no area is this more true than marriage, as you can see in Mira Nair's wonderful comedy *Monsoon Wedding*. The events leading up to Ganesh's marriage to the beautiful Leela (Ayesha Dharker) are hilarious, as the ambitious businessman Ramlogan positions his daughter to capture the rising young star.

Played by the great Indian actor Om Puri with lip-smacking satisfaction, Ramlogan makes sure Ganesh appreciates Leela's dark-eyed charm, and then demonstrates her learning by producing a large wooden sign she has lettered, with a bright red punctuation mark after every word. "Leela know a lot of punctuation marks," he boasts proudly, and soon she has Ganesh within her parentheses. The wedding brings a showdown between the two men; custom dictates that the father-in-law must toss bills onto a plate as long as the new husband is still eating his kedgeree, and Ganesh, angered that Ramlogan has stiffed him with the wedding bill, dines slowly.

The humor in *The Mystic Masseur* is generated by Ganesh's good-hearted willingness to believe in his ideas and destiny, both of which are slight. Like a thrift shop Gandhi, he sits on his veranda writing pamphlets and advising supplicants on health, wealth, and marriage. Leela meanwhile quietly takes charge, managing the family business, as Ganesh becomes the best-known Indian on Trinidad. Eventually he forms the Hindu Association, collects some political power, and is elected to Parliament, which is the beginning of his end. Transplanted from his rural base to the capital, he finds his party outnumbered by Afro-Caribbeans and condescended to by the British governors; he has traded his stature for a meaningless title, and is correctly seen by other Indians as a stooge.

The masseur's public career has lasted only from 1943 to 1954. The mistake would be to assign too much significance to Ganesh. His lack of significance is the whole point. He rises to visibility as a homegrown guru, is co-opted by the British colonial government, and by the end of the film is a nonentity shipped safely out of sight to Oxford on a cultural exchange. Critics of the film have slighted Ganesh for being a pointless man leading a marginal life; they don't sense the anger and hurt seething just below the genial surface of the novel. The young Trinidadian Indian studying at Oxford, who meets Ganesh at the train station in the opening scene, surely represents Naipaul, observing the wreck of a man who loomed large in his childhood.

Movies are rarely about inconsequential characters. They favor characters who are sensational winners or losers. But Ganesh, one senses, is precisely the character Naipaul needed to express his feelings about being an Indian in Trinidad. He has written elsewhere about the peculiarity of being raised in an Indian community thousands of miles from "home," attempting to reflect a land none of its members had ever seen. The empire created generations of such displaced communities, not least the British exiles in India, sipping Earl Grey, reading the *Times*, and saluting "God Save the Queen" in blissful oblivion to the world around them.

Ganesh gets about as far as he could get, given the world he was born into, and he is such an innocent that many of his illusions persist. Shown around the Bodleian Library in Oxford by his young guide, the retired statesman looks at the walls of books, and says, "Boy, this the center of the world! Everything begin here, everything lead back to this place." Naipaul's whole career would be about his struggle with that theory.

Mystic River ★ ★ ★ ★
R, 137 m., 2003

Sean Penn (Jimmy Markum), Tim Robbins (Dave Boyle), Kevin Bacon (Sean Devine), Laurence Fishburne (Whitey Powers), Marcia Gay Harden (Celeste Boyle), Laura Linney (Annabeth Markum), Thomas Guiry (Brendan), Emmy Rossum (Katie). Directed by Clint Eastwood and produced by Eastwood, Judie Hoyt, and Robert Lorenz. Screenplay by Brian Helgeland, based on the novel by Dennis Lehane.

Clint Eastwood's *Mystic River* is a dark, ominous brooding about a crime in the present that is emotionally linked to a crime in the past. It involves three boyhood friends in an Irish neighborhood of Boston, who were forever marked when one of them was captured by a child molester; as adults, their lives have settled into uneasy routines that are interrupted by the latest tragedy. Written by Brian Helgeland, based on the novel by Dennis Lehane, the movie uses a group of gifted actors who are able to find true human emotion in a story that could have been a whodunit, but looks too deeply and evokes too much honest pain.

The film centers on the three friends: Jimmy (Sean Penn), an ex-con who now runs the corner store; Dave (Tim Robbins), a handyman; and Sean (Kevin Bacon), a homicide detective. All are married; Jimmy to a second wife, Annabeth (Laura Linney), who helps him raise his oldest daughter and two of their own; Dave to Celeste (Marcia Gay Harden), who has given him a son; Sean to an absent, pregnant wife who calls him from time to time but never says anything. The other major character is Whitey (Laurence Fishburne), Sean's police partner.

Jimmy keeps a jealous eye on his nineteen-year-old daughter, Katie (Emmy Rossum), who works with him at the store. She's in love with Brendan (Thomas Guiry), a boy Jimmy angrily disapproves of. Theirs is a sweet puppy love; they plan to run away together, but before that can happen Katie is found brutally beaten and dead. Sean and Whitey are assigned to the case. Brendan is obviously one of the suspects, but so is Dave, who came home late the night of the murder, covered with blood and talking to his wife in anguish about a mugger he fought and may have killed.

Although elements in *Mystic River* play according to the form of a police procedural, the movie is about more than the simple question of guilt. It is about pain spiraling down through the decades, about unspoken secrets and unvoiced suspicions. And it is very much about the private loyalties of husbands and wives. Jimmy says that he will kill the person who killed his daughter, and we have no reason to doubt him, especially after he hires neighborhood thugs to make their own investigation. Laura Linney, as his wife, has a scene where she responds to his need for vengeance, and it is not unreasonable to compare her character to Lady Macbeth. Marcia Gay Harden, as Celeste, Dave's wife, slowly begins to doubt her husband's story about the mugger, and shares her doubts. We see one wife fiercely loyal, and another who suspects she has been shut out from some deep recess of her husband's soul.

Although the story eventually arrives at a solution, it is not about the solution. It is about the journey, and it provides each of the actors with scenes that test their limits. Both Penn and Robbins create urgent and breathtaking suspense as they are cross-examined by the police. There is tension between Whitey, who thinks Dave is obviously guilty, and Sean, who is reluctant to suspect a childhood friend. There are such deep pools of hatred and blood lust circling the funeral that we expect an explosion at any moment, and yet the characters are all inward, smoldering.

And always that day in the past lingers in their memories. The three boys were writing their names in wet concrete when two men in a car drove up, flashed a badge, and took one of the boys away with them. Flashbacks show that he was abused for days. Compounding his suffering was the uneasiness the other two boys always felt about him; maybe they didn't entirely understand what happened to him, but in some sense they no longer felt the same about their violated friend—whose name, half-finished, remains in the old concrete like a life interrupted in midstream.

This is Clint Eastwood's twenty-fourth film as a director, and one of the few titles where he doesn't also act. He shows here a deep rapport with the characters and the actors, who are allowed lancing moments of truth. Always an understated actor himself, he finds in his three actors pools of privacy and reserve. Robbins broods inside his own miseries and watches vampire movies on TV to find metaphors for the way he feels. Bacon hurts all the time, we feel, because of the absence of his wife. Penn is a violent man who prepares to act violently but has not, we see, found much release that way in the past.

To see strong acting like this is exhilarating. In a time of flashy directors who slice and dice their films in a dizzy editing rhythm, it is important to remember that films can look and listen and attentively sympathize with their characters. Directors grow great by subtracting, not adding, and Eastwood does nothing for show, everything for effect.   ☞

My Wife Is an Actress ★ ★ ½
R, 95 m., 2002

Charlotte Gainsbourg (Charlotte), Yvan Attal (Yvan), Terence Stamp (John), Noémie Lvovsky (Nathalie), Laurent Bateau (Vincent), Keith Allen (David), Jo McInnes (David's assistant), Ludivine Sagnier (Géraldine). Directed by Yvan Attal and produced by Claude Berri. Screenplay by Attal.

The thing about movie love scenes is that they are acting and they are not acting, both at the same time. Two actors play "characters" who kiss or caress or thrash about. They are only "acting." When the director shouts, "Cut!" they disengage and wander off to their trailers to finish the crossword puzzle. That at least is the idea they give in interviews.

But consider. Most movie actors are attractive. They come wrapped in a mystique. Everyone is curious about them, including their costars. When the director says, "Action!" and they find themselves in bed, there is the presence and warmth of the other person, the press of bosom or thigh, the pressure of a hand, the softness of lips. Does something happen that is not precisely covered by the definition of acting?

If it does not, then the actors are not humans and should not be playing them. If we in the audience sometimes feel a stirring of more than artistic interest in some of the people we see on the screen, should actors, whose experience is so much more immediate, be any different? The fact that they are not different provides the subtext for half the articles in the supermarket tabloids.

Consider all that, and I will tell you a story. I interviewed Robert Mitchum many times. He costarred with Marilyn Monroe. I never asked him anything as banal as "what was it like to kiss Marilyn Monroe?" but of course there is no woman in the history of the movies who would inspire a greater desire to ask that question. Once, though, as I was Q&Aing Mitchum at the Virginia Film Festival, somebody in the audience asked him about Marilyn.

"I loved her," he said. "I had known her since she was about fifteen or sixteen years old. My partner on the line at the Lockheed plant in Long Beach was her first husband. That's when I first met her. And I knew her all the way through. And she was a lovely girl; very, very shy. She had what is now recognized as agoraphobia. She was terrified of going out among people. At that time they just thought she was being difficult. But she had that psychological, psychic fear of appearing among people. That's why when she appeared in public, she always burlesqued herself. She appeared as you would hope that she would appear. She was a very sweet, loving, and loyal—unfortunately loyal—girl. Loyal to people who used her, and a lot who misused her."

So there you have it. Not what it was like to kiss her, but what it was like to know her. In one paragraph, probably as much truth as can be said about Monroe.

An answer like that is beyond the new movie *My Wife Is an Actress*. This is a French serio-comedy written, directed by, and starring Yvan Attal, who plays a Paris sportswriter whose wife is a famous actress. She is played by Charlotte Gainsbourg, who in real life is Attal's wife. No doubt if he were to write a serious novel about his marriage, Attal would have some truths to share, but his film feels like an arm's-length job, a comedy that deliberately avoids deep waters.

Yvan is a jealous man. He is driven to it by an unrelenting barrage of questions from members of the public, some of whom assume as a matter of course that Charlotte really does sleep with her costars. He smashes one guy in the nose, but that doesn't help, and when Charlotte goes to London to work with a big star (Terence Stamp), Yvan all but pushes her into his arms to prove his point.

Stamp, who is very good in a thankless role, plays a man so wearied by life and wear and tear that he sleeps with women more or less as a convenience. He seduces to be obliging. There is a funny moment when he propositions a woman and soberly accepts her refusal as one more interesting development, nodding thoughtfully to himself.

If the movie were all comedy, it might work better. It has an ambition to say something about its subjects, but not a willingness. It circles the possibility of mental and spiritual infidelity like a cat wondering if a mouse might still be alive. Watching it, I felt it would be fascinating to see a movie that was really, truthfully, fearlessly about this subject.

N

Napoleon Dynamite ★ ½
PG, 86 m., 2004

Jon Heder (Napoleon Dynamite), Jon Gries (Uncle Rico), Aaron Ruell (Kip Dynamite), Efren Ramirez (Pedro), Tina Majorino (Deb), Diedrich Bader (Rex), Haylie Duff (Summer). Directed by Jared Hess and produced by Jeremy Coon, Sean Covel, and Chris Wyatt. Screenplay by Jared Hess and Jerusha Hess.

There is a kind of studied stupidity that sometimes passes as humor, and Jared Hess's *Napoleon Dynamite* pushes it as far as it can go. Its hero is the kind of nerd other nerds avoid, and the movie is about his steady progress toward complete social unacceptability. Even his victory toward the end, if it is a victory, comes at the cost of clowning before his fellow students.

We can laugh at comedies like this for two reasons: because we feel superior to the characters, or because we pity or like them. I do not much like laughing down at people, which is why the comedies of Adam Sandler make me squirmy (most people, I know, laugh because they like him). In the case of Napoleon Dynamite (Jon Heder), I certainly don't like him, but then, the movie makes no attempt to make him likable. Truth is, it doesn't even try to be a comedy. It tells his story and we are supposed to laugh because we find humor the movie pretends it doesn't know about.

Napoleon is tall, ungainly, depressed, and happy to be left alone. He has red hair that must take hours in front of the mirror to look so bad. He wants us to know he is lonely by choice. He lives outside of town with his brother, Kip (Aaron Ruell), whose waking life is spent online in chat rooms, and with his grandmother, who is laid up fairly early in a dune buggy accident.

It could be funny to have a granny on a dune buggy; I smile at least at the title of the Troma film *Rabid Grannies*. But in this film the accident is essentially an aside, an excuse to explain the arrival on the farm of Napoleon's Uncle Rico (Jon Gries), a man for whom time has stood still ever since the 1982 high school sports season, when things, he still believes, should have turned out differently. Rico is a door-to-door salesman for an herbal breast enlargement potion, a product that exists only for the purpose of demonstrating Rico's cluelessness. In an age when even the Fuller Brush Man would be greeted with a shotgun (does anyone even remember him?), Rico's product exists in the twilight zone.

Life at high school is daily misery for Napoleon, who is picked on cruelly and routinely. He finally makes a single friend, Pedro (Efren Ramirez), the school's only Latino, and manages his campaign for class president. He has a crush on a girl named Deb (Tina Majorino), but his strategy is so inept that it has the indirect result of Deb going to the prom with Pedro. His entire prom experience consists of cutting in.

Watching *Napoleon Dynamite*, I was reminded of *Welcome to the Dollhouse*, Todd Solondz's brilliant 1996 film, starring Heather Matarazzo as an unpopular high school girl. But that film was informed by anger and passion, and the character fought back. Napoleon seems to passively invite ridicule, and his attempts to succeed have a studied indifference, as if he is mocking his own efforts. I'm told the movie was greeted at Sundance with lots of laughter, but then, Sundance audiences are concerned to be cool, and to sit through this film in depressed silence would not be cool, however urgently it might be appropriate.

Naqoyqatsi ★ ★ ★
PG, 89 m., 2002

A documentary directed by Godfrey Reggio and produced by Joe Beirne, Reggio, and Lawrence Taub. Screenplay by Philip Glass and Reggio.

Naqoyqatsi is the final film in Godfrey Reggio's "qatsi" trilogy, a series of impressionistic documentaries contrasting the nobility of nature with the despoliation of mankind. The titles come from the Hopi Indian language. *Koyaanisqatsi* (1983) translated as "life out of balance." *Powaqqatsi* (1988) means "life in transition." And now comes *Naqoyqatsi*, or "war as a way of life."

Like the others, *Naqoyqatsi* consists of images (450 of them, Reggio said at the Telluride premiere). We see quick streams of briefly glimpsed symbols, abstractions, digital code, trademarks, newsreels, found images, abandoned buildings, and cityscapes, and snippets of TV and photography. An early image shows the Tower of Babel; the implication is that the confusion of spoken tongues has been made worse by the addition of visual and digital languages.

Koyaanisqatsi, with its dramatic fast-forward style of hurtling images, made a considerable impact at the time. Clouds raced up mountainsides, traffic flowed like streams of light through city streets. The technique was immediately ripped off by TV commercials, so that the film's novelty is no longer obvious. Now that he has arrived at the third part of his trilogy, indeed, Reggio's method looks familiar, and that is partly the fault of his own success. Here he uses speed-up less, and relies more on quickly cut montages. It's a version of the technique used in Chuck Workman's films on the Oscarcast, the ones that marry countless shots from the movies; Reggio doctors his images with distortion, overlays, tints, and other kinds of digital alteration.

The thinking behind these films is deep but not profound. They're ritualistic grief at what man has done to the planet. "The logical flaw," as I pointed out in my review of *Powaqqatsi*, is that "Reggio's images of beauty are always found in a world entirely without man—without even the Hopi Indians. Reggio seems to think that man himself is some kind of virus infecting the planet—that we would enjoy the Earth more, in other words, if we weren't here."

Although *Naqoyqatsi* has been some ten years in the making, it takes on an especially somber coloration after 9/11. Images of marching troops, missiles, bomb explosions, and human misery are intercut with trademarks (the Enron trademark flashes past), politicians, and huddled masses, and we understand that war is now our way of life. But hasn't war always been a fact of life for mankind? We are led to the uncomfortable conclusion that to bring peace to the planet, we should leave it.

This line of reasoning may, however, be missing the point. In reviewing all three Reggio films, I have assumed he was telling us something with his images, and that I could under-

stand it and analyze it. That overlooks what may be the key element of the films, the sound tracks by composer Philip Glass (this time joined by Yo-Yo Ma, who also contributes a solo). Can it be that these films are, in the very best sense of the word, music videos? The movie is not simply "scored" by Glass; his music is a vital component of every frame, fully equal with the visuals, and you can watch these films again and again, just as you can listen to a favorite album.

Perhaps the solution is to stop analyzing the images altogether and set ourselves free from them. Just as it is a heresy to paraphrase classical music by discovering "stories" or "messages," perhaps *Naqoyqatsi* and its brothers need to be experienced as background to our own streams of consciousness—nudges to set us thinking about the same concerns that Reggio has. I have problems with *Naqoyqatsi* as a film, but as a music video, it's rather remarkable.

Narc ★ ★ ★
R, 105 m., 2003

Ray Liotta (Lieutenant Henry Oak), Jason Patric (Sergeant Nick Tellis), Chi McBride (Captain Cheevers), Busta Rhymes (Beery), Anne Openshaw (Kathryn Calvess), Richard Chevolleau (Steeds), John Ortiz (Ruiz), Thomas Patrice (Marcotte), Alan Van Sprang (Michael Calvess). Directed by Joe Carnahan and produced by Diane Nabatoff, Julius Nasso, Ray Liotta, and Michelle Grace. Screenplay by Carnahan.

Joe Carnahan's *Narc* is a cold, hard film about Detroit narcotics detectives. Ray Liotta and Jason Patric star, as a veteran whose partner has been killed, and a younger cop assigned to join him in the investigation. If many cop-partner movies have an undertone of humor, even a splash of *The Odd Couple*, this one is hard-bitten and grim: The team consists of Bad Cop and Bad Cop. The twist is that both of them are good at their work; their problem is taking the job too personally.

The film opens with a virtuoso handheld chase scene, as Nick Tellis (Patric) pursues a suspect through backyards and over fences until the chase ends in a shooting—and it's not the perp who is hit, but a pregnant woman.

Tellis is put on suspension and cools off at home with his wife and a baby he loves. It's clear this is a man with big problems involving anger and overcompensation; is there such a thing as being too dedicated as a cop?

More than a year later, his captain (Chi McBride) calls in Tellis and makes him an offer: He can be reinstated on the force if he becomes the partner of Henry Oak (Liotta). Oak's former partner, a cop named Calvess, has been murdered. The captain thinks Tellis's contacts with drug dealers and other lowlifes, plus his unique brand of dedication, are needed to track down the cop killer. He warns Tellis that Oak is a good cop but sometimes unstable, and there are quick subjective cuts to the older man beating a prisoner.

Tellis and Oak do not fit the usual pattern of cop partners in the movies. Either of them could be the lead. Neither one is supporting. As cops, they think independently and are self-starters, and cooperation doesn't come easily. Tellis is startled, too, at Oak's methods, which are quick and practical and amoral, and produce results, but are not always legal.

The movie's writer and director, Joe Carnahan, brings a rough, aggressive energy to the picture. His first film, *Blood, Guts, Bullets & Octane* (1998), was all style, but here he creates believable characters. His screenplay stays within the broad outlines of the cop-buddy formula, but brings fresh energy to the obligatory elements. It is no surprise, for example, that Tellis's wife doesn't want him back out on the streets, and that there's tension between his home life and his job. This is an ancient action cliché: A man's gotta do what a man's gotta do. But the details of the domestic scenes ring true.

In terms of its urban wasteland, the movie descends to a new level of grittiness. These streets aren't mean, they're cruel, and to work them is like being the garbageman in hell. Liotta's character stalks them as a man on a mission, driven by private agendas we only begin to suspect. The Patric character is stunned to see the other man not only violating protocol, but apparently trying to shut him out of the investigation, as if this business can only be settled privately between him and his demons.

Both Liotta and Patric have played similar roles. Patric starred in *Rush* (1992), in a brilliant performance as an undercover narcotics cop

who, along with his rookie partner (Jennifer Jason Leigh), gets hooked on drugs himself. Liotta has appeared in countless crime pictures, both as a cop and most memorably in *GoodFellas* (1990) as a cocaine-addled criminal. Here they bring a kind of rawness to the table. Liotta, heavier, wearing a beard, leaves behind his days as a handsome leading man and begins edging into interesting Brian Cox territory. Patric, ten years after *Rush*, looks less like he's playing a cop and more like he might be one.

The investigation itself must remain undescribed here. But its ending is a neat and ironic exercise in poetic justice. Pay attention during one of the very last shots, and tell me if you think the tape recorder was on or off. In a way, it makes a difference. In another way, it doesn't.

National Lampoon's Van Wilder ★
R, 95 m., 2002

Ryan Reynolds (Van Wilder), Tara Reid (Gwen), Kal Penn (Taj), Tim Matheson (Vance Wilder Sr.), Kim Smith (Casey), Daniel Cosgrove (Richard Bagg), Tom Everett Scott (Elliot Grebb), Chris Owen (Timmy [the Jumper]). Directed by Walt Becker and produced by Peter Abrams, Robert L. Levy, Jonathon Komack Martin, and Andrew Panay. Screenplay by Brent Goldberg and David Wagner.

Watching *National Lampoon's Van Wilder*, I grew nostalgic for the lost innocence of a movie like *American Pie*, in which human semen found itself in a pie. In *NatLampVW*, dog semen is baked in a pastry. Is it only a matter of time until the heroes of teenage gross-out comedies are injecting turtle semen directly through their stomach walls?

National Lampoon's Van Wilder, a pale shadow of *National Lampoon's Animal House*, tells the story of Van Wilder (Ryan Reynolds), who has been the Biggest Man on Campus for seven glorious undergraduate years. He doesn't want to graduate, and why should he, since he has clout, fame, babes, and the adulation of the entire campus (except, of course, for the professor whose parking space he swipes, and the vile fraternity boy who is his sworn enemy).

Van Wilder is essentially a nice guy, which is a big risk for a movie like this to take; he raises funds for the swimming team, tries to restrain suicidal students, and throws legendary keg parties. Ryan Reynolds is, I suppose, the correct casting choice for Van Wilder, since the character is not a devious slacker but merely a permanent student. That makes him, alas, a little boring, and Reynolds (from ABC's *Two Guys and a Girl*) brings along no zing: He's a standard leading man when the movie cries out for a manic character actor. Jack Black in this role would have been a home run.

Is Van Wilder too good to be true? That's what Gwen (Tara Reid) wonders. She's a journalism student who wants to do an in-depth piece about Van for the campus paper. Of course she's the girlfriend of the vile frat boy, and of course her investigation inspires her to admire the real Van Wilder while deploring his public image. Tara Reid is remarkably attractive, as you may remember from *Josie and the Pussycats* and *American Pie 2*, but much of the time she simply seems to be imitating still photos of Renee Zellweger smiling.

That leaves, let's see, Kal Penn as Taj, the Indian-American student who lands the job as Van Wilder's assistant, and spends much of his time using a stereotyped accent while reciting lists of synonyms for oral sex. I cannot complain, since the hero's buddy in every movie in this genre is always a sex-crazed zealot, and at least this film uses nontraditional casting. (Casting directors face a catch-22: They cast a white guy, and everybody wants to know why he had to be white. So they cast an ethnic guy, and everybody complains about the negative stereotype. Maybe the way out is to cast the ethnic guy as the hero and the white guy as the horny doofus.)

The movie is a barfathon that takes full advantage of the apparent MPAA guidelines in which you can do pretty much anything with bodily functions except involve them in healthy sex. The movie contains semen, bare breasts and butts, epic flatulence, bizarre forms of masturbation, public nudity, projectile vomiting, and an extended scene of explosive defecation with sound effects that resemble the daily duties of the Port-a-Loo serviceman, in reverse. There are also graphic shots of enormous testicles, which are allowed under the *National Geographic* loophole since they belong to Van Wilder's pet bulldog. Presumably the MPAA would not permit this if it had reason to believe there were dogs in the audience.

"On a scale of 1 to 10 shots of bourbon needed to make a pledge ralph," writes Bob Patterson of the Website Delusions of Adequacy, "this film will get a very strong five from most college-age film fans who are not offended by vulgar humor. Older filmgoers who might be offended by such offerings are encouraged to do something that is physically impossible (i.e., lift yourself up by your bootstraps)."

Although this is obviously the review the movie deserves, I confess the rating scale baffles me. Is it better or worse if a film makes you ralph? Patterson implies that older filmgoers might be offended by vulgar humor. There is a flaw in this reasoning: It is not age but humor that is the variable. Laughter for me was such a physical impossibility during *National Lampoon's Van Wilder* that had I not been pledged to sit through the film, I would have lifted myself up by my bootstraps and fled.

Never Again ★ ★
R, 97 m., 2002

Jeffrey Tambor (Christopher), Jill Clayburgh (Grace), Bill Duke (Earl), Caroline Aaron (Elaine), Eric Axen (College Girl-Boy), Michael McKean (Alex), Sandy Duncan (Natasha). Directed by Eric Schaeffer and produced by Robert Kravitz, Terence Michael, and Dawn Wolfrom. Screenplay by Schaeffer.

Here's a case of two actors who do everything humanly possible to create characters who are sweet and believable, and are defeated by a screenplay that forces them into bizarre, implausible behavior. It is not even the behavior I object to; in a raucous sex farce, it would be understandable. It is the film's refusal to come down on one side of the fence or the other: to find a tone and believe in it. It wants to be heartfelt and sincere *and* vulgar, dirty, and shocking. And it is willfully blind to human nature.

Never Again stars Jeffrey Tambor and Jill Clayburgh as Christopher and Grace, two lonely people in their fifties. She is divorced; he has never married. They both believe another romance is probably impossible. During the course of this film they will Meet Cute and have a relationship that no two people have ever or will ever have, outside the overheated imagination of Eric Schaeffer, the film's writer and director.

Christopher runs an exterminating service by day and in the evenings plays jazz piano in a Greenwich Village nightclub; the combination of those two jobs says more about an overwrought screenplay than about employment possibilities in the real world. You might assume a jazz pianist in the Village would have seen something of life and even gathered some knowledge of homosexuality, but Christopher is as naive as a thirteen-year-old, and wonders if perhaps his failure to form relationships with women is because he is gay. To test this theory, he makes a date with the least convincing transsexual in cinematic history (Michael McKean), and then, fleeing the scene but still in an investigative mood, he enters a gay bar and meets the most unconvincing male hustler in cinematic history—before eventually trying to pick up Grace, who he thinks might be a more convincing transsexual.

She is a woman, she informs him, and has simply fled to the nearest bar after an unhappy experience in her own dating career. They decide to go out for a meal, and show in a few brief scenes that a sane and plausible version of this relationship might have made a wonderful movie. But no. Schaeffer wants it both ways, and has written a screenplay that periodically runs off the rails.

The most unlikely scenes involve Clayburgh's eagerness to make up for lost time in the department of sexual experimentation. She walks into a sex shop to buy an enormous dildo, and also walks out with whips, chains, and what I guess is supposed to be an S&M uniform, although why a complete set of medieval armor would be necessary is beyond me; how about something simple, in leather or rubber? The appurtenance later pays off, so to speak, in a scene where she straps it on and can't get it off when Christopher unexpectedly comes calling with his mother. I do not pretend to know if it could possibly be true that she could not remove the offending device, but there is one thing as certain as the sun in the morning, and that is that no fifty-four-year-old woman would

open the door to her fiancé and his mother while wearing such an appliance, however well concealed by a bathrobe.

There is another scene in *Never Again* that strikes a false note. Grace walks into a beauty parlor and describes an impressive array of sexual practices in a voice clearly audible to other women in the shop, whom she does not know. I am prepared to believe that a woman will tell her hairdresser anything, but that same instinct informs me that such women speak in hushed tones, because they don't want everyone in the shop to spread gossip about events usually found in the pages of *Penthouse Forum*, if indeed that publication still exists. ("An interesting thing happened the other night between me and my boyfriend, a piano-playing exterminator. . . .")

All of this is discouraging because in scene after scene Clayburgh and Tambor show themselves ready and able to create Grace and Christopher as realistic characters. There is a remarkable scene where it appears that he's about to break up with her, and she lets him have it, in a merciless verbal dissection; it's a reminder of Clayburgh's gifts as an actress. And other scenes where his loneliness is a fact instead of a setup for gimmicks. But *Never Again* plays like a head-on collision between two ideas in conflict. Is it a movie about people, or about gags? What purpose is there in creating believable people, only to put them into situations that clash and jar? Who's in charge here? ☞

Never Die Alone ★ ★ ★ ½
R, 90 m., 2004

DMX (King David), David Arquette (Paul), Michael Ealy (Mike), Clifton Powell (Moon), Reagan Gomez-Preston (Juanita), Aisha Tyler (Nancy), Jennifer Sky (Janet), Keesha Sharp (Edna). Directed by Ernest Dickerson and produced by Earl Simmons and Alessandro Camon. Screenplay by James Gibson, based on a novel by Donald Goines.

Ernest Dickerson's *Never Die Alone* is a doom-laden morality tale centered on a character who not only refers to *Scarface*'s Tony Montana but is more evil, more vicious, more self-pitying, and more cold-blooded. This is a man named

King David, played by DMX as a midlevel drug dealer whose favorite trick is to hook a girl on cocaine and then switch her to heroin without telling her, so that she'll be completely dependent on him. If that is vile, he has a little "test" for them that is monstrous.

The movie begins with King David dead and in his coffin. I am not giving anything away; it's the first shot. Dead he may be, but he narrates the story of his own life from beyond the grave, like Tupac Shakur in *Tupac: Resurrection*. He has kept a diary on cassette tapes, and they come into the possession of an earnest white writer named Paul (David Arquette). Paul has a poster of Hemingway on the wall of his shabby rented room, and engages in the risky business of hanging out around tough types in Harlem drug bars. He's doing research, he thinks, or looking for trouble, we think.

The movie's plot is not nearly as linear and simple as I've made it sound so far. It loops back and forth through ten years of time, in flashbacks and memories, and there are several other major players. As it opens, King David has returned from Los Angeles to New York in order to "make amends" by repaying a debt to a higher-level drug kingpin named Moon (Clifton Powell), and Moon has sent his relatively untested lieutenant Mike (Michael Ealy) and another man to collect the cash payment. When that turns violent against Moon's specific instructions, it sets in motion a chain of events with beginnings that coil back through time, including the connection King David does not know he has with Mike.

Never Die Alone, written by James Gibson and based on a novel by the legendary ex-con writer Donald Goines, is not a routine story of drugs and violence, but an ambitious, introspective movie in which a heartless man tells his story without apology. The evil that he did lives after him, but there is no good to inter with his bones. What he cannot quite figure out at the end is how this white kid came into his life, and is driving him to the hospital, and seems to know his story.

There's action in the movie, but brief and brutal; this is not an action picture but a drama that deserves comparison with *Scarface* and *New Jack City*. The many characters are all drawn with care and dimension, especially the three women who have the misfortune to enter David's life; they're played by Reagan Gomez-Preston, Jennifer Sky, and Keesha Sharp. Each is onscreen relatively briefly; each makes a strong impression.

DMX is hard and cold as King David, and never more frightening than when he seems so charming to the women he encounters. It's a fearless performance, made more effective because we begin the movie by sort of liking him—so that we're being set up just like his victims. Michael Ealy, as Mike, has the difficult assignment of going through most of the movie being motivated by events we don't yet know about, so that we have to change our idea of him as the story develops. David Arquette is more the pawn of the plot than its mover, and his character functions mostly as a witness and facilitator; that's scary, because most of the time he has no idea how much danger he's in. After he inherits King David's Stutz pimpmobile, he essentially turns himself into a shooting gallery target.

The director Dickerson, who began as Spike Lee's NYU classmate and cinematographer, has done strong work before, starting with his debut film *Juice* (1992) and including the overlooked *Our America* (2002), based on the true story of two Chicago ghetto teenagers who were given a tape recorder by NPR and made an award-winning documentary. *Never Die Alone* is his best work, with the complexity of serious fiction and the nerve to start dark and stay dark, to follow the logic of its story right down to its inevitable end.

The New Guy ★ ★
PG-13, 100 m., 2002

D. J. Qualls (Dizzy/Gil), Lyle Lovett (Bear Harrison), Eddie Griffin (Luther), Eliza Dushku (Danielle), Zooey Deschanel (Nora), Parry Shen (Glen), Laura Clifton (Emily). Directed by Ed Decter and produced by Mark Ciardi, Todd Garner, and Gordon Gray. Screenplay by David Kendall.

D. J. Qualls stars in *The New Guy* as a high school misfit who switches schools and gets a fresh start. At Rocky Creek, he was the target of cruel jokes almost daily (sample: being tied to a chair while wearing false breasts), but now, at Eastland High and with a new haircut, he is seen as a cool hero. "The point is," he explains with relief, "today nobody stuffed me in my locker or singed off my ass hairs."

The movie made from this material is quirkier than I would have expected, considering that the building blocks have been scavenged from the trash heap of earlier teenage comedies. Much of the credit goes to Qualls (from *Road Trip*), who not only plays the son of Lyle Lovett in this movie but looks biologically descended from him, no mean feat. He has a goofy grin and an offhand way with dialogue that make him much more likable than your usual teenage comedy hero.

Known at one school by his nickname Dizzy and at the other by his first name Gil, Dizzy/Gil does not approach the dating game with high expectations. Here's how he asks a popular girl out on a date: "Maybe sometime if you would like to drink coffee near me, I would pay." There is a school scandal at Rocky Creek when a librarian does something painful and embarrassing I cannot describe here to that part of his anatomy I cannot name, and he ends up in prison. (His condition or crime—I am not sure—is described as Tourette's syndrome, which is either a misdiagnosis, a mispronunciation, or an example of Tourette's in action.)

Yes, prison. The movie begins with a direct-to-camera narration by Luther (Eddie Griffin), who is in prison for undisclosed reasons and is the narrator of this film for reasons even more deeply concealed. Perhaps my attention strayed, but I was unable to discern any connection between Luther and the other characters, and was baffled by how Dizzy/Gil was in prison whenever he needed to get advice from Luther, and then out again whenever it was necessary for him to rejoin the story in progress. Perhaps a subplot, or even a whole movie, is missing from the middle.

In any event, Dizzy/Gil is seen as a neat guy at the new school, especially after he unfurls a giant American flag at football practice and stands in front of it dressed as George C. Scott in *Patton* and delivers a speech so rousing that the team wins for the first time in five years. He also steals a horse and rides around on it more than is necessary.

The movie has all the shots you would expect in a movie of this sort: cheerleaders, football heroics, pratfalls. Some of them are cruel, as when a bully stuffs a midget in a trash can and rolls it downhill. Others are predictably vulgar, as when Dizzy snatches a surveillance camera from the wall and (aided by its extension cord of infinite length) uses it to send a live broadcast into every classroom of a hated teacher struggling with a particularly difficult bowel movement. Sometimes even verbal humor is attempted, as when a high school counselor (Illeana Douglas) tells our hero he is in denial, and helpfully explains, "Denial is not just a river in Egypt."

I don't know why this movie was made or who it was made for. It is, however, not assembly-line fodder, and seems occasionally to be the work of inmates who have escaped from the Hollywood High School Movie Asylum. It makes little sense, fails as often as it succeeds, and yet is not hateful and is sometimes quite cheerfully original. And D. J. Qualls is a kid you can't help but like—a statement I do not believe I have ever before made about the hero of a teenage vulgarian movie.

New York Minute ★ ½
PG, 91 m., 2004

Mary-Kate Olsen (Roxy Ryan), Ashley Olsen (Jane Ryan), Eugene Levy (Lomax), Andy Richter (Bennie Bang), Jared Padalecki (Trey), Riley Smith (Jim Wessler), Andrea Martin (Senator). Directed by Dennie Gordon and produced by Denise Di Novi, Mary-Kate Olsen, Ashley Olsen, and Robert Thorne. Screenplay by Emily Fox, Adam Cooper, and Bill Collage.

They say baseball is popular because everyone thinks they can play it. Similar reasoning may explain the popularity of the Olsen twins: Teenage girls love them because they believe they could *be* them. What, after all, do Mary-Kate and Ashley do in *New York Minute* that could not be done by any reasonably presentable female adolescent? Their careers are founded not on what they do, but on the vicarious identification of their fans, who enjoy seeing two girls making millions for doing what just about anybody could do.

The movie offers the spectacle of two cheerful and attractive seventeen-year-olds who have the maturity of silly thirteen-year-olds and romp through a day's adventures in Manhattan, a city that in this movie is populated entirely by hyperactive character actors. Nothing that happens to them has any relationship with anything else that happens to them, except for the unifying principle that it all happens to *them*. That explains how they happen to be (1) chased by a recreational vehicle through heavy traffic, (2) wading through the sewers of New York, (3) getting a beauty makeover in a Harlem salon, (4) in possession of a kidnapped dog, (5) pursued by music pirates, (6) in danger in Chinatown, and (7) ... oh, never mind.

Given the inescapable fact that they are twins, the movie of course gives them completely opposite looks and personalities, and then leads us inexorably to the moment when one will have to impersonate the other. Mary-Kate Olsen plays Roxy Ryan, the sloppy girl who skips school and dreams of getting her demo tape backstage at a "punk rock" video shoot. Ashley Olsen plays Jane Ryan, a Goody Two-shoes who will win a four-year scholarship to Oxford University if she gives the winning speech in a competition at Columbia. Perhaps in England she will discover that the university is in the town of Oxford, and so can correct friends who plan to visit her in London. (I am sure the screenwriters knew the university was in Oxford, but were concerned that audience members might confuse "going to" Oxford and "being in" Oxford, and played it safe, since London is the only city in England many members of the audience will have heard of, if indeed they have.)

But I'm being mean, and this movie is harmless, and as eager as a homeless puppy to make friends. In fact, it has a puppy. It also has a truant officer, played by Eugene Levy in a performance that will be valuable to film historians, since it demonstrates what Eugene Levy's irreducible essence is when he plays a character who is given absolutely nothing funny to say or do. His performance suggests that he stayed at home and phoned in his mannerisms. More inexplicable is Andy Richter's work as a limousine driver with sinister connections to music piracy rackets. He is given an accent, from where I could not guess, although I could guess why: At a story conference, the filmmakers

looked in despair at his pointless character and said, "What the hell, maybe we should give him an accent."

Because the movie all takes place during one day and Roxy is being chased by a truant officer, it compares itself to *Ferris Bueller's Day Off*. It might as reasonably compare itself to *The Third Man* because they wade through sewers. *New York Minute* is a textbook example of a film created as a "vehicle," but without any ideas about where the vehicle should go. The Olsen twins are not children any longer, yet not quite poised to become adults, and so they're given the props and costumes of seventeen-year-olds, but carefully shielded from the reality. That any seventeen-year-old girl in America could take seriously the rock band that Roxy worships is beyond contemplation. It doesn't even look like a band to itself.

The events involving the big speaking competition are so labored that occasionally the twins seem to be looking back over their shoulders for the plot to catch up. Of course, there is a moment when all the characters and plot strands meet on the stage of the speech contest, with the other competitors looking on in bafflement, and of course (spoiler warning, ho, ho), Jane wins the scholarship. In fact (major spoiler warning), she does so without giving the speech, because the man who donates the scholarship reads her notes, which were dropped on the stage, and *knows* it would have been the winning speech had she only been able to deliver it. Unlikely as it seems that Jane could win in such a way, this scenario certainly sidesteps the difficulty of having her deliver a speech that would sound as if she could win.

Nicholas Nickleby ★ ★ ★ ½
PG, 132 m., 2003

Charlie Hunnam (Nicholas Nickleby), Hugh Mitchell (Young Nicholas), Jamie Bell (Smike), Nathan Lane (Vincent Crummles), Barry Humphries (Mrs. Crummles), Christopher Plummer (Ralph Nickleby), Tom Courtenay (Newman Noggs), Jim Broadbent (Wackford Squeers), Edward Fox (Sir Mulberry Hawk), Timothy Spall (Charles Cheeryble), Gerald Horan (Ned Cheeryble), Juliet Stevenson (Mrs. Squeers), Romola Garai (Kate Nickleby), Anne Hathaway (Madeline Bray), Stella Gonet (Mrs.

Nickleby), Alan Cumming (Mr. Folair). Directed by Douglas McGrath and produced by Simon Channing-Williams, John Hart, and Jeff Sharp. Screenplay by McGrath, based on the novel by Charles Dickens.

Nicholas Nickleby was the third novel by Charles Dickens, following *The Pickwick Papers* and *Oliver Twist* and sharing with them a riot of colorful characters. One of them, the sadistic boarding school proprietor Wackford Squeers, was a portrait taken so much from life that it resulted in laws being passed to reform the private education industry. The novel followed a familiar Dickens pattern—a young man sets out in the world to win fortune and love despite a rogue's gallery of villains. It contained characters improbably good or despicable, and with admirable economy tied together several of the key characters in a web of melodramatic coincidences. It is not placed in the first rank of Dickens's art, but I would place it near the top for sheer readability.

The new film version by Douglas McGrath, who made *Emma* (1996), is much more reasonable than the 1980 nine-hour stage version of the Royal Shakespeare Company, which I have on laser disk and really mean to get to one of these days. The movie is jolly and exciting and brimming with life, and wonderfully well acted. McGrath has done some serious pruning, but the result does not seem too diluted; there is room for expansive consideration of such essential characters as Nicholas's vindictive Uncle Ralph (Christopher Plummer), secretly undermined by his dipsomaniac and disloyal servant Newman Noggs (Tom Courtenay). The movie gives full screen time to Wackford Squeers (Jim Broadbent, looking curiously Churchillian) and his wife (Juliet Stevenson)—and hints that psychosexual pathology inspired their mistreatment of students. Their most pathetic target, Smike (Jamie Bell, who played *Billy Elliott*), is seen as less of a caricature and more of a real victim.

To balance the scales are two of the happiest comic couples Dickens ever created: the touring theatricals Vincent and Mrs. Crummles (Nathan Lane and Barry Humphries), and the brothers Cheeryble (Timothy Spall and Gerald Horan). The Crummles rescue Nicholas (Char-

lie Hunnam) after his escape from the Squeers's school, turn him into an actor, and even find talent in the hapless Smike. Their touring company is a loving exaggeration of companies Dickens must have worked with, and is rich with such inspirations as their aging and expanding daughter the Child Phenomenon. Barry Humphries uses his alter ego, Dame Edna Everage, to play Mrs. Crummles, and if you look closely you will notice Humphries as a man, playing opposite the formidable Dame.

The Cheerybles are the lawyer brothers who agree on everything, especially that Nicholas must be hired in their firm, all of his problems solved, and his romantic future secured through a liaison with Madeline Bray (Anne Hathaway), whose tyrannical father has long ruled her life. It is particularly good to see Timothy Spall nodding and smiling as brother Charles, after seeing him so depressed in role after role.

Nicholas himself is more of a placeholder than a full-blooded character: the handsome, feckless, and earnest young man who leads us through the story as he encounters one unforgettable character after another. The most striking member of the Nickleby family is, of course, Uncle Ralph, played by Plummer in a performance so cold-blooded it actually reminded me of his stage Iago. Ralph lives only for the accumulation of money. His opinion of the poor is that poverty is their own fault, and they deserve as a result to be put to work to enrich him (in this he reflects some of the latest tax reforms). Nicholas he more or less sells to Squeers, and he lodges Mrs. Nickleby (Stella Gonet) and her daughter Kate (Romola Garai) in a hovel while Kate is put to work doing piecework. Kate is a beauty, however, and so Ralph's larger scheme is to marry her off to the vile Sir Mulberry Hawk (Edward Fox), in return for various considerations involving their business interests.

The actors assembled for *Nicholas Nickleby* are not only well cast, but well typecast. Each one by physical appearance alone replaces a page or more of Dickens's descriptions, allowing McGrath to move smoothly and swiftly through the story without laborious introductions: They are obviously who they are. The result is a movie that feels like a complete account of Dickens's novel, even though the Royal Shakespeare found an additional seven hours of inspiration.

The physical production is convincing without being too charming or too realistic. The clothes of some of the characters remind us that in « ose days their wardrobes would have consisted only of what they wore. The countryside is picturesque but falls short of greeting cards (except for the Nicklebys' cottage at the end). The story takes place at about the same time as Scorsese's *Gangs of New York*, but London is heavier on alehouses, lighter on blood in the gutters. The movie makes Dickens's world look more pleasant to inhabit than it probably was, but then so did his novels.

What animates the story is Dickens's outrage, and his good heart. *The Pickwick Papers* was essentially a series of sketches of comic characters, but in *Oliver Twist* and *Nicholas Nickleby* we find him using fiction like journalism, to denounce those who would feed on the poor and exploit the helpless. One senses that in Dickens's time there were more Uncle Ralphs than Cheerybles, but that perhaps he helped to improve the ratio.

Nine Queens ★ ★ ★
R, 114 m., 2002

Ricardo Darin (Marcos), Gaston Pauls (Juan), Leticia Bredice (Valeria), Tomas Fonzi (Federico), Ignasi Abadal (Gandolfo). Directed by Fabian Bielinsky and produced by Cecilia Bossi and Pablo Bossi. Screenplay by Bielinsky.

Fabian Bielinsky's *Nine Queens* is a con within a con within a con There comes a time when we think we've gotten to the bottom, and then the floor gets pulled out again, and we fall for another level. Since nothing is as it seems (it doesn't even seem as it seems), watching the film is like observing a chess game in which all of the pieces are in plain view but one player has figured out a way to cheat. "David Mamet might kill for a script as good," Todd McCarthy writes in *Variety*. True, although Mamet might also reasonably claim to have inspired it; the setup owes something to his *House of Games*, although familiarity with that film will not help you figure out this one.

The film starts with *a seemingly* chance meeting. Indeed, almost everything in the film is "seemingly." A young would-be con man named Juan (Gaston Pauls) is doing the $20 bill switch with a naive cashier—the switch I have never been able to figure out, where you end up with $39 while seemingly doing the cashier a favor. Juan succeeds. The cashier goes off duty. Juan is greedy, and tries the same trick on her replacement. The first cashier comes back with the manager, screaming that she was robbed. At this point Marcos (Ricardo Darin), a stranger in the store, flashes his gun, identifies himself as a cop, arrests the thief, and hauls him off.

Of course, Marcos is only seemingly a cop. He lectures Juan on the dangers of excessive greed and buys him breakfast, and then the two of them seemingly happen upon an opportunity to pull a big swindle involving the "nine queens," a rare sheet of stamps. This happens when Valeria (Leticia Bredice), seemingly Marcos's sister, berates him because one of his old criminal associates tried to con a client in the hotel where she seemingly works. The old con seemingly had a heart attack, and now the field is seemingly open for Marcos and Juan to bilk the seemingly rich and drunk Gandolfo (Ignasi Abadal).

Now before you think I've given away the game with all those "seeminglys," let me point out that they may only seemingly be seeminglys. They may in fact be as they seem. Or seemingly otherwise. As Juan and Marcos try to work out their scheme, which involves counterfeit stamps, we wonder if in fact the whole game may be a pigeon drop with Juan as the pigeon. But, no, the fake stamps are stolen, seemingly by complete strangers, requiring Marcos and Juan to try to con the owner of the *real* nine queens out of stamps they can sell Gandolfo. (Since they have no plans to really pay for these stamps, their profit would be the same in either case.)

And on and on, around and around, in an elegant and sly deadpan comedy set in modern Buenos Aires. A plot, however clever, is only the clockwork; what matters is what kind of time a movie tells. *Nine Queens* is blessed with a gallery of well-drawn character roles, including the alcoholic mark and his two bodyguards; the avaricious widow who owns the nine queens and her much younger bleached-blond boyfriend; and Valeria the sister, who opposes Marcos's seamy friends and life of crime, but might be willing to sleep with Gandolfo if she can share in the spoils.

Juan meanwhile falls for Valeria himself, and then there are perfectly timed hiccups in the plot where the characters (and we) apparently see through a deception, only to find that deeper reality explains everything—maybe. The story plays out in modern-day Buenos Aires, a city that looks sometimes Latin, sometimes American, sometimes Spanish, sometimes German, sometimes modern, sometimes ancient. Is it possible the city itself is pulling a con on its inhabitants, and that some underlying reality will deceive everyone? The ultimate joke of course would be if the Argentinean economy collapsed, so that everyone's gains, ill-gotten or not, would evaporate. But that is surely too much to hope for.

Note: Nine Queens *is like a South American version of* Stolen Summer, *the movie that won the contest sponsored by HBO, Miramax, and Matt Damon and Ben Affleck. According to* Variety, *some 350 screenplays were submitted in an Argentinean competition, Bielinsky's won, and he was given funds to film. It's illuminating that in both cases such competitions yielded more literate and interesting screenplays than the studios are usually able to find through their own best efforts.*

No Good Deed ★ ★ ★

R, 103 m., 2003

Samuel L. Jackson (Jack Friar), Milla Jovovich (Erin), Stellan Skarsgård (Tyrone), Doug Hutchison (Hoop), Joss Ackland (Mr. Quarre), Grace Zabriskie (Mrs. Quarre), Jonathan Higgins (David Brewster). Directed by Bob Rafelson and produced by Barry Berg, David Braun, Peter Hoffman, Herb Nanas, Sam Perlmutter, Andre Rouleau, and Maxime Remillard. Screenplay by Christopher Canaan and Steve Barancik, based on *The House on Turk Street* by Dashiell Hammett.

Bob Rafelson's two best movies are *Five Easy*

Pieces and *The Postman Always Rings Twice,* and *No Good Deed* is like a mingling of their themes. From *Postman* comes hard-boiled American crime fiction, and from *Five Easy Pieces* and its musical family comes the cop played by Samuel L. Jackson, a diabetic who plays the cello. He is, in fact, looking forward to a week at a "fantasy camp" where he can play with Yo-Yo Ma when fate intervenes.

Jackson's character, Jack Friar, is asked by a friend to help find her runaway daughter. He's a cop assigned to grand theft auto and usually finds runaway cars, but he postpones his vacation to ask around in the last neighborhood where the girl was seen, and that leads him to help out Mrs. Quarre, a sweet little old lady who has fallen on her steps with bags of groceries. Once inside her house, he discovers the little old lady is not sweet, and that her criminal partners think the cop is looking for them. So they tie him to a chair, where he will spend most of the movie.

The story is based on *The House on Turk Street,* a 1924 short story by Dashiell Hammett, whose work also inspired *The Maltese Falcon* and *The Thin Man.* The *noir* origins are evident in Jackson's resigned, laconic hero, and in the character of Erin (Milla Jovovich), with a blond Veronica Lake haircut, who guards Jack, talks to him, and eventually joins in a scene that improbably combines sex and the art of cello playing.

Jack Friar, who was only trying to do a good deed, has walked into the final stages of a bank robbery. A gang led by the precise Tyrone (Stellan Skarsgård) and including the violent hothead Hoop (Doug Hutchison) is about to commit a multimillion-dollar computer fraud with the help of an inside man named David (Jonathan Higgins), a bank official who thinks Erin is in love with him.

More than one man shares that misapprehension, including Hoop, who thinks he and Erin will do away with Tyrone and skip with the money. And Tyrone, who trusts Erin to stay with him. To be sure, she left him once before, but "this is how Tyrone says you shouldn't have left," Erin says, showing Jack Friar a foot with four toes.

As Erin and Jack wait in the house for the

bank robbery to take place, the old couple are at an airport. Mr. Quarre (Joss Ackland) is a feisty old fart who has a pipe collection and memories of flying a lot of missions in Korea, and has been signed up to fly the robbers to the Bahamas. Mrs. Quarre (Grace Zabriskie, who was the angry hitchhiker in *Five Easy Pieces*) is along for the ride; as they wait in the rain for their passengers to turn up, they make love in the plane, which is more than any of Erin's men can claim.

The long delay gives Jack and Erin an opportunity to share secrets. Turns out Tyrone brought Erin over from Russia, where she was a piano prodigy, which she proves with a solo. Then she releases Jack long enough for a surprisingly erotic cello duet, involving only one cello, that eludes the question: Why doesn't Jack overpower her and escape? Later, tied up again, he tries to burn through his cords by holding his feet over a flame on the kitchen range; it's surprising how painful and effective that scene is.

In a story based on double-crosses, the possibility emerges that Jack and Erin could make a deal on their own. But can Erin be trusted by anyone? The movie's ending strikes an unsentimental note that remembers the cynicism of classic *film noir*. And its look is *noir*, too; cinematographer Juan Ruiz Anchia seems inspired by the paintings of Jack Vettriano with his shadowy interiors glowing with reds, golds, and oranges.

The movie doesn't rank with Rafelson's best work, which also includes the crime melodrama *Blood and Wine* (1996), with Jack Nicholson and Jennifer Lopez. But it's an absorbing, atmospheric *noir* with nice little touches, including Skarsgård's speech patterns, the jolly greed of the Quarres, and the way that the cop and the blond relate to each other on three levels: as prisoner and captor, as man and woman, and as musicians.

Northfork ★ ★ ★ ★
PG-13, 103 m., 2003

Peter Coyote (Eddie), Anthony Edwards (Happy), Duel Farnes (Irwin), Daryl Hannah (Flower Hercules), Nick Nolte (Father Harlan), Mark Polish (Willis O'Brien), James Woods (Walter O'Brien), Claire Forlani (Mrs. Hadfield), Robin Sachs (Cup of Tea), Ben Foster (Cod), Clark Gregg (Mr. Hadfield). Directed by Michael Polish and produced and written by Mark Polish and Michael Polish.

There has never been a movie quite like *Northfork*, but if you wanted to put it on a list, you would also include *Days of Heaven* and *Wings of Desire*. It has the desolate open spaces of the first, the angels of the second, and the feeling in both of deep sadness and pity. The movie is visionary and elegiac, more a fable than a story, and frame by frame it looks like a portfolio of spaces so wide, so open, that men must wonder if they have a role beneath such indifferent skies.

The film is set in Montana in 1955, as the town of Northfork prepares to be submerged forever beneath the waters of a dam. Three two-man evacuation teams travel the countryside in their fat black sedans, persuading the lingering residents to leave. The team members have a motivation: They've all been promised waterfront property on the lake to come. Most of the residents have already pulled out, but one stubborn citizen opens fire on the evacuators, and another plans to ride out the flood waters in his ark, which does not have two of everything but does have two wives, a detail Noah overlooked.

Other lingerers include Irwin (Duel Farnes), a pale young orphan who has been turned back in by his adoptive parents (Claire Forlani and Clark Gregg) on the grounds that he is defective. "You gave us a sick child, Father," they tell Father Harlan, the parish priest (Nick Nolte). "He can't stand the journey." The priest cares for the child himself, although the lonely little kid is able to conjure up company by imagining four angels who come to console him. Or are they imaginary? They are real for little Irwin, and that should be real enough for us.

The town evokes the empty, lonely feeling you get when you make a last tour of a home you have just moved out of. There is a scene where the six evacuators line up at the counter in a diner to order soup. "Bowl or cup?" asks the waitress, and as they consider this choice with grave poker faces, we get the feeling that only by thinking very hard about soup can they avoid exploding in a frenzy of madness. One of Father Harlan's final church services is conducted after the back wall has already been removed from his church, and the landscape behind him looks desolate.

This is the third film by the Polish twins. Michael directs, Mark acts, and Mark and Michael coproduce and cowrite. Their first was the eerie, disquieting *Twin Falls Idaho*, about Siamese twins who deal with the fact that one of them is dying. The next was *Jackpot*, about a man who tours karaoke contests, looking for his big break. Now *Northfork*, which in its visual strategy presents Montana not as a scenic tourist wonderland, but as a burial ground of foolish human dreams. Indeed, one of the subplots involves the need to dig up the bodies in the local cemetery, lest the coffins bob to the surface of the new lake; Walter O'Brien (James Woods), one of the evacuators, tells his son Willis O'Brien (Mark Polish) that if they don't move the coffin of the late Mrs. O'Brien, "When this small town becomes the biggest lake this side of the Mississippi, your mother will be the catch of the day."

Funny? Yes, and so is the soup scene in the diner, but you don't laugh out loud a lot in this film because you fear the noise might echo under its limitless leaden sky. This is like a black-and-white film made in color. In some shots, only the pale skin tones contain any color at all. In talking with the Polish brothers after the film premiered at Sundance 2003, I learned that they limited all the costumes, props, and sets to shades of gray, and the cinematographer, M. David Mullen, has drained color from his film so that there is a bleakness here that gets into your bones.

Against this cold is the pale warmth of the angels, who are evoked by Irwin. To console himself for being abandoned by his adoptive parents, he believes that he is a lost angel, fallen to Earth and abducted by humans who amputated his wings. Indeed, he has scars on his shoulder blades. The angels include Flower Hercules (Daryl Hannah), who seems neither man nor woman; Cod (Ben Foster), a cowboy who never speaks; Happy (Anthony Edwards), who is almost blind, but perhaps can see some-thing through the bizarre glasses he wears, with their multiple lenses; and Cup of Tea (Robin Sachs), who talks enough to make up for Happy.

Of these the most moving is Flower Hercules, who seems to feel Irwin's loneliness and pain as her/his own. Daryl Hannah evokes a quality of care for the helpless that makes her a tender guardian angel. Since the evacuators have a stock of angel's wings, which they some-times offer as inducements to reluctant home-owners, the thought persists that angels are meant to be real in the film, just as they are in *Wings of Desire*, and only those who cannot be-lieve think Irwin has dreamed them up.

Northfork is not an entertaining film so much as an entrancing one. There were people at Sundance, racing from one indie hipness to another, who found it too slow. But the pace is well chosen for the tone, and the tone evokes the fable, and the fable is about the death of a town and of mankind's brief purchase on this barren plat of land, and it is unseemly to hurry a re-quiem. The film suggests that of the thousands who obeyed the call, "Go West, young man!" some simply disappeared into the wilderness and were buried, as Northfork is about to be buried, beneath the emptiness of it all.　☞

No Such Thing ★

R, 111 m., 2002

Sarah Polley (Beatrice), Robert John Burke (Monster), Helen Mirren (TV Producer), Julie Christie (Doctor), Baltasar Kormakur (Dr. Artaud). Directed by Hal Hartley and produced by Fridrik Thor Fridriksson, Hartley, and Cecilia Kate Roque. Screenplay by Hartley.

Hal Hartley has always marched in the avant-garde, but this time he marches alone. Follow-ers will have to be drafted. *No Such Thing* is inexplicable, shapeless, dull. It doesn't even rise to entertaining badness. Coming four years after his intriguing if unsuccessful *Henry Fool*, and filmed mostly on location in Iceland with Icelandic money, it suggests a film that was made primarily because he couldn't get any-thing else off the ground.

The film's original title was *Monster*. That

this is a better title than *No Such Thing* is beyond debate. The story involves a monstrous beast who lives on an island off the Icelandic coast, and is immortal, short-tempered, and alcoholic. As the film opens the monster (Robert John Burke) has killed a TV news crew, which inspires a cynical New York network executive (Helen Mirren) to dispatch a young reporter (Sarah Polley) to interview him. Polley's fiancé was among the monster's victims.

Her plane crashes in the ocean, she is the sole survivor and therefore makes good news herself, and is nursed back to life by Julie Christie, in a role no more thankless than the others in this film. Since the filming, Julie Christie had a face-lift and Helen Mirren won an Oscar nomination. Life moves on.

We seek in vain for shreds of recognizable human motivation. By the time she meets the monster, Polley seems to have forgotten he killed her fiancé. By the time she returns with the monster to New York, the world seems to have forgotten. The monster wants to go to New York to enlist the services of Dr. Artaud (Baltasar Kormakur), a scientist who can destroy matter and therefore perhaps can bring an end to the misery of the immortal beast. We are praying that in the case of this movie, matter includes celluloid.

Elements of the movie seem not merely half-baked, but never to have seen the inside of an oven. Helen Mirren's TV news program and its cynical values are treated with the satirical insights of callow undergraduates who will be happy with a C-plus in film class. Characterizations are so shallow they consist only of mannerisms; Mirren chain-smokes cigarettes, Dr. Artaud chain-smokes cigars, the monster swigs from a bottle. At a social reception late in the film, Sarah Polley turns up in a leather bondage dress with a push-up bra. Why, oh why?

Hal Hartley, still only forty-two, has proudly marched to his own drummer since I first met him at Sundance 1990 with *The Unbelievable Truth*, a good film that introduced two of his favorite actors, Adrienne Shelly and Robert Burke (now Robert John Burke, as the monster). Since then his titles have included *Trust*

(1991), *Simple Men* (1992), *Amateur* (1994), *Flirt* (1995), and *Henry Fool*. My star ratings have wavered around 2 or 2½, and my reviews have mostly expressed interest and hope—hope that he will define what he's looking for and share it with us.

Now I'm beginning to wonder how long the wait will be. A Hartley film can be analyzed and justified, and a review can try to mold the intractable material into a more comprehensible form. But why does Hartley make us do all the heavy lifting? Can he consider a film that is self-evident and forthcoming? One that doesn't require us to plunder the quarterly film magazines for deconstruction? I don't mind heavy lifting when a film is challenging or fun, like *Mulholland Drive*. But not when all the weight is in the packing materials.

In *No Such Thing* we have promising elements. The relationship between the monster and the TV reporter suggests *Beauty and the Beast* (more the Cocteau than the Disney version), but that vein is not mined, and the TV news satire is too callow to connect in any way with real targets. Many of the characters, like Dr. Artaud, seem like houseguests given a costume and appearing in the host's play just to be good sports. That gifted actors appear here show how desperate they are for challenging parts, and how willing to take chances. Hartley has let them down.

The Notebook ★ ★ ★ ½
PG-13, 120 m., 2004

Rachel McAdams (Young Allie Nelson), Ryan Gosling (Young Noah Calhoun), Gena Rowlands (Allie Nelson), James Garner (Noah Calhoun), Joan Allen (Allie's Mother), Heather Wahlquist (Sara Tuffington), Nancy De Mayo (Mary Allen Calhoun), Sylvia Jefferies (Rosemary). Directed by Nick Cassavetes and produced by Lynn Harris and Mark Johnson. Screenplay by Jeremy Leven and Jan Sardi, based on the novel by Nicholas Sparks.

The Notebook cuts between the same couple at two seasons in their lives. We see them in the urgency of young romance, and then we see them as old people, she disappearing into the shadows of Alzheimer's, he steadfast in his love. It is his custom every day to read to her from a notebook that tells the story of how they met and fell in love and faced obstacles to their happiness. Sometimes, he says, if only for a few minutes, the clouds part and she is able to remember who he is and who the story is about.

We all wish Alzheimer's could permit such moments. For a time, in the earlier stages of the disease, it does. But when the curtain comes down, there is never another act and the play is over. *The Notebook* is a sentimental fantasy, but such fantasies are not harmful; we tell ourselves stories every day, to make life more bearable. The reason we cried during *Terms of Endearment* was not because the young mother was dying, but because she was given the opportunity for a dignified and lucid parting with her children. In life it is more likely to be pain, drugs, regret, and despair.

The lovers are named Allie Nelson and Noah Calhoun, known as Duke. As old people they're played by Gena Rowlands and James Garner; as young people, by Rachel McAdams and Ryan Gosling. The performances are suited to the material, respecting the passion at the beginning and the sentiment at the end, but not pushing too hard; there is even a time when young Noah tells Allie, "I don't see how it's gonna work," and means it, and a time when Allie gets engaged to another man.

She's a rich kid, summering at the family's mansion in North Carolina. He's a local kid who works at the sawmill but is smart and poetic. Her parents are snobs. His father (Sam Shepard) is centered and supportive. Noah loves her the moment he sees her, and actually hangs by his hands from a bar on a Ferris wheel until she agrees to go out with him. Her parents are direct: "He's trash. He's not for you." One day her mother (Joan Allen) shows her a local working man who looks hard-used by life, and tells Allie that twenty-five years ago she was in love with him. Allie thinks her parents do not love one another, but her mother insists they do; still, Joan Allen is such a precise actress that she is able to introduce the quietest note of regret into the scene.

The movie is based on a novel by Nicholas Sparks, whose books inspired *Message in a Bottle* (1999), unloved by me, and *A Walk to Remember* (2002), which was so sweet and positive it persuaded me (as did Mandy Moore as its star). Now here is a story that could have been a tearjerker, but—no, wait, it *is* a tearjerker, it's just that it's a good one. The director is Nick Cassavetes, son of Gena Rowlands and John Cassavetes, and perhaps his instinctive feeling for his mother helped him find the way past soap opera in the direction of truth.

Ryan Gosling has already been identified as one of the best actors of his generation, although usually in more hard-edged material. Rachel McAdams, who just a few months ago was the bitchy high school queen in *Mean Girls*, here shows such beauty and clarity that we realize once again how actors are blessed by good material. As for Gena Rowlands and James Garner: They are completely at ease in their roles, never striving for effect, never wanting us to be sure we get the message. Garner is an actor so confident and sure that he makes the difficult look easy, and loses credit for his skill. Consider how simply and sincerely he tells their children: "Look, guys, that's my sweetheart in there." Rowlands, best known for high-strung, even manic characters, especially in films by Cassavetes, here finds a quiet vulnerability that is luminous.

The photography by Robert Fraisse is striking in its rich, saturated effects, from sea birds at sunset to a dilapidated mansion by candlelight to the texture of southern summer streets. It makes the story seem more idealized; certainly the retirement home at the end seems more of heaven than of earth. And the old mansion is underlined, too, first in its decay and then in its rebirth; Young Noah is convinced that if he makes good on his promise to rebuild it for Allie, she will come to live in it with him, and paint in the studio he has made for her. ("Noah had gone a little mad," the notebook says.) That she is engaged to marry another shakes him but doesn't discourage him.

We have recently read much about Alzheimer's because of the death of Ronald Reagan. His daughter Patti Davis reported that just before he died, the former president opened his eyes and gazed steadily into those of Nancy, and there was no doubt that he recognized her. Well, it's nice to think so. Nice to believe the window can open once more before closing forever.

Nowhere in Africa ★ ★ ★ ★
NO MPAA RATING, 140 m., 2003

Juliane Köhler (Jettel Redlich), Merab Ninidze (Walter Redlich), Lea Kurka (Younger Regina), Karoline Eckertz (Teenage Regina), Sidede Onyulo (Owuor [Cook]), Matthias Habich (Süsskind). Directed by Caroline Link and produced by Peter Herrmann. Screenplay by Link, based on the novel by Stefanie Zweig.

It is so rare to find a film where you become quickly, simply absorbed in the story. You want to know what happens next. Caroline Link's *Nowhere in Africa* is a film like that, telling the story of a German Jewish family that escapes from the Nazis by going to live and work on a farm in rural Kenya. It's a hardscrabble farm in a dry region, and the father, who used to be a lawyer, is paid a pittance to be the manager. At first his wife hates it. Their daughter, who is five when she arrives, takes to Africa with an immediate and instinctive love.

We see the mother and daughter, Jettel and Regina Redlich (Juliane Köhler and Lea Kurka), in their comfortable world in Frankfurt. The mother likes clothes, luxury, elegance. Her husband, Walter (Merab Ninidze), reading the ominous signs of the rise of Nazism, has gone ahead to East Africa, and now writes asking them to join him—"and please bring a refrigerator, which we will really need, and not our china or anything like that." What Jettel brings is a ballroom gown, which will be spectacularly unnecessary.

The marriage is a troubled one. Jettel thinks herself in a godforsaken place, and Walter, who works hard but is not a natural farmer, has little sympathy with her. Their sex life fades: "You only let me under your shirt when I'm a lawyer," he tells her once when his advance is turned away. But little Regina loves every moment of every day. She makes friends with the African

children her age, with that uncomplicated acceptance that children have, and seems to learn their language overnight. She picks up their lore and stories, and is at home in the bush.

Jettel, meanwhile, has a rocky start with Owuor (Sidede Onyulo), the farm cook. He is a tall, proud, competent man from the regional tribe, the Masai, who soon loves Regina like his own daughter. Jettel makes the mistake of treating him like a servant when he sees himself as a professional. He never compromises local custom regarding cooks. Asked to help dig a well, he explains, "I'm a cook. Cooks don't dig in the ground." And for that matter, "Men don't carry water."

They are outsiders here in three ways: as white people, as Germans, and as Jews. The first presents the least difficulty, because the tribal people on the land are friendly and helpful. Their status as Germans creates an ironic situation when war is declared and they are rounded up by the British colonial authorities as enemy aliens; this is absurd, since they are refugees from the enemy, but before the mistake can be corrected they are transported to Nairobi and interred—ironically, in a luxury hotel that has been pressed into service. As high tea is served to them, a British officer asks the hotel manager if the prisoners need to be treated so well. "These are our standards, and we are not willing to compromise," the manager replies proudly.

To the Africans, they are not Jews, Germans, or aliens, but simply white farmers; the rise of anticolonialism is still in the future in this district. Regina, so young when she left Europe, therefore hasn't tasted anti-Semitism until her parents send her into town to a boarding school. Now a pretty teenager (played by Karoline Eckertz), she is surprised to hear the headmaster say, "The Jews will stand outside the classroom as we recite the Lord's Prayer."

As time passes and the beauty and complexity of the land become clear to Jettel, she begins slowly to feel more at home. Her husband is vindicated in moving his family to Africa; letters arrive with sad news of family members deported to death camps. But he always considers Africa a temporary haven, and his attention is focused on a return to Europe. Each member of the Redlich family has a separate arc: The mother grows to like Africa as the father likes it less, and their daughter loves it always.

The story is told through the eyes of the daughter (Eckertz is the narrator); Caroline Link's screenplay is based on a best-selling German novel by Stefanie Zweig, who treats such matters as Jettel's brief affair with a British officer as they might have been perceived, and interpreted, by the daughter. Link's style permits the narrative to flow as it might in memory, and although there are dramatic high points (such as a fire and a plague of locusts), they are not interruptions but part of the rhythm of African life, and are joined by the sacrifice of a lamb (for rain) and an all-night ritual ceremony that the young girl will never forget.

Link's film, which won five German Oscars, including best film, won the 2003 Academy Award as best foreign film, and comes after another extraordinary film, her 1997 *Beyond Silence*, which was an Oscar nominee. That one was also about the daughter of a troubled marriage; the heroine was the hearing child of a deaf couple. I respond strongly to her interest in good stories and vivid, well-defined characters; this film is less message than memory, depending on the strength of the material to make all of the points. We feel as if we have lived it.

O

Old School ★
R, 90 m., 2003

Luke Wilson (Mitch), Will Ferrell (Frank), Vince Vaughn (Beanie), Ellen Pompeo (Nicole), Juliette Lewis (Heidi), Jeremy Piven (Gordon), Craig Kilborn (Mark), Leah Remini (Lara). Directed by Todd Phillips and produced by Daniel Goldberg, Joe Medjuck, and Phillips. Screenplay by Phillips and Scot Armstrong.

Luke Wilson, Will Ferrell, and Vince Vaughn clock in at an average age of thirty-four, which is a little old to be a frat boy. It is not their age but their longevity, however, that I question. In *Old School,* where they occupy a series of off-campus party houses, they follow lifestyles more appropriate for the college students in *Flatliners.* Anyone stuck in the jugular by an animal-disabling tranquilizer dart who then rolls into a swimming pool is not likely to have to face the kinds of questions about retirement confronting the hero of *About Schmidt.*

There is a type of older student who never seems to leave the campus. Some are actually graduate students, some are "finishing their thesis," others are gaining job experience (i.e., are bartenders or drug dealers). I graduated from Illinois, returned ten years later, and found my old friend Mike still at his usual table in the Illini Union, drinking the bottomless cup of coffee and working the crossword puzzle.

Wilson, Ferrell, and Vaughn do not play this type of student. They are not really students at all, in fact. Wilson plays a businessman who returns home early to discover that his fiancée (Juliette Lewis) is hosting an orgy. Ferrell is engaged to be married, and Vaughn is married. They stumble into founding their own fraternity after discovering by accident that you can get a lot of action if you throw nude wrestling matches in K-Y jelly.

Old School wants to be *National Lampoon's Animal House,* but then, don't they all. It assumes that the modern college campus is a hotbed, or is it a sinkhole, of moral squalor, exhibitionism, promiscuity, kinky sex, and rampant rampantness. Perhaps it is.

I have also heard, on the other hand, that the politically correct modern male undergraduate, terrified of sexual harassment charges, must have a notarized statement in hand giving him permission to even think about getting to first base, and a judge's order authorizing him to advance to second. (All women in movies set on such campuses are issued at birth a blanket license to kick groins.)

Unsure of myself, I avoid altogether the question of *Old School*'s veracity, and move on to its humor, which is easier to master because there is so little of it. This is not a funny movie, although it has a few good scenes and some nice work by Will Ferrell as an apparently compulsive nudist.

It follows the same old story about a bunch of fun-loving guys who only want to throw orgies and meet chicks, and a young fogey dean (Jeremy Piven) who wants to spoil their fun. One of the cute co-eds is played by Ellen Pompeo, who was so absolutely wonderful in *Moonlight Mile.* She should not be discouraged by this sophomore effort. Even Meryl Streep had to make a second movie after *Julia.* Oh, and I just found the title right here: *The Deer Hunter.*

The movie has been slapped together by director Todd Phillips, who careens from scene to scene without it occurring to him that humor benefits from characterization, context, and continuity. Otherwise, all you have is a lot of people acting goofy. The movie was screened before an "invited audience" in a Chicago theater, where two small groups of audience members laughed loudly at almost everything, and just about everybody else waited politely until it was over and they could leave. Critics are sometimes required to see comedies at such screenings because we can appreciate them better when we see them with a general audience, and to be sure, I learn a lot that way.

Once Upon a Time in Mexico ★ ★ ★
R, 101 m., 2003

Antonio Banderas (El Mariachi), Salma Hayek (Carolina), Johnny Depp (CIA Agent Sands), Rubén Blades (Jorge), Eva Mendes (Special Agent Ajedrez), Willem Dafoe (Barillo), Mickey Rourke (Billy), Cheech Marin (Belini). Directed by Robert Rodriguez and produced by Elizabeth Avellan, Carlos Gallardo, and Rodriguez. Screenplay by Rodriguez.

After Robert Rodriguez made his $7,000 first film, *El Mariachi* (1992), and his $3 million *Desperado* (1995), Quentin Tarantino told him they were the Mexican equivalents of Sergio Leone's first two spaghetti Westerns. After the low-budget *A Fistful of Dollars* and *For a Few Dollars More*, Leone moved up to bigger budgets for *The Good, the Bad and the Ugly* and *Once Upon a Time in the West*—and therefore, Tarantino told his friend, Rodriguez should now make *Once Upon a Time in Mexico*. And so he has, for $30 million—still a relatively modest budget, as action movies go.

Like Leone's movie, the Rodriguez epic is more interested in the moment, in great shots, in surprises and ironic reversals and close-ups of sweaty faces, than in a coherent story. Both movies feed on the music of heroism and lament. Both paint their stories in bold, bright colors. Both go for sensational kills; if Clint Eastwood kills three men with one bullet, Salma Hayek kills four men with four knives, all thrown at once.

In my review of *Desperado*, I praised Rodriguez for his technical skill and creative energy, but said he hadn't learned to structure a story so we cared about what happened. That's still true in *Once Upon a Time in Mexico*, but you know what? I didn't mind. I understood the general outlines of the story, I liked the bold strokes he uses to create the characters, and I was amused by the camera work, which includes a lot of shots that are about themselves.

The actors in a movie like this have to arrive on the screen self-contained; there are flashbacks to their earlier lives, but they explain what happened to them, not who they are. With Antonio Banderas, Salma Hayek, and Johnny Depp as his leads, and a supporting cast including Rubén Blades, Eva Mendes, Willem Dafoe, and Mickey Rourke, Rodriguez has great faces, bodies, eyes, hair, sneers, snarls, and personalities to work with. Banderas is as impassive as Eastwood, Hayek steams with passion, and Johnny Depp steams with something—maybe fermenting memories of *Pirates of the Caribbean*.

The plot is at least technically a sequel to the first two movies, once again with El Mariachi as

a troubadour with a sideline in killing (early in the movie, he cocks his guitar). I didn't remember the particulars of the first two films well enough to follow this continuation in detail, but so what? Essentially, El Mariachi (Banderas) is in self-imposed exile after the deaths of Carolina (Hayek) and their daughter. Depp, who is a CIA agent of sorts, tracks him down with the help of a talkative bartender (Cheech Marin). He wants El Mariachi to stop a plot against the president by the drug kingpin Barillo (Dafoe). Mickey Rourke's role is to carry a little dog in his arms, look sinister, and seem capable of more colorful dialogue than the screenplay provides for him. It's time for him to be rehabilitated in a lead.

There are lots of fancy shots in the movie, but nothing quite equals a sensational sequence in which Banderas and Hayek, chained together, escape from a high-rise apartment and somehow rappel to the ground with one hanging on while the other swings down to the next level. Neat.

Rodriguez is the one-man band of contemporary filmmakers, making his movies not quite by himself, but almost. His credits here say he "chopped, shot and scored" the movie, as well as writing and directing it, and he personally operated the new Sony 24-fps digital hi-def camera. As a skeptic about digital feature photography and a supporter of light through celluloid, I have to admit that this movie looks great. Maybe the camera has been improved, maybe the Boeing digital projectors are a step up from the underpowered Texas Instruments machines, but the picture is bright, crisp, and detailed. Maybe it was a little too sharp-edged, since there is something to be said for the tactile softness of celluloid, but it was impressive, and an enormous improvement over what I've seen before, including Rodriguez's own *Spy Kids 2*. (*Spy Kids 3-D* doesn't count because of the murkiness inherent in 3-D.)

What bubbles beneath all of Rodriguez's work is an impatient joy in the act of filmmaking. He started with hundreds of home movies when he was a kid, made *Desperado* for peanuts and somehow got a studio to buy it, and is still only thirty-five.

He talks about how easy digital filmmaking makes it for him and the actors—no fussing over lights, no worrying about film costs, lots of freedom to try things different ways. *Once Upon a Time in Mexico* sometimes feels as if he's winging it, but you have to admit he has an instinctive, exuberant feel for moving images. I am not sure a thoughtful and coherent story can be made using his methods, but maybe that's not what he's interested in doing.

Once Upon a Time in the Midlands
★ ★ ★
R, 104 m., 2003

Robert Carlyle (Jimmy), Rhys Ifans (Dek), Shirley Henderson (Shirley), Kathy Burke (Carol), Ricky Tomlinson (Charlie), Finn Atkins (Marlene). Directed by Shane Meadows and produced by Andrea Calderwood. Screenplay by Paul Fraser and Meadows.

Once Upon a Time in the Midlands has a score that sounds familiar, with its echoing hoof beats, harmonicas, and far-off whistles. It evokes the atmosphere of a Sergio Leone Western, sneaking up under the movie's human comedy and adding a smile. The film is set not in the West (or Spain), but in Nottingham, in the British Midlands, where its lovable working-class characters get involved in a story of love, loss, revenge, clowns, and country-and-western music.

The movie opens on the British version of the Jerry Springer show, with the love-struck Dek (Rhys Ifans) proposing marriage to his longtime live-in lover, Shirley (Shirley Henderson). To his dismay, she turns him down. Watching the show is her former husband, Jimmy (Robert Carlyle), who, as it happens, has a reason to visit their little town—he's lying low after a botched stickup. His reappearance confronts Shirley with a classic Western decision, between the respectable shopkeeper and the gunslinger from out of town.

Dek and Shirley live with Marlene (Finn Atkins), her daughter by Jimmy, which gives the snaky ex-husband an excuse to reenter their lives. He wants to reconnect with his daughter. Uh-huh. And for a time he's able to kindle once again in Shirley the excitement she once felt around this dangerous and unpredictable man. Down at his business, the Clutch Hutch, Dek fantasies about a showdown with Jimmy, but all it leads up to is a classic Western gunfight

pose with Dek holding not a revolver but a power drill.

Shirley and Dek are part of an extended family including two best friends left over from her marriage. Carol (Kathy Burke), Jimmy's foster sister, is a loud, confident woman who thinks nothing of leaping across the room to topple a man from his La-Z-Boy; her husband, Charlie (Ricky Tomlinson), is a country-and-western singer, or so he says. They provide a running commentary as Shirley tentatively decides to let Jimmy back into her life.

Dek, a gentle soul who is devastated by being turned down on national TV, is now prepared almost to surrender, since Shirley obviously doesn't love him. But her daughter Marlene does, and in her mind Dek has always been her father. That leads to scenes of surprising tenderness, in a movie that has enormous affection for all of its characters—except for Jimmy.

There's a slapstick sequence in the film: the botched robbery, which involves clowns and a Morris Mini, and it would almost break the spell except that we can just about believe these characters are goofy enough to pull off something like that (maybe they saw it in a movie?). And there's always the undertone of danger with Jimmy, who can be charming and then turn mean in an instant.

Rhys Ifans is the key player. You may remember him as Hugh Grant's Welsh roommate in *Notting Hill,* the one with such a fascination for his bodily functions. He can play peculiar, but here he plays normal, even low-key, as a guy who doubts himself so much that, if Shirley says she won't marry him, she must be right.

The movie doesn't really press its parallels with Sergio Leone; maybe the title and the music are simply supposed to suggest that even in Nottingham there can be showdowns between good and evil, and a loser can learn to stand up like a man. Some of the photography by Brian Tufano also quietly echoes the Leone look, including a lovely night exterior of the outside of a bingo parlor, outlined against the evening sky.

Note: Will American audiences have trouble with the accents? I ask because people at the screening asked me. I think it's a matter of listening to the music instead of the words. You may be a little put off at the beginning, especially

493

by Carlyle, but it's funny how as the characters develop and the story gets interesting, somehow we hear all the words and stop thinking about the accents.

One Hour Photo ★ ★ ★ ½
R, 98 m., 2002

Robin Williams (Seymour "Sy" Parrish), Connie Nielsen (Nina Yorkin), Michael Vartan (Will Yorkin), Dylan Smith (Jake Yorkin), Gary Cole (Bill Owens), Eriq La Salle (Detective Van Der Zee), Erin Daniels (Maya Burson). Directed by Mark Romanek and produced by Pamela Koffler, Christine Vachon, and Stan Wlodkowski. Screenplay by Romanek.

One Hour Photo tells the story of Seymour "Sy" Parrish, who works behind the photo counter of one of those vast suburban retail barns. He has a bland, anonymous face and a cheerful voice that almost conceals his desperation and loneliness. He takes your film, develops it, and has your photos ready in an hour. Sometimes he even gives you five-by-sevens when all you ordered were four-by-sixes. His favorite customers are the Yorkins—Nina, Will, and cute young Jake. They've been steady customers for six years. When they bring in their film, he makes an extra set of prints—for himself.

Sy follows an unvarying routine. There is a diner where he eats, alone, methodically. He is an "ideal employee." He has no friends, a coworker observes. But the Yorkins serve him as a surrogate family, and he is their self-appointed Uncle Sy. Only occasionally does the world get a glimpse of the volcanic side of his personality, as when he gets into an argument with Larry, the photo machine repairman.

The Yorkins know him by name and are a little amused by his devotion. There is an edge of need to his moments with them. If they were to decide to abandon film and get one of those new digital cameras, a prudent instinct might lead them to keep this news from Sy.

Robin Williams plays Sy, another of his open-faced, smiling madmen, like the killer in *Insomnia*. He does this so well you don't have the slightest difficulty accepting him in the role. The first time we see Sy behind his counter, neat, smiling, with a few extra pounds

from the diner routine, we buy him. He belongs there. He's native to retail.

The Yorkin family is at first depicted as ideal: models for an ad for their suburban lifestyle. Nina Yorkin (Connie Nielsen), pretty and fresh-scrubbed, has a cheery public persona. Will (Michael Vartan) is your regular clean-cut guy. Young Jake (Dylan Smith) is cute as a picture. Mark Romanek, who wrote and directed the film, is sneaky in the way he so subtly introduces discordant elements into his perfect picture. A tone of voice, a half-glimpsed book cover, a mistaken order, a casual aside . . . they don't mean much by themselves, but they add up to an ominous cloud gathering over the photo counter.

Much of the film's atmosphere forms through the cinematography by Jeff Cronenweth. His interiors at "Savmart" are white and bright, almost aggressive. You can hear the fluorescent lights humming. Through choices involving set design and lens selection, the one-hour photo counter somehow seems an unnatural distance from the other areas of the store, as if the store shuns it, or it has withdrawn into itself. Customers approach it across an exposed expanse of emptiness, with Sy smiling at the end of the trail.

A man who works in a one-hour photo operation might seem to be relatively powerless. Certainly Sy's boss thinks so. But in an era when naked baby pictures can be interpreted as child abuse, the man with access to your photos can cause you a lot of trouble. What would happen, for example, if Will Yorkin is having an affair, and his mistress brings in photos to be developed, and Uncle Sy "mistakenly" hands them to Nina Yorkin?

The movie at first seems soundly grounded in everyday reality, in the routine of a predictable job. When Romanek departs from reality, he does it subtly, sneakily, so that we believe what we see until he pulls the plug. There is one moment I will not describe (in order not to ruin it) when Sy commits a kind of social trespass that has the audience stirring with quiet surprise: surprise, because until they see the scene they don't realize that his innocent, everyday act can be a shocking transgression in the wrong context.

Watching the film, I thought of Michael

Powell's great 1960 British thriller *Peeping Tom,* which was about a photographer who killed his victims with a stiletto concealed in his camera. Sy uses a psychological stiletto, but he's the same kind of character, the sort of man you don't much notice, who blends in, accepted, overlooked, left alone so that his rich secret life can flower. There is a moment in *Peeping Tom* when a shot suddenly reveals the full depth of the character's depravity. In *One Hour Photo* a shot with a similar purpose requires only a lot of innocent family snapshots, displayed in a way that is profoundly creepy.

The movie has also been compared to *American Beauty,* another film where resentment, loneliness, and lust fester beneath the surface of suburban affluence. The difference, I think, is that the needs of the Kevin Spacey character in *American Beauty,* while frowned upon and even illegal, fall generally within the range of emotions we understand. Sy Parrish is outside that range. He was born with parts missing, and has assembled the remainder into a person who has borrowed from the inside to make the outside look okay.

On_Line ★ ★
R, 97 m., 2003

Josh Hamilton (John Roth), Harold Perrineau (Moe Curley), Isabel Gillies (Moira Ingalls), John Fleck (Al Fleming), Vanessa Ferlito (Jordan Nash), Eric Millegan (Ed Simone), Liz Owens (Angel). Directed by Jed Weintrob and produced by Tanya Selvaratnam and Adam Brightman. Screenplay by Andrew Osborne and Weintrob.

I refuse to sign up for instant messaging for the same reason I won't carry a cell phone: Don't call me, I'll call you. The characters in Jed Weintrob's *On_Line* are on call more or less all the time, living their barren lives in cyberspace, where the members of a suicide Webcam chat are bored, waiting around for someone to overdose. The film's redeeming feature is that it knows how sad these people are and finds the correct solution to their problems: They meet in the flesh.

The movie stars Josh Hamilton and Harold Perrineau as John and Moe, roommates who run an on-line sex site named InterconX. It's a little like the real-life iFriends.com; on screens that display simultaneous cybercams, its members flirt, chat, engage in virtual sex, and charge for interaction. So mesmerized is John by this process that he follows, on another screen, a twenty-four-hour live cam where Angel (Liz Owens) lives her life in public view.

This can get to be a way of life. I have a friend who became so obsessed with one woman's Webcam that he kept its window constantly open on his desktop, no doubt getting up in the night to check that she was sleeping well. This is the geek equivalent of looking in on the kids. And at Sundance 1999 I saw *Home Page,* a documentary about a pioneering on-line blogger (as they were not called then) named Justin Hall, whose life seemed to be lived just so he could report on it.

That would also describe John, who keeps his own on-line journal in which he sighs about the emptiness of his existence and the futility of it all, and whose sex life at one point is reduced to masturbating not into his own sock, which would be pathetic enough, but into his roommate's.

The movie charts its lives through a split-screen technique that resembles the Web pages where the characters hang out. Digital video is combined with screen shots in a way that is intriguing and sometimes beautiful; the way the movie chops up the screen to follow simultaneous events is a little like Ang Lee's technique in *Hulk,* and the visuals use filters, textures, and colored lighting to create an effect not unlike some of the weirder pages of the early *Wired* magazine. Even when my interest in the characters flagged, I liked looking at the movie; credit to cinematographer Toshiaki Ozawa and visual effects supervisor Christian D. Bruun.

The film's relationships suggest that although you might find a soul mate on-line, you might be better off sticking with your roommate's sock. John, for example, falls for Jordan (Vanessa Ferlito), one of the women who pays him to rent space on InterconX. When he dates her in real life, he discovers she is frighteningly real and maybe more than he can handle; we hear his thoughts while he watches her dance at a nightclub, and suspect he would be happier going home and experiencing the date on-line.

Another couple consists of an older gay man in New York (John Fleck) who develops a friendship with a teenager (Eric Millegan) who fears he is the only adolescent homosexual in Ohio. When the kid gets off the bus in New York City, I was not ready to cheer this as a victory over the loneliness of cyberspace, because I believe that teenage boys in Ohio, whatever their sexual identity, cannot solve their problems by meeting strange older men in New York. The movie is more optimistic here than I am.

The movie's weakness is in its strength. It does a good job of portraying the day-to-day life of these on-line obsessives, but we realize eventually that they are more interesting *because* they are on-line. Their problems and personalities would not necessarily be movie material if it weren't for the cyberspace overlay. When it comes to those who try to live in cyberspace, I am reminded of Dr. Johnson's comment about a dog standing on its hind legs: "It is not done well, but you are surprised to find it done at all."

Open Hearts ★ ★ ★

R, 114 m., 2003

Sonja Richter (Cecilie), Mads Mikkelsen (Niels), Paprika Steen (Marie), Nikolaj Lie Kaas (Joachim), Stine Bjerregaard (Stine), Birthe Neumann (Hanne), Niels Olsen (Finn), Ulf Pilgaard (Thomsen), Ronnie Hiort (Gustav). Directed by Susanne Bier and produced by Jonas Frederiksen and Vibeke Windelov. Screenplay by Anders Thomas Jensen.

A life can be forever changed in an instant. Joachim proposes marriage to Cecilie, they are in love, they kiss, he steps heedlessly out of the car, he is struck by another car, and is paralyzed from the neck down. All of that happens at the outset in *Open Hearts,* which is about how this instant echoes in the lives of others.

Most movies about such injuries are sentimental, like *The Other Side of the Mountain.* What I have learned from disabled friends who have had such devastating events in their lives is that sentimentality is for greeting cards. They face a new reality, and they have to be hard and brave, and sometimes they use dark humor as a relief or shield. I will never forget the puckish humor of Heather Rose, the star and author of *Dance Me to My Song,* who could control only one finger of one hand, and used it to tap out a computer message to a college audience that had just seen her film: "Let's go get pissed."

What is unusual about *Open Hearts* is how forthright it is about the reaction of Joachim (Nikolaj Lie Kaas) to his injury. We have seen him as an athlete, a rock climber, an extrovert, a man in love. But when Cecilie (Sonja Richter) is at his bedside, after he hears that he will never walk again, he turns away from her pledges of love and tells her to get lost. He is angry and doesn't even want to look at her.

This is not unreasonable. He is furious at the instant of fate that has taken his youth and his movement from him. Furious that he cannot do the things he loves. And he recoils from her love because . . . because . . . well, because it hurts him too much, and because he wants to release her from their engagement, spare her a lifetime with him on these new terms.

His anger is a stage that he has to go through. Eventually will come the other stages we hear about, involving negotiation, acceptance, and so on. Kübler-Ross's five stages for the dying get reversed for the gravely handicapped: They awaken feeling they are dead, and have to track back into accepting and embracing life.

Open Hearts is not simply about Joachim and Cecilie, however. It is about a matrix of lives affected by the accident. We meet Marie (Paprika Steen), who was driving the car that struck Joachim. While the accident was not precisely her fault, she was distracted at the time and believes she might have been able to avoid it. Her husband, Niels (Mads Mikkelsen) is by coincidence the doctor on duty in the emergency ward where Joachim is taken. He's the one who has to break the news to Cecilie.

In the weeks and months that follow, Joachim continues to be hostile to Cecilie. He issues orders that she is not to be allowed in his room. He is also startlingly hostile to a nurse, who can take it, and does, creating an intriguing dynamic. Cecilie, who has no one to confide in, begins to share her feelings with Niels, the doctor. His wife knows and approves, but does not know that Niels is falling helplessly, obsessively, in love with the younger woman.

The movie is fascinated by the nature of his love. This is not a romance, not adultery, not an affair, not any of the things that can be explained with a word. It is helpless intoxicating infatuation, so powerful he is ready to consider leaving his long and happy marriage with Marie, which has given him three children he loves.

Now it is up to us. What do we think? Two men have decided to abandon women who love them. Cecilie is in the middle—pushed away by one, loved by another. Joachim and Marie are the outsiders—he by choice, she by—well, you could call this an accident, too, a blow of fate when she does not expect it. Marie's way of dealing with Neils's new love is seen with clarity and intelligence by Susanne Bier, the director. She doesn't respond on cue with screaming and accusations, like soap opera wives, but tries to size up the new reality and see what can be saved or salvaged.

As for Joachim—well, I feel he's a rat. He should not leave his wife and children to move in with the sort-of fiancée of his patient. As Pascal once said (and Woody Allen once quoted), "The heart has its reasons of which reason knows nothing." At the end, it's all a mess. Love causes such pain and regret. Can Neils be strong and reject his love for Cecilie? Can he be as strong as Joachim? Why do we want Neils to abandon his love and Joachim to reassert his? And what is so amazingly unique about Cecilie, anyway? She is sweet and pretty but not in any way extraordinary, yet has taken possession of both these men.

It must be noted that *Open Hearts* is a Dogma film, subscribing to the Danish manifesto calling for a simpler, more direct, and less artful approach to filmmaking. This was the twenty-eighth film to receive the Dogma certificate, but I am weary of sifting each Dogma production through the same dogmatic sieve, and will simply note that it is filmed directly, intimately, without heightened effects or facile emotion-boosters. It is intensely curious about these people, sees them clearly, has no answers. I wish there were a manifesto that forgot about the stylistic stuff and simply required that.

Open Range ★ ★ ★ ½

R, 135 m., 2003

Kevin Costner (Charley Waite), Robert Duvall (Boss Spearman), Annette Bening (Sue Barlow), Abraham Benrubi (Mose), Michael Gambon (Denton Baxter), Michael Jeter (Percy), Diego Luna (Button). Directed by Kevin Costner and produced by Costner, Jake Eberts, and David Valdes. Screenplay by Craig Storper, based on the novel by Lauran Paine.

One of the many ways in which the Western has become old-fashioned is that the characters have values and act on them. Modern action movies have replaced values with team loyalty; the characters do what they do because they want to win and they want the other side to lose. The underlying text of most classic Westerns is from the Bible: "What does it profit a man if he gains the whole world, but loses his soul?" The underlying text of most modern action movies is from Vince Lombardi: "Winning isn't everything; it's the only thing."

Kevin Costner's *Open Range*, an imperfect but deeply involving and beautifully made new Western, works primarily because it expresses the personal values of a cowboy named Boss (Robert Duvall) and his employee of ten years, Charley (Costner). Boss does not believe in unnecessary violence, and is willing to put his own life at risk rather than kill someone just to be on the safe side. Charley was an expert killer during the Civil War, and has spent ten years under Boss trying to tame that side of his character. Boss is not only his friend but also his mentor and, in a sense, his spiritual leader. Charley doesn't merely work with him, but follows him as a sort of disciple.

Boss grazes his cattle on the open range. His group includes Charley, the younger man Mose (Abraham Benrubi), big and bearded, and the kid Button (Diego Luna), who would sometimes rather play with the dog than do his work. They halt outside a town, Mose is sent in on an errand, and when he doesn't return the two men ride in after him and find him in jail. The town is run by a rancher named Baxter (Michael Gambon), whose dislike of free grazers is violent, and whose payroll includes a gang of hired thugs.

When the two men free Mose and return to camp, they find the kid in bad shape. He needs to see a doctor. That means returning to the town, and they all know that to return to Baxter's domain is to risk death. "This may mean killing," Boss says. "I got no problem with that," says Charley. The subtext of the movie is that while Boss's way is best, when actual evil is encountered, Charley's way is required.

At the doctor's house, the men meet not only the doc but a woman named Sue (Annette Bening), whom they first take for his wife and later discover is his sister. Sue's and Charley's eyes meet, setting up a strong attraction that continues through the movie. She sees that he is a good man despite his rough ways and cowboy grunge. For him, this is perhaps the first good woman he has known. The movie wisely doesn't push them into a quick kiss, but underlines their awareness and reinforces it with some quiet conversations, shy and painfully sincere on Charley's part.

I can see what Costner is getting at here, and I admire his reticence, his unwillingness to push the romance beyond where it wants to go, and yet somehow the romance itself seems like an awkward fit in this story. Only a few days are involved, violence and illness overshadow everything, and it's clear that this visit will end in a gunfight. The romance, sweet and well acted as it is, seems imposed on the essential story.

The town is thoroughly cowed by Baxter. But the townspeople behave differently than they do in many Westerns, where gunfights are treated as a spectator sport. People in a settlement this size know everything that's going to happen, and as the showdown approaches, they get out of town, climbing the hill to the safety of the church. Afterward, they gather again to study and deal with the dead bodies; Costner says he saw that detail over and over in old photographs, although in many Westerns bodies seem to disappear after they serve their purpose as targets.

Most gunfights consist of the two sides blazing away at each other until the good guys win. The gunfight in *Open Range*, which is the high point of the movie, is different. Charley has been under fire, has killed, knows how men respond to the terror of being shot at. Although he and Boss (and their few confederates, including an ornery coot played by Michael Jeter) are outnumbered, Charley thinks they have a chance. In the movie's most intriguing speech, he outlines for Boss how Baxter's men are likely to react: who will freeze, who will run, who will shoot first.

All of the elements involving Boss and his men and the showdown with Baxter are achieved with the skill of a classic Western. But again at the end, the relationship between Charley and Sue seems a little forced. They have two scenes of leave-taking when one would do, possibly because their romance even at this point seems undefined and incomplete. We suspect they will meet again, although that doesn't belong in this story; for the purposes of *Open Range*, their time together is either too much or too little, and their bittersweet parting seems unsatisfying.

That is not to fault Bening's and Costner's acting in their scenes together, which is as convincing as the material permits—maybe more so. There is a lovely scene where she serves them tea, and Costner's fingers are too big to fit through the handle on his teacup. But to bring a woman into this story at all seems like a stretch, even though I can see she's supposed to underline Costner's uncertainty about his two sides, the killer side and the Boss-following side. It is Boss, after all, who sends Charley back for a proper farewell: "She's entitled to more than just your backside, walking away." What Charley tells her is to the point: "Men are gonna get killed here today, Sue, and I'm gonna kill them."

As for Duvall, here is an actor. He embodies Boss's values rather than having to explain them. His pauses are as fascinating as his actions. Consider the scene where he buys chocolates and cigars for himself and Charley: "Best smoke these while we got the chance." He is the center of the story, the man for whom values are important, and whose response to this violent situation is based on what he believes is right, not what he believes will work. "Cows is one thing," he says, "but one man telling another man where he can go in this country is something else." His character elevates *Open Range* from a good cowboy story into the archetypal region where the best Westerns exist.

Orange County ★ ★ ★
PG-13, 90 m., 2002

Colin Hanks (Shawn Brumder), Schuyler Fisk (Ashley), Catherine O'Hara (Cindy Beugler), Jack Black (Lance Brumder), John Lithgow (Bud Brumder), Kevin Kline (Marcus Skinner), Lily Tomlin (Guidance Counselor), Harold Ramis

(Don Durkett). Directed by Jake Kasdan and produced by David Gale and Scott Rudin. Screenplay by Mike White.

Orange County has the form of a teenage movie, the spirit of an independent comedy, and the subversive zeal of Jack Black, whose grin is the least reassuring since Jack Nicholson. It's one of those movies like *Ghost World* and *Legally Blonde* where the description can't do justice to the experience. It will sound like the kind of movie that, if you are over seventeen, you don't usually go to see. But it isn't.

The movie is a launching pad for three members of Hollywood's next generation. The stars are Colin Hanks (son of Tom Hanks) and Schuyler Fisk (daughter of Sissy Spacek and Jack Fisk). The director is Jake Kasdan (son of Lawrence and Meg Kasdan). All have worked before, but this is one of those happy projects where everything seems to fall naturally into place.

Hanks plays Shawn Brumder, heedless and carefree teenage Orange County surfer—until one day he finds a novel half-buried in the sand. It's by Marcus Skinner, one of those authors who can strike a kid of the right age as a conduit to truth and beauty. Shawn casts aside his old surfer lifestyle (to the grief of his pot-brained buddy) and determines to get into Stanford and study at the feet of the great Skinner (Kevin Kline).

This should be a cinch, since his test scores are very high. But he's rejected by Stanford because the daffy high school counselor (Lily Tomlin) has sent in the wrong scores under his name. This disappointment is crushing to Shawn, less disturbing to the other members of his definitively dysfunctional family. His father, Bud (John Lithgow), is workaholic and distant, his mother, Cindy (Catherine O'Hara), is—well, Catherine O'Hara, and his brother, Lance (Jack Black), is a couch potato, although potatoes may be the one substance he doesn't abuse. There is also Ashley (Schuyler Fisk), his loyal girlfriend, who believes in him, supports him, and is, in a stunning breakthrough for the teenage comedy genre, a blonde who is as intelligent as he is, maybe more.

The movie was written by Mike White, who you may remember as the author and star of *Chuck and Buck* (2000). He has one of those sideways, sardonic, nerd-savant approaches, getting a lot of his laughs by the application of logic to situations where it is not usually encountered. His characters tend to take things literally; in this case, Lance, the Jack Black character, is usually so stoned that his tunnel vision gives him an extraordinary, if misguided, clarity. Lance loves Shawn, even though he doesn't see the point of ambition or achievement, and so he offers to drive him to Palo Alto so that he can personally confront the Stanford admissions counselor.

It's around this point that we see the strategy of *Orange County*. It wants to appear to be a formula teenage screenplay (sex and dope jokes, girlfriend who is almost alienated and then reunited, personal redemption at last possible moment after maximum contrived suspense). At the same time, it goes under and over this mark: under with gags that would distinguish a Farrelly brothers picture, and over with surprisingly touching attention to Shawn's personality changes, his hopes and dreams, and especially his support from the stalwart Ashley.

The movie's cast looks like a roll call from the comedy hall of fame. If you have Harold Ramis, Jane Adams, Garry Marshall, Chevy Chase, Ben Stiller, and Mike White himself in supporting roles, and Kevin Kline (unbilled) finding just the right balance between charming nobility and weary pomposity, you have a movie that can be undone only in the making. Jake Kasdan is still in his mid-twenties, but is sure-footed and has a nice skewed sense of comic timing; this movie is a world apart from his fine first feature, *Zero Effect* (1998), a Sherlockian web that could go on the puzzler shelf with *Memento* and *Mulholland Drive*. He has also directed a lot of episodic comedy on TV (*Freaks and Geeks, Grosse Pointe*).

I was in New York when the movie was previewed for the press, and heard some idle talk about how this movie was proof that if you had the right parents you could get hired in Hollywood. True, and not true. Certainly Kasdan, Hanks, and Fisk have connections. On the other hand, studios invest real money. If your father is a famous actor, you may be able to get hired as an intern or an assistant still photographer, or get an acting job in a TV series. If you're making a feature on your own, it's because somebody with money thought you were right for the job. In this case, somebody was right.

Osama ★ ★ ★ ½
PG-13, 82 m., 2004

Marina Golbahari (Osama), Arif Herati (Espandi), Zubaida Sahar (Mother), Khwaja Nader (Mullah), Hamida Refah (Grandmother). Directed by Siddiq Barmak and produced by Barmak, Julia Fraser, Julie LeBrocquy, and Makoto Ueda. Screenplay by Barmak.

The movies are a little more than a century old. Imagine if we could see films from previous centuries—records of slavery, the Great Fire of London, the Black Plague. *Osama* is like a film from some long-ago age. Although it takes place in Afghanistan, it documents practices so cruel that it is hard to believe such ideas have currency in the modern world. What it shows is that, under the iron hand of the Taliban, the excuse of "respect" for women is used to condemn them to a lifetime of inhuman physical and psychic torture. No society that loves and respects women could treat them in this way.

The heroine of the film, Osama (Marina Golbahari), is a preadolescent in a household without a man. Under the rules of the Taliban, women are not to leave the house without a male escort or take jobs, so Osama, her mother, and grandmother are condemned to cower inside and starve, unless friends or relatives bring food. They do not. Finally the grandmother suggests that Osama cut her hair and venture out to find work, pretending to be a boy.

This story is told against a larger context of institutional sadism against women. An opening scene shows women in blue burkhas holding a demonstration—they want the right to take jobs—and being attacked by soldiers who begin with water cannons and eventually start shooting at them. Obviously, Osama is risking her life to venture out into this world, and soon she's in trouble: She is snatched away from her job and sent to a school to indoctrinate young men in the ways of the Taliban.

Then it is only a matter of time until her real sex is discovered. The punishment handed down by a judge is revealing: This child becomes one of the many wives of a dirty old man, a mullah who keeps his young women as prisoners. At that, Osama gets off lightly; another woman in the film is buried up to her neck and stoned for ... well, for behaving like a normal person in a civilized society.

The movie touches some of the same notes as *Baran* (2001), an Iranian movie about an unspoken love affair between a young Iranian worker and an Afghan immigrant who is a girl disguised as a boy. The film is not as tragic as *Osama*, in part because Iran is a country where enlightened and humanistic attitudes are fighting it out side-by-side with the old, hard ways. But in both cases Western audiences realize that to be a woman in such a society is to risk becoming a form of slave.

What is remarkable is the bravery with which filmmakers are telling this story in film after film. Consider Tahmineh Milani's *Two Women* (1999), which briefly landed her in jail under threat of death. Or Jafar Panahi's harrowing *The Circle* (2000), showing women without men trying to survive in present-day Tehran, where they cannot legally work or pause anywhere or be anywhere except inside and out of sight. The real weapons of mass destruction are ... men.

Who will go to see *Osama*? I don't know. There is after all that new Adam Sandler movie, and it's a charmer. And *The Lost Skeleton of Cadavra* is opening, for fans of campy trash. I'm not putting them down. People work hard for their money, and if they want to be entertained, that's their right. But brave, dissenting Islamic filmmakers are risking their lives to tell the story of the persecution of women, and it is a story worth knowing, and mourning. In this country Janet Jackson bares a breast and causes a silly scandal. The Taliban would have stoned her to death. If you put these things into context, the Jackson case begins to look like an affirmation of Western civilization. ☞

The Other Side of the Bed ★ ★
R, 114 m., 2003

Ernesto Alterio (Javier), Paz Vega (Sonia), Guillermo Toledo (Pedro), Natalia Verbeke (Paula), Alberto San Juan (Rafa), María Esteve (Pilar), Ramón Barea (Sagaz), Nathalie Poza (Lucia). Directed by Emilio Martínez Lázaro and produced by Tomás Cimadevilla and José

Antonio Sáinz de Vicuña. Screenplay by David Serrano.

Nobody quite makes it to the other side of the bed in the Spanish musical comedy *The Other Side of the Bed,* but that's not for lack of talking about it. Although they don't come right out and say so, I gather that this side of the bed is for heterosexuals, and that side is for homosexuals, and the movie is about a lot of people who are cheating on their partners while speculating that a lot of other people are gay.

I would like to tell you who all of these people are, but my space and your time are limited, and there are so many lovers and couples and would-be lovers and would-be couples that I was reminded of that limerick that ends,

> They argued all night
> As to who had the right
> To do what, and with which, and to
>   whom.

I'll give you just a sample. As the film opens, Pedro (Guillermo Toledo) is told by his girlfriend Paula (Natalia Verbeke) that she is in love with another and must end their relationship. Meanwhile, we discover that Paula is having a secret affair with Pedro's best friend, Javier (Ernesto Alterio), who has promised to break up with his girlfriend Sonia (Paz Vega), but lacks the nerve, possibly because he still loves her. When the men and two other friends get together to discuss their romantic miseries, one of them, of course, is keeping a big secret—and another, a macho taxi driver named Rafa (Alberto San Juan), delivers his women-hating theories and speculates that they are all lesbians at heart.

There is a lesbian in the movie, Lucia (Nathalie Poza), and she has the thankless task of standing there while other characters reveal their astonishing ignorance of lesbianism, sexuality, and indeed the nature of life on the planet that we occupy. For people who do nothing about it, these characters spend an inordinate amount of time discussing homosexuality; in this case, where there's smoke, there's smoke. Their knowledge extends to the theory that "we are all bisexual," and we keep expecting the theory to be tested in the laboratory on the other side of the bed, but this is a discussion, like what you would do if you won the lottery, that remains hypothetical and can be extended indefinitely.

The movie is a musical, which is kind of fun, with the characters expanding into song now and again. Like the heroes of a Bollywood musical from India, they seem able to materialize large numbers of backup dancers at a moment's notice. The choreography depends heavily on architecture and furniture, as the characters dance on motel balconies, lunchroom tables, etc.

All of the actors are extremely likable. And it's refreshing that the movie has a grown-up European attitude toward nudity, so that we're spared the Omniscient Bed Sheet, which always knows exactly where to fall in order to conceal a nipple. In its bright colors and zest, *The Other Side of the Bed* looks a little like an Almodóvar film—but Almodóvar knows a lot more about sexuality and, what's more important, he cares about his characters and allows them to be complicated and convincing.

Everyone in *The Other Side of the Bed,* alas, has the depth of a character in a TV commercial: They're all surface, clothes, hair, and attitude, and the men have the obligatory three-day beards. You realize after a while that it's just as well they're all so extraordinarily stupid about sex and human nature, because if they knew more, they would be wretchedly depressed about themselves.

Out of Time ★ ★ ★
PG-13, 114 m., 2003

Denzel Washington (Matt Lee Whitlock), Sanaa Lathan (Anne Merai Harrison), Dean Cain (Chris Harrison), Eva Mendes (Alex Diaz-Whitlock), John Billingsley (Chae), Alex Carter (Dr. Cabbot). Directed by Carl Franklin and produced by Jesse Beaton and Neal H. Mortiz. Screenplay by David Collard.

Denzel Washington, who played a hateful bad guy in *Training Day,* is a more sympathetic slickster in *Out of Time,* where he cheats on his wife and steals money, but has his reasons: His wife has already left him and is filing for divorce, he's cheating with his first love from high school, she's married to a wife-beater, and he steals the money to help her afford cancer therapy. So we sympathize with him as he digs himself into a hole. Any reasonable observer would consider him guilty of murder, theft, and arson—and one such observer is his estranged wife, who is also the detective assigned to the case.

Washington plays Matt Lee Whitlock, the sheriff of Banyan Key, Florida, a sleepy backwater where nothing much goes wrong. He is still on good terms with Alex (Eva Mendes), but their marriage has wound down and they're preparing for a split. That gives him time for a torrid affair with Anne Harrison (Sanaa Lathan), whose husband, Chris (Dean Cain), is a violent and jealous man. Matt narrowly avoids being caught by the husband, and that's the first of many narrow escapes in a plot that cheerfully piles on the contrivances.

Anne reveals to Matt that she's dying from lung and liver cancer. Chris has purchased a $1 million life insurance policy; she changes the beneficiary to Matt, who steals $500,000 in impounded drug loot from his office safe so that she can go to Europe for alternative therapy. The theory is that he can replace the money with the insurance payout, but alas, Anne and Chris both die in a suspicious fire, and the feds suddenly decide they need the drug money immediately. Matt seems guilty any way you look at it—his name on the insurance policy even provides a motive—and to make things worse, a neighbor saw him lurking around the house shortly before it burned down.

There are more details, many more, which I will suppress because they provide the central entertainments of the movie (what I've described is the setup, before Matt's troubles really get sticky). The movie is in the spirit of those overplotted 1940s crime movies where the hero's dilemma is so baffling that it seems impossible for him to escape; the screenplay by David Collard is inspired in part by *The Big Clock* (1948). All circumstantial evidence points to Matt; Hitchcock described this dilemma as "the innocent man wrongly accused," but the catch is, Matt isn't entirely innocent. He did steal the money, for starters.

Director Carl Franklin (*One False Move*), who also worked with Washington on *Devil in a Blue Dress* (1995), is frankly trying to manipulate the audience beyond the edge of plausibility. The early scenes seem to follow more or less possibly, but by the time Matt is hanging from a hotel balcony, or concealing incriminating telephone records, we care more about the plot

than the characters; suspension of disbelief, always necessary in a thriller, is required here in wholesale quantities. But in a movie like *Out of Time* I'm not looking for realism; I'm looking for a sense of style brought to genre material.

Washington is one of the most likable of actors, which is essential to this character, preventing us from concluding that he's getting what he deserves. Eva Mendes makes the ex-wife, Alex, into a curiously forgiving character, who feels little rancor for the straying Matt and apparently still likes him; maybe there would have been more suspense if she were furious with him. Sanaa Lathan has a tricky role as Anne—trickier the deeper we go into the plot—and is plausible at many different speeds, and Dean Cain is convincingly vile as the violent husband. John Billingsley is Chae, the local medical examiner, who is Matt's sidekick and supplies low-key, goofy support in some tight situations.

Another one of the movie's stars is its Florida location. It was photographed in and around Miami, Boca Grande, and Cortez, and reminds us how many Hollywood crime movies depend on the familiar streets of Los Angeles (or Toronto). Banyan Key seems like a real place, sleepy and laid-back, where everybody knows one another and high school romances could still smolder. As the net of evidence tightens around the sheriff, it seems more threatening because there are few places for him to hide, and few players who don't know him.

Owning Mahowny ★ ★ ★
R, 107 m, 2003

Philip Seymour Hoffman (Dan Mahowny), Minnie Driver (Belinda), John Hurt (Victor Foss), Maury Chaykin (Frank Perlin), Sonja Smits (Dana Selkirk), Ian Tracey (Ben Lock), Roger Dunn (Bill Gooden). Directed by Richard Kwietniowski and produced by Andras Hamori and Seaton McLean. Screenplay by Maurice Chauvet, based on a book by Gary Ross.

Owning Mahowny is about a man seized helplessly with tunnel vision, in the kind of tunnel that has no light at either end. He is a gambler. Cut off temporarily by his bookie, he asks incredulously, "What am I supposed to do? Go out to the track and *watch?*" Given the means to gamble, he gambles—thoughtless of the consequences, heedless of the risks, caught in the vise of a power greater than himself. Like all addictive gamblers he seeks the sensation of losing more money than he can afford. To win a great deal before losing it all back again creates a kind of fascination: Such gamblers need to confirm over and over that they cannot win.

The film is based on the true story of a Toronto bank vice president who began by stealing exactly as much as he needed to clear his debts at the track ($10,300) and ended by taking his bank for $10.2 million. So intent is he on this process that he rarely raises his voice, or his eyes, from the task at hand. Philip Seymour Hoffman, that fearless poet of implosion, plays the role with a fierce integrity, never sending out signals for our sympathy because he knows that Mahowny is oblivious to our presence. Like an artist, an athlete, or a mystic, Mahowny is alone within the practice of his discipline.

There have been many good movies about gambling, but never one that so single-mindedly shows the gambler at his task. Mahowny has just been rewarded at work with a promotion and a raise. He drives a clunker even the parking lot attendants kid him about. His suits amuse his clients. He is engaged to Belinda (Minnie Driver), a teller who is the very embodiment of a woman who might be really pretty if she took off those glasses and did something about her hair.

He is so absorbed in gambling that even his bookie (Maury Chaykin) tries to cut him off, to save himself the trouble of making threats to collect on the money Mahowny owes him. "I can't do business like this," the bookie complains, and at another point, when Mahowny is so rushed he only has time to bet $1,000 on all the home teams in the National League and all the away teams in the American, the bookie finds this a breach of ethics: He is in business to separate the gambler from his money, yes, but his self-respect requires the gambler to make reasonable bets.

When Mahowny moves up a step by stealing larger sums and flying to Atlantic City to lose them, he encounters a more ruthless and amusing professional. John Hurt plays the manager of the casino like a snake fascinated by the way a mouse hurries forward to be eaten. Hurt has seen obsessive gamblers come and go and is familiar with all the manifestations of their sickness, but this Mahowny brings a kind of grandeur to his losing.

The newcomer is quickly singled out as a high roller, comped with a luxury suite, offered French cuisine and tickets to the Pointer Sisters, but all he wants to do is gamble ("and maybe . . . some ribs, no sauce, and a Coke?"). Hurt sends a hooker to Mahowny's room, and a flunky reports back: "The only woman he's interested in is Lady Luck." Certainly Mahowny forgets his fiancée on a regular basis, standing her up, disappearing for weekends, even taking her to Vegas and then forgetting that she is upstairs waiting in their suite. (The fiancée is a classic enabler, excusing his lapses, but Vegas is too much for her; she tries to explain to him that when she saw the size of the suite she assumed they had come to Vegas to get married: "That's what normal people do in Vegas.")

It is impossible to like Mahowny, but easy to identify with him, if we have ever had obsessions of our own. Like all addicts of anything, he does what he does because he does it. "He needs to win in order to get more money to lose," one of the casino professionals observes.

Of course he will eventually be caught. He knows it, we know it, but being caught is beside the point. The point is to gamble as long as he can before he is caught. Mahowny refers at one point to having had a lot of luck, and he is referring not to winning, but to being able to finance a great deal of gambling at a level so high that, asked by a psychiatrist to rate the excitement on a scale of zero to one hundred, he unhesitatingly answers, "One hundred." And his greatest excitement in life outside of gambling? "Twenty."

Philip Seymour Hoffman's performance is a masterpiece of discipline and precision. He spends a lot of time adjusting his glasses or resting his fingers on his temples, as if to enhance his tunnel vision. He never meets the eye of the camera, or anyone else. Even when a casino security guard is firmly leading his fiancée away from his table, he hardly looks up to notice that she is there, or to say a word in her defense. He is . . . gambling. The movie has none of the false manipulation of most gambling movies, in which the actors signal their highs and lows. Hoffman understands that for this gambler, it is not winning or losing, but all process.

The movie, written by Maurice Chauvet, has been directed by Richard Kwietniowski, whose only other feature was *Love and Death on Long Island* (1998). That one also starred John Hurt, playing a reclusive British literary intellectual who becomes as obsessed as Mahowny, but with an erotic fixation. So unworldly he does not own a television and never goes to the movies, the Hurt character takes refuge from the rain in a cinema, finds himself watching a teenage comedy starring Jason Priestley, and becomes so fascinated by this young man that he keeps a scrapbook like a starstruck teenager and eventually travels to Long Island just in the hopes of meeting him. We get the impression that the Hurt character has been unaware of his homosexuality and indeed even his sexuality before being thunderstruck by this sudden fixation. In both films, Kwietniowski understands that conscious choice has little to do with his characters, that risk and humiliation are immaterial, that once they are locked in on the subjects of their obsessions, they have no choice but to hurry ahead to their dooms. ☞

P

Paid in Full ★ ★ ½
R, 93 m., 2002

Wood Harris (Ace), Mekhi Phifer (Mitch), Kevin Carroll (Calvin), Esai Morales (Lulu), Chi McBride (Pip), Cam'ron (Rico), Remo Green (Sonny), Cynthia Martells (Dora), Elise Neal (Aunt Jane), Regina Hall (Kiesha). Directed by Charles Stone III and produced by Damon Dash, Jay-Z, and Brett Ratner. Screenplay by Azie Faison Jr. and Austin Phillips.

Paid in Full tells the story of the rise and fall of a gifted young businessman. His career might have taken place at Enron, as a talented manager, staging a fake energy crisis to steal from California consumers. But opportunity finds us where we live, and Ace lives in Harlem and lacks an MBA, so he becomes a drug dealer. The skills involved are much the same as at Enron: Lie to the customers, hide or fake the income, shuffle the books, and pay off powerful friends. It is useful, in viewing a movie like *Paid in Full*, to understand that it is about business, not drugs. Breaking the law is simply an unfortunate side effect of wanting to make more money than can be done legally.

Because many drug dealers and consumers are poor and powerless, laws come down on them more ferociously than on the white-collar criminals whose misdeeds are on a larger scale. Three strikes and you're out, while three lucrative bankruptcies and you're barely up and running. *Paid in Full* might have been fascinating if it had intercut between Ace's career and the adventures of an Enron executive of about the same age. I guess in a way that's what *Traffic* did.

Paid in Full takes place in the 1980s and is based on the true stories of famous drug lords (Alpo, A. Z., Richard Porter) during that era of expanding crack addiction. Names are changed. Ace, based on A. Z. and played by Wood Harris, is a deliveryman for a dry cleaner named Pip (Chi McBride). Moving on the streets all day, it is impossible for him to miss seeing the good fortune of drug dealers, and he learns of the fortunes to be made by delivering something other than pressed pants.

He tells his story himself, in a narration like the ones in *GoodFellas* or *Casino*, and in an early scene we see money that has become so meaningless that small fortunes are bet on tossing crumpled paper at wastebaskets. When another dealer (Kevin Carroll) goes off to the pen, Ace moves quickly to grab his territory, and soon has so much money that his life demonstrates one of the drawbacks of growing up in poverty: You lack the skills to spend it fast enough. He prospers, learning from the more experienced Lulu (Esai Morales). Then another young hotshot, Rico (Cam'ron), comes along, and Ace becomes the veteran who's a target.

The movie is ambitious, has good energy, and is well acted, but tells a familiar story in a familiar way. The parallels to Brian De Palma's *Scarface* are underlined by scenes from that movie that are watched by the characters in this. The trajectory is well known: poverty, success, riches, and then death or jail. This plot describes countless lives, and is so common because the laws against drugs do such a good job of supporting the price and making the business so lucrative. The difference between drugs and corporate swindles, obviously, is that with drugs the profits are real.

Panic Room ★ ★ ★
R, 112 m., 2002

Jodie Foster (Meg Altman), Kristen Stewart (Sarah Altman), Forest Whitaker (Burnham), Jared Leto (Junior), Dwight Yoakam (Raoul), Patrick Bauchau (Stephen), Ian Buchanan (Evan), Ann Magnuson (Lydia Lynch). Directed by David Fincher and produced by Cean Chaffin, Judy Hofflund, David Koepp, and Gavin Polone. Screenplay by Koepp.

As a critic I indulge myself by scoffing at loopholes in thrillers that could not exist without them. I guess I'm seeking the ideal of a thriller existing entirely in a world of physical and psychological plausibility. *Panic Room* is about as close as I'm likely to get. Yes, there are moments when I want to shout advice at the screen, but just as often the characters are ahead of me. They also ask the same questions I'm asking, of which the most heartfelt, in a thriller, is, "Why didn't *we* do that?"

The movie, directed by David Fincher and written by David Koepp, embraces realism almost as a challenge. The movie resembles a chess game: The board and all of the pieces are in full view, both sides know the rules, and the winner will simply be the better strategist. Once we sense *Panic Room* isn't going to cheat, it gathers in tension, because the characters are operating out of their own resources, and that makes them the players, not the pawns.

Jodie Foster and Forest Whitaker star, as the chessmasters. She's Meg, a rich woman, recently divorced, who is spending her first night in a big Manhattan brownstone with her teenage daughter, Sarah (Kristen Stewart). He's Burnham, a home invader lured by tales of millions hidden in the house by its former owner. The house includes a "panic room" on the third of four stories—a reinforced retreat with independent supplies of air, electricity, and water, which can be locked indefinitely to keep the occupants safe. Burnham's day job: "I spent the last twelve years of my life building rooms like this specifically to keep out people like us."

He's talking to his partners, Junior (Jared Leto) and Raoul (Dwight Yoakam). Junior brought Burnham and Raoul onto the job, and Burnham hates it that Raoul brought along a gun. Their plan is to get in, find the money, and get out. According to Junior's information, the house is empty. It is not, and soon Meg and Sarah are locked in the safe room, the three men are outside, and it looks like a stalemate except that neither side can afford to concede.

We already know the layout of the house. We got the tour when the real-estate agent showed the women through the rooms, and again in a vertiginous shot that begins in the upstairs bedroom, swoops down two floors, zooms into the keyhole, pulls back, and careens upstairs again. The shot combines physical and virtual camera moves, a reminder that Fincher *(Seven, The Game, Fight Club)* is a visual virtuoso. He's also a master of psychological gamesmanship, and most of the movie will bypass fancy camerawork for classical intercutting between the cats and the mice (who sometimes trade sides of the board).

I have deliberately not described much of the strategy itself. That would be cheating. Once you know what everyone wants and how

the safe room works, the plot should be allowed to simply unfold. There is a neat twist in the fund of knowledge about the room; Burnham, who builds them, knows a lot more about how they work, their strengths and limitations, than Meg and Sarah, who start out basically knowing only how to run inside and lock the door.

The role of Meg was originally filled by Nicole Kidman. I learn from *Variety* that she had to drop out after a knee injury and was replaced by Foster. I have no idea if Foster is better or worse than Kidman would have been. I only know she is spellbinding. She has the gutsy, brainy resilience of a stubborn scrapper, and when all other resources fail her she can still think fast—and obliquely, like a chessmaster hiding one line of attack inside another.

The intruders are ill matched, which is the idea. Burnham has the knowledge, Junior has the plan, and Raoul has the gun. Once they are all inside the house and know the plan, therefore, Junior is not entirely necessary, unless the others are positively determined to split the loot three ways. On the other hand, Burnham hates violence, and Raoul is such a wild card he may shoot himself in the foot.

The end game in chess, for the student of the sport, is its most intriguing aspect. The loss of pieces has destroyed the initial symmetry and created a skewed board—unfamiliar terrain in which specialized pieces are required to do jobs for which they were not designed. There is less clutter; strategy must run deeper because there are fewer alternative lines. Sacrifices may be brilliant, or they may be blunders, or only apparent blunders. Every additional move limits the options, and the prospect of defeat, swift and unforeseen, hangs over the board. That is exactly the way *Panic Room* unfolds, right down to the detail that even at the end the same rules apply, and all the choices that were made earlier limit the choices that can be made now.

Party Monster ★ ★ ★
NO MPAA RATING, 98 m., 2003

Macaulay Culkin (Michael Alig), Seth Green (James St. James), Chloë Sevigny (Gitsie), Natasha Lyonne (Brooke), Justin Hagan (Freeze), Wilson Cruz (Angel Melendez), Wilmer Valderrama (Disc Jockey Keoki), Dylan McDermott (Peter Gatien). Directed by Fenton

Bailey and Randy Barbato and produced by Bailey and Barbato, Jon Marcus, Bradford Simpson, and Christine Vachon. Screenplay by Bailey and Barbato, based on the book *Disco Bloodbath* by James St. James.

Party Monster is based on a book named *Disco Bloodbath*, and there's a tug-of-war in both titles between fun and horror. Horror wins. Michael Alig, the movie's subject, looks innocent with his baby face and cute little outfits, but he is a creature of birdbrained vanity. After the drugs take over he becomes not merely dangerous but deadly, and we are reminded of George Carlin's answer when he was asked how cocaine makes you feel: "It makes you feel like having some more cocaine."

Alig is played by Macaulay Culkin, in his first movie since *Richie Rich* (1994), and it is a fearless performance as a person so shallow, narcissistic, and amoral that eventually even his friends simply stare at him in disbelief. Alig, who is now thirty-seven and serving a prison sentence for manslaughter, was a Manhattan media creature of the early 1990s, promoting parties whose primary purpose was to draw attention to their promoter. At the Limelight and other venues, including a fast-food store and the back of a trailer truck, he assembled androgynous crowds of substance abusers who desperately had fun.

Alig came to New York from South Bend, Indiana, where, needless to say, he did not fit in. Perhaps his whole identity was formed by the need to build a wall against childhood bullying, and it is possible to feel some sympathy, not for the man he became, but for the boy who had to become that man. In New York, broke but blissfully drunk on himself, he convinces club owner Peter Gatien (Dylan McDermott) to let him throw parties at the famous Limelight nightclub, and sets himself up as the next Andy Warhol. The difference (apart from the fact that Warhol was an important artist) is that Warhol defined the notion of fifteen minutes of fame, and Alig only illustrated it.

Alig has a way of instantly annexing a court of admirers. His first conquest is James St. James (Seth Green), also a party organizer, who becomes the "best friend" of a person with no gift for friendship, and who watches in dismay as Michael embraces self-destruction. Then there's Keoki (Wilmer Valderrama)—"you'll be my boyfriend." And Angel Melendez (Wilson Cruz)—"I'll make you a drug dealer." Various other moths fly into his flame, including Gitsie (Chloë Sevigny) and Brooke (Natasha Lyonne), and the grown-up and straight club owner Gatien is sometimes amazed at himself for putting up with this creature.

Michael Alig is gay as a default. Obviously he cannot be straight and be the person he is, so gay is what's left, but the movie gives the sense that sexuality is of little importance to him. Perhaps sex involves an intimacy he was uninterested in. Of course, after a certain point in his drug spiral it would have become impossible. He wanted to use not the bodies of his friends but their appearances and identities; he selects his circle as if furnishing a room.

James St. James (who wrote the book) is the relatively sane observer of the madness, a person screwed up in more conventional ways. His drugs and lifestyle are a problem, but at least there is a human being there, who attempts to reason with Michael and warn him, and who sees the train wreck coming. Fatal not to Michael but to Angel, who is killed in an agonizing way with hammer blows and injections of Drano. Yes, Alig was drugged out of his mind at the time, but if you can think of Drano while in a chemical stupor, that indicates the evil extends pretty far down your brain stem.

Culkin plays Alig as clueless to the end, living so firmly in his fantasy world that nothing can penetrate his chirpy persona. Whether this is accurate—whether indeed any of the facts in the film are accurate—is not for me to say, but it works. Seth Green is more dimensional and reachable as James, but it is Culkin's oblivious facade that makes him scary; any attempt to bring "humanity" to this character would miss the point.

That said, I am not sure what the movie accomplishes, except to portray an extreme and impenetrable personality type. The film was written and directed by Fenton Bailey and Randy Barbato, who made a 1999 documentary about Michael Alig and then decided on this fictional docudrama. Unlike such real-life crime movies as *In Cold Blood*, they find no insights into the humanity of their subject, but that may be because Alig was a cipher known only to himself (if that). The movie lacks insight and leaves us feeling sad and empty—sad for ourselves, not Alig—and maybe it had to be that way.

Passionada ★ ★ ★

PG-13, 108 m., 2003

Jason Isaacs (Charles Beck), Sofia Milos (Celia Amonte), Emmy Rossum (Vicky Amonte), Theresa Russell (Lois Vargas), Seymour Cassel (Daniel Vargas), Lupe Ontiveros (Angelica Amonte), Chris Tardio (Gianni Martinez). Directed by Dan Ireland and produced by David Bakalar. Screenplay by Jim Jermanok and Steve Jermanok.

Passionada assembles the elements for a soap opera, and turns them into a bubble bath. The movie is populated with lovable rogues, cuddly coots, passionate widows, and beloved ghosts, and is about a romance between a professional gambler and a torch singer in mourning, but somehow all of these elements fall into place; we feel surprising affection for these people from New Bedford, Massachusetts.

The movie has been directed by Dan Ireland, from a first screenplay by the brothers Jim and Steve Jermanok, whose freelance writing credits sound like homework for this story. Steve wrote the book *New England Seacoast Adventures,* and here the brothers create an emotional adventure for a down-and-out gambler and a Portuguese-American widow who sings of lost love and vows she will never marry again.

The widow is named Celia Amonte, and is played by Sofia Milos, from the TV show *CSI: Miami.* Dark of hair, eyes, and mood, she raises her teenage daughter, Vicky (Emmy Rossum), lives beneath her mother-in-law, Angelica (Lupe Ontiveros), and remains faithful to the memory of her first love, a fisherman who died at sea.

Into her life stumbles Charles Beck, played by Jason Isaacs, who plays the villain Lucius Malfoy in the *Harry Potter* films. Here he's not a villain but a luckless card-counter who has been barred from most of the casinos in North America, and has drifted into New Bedford to find support from his old gambling buddy Daniel (Seymour Cassel) and his younger wife, Lois (Theresa Russell), who is so besotted with him that she carries a cocktail kit in her purse

in case he requires a martini in a restaurant without a liquor license.

Once all of these pieces are in place, we can guess what the movie will do with them, and we will be correct. It is important that Charles stop lying about himself, that Celia move on with her life, and that Vicky, Lois, and Daniel be an amusing chorus to egg them on. Yet the movie is able to surprise us with how it arrives at a happy ending, as when Lupe Ontiveros delivers a line that we did not expect from the mother-in-law, and fills it with emotion while remaining absolutely matter-of-fact. And there is a nice twist when Vicky, Celia's daughter, proposes a deal to Charles: "Teach me to card-count, and I'll get you a date with my mom."

Sofia Milos successfully plays a character who should be all but unplayable; she sings sad love songs night after night in a local club, while never permitting love for herself. (Her singing voice is supplied by the Portuguese singer Misia.) In the economy of love stories, a widow is a wife in waiting, but the movie doesn't hurry to end her wait. Charles has too many secrets, too much baggage, too many lies to move confidently in her direction—and, besides, he likes her, and then loves her, and that will require a basic readjustment in the way he's been living his life. Isaacs's character has a way of lightly sidestepping difficult issues, in conversation and life, and it is absorbing to see him gradually realize that a moment of truth is at hand.

Strictly speaking, there is no real need for the characters of Daniel and Lois, and that has been true of many of the characters Seymour Cassel has played; he comes on to swell a progress, start a scene or two, and then the central characters march on without him. But Cassel is indispensable for bringing a relaxed, gentle humanity into a story. He provides a context and a reference for Charles; if he thinks the gambler is okay, then we can trust him with Celia. Theresa Russell is a surprising choice for the loving younger wife, until we reflect that she has long been married to the director Nicolas Roeg, twenty-nine years her senior.

Dan Ireland's first feature, *The Whole Wide World* (1996), was also about a romance between a serious young woman (Renée Zellweger) and an elusive eccentric (Vincent D'Onofrio, as the pulp fiction writer Robert E. Howard). There comes a moment when Howard is challenged to open up about elements of his life he would rather keep secret, and Charles Beck has a moment like that in *Passionada*—handled well, and without quite the payoff we expect.

The movie makes evocative use of its locations in New Bedford, the whaling port where Ishmael set sail in *Moby-Dick*. "In summer time," wrote Melville, "the town is sweet to see; full of fine maples—long avenues of green and gold." Melville did not anticipate the nearby casinos run by Indian tribes where Charles plies his trade, but the trees are still sweet to see all the same.

The Passion of the Christ ★ ★ ★ ★
R, 126 m., 2004

James Caviezel (Jesus, the Christ), Maia Morgenstern (Mary), Monica Bellucci (Mary Magdalene), Mattia Sbragia (Caiphas), Hristo Shopov (Pontius Pilate), Claudia Gerini (Pilate's Wife), Luca Lionello (Judas). Directed by Mel Gibson and produced by Bruce Davey, Gibson, and Stephen McEveety. Screenplay by Gibson and Benedict Fitzgerald.

If ever there was a film with the correct title, that film is Mel Gibson's *The Passion of the Christ*. Although the word *passion* has become mixed up with romance, its Latin origins refer to suffering and pain; later Christian theology broadened that to include Christ's love for mankind, which made him willing to suffer and die for us. The movie is 126 minutes long, and I would guess that at least 100 of those minutes, maybe more, are concerned specifically and graphically with the details of the torture and death of Jesus. This is the most violent film I have ever seen.

I prefer to evaluate a film on the basis of what it intends to do, not on what I think it should have done. It is clear that Mel Gibson wanted to make graphic and inescapable the price that Jesus paid (as Christians believe) when he died for our sins. Anyone raised as a Catholic will be familiar with the stops along the way; the screenplay is inspired not so much by the Gospels as by the fourteen Stations of the Cross. As an altar boy, serving during the Stations on Friday nights in Lent, I was encouraged to meditate on Christ's suffering, and I re-member the chants as the priest led the way from one station to another:

At the Cross, her station keeping . . .
Stood the mournful Mother weeping . . .
Close to Jesus to the last.

For us altar boys, this was not necessarily a deep spiritual experience. Christ suffered, Christ died, Christ rose again, we were redeemed, and let's hope we can get home in time to watch the Illinois basketball game on TV. What Gibson has provided for me, for the first time in my life, is a visceral idea of what the Passion consisted of. That his film is superficial in terms of the surrounding message—that we get only a few passing references to the teachings of Jesus—is, I suppose, not the point. This is not a sermon or a homily, but a visualization of the central event in the Christian religion. Take it or leave it.

David Anson, a critic I respect, finds in *Newsweek* that Gibson has gone too far. ". . . (T)he relentless gore is self-defeating," he writes. "Instead of being moved by Christ's suffering, or awed by his sacrifice, I felt abused by a filmmaker intent on punishing an audience, for who knows what sins." This is a completely valid response to the film, and I quote Anson because I suspect he speaks for many audience members, who will enter the theater in a devout or spiritual mood and emerge deeply disturbed. You must be prepared for whippings, flayings, beatings, the crunch of bones, the agony of screams, the cruelty of the sadistic centurions, the rivulets of blood that crisscross every inch of Jesus' body. Some will leave before the end.

This is not a Passion like any other ever filmed. Perhaps that is the best reason for it. I grew up on those pious Hollywood biblical epics of the 1950s, which looked like holy cards brought to life. I remember my grin when *Time* magazine noted that Jeffrey Hunter, starring as Christ in *King of Kings* (1961), had shaved his armpits. (Not Hunter's fault; the film's crucifixion scene had to be reshot because pre-view audiences objected to Jesus' hairy chest.) If it does nothing else, Gibson's film will break the tradition of turning Jesus and his disciples into neat, clean, well-barbered middle-class businessmen. They were poor men in a poor land. I debated Scorsese's *The Last Temptation of*

Christ with Michael Medved before an audience from a Christian college, and was told by an audience member that the characters were filthy and needed haircuts.

The Middle East in biblical times was a Jewish community occupied against its will by the Roman Empire, and the message of Jesus was equally threatening to both sides—to the Romans, because he was a revolutionary, and to the establishment of Jewish priests because he preached a new covenant and threatened the status quo. In the movie's scenes showing Jesus being condemned to death, the two main players are Pontius Pilate, the Roman governor, and Caiphas, the Jewish high priest. Both men want to keep the lid on, and while neither is especially eager to see Jesus crucified, they live in a harsh time when such a man is dangerous.

Pilate is seen going through his well-known doubts before finally washing his hands of the matter and turning Jesus over to the priests, but Caiphas, who also had doubts, is not seen as sympathetically. The critic Steven D. Greydanus, in a useful analysis of the film, writes: "The film omits the canonical line from John's gospel in which Caiphas argues that it is better for one man to die for the people that the nation be saved. Had Gibson retained this line, perhaps giving Caiphas a measure of the inner conflict he gave to Pilate, it could have underscored the similarities between Caiphas and Pilate and helped defuse the issue of anti-Semitism."

This scene and others might justifiably be cited by anyone concerned that the movie contains anti-Semitism. My own feeling is that Gibson's film is not anti-Semitic, but reflects a range of behavior on the part of its Jewish characters, on balance favorably. The Jews who seem to desire Jesus' death are in the priesthood, and have political as well as theological reasons for acting; like today's Catholic bishops who were slow to condemn abusive priests, Protestant TV preachers who confuse religion with politics, or Muslim clerics who are silent on terrorism, they have an investment in their positions and authority. The other Jews seen in the film are viewed positively; Simon helps Jesus to carry the cross, Veronica brings a cloth to wipe his face, Jews in the crowd cry out against his torture.

A reasonable person, I believe, will reflect that in this story set in a Jewish land, there are many characters with many motives, some good, some not, each one representing himself, none representing his religion. The story involves a Jew who tried no less than to replace the established religion and set himself up as the Messiah. He was understandably greeted with a jaundiced eye by the Jewish establishment while at the same time finding his support, his disciples, and the founders of his church entirely among his fellow Jews. The libel that the Jews "killed Christ" involves a willful misreading of testament and teaching: Jesus was made man and came to Earth *in order* to suffer and die in reparation for our sins. No race, no religion, no man, no priest, no governor, no executioner killed Jesus; he died by God's will to fulfill his purpose, and with our sins we *all* killed him. That some Christian churches have historically been guilty of the sin of anti-Semitism is undeniable, but in committing it they violated their own beliefs.

This discussion will seem beside the point for readers who want to know about the movie, not the theology. But *The Passion of the Christ*, more than any other film I can recall, depends upon theological considerations. Gibson has not made a movie that anyone would call "commercial," and if it grosses millions, that will not be because anyone was entertained. It is a personal message movie of the most radical kind, attempting to re-create events of personal urgency to Gibson. The filmmaker has put his artistry and fortune at the service of his conviction and belief, and that doesn't happen often.

Is the film "good" or "great"? I imagine each person's reaction (visceral, theological, artistic) will differ. I was moved by the depth of feeling, by the skill of the actors and technicians, by their desire to see this project through, no matter what. To discuss individual performances, such as James Caviezel's heroic depiction of the ordeal, is almost beside the point. This isn't a movie about performances, although it has powerful ones; or about technique, although it is awesome; or about cinematography (although Caleb Deschanel paints with an artist's eye); or music (although John Debney supports the content without distracting from it). It is a film about an idea. An idea that it is necessary to fully comprehend the Passion if Christianity is to make any sense. Gibson has communicated his idea with a single-minded urgency. Many will disagree. Some will agree, but be horrified by the graphic treatment. I myself am no longer religious in the sense that a long-ago altar boy thought he should be; but I can respond to the power of belief whether I agree or not, and when I find it in a film I must respect it.

Note: I said the film is the most violent I have ever seen. It will probably be the most violent you have ever seen. This is not a criticism but an observation; the film is unsuitable for younger viewers, but works powerfully for those who can endure it. The MPAA's "R" rating is definitive proof that the organization either will never give the NC-17 rating for violence alone, or was intimidated by the subject matter. If it had been anyone other than Jesus up on that cross, I have a feeling that NC-17 would have been automatic. ☞

Paycheck ★ ★
PG-13, 119 m., 2003

Ben Affleck (Michael Jennings), Uma Thurman (Rachel Porter), Aaron Eckhart (Rethrick), Paul Giamatti (Shorty), Joe Morton (Agent Dodge), Emily Holmes (Betsy), Colm Feore (Mr. Wolf), Joe Morton (Agent Dodge), Michael C. Hall (Agent Klein). Directed by John Woo and produced by Terence Chang, John Davis, Michael Hackett, and Woo. Screenplay by Dean Georgaris, based on the short story by Philip K. Dick.

Paycheck begins with a thought-provoking idea from Philip K. Dick, exploits it for its action and plot potential, but never really develops it. By the end, the film seems to have lost enthusiasm for itself, and should be scored with "Is That All There Is?" It's like an assembly of off-the-shelf parts from techno-thrillers: the vast laboratory, the cold-blooded billionaire industrialist, the hero in a situation he doesn't understand, the professional security men who line up to get bumped off by the amateur computer nerd. Because the director is John Woo, we expect a chase and a martial arts sequence, and we get them, but they're strangely detached; they feel like exercises, not exuberations.

Ben Affleck and Uma Thurman establish a strong presence as the leads, having some fun (and shedding a few tears) over the fact that they've been deeply in love but he can't re-member it. That's in the nature of Affleck's job. He plays Michael Jennings, a brilliant engineer who hires himself out to reverse-engineer new computer breakthroughs. He starts with impenetrable code or uncrackable chips, takes them apart, sees what makes them work, and reassembles them as elegant little rip-offs that sidestep copyright infringement. Because big bucks are involved in what he does, and because corporations wouldn't want a guy like this blabbing on TechTV, they write a sneaky clause into his contract: After he completes a job, his memory is wiped clean, and he's left with a gap of several weeks and a big paycheck.

For a writer with Dick's pulp origins, Michael is an ideal character type—sort of a cyber version of Johnny Dollar, the man with the action-packed expense account. Give him his salary and he's happy to walk away from the job (although we get a brief glimpse of a check that wouldn't be much of a payday for a program that essentially does the same thing as Al Pacino's software in *Simone*—creates a 3-D digital actress who looks and sounds like the real thing).

Next assignment. Michael is hired by Rethrick (Aaron Eckhart), head of the ominous Allcom. This assignment will take a little longer—three years of his life, as he tries to crack an invention that can see into the future. Yes, Rethrick wants to steal a lens so powerful that it follows the curvature of space and time right back to where it started and then some. Theory is, if you can predict the future, your stock price will go up. Yes, and you can win the lottery, too—although once the fundamental principles of stock markets and lotteries have been capsized, what do you do for an encore? See if you're going to enjoy lunch?

At a party at Rethrick's house, Michael exchanges small talk with the beautiful biologist Rachel (Uma Thurman), demonstrating once again that we should never, ever worry about the cleverness of our small talk because in the movies it can be gormless and banal and yet be repeated as a motif for an entire film. After Michael suggests that they "go somewhere else" and talk, she turns him down, and then she says, "You don't believe in second chances, do you?" Not a line to rank with "I want you to hold [the chicken salad] between your knees," but it will be repeated with variations, tears, irony, fondness, and urgency, to prove that the movie has not had its own memory erased.

The ingenious element in the plot is that when Michael's three years are up and he's free again, he discovers he has signed away millions of dollars and is left only with a manila envelope containing nineteen objects. These are apparently objects that the prewipe Michael knew he would need postwipe; he has to figure out what to use them for, and when. (Clue: He's being chased by killers at a bus station, and whoa!—He has a bus pass!) There's an echo here of *The Bourne Identity* (2002), starring Affleck's buddy Matt Damon as an amnesiac who takes possession of a Swiss safe-deposit box containing clues to several identities, perhaps including his own.

Okay, so the idea is for Michael and Rachel to stop Allcom before it can destroy the world. Destruction is likely, it's explained, because if world leaders could foresee that their enemies planned to use weapons of mass destruction, they would launch a preemptive strike to respond to the attack before it takes place. Those wacky sci-fi guys! Their way to derail this scenario, of course, involves a long motorcycle chase sequence and a martial arts battle.

Although Woo is famous for his mastery of action scenes, the motorcycle chase is played by the numbers; there hardly seems to be risk or danger involved, and the computer nerd and his biologist girlfriend don't seem particularly amazed when lots of men in black cars try to shoot them dead. Later, when Rachel does some hand-to-hand combat, we're reminded how much more convincing Thurman was in *Kill Bill*—although there's a scene involving a mechanical hand that shows some wit and gets a chuckle.

There was a basic level at which I enjoyed the movie, just for the scope of the production and the way Affleck doggedly puzzled his way through that manila envelope. But at the end we get the sense that Woo is operating with a clipboard and a checklist, making sure everyone is killed in the right order. There's simply not enough urgency involved. And the attempts of the Allcom security staff to deal with the various locks and alarms in their top-secret lab had me thinking of *Dumb and Dumber*. There are countless fascinating possibilities involved in Philip K. Dick's story, and I'm kind of

sad that the one ranking highest in the minds of the filmmakers was the opportunity to have chase scenes and blow stuff up real good.

The Perfect Score ★ ★
PG-13, 93 m., 2004

Scarlett Johansson (Francesca), Erika Christensen (Anna), Chris Evans (Kyle), Darius Miles (Desmond), Leonardo Nam (Roy), Bryan Greenberg (Matty), Fulvio Cecere (Francesca's Father), Kyle Labine (Dave), Bill Mackenzie (Bernie). Directed by Brian Robbins and produced by Roger Birnbaum, Jonathan Glickman, Robbins, and Michael Tollin. Screenplay by Mark Schwahn, Marc Hyman, and Jon Zack.

The dialogue in *The Perfect Score* mentions *The Breakfast Club*, which is nice (how come the characters in movies never seem to know there are movies—except the ones they attend but never watch?). And there are similarities between the two films, not least in the way that Scarlett Johansson, with her red lips and brunette haircut, resembles Molly Ringwald. There is also a certain seriousness linking the two films, although this one tilts toward a caper comedy.

The film takes place in Princeton, New Jersey, which in addition to being Albert Einstein's place of last employment is also home to the Princeton Testing Center, home of the SAT exam. The SATs, we learn, were once known as the Scholastic Aptitude Test, but since this name presumably reeked of common sense, it was dropped, and now "SAT" simply stands for—SAT. "Ess Ay Tee," the Website explains, making it easy for us.

We meet Kyle (Chris Evans), who for as long as he can remember has wanted to be an architect. That for him translates into being admitted to Cornell, but for Cornell, alas, he will need to score a 1,430 on his SAT, and his first score is down close to triple digits. He can take the test again, but he doubts he can improve his score.

"Kyle," says one of his buddies, "this is your dream, man. If they want to put a number on that, then the hell with them." Yeah. So Kyle and his posse decide to break into the Princeton Testing Center, steal the answers to the test, and realize their dream. And that they set out to do, in a film that sketches various motives for a half-dozen characters. You may be able to find parallels between these characters and those in *The Breakfast Club*. On the other hand, you may decide life is too short.

I wasn't thinking about *The Breakfast Club* anyway, while I watched the film. I was thinking about *Better Luck Tomorrow*, the 2002 film by Justin Lin about a group of Asian-American high school students in Orange County, who started by selling exam answers and ended up involved in drugs and murder, all without getting caught. In the original ending of the film when it played at Sundance, the central character considers turning himself in to the police, but "I couldn't let one mistake get in the way of everything I'd worked for. I know the difference between right and wrong, but I guess in the end I really wanted to go to a good college."

Lin reshot some of the film, including that ending, but I've always thought it was a good one. It shows an ability to separate achievement from morality, and places so much value on success that it finally justifies any action. Lin's young heroes, I wrote in my article about the best films of the year, have positioned themselves to take over from the fallen leaders of Enron.

I thought about the film because *The Perfect Score* considers similar material without the bite and anger and savage determination. It's too palatable. It maintains a tone of light seriousness, and it depends on the caper for too much of its entertainment value. *Better Luck Tomorrow* also has a plot that involves crime, but the difference is, *The Perfect Score* is about the intended crime and depends on it, while in *Better Luck Tomorrow* we see a process by which the behavior of the characters leads them where they never thought to go.

There is a kind of franchising of movies going on right now, in which the big studio product is like fast food: bad for you, but available on every corner. Good and challenging movies are limited to release in big cities and in a handful of independently booked cinemas. Whole states and sections of the country never see the best new films on big screens, and they're not always easy to find on video.

And that's a shame. What does it say when a dozen of the titles nominated for major Academy Awards this year did not play in a majority

of the markets? Have I drifted from the movie under review? I'm not drifting, I'm swimming.

Personal Velocity ★ ★ ★ ½
R, 86 m., 2002

Kyra Sedgwick (Delia), Parker Posey (Greta), Fairuza Balk (Paula), Nicole Murphy (May Wurtzle), Tim Guinee (Lee), Ron Leibman (Avram), Seth Gilliam (Vincent), David Warshofsky (Kurt Wurtzle), Brian Tarantina (Pete Shunt), Mara Hobel (Fay), Leo Fitzpatrick (Mylert), Wallace Shawn (Mr. Gelb), John Ventimiglia (Narrator [voice]). Directed by Rebecca Miller and produced by Alexis Alexanian, Lemore Syvan, and Gary Winick. Screenplay by Miller.

Wandering through a bookstore a few weeks ago, I picked up *The Best American Short Stories 2002*, and it launched me into a marathon of short story reading: "The O. Henry Prize Awards 2002," the collected stories of Alice Munro, Ha Jin, Michael Chabon, and William Trevor, and even one evening the works of Mr. Henry himself, long waiting on a distant shelf.

I mention this because it was a well-timed preparation for Rebecca Miller's *Personal Velocity*, which films three of her own short stories in segments of about half an hour each. This was the Grand Jury prize winner at Sundance 2002. I was in the mood for these focused, economic stories, in which we plunge into the middle of a life, witness crucial developments, and end with a moment of bittersweet insight into the character. If novels and feature films are about the arc of a life or at least a significant portion of one, short stories and films are about unexpected moments of truth: "epiphanies," James Joyce called them.

Miller's characters are Delia (Kyra Sedgwick), Greta (Parker Posey), and Paula (Fairuza Balk). These three actresses almost always appear in interesting work, often from the indie segment, and their casting is a clue about the movie: It is likely to be about specific, not generic, women, and in one way or another they will be defiantly out of step. They also share big problems about men: fathers, husbands, lovers, dates.

Delia is a battered wife, once famed as a high school slut. Greta edits cookbooks, until a famous novelist asks her to handle his next novel. Paula is running away from her life when she picks up a hitchhiker who is running away from a worse one. All three women have problems with men, and none of them find the solution in this film—which is, I think, a recommendation.

Paula's segment touched me the most. Balk's Paula is a resilient woman with much to be resilient about. She's pregnant. She has just narrowly escaped one of those senseless accidents that can forever change your life. Shaken, she gets in her car and starts driving and finds herself at her mother's home. Her mother's new husband is a jerk, and her mother won't defend her daughter against him. Paula picks up a sullen, sad, withdrawn young hitchhiker and gets a sudden insight both into what has happened to him—and how it has wounded and hardened him. What she learns is that she still has feelings, can care, is not as crippled as she thinks.

Parker Posey is a natural comedienne, and that is a gift she draws on in the not very funny story of Greta, a cookbook editor who is engaged to a fact-checker at *The New Yorker*. When the famous novelist comes along, he is looking for both an editor and a lover. Will she be loyal to her boyfriend, who her father thinks is a loser? Is the question complicated by this opportunity with a winner? Because she has never felt very deeply about anything in life, this decision looks easier to her than it should.

The first story, about Delia, stars Kyra Sedgwick as a woman who is at first intrigued when her sex life turns a little rough, until she discovers that once her husband gets the taste for hurting her, he likes it. She flees with her children, lives for a time in a friend's garage, gets a job at a diner, and then is propositioned in an oily, callow way by the owner's son (Leo Fitzpatrick). He is amazed when she calls his bluff and says yes. He is more amazed by the contemptuous, dismissive way she deals with his lust. The segment ends with her regarding him thoughtfully, as if considering her future, or her past.

These stories are commented on by a narrator (John Ventimiglia), who uses Miller's prose to draw larger lessons and look for deeper currents. Miller (the daughter of the playwright Arthur) refuses to draw morals for her characters. They are not yet through learning, and life has more lessons for them. We see them so sharply, however, in the few days we glimpse each one. The actors are gifted at establishing character with just a few well-chosen strokes (as a short story writer must also be able to do). We learn as much about each of these women in half an hour as we learn about most movie characters in two hours. More, really, because the movie doesn't pretend to solve their situations, only to dramatize them.

Much has been made of the Sundance Award–winning cinematography by Ellen Kuras, because it is digital, and cheerfully makes that obvious. No doubt the quickness and economy of digital made the film possible. But I didn't much think about the cinematography while watching the film—or if I did, I had the same thoughts I would have had while watching 35mm. My thoughts were focused on the characters. That is a compliment to Kuras and Miller. If I had been thinking about the visual medium, they would have been doing something wrong.

Peter Pan ★ ★ ★ ½
PG, 105 m., 2003

Jason Isaacs (Captain Hook/Mr. Darling), Olivia Williams (Mrs. Darling), Lynn Redgrave (Aunt Millicent), Jeremy Sumpter (Peter Pan), Rachel Hurd-Wood (Wendy Darling), Harry Newell (John Darling), Freddie Popplewell (Michael Darling), Richard Briers (Smee), Ludivine Sagnier (Tinker Bell). Directed by P. J. Hogan and produced by Lucy Fisher, Patrick McCormick, and Douglas Wick. Screenplay by Michael Goldenberg and Hogan, based on the book by J. M. Barrie.

I'm not sure how to describe this *Peter Pan* to you. It's so different from what I expected. I walked in anticipating a sweet kiddie fantasy, and was surprised to find a film that takes its story very seriously indeed, thank you, and even allows a glimpse of underlying sadness. To be Peter Pan is fun for a day or a year, but can it be fun forever? Peter is trapped in Groundhog Day, repeating the same adventures, forever faced with the tiresome Captain Hook, always shackled to Tinker Bell, who means well but would get on your nerves if you took a three-day bus trip with her.

"Peter," asks Wendy, "what are your real feelings?" Those are precisely what Peter is unable to share. This expensive production, shot in Australia and unveiling a young unknown as the beautiful Wendy, is aware of the latent sexuality between the two characters, and Peter is a little scared of that. They are at precisely the age when it is time to share their first real kiss—and they do so, astonishing the other characters (they've never seen that before—not in the cartoon, not on the stage—never!).

The movie has been directed by P. J. Hogan, best known for Julia Roberts comedies (*My Best Friend's Wedding*). Here he stays closer to the J. M. Barrie book, which is about to celebrate its centenary, and also closer to the book's buried themes, which are sidestepped by most versions of *Peter Pan*. When a muscular and bare-chested gamin appears on the windowsill of the prettiest twelve-and-a-half-year-old in London and asks her to fly away from home and family to join him with the Lost Boys in Neverland, he is exactly the kind of strange man her mother should have warned her about. When the other major player in Neverland is the one-armed Captain Hook, who takes an uncomfortably acute interest in both Peter and Wendy, there's enough inspiration here to have Freud gnawing on his cigar.

It's not that the movie is overtly sexual; it's just that the sensuality is *there,* and the other versions have pretended it was not. The live action contributes to the new focus; Peter Pan is played by Jeremy Sumpter, who was so effective in Bill Paxton's *Frailty,* and Wendy Darling is Rachel Hurd-Wood, who was selected at an open casting call and is delightful in her first role. They're attractive young people in roles that in the past have been played by such as Robin Williams and Mary Martin, and there is chemistry on the screen.

The special effects, of course, are endless, but there is a method to their excess. The movie's not simply a riot of pretty pictures, but begins with a Neverland that seems overgrown and pungent—more like Louisiana than Middle Earth. There is a vast, gloomy castle and all manner of paths into the darkness, but then scenes will turn as delicate as *A Midsummer Night's Dream*. At a point when lesser films would be giving us swashbuckling by the numbers, Peter and Wendy dance in midair, emulating the fairy ballet.

As the film narrows into its crucial themes, we realize there are two: Wendy's desire to free Peter Pan from eternal boyhood, and Hook's envy of the affection they have for each other. It is no accident that the poison made of droplets from Hook's red eye is composed of envy, malice, and disappointment.

Captain Hook and John Darling are both played by Jason Isaacs, in a dual role made traditional by decades of holiday pantomimes; each character is short on qualities the other has in abundance. Hook is all gnash and bluster, while John Darling is so shy he can hardly talk to himself in the mirror. Mrs. Darling (Olivia Williams), mother of Wendy and her two younger brothers, seems awfully composed during her long nights by the open window, waiting for her children to return, but maybe she has seen the earlier versions.

Wendy finds a role for herself in Neverland. It's touching, the way the Lost Boys so desperately want to be found, and crowd around Wendy, asking her to be their mother. (What does a mother do? "Tell us a story!" Later, when the Lost Boys join Wendy and her brothers, John and Michael, back home in their bedroom, they ask Mrs. Darling to be their mother—and she agrees, although when Smee arrives late and is motherless, the new character of Aunt Millicent (Lynn Redgrave) steps in joyfully.

It was Aunt Millicent who really started all the trouble, by observing that Wendy was not a girl anymore and offering to take her into hand and make her a woman. This offer is vaguely alarming to Wendy, and what Peter offers her is the chance to drift in her preadolescent dream forever. What she offers him is a chance to grow up. "To grow up is such a barbarous business," Hook observes. "Think of the inconvenience—and the pimples!" But to never grow up is unspeakably sad, and this is the first *Peter Pan* where Peter's final flight seems not like a victory but an escape.

Phone Booth ★ ★ ★
R, 81 m., 2003

Colin Farrell (Stu Shepard), Forest Whitaker (Captain Ramey), Katie Holmes (Pamela McFadden), Radha Mitchell (Kelly Shepard), Kiefer Sutherland (The Caller [voice]). Directed by Joel Schumacher and produced by Gil Netter and David Zucker. Screenplay by Larry Cohen.

Phone Booth is a religious fable, a showbiz fable, or both. It involves a fast-talking, two-timing Broadway press agent who is using the last phone booth in Manhattan (at 53d and Eighth) when he's pinned down by a sniper. The shooter seems to represent either God, demanding a confession of sins, or the filmmakers, having their revenge on publicists.

The man in the crosshairs is Stu Shepard (Colin Farrell), who we've already seen striding the streets, lying into his cell phone, berating his hapless gofer. Why does he now use a pay phone instead of his cellular? Because he's calling his mistress Pamela (Katie Holmes) and doesn't want the call to turn up on the monthly bill scrutinized by his wife, Kelly (Radha Mitchell).

The phone in the booth rings, and Stu follows the universal human practice of answering it. The voice is harsh, sardonic, sounds like it belongs to a man intelligent and twisted, and with a sense of humor. For the next hour or so, in a movie that is only eighty-one minutes long, Stu will be trying to keep the man on the other end from pulling the trigger. The Voice (for so we may call him) seems to know a lot about Stu—personal secrets, but also things anyone could see, like the way he rudely treated a pizza delivery man. He seems to think Stu is a reprehensible man who deserves to die—and may, unless Stu can talk or think his way out of this situation.

The movie is essentially a morality play, and it's not a surprise to learn that Larry Cohen, the writer, came up with the idea twenty years ago—when there were still phone booths and morality plays. If the movie had been conceived more recently, Stu would have been the hero for the way he lies and cheats. The movie is an instructive contrast to *People I Know*, which played at Sundance 2003 and stars Al Pacino as a press agent who doggedly tries to do the right thing despite all of his (many) sins.

The director, Joel Schumacher, discovered Colin Farrell in the tense, quirky basic training drama *Tigerland* (2000). Farrell played a recruit who was too smart and too verbal to be a good trainee, and stirred up trouble in a fraught situation. Now comes a similar character, further twisted by civilian life. The movie is Farrell's to win or lose, since he's on-screen most of the time, and he shows energy and intensity.

As the crisis builds in tension, he forms a rapport with Captain Ramey (Forest Whitaker), a cop experienced at hostage situations, who at first believes Stu might be the perp and not the victim. The two actors have to communicate nonverbally to keep the sniper from realizing what's happening, and the movie shows them figuring that out.

The movie was premiered at Toronto 2002, scheduled for immediate release, and then yanked when the Beltway Sniper went into action. Then it opened during the Iraqi war. Hard to pick a safe opening date these days. Schumacher is the director of many blockbuster titles, like two of the *Batman* movies, but he sometimes leaves the big budgets behind (he shot *Phone Booth* on one set in ten days).

For the voice of his sniper, he calls on Kiefer Sutherland, who also starred in Schumacher's *The Lost Boys* (1987), *Flatliners* (1990), and *A Time to Kill* (1996) and here takes the mostly (but not quite entirely) invisible role as a very useful favor to Schumacher—because if the voice doesn't work, neither does the movie. It does. I especially like the way the caller taunts Stu: "Do you see the tourists with their video cameras, hoping the cops will shoot so they can sell the tape?"

The Pianist ★ ★ ★ ½
R, 148 m., 2002

Adrien Brody (Wladyslaw Szpilman), Daniel Caltagirone (Majorek), Thomas Kretschmann (Captain Wilm Hosenfeld), Frank Finlay (Father), Maureen Lipman (Mother), Emilia Fox (Dorota), Ed Stoppard (Henryk), Julia Rayner (Regina). Directed by Roman Polanski and produced by Robert Benmussa, Polanski, and Alain Sarde. Screenplay by Ronald Harwood, based on the book by Wladyslaw Szpilman.

The title is an understatement, and so is the

film. Roman Polanski's *The Pianist* tells the story of a Polish Jew, a classical musician, who survived the Holocaust through stoicism and good luck. This is not a thriller, and avoids any temptation to crank up suspense or sentiment; it is the pianist's witness to what he saw and what happened to him. That he survived was not a victory when all whom he loved died; Polanski, in talking about his own experiences, has said that the death of his mother in the gas chambers remains so hurtful that only his own death will bring closure.

The film is based on the autobiography of Wladyslaw Szpilman, who was playing Chopin on a Warsaw radio station when the first German bombs fell. Szpilman's family was prosperous and seemingly secure, and his immediate reaction was, "I'm not going anywhere." We watch as the Nazi noose tightens. His family takes heart from reports that England and France have declared war; surely the Nazis will soon be defeated, and life will return to normal.

It does not. The city's Jews are forced to give up their possessions and move to the Warsaw Ghetto, and there is a somber shot of a brick wall being built to enclose it. A Jewish police force is formed to enforce Nazi regulations, and Szpilman is offered a place on it; he refuses, but a good friend, who joins, later saves his life by taking him off a train bound for the death camps. Then the movie tells the long and incredible story of how Szpilman survived the war by hiding in Warsaw, with help from the Polish resistance.

Szpilman is played in the film by Adrien Brody, who is more gaunt and resourceless than in Ken Loach's *Bread and Roses* (2000), where he played a cocky Los Angeles union organizer. We sense that his Szpilman is a man who came early and seriously to music, knows he is good, and has a certain aloofness to life around him. More than once we hear him reassuring others that everything will turn out all right; this faith is based not on information or even optimism, but essentially on his belief that, for anyone who plays the piano as well as he does, it must.

Polanski himself is a Holocaust survivor, saved at one point when his father pushed him through the barbed wire of a camp. He wandered Krakow and Warsaw, a frightened child, cared for by the kindness of strangers. His own survival (and that of his father) are in a sense as random as Szpilman's, which is perhaps why he was attracted to this story. Spielberg tried to enlist Polanski to direct *Schindler's List*, but he refused, perhaps because Schindler's story involved a man who deliberately set out to frustrate the Holocaust, while from personal experience he knew that fate and chance played an inexplicable role in most survivals.

The film was shot in Poland (where he had not worked since his film *Knife in the Water*, in 1962), and also in Prague and in a German studio. On giant sets he re-creates a street overlooked by the apartment where Szpilman is hidden by sympathizers; from his high window the pianist can see the walls of the ghetto and make inferences about the war, based on the comings and goings at the hospital across the street. Szpilman is safe enough here for a time, but hungry, lonely, sick, and afraid, and then a bomb falls and he discovers with terror that the running water no longer works. By now it is near the end of the war and the city lies in ruins; he finds some rooms standing in the rubble, ironically containing a piano that he dare not play.

The closing scenes of the movie involve Szpilman's confrontation with a German captain named Wilm Hosenfeld (Thomas Kretschmann), who finds his hiding place by accident. I will not describe what happens, but will observe that Polanski's direction of this scene, his use of pause and nuance, is masterful.

Some reviews of *The Pianist* have found it too detached, lacking urgency. Perhaps that impassive quality reflects what Polanski wants to say. Almost all of the Jews involved in the Holocaust were killed, so all of the survivor stories misrepresent the actual event by supplying an atypical ending. Often their buried message is that by courage and daring, these heroes saved themselves. Well, yes, some did, but most did not and—here is the crucial point—most could not. In this respect Tim Blake Nelson's *The Grey Zone* (2002) is tougher and more honest, by showing Jews trapped within a Nazi system that removed the possibility of moral choice.

By showing Szpilman as a survivor but not a fighter or a hero—as a man who does all he can to save himself, but would have died without enormous good luck and the kindness of a few non-Jews—Polanski is reflecting, I believe, his own deepest feelings: that he survived, but need not have, and that his mother died, and left a wound that has never healed.

After the war, we learn, Szpilman remained in Warsaw and worked all of his life as a pianist. His autobiography was published soon after the war, but was suppressed by Communist authorities because it did not hew to the party line (some Jews were flawed and a German was kind). Republished in the 1990s, it caught Polanski's attention and resulted in this film, which refuses to turn Szpilman's survival into a triumph and records it primarily as the story of a witness who was there, saw, and remembers.

The Piano Teacher ★ ★ ★ ½
NO MPAA RATING, 130 m., 2002

Isabelle Huppert (Erika Kohut), Benoit Magimel (Walter Klemmer), Annie Girardot (The Mother), Susanne Lothar (Mrs. Schober), Udo Samel (Dr. Blonskij), Anna Sigalevitch (Anna Schober), Cornelia Kondgen (Mme. Blonskij), Thomas Weinhappel (Baritone). Directed by Michael Haneke and produced by Viet Heiduschka. Screenplay by Haneke, based on the novel by Elfriede Jelinek.

There is a self-assurance in Isabelle Huppert that defies all explanation. I interviewed her in 1977, asking her how she got her start in the movies. She knocked on the door of a Paris studio, she said, and announced, "I am here." Was she kidding? I peered at her. I thought not.

In Michael Haneke's *The Piano Teacher*, which won three awards at Cannes 2001 (best actress, actor, and film), she plays a bold woman with a secret wound. She is Erika Kohut, fortyish, a respected instructor at a conservatory of music in Vienna. Demanding, severe, distant, unsmiling, she leads a secret life of self-mutilation. That she sleeps in the same bed with her domineering mother is no doubt a clue—but to what?

Erika is fascinated with the sexual weaknesses and tastes of men. There is a scene where she visits a porn shop in Vienna, creating an uncomfortable tension by her very presence. The male clients are presumably there to indulge their fantasies about women, but faced with a real one, they look away, disturbed or

ashamed. If she were obviously a prostitute they could handle that, but she's apparently there to indulge her own tastes, and that takes all the fun out of it, for them. She returns their furtive glances with a shriveling gaze.

She has a handsome young student named Walter (Benoit Magimel). She notices him in a particular way. They have a clash of wills. He makes it clear he is interested in her. Not long after, in one of the school's rest rooms, they have a sexual encounter—all the more electrifying because while she shocks him with her brazen behavior, she refuses to actually have sex with him. She wants the upper hand.

What games does she want to play? A detailed and subtle plan of revenge against her mother is involved, and Walter, who is not really into sadomasochism, allows himself to be enlisted out of curiosity, or perhaps because he hopes she will yield to him at the end of the scenario. Does it work out that way? Some audience members will dislike the ending, but with a film like this any conventional ending would be a cop-out.

Most sexual relationships in the movies have a limited number of possible outcomes, but this one is a mystery. Another mystery is, what's wrong with Erika? She is not simply an adventuress, a sexual experimenter, a risk taker. Some buried pathology is at work. Walter's idle thoughts about an experienced older woman have turned into nightmares about experiences he doesn't even want to know about.

Huppert often plays repressed, closed-off, sexually alert women. At forty-seven, she looks curiously as she did at twenty-two; she is thin, with fine, freckled skin that does not seem to weather, and seems destined to be one of those women who was never really young and then never really ages. Many of her roles involve women it is not safe to scorn. Magimel won his best actor award for standing up to her force. He doesn't play the standard movie character we'd expect in this role (the immature twentysomething boy who flowers under the tutelage of an older woman). Instead, he's a capable, confident young man who thinks he has met hidden wildness and then finds it is madness.

The movie seems even more highly charged because it is wrapped in an elegant package. These are smart people. They talk about music as if they understand it, they duel with their minds as well as their bodies, and Haneke photographs them in two kinds of spaces: Sometimes they're in elegant, formal conservatory settings, and at other times in frankly vulgar places where quick release can be snatched from strangers. There is an old saying: Be careful what you ask for, because you might get it. *The Piano Teacher* has a more ominous lesson: Be especially careful with someone who has asked for you.

Pieces of April ★ ★ ★
PG-13, 81 m., 2003

Katie Holmes (April Burns), Patricia Clarkson (Joy Burns), Oliver Platt (Jim Burns), Derek Luke (Bobby), Alison Pill (Beth Burns), Alice Drummond (Grandma Dottie), John Gallagher Jr. (Timmy Burns), Sean Hayes (Wayne). Directed by Peter Hedges and produced by Alexia Alexanian, John S. Lyons, and Gary Winick. Screenplay by Hedges.

Thanksgiving is not a conventional religious or political holiday but consists simply of families gathering to love one another and express gratitude. That's the tricky part. There are no theologies to fall back on. It has inspired a uniquely North American group of films. Most of the families in them are troubled, but there is usually a reconciliation, comforting to everyone except the turkey.

The best Thanksgiving film is Woody Allen's *Hannah and Her Sisters,* and the most entertaining are *Planes, Trains and Automobiles* and *What's Cooking?* The most depressing is *The Ice Storm,* and the best single line is by Lou Jacobi in *Avalon:* "You cut the turkey without me?" The spirit of the genre is summed up in *Home for the Holidays* when two family members are fighting on the lawn while the father hoses them down. Seeing the neighbors gawking across the street, the father snarls, "Go back to your own goddamn holidays!"

Peter Hedges's *Pieces of April* ends prematurely and has a side plot that's a distraction and a cheat, but it contains much good humor and works anyway. It consists of two and a half parallel stories. Story one: The Burns family is driving from the suburbs to New York to have Thanksgiving dinner with a troublesome daughter. Story two: The daughter, who has never cooked a Thanksgiving dinner before, is trying to cope despite a broken oven. Story two and a half: Her boyfriend disappears on a mission that is unnecessary, distracting, and misleading.

Katie Holmes plays April Burns, the tattooed daughter who has been the family's despair. Derek Luke is her boyfriend, a sweet guy whose subplot hints he's up to no good, but that's just a cheap tease. Driving into the city are Jim Burns (Oliver Platt), wife Joy (Patricia Clarkson), daughter Beth (Alison Pill), son Timmy (John Gallagher Jr.), and Grandma Dottie (Alice Drummond), who is in that stage of movie-induced Alzheimer's that allows her to provide perfectly timed zingers when necessary.

The movie belongs to April and her mother. Joy is dying of breast cancer and this may be her final Thanksgiving, but she uses her mortality as a springboard for brave humor; at one point, she asks for silence to reflect on an approaching crisis. "We all have to give a lot of thought . . ." she says, and they wait for a declaration about her impending death, "to how we are going to hide the food we don't eat."

In April's apartment, all is chaos. She's gone through a punk/Goth rebellion, but a yearning for family ritual runs deep, and her new boyfriend has helped her believe that she has a home she can invite her family to. The turkey is the problem. April's oven is broken, and that sends her on a quest through her building for someone with an oven she can borrow. Most of the neighbors are suspicious or hostile, but there's a Chinese family that illustrates the same message as *What's Cooking?:* Thanksgiving is a reminder that all Americans, even Native Americans, are immigrants to this continent.

There's lots of humor in the car with the dysfunctional Burnses. Beth is outraged that they're visiting her sister; April was the apple of the family eye before she went wrong, and Beth feels threatened that she seems about to go right again. Young Timmy is a pothead whose supply of grass provides comfort to his dying mom, who after a few inhales likes the rapper on the radio. Jim, the dad, tries to put down rebellion and see the bright side: "This new guy, Bobby, sounds very promising. Apparently he reminds her of me." A measure of the family's goofiness comes when they stop to conduct a burial service for an animal they've run over.

Their eulogy: "We're sorry we didn't know you. We hope it was quick."

The wild card is Bobby, the boyfriend, and here Hedges, the writer-director, halfheartedly tries to do something that doesn't work and is a little offensive. Bobby is middle-class, kind, soft-spoken, and a good influence on April, but the screenplay sends him out of the apartment on an obscure mission and hints that it may involve something illegal or dangerous; his behavior and deliberately misleading dialogue plays on clichés about young black men.

And consider the scene where he first encounters April's family. He's bleeding and looks dangerous and they think they're under attack. Bobby's behavior indicates an undigested idea of who the character is and how it would be funny to portray him. It's not mean-spirited so much as half-assed; Hedges has a confused idea that it would be funny to play on negative associations about young black men, to make it a joke when we find out how nice Bobby is. Not funny.

The movie ends rather abruptly, as if it ran out of money. Maybe it did; it was shot on digital for $200,000 in three weeks (and looks remarkably good given those constraints). The closing montage of photographs looks uncannily like a way to represent a scene Hedges didn't have time to shoot (the eighty-one-minute running time is another hint). Despite its flaws, *Pieces of April* has a lot of joy and quirkiness; it's well intentioned in its screwy way, with flashes of human insight, and actors who can take a moment and make it glow. You forgive the lapses. You have the feeling that Hedges sees the same stuff that bothers you and it makes him squirm, too; a movie made this close to the line has no room for second thoughts.

Hedges is a novelist who wrote the screen adaptation for his own wonderful *What's Eating Gilbert Grape* in 1993, and adapted Nick Hornby's *About a Boy* (2002) for the screen, winning an Oscar nomination in the process. He has a feeling for his characters and tries to find humor in true observation. *Pieces of April* was a success at Sundance 2003, where Patricia Clarkson was honored for her acting. The movie is an enjoyable calling card that will set the stage, I suspect, for a new Hedges movie made with more resources and under less time pressure, and that is a movie I am looking forward to seeing.

Pirates of the Caribbean: The Curse of the Black Pearl ★ ★ ★
PG-13, 134 m., 2003

Johnny Depp (Captain Jack Sparrow), Geoffrey Rush (Captain Barbossa), Orlando Bloom (Will Turner), Keira Knightley (Elizabeth Swann), Jack Davenport (Commodore Norrington), Jonathan Pryce (Governor Weatherby Swann). Directed by Gore Verbinski and produced by Jerry Bruckheimer. Screenplay by Ted Elliott and Terry Rossio.

There's a nice little 90-minute B movie trapped inside the 134 minutes of *Pirates of the Caribbean: The Curse of the Black Pearl,* a movie that charms the audience and then outstays its welcome. Although the ending leaves open the possibility of a sequel, the movie feels like it already includes the sequel; maybe that explains the double-barreled title. It's a good thing that Geoffrey Rush and Johnny Depp are on hand to jack up the acting department. Their characters, two world-class goofballs, keep us interested even during entirely pointless swordfights.

Pointless? See if you can follow me here. Captain Jack Sparrow (Depp) has a deep hatred for Captain Barbossa (Rush), who led a mutiny aboard Sparrow's pirate ship, the *Black Pearl,* and left Captain Jack stranded on a deserted island. Barbossa and his crew then ran afoul of an ancient curse that turned them into the Undead. By day they look like normal if dissolute humans, but by the light of the moon they're revealed as skeletal cadavers.

Now here's the important part: Because they're already dead, they cannot be killed. Excuse me for supplying logic where it is manifestly not wanted, but doesn't that mean there's no point in fighting them? There's a violent battle at one point between the *Black Pearl* crew and sailors of the Royal Navy, and unless I am mistaken the sailors would all eventually have to be dead, because the skeletons could just keep on fighting forever until they won. Yes?

The only reason I bring this up is that the battle scenes actually feel as if they go on forever. It's fun at first to see a pirate swordfight, but eventually it gets to the point where the sword clashing, yardarm swinging, and timber shivering get repetitious. I also lost count of how many times Jack Sparrow is the helpless captive of both the British and the pirates, and escapes from the chains/brig/noose/island.

And yet the movie made me grin at times and savor the daffy plot and enjoy the way Depp and Rush fearlessly provide performances that seem nourished by deep wells of nuttiness. Depp in particular seems to be channeling a drunken drag queen, with his eyeliner and the way he minces ashore and slurs his dialogue ever so insouciantly. Don't mistake me: This is not a criticism, but admiration for his work. It can be said that his performance is original in its every atom. There has never been a pirate, or for that matter a human being, like this in any other movie. There's some talk about how he got too much sun while he was stranded on that island, but his behavior shows a lifetime of rehearsal. He is a peacock in full display.

Consider how boring it would have been if Depp had played the role straight, as an Errol Flynn or Douglas Fairbanks (Sr. or Jr.) might have. To take this material seriously would make it unbearable. Captain Sparrow's behavior is so rococo that other members of the cast actually comment on it. And yet because it is consistent and because you can never catch Depp making fun of the character, it rises to a kind of cockamamy sincerity.

Geoffrey Rush is relatively subdued—but only by contrast. His Barbossa, whose teeth alone would intimidate a congregation of dentists, brings gnashing to an art form. Only the film's PG-13 rating prevents him from doing unthinkable things to the heroine, Elizabeth Swann (Keira Knightley), whose blood, it is thought, can free the captain and his crew from the curse of the *Black Pearl*. Elizabeth is the daughter of the governor (Jonathan Pryce) of Port Royal, a British base in the Caribbean, and seems destined to marry Commodore Norrington (Jack Davenport), a fate that we intuit would lead to a lifetime of conversations about his constipation.

She truly loves the handsome young swordsmith Will Turner (Orlando Bloom), whom she met when they were both children, after spotting him adrift on a raft with a golden pirate medallion around his neck, which turns out to hold the key to the curse. Jack Sparrow takes a fatherly interest in young Turner, especially when he discovers who his father was . . . and that is quite enough of the plot.

Orlando Bloom is well cast in a severely limited role, as the heroic straight arrow. He has the classic profile of a silent film star. Keira Knightley you will recall as the best friend of the heroine in *Bend It Like Beckham,* where she had a sparkle altogether lacking here. Truth be told, she doesn't generate enough fire to explain why these swashbucklers would risk their lives for her, and in close-up seems composed when she should smolder. Parminder K. Nagra, the star of *Beckham,* might have been a more spirited choice here.

The movie is based on the theme park ride at Disney World, which I have taken many times. It is also inspired (as the ride no doubt was) by the rich tradition of pirate movies and excels in such departments as buried treasure, pirates' caves, pet parrots, and walking the plank, although there is a shortage of eye patches and hooks. The author Dave Eggers has opened a pirates' store, complete with planks measured and made to order, and the movie plays like his daydreams. ☞

Poolhall Junkies ★ ★ ★
R, 94 m., 2003

Gregory "Mars" Callahan (Johnny Doyle), Chazz Palminteri (Joe), Rick Schroder (Brad), Rod Steiger (Nick), Michael Rosenbaum (Danny Doyle), Alison Eastwood (Tara), Christopher Walken (Mike). Directed by Gregory "Mars" Callahan and produced by Karen Beninati, Vincent Newman, and Tucker Tooley. Screenplay by Chris Corso and Callahan.

One of the things I like best about *Poolhall Junkies* is its lack of grim desperation. Its characters know that pool is a game, and do not lead lives in which every moment is a headbutt with fate. Yes, there are fights, weapons are drawn, and old scores are settled, but the hero's most important bet is made to help his girl get a job she wants, the two archrivals are clearly destined to become friends, and Christopher Walken gets to deliver one of his famous monologues. He starts out, "Have you ever watched one of those animal channels?" and we are grinning already.

This is a young man's film, humming with the fun of making it. It was directed and cowritten by Gregory "Mars" Callahan, who also plays the leading role, Johnny Doyle, who was so good when he was a kid that "the cue was part of his arm and the balls had eyes." He never wanted to grow up to be a pool hustler. He wanted to join the pro tour. He's a good player, but he's not one of those nuts whose eyeballs spin like pinwheels when he's lining up a shot.

Johnny was more or less abandoned by his parents, and adopted by Joe (Chazz Palminteri), a manager of young pool talent. Joe likes taking his cut from the kid's earnings, and Johnny grows up before he discovers that Joe destroyed his invitation to join the pros. That leads to a scene in which Joe breaks the kid's hand, but not his thumb, and then seeks more revenge by taking a new protégé named Brad (Rick Schroder) under his management. Joe also involves Johnny's kid brother Danny (Michael Rosenbaum) in big trouble.

Johnny has a girlfriend named Tara (Alison Eastwood), who's in law school and doesn't approve of pool hustling, so Johnny gets a job as a construction carpenter, but the nails do not have eyes. Johnny and Tara are invited to a party at the home of a rich lawyer, where they meet her uncle Mike (Walken), one of the few actors in movie history who always draws a quiet rustle of pleasure from the audience the first time he appears on the screen.

And so on. The plot you are already generally familiar with. There will be high-stakes games of pool with lives and fortunes, etc., hanging in the balance. That goes with the territory. *Poolhall Junkies* is a pleasure not because it rivets us with unbearable poolhall suspense, but because it finds a voluptuous enjoyment in the act of moviemaking. You get the sense that "Mars" Callahan, whom I have never met, woke during the night to hug himself that he was getting to make this movie.

Poolhall Junkies has big moments of inspiration, like the Walken speech and a couple of other monologues. It has movie-fan moments, as when Rod Steiger, as the manager of a poolhall, gets to stick out his lower jaw and lay it on the line (this was Steiger's final role). It has

Callahan as a serious kid with chiseled dark Irish features, who is cool like McQueen was cool—no big thing, just born that way.

And then it has, well, this corny stuff that Callahan kept in the screenplay because he's no doubt the kind of guy who doesn't like to walk into a bar without a joke to tell. There's a lawyer joke ("What do you call it when you have 10,000 lawyers buried up to their necks in the sand?"). And the oldest trick bet in the book ("I'll bet you I can tell you where you got your shoes"). And a barroom hustle recycled directly out of Steve Buscemi's *Trees Lounge* ("I'll bet I can drink both of these pints faster than you can drink both of those shots"). I mean, come on.

These little hustles set up bigger ones that are also the oldest gags in the book, but the movie delivers on them and has fun while it's doing it. Callahan plays the character of Johnny Doyle not to convince you he's the meanest mother in the city, but simply to demonstrate that it would not be wise to bet large sums of money against him in the game of pool. There is an innocence at work here that reminds me of young Sylvester Stallone, who gave Rocky Balboa pet turtles named Cuff and Link.

Is this a great movie? Not at all. Is it more or less consistently entertaining? Yes. Do Walken and Palminteri do things casually that most actors could not do at all? Yes. Did I feel afterward as if I had been dragged through the blood and grime of the mean streets? No, but I felt like I had a good time at the movies.

Possession ★ ★ ★ ½
PG-13, 102 m., 2002

Gwyneth Paltrow (Maud Bailey), Aaron Eckhart (Roland Michell), Jeremy Northam (Randolph Henry Ash), Jennifer Ehle (Christabel LaMotte), Lena Headey (Blanche Glover), Trevor Eve (Professor Morton Cropper), Toby Stephens (Fergus Wolfe), Anna Massey (Lady Bailey), Holly Aird (Ellen), Felicity Brangan (Lucy). Directed by Neil LaBute and produced by Barry Levinson and Paula Weinstein. Screenplay by David Henry Hwang, Laura Jones, and LaBute, based on the novel by A. S. Byatt.

A visiting American scholar is paging through an old volume at the British Museum when he comes upon a letter stuffed between the pages—a love letter, it would appear, from Queen Victoria's poet laureate, addressed to a woman not his wife. The poet has been held up for more than a century as a model of marital fidelity. The letter is dynamite. The scholar slips the letter out of the book and into his portfolio, and is soon displaying it, with all the pride and uncertainty of a new father, to a British woman who knows (or thought she knew) everything about the poet.

The American, named Roland Michell (Aaron Eckhart), is professionally ambitious but has a block against personal intimacy. The British expert, named Maud Bailey (Gwyneth Paltrow), is suspicious of love, suspicious of men, suspicious of theories that overturn a century of knowledge about her specialty. Together, warily, edgily, they begin to track down the possibility that the happily married Randolph Henry Ash did indeed have an affair with the nineteenth-century feminist and lesbian Christabel LaMotte. Two modern people with high walls of privacy are therefore investigating two Victorians who in theory never even met.

This setup from A. S. Byatt's 1990 Booker Award–winning novel would seem like the last premise in the world to attract the director Neil LaBute, whose In the Company of Men and Your Friends and Neighbors were about hard-edged modern sexual warfare. But look again at the romantic fantasies in his overlooked Nurse Betty (2000) about a housewife in love with a soap opera character and a killer in love with a photograph of the housewife, and you will see the same premise: Love, fueled by imagination, tries to leap impossible divides.

The film, written by David Henry Hwang, Laura Jones, and LaBute, uses a flashback structure to move between the current investigation and the long-ago relationship. Jeremy Northam plays Ash, an upright public figure, and Jennifer Ehle is Christabel, a pre-Raphaelite beauty who lives with the darkly sensuous Blanche Glover (Lena Headey). The nature of their relationship is one of the incidental fascinations of the movie: At a time before lesbianism was widely acknowledged, female couples were commonly accepted and the possibility of a sexual connection didn't necessarily occur. Blanche is the dominant and possessive one, and Christabel is

perhaps not even essentially lesbian, but simply besotted with friendship. When she and Ash make contact, it is Blanche, not Ash's unbending wife, who is the angered spouse.

In the way it moves between two couples in two periods, Possession is like Karel Reisz's The French Lieutenant's Woman (1981). That film, with a screenplay by Harold Pinter, added a modern couple that didn't exist in the John Fowles novel, and had both couples played by Meryl Streep and Jeremy Irons. The notion of two romances on parallel trajectories is common to both films, and intriguing because there seem to be insurmountable barriers in both periods.

Ash and Christabel are separated by Victorian morality, his marriage, and her relationship. The moderns, Maud and Roland, seem opposed to any idea of romance; she has her own agenda, and he is reticent to a fault. "You have nothing to fear from me," he tells her early on, because he avoids relationships. Later, when they find themselves tentatively in each other's arms, he pulls back: "We shouldn't be doing this; it's dangerous."

This might be convincing if Roland and Maud looked like our conventional idea of literary scholars: Mike White, perhaps, paired with Lili Taylor. That they are both so exceptionally attractive is distracting; Paltrow is able to project a certain ethereal bookishness, but a contemporary man with Eckhart's pumped-up physique and adamant indifference to Paltrow would be read by many observers as gay. That he is not—that his reticence is a quirk rather than a choice—is a screenplay glitch we have to forgive.

We do, because the movie is not a serious examination of scholarship or poetry, but a brainy romance. In a world where most movie romances consist of hormonal triggers and plumbing procedures, it's sexy to observe two couples who think and debate their connections, who quote poetry to one another, who consciously try to enhance their relationships by seeking metaphors and symbols they can attach to. Romance defined by the body will decay with the flesh, but romance conceived as a grand idea—ah, now that can still fascinate people a century later.

LaBute is a director who loves the spoken word. No surprise that between movies he writes and directs plays. I suspect he would be incapable of making a movie about people who had nothing interesting to say to one another. What he finds sexy is not the simple physical fact of two people, but the scenario they write around themselves; look at the way the deaf woman in *In the Company of Men* so completely defeats both men by discovering their ideas of themselves and turning those ideas against them. By the end of the movie, with the egos of both men in shards at her feet, the woman seems more desirable than we could have imagined possible.

What happens in *Possession* is not the same, but it is similar enough to explain LaBute's interest in the story. He likes people who think themselves into and out of love, and finds the truly passionate (like Blanche) to be the most dangerous. He likes romances that exist out of sight, denied, speculated about, suspected, fought against. Any two people can fall into each other's arms and find that they enjoy the feeling. But to fall into someone else's mind — now that can be dangerous.

The Prince & Me ★ ★ ½

PG, 111 m., 2004

Julia Stiles (Paige Morgan), Luke Mably (Prince Edvard), Ben Miller (Soren), James Fox (King Haraald), Miranda Richardson (Queen Rosalind), Eliza Bennett (Princess Anabella), Alberta Watson (Amy Morgan), John Bourgeouis (Ben Morgan). Directed by Martha Coolidge and produced by Mark Amin. Screenplay by Jack Amiel, Michael Begler, and Katherine Fugate.

The Prince & Me recycles a story so old that it must satisfy some basic yearning in the human psyche—or at least that portion of the psyche installed in teenage girls. It is, as you have probably guessed, about a romance between a prince and a commoner—in this case, between the future king of Denmark and a Wisconsin farm girl. He enrolls in a Wisconsin university, they fall into hate and then into love, but when she follows him back to Denmark she has to ask herself if she really wants to be the future queen.

If the story felt more than usually familiar, maybe it's because I saw *Win a Date with Tad*

Hamilton! In that version, a small-town girl won a date with a big Hollywood star, flew to Los Angeles, and in her simplicity and sincerity inspired the star to fall in love. But was she really cut out to be a movie star's wife? In both cases, the movies start by establishing the men as targets of paparazzi because of their steamy romantic lives; in both cases, the men are won over by the freshness of a woman unlike any they have ever dated.

The Prince & Me is an efficient, sweet, sometimes charming PG-rated version of the story, ideal for girls of a certain age but perhaps not for everybody else. It stars Julia Stiles as Paige Morgan, a serious, focused student of biochemistry, who was raised on an organic dairy farm and is famous as "the last unengaged girl in town." Stiles is gifted at conveying intelligence, which is a mixed blessing here; any smarter, and she'd realize she was in a movie.

Luke Mably plays Prince Edvard of Denmark, a.k.a. "Eddie," who flies to Wisconsin to escape the paparazzi and also because he saw a video in which Wisconsin college girls flash their boobs for the camera, and he assumes this is typical behavior in Wisconsin. This is such a stupid motivation for the prince's trip that it throws the character a little out of balance; it takes him several scenes in Wisconsin to reestablish himself as a person of normal intelligence.

Eddie arrives incognito with his valet Soren (Ben Miller) in tow, but because his parents have cut off his allowance he's short on funds and has to take a job in the campus cafeteria where Paige works. They clash almost at once, and find a temporary truce when she can help him with chemistry and he can help her with Shakespeare (he knows a lot about princes of Denmark). This stretch of the film is fun because it's based on tension; not so much fun is the formulaic part where she discovers his true identity, is angry at the deception, he returns to his father's sickbed, she follows him to Denmark, he proposes marriage, and so forth.

The movie does struggle to make something interesting of the royal family. The king (Edward Fox) and queen (Miranda Richardson) are played by fine actors who bring dimension and conviction to their roles; they are not simply marching through clichés. The queen's initial disapproval of Paige and her gradual acceptance are well handled. But the plot jerks Paige and Eddie back and forth romantically so many times we lose patience with it; we know, because the story is so familiar, that she must accept his proposal, then have second thoughts, then . . . well, you know.

As pure escapism, there are some sublime moments. I like the one where the queen takes Paige into the royal vault to show her the crown jewels, and ask her to pick out something to wear to the coronation ball. As Paige's eyes sweep the glittering shelves, there is a certain intake of breath among some of the women in the audience, and I was reminded of a similar moment in *The Greek Tycoon* when Aristotle Onassis outlines their marriage contract to Jackie Kennedy, and adds, "plus a million dollars a month walking-around money."

So there's good stuff here, and the stars are likable, but the director, Martha Coolidge, throws so many logical roadblocks in our path that we keep getting distracted from the story. When Paige arrives unannounced in Denmark and stands in the crowd at a royal parade, Eddie sees her and sweeps her up on his horse as the Danes shout, "Paige! It's Paige!" That's because they know her from photos the paparazzi took in Wisconsin. Okay, but how about later, when Eddie is giving his first speech as king, and Paige walks through the middle of the crowd and *no one* notices her, just because at that point the plot doesn't want them to? Despite the fact that she's now infinitely more famous in Denmark as the girl who accepted Eddie's proposal and then rejected it?

Quibble, quibble. The movie's target audience won't care. Others will. *The Prince & Me* has the materials to be a heartwarming mass-market love story, but it doesn't assemble them convincingly. *Win a Date with Tad Hamilton!* is less obviously blessed, but works better. Strange, how the girl's parents in both movies seem to have been assembled from the same kit.

Pumpkin ★ ★ ★ ½
R, 113 m., 2002

Christina Ricci (Carolyn McDuffy), Hank Harris (Pumpkin Romanoff), Brenda Blethyn (Judy Romanoff), Dominique Swain (Jeanine Kryszinsky), Marisa Coughlan (Julie Thurber), Sam Ball (Kent Woodlands), Harry J. Lennix (Robert Meary), Michelle Krusiec (Anne Chung). Directed by Anthony Abrams and Adam Larson Broder and produced by Karen Barber, Albert Berger, Christina Ricci, Andrea Sperling, and Ron Yerxa. Screenplay by Broder.

Pumpkin defies description. Maybe it doesn't need a category—it needs a diagnosis. Relentlessly, and sometimes brilliantly, it forces us to decide what we really think, how permissive our taste really is, how far a black comedy can go before it goes too far. It's like a teenage sex comedy crossed with the darkest corners of underground comics. We laugh in three ways: with humor, with recognition, and with disbelief.

The film stars Christina Ricci as Carolyn McDuffy, the peppiest member of a sorority house that dreams of being named Sorority of the Year. To get extra points, the house arranges to coach "special people"—handicapped and retarded athletes—and all of the girls are lined up eagerly when the buses arrive with their tutorial victims. One of them is Pumpkin Romanoff (Hank Harris), who seems to be both mentally and physically challenged, although the movie refuses to permit a verdict about his intelligence level. At first Carolyn is too awkward and embarrassed to deal with Pumpkin—everything she says seems to be offensive—but then she finds she can't get him out of her mind. Pumpkin, of course, has fallen instantly in love with her.

Carolyn has a boyfriend, a BMOC and tennis champion named Kent Woodlands (Sam Ball), who in his own way is also handicapped: He's too handsome, with the improbable good looks of a silent screen idol. But she begins to spend more time with Pumpkin, who at first seems ill-equipped for his chosen sport of discus throwing (he can't stand or throw), but works out tirelessly in his backyard to get in shape.

Pumpkin's mother, Judy (Brenda Blethyn), is an alcoholic who coddles her son and then puts him down. She sees Carolyn as a threat, and when she finds the two in bed together she calls her a slut and a pedophile. This raises an interesting point, since Pumpkin is apparently about fifteen or sixteen, but sex between older women and younger men seems permitted in

525

the movies even though it's taboo the other way around.

Carolyn eventually begins to see the hypocrisy of the Greek system, the shallowness of Kent, and the truly special qualities of Pumpkin. Yes, and there is even a scene where Pumpkin gets an ovation for a discus throw. But this is not one of those heartwarming stories about overcoming obstacles. *Pumpkin* creates inspirational moments only to undermine them, and doubts all good motives. Consider the way the sororities compete for the black and Filipino girls who are going through rush, because they want to add "diversity," and besides, the Filipino "looks almost white." Consider the way Carolyn's Asian sorority sister, Anne Chung (Michelle Krusiec), is never referred to without the word "even" in front of her name: "You can go to the prom with any of the sisters," house president Julie Thurber (Marisa Coughlan) tells Kent. "Even Anne Chung."

The movie takes side shots at other campus targets. Carolyn takes a poetry workshop taught by a black professor (Harry J. Lennix), who announces poetry cannot be taught and that he hates to grade papers, but that, not to worry, "you'll get your stupid credit." Carolyn composes for this class an "Ode to Pasadena" that must be heard to be believed. When she decides to take a stand and leave school, she announces she'll go to "community college," only to discover she has too many credits and has to settle for Long Beach Tech. In her rooming house at Long Beach, the students eat beans, not lamb chops, her favorite at the sorority house.

The climax of the movie involves a fight between Pumpkin and Kent that goes beyond the usual boundaries of commercial comedies, and a car crash that is a deliberate exercise in mocking special effects and stunt explosions. Everything in the movie mocks itself. Even the last shot calls Carolyn's final sincerity into question. But I can say this: *Pumpkin* is alive, and takes chances, and uses the wicked blade of satire in order to show up the complacent political correctness of other movies in its campus genre. It refuses to play it safe. And there is courage in the performances—for example, in the way Sam Ball deals with what happens to his character. Or in the way Christina Ricci sails fearlessly into the risky

material. *Pumpkin* may make you mad, but at least you're not angry because it wasn't trying.

Punch-Drunk Love ★ ★ ★ ½
R, 89 m., 2002

Adam Sandler (Barry Egan), Emily Watson (Lena Leonard), Philip Seymour Hoffman (Dean Trumbell), Luis Guzmán (Lance), Mary Lynn Rajskub (Elizabeth), Ashley Clark (Latisha), Julie Hermelin (Kathleen). Directed by Paul Thomas Anderson and produced by Anderson, Daniel Lupi, and Joanne Sellar. Screenplay by Anderson.

There is a new Adam Sandler on view in *Punch-Drunk Love*—angry, sad, desperate. In voice and mannerisms he is the same childlike, love-starved Adam Sandler we've seen in a series of dim comedies, but this movie, by seeing him in a new light, encourages us to look again at those films. Given a director and a screenplay that see through the Sandler persona, that understand it as the disguise of a suffering outsider, Sandler reveals depths and tones we may have suspected but couldn't bring into focus.

The way to criticize a movie, Godard famously said, is to make another movie. In that sense *Punch-Drunk Love* is film criticism. Paul Thomas Anderson says he loves Sandler's comedies—they cheer him up on lonely Saturday nights—but as the director of *Boogie Nights* and *Magnolia*, he must have been able to sense something missing in them, some unexpressed need. The Sandler characters are almost oppressively nice, like needy puppies, and yet they conceal a masked hostility to society, a passive-aggressive need to go against the flow, a gift for offending others while in the very process of being ingratiating.

In *Punch-Drunk Love*, Sandler plays Barry Egan, an executive in a company with a product line of novelty toiletries. Barry has seven sisters, who are all on his case at every moment, and he desperately wishes they would stop invading his privacy, ordering him around and putting him down. He tries at a family gathering to be congenial and friendly, but we can see the tension in his smiling lips and darting eyes, and suddenly he explodes, kicking out the glass patio doors.

This is a pattern. He presents to the world a face of cheerful blandness, and then erupts in terrifying displays of frustrated violence. He does not even begin to understand himself. He seems always on guard, unsure, obscurely threatened. His outbursts here help to explain the curiously violent passages in his previous film, *Mr. Deeds,* which was a remake of a benign Frank Capra comedy. It's as if Sandler is Hannibal Lecter in a Jerry Lewis body.

Most of Sandler's plots are based on predictable, production-line formulas, and after *Punch-Drunk Love* I may begin seeing them as traps containing a resentful captive. The quirky behavior may be a way of calling out for help. In *Big Daddy,* for example, the broad outlines are familiar, but not the creepy way his character trains his adopted five-year-old to be hostile. At one point, ho, ho, they toss tree branches into the path of middle-aged in-line skaters, causing some nasty falls. The hostility veiled as humor in the typical Sandler comedy is revealed in *Punch-Drunk Love* as—hostility.

The film is exhilarating to watch because Sandler, liberated from the constraints of formula, reveals unexpected depths as an actor. Watching this film, you can imagine him in Dennis Hopper roles. He has darkness, obsession, and power. His world is hedged around with mystery and challenge. Consider an opening scene, when he is at work hours before the others have arrived and sees a harmonium dumped in the street in front of his office. It is at once the most innocent and ominous of objects; he runs from it and then peeks around a corner to see if it is still there.

In the Paul Thomas Anderson universe, people meet through serendipity and need, not because they are fulfilling their plot assignments. Barry meets Lena Leonard (Emily Watson), a sweet executive with intently focused eyes, who asks him to look after her broken-down car and later goes out on a dinner date with him. They like each other right away. During the dinner he gets up from his table, goes to the men's room, and in a blind rage breaks everything he can. "Your hand is bleeding," she gently observes, and after they are thrown out of the restaurant she carries on as if the evening is still normal.

Barry is meanwhile enraged by an ongoing battle he is having with a Utah phone sex company. He called the number and was billed for the call, but he was unable to talk easily with the woman at the other end, or even quite conceive of what she wanted him to do. Then she pulled a scam using his credit card number, and this leads to mutual threats and obscenities over the phone, and to a visit from the porn company's "four blond brothers," who want to intimidate him and extract cash.

Barry is frightened. He knows Lena is going on a business trip to Hawaii. They definitely have chemistry. This would be an ideal time to get off the mainland. He has discovered a loophole in a Healthy Choice promotion that will allow him to earn countless American Airlines frequent-flier miles at very little cost. (This part of the story is based on fact.) It is typical of an Anderson film that Barry, having hit on his mileage scheme, cannot use his miles so quickly, and so simply buys a ticket to Honolulu and meets Lena for a picture-postcard rendezvous on Waikiki Beach. Here and elsewhere, Anderson bathes the screen in romantic colors and fills the sound track with lush orchestrations.

I feel liberated in films where I have absolutely no idea what will happen next. Lena and Barry are odd enough that anything could happen in their relationship. A face-to-face meeting with the Utah porn king (Anderson regular Philip Seymour Hoffman) and another meeting with the four blond brothers are equally unpredictable. And always there is Barry's quick, terrifying anger, a time bomb ticking away beneath every scene.

Punch-Drunk Love is above all a portrait of a personality type. Barry Egan has been damaged, perhaps beyond repair, by what he sees as the depredations of his domineering sisters. It drives him crazy when people nose into his business. He cannot stand to be trifled with. His world is entered by alarming omens and situations that baffle him. The character is vividly seen and the film sympathizes with him in his extremity. Paul Thomas Anderson has referred to *Punch-Drunk Love* as "an art house Adam Sandler film." It may be the key to all of the Adam Sandler films, and may liberate Sandler for a new direction in his work. He can't go on making those moronic comedies forever, can he? Who would have guessed he had such uncharted depths?

The Punisher ★ ★
R, 124 m., 2004

Thomas Jane (Frank Castle [Punisher]), John Travolta (Howard Saint), Will Patton (Quentin Glass), Laura Harring (Livia Saint), Rebecca Romijn-Stamos (Joan), Samantha Mathis (Maria Castle), John Pinette (Mr. Bumpo), Ben Foster (Spacker Dave), Marcus Johns (Will Castle), Roy Scheider (Mr. Castle). Directed by Jonathan Hensleigh and produced by Avi Arad and Gale Anne Hurd. Screenplay by Michael France and Hensleigh, based on the comic book by Gerry Conway, Garth Ennis, Johnny Romita, and Michael Tolkin.

The Punisher is a long, dark slog through grim revenge. Unlike most movies based on comic book heroes, it doesn't contain the glimmer of a smile, and its hero is a depressed alcoholic—as well he might be, since his entire family, including wife, child, father, and even distant cousins have been massacred before his eyes. As he seeks vengeance, he makes the Charles Bronson character in *Death Wish* look relatively cheerful and well adjusted.

I wonder if the filmmakers understand quite how downbeat and dark their movie is? It opens with an FBI sting that leads to the death of a mobster's son. The operation, we learn, was the last assignment before retirement for agent Frank Castle (Thomas Jane). The criminal, a wealthy, high-profile money launderer named Mr. Saint (John Travolta), orders Castle's death, and then his wife, Livia (Laura Harring), adds, "His family. His whole family."

This sets up a sequence from which the movie hardly recovers. Castle has a romantic walk on the beach with his wife, Maria (Samantha Mathis), a hug with his child, and sentimental moments as his father (Roy Scheider) speaks at a family reunion. Then Saint's gunmen mow down the entire family in a series of gruesome vignettes, not neglecting to linger on the death of wife and child after their pitiful attempt to flee.

Castle kills a few of the attackers, but is cornered on a pier, shot repeatedly, doused with gasoline, blown up, and lands in the water. This establishes a pattern for the movie: No one is killed only once. (Later in the film, a target is shot, chained to the back of a car and dragged into a car lot where all of the cars explode.) Miraculously, Castle survives and is nursed back to health by one of those useful clichés, the black loner who lives by himself on an island and possesses the wisdom of the ages.

The rest of the movie involves his recovery, his preparations, and his methodical revenge against Mr. Saint and all of his people. Several colorful supporting characters are introduced, especially the three oddballs who live in the shabby rooming house Castle occupies. They are Joan (Rebecca Romijn-Stamos), a sexy but frightened woman with an abusive boyfriend; Mr. Bumpo (John Pinette), a tubby sissy, and Spacker Dave (Ben Foster), who is pierced in ways you don't even want to think about. We have all been indoctrinated in the notion that "we are family!" and these three attempt to include Castle in their circle despite his need to isolate, drink, kill, and brood. There is something a little odd when he's invited over for ice cream and cake.

The movie is relentless in its violence. There is a scene where Spacker Dave is tortured by having his piercings removed with pliers; the scene breaks the fabric of the film and moves into a different and macabre arena. *The Punisher* opened on the same weekend as another movie about a gruesome massacre and an elaborate revenge, *Kill Bill: Vol. 2,* but they are as different as night and day; *Kill Bill* vibrates with humor, irony, over-the-top exaggeration, and the joy of filmmaking. *The Punisher* is so grim and cheerless you wonder if even its hero gets any satisfaction from his accomplishments.

That said, I have to note that the film, directed by Jonathan Hensleigh, is consistently well acted, and has some scenes of real power. That the Punisher is a drear and charmless character does not mean that Thomas Jane doesn't play him well: He goes all the way with the film's dark vision, and is effective in the action scenes. John Travolta, as Mr. Saint, finds a truth you would not think was available in melodrama of this sort; his grief over his son and possessive jealousy over his wife are compelling.

The film doesn't simply set up Saint as a bad guy and a target, but devotes attention to the character, and develops an intriguing relationship between Saint and his right-hand man Quentin Glass (the always effective Will Patton). The Punisher is able to use Saint's jealousy to drive a wedge between the two men, but here's the strange thing: What happens between Saint and Glass is convincing, but what the Punisher does to sabotage their relationship is baffling and ludicrous, involving false fire hydrants and the improbable detail that Saint would allow his wife to go to the movies alone after he knows the Punisher is alive and at war.

Right down the line, the performances are strong. Even the three misfits in the run-down rooming house are given the dimension and screen time to become interesting. The screenplay, by Michael France and Jonathan Hensleigh, based on the Marvel comic, doesn't simply foreground the Punisher and make everyone else into one-dimensional cartoons. There's so much that's well done here that you sense a good movie slipping away. That movie would either be lighter than this one or commit to its seriousness, like *Scarface*. This one loses control of its mood and doesn't know what level of credibility it exists on. At the end, we feel battered down and depressed, emotions we probably don't seek from comic book heroes.

Q

Queen of the Damned ★ ★
R, 101 m., 2002

Stuart Townsend (Lestat de Lioncourt), Aaliyah (Akasha), Marguerite Moreau (Jesse Reeves), Vincent Perez (Marius), Paul McGann (David Talbot), Lena Olin (Maharet), Christian Manon (Mael), Claudia Black (Pandora). Directed by Michael Rymer and produced by Jorge Saralegui. Screenplay by Scott Abbott and Michael Petroni, based on the novels *The Vampire Chronicles* by Anne Rice.

Vampires are always in pose mode, which tends to make vampire movies into comedies. The stark horror of *Nosferatu* has long since dribbled down into overwrought melodrama. The buried message of many scenes is: "Regard me well, for here I am, and I am thus." A lot of the dialogue is declamatory, and many sentences are versions of, "Together, we (will, can, must) (rule, change, destroy) the (world, our victims, the people in this bar)."

Queen of the Damned, based on Anne Rice's endless Vampire Chronicles, happily occupies this mode. It is happy to be goofy. *Interview With the Vampire,* Neil Jordan's glossy 1994 version of the earlier Rice novel, was more ambitious and anchored—even sad. This sequel, also about the vampire Lestat, is filled with characters who seem to have taken Gene Simmons as their role model.

The movie stars Stuart Townsend as Lestat, in the role played last time by Tom Cruise. The world got to be too much for him, Lestat explains, and so he withdrew from it and went to sleep 200 years ago. But then "the world didn't sound like the place I had left—but something different, better." Cut to a montage of musical groups, and Lestat pushes back the stone lid of his crypt and materializes during a rehearsal of a rock band. When they ask who he is, he smiles and casts centuries of tradition to the winds: "I am . . . the Vampire Lestat!"

Soon he's a rock god, the lead singer of a Goth band. Other characters emerge. We meet Jesse (Marguerite Moreau), researcher for a London vampire study institute. She likes to play with danger, and even cruises a vampire bar Lestat told her about. We meet the fey Marius (Vincent Perez), the older vampire who turned Lestat on, or out. And Maharet (Lena Olin), who I think is supposed to be a good vampire, or at least one who wishes the others would follow the rules. Along the way we are given vampire feeding lessons: "You must never take the last drop or it will draw you in and you die."

Most noticeably we meet Queen Akasha, the title character, played by Aaliyah, the singer who was killed in a 2001 air crash. She appears first as a statue in a phantasmagorical Egyptian cryptlike shrine, where Lestat plays his violin so fiercely that parts of her stone body seem to glow back into life. She "drank the world dry when she ruled Egypt," Marius tells Lestat. (Historical footnote: The first movie to make the queen of the Egyptians black also makes her a vampire. Is this progress?) Soon Akasha is alive all over, and has the hots for Lestat, making plans about how, together, they will rule the world.

Since this will be her only starring movie role, it's sad that her character has such a narrow emotional range. The Lestat-Akasha romance suffers by being conducted in declarative mode, with Akasha addressing her lover with the intimacy Queen Victoria would have lavished on her footman. Lestat digs her, though, because when he drinks her blood it makes him wild. Nothing good can come of this.

A more intriguing relationship is between Lestat and Marius, who seems to have a thing for him. Marius reappears in Lestat's life after so many centuries that Lestat comments on his outdated apparel. "How did you manage to slip through the fifties in red velvet?" he asks, forgetting that he slept through the 1950s himself and has probably not made much of a study of the decade's clothing styles. He welcomes Marius to Los Angeles and shows him the world from a perch on a painter's scaffold that hangs directly in front of Lestat's leather-clad crotch on a giant Sunset Boulevard outdoor advertisement. We get the feeling Marius would enjoy the view more if he turned around.

There is a showdown. Queen Akasha's subjects, fellow vampires, revolt against her tyrannical rule when she reveals her plans to rule, etc., the world, etc., together, etc., with Lestat.

The others hope to drink all of her blood, so that even if they die, she dies too. But Akasha is not without her defenses. All she has to do is point at enemies and they burst into flame, curl up into charred shadows of themselves, and float upward just like the wrapper from an Amaretti di Saronno cookie.

The movie doesn't reach the level of camp goofiness attained by films like *The Mummy Returns* and *Lara Croft: Tomb Raider*, perhaps because the filmmakers labor under the impression that Anne Rice's works must be treated respectfully. The key to a movie like this is to ask yourself, if these characters were not vampires, what would be interesting about them? The answer is, together they couldn't even rule the people in this bar.

The Quiet American ★ ★ ★
R, 118 m., 2003

Michael Caine (Thomas Fowler), Brendan Fraser (Alden Pyle), Do Thi Hai Yen (Phuong), Rade Serbedzija (Inspector Vigot), Tzi Ma (Hinh), Robert Stanton (Joe Tunney), Holmes Osborne (Bill Granger), Quang Hai (The General), Ferdinand Hoang (Mr. Muoi). Directed by Phillip Noyce and produced by Staffan Ahrenberg and William Horberg. Screenplay by Christopher Hampton and Robert Schenkkan, based on the novel by Graham Greene.

The Englishman is sad and lonely. He suffers from the indignity of growing too old for romance while not yet free of yearning. He is in love for one last time. He doesn't even fully understand it is love until he is about to lose it. He is a newspaper correspondent in Saigon, and she is a dance-hall girl thirty or forty years younger. She loves him because he pays her to. This arrangement suits them both. He tells himself he is "helping" her. Well, he is, and she is helping him.

His name is Fowler, and he is played by Michael Caine in a performance that seems to descend perfectly formed. There is no artifice in it, no unneeded energy, no tricks, no effort. It is there. Her name is Phuong (Do Thi Hai Yen), and like all beautiful women who reveal little of their true feelings, she makes it possible for him to project his own upon her. He loves her for what he can tell himself about her.

Between them steps Alden Pyle (Brendan Fraser), the quiet young American who has come to Vietnam, he believes, to save it. Eventually he also believes he will save Phuong. Young men, like old ones, find it easy to believe hired love is real, and so believe a girl like Phuong would prefer a young man to an old one, when all youth represents is more work.

Graham Greene's novel *The Quiet American* (1955) told the story of this triangle against the background of America's adventure in Vietnam in the early 1950s—when, he shows us, the CIA used pleasant, presentable agents like Pyle to pose as "aid workers" while arranging terrorist acts that would justify our intervention there.

The novel inspired a 1958 Hollywood version in which the director Joseph Mankiewicz turned the story on its head, making Fowler the bad guy and Pyle the hero. Did the CIA have a hand in funding this film? Stranger things have happened: The animated version of *Animal Farm* (1954) was paid for by a CIA front, and twisted Orwell's fable about totalitarianism both East and West into a simplistic anti-Communist cartoon.

Now comes another version of *The Quiet American*, this one directed by the Australian Phillip Noyce and truer to the Greene novel. It is a film with a political point of view, but often its characters lose sight of that in their fascination with each other and with the girl. A question every viewer will have to answer at the end is whether a final death is the result of moral conviction or romantic compulsion.

The film is narrated by Caine's character in that conversational voice weary with wisdom; we are reminded of the tired cynicism of the opening narration in the great film of Greene's *The Third Man*. Pyle has "a face with no history, no problems," Fowler tells us; his own face is a map of both. "I'm just a reporter," he says. "I offer no point of view, I take no action, I don't get involved." Indeed, he has scarcely filed a story in the past year for his paper, the *Times* of London; he is too absorbed in Phuong and opium.

The irony is that Pyle, whom he actually likes at first, jars him into action and involvement. What he finally cannot abide is the younger man's cheerful certainty that he is absolutely right: "Saving the country and saving a woman would be the same thing to a man like that."

As luck would have it, *The Quiet American* was planned for release in the autumn of 2001. It was shelved after 9/11, when Miramax president Harvey Weinstein decided, no doubt correctly, that the national mood was not ripe for a film pointing out that the United States is guilty of terrorist acts of its own. Caine appealed to Weinstein, who a year later allowed the film to be shown at the Toronto Film Festival, where it was well received by the public and critics.

It would be unfortunate if people went to the movie, or stayed away, because of its political beliefs. There is no longer much controversy about the CIA's hand in stirring the Vietnam pot, and the movie is not an exposé but another of Greene's stories about a worn-down, morally exhausted man clinging to shreds of hope in a world whose cynicism has long since rendered him obsolete. Both men "love" Phuong, but for Pyle she is less crucial. Fowler, on the other hand, admits: "I know I'm not essential to Phuong, but if I were to lose her, for me that would be the beginning of death." What Phuong herself thinks is not the point with either man, since they are both convinced she wants them.

Fraser, who often stars as a walking cartoon *(Dudley Do-Right, George of the Jungle)*, has shown in other pictures, like *Gods and Monsters,* that he is a gifted actor, and here he finds just the right balance between confidence and blindness: What he does is evil, but he is convinced it is good, and has a simple, sunny view that maddens an old hand like Fowler. The two characters work well together because there is an undercurrent of commonality: They are both floating in the last currents of colonialism, in which life in Saigon can be very good, unless you get killed.

Phillip Noyce made two great pictures close together, this one and *Rabbit-Proof Fence.* He feels anger as he tells this story, but he conceals it, because the story as it stands is enough. Some viewers will not even intercept the political message. It was that way with Greene: The politics were in the very weave of the cloth, not worth talking about. Here, in a rare Western feature shot in Vietnam, with real locations and sets that look well-worn enough to be real, with wonderful performances, he suggests a worldview more mature and knowing than the simplistic pieties that provide the public face of foreign policy.

Quitting ★ ★ ½
R, 112 m., 2002

Jia Hongsheng (Hongsheng), Jia Fengsen (Hongsheng's Father), Chai Ziurong (Hongsheng's Mother), Wang Tong (Hongsheng's Sister), Shun Xing (Jia's Roommate), Li Jie (Hongsheng's Musician Friend), Zhang Yang (Director). Directed by Zhang and produced by Peter Loehr. Screenplay by Zhang and Huo Xin.

Quitting is not so much a movie about drug addiction as a movie about sentimentalized Chinese ideas of drug addiction. It is a brave experiment, based on life and using actors who play themselves, but it buys into the whole false notion that artists are somehow too brilliant to be sober—that drugs and booze are almost necessary to tame their creativity, dull their pain, and allow them to tolerate life with the clods around them. Thus the "cure" is not so much to stop using as to stop dreaming; one must become boring to become clean and sober.

Astonishing, how persistent this idea is, since there is nothing more boring than a drunk or an addict, repeating the same failed pattern every day. But China does not embrace the useful disease model of addiction, and in a hospital where the hero is sent, a fellow patient explains, "The Soviets called it hysteria, but the Chinese called it dementia." Addiction is neither. In most cases, it is simply a habitual inability to avoid getting wasted.

If *Quitting* embraced Western ideas, its hero would no doubt quickly find himself attending AA meetings, and while that might be better for his health it might not be better for this movie. *Quitting* stars Jia Hongsheng, who starred in Chinese movies and on television circa 1990, and then, while appearing in the title role of *Kiss of the Spider Woman* on stage in 1992, quickly progressed from pot through heroin into professional and personal dysfunction.

Eventually he had to move in with his sister. He became a recluse and rejected all work offers. His parents, who were provincial actors, moved to Beijing to take care of him, and the four family members found themselves trapped in an apartment with his disease. Although this is a showbiz family, the parents come from a backwater; Hongsheng believes he receives secret messages from John Lennon, while his father has not even heard of the "Bittles."

Jia Hongsheng plays himself in this story. The parents and other characters play themselves, and the director of the film, Zhang Yang, was the real-life stage director of *Kiss of the Spider Woman*. This gives the film an eerie intrinsic interest: They act in scenes based on remembered pain. This is, however, not a documentary, and a startling shot late in the film underlines the fact that it is artistry, not fact.

The movie's pumped-up scenes of domestic anguish are the least convincing, and when Hongsheng hangs up on TV producers or hides in his room, he is less a suffering person than an addict acting out a tiresome script. When, however, he sits on the grass under a highway overpass with his father and they both drink beer, there is a kind of unforced communion; the father, who has a drinking problem, has promised his wife not to drink, and so as they play hooky together they have a moment of peace.

Zhang Yang's previous film was the popular *Shower* (1999), about a successful son who returns from the provinces to Beijing, where his elderly father and retarded brother run a bathhouse. That film was a warm human comedy, but has connections with *Quitting;* the director cares about how fathers and sons can seem so different and be so much the same.

R

Rabbit-Proof Fence ★ ★ ★ ½
PG, 94 m., 2002

Everlyn Sampi (Molly), Tianna Sansbury (Daisy),
Laura Monaghan (Gracie), David Gulpilil
(Moodoo), Ningali Lawford (Molly's Mother),
Myarn Lawford (Molly's Grandmother),
Deborah Mailman (Mavis), Jason Clarke
(Constable Riggs), Kenneth Branagh
(A. O. Neville). Directed by Phillip Noyce
and produced by Noyce, Christine Olsen, and
John Winter. Screenplay by Olsen, based on
the book by Doris Pilkington Garimara.

The most astonishing words in *Rabbit-Proof Fence* come right at the end, printed on the screen as a historical footnote. The policies depicted in the movie were enforced by the Australian government, we are told, until 1970. Aboriginal children of mixed race were taken by force from their mothers and raised in training schools that would prepare them for lives as factory workers or domestic servants. More than a century after slavery was abolished in the Western world, a Western democracy was still practicing racism of the most cruel description.

The children's fathers were long gone—white construction workers or government employees who enjoyed sex with local Aborigine women and then moved on. But why could the mixed-race children not stay where they were? The offered explanations are equally vile. One is that a half-white child must be rescued from a black society. Another was that too many "white genes" would, by their presumed superiority, increase the power and ability of the Aborigines to cause trouble by insisting on their rights. A third is that, by requiring the lighter-skinned children to marry each other, blackness could eventually be bred out of them. Of course it went without saying that the "schools" they were held in prepared them only for menial labor.

The children affected are known today in Australia as the Stolen Generations. The current Australian government of Prime Minister John Howard still actually refuses to apologize for these policies. Trent Lott by comparison is enlightened.

Phillip Noyce's film is fiction based on fact. The screenplay by Christine Olsen is based on a book by Doris Pilkington Garimara, telling the story of the experiences of her mother, Molly, her aunt Daisy, and their cousin Gracie. Torn from their families by government officials, they were transported some 1,500 miles to a training school, where they huddled together in fear and grief, separated from everyone and everything they had ever known. When they tried to use their own language, they were told to stop "jabbering."

At the time of the adventures in the movie, Molly (Everlyn Sampi) is fourteen, Daisy (Tianna Sansbury) is eight, and Gracie (Laura Monaghan) is ten. The school where they are held is not a Dickensian workhouse; by the standards of the time it is not unkind (that it inflicts the unimaginable pain of separation from family and home does not figure into the thinking of the white educators, who consider they are doing a favor). The girls cannot abide this strange and lonely place. They run away and start walking toward their homes. It will be a journey of 1,500 miles. They have within their heads an instinctive map of the way, and are aided by a fence that stretches for hundreds of miles across the outback, to protect farmlands from a pestilence of rabbits.

The principal white character in the movie is A. O. Neville (Kenneth Branagh), who in 1931 was the administrator of the relocation policies and something of an amateur eugenicist with theories of race and breeding that would have won him a ready audience in Nazi Germany. That Australians could have accepted thinking such as his, and indeed based government policy on it, indicates the sorry fact that many of them thought Aborigines were a step or two down the evolutionary ladder from modern Europeans. That the Aboriginal societies of Australia and New Zealand were remarkably sophisticated was hard for the whites to admit—especially because, the more one credited these native races, the more obvious it was that the land had been stolen from their possession.

As the three girls flee across the vast landscape, they are pursued by white authorities and an Aboriginal tracker named Moodoo

(David Gulpilil), who seems not especially eager to find them. Along the way they are helped by the kindness of strangers, even a white woman. This journey, which evokes some of the same mystery of the Outback as many other Australian films (notably *Walkabout*), is beautiful, harrowing, and sometimes heartbreaking.

The three young stars are all Aboriginals, untrained actors, and Noyce is skilled at the way he evokes their thoughts and feelings. Narration helps fill gaps and supplies details that cannot be explained on-screen. The end of the journey is not the same for all three girls, and there is more heartbreak ahead, which it would be wrong for me to reveal. But I must say this. The final scene of the film contains an appearance and a revelation of astonishing emotional power; not since the last shots of *Schindler's List* have I been so overcome with the realization that real people, in recent historical times, had to undergo such inhumanity.

Radio ★ ★ ★
PG, 109 m., 2003

Cuba Gooding Jr. (James "Radio" Kennedy), Ed Harris (Coach Harold Jones), Alfre Woodard (Principal Daniels), Debra Winger (Linda Jones), S. Epatha Merkerson (Maggie), Riley Smith (Johnny Clay), Sarah Drew (Mary Helen Jones), Chris Mulkey (Frank Clay). Directed by Michael Tollin and produced by Brian Robbins and Tollin. Screenplay by Mike Rich and Gary Smith.

I don't know the slightest thing about the true story that inspired *Radio,* and I don't really want to, because the movie has convinced me that it's pretty close to real life. I believe that because (1) the closing credits include footage of the real Radio Kennedy and Coach Jones and (2) because the movie isn't hyped up with the usual contrivances. Here is a film about football that doesn't even depend for its climax on the Big Game.

There are scenes that in another movie might have seemed contrived—the way the local boosters's club gathers after every game in the downtown barbershop, for example, to get the coach's report and grill him. Isn't this the sort of thing that happens only in movie small towns? Just like there's always a diner filled with regulars who apparently sit there twenty-four hours a day waiting to act as the local Greek chorus?

Maybe, but by the end of *Radio* I was half-convinced that if I were to visit Anderson, South Carolina, on the night of a high school game, I could walk downtown and see the boosters right there through the barbershop window.

The movie is based on a *Sports Illustrated* story about the way a series of Anderson teams and coaches have adopted James "Radio" Kennedy, a mentally disabled local man, as a team mascot and cheerleader. He is much beloved, and we sense that his good heart and cheer needed only the right opportunity to give him this mission in life. The movie focuses in fictional form on Radio's first season with the team, and about the bond that forms between the youngish man (Cuba Gooding Jr.) and lean, no-nonsense Coach Harold Jones (Ed Harris).

Radio, when first seen, goes on his harmless daily rounds through the town, pushing a shopping cart filled with treasures and listening to a beloved portable radio. One day a few football players lock him in an equipment shed and throw footballs at it, frightening him, and after Jones rescues Radio he becomes committed to a project—an obsession, really—to involve Radio with the team.

Jones's wife, Linda (Debra Winger), of course has the obligatory scenes complaining that his mind is always on his work. His daughter, Mary Helen Jones (Sarah Drew), of course has the obligatory scenes in which she stays out too late and gives other signs of needing more of her father's attention. But here's an unexpected thing: Not much is made in the obligatory way of these subplots, because Jones is a nice guy and his family understands him and the daughter sort of solves her own problems.

There are villains of a sort. Johnny Clay (Riley Smith) is the star player who instinctively picks on Radio, maybe because his dad, Frank (Chris Mulkey), is also a bully (does it go without saying that Frank is the town banker, and a big cheese in the booster club?). Frank thinks Radio is a "distraction" to the team, but Radio is so beloved and Coach Jones such a big-hearted man that even the villains seem to be going through the motions just to be good sports and lend the film some drama.

Radio is such a sweet expression of the better side of human nature, indeed, that it's surprising to find it in theaters and not on one of the more innocuous cable channels. In Gooding and Harris it has top-line talent, and a screenplay by Mike Rich (who wrote *Finding Forrester*) and Gary Smith (who wrote the *SI* story). Director Michael Tollin (*Summer Catch,* unreviewed by me) tells his story as simply and directly as he can, with no fancy stuff, and what we get is just what we're promised: a story about a town that adopts a disadvantaged young man for its benefit and his own. Radio teaches the town, Jones says, by treating everyone the way we should all treat one another; the young man is incapable of meanness, spite, or dishonesty.

The role is tricky for an actor; Gooding wants to make Radio lovable without being grotesquely cute, and mostly he succeeds, although Gooding is by instinct an expansive actor (the kind of man you imagine underlines his signature), and maybe a calmer actor like Ice Cube would have been a good choice. It was enough for Gooding to make me like Radio; in a few scenes I think he wanted me to pet him. Ed Harris is well cast in a role like Coach Jones, because he brings along confident, masculine authority without even having to think about it. The other actors are pretty much pro forma; Alfre Woodard plays the sensible high school principal, S. Epatha Merkerson is convincing as Radio's loving mom, and Debra Winger is strong in a small role that makes me want to see her in a larger one.

Now if the movie's story sounds too good to be true, that's probably how you'll find it. There is no cynicism in *Radio,* no angle or edge. It's about what it's about, with an open, warm, and fond nature. Every once in a while human nature expresses itself in a way we can feel good about, and this is one of those times. For families, for those who find most movies too cynical, for those who want to feel good in a warm and uncomplicated way, *Radio* is a treasure. Others may find it too slow or sunny or innocent. You know who you are.

Raising Helen ★ ★

PG-13, 119 m., 2004

Kate Hudson (Helen Harris), John Corbett (Pastor Dan), Joan Cusack (Jenny), Hector Elizondo (Mickey Massey), Helen Mirren (Dominique), Hayden Panettiere (Audrey), Spencer Breslin (Henry), Abigail Breslin (Sarah), Sakina Jaffrey (Nilma Prasad), Felicity Huffman (Lindsay). Directed by Garry Marshall and produced by Ashok Amritraj and David Hoberman. Screenplay by Jack Amiel and Michael Begler.

Raising Helen is a perfectly pleasant comedy in which nice people do good things despite challenges that are difficult but not excessive. As a pilot for a TV sitcom it would probably be picked up, but it's not compelling enough to involve a trip to the movies. From beginning to end, we've been there, seen that.

Kate Hudson, who stars, seems to be following in the footsteps of her mother, Goldie Hawn; both have genuine talent, but choose too often to bury themselves in commercial formulas. Hudson plays Helen Harris, a high-powered Manhattan career woman who works as the personal assistant to the head (Helen Mirren) of a famous modeling agency. She works hard, is on call 24-7, and even when she parties she's talent-scouting. She has a sister named Jenny (Joan Cusack) who lives in the suburbs and raises her children as a disciplined time-and-motion study. Jenny's house, Helen observes, looks like a showroom at Pottery Barn.

Tragedy strikes. Their sister Lindsay (Felicity Huffman) and her husband are killed in an accident, and in her will Lindsay leaves custody of her small son and daughter not to Jenny the perfect homemaker, but to Helen the fast-track girl. How can this be? Helen and Jenny are both appalled, but Helen takes on the task of raising little Henry and Sarah, played by real-life siblings Spencer and Abigail Breslin.

If Helen has any notions that she can be a mom and keep her agency job, she's disabused by Mirren, who expects total dedication. Soon Helen has lost her job, moved her little family to a lower-middle-class neighborhood in Queens, and enrolled the kids in a nearby Lutheran school run by Pastor Dan (John Corbett), who is single and therefore preordained to fall in love with Helen, although not before many plot-laden details have been worked through. She gets a job in a car dealership run by the unfailingly dynamic Hector Elizondo.

The movie, directed by Garry Marshall

(Pretty Woman), is not unaware of the lifestyle differences between single Manhattan career women and receptionists in Queens. Not even after Helen unloads an eyesore green Lincoln and is promoted to sales does she have the money, or the skills, to make things work—even though she learns fast. But she's let off fairly easily. The movie exists in the kind of economy where one working-class paycheck can just about support a family, and where city kids go to the wholesome parochial school down the street. Times are harder now, but the movie doesn't know it—can't afford to, if its sunny disposition is to prevail.

Most of Helen's lessons in survival come not from her sister, a forbiddingly humorless caricature, but from her across-the-hall Indian neighbor Nilma Prasad (Sakina Jaffrey), who, just like all neighbors in sitcoms, is willing to drop her own life at a moment's notice to play a supporting role in the heroine's; she channels Ethel Mertz.

The romance between Helen and Pastor Dan progresses with agonizing slowness, complicated by Helen's belief that Lutheran ministers cannot marry (her attempts to fake Lutheranism to get her kids into the school are amusing, but could have been subtler). Finally, Pastor Dan breaks the ice: "I'm a sexy man of God, and I know it." Then there are the scenes where the kids resent this man who seems about to replace their father, and the obligatory group visit to the zoo, scored with the obligatory use of Simon and Garfunkel's "At the Zoo."

Garry Marshall is a smart director with more of a comic edge than this movie allows him. I wonder if at any point he considered darkening the material even a little, and making Hudson's character a shade more desperate and less Lucy-like. There's nothing at risk in *Raising Helen*. We're not even surprised the kids go to Helen and not her sister, because the sister is written in a way that makes her impossible as a parental candidate.

Pastor Dan is the conveniently available, nearby eligible male, but somehow we doubt there are many ordained Lutheran bachelors in Queens; why not rotate the plot toward more complexity? Surely that nice Mrs. Prasad across the hall has a brother who is a widower with two children of his own? To obtain comedy, you don't give Helen problems and then supply a man who solves them; you supply a man who brings in additional problems. I can imagine this premise being passed through the imagination of a director like Gurinder Chadha *(Bend It Like Beckham, What's Cooking?)* and emerging fresh and exciting. *Raising Helen* is tame and timid from beginning to end, and relentlessly conventional. Because Helen takes no real risks, because she lives surrounded by the safeguards of formula fiction, the movie is fated from its first shot to be obedient to convention.

Raising Victor Vargas ★ ★ ★ ½
R, 88 m., 2003

Victor Rasuk (Victor Vargas), Judy Marte (Judy Ramirez), Melonie Diaz (Melonie), Altagracia Guzman (Grandma), Silvestre Rasuk (Nino Vargas), Krystal Rodriguez (Vicki Vargas), Kevin Rivera (Harold), Wilfree Vasquez (Carlos). Directed by Peter Sollett and produced by Sollett, Scott Macaulay, Robin O'Hara, and Alain de la Mata. Screenplay by Sollett.

Raising Victor Vargas tells the heartwarming story of first love that finds a balance between lust and idealism. Acted by fresh-faced newcomers who never step wrong, it sidesteps the clichés of teenage coming-of-age movies and expands into truth and human comedy. It's the kind of movie you know you can trust, and you give yourself over to affection for these characters who are so lovingly observed.

We meet the Vargas family, who live on the Lower East Side of New York. Grandma (Altagracia Guzman) came from the Dominican Republic. She is raising her three grandchildren: Victor (Victor Rasuk), Nino (Silvestre Rasuk), and Vicki (Krystal Rodriguez). Victor, who is about sixteen, fancies himself a ladies' man but is not as experienced as he seems. Nino looks up to him. Vicki, who is plump and seems to live on the sofa, is fed up with both boys—and Grandma lives in fear of the hazards that surround them.

In another movie those hazards might involve gangs, drugs, and guns. Not in *Raising Victor Vargas*, which eliminates the usual urban dangers and shows us a home where the values may be old-fashioned but have produced three basically good kids. It's refreshing to find a movie where a Latino family in a poor neighborhood is not portrayed with the usual tired conventions about poverty and crime, but is based on love and strong values. It's only natural that Nino reveals himself as a moderately talented pianist.

If Victor thinks constantly about dating and sex, what boy his age doesn't? As the film opens, he is interrupted during the conquest of Fat Donna, who lives upstairs. It would appear, however, that the interruption came just in time to qualify him still as a virgin. Fat Donna is apparently a neighborhood legend, and although he swears her to secrecy the gossip quickly spreads and his sister cheerfully informs him, "You'll always be known as Fat Donna's boy."

This causes him no small agony, because at the swimming pool he sees the girl of his dreams: Judy Ramirez (Judy Marte), who seems beautiful and elegant and forever inaccessible. The movie's romantic plot involves a complicated scheme in which he convinces Judy's younger brother to arrange an introduction in return for Victor's influence in helping the younger brother meet his sister, Vicki. Meanwhile, Victor's friend Harold falls for Judy's friend Melonie (Melonie Diaz), who seems to be a classic type—the plain girl who is the popular girl's best friend. But then, in a movie tradition that I continue to love, Melonie takes off her glasses and lets down her hair.

The movie is not simply about these three inexperienced and uncertain pairs of lovers. If it were, it would be a typical teenage comedy. It is much deeper and more knowing than that, especially in the way it shows Grandma waging a losing battle to maintain her idea of the family's innocence. Although Victor is a good boy, Grandma imagines his life as a hotbed of sin, and the city as the devil's workshop. When Victor invites Judy to dinner it is a disaster because Grandma has not even suspected their friendship.

There is a delicate progress in the relationship of the two young lovers. Judy for a long time plays hard to get; she's determined to resist the relentless male lust all around her, and demands respect and attention from the boy who will win her heart. Victor is not strong in these qualities, but in a subtle and moving way

he begins to learn about them, and the tentative progress of their love is a tender delight.

It is also touching that while Victor, Nino, and Vicki are exasperated by their grandmother's old world ways, they love her and need her. And the film is careful not to make Grandma into a caricature: What she does, she does from love, and when there is a crisis involving a social worker, which threatens the family, Victor finds a silent and tactful way to end it. The screenplay finds reconciliation in a touching story Grandma tells about her childhood.

I was in a discussion the other day about whether a movie can be erotic. Sexual, yes, and explicit, yes—but truly erotic? To achieve that, a film must abandon the details of sexual congress and focus instead on the personalities of its characters. When Victor and Judy finally kiss in this movie, it is a moment more real and joyous than miles of "sex scenes," because by then we know who they are, how they have traveled together to this moment, and what it means to them.

Raising Victor Vargas was written and directed by Peter Sollett. It grew from an award-winning short subject he made with the same actors, who are not experienced professionals but are fresh and true in a way that suggests they're the real thing, and will have fruitful careers.

Note: Like so many movies dealing intelligently with teenage sexuality, Raising Victor Vargas *has been rated R by the MPAA, which awards the PG-13 to comedies celebrating cheap vulgarity, but penalizes sincere expressions of true experience and real-life values.*

Rana's Wedding ★ ★ ★
NO MPAA RATING, 90 m., 2004

Clara Khoury (Rana), Khalifa Natour (Khalil), Ismael Dabbag (Ramzy), Walid Abed Elsalam (Marriage Official), Zuher Fahoum (Father), Bushra Karaman (Grandmother). Directed by Hany Abu-Assad and produced by Bero Beyer and George Ibrahim. Screenplay by Ihab Lamey and Liana Badr.

Rana's father is going to the airport at 4 P.M., and she can either get married or leave the country with him. He supplies her with a list of eligible bachelors who have asked for her hand in marriage. But she is in love with Khalil. Can she find him, ask him to marry her, find a registrar, get her hair done, gather the relatives, and get married—all before 4 o'clock?

This could be the description of a Hollywood romantic comedy. And indeed it is a romantic comedy of sorts, as romance and comedy survive in the midst of the conflict between Palestinians and Israelis. The movie takes place on both sides of the armed border separating Jerusalem and the Palestinian settlement of Ramallah, and although the comedy occupies the foreground, the background is dominated by checkpoints and armed soldiers, street funerals and little boys throwing rocks, bulldozers tearing down buildings and a general state of siege.

Rana (Clara Khoury) is a Palestinian who is seventeen; her lover, Khalil (Khalifa Natour), a theater director, seems to be around forty. Although her father has grave doubts about their marriage, they cite Islamic law that allows them to wed if they inform the father in the presence of a registrar. Her problem is to find her lover, find the registrar, find her father, and get them all together in the same place at the same time. This involves several trips back and forth through armed roadblocks that quietly make the point that Palestinians spend all day every day facing hostility and suspicion.

What's interesting is that the movie, made by the Netherlands-based Palestinian filmmaker Hany Abu-Assad, makes little overt point of its political content; the politics are the air that the characters breathe, but the story is about their short-term romantic goals. And those are made more complicated because Rana is not a simple woman. She changes her mind, she gets jealous, she risks missing the deadline in order to get her hair done, she sometimes seems older, sometimes like a child.

The premise is a little hard to accept: Has her father actually sent her a note on the morning when he is to leave the country, setting the 4 P.M. deadline? She seems very independent; is there any way she can stay behind? Could she have considered marriage days or weeks earlier, or has all of this come about at the last moment? And what, exactly, is her father's reasoning? Al-though we see him briefly, we have no real ideas about who he is and how he thinks.

It is also rather startling that Khalil is prepared to get married at a moment's notice. Rana finally tracks him down on the stage of a theater in the Palestinian sector, where he's asleep with some of his cast; the roadblocks make that easier than going home. She awakens him with the news that they are to get married this very day, and he takes it fairly well, I'd say. Enlisting a friend with a yellow VW beetle, he sets off with Rana on a mission to find the registrar (who is not at home, of course) and meet the deadline.

We have to accept this unlikely plot, I suppose, because there it is—a device to add suspense. More suspense comes because Rana sometimes seems in no hurry. But the strength of the movie comes in its observation of details, as when Rana sees small boys throwing rocks at a barricade, and Israeli soldiers firing back; this scene, and other border scenes, look like real life captured by the film, although I have no way of knowing if that's true. There's also a scene where Rana and Khalil stop for a quiet talk, and notice a security camera pointed at them, and when Rana forgets the plastic carryall with her possessions in it, and runs back to find she's too late: the police, thinking it might contain a bomb, have just blown it up with a remote-controlled cannon.

There are, of course, two sides to such an experience; if Palestinians use hidden explosives and suicide bombers, then the Israelis of course must try to prevent them. But the movie doesn't preach; it simply observes. This is how daily life is. The movie is passable as a story but fascinating as a document. It gives a more complete visual picture of the borders, the Palestinian settlements, and the streets of Jerusalem than we ever see on the news, and we understand that the Palestinians are not all suicide bombers living in tents, as the news sometimes seems to imply, but in many cases middle-class people like Rana and her circle, sharing the same abilities and aspirations as their neighbors. I think the point is to show how their conditions of life are like a water torture, breaking them down a drop at a time, reminding them that having lived in this place for a long time, they are nevertheless homeless.

Rare Birds ★ ★ ★
R, 104 m., 2003

William Hurt (Dave), Andy Jones (Phonse), Molly Parker (Alice). Directed by Sturla Gunnarsson and produced by Paul Pope and Janet York. Screenplay by Edward Riche, based on his novel.

People who live at the edge of the sea sometimes have a restless look in their eyes, as if they have gone as far as they can go, and it is not far enough. Consider Dave Purcell (William Hurt), who has opened a fine dining restaurant named The Auk on a rocky seaside outcrop of Newfoundland, far from large numbers of fine diners. He is a quiet, moody perfectionist, his food is splendid, his business is lousy, and he is going broke. There is also the matter of his addiction to drugs and alcohol, which he is struggling to overcome.

Dave's best friend is Phonse (Andy Jones), an optimistic codger who comes up with a scheme to help business: They'll report the sighting of a rare duck, the area will be swamped with bird-watchers, and even birders have to eat, no? This fraud works so well that Dave can no longer run The Auk as a one-man show, and hires a waitress. This is Alice (Molly Parker), and soon the two are in love. (There was once a Mrs. Purcell, whose love for Dave did not extend to joining him on the rocky Newfoundland outcrop, etc.)

Sturla Gunnarsson's *Rare Birds,* adapted by Edward Riche from his novel, is a sweetheart of a film, whimsical and touching. It positions itself somewhere between a slice of life and a screwball comedy. Hurt plays Dave tenderly, as an inward and unsocial man who apparently enjoys running his restaurant in complete privacy. His life is complicated enormously not only by the rush of business and the arrival of Alice, but also by Phonse's discovery of a large amount of cocaine floating in the bay. Can this be resold? Can Dave stay away from it?

There are, we should note, men skulking about who are obviously not bird fanciers. Dave might not notice them. Phonse does. He is obsessed with the possibilities of marketing a "recreational submarine," and thinks maybe they're industrial spies. Of course, they could also be narcs. This plot gets a little overheated

by the end of the film; I could have done with less action and more whimsy, but Hurt stays true to his character and the film weaves a goofy spell.

The film was made in 2001 by Gunnarsson, whose previous work was the wonderful *Such a Long Journey,* inspired by the novel by Rohinton Mistry. *Rare Birds* was scheduled for its world premiere at the Toronto Film Festival on September 11, 2001. That premiere never happened, the public did not see the film, and its fate was forever changed; a few critics were able to attend a makeup screening in a little twenty-seat theater. It's now in limited theatrical release, and also available on tape and DVD. Best to see it in a theater; The Auk may be in an unlikely location, but it has a magnificent view.

Read My Lips ★ ★ ★ ½
NO MPAA RATING, 115 m., 2002

Vincent Cassel (Paul Angeli), Emmanuelle Devos (Carla Bhem), Olivier Gourmet (Marchand), Olivier Perrier (Masson), Olivia Bonamy (Annie), Bernard Alane (Morel). Directed by Jacques Audiard and produced by Jean-Louis Livi and Philippe Carcassonne. Screenplay by Audiard and Tonino Benacquista.

Carla is an office worker whose hearing is impaired, and who can read lips. This skill is crucial in a late scene in *Read My Lips,* a thriller crossed with a psychosexual study. Without giving away surprises, I can say that by reading the lips of Paul, her partner in crime, she is able to reverse a tricky situation. But *Read My Lips* is not a simpleminded movie in which merely being *able* to read lips saves the day. In this brilliant sequence she reads his lips and that *allows* them to set into motion a risky chain of events based on the odds that the bad guys will respond predictably.

By this point in the movie, we are deep into crime, double crosses, beatings, and murder, but *Read My Lips* begins as the story of an office worker—one of those hapless souls who is hardly noticed by the coworkers who leave their half-empty coffee cups on her desk. Carla (Emmanuelle Devos) is in her thirties, with ordinary looks; she seems to exist as an invisible service to others. She has no social life, has neighbors who dump their kids for baby-sitting, and lives in a world of shouts and whispers, depending on the function of her hearing aids. Apparently (it is a little unclear) she was once more deaf than she is now, and is improving.

Carla would like a guy. Her boss suggests she hire an assistant, and immediately we sense her mind at work. What kind of an assistant would she like? A man. What attributes should he have? Nice hands. She eventually hires the spectacularly shaky job candidate Paul (Vincent Cassel), who is fresh out of jail, sleeps rough, has one set of clothes, and, I guess, nice hands. He owes his job to her, and so she treats him a little like the others in the office treat her. There is a sexual undercurrent, complicated because they are both unwilling to seem needy.

Paul has not completely cut his connections to the criminal element in the French city where they live. He moonlights as a bartender, has snaky deals on the side, and finds out almost by accident about a bag of loot that's ripe for the stealing. He can't pull off the job by himself, and enlists Carla, who turns out to have that combination of cunning and hostility that makes successful criminals. Spying on the men with the money, who belong to a dangerous local gang, she perches on a rooftop and uses binoculars to read their lips and discover their plans.

The details of the heist are nicely worked out, and original, as these things go. But the heist is not the point of *Read My Lips*. It is more of a maguffin. The bag and the bad guys are simply the props to justify the way Paul and Carla take their relationship to a new level—how they find, in this dangerous enterprise, a way to use unsuspected skills and discover deep compatibility. Neither Carla, in her office, nor Paul, in his desultory lawlessness, would have ever broken loose and discovered their true potential without the other.

That discovery provides another example of the depth of the screenplay, by director Jacques Audiard and Tonino Benacquista. Just as the lip-reading is not a payoff but a setup, so the relationship of Carla and Paul is not about obvious sex but about a communion of two souls—and sex. A lesser movie would have had them in bed by the halfway mark, in an obligatory sex scene of little motivation, interest, or purpose. Instead, *Read My Lips* is really interested in these two characters. At first they have

a simultaneous attraction and repulsion; each finds it sexy that the other one behaves with a certain competitive hostility. Then they share the goal of the crime, which has its own fascination and fulfills both of their natures. And only then, through that experience, do they make a delightful discovery that at deeply buried levels they are connected, in a world where they have never met anyone who feels as they feel.

It is nothing to discover that another person turns you on; that's commonplace. But to discover that you and another person are mutually turned on by deep instincts you bring out in each other—instincts involving the very way you live your lives—is rare, and makes you tremble with joy and risk the unthinkable. The movie is not about deafness, lip-reading, crime, or sex, but about that discovery; the plot simply provides the rails on which it rides.

Real Women Have Curves ★ ★ ★ ½
PG-13, 90 m., 2002

America Ferrera (Ana), Lupe Ontiveros (Carmen), Ingrid Oliu (Estela), George Lopez (Mr. Guzman), Brian Sites (Jimmy). Directed by Patricia Cardosa and produced by Effie Brown and George LaVoo. Screenplay by Josefina Lopez and LaVoo, based on a play by Lopez.

Ana's boyfriend Jimmy tells her, "You're not fat. You're beautiful." She is both. *Real Women Have Curves* doesn't argue that Ana is beautiful on the "inside," like the Gwyneth Paltrow character in *Shallow Hal,* but that she is beautiful inside and out—love handles, big boobs, round cheeks, and all. "Turn the lights on," she shyly tells Jimmy. "I want you to see me. See, this is what I look like."

Ana has learned to accept herself. It is more than her mother can do. Carmen (Lupe Ontiveros) is fat, too, and hates herself for it, and wants her daughter to share her feelings. Ana is smart and could get a college scholarship, but Carmen insists she go to work in a dress factory run by a family member: It's her duty to the family, apparently, to sacrifice her future. The fact that the dress factory is pleasant and friendly doesn't change the reality that it's a dead end; you are at the wrong end of the economy when you make dresses for $18 so that they can be sold for $600.

Ana is a Mexican-American, played by America Ferrera, an eighteen-year-old in her first movie role. Ferrera is a wonder: natural, unforced, sweet, passionate, and always real. Her battle with her mother is convincing in the movie because the director, Patricia Cardosa, doesn't force it into shrill melodrama, but keeps it within the boundaries of a plausible family fight. It is a tribute to the great Lupe Ontiveros that Carmen is able to suggest her love for her daughter, even when it is very hard to see.

There have been several movies recently about the second generation of children of emigrants—Indian, Filipino, Chinese, Korean, Vietnamese—and they follow broad outlines borrowed from life. The parents try to enforce conditions of their homeland on the kids, who are becoming Americanized at blinding speed. While Carmen is insisting on her daughter's virginity, Ana is buying condoms. She insists on a view of her life that is not her parents'. That includes college.

If this movie had been made ten years ago, it might have been shrill, insistent, and dramatic—overplaying its hand. Cardosa and her writers, Josefina Lopez and George LaVoo, are more relaxed, more able to feel affection for all of the characters. Yes, her parents want Ana to work in the dress shop of their older daughter, and yes, they fear losing her—because they sense if she goes away to college she will return as a different person. But the parents are not monsters, and we sense that their love will prevail over their fears.

The film focuses on Ana at a crucial moment, right after high school, when she has decided with a level head and clear eyes to come of age on her own terms. Her parents would not approve of Jimmy, an Anglo, but Ana knows he is a good boy and she feels tender toward him. She also knows he will not be the last boy she dates; she is mature enough to understand herself and the stormy weathers of teenage love. When they have sex, there is a sense in which they are giving each other the gift of a sweet initiation, with respect and tenderness, instead of losing their innocence roughly to strangers in a way without love.

The film's portrait of the dressmaking factory is done with great good humor. Yes, it is very hot there. Yes, the hours are long and the pay is poor. But the women are happy to have jobs and paychecks, and because they like one another there is a lot of laughter. That leads to one of the sunniest, funniest, happiest scenes in a long time. On a hot day, Ana takes off her blouse, and then so do the other women, giggling at their daring, and the music swells up as their exuberance flows over. They are all plump, but Ana, who has a healthy self-image, leads them in celebrating their bodies.

I am so relieved that the MPAA rated this movie PG-13. So often they bar those under seventeen from the very movies they could benefit from the most. *Real Women Have Curves* is enormously entertaining for moviegoers of any age (it won the Audience Award at Sundance 2002). But for young women depressed because they don't look like skinny models, this film is a breath of common sense and fresh air. *Real Women Have Curves* is a reminder of how rarely the women in the movies are real. After the almost excruciating attention paid to the world-class beauties in a movie like *White Oleander* (a film in which the more the women suffered the better they looked), how refreshing to see America Ferrera light up the room with a smile from the heart.

The Reckoning ★ ★ ★
R, 112 m., 2004

Willem Dafoe (Martin), Paul Bettany (Nicholas), Gina McKee (Sarah), Brian Cox (Tobias), Ewen Bremner (Damian), Vincent Cassel (Lord de Guise), Simon McBurney (Stephen), Elvira Minguez (Martha). Directed by Paul McGuigan and produced by Caroline Wood. Screenplay by Mark Mills, based on the novel *Morality Play* by Barry Unsworth.

In England circa 1380, a troupe of traveling actors makes its way across the medieval landscape, where to go twenty miles from home was to enter a world of strangers. In London at about the same time, Geoffrey Chaucer was writing about another group on the road—pilgrims on their way to Canterbury. His Knight, learning from the journey, declared:

This world is but a thoroughfare full of woe,
And we be pilgrims, passing to and fro.
Death is an end to every worldly sore.

The actors arrive at much the same conclusion in *The Reckoning*, when they arrive at a village where a murder trial is under way. A mute woman (Elvira Minguez) has been charged with the death of a local boy, and been sentenced to death as a witch. The actors by their nature are more worldly and sophisticated than the village folk, and after questioning the woman through sign language, they begin to doubt her guilt.

It is at first no affair of theirs, however, and they unload their props and costumes from a lumbering covered wagon and stage the wheezer they've been touring with: a morality tale about Adam and Eve. That this is probably the first play ever seen by the locals does not give it the virtue of novelty; it is ever so much more entertaining to hang witches than to attend allegory. In desperation, the players decide to devise a play based on the murder case, and the more they discover, the more they doubt the woman's guilt. The village in fact is a hotbed of sin and suspicion, and only a conspiracy of fear has kept the lid on. The actors are stirring the pot.

Ah, but there's a twist. One of the troupe, Nicholas (Paul Bettany, the surgeon in *Master and Commander*), is not an actor at all, but a priest who was discovered at the wrong kind of devotions with a wife from his congregation—not the Wife of Bath, alas, or he might have gotten away with it. Fleeing for his life, he is taken on by the troupe, whose leader, Martin (Willem Dafoe), agrees to shelter him. Martin's sister Sarah (Gina McKee) is intrigued by Nicholas's aura of sensual guilt, but the veteran actor Tobias (Brian Cox) thinks they have enough mouths to feed without a freeloader. These tensions all play a role when the troupe begins to suspect a village scandal, and Lord Robert de Guise (Vincent Cassel) orders them to leave.

The Reckoning has been directed, perhaps incredibly, by Paul McGuigan, the Scots filmmaker whose previous work (*Gangster No. 1*) did not seem to point him in this direction. And yet the previous movie shows the same taste for dissecting the evil beneath the skin.

Basing his film on the novel *Morality Play* by Barry Unsworth and a screenplay by Mark Mills, McGuigan shows a world in which characters project a rigid self-confidence which, when cracked, reveals venom.

The medieval world of the film has been convincingly re-created (it was photographed in Spain), and the ambience and plot suggest connections with three other medieval mystery films: *The Name of the Rose*, about a murder at a monastery, *The Return of Martin Guerre*, about a man who may be Martin or may have murdered him, and Bergman's *The Virgin Spring*, about a girl murdered by itinerant farmworkers. In those years, superstition and ignorance were the key elements in any criminal investigation.

The Reckoning has just a little too much of the whodunit and the thriller and not enough of the temper of its clash between cultures, but it works, maybe because the simplicity of the underlying plot is masked by the oddness of the characters. Willem Dafoe is invaluable in an enterprise like this, always seeming to speak from hard experience, giving mercy because he has needed it. Bettany plays the priest as a man left rudderless by his loss of status, and Cox plays the kind of malcontent who, on a modern movie location, would be angry about the quality of the catering. Given the vast scale of a quasi-medieval epic like *The Lord of the Rings*, it is refreshing to enter the rude poverty of the real Middle Ages, where both the peasant and his lord lived with death and disease all around, and trusted sorcery and superstition to see them through.

The Recruit ★ ★ ½
PG-13, 105 m., 2003

Al Pacino (Walter Burke), Colin Farrell (James Clayton), Bridget Moynahan (Layla Moore), Gabriel Macht (Zack). Directed by Roger Donaldson and produced by Roger Birnbaum, Jeff Apple, and Gary Barber. Screenplay by Roger Towne, Kurt Wimmer, and Mitch Glazer.

The Recruit reveals that the training process of the Central Intelligence Agency is like a fraternity initiation, but more dangerous. At one point would-be agents are given a time limit to walk into a singles bar and report back to the parking lot with a partner willing to have sex with them. Uh-huh. As for the Company's years of embarrassments and enemy spies within the ranks? "We reveal our failures but not our successes," the senior instructor tells the new recruits. Quick, can you think of any event in recent world history that bears the stamp of a CIA success?

The senior instructor is Walter Burke, played by Al Pacino in a performance that is just plain fun to watch, gruff, blunt, with a weathered charm. He recruits an MIT whiz kid named James Clayton (Colin Farrell), who turns down a big offer from Dell Computers because he wants to know more about the fate of his late father, a CIA agent. Or maybe because he uses a Macintosh.

Clayton is taken to The Farm, a rustic hideaway somewhere in Ontario, doubling for Virginia, where during the entrance exam he locks eyes with the lovely and fragrant Layla (Bridget Moynahan). He also meets Zack (Gabriel Macht), a former Miami cop who speaks English, Spanish, and Farsi.

The training process involves a series of Bondian sequences in which the agents learn such skills as blowing up cars: (a) Throw bomb under car; (b) detonate. They are also taught about biodegradable listening devices, weapons usage, and how to shadow someone. And they are told of an agency superweapon that (I think I heard this right) can plug into an electric socket and disable every digital device connected to the grid. Agents: Be sure Mr. Coffee has completed his brewing cycle before employing weapon.

The early scenes in the film are entertaining, yes, because Pacino works his character for all its grizzled charm, and Colin Farrell is not only enormously likable but fascinates us with his permanent four-day beard. His chemistry with Layla is real enough, but come on: When he walks into that bar to pick up someone, doesn't it occur to him that it is hardly a coincidence that Layla is already there? Mata Hari would make mincemeat of this guy, but the girl shows promise; as Marlene Dietrich usefully observed, "It took more than one man to change my name to Shanghai Lily."

Still, it's intriguing to see these young trainees learning their job, and to hear Pacino's observations, which are epigrammatic ("I don't have answers. Only secrets"), hard-boiled ("They show you your medal. You don't even get to take it home"), complacent ("Our cause is just"), and helpful ("Nothing is what it seems. Trust no one"). Pacino's character wisely sticks to political generalities so that the film can play in foreign markets; the closest it comes to current events is in the mention of Farsi, which is the language of Iran, although, as Michael Caine likes to say, not many people know that.

The first two acts of the film are fun because they're all setup and buildup, and because the romance between James and Layla is no more cornball and contrived than it absolutely has to be. The third act is a mess. It saddles Pacino with the thankless role of the Talking Killer (not that he necessarily kills). That's the guy who has to stand there and explain the complexities of the plot when any real CIA veteran would just blow the other guy away. By the time Pacino wraps things up, we're realizing that the mantras "Nothing is what it seems" and "Trust no one," if taken seriously, reveal the entire plot. There is, however, a neat little misunderstanding at the end that earns a chuckle.

The movie was directed by Roger Donaldson, who does political thrillers about as well as anyone; his *Thirteen Days* (2001), about the Cuban missile crisis, and *No Way Out* (1987), about a scandal in the Department of Defense, were gripping and intelligent, and *The Recruit* is so well directed and acted that only a churl such as myself would question its sanity. It's the kind of movie you can sit back and enjoy, as long as you don't make the mistake of thinking too much.

Red Betsy ★ ★ ★

PG, 98 m., 2003

Alison Elliott (Winifred Rounds), Leo Burmester (Emmet Rounds), Lois Smith (Helen Rounds), Chad Lowe (Orin Sanders), William Wise (Grandpa Charles), Isa Thomas (Grandma K), Brent Crawford (Dale Rounds), Courtney Jines (Jane Rounds). Directed by Chris Boebel and produced by James Calabrese. Screenplay by Boebel, based on a short story by Charles Boebel.

Red Betsy takes place in a corner of rural

Wisconsin, and it contains more truth about World War II than *Pearl Harbor* even dreamed of. There are no battle scenes in this movie, no special effects—not even any airplanes, except for one powered with a Model A engine from a junkyard. The movie sees World War II and the following years through the eyes of those who went away and those who stayed at home, and it tells one small true story that represents the incalculable effect of the war.

The movie opens in 1941, on a farm near Delafield, Wisconsin, where a small group has gathered to watch nervously as a little red airplane prepares to take off from a flat field. "Don't worry, Mom; it's guaranteed to fly," says Dale Rounds (Brent Crawford), not very reassuringly, and his plane does fly; he circles overhead in the *Red Betsy*, in what will be the most glorious moment of his short life.

Dale is engaged to Winifred (Alison Elliott). They plan to go to school in Madison in the fall, but he hasn't quite gotten around to breaking the news to his parents, Emmet and Helen (Leo Burmester and Lois Smith). Emmet is crusty and old-fashioned, and expects the young couple to move into the Little House on the property and work the farm until he dies, then they can move into the Big House and Dale can take over. Helen says she'll break the news to her husband. She's had a lot of practice at telling him things he doesn't want to hear. He accepts the plans—not cheerfully, but he accepts them.

(Spoiler warning.) The happiness of the wedding day is brief. Helen dies suddenly and leaves Emmet alone and feeling abandoned. Pearl Harbor is attacked, and Dale can't wait to sign up. Winifred agrees uneasily to move into the Little House, "just for a year," look after Emmet, and wait for Dale to return. Within a few months a telegram arrives with the news that Dale has been killed in action in the Pacific; another piece of news is that Winifred is pregnant.

All of that is prologue to the real subject of the movie, which involves those whose lives were changed by the war, and how they coped. Emmet doesn't need much looking after. He runs the farm as always, and has nothing but scorn for the tree-trimmers of the Rural Electrification Authority, who plan to bring electricity to the district. By 1949, Winifred is teaching in the local school, and she and her daughter, Jane, are still living in the Little House.

There were countless stories like this. Born in downstate Illinois seven months after Pearl Harbor, I grew up hearing about fiancés and sons killed in the war, and saw their pictures—so young and serious in uniform—on the living-room mantel. My aunt never married after her boyfriend died aboard the USS *Indianapolis*. People carried on with their lives and coped, and *Red Betsy* is about that—how the years pass, how Winifred changes and adapts to a life she never imagined, how Jane grows up, how Emmet wages his lonely war against everything that has changed the serenity and predictability that ruled his life for so long.

The movie isn't too sentimental. It is told in the direct terms that we use to relate family stories; they're sad, but we've told them many times and they no longer make us cry. The director is Chris Boebel, a graduate of the NYU film school, and he wrote the screenplay with his father, Charles, an English teacher. It's based on one of the father's short stories. The family comes from rural Wisconsin stock, and Chris's grandmother still lives on a farm. This is not the country postcard of Hollywood fantasies, but just a working farm in a district where there are few enough people that every personality seems backlighted.

Their faces are important in the movie. Although all the leads are professional actors (Lois Smith is the Oscar-nominated Steppenwolf Theatre Company legend, Burmester was in *Gangs of New York*, Elliott is a veteran, and Chad Lowe plays an REA official), they're unaffected and understated; they've observed how midwestern farm people are embarrassed by making displays of themselves. I don't know if the extras in the wedding scene are locals, and I don't need to know, because I can see that they are. I like the way Alison Elliott, as Winifred, really does stand out in the crowd, with her red lipstick, her stylish 1940s dresses, her cigarettes sneaked with a girlfriend on the screened-in porch. I can look at Winifred and look at Emmet and know precisely how and why they will never really understand each other.

And yet the years bring accommodations, and the new becomes routine, and if people want to do the right thing, sooner or later they work their way around to it. That's what *Red Betsy* is about. How long has it been since you saw a movie about that?

Red Dragon ★ ★ ★ ½

R, 124 m., 2002

Anthony Hopkins (Hannibal Lecter), Edward Norton (Will Graham), Ralph Fiennes (Francis Dolarhyde), Harvey Keitel (Jack Crawford), Emily Watson (Reba McClane), Mary-Louise Parker (Molly Graham), Philip Seymour Hoffman (Freddy Lounds). Directed by Brett Ratner and produced by Dino De Laurentiis and Martha Schumacher. Screenplay by Ted Tally, based on the book by Thomas Harris.

Red Dragon opens with the pleasure of seeing Hannibal Lecter as he was before leaving civilian life. The camera floats above a symphony orchestra and down into the audience, and we spot Lecter almost at once, regarding with displeasure an inferior musician. Interesting, how the director forces our attention just as a magician forces a card: We notice Lecter because he is located in a strong place on the screen, because his face is lighted to make him pop out from the drabness on either side, and because he is looking directly at the camera.

I felt, I confess, a certain pleasure to find him in the audience. Hannibal Lecter is one of the most wicked villains in movie history, and one of the most beloved. We forgive him his trespasses because (1) they are forced upon him by his nature; (2) most of the time he is helplessly imprisoned, and providing aid to the FBI, or seeming to, after his peculiar fashion; and (3) he is droll and literate, dryly humorous, elegantly mannered. In these days of movie characters who obediently recite the words the plot requires of them, it's a pleasure to meet a man who can hold up his end of the conversation.

The opening, with Hannibal still in civilian life, allows a tense early scene in which the doctor (Anthony Hopkins) receives a late-night visitor, FBI agent Will Graham (Edward Norton). Graham has been assisted by Lecter in examining a series of crimes which, he has just realized, involved cannibalism—and now, as he regards the doctor in the gloom of the shadowed study, it occurs to him, just as it simultaneously occurs to Lecter, that it is clear to both of them who this cannibal might be.

Flash-forward several years. Lecter is in prison, Graham has taken early retirement, but now his old FBI boss (Harvey Keitel) wants to recruit him to solve a pair of serial killings, this time by a man dubbed the Tooth Fairy because he leaves an unmistakable dental imprint at the scenes of his crimes. Graham resists, but photos of the dead families and a poignant look at his own living family do the trick, and he joins the case as a freelance adviser. This requires him to examine crime scenes by creeping through them in pitch darkness in the middle of the night, although there is no reason he could not visit at noon (except, of course, that he wants to share the killer's point of view, and also because the film seeds the darkness with potential danger).

The director is Brett Ratner, who has not achieved the distinction of the three previous directors of Hannibal Lecter movies (Jonathan Demme on *The Silence of the Lambs*, Ridley Scott on *Hannibal*, and Michael Mann on *Manhunter*, the first version of *Red Dragon*, made in 1986). Ratner's credits have included the *Rush Hour* pictures, *The Family Man*, and *Money Talks*, some with their merits, none suggesting he was qualified to be Lecter's next director.

To my surprise, he does a sure, stylish job, appreciating the droll humor of Lecter's predicament, creating a depraved new villain in the Tooth Fairy (Ralph Fiennes), and using the quiet, intense skills of Edward Norton to create a character whose old fears feed into his new ones. There is also humor, of the uneasy he-can't-get-away-with-this variety, in the character of a nosy scandal-sheet reporter (Philip Seymour Hoffman). The screenplay by Ted Tally, who wrote *Lambs*, also supplies a blind girl in peril (Emily Watson), and blind girls have worked dependably since the days of silent pictures.

A movie like *Red Dragon* is all atmosphere and apprehension. Ratner doesn't give us as much violence or as many sensational shocks as Scott did in *Hannibal*, but that's a plus: Lecter is a character who commands contemplation and unease, and too much action just releases the tension. To be sure, Scott was working with a Thomas Harris novel that itself went so high over the top (remember the quadriplegic murdered with an electric eel?) that much of it could not be filmed. But this movie, based on Harris's first novel, has studied *The Silence of the Lambs* and knows that the action comes second to general creepiness.

There are stabbings, shootings, fires, explosions, tortures, mutilations, and a flaming corpse in a wheelchair, but within reason.

As the Tooth Fairy figure, named Francis Dolarhyde, Ralph Fiennes comes as close as possible to creating a sympathetic monster. What he does is unspeakable. What has been done to him is unspeakable. Dolarhyde himself is horrified by his potential, and the character of the blind girl is not merely a cheap gimmick (although it is that, too), but a device that allows him to ask just how far he is prepared to go. We are reminded of another monster and another blind person, in *Bride of Frankenstein* (1932), and in both cases the monster feels relief because the blind cannot see that he is a monster. (In photos of a crime scene, ex-agent Graham notices that mirrors have been broken and shards of the glass put in the eye sockets of victims—perhaps because the Tooth Fairy cannot stand to look at himself, but is driven to a frenzy when others can look at him.)

The movie has been photographed by Dante Spinotti, who also filmed Michael Mann's more cool, stylized version, and here he provides darkness and saturated colors. The Lecter world is one of dampness, lowering clouds, early sunsets, chill in the bones. Lecter himself, when he appears, is like a little fire we can warm ourselves before; he smiles benevolently, knows all, accepts his nature, offers to help, and more often than not has another macabre scheme under way. The early passages of this movie benefit from our knowledge that Lecter will sooner or later appear; it's as if the plot is tiptoeing toward a ledge.

The Lecter character, and the agents who deal with him and the monsters who take him as a role model, create an atmosphere that encourages style in the filmmaking. It is much the same with the best upper-class crime novels. There is violence, yes, but also a lot of carefully described atmosphere, as we enter the attractive lives of the rich and vicious: Consider Nero Wolfe, who, like Hannibal Lecter, hates to interrupt dinner with a murder.

Red Trousers: The Life of the Hong Kong Stuntmen ★ ★

R, 93 m., 2004

Robin Shou (Himself), Beatrice Chia (Silver),

Keith Cooke (Kermuran), Hakim Alston (Eyemarder), Ridley Tsui (Himself), Craig Reid (Jia Fei). A documentary directed and produced by Robin Shou. Screenplay by Shou.

There's no room for the concept of workman's compensation in the world of the Hong Kong stuntman. Although certain stunts involve an 80 percent chance of a trip to the hospital, that's all in a day's work, and the stuntman who complains risks losing face with his employers—and his fellow stuntmen.

So we learn in *Red Trousers: The Life of the Hong Kong Stuntmen,* a rambling and frustrating documentary that nevertheless contains a lot of information about the men and women who make the Hong Kong action film possible. Not for them the air bags and safety precautions of Hollywood stuntmen. Quite often, we're stunned to learn, their stunts are done exactly as they seem: A fall from a third-floor window, for example, involves a stuntman falling from a third-floor window.

There is a sequence in the film where a stuntman is asked to fall off a railing, slide down a slanting surface to a roof, and bounce off the roof to the floor below. It is rehearsed with pads on the floor. When the shot is ready, the director tells his stuntman, "No pads. Concrete floor." And when the stuntman lands on the concrete incorrectly the first time, he insists on doing the stunt again: "I came off the roof at the wrong angle. This time I will get it right."

Are stuntmen ever killed? No doubt they are, but you will not hear about it in this doc, directed by the onetime stuntman and current actor and director Robin Shou *(Mortal Kombat).* We do learn of a stuntman who was gravely injured when his wire snapped and he fell from a great height to land on jagged rocks. We see the shot as the wire snaps, and then the cameras keep rolling, Jackie Chan–style, as the crew race over to the man, who is screaming in pain. There's a call for pads to put him on, and then he's carried off on the shoulders of five or six crew members. We realized with astonishment that there is no medical team standing by, no ambulance, no provision at all should the stunt go wrong.

Later, visiting the injured stuntman in his village, we learn that he needed many operations over a period of two years on a shattered leg, but thank goodness his facial cuts didn't leave scars. He was paid $25 a day for two days of work, he observes. What about compensation? No mention. Good thing they have socialized medicine.

Wires are, of course, often used in stunts, to make the characters appear to defy gravity, but it would be wrong to assume they make stunts any easier. We see stunts where the wires are used to slam a stuntman against a wall, or spin him into a fall. The wires do not break the impact or slow the fall.

We hear a lot about how carefully Hollywood stuntmen prepare their "gags," but consider a scene in this movie where a stuntman jumps off a highway overpass, lands on top of a moving truck, and then rolls off the truck onto the top of a van before falling to the highway. How was the stunt done? Just as it looks. "My call was for 5:30 and the stunt was finished by 5:45," the stuntman reports cheerfully. Good thing the truck and the van were in the right places, or he might have been run over, or have fallen from the overpass to the pavement.

There are a lot of interviews with stuntmen in the movie, who repeat over and over how they love their work, how excited they are to be in the movies, how of course they're frightened but it's a matter of pride to do a stunt once you have agreed to it—if word gets around that they've balked, the jobs might dry up. They take pride in the fact that Hong Kong stuntmen are allowed to make physical contact with the stars, while in Hollywood, the stars must never be touched.

All of this has a fascination, and yet *Red Trousers* is a jumbled and unsatisfying documentary. It jumps from one subject to another, it provides little historical context, it shows a lot of stunts being prepared and executed but refuses to ask the obvious questions in our minds: Are there no laws to protect injured stuntmen? Are they forced to sign releases? How many are killed or crippled? Why not use more safety measures?

Instead, Shou devotes way too much screen time to scenes from *Lost Time* (2001), a short action film he directed. Yes, we see stunts in preparation and then see them used in the movie, but sometimes he just lets the movie

run, as if we want to see it. He explains that the term "red trousers" originated with the uniforms of students at the Beijing Opera School, which produced many of the early stuntmen, and shows us students of the opera school today; they begin as children, their lives controlled from morning to night, just as depicted in Kaige Chen's great Chinese film *Farewell, My Concubine* (1993). He interviews some of the students, who are still children, and as they affirm their ambitions and vow their dedication, we glimpse a little of where the stuntman code comes from. But if the wire breaks some day, they may, during the fall, find themselves asking basic questions about their working conditions.

Reign of Fire ★
PG-13, 100 m., 2002

Matthew McConaughey (Denton Van Zan), Christian Bale (Quinn Abercromby), Izabella Scorupco (Alex), Gerard Butler (Creedy), Randall Carlton (Tito), Doug Cockle (Goosh), Duncan Keegan (Michael), Rory Keenan (Devon), Alice Krige (Dragon Slayer's Mother). Directed by Rob Bowman and produced by Gary Barber, Roger Birnbaum, Lili Fini Zanuck, and Richard D. Zanuck. Screenplay by Gregg Chabot, Kevin Peterka, and Matt Greenberg.

One regards *Reign of Fire* with awe. What a vast enterprise has been marshaled in the service of such a minute idea. Incredulity is our companion, and it is twofold: We cannot believe what happens in the movie, and we cannot believe that the movie was made.

Of course, in a story involving mankind's battle with fire-breathing dragons in the year 2020, there are a few factual matters you let slide. But the movie makes no sense on its own terms, let alone ours. And it is such a grim and dreary enterprise. One prays for a flower or a ray of sunshine as those grotty warriors clamber into their cellars and over their slag heaps. Not since *Battlefield Earth* has there been worse grooming.

The story: A tunnel beneath London breaks open an underground cavern filled with long-dormant fire-breathing dragons. They fly to the surface and attack mankind. When one is destroyed, countless more take its place. Man's weapons only increase the damage. Soon civilization has been all but wiped out; the heroes of the film cower in their underground hiding places and dream of defeating the dragons.

Along comes Van Zan (Matthew McConaughey), the Dragon Slayer. He is bald and bearded, and his zealot's eyes focus in the middle distance as he speaks. He's the kind of tough guy who smokes cigar butts. Not cigars. Butts. He has a disagreement with Quinn Abercromby (Christian Bale), the leader of the group. I am not sure why they so ferociously oppose each other, but I believe their quarrel comes down to: Van Zan thinks they have to fight the dragons, and Quinn thinks they have to fight the dragons but they have to look out real good, because those are dangerous dragons and might follow them home.

There's not much in the way of a plot. Alex (Izabella Scorupco) gets grubby and distraught while standing between the two men and trying to get them to stop shouting so much and listen to her scientific theories. Meanwhile, dragons attack, their animated wings beating as they fry their enemies. Their animation is fairly good, although at one point a dragon in the background flies past the ruined dome of St. Paul's, and you can see one through the other, or vice versa.

I'm wondering why, if civilization has been destroyed, do they have electricity and fuel? Not supposed to ask such questions. They're like, how come everybody has cigarettes in *Water World*? Van Zan figures out that the dragon's fire comes from the way they secrete the ingredients for "natural napalm" in their mouths. His plan: Get real close and fire an explosive arrow into their open mouth at the crucial moment, causing the napalm to blow up the dragon.

He has another bright idea. (Spoiler warning.) All of the dragons they see are females. Many of them carry eggs. Why no males? Because, Van Zan hypothesizes, the dragons are like fish and it only takes a single male to fertilize umpteen eggs. "We kill the male, we kill the species," he says.

Yeah, but . . . there are dragons everywhere. Do they only have one male, total, singular? How about those eggs? Any of them male? And

also, after the male is dead, presumably all of the females are still alive, and they must be mad as hell now that they're not getting any action. How come they stop attacking?

I know I have probably been inattentive, and that some of these points are solved with elegant precision in the screenplay. But please do not write to explain, unless you can answer me this: Why are the last words in the movie "Thank God for evolution"? Could it be a ray of hope that the offspring of this movie may someday crawl up onto the land and develop a two-celled brain?

Resident Evil ★

R, 100 m., 2002

Milla Jovovich (Alice/Janus Prospero/Marsha Thompson), Michelle Rodriguez (Rain Ocampo), Eric Mabius (Matt), James Purefoy (Spence Parks), Colin Salmon (James P. Shade), Marisol Nichols (Dana), Joseph May (Blue). Directed by Paul Anderson and produced by Anderson, Jeremy Bolt, Bernd Eichinger, and Samuel Hadida. Screenplay by Anderson.

Resident Evil is a zombie movie set in the twenty-first century and therefore reflects several advances over twentieth-century films. For example, in twentieth-century slasher movies, knife blades make a sharpening noise when being whisked through thin air. In the twenty-first century, large metallic objects make crashing noises just by being looked at.

The vast Umbrella Corporation, whose secret laboratory is the scene of the action, specializes in high-tech weapons and genetic cloning. It can turn a little DNA into a monster with a nine-foot tongue. Reminds me of the young man from Kent. You would think Umbrella could make a door that doesn't make a slamming noise when it closes, but its doors make slamming noises even when they're open. The narration tells us that Umbrella products are in "90 percent of American homes," so it finishes behind Morton salt.

The movie is *Dawn of the Dead* crossed with *John Carpenter's Ghosts of Mars,* with zombies not as ghoulish as the first and trains not as big as the second. The movie does however have Milla Jovovich and Michelle Rodriguez.

According to the Internet Movie Database, Jovovich plays "Alice/Janus Prospero/Marsha Thompson," although I don't believe anybody ever calls her anything. I think some of those names come from the original video game. Rodriguez plays "Rain Ocampo," no relation to the Phoenix family. In pairing classical and literary references, the match of Alice and Janus Prospero is certainly the best name combo since Huckleberry P. Jones/Pa Hercules was portrayed by Ugh-Fudge Bwana in *Forbidden Zone* (1980).

The plot: Vials of something that looks like toy coils of plastic DNA models are being delicately manipulated behind thick shields in an airtight chamber by remote-controlled robot hands; when one of the coils is dropped, the factory automatically seals its exits and gasses and drowns everyone inside. Umbrella practices zero tolerance. We learn that the factory, code named The Hive, is buried half a mile below the surface. Seven investigators go down to see what happened. Three are killed, but Alice/Janus Prospero/Marsha, Rain Ocampo, Matt, and Spence survive in order to be attacked for sixty minutes by the dead Hive employees, who have turned into zombies. Meanwhile, the monster with the nine-foot tongue is mutating. (Eventually, its tongue is nailed to the floor of a train car and it is dragged behind it on the third rail. I hate it when that happens.)

These zombies, like the *Dawn of the Dead* zombies, can be killed by shooting them, so there is a lot of zombie shooting, although not with the squishy green-goo effect of George Romero's 1978 film. The zombies are like vampires, since when one bites you it makes you a zombie. What I don't understand is why zombies are so graceless. They walk with the lurching shuffle of a drunk trying to skate through urped Slurpees to the men's room.

There is one neat effect when characters unwisely venture into a corridor and the door slams shut on them. Then a laser beam passes at head level, decapitating one. Another beam whizzes past at waist level, cutting the second in two while the others duck. A third laser pretends to be high but then switches to low, but the third character outsmarts it by jumping at the last minute. Then the fourth laser turns into a grid that dices its victim into pieces the size of a Big Mac. Since the grid is inescapable, what were the earlier lasers about? Does the corridor have a sense of humor?

Alice/Janus Prospero/Marsha Thompson and her colleagues are highly trained scientists, which leads to the following exchange when they stare at a pool of zombie blood on the floor.

Alice/J.P./M.T./Rain (I forget which): "It's coagulating!"
Matt/Spence (I forget which): "That's not possible!"
"Why not?!?"
"Because blood doesn't do that until you're dead!"

How does the blood on the floor know if you're dead? The answer to this question is so obvious I am surprised you would ask. Because it is zombie blood.

The characters have no small talk. Their dialogue consists of commands, explanations, exclamations, and ejaculations. Yes, an ejaculation can be dialogue. If you live long enough you may find that happening frequently.

Oh, and the film has a Digital Readout. The Hive is set to lock itself forever after sixty minutes have passed, so the characters are racing against time. In other words, after it shuts all of its doors and gasses and drowns everybody, it waits sixty minutes and *really* shuts its doors—big time. No wonder the steel doors make those slamming noises. In their imagination, they're practicing. Creative visualization, it's called. I became inspired, and visualized the theater doors slamming behind me.

Respiro ★ ★ ★
PG-13, 90 m., 2003

Valeria Golino (Grazia), Vincenzo Amato (Pietro), Francesco Casisa (Pasquale), Veronica D'Agostino (Marinella), Filippo Pucillo (Filippo). Directed by Emanuele Crialese and produced by Dominic Process. Screenplay by Crialese.

That there is something not right about Grazia, all the village agrees. "Bring her shot!" her husband calls out at fraught moments, and the children and neighbors hold her down while he jabs her with a needle filled with—what? It calms her down, anyway. There is said to be a doctor in Milan who could help her, but when the entire village unites in favor of the Milan trip, Grazia runs away and is thought to be dead in the sea.

The village is angry at her because Grazia opened the doors of an old stone building and released dozens of stray dogs to run about the streets. Whether they were rabid or just homeless is not clear, and why they were being held instead of put down is not explained, but the men of the village are resourceful, and take to their rooftops with rifles to shoot all the dogs. Then it becomes clear that Grazia must go to Milan: "This can't go on."

The village is on the Italian island of Lampedusa, not far from Tunisia. Whether *Respiro* paints an accurate portrait of its society, I cannot say. Fishing and canning are the local industries, everybody lives in everybody else's pockets, and the harsh sun beats down on a landscape of rock and beach, sea and sky, and sand-colored homes surrounded by children and Vespas.

In this world Grazia (Valeria Golino) is a legend. Young-looking to be the mother of three children, one a teenager, she is married to Pietro (Vincenzo Amato), a handsome fisherman who loves her, but is understandably disturbed when his boat passes a beach where Grazia is swimming nude with their children. More accurately, she is nude, and her son Pasquale (Francesco Casisa) wants her to put her clothes back on and come home with him.

Pasquale tries to protect his mother. She has what we in the audience diagnose as manic depression, although the movie never declares itself. Mostly she's in the manic phase, too happy, too uncontrolled, burning with a fierce delight that wears out everyone else. Rather than go to Milan, she runs away, and Pasquale helps her hide in a cave he knows, and brings her food while the village searches for her and Pietro grows bereft.

But the story of Grazia is only one of the pleasures of *Respiro*, which won the grand prize in the Critics' Week program at Cannes 2002. The movie, written and directed by the New York University graduate Emanuele Crialese, has a feeling for the rhythms of life on the island, and especially for the way the boys— Grazia's two sons and others—run wild as boys will. We see them trapping birds and cooking them for a treat, dep[...] ing tribes constantly [...] to returning fishing [...] a few fish they can [...] chances at winnin[...]

When the boys [...] their bearded and sun-bronzed [...] thers behave as all fathers do everywhere, a[...] set up the train "for the kids" because they want to play with it themselves. In the middle of this enterprise, Grazia lures Pietro away for a "nap." It's clear they are still passionately in love. Sex indeed is not far from the surface in this family, and the teenage daughter, Marinella (Veronica D'Agostino), flirts with the new policeman in town, who seems a good deal less sure of his moves than she is.

That's why it's all the more sad when Grazia disappears and Pasquale helps in her deception. Pietro mourns on the beach while Grazia is not far away, living in the cave. How could she do such a heartless thing? Well, because she really does need the man in Milan, although the movie sidesteps that inescapable reality with an ending both poetic and unlikely.

Respiro is a cheerful, life-affirming film, strong in its energy, about vivid characters. It uses mental illness as an entertainment, not a disease. As I watched it, I wondered—do such people really live on Lampedusa, and is this film an accurate reflection of their lives? I have no idea. I tend to doubt it. But perhaps it doesn't matter, since they exist for the ninety minutes of this film, and engage us with their theatricality. Grazia needs help, but her island will not be such a lively place to live if she gets it.

The Return ★ ★ ★
NO MPAA RATING, 106 m., 2004

Vladimir Garin (Andrey), Ivan Dobronravov (Ivan), Konstantin Lavronenko (Father), Natalia Vdovina (Mother). Directed by Andrey Zvyagintsev and produced by Dmitry Lesnevsky. Screenplay by Vladimir Moiseenko and Alexander Novototsky.

Here is the latest and most disturbing of three films about children and their ominous fathers. Bill Paxton's *Frailty* was about two brothers who are fearful about their father's conviction that an angel of God has assigned him to kill possessed among us. *I'm Not Scared,* ...ele Salvatores of Italy, was about a ...boy who stumbles upon a chained kid-...victim and gradually realizes his father is ...e kidnapper. Now we have *The Return,* from Russia, which is all the more frightening because two young brothers never do fully understand their father's alarming behavior. It is a Kafkaesque story, in which ominous things follow each other with a certain internal logic, but make no sense at all.

As the movie opens, Andrey (Vladimir Garin) and his younger brother Ivan (Ivan Dobronravov) return home one day to hear their mother whisper, "Quiet! Dad's sleeping." This is a father they have not seen for years, if ever, and the movie gives us no explanation for his absence. Almost immediately he proposes a fishing trip, and the boys are less than overjoyed at this prospect of leaving home with a man who is essentially a stranger.

The father (Konstantin Lavronenko) drives them to a lakeside. He attempts to impose stern discipline in the car, but this seems less the result of cruelty than because of his awkwardness around young boys. Indeed, the movie's refusal to declare the father a villain adds to the ambiguity; eventually he creates a disturbing situation, but does he act by design, compulsion, or impulse? And what are his motives?

Whatever they are, it's clear that catching fish is not one of them. There is an ominous scene under a lowering sky and scattered rain, as he and the boys row a small boat to an island far away in the middle of the lake. On the island, the boys explore, and there is a tower that tests their fear of heights. They spy on their father, and see him retrieve a small buried trunk. What's in it? We think perhaps he is a paroled convict, returning for his loot. Or a man who has learned of buried treasure. Or . . .

Doesn't matter. The box, which has caused so much trouble, is lost to history by the end of the film, along with the reason why the father thought he needed to bring his two sons along. Was he acting from some kind of stunted impulse to make up time with his boys? Was he subjecting them to an experience he had undergone? Are they safe with him?

The Return, directed by Andrey Zvyagintsev and cowritten by Vladimir Moiseenko and Alexander Novototsky, does not conceal information from the audience, which would be a technique of manipulation—but from the young boys, which is a technique of drama. The movie is not about the father's purpose but the boys' confusion and alarm. Like the other two films I mentioned, it eventually arrives at the point where the boys must decide whether or not to act, and here the interior dynamic of their own relationship is more important than how they feel about their father.

Zvyagintsev films on chilly, overcast days, on an island that in this season is not a vacation spot. His cinematographer, Mikhail Kritchman, denatures the color film stock to deny us cheer. We do not like this island, or trust this father, or like the looks of the boat—which for a long time is left untethered on the beach, so that there's a constant underthought that it might float away. What finally happens is not anything we could have anticipated, except to observe that something like that seemed to be hanging in the damp, cold air.

Note: An additional sadness creeps into the film if we know that Vladimir Garin, the older of the two boys, drowned not long after the film was completed, in a situation not unlike one in the film.

Return to Never Land ★ ★ ★

G, 76 m., 2002

With the voices of: Blayne Weaver (Peter Pan), Harriet Owen (Jane), Corey Burton (Captain Hook), Jeff Bennett (Smee/Starkey and Wibbles), Kath Soucie (Wendy/Narrator), Andrew McDonough (Danny). An animated film directed by Robin Budd and Donovan Cook and produced by Christopher Chase and Dan Rounds. Screenplay by Carter Crocker and Temple Matthews.

The opening titles tell us this is "Peter Pan in Return to Never Land," and indeed, why can't an animated character be a movie star? Years have passed since the end of the first story— London is reeling under the Blitz—and Wendy has grown up, married, and produced a daughter, Jane. But Peter Pan, Tinker Bell, the Lost Boys, and Captain Hook all remain unchanged in Never Land.

During all of those years Hook has continued to search for his lost treasure, which was, he believes, stolen by Peter and hidden somewhere on the island. As the film opens, Jane indulges her mother's stories about fairies that can fly. She doesn't believe them, but is persuaded when kidnapped by Hook and his men—who fly in their pirate ship over London, luckily without engaging any antiaircraft batteries.

Hook believes Jane may be the key to finding the treasure—or at the least a way to pry the secret out of Peter. We can almost sympathize with his impatience. The original *Peter Pan* hurtled through its narrative, and then left him on hold for twenty-five years, gnashing his teeth and spinning his wheels. All the same, Never Land rules apply, and at one point Tinker Bell is grounded because, yes, Jane doesn't believe in fairies.

Of the voice-over talent, Corey Burton is almost inevitably the star, because he's assigned Captain Hook, one of those roles that sort of directs itself. Blayne Weaver is fine as Peter Pan, but it's interesting that none of the voice talents sing any of the movie's songs; they appear on the sound track as commentaries or parallels to the action.

Return to Never Land is a bright and energetic animated comedy, with all the slick polish we expect from Disney, but it's not much more. This one feels like it had a narrow escape from the direct-to-video market. It's not a major item like *Monsters, Inc.* and lacks the in-jokes and sly references that allow a movie like that to function on two levels. It's more of a Saturday afternoon stop for the kiddies—harmless, skillful, and aimed at grade-schoolers.

The Revolution Will Not Be Televised
★ ★ ★ ½
NO MPAA RATING, 74 m., 2003

Featuring Hugo Chavez, Pedro Carmona, Jesse Helms, Colin Powell, and George Tenet. A documentary directed by Kim Bartley and Donnacha O'Briain and produced by David Power.

Was the United States a shadowy presence in the background of the aborted coup in Venezuela in 2002? The democratically elected government of Hugo Chavez was briefly overthrown by a cabal of rich businessmen and army officers, shortly after their representatives had been welcomed in the White House. Oh, the United States denied any involvement in the episode; there's Colin Powell on TV, forthrightly professing innocence. But earlier we heard ominous rumblings from Jesse Helms, Ari Fleischer, and George Tenet, agreeing that Chavez was no friend of the United States, and after the coup there was no expression of dismay from Washington, no announcement that we would work to restore the elected government.

Why was Chavez not our friend? It all comes down to oil, as it so often does these days. Venezuela is the fourth-largest oil-producing nation in the world, and much of its oil comes to the United States. Its price has been guaranteed by the cooperation of the nation's ruling class. Chavez was elected primarily by the poor. He asked a simple question: Since the oil wells have always been nationalized and the oil belongs to the state, why do the profits flow directly to the richest, whitest 20 percent of the population, while being denied to the poorer, darker 80 percent? His plan was to distribute the profits equally among all Venezuelans.

This was, you may agree, a fair and obvious solution. But not to the 20 percent, of course. And not to other interested parties, including our friends the Saudis, whose people get poorer as the sheiks get richer. Charging Chavez with being a Communist who wanted to bring Castroism to Venezuela, the rich and powerful staged a coup on April 12, 2002. Chavez was put under arrest and held on an island, and the millionaire businessman Pedro Carmona was sworn in as president. This was in violation of the constitution, but he blandly assured TV audiences he was in power because "of a mandate better than any referendum." There was no disagreement from Washington.

Incredibly, the coup failed. Hundreds of thousands of Chavez supporters surrounded the presidential palace, and the loyal presidential guard put the interlopers under arrest. Although the state-run Channel 8 was taken off the air and the private channels told lies and showed falsified news footage, Venezuelans learned from CNN and other cable channels that Chavez had not resigned and a coup had taken place; they demanded his return, and a few days later he arrived by helicopter at the presidential palace and resumed office.

These events are recounted in *The Revolution Will Not Be Televised*, a remarkable documentary by two Irish filmmakers. It is remarkable because the filmmakers, Kim Bartley and Donnacha O'Briain, had access to virtually everything that happened within the palace during the entire episode. They happened to be in Caracas to make a doc about Chavez, they had access to his cabinet meetings, they were inside the palace under siege, they faced a tense deadline after which it would be bombed, they stayed after Chavez gave himself up to prevent the bombing, and they filmed the new government. There are astonishing shots, such as the one where Chavez's men, now back in power, go down to the basement to confront coup leaders who have been taken prisoner. Why no one on either side thought to question the presence of the TV crew is a mystery, but they got an inside look at the coup—before, during, and after—that is unique in film history.

Film can be made to lie. Consider footage shown on the private TV channels to justify the coup. Learning that the right wing was sponsoring a protest march against Chavez, his supporters also marched on the palace. Scuffles broke out, and then concealed snipers began to fire on the Chavez crowd. Some in the crowd fired back. Although the dead and wounded were Chavez supporters, the private TV showed footage of them firing, and said they were firing at the anti-Chavez protest march. Bartley and O'Briain use footage of the same moment, from another angle, to show that there is no protest march in view, and that the fire is aimed at snipers above the parade route. That this deception was deliberate is confirmed by a producer for the private TV channels, who resigned in protest and explains how the footage was falsified. (Private TV did have one interesting slip; in a talk show the morning after the coup, one of its elated leaders talks frankly about the plan to disrupt the Chavez march and overthrow the government, while others on the program look like they'd like to throttle him.)

If private TV lied to the nation in support of the coup, the doc itself is clearly biased in favor

of Chavez—most clearly so in depicting his opponents. When the right-wing leaders are introduced, it's in slo-mo, with ominous music and funereal drums. He may have articulate opponents in Venezuela, but the only ones we see are inane society people who warn each other, "Watch your servants!" Does everyone on the right in Venezuela dress like (a) an undertaker, (b) a military officer, or (c) a disco guest circa 1990?

Interestingly, there was relative civility on both sides. Chavez and his cabinet were arrested, but not harmed. After Chavez regained power, he said there would be no "witch hunt" of those who opposed him; although Carmona fled to Miami, several of the coup's military leaders (stripped of rank) remained in Venezuela and still continue as members of the opposition. This shows remarkable confidence on the part of Chavez, and a commitment to the democratic process.

It is, of course, impossible to prove that the coup was sponsored by the CIA or any other U.S. agency. But what was the White House thinking when it welcomed two antigovernment leaders who soon after were instrumental in the coup? Not long ago, reviewing another film, I wrote about the CIA-sponsored overthrow of Chile's democratically elected president, Salvador Allende. I got a lot of e-mail telling me the CIA had nothing to do with it. For anyone who believes that, I have a bridge I'd like to sell them.

Note: The last words in George Orwell's notebook were: "At age 50, every man has the face he deserves." Although it is outrageously unfair and indefensibly subjective of me, I cannot prevent myself from observing that Chavez and his cabinet have open, friendly faces, quick to smile, and that the faces of his opponents are closed, shifty, hardened. ☞

The Ring ★ ★
PG-13, 115 m., 2002

Naomi Watts (Rachel Keller), Martin Henderson (Noah), Brian Cox (Richard Morgan), David Dorfman (Aidan Keller), Lindsay Frost (Ruth), Amber Tamblyn (Katie), Rachael Bella (Becca), Daveigh Chase (Samara Morgan), Richard Lineback (Innkeeper). Directed by Gore Verbinski and produced by Laurie MacDonald and Walter F. Parkes. Screenplay by Hiroshi Takahashi and Ehren Kruger, based on the novel by Kôji Suzuki.

Rarely has a more serious effort produced a less serious result than in *The Ring*, the kind of dread dark horror film where you better hope nobody in the audience snickers, because the film teeters right on the edge of the ridiculous.

Enormous craft has been put into the movie, which looks just great, but the story goes beyond contrivance into the dizzy realms of the absurd. And although there is no way for everything to be explained (and many events lack any possible explanation), the movie's ending explains and explains and *explains,* until finally you'd rather just give it a pass than sit through one more tedious flashback.

The story involves a video that brings certain death. You look at it, the phone rings, and you find out you have seven days to live. A prologue shows some teenage victims of the dread curse, and then newspaper reporter Rachel Keller (Naomi Watts) gets on the case, helped by eerie drawings by her young son, Aidan (David Dorfman).

The story has been recycled from a popular Japanese thriller by Kôji Suzuki, which was held off the market in this country to clear the field for this remake. Alas, the same idea was ripped off in August 2002 by *FearDotCom,* also a bad movie, but more plain fun than *The Ring,* and with a climax that used brilliant visual effects while this one drags on endlessly.

I dare not reveal too much of the story, but will say that the video does indeed bring death in a week, something we are reminded of as Rachel tries to solve the case while titles tick off the days. A single mom, she enlists Aidan's father, a video geek named Noah (Martin Henderson), to analyze the deadly tape. He tags along for the adventure, which inevitably leads to their learning to care for each other, I guess, although the movie is not big on relationships. Her investigation leads her to a remote cottage on an island, and to the weird, hostile man (Brian Cox) who lives there. And then the explanations start to pile up.

This is Naomi Watts's first move since *Mulholland Drive,* and I was going to complain that we essentially learn nothing about her character, except that she's a newspaper reporter—but then I remembered that in *Mulholland Drive* we essentially learned nothing except that she was a small-town girl in Hollywood, and by the end of the movie we weren't even sure we had learned that. *Mulholland Drive* however, evoked juicy emotions and dimensions that *The Ring* is lacking, and involved us in a puzzle that was intriguing instead of simply tedious.

There are a couple of moments when we think *The Ring* is going to end, and it doesn't. One is that old reliable where the heroine, soaking wet and saved from death, says, "I want to go home," and the hero cushions her head on his shoulder. But no, there's more. Another is when Aidan says, "You didn't let her out, did you?" That would have been a nice ironic closer, but the movie spells out the entire backstory in merciless detail, until when we're finally walking out of the theater, we're almost ashamed to find ourselves wondering, hey, who was that on the phone?

Rivers and Tides: Andy Goldsworthy Working with Time ★ ★ ★ ½
NO MPAA RATING, 90 m., 2003

A documentary about Scottish environmental artist Andy Goldsworthy. Directed by Thomas Riedelsheimer and produced by Annedore von Donop. Screenplay by Riedelsheimer.

Have you ever watched—no, better, have you ever *been* a young child intent on building something out of the materials at hand in the woods, or by a stream, or at the beach? Have you seen the happiness of an adult joining kids and slowly slipping out of adulthood and into the absorbing process of this . . . and now . . . and over here . . . and build this up . . . and it should go like this?

The artist Andy Goldsworthy lives in that world of making things. They have no names; they are Things. He brings order to leaves or twigs or icicles and then surrenders them to the process of nature. He will kneel for hours by the oceanside, creating a cairn of stones that balances precariously, the weight on the top holding the sides in place, and then the tide will come in and wash away the sand beneath, and the cairn will collapse, as it must, as it should.

"The very thing that brought the thing to be is the thing that will cause its death," Goldsworthy explains, as his elegant, spiraled constructions once again become random piles of stones on the beach. As with Andy's stones, so with our lives.

Rivers and Tides: Andy Goldsworthy Working with Time is a documentary that opened in San Francisco in mid-2002 and just kept running, moving from one theater to another, finding its audience not so much through word of mouth as through hand-on-elbow, as friends steered friends into the theater, telling them that this was a movie they had to see. I started getting E-mail about it months ago. Had I seen it? I hadn't even heard of it.

It is a film about a man wholly absorbed in the moment. He wanders woods and riverbanks, finding materials and playing with them, fitting them together, piling them up, weaving them, creating beautiful arrangements that he photographs before they return to chaos. He knows that you can warm the end of an icicle just enough to make it start to melt, and then hold it against another icicle, and it will stick. With that knowledge, he makes an ice sculpture, and then it melts in the sun and is over.

Some of his constructions are of magical beauty, as if left behind by beings who disappeared before the dawn. He finds a way to arrange twigs in a kind of web. He makes a spiral of rocks that fans out from a small base and then closes in again, a weight on top holding it together. This is not easy, and he gives us pointers: "Top control can be the death of a work."

Often Andy will be . . . almost there . . . right on the edge . . . holding his breath as one last piece goes into place . . . and then the whole construction will collapse, and he will look deflated, defeated for a moment ("Damn!"), and then start again: "When I build something I often take it to the very edge of its collapse, and that's a very beautiful balance."

His art needs no explanation. We go into modern art galleries and find work we cannot comprehend as art. We see Damien Hirst's sheep, cut down the middle and embedded in plastic, and we cannot understand how it won the Turner Prize (forgetting that no one thought Turner was making art, either). We suppose that concepts and statements are involved.

But with Andy Goldsworthy, not one word of explanation is necessary because every single one of us has made something like his art. We have piled stones or made architectural constructions out of sand, or played Pick-Up Stix, and we know *exactly* what he is trying to do—and why. Yes, why, because his art takes him into that zone where time drops away and we forget our left-brain concerns and are utterly absorbed by whether this . . . could go like this . . . without the whole thing falling apart.

The documentary, directed, photographed, and edited by Thomas Riedelsheimer, a German filmmaker, goes home with Goldsworthy to Penpont, Scotland, where we see him spending some time with his wife and kids. It follows him to a museum in the south of France, and to an old stone wall in Canada that he wants to rebuild in his own way. It visits with him old stone markers high in mountains, built by early travelers to mark the path.

And it offers extraordinary beauty. We watch as he smashes stones to release their content, and uses that bright red dye to make spectacular patterns in the currents and whirlpools of streams. We see a long rope of linked leaves, bright green, uncoil as it floats downstream. Before, we saw only the surface of the water, but now the movement of the leaves reveals its current and structure. What a happy man. Watching this movie is like daydreaming.

Road to Perdition ★ ★ ★
R, 119 m., 2002

Tom Hanks (Michael Sullivan), Paul Newman (John Rooney), Tyler Hoechlin (Michael Sullivan Jr.), Jude Law (Maguire, aka The Reporter), Anthony LaPaglia (Al Capone), Daniel Craig (Connor Rooney), Stanley Tucci (Frank Nitti), Jennifer Jason Leigh (Annie Sullivan). Directed by Sam Mendes and produced by Mendes, Dean Zanuck, and Richard D. Zanuck. Screenplay by David Self, based on the graphic novel by Max Allan Collins and Richard Piers Rayner.

Road to Perdition is like a Greek tragedy, dealing out remorseless fates for all the characters. Some tragedies, like "Hamlet," are exhilarating, because we have little idea how quirks of character will bring about the final doom. But the impact of Greek tragedy seems muted to me, because it's preordained. Since *Road to Perdition* is in that tradition, it loses something. It has been compared to *The Godfather*, but *The Godfather* was about characters with free will, and here the characters seem to be performing actions already long since inscribed in the books of their lives.

Yet the movie has other strengths to compensate for the implacable progress of its plot. It is wonderfully acted. And no movie this year will be more praised for its cinematography; Conrad L. Hall's work seems certain to win the Academy Award. He creates a limbo of darkness, shadow, night, fearful faces half-seen, cold, and snow. His characters stand in downpours, the rain running off the brims of their fedoras and soaking the shoulders of their thick wool overcoats. Their feet must always be cold. The photography creates a visceral chill.

The story involves three sets of fathers and sons—two biological, the third emotional—and shows how the lives they lead make ordinary love between them impossible. Tom Hanks plays Michael Sullivan, an enforcer for a suburban branch of the Chicago mob, circa 1931. Tyler Hoechlin plays his son Michael Jr., a solemn-eyed twelve-year-old. After his brother, Peter, asks, "What does Dad do for a job?" Michael Jr. decides to find out for himself. One night he hides in a car, goes along for the ride, and sees a man killed. Not by his father, but what difference does it make?

Sullivan works for John Rooney (Paul Newman), the mob boss, who is trim and focused and uses few words. John's son Connor (Daniel Craig) is a member of the mob. Sullivan finds out that Connor has been stealing from his father, and that sets up the movie's emotional showdown, because Sullivan thinks of John like his own father, and John speaks of Sullivan as a son. "Your mother knows I love Mr. Rooney," Michael Sr. tells his son. "When we had nothing, he gave us a home."

Men who name their sons after themselves presumably hope the child will turn out a little like them. This is not the case with Michael Sr., who has made a pact with evil in order to support his wife (Jennifer Jason Leigh) and two boys in comfort. Unlike Rooney, he doesn't want

his son in the business. The movie's plot asks whether it is possible for fathers to spare their sons from the costs of their sins. It also involves sons who feel they are not the favorite. "Did you like Peter better than me?" Michael Jr. asks his father, after his little brother has been killed. And later Sullivan goes to see Mr. Rooney, and cannot understand why Rooney would prefer his son Connor, who betrayed and stole from him, to his loyal employee who is "like a son."

The movie is directed by Sam Mendes, from a graphic novel by Max Allan Collins and Richard Piers Rayner, much revised by screenwriter David Self. This is only Mendes's second film, but recall that his first, *American Beauty*, won Oscars in 1999 for best picture, director, actor, screenplay—and cinematography, by Conrad Hall. Both films involve men in family situations of unbearable pain, although the first is a comedy (of sorts) and this one certainly is not. Both involve a father who, by leading the life he chooses, betrays his family and even endangers them. Both involve men who hate their work.

The key relationships are between Hanks and Newman, and Hanks and Tyler Hoechlin, the newcomer who plays his son. Newman plays Mr. Rooney as a man who would prefer that as few people be harmed as necessary, but he has an implacable definition of "necessary." He is capable of colorful Corleone-style sayings, as when he declares that his mob will not get involved in labor unions: "What men do after work is what made us rich. No need to screw them at work." Against this benevolence we must set his trade in booze, gambling, and women, and his surgical willingness to amputate any associate who is causing difficulty.

The Hanks character sees the good side of Mr. Rooney so willfully that he almost cannot see the bad. Even after he discovers the worst, he feels wounded more than betrayed. He's a little naive, and it takes Rooney, in a speech Newman delivers with harsh clarity, to disabuse him. Called a murderer, Rooney says: "There are *only* murderers in this room, Michael. Open your eyes. This is the life we chose. The life we lead. And there is only one guarantee—none of us will see heaven."

Sullivan wants his son to see heaven, and that sets up their flight from Rooney justice. Father and son flee, pursued by a hit man (Jude

Law) who supplements his income by selling photographs of the people he has killed. The plot all works out in an ending that may seem too neat, unless you reflect that in tragedy there is a place of honor for the *deus ex machina*—the god being lowered by the machinery of the plot into a scene that requires solution.

I mentioned the rain. This is a water-soaked picture, with melting snow on the streets and dampness in every room. That gives Conrad Hall the opportunity to develop and extend one of his most famous shots. In *In Cold Blood* (1967), he has a close-up of Robert Blake, as a convicted killer on the night of his death. He puts Blake near a window, and lights his face through the windowpane, as raindrops slide down the glass. The effect is of tears on his face. In *Road to Perdition,* the light shines through a rain-swept window onto a whole room that seems to weep.

After I saw *Road to Perdition,* I knew I admired it, but I didn't know if I liked it. I am still not sure. It is cold and holds us outside. Yes, there is the love of Hanks for his son, but how sadly he is forced to express it. The troubles of the mob seem caused because Rooney prefers family to good management, but Michael Sullivan's tragedy surely comes because he has put it the other way around—placing Rooney above his family. The movie shares with *The Godfather* the useful tactic of keeping the actual victims out of view. There are no civilians here, destroyed by mob activities. All of the characters, good and bad, are supplied from within the mob. But there is never the sense that any of these characters will tear loose, think laterally, break the chains of their fate. Choice, a luxury of the Corleones, is denied to the Sullivans and Rooneys, and choice or its absence is the difference between Sophocles and Shakespeare. I prefer Shakespeare.

Roger Dodger ★ ★ ★

R, 104 m., 2002

Campbell Scott (Roger), Jesse Eisenberg (Nick), Isabella Rossellini (Joyce), Elizabeth Berkley (Andrea), Jennifer Beals (Sophie), Ben Shenkman (Donovan), Mina Badie (Donna). Directed by Dylan Kidd and produced by Anne Chaisson, Kidd, and George VanBuskirk. Screenplay by Kidd.

Roger is an advertising executive who explains that his technique is to make consumers feel miserable so they can restore their happiness by buying the sponsor's product. In his private life, Roger is the product, trying to make women feel miserable about themselves and then offering himself as the cure. Roger is an optimist who keeps on talking, just as if his approach works.

As *Roger Dodger* opens, Roger (Campbell Scott) has just been dumped by his lover, Joyce (Isabella Rossellini), who is also his boss and makes him feel miserable with admirable economy of speech: "I am your boss. You work for me. I have explained to you that I do not wish to see you socially any longer. Find a way to deal with it." Roger can't quite believe her. Indeed, he attends a party at her house that he has specifically not been invited to. He's an optimist in the face of setbacks, a con man who has conned himself.

Into his office and life one day walks his nephew Nick (Jesse Eisenberg), who is sixteen. Roger isn't on speaking terms with Nick's mother, but Nick is another matter, a young man who asks for guidance that Roger feels himself uniquely equipped to provide. Nick knows little of women and wants advice, and Roger starts with theory and then takes Nick nightclub-hopping so they can work on the practice. During one incredibly lucky evening, they meet Andrea and Sophie (Elizabeth Berkley and Jennifer Beals), who are intrigued by Nick's innocence, charmed by his honesty, and delighted by his wit. The kid's naïveté acts like a mirror in which they can study their own attitudes. Roger the coach finds himself on the sidelines.

The movie, written and directed by Dylan Kidd, depends on its dialogue and, like a film by David Mamet or Neil LaBute, has characters who use speech like an instrument. The screenplay would be entertaining just to read, as so very few are. Scott, who usually plays more conventional roles, emerges here as acid and sardonic, with a Shavian turn to his observations, and although his advice is not very useful it is entertaining.

The problem of Nick's young age is one that

several other movies, notably *Tadpole,* have negotiated lately. Apparently when it comes to the age of consent for sex, in the movies young males don't count. If an innocent sixteen-year-old girl were taken to a nightclub by her aunt and set up with a couple of thirty-something guys, the MPAA would be outraged and Hollywood terrified. But turn the tables and somehow the glint in Nick's eye takes care of everything.

Roger Dodger effectively deflects criticism in this area by making Roger the victim and the subject. While Nick is funny and earnest and generates many laughs, the movie is really about Roger—about his attempts to tutor his nephew in a lifestyle that has left the older man lonely and single. The film is not just a lot of one-liners, but has a buried agenda, as the funny early dialogue slides down into confusion and sadness. There is a lesson here for Nick, but not the one Roger is teaching.

Rollerball ½★

PG-13, 98 m., 2002

Chris Klein (Jonathan Cross), Jean Reno (Alexi Petrovich), LL Cool J (Marcus Ridley), Rebecca Romijn-Stamos (Aurora), Naveen Andrews (Sanjay), Paul Heyman (Announcer). Directed by John McTiernan and produced by McTiernan, Charles Roven, and Beau St. Clair. Screenplay by William Harrison, Larry Ferguson, and John Pogue, based on the short story by Harrison.

Rollerball is an incoherent mess, a jumble of footage in search of plot, meaning, rhythm, and sense. There are bright colors and quick movement on the screen, which we can watch as a visual pattern that, in entertainment value, falls somewhere between a kaleidoscope and a lava lamp.

The movie stars Chris Klein, who shot to stardom, so to speak, in the *American Pie* movies and inhabits his violent action role as if struggling against the impulse to blurt out, "People, why can't we all just get along?" Klein is a nice kid. For this role, you need someone who has to shave three times a day.

The movie is set in 2005 in a Central Asian republic apparently somewhere between Uzbekistan and Mudville. Jean Reno plays Petro-

vich, owner of "the hottest sports start-up in the world," a Rollerball league that crowds both motorcycles and roller skaters on a figure-eight track that at times looks like Roller Derby crossed with demo derby, at other times like a cruddy video game. The sport involves catching a silver ball and throwing it at a big gong so that showers of sparks fly. One of the star players confesses she doesn't understand it, but so what: In the final game Petrovich suspends all rules, fouls, and penalties. This makes no difference that I could see.

Klein plays Jonathan Cross, an NHL draft pick who has to flee America in a hurry for the crime of racing suicidally down the hills of San Francisco flat on his back on what I think is a skateboard. His best friend is Marcus Ridley (LL Cool J), who convinces him to come to Podunkistan and sign for the big bucks. Jonathan is soon attracted to Aurora (Rebecca Romijn-Stamos, from *X-Men*).

"Your face isn't nearly as bad as you think," he compliments her. She has a scar over one eye, but is otherwise in great shape, as we can see because the locker rooms of the future are co-ed. Alas, the women athletes of the future still turn their backs to the camera at crucial moments, carry strategically placed towels, stand behind furniture, and in general follow the rules first established in 1950s nudist volleyball pictures.

I counted three games in the Rollerball season. The third is the championship. There is one road trip, to a rival team's Rollerball arena, which seems to have been prefabricated in the city dump. The games are announced by Paul Heyman, who keeps screaming, "What the hell is going on?" There is no one else in the booth with him. Yet when Aurora wants to show Jonathan that an injury was deliberate, she can call up instant replays from all the cameras on equipment thoughtfully provided in the locker room.

The funniest line in the movie belongs to Jean Reno, who bellows, "I'm this close to a North American cable deal!" North American cable carries Battling Bots, Iron Chefs, Howard Stern, and monster truck rallies. There isn't a person in the audience who couldn't get him that deal. Reno also has the second funniest line. After Jonathan engages in an all-night 120-mph motorcycle chase across the frozen steppes of Bankruptistan, while military planes drop armed Jeeps to chase him, and after he sees his best pal blown to bits *after* leaping across a suspension bridge that has been raised in the middle of the night for no apparent reason, Reno tells him, "Play well tonight."

Oh, and I almost forgot Aurora's breathless discovery after the suspicious death of one of the other players. "His chin strap was cut!" she whispers fiercely to Jonathan. Neither she nor he notices that Jonathan makes it a point never to fasten his own chin strap at any time during a game.

Someday this film may inspire a long, thoughtful book by John Wright, its editor. My guess is that something went dreadfully wrong early in the production. Maybe dysentery or mass hypnosis. And the director, John McTiernan *(Die Hard)*, was unable to supply Wright with the shots he needed to make sense of the story. I saw a Russian documentary once where half the shots were blurred and overexposed because the KGB attacked the negative with X rays. Maybe this movie was put through an MRI scan. Curiously, the signifiers have survived, but not the signified. Characters set up big revelations and then forget to make them. And the long, murky night sequence looks like it was shot, pointlessly, with the green-light NightShot feature on a consumer video camera.

One of the peculiarities of television of the future is a device titled "Instant Global Rating." This supplies a digital readout of how many viewers there are (except on North American cable systems, of course). Whenever something tremendously exciting happens during a game, the rating immediately goes up. This means that people who were not watching somehow sensed they had just missed something amazing, and responded by tuning in. When *Rollerball* finally does get a North American cable deal, I predict the ratings will work in reverse.

The Rookie ★ ★

G, 129 m., 2002

Dennis Quaid (Jimmy), Rachel Griffiths (Lorri), Jay Hernandez ("Wack" Campos), Beth Grant (Olline), Brian Cox (Jim Sr.). Directed by John Lee Hancock and produced by Gordon Gray, Mark Ciardi, and Mark Johnson. Screenplay by Mike Rich.

The Rookie combines two reliable formulas: the Little Team That Goes to State and the Old-Timer Who Realizes His Youthful Dream. When two genres approach exhaustion, sometimes it works if they prop each other up. Not this time, not when we also get the Dad Who Can't Be Pleased However Hard His Son Tries, and the Wife Who Wants Her Husband to Have His Dream but Has a Family to Raise. The movie is so resolutely cobbled together out of older movies that it even uses a totally unnecessary prologue, just because it seems obligatory.

We begin in the wide open spaces of west Texas, where wildcat oil prospectors have a strike in the 1920s. The little town of Big Lake springs up, and in the shadow of one of the rickety old derricks a baseball diamond is scratched out of the dust. Supporting this enterprise, we're told, is St. Rita, "patron saint of hopeless causes." I thought that was St. Jude, but no, the two saints share the same billing. Certainly St. Rita is powerful enough to deal with baseball, but it would take both saints in harness to save this movie.

The story leaps forward in time to the recent past, as we follow a career navy officer (Brian Cox) who moves with his family from town to town while his son, little Jimmy, pounds his baseball mitt and is always getting yanked off his latest team just when it starts to win.

Now it's the present and the Little Leaguer has grown up into big Jimmy (Dennis Quaid), coach of the Big Lake High School baseball team. He's married to Lorri (Rachel Griffiths), they have an eight-year-old, and he has all but forgotten his teenage dream of pitching in the majors. By my calculations thirty years have passed, but his dad, Jim Sr., looks exactly the same age as he did when Jimmy was eight, except for some gray hair, of course. Brian Cox is one of those actors like Walter Matthau who has always been about the same age. I was so misled by the prologue I thought maybe Jim and Jim Sr. were connected in some way with the wildcatters and St. Rita, but apparently the entire laborious prologue is meant simply to establish that baseball was played in Big Lake before Jimmy and Lorri moved there.

All movies of this sort are huggable. They're about nice people, played by actors we like, striving for goals we can identify with. Dennis Quaid is just plain one of the nicest men in the movies, with that big goofy smile, but boy, can he look mean when he narrows his eyes and squints down over his shoulder from the pitching mound.

Faithful readers will know that I have a special regard for Rachel Griffiths, that most intelligent and sexy actress, but what a price she has had to pay for her stardom on HBO's *Six Feet Under.* Instead of starring roles in small, good movies *(My Son the Fanatic, Hilary and Jackie, Me Myself I),* she now gets the big bucks on TV, but her work schedule requires her to take supporting roles in movies that can be slotted into her free time. So here she plays the hero's faithful wife, stirring a pot and buttoning the little boy's shirt, her scenes basically limited to pillow talk, telephone conversations, sitting in the stands and, of course, presenting the hero with the choice of his dream or his family.

The high school team comes from such a small school that, as nearly as I can see, they have only nine members and no subs (Jimmy's eight-year-old is the batboy). It's captained by "Wack" Campos (Jay Hernandez), who is good in the standard role of coach's alter ego. Every single game in the movie, without exception, goes according to the obvious demands of the screenplay, but there is a surprise development when Jimmy pitches batting practice and they're amazed by the speed he still has on his fastball. They make him a deal: If they get to district finals or even state, Jimmy has to try out for the majors again. Is there anyone alive who can hear these lines and not predict what will happen between then and the end of the movie?

The Rookie is comforting, even soothing, to those who like the old songs best. It may confuse those who, because they like the characters, think it is good. It is not good. It is skillful. Learning the difference between good movies and skillful ones is an early step in becoming a moviegoer. *The Rookie* demonstrates that a skillful movie need not be good. It is also true that a good movie need not be skillful, but it takes a heap of moviegoing to figure that one out. And pray to St. Rita.

Rugrats Go Wild! ★ ★
PG, 81 m., 2003

With the voices of: Michael Bell (Drew Pickles/Chaz Finster), Jodi Carlisle (Marianne Thornberry), Nancy Cartwright (Chuckie Finster), Lacey Chabert (Eliza Thornberry), Melanie Chartoff (Didi Pickles), Cheryl Chase (Angelica C. Pickles), Tim Curry (Sir Nigel Thornberry), Elizabeth Daily (Tommy Pickles), Danielle Harris (Debbie Thornberry), Bruce Willis (Spike). Directed by John Eng and Norton Virgien and produced by Gabor Csupo and Arlene Klasky. Screenplay by Kate Boutilier.

The Rugrats meet the Thornberrys in *Rugrats Go Wild!* a merger of the two popular Nickelodeon franchises that confirms our suspicion that Angelica Pickles can shout down anybody, even Debbie Thornberry. The movie has so much shouting, indeed so much noise in general, that I pity parents who will have to listen to it again and again and again after the DVD comes home and goes into an endless loop. The most persuasive argument for the animation of Hayao Miyazaki is that it's sometimes quiet and peaceful.

In the movie, the Pickles family goes on a cruise—not on the magnificent ocean liner that's pulling out just as they arrive at the dock, but on a leaky gutbucket that soon runs into big trouble, as the movie sails into *Perfect Storm* territory with a wall of water that towers above them.

Marooned by the storm on a deserted island, they discover it isn't deserted when they stumble upon Debbie Thornberry sunning herself beside the family's luxury camper. Yes, the Wild Thornberrys are on the island to film a documentary, and Sir Nigel and family more or less rescue the Pickles family, not without many adventures. One intriguing development: Spike, the Pickles's dog, talks for the first time, thanks to the ability of little Eliza Thornberry to speak with animals. (Spike's voice is by Bruce Willis.)

I sat watching the movie and was at a loss for an entry point. Certainly this is not a film an adult would want to attend without a child; unlike *Finding Nemo,* for example, it doesn't play on two levels, but just on one: shrill, nonstop action. That doesn't mean it lacks humor and charm, just that it pitches itself on the level of

561

the Nickelodeon show instead of trying to move it beyond the target audience.

That's what I think, anyway, but as an adult, am I qualified to judge this film? Not long ago I (and 80 percent of the other critics in America) disliked Eddie Murphy's *Daddy Day Care*, only to be reprimanded by Al Neuharth, founder of *USA Today*, who wrote a column saying we critics were out of touch because he went with his children, aged five to twelve, and they liked it.

I offered Mr. Neuharth a list of a dozen other films his kids would probably like infinitely more, and which would also perhaps challenge and enlighten them, instead of simply bludgeoning them with sitcom slapstick. But on the off chance he was right, I took my grandsons, Emil, aged nine, and Taylor, age five, along with me to *Rugrats Go Wild!* and afterward asked them to rate it on a scale of one to ten.

They both put it at five. "Not as much fun as the TV show," said Emil. "Angelica didn't get to do as much funny stuff." What did they think about the Pickles family meeting the Thornberrys? They were unmoved, not to say indifferent.

My own feeling is that the film is one more assault on the notion that young American audiences might be expected to enjoy films with at least some subtlety and depth and pacing and occasional quietness. The filmmakers apparently believe their audience suffers from ADD, and so they supply breakneck action and screaming sound volumes at all times. That younger viewers may have developed ADD from a diet of this manic behavior on television is probably a fruitful field for study.

Note: The movie is presented in "Odorama." At most screenings, including the one I attended, audience members are given scratch-and-sniff cards with six scents, keyed to numbers that flash on the screen. We can smell strawberries, peanuts, tuna fish, etc. Scratching and sniffing, I determined that the root beer smells terrific, but the peanut butter has no discernible smell at all. The kids around me seemed pretty underwhelmed by this relic from the golden age of exploitation, which was last used by John Waters with his Polyester (1981).

The Rules of Attraction ★ ★
R, 110 m., 2002

James Van Der Beek (Sean Bateman), Shannyn Sossamon (Lauren Hynde), Ian Somerhalder (Paul Denton), Jessica Biel (Lara Holleran), Kip Pardue (Victor Johnson), Kate Bosworth (Kelly), Thomas Ian Nicholas (Mitchell Allen), Joel Michaely (Raymond). Directed by Roger Avary and produced by Greg Shapiro. Screenplay by Avary, based on the novel by Bret Easton Ellis.

I did not like any of the characters in *The Rules of Attraction*. I cringe to write those words, because they imply a superficial approach to the film. Surely there are films where I hated the characters and admired the work? *In the Company of Men*? No, that gave me a victim to sympathize with. There is no entry portal in *The Rules of Attraction*, and I spent most of the movie feeling depressed by the shallow, selfish, greedy characters. I wanted to be at another party.

Leaving the movie, I reflected that my reaction was probably unfair. *The Rules of Attraction* was based on a novel by Bret Easton Ellis, and while life is too short to read one of his books while a single work of Conrad, Faulkner, or Bellow eludes me, I am familiar enough with his world (through the movies) to know that he agrees his characters are shallow, selfish, and greedy, although perhaps he bears them a certain affection, not least because they populate his books. So I went to see the movie a second time, and emerged with a more evolved opinion: *The Rules of Attraction* is a skillfully made movie about reprehensible people.

The writer-director is Roger Avary, who directed *Killing Zoe* and coauthored Quentin Tarantino's *Pulp Fiction*. (Whether he cast James Van Der Beek as his lead because he looks more like Tarantino than any other working actor, I cannot guess.) In all of his work Avary is fond of free movement up and down the time line, and here he uses an ingenious approach to tell the stories of three main characters who are involved in, I dunno, five or six pairings. He begins with an "End of the World" party at Camden College, the ultimate party school, follows a story thread, then rewinds and follows another. He also uses fast-forward brilliantly to summarize a European vacation in a few hilarious minutes.

The yo-yo time line works because we know, or quickly learn, who the characters are, but sometimes it's annoying, as when we follow one sex romp up to a certain point and then return to it later for the denouement. This style may at times reflect the confused state of mind of the characters, who attend a college where no studying of any kind is ever glimpsed, where the only faculty member in the movie is having an affair with an undergraduate, and where the improbable weekend parties would put the orgies at Hef's pad to shame.

The parties are a lapse of credibility. I cannot believe, for example, that large numbers of coeds would engage in topless lesbian breast play at a campus event, except in the inflamed imaginations of horny undergraduates. But assuming that they would: Is it plausible that the horny undergraduates wouldn't even *look* at them? Are today's undergraduate men so (choose one) blasé, politically correct, or emasculated that, surrounded by the enthusiastic foreplay of countless half-naked women, they would blandly carry on their conversations?

This is not to imply that *The Rules of Attraction* is in any sense a campus sex-romp comedy. There is comedy in it, but so burdened are the students by their heavy loads of alcoholism, depression, drug addiction, and bisexual promiscuity that one yearns for them to be given respite by that cliché of the 1960s, the gratuitous run through meadows and woods. These kids need fresh air.

In the movie, James Van Der Beek plays drug dealer Sean Bateman, who desperately wants to sleep with chic, elusive Lauren (Shannyn Sossamon). She once dated Paul (Ian Somerhalder), who is bisexual and who wants to sleep with Sean, who is straight, but right now if Lauren had her druthers she would bed Victor (Kip Pardue), who stars in the sped-up European trip and slept with half of Europe. (The sexual orientations of most of the major characters come down to: When they're not with the sex they love, they love the sex they're with.) Many but not all of these desired couplings take place, there are distractions from still other willing characters, and a sad suicide involving a character I will not divulge, except to say that when we see how miserable she was in flashbacks to various earlier events, we wonder why,

on a campus where promiscuity is epidemic, she had the misfortune to be a one-guy woman.

Avary weaves his stories with zest and wicked energy, and finds a visual style that matches the emotional fragmentation. I have no complaints about the acting, and especially liked the way Shannyn Sossamon kept a kind of impertinent distance from some of the excesses. But by the end, I felt a sad indifference. These characters are not from life, and do not form into a useful fiction. Their excesses of sex and substance abuses are physically unwise, financially unlikely, and emotionally impossible. I do not censor their behavior, but lament the movie's fascination with it. They do not say and perhaps do not think anything interesting. The two other Bret Easton Ellis movies (*Less Than Zero* and *American Psycho*) offered characters who were considerably more intriguing. We had questions about them; they aroused our curiosity. The inhabitants of *The Rules of Attraction* are superficial and transparent. We know people like that, and hope they will get better.

Runaway Jury ★ ★ ★
PG-13, 127 m., 2003

John Cusack (Nicholas Easter), Gene Hackman (Rankin Fitch), Dustin Hoffman (Wendell Rohr), Rachel Weisz (Marlee), Bruce Davison (Durwood Cable), Bruce McGill (Judge Harkin), Jeremy Piven (Lawrence Greer), Nick Searcy (Doyle), Cliff Curtis (Frank Herrera). Directed by Gary Fleder and produced by Fleder, Christopher Mankiewicz, and Arnon Milchan. Screenplay by Brian Koppelman, David Levien, Rick Cleveland, and Matthew Chapman, based on the novel by John Grisham.

Although the jury selection process is intended to weed out bias among prospective jurors, it's an open secret that both sides look for bias—in their own favor, of course. There's an argument that juries would be more fairly selected by a random process, and *Runaway Jury* plays like the poster child for that theory. The new John Grisham thriller is about a jury consultant who tries to guarantee a friendly panel, and a juror who does a little freelance jury consulting on his own.

The case involves a widow who is suing a gun

manufacturer because her husband was killed in an office massacre involving an easily obtained weapon. The widow has hired the traditional, decent Wendell Rohr (Dustin Hoffman) to represent her, and the gun manufacturer is defended by a lawyer named Durwood Cable (Bruce Davison), who is the instrument of the evil, brilliant jury consultant Rankin Fitch (Gene Hackman).

Fitch has been hired by the reptilian head of the gun company to find a jury stacked in the company's favor. The most interesting sequence in the movie, a virtuoso montage of image, dialogue, and music by the director Gary Fleder, shows him doing just that. Fitch stands in front of an array of computer and television monitors, apparently able to summon at will the secrets of all the prospective jurors. I was reminded a little of Tom Cruise manipulating those floating digital images in *Minority Report*. Spying on dozens of jury pool members is probably not legal, especially when blackmailable information is obtained, but apart from that—wouldn't it cost millions, and could it be done in such a short time?

Such quibbles disappear in the excitement of the chase, as Fitch presides over his screens like an orchestra conductor, offering pithy comments on possible jurors and their faults. "I hate Baptists as much as I hate Democrats," he says. I don't know who that means he likes (atheist Republicans?), but Hackman can sell a line like that and make us believe Fitch can see into jurors' souls.

There is, however, one juror who gets on the panel despite Fitch's grave misgivings. This is Nicholas Easter (John Cusack), a feckless young man who seems to come from nowhere and appears to be trying to get off the jury (he feeds the judge a rambling explanation about the video game contest he's involved in). Easter's evasions inspire the judge (Bruce McGill) to lecture him on doing his duty, and puts indirect pressure on both sides to accept him.

(Spoiler warning.) Easter, as it turns out, is involved in a freelance arrangement with his woman friend Marlee (Rachel Weisz) to sell the jury to the highest bidder. He'll work on the inside, she'll handle the negotiations, and the highest bidder gets the verdict. This is an ingenious plot device, saving the movie from being a simple confrontation between good and evil and adding a wild card, forcing both sides to choose their own morality. Will the decent Wendell Rohr pay in order to win the verdict he believes his client deserves? Will the devious Durwood Cable add this expense to the massive Fitch operation? Can Easter sway a jury that Fitch thinks he has hand-picked for acquittal? These questions are so absorbing that we neglect to ask ourselves how Easter could be so sure of being called up for jury duty in the first place. If I missed the explanation, it must have been a doozy.

The movie hums along with a kind of sublime craftsmanship, fueled by the consistent performances of Hackman and Hoffman (in their first film together), the remarkable ease of John Cusack (the most relaxed and natural of actors since Robert Mitchum), and the juicy typecasting in the supporting roles. Several jury members are given back stories (there's a marine veteran, played by Cliff Curtis, who thinks the case is nonsense), and a little jury rebellion that leads to their defiant reciting of the Pledge of Allegiance in the courtroom. McGill, as the judge, treats them like an unruly gradeschool class.

The movie's ending is underwhelming. There's a whole lot of explaining going on, as we discover everyone's hidden motives long after they've ceased to be relevant. And there's not enough behind-the-scenes stuff in the jury room showing Easter at work (what we see is a study in applied psychology). The jury room itself looks curiously like the one in *12 Angry Men*, reminding us of a movie where the jury really did decide a case. Here the jury is getting the case decided for it. "There are some things," say the movie's ads, "that are too important to be left to juries."

The Rundown ★ ★ ★ ½
PG-13, 104 m., 2003

Dwayne Johnson [The Rock](Beck), Seann William Scott (Travis), Rosario Dawson (Mariana), Christopher Walken (Hatcher), Stephen Bishop (Quarterback), Ewen Bremner (Declan), Jeff Chase (Kambui), Jon Gries (Harvey), William Lucking (Billy Walker). Directed by Peter Berg and produced by Marc

Abraham, Karen Glasser, and Kevin Misher. Screenplay by R. J. Stewart and James Vanderbilt.

Early in *The Rundown*, The Rock is entering a nightclub to confront some tough guys, and he passes Arnold Schwarzenegger on the way out. "Have a good time," Arnold says. It's like he's passing the torch. Whether The Rock will rival Schwarzenegger's long run as an action hero is hard to say—but on the basis of *The Rundown*, he has a good chance. I liked him in his first starring role, *The Scorpion King* (2002), but only up to a point: "On the basis of this movie," I wrote, "he can definitely star in movies like this." That's also true on the basis of *The Rundown*—but it's a much better movie, and he has more to do.

He plays a man named Beck, a "retrieval expert" who in the early scene is trying to retrieve a bad debt from an NFL quarterback. He does, beating up the entire defensive line in the process. Then his boss sends him on another mission—to bring back his son, who is somewhere in the Amazon. The moment I heard "Amazon" I perked up, because I'm getting tired of action movies shot entirely within Los Angeles County. Hawaii doubles for South America in the movie, and does a great job of it, apparently aided at times by computer effects; and the jungle locations give the film a texture and beauty that underlines the outsized characters.

Beck's mission takes him to a town named El Dorado, run by the evil Hatcher (Christopher Walken, whose first appearance, as usual, cheers up the audience). Beck's quarry is Travis Walker, a feckless fortune hunter played by Seann William Scott, who, yes, is the same Seann William Scott who plays Stiffler in the *American Pie* series. Here he has the same cocky in-your-face personality, has added a beard, and is once again a natural comic actor.

So is The Rock, within the limits set by his character (there is some kind of a sliding scale in action pictures in which the star can be funny up to a point, but the second banana can go beyond that point). I liked, for example, Beck's call to his boss before beating up half the NFL team: He doesn't want to pound on them because "They may have a chance to repeat."

Just about the first person Beck meets in El Dorado is the bartender Mariana, played by Rosario Dawson, who later sees a lot of action and is convincing in it, reminding me a little of Linda Hamilton in *The Terminator*. "Have more beautiful lips ever been photographed?" I asked in my review of her performance in *Chelsea Walls*. On the basis of her performance here, I suggest that the answer is no.

Walken's character runs El Dorado as the kind of company town where all your wages go right back into the pocket of the boss (you have to rent your shovel by the day). Dawson's character doesn't like this, but I will not reveal more. Scott's character wants to find and steal a priceless Indian relic that will free the Indians in some unspecified way, but not if he sells it on eBay first. The Rock's character gets in the middle.

It goes without saying that Beck and Travis have to get lost in the jungle at some point, but how to arrange this? The film is admirably direct: Beck causes a Jeep to crash, and he and Travis roll down a hillside that is about nine miles long. I was reminded of the similar scene in *Romancing the Stone*, and indeed the two movies have a similar comic spirit. Once in the jungle they have all sorts of harrowing adventures, and I enjoyed it that real things were happening, that we were not simply looking at shoot-outs and chases, but at intriguing and daring enterprise.

So determined is the film to avoid shoot-outs on autopilot that Beck makes it a point not to use firearms. "Guns take me to a place I don't want to go," he says. When the chips are down and the going is very heavy, however, he reconsiders. There's a lurid, overheated montage showing close-ups of guns and ammo and close-ups of The Rock's eyes, and the pressure to pick up a gun builds and builds until it's like the drunk in *The Lost Weekend* contemplating falling off the wagon.

Christopher Walken has a specialty these days: He walks on-screen and delivers a febrile monologue that seems to come from some steamy bog in his brain. In *Poolhall Junkies*, he had a riff about the law of the wild. In *Gigli* he wondered if aliens had kidnapped the judge's brother. Here he tells a torturous parable about the Tooth Fairy, which the locals have a lot of trouble understanding. He also has a hat that reminds me of the hat rule: Hero wears normal hat, sidekick wears funny hat, villain wears ugly hat.

The movie was directed by Peter Berg, the actor, whose first directorial job was *Very Bad Things* (1998), a movie I thought was a very bad thing. Since I am quoting my old reviews today, let it be noted that I wrote in my review of that one: "Berg shows that he can direct a good movie, even if he hasn't." Now he has.

Russian Ark ★ ★ ★ ★
NO MPAA RATING, 96 m., 2002

Sergey Dontsov (The Marquis), Mariya Kuznetsova (Catherine the Great), Leonid Mozgovoy (The Spy), Mikhail Piotrovsky (Himself), David Giorgobiani (Orbeli), Aleksandr Chaban (Boris Piotrovsky), Lev Yeliseyev (Himself), Oleg Khmelnitsky (Himself), Maksim Sergeyev (Peter the Great). Directed by Aleksandr Sokurov and produced by Andrey Deryabin, Jens Meuer, and Karsten Stöter. Screenplay by Anatoly Nikiforov, Boris Khaimsky, Svetlana Proskurina, and Sokurov.

Every review of *Russian Ark* begins by discussing its method. The movie consists of one unbroken shot lasting the entire length of the film, as a camera glides through the Hermitage, the repository of Russian art and history in St. Petersburg. The cinematographer, Tilman Buttner, using a Steadicam and high-definition digital technology, joined with some 2,000 actors in a high-wire act in which every mark and cue had to be hit without fail; there were two broken takes before the third time was the charm.

The subject of the film, which is written, directed, and (in a sense) hosted by Aleksandr Sokurov, is no less than three centuries of Russian history. The camera doesn't merely take us on a guided tour of the art on the walls and in the corridors, but witnesses many visitors who came to the Hermitage over the years. Apart from anything else, this is one of the best-sustained *ideas* I have ever seen on the screen. Sokurov reportedly rehearsed his all-important camera move again and again with the cinematographer, the actors, and the invisible sound and lighting technicians, knowing

that the Hermitage would be given to him for only one precious day.

After a dark screen and the words "I open my eyes and I see nothing," the camera's eye opens upon the Hermitage and we meet the Marquis (Sergey Dontsov), a French nobleman who will wander through the art and the history as we follow him. The voice we heard, which belongs to the never-seen Sokurov, becomes a foil for the Marquis, who keeps up a running commentary. What we see is the grand sweep of Russian history in the years before the Revolution, and a glimpse of the grim times afterward.

It matters little, I think, if we recognize all of the people we meet on this journey; such figures as Catherine II and Peter the Great are identified (Catherine, like many another museum visitor, is searching for the loo), but some of the real people who play themselves, like Mikhail Piotrovsky, the current director of the Hermitage, work primarily as types. We overhear whispered conversations, see state functions, listen as representatives of the Shah apologize to Nicholas I for the killing of Russian diplomats, even see little flirtations.

And then, in a breathtaking opening-up, the camera enters a grand hall and witnesses a formal state ball. Hundreds of dancers, elaborately costumed and bejeweled, dance to the music of a symphony orchestra, and then the camera somehow seems to float through the air to the orchestra's stage and moves among the musicians. An invisible ramp must have been put into place below the camera frame for Buttner and his Steadicam to smoothly climb.

The film is a glorious experience to witness, not least because, knowing the technique and understanding how much depends on every moment, we almost hold our breath. How tragic if an actor had blown a cue or Buttner had stumbled five minutes from the end! The long, long single shot reminds me of a scene in *Nostalgia*, the 1982 film by Russia's Andrei Tarkovsky, in which a man obsessively tries to cross and recross a littered and empty pool while holding a candle that he does not want to go out: The point is not the action itself, but its duration and continuity.

It will be enough for most viewers, as it was for me, to simply view *Russian Ark* as an original and beautiful idea. But Stanley Kauffmann raises an inarguable objection in his *New Republic* review, when he asks, "What is there intrinsically in the film that would grip us if it had been made—even excellently made—in the usual edited manner?" If it were not one unbroken take, if we were not continuously mindful of its 96 minutes—what then? "We sample a lot of scenes," he writes, "that in themselves have no cumulation, no self-contained point. . . . Everything we see or hear engages us only as part of a directorial tour de force."

This observation is true, and deserves an answer, and I think my reply would be that *Russian Ark,* as it stands, is enough. I found myself in a reverie of thoughts and images, and sometimes, as my mind drifted to the barbarity of Stalin and the tragic destiny of Russia, the scenes of dancing became poignant and ironic. It is not simply what Sokurov shows about Russian history, but what he does not show—doesn't need to show, because it shadows all our thoughts of that country. Kauffmann is right that if the film had been composed in the ordinary way out of separate shots, we would question its purpose. But it is not, and the effect of the unbroken flow of images (experimented with in the past by directors like Hitchcock and Max Ophuls) is uncanny. If cinema is sometimes dreamlike, then every edit is an awakening. *Russian Ark* spins a daydream made of centuries.

S

The Saddest Music in the World
★ ★ ★ ½
NO MPAA RATING, 99 m., 2004

Mark McKinney (Chester Kent), Isabella Rossellini (Lady Port-Huntly), Maria de Medeiros (Narcissa), David Fox (Fyodor), Ross McMillan (Roderick/Gavrillo). Directed by Guy Maddin and produced by Niv Fichman, Daniel Iron, and Jody Shapiro. Screenplay by Maddin and George Toles, based on an original screenplay by Kazuo Ishiguro.

So many movies travel the same weary roads. So few imagine entirely original worlds. Guy Maddin's *The Saddest Music in the World* exists in a time and place we have never seen before, although it claims to be set in Winnipeg in 1933. The city, we learn, has been chosen by the *London Times,* for the fourth year in a row, as "the world capital of sorrow." Here Lady Port-Huntly (Isabella Rossellini) has summoned entries for a contest which will award $25,000 "in depression-era dollars" to the performer of the saddest music.

This plot suggests, no doubt, some kind of camp musical, a sub–Monty Python comedy. What Maddin makes of it is a comedy, yes, but also an eerie fantasy that suggests a silent film like *Metropolis* crossed with a musical starring Nelson Eddy and Jeannette McDonald, and then left to marinate for long forgotten years in an enchanted vault. The Canadian filmmaker has devised a style that evokes old films from an alternate time line; *The Saddest Music* is not silent and not entirely in black and white, but it looks like a long-lost classic from decades ago, grainy and sometimes faded; he shoots on 8mm film and video, and blows it up to look like a memory from cinema's distant past.

The effect is strange and delightful; somehow the style lends quasi-credibility to a story that is entirely preposterous. Because we have to focus a little more intently, we're drawn into the film, surrounded by it. There is the sensation of a new world being created around us. The screenplay is by the novelist Kazuo Ishiguro, who wrote the very different *Remains of the Day.* Here he creates, for Maddin's visual style, a fable that's *Canadian Idol* crossed with troubled dreams.

Lady Port-Huntly owns a brewery, and hopes the contest will promote sales of her beer. Played by Rossellini in a blond wig that seems borrowed from a Viennese fairy tale, she is a woman who has lost her legs and propels herself on a little wheeled cart until being supplied with fine new glass legs, filled with her own beer.

To her contest come competitors like the American Chester Kent (Mark McKinney of *The Kids in the Hall*), looking uncannily like a snake-oil salesman, and his lover, Narcissa (Maria de Medeiros), who consults fortune-tellers on the advice of a telepathic tapeworm in her bowels. If you remember de Medeiros and her lovable little accent from *Pulp Fiction* (she was the lover of Bruce Willis's boxer), you will be able to imagine how enchantingly she sings "The Song Is You."

Kent's brother Roderick (Ross McMillan) is the contestant from Serbia. Their father, Fyodor (David Fox), enters for Canada, singing the dirge "Red Maple Leaves." One night while drunk, he caused a car crash and attempted to save his lover by amputating her crushed leg—but, alas, cut off the wrong leg, and is finally seen surrounded by legs. And that lover, dear reader, was Lady Port-Huntly.

Competitors are matched off two by two. "Red Maple Leaves" goes up against a pygmy funeral dirge. Bagpipers from Scotland compete, as does a hockey team that tries to lift the gloom by singing "I Hear Music." The winner of each round gets to slide down a chute into a vat filled with beer. As Lady Port-Huntly chooses the winners, an unruly audience cheers. Suspense is heightened with the arrival of a cellist whose identity is concealed by a long black veil.

You have never seen a film like this before, unless you have seen other films by Guy Maddin, such as *Dracula: Pages from a Virgin's Diary* (2002), or *Archangel* (1990). Although his *Tales from the Gimli Hospital* was made in 1988, his films lived on the fringes, and I first became aware of him only in 2000, when he was one of the filmmakers commissioned to make a short for the Toronto Film Festival. His *The Heart of the World*, now available on DVD with *Archangel* and *Twilight of the Ice Nymphs* (1997), was a triumph, selected by some critics as the best film in the festival. It, too, seemed to be preserved from some alternate universe of old films.

The more films you have seen, the more you may love *The Saddest Music in the World*. It plays like satirical nostalgia for a past that never existed. The actors bring that kind of earnestness to it that seems peculiar to supercharged melodrama. You can never catch them grinning, although great is the joy of Lady Port-Huntly when she poses with her sexy new beer-filled glass legs. Nor can you catch Maddin condescending to his characters; he takes them as seriously as he possibly can, considering that they occupy a mad, strange, gloomy, absurd comedy. To see this film, to enter the world of Guy Maddin, is to understand how a film can be created entirely by its style, and how its style can create a world that never existed before, and lure us, at first bemused and then astonished, into it.

Safe Conduct ★ ★ ★ ★
NO MPAA RATING, 170 m., 2003

Jacques Gamblin (Jean Devaivre), Denis Podalydès (Jean Aurenche), Charlotte Kady (Suzanne Raymond), Marie Desgranges (Simone Devaivre), Ged Marlon (Jean-Paul Le Chanois), Philippe Morier-Genoud (Maurice Tourneur), Laurent Schilling (Charles Spaak), Maria Pitarresi (Reine Sorignal). Directed by Bertrand Tavernier and produced by Frédéric Bourboulon and Alain Sarde. Screenplay by Jean Cosmos and Tavernier, based on the book by Jean Devaivre.

More than 200 films were made in France during the Nazi Occupation, most of them routine, a few of them good, but none of them, Bertrand Tavernier observes, anti-Semitic. This despite the fact that anti-Semitism was not unknown in the French films of the 1930s. Tavernier's *Safe Conduct* tells the story of that curious period in French film history through two central characters, a director and a writer, who made their own accommodations while working under the enemy.

The leading German-controlled production company, Continental, often censored scenes it objected to, but its mission was to foster the illusion of life as usual during the Occupation; it would help French morale, according to this theory, if French audiences could see new French films, and such stars as Michel Simon and Danielle Darrieux continued to work.

Tavernier considers the period through the lives of two participants, the assistant director Jean Devaivre (Jacques Gamblin) and the writer Jean Aurenche (Denis Podalydès). The film opens with a flurry of activity at the hotel where Aurenche is expecting a visit from an actress; the proprietor sends champagne to the room, although it is cold and the actress would rather have tea. Aurenche is a compulsive womanizer who does what he can in a passive-aggressive way to avoid working for the Germans while not actually landing in jail. Devaivre works enthusiastically for Continental as a cover for his activities in the French Resistance.

Other figures, some well known to lovers of French cinema, wander through: We see Simon so angry at the visit of a Nazi "snoop" that he cannot remember his lines, and Charles Spaak (who wrote *The Grand Illusion* in 1937) thrown into a jail cell, but then, when his screenwriting skills are needed, negotiating for better food, wine, and cigarettes in order to keep working while behind bars.

Like Francois Truffaut's *The Last Metro* (1980), the movie questions the purpose of artistic activity during wartime. But Truffaut's film was more melodramatic, confined to a single theater company and its strategies and deceptions, while Tavernier is more concerned with the entire period of history.

The facts of the time seem constantly available just beneath the veneer of fiction, and sometimes burst through, as in a remarkable aside about Jacques Dubuis, Devaivre's brother-in-law; after he was arrested as a Resistance member, the film tells us, Devaivre's wife never saw her brother again—except once, decades later, as an extra in a French film of the period.

We see the moment in a film clip, as the long-dead man collects tickets at a theater. There was debate within the film community about collaborating with the Nazis, and some, like Devaivre, risked contempt for their cooperative attitude because they could not reveal their secret work for the Resistance. Tavernier shows him involved in a remarkable adventure, one of those wartime stories so unlikely they can only be true. Sent home from the set with a bad cold, he stops by the office and happens upon the key to the office of a German intelligence official who works in the same building. He steals some papers, and soon, to his amazement, finds himself flying to England on a clandestine flight to give the papers and his explanation to British officials. They fly him back; a train schedule will not get him to Paris in time, and so he rides his bicycle all the way, still coughing and sneezing, to get back to work. Everyone thinks he has spent the weekend in bed.

You would imagine a film like this would be greeted with rapture in France, but no. The leading French film magazine, *Cahiers du Cinema,* has long scorned the filmmakers of this older generation as makers of mere "quality," and interprets Tavernier's work as an attack on the New Wave generation that replaced them. This is astonishingly wrongheaded, since Tavernier (who worked as a publicist for such New Wavers as Godard and Chabrol) is interested in his characters not in terms of the cinema they produced but because of the conditions they survived, and the decisions they made.

Writing in the *New Republic,* Stanley Kauffmann observes: "Those who now think that these film people should have stopped work in order to impede the German state must also consider whether doctors and plumbers and teachers should also have stopped work for the same reason." Well, some would say yes. But that could lead to death, a choice it is easier to urge upon others than to make ourselves.

What Tavernier does here is celebrate filmmakers who did the best they could under the circumstances. Tavernier knew many of these characters; Aurenche and Pierre Bost, a famous screenwriting team, wrote his first film, *The Clockmaker of St. Paul,* and Aurenche worked on several others. In the film's closing moments, we hear Tavernier's own voice in narration, saying that at the end of his life, Aurenche told him he would not have done anything differently.

The Safety of Objects ★ ★

R, 121 m., 2003

Glenn Close (Esther Gold), Dermot Mulroney (Jim Train), Jessica Campbell (Julie Gold), Patricia Clarkson (Annette Jennings), Joshua Jackson (Paul Gold), Moira Kelly (Susan Train), Robert Klein (Howard Gold), Timothy Olyphant (Randy), Alex House (Jake Train), Mary Kay Place (Helen). Directed by Rose Troche and produced by Dorothy Berwin and Christine Vachon. Screenplay by Troche, based on stories by A. M. Homes.

Side by side on a shady suburban street, in houses like temples to domestic gods, three families marinate in misery. They know one another, but what they don't realize is how their lives are secretly entangled. We're intended to pity them, although their troubles are so densely plotted they skirt the edge of irony; this is a literate soap opera in which beautiful people have expensive problems and we wouldn't mind letting them inherit some undistinguished problems of our own.

To be sure, one of the characters has a problem we don't envy. That would be Paul Gold (Joshua Jackson), a bright and handsome teenager who has been in a coma since an accident. Before that he'd been having an affair with the woman next door, Annette Jennings (Patricia Clarkson), so there were consolations in his brief conscious existence.

Now his mother, Esther (Glenn Close), watches over him, reads to him, talks to him, trusts he will return to consciousness. His father, Howard (Robert Klein), doesn't participate in this process, having written off his heir as a bad investment, but listen to how Esther talks to Howard: "You never even put your eyes on him. How do you think that makes him feel?" The dialogue gets a laugh from the heartless audience, but is it intended as funny, thoughtless, ironic, tender, or what? The movie doesn't give us much help in answering that question.

In a different kind of movie, we would be deeply touched by the mother's bedside vigil. In a *very* different kind of movie, like Pedro

Almodóvar's *Talk to Her*, which is about two men at the bedsides of the two comatose women they love, we would key in to the weird-sad tone that somehow rises above irony into a kind of sincere, melodramatic excess. But here—well, we know the Glenn Close character is sincere, but we can't tell what the film thinks about her, and we suspect it may be feeling a little more superior to her than it has a right to.

Written and directed by Rose Troche, based on stories by A. M. Homes, *The Safety of Objects* hammers more nails into the undead corpse of the suburban dream. Movies about the Dread Suburbs are so frightening that we wonder why everyone doesn't flee them, like the crowds in the foreground of Japanese monster movies.

The Safety of Objects travels its emotional wastelands in a bittersweet, elegiac mood. We meet a lawyer named Jim Train (Dermot Mulroney), who is passed over for partnership at his law firm, walks out in a rage, and lacks the nerve to tell his wife, Susan (Moira Kelly). Neither one of them knows their young child, Jake (Alex House), is conducting an affair—yes, an actual courtship—with a Barbie doll.

Next door is Helen (Mary Kay Place), who, if she is really going to spend the rest of her life picking up stray men for quick sex, should develop more of a flair. She comes across as desperate, although there's a nice scene where she calls the bluff of a jerk who succeeds in picking her up—and is left with the task of explaining why, if he really expected to bring someone home, his house is such a pigpen.

Let's see who else lives on the street. Annette, the Clarkson character, makes an unmistakable pitch to a handyman, who gets the message, rejects it, but politely thanks her for the offer. Annette is pathetic about men: She forgives her ex-husband anything, even when he skips his alimony payments, and lets a child get away with calling her a loser because she can't afford summer camp.

What comes across is that all of these people are desperately unhappy, are finding no human consolation or contact at home, are fleeing to the arms of strangers, dolls, or the comatose, and place their trust, if the title is to be believed, in the safety of objects. I don't think that means objects will protect them. I think it means they can't hurt them.

Strewn here somewhere are the elements of an effective version of this story—an *Ice Storm* or *American Beauty*, even a *My New Gun*. But Troche's tone is so relentlessly, depressingly monotonous that the characters seem trapped in a narrow emotional range. They live out their miserable lives in one lachrymose sequence after another, and for us there is no relief. *The Safety of Objects* is like a hike through the swamp of despond, with ennui sticking to our shoes.

The Salton Sea ★ ★ ★
R, 103 m., 2002

Val Kilmer (Danny/Tom), Vincent D'Onofrio (Pooh-Bear), Adam Goldberg (Kujo), Luis Guzman (Quincy), Doug Hutchison (Morgan), Anthony LaPaglia (Garcetti), Glenn Plummer (Bobby), Peter Sarsgaard (Jimmy the Finn), Deborah Kara Unger (Colette). Directed by D. J. Caruso and produced by Ken Aguado, Frank Darabont, Eriq LaSalle, and Butch Robinson. Screenplay by Tony Gayton.

The Salton Sea is a low-life black comedy drawing inspiration from *Memento, Pulp Fiction*, and those trendy British thrillers about drug lads. It contains one element of startling originality: its bad guy, nicknamed Pooh-Bear and played by Vincent D'Onofrio in a great, weird, demented giggle of a performance; imagine a Batman villain cycled through the hallucinations of *Requiem for a Dream*.

The movie opens with what looks like a crash at the intersection of film and *noir:* Val Kilmer sits on the floor and plays a trumpet, surrounded by cash, photos, and flames. He narrates the film and makes a laundry list of biblical figures (Judas, the prodigal son) he can be compared with. As we learn about the murder of his wife and the destruction of his life, I was also reminded of Job.

Kilmer plays Danny Parker, also known as Tom Van Allen; his double identity spans a life in which he is both a jazz musician and a meth middleman, doing speed himself, inhabiting the dangerous world of speed freaks ("tweakers") and acting as an undercover agent for the cops. His life is so arduous we wonder, not for the first time, why people go to such extraordinary efforts to get and use the drugs that make them so unhappy. He doesn't use to get high, but to get from low back to bearable.

The plot involves the usual assortment of lowlifes, scum, killers, bodyguards, dealers, pathetic women, two-timing cops, and strung-out addicts, all employing Tarantinian dialogue about the flotsam of consumer society (you'd be surprised to learn what you might find under Bob Hope on eBay). Towering over them, like a bloated float in a nightmarish Thanksgiving parade, is Pooh-Bear, a drug dealer who lives in a fortified retreat in the desert and brags about the guy who shorted him $11 and got his head clamped in a vise while his brains were removed with a handsaw.

D'Onofrio is a gifted actor and his character performances have ranged from Orson Welles to Abbie Hoffman to the twisted killer with the bizarre murder devices in *The Cell*. Nothing he has done quite approaches Pooh-Bear, an overweight good ol' boy who uses his folksy accent to explain novel ways of punishing the disloyal, such as having their genitals eaten off by a rabid badger. He comes by his nickname because cocaine abuse has destroyed his nose, and he wears a little plastic job that makes him look like Pooh.

The Salton Sea is two movies fighting inside one screenplay. Val Kilmer's movie is about memory and revenge, and tenderness for the abused woman (Deborah Kara Unger) who lives across the hall in his fleabag hotel. Kilmer plays a fairly standard middleman between dealers who might kill him and cops who might betray him. But he sometimes visits a world that is essentially the second movie, a nightmarish comedy. Director D. J. Caruso and writer Tony Gayton *(Murder by Numbers)* introduce scenes with images so weird they're funny to begin with, and then funnier when they're explained. Consider Pooh-Bear's hobby of restaging the Kennedy assassination with pet pigeons in model cars. Note the little details like the pink pillbox hat. Then listen to his driver/bodyguard ask what "JFK" stands for.

On the basis of this film, meth addiction is such a debilitating illness that it's a wonder its victims have the energy for the strange things the screenplay puts them up to. We meet, for example, a dealer named Bobby (Glenn Plummer), whose girlfriend's writhing legs extend frantically from beneath the mattress he sits on, while he toys with a compressed-air spear gun. Bobby looks like a man who has earned that good night's sleep.

The Salton Sea is all pieces and no coherent whole. Maybe life on meth is like that. The plot does finally explain itself, like a dislocated shoulder popping back into place, but then the plot is off the shelf; only the characters and details set the movie aside from its stablemates. I liked it because it was so endlessly, grotesquely, inventive: Watching it, I pictured Tarantino throwing a stick into a swamp, and the movie swimming out through the muck, retrieving it, and bringing it back with its tail wagging.

The Santa Clause 2 ★ ★ ★
G, 95 m., 2002

Tim Allen (Scott/Santa), Judge Reinhold (Neil), Wendy Crewson (Laura Miller), Elizabeth Mitchell (Carol Newman), David Krumholtz (Bernard), Eric Lloyd (Charlie Calvin), Spencer Breslin (Curtis), Liliana Mumy (Lucy). Directed by Michael Lembeck and produced by Robert F. Newmyer, Brian Reilly, and Jeffrey Silver. Screenplay by Don Rhymer, Cinco Paul, Ken Daurio, Ed Decter, and John J. Strauss.

There ain't no sanity clause!

—Chico Marx

True, but there is a *Santa Clause 2*, which requires that Santa get married or else. This information is revealed at the North Pole at the worst possible time, during the pre-Christmas manufacturing rush, when air force listening planes hear what sounds like "tiny hammers" from beneath the snow. The current occupant of the Santa suit is happy supervising his elves and perfecting his chimney-craft, when he's informed of a loophole in his contract: If he doesn't produce a Mrs. Claus in twenty-eight days, he'll stop being Santa and (I'm not real sure about this) the office may even entirely disappear, casting the world's children into gloom.

Already, Santa is thinner, the red suit looks baggy, and the white beard seems to be shedding. The outlook is grim. We recognize Santa from *The Santa Clause*, the 1994 movie that explained how he got the job in the first place. As you may (or very likely may not) recall, Scott Calvin (Tim Allen) was a divorced man who, in attempting to join in the holiday spirit, accidentally . . . well, killed Santa Claus. And then found a card informing him that now *he* was Santa Claus.

In the years that have passed, Scott's ex-wife, Laura (Wendy Crewson), and her nice new husband, Neil (Judge Reinhold), have continued to raise Scott's son, Charlie, but now the kid is involved in a high school graffiti prank, and the elves have to break the news to Santa: Charlie has switched lists, from "nice" to "naughty." In a panic, Scott/Santa flies back home to counsel his son and perhaps find a wife, while the North Pole is put under the command of a cloned Santa who soon uses toy soldiers to stage a military coup and establish a dictatorship.

Santa Clause 2 is more of the same tinsel-draped malarkey that made the original film into a big hit, but it's more engaging, assured, and funny, and I like it more. The first movie seemed too desperately cheery; this one has a nice acerbic undertone, even though there is indeed a romance in the works for Santa and Principal Newman (Elizabeth Mitchell), whose experience with corridor passes may come in handy if she has to supervise millions of elves.

The movie is not a special-effects extravaganza like *The Grinch,* but in a way that's a relief. It's more about charm and silliness than about great, hulking, multimillion-dollar high-tech effects. The North Pole looks only a little more elaborate than a department store window, the Clone Santa's troops look like refugees from the March of the Wooden Soldiers, and Santa's mode of transportation is a reindeer named Comet who is not the epitome of grace.

One new touch this time is the Board Meeting of Legendary Characters, which Santa chairs, with members including the Sandman, the Tooth Fairy, Mother Nature, the Easter Bunny, etc., many of them played by well-known actors I will leave you to discover for yourself. I suppose it makes sense that all of these characters would exist in the same universe, and when the Tooth Fairy saves the day, it is through the film's profound understanding of the rules of tooth fairydom.

I almost liked the original *Santa Clause,* but wrote that "despite its charms, the movie didn't push over the top into true inspiration." Now here is *The Santa Clause 2,* which kind of does push over the top, especially with the Clone Santa subplot, and is all-around a better film, although I believe that any universe that includes the Tooth Fairy and the Sandman could easily accommodate, and benefit from, the Marx brothers.

Saved! ★ ★ ★ ½
PG-13, 92 m., 2004

Jena Malone (Mary), Mandy Moore (Hilary Faye), Macaulay Culkin (Roland), Patrick Fugit (Patrick), Martin Donovan (Pastor Skip), Mary-Louise Parker (Lillian), Eva Amurri (Cassandra), Chad Faust (Dean). Directed by Brian Dannelly and produced by Michael Stipe, Sandy Stern, Michael Ohoven, and William Vince. Screenplay by Dannelly and Michael Urban.

Saved! is a satire aimed at narrow-minded Christians, using as its weapon the values of a more tolerant brand of Christianity. It is also a high school comedy, starring names from the top shelf of teenage movie stars: Mandy Moore *(The Princess Diaries),* Jena Malone *(Donnie Darko),* Patrick Fugit *(Almost Famous),* and Macaulay Culkin, who is twenty-three but looks younger than anyone else in the cast. That Hollywood would dare to make a comedy poking fun at the excesses of Jesus people is, I think, an encouraging sign; we have not been entirely intimidated by the religious right.

The film follows the traditional pattern of many other teenage comedies. There's a clique ruled by the snobbiest and most popular girl in school, and an opposition made up of outcasts, nonconformists, and rebels. We saw this formula in *Mean Girls.* What's different this time is that the teen queen, Hilary Faye, is the loudest Jesus praiser at American Eagle Christian High School, and is played by Mandy Moore, having a little fun with her own good-girl image.

Her opposition is a checklist of kids who do not meet with Hilary Faye's approval. That would include Dean (Chad Faust), who thinks he may be gay; Cassandra (Eva Amurri), the only Jew in school and an outspoken rebel, and Roland (Culkin), Hilary Faye's brother, who is in a wheelchair but rejects all forms of sympathy and horrifies his sister by becoming Cassandra's boyfriend. There's also Patrick (Fugit), member of a Christian skateboarding team and the son of Pastor Skip (Martin Donovan), the school's principal. Patrick is thoughtful and introspective, and isn't sure he agrees with his father's complacent morality.

The heroine is Mary (Jena Malone), whose mother, Lillian (Mary-Louise Parker), has recently been named the town's No. 1 Christian Interior Decorator. Mary's boyfriend is Dean (Chad Faust, an interesting name in this context). One day they're playing a game that involves shouting out secrets to each other while underwater in the swimming pool, and Dean bubbles: "I think I'm gay!" Mary is shocked, bangs her head, thinks she sees Jesus (he's actually the pool maintenance guy), and realizes it is her mission to save Dean. That would involve having sex with him, she reasons, since only such a drastic act could bring him over to the hetero side. She believes that under the circumstances, Jesus will restore her virginity.

Jesus does not, alas, intervene, and Mary soon finds herself staring at the implacable blue line on her home pregnancy kit. Afraid to tell her mother, she visits Planned Parenthood, and is spotted by Cassandra and Roland.

Cassandra: There's only one reason
    Christian girls come downtown to the
    Planned Parenthood!
Roland: She's planting a pipe bomb?

You see what I mean. The first half of this movie is astonishing in the sharp-edged way it satirizes the knee-jerk values of Hilary Faye and her born-again friends. Another target is widower Pastor Skip, who is attracted to Mary's widowed mother, Lillian; she likes him, too, but they flirt in such a cautious way we wonder if they even realize what they're doing. A big complication: Skip is married, and his estranged wife is doing missionary work in Africa, making his feelings a torment.

At the time Mary sacrifices her virginity to conquer Dean's homosexuality, she's a member of Hilary Faye's singing trio, the Christian Jewels, and a high-ranking celebrity among the school's Jesus boosters. But the worldly Cassandra spots her pregnancy before anyone else does, and soon the unwed mother-to-be is hanging out with the gay, the Jew, and the kid in the wheelchair. They're like a hall of fame of outsiders.

Dean's sexuality is discovered by his parents, and he's shipped off to Mercy House, which specializes in drug detox and "degayification." Once again the screenplay, by director Brian Dannelly and Michael Urban, is pointed: "Mercy House doesn't really exist for the people that go there, but for the people who send them," says Patrick, who is having his own rebellion against Pastor Skip, and casts his lot with the rebels.

Now if the film were all pitched on this one note, it would be tiresome and unfair. But having surprised us with its outspoken first act, it gets religion of its own sort in the second and third acts, arguing not against fundamentalism but against intolerance; it argues that Jesus would have embraced the cast-outs and the misfits, and might have leaned toward situational ethics instead of rigid morality. Doesn't Mary, after all, think she's doing the right thing when she sleeps with Dean? (What Dean thinks remains an enigma.)

Saved! is an important film as well as an entertaining one. At a time when the FCC is enforcing a censorious morality on a nation where 8.5 million listeners a day are manifestly not offended by Howard Stern, here is a movie with a political message: Jesus counseled more acceptance and tolerance than some of his followers think. By the end of the movie, mainstream Christian values have not been overthrown, but demonstrated and embraced. Those who think Christianity is just a matter of enforcing their rule book have been, well, enlightened. And that all of this takes place in a sassy and smart teenage comedy is, well, a miracle. Oh, and *mirabile dictu*, some of the actors are allowed to have pimples. ☞

Scary Movie 3 ★ ½
PG-13, 90 m., 2003

Anna Faris (Cindy Campbell), Charlie Sheen (Tom Logan), Regina Hall (Brenda Meeks), Denise Richards (Annie Logan), Jeremy Piven (Ross Giggins), Queen Latifah (Shaniqua), Eddie Griffin (Orpheus), Anthony Anderson (Mahalik), Simon Rex (George). Directed by

David Zucker and produced by Robert K. Weiss and Zucker. Screenplay by Brian Lynch, Craig Mazin, Pat Proft, Kevin Smith, and Zucker.

Scary Movie 3 understands the concept of a spoof but not the concept of a satire. It clicks off several popular movies *(Signs, The Sixth Sense, The Matrix, 8 Mile, The Ring)* and recycles scenes from them through a spoofalator, but it's feeding off these movies, not skewering them. The average issue of *Mad* magazine contains significantly smarter movie satire, because Mad goes for the vulnerable elements, and *Scary Movie 3* just wants to quote and kid.

Consider the material about *8 Mile.* Eminem is talented and I liked his movie, but he provides a target that *Scary Movie 3* misses by a mile. The Eminem clone is played by Simon Rex, whose material essentially consists of repeating what Eminem did in the original movie, at a lower level. He throws up in the john (on somebody else, ho, ho), he duels onstage with a black rapper, he preempts criticism by attacking himself as white, he pulls up the hood on his sweatshirt and it's shaped like a Ku Klux Klan hood, and so on. This is parody, not satire, and no points against Eminem are scored.

Same with the crop circles from *Signs,* where farmer Tom Logan (Charlie Sheen) finds a big crop circle with an arrow pointing to his house and the legend ATTACK HERE. That's level one. Why not something about the way the movie extended silence as far as it could go? His parting scene with his wife (Denise Richards), who is being kept alive by the truck that has her pinned to a tree, is agonizingly labored.

The Ring material is barely different from *The Ring* itself; pop in the cassette, answer the phone, be doomed to die. *The Sixth Sense* stuff is funnier, as a psychic little kid walks through the movie relentlessly predicting everyone's secrets. Funny, but it doesn't build. Then there's an unpleasant scene at the home of news reader Cindy Campbell (Anna Faris), involving a salivating priest who arrives to be a baby-sitter for her young son (ho, ho).

The movie is filled with famous and semi-famous faces, although only two of them work for their laughs and get them. That would be in the pre–opening credits, where Jenny McCarthy and Pamela Anderson take the dumb blond shtick about as far as it can possibly go, while their push-up bras do the same thing in another department.

Other cameos: Queen Latifah, Eddie Griffin, William Forsythe, Peter Boyle, Macy Gray, George Carlin, Ja Rule, Master P, and Leslie Nielsen, the Olivier of spoofs, playing the president. But to what avail? The movie has been directed by David Zucker, who with his brother Jerry and Jim Abrahams more or less invented the genre with the brilliant *Airplane!* (1980). Maybe the problem isn't with him. Maybe the problem is that the genre is over and done with and dead. *Scream* seemed to point in a new and funnier direction—the smart satire—but *Scary Movie 3* points right back again. It's like it has its own crop circle, with its own arrow pointing right at itself.

School of Rock ★ ★ ★ ½
PG-13, 108 m., 2003

Jack Black (Dewey Finn), Joan Cusack (Rosalie Mullins), Mike White (Ned Schneebly), Sarah Silverman (Patty), Joey Gaydos (Zack), Miranda Cosgrove (Summer), Maryam Hassan (Tomika), Kevin Clark (Kevin), Rebecca Brown (Katie), Robert Tsai (Lawrence),Brian Falduto (Billy). Directed by Richard Linklater and produced by Scott Rudin. Screenplay by Mike White.

Jack Black is a living, breathing, sweating advertisement for the transformative power of rock and roll in *School of Rock,* the first kid movie that parents will like more than their children. He plays Dewey Finn, failed rocker, just kicked out of the band he founded. Rock is his life. When he fakes his way into a job as a substitute fifth-grade teacher, he ignores the lesson plans and turns the class into a rock band; when the kids ask about tests, he promises them that rock "will test your head, and your mind, and your brain, too."

Now that's a cute premise, and you probably think you can guess more or less what the movie will be like. But you would be way wrong, because *School of Rock* is as serious as it can be about its comic subject, and never condescends to its characters or its audience. The kids aren't turned into cloying little clones, but remain stubborn, uncertain, insecure, and kidlike.

And Dewey Finn doesn't start as a disreputable character and then turn gooey. Jack Black remains true to his irascible character all the way through; he makes Dewey's personality not a plot gimmick, but a way of life.

If quirky, independent, grown-up outsider filmmakers set out to make a family movie, this is the kind of movie they would make. And they did. The director is Richard Linklater (*Dazed and Confused, Before Sunrise*), the indie genius of Austin, Texas, who made *Waking Life* in his garage and revolutionized animation by showing that a commercial film could be made at home with a digital camera and a Macintosh. The writer and costar is Mike White, who since 2000 has also written *Chuck and Buck, Orange County* (which costarred Black as a rebel couch potato), and the brilliant *The Good Girl*, with Jennifer Aniston as a married discount clerk who falls in love with the cute checkout kid.

White's movies lovingly celebrate the comic peculiarities of everyday people, and his Dewey Finn is a goofy original—a slugabed who complains, when his roommate (White) asks for the rent, "I've been mooching off of you for years!" He truly believes that rock, especially classic rock, will heal you and make you whole. His gods include Led Zeppelin, The Ramones, and The Who. His own career reaches a nadir when he ends a solo by jumping ecstatically off the stage and the indifferent audience lets him fall to the floor.

He needs money. A school calls for his roommate, he fakes his identity, and later that day is facing a suspicious group of ten-year-olds and confiding, "I've got a terrible hangover." It's an expensive private school, their parents pay $15,000 a year in tuition, and Summer (Miranda Cosgrove), the smarty-pants in the front row, asks, "Are you gonna teach us anything, or are we just gonna sit here?"

The class files out for band practice, Dewey listens to their anemic performance of classical chestnuts, and has a brainstorm: He'll convert them into a rock group and enter them in a local radio station's Battle of the Bands.

The movie takes music seriously. Dewey assigns instruments to the talented students, including keyboardist Lawrence (Robert Tsai), lead guitarist Zack (Joey Gaydos), drummer Kevin (Kevin Clark), and backup singer Tomika (Maryam Hassan), who is shy because of her weight. "You have an issue with *weight?*" Dewey asks. "You know who else has a weight issue? *Me!* But I get up there on the stage and start to sing, and people *worship* me!"

There's a job for everyone. Billy (Brian Falduto) wants to be the band's designer, and produces glitter rock costumes that convince Dewey the school uniforms don't look so bad. Busybody Summer is made the band's manager. Three girls are assigned to be groupies, and when they complain that groupies are sluts, Dewey defines them as more like cheerleaders.

Of course there is a school principal. She is Rosalie Mullins (Joan Cusack), and, miraculously, she isn't the standard old prune that movies like this usually supply, but a good soul who loves her school and has been rumored to be capable, after a few beers, of getting up on the table and doing a Stevie Nicks imitation. The big payoff is the Battle of the Bands, and inevitably all of the angry parents are in the front row, but the movie stays true, if not to its school, at least to rock and roll, and you have a goofy smile most of the time.

I saw a family film named *Good Boy!* that was astonishingly stupid, and treated its audience as if it had a tragically slow learning curve and was immune to boredom. Here is a movie that proves you can make a family film that's alive and well acted and smart and perceptive and funny—and that rocks.

Note: I have absolutely no clue why the movie is rated PG-13. There's "rude humor and some drug references," the MPAA says. There's not a kid alive who would be anything but delighted by this film. It belongs on the MPAA's List of Shame with Whale Rider and Bend It Like Beckham, two other PG-13 films perfect for the family. ☞

Scooby-Doo ★
PG, 87 m., 2002

Matthew Lillard (Norville "Shaggy" Rogers), Freddie Prinze Jr. (Fred Jones), Sarah Michelle Gellar (Daphne Blake), Linda Cardellini (Velma Dinkley), Rowan Atkinson (Mondavarious), Isla Fisher (Mary Jane), Andrew Bryniarski

(Henchman). Directed by Raja Gosnell and produced by Charles Roven. Screenplay by James Gunn, based on characters created by Willam Hanna and Joseph Barbera.

I am not the person to review this movie. I have never seen the *Scooby-Doo* television program, and on the basis of the film I have no desire to start now. I feel no sympathy with any of the characters, I am unable to judge whether the live-action movie is a better idea than the all-cartoon TV approach, I am unable to generate the slightest interest in the plot, and I laughed not a single time, although I smiled more than once at the animated Scooby-Doo himself, an island of amusement in a wasteland of feckless-ness.

What I can say, I think, is that a movie like this should in some sense be accessible to a nonfan like myself. I realize that every TV cartoon show has a cadre of fans that grew up with it, have seen every episode many times, and are alert to the nuances of the movie adaptation. But those people, however numerous they are, might perhaps find themselves going to a movie with people like myself—people who found, even at a very young age, that the world was filled with entertainment choices more stimulating than *Scooby-Doo*. If these people can't walk into the movie cold and understand it and get something out of it, then the movie has failed except as an in-joke.

As for myself, scrutinizing the screen help-lessly for an angle of approach, one thing above all caught my attention: the director, Raja Gosnell, has a thing about big boobs. I say this not only because of the revealing low-cut costumes of such principals as Sarah Michelle Gellar, but also because of the number of busty extras and background players, who drift by in crowd scenes with what Russ Meyer used to call "cleavage cantilevered on the same principle that made the Sydney Opera House possible." Just as Woody Allen's *Hollywood Ending* is a comedy about a movie director who forges ahead even though he is blind, *Scooby-Doo* could have been a comedy about how a Russ Meyer clone copes with being assigned a live-action adaptation of a kiddie cartoon show.

I did like the dog. Scooby-Doo so thoroughly

upstages the live actors that I cannot understand why Warner Bros. didn't just go ahead and make the whole movie animated. While Matthew Lil-lard, Sarah Michelle Gellar, and Linda Cardellini show pluck in trying to outlast the material, Freddie Prinze Jr. seems completely at a loss to account for his presence in the movie, and the squinchy-faced Rowan *(Mr. Bean)* Atkinson plays the villain as a private joke.

I pray, dear readers, that you not send me mail explaining the genius of *Scooby-Doo* and attacking me for being ill prepared to write this review. I have already turned myself in. Not only am I ill prepared to review the movie, but I venture to guess that anyone who is not literally a member of a *Scooby-Doo* fan club would be equally incapable. This movie exists in a closed universe, and the rest of us are aliens. The Internet was invented so that you can find someone else's review of *Scooby-Doo*. Start surfing.

Scooby-Doo 2: Monsters Unleashed
★ ★
PG, 93 m., 2004

Freddie Prinze Jr. (Fred), Sarah Michelle Gellar (Daphne), Matthew Lillard (Shaggy), Linda Cardellini (Velma), Seth Green (Patrick), Peter Boyle (Old Man Wickles), Tim Blake Nelson (Jacobo), Alicia Silverstone (Heather). Directed by Raja Gosnell and produced by Charles Roven and Richard Suckle. Screenplay by James Gunn.

The Internet was invented so that you can find someone else's review of Scooby-Doo. *Start surfing.*

Those were the closing words of my 2002 re-view of the original *Scooby-Doo*, a review that began with refreshing honesty: "I am not the person to review this movie." I was, I reported, "unable to generate the slightest interest in the plot, and I laughed not a single time, although I smiled more than once at the animated Scooby-Doo himself, an island of amusement in a wasteland of fecklessness."

Whoa, but I was in a bad mood that day. I gave the movie a one-star rating. Now I am faced with *Scooby-Doo 2*. There is a subtitle: *Monsters Unleashed*. As the story commences, our heroes in Mystery Inc. are attending the opening night of a museum exhibiting souvenirs from all of the cases they have solved. The event turns into a disaster when one of the monster costumes turns out to be inhabited and terrorizes the charity crowd.

Now I don't want you to think I walked into 2 with a chip on my shoulder because of the 2002 film. I had completely forgotten the earlier film, and so was able to approach the sequel with a clean slate. I viewed it as the second movie on a day that began with a screening of *Taking Lives*, with Angelina Jolie absorbing vibes from the graves of serial killer victims. The third movie was Bresson's 1966 masterpiece *Au Hasard Balthazar*, which could have been called *The Passion of the Donkey*. So you see, we have to shift gears quickly on the film crit beat.

What I felt as I watched *Scooby-Doo* was not the intense dislike I had for the first film, but a kind of benign indifference. There was a lot of eye candy on the screen, the colors were bright, the action was relentless, Matthew Lillard really is a very gifted actor, and the animated Scooby-Doo is so jolly I even liked him in the first movie. This film is no doubt ideally constructed for its target audience of ten-year-olds and those who keenly miss being ten-year-olds.

Once again, to quote myself, I am not the person to review this movie, because the values I bring to it are irrelevant to those who will want to see it. This is a silly machine to whirl goofy antics before the eyes of easily distracted audiences, and it is made with undeniable skill. Watching it is a little like watching synchronized swimming: One is amazed at the technique and discipline lavished on an enterprise that exists only to be itself.

But a little more about the movie. The original cast is back, led by Lillard as Scooby-Doo's friend Shaggy, and containing Freddie Prinze Jr., Sarah Michelle Gellar, and Linda Cardellini. Alicia Silverstone plays a trash-TV reporter who is determined to debunk the myth of Mystery Inc. The always reliable Peter Boyle is mean Old Man Wickles, who, if he is not involved in skullduggery, is in the movie under false pretenses. Seth Green is funny as the museum curator. And there are a lot of cartoon monsters.

Is this better or worse than the original? I have no idea. I'll give it two stars because I

didn't feel anything like the dislike I reported after the first film, but no more than two, because while the film is clever it's not really trying all that hard. I think the future of the republic may depend on young audiences seeing more movies like *Whale Rider* and fewer movies like *Scooby-Doo 2*, but then that's just me.

The Scorpion King ★ ★ ½
PG-13, 94 m., 2002

The Rock (Mathayus), Steven Brand (Memnon), Michael Clarke Duncan (Balthazar), Kelly Hu (The Sorceress), Bernard Hill (Philos), Grant Heslov (Arpid), Peter Facinelli (Takmet), Ralf Moeller (Thorak). Directed by Chuck Russell and produced by Stephen Sommers, Sean Daniel, James Jacks, and Kevin Misher. Screenplay by Sommers, William Osborne, and David Hayter, based on a story by Sommers and Jonathan Hales.

"Where do you think you are going with my horse?"

"To Gomorrah. Nothing we can say will stop him."

—Dialogue in *The Scorpion King*

And a wise move, too, because *The Scorpion King* is set "thousands of years before the Pyramids," so property values in Gomorrah were a good value for anyone willing to buy and hold. Here is a movie that embraces its goofiness like a Get Out of Jail Free card. The plot is recycled out of previous recycling jobs, the special effects are bad enough that you can grin at them, and the dialogue sounds like the pre-Pyramidal desert warriors are channeling a Fox sitcom (the hero refers to his camel as "my ride").

The film stars The Rock, famous as a WWF wrestling star (Vince McMahon takes a producer's credit), and on the basis of this movie, he can definitely star in movies like this. This story takes place so long ago in prehistory that The Rock was a hero and had not yet turned into the villain of *The Mummy Returns* (2001), and we can clearly see his face and muscular physique—an improvement over the earlier film, in which his scenes mostly consisted of his face being attached to a scorpion so large it looked like a giant lobster. How gigantic was the lobster? It would take a buffalo to play the Turf.

The story: An evil Scorpion King named Memnon (Steven Brand) uses the talents of a sorceress (Kelly Hu) to map his battle plans, and has conquered most of his enemies. Then we meet three Arkadians, professional assassins who have been "trained for generations in the deadly art," which indicates their training began even before they were born. The Arkadian leader Mathayus, played by The Rock, is such a powerful man that early in the film he shoots a guy with an arrow and the force of the arrow sends the guy crashing through a wall and flying through the air. (No wonder he warns, "Don't touch the bow.")

How The Rock morphs from this character into the *Mummy Returns* character is a mystery to me, and, I am sure, to him. Along the trail Mathayus loses some allies and gains others, including a Nubian giant (Michael Clarke Duncan), a scientist who has invented gunpowder, a clever kid, and a wisecracking horse thief. The scene where they vow to kill the Scorpion King is especially impressive, as Mathayus intones, "As long as one of us still breathes, the sorcerer will die!" See if you can spot the logical loophole.*

Mathayus and his team invade the desert stronghold of Memnon, where the sorceress, who comes from or perhaps is the first in a long line of James Bond heroines, sets eyes on him and wonders why she's bothering with the scrawny king. Special effects send Mathayus and others catapulting into harems, falling from castle walls, and narrowly missing death by fire, scorpion, poisonous cobra, swordplay, arrows, explosion, and being buried up to the neck in the sand near colonies of fire ants. And that's not even counting the Valley of the Death, which inspires the neo-Mametian dialogue: "No one goes to the Valley of the Death. That's why it's called the Valley of the Death."

Of all the special effects in the movie, the most impressive are the ones that keep the breasts of the many nubile maidens covered to within one centimeter of the PG-13 guidelines. Kelly Hu, a beautiful woman who looks as if she is trying to remember the good things her agent told her would happen if she took this role, has especially clever long flowing hair, which cascades down over her breasts instead of up over her head even when she is descending a waterfall.

Did I enjoy this movie? Yeah, I did, although not quite enough to recommend it, because it tries too hard to be hyper and not hard enough to be clever. It is what it is, though, and is pretty good at it. Those who would dislike the movie are unlikely to attend it (does anybody go to see The Rock in *The Scorpion King* by accident?). For its target audience, looking for a few laughs, martial arts and stuff that blows up real good, it will be exactly what they expected. It has high energy, the action never stops, the dialogue knows it's funny, and The Rock has the authority to play the role and the fortitude to keep a straight face. I expect him to become a durable action star. There's something about the way he eats those fire ants that lets you know he's thinking, "If I ever escape from this predicament, I'm gonna come back here and fix me up a real mess of fire ants, instead of just chewing on a few at a time."

Now see if you can spot the logical error in my question.

Scotland, PA. ★ ★ ½
R, 102 m., 2002

James LeGros (Joe "Mac" McBeth), Maura Tierney (Pat McBeth), Christopher Walken (Lieutenant Ernie McDuff), Kevin Corrigan (Anthony "Banco" Banconi), James Rebhorn (Norm Duncan), Tom Guiry (Malcolm Duncan), Andy Dick (Hippie Jesse), Amy Smart (Hippie Stacy), Timothy "Speed" Levitch (Hippie Hector), Josh Pais (Doug McKenna), Geoff Dunsworth (Donald Duncan). Directed by Billy Morrissette and produced by Richard Shepard and Jonathan Stern. Screenplay by Morrissette, based on *Macbeth* by Shakespeare.

Scotland, PA. translates Shakespeare's *Macbeth* into a comedy set in a Pennsylvania fast-food burger stand, circa 1975. Lady Macbeth rubs unhappily at a grease burn on her hand, the three witches become three local hippies, and poor Duncan, the manager, isn't attacked with a knife but is pounded on the head with a skillet. If you know *Macbeth*, it's funny. Anyone who doesn't is going to think these people are acting mighty peculiar.

Like all good satire, this one is based on

venom and loathing. I learn that Billy Morrissette, the writer-director, first began to think of burger stands in Macbethian terms while working in one some twenty years ago. He shared his thoughts with his girlfriend, Maura Tierney, who became his wife, and appropriately plays Lady Macbeth, a.k.a. Mrs. McBeth, in this movie.

The story: "Mac" McBeth (James LeGros) and his wife, Pat, slave unhappily in Duncan's, a fast-food outlet run by Norm Duncan (James Rebhorn). Mac lives with the dream that he will someday be manager. His current boss is Doug McKenna (Josh Pais), who is ripping off Duncan and pocketing receipts. The McBeths tell Duncan about the theft, expecting Mac will be named the new manager. But, no, Duncan picks his two sons, Malcolm (Tom Guiry) and Donald (Geoff Dunsworth) as his heirs.

This is not right, Pat McBeth hisses fiercely to her husband. Especially not after Mac has increased sales by introducing the concept of a drive-through line to Scotland, Pa. Pat badgers her husband to kill Duncan and buy the eatery from his indifferent sons. "We're not bad people, Mac," she argues. "We're just underachievers who have to make up for lost time."

Macbeth is Shakespeare's most violent play, and *Scotland, PA.* follows cheerfully in that tradition; after Duncan is pounded on the head, what finishes him off is a headfirst dive into the french-fry grease. The case is so suspicious that the local cops call in Lieutenant Ernie McDuff (Christopher Walken), who affects a kind of genial absentmindedness as a cover for his investigation. "This place really looks great," he tells the proud couple at the grand opening of their McBeth's. "Of course, the last time there was a dead body in the fryer."

Morrissette uses the Shakespeare parallels whenever he can (there is, of course, a ghost at McBeth's opening), and Tierney, in the juiciest role, actually evokes some of the power of the original Lady Macbeth, especially in the way she deals with the torment of her blistered hands. And James LeGros is as feckless and clueless as Shakespeare's Macbeth—easily led, easily deceived, easily disheartened.

The buried joke in many parodies is that events must happen because they did in the original. That works here to explain the remorseless procession of bloody and creepy events. We're expected to engage with the movie on two levels—as itself, and as a parallel to Shakespeare. While modern retellings of Shakespeare often work (as in the Michael Almereyda–Ethan Hawke *Hamlet* or Tim Blake Nelson's *O*), a parody is another matter; like an update, it deprives itself of the purpose of the original. It's even more complicated when the maker of the parody doesn't despise the original, but clearly likes it. Morrissette hates fast food, not *Macbeth*.

I enjoyed the movie in a superficial way, while never sure what its purpose was. I have the curious suspicion that it will be enjoyed most by someone who knows absolutely nothing about Shakespeare, and can see it simply as the story of some very strange people who seem to be reading from the same secret script.

The Scoundrel's Wife ★ ★ ½
R, 99 m., 2003

Tatum O'Neal (Camille Picou), Julian Sands (Dr. Lenz), Tim Curry (Father Antoine), Lacey Chabert (Florida Picou), Eion Bailey (Ensign Jack Burwell), Patrick McCollough (Blue Picou). Directed by Glen Pitre and produced by Peggy Rajski and Jerry Daigle. Screenplay by Michelle Benoit and Pitre.

The Scoundrel's Wife takes place in the small but real bayou fishing village of Cut Off, Louisiana, during World War II. German submarines have been sighted offshore, and the Coast Guard suspects local shrimp boat operators of trading with the enemy. If the premise seems far-fetched, the movie's closing titles remind us that some 600 vessels were attacked by U-boats in American coastal waters, and the movie's plot is inspired by stories heard in childhood by the director, Glen Pitre, who lives in Cut Off to this day.

Pitre is a legendary American regional director, a shrimper's son who graduated from Harvard and went back home to Louisiana to make movies. His early films were shot in the Cajun dialect, starred local people, and played in local movie houses where they quickly made back their investment. I met him at Cannes and again at the Montreal festival—French enclaves where he was being saluted as arguably the world's only Cajun-language filmmaker.

He broke into the mainstream with *Belizaire the Cajun* (1986), starring Armand Assante as a Cajun who defends his people's homes against marauding bands of Anglo rabble-rousers. Found guilty of murder, he stands on a scaffold between two (symbolic?) thieves and tries to talk his way free. He's sort of a bayou version of Gandhi, restraining his anger, able to see the comic side of his predicament, possessed of physical strength and quiet charm.

Now Pitre is back with *The Scoundrel's Wife*, again filmed near home, with local extras joining such stars as Tatum O'Neal, Julian Sands, Tim Curry, Lacey Chabert, and Eion Bailey (of *Band of Brothers*). The film is frankly melodramatic and the climax is hard to believe, but the movie has such a fresh sense of place and such a keen love for its people that it has genuine qualities despite its narrative shortcomings.

O'Neal stars, in her first role since *Basquiat* (1996), as Camille Picou, the widow of a shrimp boat captain who was making ends meet by smuggling in Chinese aliens. He may have been guilty of the murder of some of them, and Camille may have been an accomplice—at least that's what the local people think. She's raising her two teenagers, her son, Blue (Patrick McCollough), and daughter, Florida (Chabert), when World War II begins, and the Coast Guard entrusts a local boy, the untested young ensign Jack Burwell (Bailey), to monitor fishing activities and keep an eye out for spies.

Are there spies in Cut Off? There are certainly suspicious characters. One of them is the German refugee Dr. Lenz (Julian Sands), said to be Jewish, who has settled in as the only local doctor. Another, oddly enough, is the local priest, Father Antoine (Tim Curry), who is charmingly drunk much of the time but also spends ominous evenings in the cemetery, using an iron cross as an antenna for his shortwave radio.

Whether the priest is a spy (and whether the doctor is all he says he is) will not be discussed here. There are two possible romances in the film, one between the widow Picou and the German, the other between the ensign and young Florida. There is also much malicious gossip, all adding up to a scene in the doctor's front yard when a lynch crowd turns up and seems remarkably easy to convince of first one story and then another.

Objectively, *The Scoundrel's Wife* has prob-lems, and there will not be a person in the audience convinced of what happens in the last scene. But I just fired off a note to a campus film critic who was being urged to write more objectively, and asked him, what is a review if not subjective? So let me confess my subjectivity.

I like the bayou flavor of this film, and the fact that it grows from a local story that has been retailed, no doubt, over hundreds of bowls of gumbo. I like the quiet dignity O'Neal brings to her guilt-ridden widow, and I like Curry's willingness to make his priest a true eccentric, instead of trying to hunker down into some bayou method performance. I like the soft, humid beauty of Uta Briesewitz's photography. And if the ending does not convince, well, a lot of family legends do not bear close scrutiny. The movie is finally just a little too ungainly, too jumbled at the end, for me to recommend, but it has heart, and I feel a lot of affection for it.

The Sea ★ ★
NO MPAA RATING, 109 m., 2003

Gunnar Eyjolfsson (Thordur), Hilmir Snaer Gudnason (Agust), Helene De Fougerolles (Francoise), Kristbjorg Kjeld (Kristin), Sven Nordin (Morten), Gudrun S. Gisladottir (Ragnheidur), Sigurdur Skulason (Haraldur), Elva Osk Olafsdottir (Aslaug), Nina Dogg Filippusdottir (Maria), Herdis Thorvaldsdottir (Kata). Directed by Baltasar Kormakur and produced by Kormakur and Jean-Francois Fonlupt. Screenplay by Kormakur and Olafur Haukur Simonarson, based on a play by Simonarson.

How to spot a film inspired by *King Lear*: An old fart summons home three children amid hints of dividing the kingdom. Once we've spotted this early telltale clue, there can't be many surprises. Each child will fail to do or say what is expected, and the odds are good the O.F. will eventually be wandering in some kind of a wilderness. I've seen the story set in Japan and a farm in Iowa, and now here is *The Sea*, which begins with the Lear figure thundering against changes in the Icelandic fishing industry.

The patriarch is Thordur (Gunnar Eyjolfsson), who owns a fish processing factory in a fading Icelandic fishing village, and refuses to change his ways. His fish are still cleaned by hand, by local women in spotless uniforms, and he rails against the mechanized factory ships that process and ice the fish at sea. He is also loyal to the aging operators of the port's small fishing boats, which are no longer economic.

Still, there is money to be made, or salvaged, from the family business, especially if Thordur sells out to his hated rival and there is a redistribution of local fishing quotas. That is what, in various ways, his desperately neurotic and unhappy family hopes will happen.

We meet the three children, Agust (Hilmir Snaer Gudnason), Haralder (Sigurdur Skulason), and the daughter, Ragnheidur (Gudrun S. Gisladottir). Each is unhappy in a different way. Agust has been living in Paris with his pregnant girlfriend, Maria (Nina Dogg Filippusdottir), squandering his business-school tuition on *la vie bohème*. Haraldur has to endure his harpy of a wife, Aslaug (Elva Osk Olafsdottir), a drunk who runs a sexy lingerie shop. And Ragnheidur, who as the youngest daughter might be suspected of Cordelia tendencies, is a would-be filmmaker in an unhappy marriage.

Ah, but there are more characters. Thordur's wife, Kristin (Kristbjorg Kjeld), is the sister of his first wife, who died in a way that still inspires festering bitterness. And we meet Thordur's old mother, who specializes in spitting out the painful truth at the wrong moment; and various former mistresses, colorful cops, crotchety fishermen, and disloyal business associates.

The characters in Baltasar Kormakur's film are thoroughly wretched, but lack the stature of tragic heroes and are mainly sniveling little rats. They hate their father and each other. The father is clearly wrong about the fishing business, and probably knows it, but hangs onto his old ways out of sheer bloody-mindedness, or to make his family miserable. Since there seems to be no joy in the little village except the kinds that can be purchased with money, it seems ill-mannered of old Thordur to refuse to cash in, and merely sensible of Agust to relocate to Paris.

The Sea is overcrowded and overwritten, with too many shrill denunciations and dramatic surprises; we don't like the characters and, worse, they don't interest us. Surprisingly, the film was nominated by Iceland for this year's Best Foreign Film Oscar. I am surprised

because in July 2002 at the Karlovy Vary film festival, I saw a much better film about Icelandic families named *The Seagull's Laughter*, a human comedy about a teenage girl whose life is changed by the return home of a sexy local woman, a bit of a legend who has lived abroad for years. It has the grace and humanity that the lumbering *The Sea* is lacking.

Seabiscuit ★ ★ ★ ½
PG-13, 140 m., 2003

Tobey Maguire (Red Pollard), Jeff Bridges (Charles Howard), Chris Cooper (Tom Smith), Gary Stevens (George Woolf), Elizabeth Banks (Marcela Howard), William H. Macy (Tick Tock McGlaughlin), Eddie Jones (Samuel Riddle). Directed by Gary Ross and produced by Kathleen Kennedy, Frank Marshall, Ross, and Jane Sindell. Screenplay by Ross, based on the book by Laura Hillenbrand.

Seabiscuit was a small horse with a lazy side. Sleeping and eating were his favorite occupations early in life, and he wasn't particularly well behaved. That was before he met three men who would shape him into the best-loved sports legend of the 1930s: the owner Charles Howard, who had a knack for spotting potential in outcasts, the trainer Tom Smith, who was called a screwball for thinking he could heal horses other trainers would have shot, and the jockey Red Pollard, who started out as an exercise boy and stable cleaner because in the depression he would settle for anything.

Seabiscuit, based on the best-seller by Laura Hillenbrand, tells the stories of these three men and the horse against the backdrop of the times. The depression had brought America to its knees. The nation needed something to believe in. And in the somewhat simplified calculus of the movie, both Seabiscuit and Roosevelt's New Deal, more or less in that order, were a shot in the American arm. If an underdog like Seabiscuit could win against larger and more famous horses with distinguished pedigrees, then maybe there was a chance for anyone.

The story has the classic structure of a sports movie, with a setback right before the big race at the end, but, like Seabiscuit, it's a slow starter. There is a leisurely introduction to the times and the three men before the horse makes its appearance, and we see once again the classic battle between the automobile and the horse. Charles Howard (Jeff Bridges) begins as a bicycle salesman, is asked to repair a Stanley Steamer, takes it apart and makes some improvements, and before long is a millionaire who buys a farm and turns the stables into a garage.

After a family tragedy, however, he changes directions and becomes a horse owner and breeder. And there are sequences showing how he encounters Pollard (Tobey Maguire) and Smith (Chris Cooper). Soon he has everything in place except a horse, and Smith has unaccountable faith in Seabiscuit. It has to do with the horse's heart.

The movie doesn't make the mistake of treating the horse like a human. It is a horse all the time, a horse with the ability to run very fast and an inability to lose, when guided by Smith's strategy and Pollard's firm love. The movie's races are thrilling because they must be thrilling; there's no way for the movie to miss on those, but writer-director Gary Ross and his cinematographer, John Schwartzman, get amazingly close to the action; it's hard for us to figure out where the camera is, since we seem to be suspended at times between two desperately striving horses and their jockeys.

The movie gives me a much better sense of how difficult and dangerous it is to ride one of those grand animals in a race. The jockeys are sometimes friends, sometimes mortal enemies, and they often shout at one another during races. Sometimes this works, sometimes it is a little improbable, as when Red says "good-bye" to a friend as Seabiscuit shifts into winning gear.

As horses compete, so do owners. After Seabiscuit has conquered all of the champion horses of the West, Charles Howard begins a strategy to force a match race between his horse and War Admiral, the eastern champion and Triple Crown winner owned by Samuel Riddle (Eddie Jones). He goes on a whistle-stop campaign across the country (this seems to anticipate Truman's 1948 campaign) and builds up such an overwhelming groundswell of public sentiment that Riddle caves in and agrees—on his terms, of course, which makes the race all the more dramatic. The radio broadcast of that historic race was heard, we are told, by the largest audience in history. Businesses closed for the afternoon so their employees could tune in.

If *Seabiscuit* has a weakness, it's the movie's curious indifference to betting. Horses race and bettors bet, and the relationship between the two is as old as time, except in this movie, where the Seabiscuit team seems involved in pure sport and might even be shocked! shocked! to learn that there is gambling at the track. Since a subplot about betting would no doubt be a complicated distraction, perhaps this is not such a loss.

I liked the movie a whole lot without quite loving it, maybe because although I can easily feel love for dogs, I have never bonded much with horses. I was happy for Seabiscuit without being right there with him every step of the way. The character I liked the best was Tom Smith, and once again Chris Cooper shows himself as one of the most uncannily effective actors in the movies. Here he seems old, pale, and a little worn out. In *Adaptation,* he was a sunburned swamp rat. In John Sayles's *Lone Star* he was a ruggedly handsome Texas sheriff. How does he make these transformations? Here, with a few sure movements and a couple of quiet words, he convinces us that what he doesn't know about horses isn't worth knowing.

Tobey Maguire and Jeff Bridges are wonderful, too, in the way they evoke their characters; Maguire as a jockey who commits his whole heart and soul, Bridges as a man who grows wiser and better as he ages. And then there is William H. Macy as Tick Tock McGlaughlin, a manic radio announcer who throws in corny sound effects and tortured alliterations as he issues breathless bulletins from the track. If Tick Tock McGlaughlin did not exist in real life, I don't want to know it.

Seabiscuit will satisfy those who have read the book, and I imagine it will satisfy those like myself, who have not. I have recently edged into the genre of racing journalism, via *My Turf* by William A. Nack, the great writer for *Sports Illustrated.* I was at a reading where he made audience members cry with his description of the death of Secretariat, and I saw people crying after *Seabiscuit,* too. More evidence for my theory that people more readily cry at movies not because of sadness, but because of goodness and courage.

The Seagull's Laughter ★ ★ ★ ½

NO MPAA RATING, 102 m., 2004

Margrét Vilhjálmsdóttir (Freya), Ugla Egilsdóttir (Agga), Heino Ferch (Björn Theódór), Hilmir Snær Guönason (Magnús), Kristbjörg Kjeld (Grandma), Edda Bjorg Eyjólfsdóttir (Dodo), Guölaug Ólafsdóttir (Ninna), Eyvindur Erlendsson (Granddad). Directed by Ágúst Guömundsson and produced by Kristin Atladóttir. Screenplay by Guömundsson, based on the novel by Kristin Marja Baldursdóttir.

The most beautiful woman in the Icelandic village of Hafnarfjordur ran off to New York with an American serviceman, or so it is said, and now returns to her hometown without her husband but with seven trunks of sexy dresses. Is she a widow, as she claims, or did she never marry the serviceman, or did he come to a bad end? Freya is the kind of woman who inspires such speculation, especially in the inflamed imagination of her eleven-year-old cousin Agga, who adores and hates her, sometimes at the same time.

The Seagull's Laughter, an uncommonly engaging comedy with ripe, tragic undertones, begins with the fact that everybody in town lives in everybody else's pockets. There are few secrets. Certainly Freya (Margret Vilhjálmsdóttir) is a sex bomb in search of a husband, and there are only two eligible men in the village: an engineer who lives with his mother and is engaged to the mayor's daughter, and a young policeman. The engineer has the better job and house, and so the mayor's daughter must go.

All of this is seen through the eyes of Agga, played by Ugla Egilsdóttir with such spirit and deviousness that when I was on the jury at the Karlovy Vary festival in 2002, we gave her the best actress award. She is on the trembling edge of adolescence, and her ambiguous feelings about sexuality cause her to worship the older woman while at the same time trying to frame her with arson, murder, and other crimes, during regular visits to the young cop. He dismisses her breathless eyewitness reports as the fantasies of an overwrought would-be Nancy Drew, but the movie suggests some of her reports—especially involving the mysterious fire

that kills the wife-beating husband of Freya's best friend—may contain bits of truth.

Freya has essentially returned from America with no prospects at all. She takes a job in the chemist's shop, and finds popularity with the local drunks by selling them rubbing alcohol. She has moved into her grandfather's house, displacing the resentful Agga from her bed, and joins a matriarchy. The grandfather is almost always away at sea, and his house is ruled by his wife, Agga's grandmother, who also provides a home for her daughters, Dodo and Ninna, and her pipe-smoking sister-in-law, Kidda. Death is a fact in this home; Kidda's husband has died, and so have young Agga's parents. (When the police arrive at the door and ask to speak with her mother, she calmly tells them, "That will be difficult. She's dead.") The women are supportive of Freya and delighted by all of her dresses; they hold a spontaneous dress-up parade, and end by admiringly measuring her waist, bustline, and long hair.

Freya captures the eye of the engineer, Björn Theódór (Heino Ferch), at a village dance, spirits him away, and doesn't return, Agga breathlessly tattles to the policeman, until 5 A.M. ("Five thirteen," he corrects her). Freya tells Agga how they spent the night, leaving out the detail of their lovemaking, but speaking of the softness of long summer nights, the look of the sea, and the stroll they took on the path through the . . . well, through the fish-drying racks.

The racks come up later, after winter sets in and Freya begins to take long, despairing walks in the snow. She hates Iceland, she cries out: the cold and the snow and the seagulls laughing at her, and the smell of fish. But home is where, when you have to go there, they have to take you in.

The understory involves Agga's gradual transition into womanhood. Watching Freya, sometimes spying on her, she gets insights into the adult world and translates them into bulletins for the young cop. She plays both sides of the street, at one point forging a letter to keep Freya and the engineer in contact. And she learns hard lessons when Freya's best friend is mistreated by her husband and threatens suicide, and Freya calms her in an extraordinary scene by getting on her hands and knees, letting down her long hair, creeping to the friend, and calming her with its smell. This seems to refer to a childhood memory, and has an unexpected emotional impact.

The movie balances between dark and light, between warmth and cold, like an Icelandic year. It's scored with Glenn Miller and other swing bands from the war era, and opens and closes with the 1950s hit "Sh-boom." The message I think is that tragedy is temporary and the dance of life goes on. Soon it will be Agga's turn to choose a partner.

The Sea Is Watching ★ ★ ½
R, 119 m., 2003

Misa Shimizu (Kikuno), Nagiko Tono (O-Shin), Masatoshi Nagase (Ryosuke), Hidetaka Yoshioka (Fusanosuke), Eiji Okuda (Ginji), Renji Ishibashi (Zenbei), Miho Tsumiki (Okichi), Michiko Kawai (Osono). Directed by Kei Kumai and produced by Naoto Sarukawa. Screenplay by Akira Kurosawa, based on the novel by Shugoro Yamamoto.

Prostitutes are a great convenience in stories, allowing the author to dispense with courtship and begin immediately with sex and intrigue. Little wonder, then, that the Japanese master Akira Kurosawa, who rarely focused on women in his movies and said he did not much understand them, would use a brothel as the setting for his screenplay *The Sea Is Watching*. Based on a novel by Shugoro Yamamoto, left unfilmed when Kurosawa died in 1998, it has been directed by Kei Kumai as a film that seems more melodramatic and sentimental than Kurosawa's norm. Perhaps when you do not really understand someone, in fiction or in life, you are a little nicer to them.

The movie is set in the Edo period, circa 1850, in a village that would later become Tokyo. Into a brothel one night stumbles a callow young samurai named Fusanosuke (Hidetaka Yoshioka), who has disgraced himself by getting drunk, killing a man, and losing his sword. A prudent prostitute would show him the door, but O-Shin (Nagiko Tono) feels tender and protective, and besides, as her fellow prostitutes

never tire of telling her, she's a sucker for a hard-luck story. She disguises the samurai to protect him from the dead man's friends, and after he is banished from his father's house he returns to O-Shin again and again for long, heartfelt conversations—and no sex.

O-Shin's best friend in the house is Kikuno (Misa Shimizu), who is protective of the girl and worried about her tendency to mix business with pleasure. It appears, though, that O-Shin might achieve what few prostitutes could in Japan's feudal society, and make a marriage with a nice man. The other girls in the house begin to service her clients so that she can cleanse herself, in a sense, by a period of celibacy.

There are other men whom O-Shin also feels tenderness for. One of them is Ginji (Eiji Okuda), an elderly businessman who wants O-Shin to come and live with him, and whose offer is probably more sincere and practical than the romantic delusions she harbors about Fusanosuke.

The movie does a good job of evoking daily life in the brothel, which meets not only the sexual needs of its clients but also, and perhaps more urgently, their need for a place to escape from the rigors of the caste system and find sympathetic conversation. We also see something of the district, which is separated from the main town by the river, and is understood by everyone to be a haven of vice. When O-Shin discovers rather cruelly what a shallow and feckless creature Fusanosuke really is, there is yet a third client who touches her heart, and he could be real trouble. This is Ryosuke (Masatoshi Nagase).

We are always aware of the nearby presence of the sea—today's Tokyo Bay. And when a great, cleansing, violent typhoon roars in and the district is evacuated, Kikuno refuses to leave because she has been entrusted with the house keys by the madam; O-Shin stays with her out of loyalty and a general indifference to life. As they sit on the roof beam of the house, surrounded by floodwaters, they find out at last if anyone cares enough to come and rescue them.

It must not be a coincidence that Kurosawa named his heroine O-Shin, creating an English pun on "ocean." But the connection between O-Shin and the rising sea is murky to me, unless perhaps they share an underlying sympathy so that the sea comes, in a sense, to her rescue. The movie is slow and unabashedly melodramatic. Without looking at the credits I would never have identified it as Kurosawa's work, but it has a sweetness and a directness that's appealing. It might never have been made without Kurosawa's name attached to it, and that is true as well of the master's own last film, *Madadayo* (1993), a touching elegy about an old professor honored by his students. But Kurosawa was a great artist, and so even his lesser work is interesting—just as we would love to find one last lost play, however minor, by his hero Shakespeare.

Secondhand Lions ★ ★ ★
PG, 107 m., 2003

Michael Caine (Garth), Robert Duvall (Hub), Haley Joel Osment (Walter), Kyra Sedgwick (Mae), Emmanuelle Vaugier (Princess Jasmine). Directed by Tim McCanlies and produced by David Kirschner, Scott Ross, and Corey Sienega. Screenplay by McCanlies.

Secondhand Lions is about the uncles every boy should have, and the summer every boy should spend. No uncles or summers like this ever existed, but isn't it nice to think that Uncle Garth and Uncle Hub are waiting there on their Texas ranch, shooting at fish and salesmen, and waiting for their twelve-year-old nephew to be dumped on them?

They are two completely inexplicable and unlikely characters, and we doubt we can believe anything we learn about them, but in the hands of those sainted actors Robert Duvall and Michael Caine they glow with a kind of inner conviction even while their stories challenge even the kid's credulity. Maybe Hub really was a foreign legionnaire and led thousands of men into battle and won and lost a dozen fortunes, and maybe he really was in love with a desert princess named Jasmine, and then again maybe he's just been sitting there on the porch with Garth making up tall tales for gullible nephews.

The nephew's name is Walter, and he is played by Haley Joel Osment, the child actor from *The Sixth Sense* and *A.I.: Artificial Intelligence,* now on the edge of adolescence but still

with that clear-eyed directness that cuts right to the heart of a scene. Some actors have trouble standing up to that kind of unadorned presence, but Caine and Duvall are not ordinary, and they look the kid straight in the eye and tell him exactly what he needs to know.

Walter is dumped with the uncles after his mother, Mae (Kyra Sedgwick), decides to attend court reporting school and ends up engaged to a guy in Vegas. Things like that are always happening to her. Walter's first impression of Garth and Hub is a fearful one; they seem carved from a block of American Gothic, and sit in their high-backed chairs on the porch like men who are prepared to wait for death no matter how long it takes. The summer will, however, not be boring, Walter understands, when the uncles start firing shotguns at unwanted visitors.

They have a lot of traffic on the farm because word has it they've got millions stashed away somewhere. Maybe they used to work with Al Capone (one local rumor), or maybe they kept one of those dozen fortunes Hub won, or maybe there aren't any millions at all. Hub and Garth go through life like a double act, feeding each other straight lines as they plant a garden that is unexpectedly heavy on corn, or order a used circus lion to be delivered to the farm. (A giraffe also shows up, but the movie loses track of him.)

The plot, such as it is, is hardly necessary. Yes, Mae turns up with the fiancé from Vegas, and yes, he wants to get his hands on the money, but of course Hub can handle him. Even on the day he collapses and then checks himself out of the hospital, we see him punch out four louts in a local saloon, and then give them the special speech he always gives to young men. It has to do with being able to believe in something even if it's not true, because the believing part is what's important.

The movie, written and directed by Tim McCanlies, is a gentle and sweet whimsy, attentive to the love between the two brothers, respectful of the boy's growth and curiosity. There are flashbacks to the story of Princess Jasmine and her jealous lover, and it appears that Hub as a swordsman would have shamed Zorro. True? Who cares, as long as you believe it is.

Watching the movie, I was reminded of *Un-*

strung Heroes (1995), the Diane Keaton film about a young boy who goes to live with his uncles, who are world-class eccentrics. That movie was based on a memoir by Franz Lidz; Tim McCanlies, who wrote and directed *Secondhand Lions,* seems to have made it up, although his friend Harry Knowles thinks maybe it's inspired by the childhood of Bill Watterson, the creator of *Calvin & Hobbes.* Certainly young Walter grows up to become a cartoonist whose characters include a couple of goofy but heroic uncles and a used lion. To have the kind of childhood you can use as inspiration for a comic strip should be the goal of every kid.

Secretary ★ ★ ★
R, 104 m., 2002

James Spader (E. Edward Grey), Maggie Gyllenhaal (Lee Holloway), Jeremy Davies (Peter), Lesley Ann Warren (Joan Holloway), Stephen McHattie (Burt Holloway), Amy Locane (Theresa). Directed by Steven Shainberg and produced by Shainberg, Andrew Fierberg, and Amy Hobby. Screenplay by Erin Cressida Wilson, based on the story by Mary Gaitskill.

Secretary approaches the tricky subject of sadomasochism with a stealthy tread, avoiding the dangers of making it either too offensive or too funny. Because S&M involves postures that are absorbing for the participants but absurd to the onlooker, we tend to giggle at the wrong times. Here is a film where we giggle at the right times. The director, Steven Shainberg, has succeeded by focusing intently on his characters, making them quirky individuals rather than figures of fun.

The movie, to begin with, is well cast. There may be better actors than James Spader and Maggie Gyllenhaal, but for this material, I cannot think who they are. About Spader there always seems to be some inarticulated secret hovering, and Gyllenhaal avoids numerous opportunities to make her character seem pathetic, and makes her seem plucky instead—intent on establishing herself and making herself necessary.

Spader plays Mr. Grey, a lawyer whose office looks like the result of intense conversations with an interior designer who has seen too many Michael Douglas movies. Mr. Grey has such bad luck with secretaries that he has an illuminated help-wanted sign out front he can light up, like the VACANCY sign at a motel. Gyllenhaal plays Lee Holloway, who has the illness of self-mutilation and comes from a neurotic family. Released from treatment, Lee takes typing classes, goes looking for work, and has an interview with Mr. Grey. Something unspoken passes between them, and they know they are thinking about the same thing.

Lee is submissive. Spader is dominant and obsessive (he has a fetish for lining up red markers in his desk drawer). He demands perfection, she falls short of the mark, he punishes her, and this becomes a workable relationship. When he loses interest for a time and stops correcting her mistakes, she grows disconsolate; when he sharply calls her back into his office, she is delighted.

The movie does not argue that S&M is good for you, but has a more complex dynamic. By absorbing so much of Mr. Grey's time and attention, Lee, who has abysmal self-esteem, feels that attention is being paid to her. Mr. Grey notices her. He thinks about her. He devises new games for them. He never threatens serious hurt or harm, but instead tends toward role-playing and ritual. What they discover is that, in the long run, S&M is more fun (and less trouble) for the M than for the S. "We can't go on like this twenty-four hours a day," Mr. Grey complains at one point. Lee doesn't see why not.

Jeremy Davies plays Peter, the other key role, sincere to the point of being inarticulate, who for a time dates Lee. Mr. Grey looks on jealously as they do their laundry together, and is faced with the possibility that he might lose his agreeable secretary. That would be the final straw, since we sense that Mr. Grey is in much worse shape than Lee was ever in. His obsessive-compulsive behavior is driving him nuts, not to mention his clients. Stories about S&M often have an ironic happy ending, but this one, based on a short story by Mary Gaitskill, seems sincere enough: They've found a relationship that works. For them.

The movie's humor comes through the close observation of behavior. It allows us to understand what has happened without specifying it. The lawyer and secretary have subtle little signals by which they step out of their roles and sort of wink, so they both know that they both know what they're doing. Their behavior, which is intended to signify hostility, eventually grows into a deeper recognition of each other's natures and needs. That, of course, leads to affection, which can be tricky, but not for them, because both suspect there is no one else they're ever likely to meet who will understand them quite so completely.

Secret Ballot ★ ★ ★
G, 105 m., 2002

Nassim Abdi (Woman), Cyrus Abidi (Soldier). Directed by Babak Payami and produced by Marco Muller and Payami. Screenplay by Payami.

Secret Ballot is a quixotic new Iranian comedy about a female election agent who is sent to a remote island to collect ballots in a national election. Because we never find out who or what is being elected, there has been much puzzlement among critics about what the election symbolizes. I believe the message is in the messenger: The agent is a *woman*.

"It's election day, don't you know?" the woman tells a bored soldier assigned to drive her around. "There's a letter. You have to guard the ballots."

The soldier studies the letter. "It says an agent will come, not a woman."

"I'm in charge here, mister. I have orders. You must obey or I'll see to it you remain a soldier forever."

Strong words in a culture where the rights of women are limited. I was reminded of *In the Heat of the Night,* in which the whole point is that the Sidney Poitier character insists on being treated with respect. This movie could be titled "They Call Me MISS Election Agent." The plot is secondary to the fact of the character's gender, and in Iran this movie must play with a subtext we can only guess.

But what else is going on? Is the movie intended to show us (a) that democracy exists in Iran, (b) that it is struggling to be born, or (c) that most people find it irrelevant to their daily lives? There's a little of all three during the long day the solider and the woman (both unnamed) spend together. Some citizens, asked to choose two of ten names on the ballot, complain they've never heard of any of them. A fierce old lady shuts her door to the team, but later sends them food, and her courier observes, "Granny Baghoo has her own government here." A man in charge of a solar energy station expresses his opinion with admirable clarity: "I know no one but God almighty, who makes the sun come up. If I vote for anyone, it must be God."

If the woman is the Poitier character, the soldier is like the sheriff played by Rod Steiger. He starts out strongly disapproving of a female agent, but during the course of the day begins to find her persuasive, intriguing, and sympathetic. By the end of the day, when he casts his ballot, it is for her, and we're reminded of the sheriff's little smile as Mister Tibbs gets back on the train.

The director, Babak Payami, has a visual style that is sometimes astonishing, sometimes frustrating, sometimes both. The first shot is of a plane dropping a box by parachute over a dry, empty plain. The camera pans with exquisite subtlety to reveal . . . a bed? Can it be a bed, in the middle of this wilderness? We see that it is. In this hot climate, they sleep outdoors.

As the soldier drives the agent around the island, events do not build so much as accumulate. Mourners in a cemetery tell her women are not allowed inside. Symbol quandary: (a) The fading patriarchy is buried there, or (b) women cannot even die as equals? In the middle of a deserted, unpopulated plain, the soldier brings the jeep to a halt before a red traffic light. Symbol quandary: (a) Outmoded laws must be ignored, or (b) in a democracy the law must be respected everywhere?

As the woman continues her discouraging attempt to involve indifferent islanders in the vote, we are reminded of Dr. Johnson's famous observation in the eighteenth century, when women were as much without rights in England as they are today in the Middle East. After hearing a woman deliver a sermon, he told Mr. Boswell: "It is not done well, but one is surprised to find it done at all."

Watching the movie, I reflected on a persistent subgenre of Iranian cinema, in which characters drive or walk endlessly through enigmatic landscapes, holding conversations of debatable meaning. Kiarostami's *Taste of Cherry* (1997), a Cannes winner much prized by many critics, not by me, follows that pattern. *Secret Ballot* brings to it much more interest and life. Perhaps the lack of cities, names, relationships, and plots provides a certain immunity: A film cannot be criticized for being about what it does not contain.

The Secret Lives of Dentists ★ ★ ★
R, 104 m., 2003

Campbell Scott (David Hurst), Hope Davis (Dana Hurst), Denis Leary (Slater), Robin Tunney (Laura). Directed by Alan Rudolph and produced by Campbell Scott and George Van Buskirk. Screenplay by Craig Lucas, based on the novel *The Age of Grief* by Jane Smiley.

They met in dental school, where he was awed by her brilliance, and now they share a practice and a family. Their three daughters are a handful, especially the little one, who is going through a phase of preferring daddy to mommy, but slaps daddy whenever she gets the chance. They are happy, apparently, but something strange is going on under the surface of this marriage, and one day David accidentally glimpses his wife sharing a tender and loving moment with another man.

What should he do then? Alan Rudolph's *The Secret Lives of Dentists* is about a quiet, inward man. David (Campbell Scott) is a good father and certainly loves his wife, but when Dana (Hope Davis) tries to talk to him he seems to be asleep. She says she wishes they were closer: "You scare me a little." And yet what about her affair? For the time being, David determines to say nothing and do nothing, and hope that, whatever it is, it plays itself out and Dana comes back to him—to them.

David has the kind of patient a dentist must dread: a cocky wiseass named Slater (Denis Leary) who masks his fear with hostility, hates dentists, is keeping an appointment made by his ex-wife. David fills a cavity, only to be confronted at the community opera by Slater, who holds up a filling that dropped out and informs the audience that David is a lousy dentist. This is on the same night he saw his wife with the strange man. Not a good night.

The story advances through a mixture of everyday realism and fantasy. We get a deep, real, convincing portrait of a family going through a period of crisis (the family doctor insists on diagnosing all of the children's illnesses as emotional reactions to tension between the parents). We see meals served, fights stopped, love expressed, weekends planned. At the same time, Slater begins to turn up in David's mind as an imaginary guest, and we see him, too—standing in the kitchen, offering free advice in the dining room, even sliding out from under the bed.

Slater hates his ex-wife and thinks women have it coming to them. He advises David to cut and run. David tries to explain himself: He won't confront Dana about her affair because he doesn't want to have to do something about it. Perhaps he is afraid that, if forced, she will chose her lover instead of her husband.

Whether she chooses, and whether he acts, you will have to discover for yourself. What you will find is a film with an uncanny feeling for the rhythms of daily life, acted by Scott and Davis with attention to those small inflections of speech that can turn words into weapons. There is also a lot of physical acting; the youngest child, in particular, has a great need to be held and touched and hauled around in her parents' arms. And then there are the five days of the flu, as first one and then another family member develops a fever and starts throwing up. Scott is wonderful here in the way he shows his character caring for the family while coming apart inside.

I suppose the Slater character is essential to Rudolph's idea of the movie, which is based on the novel *The Age of Grief* by Jane Smiley. To introduce Slater's imaginary presence is a risk, and a reach, and I suppose it deserves credit, especially since Leary plays the character about as well as he can probably be played. But I wanted less, in a way. I wanted to lose the whole fantasy overlay and stay with the movie's strength, which is to show the everyday life of a family in crisis. There are real feelings here, which go deep and are truly felt, and the whole Slater apparatus is only a distraction. *The Secret Lives of Dentists* tries hard to be a good film, but if it had relaxed a little, it might have been great.

Secret Things ★ ★ ★
NO MPAA RATING, 115 m., 2004

Coralie Revel (Natalie), Sabrina Seyvecou (Sandrine), Roger Mirmont (Delacroix), Fabrice Deville (Christophe), Blandine Bury (Charlotte), Olivier Soler (Cadene), Viviane Theophildes (Mme. Mercier). Directed by Jean-Claude Brisseau and produced by Brisseau and Jean-Francois Geneix. Screenplay by Brisseau.

Secret Things is a rare item these days: an erotic film made well enough to keep us interested. It's about beautiful people, has a lot of nudity, and the sex is as explicit as possible this side of porno. If you enjoyed *Emmanuelle,* you will think this is better. And, like Bertolucci's more considerable film *The Dreamers,* it will remind you of the days when movies dealt as cheerfully with sex as they do today with action. Of course, it is French.

What is amazing is how seriously the French take it. I learn from *Film Journal International* that *Secret Things* was named Film of the Year by *Cahiers du Cinema,* the magazine that brought Godard, Truffaut, Chabrol, and Rohmer into the world, and became the bible of the auteur theory. But then *Cahiers* has long been famous for jolting us out of our complacency by advocating the outrageous.

The movie is an erotic thriller that opens with a woman alone on a sofa, doing what such women do on such sofas in such movies. The camera slowly draws back to reveal the location: a strip club. We hear the voice of the narrator, Sandrine (Sabrina Seyvecou), who is a bartender in the club and new to this world; she needed the job. When she seems reluctant to have sex with the customers, the performer, named Natalie (Coralie Revel), tells her that is her right, and they are both fired.

Sandrine cannot go to her flat because she is behind on the rent. Natalie invites her to spend the night with her. You see how these situations develop in erotic fiction. They have a tête-à-tête, and vice versa. We hear frank, revealing,

and well-written dialogue about their sexual feelings. Natalie is a realist about sex, she says. When it comes to pleasure, she is more interested in herself than in her partners, who are nonparticipants in the erotic theater of her mind. What turns her on is being watched by strangers, and although Sandrine is shocked at first, in no time at all they are doing things in a Metro station that would get you arrested if you were not in a movie.

"Let's climb the social ladder," Natalie suggests to Sandrine. They target a small but wealthy company whose cofounder is about to die. His son, a notorious rake and pervert, will inherit. Sandrine gets a job as a secretary and is provocative in just such a way as to attract the attention of the other cofounder, Delacroix (Roger Mirmont). Soon she is his private secretary, and almost immediately his lover; her boldness in seducing him shows a nerve that is almost more interesting than her technique. She has him so completely in her power, she feels sorry for the poor guy.

Sandrine arranges for Natalie to be hired by the company, and soon they have both fallen into the orbit of Christophe (Fabrice Deville), the son and heir. This is a disturbed man. As a child, he watched his mother die and sat for days beside her body. As an adult, he has been such a cruel lover that not one but two women committed suicide by setting themselves afire in front of him. He has a sister, Charlotte (Blandine Bury), and feels about her as such men do in such movies.

If the film is erotic on the surface, its undercurrent is as hard and cynical as *In the Company of Men.* The difference is that, this time, women are planning the cruel jokes and deceptions—or they would like to think they are. The writer and director, Jean-Claude Brisseau, devises an ingenious plot that involves corporate intrigue and blackmail, double-crossing and sabotage, and sex as the key element in the control of the country.

And all the time, Sandrine's narration adds another element. She is detached, observant, and a little sad in her comments on the action; unlike an American narrator, who would try to be steamy, she talks to us like one adult to another, commenting on what she really felt, who she felt sorry for, what she regretted having to do, and who she trusted but shouldn't have. The ending, which resolves all the plotting and intrigue with clockwork precision, is ironic not like a Hitchcock film, but like a French homage to Hitchcock; Truffaut's *The Bride Wore Black*, perhaps.

The film is well made, well acted, cleverly written, photographed by Wilfrid Sempe as if he's a conspirer with the sexual schemers. There's an especially effective scene where Natalie stands behind an open door and drives poor Delacroix frantic as coworkers pass by right outside. The movie understands that even powerful men can be rendered all but helpless by women with sufficient nerve. *Secret Things* is not the film of the year, or even of the fortnight, but it is a splendid erotic film with a plot so cynical that we're always kept a little off balance.

Secret Window ★ ★ ★
PG-13, 106 m., 2004

Johnny Depp (Mort Rainey), John Turturro (John Shooter), Maria Bello (Amy Rainey), Timothy Hutton (Ted), Charles S. Dutton (Ken Karsch), Len Cariou (Sheriff). Directed by David Koepp and produced by Gavin Polone. Screenplay by Koepp, based on a Stephen King novella.

The first shot after the credits of *Secret Window* is an elaborate one. It begins with a view across a lake to a rustic cabin. Then the camera moves smoothly in to the shore and across the grounds and in through a window of the cabin, and it regards various rooms before closing in on a large mirror that reflects a man asleep on a couch.

The framing narrows until we no longer see the sides of the mirror, only the image. And then we realize we aren't looking at a reflection, but are in fact now in the real room. Not possible logically, but this through-the-looking-glass shot, along with a wide-brimmed black hat and some Pall Mall cigarettes, are the only slight ripples in the smooth surface of the movie's realism.

The movie stars Johnny Depp in another of those performances where he brings a musing eccentricity to an otherwise straightforward role. He plays Mort Rainey, a best-selling novelist of crime stories; like the hero of *Misery*, he reminds us that the original story is by Stephen King. The computer on his desk in the loft contains one paragraph of a new story, until he deletes it. He spends a lot of time sleeping, and has possibly been wearing the same ratty bathrobe for months. His hair seems to have been combed with an eggbeater, but of course with Johnny Depp you never know if that's the character or the actor.

A man appears at his door. He is tall and forbidding, speaks with a Mississippi accent, wears the wide-brimmed black hat, and says, "You stole my story." This is John Shooter (John Turturro), a writer who leaves behind a manuscript that is, indeed, almost word for word the same as Rainey's story *Secret Window*. The plot deals with a man who has been betrayed by his wife, murders her, and buries her in her beloved garden—where, after a time, she will be forgotten, "perhaps even by me." Rainey knows he did not steal the story, but Shooter is an angry and violent man who stalks the author and causes bad things to happen: a screwdriver through the heart of his beloved dog, for example. Shooter says he wrote his story in 1997, and Rainey has his comeback: He wrote his in 1994, and thinks he has an old issue of *Ellery Queen's Mystery Magazine* to prove it.

But that leads him back into the world of his estranged wife, Amy (Maria Bello), who is living with her new lover (Timothy Hutton). She has the big house in town, and that's why Rainey is living in sloth and despond in the lake cottage. To tell more would be wrong, except to note Rainey's decision to hire an ex-cop (Charles S. Dutton) as a bodyguard, and to complain to the local sheriff (Len Cariou), an arthritic whose hobby is knitting.

Rainey appears to be the classic Hitchcock hero, an innocent man wrongly accused. He has been cheated on by his wife, and now this nut from nowhere is threatening his life because of a story he did not steal. The situation is magnified nicely by the location at the isolated cottage, which leaves many opportunities for disturbing sounds, strange omens, broken lightbulbs, threatening letters, and Shooter himself, who appears at disconcerting moments and seems to be stalking Rainey wherever he goes.

All of this could add up to a straight-faced thriller about things that go boo in the night, but Johnny Depp and director David Koepp (who wrote *Panic Room* and directed *Stir of Echoes*) have too much style to let that happen. Like many men who have lived alone for a long time, Rainey carries on a running conversation with himself—dour, ironic, sometimes amused. He talks to the dog until the dog is killed. Aroused from a nap, he stumbles through a confused investigation, asks himself, "Now, where was I?" and returns to the same position on the couch.

Even his friends are entertaining. When he talks with the ex-cop, they use a chess clock, banging their button when the other guy starts talking. Maybe this has something to do with billing arrangements, or maybe they're just competitive. Probably the latter, since bodyguards are always on duty.

The story is more entertaining as it rolls along than it is when it gets to the finish line. But at least King uses his imagination right up to the end, and spares us the obligatory violent showdown that a lesser storyteller would have settled for. A lot of people were outraged that he was honored at the National Book Awards, as if a popular writer could not be taken seriously. But after finding that his book *On Writing* had more useful and observant things to say about the craft than any book since Strunk and White's *The Elements of Style*, I have gotten over my own snobbery.

King has, after all, been responsible for the movies *The Shawshank Redemption, The Green Mile, The Dead Zone, Misery, Apt Pupil, Christine, Hearts in Atlantis, Stand by Me,* and *Carrie. Secret Window* is somewhere in the middle of that range storywise, and toward the top in Depp's performance. And we must not be ungrateful for *Silver Bullet*, which I awarded three stars because it was "either the worst movie ever made from a Stephen King story, or the funniest," and you know what side of that I'm gonna come down on.

Seeing Other People ★ ★ ½
R, 90 m., 2004

Jay Mohr (Ed), Julianne Nicholson (Alice), Lauren Graham (Claire), Bryan Cranston (Peter), Josh Charles (Lou), Andy Richter (Carl), Matthew Davis (Donald), Jill Ritchie (Sandy), Helen Slater (Penelope). Directed by Wallace Wolodarsky and produced by Gavin Polone. Screenplay by Maya Forbes and Wolodarsky.

Alice and Ed are happy. They've been happy for five years. They're engaged to be married. But then Alice begins to mope. She wonders if she's been unfairly shortchanged in the sexual experience sweepstakes, since before Ed she slept with only three guys, and two of them don't count, one because he was not a guy. So she makes a modest proposal: They should both fool around a little before they get married. That will jump-start their own fairly tame sex life, and reconcile her to a lifetime of faithfulness.

Seeing Other People takes her suggestion and runs with it through several sexual encounters, arriving at the conclusion that the biggest danger of meaningless sex is that it can become meaningful. It isn't a successful movie, but is sometimes a very interesting one, and there is real charm and comic agility by the two leads, Julianne Nicholson and Jay Mohr. There is also finally a role for which Andy Richter seems ideally cast.

The movie has to overcome one problem: We like Ed and Alice. Their friends like them. They seem intended for each other. They aren't sitcom types, but solid, loyal, comfortable, smart people; Alice reminds me a little of Nicholson's great performance in *Tully* (2000) as a veterinarian who knows who she wants to marry and captures him with infinite subtlety and tenderness.

Here she suggests the rules. They will be completely honest with each other. They will be honest with their partners. They will somehow know when to stop. Alice takes the first leap: "I made out with someone," she tells Ed. "Made out?" "Yeah, like . . . made out." As she describes her experience, they grow excited, and have, they tell friends the next day, the best sex they've had—ever. It'll be downhill from there, as Alice meets a contractor named Donald (Matthew Davis) and Ed meets a waitress named Sandy (Jill Ritchie). Neither Sandy nor Donald see themselves as one-night stands, and are not content to play walk-through roles in the sexual adventures of an engaged couple.

Other characters include Alice's sister (Lauren Graham) and brother-in-law (Bryan Cranston), and Ed's two best friends, played by Josh Charles as a sexual cynic, and Andy Richter as a sincere, salt-of-the-earth guy who just absolutely knows no good can come of this experiment.

Seeing Other People is not so much about sex

as about its consequences, and although we see some heaving blankets, what the characters mostly bare are their souls. I liked it best in the tentative early stages, when Ed and Alice were unsure about their decision, not very brave about acting on it, and fascinated by talking about it. Then the movie starts working out various permutations of possible couples, and we get a traffic jam. I don't want to give away all the secrets, but Alice gets into bed with one person she should not, would not, and probably could not get into bed with—not if she's the person she seems to be.

There's a quiet joke in the fact that Alice wants to fool around and Ed is reluctant to go along. And there's a nice irony when Alice decides to call off the experiment just when Sandy has promised Ed a three-way with her college roommate. Ed perseveres, only to learn what many have discovered before him, that three-way sex tends to resemble a three-car race where one car is always in the pits.

This is not a boring movie, and the dialogue has a nice edge to it. It was written by a married couple, Maya Forbes and Wallace Wolodarsky, and directed by Wolodarsky; his credits include *The Simpsons* and hers include *The Larry Sanders Show*. I liked the way they had Alice and Ed actually discuss their experiment, instead of simply presenting it as a comic setup. But I don't know if the filmmakers ever decided how serious the movie should be, and so fairly harrowing moments of truth alternate with slapstick (man escapes through bedroom window as wife enters through door, etc.). And there are so many different pairings to keep track of that the movie loses focus and becomes a juggling act. Too bad, because in their best scenes together Nicholson and Mohr achieve a kind of intimacy and immediate truth that is hard to find, and a shame to waste.

September 11 ★ ★ ★

NO MPAA RATING, 135 m., 2003

Segments directed by Alejandro Gonzalez Inarritu, Ken Loach, Mira Nair, Amos Gitai, Youssef Chahine, Danis Tanovic, Samira Makhmalbaf, Claude Lelouch, Shohei Imamura, Sean Penn, and Idrissa Ouedraogo, and produced by Alain Brigand.

The recent release of the audio recordings of calls from the doomed World Trade Center adds an eerie timeliness to *September 11*, a film in which eleven directors from around the world contribute eleven segments of eleven minutes each. Voices and sounds without pictures force us to internalize a catastrophe almost impossible to visualize.

That's illustrated in the best of the segments, an overpowering film by Alejandro Gonzalez Inarritu of Mexico, best known for *Amores Perros*. He keeps his screen entirely black for most of the eleven minutes, occasionally interrupting it with flashes of bodies falling from the burning World Trade Center. We realize after a while that the muffled thuds on the sound track are the bodies landing.

The sound track begins and ends with a collage of excited voices, and during the eleven minutes we also hear snatches of newscasts and part of a cell phone call from a passenger on one of the hijacked airplanes ("We have a little problem on the plane, and I wanted to say I love you . . ."). Toward the end, there is the sound of fearsome hammering, and we realize with a chill that this is the sound of the floors collapsing, one on top of another, growing louder. It must have been recorded from a radio inside the building; it is the last thing the terrified people inside the towers heard. This film is so strong because it allows us to use our imaginations. It generates almost unbearable empathy.

Another of the best films is by Ken Loach of Great Britain, who films a Chilean writing a letter to Americans in which he offers his sympathy. Then he recalls that on another Tuesday, September 11—this one in 1973—the democratically elected government of Chile was overthrown by a CIA-funded military coup, President Salvador Allende was murdered, and the right-wing dictator Augusto Pinochet was installed as the U.S. puppet to rule over a reign of torture and terror. I wrote in my notes: "Do unto others as you would have them do unto you."

The third powerful film is by Mira Nair of India, who tells the true story of a Pakistani mother in New York whose son got on the subway to go to medical school and never returned. She was questioned by the FBI, her son was named as a suspected terrorist, and only six months later was his body found in the rubble, where, as a trained medic, he had gone to help. His hero's coffin was draped in the American flag.

One of the most sympathetic films comes from Iran. Samira Makhmalbaf's film shows a teacher trying to explain to her students—Afghan refugees in Iran—what has happened in New York. The kids get into a discussion about God, and whether he would kill some people to make others; "God isn't crazy," one child finally decides. None of the children can imagine a tall building, so the teacher takes them to stand beneath a smokestack, and the smoke from the top makes an eerie mirror of the catastrophe.

Other films miss the mark. Amos Gitai of Israel shows a TV news reporter broadcasting live from the scene of a suicide bombing when she is taken off the air because of the news from New York. This situation could have generated an interesting film, but the reporter is depicted as so self-centered and goofy that the piece derails. A film by Egypt's Youssef Chahine also has an interesting premise—a director is visited by the ghost of a U.S. Marine who was killed in the Beirut bombing—but the piece is unfocused, half-realized.

The only note of humor comes in a charming film by Idrissa Ouedraogo, from Burkina Faso in Africa, where five poor boys believe they have spotted Osama bin Laden in their town, and plot to capture him and win the $25 million reward. They are not entirely off the track; the actor hired to play Bin Laden could be his double.

Other films are from Bosnia's Danis Tanovic, who shows women continuing to march with the names of their dead despite the deaths in New York; Japan's Shohei Imamura, who shows a man who survived the atomic bombing but has become convinced he is a snake; Sean Penn of the United States, who stars Ernest Borgnine as an old man who rejoices when his dead wife's flowers bloom, not realizing they get sunlight because the towers have fallen; and France's Claude Lelouch, with a sentimental piece about a deaf woman who does not realize what has happened until her boyfriend returns alive, covered with dust.

Emerging from *September 11*, shaken particularly by Inarritu's use of sound with a mostly black screen, I could not help wondering:

Would it have killed one of these eleven directors to make a clear-cut attack on the terrorists themselves? 9/11 was a savage and heartless crime, and after the symbolism and the history and the imagery and the analysis, that is a point that must be made.

Sex and Lucía ★ ★ ★

NO MPAA RATING, 128 m., 2002

Paz Vega (Lucía), Tristán Ulloa (Lorenzo), Najwa Nimri (Elena), Daniel Freire (Carlos/Antonio), Javier Cámara (Pepe), Elena Anaya (Belén), Silvia Llanos (Luna), Juan Fernández (Chief). Directed by Julio Medem and produced by Fernando Bovaira and Enrique López Lavigne. Screenplay by Medem.

One of the characters in *Sex and Lucía* is writing a novel. Many of the things that happen in the novel have happened to him. Or he imagines they have, or will. Or they are all only in the novel. It is being read by one of the women who is a character in it. Meanwhile, the audience knows of connections between the characters that they themselves do not suspect. And then there are additional connections because the same actor plays two roles—one real, I guess, and the other . . . well, real too, I guess.

To describe the plot is not possible in a limited space, and besides, I'm not sure I'm up to it. I doubt that anyone seeing this film will completely understand it after one viewing, but that doesn't mean you have to see it twice—it simply means that confusion is part of the effect. The Spanish director, Julio Medem, made a lovely film named *The Lovers of the Arctic Circle* (1998), which was a palindrome—a story that began at both ends and met at the middle (his characters were named, inevitably, Ana and Otto). He likes to toy with the mind of the audience, and he's good at it.

Let's try for a bare outline. We meet Lucía (Paz Vega), a waitress who gets a telephone call leading her to believe her lover has been killed in an accident. He is Lorenzo (Tristán Ulloa). Distraught, she goes to an island he often talked about, and there she meets Carlos (Daniel Freire), a scuba diver who steers her toward a guest house occupied by Elena (Najwa Nimri).

We know, because of a prologue, that Elena

is the mother of a daughter by Lorenzo. They met for one magic night on the island and did not exchange names. Hold that for a second, while we flash back six years to the first meeting between Lorenzo and Lucía, who tells him she admires his novel and is in love with him. They become passionate lovers, but eventually he turns sour as he gets bogged down in his second novel. This novel is about how his friend's sister has met Elena, put together the relevant dates and clues, and concluded that Elena's child is Lorenzo's. Lorenzo then goes to see the child, who is being looked after by the sexy Belén (Elena Anaya), who is, I think, Elena's roommate. But there is some confusion here; the scenes where he meets her may exist only in the novel, and Elena may be on the island. On the other hand . . .

But you see how it is. We bookmark the characters, they turn up in various combinations, and Medem describes them as unattached triangles that do not know about one another.

So much for Lucía. What about sex? The movie is an adult film in the 1970s meaning of that term, and has a good deal of sex and nudity, some of it gratuitous, although sometimes, as in this story, gratuitous sex is the most fun. To give you an idea of the film's complications, Carlos the scuba diver is played by the same actor as Antonio, who is the boyfriend of Belén's mother, a former porn actress.

What is the point of all of this? To absorb us, I think. To engage us. The characters are freed by the very absurdity of the plot. They are not required to march lockstep toward a conclusion based on the diminishing number of alternatives left to them. Even at the end of the film, they are drowning in alternatives. And the film itself tells us it has a hole in the middle and then starts over again—as indeed it does, since Lucía falls into a hole and nothing is ever heard again about it.

In notes about the movie, Julio Medem says he wrote a screenplay and then a novel, and then wrote the novel into the screenplay, and so forth. Despite his love of the labyrinthine, he can build a scene, and even if the story parts do not fit, every scene plays strongly in and of itself. The parts work even if the whole leaves me uncertain. Many movies are certain about their whole, but are made of careless parts. Forced to choose, I would take the parts.

Note: The film's digital photography is inadequate to the task of filming under the bright sun of the island. A portentous zoom to the sun is almost ruined because the image is so overexposed you hardly notice the sun. Since voluptuous visuals were obviously part of Medem's plan, he should have used film. Digital is still too anorexic for his purposes.

Sex with Strangers ★ ★
NO MPAA RATING, 105 m., 2002

A documentary directed and produced by Joe and Harry Gantz.

The most intriguing element of *Sex with Strangers* involves not the sex, but the strangers. Here are people who do not allow the use of their last names, yet they cheerfully have sex in front of the camera—and even willingly participate in scenes that make them look cruel, twisted, reckless, and perhaps deranged. We know from the Springer show that shame is no barrier when it comes to collecting your fifteen minutes of fame. But these people act like this, we realize, even when the cameras aren't on. They live this way.

The movie has been produced and directed by Joe and Harry Gantz, who do the *Taxicab Confessions* program for HBO. They follow two couples and a sad threesome through their adventures in the swinging lifestyle, in a documentary that strongly suggests the screwing they're getting isn't worth the screwing they're getting. Even assuming they have an insatiable appetite for sex with strangers, how do they develop an appetite for trolling through the roadside bars of the nation, picking up the kinds of people who can be picked up there? Groucho Marx wouldn't belong to any club that would have him as a member. The stars of this film might be wise not to sleep with anyone who would sleep with them.

We meet James and Theresa, Shannon and Gerard, and Calvin and Sarah and Julie. James and Theresa have it all figured out. They even have their own business cards. They cruise the back roads of the nation, pulling up to bars in their motor home, meeting new friends inside, and inviting them out to the Winnebago for a swap meet. Shannon and Gerard are more complicated: She seems deeply neurotic about the lifestyle, he wants to swing without her, they have a child whom they try to insulate from Mommy and Daddy's ever-changing new friends, and there's even a scene where they chat about their lifestyle with her mother, getting points for "openness" when they should be penalized for inflicting their secrets upon the poor woman.

Now, as for Calvin. He uses the rhetoric of the lifestyle primarily, we suspect, as a way to justify sleeping with both Sarah and Julie, neither one of whom is particularly enthusiastic about his hobby. He wants it all, but isn't a good sport when Sarah and Julie slip off without the middleman.

Although mate-swappers would have you believe that they are open and willing participants in their lifestyle, the evidence on screen suggests that men are a good deal more keen about the practice than women, perhaps because there is an intrinsic imbalance in the pleasures to be had from quickie anonymous sex.

When I first saw the movie, I had fundamental questions about how much of it could be trusted. On *Ebert & Roeper*, I said: "There's a scene where James and Theresa are in a club and they meet another couple and they ask the other couple, 'Do you want to swing?' And the other couple says, 'Sure.' And they say, 'Oh, we have our motor home right outside.' And so they go outside, the two couples, *and the camera*. And I'm wondering: Let's say I wanted to be a swinger, and I've just met two people who are going to take me into their motor home. Am I going to wonder about the fact that this happens to be *videotaped* while it's happening? When I saw scenes like that, I thought, this has all been rehearsed. It's a setup."

After the show played, I got an e-mail from Joe Gantz, who assured me that all of the scenes in the movie do indeed reflect reality. One key to their footage is that they always have two cameras running all the time, to supply cutaways and reaction shots. Another is that, by definition, they show only couples who agreed to be photographed. If a hypothetical couple got to the motor home and balked at the cameras, they wouldn't be in the movie.

That leads me back to where I began, to curiosity about the mind-set of the people in the film. By openly swapping mates, they have already abandoned conventional notions of privacy and modesty. Perhaps it is only a small additional step to do it on camera. But I didn't find much fascination in the swinging. What they're doing is a matter of plumbing arrangements and mind games, of no erotic or sensuous charge. But *that* they are doing it is thought-provoking. What damage had to be done to their self-esteem, and how, to lead them to this point?

Shanghai Knights ★ ★ ★
PG-13, 107 m., 2003

Jackie Chan (Chon Wang), Owen Wilson (Roy O'Bannon), Aaron Johnson (Charlie), Thomas Fisher (Artie Doyle), Aidan Gillen (Rathbone), Fann Wong (Chon Lin), Donnie Yen (Wu Chow), Oliver Cotton (Jack the Ripper). Directed by David Dobkin and produced by Roger Birnbaum, Gary Barber, and Jonathan Glickman. Screenplay by Alfred Gough and Miles Millar.

Shanghai Knights has a nice mix of calculation and relaxed goofiness, and in Jackie Chan and Owen Wilson it once again teams up two playful actors who manifestly enjoy playing their ridiculous roles. The world of the action comedy is fraught with failure, still more so the period-Western-kung-fu comedy, but here is a movie, like its predecessor *Shanghai Noon* (2000), that bounds from one gag to another like an eager puppy.

The movie opens with the obligatory action prologue required in the Screenwriter's Code: The Great Seal of China is stolen by sinister intruders, and its guardian killed. The guardian, of course, is the father of Chon Wang (Jackie Chan), who, as we join him after the titles, is sheriff of Carson City, Nevada, and busy ticking off the names of the bad guys he has apprehended. Hearing of the tragedy from his beautiful sister, Chon Lin (Fann Wong), Wang hurries to New York to join up with his old comrade in arms Roy O'Bannon (Owen Wilson).

The movie's plot is entirely arbitrary. Nothing has to happen in Nevada, New York, or its ultimate location, London, although I suppose the setup does need to be in China. Every new scene simply establishes the setting for comedy, martial arts, or both. Because the comedy is fun in a broad, genial way, and because Jackie Chan and his costars (including Fann Wong) are martial arts adepts, and because the director, David Dobkin, keeps the picture filled with energy and goodwill, the movie is just the sort of mindless entertainment we're ready for after all of December's distinguished and significant Oscar finalists.

The plot moves to London because, I think, that's where the Great Seal and the evil plotters are, and even more because it needs fresh locations to distinguish the movie from its predecessor. The filmmakers click off locations like Sheriff Chan checking off the bad guys: the House of Lords, Buckingham Palace (fun with the poker-faced guards), Whitechapel and an encounter with Jack the Ripper, Big Ben (homage to Harold Lloyd), Madame Tussaud's. Charlie Chaplin and Arthur Conan Doyle make surprise appearances, surprises I will not spoil.

For Jackie Chan, *Shanghai Knights* is a comeback after the dismal *The Tuxedo* (2002), a movie that made the incalculable error of depriving him of his martial arts skills and making him the captive of a cybernetic suit. Chan's character flip-flopped across the screen in computer-generated action, which is exactly what we don't want in a Jackie Chan movie. The whole point is that he does his own stunts and the audience knows it.

They know it, among other reasons, because over the closing credits there are always outtakes in which Jackie and his costars miss cues, fall wrong, get banged and bounced on assorted body parts, and break up laughing. The outtakes are particularly good this time, even though I cannot help suspecting (unfairly, maybe) that some of them are just as staged as the rest of the movie.　　　☞

Shaolin Soccer ★ ★ ★
PG-13, 87 m., 2004

Stephen Chow (Sing), Vicki Zhao (Mui), Man Tat Ng (Golden Leg Fung), Patrick Tse (Hung), Yut Fei Wong (Iron Head). Directed by Stephen Chow and produced by Kwok-fai Yeung. Screenplay by Chow and Kan-Cheung Tsang.

Shaolin Soccer is like a poster boy for my theory of the star rating system. Every month or so, I get an anguished letter from a reader wanting to know how I could possibly have been so ignorant as to award three stars to, say, *Hidalgo* while dismissing, say, *Dogville* with two stars. This disparity between my approval of kitsch and my rejection of angst reveals me, of course, as a superficial moron who will do anything to suck up to my readers.

What these correspondents do not grasp is that to suck up to *my* demanding readers, I would do better to praise *Dogville*. It takes more nerve to praise pop entertainment; it's easy and safe to deliver pious praise of turgid deep thinking. It's true, I loved *Anaconda* and did not think *The United States of Leland* worked, but does that mean I drool at the keyboard and prefer man-eating snakes to suburban despair?

Not at all. What it means is that the star rating system is relative, not absolute. When you ask a friend if *Hellboy* is any good, you're not asking if it's any good compared to *Mystic River,* you're asking if it's any good compared to *The Punisher.* And my answer would be, on a scale of one to four, if *Superman* (1978) is four, then *Hellboy* is three and *The Punisher* is two. In the same way, if *American Beauty* gets four stars, then *Leland* clocks in at about two.

And that is why *Shaolin Soccer,* a goofy Hong Kong action comedy, gets three stars. It is piffle, yes, but superior piffle. If you are even considering going to see a movie where the players zoom fifty feet into the air and rotate freely in violation of everything Newton held sacred, then you do not want to know if I thought it was as good as *Lost in Translation.*

Shaolin Soccer has become a legend. It's the top-grossing action comedy in Hong Kong history, and was a big hit at Toronto 2002 (although, for some reason, I didn't see it; I must have been sidetracked by *Bowling for Columbine*). Miramax bought it, and shelved it for two years, apparently so Harvey Weinstein could cut it by thirty minutes, get rid of the English dubbing, restore the subtitles, and open it one week after his own *Kill Bill: Vol. 2*. To put this movie up against Tarantino is like sending Simon Cowell against William H. Rehnquist, but Simon has his fans.

The movie has been directed and cowritten by Stephen Chow, who stars as Sing, a martial arts master turned street cleaner, who uses his skills in everyday life and is in love with Mui (Vicki Zhao), who sells buns from her little street stand and combs her hair forward to conceal a complexion that resembles pizza with sausage and mushrooms. It is a foregone conclusion that by the end of this film Mui will be a startling beauty. Less predictable is that Sing recruits seven soccer players from his former monastery to form a soccer team.

His inspiration to do this is Fung (Man Tat Ng), known as the Golden Leg because he was, years ago, a great soccer hero until his leg was broken by Hung (Patrick Tse). Hung now rules the soccer world as owner of Team Evil (yes, Team Evil), while Fung drags his leg like the Hunchback of Notre Dame. It is another foregone conclusion that Team Evil will meet the Shaolin soccer team formed by Fung and Sing in a thrilling match played before what looks like a vast crowd that has been borrowed from a computer game.

The game doesn't follow any known rules of soccer, except that there is a ball and a goal. As the players swoop high into the air and do acrobatics before kicking the ball, I was reminded more of Quidditch. There is also the matter of ball velocity. The players can kick the ball so hard that it actually catches fire as it rockets through the air, or digs a groove in the ground as it plows toward the goal.

Since the game is impossible and it is obvious Team Evil will lose, there's not much suspense, but there is a lot of loony comedy, a musical number, and the redemption of the Poor Spotted Little Bun Girl. As soccer comedies go, then, I say three stars. It's nowhere near as good as *Bend It Like Beckham* (2002), of course, but *Beckham* is in a different genre, the coming-of-age female-empowerment film. It's important to keep these things straight.

The Shape of Things ★ ★ ★ ½
R, 96 m., 2003

Paul Rudd (Adam), Rachel Weisz (Evelyn), Gretchen Mol (Jenny), Fred Weller (Phillip). Directed by Neil LaBute and produced by LaBute, Gail Mutrux, Philip Steuer, and Rachel Weisz. Screenplay by LaBute.

The world of Neil LaBute is a battleground of carnage between the sexes. Men and women distrust one another, scheme to humiliate one another, are inspired to fearsome depths of cruelty. Their warfare takes place in the affluent habitats of the white upper-middle class—restaurants, bookstores, coffee shops, corporate offices, campuses, museums, and apartments of tasteful sterility. Although one of his gender wars films was shot in Fort Wayne, Indiana, and the other two in southern California, there is no way to tell that from the information on the screen. All of his characters seem to live in clean, well-lighted, interchangeable places.

The Shape of Things is the third of these films. First came *In the Company of Men* (1997) and *Your Friends and Neighbors* (1998). Then there were two mainstream films, *Nurse Betty* (2000) and *Possession* (2002). Now we are back in the world of chamber dramas involving a handful of intimately linked characters. The first film was driven by a man of ferocious misanthropy. The second involved characters whose everyday selfishness and dishonesty were upstaged by a character of astonishing cruelty. In *The Shape of Things*, while the two couples have their share of character defects, they seem generally within the norm, until we fully understand what has happened.

In a museum, we see Evelyn (Rachel Weisz) step over a velvet rope to take Polaroids of a male nude statue—or, more specifically, of a fig leaf added at a later date. The museum guard, named Adam (Paul Rudd), asks her to step outside the rope, but eventually steps inside it himself, to plead with her not to cause trouble just before his shift ends. He's a student, working part-time.

They begin to see each other. She's a graduate student, working on a project that she describes, as she describes a great many things, as a "thingy." Eventually we meet an engaged couple, Jenny (Gretchen Mol) and Phillip (Fred Weller), who are friends of Adam's. Over a period of months, they notice changes in him. He loses weight. Gets a haircut. Rids himself of a nerdy corduroy jacket that, we learn, Phillip has been urging him to throw away since freshman year. He even has a nose job, which he tries to explain as an accidental injury.

What, or who, is responsible for these changes? Can it be Evelyn, who is now Adam's girlfriend? Adam denies it, although it is not unknown for a woman to make over the new man in her life, and even Jenny observes that most men have traits that stand between them and perfection—traits women are quick to observe and quite willing to change.

The movie unfolds as a series of literate conversations between various combinations of these four articulate people. Their basic subject is one another. They are observant about mannerisms, habits, values, and changes, and feel licensed to make suggestions. There is even a little low-key sexual cheating, involving kissing, and low-key emotional assaults, involving telling about the kissing.

And then . . . but I will not say one more word because the rest of the movie is for you to discover. Let it simply be said that there are no free passes in LaBute's class in gender studies.

The Shape of Things builds a sense of quiet dread under what seems to be an ordinary surface. Characters talk in a normal way, and we suspect that their blandness disguises buried motives. Often they are quite happy to criticize each other, and none of them takes criticism well. These characters are perhaps in training to become the narcissistic, self-absorbed monsters in *Your Friends and Neighbors.*

LaBute has that rarest of attributes, a distinctive voice. You know one of his scenes at once. His dialogue is the dialogue overheard in trendy midscale restaurants, with the words peeled back to suggest the venom beneath. He also has a distinctive view of life, in which men and women are natural enemies—and beyond that,

every person is an island surrounded by enemies. This seems like a bleak and extreme view, and yet what happens in his films often feels like the logical extension of what happens to us or around us every day. It is the surface normality of the characters and their world that is scary.

LaBute has been compared to David Mamet, and no doubt there was an influence, seen in the devious plots and the precisely heard, evocative language. But Mamet is much more interested in plotting itself, in con games and deceptions, while in LaBute there is the feeling that some kind of deeper human tragedy is being enacted; his characters deceive and wound one another not for gain or pleasure, but because that is their nature.

Actors have a thankless task in a film like this. All four players are well cast in roles that ask them to avoid "acting" and simply exist on a realistic, everyday level. Like the actors in a Bresson film, they're used for what they intrinsically represent, rather than for what they can achieve through their art. They are like those all around us, and like us, except that LaBute is suspicious of their hidden motives. One person plays a cruel trick in *The Shape of Things*, but we get the uneasy sense that, in LaBute's world, any one of the four could have been that person.

Shattered Glass ★ ★ ★ ½
PG-13, 99 m., 2003

Hayden Christensen (Stephen Glass), Peter Sarsgaard (Chuck Lane), Chloë Sevigny (Caitlin Avey), Melanie Lynskey (Amy Brand), Steve Zahn (Adam Penenberg), Hank Azaria (Michael Kelly), Rosario Dawson (Andie Fox), Luke Kirby (Rob Gruen). Directed by Billy Ray and produced by Craig Baumgarten, Marc Butan, Tove Christensen, Gaye Hirsch, and Adam Merims. Screenplay by Ray, based on the article by Buzz Bissinger.

"Are you mad at me?" Stephen Glass asks. He's like a puppy who's made a mess on the carpet but knows he's cute and all of the kids are crazy about him. The kids in this case are his fellow staffers at the *New Republic,* and the mess consists of twenty-seven steaming piles of fabricated falsehoods that he deposited on its pages.

You may remember some of Glass's stories. I know I did. I loved his piece about the young hacker who terrified corporations with raids on their computers, and then sold them his expertise to shoot down other hackers. This guy was so successful he had his own agent. Then there was the gathering of Young Republicans at a Washington hotel, partying all night like drunken fraternity boys. And the convention of the political novelties industry, with display tables of racist, homophobic, and anti-Clinton T-shirts, bumper stickers, and books.

Terrific stories. Problem is, Stephen Glass (Hayden Christensen) made them all up. Without realizing it, The *NR* had started publishing fiction. Magazines employ fact-checkers to backstop their writers, and they're a noble crowd, but sometimes they check the trees and not the forest; it doesn't occur to them that a piece might be a total fraud.

The first puncture of Stephen Glass's balloon came from Adam Penenberg (Steve Zahn), who as a writer for the Web-based Forbes Digital Tool was several steps down the ladder from the *New Republic*'s superstar. But when he tries to follow up on that rich hacker with his own agent, he can't find him—or his agent, or the company that hired him, or his Website, or anything. When he calls the *NR*, his query lands on the desk of Charles Lane (Peter Sarsgaard), the magazine's new editor. Lane has enough to worry about: He has recently replaced the beloved Michael Kelly, he lacks Kelly's charisma, and the staffers instinctively side with Glass against the cool, distant Lane.

When you hear about a case like this, or the similar fraud committed against the *New York Times* by Jayson Blair, you wonder how a world-class publication gets itself conned by some kid. Maybe the key word is "kid." Maybe the hotshot newcomers generate an attractive aura around themselves so that editors would rather jump on the bandwagon than seem like old fogeys.

Shattered Glass, written and directed by Billy Ray and based on a *Vanity Fair* article by Buzz Bissinger, relates the rise and fall of the young charmer in terms of the office culture at the *New Republic*, which is written by and for smart people and, crucially, doesn't use photographs.

("Photos would have saved us," one staffer notes, "because there wouldn't have been any." There were, however, photos with Jayson Blair's stories—it's just that the photographer could never seem to find him at the scene of the story.)

The movie is smart about journalism because it is smart about offices; the typical newsroom is open space filled with desks, and journalists are actors on this stage; to see a good writer on deadline with a big story is to watch not simply work, but performance.

Stephen Glass was a better actor than most, playing the role of a whiz kid with bashful narcissism. There is a fascinating and agonizing sequence during which Lane tries to pin down the slippery details of a Glass story, and Glass tries to wriggle free. Phone numbers go missing, files are left at home, phone calls aren't answered, and as it becomes obvious to Lane that the story will not hold water, a kind of dread begins to grow.

We like Glass, too, and we can see he's trapped; he channels those nightmares we all have about flunking the big exam. There are a couple of times when Lane seems to have him nailed down and he squirms free with a desperate but brilliant improvisation, and we're reminded of Frank Abagnale Jr., the hero of *Catch Me If You Can*, who found an addictive joy in getting praise he did not deserve.

Glass's fellow workers admire him because (a) he's turning in work they would have died to have written, and (b) he doesn't rub it in. Two of his most admiring colleagues, Caitlin Avey (Chloë Sevigny) and Amy Brand (Melanie Lynskey), feel protective toward him; like sisters, they worry that he works too hard, pushes himself, doesn't take credit, doesn't know how good he is. A more typical newsroom colleague is Andie Fox, played by Rosario Dawson over at Forbes Digital Tool; she senses that Penenberg (Zahn) is onto a really big story, wants a piece of it, and keeps trying to elbow in.

Because *Shattered Glass* is cast so well, with actors who seem to instinctively embody their parts, it's worth another look at some of Billy Ray's choices. Hayden Christensen, who makes Glass's career believable by being utterly plausible himself, played young Anakin Skywalker in *Star Wars: Attack of the Clones*. Steve Zahn often plays clueless losers, and Rosario Dawson specializes in sex and action roles; not here.

Chloë Sevigny is a versatile actress, but you might not have thought of her as a *New Republic* staffer until you see her here, and she's pitch-perfect. Peter Sarsgaard has the balancing act as a new editor who happens to be right but is under enormous pressure to be wrong.

Shattered Glass deserves comparison with *All the President's Men* among movies about journalism, but it's about a type known in many professions: The guy who seems to be pursuing the office agenda when actually he's pursuing his own. Filled with a vision of his own success, charming and persuasive, smart, able to create whole worlds from fictions that work as well as facts, he has an answer for everything until someone finally thinks to ask the fundamental question: Is it all a fraud, right down to the bone?

In recent years we have seen vast corporations built on lies and political decisions based more on wishes than facts. The engineers of those deceptions have all been enormously likable, of course. They need to be. We are saved, from time to time, not so much by the rectitude of the Charles Lanes as by the dogged curiosity of the Adam Penenbergs.

Showtime ★ ★

PG-13, 95 m., 2002

Robert De Niro (Mitch), Eddie Murphy (Trey), Rene Russo (Chase Renzi), William Shatner (Himself), Frankie Faison (Captain Winship). Directed by Tom Dey and produced by Jane Rosenthal and Jorge Saralegui. Screenplay by Keith Sharon, Alfred Gough, and Miles Millar, based on a story by Saralegui.

The cop buddy comedy is such a familiar genre that a movie can parody it and occupy it at the same time. The characters in *Showtime* do it as a kind of straddle, starting out making fun of cop buddy clichés and ending up trapped in them. The movie's funny in the opening scenes and then forgets why it came to play.

We meet two cops: Mitch (Robert De Niro), who never had to choose between a red wire and a green wire, and Trey (Eddie Murphy), who is a cop but would rather play one on TV. You can guess from the casting that the movie will have energy and chemistry, and indeed while I watched it my strongest feeling was

affection for the actors. They've been around so long, given so much, are so good at what they do. And Rene Russo, as the TV producer who teams them on a reality show, is great at stalking in high heels as if this is the first time she's ever done it without grinding a body part beneath them.

Mitch wants only to do his job. Trey is a hot dog who has learned more from TV than at the police academy. Making a drug bust, he knowledgeably tastes the white powder and finds it's cocaine. "What if it's cyanide?" Mitch asks (or anthrax, we're thinking). "There's a reason real cops don't taste drugs."

We meet Chase Renzi (Russo), TV producer with a problem: Her report on exploding flammable baby pajamas didn't pan out. She's electrified when she sees TV footage of Mitch getting angry with a TV cameraman and shooting his camera. The network sues. Mitch is threatened with suspension, just like in all the *Dirty Harry* movies, but offered an ultimatum: Star in a new reality show with Trey ("You do the show; they drop the suit").

Mitch grudgingly agrees, and some of the best scenes involve the callow Trey instructing the hard-edged Mitch in the art of acting (this is a flip of John Wayne tutoring James Caan in *El Dorado*). During these scenes we're seeing pure De Niro and Murphy, freed from effects and action, simply acting. They're good at it.

Enter a bad guy with a big gun. A gun so big we are surprised not by its power but by the fact that anyone can lift it. An expert testifies: "This gun is like the fifty-foot shark. We know it's there, but nobody has ever seen it." Most of the second half of the movie involves Mitch and Trey chasing down the gun and its owners, who use it in a series of daring robberies. This we have seen before. Oh yes.

The movie was directed by Tom Dey, whose only previous film was *Shanghai Noon* (2000), a buddy movie pairing a Chinese martial arts fighter and a train robber. I learn from the Internet Movie Database that he studied film at Brown University, the Centre des Etudes Critiques in Paris, and the American Film Institute. He probably knows what's wrong with this movie more than I do.

But making movies is an exercise in compromise no less appalling than the making of the "reality" TV show in *Showtime.* My guess:

The screenplay ("by Keith Sharon, Alfred Gough, and Miles Millar, based on a story by Jorge Saralegui") was funnier and more satirical until the studio began to doubt the intelligence of the potential audience, and decided to shovel in more action as insurance. As we all know, the first rule of action drama is that when a gun as legendary as a fifty-foot shark comes on-screen in the first act, somebody eventually finds a spent shell casing the size of a shot glass.

Note: Most of the computers in movies for several years have been Macintoshes, maybe because the Mac is the only computer that doesn't look like every other computer and therefore benefits from product placement. But this is the first movie in which an entire iMac commercial runs on TV in the background of a shot.

Shrek 2 ★ ★ ★
PG, 105 m., 2004

With the voices of: Mike Myers (Shrek), Eddie Murphy (Donkey), Cameron Diaz (Princess Fiona), John Cleese (King Harold), Julie Andrews (Queen Lillian), Jennifer Saunders (Fairy Godmother), Antonio Banderas (Puss-in-Boots), Rupert Everett (Prince Charming), Larry King (The Ugly Stepsister). An animated film directed by Andrew Adamson, Kelly Asbury, and Conrad Vernon and produced by David Lipman, Aron Warner, and John H. Williams. Screenplay by J. David Stem, Joe Stillman, and David N. Weiss, based on the characters by William Steig.

Shrek 2 is bright, lively, and entertaining, but it's no *Shrek*. Maybe it's too much to expect lightning to strike twice. *Shrek* was so original in its animation and such an outpouring of creative imagination that it blindsided us; *Shrek 2* is wonderful in its own way, but more earthbound. It's more fun to see Shrek battle a dragon than to watch him meeting his new in-laws.

Shrek (voiced again by Mike Myers) actually seems teetering on the brink of middle-class respectability in the sequel. There's nothing like a good woman to tame an ogre. His outsider status as the loner in the swamp has changed dramatically through his romance with Princess Fiona (Cameron Diaz), although his table manners could stand improvement when he has dinner with her parents, King Harold (John Cleese) and Queen Lillian (Julie Andrews).

In the first film, as you may remember, Fiona's curse was that she had been taken captive by a dragon, but could be freed if the dragon was slain and she was kissed by the hero who did the deed. Ideally, that would be Prince Charming (Rupert Everett), but in *Shrek 2*, when he finally arrives in the neighborhood he discovers to his intense disappointment that the ogre has already dispatched the dragon and wed the princess—and that Shrek's kiss dramatically transformed Fiona. No longer petite, she is tall and broad and green, and an ogre.

A summons comes from the Kingdom of Far Far Away: Her parents want to meet her new husband. This involves a very long journey by Shrek, Fiona, and Donkey (Eddie Murphy), who insists on coming along. Donkey is the comic high point of the movie, with Murphy's nonstop riffs and inability to guess when he is not welcome. "The trick isn't that he talks," Shrek observed in the first movie. "The trick is to get him to shut up." The kingdom is indeed far, far away, which gives Donkey endless opportunities to ask, "Are we there yet?"

Their arrival at the castle of Fiona's parents provides big laughs; Harold and Lillian are shocked to find that their daughter has not only married an ogre, but also become one. A basket of doves is released to celebrate their arrival, and one of them is so astonished it flies bang into the castle wall, and drops dead at Harold's feet. Eventually the plot leads us into the environs of the Fairy Godmother (Jennifer Saunders), a sinister figure who operates a vast factory manufacturing potions and hexes. Is it possible that her Happily Ever After potion could transform ogres into humans? Not if she can help it; she wants to get rid of Shrek and marry Fiona to Prince Charming, according to her original plan.

The screenplay, by J. David Stem, Joe Stillman, and David N. Weiss, has the same fun *Shrek* did in playing against our expectations. Who would anticipate a fight between the ogre and his bride, with Shrek marching out of the house? What about the arrivals ceremony at the matrimonial ball, with all of the kingdom's celebrities walking down a red carpet while an unmistakable clone of Joan Rivers does the commentary? And there's real sweetness when Shrek and Fiona start smooching.

The movie has several songs, none of which I found very memorable, although of course I am the same person who said the Simon and Garfunkel songs in *The Graduate* were "instantly forgettable." The first song, "Accidentally in Love," explains how Shrek and Fiona fell for each other. It's cut like a music video, which is okay, but I think it comes too early in the film, before we really feel at home with the narrative.

A few minor characters from the first film, like the Gingerbread Man and the Three Blind Mice, return for the sequel, and there's a new major character: Puss-in-Boots, a cat who seems to have been raised on Charles Boyer movies, and is voiced by Antonio Banderas. Donkey and Puss build an enormous mutual resentment, because each one thinks he's the star.

Sequels have their work cut out for them. Some people think *Godfather, Part II* is better than *The Godfather,* but the first film loomed so tall in my mind that I gave "Part II" only three stars. In the same way, perhaps I would have liked *Shrek 2* more if the first film had never existed. But I'll never know. Still, *Shrek 2* is a jolly story, and Shrek himself seems durable enough to inspire *Shrek 3* with no trouble at all. Maybe it will be *Shrek Meets Cheaper by the Dozen.*

Signs ★ ★ ★ ★
PG-13, 120 m., 2002

Mel Gibson (Graham Hess), Joaquin Phoenix (Merrill Hess), Rory Culkin (Morgan Hess), Abigail Breslin (Bo Hess), Cherry Jones (Officer Caroline Paski), Patricia Kalember (Colleen Hess). Directed by M. Night Shyamalan and produced by Frank Marshall, Sam Mercer, and Shyamalan. Screenplay by Shyamalan.

M. Night Shyamalan's *Signs* is the work of a born filmmaker, able to summon apprehension out of thin air. When it is over, we think not how little has been decided, but how much has been experienced. Here is a movie in which the plot is the rhythm section, not the melody. A movie that stays free of labored explanations

and a forced climax, and is about fear in the wind, in the trees, in a dog's bark, in a little girl's reluctance to drink the water. In signs.

The posters show crop circles, those huge geometric shapes in fields of corn and wheat, which were seen all over the world in the 1970s. Their origin was explained in 1991 when several hoaxers came forward and demonstrated how they made them; it was not difficult, they said. Like many supernatural events, however, crop circles live on after their unmasking, and most people today have forgotten, or never knew, that they were explained. *Signs* uses them to evoke the possibility that . . . well, the possibility of anything.

The genius of the film, you see, is that it isn't really about crop circles, or the possibility that aliens created them as navigational aids. I will not even say whether aliens appear in the movie, because whether they do or not is beside the point. The purpose of the film is to evoke pure emotion through the use of skilled acting and direction, and particularly through the sound track. It is not just what we hear that is frightening. It is the way Shyamalan has us listening intensely when there is nothing to be heard. I cannot think of a movie where silence is scarier, and inaction is more disturbing.

Mel Gibson stars, as Father Graham Hess, who lives on a farm in Bucks County, Pennsylvania. We discover he is a priest only belatedly, when someone calls him "father." "It's not 'father' anymore," he says. Since he has two children, it takes us a beat to compute that he must be Episcopalian. Not that it matters, because he has lost his faith. The reason for that is revealed midway in the film, a personal tragedy I will not reveal.

Hess lives on the farm with his brother Merrill (Joaquin Phoenix) and his children, Morgan and Bo (Rory Culkin and Abigail Breslin). There is an old-fashioned farmhouse and barn, and wide cornfields, and from the very first shot there seems to be something . . . out there, or up there, or in there. Hess lives with anxiety gnawing at him. The wind sounds strange. Dogs bark at nothing. There is something *wrong*. The crop circles do not explain the feelings so much as add to them. He catches a glimpse of something in a corn field. Something wrong.

The movie uses TV news broadcasts to report on events around the world, but they're not the handy CNN capsules that supply just what the plot requires. The voices of the anchors reveal confusion and fear. A video taken at a birthday party shows a glimpse of the most alarming thing. "The history of the world's future is on TV right now," Morgan says.

In a time when Hollywood mistakes volume for action, Shyamalan makes quiet films. In a time when incessant action is the style, he persuades us to pay close attention to the smallest nuances. In *The Sixth Sense* (1999) he made a ghost story that until the very end seemed only to be a personal drama—although there was something there, some buried hint, that made us feel all was not as it seemed. In *Unbreakable* (2000) he created a psychological duel between two men, and it was convincing even though we later discovered its surprising underlying nature, and all was redefined.

In *Signs*, he does what Hitchcock said he liked to do, and plays the audience like a piano. There is as little plot as possible, and as much time and depth for the characters as he can create, all surrounded by ominous dread. The possibility of aliens is the catalyst for fear, but this family needs none, because it has already suffered a great blow.

Instead of flashy special effects, Shyamalan creates his world out of everyday objects. A baby monitor that picks up inexplicable sounds. Bo's habit of leaving unfinished glasses of water everywhere. Morgan's bright idea that caps made out of aluminum foil will protect their brains from alien waves. Hess's use of a shiny kitchen knife, not as a weapon, but as a mirror. The worst attack in the film is Morgan's asthma attack, and his father tries to talk him through it, in a scene that sets the entire movie aside and is only about itself.

At the end of the film, I had to smile, recognizing how Shyamalan has essentially ditched a payoff. He knows, as we all sense, that payoffs have grown boring. The mechanical resolution of a movie's problems is something we sit through at the end, but it's the setup and the buildup that keep our attention. *Signs* is all buildup. It's still building when it's over. ☞

Simøne ★ ★
PG-13, 117 m., 2002

Al Pacino (Viktor Taransky), Catherine Keener (Elaine), Evan Rachel Wood (Lainey Taransky), Rachel Roberts (Simøne), Jay Mohr (Hal Sinclair), Pruitt Taylor Vince (Max Sayer), Winona Ryder (Nicola Anders), Elias Koteas (Hank Aleno). Directed and produced by Andrew Niccol. Screenplay by Niccol.

Simøne tells the story of a director at the end of his rope who inherits a mad inventor's computer program that allows him to create an actress out of thin air. She becomes a big star and the center of a media firestorm, and he's trapped: The more audiences admire her, the less he can reveal she is entirely his work. The movie sets this dilemma within a cynical comedy about modern Hollywood; it's fitfully funny but never really takes off. Out of the corners of our eyes we glimpse the missed opportunities for some real satirical digging.

Al Pacino plays the director, Viktor Taransky, once brilliant, recently the author of a string of flops. Only his young daughter, Lainey (Evan Rachel Wood), still believes in him—a little. His ex-wife, Elaine (Catherine Keener), the head of the studio, has lost all hope for his career and pulls the plug on his latest project when the temperamental star (Winona Ryder) blows up.

Into the life of this desperate man comes another one (Elias Koteas), who has devised a computer program that creates "synthespians." Viktor isn't interested—but then, when the wizard leaves him the program in his will, he starts noodling around with the software and the beautiful, talented, and (above all) cooperative Simøne is the result. She needs, Viktor exults, no hairdresser, makeup, driver, car, trailer, stand-in or stuntwoman—no, not even for the fall from the plane. She is always on time, never complains, says the words just as they're written, and has no problem with nudity.

Viktor creates Simøne's performance on a computer that stands all alone in the middle of an otherwise empty sound stage. The other actors in the movie are told Simøne will be added to their scenes electronically. The premiere of the first movie is a huge success, and of course paparazzi from the supermarket tabloids stalk Viktor in hopes of photographing Simøne. No luck.

The movie was written, produced, and directed by Andrew Niccol, who wrote *The Truman Show* and wrote and directed *Gattaca,* both films about the interface between science and personality. *Simøne* is not in that league. He wants to edge it in the direction of a Hollywood comedy, but the satire is not sharp enough and the characters, including the ex-wife, are too routine.

And there's a bigger problem: Simøne always remains . . . just Simøne. The computer image always looks as if it's about to come to life and never does. One can imagine software bugs that recklessly import other on-line personalities into Simøne: Matt Drudge, for example, or Harry Knowles, or Danni Ashe. One can imagine Simøne suddenly being possessed by Lara Croft, tomb raider, and breaking up a serious dramatic scene with video-game violence. One can imagine . . . well, almost anything except that she remains a well-behaved program. When Simøne "appears" on a chat show, for example, it's kind of funny that she sticks to well-worn subjects like dolphins and smoking, but why not go the extra mile and put her on the Howard Stern show?

Pacino, that splendid actor, does what he can to bring Viktor to life. But the screenplay's too narrow, and prevents him from taking the character beyond a certain point. Most of the big events are handled with sitcom simplicity, and the hungry gossip reporters are presented as they always are, a howling pack with no wit or originality. Even Catherine Keener, as the studio head, simply plays an ex-wife who is a studio head: There's no twist, nothing unexpected.

The problem, I think, is that in aiming for too wide an audience, Niccol has made too shallow a picture. *The Truman Show* and *Gattaca* pushed their premises; *Simøne* settles for the predictable. The story elements echo the sad experience of the team assembled to make *Final Fantasy,* the summer of 2001 sci-fi movie that failed at the box office. That movie was made up entirely of "real" characters generated by computers, including Aki Ross, the heroine, who, all things considered, is a more intriguing woman than Simøne (whose appearance is provided by the actress Rachel Roberts). The *Final Fantasy* team labored four years and achieved everything they dreamed of, and were rejected by the public. Much more interesting than a director who has unimaginable success fall into his lap.

Sinbad: Legend of the Seven Seas
★ ★ ★ ½
PG, 85 m., 2003

With the voices of: Brad Pitt (Sinbad), Catherine Zeta-Jones (Marina), Joseph Fiennes (Proteus), Michelle Pfeiffer (Eris), Dennis Haysbert (Kale). Directed by Patrick Gilmore and Tim Johnson and produced by Jeffrey Katzenberg and Mireille Soria. Screenplay by John Logan.

Sinbad: Legend of the Seven Seas plays like a fire sale in three departments of the genre store: Vaguely Ancient Greek, Hollywood Swashbuckler, and Modern Romance. That it works is because of the high-energy animation, some genuinely beautiful visual concepts, and a story that's a little more sensuous than we expect in animation.

Sinbad, whose voice is by Brad Pitt, is a sailor and pirate whose name and legend have been stretched to accommodate an astonishing range of movie adventures. This time we learn he was a resident of Syracuse, a commoner friend of Prince Proteus (Joseph Fiennes), and left town after his first look at Proteus's intended, Marina (Catherine Zeta-Jones). "I was jealous for the first time," he remembers.

Sinbad runs away and finds a career commanding a pirate vessel with his first mate, a stalwart giant named Kale (Dennis Haysbert). They have indeed sailed the seven seas, all right, if we're to believe his talk of retirement in Fiji. Considering how far Fiji was from Greece in the centuries before the Suez Canal, we rather doubt he has really been there, but no matter: Maybe he's been talking to Realtors.

As the film opens, Sinbad's pirate ship attacks a ship commanded by Proteus, who is in possession of the *Book of Peace*, a sacred volume of incalculable value to the future of Syracuse. This attempted theft goes ahead despite the fact that the two men are old friends and happy to see each other; a pirate is never off duty. Sinbad's scheme is interrupted by Eris (Michelle Pfeiffer), the goddess of chaos, who likes to mix things up and creates a gigantic sea monster to threaten both ships. The battle with the seemingly indestructible monster is one of several astonishing sequences in the film; the others involve sailing off the edge of the world; Tartarus, the realm of the dead, which awaits them over the edge; and a winter vastness presided over by an awesome snowbird. These scenes are animated so fluidly and envision strange sights so colorfully that there is real exhilaration.

The story, directed by Patrick Gilmore and Tim Johnson and written by John Logan, involves the shape shifting, deceptions, switches, and parental ultimatums much beloved by legend. It also exploits the tendency throughout Greek legend for the gods to interfere in the affairs of man. As flies to wanton boys are, Sinbad is to Eris. Although Sinbad did not actually steal the *Book of Peace*, the meddlesome Eris impersonates him and he seems to steal it, and Sinbad is taken prisoner and condemned to die by King Dymas, father of Proteus. Sinbad protests his innocence; Proteus believes him and offers himself as hostage to free Sinbad to sail off in search of the book. There's a ten-day deadline.

Here's where the sensuous stuff ramps up. Marina, who says she has always wanted to go away to sea, stows away on Sinbad's ship, and that comes in handy when all of the sailors on board are bewitched by seductive Sirens. A female immune to their charms, Marina takes the helm, saves the ship, and furthers the inevitable process by which she falls in love with Sinbad, who, as the character with his name in the title, of course must get the girl.

The scene where the ship sails off the edge of the world to the land of Tartarus involves physics of a nature that Archimedes, a famous native son of Syracuse, would probably not have approved, but what wondrous visuals, and what a haunting realm they discover, filled with the hulls of wrecked ships and the bones of doomed sailors. *Sinbad* is rich with ideas and images, and it exploits the resources of mythology to create such creatures as the snowbird, who at one point locks Syracuse in a grip of ice.

Syracuse itself, for that matter, is a magically seen place, a city of towering turrets atop a mountain range. When Sinbad returns, it is to deal with the crucial question of whether Marina will return to her betrothed or stay with him. This is handled with great tact in a conversation in which both men agree that her basic motivation is to sail away and see the world, although she also, I suspect, has a burning desire to see the bunk in Sinbad's cabin.

Sinbad: Legend of the Seven Seas is another worthy entry in the recent renaissance of animation, and in the summer that also gave us *Finding Nemo*, it's a reminder that animation is the most liberating of movie genres, freed of gravity, plausibility, and even the matters of lighting and focus. There is no way that Syracuse could exist outside animation, and as we watch it, we are sailing over the edge of the human imagination.

Since Otar Left ★ ★ ★
NO MPAA RATING, 102 m., 2004

Esther Gorintin (Eka [Grandmother]), Nino Khomassouridze (Marina [Daughter]), Dinara Droukarova (Ada [Granddaughter]), Temour Kalandadze (Tenguiz), Roussoudan Bolkvadze (Roussiko), Sacha Sarichvili (Alexo), Dputa Skhirtladze (Niko). Directed by Julie Bertuccelli and produced by Yael Fogiel. Screenplay by Bertuccelli, Bernard Renucci, and Roger Bohbot.

Since Otar Left tells a story of conventional melodrama and makes it extraordinary because of the acting. The characters are so deeply known, so intensely observed, so immediately alive to us, that the story primarily becomes the occasion for us to meet them. Nothing at the plot level engaged me much, not even the ending, which is supposed to be so touching. But I was touched deeply, again and again, simply by watching these people live their lives.

Three women live in a book-lined flat in Tbilisi, the capital of the one-time Soviet republic of Georgia. Eka is the grandmother, very old, very determined (she is played by Esther Gorintin, who was eighty-five when she began her acting career five years ago). Marina (Nino Khomassouridze) is her daughter, around fifty, a woman of quick peremptory dismissals and sudden rushes of feeling. Ada (Dinara Droukarova), late twenties, is Marina's daughter, a student of literature, bored with her life.

We gather that Eka was French, moved to Georgia with her Soviet husband, was a committed Communist. She still thinks Stalin was a great man. Marina says he was a murderer. Ada looks incredulous that they are still having this argument. The cramped quarters are made into an arena when Eka turns up her television, and both Marina and Ada crank up their CD players.

But look at the way these actresses move. Every step, every gesture, suggests long familiarity with these lives. A visit to the post office observes the body language of people long buried in their jobs. The way that Marina discards her fork as the three women have tea says everything about her impatience. The women use verbal and physical shorthand to illuminate what goes without saying. Eka is always certain of herself. Marina is never satisfied ("I wish I loved you," she says to her patient man friend). Ada is fed up and trapped.

The crowded flat is dominated by the person who isn't there—Otar, Eka's son, who has moved to Paris to look for work. He telephones, but the lines fail. He sends money, but the postal service is uncertain. Things worked better in Stalin's day, Eka is certain. When news comes that Otar has been killed in an accident, Marina decides they will not tell old Eka, to spare her. This leads to a deception, the details of which are familiar from similar films.

What is not familiar, what becomes increasingly fascinating, is the direct and relentless way Eka marches toward the truth. She determines to go to Paris to visit her son, takes along the other two, finds them missing from their hotel room, and mutters "Those two are leading me on."

What is clear is that this old woman has a life and will of her own. There is a wonderful scene while she is still at home in Georgia. She leaves the house alone, looks up some information in the library, buys two cigarettes, and smokes them while riding on a Ferris wheel. With a lesser actor or character, this would be a day out for a lovable granny. With Esther Gorintin playing Eka, it is the day of a woman who thinks she has it coming to her.

What happens, and how, need not concern us. What I remember is the way Julie Bertuccelli, the director and cowriter, sees right into the beings of her characters. Consider two scenes in which the old woman gets a foot massage. In one, her granddaughter absently massages her foot while reading aloud from Proust. In the other, her daughter, usually so wounded and stern, giggles helplessly while tickling her feet, and old Eka laughs and squirms like a child. After seeing this movie, you watch another one with less gifted actors, and the characters seem to have met each other for the first time on the set, earlier that day.

The Singing Detective ★ ★ ★
R, 109 m., 2003

Robert Downey Jr. (Dan Dark), Robin Wright Penn (Nicola/Nina/Blond), Mel Gibson (Dr. Gibbon), Jeremy Northam (Mark Binney), Katie Holmes (Nurse Mills), Adrien Brody (First Hood), Jon Polito (Second Hood), Carla Gugino (Betty Dark/Hooker), Saul Rubinek (Skin Specialist), Alfre Woodard (Chief of Staff). Directed by Keith Gordon and produced by Bruce Davey, Mel Gibson, and Steven Haft. Screenplay by Dennis Potter.

He calls himself "a human pizza." His skin looks like sausage and mushrooms with extra tomato sauce and an occasional eruption of cheese. He is in excruciating pain but surprisingly articulate about it, considering that his lips are so chapped they can hardly move. During a painful treatment, he announces, "I'm gonna go back to my bed. It's vivid and exciting there."

It certainly is. To escape from his agony, he evokes daydreams from a pulp novel he once wrote, luridly populated by *noir* characters who look just like people in his own life—his mother, his nurse, himself. He varies this sometimes by visualizing song-and-dance numbers done in the style of 1950s musicals. In the middle of a difficult medical procedure, the hospital staff or his visitors are likely to break into choreographed versions of '50s hits like "Walking in the Rain," "Doggie in the Window," or "At the Hop."

Keith Gordon's *The Singing Detective* involves the world of Dan Dark (Robert Downey Jr.), once a writer, now living in a world so encompassed by pain that it has become the single fact of his life. The movie is based on an eight-hour BBC series that ran in 1986; both were written by Dennis Potter, whose own psoriasis was nearly unbearable. We know the story was autobiographical, but now it seems to be based on two lives: Potter's and Downey's. What horrors Downey has endured during his struggle with addiction we can easily imagine. Dan Dark's sardonic view of the world and his insulting, sarcastic manner of speech is a defense mechanism familiar to anyone who has known a user.

The film played at Sundance 2003, where the buzz decided it didn't work. I am as guilty as anyone of employing the concept of a film "working," but in this case I wonder how anyone *thought* it would work. It can't be the eight-hour series because it's two hours long. It can't misrepresent Potter's vision because it is his vision; this was the last big project he worked on before he died, and he wanted to see a feature-length movie version of what in some ways was his life story. Of course the medical details don't "work" with the pulp detective story, nor do the musical numbers "work" anywhere, but wouldn't it take a facile compromise to make them fit smoothly together? Here is a character in agony, who deliberately breaks the reality of his world to escape to a more bearable one.

It might be more useful to ask, who would want to see this movie, and why? When I saw it at Sundance, my attention was divided because I was trying to process the meaning of the jagged structure. Seeing it again, knowing what to expect, I found it a more moving experience. I knew, for example, that the *film noir* sequences were not simply pulp escapism, but represented Dan Dark's lurid resentments against people he hated, such as his mother (Carla Gugino) and his cheating wife (Robin Wright Penn).

The movie does not propose to be a comedy, a musical, a *film noir* story, or a medical account. It proposes to be a subjective view of suffering and the ways this character tries to cope with it. Understand that, and the pieces fall into place. Hospitals have a chart with numbers from 1 to 8 and ask you to "rate" the level of your pain. For Dan Dark such a chart is a ghastly joke.

The Singing Detective is a movie about a man who has been failed by science and drugs, and turns in desperation to his mind, seeking temporary insanity as a release. His sharp intelligence is an asset. He knows the 1950s songs are trash, and that's the point; you don't throw songs you love onto the bonfire. Eventually, slowly, he begins to get better. Perhaps his skin condition was partly psychosomatic after all. Or perhaps he simply healed himself, mind over matter. Norman Cousins wrote a book about how he cured himself by laughter. Dennis Potter and his surrogate Robert Downey Jr. seem to be trying anger and resentment as a cure. If it works, don't fix it.

Skins ★ ★ ★
R, 87 m., 2002

Graham Greene (Mogie Yellow Lodge), Eric Schweig (Rudy Yellow Lodge), Gary Farmer (Verdell Weasel Tail), Noah Watts (Herbie), Michelle Thrush (Stella), Lois Red Elk (Aunt Helen), Elaine Miles (Rondella), Nathaniel Arcand (Teen Mogie), Chaske Spencer (Teen Rudy). Directed by Chris Eyre and produced by Jon Kilik and David Pomier. Screenplay by Jennifer D. Lyne, based on the novel *Skins* by Adrian C. Louis.

Skins tells the story of two brothers, both Sioux, one a cop, one an alcoholic "whose mind got short-circuited in Vietnam." They live on the Pine Ridge Reservation, in the shadow of Mount Rushmore and not far from the site of the massacre at Wounded Knee. America's founding fathers were carved, the film informs us, into a mountain that was sacred to the Sioux, and that knowledge sets up a final scene of uncommon power.

The movie is almost brutal in its depiction of life at Pine Ridge, where alcoholism is nine times the national average and life expectancy

50 percent. Director Chris Eyre, whose previous film was the much-loved *Smoke Signals* (1998), has turned from comedy to tragedy and is unblinking in his portrait of a community where poverty and despair are daily realities.

Rudy Yellow Lodge (Eric Schweig), the policeman, is well liked in a job that combines law enforcement with social work. His brother, Mogie (Graham Greene), is the town drunk, but his tirades against society reveal the eloquence of a mind that still knows how to see injustice. Mogie and his buddy Verdell Weasel Tail (Gary Farmer) sit in the sun on the town's main street, drinking and providing a running commentary that sometimes cuts too close to the truth.

Flashbacks show that both brothers were abused as children by an alcoholic father. Mogie probably began life with more going for him, but Vietnam and drinking have flattened him, and it's his kid brother who wears the uniform and draws the paycheck. Those facts are established fairly early, and we think we can foresee the movie's general direction, when Eyre surprises us with a revelation about Rudy: He is a vigilante.

A man is beaten to death in an abandoned house. Rudy discovers the two shiftless kids who did it, disguises himself, and breaks their legs with a baseball bat. Angered by white-owned businesses across the reservation border that make big profits selling booze to the Indians on the day the welfare checks arrive, he torches one of the businesses—only to find he has endangered his brother's life in the process. His protest, direct and angry, is as impotent as every other form of expression seems to be.

When *Skins* premiered at Sundance last January, Eyre was criticized by some for painting a negative portrait of his community. Justin Lin, whose *Better Luck Tomorrow* showed affluent Asian-American teenagers succeeding at a life of crime, was also attacked for not taking a more positive point of view. Recently the wonderful comedy *Barbershop* has been criticized because one character does a comic riff aimed at African-American icons.

In all three cases, the critics are dead wrong because they would limit the artists in their community to impotent feel-good messages

instead of applauding their freedom of expression. In all three cases, the critics are also tone-deaf because they cannot distinguish *what* the movies depict from *how* they depict it. That is particularly true with some of the critics of *Barbershop*, who say they have not seen the film. If they did, the audience's joyous laughter might help them understand the context of the controversial dialogue, and the way in which it is answered.

Skins is a portrait of a community almost without resources to save itself. We know from *Smoke Signals* that Eyre also sees another side to his people, but the anger and stark reality he uses here are potent weapons. The movie is not about a crime plot, not about whether Rudy gets caught, not about how things work out. It is about regret. Graham Greene achieves the difficult task of giving a touching performance even though his character is usually drunk, and it is the regret he expresses, to his son and to his brother, that carries the movie's burden of sadness. To see this movie is to understand why the faces on Mount Rushmore are so painful and galling to the first Americans. The movie's final image is haunting.

Slackers no stars
R, 87 m., 2002

Devon Sawa (Dave), Jason Schwartzman (Ethan), James King (Angela), Jason Segel (Sam), Michael C. Maronna (Jeff), Laura Prepon (Reanna), Mamie Van Doren (Mrs. Van Graaf). Directed by Dewey Nicks and produced by Neal H. Moritz and Erik Feig. Screenplay by David H. Steinberg.

Slackers is a dirty movie. Not a sexy, erotic, steamy, or even smutty movie, but a just plain dirty movie. It made me feel unclean, and I'm the guy who liked *There's Something About Mary* and both *American Pie* movies. Oh, and *Booty Call*. This film knows no shame.

Consider a scene where the heroine's roommate, interrupted while masturbating, continues even while a man she has never met is in the room. Consider a scene where the hero's roommate sings a duet with a sock puppet on his penis. Consider a scene where we cut away from the hero and the heroine to join two roommates just long enough for a loud fart, and then cut back to the main story again.

And consider a scene where Mamie Van Doren, who is seventy-one years old, plays a hooker in a hospital bed who bares her breasts so that the movie's horny creep can give them a sponge bath. On the day when I saw *Slackers*, there were many things I expected and even wanted to see in a movie, but I confess Mamie Van Doren's breasts were not among them.

The movie is an exhausted retread of the old campus romance gag where the pretty girl almost believes the lies of the reprehensible schemer, instead of trusting the nice guy who loves her. The only originality the movie brings to this formula is to make it incomprehensible, through the lurching incompetence of its story structure. Details are labored while the big picture remains unpainted.

Slackers should not be confused with Richard Linklater's *Slacker* (1991), a film that will be treasured long after this one has been turned into landfill. *Slackers* stars the previously blameless Devon Sawa *(SLC Punk! Final Destination)* and Jason Schwartzman *(Rushmore)* as rivals for the attention of the beautiful Angela (James King, who despite her name is definitely a girl). Schwartzman plays Ethan, campus geek; Sawa is Dave, a professional cheater and con man. Ethan obsesses over Angela and blackmails Sawa by threatening to expose his exam-cheating scheme. He demands that Dave "deliver" the girl to him.

This demand cannot be met for a number of reasons. One of them is that Ethan is comprehensively creepy (he not only has an Angela doll made from strands of her hair, but does things with it I will not tire you by describing). Another reason is that Angela falls for Dave. The plot requires Angela to temporarily be blinded to Ethan's repulsiveness and to believe his lies about Dave. These goals are met by making Angela remarkably dense, and even then we don't believe her.

Watching *Slackers*, I was appalled by the poverty of its imagination. There is even a scene where Ethan approaches a girl from behind, thinking she is Angela, and of course she turns around and it is not Angela, but a girl who wears braces and smiles at him so widely

and for so long we can almost hear the assistant director instructing her to be sure the camera can see those braces.

But back to the dirt. There is a kind of one-upmanship now at work in Hollywood, inspired by the success of several gross-out comedies, to elevate smut into an art form. This is not an entirely futile endeavor; it can be done, and when it is done well, it can be funny. But most of the wanna-bes fail to understand one thing: It is funny when a character is offensive *despite* himself, but not funny when he is *deliberately* offensive. The classic "hair gel" scene involving Ben Stiller and Cameron Diaz in *There's Something About Mary* was funny because neither one had the slightest idea what was going on.

Knowing that this movie will be block-booked into countless multiplexes, pitying the audiences that stumble into it, I want to stand in line with those kids and whisper the names of other movies now in release: *Monster's Ball, Black Hawk Down, Gosford Park, The Royal Tenenbaums, A Beautiful Mind, The Count of Monte Cristo*. Or even *Orange County*, also about screwed-up college students, but in an intelligent and amusing way. There are a lot of good movies in theaters right now. Why waste two hours (which you can never get back) seeing a rotten one?

The Sleepy Time Gal ★ ★ ★ ½
R, 94 m., 2002

Jacqueline Bisset (Frances), Martha Plimpton (Rebecca), Nick Stahl (Morgan), Amy Madigan (Maggie), Seymour Cassel (Bob), Peggy Gormley (Betty), Frankie Faison (Jimmy Dupree), Carmen Zapata (Anna). Directed by Christopher Münch and produced by Ruth Charny and Münch. Screenplay by Münch.

Oh, what a sad story this is, about a woman who never accepted anything good in her life because she was hoping for something better. Now she is dying, and in her quiet and civilized way is trying to double back and see what can be retrieved. We think we'll have enough time to tidy up the loose ends, and then death slams down.

The Sleepy Time Gal stars Jacqueline Bisset as Frances, a woman who in some ways has led an admirable life. She made her own way. Very early, she was the late-night disc jockey on a Florida radio station, and her later jobs reflected various causes or passing fancies. She was married twice, had a son by each marriage—and she also, we learn, had a daughter by a third man, and gave her up for adoption. She has not been an attentive mother. One of the sons faithfully attends her bedside, but he observes, "She doesn't really know very much about me"—perhaps not even that he is gay. The other son phones in from London, but will not supply a return number. She wishes she could contact the daughter.

We meet that daughter early in the film. She is Rebecca (Martha Plimpton), raised by foster parents in Boston, now a corporate lawyer. She travels to Daytona Beach to buy a radio station for her employer and has the taxi stop outside a hospital there—the hospital, she knows, where she was born. She looks at it, but what can it tell her? Drive on.

The radio station for many years played rhythm and blues; it was a "race station" when such stations were unknown, says its proud owner Jimmy (Frankie Faison). He wants to give its record collection to the local community college. "I'll be damned if I know what it is that makes this deal so sad," Rebecca says, but Jimmy is not sad; he plans to travel with his wife, maybe to Malaysia. She asks him why he never moved to a bigger market. There were a lot of reasons, he says, and one of them was love. He loved the announcer who was known as the Sleepy Time Gal. Rebecca, looking at her photograph, has no way of knowing it is her mother. That night Rebecca sleeps with Jimmy, who has no way of knowing she is the daughter of the Sleepy Time Gal.

The film is written and directed by Christopher Münch, who made *The Hours and Times* (1991), about a trip to Spain during which John Lennon experiments with homosexuality. In *The Sleepy Time Gal,* he does an unexpected thing. He shows us a story that is not completed and, because of death, will never be completed. Movies are fond of deathbed scenes in which all matters are sealed and wounds cured,

but sometimes, with plain bad timing, people just die and leave matters undetermined. Frances has led an interrupted life and her death will not be tidy either.

Consider one of the most beautiful and mysterious scenes in the movie, where she visits the Pennsylvania farm of a former lover and his wife. She is in remission at the time. Bob and Betty (Seymour Cassel and Peggy Gormley) have been happily married for thirty years. But always Betty has known that Frances occupies emotional ground in her husband's mind. She doesn't know they had a daughter, but she senses their feeling for each other and feels no jealousy. That Bob still loves Frances is clear from the first time we see him, in an extraordinary close-up. I have seen Seymour Cassel in countless roles over the years, but did not guess he had a smile like the one he uses to greet Frances at the airport—the smile of a man who is happy as a puppy dog to see her. This smile replaces twenty minutes of exposition.

But see how the visit goes. Listen to the conversation between Frances and Betty, and listen later to how it is recycled in the book Betty writes, which glimpses the love of Bob and Frances from outside. The book is only guessing, but becomes all that remains of that love. Frances flees from Pennsylvania as she has fled, we suspect, from everything: She is not a bad woman, but she mistrusts happiness and is frightened of belonging to anyone.

After the grace of remission, she begins to fail, and the watch at the deathbed is by her son Morgan (Nick Stahl) and nurse Maggie (Amy Madigan). They deal with her and comfort her. They care for her. But this is a difficult woman to deal with. Meanwhile, on the East Coast, Rebecca continues her search for her birth parents. *The Sleepy Time Gal* is not, however, about a deathbed reunion; having given away this child, Frances finds she cannot get her back again at her own convenience.

Münch's screenplay is tenderly observant of his characters. Münch watches them as they float within the seas of their personalities. His scenes are short and often unexpected. The story unfolds in sidelong glances. His people are all stuck with who they are, and speak in thoughtful, well-considered words, as if afraid of being misquoted by destiny.

Life's missed opportunities, at the end, may seem more poignant to us than those we embraced—because in our imagination they have a perfection that reality can never rival. Bob and Frances might never have built a happy marriage ("We felt the pull of our own futures away from each other," she remembers), but their thirty years of unrealized romance has a kind of perfection. Bob's wife understands that, and remembers them both with love. She writes a book. Rebecca, who by now knows who she is and who Bob was, attends a book signing and meets her, but does not introduce herself. So one life slips past another, all of us focused on our plans for eventual perfection.

A Slipping-Down Life ★ ★ ★
R, 111 m., 2004

Lili Taylor (Evie Decker), Guy Pearce (Drumstrings Casey), John Hawkes (David Elliot), Sara Rue (Violet), Irma P. Hall (Clotelia), Tom Bower (Mr. Decker), Shawnee Smith (Faye-Jean), Veronica Cartwright (Mrs. Casey). Directed by Toni Kalem and produced by Richard Raddon. Screenplay by Kalem, based on the novel by Anne Tyler.

I first became aware of Lili Taylor in *Mystic Pizza* (1988), a star-making film that also introduced Julia Roberts. She plays the girl who walks away from the altar because her husband-to-be doesn't believe in sex before marriage and she doesn't think it's worth marrying him just to get him into bed. That kind of almost-logical circular reasoning is common in her characters; you can see it in other Taylor masterpieces, like *Dogfight* (1991), *Household Saints* (1993), *Girls Town* (1996), her great work in *I Shot Andy Warhol* the same year, and in *Casa de los Babys* (2003).

I don't suppose Taylor was born to play Evie Decker, the heroine of *A Slipping-Down Life*, but I can't imagine any other actress getting away with this role. She has a kind of solemnity she can bring to goofy characters, elevating them to holy (and usually lovable) fools. Here she plays a young woman from a small town who is lonely and isolated and lives with her father, who loves her but spends his evenings talking to ham radio operators in Moscow. She needs for something to happen to her.

Something does. She hears a rock singer on the radio one night. His off-balance ad lib philosophizing turns off the disc jockey, but sends her out to a local bar to see him in person. He becomes to her a demigod, a source of light and wisdom, but she is too inept to attract his attention. So she goes into the rest room and uses a piece of a broken bottle to carve his name into her forehead.

His name is Drumstrings Casey. She just carves the "Casey." "Why didn't you use my first name?" he asks her. "I didn't have room on my forehead," she says. "They call me Drum," he says. "I wish I'd known that," she says. There is another problem: She carved the name backward, because that way it looked right in the mirror. But at least when she looks at herself in the mirror it looks okay to her.

Drumstrings is played by Guy Pearce, of *Memento* and *L.A. Confidential*. He fits easily into the role of a third-rate, small-town rock god. When his agent finds out what Evie did, he talks Drumstrings into coming to the hospital to get his picture taken with her, and the publicity leads to an offer to have her appear at his concerts, to drum up business. This works well enough that he gets a gig in a nearby town, and doesn't invite her along, which breaks her heart. But somehow without that crazy girl in the audience, Drumstrings has an off night, and realizes he needs her.

The movie, written by the director Toni Kalem and based on a novel by Anne Tyler, performs a delicate maneuver as it slips along. The film opens with Evie totally powerless and miserable, and with Drumstrings holding all the cards. But her self-mutilation empowers her, and it provides a way for her to hold Drum's attention long enough for him to begin to like her. What she doesn't understand at first is that he's holding cards as bad as her own.

The film is like a tightrope walk across possible disasters. It could so easily go wrong. The plot itself is not enough to save it; indeed, this plot in the wrong hands could be impossible. But Kalem, an actress herself, understands how mood and nuance shape film stories; it's not what it's about, but how it's about it. Lili Taylor never overplays, never asks us to believe anything that isn't right there for us to see and hear. She changes by almost invisible steps into a woman who knows what she wants in a man and in marriage, and is able to communicate that to Drumstrings in a way he can, eventually, imperfectly, understand.

The supporting performances are like sturdy supports when the movie needs them. Tom Bower plays Evie's father as a man who has receded into his own loneliness. Irma P. Hall plays their maid, who is the de facto head of the household. John Hawkes is Drumstring's manager, who understands managing and publicity only remotely, but with great enthusiasm. Drum's mother (Veronica Cartwright) does not consider it a plus that this woman has carved her son's name into her forehead. Backward.

The movie is not a great dramatic statement, but you know that from the modesty of the title. It is about movement in emotional waters that had long been still. Taylor makes it work because she quietly suggests that when Evie's life has stalled, something drastic was needed to shock her back into action, and the carving worked as well as anything. Besides, when she combs her bangs down, you can hardly see it.

Solaris ★ ★ ★ ½
PG-13, 98 m., 2002

George Clooney (Chris Kelvin), Natascha McElhone (Rheya Kelvin), Jeremy Davies (Snow), Viola Davis (Helen Gordon), Ulrich Tukur (Gibarian). Directed by Steven Soderbergh and produced by James Cameron, Jon Landau, and Rae Sanchini. Screenplay by Soderbergh, based on the novel by Stanislaw Lem.

Solaris tells the story of a planet that reads minds and obliges its visitors by devising and providing people they have lost, and miss. The catch-22 is that the planet knows no more than its visitors know about these absent people. As the film opens, two astronauts have died in a space station circling the planet, and the two survivors have sent back alarming messages. A psychiatrist named Chris Kelvin (George Clooney) is sent to the station, and when he awakens after his first night on board, his wife, Rheya (Natascha McElhone), is in bed with him. Some time earlier, on Earth, she had committed suicide.

"She's not human," Kelvin is warned by Dr. Helen Gordon (Viola Davis), one of the surviving crew members. Kelvin knows this materialization cannot be his wife, yet is confronted with a person who seems palpably real, shares memories with him, and is flesh and blood. The other survivor, the goofy Snow (Jeremy Davies), asks, "I wonder if they can get pregnant?"

This story originated with a Polish novel by Stanislaw Lem, which is considered one of the major adornments of science fiction. It was made into a 1972 movie of the same name by the Russian master Andrei Tarkovsky. Now Steven Soderbergh has retold it in the kind of smart film that has people arguing about it on their way out of the theater.

The movie needs science fiction to supply the planet and the space station, which furnish the premise and concentrate the action, but it is essentially a psychological drama. When Kelvin arrives on the space station, he finds the survivors seriously spooked. Soderbergh directs Jeremy Davies to escalate his usual style of tics and stutters to the point where a word can hardly be uttered without his hands waving to evoke it from midair.

Even scarier is Gordon, the scientist played by Viola Davis, who has seen whatever catastrophe overtook the station and does not consider Kelvin part of the solution. In his gullibility, will he believe his wife has somehow really been resurrected? And . . . what does the planet *want*? Why does it do this? As a favor, or as a way of luring us into accepting manifestations of its own ego and need? Will the human race eventually be replaced by the Solaris version?

Clooney has successfully survived being named *People* magazine's sexiest man alive by deliberately choosing projects that ignore that image. His alliance with Soderbergh, both as an actor and coproducer, shows a taste for challenge. Here he is intelligent, withdrawn, sad, puzzled. Certain this seems to be his wife, and although he knows intellectually that she is not, still—to destroy her would be . . . inhuman. The screenplay develops a painful paradox out of that reality.

The genius of Lem's underlying idea is that the duplicates, or replicants, or whatever we choose to call them, are self-conscious and seem to carry on with free will from the moment they are evoked by the planet. Rheya, for example, says, "I'm not the person I remember. I don't remember experiencing these things." And later, "I'm suicidal because that's how you remember me."

In other words, Kelvin gets back not his dead wife, but a being who incorporates all he knows about his dead wife, and nothing else, and starts over from there. She has no secrets because he did not know her secrets. If she is suicidal, it is because he thought she was. The deep irony here is that all of our relationships in the real world are exactly like that, even without the benefit of Solaris. We do not know the actual other person. What we know is the sum of everything we think we know about them. Even empathy is perhaps of no use; we think it helps us understand how other people feel, but maybe it only tells us how we would feel, if we were them.

At a time when many American movies pump up every fugitive emotion into a clanging assault on the audience, Soderbergh's *Solaris* is quiet and introspective. There are some shocks and surprises, but this is not *Alien*. It is a workshop for a discussion of human identity. It considers not only how we relate to others, but how we relate to our ideas of others—so that a completely phony, nonhuman replica of a dead wife can inspire the same feelings that the wife herself once did. That is a peculiarity of humans: We feel the same emotions for our ideas as we do for the real world, which is why we can cry while reading a book, or fall in love with movie stars. Our idea of humanity bewitches us, while humanity itself stays safely sealed away into its billions of separate containers, or "people."

When I saw Tarkovsky's original film, I felt absorbed in it, as if it were a sponge. It was slow, mysterious, confusing, and I have never forgotten it. Soderbergh's version is more clean and spare, more easily readable, but it pays full attention to the ideas and doesn't compromise. Tarkovsky was a genius, but one who demanded great patience from his audience as he ponderously marched toward his goals. The Soderbergh version is like the same story freed from the weight of Tarkovsky's solemnity. And it evokes one of the rarest of movie emotions, ironic regret.

Something's Gotta Give ★ ★ ★ ½
PG-13, 124 m., 2003

Jack Nicholson (Harry Sanborn), Diane Keaton (Erica Barry), Amanda Peet (Marin Barry), Keanu Reeves (Julian Mercer), Frances McDormand (Zoe), Jon Favreau (Leo). Directed by Nancy Meyers and produced by Bruce A. Block and Meyers. Screenplay by Meyers.

"Some say I'm an expert on the younger woman—since I've been dating them for forty years."

Who's talking here? Jack Nicholson, or the character he plays in *Something's Gotta Give*? Maybe it doesn't make any difference. After playing an older man entirely unlike himself in *About Schmidt*, Nicholson here quite frankly and cheerfully plays a version of the public Jack, the guy who always seems to be grinning like he got away with something. This has inspired scoldings from the filmcrit police ("This is Jack playing 'Jack,' " says *Variety*), but who would you rather have playing him? Nicholson's quasi-autobiographical role is one of the pleasures of the film.

Nicholson's character, named Harry Sanborn, is a rich music executive who is currently dating the nubile young Marin Barry (Amanda Peet). She takes him for a weekend to her mother's home in the Hamptons—where, horrors, he is found raiding the refrigerator in the middle of the night by her mother, Erica (Diane Keaton), and Aunt Zoe (Frances McDormand). Erica is a famous playwright, too worldly to object to her grown daughter's taste in men, and the four spend the weekend together. We learn that Harry and Marin have not yet actually had sex, and alas, as they circle for a landing Harry is seized with chest pains and rushed to the hospital.

Only in the Hamptons would the doctor be handsome Julian Mercer (Keanu Reeves), who is instantly smitten by the sexy older woman.

He prescribes bed rest for Harry, who takes refuge in Erica's guest room as the others return to the city. And that's the setup for a witty sitcom, written and directed by Nancy Meyers, who in movies like *Baby Boom* and *What Women Want* has dealt skillfully with the sexual adventures of characters whose ages fall between those who remember where they were when John Kennedy was shot, and when John Lennon was shot. It is more or less foreordained that Harry and Erica will fall in love, despite his taste for younger women. The twist is that Dr. Mercer also falls in love with Erica, supplying her with two possible lovers at a time in her life when she thought she'd gone into sexual retirement.

How, why, and whether Harry and Julian do or don't become Erica's lovers is entirely a matter of sitcom accounting, and need not concern us. What's intriguing about the movie is what they say in between. Meyers gives them more and smarter dialogue than we expect in a romantic comedy, because if Erica and Harry are ever to have sex, they're going to have to talk themselves into it. She has strong opinions about this man whose lifestyle is so notorious he made the cover of *New York* magazine as "The Escape Artist." And Harry, shocked by his sudden brush with mortality, finds that for the first time in his life he needs someone he can actually talk with in the middle of the night.

The movie is true enough to its characters that at one point, when Harry and Erica both find themselves crying at the same time, we find ourselves surprisingly moved by this recognition of their humanity. And when Harry goes back to his old ways, as we know he must, we're moved again, this time by how lonely he feels, and how sad it is when he plays his old tapes. Harry and Erica are convincing characters, at least in the world of romantic comedy.

It's Dr. Mercer who seems like nothing more than a walking plot complication. We don't believe or understand his relationship with Erica, and it must be said that a young man who would propose to a woman twenty-five years his senior, fly to Paris with her, plan marriage, and yet immediately surrender her to his rival without a struggle (out of good manners and breeding, it would seem) has desires that are all

too easily contained. There is sexual mystery surrounding the whole situation. Harry doesn't know (for sure) whether Erica and young Dr. Mercer have had sex, which perhaps makes the situation easier for him; in the Hamptons, a virgin is anyone who hasn't slept with anyone you know since you met them.

A movie like this depends crucially on its stars. To complain that Nicholson is playing "himself"—or that Keaton is also playing a character very much like her public persona— is missing the point. Part of the appeal depends on the movie's teasing confusion of reality and fiction. Harry defends himself by telling Erica, "I have never lied to you. I have always told you some version of the truth," and we smile at the backward morality in that statement; we wonder if Nicholson himself contributed that line to the screenplay. We are meant to wonder.

The film's nudity observes the usual double standard; we get three opportunities for a leisurely study of Nicholson's butt, but the nude shot of Diane Keaton is so brief it falls only a frame this side of subliminal. Their faces are more interesting, anyway. "At fifty," Orwell tells us, "every man has the face he deserves." I don't know what Harry and Erica did to deserve theirs, but they didn't skip any payments. They bring so much experience, knowledge, and humor to their characters that the film works in ways the screenplay might not have even hoped for.

Note: The paintings in the Hamptons house are by Jack Vettriano, and the drawings are by Paul Cox. I have not reason for telling you that, but I couldn't stop myself. ☞

The Son ★ ★ ★ ★
NO MPAA RATING, 103 m., 2003

Olivier Gourmet (Olivier), Morgan Marinne (Francis), Isabella Soupart (Magali), Remy Renaud (Philippo), Nassim Hassaini (Omar), Kevin Leroy (Raoul), Felicien Pitsaer (Steve). Directed by Jean-Pierre Dardenne and Luc Dardenne and produced by the Dardennes and Denis Freyd. Screenplay by the Dardennes.

The Son is complete, self-contained, and final. All the critic can bring to it is his admiration.

It needs no insight or explanation. It sees everything and explains all. It is as assured and flawless a telling of sadness and joy as I have ever seen.

I agree with Stanley Kauffmann, in the *New Republic,* that a second viewing only underlines the film's greatness, but I would not want to have missed my first viewing, so I will write carefully. The directors, Jean-Pierre Dardenne and Luc Dardenne, do not make the slightest effort to mislead or deceive us. Nor do they make any effort to explain. They simply (not so simply) show, and we lean forward, hushed, reading the faces, watching the actions, intent on sharing the feelings of the characters.

Let me describe a very early sequence in enough detail for you to appreciate how the Dardenne brothers work. Olivier (Olivier Gourmet), a Belgian carpenter, supervises a shop where teenage boys work. He corrects a boy using a power saw. We wonder, because we have been beaten down by formula films, if someone is going to lose a finger or a hand. No. The plank is going to be cut correctly.

A woman comes into the shop and asks Olivier if he can take another apprentice. No, he has too many already. He suggests the welding shop. The moment the woman and the young applicant leave, Olivier slips from the shop and, astonishingly, scurries after them like a feral animal and spies on them through a door opening and the angle of a corridor. A little later, strong and agile, he leaps up onto a metal cabinet to steal a look through a high window.

Then he tells the woman he will take the boy after all. She says the boy is in the shower room. The handheld camera, which follows Olivier everywhere, usually in close medium shot, follows him as he looks around a corner (we intuit it is a corner; two walls form an apparent join). Is he watching the boy take a shower? Is Olivier gay? No. We have seen too many movies. He is simply looking at the boy asleep, fully clothed, on the floor of the shower room. After a long, absorbed look he wakes up the boy and tells him he has a job.

Now you must absolutely stop reading and go see the film. Walk out of the house today, tonight, and see it, if you are open to simplicity, depth, maturity, silence, in a film that sounds in the echo chambers of the heart. *The Son* is a great film. If you find you cannot respond to it, that is the degree to which you have room to grow. I am not being arrogant; I grew during this film. It taught me things about the cinema I did not know.

What did I learn? How this movie is only possible because of the way it was made, and would have been impossible with traditional narrative styles. Like rigorous documentarians, the Dardenne brothers follow Olivier, learning everything they know about him by watching him. They do not point, underline, or send signals by music. There are no reaction shots because the entire movie is their reaction shot. The brothers make the consciousness of the Olivier character into the auteur of the film.

. . . So now you have seen the film. If you were spellbound, moved by its terror and love, struck that the visual style is the only possible one for this story, then let us agree that rarely has a film told us less and told us all, both at the once.

Olivier trains wards of the Belgian state—gives them a craft after they are released from a juvenile home. Francis (Morgan Marinne) was in such a home from his eleventh to sixteenth years. Olivier asks him what his crime was. He stole a car radio.

"And got five years?"

"There was a death."

"What kind of a death?"

There was a child in the car, whom Francis did not see. The child began to cry and would not let go of Francis, who was frightened and "grabbed him by the throat."

"Strangled him," Olivier corrects.

"I didn't mean to," Francis says.

"Do you regret what you did?"

"Obviously."

"Why obviously?"

"Five years locked up. That's worth regretting."

You have seen the film and know what Olivier knows about this death. You have seen it and know the man and boy are at a remote lumberyard on a Sunday. You have seen it and know how *hard* the noises are in the movie, the heavy planks banging down one upon another. How it hurts even to hear them. The film does not use these sounds or the towers of lumber to create suspense or anything else. It simply respects the nature of lumber, as Olivier does and is teaching Francis to do. You expect, because you have been trained by formula films, an accident or an act of violence. What you could not expect is the breathtaking spiritual beauty of the ending of the film, which is nevertheless no less banal than everything that has gone before.

Olivier Gourmet won the award for best actor at Cannes 2002. He plays an ordinary man behaving at all times in an ordinary way. Here is the key: *Ordinary for him.* The word for his behavior—not his performance, his behavior—is "exemplary." We use the word to mean "praiseworthy." Its first meaning is "fit for imitation."

Everything that Olivier does is exemplary. Walk like this. Hold yourself just so. Measure exactly. Do not use the steel hammer when the wooden mallet is required. Center the nail. Smooth first with the file, then with the sandpaper. Balance the plank and lean into the ladder. Pay for your own apple turnover. Hold a woman who needs to be calmed. Praise a woman who has found she is pregnant. Find out the truth before you tell the truth. Do not use words to discuss what cannot be explained. Be willing to say, "I don't know." Be willing to have a son and teach him a trade. Be willing to be a father.

A recent movie got a laugh by saying there is a rule in *The Godfather* to cover every situation. There can never be that many rules. *The Son* is about a man who needs no rules because he respects his trade and knows his tools. His trade is life. His tools are his loss and his hope.

A Song for Martin ★ ★ ★ ½
PG-13, 118 m., 2002

Sven Wollter (Martin), Viveka Seldahl (Barbara), Reine Brynolfsson (Biederman), Lisa Werlinder (Elisabeth), Linda Källgren (Karin), Peter Engman (Philip), Klas Dahlstedt (Erik), Kristina Törnqvist (Dr. Gierlich). Directed by Bille August and produced by August, Lars Kolvig, Michael Lundberg, and Michael Obel. Screenplay by August, based on the novel by Ulla Isaksson.

A Song for Martin tells the story of two people who find sudden, delirious love, and then lose it in one of the most painful ways possible, because of Alzheimer's disease. Their love and loss is all the more poignant because they are such warm, creative people—and perhaps because we sense an ease and acceptance between the two actors, Sven Wollter and Viveka Seldahl, who were married in real life. That she died not long after the movie was made adds another dimension of poignance.

The film, directed by Bille August *(Pelle the Conqueror)*, takes place in cultural circles in Gothenburg, Sweden. Martin, played by Wollter, is a famous conductor and composer, and Barbara (Seldahl) is his first violinist. One day she points out an error to him, he is grateful, they walk back to a hotel together, there is eye contact, and before long they are involved in a romance that must have been smoldering for years. Martin's manager Biederman (Reine Brynolfsson) is quick to spot the situation, and dubious ("Do you think it's wise to fiddle with the fiddler?"), but soon Martin and Barbara have divorced their current spouses and are married and on a passionate honeymoon in Morocco.

The movie probably makes a mistake in giving them both earlier marriages, since leaving those partners raises questions the movie never really deals with. Better to have them meet with their hands free, especially since the movie is not about former marriages but about a good one that turns sad.

The signs of Alzheimer's are at first isolated. Martin forgets Biederman's name. He is sometimes confused. Progress on composing an opera becomes uncertain. "It's as if something fell inside my head," he tells Barbara. The disease progresses, probably more quickly than it would in real life, and there are fairly melodramatic episodes, as when he forgets his purpose on the podium or uses a potted tree for a urinal in a restaurant.

The movie is not about Alzheimer's so much as about loss. Barbara takes them back to the same Moroccan hotel where they had their honeymoon, hoping to reawaken his memories, but it's a disaster, and leads to a scene where he tries to drown them both, in a combination of fear, confusion, and anger. Sometimes she gets angry at him. "All I ask," she tells him, "is a little of the charm you turn on for everyone else." But the man who was Martin is disappearing before her very eyes.

For me the center of the film is the performance by Viveka Seldahl. She is a pretty woman with a warm smile, and she embodies the feelings of Barbara so completely that the pain of her loss becomes palpable. The movie is more honest about Alzheimer's, I think, than *Iris,* the film about the novelist Iris Murdoch, who also had the disease. *A Song for Martin* starts at the beginning and goes straight through to the inevitable end, unblinkingly. It doesn't relieve the pressure, as *Iris* does, with flashbacks to happier days. What it knows is that the happier days are behind, and the person who lived them is disappearing. That the body of that person remains present and alive is a particular grief for the survivors.

Songs from the Second Floor ★ ★ ★

NO MPAA RATING, 98 m., 2000

Lars Nordh (Kalle), Stefan Larsson (Stefan), Torbjörn Fahlstrom (Pelle), Sten Andersson (Lasse), Lucio Vucina (Magician), Hanna Eriksson (Mia), Peter Roth (Tomas), Tommy Johansson (Uffe). Directed by Roy Andersson and produced by Lisa Alwert and Andersson. Screenplay by Andersson.

In a sour gray city, filled with pale drunken salarymen and parading flagellants, everything goes wrong, pain is laughed at, businesses fail, traffic seizes up, and a girl is made into a human sacrifice to save a corporation. Roy Andersson's *Songs from the Second Floor* is a collision at the intersection of farce and tragedy—the apocalypse, as a joke on us.

You have never seen a film like this before. You may not enjoy it, but you will not forget it. Andersson is a deadpan Swedish surrealist who has spent the last twenty-five years making "the best TV commercials in the world" (Ingmar Bergman), and now bites off the hand that fed him, chews it thoughtfully, spits it out, and tramples on it. His movie regards modern capitalist society with the detached hilarity of a fanatic saint squatting on his pillar in the desert.

I saw it at the 2000 Cannes Film Festival. Understandably, it did not immediately find a distributor. Predictably, audiences did not flock to it. When I screened it at my 2001 Overlooked Film Festival, there were times when the audience laughed out loud, times when it squinted in dismay, times when it watched in disbelief.

When two of the actors came out onstage afterward, it was somehow completely appropriate that one of them never said a word.

I love this film because it is completely new, starting from a place no other film has started from, proceeding implacably to demonstrate the logic of its despair, arriving at a place of no hope. One rummages for the names of artists to evoke: Bosch, Tati, Kafka, Beckett, Dali. It is "slapstick Ingmar Bergman," says J. Hoberman in the *Village Voice.* Yes, and tragic Groucho Marx.

The film opens ironically with a man in a tanning machine—ironic, because all of the other characters will look like they've spent years in sunless caves. It proceeds with a series of set pieces in which the camera, rarely moving, gazes impassively at scenes of absurdity and despair. A man is fired and clings to the leg of his boss, who marches down a corridor dragging him behind. A magician saws a volunteer in two. Yes. A man with the wrong accent is attacked by a gang. A man burns down his own store and then assures insurance inspectors it was arson, but as they talk we lose interest, because outside on the street a parade of flagellants marches past, whipping themselves in time to their march.

There is the most slender of threads connecting the scenes—the arsonist is a continuing character—but Andersson is not telling a conventional story. He is planting his camera here and there in a city that has simply stopped working, has broken down and is cannibalizing itself. It is a twentieth-century city, but Andersson sees it as an appropriate backdrop for the plague or any other medieval visitation. And its citizens have fallen back on ancient fearful superstition to protect themselves.

Consider the scene where clerics and businessmen, all robed for their offices, gather in a desolate landscape as a young woman walks the plank to her death below. Perhaps the sacrifice of her life will placate the gods who are angry with the corporation. We watch this scene and we are forced to admit that corporations are capable of such behavior: that a tobacco company, for example, expects its customers to walk the plank every day.

Is there no hope in this devastation? A man who corners the market in crucifixes now bitterly tosses out his excess inventory. "I staked everything on a loser," he complains. Does that make the movie anti-Christian? No. It is not anti-anything. It is about the loss of hope, about the breakdown of all systems of hope. Its characters are piggish, ignorant, clueless salarymen who, without salaries, have no way to be men. The movie argues that in an economic collapse our modern civilization would fall from us, and we would be left wandering our cities like the plague victims of old, seeking relief in drunkenness, superstition, sacrifice, sex, and self-mockery.

Oh, but yes, the film is often very funny about this bleak view. I have probably not convinced you of that. It's funny because it stands back and films its scenes in long shot, the camera not moving, so that we can distance ourselves from the action—and we remember the old rule from the silent days: Comedy in long shot, tragedy in close-up. Close shots cause us to identify with the characters, to weep and fear along with them. Long shots allow us to view them objectively, within their environment. *Songs from the Second Floor* is a parade of fools marching blindly to their ruin, and for the moment, we are still spectators and have not been required to join the march. The laughter inspired by the movie is sometimes at the absurd, sometimes simply from relief.

The Son's Room ★ ★ ★ ½
R, 99 m., 2002

Nanni Moretti (Giovanni), Laura Morante (Paola), Jasmine Trinca (Irene), Giuseppe Sanfelice (Andrea), Sofia Vigliar (Arianna), Silvio Orlando (Oscar), Claudia Della Seta (Raffaella), Stefano Accorsi (Tommaso). Directed by Nanni Moretti and produced by Angelo Barbagallo and Moretti. Screenplay by Moretti, Linda Ferri, and Heidrun Schleef.

The Son's Room follows an affluent Italian family through all the stages of grieving. When the teenage son dies in a diving accident, his parents and sister react with instinctive denial, followed by sorrow, anger, the disintegration of their own lives, the picking up of the pieces, and finally a form of acceptance. Because all of these stages are reflected in the clearly seen details of everyday life, the effect is very touching.

The film has been written and directed by Nanni Moretti, whose 1994 film *Caro Diario (Dear Diary)* was about his own death sentence: Based on fact, it related his feelings when he was diagnosed with cancer and told (mistakenly) that he had a year to live. That film was not quite successful, an uneasy truce between Woody Allen and Elisabeth Kübler-Ross, but *The Son's Room* has a relaxed tenderness and empathy. He got the idea for the story, he has said, when he learned that he and his wife were expecting a son.

Moretti stars as Giovanni, a psychiatrist whose patients rehearse the same problems hour after hour in his office. Can he help them? That's a question he eventually has to ask himself. At home, there is a problem when his son Andrea (Giuseppe Sanfelice) is accused of having stolen a fossil from the school science lab. He denies the charge. Giovanni and his wife, Paola (Laura Morante), get involved, visit the parents of his son's accuser. We see that this is a happy family; the sister Irene (Jasmine Trinca) is on a basketball team, the son studies Latin, and when the parents overhear a conversation indicating that Andrea smokes pot, they are not too concerned. There is a lovely scene where all four sing together during a car trip.

Then the accident takes place, and has the effect of sending mother, father, and daughter spinning into their own private corners. For the father, this means impatience with his clients, and resentment against one whose call on a Sunday derailed Giovanni's plans to go jogging with his son—thus freeing the boy to go diving, and indirectly leading to his death. Grieving mixes with pain as Giovanni imagines the way the day *should* have unfolded, with the two of them on a run, and the son still alive at the end.

We know from the fable of the appointment in Samarra that it is no use trying to outsmart fate, but it is human nature to try—and to torture ourselves when we fail. For Irene, the sister, grief and anger cause her to fight during a basketball game. For Giovanni, they lead to questions about his practice. And then . . . a letter arrives, from Arianna (Sofia Vigliar). It is addressed to the dead Andrea, whom she met for only one day. But somehow there was a connection between them, and she hopes to see him again.

The Son's Room uses this letter, and Arianna's eventual appearance, as its means of resolving the story. To explain how this is done would be unsatisfactory, because Moretti is more concerned with tones and nuances than plot points, and the gradual way Arianna becomes the instrument of acceptance is quietly touching. She represents life that must go on—just as Auden in his poem observes that although Icarus falls into the sea, farmers still plow their fields and dogs go on their doggy errands. Curious, how a late shot of people at dawn says so much by saying nothing at all.

The Son's Room won the Palme d'Or, or top prize, at Cannes. It was a popular choice—too popular, sniffed some, who objected to its mainstream style and frank sentimentality. Yes, but not all movies can be stark, difficult, and obscure. Sometimes in a quite ordinary way a director can reach out and touch us.

Sorority Boys ½★

R, 96 m., 2002

Barry Watson (Dave/Daisy), Harland Williams (Doofer/Roberta), Michael Rosenbaum (Adam/Adina), Melissa Sagemiller (Leah), Heather Matarazzo (Katie). Directed by Wallace Wolodarsky and produced by Larry Brezner and Walter Hamada. Screenplay by Joe Jarvis and Greg Coolidge.

One element of *Sorority Boys* is undeniably good, and that is the title. Pause by the poster on the way into the theater. That will be your high point. It has all you need for a brainless, autopilot, sitcom ripoff: a high concept that is right there in the title, easily grasped at the pitch meeting. The title suggests the poster art, the poster art gives you the movie, and story details can be sketched in by study of *Bosom Buddies, National Lampoon's Animal House,* and the shower scenes in any movie involving girls' dorms or sports teams.

What is unusual about *Sorority Boys* is how it caves in to the homophobia of the audience by not even *trying* to make its cross-dressing heroes look like halfway, even tenth-of-the-way, plausible girls. They look like college boys wearing cheap wigs and dresses they bought at Goodwill. They usually need a shave. One keeps his retro forward-thrusting sideburns and just combs a couple of locks of his wig

forward to "cover" them. They look as feminine as the sailors wearing coconut brassieres in *South Pacific.*

Their absolute inability to pass as women leads to another curiosity about the movie, which is that all of the other characters are obviously mentally impaired. How else to explain fraternity brothers who don't recognize their own friends in drag? Sorority sisters who think these are real women and want to pledge them on first sight? A father who doesn't realize that's his *own son* he's trying to pick up?

I know. I'm being too literal. I should be a good sport and go along with the joke. But the joke is not funny. The movie is not funny. If it's this easy to get a screenplay filmed in Hollywood, why did they bother with that Project Greenlight contest? Why not ship all the entries directly to Larry Brezner and Walter Hamada, the producers of *Sorority Boys,* who must wear Santa suits to work?

The plot begins with three members of Kappa Omicron Kappa fraternity, who are thrown out of the KOK house for allegedly stealing party funds. Homeless and forlorn, they decide to pledge the Delta Omicron Gamma house after learning that the DOGs need new members. Dave (Barry Watson) becomes Daisy and is soon feeling chemistry with the DOG president, Leah (Melisa Sagemiller), who is supposed to be an intellectual feminist but can shower nude with him and not catch on he's a man.

Harland Williams and Michael Rosenbaum play the other two fugitive KOKs—roles that, should they become stars, will be invaluable as a source of clips at roasts in their honor. Among the DOGs is the invaluable Heather Matarazzo, who now has a lock on the geeky plain girl roles, even though she is in actual fact sweet and pretty. Just as Latina actresses have risen up in arms against Jennifer Connelly for taking the role of John Forbes Nash's El Salvadoran wife in *A Beautiful Mind,* so ugly girls should picket Heather Matarazzo.

Because the intelligence level of the characters must be low, very low, very very low, for the masquerade to work, the movie contains no wit, only labored gags involving falsies, lipstick, unruly erections, and straight guys who don't realize they're trying to pick up a man. (I imagine yokels in the audience responding with the Gradually Gathering Guffaw as they catch on. "Hey, Jethro! He don't know she's a guy! Haw! Haw! Haw!") The entire movie, times ten, lacks the humor of a single line in the Bob Gibson/Shel Silverstein song "Mendocino Desperados" ("She was a he, but what the hell, honey / Since you've already got my money . . .").

I'm curious about who would go to see this movie. Obviously moviegoers with a low opinion of their own taste. It's so obviously what it is that you would require a positive desire to throw away money in order to lose two hours of your life. *Sorority Boys* will be the worst movie playing in any multiplex in America this weekend, and, yes, I realize *Crossroads* is still out there.

Spartan ★ ★ ★ ★
R, 106 m., 2004

Val Kilmer (Robert Scott), Derek Luke (Curtis), William H. Macy (Stoddard), Ed O'Neill (Burch), Tia Texada (Jackie Black), Kristen Bell (Laura Newton). Directed by David Mamet and produced by Art Linson, David Bergstein, Elie Samaha, and Moshe Diamant. Screenplay by Mamet.

Spartan opens without any credits except its title, but I quickly knew it was written by David Mamet because nobody else hears and writes dialogue the way he does. That the film tells a labyrinthine story of betrayal and deception, a con within a con, also stakes out Mamet territory. But the scope of the picture is larger than Mamet's usual canvas: This is a thriller on a global scale, involving the Secret Service, the FBI, the CIA, the White House, a secret Special Ops unit, and Middle Eastern kidnappers. Such a scale could lend itself to one of those big, clunky action machines based on 700-page best-sellers that put salesmen to sleep on airplanes. But no. Not with Mamet, who treats his action plot as a framework for a sly, deceptive exercise in the gradual approximation of the truth.

Before I get to the plot, let me linger on the dialogue. Most thrillers have simpleminded characters who communicate to each other in primary plot points ("Cover me." "It goes off in ten minutes." "Who are you working for?") *Spartan* begins by assuming that all of its char-

acters know who they are and what they're doing, and do not need to explain this to us in thriller-talk. They communicate in elliptical shorthand, in shoptalk, in tradecraft, in oblique references, in shared memories; we can't always believe what they say, and we don't always know that. We get involved in their characters and we even sense their rivalries while the outline of the plot is still murky. How murky we don't even dream.

Val Kilmer, in his best performance since *Tombstone,* plays a Special Ops officer named Scott, who as the movie opens is doing a field exercise with two trainees: Curtis (Derek Luke) and Jackie Black (Tia Texada). He's called off that assignment after the daughter of the president is kidnapped. The Secret Service was supposed to be guarding her, but . . . what went wrong is one of the movie's secrets. Ed O'Neill plays an agent in charge of the search for the daughter, William H. Macy is a political operative from the White House, and it turns out that the daughter, Laura Newton (Kristen Bell), was taken for reasons that are not obvious, by kidnappers you would not guess, who may or may not know she is the president's daughter. Kilmer's assignment: go anywhere and get her back by any means necessary. Curtis and Jackie want to get involved, too, but Kilmer doesn't want them, which may not be the final word on the subject.

And that is quite enough of the plot. It leaves me enjoying the way Mamet, from his earliest plays to his great films like *House of Games, Wag the Dog, Homicide,* and *The Spanish Prisoner,* works like a magician who uses words instead of cards. The patter is always fascinating, and at right angles to the action. He's like a magician who gets you all involved in his story about the king, the queen, and the jack, while the whole point is that there's a rabbit in your pocket. Some screenwriters study Robert McKee. Mamet studies magic and confidence games. In his plots, the left hand makes a distracting movement, but you're too smart for that, and you quick look over at the right hand to spot the trick, while meantime the left hand does the business while still seeming to flap around like a decoy.

The particular pleasure of *Spartan* is to watch the characters gradually define themselves and the plot gradually emerge like your face in a steamy mirror. You see the outlines, and then your nose, and then you see that somebody is standing behind you, and then you see it's you, so who is the guy in the mirror? Work with me here. I'm trying to describe how the movie operates without revealing what it does.

William H. Macy, who has been with Mamet since his earliest theater days, is an ideal choice for this kind of work. He always seems like the ordinary guy who is hanging on for retirement. He's got that open, willing face, and the flat, helpful voice with sometimes the little complaint in it, and in *Spartan* he starts out with what looks like a walk-on role (we're thinking David found a part for his old pal) and ends up walking away with it. Val Kilmer, a versatile actor who can be good at almost anything (who else has played Batman and John Holmes?), here plays lean and hard, Sam Jackson style. His character is enormously resourceful with his craft, but becomes extremely puzzled about what he can do safely, and who he can trust. Derek Luke, a rising star with a quiet earnestness that is just right here, disappears for a long stretch and then finds out something remarkable, and Tia Texada, in the Rosario Dawson role, succeeds against all odds in actually playing a woman soldier instead of a sexy actress playing a woman soldier.

I like the safe rooms with the charts on the walls, and I like the casual way that spycraft is explained by being used, and the way Mamet keeps pulling the curtain aside to reveal a new stage with a new story. I suppose the last scene in the film will remind some of our friend the *deus ex machina*, but after reflection I have decided that, in that place, at that time, what happens is about as likely to happen as anything else, maybe likelier.

Spellbound ★ ★ ★

G, 95 m., 2003

The Spellers: Harry Altman, Angela Arenivar, Ted Brigham, April DeGideo, Neil Kadakia, Nupur Lala, Emily Stagg, Ashley White. A documentary directed by Jeffrey Blitz and produced by Blitz and Sean Welch.

It is useful to be a good speller, up to a point. After that point, you're just showing off. The eight contestants in *Spellbound*, who have come from all over the country to compete in the 1999 National Spelling Bee, are never likely to need words such as "opsimath" in their daily rounds, although "logorrhea" might come in handy. As we watch them drilling with flash cards and work sheets, we hope they will win, but we're not sure what good it will do them.

And yet for some of them, winning the bee will make a substantial difference in their lives—not because they can spell so well, but because the prizes include college scholarships. Take Angela Arenivar, for example. She makes it all the way to the finals in Washington, D.C., from the Texas farm where her father works as a laborer. He originally entered the country illegally, still speaks no English, and is proud beyond all words of his smart daughter.

We cheer for her in the finals, but then we cheer for all of these kids, because it is so easy to remember the pain of getting something wrong in front of the whole class. None of these teenagers is good only at spelling. Jeffrey Blitz takes his documentary into their homes and schools, looks at their families and ambitions, and shows us that they're all smart in a lot of other ways—including the way that makes them a little lonely at times.

Consider Harry Altman. He is a real kid, but has so many eccentricities that he'd be comic relief in a teenage comedy. His laugh would make you turn around in a crowded room. He screws his face up into so many shapes while trying to spell a word that it's a wonder the letters can find their way to the surface. High school cannot be easy for Harry, but he will have his revenge at the twentieth class reunion, by which time he will no doubt be a millionaire or a Nobel winner, and still with that unlikely laugh.

To be smart is to be an outsider in high school. To be seen as smart is even worse (many kids learn to conceal their intelligence). There is a kind of rough populism among adolescents that penalizes those who try harder or are more gifted. In talking with high school kids, I find that many of them go to good or serious movies by themselves, and choose vulgarity and violence when going with their friends. To be a kid and read good books and attend good movies sets you aside. Thank God you have the books and the movies for company—and now the Internet, where bright teenagers find each other.

In *Spellbound*, which was one of this year's

Oscar nominees, Blitz begins with portraits of his eight finalists and then follows them to Washington, where they compete on ESPN in the bee, which was founded years ago by Scripps-Howard newspapers. The ritual is time-honored. The word is pronounced and repeated. It may be used in a sentence. Then the contestant has to repeat it, spell it, and say it again.

We've never heard most of the words (cabotinage?). General spelling rules are useful only up to a point, and then memory is the only resource. Some of these kids study up to eight hours a day, memorizing words they may never hear, write, or use. Even when they think they know a word, it's useful to pause and be sure, because once you get to the end of a word you can't go back and start again. You don't win because of your overall score, but because you have been perfect longer than anyone else; the entire bee is a sudden-death overtime.

Oddly enough, it's not tragic when a kid loses. Some of them shrug or grin, and a couple seem happy to be delivered from the pressure and the burden. One girl is devastated when she misspells a word, but we know it's because she knew it, and knew she knew it, and still got it wrong. They're all winners, in a way, and had to place first in their state or regional contests to get to Washington. When the finalist Nupur Lala, whose parents came from India, returns home to Florida, she's a local hero, and a restaurant hails her on the sign out in front: "Congradulations, Nupur!"

Spider ★ ★ ★
R, 98 m., 2003

Ralph Fiennes (Dennis "Spider" Cleg), Miranda Richardson (Yvonne/Mrs. Cleg), Gabriel Byrne (Bill Cleg), Lynn Redgrave (Mrs. Wilkinson), John Neville (Terrence), Bradley Hall (Young Spider), Gary Reineke (Freddy), Philip Craig (John). Directed by David Cronenberg and produced by Catherine Bailey, Cronenberg, and Samuel Hadida. Screenplay by Patrick McGrath, based on his novel.

He looked like a man cut away from the stake, when the fire has overrunningly wasted all the limbs without consuming them. . . .

So Ahab is described in *Moby-Dick*. The de-

scription matches Dennis Cleg, the subject (I hesitate to say "hero") of David Cronenberg's *Spider*. Played by Ralph Fiennes, he is a man eaten away by a lifetime of inner torment; there is not one ounce on his frame that is not needed to support his suffering. Fiennes, so jolly as J. Lo's boyfriend in *Maid in Manhattan*, looks here like a refugee from the slums of hell.

We see him as the last man off a train to London, muttering to himself, picking up stray bits from the sidewalk, staring out through blank, uncomprehending eyes. He finds a boardinghouse in a cheerless district, and is shown to a barren room by the gruff landlady (Lynn Redgrave). In the lounge he meets an old man who explains kindly that the house has a "curious character, but one grows used to it after a few years."

This is a halfway house, we learn, and Spider has just been released from a mental institution. In the morning the landlady bursts into his room without knocking—just like a mother, we think, and indeed later he will confuse her with his stepmother. For that matter, his mother, his stepmother, and an alternate version of the landlady are all played by the same actress (Miranda Richardson); we are meant to understand that her looming presence fills every part of his mind that is reserved for women.

The movie is based on an early novel by Patrick McGrath. It enters into the subjective mind of Spider Cleg so completely that it's impossible to be sure what is real and what is not. We see everything through Spider's eyes, and he is not a reliable witness. He hardly seems aware of the present, so traumatized is he by the past. Whether they are trustworthy or not, his childhood memories are the landscape in which he wanders.

In flashbacks, we meet his father, Bill Cleg (Gabriel Byrne) and mother (Richardson). Then we see his father making a rendezvous in a garden shed with Yvonne (also Richardson), a tramp from the pub. The mother discovers them there, is murdered with a spade, and buried right then and there in the garden, with the little boy witnessing everything. Yvonne moves in, and at one point tells young Dennis, "Yes, it's true he murdered your mother. Try and think of me as your mother now."

Why are the two characters played by the

same actress? Is this an artistic decision, or a clue to Spider's mental state? We cannot tell for sure, because there is almost nothing in his life that Spider knows for sure. He is adrift in fear. Fiennes plays the character as a man who wants to take back every step, reconsider every word, question every decision. There is a younger version of the character, Spider as a boy, played by Bradley Hall. He is solemn and wide-eyed, is beaten with a belt at one point, has a childhood that functions as an open wound. We understand that this boy is the most important inhabitant of the older Spider's gaunt and wasted body.

The movie is well-made and -acted, but it lacks dimension because it essentially has only one character, and he lacks dimension. We watch him and perhaps care for him, but we cannot identify with him, because he is no longer capable of change and decision. He has long since stopped trying to tell apart his layers of memory, nightmare, experience, and fantasy.

He is alone and adrift. He wanders through memories, lost and sad, and we wander after him, knowing, somehow, that Spider is not going to get better—and that if he does, that would simply mean the loss of his paranoid fantasies, which would leave him with nothing. Sometimes people hold onto illnesses because they are defined by them, given distinction, made real. There seems to be no sense in which Spider could engage the world on terms that would make him any happier.

There are three considerable artists at work here: Cronenberg, Fiennes, and Richardson. They are at the service of a novelist who often writes of grotesque and melancholy characters; he is Britain's modern master of the gothic. His Spider Cleg lives in a closed system, like one of those sealed glass globes where little plants and tiny marine organisms trade their energy back and forth indefinitely. In Spider's globe he feeds on his pain and it feeds on him. We feel that this exchange will go on and on, whether we watch or not. The details of the film and of the performances are meticulously realized; there is a reward in seeing artists working so well. But the story has no entry or exit, and is cold, sad, and hopeless. Afterward, I felt more admiration than gratitude.

Spider-Man ★ ★ ½
PG-13, 121 m., 2002

Tobey Maguire (Spider-Man/Peter Parker), Willem Dafoe (Green Goblin/Norman Osborn), Kirsten Dunst (Mary Jane Watson), James Franco (Harry Osborn), Cliff Robertson (Ben Parker), Rosemary Harris (May Parker), J. K. Simmons (J. Jonah Jameson), Joe Manganiello (Flash Thompson). Directed by Sam Raimi and produced by Laura Ziskin, Ian Brice, and Avi Arad. Screenplay by David Koepp, based on the Marvel comic by Stan Lee and Steve Ditko.

Imagine *Superman* with a Clark Kent more charismatic than the Man of Steel, and you'll understand how *Spider-Man* goes wrong. Tobey Maguire is pitch-perfect as the socially retarded Peter Parker, but when he becomes Spider-Man, the film turns to action sequences that zip along like perfunctory cartoons. Not even during Spidey's first experimental outings do we feel that flesh and blood are contending with gravity. Spidey soars too quickly through the skies of Manhattan; he's as convincing as Mighty Mouse.

The appeal of the best sequences in the Superman and Batman movies is that they lend weight and importance to comic-book images. Within the ground rules set by each movie, they even have plausibility. As a reader of the Spider-Man comics, I admired the vertiginous frames showing Spidey dangling from terrifying heights. He had the powers of a spider and the instincts of a human being, but the movie is split between a plausible Peter Parker and an inconsequential superhero.

Consider a sequence early in the film, after Peter Parker is bitten by a mutant spider and discovers his new powers. His hand is sticky. He doesn't need glasses anymore. He was scrawny yesterday, but today he's got muscles. The movie shows him becoming aware of these facts, but insufficiently amazed (or frightened) by them. He learns how to spin and toss webbing, and finds that he can make enormous leaps. And then there's a scene where he's like a kid with a new toy, jumping from one rooftop to another, making giant leaps, whooping with joy.

Remember the first time you saw the characters defy gravity in *Crouching Tiger, Hidden Dragon*. They transcended gravity, but they didn't dismiss it: They seemed to possess weight, dimension, and presence. Spider-Man, as he leaps across the rooftops, is landing too lightly, rebounding too much like a bouncing ball. He looks like a video-game figure, not like a person having an amazing experience.

The other superbeing in the movie is the Green Goblin, who surfs the skies. He, too, looks like a drawing being moved quickly around a frame, instead of like a character who has mastered a daring form of locomotion. He's handicapped, also, by his face, which looks like a high-tech action figure with a mouth that doesn't move. I understand why it's immobile (we're looking at a mask), but I'm not persuaded; the movie could simply ordain that the Green Goblin's exterior shell has a face that's mobile, and the character would become more interesting. (True, Spider-Man has *no* mouth, and Peter Parker barely opens his—the words slip out through a reluctant slit.)

The film tells Spidey's origin story—who Peter Parker is, who Aunt May (Rosemary Harris) and Uncle Ben (Cliff Robertson) are, how Peter's an outcast at school, how he burns with unrequited love for Mary Jane Watson (Kirsten Dunst), how he peddles photos of Spider-Man to cigar-chomping editor J. Jonah Jameson (J. K. Simmons).

Peter Parker was crucial in the evolution of Marvel comics because he was fallible and had recognizable human traits. He was a nerd, a loner, socially inept, insecure, a poor kid being raised by relatives. Tobey Maguire gets all of that just right, and I enjoyed the way Dunst is able to modulate her gradually increasing interest in this loser who begins to seem attractive to her. I also liked the complexity of the villain, who in his Dr. Jekyll manifestation is brilliant tycoon Norman Osborn (Willem Dafoe) and in his Mr. Hyde persona is a cackling psychopath. Osborn's son, Harry (James Franco), is a rich kid, embarrassed by his dad's wealth, who is Peter's best and only friend, and Norman is affectionate toward Peter even while their alter egos are deadly enemies. That works,

and there's an effective scene where Osborn has a conversation with his invisible dark side.

The origin story is well told, and the characters will not disappoint anyone who values the original comic books. It's in the action scenes that things fall apart. Consider the scene where Spider-Man is given a cruel choice between saving Mary Jane or a cable car full of schoolkids. He tries to save both, so that everyone dangles from webbing that seems about to pull loose. The visuals here could have given an impression of the enormous weights and tensions involved, but instead the scene seems more like a bloodless storyboard of the idea. In other CGI scenes, Spidey swoops from great heights to street level and soars back up among the skyscrapers again with such dizzying speed that it seems less like a stunt than like a fast-forward version of a stunt.

I have one question about the Peter Parker character: Does the movie go too far with his extreme social paralysis? Peter tells Mary Jane he just wants to be friends. "Only a friend?" she repeats. "That's all I have to give," he says. How so? Impotent? Spidey-sense has skewed his sexual instincts? Afraid his hands will get stuck?

Spider-Man 2 ★ ★ ★ ★
PG-13, 125 m., 2004

Tobey Maguire (Peter Parker/Spider-Man), Kirsten Dunst (Mary Jane Watson), Alfred Molina (Dr. Otto Octavius/Doc Ock), James Franco (Harry Osborn), Rosemary Harris (Aunt May), J. K. Simmons (J. Jonah Jameson). Directed by Sam Raimi and produced by Avi Arad and Laura Ziskin. Screenplay by Alvin Sargent, Michael Chabon, Miles Millar, and Alfred Gough, based on the comic book by Stan Lee and Steve Ditko.

Now this is what a superhero movie should be. *Spider-Man 2* believes in its story in the same way serious comic readers believe, when the adventures on the page express their own dreams and wishes. It's not camp and it's not nostalgia, it's not wall-to-wall special effects and it's not pickled in angst. It's simply and poignantly a realization that being Spider-Man is a burden that

Peter Parker is not entirely willing to bear. The movie demonstrates what's wrong with a lot of other superhero epics: They focus on the super-powers and short-change the humans behind them (has anyone ever been more boring than Clark Kent or Bruce Wayne?).

Spider-Man 2 is the best superhero movie since the modern genre was launched with *Superman* (1978). It succeeds by being true to the insight that allowed Marvel Comics to upturn decades of comic book tradition: Readers could identify more completely with heroes like themselves than with remote, godlike paragons. Peter Parker was an insecure high school student, in grade trouble, inarticulate in love, unready to assume the responsibilities that came with his unexpected superpowers. It wasn't that Spider-Man could swing from sky-scrapers that won over his readers; it was that he fretted about personal problems in the thought balloons above his Spidey face mask.

Parker (Tobey Maguire) is in college now, studying physics at Columbia, more helplessly in love than ever with Mary Jane Watson (Kirsten Dunst). He's on the edge of a break-down: He's lost his job as a pizza deliveryman, Aunt May faces foreclosure on her mortgage, he's missing classes, the colors run together when he washes his Spider-Man suit at the Laundromat, and after his web-spinning ability inexplicably seems to fade, he throws away his beloved uniform in despair. When a bum tries to sell the discarded Spidey suit to Jonah Jameson, editor of the *Daily Bugle,* Jameson offers him $50. The bum says he could do better on eBay. Has it come to this?

I was disappointed by the original *Spider-Man* (2002), and surprised to find this film working from the first frame. Sam Raimi, the director of both pictures, this time seems to know exactly what he should do, and never steps wrong in a film that effortlessly combines special effects and a human story, keeping its parallel plots alive and moving. One of the keys to the movie's success must be the contribution of novelist Michael Chabon to the screenplay; Chabon understands in his bones what comic books are, and why. His inspired 2000 novel, *The Amazing Adventures of Kavalier and Clay,* chronicles the birth of a 1940s comic book su-perhero and the young men who created him; Chabon worked on the screen story that fed

into Alvin Sargent's screenplay. *See entry in the Answer Man section.*

The seasons in a superhero's life are charted by the villains he faces (it is the same with James Bond). *Spider-Man 2* gives Spider-Man an enemy with a good nature that is overcome by evil. Peter Parker admires the famous Dr. Otto Octavius (Alfred Molina), whose labora-tory on the banks of the East River houses an experiment that will either prove that fusion can work as a cheap source of energy, or vapor-ize Manhattan. To handle the dangerous mate-rials of his experiments, Octavius devises four powerful tentacles that are fused to his spine and have cyber-intelligence of their own; a chip at the top of his spine prevents them from over-riding his orders, but when the chip is de-stroyed the gentle scientist is transformed into Doc Ock, a fearsome fusion of man and ma-chine, who can climb skyscraper walls by dri-ving his tentacles through concrete and bricks. We hear him coming, hammering his way to-ward us like the drums of hell.

Peter Parker meanwhile has vowed that he cannot allow himself to love Mary Jane because her life would be in danger from Spider-Man's enemies. She has finally given up on Peter, who is always standing her up; she announces her engagement to no less than an astronaut. Peter has heart-to-hearts with her and with Aunt May (Rosemary Harris), who is given full screen time and not reduced to an obligatory cameo. And he has to deal with his friend Harry Osborn (James Franco), who likes Peter but hates Spider-Man, blaming him for the death of his father (a.k.a. the Green Goblin, although much is unknown to the son).

There are special effects, and then there are special effects. In the first movie I thought Spider-Man seemed to move with all the real-ism of a character in a cartoon. This time, as he swings from one skyscraper to another, he has more weight and dimension, and Raimi is able to seamlessly match the CGI and the human actors. The f/x triumph in the film is the work on Doc Ock's four robotic tentacles, which move with an uncanny life, reacting and re-sponding, doing double-takes, becoming char-acters of their own.

Watching Raimi and his writers cut between the story threads, I savored classical workman-ship: The film gives full weight to all of its elements, keeps them alive, is constructed with such skill that we care all the way through; in a lesser movie from this genre, we usually perk up for the action scenes but wade grimly through the dialogue. Here both stay alive, and the dialogue is more about emotion, love, and values, less about long-winded explanations of the inexplicable (it's kind of neat that Spider-Man never does find out why his web-throwing ability sometimes fails him).

Tobey Maguire almost didn't sign for the sequel, complaining of back pain; Jake Gyllenhaal, another gifted actor, was reportedly in the wings. But if Maguire hadn't returned (along with Spidey's throwaway line about his aching back), we would never have known how good he could be in this role. Kirsten Dunst is valuable, too, bringing depth and heart to a girlfriend role that in lesser movies would be conventional. When she kisses her astronaut boyfriend upside-down, it's one of those perfect moments that rewards fans of the whole saga; we don't need to be told she's remembering her only kiss from Spider-Man.

There are moviegoers who make it a point of missing superhero movies, and I can't blame them, although I confess to a weakness for the genre. I liked both of *The Crow* movies, and *Daredevil, The Hulk,* and *X2,* but not enough to recommend them to friends who don't like or understand comic books. *Spider-Man 2* is in another category: It's a real movie, full-blooded and smart, with qualities even for those who have no idea who Stan Lee is. It's a superhero movie for people who don't go to superhero movies, and for those who do, it's the one they've been yearning for. ☞

Spirit: Stallion of the Cimarron
★ ★ ★
G, 82 m., 2002

With the voices of: Matt Damon (Narrator), James Cromwell (Cavalry Colonel), Daniel Studi (Little Creek). Directed by Kelly Asbury and Lorna Cook and produced by Mireille Soria and Jeffrey Katzenberg. Screenplay by John Fusco.

The animals do not speak in *Spirit: Stallion of the Cimarron,* and I think that's important to the film's success. It elevates the story from a children's fantasy to one wider audiences can enjoy, because although the stallion's adventures are admittedly pumped-up melodrama, the hero is nevertheless a horse and not a human with four legs. There is a whole level of cuteness that the movie avoids, and a kind of narrative strength it gains in the process.

The latest release from DreamWorks tells the story of Spirit, a wild mustang stallion, who runs free on the great western plains before he ventures into the domain of man and is captured by U.S. Cavalry troops. They think they can tame him. They are wrong, although the gruff-voiced colonel (voice by James Cromwell) makes the stallion into a personal obsession.

Spirit does not want to be broken, shoed, or inducted into the army, and his salvation comes through Little Creek (voice by Daniel Studi), an Indian brave who helps him escape and rides him to freedom. The pursuit by the cavalry is one of several sequences in the film where animation frees chase scenes to run wild, as Spirit and his would-be captors careen down canyons and through towering rock walls, duck under obstacles and end up in a river.

Watching the film, I was reminded of Jack London's classic novel *White Fang,* so unfairly categorized as a children's story even though the book (and the excellent 1991 film) used the dog as a character in a parable for adults. White Fang and Spirit represent holdouts against the taming of the frontier; invaders want to possess them, but they do not see themselves as property.

All of which philosophy will no doubt come as news to the cheering kids I saw the movie with, who enjoyed it, I'm sure, on its most basic level, as a big, bold, colorful adventure about a wide-eyed horse with a stubborn streak. That Spirit does not talk (except for some minimal thoughts that we overhear on voice-over) doesn't mean he doesn't communicate, and the animators pay great attention to body language and facial expressions in scenes where Spirit is frightened of a blacksmith, in love with a mare, and the partner of the Indian brave (whom he accepts after a lengthy battle of wills).

There is also a scene of perfect wordless communication between Spirit and a small Indian child who fearlessly approaches the stallion at a time when he feels little but alarm about humans. The two creatures, one giant, one tiny, tentatively reach out to each other, and the child's absolute trust is somehow communicated to the horse. I remembered the great scene in *The Black Stallion* (1979) where the boy and the horse edge together from the far sides of the wide screen.

In the absence of much dialogue, the songs by Bryan Adams fill in some of the narrative gaps, and although some of them simply comment on the action (a practice I find annoying), they are in the spirit of the story. The film is short at eighty-two minutes, but surprisingly moving, and has a couple of really thrilling sequences, one involving a train wreck and the other a daring leap across a chasm. Uncluttered by comic supporting characters and cute sidekicks, *Spirit* is more pure and direct than most of the stories we see in animation—a fable I suspect younger viewers will strongly identify with.

Spirited Away ★ ★ ★ ★
PG, 124 m., 2002

With the voices of: Daveigh Chase (Chihiro), Suzanne Pleshette (Yubaba), Jason Marsden (Haku), Susan Egan (Lin), David Ogden Stiers (Kamaji), Michael Chiklis (Chihiro's Father), Lauren Holly (Chihiro's Mother), John Ratzenberger (Assistant Manager). Directed by Hayao Miyazaki (U.S. production directed by Kirk Wise) and produced by Toshio Suzuki and Donald W. Ernst. Screenplay by Miyazaki, Cindy Davis Hewitt, and Donald H. Hewitt.

Spirited Away has been compared to *Alice in Wonderland*, and indeed it tells of a ten-year-old girl who wanders into a world of strange creatures and illogical rules. But it's enchanting and delightful in its own way, and has a good heart. It is the best animated film of recent years, the latest work by Hayao Miyazaki, the Japanese master who is a god to the Disney animators.

Because many adults have an irrational reluctance to see an animated film from Japan (or anywhere else), I begin with reassurances: It has been flawlessly dubbed into English by John Lasseter (*Toy Story*), it was cowinner of this year's Berlin Film Festival against "regular" movies, it passed *Titanic* to become the top-grossing film in Japanese history, and it is the first film ever to make more than $200 million before opening in America.

I feel like I'm giving a pitch on an infomercial, but I make these points because I come bearing news: This is a wonderful film. Don't avoid it because of what you think you know about animation from Japan. And if you only go to Disney animation—well, this is being released by Disney.

Miyazaki's works (*My Neighbor Totoro, Kiki's Delivery Service, Princess Mononoke*) have a depth and complexity often missing in American animation. Not fond of computers, he draws thousand of frames himself, and there is a painterly richness in his work. He's famous for throwaway details at the edges of the screen (animation is so painstaking that few animators draw more than is necessary). And he permits himself silences and contemplation, providing punctuation for the exuberant action and the lovable or sometimes grotesque characters.

Spirited Away is told through the eyes of Chihiro (voice by Daveigh Chase), a ten-year-old girl, and is more personal, less epic, than *Princess Mononoke*. As the story opens, she's on a trip with her parents, and her father unwisely takes the family to explore a mysterious tunnel in the woods. On the other side is what he speculates is an old theme park; but the food stalls still seem to be functioning, and as Chihiro's parents settle down for a free meal, she wanders away and comes upon the film's version of Wonderland, which is a towering bathhouse.

A boy named Haku appears as her guide, and warns her that the sorceress who runs the bathhouse, named Yubaba, will try to steal her name and thus her identity. Yubaba (Suzanne Pleshette) is an old crone with a huge face; she looks a little like a Toby mug, and dotes on a grotesquely huge baby named Bou. Ominously, she renames Chihiro, who wanders through the structure, which is populated, like *Totoro*, with little balls of dust that scurry and scamper underfoot.

In the innards of the structure, Chihiro comes upon the boiler room, operated by a man named Kamaji (David Ogden Stiers), who is dressed in a formal coat and has eight limbs, which he employs in a bewildering variety of ways. At first he seems as fearsome as the world he occupies, but he has a good side, is no friend of Yubaba, and perceives Chihiro's goodness.

If Yubaba is the scariest of the characters and Kamaji the most intriguing, Okutaresama is the one with the most urgent message. He is the spirit of the river, and his body has absorbed the junk, waste, and sludge that has been thrown into it over the years. At one point he actually yields up a discarded bicycle. I was reminded of a throwaway detail in *My Neighbor Totoro*, where a child looks into a bubbling brook, and there is a discarded bottle at the bottom. No point is made; none needs to be made.

Japanese myths often use shape-shifting, in which bodies reveal themselves as facades concealing a deeper reality. It's as if animation was invented for shape-shifting, and Miyazaki does wondrous things with the characters here. Most alarming for Chihiro, she finds that her parents have turned into pigs after gobbling up the free lunch. Okutaresama reveals its true nature after being freed of decades of sludge and discarded household items. Haku is much more than he seems. Indeed, the entire bathhouse seems to be under spells affecting the appearance and nature of its inhabitants.

Miyazaki's drawing style, which descends from the classical Japanese graphic artists, is a pleasure to regard, with its subtle use of colors, clear lines, rich detail, and its realistic depiction of fantastical elements. He suggests not just the appearances of his characters, but their natures. Apart from the stories and dialogue, *Spirited Away* is a pleasure to regard just for itself. This is one of the year's best films.

Spun ★ ★ ★

R, 101 m., 2003

Jason Schwartzman (Ross), Mickey Rourke (Cook), Brittany Murphy (Nikki), John Leguizamo (Spider Mike), Mena Suvari (Cookie), Patrick Fugit (Frisbee), Peter Stormare (Cop No. 1), Alexis Arquette (Cop No. 2), Chloe Hunter (April). Directed by Jonas Akerlund and produced by Chris Hanley, Fernando Sulichin, Timothy Wayne Peternel, and Danny Vinik. Screenplay by Will De Los Santos and Creighton Vero.

Spun is a movie about going around and around and around on speed. Sometimes it can be exhausting to have a good time. The characters live within the orbit of Cook, who converts enormous quantities of nonprescription pills into drugs, and Spider Mike, who sells these and other drugs to people who usually can't pay him, leading to a lot of scenarios in which bodily harm is threatened in language learned from TV.

Because Cook is played with the studied weirdness of Mickey Rourke and Spider Mike with the tireless extroversion of John Leguizamo, *Spun* has an effortless wickedness. Rourke in particular has arrived at that point where he doesn't have to play heavy because he is heavy. Leguizamo has the effect of trying to talk himself into and out of trouble simultaneously.

Their world includes characters played by Jason Schwartzman (from *Rushmore*), Mena Suvari (from *American Beauty*), Patrick Fugit (from *Almost Famous*), and Brittany Murphy (from *8 Mile* and *Just Married*). Uncanny, in a way, how they all bring along some of the aura of their famous earlier characters, as if this were a doc about Hollywood youth gone wrong.

Brittany Murphy made quite an impact at the Independent Spirit Awards by being unable to master the concept of reading the five nominees *before* opening the envelope, despite two helpful visits from the stage manager and lots of suggestions from the audience, but with Murphy, you always kind of wonder if she doesn't know exactly what she's doing.

Here she plays Nikki, Cook's girlfriend, which is the kind of situation you end up in when you need a lot of drugs for not a lot of money. She depends on Ross (Schwartzman) to chauffeur her everywhere in his desperately ill Volvo, sometimes taking him off on long missions through the city. These journeys have a queasy undertone since we know (although Ross sometimes forgets) that he has left his own current stripper girlfriend handcuffed to a bed. April (Chloe Hunter), the handcuffed girlfriend, is all the more furious because she realizes Ross is not sadistic but merely confused and absent-minded.

The movie plays like a dark screwball comedy in which people run in and out of doors, get involved with mistaken identities, and desperately try to keep all their plates in the air. The film's charm, which is admittedly an acquired and elusive taste, comes from the fact that *Spun* does not romanticize its characters, does not enlarge or dramatize them, but seems to shake its head incredulously as these screwups persist in ruinous and insane behavior.

Leguizamo is fearless when it comes to depictions of sexual conduct. You may recall him as the transvestite Miss Chi-Chi Rodriguez in *To Wong Foo, Thanks for Everything! Julie Newmar* (1995), or more probably as the energetic Toulouse-Lautrec in *Moulin Rouge*, and he toured in his stage show *John Leguizamo's Sexaholixs*. In *Spun* he demonstrates that although black socks have often played important roles in erotic films, there are still frontiers to be explored. What I have always enjoyed about him is the joy and abandon with which he approaches the right kind of role, as if it is play, not work. Here his energy inspires the others, causing even Patrick Fugit's slothful Frisbee to stir.

The movie is like the low-rent, road show version of those serious drug movies where everybody is macho and deadly. The characters in *Narc* would crush these characters under their thumbs. *Spun* does have two drug cops, played by Peter Stormare and Alexis Arquette, but they work for some kind of TV reality show, are followed by cameras, and are also strung out on speed.

The director, Jonas Akerlund, comes from Sweden via commercials and music videos, and has obviously studied *Requiem for a Dream* carefully, since he uses the same kind of speeded-up visual disconnections to suggest life on meth. His feel for his characters survives his technique, however, and it's interesting how this story and these people seem to have been living before the movie began and will continue after it is over; instead of a plot, we drop in on their lives. When Cook starts the mother of all kitchen fires, for example, he walks toward the camera (obligatory fireball behind him), already looking for a new motel room.

Spy Kids 2: The Island of Lost Dreams
★ ★ ★
PG, 86 m., 2002

Antonio Banderas (Gregorio Cortez), Carla Gugino (Ingrid Cortez), Alexa Vega (Carmen Cortez), Daryl Sabara (Juni Cortez), Steve Buscemi (Romero), Matthew O'Leary (Gary Giggles), Emily Osment (Gerti Giggles), Bill Paxton (Dinky Winks), Ricardo Montalban (Grandpa), Holland Taylor (Grandma). Directed by Robert Rodriguez and produced by Elizabeth Avellan and Rodriguez. Screenplay by Rodriguez.

Spy Kids 2: The Island of Lost Dreams uses the same formula as the wonderful 2001 picture: bright colors, weird gimmicks, fanciful special effects, goofy villains, sassy dialogue, and lots of moxie. The second installment is a galloping adventure pitting Carmen and Juni Cortez (Alexa Vega and Daryl Sabara), the two original spy kids, against the snot-nosed Gary and Gerti Giggles (Matthew O'Leary and Emily Osment), whose dad has staged a sneaky takeover of the federal spy agency. Soon they're on an invisible island ruled by Romero (Steve Buscemi), a not-quite-mad scientist with a gizmo that could control, or destroy, the world.

Director Robert Rodriguez wrote, directed, edited, and even did some of the digital photography. He seems to have chosen his color palette from those brightly painted little Mexican sculptures you see in gift shops, the ones that have so much energy they make you smile. The whole film has a lively Mexican-American tilt, from the Hispanic backgrounds of the young actors to the surprise appearance of none other than Ricardo Montalban, as Grandpa, in a wheelchair with helicopter capabilities.

The opening sequence is inspired; Carmen and Juni visit a theme park, where the owner (Bill Paxton) proudly explains his great new rides. These rides are so extravagantly, recklessly over the top that I was laughing; we see the Whipper Snapper (customers ride in cars at the end of long ropes that are snapped like whips), the Vomiter (Paxton gets out his umbrella to shield himself from the inevitable customer reaction), and the Juggler, a ride that literally juggles cars containing the patrons.

The daughter of the president of the United States is among the park's guests, and she's a little brat who soon finds herself teetering dangerously on a ledge of the Juggler, while the Spy Kids and the Giggles team compete to rescue her. The Spy Kids save the day, but the Giggleses get the credit, setting off a rivalry that leads to the Island of Lost Dreams.

Just like in the Bond pictures, nothing less than the survival of the world is at stake, but Buscemi plays Romero the scientist as a conflicted character, basically a nice guy who wants to be left alone to tinker with his planet-destroying inventions. The chase to the island involves an undersea journey by the Spy Kids, and, just like in the first movie, pursuit by their worried parents. (The exasperation the kids feel because of their parents' overprotectiveness is mirrored when the grandparents [Montalban and Holland Taylor] come onboard the pursuit sub to give unwanted advice to mom and dad Cortez.)

I liked the special effects, especially a green-and-gold sea monster that was kind of beautiful in its own way, and a many-legged spider man who turns out to have a good heart. The movie is filled with lots of other gimmicks, including Juni's favorite device, a Palm Pilot that has morphed into a personal valet, and creeps across his coat on spider legs to knot his tie.

The dialogue has a certain self-kidding element, as in an exchange where the Kids are searching for the Transmooger, the device that can destroy the world. "There it is!" Carmen shouts. "How do you know?" asks Juni. "Because it's big and round and in the middle of the room."

With Spy Kids 2: The Island of Lost Dreams, the Spy Kids franchise establishes itself as a durable part of the movie landscape: a James Bond series for kids. One imagines Spy Kids 9, with Alexa Vega and Daryl Sabara promoted to the roles of the parents, Antonio Banderas and Carla Gugino as the grandparents, and kids yet unborn in the title roles.

Standing in the Shadows of Motown
★ ★ ★
PG, 116 m., 2002

A documentary featuring Richard "Pistol" Allen, Jack "Black Jack" Ashford, Bob Babbitt, Johnny Griffith, Joe Hunter, Uriel Jones, Joe Messina, Eddie "Chank" Willis, Benny "Papa Zita" Benjamin, James "Igor" Jamerson, Eddie "Bongo" Brown, Earl "Chunk of Funk" Van Dyke, Robert White, Joan Osborne, Gerald Levert, Me'Shell NdegéOcello, Bootsy Collins,

Ben Harper, Chaka Khan, Montell Jordan, and Tom Scott. Directed by Paul Justman and produced by Justman, Sandford Passman, and Allan Slutsky. Screenplay by Walter Dallas and Ntozake Shange, based on the book Standing in the Shadows of Motown by Slutsky.

Think of the Supremes, Gladys Knight, Smokey Robinson, Marvin Gaye, Martha Reeves, Stevie Wonder, and the Temptations. You hold decades of pop music history in your mind: the Motown Sound. Now ask who the instrumentalists were on their records. Or don't even bother, because the question is asked and answered in the affectionate new documentary Standing in the Shadows of Motown. In the movie, fans are asked: Who played on the recordings with those artists? Who, for example, was behind Gladys Knight? "The Pips?" asks one Motown fan.

No, it wasn't the Pips, the Miracles, or the Vandellas. The musicians who played behind all of the Motown stars on their studio recordings were the Funk Brothers. The Funk Brothers? Paul Justman's documentary, based on a book by Allan Slutsky, gives belated praise for Motown's house musicians, the men who played under all the Motown hits recorded in Detroit.

The hero of the Funk Brothers themselves seems to have been the late James Jamerson, the bass player who used only one finger but seemed able to keep two times at once. Their stories about him are legion. The other original Funks were drummer Benny Benjamin, pianist Joe Hunter, and guitarists Eddie Willis and Joe Messina. The movie talks with or about perhaps a dozen other musicians who played on many or most of the Motown records, but it's difficult to keep them straight—because, of course, they were not famous.

And yet the Motown Sound was, quite simply, their sound. No disrespect to the singers, but, as drummer Steve Gordon observes, "You could have had Deputy Dawg singin' on some of this stuff." The documentary argues that they played on hits that sold more records than the Beatles, Elvis, the Beach Boys, and the Rolling Stones combined—but were almost anonymous.

The first Motown sides were cut in Studio A, which was simply the garage of Berry Gordy, the label's founder. It was down four steps from his kitchen and originally had a dirt floor. Along with the Sun studios in Memphis, it was one of the birthplaces of the last half-century of American hit music. The movie returns to that location ("Hitsville, USA") for sessions in which the surviving Funk Brothers remember the good times and bad, and the very sound of the studio itself.

Sessions would last all day and into the night. A producer would come in with a song and a few chords, and they'd play with it, adapting it to the house style, adding a touch here, a riff there, until it emerged as the big, bold, and sometimes almost unreasonably happy Motown Sound. In one of the movie's best sequences, we see them cobbling a song together almost from scratch. Sometimes, they remember, they were so overworked they'd hide out in a nearby funeral parlor, where Gordy wouldn't think to look for them.

The sound was born in and nurtured by a series of Detroit clubs, places like the Chit Chat and 20 Grand, now closed, where the Funks and other musicians got their start and returned to their roots. Separately they were great and together they were beyond great; it's clear that working steadily behind literally hundreds of hits fused them into a group that all but thought with one mind. As they remember those days, they're like military veterans or the members of a World Series team, and we realize nothing that came after ever held the same joy for them.

The Motown Sound came to an end in 1972, when Gordy moved the label from Detroit to Los Angeles with "no warning and no acknowledgement." The Funks found out from a notice tacked to the door. Some of them followed Motown to the coast, but the magic was gone, and the movie doesn't ask the obvious question: Why didn't some of the singers they worked with know how important they were and demand them, or return to Detroit to record with them?

Standing in the Shadows of Motown interlaces interviews with the surviving Funk Brothers with new performances of many of the hit songs, and some sequences in which events of the past are re-created. The flashback sequences are not especially effective, but are probably better than more talking heads. Or maybe not. The contemporary performers who sing in

front of the Funks include Joan Osborne, Ben Harper, Me'Shell NdegéOcello, Montell Jordan, Gerald Levert, Chaka Khan, and the flamboyant Bootsy Collins, who upstages the Funks, not to his own advantage.

What's interesting about these performances is that the singers make no attempt to imitate the original artists, and yet the Funks turn the songs into soundalikes anyway. Is it possible those great Motown stars were more or less created by these unsung musicians? The Funks think that is a distinct possibility. Of course, the backup singers had a lot to do with it, too, and this movie never gets around to them. They're in the shadows of the shadows.

Starsky & Hutch ★ ★ ★
PG-13, 97 m., 2004

Ben Stiller (Dave Starsky), Owen Wilson (Ken Hutchinson), Snoop Dogg (Huggy Bear), Vince Vaughn (Reese Feldman), Juliette Lewis (Kitty), Fred Williamson (Captain Doby). Directed by Todd Phillips and produced by William Blinn, Stuart Cornfeld, Akiva Goldsman, Tony Ludwig, and Alan Riche. Screenplay by John O'Brien, Phillips, Scot Armstrong, and Stevie Long.

As Hollywood works its way through retreads of TV series from the 1960s and 1970s, I find I can approach each project with a certain purity, since I never saw any of the original shows. Never saw a single *Starsky and Hutch*. Not one episode of *I Spy*. No *Mod Squad*. No *Charlie's Angels*. What was I doing instead, apart from seeing thousands of movies? Avoiding episodic television like a communicable disease, and improving myself with the great literature of the ages. Plus partying.

So here is *Starsky & Hutch*, adding the ampersand for a generation too impatient for "and." It's a surprisingly funny movie, the best of the 1970s recycling jobs, with one laugh ("Are you okay, little pony?") almost as funny as the moment in *Dumb and Dumber* when the kid figured out his parakeet's head was Scotch-taped on.

Ben Stiller and Owen Wilson star, in their sixth movie together. They use the same comic contrasts that worked for Hope and Crosby and Martin and Lewis: one is hyper and the other is sleepy-eyed and cool. In a genial spoof of the cop buddy genre, they're both misfits on the Bay City police force. Starsky (Stiller) is the kind of cop who would ask another cop if he had a license for his firearm. Hutch (Wilson) has done nothing useful at all for months, aside from enriching himself illegally by stealing from dead bodies. Their captain (Fred Williamson) thinks they deserve each other, and makes them partners in a scene where Hutch immediately insults Starsky's perm.

The bad guy is Reese Feldman (Vince Vaughn), coils of cigarette smoke constantly rising in front of his face. He's a big-time cocaine dealer who has invented, or discovered, a form of cocaine that has no taste or smell and can fool police dogs. He's also a vicious boss who kills an underling in the opening scene and pushes him off his yacht. Discovery of the floater gives Starsky and Hutch their first big case, although they almost blow it, since Hutch's first suggestion is to push it back out to sea and hope it floats to the next precinct.

Although the plot survives sporadically, the movie is mostly about the rapport between Stiller and Wilson, who carry on a running disagreement about style while agreeing on most other issues, such as the importance of partying with sexy cheerleaders as part of their investigation. Carmen Electra and Amy Smart are the cheerleaders, improbably attracted to the guys, and there's a very funny scene where Wilson croons a minor David Soul hit from the 1970s while a psychedelically fueled cartoon bird chirps on his shoulder.

The movie doesn't make the mistake of relying entirely on its stars. Apart from Vaughn and the cheerleaders, the supporting cast benefits mightily from Juliette Lewis, as Vaughn's mistress, and Snoop Dogg as Huggy Bear, a combo pimp/superfly/police informer whose outfits are like retro cubed. Will Ferrell turns up in a weird cameo as a jailhouse source whose sexual curiosity falls far outside anything either Starsky and Hutch had ever imagined ("arch your back and look back at me over your shoulder, like a dragon").

Another character is Starsky's beloved brightred, supercharged Ford Gran Torino, which he drives like a madman while obsessing about the smallest scratch. The closing stunt involves something we've been waiting to happen in car stunt scenes for a very long time.

The film's director is Todd Phillips, of *Road Trip* and *Old School*. I was not a big fan of either movie, but they both contained real laughs, and now in *Starsky & Hutch* he reaches critical mass. Will the movie inspire me to watch reruns of the original series? No. I want to quit while I'm ahead.

Star Trek: Nemesis ★ ★
PG-13, 116 m., 2002

Patrick Stewart (Captain Picard), Jonathan Frakes (Commander Riker), Brent Spiner (Data), LeVar Burton (Geordi La Forge), Michael Dorn (Worf), Gates McFadden (Dr. Crusher), Marina Sirtis (Deanna Troi), Tom Hardy (Praetor Shinzon), Ron Perlman (Reman Viceroy). Directed by Stuart Baird and produced by Rick Berman. Screenplay by John Logan.

I'm sitting there during *Star Trek: Nemesis*, the tenth *Star Trek* movie, and I'm smiling like a good sport and trying to get with the dialogue about the isotronic Ruritronic signature from planet Kolarus III, or whatever the hell they were saying, maybe it was "positronic," and gradually it occurs to me that Star Trek is over for me. I've been looking at these stories for half a lifetime, and, let's face it, they're out of gas.

There might have been a time when the command deck of *Starship Enterprise* looked exciting and futuristic, but these days it looks like a communications center for security guards. Starships rocket at light speed halfway across the universe, but when they get into battles the effect is roughly the same as onboard a World War II bomber. Fearsome death rays strike the *Enterprise*, and what happens? Sparks fly out from the ceiling and the crew gets bounced around in their seats like passengers on the No. 36 bus. This far in the future they wouldn't have sparks because they wouldn't have electricity, because in a world where you can beam matter—*beam* it, mind you—from here to there, power obviously no longer lives in the wall and travels through wires.

I've also had it with the force shield that protects the *Enterprise*. The power on this thing is always going down. In movie after movie after movie I have to sit through sequences during which the captain is tersely informed that the front shield is down to 60 percent, or the back shield is down to 10 percent, or the side shield is leaking energy, and the captain tersely orders that power be shifted from the back to the sides or all put in the front, or whatever, and I'm thinking, life is too short to sit through ten movies in which the power is shifted around on these shields. The shields have been losing power for decades now, and here it is the Second Generation of *Star Trek*, and they still haven't fixed them. Maybe they should get new batteries.

I tried to focus on the actors. Patrick Stewart, as Captain Picard, is a wonderful actor. I know because I have seen him elsewhere. It is always said of Stewart that his strength as an actor is his ability to deliver bad dialogue with utter conviction. I say it is time to stop encouraging him. Here's an idea: Instead of giving him bad dialogue, why not give him good dialogue and see what he can do with that? Here is a man who has played Shakespeare.

The plot of *Star Trek: Nemesis* involves a couple of strands, one involving a clone of Data, which somehow seems redundant, and another involving what seems to be a peace feeler from the Romulan empire. In the course of the movie the Romulan Senate is wiped out by a deadly blue powder and the sister planet, Remus, stages an uprising, or something, against being made to work as slaves in the mines. Surely slavery is not an efficient economic system in a world of hyperdrives, but never mind: Turns out that Picard shares something unexpected with his rival commander, although you can no doubt guess what it is, since the movie doesn't work you very hard.

There is a scene in the movie in which one starship rams another one. You would think this would destroy them both, and there are a lot of sparks and everybody has to hold onto their seats, but the *Star Trek* world involves physical laws that reflect only the needs of the plot. If one ship rammed another and they were both destroyed and everyone died, and the movie ended with a lot of junk floating around in space, imagine the faces of the people in the audience.

I think it is time for *Star Trek* to make a mighty leap forward another 1,000 years into the future, to a time when starships do not look like rides in a 1970s amusement arcade, when aliens do not look like humans with funny foreheads, and when wonder, astonishment, and literacy are permitted back into the series. *Star Trek* was kind of terrific once, but now it is a copy of a copy of a copy.

Star Wars: Episode II—Attack of the Clones ★ ★
PG, 124 m., 2002

Ewan McGregor (Obi-Wan Kenobi), Natalie Portman (Senator Padmé Amidala), Hayden Christensen (Anakin Skywalker), Christopher Lee (Count Dooku), Ian McDiarmid (Palpatine), (voice of) Frank Oz (Yoda), Samuel L. Jackson (Mace Windu), Pernilla August (Shmi Skywalker), Jack Thompson (Cliegg Lars), Temuera Morrison (Jango Fett), Jimmy Smits (Senator Bail Organa). Directed by George Lucas and produced by Rick McCallum. Screenplay by Lucas and Jonathan Hales.

It is not what's there on the screen that disappoints me, but what's not there. It is easy to hail the imaginative computer images that George Lucas brings to *Star Wars: Episode II—Attack of the Clones*. To marvel at his strange new aliens and towering cities and sights such as thousands of clones all marching in perfect ranks into a huge spaceship. To see the beginnings of the dark side in young Anakin Skywalker. All of those experiences are there to be cheered by fans of the *Star Wars* series, and for them this movie will affirm their faith.

But what about the agnostic viewer? The hopeful ticket-buyer walking in not as a cultist but as a moviegoer hoping for a great experience? Is this *Star Wars* critic-proof and scoff-resistant? Yes, probably, at the box office. But as someone who admired the freshness and energy of the earlier films, I was amazed, at the end of *Episode II*, to realize that I had not heard one line of quotable, memorable dialogue. And the images, however magnificently conceived, did not have the impact they deserved. I'll get to them in a moment.

The first hour of *Episode II* contains a sensational chase through the skyscraper canyons of a city, and assorted briefer shots of spaceships and planets. But most of that first hour consists of dialogue, as the characters establish plot points, update viewers on what has happened since *Episode I*, and debate the political crisis facing the Republic. They talk and talk and talk. And their talk is in a flat utilitarian style: They seem more like lawyers than the heroes of a romantic fantasy.

In the classic movie adventures that inspired *Star Wars,* dialogue was often colorful, energetic, witty, and memorable. The dialogue in *Episode II* exists primarily to advance the plot, provide necessary information, and give a little screen time to continuing characters who are back for a new episode. The only characters in this stretch of the film who have inimitable personal styles are the beloved Yoda and the hated Jar Jar Binks, whose idiosyncrasies turned off audiences for *Phantom Menace.* Yes, Jar Jar's accent may be odd and his mannerisms irritating, but at least he's a unique individual and not a bland cipher. The other characters—Obi-Wan Kenobi, Padme Amidala, Anakin Skywalker—seem so strangely stiff and formal in their speech that an unwary viewer might be excused for thinking they were the clones, soon to be exposed.

Too much of the rest of the film is given over to a romance between Padme and Anakin in which they're incapable of uttering anything other than the most basic and weary romantic clichés, while regarding each other as if love was something to be endured rather than cherished. There is not a romantic word they exchange that has not long since been reduced to cliché. No, wait: Anakin tells Padme at one point: "I don't like the sand. It's coarse and rough and irritating—not like you. You're soft and smooth." I hadn't heard that before.

When it comes to the computer-generated images, I feel that I cannot entirely trust the screening experience I had. I could see that in conception many of these sequences were thrilling and inventive. I liked the planet of rain, and the vast coliseum in which the heroes battle strange alien beasts, and the towering Senate chamber, and the secret factory where clones were being manufactured.

But I felt like I had to lean with my eyes toward the screen in order to see what I was being shown. The images didn't pop out and smack me with delight, the way they did in earlier films. There was a certain fuzziness, an indistinctness that seemed to undermine their potential power.

Later I went on the Web to look at the trailers for the movie, and was startled to see how much brighter, crisper, and more colorful they seemed on my computer screen than in the theater. Although I know that video images are routinely timed to be brighter than movie images, I suspect another reason for this. *Episode II* was shot entirely on digital video. It is being projected in digital video on nineteen screens, but on some 3,000 others, audiences will see it as I did, transferred to film.

How it looks in digital projection I cannot say, although I hope to get a chance to see it that way. I know Lucas believes it looks better than film, but then he has cast his lot with digital. My guess is that the film version of *Episode II* might jump more sharply from the screen in a small multiplex theater. But I saw it on the largest screen in Chicago, and my suspicion is, the density and saturation of the image was not adequate to imprint the image there in a forceful way.

Digital images contain less information than 35mm film images, and the more you test their limits, the more you see that. Not long ago I saw *Patton* shown in 70mm Dimension 150, and it was the most astonishing projection I had ever seen—absolute detail on a giant screen, which was 6,000 times larger than a frame of the 70mm film. That's what large-format film can do, but it's a standard Hollywood has abandoned (except for IMAX), and we are being asked to forget how good screen images can look—to accept the compromises. I am sure I will hear from countless fans who assure me that *Episode II* looks terrific, but it does not. At least, what I saw did not. It may look great in digital projection on multiplex-size screens, and I'm sure it will look great on DVD, but on a big screen it lacks the authority it needs.

I have to see the film again to do it justice. I'm sure I will greatly enjoy its visionary sequences on DVD; I like stuff like that. The dialogue is another matter. Perhaps because a movie like this opens everywhere in the world on the same day, the dialogue has to be dumbed down for easier dubbing or subtitling. Wit, poetry, and imagination are specific to the languages where they originate, and although translators can work wonders, sometimes you get the words but not the music. So it's safer to avoid the music.

But in a film with a built-in audience, why

not go for the high notes? Why not allow the dialogue to be inventive, stylish, and expressive? There is a certain lifelessness in some of the acting, perhaps because the actors were often filmed in front of blue screens so their environments could be added later by computer. Actors speak more slowly than they might—flatly, factually, formally, as if reciting. Sometimes that reflects the ponderous load of the mythology they represent. At other times it simply shows that what they have to say is banal. *Episode II—Attack of the Clones* is a technological exercise that lacks juice and delight. The title is more appropriate than it should be.

* * *

I did go back a few days later to see the movie digitally projected.

After seeing the new *Star Wars* movie projected on film, I wrote that the images had "a certain fuzziness, an indistinctness that seemed to undermine their potential power." But I knew the film had been shot on digital video, and that George Lucas believed it should preferably be seen, not on film, but projected digitally. Now I've been able to see the digital version, and Lucas is right: *Star Wars: Episode II—Attack of the Clones* is sharper, crisper, brighter, and punchier on digital than on film.

This will come as melancholy news, I suppose, to the vast majority of fans destined to see the movie through a standard film projector. Although an accurate count is hard to come by, there are apparently about 20 screens in America showing *Episode II* with a digital projector, and about 3,000 showing it on film. Lucas is so eager to promote his vision of the digital future that he is willing to penalize his audience, just to prove a point.

But he *does* prove the point. On Sunday I returned to Chicago's McClurg Court theater, where I had seen *Episode II* on film the previous Tuesday. On Wednesday, technicians from Boeing Digital Cinema swooped down on the theater to install a new Texas Instruments digital projector, and that's how I saw the film a second time—sitting in almost exactly the same seat.

Watching it on film, I wrote: "I felt like I had to lean with my eyes toward the screen in order to see what I was being shown." On digital, the images were bright and clear. Since the movie was being projected on film on another Mc-

Clurg screen (both screenings were part of a charity benefit) I slipped upstairs, watched a scene on film, and then hurried downstairs to compare the same scene on video. The difference was dramatic: more detail, more depth, more clarity.

Readers familiar with my preference for film over video projection systems will wonder if I have switched parties. Not at all. It's to be expected that *Episode II* would look better on digital, because it was entirely filmed on digital. Therefore, the digitally projected version is generation one, and the film version is one generation further from the source. Lucas is right as far as a computer-aided special-effects movie like *Episode II* goes, but may be wrong for the vast majority of movies that depict the real world on celluloid.

It is important to understand that *Episode II* is essentially an animated film with humans added to it. This is the flip side of *Who Framed Roger Rabbit,* which was a live-action film with cartoon characters laid on top. Most of the non-human screen images in *Episode II,* and some of the characters (Yoda, Jar Jar Binks) are created entirely in computers. Even in scenes dominated by humans, the backgrounds and locations are often entirely computer-generated.

Whether this is an advance is debatable. I am receiving mail from readers who prefer the earlier *Star Wars* effects, using models, back projection, puppets, and the like. They also question *Spider-Man,* where Spidey's action sequences are animated using CGI, or Computer-Generated Imagery. David Soto of Santa Ana, California, writes: "I liked it, although I wanted to love it. One thing I noticed—for a second I had the impression I was watching a Power Rangers episode." He said CGI made everything "look so fast, so weightless, so unreal."

I agree. In *Episode II,* this is true of the most popular scene in the movie, where Yoda abandons his contemplative and sedentary lifestyle and springs into action. Yes, it's fun to see the surprise Yoda has up his sleeve, but in the scene itself he turns from a substantial, detailed, "realistic" character into a bouncing blob of Yodaness, moving too quickly to be perceived in any detail.

The debate about CGI versus traditional effects will be fueled by *Episode II* and *Spider-*

Man. The debate about digital projection is just beginning. My feeling is that movies shot on digital look better projected on video, and that movies shot on film look better projected on film. Of course, every theater, every print, and every projector is different, so results may vary.

What I dislike about Lucas's approach is that he wants to change the entire world of film to suit his convenience. Because his movies are created largely on computers, it suits him to project them digitally. Because the *Star Wars* franchise is so hugely profitable, he hopes he has the clout to swing the movie world behind him—especially since well-funded Boeing and Texas Instruments stand to make millions by grabbing the projection franchise away from film. A century of cinematic tradition may be shown to the exit by Head Usher Jar Jar, while Yoda consoles us with the Force.

The Statement ★ ★

R, 120 m., 2004

Michael Caine (Pierre Brossard), Tilda Swinton (Anne-Marie Livi), Jeremy Northam (Colonel Roux), Charlotte Rampling (Nicole), Noam Jenkins (Michael Levy), Matt Craven (David Manenbaum), Alan Bates (Armand Bertier). Directed by Norman Jewison and produced by Jewison and Robert Lantos. Screenplay by Ronald Harwood, based on a novel by Brian Moore.

Michael Caine is such a lovely actor. In a movie like *The Statement*, where he is more or less adrift among competing themes, it's a pleasure to watch him craft a character we can care about even when the story keeps throwing him curves. He has such patience with a moment, such an ability to express weariness or fear without seeming to try. Here he plays a weak man baffled by life and by his own motives, and he arouses so much sympathy that even though he's supposed to be the villain, the movie ends up with substitute villains who are shadowy and ill-explained.

Caine plays Pierre Brossard, a Frenchman who was involved in the execution of Jews during World War II. Wanted as a war criminal, he has been living in hiding ever since, in a series of Roman Catholic monasteries and other safe houses. It's explained that he is a member of an ultrasecret Catholic society that protects its own, and that presents one of the movie's many hurdles: Although the story is based on fact, the movie never convinced me of its truth.

The screenplay, by Ronald Harwood (*The Pianist*), based on a novel by Brian Moore, is inspired by the real-life Paul Touvier, who executed Jewish hostages and then was protected for many years by an informal network of right-wing Catholics. Would a series of abbots and cardinals place the church at risk for this insignificant man for years after the war has ended? Yes, apparently, some did; but a movie must seem to be based on its own facts, not those in research consulted by the screenwriters. The situation on screen is not made to seem real.

Caine himself is virtually made to play two different characters. Early in the film we see him cool and merciless as he perceives that he is being followed, and calmly kills the man who wants to kill him. Later, we see him weak, pathetic, and confused. Perhaps he contains both men, but the movie seems to write the character first one way and then the other, showing not contrasts but simply contradictions.

Scene after scene works on its own terms. The director, Norman Jewison, has skill and conscience and obviously feels for the material, even if he hasn't found the way to tell it. There is a confrontation, for example, between Brossard and his estranged wife (Charlotte Rampling), which for edge and emotional danger could come from Le Carré or Graham Greene, but in *The Statement* it works on its own terms but doesn't fit into the whole, giving us one more facet of a personality that doesn't seem to fit together in any sensible way.

Presumably the moral thrust of the movie is against elements within the Church that supported anti-Semitism and continued to protect war criminals after the war. That there were such elements, and that the real Touvier was such a criminal, is beyond doubt. But then why does the movie supply a murky third element—a conspiracy to murder Brossard and pin the death on Zionists? The film fails to explain who these conspirators are, or to make clear exactly what they hope to achieve. We are not even quite sure which side they are on: Do

637

they want to attack anti-Semites, or protect the Church, or support Israel, or what? I don't require that a movie have a message, but in a message movie it is helpful to know what the message is.

Stateside ★ ★

R, 96 m., 2004

Rachel Leigh Cook (Dori Lawrence), Jonathan Tucker (Mark Deloach), Agnes Bruckner (Sue Dubois), Joe Mantegna (Mr. Deloach), Carrie Fisher (Mrs. Dubois), Diane Venora (Mrs. Hengen), Ed Begley Jr. (Father Concoff), Val Kilmer (SDI Skeer). Directed by Reverge Anselmo and produced by Robert Greenhut and Bonnie Wells-Hlinomaz.

Stateside tells the story of a rich kid who joins the marines to stay out of jail, and then finds himself in love with a famous actress and rock singer who is being treated for schizophrenia. Stated as plainly as that, the plot could have been imported from a soap opera, but the writer-director, Reverge Anselmo, assures us it is "based on a true story." Perhaps. Certainly he rotates it away from sensationalism, making it the story of an irresponsible kid who is transformed by boot camp and then becomes obsessed with what he sees as his duty to the actress.

The kid is named Mark (Jonathan Tucker). He goes to an upscale Catholic high school, drinks too much one night, and is driving a car that broadsides the car of the headmaster, Father Concoff (Ed Begley Jr.). The priest is paralyzed from the waist down, but doesn't sue (he explains why, but so enigmatically it doesn't work). Mark's millionaire father (Joe Mantegna) pulls strings to have the charges dropped in exchange for Mark enlisting in the marines.

Mark goes to Parris Island for basic training, under the command of a drill instructor named Skeer (Val Kilmer). Skeer doesn't like the rich kid and makes it hard on him; the kid puts his head down and charges through, emerging at the end of the ordeal as what Skeer, if not all of the rest of us, would consider a success.

Home on leave before more training, he visits his girlfriend. That would be Sue (Agnes Bruckner), who lost her front teeth in the crash, but lost her freedom after her mother (Carrie Fisher) found some sexually explicit letters she wrote. The letters are obviously evidence of madness, so she's institutionalized, in the Connecticut version of *The Magdalene Sisters*. When Mark visits her, he meets her roommate, Dori (Rachel Leigh Cook), and they fall in love.

All of this sounds simpler than the movie makes it. The opening scenes are disjointed and confusing, and it doesn't help that the characters sometimes seem to be speaking in poetic code. We meet Dori early in the film, before Mark does, when she has a breakdown onstage and walks away from her band. But the movie doesn't make it clear who she is or what has happened, and we piece it together only later.

Famous as she is, she is also troubled, and Mark's steadfast loyalty and level gaze win her heart. She wouldn't ordinarily date a man from boot camp, even a rich one, but Mark's letters tell her he will stand by her, and she believes him. So do we, after he manages to balance the marines with trips home, springing her at various times from mental institutions and hospitals. These moments of freedom are heady for her, and she enjoys getting out from under her medication too. But her therapist (Diane Venora) solemnly explains to Mark that he is bad for Dori, that she needs her medication, that she can be a danger to herself. One conversation between them is especially well handled.

The point of the movie, I think, is that the marines make Mark into a man, but he takes his newfound self-confidence and discipline and uses it to commit to a lost cause. He doggedly persists in his devotion to Dori because he loves her, yes, but also because her helplessness makes him feel needed, and her illness is a test of his resolve.

Perhaps the movie is based on more of the true story than was absolutely necessary. Toward the end of the film, Mark is part of the marine landing in Lebanon, and returns home gravely wounded. This happens too late in the film for the consequences to be explored, especially in terms of his relationship with Dori. *Stateside* might have been wiser to bring the Mark-Dori story to some kind of a bittersweet conclusion without opening a new chapter that it doesn't ever really close.

The performances are strong, although undermined a little by Anselmo's peculiar style of dialogue, which sometimes sounds more like experimental poetry or song lyrics than like speech. It is also hard to know how to read Dori; we believe the therapist who says she is very ill, but her illness is one of those movie conveniences in which she is somehow usually able to do or say what the screenplay requires. There's also the enigma of Mark's father, played by Mantegna as a remote, angry man who carts an oxygen bottle around with him. We sense there's more Anselmo wants to say about the character than he has time for. *Stateside* plays like urgent ideas for a movie that Anselmo needed to make, but they're still in note form.

The Station Agent ★ ★ ★ ½
R, 88 m., 2003

Peter Dinklage (Finbar McBride), Patricia Clarkson (Olivia Harris), Bobby Cannavale (Joe Oramas), Michelle Williams (Emily), Raven Goodwin (Cleo), Paul Benjamin (Henry Styles). Directed by Thomas McCarthy and produced by Robert May, Mary Jane Skalski, and Kathryn Tucker. Screenplay by McCarthy.

"It's really funny how people see me and treat me, since I'm really just a simple, boring person."

So says Finbar McBride, the hero of *The Station Agent.* Nothing in life interests him more than trains. Model trains, real trains, books about trains. He likes trains. Finbar is a dwarf, and nothing about him interests other people more than his height. It's as if he's always walking in as the next topic of conversation. His response is to live in solitude. This works splendidly as a defense mechanism, but leaves him deeply lonely, not that he'd ever admit it.

Finbar is a character of particular distinction, played by Peter Dinklage as a man who is defiantly himself. Rarely have I seen a movie character more *present* in every scene. He is the immovable object, resisting approaches by strangers, and at first no one can get through his defenses except for a little African-American girl who looks straight at him and is not intimidated and will not be dismissed.

As the movie opens, Finbar is working in a model train store owned by apparently his only friend in the world, Henry Styles (Paul Benjamin). Henry drops dead, and Finbar inherits from him an abandoned train station near a town with the unlikely but real name of New-foundland, New Jersey. Nothing prevents Finbar from moving immediately to New Jersey and living in the station, and so he does, exciting enormous curiosity from Joe Oramas (Bobby Cannavale), who runs a roadside coffee wagon on a road where hardly anyone ever seems to stop for coffee. Joe has unlimited time on his hands, is lonely in a gregarious rather than a reclusive way, and forces himself into Finbar's life with relentless cheerfulness. Cannavale is such an eruption of energy that the two quieter characters almost have to shield themselves from him. There's humor in Finbar's persistent attempts to slam the door on a man who totally lacks the ability to be rejected.

There is a third lonely soul in Newfoundland. She is Olivia Harris (Patricia Clarkson), who is going through a divorce and is in mourning for the death of her child. Olivia is a very bad driver. As Finbar walks to the convenience store one morning, she nearly hits him with her car. At the store, he has to endure posing for a snapshot taken by the clerk. Walking back home, he's nearly hit by her a second time, and takes a tumble into the ditch.

That would be a slapstick scene in another kind of movie, but writer-director Thomas McCarthy is aiming a bit more deeply. Yes, this is a comedy, but it's also sad, and finally it's simply a story about trying to figure out what you love to do and then trying to figure out how to do it. Joe has that part mastered, since the coffee wagon represents a lifestyle so perfect that the only way to improve it would be if, say, a dwarf moved into the train station. Finbar thinks he has life mastered—he thinks all he wants to do is sit in his train station and think about trains—but perhaps there are possibilities of friendship and sex that he has not considered.

Finbar is a handsome man, which does not escape the attention of a local librarian named Emily (Michelle Williams). But she wants him not for his mind, or his trains, but for his body, and he is not interested in satisfying that kind of curiosity. Olivia is a more complex case, since perhaps she sees in the little man her lost child, or perhaps that is only the avenue into what she really sees. It is a great relief in any event that *The Station Agent* is not one of those movies in which the problem is that the characters have not slept with each other and the solution is that they do. It's more about the enormous unrealized fears and angers that throb beneath the surfaces of their lives; Finbar and Olivia could explode in one way or another at any moment, and the hyperactive Joe is capable of anything.

The movie's island of sanity is Cleo (Raven Goodwin), whom you may remember as the young adopted girl in *Lovely and Amazing*. Goodwin, like Dinklage, has a particular and unshakable presence on the screen, and I hope the movies do not misplace her, as they do so many child actors. As she regards Finbar and asks him if he is a midget ("No. A dwarf"), we realize that Finbar hates such questions, but is happy to answer hers, because he understands that Cleo is simply gathering information.

There was a documentary on cable about little people, describing their lives in their own words, and its subtext seemed to be: "Yes, I'm short. Get over it." I remember my face burning with shame early one morning when I was six years old and went with my father to where the circus was setting up. I gawked through a flap in the dining tent at the circus giant, and he scowled and said, "Can't you find anything else to stare at?" and I learned something that I never had to be taught again.

The Station Agent makes it clear that too many people make it all the way to adulthood without manners enough to look at a little person without making a comment. It isn't necessarily a rude comment—it's that any comment at all is rude. In a way, the whole movie builds up to a scene in a bar. A scene that makes it clear why Finbar does not enjoy going to bars. The bar contains a fair number of people so witless and cruel that they must point and laugh, as if Finbar has somehow chosen his height in order to invite their moronic behavior. Finally he climbs up on a table and shouts, "Here I am! Take a look!" And that is the moment you realize there is no good reason why Peter Dinklage could not play Braveheart.

Stealing Harvard ★
PG-13, 82 m., 2002

Jason Lee (John Plummer), Tom Green (Duff), Leslie Mann (Elaine), Dennis Farina (Mr. Warner), Megan Mullally (Patty), John C. McGinley (Detective Charles), Chris Penn (David), Tammy Blanchard (Noreen). Directed by Bruce McCulloch and produced by Susan Cavan. Screenplay by Peter Tolan.

The laugh in *Stealing Harvard* comes early, when we see the name of the company where the hero works. It's a home health-care corporation named Homespital. That made me laugh. It made me smile again when the name turned up later. And on the laugh meter, that's about it. This is as lax and limp a comedy as I've seen in a while, a meander through worn-out material.

Jason Lee, who can be engaging in the right material (like *Chasing Amy* and *Almost Famous*), is bland and disposable here, as John Plummer, a young Homespital executive. The firm is owned by his fiancée's father (Dennis Farina), who subjects John to savage cross-examinations on whether he has slept with his daughter. He lies and says he hasn't. He might be telling the truth if he said he wishes he hadn't, since the fiancée, Elaine (Leslie Mann), inexplicably weeps during sex.

Despite his foray into the middle classes, John has not forgotten his superslut sister Patty (Megan Mullally), who despite a life of untiring promiscuity, has a daughter, Noreen (Tammy Blanchard), who has been accepted by Harvard. Carefully preserved home videos show John promising to help with her tuition, and as it happens Noreen needs $29,000—almost exactly the amount Elaine has insisted John have in the bank before she will marry him.

Crime is obviously the way to raise the money, according to John's best pal, Duff (Tom Green), who suggests a break-in at a house where the safe seems to stand open. The owner is, alas, at home, and there is a painfully unfunny sequence in which he forces John to dress in drag and "spoon" to remind him of his late wife. There's another botched robbery in which John and Duff, wearing ski masks, argue over which one gets to call himself Kyle, and so on.

Seeing Tom Green reminded me, how could it not, of his movie *Freddy Got Fingered* (2001), which was so poorly received by film critics that it received only one lonely, apologetic positive review on the Tomatometer. I gave it—let's see—no stars. Bad movie, especially the scene where Green was whirling the newborn infant around his head by its umbilical cord.

But the thing is, I remember *Freddy Got Fingered* more than a year later. I refer to it sometimes. It is a milestone. And for all its sins it was at least an ambitious movie, a go-for-broke attempt to accomplish something. It failed, but it has not left me convinced that Tom Green doesn't have good work in him. Anyone with his nerve and total lack of taste is sooner or later going to make a movie worth seeing.

Stealing Harvard, on the other hand, is a singularly unambitious product, content to paddle lazily in the shallows of sitcom formula. It has no edge, no hunger to be better than it is. It ambles pleasantly through its inanity, like a guest happy to be at a boring party. When you think of some of the weird stuff Jason Lee and Tom Green have been in over the years, you wonder what they did to amuse themselves during the filming.

The Stepford Wives ★ ★ ★
PG-13, 93 m., 2004

Nicole Kidman (Joanna Eberhart), Matthew Broderick (Walter Kresby), Bette Midler (Bobbie Markowitz), Jon Lovitz (Dave Markowitz), Roger Bart (Roger Bannister), David Marshall Grant (Jerry Harmon), Faith Hill (Sarah Sunderson), Glenn Close (Claire Wellington), Christopher Walken (Mike Wellington). Directed by Frank Oz and produced by Donald De Line, Gabriel Grunfeld, Scott Rudin, and Edgar J. Scherick. Screenplay by Paul Rudnick, based on the book by Ira Levin.

The Stepford Wives depends for some of its effect on a plot secret that you already know, if you've been paying attention at any time since the original film version was released in 1975. If you don't know it, stay away from the trailer, which gives it away. It's an enticing premise, an opening for wicked feminist satire, but the 1975 movie tilted toward horror instead of comedy. Now here's a version that tilts the other way, and I like it a little better.

The experience is like a new production of a well-known play. The original suspense has evaporated, and you focus on the adaptation and acting. Here you can also focus on the new screenplay by Paul Rudnick, which is rich with zingers. Rudnick, having committed one of the worst screenplays of modern times (*Isn't She Great,* the Jacqueline Susann story), redeems himself with barbed one-liners; when one of the community planners says he used to work for AOL, Joanna asks, "Is that why the women are so slow?"

Nicole Kidman stars, as Joanna Eberhart, a high-powered TV executive who is fired after the victim of one of her reality shows goes on a shooting rampage. Her husband, Walter (Matthew Broderick), resigns from the same network, where he worked under her, and moves with his wife and two children to the gated community of Stepford, Connecticut.

It's weird there. The women all seem to be sexy clones of Betty Crocker. Glenn Close is Claire Wellington, the real-estate agent, greeter, and community cheerleader, and she gives Joanna the creeps (she's "flight attendant friendly"). Nobody in Stepford seems to work; they're so rich they don't need to, and the men hang out at the Men's Association while the women attend Claire's exercise sessions. In Stepford, the women dress up and wear heels even for aerobics (no sweaty gym shorts), and Claire leads them in pantomimes of domestic chores ("Let's all be washing machines!").

Walter loves it in Stepford. Joanna hates it. She bonds with Bobbie Markowitz (Bette Midler), author of a best-selling memoir about her mother, *I Love You, But Please Die.* Her house is a pigpen. Every other house in Stepford is spotlessly clean, even though there seem to be no domestic servants; the wives cheerfully do the housework themselves. They also improve themselves by attending Claire's book club. A nice example of Rudnick's wit: When Joanna shares that she has finished volume two of Robert Caro's biography of Lyndon Johnson, Claire takes a beat, smiles bravely, and suggests they read *Christmas Keepsakes* and discuss celebrating Jesus' birthday with yarn.

Christopher Walken is Claire's husband and seems to be running Stepford; it's the kind of creepy role that has Walken written all over it, and he stars in a Stepford promotional film that showcases another one of his unctuous explanations of the bizarre. A new touch this time: Stepford has a gay couple, and Roger (Roger Bart), the "wife," is flamboyant to begin with, until overnight, strangely, he becomes a serious-minded congressional candidate.

What's going on here? You probably know, but I can't tell you. When Ira Levin's original novel was published in 1972, feminism was newer, and his premise satirized the male desire for tame, sexy wives who did what they were told and never complained. Rudnick and director Frank Oz don't do anything radical with the original premise (although they add some post-1972 touches like the Stepford-style ATM machine), but they choose comedy over horror, and it's a wise decision. Kidman plays a character not a million miles away from her husband-killer in *To Die For*, even though this time she's the victim. Bette Midler is defiantly subversive as the town misfit. And Walken is . . . Walken.

The movie is surprisingly short, at 93 minutes including end titles (the 1975 film was 115 minutes long). Maybe it needs to be short. The secret is obvious fairly early (a woman goes berserk and when Walter says she was probably just sick, Joanna says, "Walter, she was sparking!"). It could probably work as a springboard for heavy-duty social satire, but that's not what audiences expect from this material, and Rudnick pushes about as far as he can without tearing the envelope. Some movies are based on short stories, some on novels. *The Stepford Wives* is little more than an anecdote, and like all good storytellers, Oz and Rudnick don't meander on their way to the punch line.　　　　　　　☞

Stevie ★ ★ ★ ½
NO MPAA RATING, 140 m., 2003

A documentary directed by Steve James and produced by James, Adam Singer, and Gordon Quinn.

Stevie is a brave and painful film, the story of a man who goes looking for the youngster he met ten years earlier through the Big Brother program. He finds that the news about him is not good, and will get worse. This is a story involving a family so dysfunctional it seems almost to exist for the purpose of wounding and warping this child, Stephen Fielding. As he was wounded, so he has wounded others. That's often the way it goes. They say that child abusers were almost always abused as children. Stevie could be Exhibit A.

The movie is by Steve James, who directed the great documentary *Hoop Dreams* (1994).

For years people asked him, "Whatever happened to those kids?"—to the two young basketball players he followed from eighth grade to adulthood. James must often have wondered about the kid nobody ever asked about, Stevie. While he was a student at Southern Illinois University, Steve was a Big Brother to Stevie, but he lost touch in 1985 after graduating. Ten years later, he went back downstate to the little town of Pomona, ten or fifteen miles down the road from Carbondale, to seek out Stevie.

That must have taken some courage, and even on his first return James must have suspected that this story would not have a happy ending. But it has so much truth, as it shows an unhappy childhood reaching out through the years and smacking down its adult survivor.

Here are a few facts, for orientation. Stevie Fielding was not wanted. He was born out of wedlock, does not know who his father is, was raised by a mother who didn't want him, was beaten by her. When she did marry, she turned him over to her new husband's mother to raise. He also made a circuit of foster homes and juvenile centers, where he was raped and beaten regularly.

When we meet Stevie again he is twenty-three and not doing well. His tattoos and Harley T-shirt express a bravado he does not possess, and he makes a poor impression with haystack hair, oversized thick glasses, and bad teeth. The most important person in his life is his girlfriend, Tonya Gregory, who on first impression seems slow, but who on longer acquaintance reveals herself to be smart about Stevie, and loyal to him. His stepsister Brenda is also a support, a surrogate mother who seems the best-adjusted member of his family, perhaps because, as her husband tells us, "They didn't beat her."

Stevie freely expresses hatred for his mother, Bernice ("Someday I am going to kill her"), and she is one of the villains of the piece, but having stopped drinking, she feels remorse and even blames herself, to a degree, for Stevie's problems—especially the latest one. Between 1995, when Steve James first revisits Stevie, and 1997, when production proper started on this documentary, Stevie was charged with molesting an eight-year-old girl.

Stevie says he is innocent. Even Tonya thinks

he is guilty. We do not forgive him this crime because of his tragic childhood, but it helps us understand it—even predict it, or something like it. And as he goes through the court system, Tonya stands by him, Brenda helps him as much as she can, and Bernice, his mother, seems slowly to change for the better—to move in the direction she might have taken if it had not been for her own troubles.

There is no sentimentality in *Stevie*, no escape, no release. "The film does not come to a satisfying ending," writes the critic David Poland. He wanted more of a "lift," and so, I suppose, did I—and Steve James. But although *Hoop Dreams* ended in a way that a novelist could not have improved upon, *Stevie* seems destined to end the way it does, and is the more courageous and powerful for it. A satisfying ending would have been a lie. Most of us are blessed with happy families. Around us are others, nursing deep hurts and guilts and secrets—punished as children for the crime of being unable to fight back.

To watch *Stevie* is to wonder if anything could have been done to change the course of this history. Steve James's Big-Brothering was well intentioned, and his wife, a social worker, believes in help from outside. But this extended family seems to form a matrix of pain and abuse that goes around and around in each generation, and mercilessly down through time to the next. To be born into the family is to have a good chance of being doomed, and Brenda's survival is partly because she got out fast, married young, and kept her distance.

Philip Larkin could have been thinking of this family in his most famous poem, whose opening line cannot be quoted here, but which ends:

Man hands on misery to man.
It deepens like a coastal shelf.
Get out as early as you can,
And don't have any kids yourself.

Search the Web using the first two lines, and you will find a poem that Stevie Fielding might agree with.

Stolen Summer ★ ★ ★

PG, 91 m., 2002

Aidan Quinn (Joe O'Malley), Bonnie Hunt (Margaret O'Malley), Adi Stein (Pete O'Malley), Kevin Pollak (Rabbi Jacobsen), Mike Weinberg (Danny Jacobsen), Lisa Dodson (Mrs. Jacobsen), Brian Dennehy (Father Kelly), Eddie Kaye Thomas (Patrick O'Malley), Ryan Kelley (Seamus O'Malley). Directed by Pete Jones and produced by Ben Affleck, Matt Damon, and Chris Moore. Screenplay by Jones.

Gene Siskel proposed an acid test for a movie: Is this film as good as a documentary of the same people having lunch? At last, with *Stolen Summer*, we get a chance to decide for ourselves. The making of the film has been documented in the HBO series *Project Greenlight*, where we saw the actors and filmmakers having lunch, contract disputes, story conferences, personal vendettas, location emergencies, and even glimpses of hope.

Movies are collisions between egos and compromises. With some there are no survivors. *Stolen Summer* is a delightful surprise because despite all the backstage drama, this is a movie that tells stories that work—is charming, is moving, is funny, and looks professional. That last point is crucial, because as everyone knows, director Pete Jones and his screenplay were chosen in a contest sponsored by Miramax and actors Ben Affleck and Matt Damon. Miramax gave them a break with their screenplay *Good Will Hunting*, and they wanted to return the favor.

Stolen Summer takes place on the South Side of Chicago in the summer of 1976, when an earnest second-grader named Pete O'Malley (Adi Stein) listens in Catholic school and believes every word about working his way into heaven. Seeking advice from a slightly older brother about how to guarantee his passage to paradise, Pete is startled to learn that the Jews are not seeking to be saved through Jesus. So Pete sets up a free lemonade stand in front of the local synagogue, hoping to convert some Jews and pay for his passage.

There is already a link between Pete's family and that of Rabbi Jacobsen (Kevin Pollak). Pete's dad, Joe (Aidan Quinn), is a fireman who dashed into a burning home and rescued the Jacobsens' young son Danny (Mike Weinberg), who is about Pete's age. Pete has already met the rabbi and now becomes best friends with his son. Although Danny is not much interested in the theology involved, he joins Pete's "quest" to get them both into the Roman Catholic version of heaven. Is Pete's obsession with church rules and heaven plausible for a second-grader? Having been there, done that, I can state that this was not an unknown stage for Catholic school kids to go through, and that I personally knelt in prayer on behalf of my Protestant playmates, which they found enormously entertaining.

The touchier question of "converting the Jews" is handled by the movie so tactfully that it is impossible not to be charmed. The key performance here is by Kevin Pollak, as a rabbi whose counterpoint to Pete's quest involves understated reaction shots and instinctive sympathy and humor. When the Jacobsens invite Pete over for lunch, he makes the sign of the cross, and when the rabbi asks why he's doing it (the unstated words are "at our table"), Pete explains solemnly, "It's like picking up the phone and being sure God is there." Earlier, during his first visit inside the synagogue, Pete is surprised to find no crucifix hanging from the ceiling, and confides to the rabbi: "Sometimes I think of climbing up and loosening the screws and letting him go."

The movie cuts between Pete's quest, which is admittedly a little cutesy, and the completely convincing marriage of his parents, Joe and Margaret (Bonnie Hunt). These are (I know) actors who grew up in Chicago neighborhoods and were raised (I believe) as Catholics, and they are pitch-perfect. Note the scene where Hunt is driving most of her eight kids to Mass and the troublesome Seamus is making too much noise in the backseat. Still driving, she reaches out to him and beckons him closer, saying, "Come closer . . . come on, come on, I'm not going to hit you," and then smacks him up alongside the head. Every once in a while a movie gives you a moment of absolute truth.

Danny has leukemia, which he explains solemnly to Pete, who is fascinated. Danny's mother is worried about her young son spending so much time with Pete, but the rabbi observes it may be Danny's last chance to act like a normal kid. The "quest" involves such tests as swimming out to a buoy in Lake Michigan, and while we doubt that, even in innocent 1976, second-graders were going to the beach

by themselves, we understand the dramatic purpose.

The most fraught scenes in the movie involve the synagogue's decision to thank the O'Malley family after Joe risked his life to save Danny. They settle on a scholarship for Patrick, the oldest O'Malley boy, and the rabbi is startled when Joe turns it down in anger. Joe tells his wife: "It's about the Jews helping out some poor Roman Catholic family so they can go on TV and get free publicity." Is this anti-Semitism? No, I think it's tribalism, and Joe O'Malley would say the same thing about the Episcopalians, the Buddhists, or the Rotary Club. Bonnie Hunt's response is magnificent: If Joe doesn't let his son accept the scholarship, "So help me God, when you come home at night, the only thing colder than your dinner will be your bed."

Stolen Summer is a film combining broad sentiment with sharp observation, although usually not in the same scenes. I don't know if writer-director Jones came from a large Irish-American family on the South Side, but do I even need to ask? The movie even has Brian Dennehy, patron saint of the Chicago stage, as the parish priest. In a time when so many big-budget mainstream movies are witless and heartless, *Stolen Summer* proves that studios might do just about as well by holding a screenplay contest and filming the winner.

The Stoneraft ★ ★ ★
NO MPAA RATING, 117 m., 2003

Ana Padrão (Joana), Gabino Diego (Jose), Icíar Bollain (Maria), Diogo Infante (Joaquim), Federico Luppi (Pedro). Directed and produced by George Sluizer. Screenplay by Yvette Biro and Sluizer, based on the novel by José Saramago.

Certain unexpected shots send an uneasy shudder through the audience. In *Close Encounters* there was the pickup truck waiting at the train crossing when two headlights appeared in the rear window and then, inexplicably, began to rise vertically. In George Sluizer's new film *The Stoneraft*, a dog trots doggily through a country field, and then for no reason leaps across a patch of ground, and continues on his doggy way. A second later, a crack opens up in the ground right where he jumped. How did the dog know?

The film is a low-key disaster picture, made about characters who are inward, thoughtful, talkative. It's about the Iberian Peninsula breaking loose from Europe and sending Spain and Portugal very quickly out into the Atlantic toward a collision with the Azores.

Like all disaster movies, it follows the larger story through several smaller ones. There are five of them, drawn together finally by the dog. Jose (Gabino Diego) discovers that he is being followed everywhere by a flock of birds. Joana (Ana Padrão) uses a stick to idly trace a line in the earth, and finds she cannot erase the line. Joaquim (Diogo Infante) picks up a heavy stone and heaves it into the sea, only to watch amazed as it skips over the waves like a pebble. Maria (Icíar Bollain) starts to unravel a knitted blue sock that has gone wrong, and discovers that her task is never done: "No matter how long I work, there is still more wool." An older man named Pedro (Federico Luppi) can feel the earth trembling even if no one else can.

These people end up in an increasingly crowded Citroën 2CV, driving toward the collision coast as crowds flee in the opposite direction. Eventually the car breaks down and they switch to a horse cart. Some villages are being looted by mobs; in others, people dance in the streets, for tomorrow they may die.

Television covers the fallout. Britain reasserts its claim to Gibraltar. Americans arrive to try to close the widening rift with cables and earth-moving machinery. Governments resign. No one has an explanation, although many believe the film's five heroes may have had something to do with it.

Sluizer is the same director who made *The Vanishing* (1993), one of the best thrillers ever made, about a man whose wife disappears at a highway rest stop. He later remade it in a Hollywood version that vulgarized his own material. This time, he has reversed the process, taking the tacky American disaster movie and translating it into a quieter and more elegant European version.

It's amusing how few special effects he gets away with. Two entire nations break off from Europe and set sail, and he covers it with a trench in the ground, a flock of birds, a ball of blue wool, and a trained dog. The effect is uncanny and haunting, and I was reminded a little of *On the Beach* (1959), in which the nuclear destruction of the Northern Hemisphere is observed from Australia via low-tech shortwave broadcasts and hearsay reports.

The movie is meant partly as satire; after years of reports about nations breaking away from the EUC, here are two that literally do. There's some social observation: Why does the public assume the man followed by birds represents the cause, not the solution? Much of the story is told at the pace of a leisurely day in the country, as the five characters and the dog muse about the curious turn of events. Is it possible that the small actions of these people could have set into motion the partitioning of subcontinents? After all, doesn't chaos theory teach us that the beating of a butterfly's wings in Asia could theoretically begin a chain of events leading to a hurricane in . . . the Azores, wasn't it?

Stone Reader ★ ★ ★ ½
PG-13, 128 m., 2003

With Carl Brandt, Frank Conroy, Bruce Dobler, Robert C. S. Downs, Robert Ellis, Leslie Fiedler, Ed Gorman, Robert Gottlieb, Dan Guenther, John Kashiwabara, Mark Moskowitz, Dow Mossman, William Cotter Murray, John Seelye. Directed by Mark Moskowitz and produced by Moskowitz and Robert M. Goodman. Screenplay by Moskowitz.

In 1972, a man reads a review of a new novel named *The Stones of Summer* in the *New York Times*. The reviewer believes it is one of the most extraordinary novels of its generation—a masterpiece. The man buys the novel, can't get into it, puts it on the shelf, moves it around with his books for years, and finally reads it. He thinks it's a masterpiece, too. He goes on the Internet to find out what else the author, Dow Mossman, has written. Mossman has written nothing—has disappeared, it would appear, from the face of the Earth.

Stone Reader is the story of the reader's quest for that missing writer. Mark Moskowitz, whose day job is directing political commercials, embarks on a quixotic quest for Dow

Mossman, finds him after much difficulty, and discovers why he has been silent for thirty years, and what he has been up to. It will occur to any attentive viewer of the film that Moskowitz could have found Mossman more quickly and easily than he does—that at times he is stretching out the search for its own sake—but then the movie is not really about Mossman anyway. It is about a reader who goes in search of other readers, and it is a love poem to reading.

It is the kind of movie that makes you want to leave the theater and go directly to a bookstore. Maybe to buy *The Stones of Summer*, which got a new edition in autumn 2003, but also to buy—well, it reawakened my interest in Joseph Heller's *Something Happened*, which has been lost in the shadow of his *Catch-22*, and it observes correctly that Kerouac's *On the Road* is a better novel than a lot of people think it is, and it reminded me of Frederick Exley's *A Fan's Notes*, which has been described as the kind of book that, when you meet someone at a party who has also read it, forces you to seek out a quiet corner to talk urgently about it, with much laughter and shaking of heads.

Moskowitz, who narrates the movie and appears in much more of it than Dow Mossman, is a Woody Allenish character who makes the filming into the subject of the film. At one point, he phones his mother for advice on what he should ask Mossman. (At another, he asks her what sort of kid he was at eighteen, when he first bought the novel, and she remembers: "You had a beard, and you used to like to wear only the linings of coats.") When he encounters a fresh interview subject, he is likely to produce a box jammed with books and stack them up between them, reciting the titles like a litany of touchstones. I do not travel around with boxes of books, but get me in conversation with another reader, and I'll recite titles, too. Have you ever read *Quincunx*? *The Raj Quartet*? *A Fine Balance*? Ever heard of that most despairing of all travel books, *The Saddest Pleasure*, by Moritz Thomsen? Does anybody hold up better than Joseph Conrad and Willa Cather? Know any Yeats by heart? Surely P. G. Wodehouse is as great at what he does as Shakespeare was at what he did.

Shakespeare, as it turns out, has been one of Dow Mossman's companions during his missing years. Without telling you very much about where he is now or why he didn't write another novel or what his work has been since 1972, I can nevertheless evoke his presence as a person you would very much like to talk books with. He turns out not to be a tragic recluse, a sad alcoholic, or a depressive, but a man filled with words and good cheer. When he came to my Overlooked Film Festival, where the film played in April, he and the French director Bertrand Tavernier seemed always to be in a corner together, trading enthusiasm about books.

Mark Twain is one of his heroes, and he can cite the chapter of Twain's autobiography that you must read. He is awestruck by Casanova's memoirs. He hated *Shakespeare in Love* because of those scenes where Shakespeare crumpled up a page of foolscap in frustration and threw it away: Paper was too expensive to throw away in those days, Mossman observes, and he is convinced Shakespeare created his plays in his mind while walking around London, and then taught them to his players. Since many of the plays show evidence of being based on actors' prompt copies and scholars can sometimes identify the actor-source who may have been more familiar with some scenes than others, he may be right.

Doesn't matter. What matters is listening to him talk about books with Moskowitz. In the scene where Moskowitz first encounters him, they are soon talking about Shakespeare, not Mossman. Here, we feel, is a man who should appear regularly on National Public Radio, just talking about books he loves.

Before he finds Mossman, Moskowitz interviews several men of letters (no women). Some of them, he hopes, might remember *The Stones of Summer*—such as Robert Gottlieb, the famous editor, or John Kashiwabara, who designed the book cover, or Frank Conroy, who was Mossman's adviser at the University of Iowa. John Seelye, who wrote the original review for the *New York Times*, remembers the book. The late Leslie Fiedler, a towering literary critic, has never heard of it — but Moskowitz interviews him anyway, about the phenomenon of one-book novelists. (Some writers who write many books, like Kerouac, Salinger, Malcolm Lowry, and James T. Farrell, are nevertheless really one-book novelists, they decide.)

Stone Reader is a meandering documentary,

frustrating when Moskowitz has Mossman in his sights and *still* delays bagging him while talking to other sources. But at the end, we forgive his procrastination (and remember, with Laurence Sterne and *Tristam Shandy,* that procrastination can be an art if it is done delightfully). Moskowitz has made a wonderful film about readers and reading, writers and writing. Now somebody needs to go to Cedar Rapids and make a whole documentary about Dow Mossman. Call it *The Stone Writer.*

The Story of the Weeping Camel ★ ★ ★
PG, 90 m., 2004

Janchiv Ayurzana (Janchiv [Great Grandfather]), Chimed Ohin (Chimed [Great Grandmother]), Amgaabazar Gonson (Amgaa [Grandfather]), Zeveljamz Nyam (Zevel [Grandmother]), Ikhbayar Amgaabazar (Ikchee [Father]), Odgerel Ayusch (Odgoo [Mother]), Enkhbulgan Ikhbayar (Dude [Older Brother]), Uuganbaatar Ikhbayar (Ugna [Younger Brother]), Guntbaatar Ikhbayar (Guntee [Baby Brother]), Ingen Temee (Mother Camel), Botok (Baby Camel). Directed by Byambasuren Davaa and Luigi Falorni and produced by Tobias Siebert. Screenplay by Davaa and Falorni.

On the edges of the Gobi Desert live to this day nomadic herders who travel with their animals and exist within an ancient economy that requires no money. *The Story of the Weeping Camel,* which despite its title is a joyous movie, tells the story of one of those families, and of their camel, which gives birth to a rare white calf and refuses to nurse it. It is a terrible thing to hear the cry of a baby camel rejected by its mother.

The movie has been made in the same way that Robert Flaherty made such documentaries as *Nanook of the North, Man of Aran,* and *Louisiana Story.* It uses real people in real places, and essentially has them play themselves in a story inspired by their lives. That makes it a "narrative documentary," according to the filmmakers. A great many documentaries are closer to this model than their makers will admit; even *cinema verité* must pick and choose from the available footage and reflect a point of view.

We meet four generations of the same family. Do not think of them as primitive; it takes

great wisdom to survive in their manner. I learn from the press materials that the older brother, Dude (Enkhbulgan Ikhbayar), went away to boarding school but then returned to his family because he enjoyed the way of life. Certainly these people live close to the land and to their animals, and their yurts are masterpieces of construction—sturdy, portable homes that can be carried on the back of a camel, but are sturdy enough to withstand winter storms.

It is spring when the movie begins, and a mother camel (Ingen Temee) has just given painful birth to her white calf (Botok). It is only reasonable to supply the names of these animals, since they are so much a part of their nomad families. Does the mother refuse her milk because the calf looks strange to her, or because of her birth agony? No matter; unless the calf is fed, it will die, and the family needs it.

When bottle-feeding fails, Dude and his younger brother Ugna (Uuganbaatar Ikhbayar) travel by camel some fifty kilometers to the nearest town to bring back a musician who will play a traditional song to the camel and perhaps persuade it to relent. While in the village, they watch television and brush against other artifacts of modern life with curiosity, but without need.

The musician accompanies them to the village. He plays the traditional song. Legend has it that if a camel finally agrees to nurse her young, this will cause her to weep. There are also a few damp eyes among members of the family. All of this is told in a narrative that is not a cute true-life animal tale, but an observant and respectful record of the daily rhythms and patterns of these lives. We sense the dynamics among the generations, how age is valued and youth is cherished, how the lives of these people make sense to them in a way that ours never will, because they know why they do what they do, and what will come of it. The causes and effects of their survival are visible, and they are responsible.

The filmmakers are Byambasuren Davaa and Luigi Falorni. They cowrote and directed; he photographed. They met at the Munich Film School, where she told him that her grandparents had been herders. Their film was shot on location in about a month, and has an authenticity in its very bones. In a commercial movie, sentiment would rule, and we would feel sorry for the cute baby camel. Well, yes, we feel sorry for the calf in *The Story of the Weeping Camel,* but we also understand that the camel represents wealth and survival for its owners, and in what they do, they're thinking, as they should, more about themselves than about the camel.

I believe this film would be fascinating for smart children, maybe the same ones who liked *Whale Rider,* because so much of it is told through the eyes of the younger brother. Although the desert society is alien to everything we know, in another way it is instantly understandable, because we know about parents and grandparents, about working to put food on the table, about the need of babies to nurse. Here is a film that is about life itself, and about those few humans who still engage it at first hand.

Note: Two other splendid documentaries cover similar ground. Taiga *(1995), the remarkable eight-hour documentary by Ulrike Ottinger, lives and travels with nomads for a year, and witnesses their private lives and religious ceremonies.* Genghis Blues *is the wonderful 1999 documentary about a blind San Francisco blues singer who hears Tuvan throat singing on the radio, teaches himself that difficult art, and journeys to Tuva, which is between Mongolia and Siberia, to enter a throat-singing contest.*

Storytelling ★ ★ ★ ½
R, 87 m., 2002

Fiction
Selma Blair (Vi), Leo Fitzpatrick (Marcus), Robert Wisdom (Mr. Scott).
Nonfiction
Mark Webber (Scooby), John Goodman (Marty), Julie Hagerty (Fern), Jonathan Osser (Mikey), Noah Fleiss (Brady), Lupe Ontiveros (Consuelo), Paul Giamatti (Toby). Directed by Todd Solondz and produced by Ted Hope and Christine Vachon. Screenpaly by Solondz.

For some artists, especially younger ones, the creative impulse is linked directly to the genitals: They create because they hope it makes them sexually attractive. This is a truth so obvious it is rarely mentioned in creative writing circles, although writers as various as Philip Roth, Thomas Wolfe, and Martin Amis have built their careers on it. *Storytelling,* the in-your-face new film by Todd Solondz, is a confessional in which Solondz explores his own methods and motives, and tries to come clean.

The movie contains two stories. The first, *Fiction,* is about a college creative writing student (Selma Blair) whose boyfriend (Leo Fitzpatrick) has cerebral palsy. "You wanna hear my short story now?" he asks her immediately after sex, and it is clear he is trading on sex as a way to win an audience. Although he is the "cripple," that gives him an advantage in her politically correct cosmos, and he milks it. Later, when they've broken up, he observes sadly, "The kinkiness has gone. You've become kind."

She moves on to a one-night stand with her writing professor (Robert Wisdom), a forbidding black man whose tastes run toward rough rape fantasies. She goes looking for trouble, but finds she doesn't like it, and writes a tearful, defiant story about their encounter. When the other students tear it to shreds, she weeps, "But it's the truth!"

All three of these characters are using the pose of "writer" as a way to get sex, get their work read, or both, sometimes at the same time. *Nonfiction,* the longer second section of the film, opens with a would-be documentary filmmaker named Toby (Paul Giamatti) looking at the high school yearbook photo of a girl he now remembers yearningly. Calling her, he finds she is married and has a family, and immediately decides he is making a documentary about an American family and needs hers.

This family, the Livingstons, is Jewish, lives in the suburbs, and is a seething zone of resentment and rage. The father (John Goodman) presides over the dinner table like an enforcer; the mother (Julie Hagerty) is a twittering mass of reconciliation. Scooby (Mark Webber), the oldest son, smokes pot, is sullen, hides in his room. Brady (Noah Fleiss), the middle son, plays football and speculates that Scooby is a "homo." Mikey (Jonathan Osser), the youngest son, has earnest conversations with the El Salvadoran maid, Consuelo (Lupe Ontiveros). She hates the family and her job. Mikey wants to be nice to her but is clueless ("But Consuelo, even though you're poor, don't you have any hobbies or interests or anything?"). When he finds her weeping because her son has been executed for murder, he expresses polite regret before asking her to clean up some grape juice he has spilled. Later, he hypnotizes his father and instructs him to fire her.

Dinner conversation at the Livingstons' is fraught with hazards. When the Holocaust comes up, it is Scooby who observes that since it forced an ancestor to escape to America, "If it wasn't for Hitler, none of us would ever have been born." This gets him immediately banished from the table, a fate that hangs over every meal as the father angrily monitors the conversation.

Alert readers will have noticed that *Storytelling* seems to be working from a list of sensitive or taboo subjects: physical disability, race, rape, facile charges of racism, exploitation of the poor, the Holocaust, homosexuality. I will not reveal the identity of the character who goes into a coma and is apparently braindead; I will observe that this development cheers the editor of Toby's documentary, who tells him it's just what his film needs.

One character does attack Toby's documentary, telling him it's "glib and facile to make fun of these people." "I'm not making fun of them," Toby says. "I love them." Toby, of course, represents Solondz, whose two previous films *(Welcome to the Dollhouse* and *Happiness)* were attacked for making glib and facile fun of the characters. So has this one; Ed Gonzalez of *Slant* refers to Solondz's "cowardly apologias." In a Solondz film there's always a delicate line to be walked between social satire on the one hand and a geek show on the other.

I think Solondz is not cowardly but brave, and does his bourgeois-mugging in full view, instead of concealing it. We live in a time when many comedies mock middle-class American suburban life, but Solondz is one director who does it out in the open, to extremes, pushing the envelope, challenging us to decide what we think. And because his timing is so precise and his ear for dialogue so good, he sometimes tricks us into laughing before we have time to think, gee, we shouldn't be laughing at that.

I saw *Storytelling* at Cannes 2001 and wrote that I wanted to see it again before deciding what I thought about it. I saw it again, and still felt I had to see it again. I saw it a third time. By then I had moved beyond the immediate shock of the material and was able to focus on what a well-made film it was; how concisely Solondz gets the effects he's after.

I was also forced to conclude that I might *never* know for sure what I thought about it— that it was a puzzle without an answer, a demonstration that there are some areas so fraught and sensitive that most people just hurry past them with their eyes averted. By not averting his eyes, Solondz forces us to consider the unthinkable, the unacceptable, the unmentionable. He should not be penalized for going further than the filmmakers who attack the same targets but have better manners—or less nerve.

Note: During the sex scene between the professor and his student, a bright red quadrangle obscures part of the screen. When I saw the movie at Cannes, the audience could see the two characters—graphically, but not in explicit pornographic detail. The MPAA refused to give the film an R rating because of that scene. Solondz refused to cut it, and used the red blocking as a way of underlining the MPAA's censorship. Good for him. And one more reminder that the MPAA and Jack Valenti oppose a workable adult rating for America.

Strayed ★ ★ ★

NO MPAA RATING, 95 m., 2004

Emmanuelle Béart (Odile), Gaspard Ulliel (Yvan), Grégoire Leprince-Ringuet (Philippe), Clémence Meyer (Cathy), Jean Fornerod (Georges), Samuel Labarthe (Robert). Directed by André Téchiné and produced by Jean-Pierre Ramsay-Levi. Screenplay by Gilles Taurand and Téchiné, based on the novel *The Boy with Gray Eyes* by Gilles Perrault.

Who is this Yvan, this boy with the shaved head who has crawled out of the mud to lead them to safety? And why should she trust him? Odile (Emmanuelle Béart) is a bourgeois Parisian woman with two children and no way to protect them, and Yvan (Gaspard Ulliel) has a toughness that is reassuring and at the same time menacing. She really has no choice but to follow him into the forest, after Nazi planes have strafed and bombed the column of refugees streaming south from Paris.

It is 1940, and all of the certainties of Odile's life have evaporated. She is a pretty widow in her late thirties, a teacher, who fled Paris and joined the flight from the Germans with her thirteen-year-old son, Philippe, and her daughter, Cathy, who is seven. Her children trust her, but she doesn't trust herself, because her experience and values are irrelevant in this sudden war. "It's every man for himself," someone shouts on the road, not originally but cogently, as bullets kill some and spare others.

Yvan is tough and sure of himself, and her instincts as a teacher tell her he is dangerous. The teenager Philippe is frightened but more realistic; he believes they need this strange young man. Yvan has a sweet side, and seems to want to help them; there is perhaps even the suggestion that he needs this family to replace one he lost, and he needs this chance to be helpful and competent. Or perhaps the fact that Philippe secretly bribed him with his father's watch convinced him to stay; we never know for sure what he's thinking.

Strayed begins and ends with facts of war, but it is really a film about the nature of male and female, about middle-class values and those who cannot afford them, about how helpless we can be when the net of society is broken. The French director André Téchiné, no sentimentalist, creates a separate world for his four characters, and the war goes on elsewhere.

Separated from the other refugees, they walk through a forest of such beauty that war seems impossible, and they sleep under the stars. The next day, they come upon a country home, comfortable, isolated, and tempting. The owners have fled. Yvan believes they should break in and stay there for a while; the roads are mobbed, there is no sure safety in the south, and no one will look for them here. Odile argues that the house is private property. Her bourgeois instincts are so strong that she would sleep with her children in the woods, or try to rejoin the exodus, rather than break in. For Yvan, there is no choice: They must survive.

We realize that the war is very new to her, that she clings to the certainties of her ordered life and must learn that the rules have changed. They break in, of course. There is a wine cellar, many bedrooms, some food. Yvan hunts for game. Odile establishes a domestic routine. They could almost be on holiday, the children vibrating with the sense of adventure, Odile putting good French food on the table, and

Yvan . . . Yvan . . . enjoying it too, but on guard, and always aware of their danger. Their danger and, we sense, his own.

When you put a beautiful woman and a forceful young man in an isolated situation where they must live closely together, sexual tension coils under the surface. At first it is not obvious, because Odile's bourgeois certainties make it impossible that she could sleep with a rough working-class stranger twenty years younger. And there are the children, although Philippe admires Yvan: Here is an older brother, or perhaps a father figure, who can protect them when his own father has failed.

There are certain mysteries, which I will not reveal, involving secrets Odile keeps from Yvan and those he keeps from her, and certain questions about how long they should stay in the house—questions that seem to depend, in Yvan's mind, on more than the simple matter of survival. There are things Philippe observes and keeps to himself. And always there is the knowledge between Odile and Yvan that they could sleep together, that the nature of their relationship is shifting, that the war has changed the rules and that Yvan has become necessary to her family.

We sense the story will not end here, and we know this temporary family cannot live in this house forever, with time suspended. We are not sure how near a town might be, and Odile wonders why the telephone doesn't work. Someone will find them, and what will happen then? Those questions occur to us as they occur to the characters, adding an urgency, an unreality, as the days pass comfortably. Téchiné, a master of buried power struggles, increases the level of uncertainty and apprehension until we know something must happen, and then something does, and the essential natures of Yvan and Odile, and their way their society formed them, becomes clear.

Stuart Little 2 ★ ★ ★
PG, 78 m., 2002

Geena Davis (Eleanor Little), Hugh Laurie (Fredrick Little), Jonathan Lipnicki (George Little). And the voices of: Michael J. Fox (Stuart Little), Nathan Lane (Snowbell), Melanie Griffith (Margalo), James Woods (Falcon). Directed by Rob Minkoff and produced by Lucy

Fisher and Douglas Wick. Screenplay by Bruce Joel Rubin and Wick, based on characters from the book *Stuart Little* by E. B. White.

Faithful readers will know that I question the logic of a human-size family with a son who is two inches tall, particularly when the son is a mouse. In watching the first *Stuart Little* (1999), I cringed every time the heavy footfall of one of his parents landed near little Stuart. The mouse is cute, but he was born to be squished.

I vowed to approach *Stuart Little 2* afresh. I would go into full-blown suspension-of-disbelief mode. If there must be a movie about a mouse-child in the real world, then I must accept it—even if the film toys with my fears by putting Stuart into a soccer game with full-size kids. Even Stuart's mom (Geena Davis) gets the shivers at "the thought of all those boys running around with those cleats in their shoes."

Stuart's dad (Hugh Laurie) is more optimistic, believing that a Little can do anything he sets his mind to, and sending the little tyke on dangerous missions, as when he is lowered down the kitchen drain to look for his mother's diamond ring. For that matter, Stuart's daily commute to school in his tiny little red sports car must not be without its hazards.

Stuart Little 2 is not indifferent to the problems involved, not least the compositional problems faced by Steve Poster, its cinematographer, in framing both the six-foot Davis and the two-inch Stuart in the same shot. It provides Stuart (voice by Michael J. Fox) with a friend about his own size, a yellow bird named Margalo (voice by Melanie Griffith). She falls from the sky with a wounded wing, lands in Stuart's sports car, is taken home for first aid, and soon becomes his chum.

There is even a hint of cross-species romance, as Stuart and Margalo go on a date to the drive-in movies (by parking his red sportster in front of the TV). The movie they're watching is Hitchcock's *Vertigo*, about a man who falls in love with a woman who is deceiving him, but Stuart doesn't take the hint, and is blindsided when it turns out (spoiler warning) that Margalo is a con artist, teamed up with a snarky falcon (voice by James Woods). The falcon's advice: "Don't ever make a friend I can eat."

By this point the movie has located itself pretty much two inches above ground level, although there are important roles for the family cat, Snowbell (voice by Nathan Lane), and the family son, George (Jonathan Lipnicki). There's an exciting sequence involving entrapment in a skyscraper, entombment in a garbage barge, and an aerial dogfight between the falcon and Stuart, piloting a model airplane.

Yes, reader, I enjoyed the movie, in its innocent way. It has some of the same charm, if not the same genius, as the movies about Babe the pig. The film imagines Manhattan as a sunny, peaceful place where no one is surprised to see a mouse driving a car, and where the parents are so optimistic that when Stuart goes missing they drive around looking for him—as if you could see a two-inch mouse from the middle of New York traffic.

Of the voices, Melanie Griffith makes Margalo lovable and as sexy as a little yellow bird can be, and Nathan Lane does a virtuoso job with Snowbell, the only cat with dialogue by Damon Runyon. Michael J. Fox's Stuart is stalwart and heroic—the Braveheart of mice. As for the parents, Geena Davis and Hugh Laurie deserve some kind of award for keeping straight faces. My only question involves the sweet scene at the end, when Margalo bids them farewell to join the southward migration of geese in the autumn. I think there is a good chance she is a canary, and they don't migrate.

Stuck on You ★ ★ ★
PG-13, 118 m., 2003

Matt Damon (Bob), Greg Kinnear (Walt), Cher (Herself), Eva Mendes (April), Seymour Cassel (Morty), Wen Yann Shih (May), Ray "Rocket" Valliere (Rocket), Jay Leno (Himself), Jack Nicholson (Himself), Meryl Streep (Herself), Griffin Dunne (Himself). Directed by Bobby Farrelly and Peter Farrelly and produced by Bobby Farrelly, Peter Farrelly, Bradley Thomas, and Charles B. Wessler. Screenplay by Bobby Farrelly and Peter Farrelly.

Bob and Walter are joined at the hip, and they like it that way. Their life has become a double act, and they're so efficient behind the counter of their diner in Martha's Vineyard that customers get a free burger if they have to wait more than three minutes. There are, of course, difficulties involved with being conjoined twins, but they're amiable souls and have learned to accommodate each other. Bob (Matt Damon) would happily stay on the island for a lifetime, but Walt (Greg Kinnear) is restless and has ambitions; he wants to be an actor. This has already led to an annual crisis involving the local amateur production; as Walt acts, Bob battles stage fright.

Stuck on You is the new movie by the Farrelly brothers, who have earlier dealt with schizophrenics *(Me, Myself and Irene)*, fat people *(Shallow Hal)*, a one-handed bowler *(Kingpin)*, stupidity *(Dumb and Dumber)*, and hair gel *(There's Something About Mary)*. Their next film, *The Ringer*, will be about an imposter who tries to crash the Special Olympics. The subjects of their comedies are defiantly non-P.C., but their hearts are in the right place, and it's refreshing to see a movie that doesn't dissolve with embarrassment in the face of handicaps.

Walter and Bob are a case study of how to live happily while bonded for life to another person. An operation to separate them would be risky, because their shared liver is mostly on Bob's side, and Walt's chances of survival would only be 50-50. Thus, when Walt determines that he must go to Hollywood to try his fortunes as an actor, Bob is a good sport and sadly says good-bye to the gang at the burger bar.

Up until now they have done everything together, including sports; being conjoined is an advantage in baseball, where the twins stand on the mound, one staring down the hitter while the other catches a runner off base. But in Hollywood life changes, because Walt has an immediate stroke of good luck in his career, while Bob is reduced, literally, to a bystander.

Walt's break comes through a lucky meeting with Cher, who is auditioning for a new TV series she hates and wants to get out of. She thinks maybe a conjoined twin would be the ideal costar to sink the ratings. Some of the movie's funniest scenes involve Walt acting with Cher while Bob stands behind scenery or is removed by special effects—but when the press discovers that Cher's costar is a still-joined twin, the ratings go through the roof.

Meanwhile, romance beckons. Bob has been flirting with an online Los Angeles pen pal for three years, but when he meets May (Wen Yann Shih), he's too shy to reveal his condition; keeping the secret involves contortions, evasions,

and misunderstandings, mostly based on the fact that Walt always seems to be right there at Bob's side. Walt, meanwhile, strikes up a friendship with a poolside babe at their motel. She's April (Eva Mendes), a dumb brunette who interprets everything in southern California terms; seeing the bridge of flesh that joins the brothers at the hip, she casually asks them, "So—where'd you get this done?" Mendes adds this role of broad comedy to her dramatic work as Denzel Washington's wife in *Out of Time* and an action role in *2 Fast 2 Furious*, showing herself at home across a range of genres.

The movie's showbiz milieu is much helped by the appearance of famous stars in cameo roles. Jack Nicholson turns up briefly, Jay Leno interviews both twins at once, Cher pokes fun at her own image, Griffin Dunne is the self-important director of her TV show, and Meryl Streep is the very definition of a good sport in a surprise appearance late in the film.

Many of the characters are challenged minorities in one way or another, including Morty (Seymour Cassel), who lives in a retirement home, uses a scooter to get around, but still chain smokes cigars and considers himself a full-service agent. There's a scene where the brothers reduce his fee by pointing out he will, after all, be representing only one of them.

The movie is funny, but also kindhearted. Much screen time is given to Rocket (Ray "Rocket" Valliere), a waiter in the burger joint. He's a mentally challenged friend of the Farrellys, who makes it clear here why they like him. Their approach to handicaps is open and natural, and refreshing compared to the anguished, guilt-laden treatment usually given to handicapped characters in movies. The fact that Walt hopes to be a movie star is less amazing, really, than that the Farrellys had the nerve to make a comedy about it.

The Sum of All Fears ★ ★ ★ ½
PG-13, 127 m., 2002

Ben Affleck (Jack Ryan), Morgan Freeman (Bill Cabot), James Cromwell (President Fowler), Liev Schreiber (John Clark), Alan Bates (Richard Dressler), Philip Baker Hall (Defense Secretary Becker), Bruce McGill (Security Adviser Revel), Jamie Harrold (Dillon), Ciaran Hinds (President Nemerov), Bridget Moynahan (Cathy Muller).

Directed by Phil Alden Robinson and produced by Mace Neufeld. Screenplay by Paul Attanasio and Daniel Pyne, based on the novel by Tom Clancy.

Oh, for the innocent days when a movie like *The Sum of All Fears* could be enjoyed as a "thriller." In these dark times it is not a thriller but a confirmer, confirming our fears that the world is headed for disaster. The film is about the detonation of a nuclear device in an American city. No less an authority than Warren Buffett recently gave a speech in which he flatly stated that such an event was "inevitable." Movies like *Black Sunday* could exorcise our fears, but this one works instead to give them form.

To be sure, Tom Clancy's horrifying vision has been footnoted with the obligatory Hollywood happy ending, in which world war is averted and an attractive young couple pledge love while sitting on a blanket in the sunshine on the White House lawn. We can walk out smiling, unless we remember that much of Baltimore is radioactive rubble. Human nature is a wonderful thing. The reason the ending is happy is because we in the audience assume we'll be the two on the blanket, not the countless who've been vaporized.

The movie is based on another of Tom Clancy's fearfully factual stories about Jack Ryan, the CIA agent, this time a good deal younger than Harrison Ford's Ryan in *A Clear and Present Danger,* and played by Ben Affleck. It follows the ancient convention in which the hero goes everywhere important and personally performs most of the crucial actions, but it feels less contrived because Clancy has expertise about warfare and national security issues; the plot is a device to get us from one packet of information to another.

The story: In 1973, an Israeli airplane carrying a nuclear bomb crashes in Syria. Many years later, the unexploded bomb is dug up, goes on the black market, and is sold to a right-wing fanatic who has a theory: "Hitler was stupid. He fought America and Russia, instead of letting them fight one another." The fanatic's plan is to start a nuclear exchange between the superpowers, after which Aryan fascists would pick up the pieces.

The use of the neo-Nazis is politically cor-rect: Best to invent villains who won't offend any audiences. This movie can play in Syria, Saudi Arabia, and Iraq without getting walk-outs. It's more likely that if a bomb ever does go off in a big city, the perpetrators will be True Believers whose certainty about the next world gives them, they think, the right to kill us in this one.

In the film, Ryan becomes a sort of unofficial protégé of Bill Cabot (Morgan Freeman), a high-level CIA official and good guy who maintains a "back channel" into the Kremlin to avoid just such misunderstandings as occur. Ryan and Cabot fly to Moscow when a new president assumes power, and the new Soviet leader (Ciaran Hinds) is shown as a reasonable man who must take unreasonable actions (like invading Chechnya) to placate the mili-tarists in his government.

America is being run by President Fowler (tall, Lincolnesque James Cromwell), who is surrounded by advisers cast with some of the most convincing character actors in the movies: Philip Baker Hall, Alan Bates, Bruce McGill, etc. Crucial scenes take place aboard *Air Force One* after Baltimore has been bombed, and we see the president and his cab-inet not in cool analytical discussions but all shouting at once. Somehow I am reassured by the notion that our leaders might be really upset at such a time; anyone who can be dis-passionate about nuclear war is probably able to countenance one.

There are some frightening special effects in the movie, which I will not describe, be-cause their unexpected appearance has such an effect. There are also several parallel story lines, including one involving a particularly skilled dirty-tricks specialist named John Clark (Liev Schreiber) who I am glad to have on our side. There are also the usual frustrations in which the man with the truth can't get through because of bureaucracy.

Against these strengths are some weaknesses. I think Jack Ryan's one-man actions in post-bomb Baltimore are unlikely and way too well-timed. I doubt he would find evildoers still hanging around the scene of their crime. I am not sure all of the threads—identifying the plu-tonium, finding the shipping manifest and in-voice, tracking down the guy who dug up the bomb—could take place with such gratifying precision. And I smile wearily at the necessity of supplying Jack with a girlfriend (Bridget Moynahan), who exists only so that she can (1) be impatient when he is called away from dates on official business; (2) disbelieve his alibis; (3) be heroic; (4) be worried about him; (5) be smudged with blood and dirt; and (6) populate the happy ending. We are so aware of the character's function that we can hardly believe her as a person.

These details are not fatal to the film. Director Phil Alden Robinson and his writers, Paul Attanasio and Daniel Pyne, do a spellbinding job of cranking up the tension; they create a portrait of convincing realism, and then they add the other stuff because, well, if anybody ever makes a movie like this without the obligatory Hollywood softeners, audiences might flee the theater in despair. My own fear is that in the postapocalyptic future, *The Sum of All Fears* will be seen as touchingly optimistic.

Sunshine State ★ ★ ★ ½
PG-13, 141 m., 2002

Edie Falco (Marly Temple), Angela Bassett (Desiree Perry), Jane Alexander (Delia Temple), Ralph Waite (Furman Temple), James McDaniel (Reggie Perry), Timothy Hutton (Jack Meadows), Mary Alice (Eunice Stokes), Bill Cobbs (Dr. Lloyd), Mary Steenburgen (Francine Pickney), Tom Wright (Flash Phillips), Alan King (Murray Silver). Directed by John Sayles and produced by Maggie Renzi. Screenplay by Sayles.

John Sayles's *Sunshine State* looks at first like the story of clashes between social and economic groups: between developers and small landowners, between black and white, between the powerful and their workers, between the Chamber of Commerce and local reality. It's set on a Florida resort island, long stuck in its ways, that has been targeted by a big development company. But this is not quite the story the setup seems to predict.

If the movie had been made twenty or thirty years ago, the whites would have been racists, the blacks victims, and the little businessmen would have struggled courageously to hold out against the developers. But things do change in our country, sometimes slowly for the better,

and *Sunshine State* is set at a point in time when all of the players are a little more reconciled, a little less predictable, than they would have been. You can only defend a position so long before the needs of your own life begin to assert themselves.

The island, named Plantation Island, consists of Delrona Beach, a small community of retirees and retail stores, and Lincoln Beach, an enclave of prosperous African-Americans. Both groups have been targeted by a big land development company probably owned by a white-haired golfer named Murray Silver (Alan King), although he exists so far above the world of the little people that it's hard to be sure. The company wants to buy up everything and turn it into a high-rise "beach resort community."

That would doom the Sea-Vue Motel and restaurant, which is run by Marly Temple (Edie Falco, of *The Sopranos*). The motel was built by her parents, Furman and Delia (Ralph Waite and Jane Alexander), and is Furman's life work. But it is not Edie's dream. In a movie made twenty years ago, she would be fighting against the capitalist invaders, but, frankly, she *wants* to sell—and she even begins a little romance with Jack (Timothy Hutton), the architect sent in to size things up.

Over on the Lincoln Beach side, Eunice Stokes (Mary Alice) lives in her tidy white house with a sea view. When she bought this house, it represented a substantial dream for an ambitious black couple; today, it looks a little forlorn. For the first time in years, her daughter Desiree (Angela Bassett) has come to visit. Desiree got pregnant at fifteen with the Florida Flash (Tom Wright), a football hero, and was sent away because Eunice was too proud of her middle-class respectability to risk scandal. Desiree has prospered on TV in Boston and returns with an anesthetist husband.

The Florida Flash, meanwhile, has not prospered. He had an injury on his way to the Heisman Trophy and now sells used cars. Success seems to go wrong on this island; while Francine (Mary Steenburgen), the bubbly Chamber of Commerce pageant chairman, narrates a story of pirates and treasure, her husband tries to kill himself, although neither hanging nor a nail gun does the trick. He's got business difficulties.

Because we are so familiar with the conventional approach to a story like this, it takes time to catch on that Sayles is not repeating the old progressive line about the little guy against big capital. He has made a more observant, elegiac, sad movie, about how the dreams of the parents are not the dreams of the children.

Because Furman wanted a motel, Marly has to work long hours to run it. Because Eunice wanted respectability, Desiree had to run away from home. Because the Chamber of Commerce wants a pageant about "local history," Francine has to concoct one. (The island's real history mostly involves "mass murder, rape, and slavery," she observes, so they'll "Disney-fy it a little bit.") Even the outside predators are not so bad. Timothy Hutton, as the architect, is not typecast as an uncaring pencil pusher who wants to bulldoze the beach, but as a wage earner who moves from one job to another, living in motels, without a family, always on assignment.

Sayles pulls another surprise. His characters are not unyielding. Consider the scene where Marly tells her father she's had it with the motel. Consider the scene where her mother, an Audubon Society stalwart, observes that there might be an angle in selling birdlands and giving the money to the society. Consider Eunice's need to reconsider her daughter's needs and behavior. Look at the daughter's difficulty in reconciling memories of the Florida Flash with the car salesman she sees before her. And consider how at the end of the film, fate and history turn out to play a greater role than any of the great plans.

Sayles's film moves among a large population of characters with grace, humor, and a forgiving irony. The performances by Angela Bassett, Edie Falco, and Mary Alice are at the heart of the story, and there are moments when other characters can illuminate themselves with one flash of dialogue, as Ralph Waite does one day in considering the future of the motel. Some of the characters seem to have drifted in from Altman Land, especially Mary Steenburgen's, whose narration of the pageant is a wildly irrelevant counterpoint to the island's reality. Others, like Tim Hutton's sad architect, seem to have much more power than they do. And what about Alan King and his golfing buddies? They show that if you have enough money and power, you don't need to get your hands dirty making more (others will do that for you), and you can be genial and philosophical—a sweet, colorful character, subsidized by the unhappiness of others.

Sunshine State is not a radical attack on racism and big business, not a defense of the environment, not a hymn in favor of small communities over conglomerates. It is about the next generation of those issues and the people they involve. Racism has faded to the point where Eunice's proud home on Lincoln Beach no longer makes the same statement. Big business is not monolithic but bumbling. The little motel is an eyesore. The young people who got out, like Desiree, have prospered. Those who stayed, like Marly, have been trapped. And the last scene of the film tells us, I think, that we should hesitate to embrace the future in this nation until we have sufficiently considered the past.

Super Size Me ★ ★ ★
NO MPAA RATING, 96 m., 2004

A documentary directed by Morgan Spurlock and produced by Spurlock. With Dr. Daryl Isaacs, Ronald McDonald, and Dr. Lisa Ganjhu.

Of course it is possible to eat responsibly at McDonald's, as spokesmen for the chain never tire of reminding us. Fast food is simply one element of a balanced nutritional plan. Of course, it's the *unbalanced element* unless you order the fish filet sandwich with no mayonnaise and one of those little salads with the lo-cal dressing; then you'll be fine, except for the refined white flour in the bun and the high intake of sodium. Eating responsibly at McDonald's is like going to a strip club for the iced tea.

I say this having eaten irresponsibly at McDonald's since I was in grade school, and one of the very first McDonald's outlets in the nation opened in Urbana, Illinois. Hamburgers were fifteen cents; fries were a dime. Make it two burgers and we considered that a meal. Today it is possible to ingest thousands of calories at McDonald's and zoom dangerously over your daily recommended limits of fat, sugar, and salt. I know because Morgan Spurlock proves it in *Super Size Me.*

This is the documentary that caused a sensation at Sundance 2004 and allegedly inspired McDonald's to discontinue its "supersize" promotions as a preemptive measure. In it, Spurlock vows to eat three meals a day at McDonald's for one month. He is examined by three doctors at the beginning of the month and found to be in good health. They check him again regularly during the filming, as his weight balloons thirty pounds, his blood pressure skyrockets, his cholesterol goes up sixty-five points, he has symptoms of toxic shock to his liver, his skin begins to look unhealthy, his energy drops, he has chest pains, and his girl-friend complains about their sex life. At one point his doctors advise him to abandon McDonald's before he does permanent damage. The doctors say they have seen similar side effects from binge drinkers, but never dreamed you could get that way just by eating fast food.

It's amazing, what you find on the menu at McDonald's. Let's say you start the day with a sausage and egg McMuffin. You'll get ten grams of saturated fat—50 percent of your daily rec-ommendation, not to mention 39 percent of your daily sodium intake. Add a Big Mac and medium fries for lunch, and you're up to 123 percent of your daily saturated fat recommen-dation and 96 percent of your sodium. For din-ner, choose a quarter-pounder with cheese, add another medium order of fries, and you're at 206 percent of daily saturated fat and 160 per-cent of sodium. At some point add a strawberry shake to take you to 247 percent of saturated fat and 166 percent of sodium. And remember that most nutritionists recommend less fat and salt than the government guidelines.

There is a revisionist interpretation of the film, in which Spurlock is identified as a self-promoter who, on behalf of his film, ate more than any reasonable person could consume in a month at McDonald's. That is both true and not true. He does have a policy that whenever he's asked if he wants to "supersize it," he must reply "yes." But what he orders for any given meal is not uncommon, and we have all known (or been) customers who ordered the same items. That anyone would do it three times a day is unlikely. Occasionally you might want to go upscale at someplace like Outback, where the Bloomin' Onion Rings all by themselves provide more than a day's worth of fat and sodium, and 1,600 calories. Of course, they're supposed to be shared. For best results, share them with everyone else in the restaurant.

We bear responsibility for our own actions, so . . . is it possible to go to McDonald's and order a healthy meal? A Chicago nutritionist told a *Sun-Times* reporter that of course Spur-lock put on weight, because he was eating 5,000 calories a day. She suggested a McDonald's three-meal menu that would not be fattening, but as I studied it, I wondered: How many cus-tomers consider a small hamburger, small fries and a diet Coke as their dinner? When was the last time you even *ordered* a small hamburger (that's not a quarter-pounder) at McDonald's? Don't all raise your hands at once.

Oh, I agree with the nutritionist that her recommended three meals would not add weight; her daily caloric intake totaled 1,460 calories, which is a little low for a child under four, according to the USDA. But even her menu would include fifty-four grams of fat (fifteen saturated), or about one-third of calo-ries (for best heart health, fat should be down around 20 percent). And her diet included an astonishing 3,385 megagrams of sodium (daily recommendation: 1,600 megagrams to 2,400 megagrams). My conclusion: Even the nutri-tionist's bare-bones 1,460-calorie McDonald's menu is dangerous to your health.

I approached *Super Size Me* in a very partic-ular frame of mind because in December 2002, after years of fooling around, I began seriously following the Pritikin program of nutrition and exercise, and I have lost about eighty-six pounds. Full disclosure: Fifteen of those pounds were probably lost as a side effect of surgery and radiation; the others can be ac-counted for by Pritikin menus and exercise (the 10,000 Step-a-Day Program plus weights two or three times a week). So of course that makes me a true believer.

You didn't ask, but what I truly believe is that unless you can find an eating program you can stay on for the rest of your life, dieting is a waste of time. The pounds come back. Instead of ex-treme high-protein or low-carb diets with all their health risks, why not exercise more, avoid refined foods, and eat a balanced diet of fruits and veggies, whole grains, fish, and a little meat, beans, soy products, low-fat dairy, low fat, low salt? Of course, I agree with McDonald's that a visit to Mickey D's can be part of a responsible nutritional approach. That's why I've dined there twice in the last seventeen months.

Super Troopers ★ ★ ½
R, 103 m., 2002

Jay Chandrasekhar (Thorny), Kevin Heffernan (Farva), Steve Lemme (Mac), Paul Soter (Foster), Erik Stolhanske (Rabbit), Brian Cox (Captain John O'Hagan), Daniel von Bargen (Chief Grady), Marisa Coughlan (Ursula), Lynda Carter (Governor Jessman). Directed by Jay Chandrasekhar and produced by Richard Perello. Screenplay by Broken Lizard (Jay Chandrasekhar, Kevin Heffernan, Steve Lemme, Paul Soter, and Erik Stolhanske).

Super Troopers plays like it was directed as a do-it-yourself project, following instructions that omitted a few steps, and yet the movie has an undeniable charm. Imagine a group of Vermont state troopers treating their job like an opportunity to stage real-life *Candid Camera* situations. Now imagine that all of the troopers have ambitions to be stand-up comics. And that they were inspired to get into the force by watching *Police Academy* movies. But that they are basically good guys. That kind of describes it.

The movie is set in Spurbury, Vermont, where there isn't enough crime to go around. That causes a bitter rivalry between the state troopers, led by Captain O'Hagan (Brian Cox), and the city police, led by Chief Grady (Daniel von Bargen). When a dead body turns up in a Winebago and drug smuggling seems to be involved, the two forces compete for clues, arrests, and especially for funds. The state police post, indeed, has been threatened with a complete shutdown by the budget-minded governor (Lynda Carter).

Perhaps because these may be the last weeks they can spend working together, or perhaps simply because they're fundamentally goofy, the troopers pass their days blowing the minds of people they stop on the highway.

> Trooper: Do you know how fast you were going?
> Terrified kid whose friends are stoned: Sixty-five?
> Trooper: Sixty-three.

Other nice touches include (a) using the loudspeaker to instruct a driver to pull over after he has already pulled over, and (b) casually saying "meow" in the middle of a conversation with a curbed driver.

Captain O'Hagan is understandably distressed at the bizarre behavior of his men, and worried about the possible closing of the post. A drug bust would save the day, but his men seem fairly unfocused as they look into a promising case. "Are you suggesting," the local chief asks the troopers, "that a cartoon monkey is bringing drugs into our town?" Well, no, but it's a long story.

There's romantic intrigue when a sweet and sexy local cop named Ursula (Marisa Coughlan) starts to date a trooper named Foster (Paul Soter). This goes against the rules and undermines the rivalry, but may provide a solution to the drug mystery. Foster, however, is not too bright, as when he suggests that he and Ursula get into the backseat of the cruiser. He has forgotten that once you are in the backseat of a cruiser, someone else has to let you out.

During their sessions in local diners, which are long and frequent, the cops trade dialogue like members of a comedy troupe, which indeed they are. The name of their troupe is Broken Lizard, it shares credit for the screenplay, and the director is Jay Chandrasekhar. He also plays the trooper named Thorny. Vermonters find it obvious that he is of ethnic origin, but are baffled by the challenge of identifying his ethnic group, and there's a running gag as he remains poker-faced while people assume he's Mexican, Arabic, Indian or . . . something.

Broken Lizard, I learn, began as an undergraduate troupe at Colgate in 1989, raised $200,000 to make a movie named *Puddle Cruiser* and, instead of making a distribution deal, did a campus tour to show it. *Super Troopers* aims higher, and may spin off a Fox TV sitcom which, on the basis of this film, might work.

Super Troopers has kind of a revue feel. There is a plot, which somehow arrives at a conclusion, but the movie doesn't tell a story so much as move from one skit to another, with a laid-back charm that is more relaxed and self-confident than the manic laffaminit style of the *Police Academy* pictures. No movie is altogether uninspired that includes lines like, "Desperation is a stinky cologne." I can't quite recommend it—it's too patched together—but I almost can; it's the kind of movie that makes you want to like it.

S.W.A.T. ★ ★ ★
PG-13, 111 m., 2003

Samuel L. Jackson (Hondo Harrelson), Colin Farrell (Jim Street), Brian Gamble (Jeremy Renner), Michelle Rodriguez (Chris Sanchez), James Todd Smith [LL Cool J] (David "Deke" Kay), Olivier Martinez (Alex). Directed by Clark Johnson and produced by Dan Halsted, Chris Lee, and Neal H. Moritz. Screenplay by David Ayer and David McKenna.

Half an hour into watching *S.W.A.T.*, I realized the movie offered pleasures that action movies hardly ever allow themselves anymore:

1. The characters had dialogue and occupied a real plot, which involved their motivations and personalities.

2. The action scenes were more or less believable. The cops didn't do anything that real cops might not really almost be able to do, if they had very, very good training.

I started taking notes along these lines, and here are a few of my jottings:

"When a cop shoots at a robber in a hostage situation, the hostage is wounded."

"The chief punishes two hotshots with demotions instead of pulling their badges and guns and kicking them off the force."

"When the bad guy steals a cop car, we expect a chase, but he backs up and crashes it within a block."

"When the chase leads down to the Los Angeles subway system, the cops approach a stopped train, board it, and look for their quarry. Astonishingly, there is not a fight scene atop a speeding train."

"In a S.W.A.T. team training scene, the trainees are running toward a target while shooting, and somebody asks, 'No rolls?' The veteran cop in charge replies: 'They only roll in John Woo movies—not in real life.'"

That's the point with *S.W.A.T.* This isn't a John Woo movie, or *Bad Boys 2*, or any of the other countless movies with wall-to-wall action and cardboard characters. It isn't exactly real life, either, and I have to admit some of the stunts and action scenes are a shade unlikely, but the movie's ambition is essentially to be the same kind of police movie they used to make before special effects upstaged human beings.

The result is one of the best cop thrillers since *Training Day.* Samuel L. Jackson and Colin Farrell costar, playing the time-honored roles of veteran officer and young hothead. Michelle Rodriguez and James Todd Smith (a.k.a. LL Cool J), both effective actors, give depth to the S.W.A.T. team. And Olivier Martinez, who played Diane Lane's lover in *Unfaithful,* is the smirking playboy arms dealer who offers a $100 million reward to anyone who springs him from custody.

The plot begins with a hostage situation gone wrong. A S.W.A.T. team member (Brian Gamble) disobeys orders, enters a bank, and wounds a hostage. He and his partner, Jim Street (Farrell), are offered demotions. Street accepts; his partner leaves the force. But Street, a talented officer and a great shot, is spotted by the legendary veteran Hondo Harrelson (Samuel L. Jackson) and chosen for his hand-picked elite S.W.A.T. team.

One of the pleasures of the movie is the training sequence, where Jackson leads his team through physical and mental maneuvers. Many recent action movies have no training scenes because, frankly, you can't train to do their impossible stunts—you need an animator to do them for you.

A routine traffic bust leads to the unexpected arrest of Alex (Olivier Martinez), an internationally wanted fugitive. Alex offers the $100 million reward on television, the cops assume there will be a lot of escape masterminds hoping to collect the reward, and it's up to Hondo and his team to safely escort the prisoner to a federal penitentiary.

That it does not go smoothly goes without saying. I'm not arguing that the last forty-five minutes of the movie are, strictly speaking, likely or even plausible, but nothing violates the laws of physics and you can kind of see how stuff like that might sort of happen, if you get my drift.

S.W.A.T. is a well-made police thriller, nothing more. No Academy Awards. But in a time when so many action pictures are mindless assaults on the eyes, ears, and intelligence, it works as superior craftsmanship. The director, Clark Johnson, is a veteran of TV, both as an actor and director, and supplies a well-made film that trusts its story and actors. What a pleasure, after movies that merely wanted to make my head explode.

The Sweetest Thing ★ ½
R, 84 m., 2002

Cameron Diaz (Christina), Christina Applegate (Courtney), Thomas Jane (Peter), Selma Blair (Jane), Jason Bateman (Roger), Parker Posey (Judy). Directed by Roger Kumble and produced by Cathy Konrad. Screenplay by Nancy M. Pimental.

I like Cameron Diaz. I just plain like her. She's able to convey bubble-brained zaniness about as well as anyone in the movies right now, and then she can switch gears and give you a scary dramatic performance in something like *Vanilla Sky*. She's a beauty, but apparently without vanity; how else to account for her appearance in *Being John Malkovich*, or her adventures in *There's Something About Mary*? I don't think she gets halfway enough praise for her talent.

Consider her in *The Sweetest Thing*. This is not a good movie. It's deep-sixed by a compulsion to catalog every bodily fluids gag in *There's Something About Mary* and devise a parallel clone-gag. It knows the words but not the music; while the Farrelly brothers got away with murder, *The Sweetest Thing* commits suicide.

And yet there were whole long stretches of it when I didn't much care how bad it was—at least, I wasn't brooding in anger about the film—because Cameron Diaz and her costars had thrown themselves into it with such heedless abandon. They don't walk the plank, they tap-dance.

The movie is about three girls who just wanna have fun. They hang out in clubs, they troll for cute guys, they dress like *Maxim* cover girls, they study paperback best-sellers on the rules of relationships, and frequently (this comes as no surprise), they end up weeping in each other's arms. Diaz's running mates, played by Christina Applegate and Selma Blair, are pals and confidantes, and a crisis for one is a crisis for all.

The movie's romance involves Diaz meeting Thomas Jane in a dance club; the chemistry is right but he doesn't quite accurately convey that the wedding he is attending on the weekend is his own. This leads to Diaz's ill-fated expedition into the wedding chapel, many misunderstandings, and the kind of Idiot Plot dialogue in which all problems could be in-stantly solved if the characters were not studiously avoiding stating the obvious.

The plot is merely the excuse, however, for an astonishing array of sex and body plumbing jokes, nearly all of which dream of hitting a home run like *There's Something About Mary*, but do not. Consider *Mary*'s scene where Diaz has what she thinks is gel in her hair. Funny—because she doesn't know what it really is, and we do. Now consider the scene in this movie where the girls go into a men's room and do not understand that in a men's room a hole in the wall is almost never merely an architectural detail. The payoff is sad, sticky, and depressing.

Or consider a scene where one of the room-mates gets "stuck" while performing oral sex. This is intended as a rip-off of the "franks and beans" scene in *Mary*, but gets it all wrong. You simply cannot (I am pretty sure about this) get stuck in the way the movie suggests—no, not even if you've got piercings. More to the point, in *Mary* the victim is unseen, and we picture his dilemma. In *Sweetest Thing*, the victim is seen, sort of (careful framing preserves the R rating), and the image isn't funny. Then we get several dozen neighbors, all singing to inspire the girl to extricate herself; this might have looked good on the page, but it just plain doesn't work, especially not when embellished with the sobbing cop on the doorstep, the gay cop, and other flat notes.

More details. Sometimes it is funny when people do not know they may be consuming semen (as in *American Pie*) and sometimes it is not, as in the scene at the dry cleaners in this movie. How can you laugh when what you really want to do is hurl? And what about the scene in the ladies' room, where the other girls are curious about Applegate's boobs and she tells them she paid for them and invites them to have a feel, and they do, like shoppers at K-mart? Again, a funny concept. Again, destroyed by bad timing, bad framing, and overkill. Because the director, Roger Kumble, doesn't know how to set it up and pay it off with surgical precision, he simply has women pawing Applegate while the scene dies. An unfunny scene only grows worse by pounding in the concept as if we didn't get it.

So, as I say, I like Cameron Diaz. I like everyone in this movie (I must not neglect the invaluable Parker Posey, as a terrified bride). I like their energy. I like their willingness. I like the opening shot when Diaz comes sashaying up a San Francisco hill like a dancer from *In Living Color* who thinks she's still on the air. I like her mobile, comic face—she's smart in the way she plays dumb. But the movie I cannot like, because the movie doesn't know how to be liked. It doesn't even know how to be a movie.

Sweet Home Alabama ★ ★ ★
PG-13, 102 m., 2002

Reese Witherspoon (Melanie Carmichael), Josh Lucas (Jake Perry), Patrick Dempsey (Andrew Hennings), Fred Ward (Earl Smooter), Mary Kay Place (Pearl Smooter), Jean Smart (Stella Perry), Candice Bergen (Kate Hennings). Directed by Andy Tennant and produced by Stokely Chaffin and Neal H. Moritz. Screenplay by C. Jay Cox.

Among the pieties that Hollywood preaches but does not believe is the notion that small towns are preferable to big cities. Film after film rehearses this belief: Big cities are repositories of greed, alienation, and hypocrisy, while in a small town you will find the front doors left unlocked, peach pies cooling on the kitchen windowsill, and folks down at the diner who all know your name. *Sweet Home Alabama* is the latest, admittedly charming, recycling of this ancient myth.

The fact is that few people in Hollywood have voluntarily gone home again since William Faulkner fled back to Mississippi. The screenwriters who retail the mirage of small towns are relieved to have escaped them. I await a movie where a New Yorker tries moving to a small town and finds that it just doesn't reflect his warmhearted big-city values.

Reese Witherspoon, who is the best reason to see *Sweet Home Alabama,* stars as Melanie Carmichael, a small-town girl who moves to the Big Apple and while still in her twenties becomes a famous fashion designer. She's in love with Andrew (Patrick Dempsey), a JFK Jr. look-alike whose mother (Candice Bergen) is mayor of New York. After he proposes to her in Tiffany's, which he has rented for the occasion, she flies back home to Alabama to take care of unfinished business.

She especially doesn't want Andrew to discover that she is already married to a local boy, and that her family doesn't own a moss-dripped plantation. Her folks live in a luxury mobile home with lots of La-Z-Boys and knitted afghans (La-Z-Boy: the sign of a home where the man makes the decisions). Her husband, Jake (Josh Lucas), was her high school sweetheart, but, looking ahead at a lifetime of dirty diapers and dishes with a loser, she fled north. His plan: Prove himself to earn her respect and get her back again. That's why he's never given her the divorce.

When Melanie returns home, she's greeted by the locals, who remember her high school hijinks (like tying dynamite to a stray cat, ho, ho). Her parents (Fred Ward and Mary Kay Place), who spin away their days lounging around the double-wide practicing sitcom dialogue, look on with love and sympathy, because they know that sooner or later she'll realize that home is right here. A clue comes when the Candice Bergen character advises her prospective in-laws to "go back to your double-wide and fry something."

The Lucas character is more complex, as he needs to be, because the screenplay requires him to keep a secret that common sense insists he divulge immediately. He must meanwhile undergo a subtle transformation so that when we first meet him we think he's a redneck hayseed, and then later he has transmogrified into a sensitive, intelligent, caring male. Oh, and his coon dog still likes her.

The JFK Jr. guy, in the meantime, cannot be permitted to become a total jerk, because the movie's poignancy factor demands that he be understanding, as indeed he would be, with a Jackie look-alike mom who is mayor of New York, a city where, in this movie, nothing bad has happened in recent memory.

So okay, we understand how the formula works, even without learning that C. Jay Cox, the screenwriter, is a student of writing coach Syd Field's theories (i.e., analyze successful movies and copy their structures). We know that the movie absolutely requires that Melanie reject bright lights, big city, and return to the embrace of her hometown. And we know the odds are low that Melanie will get the divorce, return to New York, and marry the mayor's son. (Anyone who thinks I have just committed a spoiler will be unaware of all movies in this genre since *Ma and Pa Kettle*.)

But answer me this. What about Melanie as a person, with her own success and her own ambition? Would a woman with the talent and ambition necessary to become world-famous in the fashion industry before the age of thirty be able, I ask you, be willing, be prepared, to renounce it all to become the spouse of a man who has built a successful business as a (let's say) glassblower?

The chances of that happening are, I submit, extremely thin, and that is why *Sweet Home Alabama* works. It is a fantasy, a sweet, light-hearted fairy tale with Reese Witherspoon at its center. She is as lovable as Doris Day would have been in this role (in fact, Doris Day *was* in this role, in *Please Don't Eat the Daisies*). So I enjoyed Witherspoon and the local color, but I am so very tired of the underlying premise. Isn't it time for the movies to reflect reality, and show the Melanies of the world fleeing to New York as fast as they can? Even if Syd Field flunks you?

Sweet Sixteen ★ ★ ★ ½
R, 106 m., 2003

Martin Compston (Liam), Annmarie Fulton (Chantelle), William Ruane (Pinball), Michelle Abercromby (Suzanne), Michelle Coulter (Jean), Gary McCormack (Stan), Tommy McKee (Rab), Calum McAllees (Calum). Directed by Ken Loach and produced by Rebecca O'Brien. Screenplay by Paul Laverty.

Sweet Sixteen is set in Scotland and acted in a local accent so tricky it needs to be subtitled. Yet it could take place in any American city, in this time of heartless cuts in social services and the abandonment of the poor. I saw the movie at about the same time our lawmakers attacked the pitiful $400 child tax credit, while transferring billions from the working class to the richest 1 percent. Such shameless greed makes me angry, and a movie like *Sweet Sixteen* provides a social context for my feelings, showing a decent kid with no job prospects and no opportunities, in a world where only crime offers a paying occupation.

Yes, you say, but this movie is set in Scotland, not America. True, and the only lesson I can learn from that is that in both countries too many young people correctly understand that society has essentially written them off.

The director of *Sweet Sixteen*, Ken Loach, is political to the soles of his shoes, and his films are often about the difficulties of finding dignity as a working person. His *Bread and Roses* (2000) starred the future Oscar winner Adrien Brody as a union activist in Los Angeles, working to organize a group of nonunion office cleaners and service employees. In *Sweet Sixteen*, there are no jobs, thus no wages.

The movie's hero is a fifteen-year-old named Liam (Martin Compston) who has already been enlisted into crime by his grandfather and his mother's boyfriend. We see the three men during a visit to his mother in prison, where Liam is to smuggle drugs to her with a kiss. He refuses: "You took the rap once for that bastard." But the mother is the emotional and physical captive of her boyfriend, and goes along with his rules and brutality.

The boy is beaten by the two older men, as punishment, and his precious telescope is smashed. He runs away, finds refuge with his seventeen-year-old sister, Chantelle (Annmarie Fulton), and begins to dream of supporting his mother when she is released from prison. He finds a house trailer on sale for 6,000 pounds, and begins raising money to buy it.

Liam and his best friend, Pinball (William Ruane), have up until now raised money by selling stolen cigarettes, but now he moves up a step, stealing a drug stash from the grandfather and the boyfriend and selling it himself. Eventually he comes to the attention of a local crime lord, who offers him employment—but with conditions, he finds out too late, that are merciless.

Some will recall Loach's great film *Kes* (1969), about a poor English boy who finds joy in training a pet kestrel—a season of self-realization, before a lifetime as a miner down in the pits. *Sweet Sixteen* has a similar character; Liam is sweet, means well, does the best he can given the values he has been raised with. He never quite understands how completely he is a captive of a system that has no role for him.

Yes, he could break out somehow—but we can see that so much more easily than he can.

His ambition is more narrow. He dreams of establishing a home where he can live with his mother, his sister, and his sister's child. But the boyfriend can't permit that; it would underline his own powerlessness. And the mother can't make the break with the man she has learned to be submissive to.

The movie's performances have a simplicity and accuracy that are always convincing. Martin Compston, who plays Liam, is a local seventeen-year-old discovered in auditions at his school. He has never acted before, but is effortlessly natural. Michelle Coulter, who plays his mother, is a drug rehab counselor who has also never acted before, and Annmarie Fulton, who plays the sister Chantelle, has studied acting but never appeared in a film.

By using these inexperienced actors (as he often does in his films), Loach gets a spontaneous freshness; scenes feel new because the actors have never done anything like them before, and there are no barriers of style and technique between us and the characters. At the end of *Sweet Sixteen*, we see no hope in the story, but there is hope in the film itself, because to look at the conditions of Liam's life is to ask why, in a rich country, his choices must be so limited. The first crime in his criminal career was the one committed against him by his society. He just followed the example.

Note: The flywheels at the MPAA still follow their unvarying policy of awarding the PG-13 rating to vulgarity and empty-headed violence (2 Fast 2 Furious), while punishing with the R any film like this, which might actually have a useful message for younger viewers.

Swept Away ★
R, 82 m., 2002

Madonna (Amber Leighton), Adriano Giannini (Giuseppe), Bruce Greenwood (Anthony Leighton), Elizabeth Banks (Debi), David Thornton (Mike), Jeanne Tripplehorn (Marina), Michael Beattie (Todd). Directed by Guy Ritchie and produced by Matthew Vaughn. Screenplay by Ritchie.

Swept Away is a deserted island movie during which I desperately wished the characters had chosen one movie to take along if they were stranded on a deserted island, and were showing it to us instead of this one.

The movie is a relatively faithful remake of an incomparably superior 1976 movie with the lovely title, *Swept Away by an Unusual Destiny in the Blue Sea of August.* It knows the words but not the music. It strands two unattractive characters, one bitchy, one moronic, on an island where neither they, nor we, have anyone else to look at or listen to. It's harder for them than it is for us, because they have to go through the motions of an erotic attraction that seems to have become an impossibility the moment the roles were cast.

Madonna stars as Amber, the spoiled rich wife of a patient and long-suffering millionaire. They join two other couples in a cruise on a private yacht from Greece to Italy. The other five passengers recede into unwritten, even unthought-about roles, while Amber picks on Giuseppe (Adriano Giannini), the bearded deckhand. She has decided he is stupid and rude, and insults him mercilessly. So it was in the earlier film, but in this version Amber carries her behavior beyond all reason, until even the rudest and bitchiest rich woman imaginable would have called it a day.

Amber orders Giuseppe to take her out in the dinghy. He demurs: It looks like a storm. She insists. They run out of gas and begin to drift. She insults him some more, and when he succeeds after great effort in catching a fish for them to eat, she throws it overboard. Later she succeeds in putting a hole in the dinghy during a struggle for the flare gun. They drift at sea until they wash up on a deserted island, where the tables are turned and now it is Giuseppe who has the upper hand. Her husband's wealth is now no longer a factor, but his survival skills are priceless.

All of this is similar to the 1976 movie, even the business of the fish thrown overboard. What is utterly missing is any juice or life in the characters. Giancarlo Giannini and Mariangela Melato became stars on the basis of the original *Swept Away,* which was written and directed by Lina Wertmüller, one of the most successful Italian directors of the 1970s. She was a leftist but not a feminist, and aroused some controversy with a story where it turned out the rich woman liked being ordered around and slapped a little—liked it so much she encouraged the sailor to experiment with practices he could not even pronounce.

This new *Swept Away* is more sentimental, I'm afraid, and the two castaways fall into a more conventional form of love. I didn't believe it for a moment. They have nothing in common, but worse still, neither one has any conversation. They don't say a single interesting thing. That they have sex because they are stranded on the island I can believe. That they are not sleeping in separate caves by the time they are rescued I do not.

The problem with the Madonna character is that she starts out so hateful that she can never really turn it around. We dislike her intensely and thoroughly, and when she gets to the island we don't believe she has learned a lesson or turned nice—we believe she is behaving with this man as she does with all men, in the way best designed to get her what she wants. As for the sailor, does he *really* love her, as he says in that demeaning and pitiful speech toward the end of the film? What is there to love? They shared some interesting times together, but their minds never met.

The ending is particularly unsatisfactory, depending as it does on contrived irony that avoids all of the emotional issues on the table. If I have come this far with these two drips, and sailed with them, and been shipwrecked with them, and listened to their tiresome conversations, I demand that they arrive at some conclusion more rewarding than a misunderstanding based upon a misdelivered letter. This story was about something when Lina Wertmüller directed it, but now it's not about anything at all. It's lost the politics and the social observation and become just another situation romance about a couple of saps stuck in an inarticulate screenplay.

Swimming ★ ★ ★
NO MPAA RATING, 98 m., 2002

Lauren Ambrose (Frankie Wheeler), Joelle Carter (Josee), Jennifer Dundas (Nicola Jenrette), Jamie Harrold (Heath), Josh Pais (Neil Wheeler), Anthony Ruivivar (Kalani). Directed by Robert J. Siegel and produced by Linda Moran and Siegel. Screenplay by Liza Bazadona, Siegel, and Grace Woodard.

Swimming is above all about a young woman's face, and by casting an actress whose face projects that woman's doubts and yearnings, it succeeds. The face belongs to Lauren Ambrose, who you may know as the young redhead on *Six Feet Under*. She plays Frankie, a teenage girl whose parents took early retirement, leaving the family burger stand on the boardwalk in Myrtle Beach, South Carolina, to Frankie and her older married brother, Neil (Josh Pais).

The movie's plot, I fear, is an old reliable: After this summer, nothing will ever be the same again. What saves it is that this summer is unlike other summers we've seen in coming-of-age movies. It's different because Frankie holds her own counsel, doesn't easily reveal her feelings, and is faced with choices that she's not even sure she has to make.

Frankie is a tomboy, invariably dressed in bib overalls and T-shirts, her hair tousled, her face freckled, with apple cheeks. Sexuality for her is an unexplored country. Her best friend is Nicola (Jennifer Dundas), who runs a piercing stand next to the burger joint. (So sincere is Nicola's dedication to piercing that when she gets a cut on her forehead she decides a scar would be cool.) Nicola dresses in an attempt to come across as a sexy blonde, but is loyal: When two cute guys in a car want her to come along but tell her, "lose your friend," she won't play.

One day Josee (Joelle Carter) appears in town. Ostensibly the girlfriend of the hunky lifeguard, she gets a job at the burger joint even though Neil decides she is "the worst waitress I have ever seen." Josee is a sexual creature, who one day out of the blue tells Frankie: "Frankie? I think I want you. I want your body." Frankie's reaction to this news is not to react at all. Life continues as before, but with confusing desire simmering beneath the surface. It is possible that Josee is the first person to ever express a desire for Frankie, and by doing so she has activated Frankie's ability to feel desirable.

The summer brings other possibilities. Nicola meets Kalani (Anthony Ruivivar), a

Marine from Hawaii with an imaginary friend, Ted. Frankie meets Heath (Jamie Harrold), a gawky loner who lives in a van with his dogs and sells tie-dyed T-shirts, which he dyes himself at a local Laundromat. Nicola begins to resent all the time Frankie spends with Josee, and tells her something she doesn't want to know: Josee is cheating with Neil, who has a young family.

Swimming could unfold as a sitcom, or as a desperately sincere drama, but director Robert J. Siegel and his cowriters, Liza Bazadona and Grace Woodard, go for something more delicate and subtle. They use Ambrose's ability to watch and think and not commit, and they allow the summer's choices and possibilities to unfold within her as if her sexuality is awakening and stretching for the first time. What happens, and why, is sweet and innocent, and not pumped up for effect.

Lauren Ambrose's effect in the film reminded me of another early performance many years ago: the work by Cathy Burns in Frank Perry's *Last Summer* (1969). She, too, played a tomboy whose sexuality was unawakened, a member of a group with another young woman (Barbara Hershey) who was sexier and bolder, whose first romance was based more on admiration than lust ("You're so masterful," she tells the boy she admires). Often the movies are no more than opportunities for us to empathize with people we find ourselves in sympathy with. Ambrose has an extraordinary ability to make us like her and care for her, and that is the real subject of the movie—in which, by the way, she never does go swimming.

Swimming Pool ★ ★ ★
R, 102 m., 2003

Charlotte Rampling (Sarah Morton), Ludivine Sagnier (Julie), Charles Dance (John Bosload), Marc Fayolle (Marcel, the Keeper), Jean-Marie Lamour (Franck, the Bartender), Mireille Mossé (Marcel's Daughter). Directed by François Ozon and produced by Olivier Delbosc and Marc Missonnier. Screenplay by Emmanuéle Bernheim and Ozon.

"She threw me a look I caught in my hip pocket," Robert Mitchum's private eye says of Charlotte Rampling's femme fatale in *Farewell,*

My Lovely (1975). You don't know what that means, but you know exactly what it means. Rampling has always had the aura of a woman who knows things you would like to do that you haven't even thought of. She played boldly sexual roles early in her career, as in *The Night Porter* (1974), and now, in *Swimming Pool,* a sensuous and deceptive new thriller, she becomes fascinated by a young female predator.

Rampling plays Sarah Morton, a British crime writer whose novels seem to exist somewhere between those of P. D. James and Ruth Rendell. Now she is tired and uncertain, and her publisher offers her a holiday at his French villa. She goes gratefully to the house, shops in the nearby village, and finds she can write again. She is alone except for a taciturn caretaker, who goes into the village at night to live with his daughter, a dwarf who seems older than he is.

Then an unexpected visitor turns up: Julie (Ludivine Sagnier), the daughter her publisher didn't think to tell her about. Sarah is annoyed. Her privacy has been violated. Her privacy and her sense of decorum. Julie is gravid with self-confidence in her emerging sexuality, appears topless at the villa's swimming pool, brings home men to sleep with—men who have nothing in common except Julie's willingness to accommodate them. Sarah is surprised, intrigued, disapproving, curious. She looks down from high windows, spying on the girl who seems so indifferent to her opinion. Eventually she even steals glimpses of the girl's diary.

There is a waiter in the town named Franck (Jean-Marie Lamour), whom Sarah has chatted with and who is perhaps not unaware of her enduring sexuality. But he becomes one of Julie's conquests, too—maybe because Julie senses the older woman's interest in him.

At this point the film takes a turn toward violence, guilt, panic, deception, and concealment, and I will not take the turn with it, because a film like this must be allowed to have its way with you. Let us say that François Ozon, the director and cowriter (with Emmanuéle Bernheim), understands as Hitchcock did the small steps by which a wrong decision grows in its wrongness into a terrifying paranoid nightmare. And how there is nothing more disturbing than trying to conceal a crime that cries out to be revealed.

There is one moment late in the film that displays Rampling's cool audacity more than any other. The caretaker is about to investigate something that is best not investigated. What she does to startle and distract him I will not hint at, but what a startling moment, and what boldness from Rampling!

Ozon is a director who specializes in films where the absent is more disturbing than the present. Rampling starred in his *Under the Sand* (2000), a film about a husband who apparently drowns and a wife who simply refuses to accept that possibility. He also made the terrifying fifty-seven-minute film *See the Sea* (1997), in which the mother of an infant befriends a young woman hitchhiker and begins to feel that it was a dangerous mistake.

Swimming Pool is more of a conventional thriller than those two—or if it is unconventional, that is a development that doesn't affect the telling of most of the story. After it is over you will want to go back and think things through again, and I can help you by suggesting there is one, and only one, interpretation that resolves all of the difficulties, but if I told you, you would have to kill me.

Sylvia ★ ★ ★

R, 110 m., 2003

Gwyneth Paltrow (Sylvia Plath), Daniel Craig (Ted Hughes), Blythe Danner (Aurelia Plath), Lucy Davenport (Doreen), Michael Gambon (Professor Thomas), Jared Harris (Al Alvarez), Eliza Wade (Frieda Hughes), Amira Casar (Assia Wevill). Directed by Christine Jeffs and produced by Alison Owen. Screenplay by John Brownlow.

> *Fame will come. Fame especially for you.*
> *Fame cannot be avoided. And when it*
>   *comes*
> *You will have paid for it with your happiness,*
> *Your husband and your life.*

So (perhaps) the spirit of the Ouija board whispered to Sylvia Plath, one evening when she and Ted Hughes were spelling out their futures and she suddenly refused to continue. Hughes uses the speculation to close his poem "Ouija" in *Birthday Letters,* the book of poetry

he wrote about his relationship with Plath. It was started after her suicide in 1963 and published after his death in 1998. It broke his silence about Sylvia, which persisted during years when the Plath industry all but condemned him of murder.

But if there was ever a woman who seemed headed for suicide with or without this husband or any other, that woman must have been Plath, and there is a scene in *Sylvia* where her mother warns Hughes of that, not quite in so many words. "The woman is perfected," Plath wrote in a poem named "Edge." "Her dead body wears the smile of accomplishment." Of course, it is foolhardy to snatch words from a poem and apply them to a life as if they make a neat fit, but "Edge" was her last poem, written on February 5, 1963, and six days later she left out bread and milk for her children, sealed their room to protect them, and put her head in the gas oven.

Christine Jeffs's *Sylvia* is the story of the short life of Plath (1932–1963), an American who came as a student to Cambridge, met the young poet Ted Hughes at a party, was kissed by him before the evening had ended, and famously bit his cheek, drawing blood. It was not merely love at first sight, but passion, and the passion continued as they moved back to Massachusetts, where she was from, and where he taught. Then back to England, and to a lonely cottage in the country, and to the birth of their children, and to her (correct) suspicion that he was having an affair, and to their separation, and to February 11, 1963. He was famous before she was, but the posthumous publication of *Ariel,* her final book of poems, brought greater fame to her. In the simplistic accounting that governs such matters, her death was blamed on his adultery, and in the thirty-five years left to him he lived with that blame.

Hughes became Britain's poet laureate. He married the woman he was having the affair with (she died a suicide, too). He burned one of Plath's journals—he didn't want the children to see it, he said—and was blamed for covering up an indictment of himself. He edited her poetry. He saw her novel *The Bell Jar* to press, and kept his silence. *Birthday Letters* is all he had to write about her. When you read the book you can feel his love, frustration, guilt, anger, sense of futility. When you read her poetry, you experience the clear, immediate voice of a great poet more fascinated by death than life. "Somebody's done for," she wrote in the last line of "Death & Co." (November 14, 1962), and although that line follows bitter lines that are presumably about Hughes, there is no sense that he's done for. It's her.

A movie about their lives was probably inevitable. It will be bracketed with *Iris,* the 2001 film about the British novelist Iris Murdoch, who died of Alzheimer's. I deplored the way that that movie made so much of Iris the wild young thing and Iris the tragic Alzheimer's victim, and left out the middle Iris who was a great novelist—whose work made her life worth filming in the first place. I am not so bothered by the way *Sylvia* focuses on the poet's neurosis, because her life and her work were so entwined. She wrote:

Dying
is an art, like everything else.
I do it exceptionally well.

The film stars Gwyneth Paltrow as Sylvia and Daniel Craig as Ted. They are well cast, not merely because they look something like the originals but because they sound like people who live with words and value them; there's a scene where they hurl quotations at each other, and it sounds like they know what they're doing. Paltrow's great feat is to underplay her character's death wish. There was madness in Sylvia Plath, but of a sad, interior sort, and one of the film's accomplishments is to show in a subtle way how it was so difficult for Hughes to live with her. The movie doesn't pump up the volume. Yes, she does extreme things, like burning his papers and wrecking his office, but he does extreme things, too. Adultery is an extreme thing. In this consider the scene where Hughes meets Mrs. Plath for the first time. Played by Blythe Danner (Paltrow's mother), Aurelia tells her daughter's lover that Sylvia had tried to kill herself and was a person who was capable of getting it right one of these times.

It is difficult to portray a writer's life. *Sylvia*

handles that by incorporating a good deal of actual poetry into the movie, read by or to the characters, or in voice-over. It also captures the time of their lives; they were young in the 1950s, and that was another world. England gloomed through postwar poverty, there were shortages of everything, red wine and candles made you a bohemian, poets were still considered extremely important, and Freud was being ported wholesale into literature; poets took their neuroses as their subjects. Literary criticism was taken seriously because it was written in English that could be understood and had not yet imploded into academic puzzle-making. To be good in that time was to be very good, and Plath and Hughes were both first-rate.

There are two questions the movie dodges. We don't know the precise nature of Hughes's cheating, and we don't understand how Plath felt about the children she was leaving behind—why she thought it was acceptable to leave them. The second question has no answer. The answer to the first is supplied by Hughes's critics, who accuse him of womanizing, but the film dilutes that with the suggestion that he simply could not stay in the same house any longer with Sylvia.

Imagine a hypothetical moviegoer who has not heard of Plath or Hughes or read any of their poetry. That would include almost everyone at the multiplex. Is there anything in *Sylvia* for them? Yes, in a way: a glimpse of literary lives at a time when they were more central than they are now, a touching performance by Paltrow, and a portrait of a depressive. But for those who have read the poets and are curious about their lives, *Sylvia* provides illustrations for the biographies we carry in our minds. We see the milieu, the striving, the poverty, the passion, and we hear the poetry, and in the way Paltrow's performance allows Sylvia to grow subtly distant from her daily life, we sense the approach of the end. There is not even the feeling that we are intruding, because the poems of these two poets violated their privacy in a manner both thorough and brutal.

T

Tadpole ★ ★
PG-13, 78 m., 2002

Sigourney Weaver (Eve), Aaron Stanford (Oscar Grubman), John Ritter (Stanley Grubman), Bebe Neuwirth (Diane), Robert Iler (Charlie), Adam LeFevre (Phil), Peter Appel (Jimmy), Alicia Van Couvering (Daphne Tisch), Kate Mara (Miranda Spear). Directed by Gary Winick and produced by Alexis Alexanian, Dolly Hall, and Winick. Screenplay by Heather McGowan and Niels Mueller.

Tadpole tells the story of a bright fifteen-year-old who has a crush on his stepmother and actually sleeps with her best friend, in part because the friend is wearing the stepmother's scarf and the lad is powerless over the evocative lure of her perfume. The sexual excursion is not the point of the movie, really, but the setup for its central scene, in which young Oscar has dinner with his father, his stepmother, and the friend, who wickedly threatens to reveal their secret.

Watching the movie at Sundance in January, I tried to accept this premise on its own terms, but could not. Too much has happened in the arena of sexual politics since *The Graduate,* and I kept thinking that since Oscar was fifteen and his stepmother and her friend were about forty, this plot would have been unthinkable if the genders had been reversed. The best friend, far from teasing the new sexual initiate with exposure, would have been terrified of arrest, conviction, and a jail sentence for statutory rape.

I am, I realize, hauling political correctness into a movie where it is not wanted. I know there is even a lighthearted mention of the laws involved. I know I praised *Lovely and Amazing,* which also features a romance between an adult woman and a teenage boy. But *Lovely and Amazing* is about events that happen in a plausible world (the adult is actually arrested). *Tadpole* wants only to be a low-rent *Graduate* clone.

Does it succeed on that level? Not really. True, the dinner scene has its moments, as Oscar (Aaron Stanford) squirms, his lover, Diane (Bebe Neuwirth), grins wickedly, his stepmother, Eve (Sigourney Weaver), keeps up the conversation, and his father, Stanley (John Ritter), practices a suave cluelessness that is his strategy for dealing with life. Neuwirth is really very good here, and the scene supplies the one moment when the movie seems sure of what it wants to do, and how to do it.

The rest of the movie seems perfunctory and derivative, and although I could believe that Oscar would find Eve attractive, I could not quite believe the labored conversations they have, in which he is talking on one level and she on another. It was even less credible that Eve, for a split-second, actually seems to be considering Oscar's desire seriously.

The movie, directed by Gary Winick and written by Heather McGowan and Niels Mueller, gives us Woody Allen's *Manhattan* crossed with Whit Stillman's affluent preppies. Like Stillman's *Metropolitan, Barcelona,* and *The Last Days of Disco,* it gives us a hero who is articulate, multilingual, sophisticated beyond his years, and awesomely self-confident. The difference is that Stillman was seriously intrigued by his young characters, and *Tadpole* uses Oscar primarily as an excuse for transgressive lust.

If Oscar were not forever speaking French and quoting Voltaire, we might see his passion for what it is, the invention of the filmmakers. I never really believed Oscar lusted after Eve the woman, but only after Eve the plot point—the archetypal older woman descended in an unbroken line from Mrs. Robinson.

The film has problems other than credibility. It ends with unseemly haste, it underlines its points too obviously, and its camera moves when it should be still. Some of the flaws may be excused by the filming method; *Tadpole* was filmed in two weeks for about $150,000, and the cast and crew took the minimum wage. When the film played at Sundance, there was a lot of buzz and Winick won the prize as best director. But there was also talk that the digital photography was noticeably washed-out. When Miramax bought the film (for a rumored but no doubt inflated $6 million), word was that the studio would give the visuals an overhaul. They still look unconvincing.

I am reminded of what Gene Siskel used to say whenever a hopeful director told him how little a movie cost. Gene would nod and reply, "I wish you had made it for more." I am in favor of low-budget filmmaking, but I do not consider it a virtue in itself, only a means to an end. In the case of *Tadpole,* the hurried schedule, the shaky digital video, and the lack of character development may all be connected to the fast, cheap shoot. A longer movie (this one is barely feature length at seventy-eight minutes) might have made the relationships more nuanced and convincing. In this version, we can sense the machinery beneath the skin.

Taking Lives ★ ★ ★

R, 103 m., 2004

Angelina Jolie (Illeana Scott), Ethan Hawke (James Costa), Kiefer Sutherland (Martin Asher), Olivier Martinez (Paquette), Tcheky Karyo (Leclair), Gena Rowlands (Mrs. Asher). Directed by D. J. Caruso and produced by Mark Canton and Bernie Goldmann. Screenplay by Jon Bokenkamp, based on the novel by Michael Pye.

Taking Lives is another one of those serial killer thrillers where the madman is not content with murder but must also devise an ingenious and diabolical pattern so that it can be intuited by an investigator who visits the crime scene and picks up his vibes. The vibe jockey this time is FBI agent Illeana Scott (Angelina Jolie), and the first time the other cops see her, she's on her back in the open grave of one of the victims, feeling the pain or sensing the hate or just possibly freaking out the cops so they won't take her for granted.

Although she's American, she's in Canada because her special skills have been called in by the Montreal police. Before you find it odd that the Canadian cops lack a single law enforcement person with her expertise, reflect on this: They don't even know they're not in Montreal. At almost the very moment we hear "Montreal" on the sound track, there is a beautiful shot of the Chateau Frontenac in Quebec City. This is a little like Chicago cops not noticing they are standing beneath Mount Rushmore.

But I quibble. *Taking Lives* is actually an effective thriller, on its modest but stylish level. Agent Scott quickly figures out that there's a pattern behind the killings—each victim is a few years older than the previous one, and the killer steals his identity, so he must be a person so unhappy to be himself that he has to step into a series of other lives. A moment's reflection might have informed him that his victims, were they not dead, would be keeping up with him chronologically, but maybe, you know what, he's insane.

There's a big break in the case when an artist and gallery owner named James Costa (Ethan Hawke) surprises the killer at work, and is able to supply a high-quality sketch of a suspect. Another development: Mrs. Asher (Gena Rowlands), mother of one of the supposed victims, says the dead body is not her son. Then, not long after, she sees her son quite alive on a ferry. "He's a dangerous man," she tells the cops. He was one of twins, but let's not go there.

The cops include Olivier Martinez and Tcheky Karyo, one of whom resents Scott, while the other respects her. Her methods include devising elaborate time lines of the victims and their photographs, but her greatest gift is to notice little clues. When she spots a draft beneath a bookcase, for example, Nancy Drew is the only other sleuth who would have guessed that behind the case is a hidden door to a secret room.

The movie gets a lot more complicated than I have indicated, and I will not even refer to the last act except to observe that it recycles a detail from *Fatal Attraction* in an ingenious and merciful way. The ending is, in fact, preposterous, depending as thrillers so often do on elaborate plans that depend on the killer hitting all his marks and the cops picking up on all his cues.

For that matter (I will speak cautiously), why is there a person under that bed? To kill Scott, I suppose, but when they struggle, why oh why does she not recognize him? To sacrifice this scene would have meant losing the clue of the draft under the bookcase, but with a little more imagination the hidden room could have been played for creepy chills and occult clues, and we could have lost the big *Carrie* moment. Another excellent question: How can a driver crash a speeding car and be sure who will live and who will die?

This keeps reading like a negative review. I've got to get a grip on myself. See, I *like* movies that make me ask goofy questions like this, as long as they absorb and entertain me, and have actors who can go the distance. Angelina Jolie, like Daryl Hannah, is one of those beauties you somehow never see playing a domesticated housewife. She's more of a freestanding object of wonder, a force of intrigue. Ethan Hawke has the ability to be in a thriller and yet actually seem like a real gallery owner; the art on the walls during his gallery opening looks like a group show from Mrs. Gradgrind's third-grade class, but that's contemporary art for you. And all I can say about Kiefer Sutherland, apart from praise for his good work in the past, is that he seems to have graduated from prime suspect to the parallel category of obvious suspect.

The movie was directed by D. J. Caruso, whose *The Salton Sea* (2002) included the most unforgettably weird villain in recent memory; you remember Vincent D'Onofrio's Pooh-Bear and his little plastic nose. In *Taking Lives*, he understands that a certain genre of thriller depends more upon style and tone than upon plot; it doesn't matter if you believe it walking out, as long as you were intrigued while it was happening.

Taking Sides ★ ★ ★
NO MPAA RATING, 105 m., 2003

Harvey Keitel (Major Steve Arnold), Stellan Skarsgård (Wilhelm Furtwängler), Moritz Bleibtreu (Lieutenant David Wills), Birgit Minichmayr (Emmi Straube), Oleg Tabakov (Oberst Dymshitz), Ulrich Tukur (Helmut Rode), Hanns Zischler (Rudolf Werner), August Zirner (Captain Ed Martin). Directed by István Szabó and produced by Yves Pasquier. Screenplay by Ronald Harwood, based on his play.

The death of Leni Riefenstahl was a reminder of the "de-Nazification" process in which Allied tribunals investigated possible Nazi collaborators. The subjects were not blatant war criminals like those tried at Nuremberg, yet neither were they innocent bystanders. They were German civilians of power or influence whose contribution to the war now had to be evaluated.

Some said they didn't agree with the Nazis and never joined the party, but merely continued in their civilian jobs and tried to remain outside politics. Such a man was Wilhelm Furtwängler, the conductor of the Berlin Phil-

harmonic, who was known as "Hitler's favorite conductor," just as Riefenstahl was his favorite filmmaker. *Taking Sides* is the record of Furtwängler's postwar interrogation at the hands of Steve Arnold, a U.S. Army major who in civilian life had been an insurance investigator, and who approaches the great man as if Furtwängler's restaurant had just burned down and he smelled of kerosene.

Many German artists, Jewish and not, fled their country with the rise of Hitler. Furtwängler's contemporary and rival Otto Klemperer left in 1933 and took over the podium at the Los Angeles Philharmonic. But Furtwängler (Stellan Skarsgård) remained behind, and tells Arnold (Harvey Keitel) he did it out of loyalty to his music, his orchestra, and his nation. Art for him was above politics, he said, and he never joined the Nazi Party or gave the Nazi salute. Ah, says Arnold, but you played at Hitler's birthday party. Furtwängler splits hairs: He played at an event the night before.

To remain in Germany and not be a loyal Nazi was "to walk a tightrope between exile and the gallows," he says. The impression he wants to give is that he never liked Hitler, never liked the Nazis, was loyal to the decent traditions of Germany's past. Yes, but if the Nazis had won—would he have then tried to slip out to some safe haven? That is the great question with Riefenstahl too; we can't help suspecting their postwar dislike for the Nazis was greatly amplified by their defeat.

Taking Sides, based on a play by Ronald Harwood *(The Dresser)*, has been directed by the distinguished Hungarian István Szabó, whose great *Mephisto* (1981) tells the story of an actor whose career is promoted by the Nazis he loathes; he plays the roles of his dreams but loses his soul. Szabó himself remained in Hungary during the Soviet occupation, true to his country, loyal to his art, working with the Soviets but hating them, so this material must resonate with him. *Mephisto* was at one level clearly about Soviets, not Nazis, and was about Szabó's own situation. In *Mephisto*, as the title signals, the hero sold his soul to evil. But Furtwängler is a more complicated case, and one of the problems of the film is that it doesn't clearly take sides. Another is that Furtwängler is presented as a man of pride and character, and the American comes across as a vulgar little toady who wants to impress his superiors by bagging the great man: "I'm not after small fish," he brags. "I'm after Moby-Dick." He calls the conductor a "bandleader," and says, "Musicians, morticians, they're all the same."

Major Arnold treats Furtwängler with deliberate contempt, making him wait for hours when he arrives on time for appointments and playing childish games involving the chair he sits in. Sharing his office are an aide and a secretary: Lieutenant David Wills (Moritz Bleibtreu), a German Jew in the American army, and Emmi Straube (Birgit Minichmayr), whose father was one of the Nazi officers killed in a belated uprising against Hitler. Both grew up thinking of Furtwängler as a great man, both are shocked by the contempt with which Arnold treats him, and Emmi finally announces she is leaving: "I've been questioned by the Gestapo— just like that."

Furtwängler's case is a murky one. Yes, he made anti-Semitic comments. But he also helped many Jewish musicians escape to Switzerland and the West. Yes, his recording of Beethoven's *Ninth* was played on German radio after Hitler's death. But of course it was. Yes, he was naive to think that art and politics could be kept separate. But you know how those longhairs are. The de-Nazification courts eventually cleared him, but he remained under a cloud and never toured in America.

The movie is both interesting and unsatisfying. The Keitel performance is over the top, inviting us to side with Furtwängler simply because his interrogator is so vile. There are maddening lapses, as when Furtwängler's rescue of Jewish musicians is mentioned but never really made clear. But Skarsgård's performance is poignant; it has a kind of exhausted passivity, suggesting a man who once stood astride the world and now counts himself lucky to be insulted by the likes of Major Arnold. Furtwängler chose the wrong side, and tried to have it both ways, living at arm's length with the Nazis. Klemperer left not necessarily because he was Furtwängler's moral superior, but because as a Jew it was a matter of survival. Furtwängler, ambitious, vain like many conductors, perhaps under the illusion that Hitler would win, stayed and held his nose.

At the end of a movie that never clearly chooses sides, Szabó finds the perfect image to

close with. It's from an old newsreel of the real Furtwängler, conducting the philharmonic for an audience of Nazi officers. After the concert is over, an officer approaches the podium and shakes his hand. And then Furtwängler quietly takes a handkerchief out of his pocket and wipes off his hand. Szabó shows the gesture a second time, in close-up. And there you have it. Better not to shake hands with the devil in the first place.

Talk to Her ★ ★ ★
R, 112 m., 2002

Javier Cámara (Benigno Martin), Dario Grandinetti (Marco Zuloaga), Leonor Watling (Alicia Roncero), Rosario Flores (Lydia Gonzalez), Geraldine Chaplin (Katerina Bilova), Mariola Fuentes (Rosa). Directed by Pedro Almodóvar and produced by Agustín Almodóvar. Screenplay by Almodóvar.

A man cries in the opening scene of Pedro Almodóvar's *Talk to Her,* but although unspeakably sad things are to happen later in the movie, these tears are shed during a theater performance. Onstage, a woman wanders as if blind or dazed, and a man scurries to move obstacles out of her way—chairs, tables. Sometimes she blunders into the wall.

In the audience, we see two men who are still, at this point, strangers to each other. Marco (Dario Grandinetti) is a travel writer. Benigno (Javier Cámara) is a male nurse. The tears are of empathy, and it hardly matters which man cries, because in the film both will devote themselves to caring for helpless women. What's important are the tears. If he had been the director of *The Searchers* instead of John Ford, Almodóvar told the writer Lorenza Munoz, John Wayne would have cried.

Talk to Her is a film with many themes; it ranges in tone from a soap opera to a tragedy. One theme is that men can possess attributes usually described as feminine. They can devote their lives to a patient in a coma, they can live their emotional lives through someone else, they can gain deep satisfaction from bathing, tending, cleaning up, taking care. The bond that eventually unites the two men in *Talk to Her* is that they share these abilities. For much of the movie, what they have in common is that they wait by the bedsides of women who have suffered brain damage and are never expected to recover.

Marco meets Lydia (Rosario Flores) when she is at the height of her fame, the most famous female matador in Spain. Driving her home one night, he learns her secret: She is fearless about bulls, but paralyzingly frightened of snakes. After Marco catches the snake in her kitchen (we are reminded of Annie Hall's spider), she announces she will never be able to go back into that house again. Soon after, she is gored by a bull and lingers in the twilight of a coma. Marco, who did not know her very well, paradoxically comes to know her better as he attends at her bedside.

Benigno has long been a nurse, and for years tended his dying mother. He first saw the ballerina Alicia (Leonor Watling) as she rehearsed in a studio across from his apartment. She is comatose after a traffic accident. He volunteers to take extra shifts, seems willing to spend twenty-four hours a day at her bedside. He is in love with her.

As the two men meet at the hospital and share their experiences, I was reminded of Julien and Cecilia, the characters in François Truffaut's film *The Green Room* (1978), based on the Henry James story "The Altar of the Dead." Julien builds a shrine to all of his loved ones who have died, fills it with photographs and possessions, and spends all of his time there with "my dead." When he falls in love with Cecilia, he offers her his most precious gift: He shares his dead with her. She gradually comes to understand that for him they are more alive than she is.

That seems to be the case with Benigno, whose woman becomes most real to him now that she is helpless and his life is devoted to caring for her. Marco's motivation is more complex, but both men seem happy to devote their lives to women who do not, and may never, know of their devotion. There is something selfless in their dedication, but something selfish, too, because what they are doing is for their own benefit; the patients would be equally unaware of treatment whether it was kind or careless.

Almodóvar treads a very delicate path here. He accepts the obsessions of the two men, and respects them, but as a director whose films have always revealed a familiarity with the stranger possibilities of human sexual expression, he hints, too, that there is something a little creepy about their devotion. The startling outcome of one of the cases, which I will not reveal, sets an almost insoluble moral dilemma for us. Conventional morality requires us to disapprove of actions that in fact may have been inspired by love and hope.

By Almodóvar's standards this is an almost conventional film; certainly it doesn't involve itself in the sexual revolving doors of many of his films. But there is a special-effects sequence of outrageous audacity, a short silent film fantasy in which a little man attempts to please a woman with what can only be described as total commitment.

Almodóvar has a way of evoking sincere responses from material which, if it were revolved only slightly, would present a face of sheer irony. *Talk to Her* combines improbable melodrama (gored bullfighters, comatose ballerinas) with subtly kinky bedside vigils and sensational denouements, and yet at the end we are undeniably touched. No director since Fassbinder has been able to evoke such complex emotions with such problematic material.

Tears of the Sun ★ ★ ★
R, 121 m., 2003

Bruce Willis (A. K. Waters), Monica Bellucci (Dr. Lena Hendricks), Cole Hauser (Red Atkins), Tom Skerritt (Bill Rhodes), Eamonn Walker (Zee Pettigrew), Nick Chinlund (Slo Slowenski), Fionnula Flanagan (Nurse Grace), Johnny Messner (Kelly Lake). Directed by Antoine Fuqua and produced by Ian Bryce, Mike Lobell, Arnold Rifkin, and Bruce Willis. Screenplay by Patrick Cirillo and Alex Lasker.

Tears of the Sun is a film constructed out of rain, cinematography, and the face of Bruce Willis. These materials are sufficient to build a film almost as good as if there had been a better screenplay. In a case like this, the editor often deserves the credit for concealing what is not there with the power of what remains.

The movie tells the story of a Navy Seals unit that is dropped into a Nigerian civil war zone to airlift four U.S. nationals to safety. They all work at the same mission hospital. The priest and two nuns refuse to leave. The doctor, widow of an American, is also hostile at first ("Get those guns out of my operating room!"), but then she agrees to be saved if she can also bring her patients. She cannot. There is no room on the helicopters for them, and finally Waters (Bruce Willis) wrestles her aboard.

But then he surprises himself. As the chopper circles back over the scene, they see areas already set afire by arriving rebel troops. He cannot quite meet the eyes of the woman, Dr. Lena Hendricks (Monica Bellucci). "Let's turn it around," Willis says. They land, gather about twenty patients who are well enough to walk, and call for the helicopters to return.

But he has disobeyed direct orders, his superior will not risk the choppers, and they will all have to walk through the jungle to Cameroon to be rescued. Later, when it is clear Willis's decision has placed his men and mission in jeopardy, one of his men asks, "Why'd you turn it around?" He replies: "When I figure that out, I'll let you know." And later: "It's been so long since I've done a good thing—the right thing."

There are some actors who couldn't say that dialogue without risking laughter from the audience. Willis is not one of them. His face smeared with camouflage and glistening with rain, his features as shadowed as Marlon Brando's in *Apocalypse Now,* he seems like a dark, violent spirit sent to rescue them from one hell only to lead them into another. If we could fully understand how he does what he does, we would know a great deal about why some actors can carry a role that would destroy others. Casting directors must spend a lot of time thinking about this.

The story is very simple, really. Willis and his men must lead the doctor and her patients through the jungle to safety. Rebel troops pursue them. It's a question of who can walk faster or hide better; that's why it's annoying that Dr. Hendricks is constantly telling Waters, "My people have to rest!" Presumably (a) her African patients from this district have some experience at walking long distances through the jungle, and (b) she knows they are being chased by certain death, and can do the math.

Until it descends into mindless routine action in the climactic scenes, *Tears of the Sun* is essentially an impressionistic nightmare, directed by Antoine Fuqua, the director who

emerged with the Denzel Washington cop picture *Training Day.* His cinematographers, Mauro Fiore and Keith Solomon, create a visual world of black-green saturated wetness, often at night, in which characters swim in and out of view as the face of Willis remains their implacable focal point. There are few words; Willis scarcely has 100 in the first hour. It's all about the conflict between a trained professional soldier and his feelings. There is a subtext of attraction between the soldier and the woman doctor (who goes through the entire film without thinking to button the top of her blouse), but it is wisely left as a subtext.

This film, in this way, from beginning to end, might have really amounted to something. I intuit "input" from producers, studio executives, story consultants, and the like, who found it their duty to dumb it down by cobbling together a conventional action climax. The last half-hour of *Tears of the Sun,* with its routine gun battles, explosions, and machine-gun bursts, is made from off-the-shelf elements. If we can see this sort of close combat done well in a film that is really about it, like Mel Gibson's *We Were Soldiers,* why do we have to see it done merely competently, in a movie that is not really about it?

Where the screenplay originally intended to go, I cannot say, but it's my guess that at an earlier stage it was more thoughtful and sad, more accepting of the hopelessness of the situation in Africa, where "civil war" has become the polite term for genocide. The movie knows a lot about Africa, lets us see that, then has to pretend it doesn't.

Willis, for example, has a scene in the movie where, as a woman approaches a river, he emerges suddenly from beneath the water to grab her, silence her, and tell her he will not hurt her. This scene is laughable, but effective. Laughable, because (a) hiding under the water and breathing through a reed, how can the character know the woman will approach the river at precisely that point? and (b) since he will have to spend the entire mission in the same clothes, is it wise to soak all of his gear when staying dry is an alternative?

Yet his face, so fearsome in camouflage, provides him with a sensational entrance and the movie with a sharp shudder of surprise. There is a way in which movies like *Tears of the Sun* can be enjoyed for their very texture. For the few words Willis uses, and the way he uses them. For the intelligence of the woman doctor, whose agenda is not the same as his. For the camaraderie of the Navy Seals unit, which follows its leader even when he follows his conscience instead of orders. For the way the editor, Conrad Buff, creates a minimalist mood in setup scenes of terse understatement; he doesn't hurry, he doesn't linger. If only the filmmakers had been allowed to follow the movie where it wanted to go—into some existential heart of darkness, I suspect—instead of detouring into the suburbs of safe Hollywood convention.

Ten ★ ★

NO MPAA RATING, 94 m., 2003

Mania Akbari (The Woman), Amin Maher (Her Son), Roya Arabshahi (Passenger), Katayoun Taleidzadeh (Passenger), Mandana Sharbaf (Passenger), Amene Moradi (Passenger). Directed by Abbas Kiarostami and produced by Kiarostami and Marin Karmitz. Screenplay by Kiarostami.

I am unable to grasp the greatness of Abbas Kiarostami. His critical reputation is unmatched: His *Taste of Cherry* (1997) won the Palme d'Or at Cannes, and *The Wind Will Carry Us* (1999) won the Golden Lion at Venice. And yet his films, for example his latest work *Ten*, are meant not so much to be watched as to be written about; his reviews make his points better than he does.

Any review must begin with simple description. *Ten* consists of ten scenes set in the front seat of a car. The driver is always the same. Her passengers include her son, her sister, a friend, an old woman, and a prostitute. The film is shot in digital video, using two cameras, one focused on the driver, the other on the passenger. The cameras are fixed. The film has been described as both fiction and documentary, and is both: What we see is really happening, but some of it has been planned, and Amin, for example, does not seem to be the driver's son.

Kiarostami's method, I learn from Geoff Andrew's review in *Sight & Sound*, was to audition real people, choose his actors, talk at length with them about their characters and dialogue, and then send them out in the car without him, to play their characters (or perhaps themselves) as they drove the streets and the cameras watched. Beginning with twenty-three hours of footage, he ended with this ninety-four-minute film.

Now you might agree that is a provocative and original way to make a movie. Then I might tell you that *Taste of Cherry* was also set entirely in the front seat of a car—only in that film Kiarostami held the camera and sat alternatively in the seat of the driver and the passenger. And that *The Wind Will Carry Us* was about a man driving around trying to find a place where his cell phone would work. You might observe that his method has become more daring, but you would still be left with movies about people driving and talking.

Ah, but what do we learn about them, and about modern Iran? Andrew, who thinks this is Kiarostami's best film, observes the woman complaining about Iran's "stupid laws" that forbid divorce unless she charges her husband with abuse or drug addiction. He observes that the movie shows prostitution exists in Iran, even though it is illegal. The old woman argues that the driver should try prayer, and she does, showing the nation's religious undercurrent. The friend removes her scarf to show that she has shaved her head, and this is transgressive because women are not allowed to bare their heads in public. And little Amin, the son, seems like a repressive Iranian male in training, having internalized the license of a male-dominant society to criticize and mock his mother.

All very well. But to praise the film for this is like praising a child for coloring between the lines. Where is the reach, the desire to communicate, the passion? If you want to see the themes in *Ten* explored with power and frankness in films of real power, you would turn away from Kiarostami's arid formalism and look instead at a film like Tahmineh Milani's *Two Women* (1998) or Jafar Panahi's *The Circle* (2001), which have the power to deeply move audiences, instead of a willingness to alienate or bore them.

Anyone could make a movie like *Ten*. Two digital cameras, a car, and your actors, and off you go. Of course, much would depend on the actors, what they said, and who they were playing (the little actor playing Amin is awesomely self-confident and articulate on the screen, and effortlessly obnoxious). But if this approach were used for a film shot in Europe or America, would it be accepted as an entry at Cannes?

I argue that it would not. Part of Kiarostami's appeal is that he is Iranian, a country whose films it is somewhat daring to praise. Partly, too, he has a lot of critics invested in his cause, and they do the heavy lifting. The fatal flaw in his approach is that no ordinary moviegoer, whether Iranian or American, can be expected to relate to his films. They exist for film festivals, film critics, and film classes.

The shame is that more accessible Iranian directors are being neglected in the overpraise of Kiarostami. Brian Bennett, who runs the Bangkok Film Festival, told me of attending a Tehran Film Festival with a fair number of Western critics and festival directors. "The moment a film seemed to be about characters or plot," he said, "they all got up and raced out of the room. They had it fixed in their minds that the Iranian cinema consisted of minimalist exercises in style, and didn't want to see narrative films." Since storytelling is how most films work and always have, it is a shame that Iranian stories are being shut out of Western screenings because of a cabal of dilettantes.

The Terminal ★ ★ ★ ½
PG-13, 121 m., 2004

Tom Hanks (Viktor Navorski), Catherine Zeta-Jones (Amelia Warren), Stanley Tucci (Frank Dixon), Chi McBride (Joe Mulroy), Diego Luna (Enrique Cruz), Barry Shabaka Henley (Ray Thurman), Kumar Pallana (Gupta Rajan), Zoe Saldana (Dolores Torres). Directed by Steven Spielberg and produced by Laurie MacDonald, Walter F. Parkes, and Spielberg. Screenplay by Sacha Gervasi and Jeff Nathanson.

Steven Spielberg and Tom Hanks have made, in *The Terminal,* a sweet and delicate comedy, a film to make you hold your breath, it is so precisely devised. It has big laughs, but it never seems to make an effort for them; it knows exactly, minutely, and in every detail who its hero is, and remains absolutely consistent to what he believes and how he behaves.

The hero is named Viktor Navorski. He has arrived in a vast American airport just as his nation, Krakozia, has fallen in a coup. Therefore his passport and visa are worthless, his country no longer exists, and he cannot go forward or go back. Dixon, the customs official, tells him he is free to remain in the International Arrivals Lounge, but forbidden to step foot on American soil.

This premise could have yielded a film of contrivance and labored invention. Spielberg, his actors, and writers (Sacha Gervasi and Jeff Nathanson) weave it into a human comedy that is gentle and true, that creates sympathy for all of its characters, that finds a tone that will carry them through, that made me unreasonably happy.

There is a humanity in its humor that reminds you of sequences in Chaplin or Keaton where comedy and sadness find a fragile balance. It has another inspiration, the work of the French actor-filmmaker Jacques Tati. Spielberg gives Hanks the time and space to develop elaborate situations like those Tati was always getting himself into, situations where the lives of those around him became baffling because of Tati's own profound simplicity.

In *The Terminal,* Viktor Navorski's unintended victim is Dixon, the customs and immigrations official, played by Stanley Tucci with an intriguing balance between rigidity and curiosity. He goes by the rules, but he has no great love of the rules. Sometimes the rules are cruel, but he takes no joy in the cruelty. As Navorski lingers day after day in the arrivals lounge, Dixon's impatience grows. "He's found out about the quarters," he says one day, staring grimly at a surveillance monitor. Navorski is returning luggage carts to the racks to collect the refund, and spending his profits on food.

Navorski is a man unlike any Dixon has ever encountered—a man who is exactly who he seems to be and claims to be. He has no guile, no hidden motives, no suspicion of others. He trusts. The immigration service, and indeed the American legal system, has no way of dealing with him because Viktor does not do, or fail to do, any of the things the system is set up to prevent him from doing, or not doing. He has slipped through a perfect logical loophole. *The Terminal* is like a sunny Kafka story, in which it is the citizen who persecutes the bureaucracy.

Dixon wants Navorski out of the terminal because, well, he can't live there forever, but he shows every indication of being prepared to. "Why doesn't he escape?" Dixon asks his underlings, as Navorski stands next to an open door that Dixon has deliberately left unguarded. Dixon's plan is to pass Navorski on to another jurisdiction: "You catch a small fish and unhook him very carefully. You place him back in the water, so that someone else can have the pleasure of catching him."

Dixon could arrest Navorski unfairly, but refuses to: "He has to break the law." Navorski, who speaks little English but is learning every day, refuses to break the law. He won't even lie when Dixon offers him political asylum. "Are you afraid of returning to your country?" "Not afraid," he says simply. "But aren't you afraid of *something?*" "I am afraid for . . . ghosts," says Navorski. The terminal is filled with other characters Navorski gets to know, such as Amelia the flight attendant (Catherine Zeta-Jones), who is having an affair with a married man and finds she can open her heart to this strange, simple man. And Gupta the janitor (Kumar Pallana), who leaves the floor wet and watches as passengers ignore the little yellow warning pyramids and slip and fall. "This is the only fun I have," he says. And a food services employee (Diego Luna), who is in love with an INS official (Zoe Saldana) and uses Navorski as his go-between.

These friends and others have secret social lives in the terminal, feasting on airline food, playing poker. Navorski becomes their hero when he intervenes in a heart-rending case. A Russian man has medicine he needs to take to his dying father, but Dixon says it must stay in the United States. The man goes berserk, a hostage situation threatens, but Navorski defuses the situation and finds a solution that would have pleased Solomon.

Tom Hanks does something here that many actors have tried to do and failed. He plays his entire role with an accent of varying degrees of impenetrability, and it never seems like a comic turn or a gimmick, and he never seems to be doing it to get a laugh. He gets laughs, but his acting and the writing are so good they seem to evolve naturally. That is very hard to do. He did the same thing in *Forrest Gump*, and Navorski is another character that audiences will, yes, actually love. The screenplay also sidesteps various hazards that a lesser effort would have

fallen to, such as a phony crisis or some kind of big action climax. *The Terminal* doesn't have a plot; it *tells a story.* We want to know what will happen next, and we care.

Most of this movie was shot on a set, a vast construction by production designer Alex McDowell. We're accustomed these days to whole cities and planets made of computerized effects. Here the terminal with all of its levels, with its escalators and retail shops and food courts and security lines and passenger gates actually exists. The camera of the great Janusz Kaminski can go anywhere it wants, can track and crane and pivot, and everything is real. Not one viewer in one hundred will guess this is not a real airline terminal.

Spielberg and Hanks like to work together *(Saving Private Ryan, Catch Me If You Can)*, and here they trust each other with tricky material. It is crucial, perhaps, that they're so successful as to be unassailable, which allows them to relax and take their time on a production that was burning dollars every second. Others might have heard the clock ticking and rushed or pushed, or turned up the heat by making the Dixon character into more of a villain and less of a character study. Their film has all the time in the world. Just like Viktor Navorski. He isn't going anywhere.

Terminator 3: Rise of the Machines
★ ★ ½
R, 109 m., 2003

Arnold Schwarzenegger (Terminator), Kristanna Loken (T-X), Nick Stahl (John Connor), Claire Danes (Kate Brewster), David Andrews (Robert Brewster), Mark Famiglietti (Scott Petersen). Directed by Jonathan Mostow and produced by Mario F. Kassar and Andrew G. Vajna. Screenplay by John Brancato and Michael Ferris.

In the dawning days of science fiction, there was a chasm between the concept-oriented authors and those who churned out space opera. John W. Campbell Jr.'s *Astounding Science Fiction*, later renamed *Analog* to make the point clear, was the home of the brainy stuff. Bug-eyed monsters chased heroines in aluminum brassieres on the covers of *Amazing, Imagination,* and *Thrilling Wonder Stories.*

The first two Terminator movies, especially the second, belonged to Campbell's tradition of sci-fi ideas. They played elegantly with the paradoxes of time travel, in films where the action scenes were necessary to the convoluted plot. There was actual poignancy in the dilemma of John Connor, responsible for a world that did not even yet exist. The robot Terminator, reprogrammed by Connor, provided an opportunity to exploit Isaac Asimov's Three Laws of Robotics.

But that was an age ago, in 1991. *T2* was there at the birth of computer-generated special effects, and achieved remarkable visuals, especially in the plastic nature of the Terminator played by Robert Patrick, who was made of an infinitely changeable substance that could reconstitute itself from droplets. Now we are in the latter days of CGI, when the process is used not to augment action scenes but essentially to create them. And every week brings a new blockbuster and its $50 million–plus gross, so that audiences don't so much eagerly anticipate the latest extravaganza as walk in with a show-me attitude.

Terminator 3: Rise of the Machines is made in the spirit of these slick new action thrillers and abandons its own tradition to provide wall-to-wall action in what is essentially one long chase and fight punctuated by comic, campy, or simplistic dialogue. This is not your older brother's *Terminator*. It's in the tradition of *Thrilling Wonder Stories; T2* descended from Campbell's *Analog*. The time-based paradoxes are used arbitrarily and sometimes confusingly and lead to an enormous question at the end: How, if that is what happens, are the computer-based machines of the near future created?

Perhaps because the plot is thinner and more superficial, the characters don't have the same impact, either. Nick Stahl plays John Connor, savior of mankind, in the role created by the edgier, more troubled Edward Furlong. Stahl seems more like a hero than a victim of fate, and although he tells us at the outset he lives "off the grid" and feels "the weight of the future bearing down on me," he seems more like an all-purpose action figure than a man who really (like Furlong) feels trapped by an impenetrable destiny.

Early in the film he meets a veterinarian named Kate Brewster (Claire Danes), and after they find they're on the same hit list from the killers of the future, they team up to fight back and save the planet. They are pursued by a new-model Terminator named T-X, sometimes called the Terminatrix, and played by the icy-eyed Kristanna Loken. I know these characters are supposed to be blank-faced and impassive, but somehow Robert Patrick's evil Terminator was ominous and threatening, and Loken's model is more like the mannequin who keeps on coming; significantly, she first appears in the present after materializing in a Beverly Hills shop window. The movie doesn't lavish on her the astonishing shape-shifting qualities of her predecessor.

To protect John and Kate, Terminator T-101 arrives from the future, played by Arnold Schwarzenegger, who has embodied this series from the very first. The strange thing is, this is not the same Terminator he played in *T2*. "Don't you remember me?" asks Connor. But "hasta la vista, baby" doesn't ring a bell. T-101 does, however, inexplicably remember some old Schwarzenegger movies and at one point intones, "She'll be back."

The movie has several highly evolved action set pieces, as we expect, and there's a running gag involving the cumbersome vehicles that are used. The Terminatrix commandeers a huge self-powered construction crane to mow down rows of cars and buildings, a fire truck is used at another point, and after Kate, John, and the Terminator find a caché of weapons in the coffin of John's mother, a hearse is put into play—at one point, in a development that is becoming a cliché, getting its top sheared off as it races under a truck trailer, so that it becomes a convertible hearse. (Why do movies love convertibles? Because you can see the characters.)

Kate's father is a high-up muckety-muck whose job is a cover for top-secret security work, and that becomes important when the three heroes discover that a nuclear holocaust will begin at 6:18 P.M. Can they get to the nation's underground weapons control facility in time to disarm the war? The chase leads to a genuinely creative development when a particle accelerator is used to create a magnetic field so powerful it immobilizes the Terminatrix.

The ending of the film must remain for you

to discover, but I will say it seems perfunctory—more like a plot development than a denouement in the history of humanity. The movie cares so exclusively about its handful of characters that what happens to them is of supreme importance, and the planet is merely a backdrop.

Is *Terminator 3* a skillful piece of work? Indeed. Will it entertain the Friday-night action crowd? You bet. Does it tease and intrigue us like the earlier films did? Not really. Among recent sci-fi pictures, *Hulk* is in the tradition of science fiction that concerns ideas and personalities, and *Terminator 3* is dumbed down for the multiplex hordes.

The Texas Chainsaw Massacre
no stars
R, 98 m., 2003

Jessica Biel (Erin), Jonathan Tucker (Morgan), Eric Balfour (Kemper), Andrew Bryniarski (Leatherface), Erica Leerhsen (Pepper), Mike Vogel (Andy), R. Lee Ermey (Sheriff Hoyt), Terrence Evans (Old Monty). Directed by Marcus Nispel and produced by Michael Bay and Mike Fleiss. Screenplay by Scott Kosar, based on the screenplay by Kim Henkel and Tobe Hooper.

The new version of *The Texas Chainsaw Massacre* is a contemptible film: vile, ugly, and brutal. There is not a shred of a reason to see it. Those who defend it will have to dance through mental hoops of their own devising, defining its meanness and despair as "style" or "vision" or "a commentary on our world." It is not a commentary on anything except the marriage of slick technology with the materials of a geek show.

The movie is a remake of, or was inspired by, the 1974 horror film by Tobe Hooper. That film at least had the raw power of its originality. It proceeded from Hooper's fascination with the story and his need to tell it. This new version, made by a man who has previously directed music videos, proceeds from nothing more than a desire to feed on the corpse of a once-living film. There is no worthy or defensible purpose in sight here: The filmmakers want to cause disgust and hopelessness in the audience.

Ugly emotions are easier to evoke and often more commercial than those that contribute to the ongoing lives of the beholders.

The movie begins with grainy "newsreel" footage of a 1974 massacre (the same one as in the original film; there are some changes, but this is not a sequel). Then we plunge directly into the formula of a Dead Teenager Movie, which begins with living teenagers and kills them one by one. The formula can produce movies that are good, bad, funny, depressing, whatever. This movie, strewn with blood, bones, rats, fetishes, and severed limbs, photographed in murky darkness, scored with screams, wants to be a test: Can you sit through it? There were times when I intensely wanted to walk out of the theater and into the fresh air and look at the sky and buy an apple and sigh for our civilization, but I stuck it out. The ending, which is cynical and truncated, confirmed my suspicion that the movie was made by and for those with no attention span.

The movie doesn't tell a story in any useful sense, but is simply a series of gruesome events that finally are over. It probably helps to have seen the original film in order to understand what's going on, since there's so little exposition. Only from the earlier film do we have a vague idea of who the people are in this godforsaken house, and what their relationship is to one another. The movie is eager to start the gore and unwilling to pause for exposition.

I like good horror movies. They can exorcise our demons. *The Texas Chainsaw Massacre* doesn't want to exorcise anything. It wants to tramp crap through our imaginations and wipe its feet on our dreams. I think of filmgoers on a date, seeing this movie and then—what? I guess they'll have to laugh at it, irony being a fashionable response to the experience of being had.

Certainly they will not be frightened by it. It recycles the same old tired thriller tools that have been worn out in countless better movies. There is the scary noise that is only a cat. The device of loud sudden noises to underline the movements of half-seen shadows. The van that won't start. The truck that won't start. The car that won't start. The character who turns around and sees the slasher standing right behind her. One critic writes, "Best of all, there was not a single case of 'She's only doing that [falling, going into a scary space, not picking up the gun] because she's in a thriller." Huh? Nobody does anything in this movie for any other reason. There is no reality here. It's all a thriller.

There is a controversy involving Quentin Tarantino's *Kill Bill: Volume 1*, which some people feel is "too violent." I gave it four stars, found it kind of brilliant, felt it was an exhilarating exercise in nonstop action direction. The material was redeemed, justified, illustrated, and explained by the style. It was a meditation on the martial arts genre, done with intelligence and wit. *The Texas Chainsaw Massacre* is a meditation on the geek-show movie. Tarantino's film is made with grace and joy. This movie is made with venom and cynicism. I doubt that anybody involved in it will be surprised or disappointed if audience members vomit or flee. Do yourself a favor. There are a lot of good movies playing right now that can make you feel a little happier, smarter, sexier, funnier, more excited—or more scared, if that's what you want. This is not one of them. Don't let it kill ninety-eight minutes of your life.

Thirteen ★ ★ ★ ½
R, 100 m., 2003

Evan Rachel Wood (Tracy), Nikki Reed (Evie), Holly Hunter (Melanie), Jeremy Sisto (Brady), Brady Corbet (Mason), Deborah Kara Unger (Brooke), Kip Pardue (Luke). Directed by Catherine Hardwicke and produced by Jeffrey Levy-Hinte and Michael London. Screenplay by Hardwicke and Nikki Reed.

"The two worst years of a woman's life," writes Nell Minow, "are the year she is thirteen and the year her daughter is." There are exceptions to the rule; I once attended a thirteenth birthday party at which daughter and mother both seemed to be just fine, thanks, but it is hard to imagine a worse year than the one endured by the characters in *Thirteen*. This is the frightening story of how a nice girl falls under the influence of a wild girl and barely escapes big, big, big trouble, by which I mean drugs, crime, unwanted pregnancies, and other hazards, which some teenagers seem inexplicably eager to experience.

That the horrors in this movie are worse than those found in the lives of most thirteen-year-olds, I believe and hope. It is painful enough to endure them at any age, let alone in a young and vulnerable season when life should be wondrous. But I believe such things really happen to some young teenagers, because at Sundance, I met Nikki Reed, who cowrote the screenplay when she was thirteen, and was fourteen when she played Evie, the movie's trouble maker. In real life Reed was the good girl; here, as a wild and seductive bad influence, she's so persuasive and convincing I'm prepared to believe the movie is a truthful version of real experiences.

Evie is the most popular girl in the seventh grade because of her bold personality, her clothes and accessories (mostly stolen), and her air of knowing more about sex than a thirteen-year-old should. The school's value system is suggested by the fact that some of the students are working on a "project" about J-Lo. One of Evie's admirers is Tracy (Evan Rachel Wood), a good student who hangs around with a couple of unpopular girls and wants to trade up. Evie is cruel to her ("Call me," she says, and gives her the wrong number). But when Tracy steals a purse and hands over the money, Evie takes her on a shopping spree and soon the girls are such close friends that Evie has, essentially, moved into Tracy's room.

Tracy lives with her divorced mother, Melanie, played by Holly Hunter in a performance where the character vibrates with the intensity of her life. Melanie lives in a sprawling house she can't afford, inherited from a marriage with a husband who is behind on his child support; she runs a beauty salon in her kitchen, and her house seems to be a drop zone for friends, acquaintances, their children, and their needs ("A $2 tip," she complains after one mob leaves, "and they ate half the lasagna").

Melanie is a recovering alcoholic, hanging onto AA for dear life, and with a boyfriend named Brady (Jeremy Sisto) who is in the program, too, although Melanie has painful memories from when he wasn't. Melanie is sober, but it would be fair to say her life is still unmanageable, and although she loves Tracy and protects her with a fierce mother's love, she's clueless about what's going on behind that bedroom door.

Evie's history is often described but somehow never very clear. She lives with someone named Brooke (Deborah Unger), who is not quite her mother, not quite her guardian, allegedly her cousin, more like her spaced-out roommate. Evie tells stories of violence and sexual abuse when she was young, and while we have no trouble believing such things could have happened, it's impossible to be sure when she's telling the truth.

Although Evie is trouble enough on her own, she reaches critical mass after she moves in with Tracy. Perhaps only a thirteen-year-old like Nikki Reed could have found the exact note in dialogue where the mother tries to get answers and information and is rejected and ignored like an unsolicited telephone call. You might doubt that a girl could conceal from her mother the fact that she has had her tongue and navel pierced, but this movie convinced me of that, and a lot more.

There are moments when you want to cringe at the danger these girls are in. They slip through the bedroom window and hang out on Hollywood Boulevard, they experiment sexually with kids older and tougher than they are, they all but rape "Luke the lifeguard boy" (Kip Pardue), a neighbor who accuses them, accurately, of being jailbait. They want to fly close to danger without getting hurt, and we wait for them to learn how hard and cruel the world can be.

When I met Reed at Sundance she was with the film's director, Catherine Hardwicke, who told one of those "only in southern California" stories: Hardwicke was dating Reed's father, Reed was having problems, Hardwicke suggested she keep a journal, she wrote a screenplay instead, Hardwicke collaborated on a final draft and became the director. Of Reed it can only be said that, like Diane Lane at a similar age, she has the gifts to do almost anything. Although this is Hardwicke's directing debut, she has many important credits as a production designer (*Tombstone, Three Kings, Vanilla Sky*"), and the movie is smoothly professional, especially in the way it choreographs the comings and goings in Holly Hunter's chaotic household. Hunter gave a famous performance in *Broadcast News* (1987) as a hyperactive news producer who was forever trying to keep all her plates spinning. Her problems here are similar. We know exactly how she feels as she trips on a

loose kitchen tile and starts tearing up "the goddamn $1.50-a-square-foot floor."

Who is this movie for? Not for most thirteen-year-olds, that's for sure. The R rating is richly deserved, no matter how much of a lark the poster promises. Maybe the film is simply for those who admire fine, focused acting and writing; *Thirteen* sets a technical problem that seems insoluble, and meets it brilliantly, finding convincing performances from its teenage stars, showing a parent who is clueless but not uncaring, and a world outside that bedroom window that has big bad wolves, and worse.

Note: Watching Thirteen, *I remembered another movie with the same title. David D. Williams's* Thirteen *(1997) tells the story of a thirteen-year-old African-American girl named Nina, who runs away from home and causes much concern for her mother, neighbors, and the police before turning up again. The movie is set in a more innocent place, a small Virginia town, and has a heroine who has not grown up too fast but is still partly a child, as she should be. The film, which I showed at my Overlooked Film Festival, is apparently not available on video; it would be a comfort after this one.*

Thirteen Conversations About One Thing ★ ★ ★ ★
R, 102 m., 2002

Matthew McConaughey (Troy), John Turturro (Walker), Alan Arkin (Gene), Clea DuVall (Beatrice), Amy Irving (Patricia), Barbara Sukowa (Helen), William Wise (Wade). Directed by Jill Sprecher and produced by Beni Atoori and Gina Resnick. Screenplay by Jill and Karen Sprecher.

Happiness is the subject of *Thirteen Conversations About One Thing*. For that matter, happiness is the subject of every conversation we ever have: the search for happiness, the envy of happiness, the loss of happiness, the guilt about undeserved happiness. The engine that drives the human personality is our desire to be happy instead of sad, entertained instead of bored, inspired instead of disillusioned, informed rather than ignorant. It is not an easy business.

Consider Troy (Matthew McConaughey), the prosecutor who has just won a big conviction. In the movie's opening scene, he's loud and obnoxious in a saloon, celebrating his victory. He spots a sad sack at the bar: Gene (Alan Arkin), who seems to be pessimistic about the possibility of happiness. Gene is a midlevel manager at an insurance company, has to fire someone, and decides to fire Wade, the happiest man in the department, since he can see the sunny side of anything.

Troy buys drinks for Gene. He wants everybody to be happy. Then he drives drunk, hits a pedestrian with his car, and believes he has killed her. As an assistant district attorney he knows how much trouble he's in, and instinctively leaves the scene. His problem becomes an all-consuming guilt, which spoils his ability to enjoy anything in life; he was cut in the accident, and keeps the wound open with a razor blade to punish himself.

The movie finds connections between people who think they are strangers, finding the answer to one person's problem in the question raised by another. We meet Walker (John Turturro), a sardonic college professor, who walks out on his wife (Amy Irving) and begins an affair with a woman (Barbara Sukowa). She realizes that the affair is hardly the point: Walker is going through the motions because he has been told, and believes, that this is how you find happiness. We also meet a house cleaner (Clea DuVall), who is good at her job but works for a client who can only criticize. She is injured for no reason at all, suffers great pain, does not deserve to.

The truth hidden below the surface of the story is a hard one: Nothing makes any sense. We do not get what we deserve. If we are lucky, we get more. If we are unlucky, we get less. Bad things happen to good people, and good things happen to bad people. That's the system. All of our philosophies are a futile attempt to explain it. Let me tell you a story. Not long ago I was in the middle of a cheerful conversation when I slipped on wet wax, landed hard and broke bones in my left shoulder. I was in a fool's paradise of happiness, you see, not realizing that I was working without a net—that in a second my happiness would be rudely interrupted.

I could have hit my head and been killed. Or landed better and not been injured. At best what we can hope for is a daily reprieve from all of the things that can go wrong. *Thirteen Conversations About One Thing* is relentless in the way it

demonstrates how little we control our lives. We can choose actions, but we cannot plan outcomes. Follow, for example, the consequences of Alan Arkin's decision to fire the happy man, and then see what happens to Arkin, and then see what happens to the happy man. Or watch as the Matthew McConaughey character grants reality to something he only thinks he knows. Or see how the Turturro character, so obsessed with his personal timetable, so devoted to his daily and weekly routines, is able to arrange everything to his satisfaction—and then is not satisfied.

The movie is brilliant, really. It is philosophy illustrated through everyday events. Most movies operate as if their events are necessary—that B must follow A. *Thirteen Conversations* betrays B, A, and all the other letters as random possibilities.

The film was directed by Jill Sprecher, and written with her sister, Karen. It's their second, after *Clockwatchers* (1997), the lacerating, funny story about temporary workers in an office and their strategies to prove they exist in a world that is utterly indifferent to them. After these two movies, there aren't many filmmakers whose next film I anticipate more eagerly. They're onto something. They're using films to demonstrate something to us. Movies tell narratives, and the purpose of narrative is to arrange events in an order that seems to make sense and end correctly. The Sprechers are telling us if we believe in these narratives we're only fooling ourselves.

And yet, even so, there is a way to find happiness. That is to be curious about all of the interlocking events that add up to our lives. To notice connections. To be amused or perhaps frightened by the ways things work out. If the universe is indifferent, what a consolation that we are not.

13 Going on 30 ★ ★
PG-13, 97 m., 2004

Jennifer Garner (Jenna Rink), Mark Ruffalo (Matt Flamhaff), Judy Greer (Lucy Wyman), Andy Serkis (Richard Kneeland), Kathy Baker (Beverly Rink), Phil Reeves (Wayne Rink), Christa B. Allen (Young Jenna Rink). Directed by Gary Winick and produced by Susan Arnold, Gina Matthews, and Donna Roth. Screenplay by Cathy Yuspa, Josh Goldsmith, and Niels Mueller.

Jennifer Garner is indeed a charmer, but she's the victim of a charmless treatment in *13 Going on 30*, another one of those body-switch movies (think *Big*, *Vice Versa*, *Freaky Friday*, etc.) in which a child magically occupies an adult body. The director, Gary Winick, came out of Sundance with *Tadpole* (2003), a movie in which a sixteen-year-old boy was seduced by a forty-year-old woman, and some of us wondered how well that plot would have worked with a sixteen-year-old girl and a forty-year-old man. Now Winick finds out, by supplying a thirteen-year-old girl with a thirty-year-old body and a boyfriend who's a professional hockey star. Their big makeout scene goes wrong when she thinks he's "gross," and we fade to black, mercifully, before we find out what happens then. Can you be guilty of statutory rape caused by magical body-switching?

The movie introduces us to Jenna Rink when she's a teenager (played by Christa B. Allen), who allows the most popular girls in school to push her around because she wants to be just like them. (There's a much superior version of this angle in *Mean Girls*.) She throws a party in her rec room and the girls play a nasty trick on her, which inspires her to be cruel to her only true friend, Matt, a chubby kid who lives next door and adores her.

Then she's sprinkled with magic dust (I think we have to let the movie get away with this), and discovers that she is thirty, lives in New York, is an editor of a magazine named *Poise*, and looks like Jennifer Garner. Her snotty high school classmate Lucy (Judy Greer) now works with her on the magazine, and they're friends, sort of, although the movie teaches us that career women will betray each other to get ahead.

In the best examples of this genre, there are funny scenes in which adult actors get to act as if they're inhabited by kids. Tom Hanks did this about as well as it can be done in *Big*, and I also liked Judge Reinhold in *Vice Versa*, and of course Jamie Lee Curtis in the 2003 version of *Freaky Friday*. Strangely, *13 Going on 30* doesn't linger on scenes like that, maybe because Jenna is established in a high-powered Manhattan world where she has to learn fast. The result is that most of the movie isn't really about a thirteen-year-old in an adult body, but about a power struggle at the magazine, and Jenna's attempts to renew her friendship with Matt (now played by Mark Ruffalo).

He's not cooperative. Apparently her missing seventeen years all actually occurred; it's just that she can't remember them. And after the disastrous party in the rec room, she never talked to Matt again, so why should he believe she's any different now? She's desperate, because she has no real friends, but Matt is engaged to be married, and what happens to the time line to solve that dilemma would make *Eternal Sunshine of the Spotless Mind* look as linear as a Doris Day romance.

Logical quibbles are, of course, irrelevant with a movie like this. You buy the magic because it comes with the territory. What I couldn't buy was the world of the magazine office, and the awkward scenes in which high-powered professionals don't seem to notice that they're dealing with a thirteen-year-old mind. Jenna's bright idea to redesign the magazine is so spectacularly bad that it's accepted, I suppose, only because the screenwriters stood over the actors with whips and drove them to it.

The writers, by the way, are Cathy Yuspa, Josh Goldsmith, and Niels Mueller. Yuspa and Goldsmith wrote the vastly superior office comedy *What Women Want* (2000), in which Mel Gibson was able to read the minds of the women in his office. This time there are no minds worth reading. Although we understand why Jenna is attracted to the adult Matt (who has undergone a transition from pudgy to handsome), the movie never really deals with (1) whether he fully comes to grips with the fact that this is the *same* girl he knew at thirteen, and (2) how or why or whether or when a thirteen-year-old can successfully fall in love with a thirty-year-old man, with everything that would entail (in life, anyway, if not in this movie). There are so many emotional and sexual puzzles to tap-dance around, this should have been a musical.

Till Human Voices Wake Us ★ ½
R, 101 m., 2003

Guy Pearce (Sam Franks), Helena Bonham Carter (Ruby), Lindley Joyner (Young Sam

Franks), Brooke Harman (Silvy Lewis). Directed by Michael Petroni and produced by Thomas Augsberger, Matthias Emcke, Shana Levine, Dean Murphy, Nigel Odell, and David Redman. Screenplay by Petroni.

Till Human Voices Wake Us could have been a poem by Edgar Allen Poe, a short story by Stephen King, or a *Twilight Zone* episode by Rod Serling. Poe would have liked the part where the heroine drifts on her back down the river under the starry skies. King would have the hero gasping when he finds only his coat in the boat. And Serling would have informed us, "A man named T. S. Eliot once hinted that you can drown in your sleep and not have the nightmare until you wake up in the morning."

None of these artists would have, however, made this movie. That is because film makes it literal, and the story is too slight to bear up under the weight. *The Twilight Zone* could have done it as video, because it would have represented 20 minutes of running time (instead of 101), and been photographed in that stylized 1950s black-and-white television purity where the exterior shot of every residential street seemed to leave room for a mushroom cloud.

The movie tells a story that kept its key hidden for a long time in the Australian version, which began with two young people in a rural district and only switched over, much later, to a story about two adults (Guy Pearce and Helena Bonham Carter). At least in Australia you thought for half an hour or so that the whole story was about the teenagers (Lindley Joyner and Brooke Harman). In the version shown in the rest of the world, the two stories are intercut, which of course gives away the game, since Young Sam Franks grows up to be Sam Franks, and therefore, according to the Principle of the Unassigned Character, the mysterious girl he meets on the train must therefore be . . .

I am not giving anything away. This is the first movie I have seen where the plot device is revealed by the *fact* of the first flashback. Young Sam has journeyed on into adulthood with a heavy burden of guilt, which he hints at in a lecture he gives on psychology. Freud will be of no help to him, however. Maybe Jung would have some ideas, or Dionne Warwick.

The title comes from *The Love Song of J. Alfred Prufrock*, by T. S. Eliot, which is the favorite poem of—well, I was about to say both women. It looks to me like Silvy, the young woman, is reading from the first edition, which would have been possible in Australia in those days. So is the older woman, named Ruby, at a time when the book was worth about $35,000. A book like that, you take the paperback when you go swimming.

But I am being way too cynical about a film that after all only wants to be sad and bittersweet, redemptive and healing. It doesn't really matter what your literal interpretation is for what happens in that adult summer, since there is a sense in which it doesn't really happen anyway, and the result would be the same no matter what the explanation.

There must still be a kind of moony young adolescent girl for which this film would be enormously appealing, if television has not already exterminated the domestic example of that species. The last surviving example in the wild was run over last week by a snowmobile in Yellowstone.

Timeline ★ ★
PG-13, 116 m., 2003

Paul Walker (Chris), Frances O'Connor (Kate), Gerard Butler (Andre Marek), Billy Connolly (Edward Johnston), Neal McDonough (Gorgdon), Ethan Embry (David Stern), Anna Friel (Lady Claire), David Thewlis (Robert Doniger). Directed by Richard Donner and produced by Richard Donner, Lauren Shuler Donner, and Jim Van Wyck. Screenplay by Jeff Maguire and George Nolfi, based on the novel by Michael Crichton.

Timeline is based on a Michael Crichton story that's not so much about travel between the past and the present as about travel between two movie genres. After opening on an archaeological dig (evoking memories of *Indiana Jones, The Exorcist,* and *The Omen*), it's a corporate thriller crossed with a medieval swashbuckler. The corporation has discovered a way to beam objects from one place to another, and has big plans: It wants to put Federal Express out of business. Alas, its teleportation machine intersects with a wormhole, and inadvertently sends a group of scientists back into fourteenth-century France.

So far I don't have a problem. I'll accept any premise that gets me into a good movie. But why can Crichton think of nothing more interesting for his heroes to do than immerse themselves in a medieval swashbuckler? Why travel 600 years into the past just so you can play "I Capture the Castle"? The movie follows the modern formula in which story is secondary to action, and the plot is essentially a frame for action scenes.

The movie has been directed by Richard Donner, who has given me some splendid times at the movies. His *Superman* remains one of the great superhero epics, his *Lethal Weapon* made my best-ten list, *Lethal Weapon 2* was almost as good, and he made a lighthearted version of *Maverick* with Mel Gibson that brought cheer to the Western genre. But here I think he got off on the wrong foot, with a story whose parts don't fit.

Donner and his wife, the producer Lauren Shuler Donner, attended the Chicago press screening of *Timeline* and made some comments. When filmmakers do that, I kind of want to duck behind the seat in front of me. I'd rather see the movie cold. They told of their long odyssey to get the movie made, the corporate struggles that almost sank it, the difficult locations, their determination in spite of everything. Because of those travails, I wish the movie had been a triumph, but it's not.

Donner made it a special point that the movie doesn't contain nearly as many special effects as we might assume. When besieging armies hurl fireballs into a castle, for example, those are real fireballs—not the computer-generated version, as in *Gladiator*. Twenty years ago a filmmaker might have boasted that he had used computers for his effects. Now he gets points for using the traditional methods. The problem is, unless the shots involved are so bad they call attention to themselves (and these are certainly not), it's not whether we're watching real fireballs or fake fireballs but whether we care about the fireballs.

I didn't. I felt too much of the movie consisted of groups of characters I didn't care about, running down passageways and fighting off enemies and trying to get back to the present before the window of time slams shut (there's even a big clock ticking off the seconds). Just once I'd like to see a time-travel movie inspired by true curiosity about the past, instead of by a desire to use it as a setting for action scenes. ☞

The Time Machine ★ ½
PG-13, 96 m., 2002

Guy Pearce (Alexander Hartdegen), Jeremy Irons (Uber Morlock), Sienna Guillory (Emma), Samantha Mumba (Mara), Orlando Jones (Vox), Mark Addy (Dr. Philby). Directed by Simon Wells and produced by Walter F. Parkes and David Valdes. Screenplay by John Logan, based on the novel by H. G. Wells.

The Time Machine is a witless recycling of the H. G. Wells story from 1895, with the absurdity intact but the wonderment missing. It makes use of computer-aided graphics to create a future race of grubby underground beasties who, like the characters in *Battleship Earth*, have evolved beyond the need for bathing and fingernail clippers. Because this race, the Morlocks, is allegedly a Darwinian offshoot of humans, and because they are remarkably unattractive, they call into question the theory that over a long period of time a race grows more attractive through natural selection. They are obviously the result of 800,000 years of ugly brides.

The film stars Guy Pearce as Alexander Hartdegen, a brilliant mathematician who hopes to use Einstein's earliest theories to build a machine to travel through time. He is in love with the beautiful Emma (Sienna Guillory), but on the very night when he proposes marriage a tragedy happens, and he vows to travel back in time in his new machine and change the course of history.

The machine, which lacks so much as a seat belt, consists of whirling spheres encompassing a Victorian club chair. Convenient brass gauges spin to record the current date. Speed and direction are controlled by a joystick. The time machine has an uncanny ability to move in perfect synchronization with Earth, so that it always lands in the same geographical spot, despite the fact that in the future large chunks of the Moon (or all of it, according to the future race of Eloi) have fallen to Earth, which should have had some effect on the orbit. Since it would be inconvenient if a time machine materialized miles in the air or deep underground, this is just as well.

We will not discuss paradoxes of time travel here, since such discussion makes any time travel movie impossible. Let us discuss instead an unintended journey that Hartdegen makes to 8,000 centuries in the future, when Homo sapiens have split in two, into the Eloi and Morlocks. The Morlocks evolved underground in the dark ages after the Moon's fall, and attack on the surface by popping up through dusty sinkholes. They hunt the Eloi for food. The Eloi are an attractive race of brown-skinned people whose civilization seems modeled on paintings by Rousseau; their life is an idyll of leafy bowers, waterfalls, and elegant forest structures, but they are such fatalists about the Morlocks that instead of fighting them off they all but salt and pepper themselves.

Alexander meets a beautiful Eloi woman (Samantha Mumba) and her sturdy young brother, befriends them, and eventually journeys to the underworld to try to rescue her. This brings him into contact with the Uber Morlock, a chalk-faced Jeremy Irons, who did not learn his lesson after playing an evil Mage named Profion in *Dungeons & Dragons*.

In broad outline, this future world matches the one depicted in George Pal's 1960 film *The Time Machine*, although its blond, blue-eyed race of Eloi have been transformed into dusky sun people. One nevertheless tends to question romances between people who were born 800,000 years apart and have few conversations on subjects other than not being eaten. Convenient that when humankind was splitting into two different races, both its branches continued to speak English.

The Morlocks and much of their world have been created by undistinguished animation. The Morlock hunters are supposed to be able to leap great distances with fearsome speed, but the animation turns them into cartoonish characters whose movements defy even the laws of gravity governing bodies in motion. Their movements are not remotely plausible, and it's disconcerting to see that while the Eloi are utterly unable to evade them, Hartdegen, a professor who has scarcely left his laboratory for four years, is able to duck out of the way, bean them with big tree branches, etc.

Guy Pearce, as the hero, makes the mistake of trying to give a good and realistic performance. Irons at least knows what kind of movie he's in, and hams it up accordingly. Pearce seems thoughtful, introspective, quiet, morose. Surely the inventor of a time machine should have a few screws loose, and the glint in his eye should not be from tears. By the end of the movie, as he stands beside the beautiful Eloi woman and takes her hand, we are thinking not of their future together, but about how he got from the Morlock caverns to the top of that mountain ridge in time to watch an explosion that takes only a few seconds. A Morlock could cover that distance, but not a mathematician, unless he has discovered wormholes as well.

Time Out ★ ★ ★
PG-13, 132 m., 2002

Aurelien Recoing (Vincent), Karin Viard (Muriel), Serge Livrozet (Jean-Michel), Jean-Pierre Mangeot (Father), Monique Mangeot (Mother). Directed by Laurent Cantet and produced by Caroline Benjo. Screenplay by Robin Campillo and Cantet.

Vincent loses his job. He cannot bear to confess this to his wife and children, so he invents another one, and the fictional job takes up more of his time than his family does. It is hard work to spend all day producing the illusion of accomplishment out of thin air. Ask anyone from Enron. The film *Time Out* is about modern forms of work that exist only because we say they do. Those best-sellers about modern management techniques are hilarious because the only things that many managers actually manage are their techniques.

Free from his job, Vincent is seduced by the pleasure of getting in his car and just driving around. He lives in France, near the Swiss border, and one day he wanders into an office building in Switzerland, eavesdrops on some of the employees, picks up a brochure, and tells his relatives he works in a place like this. It's an agency associated with the United Nations, and as nearly as I can tell, its purpose is to train managers who can go to Africa and train managers. This is about right. The best way to get a job through a program designed to find you a job is to get a job with the program.

Vincent, played by the sad-eyed, sincere Aurelien Recoing, is not a con man so much as a pragmatist who realizes that since his job exists mostly in his mind anyway, he might as well eliminate the middleman, his employer. He begins taking long overnight trips, sleeping in his car, finding his breakfast at cold, lonely roadside diners at daybreak. He calls his wife frequently with progress reports: The meeting went well, the client needs more time, the project team is assembling tomorrow, he has a new assignment. Since he has not figured out how to live without money, he convinces friends and relatives to invest in his fictional company, and uses that money to live on.

You would think the movie would be about how this life of deception, these lonely weeks on the road, wear him down. Actually, he seems more worn out by the experience of interacting with his family during his visits at home. His wife, Muriel (Karin Viard), a schoolteacher, suspects that something is not quite convincing about this new job. What throws her off is that there was something not quite convincing about his old job too. Vincent's father is the kind of man who, because he can never be pleased, does not distinguish between one form of displeasure and another. Vincent's children are not much interested in their dad's work.

In his travels Vincent encounters Jean-Michel (Serge Livrozet), who spots him for a phony and might have a place in his organization for the right kind of phony. Jean-Michel imports fake brand-name items. What he does is not legal, but it does involve the sale and delivery of actual physical goods. He is more honest than those who simply exchange theoretical goods; Jean-Michel sells fake Guccis, Enron sells fake dollars.

Time Out is the second film by Laurent Cantet, whose first was *Human Resources* (2000), about a young man from a working-class family who goes off to college and returns as the human resources manager at the factory where his father has worked all of his life as a punch-press operator. One of the son's tasks is to lay off many employees, including his father. The father heartbreakingly returns to his machine even after being fired, because he cannot imagine his life without a job. Vincent in a way is worse off. His job is irrelevant to his life. I admire the closing scenes of the film, which seem to ask whether our civilization offers a cure for Vincent's complaint.

Together ★ ★ ★ ½
PG, 116 m., 2003

Tang Yun (Liu Xiaochun), Liu Peiqi (Liu Cheng), Chen Hong (Lili), Wang Zhiwen (Professor Jiang), Chen Kaige (Professor Yu Shifeng), Zhang Qing (Yu Lin). Directed by Chen Kaige and produced by Chen Hong, Kaige, Li Bolun, Yan Xiaoming, and Yang Buting. Screenplay by Kaige and Xue Xiao Lu.

Here is a movie not embarrassed by strong, basic emotions like love and ambition. It has the courage to face them head-on, instead of edging up to them through irony, or disarming them with sitcom comedy. Chen Kaige's *Together* is a movie with the nerve to end with melodramatic sentiment—and get away with it, because it means it. Lots of damp eyes in the audience.

The movie tells the story of Liu Xiaochun (Tang Yun), a thirteen-year-old violin prodigy who lives in a provincial town with his father, Liu Cheng (Liu Peiqi). His father is a cook who decides Xiaochun must advance his studies in Beijing—and so he takes them both there, with his meager savings hidden in his red peasant's hat. Because he is so naive, so direct, so obviously exactly who he is, and because his son really is talented, the uncultured father is able to convince a violin teacher named Jiang (Wang Zhiwen) to take the boy as a student.

Jiang is almost a recluse, a once-talented pianist whose heart was broken by a girl, and who has retreated to a shabby apartment with his cats and his dirty laundry. As he tutors the boy, the boy tutors him, lecturing him on his hygiene and self-pity. The two become close friends, but one day Xiaochun's father decides it is time for him to move up to a better teacher—the famous Yu Shifeng, played by director Chen Kaige himself. Jiang is a realist and agrees with this change, and the leave-taking between the two friends is handled in a touching, unexpected way.

The big city is exciting for young Xiaochun, who meets a woman in her twenties named Lili, played by Chen Hong, who in real life is the director's wife. She tips him for carrying her bag, hires him to play at a party, takes him shopping, and befriends him. She is also involved in a complex and traumatic episode when the boy sells his precious violin (all that is left from his mother, he is told) to buy her a coat.

The young violinist's goal is to be chosen by Professor Yu for an important international contest. A girl named Yu Lin (Zhang Qing), another of Yu's students, is his rival, and both the professor and the girl tell him secrets that force him to reevaluate his world and values. Torn between recognition and his love for his father, he finds a solution in the last scene that is physically impossible (unless the symphony orchestra is playing very, very loudly) but is the perfect outcome for the story—an emotional high point that's dramatic and heartwarming.

The movie is also a story about the old and new China, set in old and new Beijing. Professor Jiang lives in a crowded quarter of dwellings that lean cozily on each other, its streets filled with bicycles and gossip. People know each other. Professor Yu lives in a sterile modern building with Western furnishings. When he suggests that Xiaochun leave his father and live with him, he is essentially asking him to leave an older, more human China, and enter a modern world of ambition, success, and media marketing.

Lili, the pretty neighbor, is caught between those two worlds. She is clearly a good person, yet not above using her beauty to support herself. In this PG-rated movie, however, it's a little hard to figure out exactly what her profession is. I did some Web research and discovered she is "a goodhearted neighbor [who] offers some of the film's most tender moments" (U.S. Conference of Catholic Bishops), "a gold-digging glamour-puss" (*Village Voice*), or "the proverbial hooker with the heart of gold" (*New York Post*). Morality is in the eye of the beholder.

For Chen Kaige, *Together* is a comeback after the extravagant *Temptress Moon* (1996) and *The Emperor and the Assassin* (1999). His earlier credits include *Yellow Earth*, a touching

story of a soldier collecting rural folk songs, and the masterful *Farewell My Concubine*, about two members of the Peking Opera who survive through a time of political tumult.

Together is powerful in an old-fashioned, big-studio kind of way; Hollywood once had the knack of making audience-pleasers like this, before it got too clever for its own good. Strange, but moviegoers who avoid "art films" and are simply in the mood for a good, entertaining movie would be better off with this Chinese film than with most of the multiplex specials.

Tokyo Godfathers ★ ★ ★
PG-13, 90 m., 2004

With the voices of: Toru Emori (Gin), Yoshiaki Umegaki (Hana), and Aya Okamoto (Miyuki). Directed by Satoshi Kon and produced by Masao Maruyama. Screenplay by Kon and Keiko Nobumotu.

In Japan, animation is not seen as the exclusive realm of children's and family films, but is often used for adult, science fiction, and action stories, where it allows a kind of freedom impossible in real life. Some Hollywood films strain so desperately against the constraints of the possible that you wish they'd just caved in and gone with animation (*Torque* is an example).

Now here is *Tokyo Godfathers,* an animated film both harrowing and heartwarming, about a story that will never, ever, be remade by Disney. It's about three homeless people—an alcoholic, a drag queen, and a girl of about eleven—who find an abandoned baby in the trash on a cold Christmas Eve, and try for a few days to give it a home. The title makes a nod to John Ford's *3 Godfathers* (1948), where three desperados (led by John Wayne) rescue a baby from its dying mother on Christmas Eve and try to raise it, at one point substituting axle grease for baby oil.

The three urban drifters live in a Tokyo of ice and snow, where they have fashioned a temporary shelter of cardboard and plywood, and outfitted it with all the comforts of home, like a portable stove. Here they've formed a family of sorts, but each has a story to tell, and during the movie they all tell them.

Gin, the alcoholic, claims to have been a bicycle racer who abandoned his family after losing everything by gambling. Hana, the transvestite, has felt like an outsider since birth. Miyuki, the little girl, ran away from home after a fight with her father. The others tell her she should return, but she's afraid to. And then the cries of the infant alert them, and their rescue of the little girl is a catalyst that inspires each of them to find what's good and resilient within themselves.

The movie was cowritten and directed by Satoshi Kon, whose *Perfect Blue* and *Millennium Actress* have been among the best-received and most popular anime titles. Unlike Hayao Miyazaki *(Spirited Away, My Neighbor Totoro)*, his style doesn't approach full-motion animation, but uses the simplified approach of a lot of anime, with simple backgrounds and characters who move and talk in a stylized way that doesn't approach realism. If you see this style for thirty seconds you're likely to think it's constrained, but in a feature film it grows on you and you accept it, and your imagination makes it expand into an acceptable version of the world.

The movie's story is melodrama crossed with pathos, sometimes startling hard-boiled action, and enormous coincidence. The streets of Tokyo seem empty and grim as the three godparents protect the child and eventually begin a search for its true parents. And the story involving those parents is more complicated than we imagine. There are scenes in an abandoned house, in an alley of homeless dwellings, in a drugstore, that seem forlorn and hopeless, and then other scenes of surprising warmth, leading up to a sensational ending and a quite remarkable development in which two lives are saved in a way possible only in animation.

Tokyo Godfathers is not appropriate for younger viewers, and I know there are older ones who don't fancy themselves sitting through feature-length adult animation from Japan. But there's a world there to be discovered. And sometimes, as with this film and the great *Grave of the Fireflies*, the themes are so harrowing that only animation makes them possible. I don't think I'd want to see a movie in which a real baby had the adventures this one has.

Torque ★ ★ ½
PG-13, 81 m., 2004

Martin Henderson (Cary Ford), Ice Cube (Trey Wallace), Monet Mazur (Shane), Jay Hernandez (Dalton), Christina Milian (Nina), Jaime Pressly (China), Matt Schulze (Henry). Directed by Joseph Kahn and produced by Brad Luff and Neal H. Moritz. Screenplay by Matt Johnson.

Long ago, at the dawn of motorcycle pictures, a critic who had been working for only four months encountered a film named *Hells Angels on Wheels* (1967). It was about a war between motorcycle gangs, and its cast included an actor named Jack Nicholson, whom the critic did not even name, although he found room to mention Adam Roarke, John Garwood, and Sabrina Scharf. The critic, observing that "sometimes good stuff creeps into exploitation pictures just because nobody cares enough to keep it out," made the following points:

— "The characters are authentically surly, irresponsible, mean, coarse, and human."

— Sabrina Scharf "makes you wonder how she keeps her makeup on while raising hell with the angels."

— The "accomplished camera work" includes "one shot where the camera moves in and out of focus through a field of green grass and then steals slowly across one of the big, brutal cycles. The contrast has an impact equal to David Lean's similar shots in *Doctor Zhivago* (remember the frosty window fading into the field of flowers?)."

— "The film is better than it might have been, and better than it had to be. Take it on its own terms and you might find it interesting."

Reader, that young critic was me. The film's director was Richard Rush, who went on to make *The Stunt Man*. The young cinematographer was "Leslie Kovacs," who, under his true Hungarian name of Laszló, went on to shoot *Five Easy Pieces* with Jack Nicholson, and fifty other films, including some of the best photographed of his time.

Today I went to see *Torque*, also a motorcycle picture. Whether it contains a future Nicholson is hard to say, because the dialogue is all plot-driven and as sparse as possible. But the characters are surly, irresponsible, mean, and coarse, if not human; the actresses keep their makeup on; and the look of the picture is certainly accomplished. I use the word "look" because the cinematographer has been joined by squadrons of special-effects and animation artists, platoons of stunt men, and covens of postproduction wizards.

I enjoyed the two pictures about the same. I'd rate them both two and a half stars, meaning this as faint praise, but praise nevertheless. As genre exercises they are skillful, quick, and entertaining. There is a difference, though. *Hells Angels on Wheels* was frankly intended as an exploitation picture by everyone involved, who all hoped to move up to the A-list and make better films (all except for the producer, Joe Solomon, whom we will get to in a moment). *Torque*, I fear, considers itself to be a real movie—top of the world, man! Although it's been kept on the shelf for nearly a year by Warner Bros., reportedly to avoid competing with *2 Fast 2 Furious* and *Biker Boyz*, that is a marketing judgment, not an aesthetic opinion. I suspect no one at Warners has an aesthetic opinion about *Torque*.

I spent some time with Joe Solomon once, to profile him for *Esquire*. I liked him immensely. He wasn't too big to involve himself personally in the smallest details of a production, as when he demonstrated how ice cubes could be used as a perkiness enhancer. He was never happier than when producing motorcycle pictures, and his credits included *Angels from Hell; Run, Angel, Run; Wild Wheels;* and *Nam's Angels*.

What has happened between 1967 and 2004 is that Hollywood genres have undergone a fundamental flip-flop. Low-budget pictures are now serious and ambitious and play at Sundance. Big-budget exploitation work, on which every possible technical refinement is lavished, are now flashy and dispensable and open in 3,000 multiplexes. Little did Joe Solomon suspect that he was making the major studio pictures of the future.

Now as for *Torque*. The director is Joseph Kahn, who started by directing music videos and moved to this project, I learn, after long months of frustration trying to get *Crow 4* off the ground. The first three minutes convince us we are looking at a commercial before the feature begins. Then we realize the whole movie will look like this. It's flashy, skillful work—as much CGI as real, but that's the name of the game.

The plot is about a biker (Martin Henderson) who has returned to Los Angeles from exile in Thailand. The leader of a rival gang (Ice Cube) thinks he killed his brother, and wants revenge. The two gangs clash in a series of elaborate stunt and effects sequences, including a duel between two sexy women. A Hummer is tossed into the air and spun like a top before crushing a sports car. One motorcycle chase takes place on top of a train, and then inside the train; we would care more if it were not on approximately the same level of reality as a *Road Runner* chase. One of the bikes is "built around a Rolls-Royce jet engine." It goes so fast it makes parking meters explode. The final fight sequence is so extravagantly choreographed that the props work together like a speeded-up version of a Buster Keaton sequence.

The film is better than it might have been, and better than it had to be. Take it on its own terms and you might find it interesting. Or did I say that already? One hopes that the filmmakers understand that *Torque* must be seen as the first step on their artistic journey, not its destination. ☞

Touching the Void ★ ★ ★

NO MPAA RATING, 106 m., 2004

Brendan Mackey (Simpson), Nicholas Aaron (Yates), Joe Simpson (Himself), Simon Yates (Himself). Directed by Kevin Macdonald and produced by John Smithson. Screenplay by Joe Simpson, based on his book.

For someone who fervently believes he will never climb a mountain, I spend an unreasonable amount of time thinking about mountain climbing. In my dreams my rope has come loose and I am falling, falling, and all the way down I am screaming: "Stupid! You're so stupid! You climbed all the way up there just so you could fall back down!"

Now there is a movie more frightening than my nightmares. *Touching the Void* is the most harrowing movie about mountain climbing I have seen, or can imagine. I've read reviews from critics who were only moderately stirred by the film (my friend Dave Kehr certainly kept his composure), and I must conclude that their dreams are not haunted as mine are.

I didn't take a single note during this film. I simply sat there before the screen, enthralled, fascinated, and terrified. Not for me the discussions about the utility of the "pseudo-documentary format," or questions about how the camera happened to be waiting at the bottom of the crevice when Simpson fell in. *Touching the Void* was, for me, more of a horror film than any actual horror film could ever be.

The movie is about Joe Simpson and Simon Yates, two Brits in their mid-twenties who determined to scale the forbidding west face of a mountain named Siula Grande, in the Peruvian Andes. They were fit and in good training, and bold enough to try the "one push" method of climbing, in which they carried all their gear with them instead of establishing caches along the route. They limited their supplies to reduce weight, and planned to go up and down quickly.

It didn't work out that way. Snowstorms slowed and blinded them. The ascent was doable, but on the way down the storms disoriented them and the drifts concealed the hazard of hidden crevices and falls. Roped together, they worked with one man always anchored, and so Yates was able to hold the rope when Simpson had a sudden fall. But it was disastrous: He broke his leg, driving the calf bone up through the knee socket. Both of them knew that a broken leg on a two-man climb, with rescue impossible, was a death sentence, and indeed Simpson tells us he was rather surprised that Yates decided to stay with him and try to get him down.

We know that Simpson survived, because the movie shows the real-life Simpson and Yates, filmed against plain backgrounds, looking straight on into the camera, remembering their adventure in their own words. We also see the ordeal reenacted by two actors (Brendan Mackey as Simpson, Nicholas Aaron as Yates), and experienced climbers are used as stunt doubles. The movie was shot on location in Peru and also in the Alps, and the climbing sequences are always completely convincing; the use of actors in those scenes is not a distraction because their faces are so bearded, frostbitten, and snow-caked that we can hardly recognize them.

Yates and Simpson had a 300-foot rope. Yates's plan was to lower Simpson 300 feet and wait for a tug on the rope. That meant Simpson had dug in and anchored himself and it was safe for Yates to climb down and repeat the process. A good method in theory, but then, after dark, in a snowstorm, Yates lowered Simpson over a precipice and left him hanging in midair over a drop of unknowable distance. Since they were out of earshot in the blizzard all Yates could know was that the rope was tight and not moving, and his feet were slipping out of the holes he had dug to brace them. After an hour or so he realized they were at an impasse. Simpson was apparently hanging helplessly in midair, Yates was slipping, and unless he cut the rope they would both surely die. So he cut the rope.

Simpson says he would have done the same thing under the circumstances, and we believe him. What we can hardly believe is what happens next, and what makes the film into an incredible story of human endurance.

If you plan to see the film—it will not disappoint you—you might want to save the rest of the review until later.

Simpson, incredibly, falls into a crevice but is slowed and saved by several snow bridges he crashes through before he lands on an ice ledge with a drop on either side. So there he is, in total darkness and bitter cold, his fuel gone so that he cannot melt snow, his lamp battery running low, and no food. He is hungry, dehydrated, and in cruel pain from the bones grinding together in his leg (two aspirins didn't help much).

It is clear Simpson cannot climb back up out of the crevice. So he eventually gambles everything on a strategy that seems madness itself, but was his only option other than waiting for death: He uses the rope to lower himself down into the unknown depths below. If the distance is more than 300 feet, well, then, he will literally be at the end of his rope.

But there is a floor far below, and in the morning he sees light and is able, incredibly, to crawl out to the mountainside. And that is only the beginning of his ordeal. He must somehow get down the mountain and cross a plain strewn with rocks and boulders; he cannot walk but must try to hop or crawl despite the pain in his leg. That he did it is manifest, since he survived to write a book and appear in the movie. How he did it provides an experience that at times had me closing my eyes against his agony.

This film is an unforgettable experience, directed by Kevin Macdonald (who made *One Day in September,* the Oscar-winner about the 1972 Olympiad) with a kind of brutal directness and simplicity that never tries to add suspense or drama (none is needed!), but simply tells the story, as we look on in disbelief. We learn at the end that after two years of surgeries Simpson's leg was repaired, and that (but you anticipated this, didn't you?) he went back to climbing again. Learning this, I was reminded of Boss Gettys's line about Citizen Kane: "He's going to need more than one lesson." I hope to God the rest of his speech does not apply to Simpson: ". . . and he's going to get more than one lesson."   ☞

The Tracker ★ ★ ★ ½
NO MPAA RATING, 90 m., 2004

David Gulpilil (The Tracker), Gary Sweet (The Fanatic), Damon Gameau (The Follower), Grant Page (The Veteran), Noel Wilton (The Fugitive). Directed by Rolf de Heer and produced by Bridget Ikin, Julie Ryan, and de Heer. Screenplay by de Heer.

The Tracker is one of those rare films that deserve to be called haunting. It tells the sort of story we might find in an action Western, but transforms it into a fable or parable. Four men set out into the Australian wilderness to track down an accused killer, and during the course of their journey true justice cries out to be done. The men never use their names, but the credits identify them as The Fanatic, a merciless officer; The Follower, a greenhorn new to the territory; The Veteran, an older man of few words; and The Tracker, an Aboriginal who will lead them to their quarry, also an Aboriginal.

The live action is intercut with paintings of events in the story, and the sound track includes songs about what happens. We assume the story is based on fact that became legend, and that the songs commemorate it; several critics have said the paintings are "probably Aboriginal" and done at the time (1922). Not so. The story is an original by the director, Rolf de Heer; the paintings were done on location by Peter Coad; and the songs were written by the director and Graham Tardif. They have created their own legend from their own facts, but it feels no less real; it is a distillation from Aus-

tralia's shameful history with the Aboriginals, and contains echoes of the hunt for escaped Aboriginal children in *Rabbit-Proof Fence.*

De Heer used a small crew and shot in the wilderness, camping out every night, and we see the film's events not as heightened action but as a long, slow trek across a vast landscape. It seems to be unpopulated, but no; on the first night, when the kid gets out his ukulele and starts to sing, the officer quiets him so they can hear anyone approaching. "You won't hear them," the older man says. "They're there," says the tracker.

They are there, everywhere, invisible, as spears materialize out of emptiness and pick off their horses and then one of the men. Once they come upon the camp of a small Aboriginal family group. These people are peaceful, the tracker tells the officer, but some of them are wearing discarded army uniforms, and so the officer kills them all. The greenhorn is shaken and distraught: "They were innocent." The tracker, who says what the officer likes to hear, tells him, "The only innocent black is a dead black."

This tracker is more complex than he seems. He plays a loyal army employee, but his eyes suggest other dimensions. And when one of the men is killed, how extraordinary that he recites a Catholic burial rite in Latin. He must have passed through a missionary school on his way to this day in the Outback, and is not the savage (however noble) imagined by the racist officer. At the same time, he knows his job, and when the greenhorn charges that he isn't really tracking but is only following his nose, the officer (who also knows his job) tells the tracker, "Show him," and he does—pointing out a small dislodged stone with the earth still damp where it has rested.

The tracker is played by David Gulpilil, whose career started in 1971 when he played the young Aboriginal boy who guides the lost white girl in *Walkabout.* He also played a tracker in *Rabbit-Proof Fence.* Here he has a disarming smile and an understated enthusiasm that seems genuine—to the officer, at least—while we sense a different agenda shifting beneath the surface. While it is clear that some kind of confrontation is coming, it would be unfair for me to suggest what happens.

The officer, played by Gary Sweet, is unbending and filled with certitude. There is not a doubt in his mind that he is justified in shooting innocent people, and he even claims to expect a medal. The greenhorn (Damon Gameau) is the moral weathervane; the mission at first seems justifiable, and then he wonders. The old-timer (Grant Page) is the taciturn type every society knows; he has accommodated himself to this way of doing business, but stands apart from it. Notice how while the massacre is under way, he sits on a log and smokes, and we guess something of his detachment from the way the smoke emerges as a very thin, steady stream.

The performances are all the more powerful for being in a minor key. De Heer seems determined to tell his story without calculated emotional boosts. "The brutal scenes," he told an Australian interviewer, "were basically shifted from the film itself to the paintings to make the viewer look at the death scenes and macabre scenes differently—to distance the audience." And when the officer is shouting at the family group, the volume of his dialogue is toned down and a song plays as counterpoint; here is a film about memory, sadness, tragedy, and distance, not a film that dramatizes what it laments. Truffaut said it was impossible to make an antiwar film because the action always argued for itself; de Heer may have found the answer.

The Transporter ★ ★ ½
PG-13, 92 m., 2002

Jason Statham (Frank Martin), Qi Shu (Lai), François Berléand (Tarconi), Matt Schulze (Wall Street). Directed by Corey Yuen and produced by Luc Besson and Steven Chasman. Screenplay by Besson and Robert Mark Kamen.

The marriage of James Bond and Hong Kong continues in *The Transporter,* a movie that combines Bond's luxurious European locations and love of deadly toys with all the tricks of martial arts movies. The movie stars Jason Statham (who has pumped a lot of iron since *Lock, Stock and Two Smoking Barrels*) as Frank Martin, a.k.a. the Transporter, who will transport anything at a price. His three unbreakable rules: Never change the deal, no names, and never look in the package.

Unlike Bond, Martin is amoral and works only for the money. We gather he lost any shreds of patriotism while serving in the British Special Forces, and now hires out his skills to support a lifestyle that includes an oceanside villa on the French Riviera that would retail at $30 million, minimum.

In an opening sequence that promises more than the movie is able to deliver, Martin pilots his BMW for the getaway of a gang of bank robbers. Four of them pile into the car. The deal said there would be three. "The deal never changes," Martin says, as alarms ring and police sirens grow nearer. The robbers scream for him to drive away. He shoots the fourth man. Now the deal can proceed.

And it does, in a chase sequence that is sensationally good, but then aren't all movie chase scenes sensationally good these days? There have been so many virtuoso chase sequences lately that we grow jaded, but this one, with the car bouncing down steps, squeezing through narrow lanes, and speeding backward on expressways, is up there with recent French chases like *Ronin* and *The Bourne Identity.*

The movie combines the skills and trademarks of its director, Corey Yuen, and its writer-producer, Luc Besson. The Hong Kong–based specialist in martial arts movies has forty-three titles to his credit, many of them starring Jet Li and Qi Shu. This is his English-language debut. Besson, now one of the world's top action producers (he has announced nine films for 2003 and also has *Wasabi* in current release), likes partnerships between action heroes and younger, apparently more vulnerable women. Those elements were central in his direction of *La Femme Nikita, The Professional,* and *The Fifth Element.* Now he provides Frank Martin with a young woman through the violation of Rule No. 3: Martin looks in the bag.

He has been given a large duffel bag to transport. It squirms. It contains a beautiful young Chinese woman named Lai (Qi Shu, who at age twenty-six has appeared in forty-one movies, mostly erotic or martial arts). He cuts a little hole in the bag so she can sip an orange juice, and before he remembers to consult his rules again he has brought her home to his villa and is embroiled in a plot involving gangsters from Nice and human slave cargoes from China.

The movie is by this point, alas, on autopilot. Statham's character, who had a grim fascination when he was enforcing the rules, turns into just another action hero when he starts breaking them. I actually thought, during the opening scenes, that *The Transporter* was going to rise above the genre, was going to be a study of violent psychology, like *La Femme Nikita*. No luck.

Too much action brings the movie to a dead standstill. Why don't directors understand that? Why don't they know that wall-to-wall action makes a movie *less* interesting—less like drama, more like a repetitive video game? Stunt action sequences are difficult, but apparently not as difficult as good dialogue. Unless you're an early-teens, special-effects zombie, movies get more interesting when the characters are given humanity and dimension.

Frank Martin is an intriguing man in the opening scenes, and we think maybe we'll learn something about his harsh code and lonely profession. But no: We get car leaps from bridges onto auto transporters. Parachute drops onto the tops of moving trucks. Grenades, rocket launchers, machine guns (at one point a friendly inspector asks Martin to explain 50,000 spent rounds of ammo). There is, of course, an underwater adventure, tribute to Besson's early life as the child of scuba diving instructors. At one point Martin tells Lai, "It's quiet. Too quiet." It wasn't nearly quiet enough.

Treasure Planet ★ ★ ½
PG, 95 m., 2002

With the voices of: Joseph Gordon-Levitt (Jim Hawkins [speaking]), John Rzeznik (Jim Hawkins [singing]), Brian Murray (John Silver), David Hyde Pierce (Dr. Doppler), Martin Short (B.E.N.), Emma Thompson (Captain Amelia), Roscoe Lee Browne (Arrow), Michael Wincott (Scroop). Directed by Ron Clements and John Musker and produced by Roy Conli, Clements, and Musker. Screenplay by Clements, Musker, and Rob Edwards, based on the novel *Treasure Island* by Robert Louis Stevenson.

Walt Disney's *Treasure Planet* has zest and humor and some lovable supporting characters, but do we really need this zapped-up version of the Robert Louis Stevenson classic? Eighteenth-century galleons and pirate ships go sailing through the stars, and it somehow just doesn't look right. The film wants to be a pirate movie dressed in *Star Wars* garb, but the pants are too short and the elbows stick out. For anyone who grew up on Disney's 1950 *Treasure Island*, or remembers the 1934 Victor Fleming classic, this one feels like an impostor.

I am not concerned about technical matters. I do not question why spaceships of the future would look like sailing ships of the past. I can believe they could be powered by both rockets and solar winds. It does not bother me that deep space turns out to be breathable. I do not wonder why swashbuckling is still in style in an era of ray guns and laser beams. I accept all of that. It's just that I wonder why I have to. Why not make an animated version of the classic *Treasure Island*? Why not challenge the kids with a version of an actual book written by a great writer, instead of catering to them with what looks like the prototype for a video game?

These are, I suppose, the objections of a hidebound reactionary. I believe that one should review the movie that has been made, not the movie one wishes had been made, and here I violate my own rule. But there was something in me that . . . resisted . . . this movie. I hope it did not blind me to its undeniable charms.

There is, to begin with, a likable hero named Jim Hawkins, whose speaking voice is by Joseph Gordon-Levitt and singing voice by John Rzeznik. Jim is a nice enough kid when we first see him being read to by his mother in his standard-issue Disney fatherless home. But he grows up into a troublemaker, and it is only the possession of a holographic treasure map, and the journey in this movie, that seasons him into a fine young man.

Hoping to sail away to a planet where "the treasures of a thousand worlds" have been deposited, Jim signs on as a cabin boy under the cat-eyed Captain Amelia (voice by Emma Thompson), and is soon befriended by the cook, John Silver (Brian Murray), a cyborg whose right arm contains an amazing collection of attachments and gadgets. Also onboard is the wealthy Dr. Doppler (David Hyde Pierce), who is financing the voyage. (His doglike appearance and Amelia's feline nature make us wonder, when romance blooms, whether theirs is a relationship likely to last.)

I will not be spoiling much, I assume, to suggest that John Silver is more than a cook, and less than a friend. He has mutiny in mind. And the troubles onboard the ship are backdropped by troubles in space, where a black hole threatens and there is a "space storm" as dangerous as any in the Caribbean.

It is obligatory in all Disney animated features that there be some sort of cute miniature sidekick, and the peppy little creature this time is Morph, a blue blob that can assume almost any shape, is cuddly and frisky, and takes sides. Another supporting character is B.E.N. (Martin Short), a cybernetic navigator who apparently has some fried memory boards and lots of one-liners. He would be obnoxious unless you liked creatures like him, which I do.

Disney experiments with its animation methods in the movie (which is being released simultaneously in regular theaters and on the big IMAX screens, which have recently brought such an awesome presence to *Fantasia* and *Beauty and the Beast*). The foreground characters are two-dimensional in the classical animated style, but the backgrounds are 3-D and computer-generated ("painted," the Web site assures us, but with a computer stylus rather than a brush). Some may find a clash between the two styles, but the backgrounds function as, well, backgrounds, and I accepted them without question.

I'm aware that many, maybe most, of the audience members for this film will never have heard of Robert Louis Stevenson. They may learn in the opening sequence that he once wrote a book named *Treasure Island*, but when this book is opened by Jim's mother it contains no old-fashioned words, only pop-up moving images. For these people, the loss of the story's literary roots may be meaningless. They may

wonder what old sailing ships are doing in a futuristic universe, but then there's a lot to wonder about in all animated adventures, isn't there, since none of them are plausible. My guess is that most audiences will enjoy this film more than I did. I remain stubbornly convinced that pirate ships and ocean storms and real whales (as opposed to space whales) are exciting enough. Even more exciting, because less gimmicky. But there I go again.

The Trials of Henry Kissinger ★ ★ ★
NO MPAA RATING, 80 m., 2002

A documentary directed by Eugene Jarecki and produced by Alex Gibney and Jarecki. Screenplay by Gibney, based on the book by Christopher Hitchens.

The odds are excellent that President Bush did not see this film before appointing Henry Kissinger as the head of a special commission to examine shortcomings of U.S. intelligence in the period before 9/11. *The Trials of Henry Kissinger* charges Kissinger himself with authorizing illegal terrorist acts on behalf of the United States. Did Bush put the fox in charge of the henhouse?

Yes, the film is told from a hostile point of view: It's based on a book by the New Left author Christopher Hitchens, who has made Kissinger-bashing a second career. But many of the facts in it are matters of public record. And it is widely believed, and not just on the left, that Kissinger directly or indirectly brought about the death of the democratically elected Chilean president Salvador Allende. And he is currently the defendant, as Hitchens pointed out recently on www.Slate.com, in a civil suit filed in Washington, D.C., charging that Kissinger gave the order for the assassination of the Chilean general Rene Schneider, who would not support the U.S. call for a military coup. "Every single document in the prosecution case," Hitchens notes, "is a U.S.-government declassified paper."

I am your humble scribe and have no personal knowledge of the truth or falsity of these charges. I note, however, that it may be unwise to assign a man with such a complex image to investigate terrorism. By appointing him to head the investigation into possible failures of U.S. intelligence in the months before 9/11, the president, having resisted such an investigation for more than a year, shows he doesn't really care what anyone thinks.

The Trials of Henry Kissinger, directed by Eugene Jarecki and based on Hitchens's 2001 book *The Trials of Henry Kissinger*, plays like a brief for a war crimes trial against the former secretary of state. It also plays like a roast, with easy jibes about his appetite for dating starlets and his avid careerism (at one point, we learn, he assured friends he would be the White House foreign policy adviser no matter whether Nixon or Humphrey was elected). The movie is not above cheap shots, as when it sets sequences to music.

The film's technique is partisan. It provides Kissinger's critics, including Hitchens, William Shawcross, and Seymour Hersh, with ample time to spell out their charges against Kissinger (samples: He lied to Congress about the bombing of Cambodia, and lengthened the war in Vietnam by sending a secret message to the North Vietnamese that they'd get a better deal if they waited until Nixon was in office). Then Kissinger's defenders are seen and heard, but hardly given equal time. It feels somehow as if the filmmakers have chosen just the words they want, and the context be damned; sophisticated media-watchers will note the editing tricks and suspect the film's motives.

That was also a charge against Hitchens's book: that he was such a rabid hater of Kissinger that he overstated his case, convicting Kissinger of what he suspected as well as what he could prove. More balanced criticisms of Kissinger were drowned out in the resulting controversy, and Hitchens, an easy target, drew attention away from harder targets that might have been less easily answered.

The film is nevertheless fascinating to watch as a portrait of political celebrity and ego. "Power is the greatest aphrodisiac," Kissinger famously said, and he famously proved the truth of that epigram. In the years before his marriage he was seen with a parade of babes on his arm, including Jill St. John, Candice Bergen, Samantha Eggar, Shirley MacLaine, Marlo Thomas, and, yes, Zsa Zsa Gabor. He dined out often and well in New York, Wash-

ington, D.C., and world capitals, and his outgoing social life was in distinct contrast with the buttoned-down style of his boss, Nixon.

The movie shows him as a man lustful not so much for sex as for the appearance of conquest (many of his dates were at pains to report they were deposited chastely back home at the end of the evening). He liked the limelight, the power, the access, and he successfully tended the legend that he was indispensable to American foreign policy—so much so that he got credit for some of Nixon's initiatives, such as the opening to China.

He meanwhile exercised great power, not always with discretion if the film is to be believed. There is an agonizing sound bite in which he regretfully observes that there is not always a clear choice between good and evil. Sometimes indeed evil must be done to bring about the greater good. All very well, but if the people of Chile elect a government we don't like, does that give us the right to overthrow it? And even if it does, does that make the man who thought so a wise choice to investigate our current intelligence about terrorism?

The Triplets of Belleville ★ ★ ★ ½
PG-13, 91 m., 2003

With the voices of Jean-Claude Donda, Michel Robin, Monica Viegas, M. Beatrice Bonifassi, and Charles Prevost Linton. An animated film directed by Sylvain Chomet and produced by Didier Brunner and Paul Cadieux. Screenplay by Chomet.

The Triplets of Belleville will have you walking out of the theater with a goofy damn grin on your face, wondering what just happened to you. To call it weird would be a cowardly evasion. It is creepy, eccentric, eerie, flaky, freaky, funky, grotesque, inscrutable, kinky, kooky, magical, oddball, spooky, uncanny, uncouth, and unearthly. Especially uncouth. What I did was, I typed the word "weird" and when that wholly failed to evoke the feelings the film stirred in me, I turned to the thesaurus and it suggested the above substitutes—and none of them do the trick, either.

There is not even a way I can tell you what the film is "like," because I can't think of another film "like" it. Maybe the British cartoonists Ronald Searle and Gerald Scarfe suggest the visual style. Sylvain Chomet, the writer and director, has created an animated feature of appalling originality and scary charm. It's one of those movies where you keep banging your fist against your head to stop yourself from using the word "meets," as in Monsieur Hulot meets Tim Burton, or the Marquis de Sade meets Lance Armstrong.

Most animated features have an almost grotesque desire to be loved. This one doesn't seem to care. It creates a world of selfishness, cruelty, corruption, and futility—but it's not serious about this world and it doesn't want to attack it or improve upon it. It simply wants to sweep us up in its dark comic vision.

The movie opens in France, where a small boy and his dog live in the top floor of a narrow, crooked house. The Metro roars past on schedule, and his dog races upstairs on schedule to bark at it, and the boy's grandmother gives the boy a trike and eventually a bike, and soon he is the foremost bicycle racer in the world. Meanwhile, the Metro has been replaced by an elevated highway that shoulders the house to one side, so that it leans crookedly and the stairs are dangerous for the dog to climb.

The grandmother is a ferocious trainer. A little whistle seems welded to her jaw, and she toots relentlessly as the boy pedals. Then he is kidnapped by thugs who want to use him for a private gambling operation, and the key to his rescue may be the Triplets of Belleville, who were music hall stars in the era of Josephine Baker, so how old would that make them now?

The action leaves Paris for New York, maybe, although it is more likely Montreal, where Chomet lives. Doesn't matter so much, since there has never been a city like this. Jazz joints from the 1930s exist with *noir* hideouts and bizarre tortures. After a certain point it isn't the surprises that surprise us—it's the surprises about the surprises. We take it in stride, for example, when the Triplets go fishing for frogs with dynamite. What amazes us is that one of the exploded frogs survives, and crawls desperately from a scalding pot in its bid for freedom.

I am completely failing to do justice to this film. Now you think it is about frog torture. I will get letters from PETA. What happens to the

frogs is nothing compared to what happens to the grandson, who is subjected to Rube Goldberg exercise machines, and at one point has his kneecaps vacuumed.

The movie's drawing style is haunting in a comic way. The energy of the story is inexorable. There is a concert that involves tuning bicycle wheels. Luis Buñuel wrote that when he and Salvador Dali were about to premiere their surrealist film *Un Chien Andalou*, he loaded his pockets with stones to throw at the audience in case it attacked. How can I best describe *The Triplets of Belleville* other than to suggest that Buñuel might have wanted to stone it? Some of my faithful readers went to see *Songs from the Second Floor* on my recommendation. *Triplets* comes from a similar mind-set, but is told in a manic fever, and is animated. Imagine Felix the Cat with firecrackers tied to his tail, in a story involving the French nephew and aunt of *The Reservoir Dogs*, and a score by Spike Jones. No, the other Spike Jones.

The Triumph of Love ★ ★ ★

PG-13, 107 m., 2002

Mira Sorvino (Princess/Phocion/Aspasie), Ben Kingsley (Hermocrates), Jay Rodan (Agis), Fiona Shaw (Leontine), Ignazio Oliva (Harlequin), Rachael Stirling (Hermidas/Corine), Luis Molteni (Dimas). Directed by Clare Peploe and produced by Bernardo Bertolucci. Screenplay by Peploe, Bertolucci, and Marilyn Goldin.

Mira Sorvino has a little teasing smile that is invaluable in *The Triumph of Love*, a movie where she plays a boy who does not look the slightest thing like a boy, but looks exactly like Mira Sorvino playing a boy with a teasing smile. The story, based on an eighteenth-century French play by Pierre Marivaux, is the sort of thing that inspired operas and Shakespeare comedies: It's all premise, no plausibility, and so what?

Sorvino plays a princess who goes for a stroll in the woods one day and happens upon the inspiring sight of a handsome young man named Agis (Jay Rodan) emerging naked from a swim. She knows she must have him. She also knows that he is the true possessor of her throne, that she is an usurper, and that her chances of meeting him are slim. That's because he lives as the virtual prisoner of a brother and sister, a philosopher named Hermocrates (Ben Kingsley) and a scientist named Leontine (Fiona Shaw.)

Hermocrates is a scholar of the sort who, in tales of this sort, spends much time in his study pondering over quaint and curious volumes of forgotten lore. He wears one of those skullcaps with stars and moons on it, and a long robe, and is obsessed, although not without method. His sister, past the second bloom of her youth, is ferociously dedicated to him, and together they raise the young Agis to think rationally of all things, and to avoid the distractions of women, sex, romance, and worldly things.

The scheme of the princess: She and her maid Hermidas (Rachael Stirling) will disguise themselves as young men, penetrate Hermocrates' enclave, and insinuate themselves into the good graces of the brother and sister. Then nature will take its course. This is the sort of plot, like *The Scorpion King*'s, that you either accept or do not accept; if it contained martial arts, skewerings, and explosions, no one would raise an eyebrow. Because it is elegant, mannered, and teasing, some audiences will not want to go along with the joke. Your choice.

The Triumph of Love, as a title, is literally true. Love does conquer Hermocrates, Leontine, and finally Agis. Of course it is not true love in the tiresome modern sense, but romantic love as a plot device. To win Agis, the crossdressing princess must inveigle herself into the good graces of his guardians by seducing Leontine and Hermocrates. The scene between Sorvino and Shaw is one of the most delightful in the movie, as the prim spinster allows herself reluctantly to believe that she might be irresistible—that this handsome youth might indeed have penetrated the compound hoping to seduce her. The director, Clare Peploe, stages this scene among trees and shrubbery, as the "boy" pursues the bashful sister from sun to shade to sun again.

Now comes the challenge of Hermocrates. Although there are possibilities in the notion that the philosopher might be attracted to a comely young lad, the movie departs from tradition and allows Hermocrates to see through the deception at once: He knows this visitor is a girl, accuses her of it, and is told she disguised herself as a boy only to gain access to his overwhelmingly attractive presence. Hermocrates insists she only wants access to Agis. "He is not the one my heart beats for," she says shyly, and watch Ben Kingsley's face as he understands the implications. Strange, how universal is the human notion that others should find us attractive.

Kingsley is the most versatile of actors, able to suggest, with a slant of the gaze, a cast of the mouth, emotional states that other actors could not achieve with cartwheels. There is a twinkle in his eye. He is as easily persuaded as his sister that this visitor loves him. But is it not cruel that the ripe young imposter deceives both the brother and sister, stealing their hearts as stepping-stones for her own? Not at all, because the ending, in admirable eighteenth-century style, tidies all loose ends, restores order to the kingdom, and allows everyone to live happily ever after, although it is in the nature of things that some will live happier than others.

Clare Peploe, the wife of the great Italian director Bernardo Bertolucci, was born in Tanzania, raised in Britain, educated at the Sorbonne and in Italy, began with her brother Mark as a writer on Antonioni's *Zabriskie Point*, and in addition to cowriting many of Bertolucci's films, has directed three of her own. The sleeper is *High Season* (1988), a comedy set on a Greek island and involving romance, art, spies, and a statue to the Unknown Tourist. If you know the John Huston movie *Beat the Devil* you will have seen its first cousin. With this film, once again she shows a lighthearted playfulness.

Troy ★ ★
R, 162 m., 2004

Brad Pitt (Achilles), Eric Bana (Hector), Orlando Bloom (Paris), Diane Kruger (Helen), Brian Cox (Agamemnon), Sean Bean (Odysseus), Brendan Gleeson (Menelaus), Peter O'Toole (Priam), Garrett Hedlund (Patroclus). Directed by Wolfgang Petersen and produced by Petersen, Diana Rathbun, and Colin Wilson. Screenplay by David Benioff, based on the poem "The Iliad" by Homer.

Troy is based on the poem by Homer, according to the credits. Homer's estate should sue. The movie sidesteps the existence of the Greek gods, turns its heroes into action movie clichés, and demonstrates that we're getting tired of computer-generated armies. Better a couple of hundred sweaty warriors than two masses of 50,000 men marching toward each other across a sea of special effects.

The movie recounts the legend of the Trojan War, as the fortress city is attacked by a Greek army led by Menelaus of Sparta and Agamemnon of Mycenae. The war has become necessary because of the lust of the young Trojan prince Paris (Orlando Bloom), who during a peace mission to Sparta seduces its queen, Helen (Diane Kruger). This understandably annoys her husband, Menelaus (Brendan Gleeson), not to mention Paris's brother Hector (Eric Bana), who points out, quite correctly, that when you visit a king on a peace mission it is counterproductive to leave with his wife.

What the movie doesn't explain is why Helen would leave with Paris after an acquaintanceship of a few nights. Is it because her loins throb with passion for a hero? No, because she tells him: "I don't want a hero. I want a man I can grow old with." Not in Greek myth, you don't. If you believe Helen of Troy could actually tell Paris anything remotely like that, you will probably also agree that the second night he slipped into her boudoir, she told him, "Last night was a mistake."

The seduction of Helen is the curtain-raiser for the main story, which involves vast Greek armies laying siege to the impenetrable city. Chief among their leaders is Achilles, said to be the greatest warrior of all time, but played by Brad Pitt as if he doesn't believe it. If Achilles was anything, he was a man who believed his own press releases. Heroes are not introspective in Greek drama, they do not have second thoughts, and they are not conflicted.

Achilles is all of these things. He mopes on the flanks of the Greek army with his own independent band of fighters, carrying out a separate diplomatic policy, kind of like Ollie North. He thinks Agamemnon is a poor leader with bad strategy, and doesn't really get worked up until his beloved cousin Patroclus (Garrett Hedlund) is killed in battle. Patroclus, who looks a little like Achilles, wears his helmet and armor to fool the enemy, and until the helmet is removed everyone thinks Achilles has been slain. So dramatic is that development that the movie shows perhaps 100,000 men in hand-to-hand combat, and then completely forgets them in order to focus on the Patroclus battle scene, with everybody standing around like during a fight on the playground.

Brad Pitt is a good actor and a handsome man, and he worked out for six months to get buff for the role, but Achilles is not a character he inhabits comfortably. Say what you will about Charlton Heston and Victor Mature, but one good way to carry off a sword-and-sandal epic is to be filmed by a camera down around your knees, while you intone quasi-formal prose in a heroic baritone. Pitt is modern, nuanced, introspective; he brings complexity to a role where it is not required.

By treating Achilles and the other characters as if they were human, instead of the larger-than-life creations of Greek myth, director Wolfgang Petersen miscalculates. What happens in Greek myth cannot happen between psychologically plausible characters. That's the whole point of myth. Great films like Michael Cacoyannis's *Elektra,* about the murder of Agamemnon after the Trojan War, know that and use a stark dramatic approach that is deliberately stylized. Of course, *Elektra* wouldn't work for a multiplex audience, but then maybe it shouldn't.

The best scene in the movie has Peter O'Toole creating an island of drama and emotion in the middle of all that plodding dialogue. He plays old King Priam of Troy, who at night ventures outside his walls and into the enemy camp, surprising Achilles in his tent. Achilles has defeated Priam's son Hector in hand-to-hand combat before the walls of Troy, and dragged his body back to camp behind his chariot. Now Priam asks that the body be returned for proper preparation and burial. This scene is given the time and attention it needs to build its mood, and we believe it when Achilles tells Priam, "You're a far better king than the one who leads this army." O'Toole's presence is a reminder of *Lawrence of Arabia,* which proved that patience with dialogue and character is more important than action in making war movies work.

As for the Greek cities themselves, a cliché from the old Hollywood epics has remained intact. This is the convention that whenever a battle of great drama takes place, all the important characters have box seats for it. When Achilles battles Hector before the walls of Troy, for example, Priam and his family have a sort of viewing stand right at the front of the palace, and we get the usual crowd reaction shots, some of them awkward close-ups of actresses told to look grieved.

In a way, *Troy* resembles *The Alamo.* Both are about fortresses under siege. Both are defeated because of faulty night watchmen. The Mexicans sneak up on the Alamo undetected, and absolutely nobody is awake to see the Greeks climbing out of the Trojan Horse. One difference between the two movies is that Billy Bob Thornton and the other *Alamo* actors are given evocative dialogue and deliver it well, while *Troy* provides dialogue that probably cannot be delivered well because it would sound even sillier that way.

The Truth About Charlie ★ ★ ★

PG-13, 104 m., 2002

Mark Wahlberg (Joshua Peters), Thandie Newton (Regina Lampert), Tim Robbins (Mr. Bartholomew), Joong-Hoon Park (Il-sang Lee), Lisa Gay Hamilton (Lola), Christine Boisson (Commandant Dominique), Stephen Dillane (Charlie). Directed by Jonathan Demme and produced by Demme, Peter Saraf, and Edward Saxon. Screenplay by Demme, Steve Schmidt, Jessica Bendinger, and Peter Stone.

Regina Lampert has been married for three months. She returns to Paris to find her apartment vandalized and her husband missing. A police official produces her husband's passport—and another, and another. He had many looks and many identities, and is missing in all of them. And now she seems surrounded by unsavory people with a dangerous interest in finding his $6 million. They say she knows where it is. Thank goodness for good, kind Joshua Peters, who turns up protectively whenever he's needed.

This story, right down to the names, will be familiar to lovers of *Charade,* Stanley Donen's 1963 film starring Audrey Hepburn and Cary Grant. Now Jonathan Demme recycles it in *The Truth About Charlie,* with Thandie Newton and Mark Wahlberg in the starring roles. Wahlberg will never be confused with Cary Grant but Newton, now . . . Newton, with her fragile beauty, her flawless complexion, her beautiful head perched atop that extraordinary neck . . . well, you can see how Demme thought of Hepburn when he cast her.

Charade is considered in many quarters to be a masterpiece (no less than the 168th best film of all time, according to the Internet Movie Database). I saw it recently on the sparkling Criterion DVD, enjoyed it, remember it fondly, but do not find it a desecration that Demme wanted to remake it. There are some films that are ineffably themselves, like *The Third Man,* and cannot possibly be remade. Others depend on plots so silly and effervescent that they can be used over and over as vehicles for new generations of actors. *Charade* is in the latter category. If it is true that there will never be another Audrey Hepburn, then it is, I submit, also true that there will never be another Thandie Newton.

I saw her first in *Flirting* (1991), made when she was eighteen. It was a glowing masterpiece about adolescent love. She has been in fifteen films since then, but you may not remember her. She was the lost child in Demme's *Beloved* (1998), looking like a ghost and not herself, and she played Sally Hemings, Thomas Jefferson's slave and lover, in the unsuccessful *Jefferson in Paris* (1995). I liked her in Bernardo Bertolucci's *Besieged* (1998), although the film didn't work and he photographed her with almost unseemly interest. She was in the overlooked but very good *Gridlock'd* (1997), Tupak Shakur's film. If you have seen her at all, it may have been in *Mission: Impossible II,* opposite Tom Cruise.

She carries *The Truth About Charlie,* as she must, because all of the other characters revolve around her, sometimes literally. Wahlberg has top billing, but that must be a contractual thing; she is the center of the picture, and the news is, she is a star. She has that presence and glow. The plot is essentially a backdrop, as it was in *Charade,* for Paris, suspense, romance, and star power.

I am not sure the plot matters enough to be kept a secret, but I will try not to give away too much. Essentially, Charlie was a deceptive, two-timing louse who made some unfortunate friends. Now that he has gone, several strange people emerge from the woodwork, some to threaten Regina, some, like Mr. Bartholomew (Tim Robbins), to help and advise her. There is an Asian named Il-sang Lee (Joong-Hoon Park) and a femme fatale named Lola (Lisa Gay Hamilton), and a police commandant (Christine Boisson) who appears to seek only the truth. And there is the omnipresent, always helpful Joshua Peters (Wahlberg), who was named Peter Joshua in *Charade*, but there you go.

These people all serve one function: to propel Regina past locations in Paris, from the Champs Elysees to the flea market at Clignancourt, and to accompany her through several costume changes and assorted dangers and escapes. "The history of the cinema," said Jean-Luc Godard, "is of boys photographing girls." There is more to it than that, but both *The Truth About Charlie* and *Charade* prove that is enough.

Tuck Everlasting ★ ★
PG, 90 m., 2002

Alexis Bledel (Winnie Foster), Jonathan Jackson (Jesse Tuck), William Hurt (Angus Tuck), Sissy Spacek (Mae Tuck), Scott Bairstow (Miles Tuck), Amy Irving (Augusta Foster), Victor Garber (Robert Foster), Ben Kingsley (Man in the Yellow Suit). Directed by Jay Russell and produced by Jane Startz and Marc Abraham. Screenplay by Jeffrey Lieber and James V. Hart, based on the book by Natalie Babbitt.

Tuck Everlasting is based on a novel well-known to middle school students but not to me, about a romance between two teenagers, one of whom is 104. It contains a lesson: "Do not fear death—but rather the unlived life." Wise indeed. But wiser still was Socrates, who said, "The unexamined life is not worth living." The immortals in *Tuck Everlasting* have not examined their endless lives, and the teenage mortal scarcely has a thought in her pretty little head.

The movie, shot in rural Maryland (Blair

Witch country), tells of a young woman named Winnie Foster (Alexis Bledel) who feels stifled by strict family rules. Her mother (Amy Irving) frowns disapprovingly on just about anything, but is especially certain that Winnie should never talk to strangers or walk alone in the woods. One day Winnie up and *walks* in the woods, and meets a young man named Jesse (Jonathan Jackson). He warns her against drinking from a spring at the foot of a big old tree, and then his older brother Miles (Scott Bairstow) grabs her and brings her back to their forest cottage on horseback.

These are the Tucks. Mae and Angus, Mom and Dad, are played by Sissy Spacek and William Hurt. Years ago they drank from the spring, and have become immortal. "The spring stops you right where you are," Winnie is told, and that's why Jesse has been 17 for all these years. Although this is not explained, it must stop your mental as well as your physical aging, because at 104 Jesse is not yet desperately bored by being 17.

Earlier, Angus Tuck has spied a stranger in a yellow coat skulking about, and warned the family: "Any strangers in the woods—getting too close—you know what to do. No exceptions." So it appears Winnie must die to protect the secret of the Tucks and their spring. But first Mae Tuck wants to give the poor girl a square meal, and as it becomes clear that Winnie and Jesse are soft on each other, the mean Miles teases: "Don't you wish he'd told you before he kissed you?" (His own mother says Miles is "warm as barbed wire.")

The movie has been handsomely mounted by Jay Russell, whose previous film was *My Dog Skip* (2000), a classic about childhood that was entirely lacking the feather-brained sentimentality of *Tuck Everlasting*. The new movie is slow, quiet, sweet, and maddening in the way it avoids obvious questions: Such as, if one sip from the spring grants immortality, why do the Tucks live for a century in their cottage in the woods? I know what I'd do: Spend ten years apiece in the world's most interesting places. And don't tell me they're afraid city folk will notice how old they are, since the boys live in town and Mae visits them every ten years.

The movie oozes with that kind of self-conscious piety that sometimes comes with the territory when award-winning young people's books are filmed (*Harry Potter* is an exception). The characters seem to lack ordinary human instincts, and behave according to their archetypal requirements. How else to consider the Man in the Yellow Suit (Ben Kingsley), who, if he had given the matter a moment's thought, would know he could stalk the Tucks more successfully with a brown suit? Winnie's father (Victor Garber) is a rather distant man, as befits the form for this genre, in which the women are plucky and the men are either sinister or inessential, unless they are cute teenage boys, of course.

The movie is too impressed with its own solemn insights to work up much entertainment value; is too much fable to be convincing as life; is awkward in the way it tries to convince us Winnie's in danger when we're pretty sure she's not. Even its lesson is questionable. Is it better to live fully for a finite time than to be stuck in eternity? The injunction to live life fully need not come with a time limit. That's why the outcome of the romance is so unsatisfactory. I dare not reveal what happens, except to say that it need not happen, that the explanation for it is logically porous, and that many a young girl has sacrificed more for her love. Besides, just because you're seventeen forever doesn't mean life loses all delight. You can get rid of that horse and carriage and buy a motorcycle.

Tully ★ ★ ★ ½
NO MPAA RATING, 102 m., 2000

Anson Mount (Tully Coates Jr.), Julianne Nicholson (Ella Smalley), Glenn Fitzgerald (Earl Coates), Catherine Kellner (April Reece), Bob Burrus (Tully Coates Sr.). Directed by Hilary Birmingham and produced by Birmingham and Anne Sundberg. Screenplay by Birmingham and Matt Drake, based on the short story "What Happened to Tully" by Tom McNeal.

Tully is set on a Nebraska dairy farm, one without a woman but where thoughts about women are often in the minds of the men. Tully Coates Sr. (Bob Burrus) still loves the wife who walked away from the family years ago. Tully Jr. (Anson Mount) is a ladies' man, dating a local

stripper named April (Catherine Kellner). His younger brother Earl (Glenn Fitzgerald) is quieter and more open, with a soft spot for Ella Smalley (Julianne Nicholson), who is home for the summer from studying to be a veterinarian.

In this rural community everyone knows one another. They even think they know each other's secrets, but there are dark secrets at the heart of the Tully family that only the father knows. One, revealed fairly early, is that his wife was not killed in a crash, as he told the boys, but simply abandoned them. The other I will leave for you to discover. The mother is not only alive but dying of cancer in a hospital, where $300,000 in medical bills have caused a lien to be brought against the farm: The Tullys might lose it, after their decades of hard work.

Here in Nebraska the exotic dancers are not very exotic. April is a neighbor girl, who strips in a nearby town because the money is good, but still has small-town notions about going steady. After she and Tully Jr. spend an enjoyable afternoon on the hood of his Cadillac, she claims territorial privilege: From now on, that hood is hers, and she doesn't want to hear about Tully inviting any other girl up there.

Earl has a sort of crush on Ella, who is redhaired and freckled, open-faced and clear about her own feelings. She would like to be dating Tully, but only if he can outgrow his tomcatting and see her as worthy of his loyalty. In her own way, during this summer, she will hook Tully and reel him in, and it may be years before he figures out what really happened. Julianne Nicholson is wonderful in the role, wise about men, aware of her own power.

The anchoring performance in the movie is by Bob Burrus, as the father. Long days alone in the fields have made him taciturn. The boys notice that the lights burn late in the farm office, that he is worried about something, and then they discover their line of credit is cut off at the bank.

During the course of the movie old hurts will be remembered, old secrets revealed, and new loves will form. *Tully,* directed by Hilary Birmingham, cowritten by Birmingham and Matt Drake, and based on a short story by Tom McNeal, doesn't turn those developments into a rural soap opera, but pays close and respectful attention to its characters, allowing them time to develop and deepen—so that, for example, we understand exactly what's happening when Earl warns his brother to be careful with Ella. In other words, don't treat her like another one of his conquests.

Even Ella is bemused by Tully's reputation: "What's it like to drive women crazy?" What Tully is far from understanding is that Ella knows how to drive him crazy, and there is a lovely scene when she takes him to her favorite swimming hole, and allows him to feel desire for her, and pretends that wasn't on her mind. Women know how to win the Tullys, and it's clear that the old man forgives his faithless wife and still loves her.

The movie is a matter-of-fact journal of daily farm life during its opening scenes, and its dramatic secrets are revealed only slowly. At the end, when there is a tragedy, it has been hanging there, waiting to happen, for four or five scenes. Birmingham has a writer's patience and attention to detail, and doesn't hurry things along. She knows that audiences may think they like speed, but they're more deeply moved by depth.

By the end of the film, both times I saw it, there were some tears in the audience. They confirm something I've suspected: Audiences are more touched by goodness than by sadness. Tears come not because something terrible has happened, but because something good has happened that reveals the willingness of people to be brave and kind. We might quarrel with the crucial decision at the end of *Tully*, but we have to honor it, because we know it comes from a good place. So does the whole movie.

Tupac: Resurrection ★ ★ ★ ½
R, 90 m., 2003

Tupac Shakur (Narrator). Directed by Lauren Lazin and produced by Preston Holmes, Karolyn Ali, and Lazin.

"I didn't have a record until I had a record."

So says Tupac Shakur, the gangsta rap artist who was shot down in his youth on a Las Vegas street. And, yes, it is Tupac Shakur saying it. He narrates his own story about an American life that started badly, got a lot better, and then a whole lot worse. Because he was articulate and introspective, questioned his own behavior and had a philosophical streak, and because he left behind so many hours of interviews, the makers of *Tupac: Resurrection* are able to use his voice and only his voice to tell the story of his life from his birth to beyond the grave.

Shakur was a talented child who attended the Philadelphia High School for the Performing Arts and in another world might have made another kind of music. But he came up at the defining moment of rap and embraced gangsta imagery, which became his reality. He advocated some kind of half-baked philosophy named Thug Life, which was supposed to be a code to end the anarchy of inner-city street gangs. But like the rap artist Biggie Smalls, whose murder has been linked with Shakur's in the legend of the East-West rap war, and like Sean (Puffy) Combs, who has also been associated with violence, he was not a ghetto warrior but a rich, talented performer who pretended to be a lot tougher than he was.

Tupac: Resurrection, directed by Lauren Lazin, is essentially the autobiography of a young man who suddenly has to learn how to handle fame, money, and power, and whose impulses to do the right thing are clouded by the usual problems of too much, too soon. "I was immature," he observes at one point, and later, "I tried to get humble again." He attacked Spike Lee and Eddie Murphy for no good reason. He fought with the Hughes brothers, who were trying to direct him in a movie. He was accused of rape. He did time behind bars. He was involved in gunplay. He was making millions of dollars and did not fully realize what a target that made him in a new branch of the music industry where murder was a marketing strategy.

The most important person in his life was clearly his mother, Afeni Shakur, a Black Panther who was in jail when she was pregnant with Tupac, and who later fought and won a battle with drugs; her politics and feminism helped form him, and he talks about how comfortable he is with women, how he understands them, how he was the only male in the family. In the last months of his life, his relationship with his mother is the most positive input he has—and he knows it.

He's egotistical about his success, as he makes millions for Death Row Records and its notorious proprietor, Suge Knight. One movie that ought be viewed in connection with this one is Nick Broomfield's *Biggie and Tupac* (2002), which says Knight had both rappers murdered and even fingers the hit men (off-duty Los Angeles cops on Suge's payroll). The LAPD, not surprisingly, has a different theory, but Broomfield's movie is instructive for its portrait of Suge Knight, who actually was and is the kind of hard character Shakur and Smalls posed as.

Tupac: Resurrection is about rap music, the forces that created it, and the world it then created. Shakur talks about the experiences and politics that went into his own music, in a way that casts more light on rap than anything else I've come across in a movie. Although rap is not music in the sense that you come out humming the melody, it's as genuine an American idiom as jazz or the blues, and it is primarily a medium of words, of ideology; a marriage of turntables, poetry slams, autobiography, and righteous anger.

I remember seeing Vondie Curtis-Hall's *Gridlock'd* at Sundance 1996, soon after Tupac was murdered in Vegas. I'd admired Shakur's acting in *Poetic Justice* and *Juice*, and now here, opposite the great Tim Roth, he was distinctive and memorable in what was essentially a two-character study. Consider the scene where his character, desperate to get into detox, tries to persuade Roth's character to stab him in the side, and the two get into a hopeless discussion about which side the liver is on.

In the long run Shakur might have become more important as an actor than as a singer (as Ice Cube has). As you listen to his uncanny narration of *Tupac: Resurrection*, which is stitched together from interviews, you realize you're not listening to the usual self-important vacancies from celebrity Q&As, but to spoken prose of a high order, in which analysis, memory, and poetry come together seamlessly in sentences and paragraphs that sound as if they were written. Let's assume you are a person who never intends to see a doc about rap music, but might have it in you to see one. This is the one. ☞

The Tuxedo ★ ½
PG-13, 99 m., 2002

Jackie Chan (Jimmy Tong), Jennifer Love Hewitt (Del Blaine), Jason Isaacs (Clark Devlin), Ritchie Coster (Banning), Debi Mazar (Steena), Peter Stormare (Dr. Simms), Mia Cottet (Cheryl). Directed by Kevin Donovan and produced by John H. Williams and Adam Schroeder. Screenplay by Michael Wilson and Michael Leeson.

There is an ancient tradition in action movies that the first scene is a self-contained shocker with no relevance to the rest of the plot. James Bond parachutes from a mountainside, Clint Eastwood disarms a robber, etc. Jackie Chan's *The Tuxedo* opens with a deer urinating in a mountain stream. The deer, the urine, and the stream have nothing to do with the rest of the film.

The movie's plot does involve water. The bad guy wants to add an ingredient to the world's water supply that will cause victims to dehydrate and die. To save themselves, they will have to buy the villain's pure water. Since his opening gambit is to sabotage, I repeat, the *world's* water supply, he will dehydrate everyone except those already drinking only bottled water, and so will inherit a planet of health nuts, which is just as well, since all the fish and animals and birds will dehydrate too, and everyone will have to live on PowerBars.

I have been waiting for a dehydrating villain for some time. My wife is of the opinion that I do not drink enough water. She believes the proper amount is a minimum of eight glasses a day. She often regards me balefully and says, "You're not getting enough water." In hot climates her concern escalates. In Hawaii last summer she had the grandchildren so worked up they ran into the bedroom every morning to see if Grandpa Roger had turned to dust.

The movie's villain, whose name is Banning (Ritchie Coster), has a novel scheme for distributing the formula, or virus, or secret ingredient, or whatever it is, that will make water into a dehydrating agent. He plans to use water striders, those insects that can skate across the surface of a pond. In his secret laboratory he keeps his ultimate weapon, a powerful water strider queen.

Do water striders *have* queens, like bees and ants do? For an authoritative answer I turned to Dr. May Berenbaum, head of the Department of Entomology at the University of Illinois at Urbana-Champaign, and founder of the Insect Fear Film Festival, held every year at the great university.

She says: "Water striders are true bugs (i.e., insects with piercing/sucking mouthparts) that run or skate on the surface of bodies of water, feeding on the insects that fall onto the water surface. There are about 500 species of gerrids in the world and, as far as I know, not a single one of those 500 species is eusocial (i.e., has a complex social structure with reproductive division of labor and cooperative brood care). I don't even know of an example of maternal care in the whole group. In short, the answer to your question is an emphatic 'No!' I can't wait to see this film. It definitely sounds like a candidate for a future Insect Fear Film Festival!"

More crushing evidence. Dr. Bruce P. Smith, expert entomologist at Ithaca College, tells me, "There is no known species of water striders that has queens. The most closely related insects that do are some colonial aphid species, and the most familiar (and much more distant relatives) are the ants, bees, wasps, and termites." He adds helpfully, "One mammal does have queens: the naked mole rats of Africa." Revealing himself as a student of insect films, he continues, "If my memory is correct, *Arachnophobia* has a king spider, but no queen—totally absurd!"

So there you have it. Professors Smith and Berenbaum have spoken. The evil Banning has spent untold millions on his secret plans for world domination, and thinks he possesses a water strider queen when he only has a lucky regular water strider living the life of Riley.

But back to *The Tuxedo*. Jackie Chan plays a taxi driver named Jimmy Tong, who is hired by Debi Mazar to be the chauffeur for Clark Devlin (Jason Isaacs), a multimillionaire secret agent whose $2 million tuxedo turns him into

a fighting machine (also a dancer, kung-fu expert, etc.). After Devlin is injured by a skateboard bomb, Jackie puts on the suit and soon partners with agent Del Blaine (Jennifer Love Hewitt), who realizes he has a strange accent for a man named Clark Devlin, but nevertheless joins him in battle against Banning.

The movie is silly beyond comprehension, and even if it weren't silly, it would still be beyond comprehension. It does have its moments, as when the tuxedo inadvertently coldcocks James Brown, the Godfather of Soul, and Jackie Chan has to go onstage in place of the hardest-working man in show business. He's very funny as James Brown, although not as funny as James Brown is.

There's something engaging about Jackie Chan. Even in a bad movie, I like him, because what you see is so obviously what you get. This time he goes light on the stunts, at least the stunts he obviously does himself, so that during the closing credits there are lots of flubbed lines and times when the actors break out laughing, but none of those spellbinding shots in which he misses the bridge, falls off the scaffold, etc. And some of the shots are computer-generated, which is kind of cheating, isn't it, with Jackie Chan? Luckily, special effects are not frowned upon at the Insect Fear Film Festival.

28 Days Later ★ ★ ★
R, 108 m., 2003

Cillian Murphy (Jim), Naomie Harris (Selena), Christopher Eccleston (Major Henry West), Megan Burns (Hannah), Brendan Gleeson (Frank), Noah Huntley (Mark). Directed by Danny Boyle and produced by Andrew MacDonald. Screenplay by Alex Garland.

Activists set lab animals free from their cages—only to learn, too late, that they're infected with a "rage" virus that turns them into frothing, savage killers. The virus quickly spreads to human beings, and when a man named Jim (Cillian Murphy) awakens in an empty hospital and walks outside, he finds a deserted London. In a series of astonishing shots, he wanders Piccadilly Circus and crosses Westminster Bridge with not another person in sight, learning from old wind-blown newspapers of a virus that turned humanity against itself.

So opens *28 Days Later,* which begins as a great science fiction film and continues as an intriguing study of human nature. The ending is disappointing—an action shoot-out, with characters chasing each other through the headquarters of a rogue army unit—but for most of the way, it's a great ride. I suppose movies like this have to end with the good and evil characters in a final struggle. The audience wouldn't stand for everybody being dead at the end, even though that's the story's logical outcome.

Director Danny Boyle (*Trainspotting*) shoots on video to give his film an immediate, documentary feel, and also no doubt to make it affordable; a more expensive film would have had more standard action heroes and less time to develop the quirky characters. Spend enough money on this story, and it would have the depth of *Armageddon.* Alex Garland's screenplay develops characters who seem to have a reality apart from their role in the plot—whose personalities help decide what they do and why.

Jim is the everyman, a bicycle messenger whose nearly fatal traffic accident probably saves his life. Wandering London, shouting (unwisely) for anyone else, he eventually encounters Selena (Naomie Harris) and Mark (Noah Huntley), who have avoided infection and explain the situation. (Mark: "Okay, Jim, I've got some bad news.") Selena, a tough-minded black woman who is a realist, says the virus had spread to France and America before the news broadcasts ended; if someone is infected, she explains, you have twenty seconds to kill them before they turn into a berserk, devouring zombie.

That twenty-second limit serves three valuable story purposes: (a) It has us counting "twelve . . . eleven . . . ten" in our minds at one crucial moment; (b) it eliminates the standard story device where a character can keep his infection secret; and (c) it requires the quick elimination of characters we like, dramatizing the merciless nature of the plague.

Darwinians will observe that a virus that acts within twenty seconds will not be an efficient survivor; the host population will soon be

dead—and along with it, the virus. I think the movie's answer to this objection is that the "rage" virus did not evolve in the usual way, but was created through genetic manipulation in the Cambridge laboratory where the story begins.

Not that we are thinking much about evolution during the movie's engrossing central passages. Selena becomes the dominant member of the group, the toughest and least sentimental, enforcing a hard-boiled survivalist line. Good-hearted Jim would probably have died if he hadn't met her. Eventually they encounter two other survivors: a big, genial man named Frank (Brendan Gleeson) and his teenage daughter, Hannah (Megan Burns). They're barricaded in a high-rise apartment, and use their hand-cranked radio to pick up a radio broadcast from an army unit near Manchester. Should they trust the broadcast and travel to what is described as a safe zone?

The broadcast reminded me of that forlorn radio signal from the Northern Hemisphere that was picked up in post-bomb Australia in *On the Beach.* After some discussion the group decides to take the risk, and they use Frank's taxi to drive to Manchester. This involves an extremely improbable sequence in which the taxi seems able to climb over gridlocked cars in a tunnel, and another scene in which a wave of countless rats flees from zombies.

Those surviving zombies raise the question: How long can you live once you have the virus? Since London seems empty at the beginning, presumably the zombies we see were survivors until fairly recently. Another question: Since they run in packs, why don't they attack each other? That one, the movie doesn't have an answer for.

The Manchester roadblock, which is indeed maintained by an uninfected army unit, sets up the third act, which doesn't live up to the promise of the first two. The officer in charge, Major Henry West (Christopher Eccleston), invites them to join his men at one of those creepy movie dinners where the hosts are so genial that the guests get suspicious. And then . . . see for yourself.

Naomie Harris, a newcomer, is convincing as Selena, the rock at the center of the storm. We come to realize she was not born tough, but has made the necessary adjustments to the situation. In a lesser movie there would be a love scene between Selena and Jim, but here the movie finds the right tone in a moment where she pecks him on the cheek and he blushes. There is also a touching scene where she offers Valium to young Hannah. They are facing a cruel situation. "To kill myself?" Hannah asks. "No. So you won't care as much."

The conclusion is pretty standard. I can understand why Boyle avoided having everyone dead at the end, but I wish he'd had the nerve that John Sayles showed in *Limbo* with his open ending. My imagination is just diabolical enough that when that jet fighter appears toward the end, I wish it had appeared, circled back—and opened fire. But then I'm never satisfied. *28 Days Later* is a tough, smart, ingenious movie that leads its characters into situations where everything depends on their (and our) understanding of human nature.

25th Hour ★ ★ ★ ½
R, 134 m., 2002

Edward Norton (Monty Brogan), Philip Seymour Hoffman (Jakob Elinsky), Barry Pepper (Frank Slaughtery), Rosario Dawson (Naturelle Rivera), Anna Paquin (Mary D'Annunzio), Brian Cox (James Brogan). Directed by Spike Lee and produced by Julia Chasman, Jon Kilik, Lee, and Tobey Maguire. Screenplay by David Benioff, based on his novel.

Spike Lee's *25th Hour* tells the story of a businessman's last day of freedom before the start of his seven-year prison sentence. During this day he will need to say good-bye to his girlfriend, his father, and his two best friends. And he will need to find someone to take care of his dog. The man's business was selling drugs, but his story could be a microcosm for the Enron thieves. What it has in common is a lack of remorse; the man is sorry he is going to prison, but not particularly sorry for his business practices, which he would still be engaged in if he hadn't been caught.

The man's name is Monty Brogan. He is thoughtful, well spoken, a nice guy. The first time we see him, he's rescuing a dog that has been beaten half to death. He associates with bad guys—the Russian Mafia of New York—but it's hard to picture him at work. He doesn't seem like the type, especially not on the morning of his last day, when an old customer approaches him and he wearily advises him, "Take your jones somewhere else."

Monty is played by Edward Norton as a man who bitterly regrets his greed. He should have gotten out sooner—taken the money and run. He stayed in too long, someone ratted on him, and the feds knew exactly where to look for the cocaine. He dreads prison not so much because of seven lost years, but because he fears he will be raped. His friends see his future more clearly. They are Jakob Elinsky (Philip Seymour Hoffman), a high school English teacher, and Frank Slaughtery (Barry Pepper), a Wall Street trader. Talking sadly with Jakob, Frank spells out Monty's options. He can kill himself. He can become a fugitive. Or he can do the time, but when he comes out his life will never be the same and he will not be able to put it together in any meaningful way. Frank's verdict: "It's over."

The film reflects this elegiac tone as it follows Monty's last hours of freedom. He has been lucky in his girlfriend, Naturelle (Rosario Dawson), and in his father, James (Brian Cox). Although he suspects that Naturelle could have been his betrayer, we see her as a good-hearted young woman who knows how to read him, who observes at a certain point in the evening that Monty doesn't want company. The father, a retired fireman, runs a bar on Staten Island. Most of his customers are firemen too, and the shadow of 9/11 hangs over them.

Monty has given his father money to pay off the bar's debts. He has moved with Rosario into a nice apartment. Both the father and the girl know where the money comes from. His dad disapproves of drugs, but has a curious way of forgiving his son: He blames himself. Because he was a drunk, because his wife died, it's not all Monty's fault.

The screenplay is by David Benioff, based on his own novel. It contains a brilliant sequence where Monty looks in the mirror of a rest room and spits out a litany of hate for every group he can think of in New York—every economic, ethnic, sexual, and age group gets the f-word, until finally he sees himself in the mirror, and includes himself. This scene seems so typical of Spike Lee (it's like an extension of a sequence in *Do the Right Thing*) that it's a surprise to find it's in the original novel—but then Benioff's novel may have been inspired by Lee's earlier film.

There are two other sequences where we see Lee's unique energy at work. In one of them, also from the book, the father drives Monty to prison and, in a long voice-over monologue, describes an alternative to jail. He tells his son that he could take an exit on the turnpike, head west, start over. In an extraordinary visual illustration of the monologue, we see Monty getting a job in a small town, finding a wife, starting a family, and finally, old and gray, revealing the secret of his life. Wouldn't it be nice to think so. Brian Cox's reading of this passage is another reminder that he is not only the busiest, but also the best of character actors.

The other sequence involves Jakob, the Philip Seymour Hoffman character. He is a nebbishy English teacher, single, lacking social skills, embracing his thankless job as a form of penance for having been born rich. He is attracted to one of his students, Mary D'Annunzio (Anna Paquin), but does nothing about it, constantly reminding himself that to act would be a sin and a crime. On Monty's last night he takes Naturelle, Jakob, and Frank to a nightclub, and Mary is in the crowd of girls hoping to get past the doorman. From across the street she shouts at Jakob: "Elinsky! Get me in." And we think, yes, she *would* call him by his unadorned last name—the same way she refers to him among her friends.

She does get in, and this continues a parallel story. She is precocious with sexuality yet naive with youth, and the poor schmuck Jakob is finally driven to trying to kiss her, with results that will burn forever in both of their memories. How does this story fit with Monty's? Maybe it shows that we want what we want, no matter the social price. And maybe that's the connection, too, with Frank, who invites Monty over to his big apartment in a building literally overlooking the devastation of the World Trade Center. He has never thought of moving, because the price is right. All three men are willing to see others suffer, in one way or another, or even die, so that they can have what they want. The movie suggests a thought that may not occur to a lot of its viewers: To what degree do we all live that way?

The film is unusual for not having a plot or a payoff. It is about the end of this stage of Monty's life, and so there is no goal he is striving for—unless it is closure with Naturelle and his father. He may not see them again; certainly not like this. The movie criticizes the harsh Rockefeller drug laws, which make drugs more profitable and therefore increase crime. We reflect that when Monty sold drugs, at least his customers knew exactly what they were buying and why. That makes him a little more honest than the corporate executives who relied on trust to con their innocent victims out of billions of dollars.

24 Hour Party People ★ ★ ★ ★
R, 117 m., 2002

Steve Coogan (Tony Wilson), Keith Allen (Roger Ames), Rob Brydon (Ryan Letts), Enzo Cilenti (Pete Saville), Ron Cook (Derek Ryder), Chris Coghill (Bez), Paddy Considine (Rob Gretton), Danny Cunningham (Shaun Ryder), Dave Gorman (John the Postman). Directed by Michael Winterbottom and produced by Andrew Eaton. Screenplay by Frank Cottrell Boyce.

24 Hour Party People, which tells the story of the Manchester music scene from the first Sex Pistols concert until the last bankruptcy, shines with a kind of inspired madness. It is based on fact, but Americans who don't know the facts will have no trouble identifying with the sublime posturing of its hero, a television personality named Tony Wilson, who takes himself seriously in a way that is utterly impossible to take seriously.

Wilson, a real man, is played by Steve Coogan, who plays a Wilsonoid TV personality on British TV. That sort of through-the-looking-glass mixing of reality and fancy makes the movie somehow *more* true than a factual documentary would have been. Wilson is a lanky man with the face of a sincere beagle, a flop of hair over his right eyebrow, and an ability to read banal TV copy as if it has earth-shaking profundity. He's usually the only man in the room wearing a suit and tie, but he looks like he put them on without reading the instructions. He is so heartfelt about his lunacies that we understand, somehow, that his mind deals with contradictions by embracing them.

As the film opens, Wilson is attending the first, legendary, Sex Pistols concert in Manchester, England. Here and elsewhere, director Michael Winterbottom subtly blends real newsreel footage with fictional characters so they all fit convincingly into the same shot. Wilson is transfixed by the Pistols as they sing "Anarchy in the UK" and sneer at British tradition. He tells the camera that everyone in the audience will leave the room transformed and inspired, and then the camera pans to show a total of forty-two people, two or three of them half-heartedly dancing in the aisles.

Wilson features the Pistols and other bands on his Manchester TV show. Because of a ban by London TV, his show becomes the only venue for punk rock. Turns out he was right about the Pistols. They let loose something that changed rock music. And they did it in the only way that Wilson could respect, by thoroughly screwing up everything they did, and ending in bankruptcy and failure, followed by Sid Vicious's spectacular murder-suicide flameout. The Sex Pistols became successful because they failed; if they had succeeded, they would have sold out, or become diluted or commercial. I saw Johnny Rotten a few years ago at Sundance, still failing, and it made me feel proud of him.

Tony Wilson, who preaches "anarchism" not as a political position but as an emotional state, knows he has seen the future. He joins with two partners to form Factory Records, which would become one of the most important and least financially successful recording companies in history, and joyously signs the contract in his blood (while declaring "we will have no contracts"). His bands include Joy Division (renamed New Order after the suicide of its lead singer) and Happy Mondays. His company opens a rave club, the Hacienda, which goes broke because the customers ignore the cash bars and spend all their money on Ecstasy.

Wilson hardly cares. When the club closes, he addresses the final night's crowd: "Before you leave, I ask you to invade the offices and loot them." When he meets with investors who

want to buy Factory Records, they are startled to learn he has nothing to sell—no contracts, no back catalog, nothing. "We are not really a company," he explains helpfully. "We are an experiment in human nature. I protected myself from the dilemma of selling out by having nothing to sell."

This is a lovable character, all the more so because his conversation uses the offhand goofy non sequiturs of real speech instead of being channeled into a narrow lane of movie dialogue. The writer, Frank Cottrell Boyce, gives Wilson a distinctive voice we come to love. "I went to Cambridge University!" he tells one of his broadcast bosses. "I'm a serious journalist, living in one of the most important times in human history." Yes, but the next day he's interviewing a midget elephant-trainer. He explains how the invention of broccoli funded the James Bond movies (there is a shred of truth there, actually). He quotes Plutarch and William Blake, he says one of his singers is a poet equal to Yeats, he looks at empty concert halls and observes hopefully that there were only twelve people at the Last Supper (thirteen, actually, counting the talent). And he is courageous in the face of daunting setbacks, pushing on optimistically into higher realms of failure.

The movie works so well because it evokes genuine, not manufactured, nostalgia. It records a time when the inmates ran the asylum, when music lovers got away with murder. It loves its characters. It understands what the Sex Pistols started, and what the 1990s destroyed. And it gets a certain tone right. It kids itself. At one point, Wilson looks straight at the camera and tells us that a scene is missing, "but it will probably be on the DVD."

As the screenwriter of an ill-fated Sex Pistols movie, I met Rotten, Vicious, Cook, Jones, and their infamous manager, Malcolm McLaren, and brushed the fringe of their world. I could see there was no plan, no strategy, no philosophy, just an attitude. If a book on the Sex Pistols had an upraised middle finger on the cover, it wouldn't need any words inside. And yet Tony Wilson goes to see the Pistols and sees before him a delirious opportunity to—to what? Well, obviously, to live in one of the most important times in human history, and to make your mark on it by going down in glorious flames.

21 Grams ★ ★ ★
R, 125 m., 2003

Sean Penn (Paul Rivers), Benicio Del Toro (Jack Jordan), Naomi Watts (Cristina Peck), Charlotte Gainsbourg (Mary Rivers), Melissa Leo (Marianne Jordan), Clea DuVall (Claudia), Danny Huston (Michael). Directed by Alejandro Gonzalez Inarritu and produced by Inarritu, Ted Hope, and Robert Salerno. Screenplay by Guillermo Arriaga.

21 Grams knows all about its story but only lets us discover it a little at a time. Well, every movie does that, but usually they tell their stories in chronological order, so we have the illusion that we're watching as the events happen to the characters. In this film everything has already happened, and it's as if God, or the director, is shuffling the deck after the game is over. Here is the question we have to answer: Is this approach better than telling the same story from beginning to end?

The film is by Alejandro Gonzalez Inarritu, the almost unreasonably talented Mexican filmmaker whose *Amores Perros* (2000) was an enormous success. That film intercut three simultaneous stories, all centering on a traffic accident. *21 Grams* has three stories and a traffic accident, but the stories move back and forth in time, so that sometimes we know more than the characters, sometimes they know more than we do.

While the film is a virtuoso accomplishment of construction and editing, the technique has its limitations. Even though modern physics teaches that time does not move from the past through the present into the future, entertaining that delusion is how we make sense of our perceptions. And it is invaluable for actors, who build their characters emotionally as events take place. By fracturing his chronology, Inarritu isolates key moments in the lives of his characters, so that they have to stand alone. There is a point at which this stops being a strategy and starts being a stunt.

21 Grams tells such a tormenting story, however, that it just about survives its style. It would have been more powerful in chronolog-

ical order, and even as a puzzle it has a deep effect. Remembering it, we dismiss the structure and recall the events as they happened to the characters, and are moved by its three sad stories of characters faced with the implacable finality of life.

Because the entire movie depends on withholding information and revealing unexpected connections, it is fair enough to describe the characters but would be wrong to even hint at some of their relationships. Sean Penn, Benicio Del Toro, and Naomi Watts play the key figures, and their spouses are crucial in ways that perhaps should not be described. Penn is Paul, a professor of mathematics (even that fact is withheld for a long time, and comes as a jolt because he does not seem much like one). He is dying of a heart condition, needs a transplant, and is badgered by his wife (Charlotte Gainsbourg) to donate sperm so that she can have his baby—after his death, she does not quite say.

Benicio Del Toro is Jack, a former convict who now rules his family with firm fundamentalist principles. He is using Jesus as a way of staying off drugs and alcohol; his wife (Melissa Leo) is grateful for his recovery but dubious about his cure.

The third story centers on Cristina (Naomi Watts), first seen at a Narcotics Anonymous meeting; she has a husband (Danny Huston) and two daughters, and her life seems to be getting healthier and more stable until an event takes place that eventually links all of the characters in a situation that falls halfway between tragedy and fraught melodrama.

As you watch this film you are absorbed and involved, sometimes deeply moved; acting does not get much better than the work done here by Penn, Del Toro, and Watts, and their individual moments have astonishing impact. But in the closing passages, as the shape of the underlying structure becomes clear, a vague dissatisfaction sets in. You wonder if Inarritu took you the long way around, running up mileage on his storyteller's taxi meter. Imagining how heartbreaking the conclusion would have been if we had arrived at it in the ordinary way by starting at the beginning, I felt as if an unnecessary screen of technique had been placed between the story and the audience.

Yet I do not want to give the wrong impression: This is an accomplished and effective film, despite my reservations. It grips us, moves us, astonishes us. Some of the revelations do benefit by coming as surprises. But artists often grow by learning what to leave out (the great example is Ozu). I have a feeling that Inarritu's fractured technique, which was so impressive in his first film and is not so satisfactory in this one, may inspire impatience a third time around. He is so good that it's time for him to get out of his own way.

The Twilight Samurai ★ ★ ★

NO MPAA RATING, 129 m., 2004

Hiroyuki Sanada (Seibei Iguchi), Rie Miyazawa (Tomoe Iinuma), Nenji Kobayashi (Choubei Hisasaka), Min Tanaka (Zenemon Yogo), Ren Osugi (Toyotarou Kouda), Mitsuru Fukikoshi (Michinojo Iinuma), Miki Ito (Kayana Iguchi), Erina Hashiguchi (Ito Iguchi). Directed by Yoji Yamada and produced by Hiroshi Fukazawa, Shigehiro Nakagawa, and Ichiro Yamamoto. Screenplay by Yamada Asama and Yoshitaka Asama, based on novels by Shuuhei Fujisawa.

One who is a samurai must before all things keep in mind, by day, and by night, the fact that he has to die. That is his chief business.
—Code of Bushido

The Twilight Samurai is set in Japan during the period of the Meiji Restoration, circa 1868—the same period as Kurosawa's great *Seven Samurai* and Edward Zwick's elegant *The Last Samurai*. The three films deal in different ways with a time when samurai still tried to live by the Code of Bushido, even as they faced poverty or unemployment in a changing society. *The Last Samurai* is about samurai opposing the emperor's moves to modernize Japan; ironically, we learn that the hero of *The Twilight Samurai* fought and died in that rebellion—after the story of this movie is over.

His name is Seibei (Hiroyuki Sanada), and he lives under the rule of his clan in northeast Japan, where he spends his days not in battle but as an accountant, keeping track of dried fish and other foods in storage. Seeing him bending wearily over a pile of papers, declining an invitation by his fellow workers to go out drinking, we're reminded of the hero of Kurosawa's film *Ikiru*. Seibei hurries home because

he has a senile mother and two young daughters to support, and is in debt after the death of his wife.

His story is told by director Yoji Yamada in muted tones and colors, beautifully re-creating a feudal village that still retains its architecture, its customs, its ancient values, even as the economy is making its way of life obsolete. What kind of a samurai has to pawn his sword and make do with a bamboo replacement? The film is narrated by Seibei's oldest daughter (Erina Hashiguchi), who is young in the film but an old lady on the sound track, remembering her father with love.

After working all day in the office, Seibei hurries home to grow crops to feed his family and earn extra cash. His coworkers gossip that his kimono is torn, and that he smells. One day the lord of the clan comes to inspect the food stores, notices Seibei's aroma, and reprimands him. This brings such disgrace on the family that Seibei's stern uncle reminds him, "Only a generation ago, hara-kiri would have been called for." His uncle advises him to remarry to get another worker into the home to prepare meals and do laundry. It happens that his childhood sweetheart, Tomoe (Rie Miyazawa), has just divorced her wife-beating husband, and begins to help around the house. The girls love her, but Seibei is shy and tired and cannot imagine remarrying.

The clan comes to him with an assignment: He is to kill the unruly Yogo (Min Tanaka), a samurai who has been employed by the clan for only four years, after a long, destitute time of wandering the countryside. Yogo, considered crazy, has declined the clan's suggestion that he kill himself. That seems sane enough to me, but the clan must uphold its standards even as its time is passing, and so the reluctant Seibei is bribed and blackmailed into taking on the assignment.

The closing third of the film is magnificent in the way it gathers all we have learned about Seibei and uses it to bring depth to what could have been a routine action sequence, but is much more. We see Tomoe shyly preparing him for battle ("Allow me to comb your hair"), and after a crucial conversation, he leaves her and goes to Yogo's home, where the body of an earlier emissary lies in the courtyard, covered by a swarm of flies.

I will not, of course, tell you what happens inside the house, or what happens between Seibei and Tomoe. What I can refer to is the extraordinary conversation between Seibei and Yogo, while their swords remain undrawn. "I know, you're all keyed up," Yogo says. "But I'm going to run." He has no desire to fight. He recounts his weary history as a samurai in poverty, or in bondage to a clan: "I was an errand boy, too." At one extraordinary moment he takes the ashes of his dead daughter and crunches a piece of bone between his teeth. Yogo's motive for having this conversation may not be as clear as it seems; it is up to you to decide.

Director Yoji Yamada, now seventy-three, has made at least sixty-six films, according to IMDB.com. *The Twilight Samurai*, the first to be widely released in this country, was Japan's Oscar nominee this year. He has been nominated six times since he was sixty as Japan's best director, and won once. Yet no less than forty-eight of his films were B-pictures, involving the beloved character Tora-san, popular in Japan from 1970 until the death in 1996 of Kiyoshi Atsumi, who played him. Tora-san is little known outside Japan, but for a class on Japanese cinema, I obtained one of his movies from Shochiku Studios and we watched it. Apparently they are all much the same: Tora-san, a meek, self-effacing comic figure (a little Chaplin, a little Jerry Lewis, a little Red Skelton), is a salesman who stumbles into a domestic crisis, makes it worse, and then makes it better.

One can only imagine what it would be like to direct that formula forty-eight times. Perhaps Yamada felt a little like Seibei, as he remained loyal to the studio and this character year after year. Perhaps when Seibei finds, at the end of *The Twilight Samurai*, that he may be poor and stuck in a rut but he still has greatness in him—well, perhaps that's how Yamada felt when he entered the home stretch. There is a kind of perfection in laboring humbly all your life only to show, as the end approaches, that you had greatness all along. I am half-convinced that as Seibei's daughter remembers her father's life, she is also describing Yamada's. I could probably find out if that is true, but I don't want to know. I like it better as a possibility.

Note: The Twilight Samurai *swept the 2003 Japanese Academy Awards, winning twelve categories, including best picture, director, screenplay, actor, actress, supporting actor, and cinematography.*

Twisted ★ ½
R, 96 m., 2004

Ashley Judd (Jessica Shepard), Samuel L. Jackson (John Mills), Andy Garcia (Mike Delmarco), David Strathairn (Dr. Melvin Frank), Russell Wong (Lieutenant Tong), Camryn Manheim (Lisa), Mark Pellegrino (Jimmy Schmidt). Directed by Philip Kaufman and produced by Barry Baeres, Linne Radmin, Arnold Kopelson, and Anne Kopelson. Screenplay by Sarah Thorp and Kaufman.

Phil Kaufman's *Twisted* walks like a thriller and talks like a thriller, but squawks like a turkey. And yet the elements are in place for a film that works—until things start becoming clear and mysteries start being solved and we start shaking our heads, if we are well mannered, or guffawing, if we are not.

Let me begin at the ending. The other day I employed the useful term *deus ex machina* in a review, and received several messages from readers who are not proficient in Latin. I have also received several messages from Latin scholars who helpfully translated obscure dialogue in *The Passion of the Christ* for me, and, as my Urbana High School Latin teacher Mrs. Link used to remind me, "*In medio tutissimus ibis.*"

But back to *deus ex machina*. This is a phrase you will want to study and master, not merely to amaze friends during long bus journeys but because it so perfectly describes what otherwise might take you thousands of words. Imagine a play on a stage. The hero is in a fix. The dragon is breathing fire, the hero's sword is broken, his leg is broken, his spirit is broken, and the playwright's imagination is broken. Suddenly there is the offstage noise of the grinding of gears, and invisible machinery lowers a god onto the stage, who slays the dragon, heals the hero, and fires the playwright. He is the "god from the machine."

Now travel with me to San Francisco. Ashley Judd plays Jessica Shepard, a new homicide detective who has a habit of picking up guys in bars and having rough sex with them. She drinks a lot. Maybe that goes without saying. Soon after getting her new job, she and her partner, Mike Delmarco (Andy Garcia), are assigned to a floater in the bay. She recognizes the dead man, who has been savagely beaten. It's someone she has slept with.

She reveals this information, but is kept on the case by the police commissioner (Samuel L. Jackson), who raised her as his own daughter after her own father went berserk and killed a slew of people, including her mother. The commissioner trusts her. Then another body turns up, also with the killer's brand (a cigarette burn). She slept with this guy, too. She's seeing the department shrink (David Strathairn), who understandably suggests she has to share this information with her partner. Then a third dead guy turns up. She slept with him, too. Wasn't it Oscar Wilde who said, "To kill one lover may be regarded as a misfortune. To kill three seems like carelessness"?

Detective Sheperd has a pattern. She goes home at night, drinks way too much red wine, and blacks out. The next day, her cell rings and she's summoned to the next corpse. Wasn't it Ann Landers who said that killing people in a blackout was one of the twenty danger signals of alcoholism? To be sure, Delmarco helpfully suggests at one point that she should drink less. Maybe only enough to maim?

So anyway, on a dark and isolated pier in San Francisco, three of the characters come together. I won't reveal who they are, although if one of them isn't Ashley Judd it wouldn't be much of an ending. Certain death seems about to ensue, and then with an offstage grinding noise ... but I don't want to give away the ending. Find out for yourself.

And ask yourself this question: Assuming the premise of the first amazing development, how did the San Francisco police department know exactly which dark and isolated pier these three people were on, and how did they arrive in sixty seconds (by car, truck, motorcycle, and helicopter), and how come the cops who arrived were precisely the same cops who have already been established as characters in the story? And isn't it convenient that, fast as they arrived, they considerately left time for the Talking Killer scene, in which all is explained when all the Killer has to do is blow everyone away and beat it?

The movie does at least draw a moral: *Nemo repente fuit turpissimus.*

Two Brothers ★ ★ ½
PG, 109 m., 2004

Guy Pearce (Aidan McRory), Jean-Claude Dreyfus (Eugene Normandin), Philippine Leroy-Beaulieu (Mathilde Normandin), Freddie Highmore (Raoul), Oanh Nguyen (His Excellency), Moussa Maaskri (Saladin), Vincent Scarito (Zerbino), Maï Anh Le (Naï-Rea). Directed by Jean-Jacques Annaud and produced by Annaud and Jake Eberts. Screenplay by Alain Godard and Annaud.

The brothers in *Two Brothers* are tiger cubs when we meet them, prowling the ruins of temples in the jungles of French Indochina, circa 1920. With their mother and father, Kumal and Sangha live an idyllic life, romping and wrestling and living on air, apparently, since no prey ever seems to be killed. The movie never really fesses up that tigers kill for their dinner; that would undercut its sentimentality. The result is a reassuring fairy tale that will fascinate children and has moments of natural beauty for their parents, but makes the tigers approximately as realistic as the animals in *The Lion King.*

The movie is astonishing in its photography of the two tigers, played by an assortment of trained beasts, augmented by CGI. It is less wondrous in its human story, involving such walking stereotypes as the great British hunter, the excitable French administrator, the misunderstood Indochinese prince, and the little French boy who makes friends with Sangha and sleeps with him when Sangha is at an age to be plenty old enough for his own bed, preferably behind bars.

Two Brothers was directed and cowritten by Jean-Jacques Annaud, whose international hit *The Bear* (1989) did not sentimentalize its bear cub but treated it with the respect due to an animal that earns its living under the law of the wild. In that one, the speech of the hunter (Jack Wallace) was presented not so much as language as simply the sounds that human animals make. In *Two Brothers,* the cubs may not understand English, but they get the drift. In both films, Annaud achieves almost miraculous moments, the result no doubt of a combination of training, patience, and special effects. We're usually convinced we are looking at real tiger cubs doing what they really want to do, even when it goes against their nature. Occasionally there will be a scene that stretches it, as when Kumal, who was trained in a circus to jump through a ring of fire, apparently uses telepathy to convince Sangha he can do it too.

The first half-hour or so involves only the cubs, and these scenes play like a scripted documentary. The beauty of the tigers and the exotic nature of the locations are so seductive we almost forget the movie has human stars and will therefore interrupt with a plot. But it does.

The villain, who becomes the hero, is Aidan McRory (Guy Pearce), introduced as an ivory hunter but then, after the bottom drops out of the ivory market, a tomb raider. When one of his assistants finds an ancient statue in the forest and regrets it's too heavy to bring back to Europe, McRory coldly tells him, "cut off its head." McRory is the one who kills the cubs' father and captures Kumal, selling him to a circus run by the harsh trainer Zerbino (Vincent Scarito).

Sangha is also captured, and adopted by young Raoul (Freddie Highmore), son of the French colonial administrator (Jean-Claude Dreyfus). He eventually ends up in the menagerie of a spoiled prince (Oanh Nguyen); Sangha is no longer safe as Raoul's playmate, the kid is told, "now that he has tasted blood." Apparently until that fatal taste, Sangha was a vegetarian. The prince decrees that the two tigers fight to the death in an amphitheater, but of course, being brothers, they . . . well, do more or less exactly what we expect them to do.

The story is broad melodrama that treats Sangha and Kumal as if they were almost human in their motivations and emotions. Such comforting sentiment is a luxury wild animals cannot afford. Still, along with the beauty of the animals and the photography, there are moments of genuine tension, as when McRory faces the tigers up close. That McRory does not make his own contribution to their taste for blood is because of the tiger's uncanny ability to peer deeply into the eyes of the human actors and learn there what they must do for the benefit of the movie's plot.

There is a lot in *Two Brothers* I admire. Families will not go wrong in attending this film. Some kids will think it's one of the best movies they've seen. My objections are of a sort that won't occur, I realize, to many of the viewers. But I remember *The Bear* and its brave refusal to supply its bear cub with human emotions and motivations. W. G. Sebald writes that animals and humans view one another "through a breach of incomprehension." That is profoundly true, and helpful to keep in mind when making friends with the bears at Yellowstone, or reassuring tigers that we feel their pain.

2 Fast 2 Furious ★ ★ ★
PG-13, 100 m., 2003

Paul Walker (Brian O'Connor), Tyrese (Roman Pearce), Eva Mendes (Monica Fuentes), Cole Hauser (Carter Verone), Chris "Ludacris" Bridges (Tej), James Remar (Agent Markham), Devon Aoki (Suki). Directed by John Singleton and produced by Neal H. Moritz. Screenplay by Michael Brandt and Derek Haas.

John Singleton's *2 Fast 2 Furious* tells a story so shamelessly preposterous all we can do is shake our heads in disbelief. Consider that the big climax involves a Miami drug lord who hires two street racers to pick up bags full of money in Miami and deliver them in the Keys, and adds, "You make it, I'll personally hand you one hundred G's at the finish line." Hell, for ten G's I'd rent a van at the Aventura Mall and deliver the goods myself.

But this is not an ordinary delivery. The drivers are expected to drive at speeds ranging from one hundred mph to jet-assisted takeoff velocities, which of course might attract the attention of the police, so the drug lord has to arrange a fifteen-minute "window" with a corrupt cop, whom he persuades by encouraging a rat to eat its way into his intestines. Does it strike you that this man is going to a lot of extra trouble?

Despite the persuasive rat, the cops do chase the speed racers, but the racers have anticipated this, and drive their cars into a vast garage, after which dozens or hundreds of other supercharged vehicles emerge from the garage, confusing the cops with a high-speed traffic jam. Oh, and some guys in monster trucks crush a lot of squad cars first. It is my instinct that the owners of monster trucks and street machines treat them with tender loving care, and don't casually volunteer to help out a couple of guys (one they've never seen before) by crashing their vehicles into police cars. You can get arrested for that.

Does it sound like I'm complaining? I'm not complaining. I'm grinning. *2 Fast 2 Furious* is a video game crossed with a buddy movie, a bad cop–good cop movie, a Miami drug lord movie, a chase movie, and a comedy. It doesn't have a brain in its head, but it's made with skill and style and, boy, is it fast and furious.

How much like a video game is it? The two drivers are named Brian O'Connor (Paul Walker) and Roman Pearce (Tyrese). As they race down city streets at one-fifth the speed of sound, they talk to each other. They can't hear each other, but that doesn't matter, because what they say is exactly the kind of stuff that avatars say in video games. I took some notes:

"Let's see what this thing can do!"

"Watch this, bro!"

"Let's see if you still got it, Brian!"

"How you like them apples!?"

Walker returns from the original *The Fast and the Furious* (2001), which established Vin Diesel as a star. Rather than appear in this movie, about cops infiltrating his car gang to bust the drug cartel, Diesel decided instead to make *A Man Apart*, playing a cop fighting the drug cartel. Oddly enough, *F&F2* is the better movie.

Walker's costar is Tyrese, a.k.a. Tyrese Gibson, who was so good in Singleton's *Baby Boy* (2001) and is the engine that drives *2 Fast 2 Furious* with energy and charisma. He's like an angrier Vin Diesel. Walker, who gets top billing in both movies, is pleasant but not compelling, sort of a Don Johnson lite.

Other key roles are by Cole Hauser as Carter Verone, the drug lord, whose Colombian parents didn't name him after Jimmy because he's too old for that, but possibly after Mother Maybelle; and Eva Mendes, as Monica Fuentes, the sexy undercover cop who has been on Verone's payroll for nine months and is either sleeping with him or is a sensational conversationalist.

O'Connor and Pearce are teamed up to work undercover as drivers for Verone, and promised that their records will be cleaned up if the mission succeeds. First they have to win their jobs. Verone assembles several teams of drivers and tells them he left a package in his red Ferrari at an auto pound twenty miles away. First team back with the package "gets the opportunity to work with me."

That sets off a high-speed race down Route 95 during which one car is crushed under the wheels of a truck, several more crash, and various racers and, presumably, civilians are killed. O'Connor and Pearce return with the package. As they're driving back, they don't even seem to pass the scene of the incredible carnage they caused in the opposite lanes; just as well, because at 120 mph you don't want to hit a gapers' block.

All of the chases involve the apparently inexhaustible supply of squad cars in South Florida. There's also a traffic jam in the sky, involving police and news helicopters. At one point a copter broadcaster hears a loud noise, looks up, and says, "What was that?" but we never find out what it was, perhaps because the movie is just too fast and too furious to slow down for a helicopter crash.

Two Weeks Notice ★ ★ ★

PG-13, 100 m., 2002

Sandra Bullock (Lucy Kelson), Hugh Grant (George Wade), Alicia Witt (June Carter), Dana Ivey (Ruth Kelson), Robert Klein (Larry Kelson), Heather Burns (Meryl), David Haig (Howard Wade), Dorian Missick (Tony). Directed by Marc Lawrence and produced by Sandra Bullock. Screenplay by Lawrence.

If I tell you *Two Weeks Notice* is a romantic comedy and it stars Sandra Bullock and Hugh Grant, what do you already know, and what do you need to know?

You already know: That when they meet the first time, they don't like each other. That circumstances bring them together. That they get along fine, but are sometimes scared by that, and back off a little. That they are falling in love without knowing it. That just when they're about to know it, circumstances force them apart. That they seem doomed to live separately, their love never realized. That circumstances bring them back together again. That they finally cave in and admit they're in love.

You need to know: What her job is. What his job is. What they disagree about. What their personality flaws are. And whether, just when their eyes are about to meet, it is a woman who seems to lure him away, or a man who seems to lure her away. You also need to know certain plug-in details of the movie, such as which ethnic groups and ethnic foods it will assign, and what fantasy dreams it will realize.

I have not, by making these observations, spoiled the plot of the movie. I have spoiled the plot of *every* romantic comedy. Just last week I saw *Maid in Manhattan,* and with that one you also know the same things and don't know the same things. The thing is, it doesn't matter that you know. If the actors are charming and the dialogue makes an effort to be witty and smart, the movie will work even though it faithfully follows the ancient formulas.

Romantic comedies are the comfort food of the movies. There are nights when you don't feel like a chef who thinks he's more important than the food. When you feel like sliding into a booth at some Formica joint where the waitress calls you "hon" and writes your order on a green-and-white guest check. Walking into *Two Weeks Notice* at the end of a hectic day, week, month, and year, I *wanted* it to be a typical romantic comedy starring those two lovable people, Sandra Bullock and Hugh Grant. And it was. And some of the dialogue has a real zing to it. There were wicked little one-liners that slipped in under the radar and nudged the audience in the ribs.

She plays a Harvard Law graduate who devotes her life to liberal causes, such as saving the environment and preserving landmarks. He plays a billionaire land developer who devotes his life to despoiling the environment and tearing down landmarks. They disagree about politics and everything else. He is an insufferable egotist, superficial and supercilious, amazed by his own charm and good looks. She is phobic about germs, has a boyfriend she never sees, and thinks anybody who wants to hire her wants to sleep with her.

He is also impulsive, and after she assaults him with a demand to save her favorite landmark, he hires her on the spot, promises he will not offend her sensibilities, and gives her a big salary. He does this, of course, because he plans to violate all of his promises, and because he wants to sleep with her. He may not know that, but we do.

The first half of the movie is just about perfect, of its kind, and I found myself laughing more than I expected to, and even grinning at a colleague who was one seat over, because we were both appreciating how much better the movie was than it had to be. Then a funny thing happens. The movie sort of loses its way.

This happens at about the time the billionaire, whose name is George Wade, agrees to let the lawyer, whose name is Lucy Kelson, quit and go back to her pro bono work. Her replacement is June Carter (Alicia Witt), a dazzling redhead with great legs and flattery skills. We think we know that she is going to be a rat and seduce George, and all the usual stuff. But no. She does make moves in that direction, but from instinct, not design. The fact is, she's essentially a sweet and decent person. At one point I thought I even heard her say she was married, but I must have misheard, as no romantic comedy would ever make the Other Woman technically unavailable.

Anyway, what goes wrong is not Alicia Witt's fault. She plays the role as written. It's just that, by not making her a villain, writer-director Marc Lawrence loses the momentum the formula could have supplied him. The last half of the movie basically involves the key characters being nicer than we expect them to be, more decent than we thought, and less cranked up into emotional overdrive. The result is a certain loss of energy.

I liked the movie anyway. I like the way the characters talk. I like the way they slip in political punchlines, and how some of the dialogue actually makes points about rich and poor, left and right, male and female, Democrat and Republican. The thoughts of these characters are not entirely governed by their genitals.

Sandra Bullock, who produced the film, knew just what she was doing and how to do it. Hugh Grant knew just what he was getting into. Some critics will claim they play their "usual roles," but Grant in particular finds a new note, a little more abrupt, a little more daffy than usual. And they bring to the movie what it must have: two people who we want to see kissing each other, and amusing ways to frustrate us until, of course, they finally do.

Tycoon: A New Russian ★ ★ ½
NO MPAA RATING, 128 m., 2003

Vladimir Mashkov (Platon ["Plato"]), Andrei

Krasko (Chmakov), Maria Mironova (Maria), Vladimir Golovin (Ahmet), Vladimir Goussav (Lomov), Alexandre Baluev (Koretski). Directed by Pavel Lounguine and produced by Catherine Dussart and Vladimir Grigoriev. Screenplay by Alexandre Borodianski, Lounguine, and Youli Doubov, adapted from the novel by Doubov.

Tycoon is subtitled *A New Russian*, and indeed its hero is a Russian unlike those we usually see in the movies: Plato Makovski is a killer capitalist, a onetime mathematics professor who seizes on the fall of Marxism as his opportunity to play capitalist tricks in a naive new economy. The character is based on the real-life billionaire Boris Berezovsky, who is even rumored to have financed it. Like *The Godfather*, it shows him as a crook with certain standards, surrounded by rats with none.

The movie is handicapped by a jittery editing style that prevents us from getting involved in the flow of the narrative, but it provides visuals for all those headlines about the Russian Mafia, go-go capitalists, and Moscow as Dodge City. It also suggests a series of recent Russian governments shot through with corruption and bribery, which may help explain why this was the most successful Russian film in history at the box office.

Makovski is played by Vladimir Mashkov, who in some lights looks handsome and in others feral. He has a charm based on brilliance. Most of his inner circle, like himself, came up through universities, since academia offered an alternative to bureaucracy and the army in the precollapse days. There are scenes where he dazzles the others with his audacious schemes, explaining how he will sell cars at a loss to make a profit, or pay off three debts with a nonexistent payment that circles through the debts back to the place where it does not exist.

If you don't understand that, neither do some of his admiring colleagues, but it must work, since Plato ends up fabulously wealthy. He operates not by stealth, like old-model crooks, but in the modern style of audacious publicity. Like the con men at Enron, he presents his crimes as a thriving capitalist success story, and he has access to the highest levels of the Kremlin, just as Enron had in the White House. His empire is centered in a towering

Moscow high-rise with the company name in giant letters on the roof.

All of this apparently comes to an end, however, in the assassination that opens the movie. His armored Mercedes is blown apart by an antitank missile; soon after it appears he will have to face criminal charges. ("I am a politician," he tells a TV interviewer, "and jail is part of the game.") The movie then flashes back over the past fifteen years to tell his story, using titles like "Three days before Plato's death" or "Five years before Plato's death" before each scene. These titles are of no help, because the structure makes it impossible for us to get a clear idea of chronology, and so the scenes have to be viewed as free-standing episodes involving recurring characters.

Among those characters is one of particular interest, a bulbous politician from Siberia named Lomov (Vladimir Goussav), whom Plato grooms to be the new premiere—only to be double-crossed. It's haunting, the way in which Lomov is created from nothing, grows popular through bald-faced lies, is forgiven his stupidity by an electorate tired of details, and is obedient to the interests of his billionaire backers. Lomov even becomes deluded that he has accomplished all of this on his own, and there is a strange confrontation in which he and Plato have entirely different ideas of their relationship. Plato has many other friends, including Koretski (Alexandre Baluev), a powerful minister who fights corruption mercilessly until his bribers mention the correct figure.

Another intriguing character is Chmakov (Andrei Krasko), a prosecuting judge from the provinces, brought in to investigate Plato's assassination. Although Plato and his confederates controlled an empire of bewildering size and complexity, this dogged and weary man is supposed to find the truth all by himself, and plods about in drizzly weather, looking uncannily like Mickey Spillane.

Chmakov drinks a lot, but then so does almost everyone in the movie. There isn't a major character who isn't an alcoholic, with the exception of Maria (Maria Mironova), Plato's sometime, arm's-length girlfriend. Watching this movie makes it easier to understand why the average Russian male doesn't live to be fifty: The wonder is that they live so long.

One particularly amusing character is Ahmet (Vladimir Golovin), a very old man who is brought in to deal with a gang of thugs who want 50 percent of Plato's auto dealings. He arranges a meeting for the next day. The ancient man, unprotected by bodyguards, greets the thugs in a grungy industrial area while seated behind a table with linen and crystal. He savors some caviar, informs them Plato is under his protection, and awes them into submission. It is not clear at the time whether Ahmet really is a legendary godfather or simply a bold con man. Certainly the thugs have no way of knowing.

Berezovsky, the real-life Plato, has been in trouble in recent years, including an arrest in the United Kingdom. Extradition is pending. At the end of his career Plato is lonely, isolated, and tired, and that is supposed to be the moral of the story. Yes, but since all of us face the possibility of loneliness, isolation, and exhaustion, perhaps it is better to face that fate as a billionaire.

U

Under the Tuscan Sun ★ ★ ★
PG-13, 102 m., 2003

Diane Lane (Frances Mayes), Raoul Bova
(Marcello), Sandra Oh (Patti), Vincent Riotta
(Mr. Martini), Lindsay Duncan (Katherine),
Giulia Steigerwalt (Chiara), Dan Bucatinsky
(Rodney), Valentine Pelka (Jerzy), Ralph Palka
(The German Man), Kristoffer Ryan Winters
(David). Directed by Audrey Wells and
produced by Tom Sternberg and Wells, based
on the book *Under the Tuscan Sun: At Home
in Italy* by Frances Mayes.

Under the Tuscan Sun is an alluring example of
yuppie porn, seducing audiences with a shapely
little villa in Italy. While once Katharine Hepburn journeyed to Venice, met Rosanna Brazzi,
and jumped into the Grand Canal, now Diane
Lane journeys to Tuscany and jumps into real
estate. She does find romance, to be sure, but
it's not what she's looking for and, besides, a
villa pleasures her all day long.

Lane plays Frances Mayes, a San Francisco
author who discovers her husband is cheating
on her. She gets out of the marriage, and a
friend (Sandra Oh) gives her a ticket to Italy on
a gay tour—"so nobody will hit on you," she
explains. The next thing she knows, Frances is
getting off the tour bus and making an offer on
a charming little villa that needs a lot of work.
The contessa who owns it will not sell to anybody; she demands a sign from God, but when
Frances is bombed by a pigeon, that's good
enough for the contessa.

The movie is escapist in the time-honored
Hollywood way, inviting us to share the heroine's joy as she moves in, meets the neighbors,
and hires illegal workers from Poland to rehab
the place. Diane Lane's assignment in many
scenes is simply to be delighted. Although she
wants to be alone, that would give her no one to
talk to, and so the movie surrounds her with
colorful and eccentric locals, including Katherine (Lindsay Duncan), who wears big hats and
got a lot of good advice from Fellini, and Mr.
Martini (Vincent Riotta), a friendly real estate
agent who has a crush on her. There is also a
jolly family next door with an aged grandmother who is heartbroken after being dumped
by an e-mail lover from Ecuador.

The movie is inspired by *Under the Tuscan
Sun: At Home in Italy,* a best-seller by Frances
Mayes, unread by me. I gather that Mayes in real
life did not have the divorce, etc., and I suspect
she also did not experience certain events that
are obligatory in movies of this sort, including
the accidentally collapsing ceiling and the violent thunderstorm. As lightning flashed, windows banged open, rain poured in, and the
heavens vented their fury, it occurred to me
what convenient storytelling devices thunder-
storms are: They allow heroines to get wet, run
from room to room in desperation, be surrounded by drama, and wake up the next
morning to a perfect day—all for free, without
the slightest need to establish why the storm
started or stopped. Any screenwriter seeking an
exciting transition between two plot points is
safe with a thunderstorm, which doesn't require
dialogue or change anything, but gives the audience the impression something is happening.

So, yes, the movie is basically paint-by-numbers. The first time Frances sees the villa, it
looks not so much run-down, but more like a
crew of prop men had worked for a week to
supply crooked shutters, peeling paint, and
overgrown gardens. By the end, when it looks
like a photo from *Conde Nast Traveler,* it looks
as if the same prop men have been working
with Martha Stewart. But that's the whole
point: We don't want a realistic movie about illegal Polish workmen rehabbing a yuppie's new
house (although such a movie exists: Jerzy
Skolimowski's *Moonlighting,* from 1982). We
want a fantasy in which after the colorful setbacks, the house emerges magically from its cocoon, and so does the heroine.

What redeems the film is its successful escapism and Diane Lane's performance. They
are closely linked. Consider first Diane Lane.
Some people are fortunate to have faces that
can be decoded as a sign of good character. This
has nothing to do with "beauty" and more to
do with ineffables like smiles and eyes. Diane
Lane involves us, implicates us. We don't stand
outside her performance, and neither does she.
We sign on for the ride, and when clichés hap-

pen (like the thunderstorm), in a way we're watching Diane Lane surviving the scene rather than her character surviving the storm. The dynamic is the same. She persuades us that she deserves to be happy. When her character has sex for the first time in a long time, the movie is shy about showing the sex but bold about showing her reaction, as she comes home, bounces up and down on her bed, pumps her fist in the air, and shouts, "Yes! Yes! I still got it!" More movie characters feel like that than ever admit it.

Of the supporting cast, I can say that Vincent Riotta can occasionally be seen winking from behind the ethic stereotypes, that Sandra Oh has that wonderful air of no-nonsense friendship, but that Frances's whirlwind lover Marcello (Raoul Bova) needn't have been so obviously ripped from the bodice of a romance novel.

That leaves Katherine (Lindsay Duncan), who dresses like the flamboyant mistress played by Sandra Milo in Fellini's 8½, turns up everywhere the plot requires her, shares memories of Fellini which, if they are true, would make her seventyish, and is inexplicable and therefore intriguing. There is absolutely no reason for this character to be in the movie, and really no explanation for who she is and what she wants. We keep waiting for the plot to give her something to do, but she exists firmly at the level of comic relief and ambiguous sexual implication. She's better than a thunderstorm, and I would not do without her.

Underworld ★ ★

R, 121 m., 2003

Kate Beckinsale (Selene), Scott Speedman (Michael), Shane Brolly (Kraven), Michael Sheen (Lucian), Bill Nighy (Viktor), Erwin Leder (Singe), Sophia Myles (Erika). Directed by Len Wiseman and produced by Gary Lucchesi, Tom Rosenberg, and Richard S. Wright. Screenplay by Danny McBride.

Umberto Eco, the distinguished writer from Italy, offered a definition of pornography that has stood the test of time. A porno movie, he said, is a movie where you become acutely aware that the characters are spending too much time getting in and out of cars and walk-

ing in and out of doors. Eco's wisdom came to mind when Todd McCarthy, writing in *Variety*, observed of *Underworld* that "there may be more openings and closings of doors in this picture than in the entire oeuvre of Ernst Lubitsch." That is not the sort of detail that should occur to you while you're watching a movie about a war between werewolves and vampires.

But *Underworld* is all surfaces, all costumes and sets and special effects, and so you might as well look at the doors as anything else. This is a movie so paltry in its characters and shallow in its story that the war seems to exist primarily to provide graphic visuals. Two of those visuals are Kate Beckinsale, who plays Selene, a vampire with (apparently) an unlimited line of credit at North Beach Leather, and Scott Speedman as Michael, a young intern who is human, at least until he is bitten by a werewolf—and maybe even after, since although you become a vampire after one bites you, I am uncertain about the rules regarding werewolves.

Hold on, I just Googled it. A werewolf bite does indeed turn you into a werewolf, according to a Website about the computer game Castlevania, which helpfully goes on to answer the very question I was going to ask next: "What would be the result if a werewolf bites a vampire? It is called a were-pire or wolf zombie . . ." The reason intern Michael is bitten by the werewolf Lucian, I think, is because the werewolves want to create a new hybrid race and gang up on the vampires.

All of this is an emotional drain on Selene, who finds herself in love with a werewolf at the same time that her vampire kingdom is in grave danger. Exactly why she falls in love with Michael, or whether love bites are allowed in their foreplay, is not very clear, probably because romance and sex inevitably involve dialogue, and dialogue really slows things down. This is not a movie that lingers for conversation; its first words, "You're acting like a pack of rabid dogs," occur after fifteen minutes of nonstop and senseless action in a fight scene involving characters we have not been introduced to.

Selene is being challenged for leader of the vampires by Kraven (Shane Brolly), who, as you might have guessed from his name, is a villain, just as you can guess from his name that Viktor (Bill Nighy) is not. Viktor, in fact, is deep in a sleep of centuries when he's awakened prematurely by Selene, who needs his advice to deal with the werewolf/human/Kraven situation. The gradual transformation in appearance of the reawakened Viktor is an intriguing special-effects exercise; he begins as a terminal case of psoriasis and ends as merely cheerfully cadaverous.

Underworld is the directing debut of Len Wiseman, an art director *(Stargate, Independence Day)* who can stage great-looking situations but has few ideas about characters and plots. It's so impossible to care about the characters in the movie that I didn't care if the vampires or werewolves won. I might not have cared in a better movie, either, but I might have been willing to pretend.

Undisputed ★ ★ ★
R, 96 m., 2002

Wesley Snipes (Monroe Hutchens), Ving Rhames (James "Iceman" Chambers), Peter Falk (Emmanuel "Mendy" Ripstein), Fisher Stevens (James Kroycek), Michael Rooker (Prison Guard), Wes Studi (Mingo Sixkiller). Directed by Walter Hill and produced by David Giler, Hill, Brad Krevoy, and Andrew Sugerman. Screenplay by Hill and Giler.

Walter Hill's *Undisputed* is like a 1940s Warner Bros. B picture, and I mean that as a compliment. With efficiency and laconic skill it sets up the situation, peoples it with clearly drawn characters, and heads for a showdown. There is a kind of pleasure to be had from its directness, from its lack of gimmicks, from its classical form. And just like in the Warner pictures, there is also the pleasure of supporting performances from character actors who come onstage, sing an aria, and leave.

The movie stars Ving Rhames as "Iceman" Chambers, heavyweight champion of the world, recently convicted of rape in a plot obviously inspired by Mike Tyson's misadventures. He's sentenced to the maximum-security Sweetwater Prison in the Mojave Desert, which has an active boxing program. The Sweetwater champion is Monroe Hutchens (Wesley Snipes), and a showdown between the two men is inevitable.

First, though, Iceman has to challenge the leader of the most powerful gang behind bars,

and spend some time in solitary as punishment. If he hadn't done that, he explains, he'd be dead. And Monroe has to hear stories about how he's not the undisputed champion any longer.

Also resident in this prison is Emmanuel "Mendy" Ripstein (Peter Falk), an aging Mafioso who still wields enormous clout inside and beyond the prison walls. He even has his own personal assistant. Ripstein is a fight fan. He agrees with the prevailing opinion that there must be a bout to settle the prison championship, and arranges odds with his Vegas contacts. There will even be a payoff for the two fighters, and Snipes is adamant in negotiating a bigger percentage for himself. The Iceman seems more concerned with survival, and Rhames has a direct, unaffected way with his dialogue that is quietly convincing.

The Falk character is a piece of work. He's like a distillation of Falkness. He squints, he talks out of the side of his mouth, he has a tough-guy accent, he has a way of implying authority. And then he has his aria. This is an unbroken monologue that goes for a minute or two (maybe longer—I was laughing too hard to count), and it is variations on the two themes of the f-word and his wife's bad advice. It touches on the competing charms of California and Florida, comments on state and federal legal details, and rises to a kind of musical grandeur. The screenplay is by Walter Hill and David Giler, who worked together on the *Alien* pictures, but whether they or Falk wrote this monologue is hard to say; it seems to rise from another dimension.

Michael Rooker *(Henry: Portrait of a Serial Killer)* has an important role as the prison guard who coordinates the boxing matches, protected by the benign detachment of the warden. He sets a date for the match, and then the two boxers go into more or less routine training sessions, leading up to the big fight, which is held inside a steel cage. The fight scenes are well choreographed and convincing, and Snipes and Rhames are completely plausible as boxers.

Walter Hill has devoted his career to men's action pictures. He pitted Charles Bronson and James Coburn against each other in his first picture, *Hard Times* (1975), and reinvented the cop buddy movie with Nick Nolte and Eddie Murphy in *48 HRS.* (1982). One day I met the sound men on *Hard Times* and watched them pounding a leather sofa with Ping-Pong paddles to create the sounds of blows landing; *Undisputed* evokes the same cheerful spirit.

Some critics of the movie complain that there is no hero, since the Iceman has been convicted of rape and Monroe of murder. That is more of a strength than a weakness, depriving us of an obvious favorite and creating a fight in which it is plausible to expect either boxer could win. Of course, Monroe is the underdog, which counts for something, but when you think how obviously the deck is stacked in most boxing movies, this one has a right to call itself suspenseful. On the other hand, with mob involvement, the fight could be fixed. Falk, as Ripstein, has a lovely scene where he expresses himself on that possibility.

Unfaithful ★ ★ ★

R, 123 m., 2002

Diane Lane (Connie Sumner), Richard Gere (Edward Sumner), Olivier Martinez (Paul Martel), Erik Per Sullivan (Charlie Sumner), Myra Lucretia Taylor (Gloria), Michelle Monaghan (Lindsay), Chad Lowe (Bill Stone). Directed by Adrian Lyne and produced by Lyne and G. Mac Brown. Screenplay by Alvin Sargent and William Broyles Jr., based on the film by Claude Chabrol.

"The heart has its reasons," said the French philosopher Pascal, quoted by the American philosopher Woody Allen. It is a useful insight when no other reasons seem apparent. Connie Sumner's heart and other organs have their reasons for straying outside a happy marriage in *Unfaithful*, but the movie doesn't say what they are. This is not necessarily a bad thing, sparing us tortured Freudian explanations and labored plot points. It is almost always more interesting to observe behavior than to listen to reasons.

Connie (Diane Lane) and her husband, Edward (Richard Gere), live with their nine-year-old son, Charlie (Erik Per Sullivan), in one of those Westchester County houses that have a room for every mood. They are happy together, or at least the movie supplies us with no reasons why they are unhappy. One windy day she drives into New York, is literally blown

down on top of a rare book dealer named Paul Martel (Olivier Martinez), and is invited upstairs for Band-Aids and a cup of tea. He occupies a large flat filled with shelves of books and art objects.

Martel is your average Calvin Klein model as a bibliophile. He has the Spanish looks, the French accent, the permanent three-day beard, and the strength to suspend a woman indefinitely in any position while making love. He is also cool in his seduction methods. Instead of making a crude pass, he asks her to accept a book as a gift from him, and directs her down an aisle to the last book on the end of the second shelf from the top, where he tells her what page to turn to, and then joins her in reciting the words there: "Be happy for this moment, for this moment is your life."

Does it occur to Connie that Martel planted that book for just such an occasion as this? No, because she likes to be treated in such a way, and soon she's on the phone with a transparent ruse to get up to his apartment again, where Martel overcomes her temporary stall in bed by commanding her: "Hit me!" That breaks the logjam, and soon they're involved in a passionate affair that involves arduous sex in his apartment and quick sex in rest rooms, movie theaters, and corridors. (The movie they go see is Tati's *Monsieur Hulot's Holiday*, which, despite its stature on my list of The Great Movies, fails to compete with furtive experiments that would no doubt have Hulot puffing furiously at his pipe.)

Edward senses that something is wrong. There are clues, but mostly he picks up on her mood, and eventually hires a man to shadow her. Discovering where Martel lives, he visits there one day, and what happens then I will not reveal. What does *not* happen then, I am happy to reveal, is that the movie doesn't turn into a standard thriller in which death stalks Westchester County and the wife and husband fear murder by each other, or by Martel.

That's what's intriguing about the film: Instead of pumping up the plot with recycled manufactured thrills, it's content to contemplate two reasonably sane adults who get themselves into an almost insoluble dilemma. *Unfaithful* contains, as all movies involving suburban families are required to contain, a scene where the parents sit proudly in the audience while their child performs bravely in a school play. But there are no detectives lurking in the shadows to arrest them, and no killers skulking in the parking lot with knives or tire irons. No, the meaning of the scene is simply, movingly, that these two people in desperate trouble are nevertheless able to smile at their son on the stage.

The movie was directed by Adrian Lyne, best known for higher-voltage films like *Fatal Attraction* and *Indecent Proposal.* This film is based on *La Femme Infidele* (1969) by Claude Chabrol, which itself is an update of *Madame Bovary.* Lyne's film is juicier and more passionate than Chabrol's, but both share the fairly daring idea of showing a plot that is entirely about illicit passion and its consequences in a happy marriage. Although cops turn up from time to time in *Unfaithful,* this is not a crime story, but a marital tragedy.

Richard Gere and Diane Lane are well suited to the roles, exuding a kind of serene materialism that seems happily settled in suburbia. It is all the more shocking when Lane revisits Martel's apartment because there is no suggestion that she is unhappy with Gere, starved for sex, or especially impulsive. She goes back up there because—well, because she wants to. He's quite a guy. On one visit he shows her *The Joy of Cooking* in Braille. And then his fingers brush hers as if he's reading *The Joy of Sex* on her skin.

The United States of Leland ★ ★
R, 108 m., 2004

Don Cheadle (Pearl Madison), Ryan Gosling (Leland P. Fitzgerald), Chris Klein (Allen Harris), Jena Malone (Becky Pollard), Lena Olin (Marybeth Fitzgerald), Kevin Spacey (Albert T. Fitzgerald), Martin Donovan (Harry Pollard), Ann Magnuson (Karen Pollard), Michelle Williams (Julie Pollard), Kerry Washington (Ayesha). Directed by Matthew Ryan Hoge and produced by Bernie Morris, Jonah Smith, Kevin Spacey, and Palmer West. Screenplay by Hoge.

Early in *The United States of Leland,* a teenager named Leland stabs an autistic boy twenty times, is arrested for the murder, and explains why he committed it: "Because of the sadness." The movie will cycle through many characters

and much fraught dialogue to explain this statement, but it never seems sure what it thinks about Leland's action. I believe it is as cruel and senseless as the killings in *Elephant,* but while that film was chillingly objective, this one seems to be on everybody's side. It's a moral muddle.

Leland P. Fitzgerald (Ryan Gosling) is the alienated child of a distant mother (Lena Olin) and an absent father who is a famous novelist (Kevin Spacey). Much is made of his father's decision to send his son on a trip every year—to Paris, to Venice—but not to meet him there. Leland has recently broken up with Becky (Jena Malone), the drug-addicted sister of the murdered boy, but that doesn't seem to be the reason for his action.

We meet the victim's other sister, Julie (Michelle Williams), and her boyfriend, Allen (Chris Klein). They're also in a rocky time in their romance, but we can't be sure that's what prompts Allen to the action he takes in the film. The dead boy's parents are Harry and Karen Pollard (Martin Donovan and Ann Magnuson), and while they are bereft, they express themselves in ways borrowed from docudramas.

There are two perfectly crafted performances in the movie, by Spacey as Albert Fitzgerald, the novelist who flies in from Europe, and by Don Cheadle as Pearl Madison, a high school teacher in the juvenile detention facility where Leland is held. Pearl, who perhaps sees a book in the murder, encourages Leland to open up about his feelings, and much of the movie is narrated by Leland from writings in his journal.

Some of the scenes in the movie, written and directed by Matthew Ryan Hoge, are so perfectly conceived that they show up the rest. When the novelist and the teacher meet in a hotel bar, it's an opportunity for Spacey to exercise his gift for understated irony ("There are no private spaces in my son's heart reserved for me"), and for Cheadle to show a man conflicted between his real concern for Leland and his personal awe at meeting the great writer. Ryan Gosling, a gifted actor, does everything that can be done with Leland, but the character comes from a writer's conceits, not from life.

The movie circles through characters and

subplots on its way to its final revelations, and some of the subplots are blatantly unnecessary. Why, for example, must Cheadle's character have an affair with a coworker (Kerry Washington) and then try to explain it to his apparently estranged girlfriend? What does this have to do with anything? Why, really, does Spacey's character fly in if he is only going to sit in a hotel bar and exude literate bitterness? Perhaps to show that his emotional distance from his son helped lead to the murder? But no, because Leland's problem is not alienation, but an excess of empathy.

Lost in all of this is the fate of the murdered boy. The character and his autism are used as plot points, and there is little concern about his fate except as it helps set the story into motion and provide the inspiration for Leland's action. Subplots involving his sisters, their problems, their romances, and their boyfriends are made more confusing because the movie makes it difficult for us to be sure who they are; for a long time we're not sure they're sisters. That's not subtle writing, but needless confusion.

The reason for Leland's action, when we understand it, has a clarity and simplicity that would be at home in a short story. The problem is that the movie follows such a tortured path in arriving at it that, at the end, his motive is not so much a moment of insight as a plot point. And there is another murder in the movie that had me leaving the theater completely uncertain about how I was intended to feel about it. Is it that the first murder, however tragically mistaken, was at least committed with loftier motives than the second? Or what?

Uptown Girls ★ ★ ★
PG-13, 93 m., 2003

Brittany Murphy (Molly Gunn), Dakota Fanning (Ray Schleine), Heather Locklear (Roma Schleine), Jesse Spencer (Neal), Marley Shelton (Ingrid), Donald Faison (Huey). Directed by Boaz Yakin and produced by Allison Jacobs, John Penotti, and Fisher Stevens. Screenplay by Julia Dahl, Mo Ogrodnik, and Lisa Davidowitz, based on the story by Jacobs.

The theory is that Brittany Murphy is trying to channel Marilyn Monroe, but as I watched *Uptown Girls* another name came to mind: Lucille

Ball. She has a kind of divine ineptitude that moves beyond Marilyn's helplessness into Lucy's dizzy lovability. She is like a magnet for whoops! moments.

I remember her as a presenter at the 2003 Independent Spirit Awards, where her assignment was to read the names of five nominees, open an envelope, and read the winner. This she was unable to do, despite two visits by a stage manager who whispered helpful suggestions into her ear. She kept trying to read every nominee as the winner, and when she finally arrived triumphantly at the real winner, she inspired no confidence that she had it right.

Some thought she was completely clueless, or worse. I studied her timing and speculated that she knew exactly what she was doing, and that while it took no skill at all to get it right, it took a certain genius to get it so perfectly wrong. She succeeded in capturing the attention of every person in that distracted and chattering crowd, and I recalled Lucy shows where everyone in a restaurant would suddenly be looking at her.

Uptown Girls gives Murphy an opportunity to channel Lucy at feature length. She plays an improbable character in an impossible story, but of course she does. She is Molly Gunn, whose father was a rock star until both parents were killed in a plane crash, leaving her with a collection of guitars and a trust fund administered by someone named Bob. As the story opens, Bob has disappeared with all of her money and she is forced to work for the first time in her life. This does not come easy to a girl whose only skills are as a consumer.

She gets a job as the nanny of an eight-year-old girl named Ray (Dakota Fanning), who seems so old and wise that when she tells Molly, "Act your age," we see what she means. Ray is a dubious little adult in a child's body, and although her family is rich she has never enjoyed any of the usual rich kid pleasures.

"You've never been to Disneyland?" asks Molly.

"Alert the media," says Ray.

Molly still makes some effort to preserve her pre-Ray, prepoverty lifestyle, and this includes an infatuation with a young singer named Neal (Jesse Spencer), who keeps his distance. He is only 274 days sober, he tells her, and has been advised to stay celibate for his first year. This turns out to be less than the truth, in a plot twist involving Ray's worldly mother Roma (Heather Locklear, yes, Heather Locklear as the mother, and how time flies).

Ray is a hypochrondiac who travels with her own soap and monitors her medications and whose basic inability is to act like a kid. Molly has never grown up. Although this scenario is as contrived as most such movie plots, there is a way in which it works because Ray does seem prematurely old and Molly does seem eternally childlike; in the case of Dakota Fanning I think we are looking at good acting, and in Brittany Murphy's case I think we are seeing something essential in her nature. Even in *8 Mile*, where she played Eminem's girlfriend in a landscape of urban grunge, there was a part of her that was identical with Molly's crush on Neal the singer.

I dismiss all cavils about the movie's logic and plausibility as beside the point. This is not a movie about plot but about personalities. Molly Gunn is a comic original, vulnerable and helpless, well-meaning and inept, innocent and guileless—or, more accurately, a person of touchingly naive guile. Murphy's performance has a kind of ineffable, mischievous innocence about it.

I also enjoyed the movie's emotional complexity. *Uptown Girls* could have been a simpleminded, relentlessly cheerful formula picture. There is an underlying formula there, of course, with all problems resolved at the end, but Ray is anything but another cookie-cutter little movie girl, and Molly's problems at times are really daunting. The surprise she gets about Neal's behavior is not the sort of thing that usually happens in this genre. The director is Boaz Yakin, who made the searing movie *Fresh* in 1994. That one, too, was about a young kid with a lot of adult wisdom and an underlying sadness. *Uptown Girls*, on a completely different wavelength, suggests some of the same undertones. The screenplay, by Julia Dahl, Mo Ogrodnik, and Lisa Davidowitz, based on a story by the producer, Allison Jacobs, takes what we might expect from this material and rotates it into a slightly darker dimension, where Brittany Murphy's Lucy act is not merely ditzy, but even a little brave.

V

Valentin ★ ★ ★
PG-13, 86 m., 2004

Rodrigo Noya (Valentin), Julieta Cardinali (Leticia), Carmen Maura (His Grandmother), Alejandro Agresti (His Father), Mex Urtizberea (Rufo). Directed by Alejandro Agresti and produced by Laurens Geels, Thierry Forte, and Julio Fernandez. Screenplay by Agresti.

Valentin is a nine-year-old boy who is solemn and observant, and peers out at the world through enormous glasses that correct his wandering eye. He lives with his grandmother in Buenos Aires in the late 1960s. His mother is not on the scene. His father appears from time to time with a girlfriend, usually a new one. Valentin spends a lot of time "building stuff for astronauts" and observing the adults in his life with analytical zeal.

He narrates his own story, but here's an interesting touch: The voice belongs to the young actor (Rodrigo Noya), but the sensibility is that of an adult remembering his childhood. There is an interesting explanation. The movie was written and directed by Alejandro Agresti, who tells us it is his own life story. Interesting that he plays the father who causes this little boy so much grief.

Valentin's grandmother (Carmen Maura) is not a lovable movie granny. She does what is necessary for the boy, is miserly with her affections, is trying to stage-manage her son into a second marriage. One day his father comes home with a girlfriend Valentin likes. This is Leticia (Julieta Cardinali), and she likes Valentin too. They get along famously, until one day he makes the mistake of telling her disturbing things about his father. She makes the mistake of repeating them to his father. As a result, Leticia breaks up with his father, and his father is angry with Valentin.

The movie sets its story against an Argentina carefully remembered by Agresti. Buenos Aires looks and sounds cosmopolitan and embracing, and there is a leisurely feeling to the streets and cafés, especially one in which Valentin observes a man sitting and reading and smoking, day after day. This is Rufo (Mex Urtizberea), a musician, who gives Valentin some piano lessons and becomes his confidant. "Rufo gave me the feeling I was older and more useful," he explains.

Valentin feels that since the adult world handles its affairs badly, he must sometimes take things into his own hands. When he decides his grandmother is ill, he convinces a doctor to visit her. Later, he gives the doctor a painting as a present. Outside events penetrate unevenly into his mind; he is up-to-date on the astronauts, but not so sure what it means when Che Guevara is killed. In church, people walk out of a sermon about Che; at home, anti-Semitism is prevalent, even though Valentin's mother was Jewish (we begin to suspect why she may have left the family).

I am not always sure what I mean when I praise a child actor, especially one as young as Rodrigo Noya. Certainly, casting has a lot to do with his appeal; he looks the part and exudes a touching solemnity. But there is more. There's something about this kid, and the way he talks and listens and watches people, that is very convincing. Perhaps it helped that he was directed by a man who was once Valentin himself. The film is warm and intriguing, and he is the engine that pulls us through it. We care about what happens to him; high praise.

By the end of the film, Valentin feels, with some reason, that he has been set adrift by the adult world. But he is smart and resourceful, and he has a simple but effective working knowledge of human nature. What he does and how he does it, and who he does it for I will leave for you to discover, since the movie's closing scenes are filled with a sublime serendipity. Let me just say he earns his name.

Van Helsing ★ ★ ★
PG-13, 131 m., 2004

Hugh Jackman (Gabriel Van Helsing), Kate Beckinsale (Anna Valerious), Richard Roxburgh (Count Dracula), Shuler Hensley (Frankenstein's Monster), David Wenham (Carl), Will Kemp (Velkan Valerious), Kevin J. O'Connor (Igor), Samuel West (Dr. Frankenstein), Robbie Coltrane (Mr. Hyde). Directed by Stephen Sommers and produced by Bob Ducsay and Sommers. Screenplay by Sommers.

The zombies were having fun,
The party had just begun,
The guests included Wolf Man,
Dracula and his son.
        — "Monster Mash" by Bobby Pickett

Strange that a movie so eager to entertain would forget to play *Monster Mash* over the end credits. There have been countless movies uniting two monsters (*Frankenstein Meets the Wolf Man, King Kong vs. Godzilla,* etc.), but *Van Helsing* convenes Frankenstein, his Monster, Count Dracula, the Wolf Man, Igor, Van Helsing the vampire hunter, assorted other werewolves, werebats and vampires, and even Mr. Hyde, who as a bonus seems to think he is the Hunchback of Notre Dame.

The movie is like a greatest hits compilation; it's assembled like Frankenstein's Monster, from spare parts stitched together and brought to life with electricity, plus lots of computer-generated images. The plot depends on Dracula's desperate need to discover the secret of Frankenstein's Monster because he can use it to bring his countless offspring to life. Because Dracula (Richard Roxburgh) and his vampire brides are all dead, they cannot give birth, of course, to live children. That they give birth at all is somewhat remarkable, although perhaps the process is unorthodox, since his dead offspring hang from a subterranean ceiling wrapped in cocoons that made me think, for some reason, of bagworms, which I spent many a summer hand-picking off the evergreens under the enthusiastic direction of my father.

Van Helsing (Hugh Jackman, Wolverine in the X-Men movies) is sometimes portrayed as young, sometimes old in the Dracula movies. Here he's a professional monster-killer with a *Phantom of the Opera* hat, who picks up a dedicated friar named Carl (David Wenham) as his sidekick. His first assignment is to track down Mr. Hyde (Robbie Coltrane), who now lives in Notre Dame cathedral and ventures out for murder. That job doesn't end as planned, so Van Helsing moves on to the Vatican City to get new instructions and be supplied with high-tech weapons by the ecclesiastical equivalent of James Bond's Q.

Next stop: Transylvania, where the movie opened with a virtuoso black-and-white sequence showing a local mob waving pitchforks and torches and hounding Frankenstein's Monster into a windmill that is set ablaze. We know, having seen the old movies, that the Monster will survive, but the mob has worked itself into such a frenzy that when Van Helsing and Carl arrive in the village, they are almost forked and burnt just on general principles. What saves them is an attack by three flying vampiresses, who like to scoop up their victims and fly off to savor their blood; Van Helsing fights them using a device that fires arrows like a machine gun.

And that leads to his meeting the beautiful Anna Valerious (Kate Beckinsale), who with her brother, Velkan (Will Kemp), represents the last of nine generations of a family that will never find eternal rest until it vanquishes Dracula. (Conveniently, if you kill Dracula, all the vampires he created will also die.) Anna is at first suspicious of Van Helsing, but soon they are partners in vengeance, and the rest of the plot (there is a whole lot of it) I will leave you to discover for yourselves.

The director, Stephen Sommers, began his career sedately, directing a very nice *Adventures of Huckleberry Finn* (1993) and the entertaining *Jungle Book* (1994). Then Victor Frankenstein must have strapped him to the gurney and turned on the juice, because he made a U-turn into thrillers, with *Deep Rising* (1998), where a giant squid attacks a cruise ship, and *The Mummy* (1999) and *The Mummy Returns* (2001, introducing The Rock as the Scorpion King). Now comes *Van Helsing,* which employs the ultimate resources of CGI to create a world that is violent and hectic, bizarre and entertaining, and sometimes very beautiful.

CGI can get a little boring when it allows characters to fall hundreds of feet and somehow survive, or when they swoop at the ends of ropes as well as Spiderman, but without Spidey's superpowers. But it can also be used to create a visual feast, and here the cinematography by Allen Daviau (*E.T.*) and the production design by Allen Cameron join with Sommers's imagination for spectacular sights. The best is a masked ball in Budapest, which is part real (the musicians balancing on balls, the waiters circling on unicycles) and part fabricated in the computer. Whatever. It's a remarkable scene, and will reward study on the DVD. So will the extraordinary coach chase.

I also liked the movie's re-creation of Victor Frankenstein's laboratory, which has been a favorite of production designers, art directors, and set decorators since time immemorial (Mel Brooks's *Young Frankenstein* recycled the actual sets built for James Whale's *The Bride of Frankenstein*). Here Frankenstein lives in a towering Gothic castle just down the road from Dracula, and the mechanism lifts the Monster to unimaginable heights to expose him to lightning bolts. There are also plentiful crypts, stygian passages, etc., and a library in which a painting revolves, perhaps in tribute to Mel Brooks's revolving bookcase.

The screenplay by Sommers has humor, but restrains itself; the best touches are the quiet ones, as when the friar objects to accompanying Van Helsing ("But I'm not a field man") and when the Monster somewhat unexpectedly recites the 23rd Psalm. At the outset, we may fear Sommers is simply going for f/x overkill, but by the end he has somehow succeeded in assembling all his monsters and plot threads into a high-voltage climax. *Van Helsing* is silly, and spectacular, and fun.

Veronica Guerin ★ ★ ★

R, 98 m., 2003

Cate Blanchett (Veronica Guerin), Gerard McSorley (John Gilligan), Ciaran Hinds (John Traynor), Brenda Fricker (Bernie Guerin), Don Wycherley (Chris Mulligan), Barry Barnes (Graham Turley), Simon O'Driscoll (Cathal Turley), Emmet Bergin (Aengus Fanning), Gerry O'Brien (Martin Cahill). Directed by Joel Schumacher and produced by Jerry Bruckheimer. Screenplay by Carol Doyle and Mary Agnes Donoghue.

Veronica Guerin may or may not have been a great journalist, but she was certainly a brave and foolish one. Disturbed by the sight of gangs selling drugs to children and teenagers in the Dublin of the 1990s, she began a high-profile, even reckless campaign to expose them. Was she surprised when her campaign ended with her own murder? She must have been, or she would have gone about it differently. That she struck a great blow against the Irish drug traffic

is without doubt, but perhaps she could have done so and still survived to raise her son.

Cate Blanchett plays Guerin in a way that fascinated me for reasons the movie probably did not intend. I have a sneaky suspicion that director Joel Schumacher and his writers (Carol Doyle and Mary Agnes Donoghue) think of this as a story of courage and determination, but what I came away with was a story of bone-headed egocentrism. There are moments when Guerin seems so wrapped up in her growing legend and giddy with the flush of the hunt that she barely notices her patient husband, who seems quite gentle, under the circumstances, and his suggestions that she consider the danger she's in and think of their child.

Daily journalism in Britain and Ireland is miles more aggressive than in North America, no doubt because there is a truly competitive press. All of Dublin's papers are national, there are additional titles on Sundays, and, not incidentally, the Irish are great readers. It is unthinkable that an Irish politician would boast that he never reads the papers. Guerin was a well-known writer for the *Sunday Independent*—"a rag," she says at one point, unfairly. Her good looks and unbuttoned personality were popular. Sunday journalists go for the home run, and she hit hers in 1994 when young addicts told her of the gangs that used them as retailers in the housing projects.

Appalled, she tries to backtrack from the poor street sellers to the rich men who presumably lurk at a safe remove. The movie knows more than she does about the gangs, and intercuts her investigation with horrifying violence used by the gangs to maintain discipline. You may remember John Boorman's *The General* (1998), starring Brendan Gleeson as Martin Cahill, a criminal Robin Hood of sorts (he stole from the rich and gave to himself). In that film, he nails a suspected stool pigeon to a snooker table; in *Veronica Guerin*, the same character, now played by Gerry O'Brien, is nailing someone to the floor. He should have been called The Carpenter.

Cahill eventually got into trouble by interfering with the IRA's drug trade, but that hot potato goes unreported by Guerin, in part because she has an inside source feeding her information about the Dublin mob. This is a very nervous midlevel crook named John Traynor

(Ciaran Hinds) who has a bit of a crush on her, actually worries about her safety, and couples his information with warnings that she is in very real danger. Traynor tries to play a double game and ends by outsmarting himself without helping her.

Cate Blanchett dominates the material with a headstrong, extroverted performance. Her Veronica Guerin is heady with excitement, and it doesn't hurt that enormous billboards promote the investigation by the *Independent*'s star journalist. Her editors look alternately grateful and alarmed when she breezes in with another scoop, and we get the feeling she considers her press card to be a guarantee of immunity—or at least, a bulletproof vest. We know Veronica is going to die because that happens in the first five minutes of the movie. All the rest is flashback, showing how she arrived at the day of her death. We cringe at the flamboyant risks she takes—as when she actually walks into the house of an Irish Mafia kingpin and asks him why he sells drugs to children. The film develops an undertone of horror; it's like watching fate unfold.

A lot of critics in England disliked it, which is valid enough, but some of them seemed to confuse Guerin's journalism and Blanchett's performance. The film ends with the obligatory public funeral, grateful proles lining the streets while type crawls up the screen telling how much Guerin's antidrug crusade accomplished. These are standard prompts for us to get a little weepy at the heroism of this brave martyr, but actually I think Blanchett and Schumacher have found the right note for their story. Their Veronica Guerin dies, essentially, because the excitement of a great story robs her of all common sense. Oh, certainly, she felt outrage and anger, and so should she have, but it was so much fun to skewer these hard, evil men. And then they did what everyone has been telling her for weeks they would do, and she was dead.

View from the Top ★ ★ ★
PG-13, 87 m., 2003

Gwyneth Paltrow (Donna), Mark Ruffalo (Ted), Christina Applegate (Christine), Mike Myers (John Whitney), Candice Bergen (Sally), Kelly Preston (Sherry), Rob Lowe (Copilot Steve). Directed by Bruno Barreto and produced by Matthew Baer, Bobby Cohen, and Brad Grey. Screenplay by Eric Wald.

View from the Top stars Gwyneth Paltrow in a sweet and sort of innocent story about a small-town girl who knows life holds more for her, and how a job as a flight attendant becomes her escape route. Along the way she meets friends who help her and friends who double-cross her, a guy who dumps her, and a guy she dumps. And she finds love. What more do you want from a movie?

I confess I expected something else. Flight attendants have been asking me for weeks about this movie, which they are in a lather to see. It may be closer to their real lives than they expect. I anticipated an updated version of *Coffee, Tea or Me?* but what I got instead was *Donna the Flight Attendant*. The movie reminded me of career books I read in the seventh grade with titles like *Bob Durham, Boy Radio Announcer*. It's a little more sophisticated, of course, but it has the same good heart, and a teenager thinking of a career in the air might really enjoy it.

So did I, in an uncomplicated way. Paltrow is lovable in the right roles, and here she's joined by two others who are sunny on the screen: Candice Bergen, as the best-selling author/flight attendant who becomes her mentor, and Mark Ruffalo (from *You Can Count on Me*) as the law student who wants to marry her. The movie knows a secret; most careers do not involve clawing your way to the top, but depend on the kindness of the strangers you meet along the way, who help you just because they feel like it.

We meet Donna (Paltrow) as the daughter of a much-married former exotic dancer from Silver Springs, Nevada. She seems doomed to a life working at the mall until she sees a TV interview with the best-selling Bergen, whose book inspires Donna to train as a flight attendant. Her first stop is a puddle jumper named Sierra Airlines, which flies mostly to and from Fresno, but then she enrolls in training at Royalty Airlines, where the instructor (Mike Myers) is bitter because his crossed eye kept him from flying. Myers finds a delicate balance between lampoon and poignancy—and that's some balance.

Ruffalo plays the sometime law student who

comes into her life in Nevada and then again in Cleveland, where she's assigned not to Royalty's transatlantic routes but to the discount Royalty Express. Her first flight is comic (she runs down the aisle screaming, "We're gonna crash!") and then we follow her through intrigues and romantic episodes that lead to a lonely Christmas in Paris when she decides life *still* has to offer more than this.

The movie, directed by Bruno Barreto and written by Eric Wald, is surprising for what it doesn't contain: no scenes involving mile-high clubs, lecherous businessmen, or randy pilots, but the sincere story of a woman who finds her career is almost but not quite enough. Adult audiences may be underwhelmed. Not younger teenage girls, who will be completely fascinated.

W

Waking Up in Reno ★ ½
R, 100 m., 2002

Billy Bob Thornton (Lonnie Earl), Charlize Theron (Candy), Patrick Swayze (Roy), Natasha Richardson (Darlene), Brent Briscoe (Russell Whitehead), Mark Fauser (Boyd). Directed by Jordan Brady and produced by Ben Myron, Robert Salerno, and Dwight Yoakam. Screenplay by Brent Briscoe and Mark Fauser.

Waking Up in Reno is another one of those road comedies where southern roots are supposed to make boring people seem colorful. If these characters were from Minneapolis or Denver, no way anyone would make a film about them. But because they're from Little Rock, Arkansas, and wear stuff made out of snakeskin and carry their own cases of Pabst into the hotel room, they're movie-worthy.

Well, they could be, if they had anything really at risk. But the movie is way too gentle to back them into a corner. They're nice people whose problems are all solved with sitcom dialogue, and the profoundly traditional screenplay makes sure that love and family triumph in the end. Surprising that Billy Bob Thornton, Charlize Theron, Natasha Richardson, and Patrick Swayze would fall for this, but Swayze *did* make *Road House*, so maybe it's not so surprising in his case.

Thornton stars as Lonnie Earl, a Little Rock car dealer who appears in his own commercials and cheats on his wife, Darlene (Richardson). He cheats with Candy (Theron), the wife of his best friend, Roy (Swayze). Actually, they only cheat twice, but if that's like only being a little bit pregnant, maybe she is.

The two couples decide to pull a brand-new SUV off of Lonnie Earl's lot and take a trip to Reno, with stops along the way in Texas (where Lonnie Earl wants to win a seventy-two-ounce steak-eating contest) and maybe at the Grand Canyon. Others have their dreams, too; Darlene has always had a special place in her heart for Tony Orlando, ever since she saw him on the Jerry Lewis telethon. And that's the sort of dialogue detail that's supposed to tip us off how down-home and lovable these people are: They like Tony Orlando, they watch Jerry Lewis.

We sense that director Jordan Brady and writers Brent Briscoe and Mark Fauser don't like Tony Orlando and Jerry Lewis as much as the characters do, but the movie's not mean enough to say so, and so any comic point is lost.

That kind of disconnect happens all through the movie: The filmmakers create satirical characters and then play them straight. We're actually expected to sympathize with these caricatures, as Lonnie Earl barely survives the seventy-two-ounce steak and they arrive in Reno for run-ins with the hotel bellboys and the hooker in the bar.

Consider the scene where the helpful bellboy hauls their luggage into their suite and then loiters suggestively for a tip. "Oh, I get it," says Lonnie Earl. "You want your dollar." And he gives him one. The problem here is that no real-life Little Rock car dealer would conceivably believe that the correct tip for luggage for four people would be one dollar. Lonnie Earl must be moderately wealthy, has traveled, has tipped before, is not entirely clueless. But the movie shortchanges his character to get an easy (and very cheap) laugh.

The action in Reno mostly centers around Candy's attempts to get pregnant, her monitoring of her ovular temperature, Roy's obligation to leap into action at every prompt, and the revelation that . . . well, without going into details, let's say secrets are revealed that would more wisely have been left concealed, and that Lonnie Earl, Roy, Candy, and Darlene find themselves in a situation that in the real world could lead to violence but here is settled in about the same way that the Mertzes worked things out with Lucy and Desi.

Yes, the characters are pleasant. Yes, in some grudging way we are happy that they're happy. No, we do not get teary-eyed with sentiment when the movie evokes the Grand Canyon in an attempt to demonstrate that the problems of four little people don't amount to a hill of beans. At the end of the movie titled *Grand Canyon* (1992), I actually was emotionally touched as the characters looked out over the awesome immensity. But then they were real characters, and nothing in *Waking Up in Reno* ever inspired me to think of its inhabitants as anything more than markers in a screenplay.

Walking Tall ★ ★
PG-13, 85 m., 2004

The Rock (Chris Vaughn), Neal McDonough (Jay Hamilton Jr.), Johnny Knoxville (Ray Templeton), John Beasley (Chris Vaughn Sr.), Barbara Tarbuck (Connie Vaughn), Kristen Wilson (Michelle), Khleo Thomas (Pete), Ashley Scott (Deni), Michael Bowen (Sheriff Watkins). Directed by Kevin Bray and produced by Ashok Amritraj, Jim Burke, Lucas Foster, and David Hoberman. Screenplay by David Klass, Channing Gibson, Brian Koppelman, and David Levien.

I didn't see the original *Walking Tall.* I was "out of town at the time," I explained in my review of *Walking Tall, Part 2.* Sounds reasonable. But I suspect the earlier film was tilted more toward populism and less toward superhero violence than the new *Walking Tall,* which is "dedicated to the memory of Buford Pusser," but turns the story into a cartoon of retribution and revenge.

The Rock stars as a war hero named Chris Vaughn who returns to his southern hometown and finds that the mill has closed, a casino has opened, and kids are addicted to drugs. His character is named Chris Vaughn and not Buford Pusser, possibly because The Rock, having gone to a great deal of trouble to adopt a name both simple and authoritative, could not envision himself being called "Buford" or "Sheriff Pusser" for any amount of money.

He finds that an old high school nemesis named Jay Hamilton Jr. (Neal McDonough) has closed the mill, opened the casino, and manufactures the drugs. We know Jay is the villain because he has that close-cropped, curly, peroxided hair that works like a name tag that says, "Hi! I'm the Villain!" Outraged by the corruption that has descended upon his town, The Rock picks up the famous Buford Pusser Model Oak Club, smashes up the casino, defends himself in court, and makes such an impassioned speech that he has soon been elected sheriff. I love those movie trials in which cases are settled not according to guilt and innocence and the law, but according to who is *really* right and *deserves* to go free.

Sheriff Vaughn hires an old high school pal named Ray Templeton to be his deputy. The role is played by Johnny Knoxville, famous for *Jackass,* who is, in fact, completely convincing

and probably has a legitimate movie career ahead of him and doesn't have to stuff his underpants with dead chickens and hang upside down over alligator ponds anymore.

The scenes establishing all of these events are handled efficiently and have a certain interest, but then the movie, alas, goes on autopilot with a series of improbable fight scenes that are so heavy on stunts and special effects that we might as well be watching a cartoon. This is an action movie, pure and simple, and one can only wonder what the late Buford Pusser would have made of it. Maybe he would have advised Sheriff Vaughn that times have changed and he should forget the oak club and get himself an AK-47.

The Rock comes out of the movie more or less intact, careerwise. I've felt from the beginning that he had the makings of a movie star, and I still think so; he has a kind of inner quiet that allows him to inhabit preposterous scenes without being overwhelmed by them. His acting style is flat and uninflected, authoritative without pushing it; he's a little like John Wayne that way. Also like Wayne, he's a big, physically intimidating man who is able to suggest a certain gentleness; he's not inflamed, not looking for a fight, not shoving people around, but simply trying to right wrongs. I seriously doubt that he could play a convincing villain. Not even with a name tag.

A Walk to Remember ★ ★ ★
PG, 100 m., 2002

Mandy Moore (Jamie Sullivan), Shane West (Landon Carter), Daryl Hannah (Cynthia Carter), Peter Coyote (Reverend Sullivan), Lauren German (Belinda), Clayne Crawford (Dean). Directed by Adam Shankman and produced by Denise Di Novi and Hunt Lowry. Screenplay by Karen Janszen, based on the novel by Nicholas Sparks.

A Walk to Remember is a love story so sweet, sincere, and positive that it sneaks past the defenses built up in this age of irony. It tells the story of a romance between two eighteen-year-olds that is summarized when the boy tells the girl's doubtful father: "Jamie has faith in me. She makes me want to be different. Better." After all of the vulgar crudities of the typical modern teenage movie, here is one that looks closely, pays attention, sees that not all teenagers are as cretinous as Hollywood portrays them.

Mandy Moore, a natural beauty in both face and manner, stars as Jamie Sullivan, an outsider at school who is laughed at because she stands apart, has values, and always wears the same ratty blue sweater. Her father (Peter Coyote) is a local minister. Shane West plays Landon Carter, a senior boy who hangs with the popular crowd but is shaken when a stupid dare goes wrong and one of his friends is paralyzed in a diving accident. He dates a popular girl and joins in the laughter against Jamie. Then, as punishment for the prank, he is ordered by the principal to join the drama club: "You need to meet some new people."

Jamie's in the club. He begins to notice her in a new way. He asks her to help him rehearse for a role in a play. She treats him with level honesty. She isn't one of those losers who skulks around feeling put-upon; her self-esteem stands apart from the opinion of her peers. She's a smart, nice girl, a reminder that one of the pleasures of the movies is to meet good people.

The plot has revelations that I will not betray. Enough to focus on the way Jamie's serene example makes Landon into a nicer person—encourages him to become more sincere and serious to win her respect. There are setbacks along the way, as in a painful scene at school where she approaches him while he's with his old friends and says, "See you tonight," and he says, "In your dreams." When he turns up at her house, she is hurt and angry, and his excuses sound lame even to him.

The movie walks a fine line with the Peter Coyote character, whose church Landon attends. Movies have a way of stereotyping reactionary Bible-thumpers who are hostile to teen romance. There is a little of that here; Jamie is forbidden to date, for example, although there's more behind her father's decision than knee-jerk strictness. But when Landon goes to the Reverend Sullivan and asks him to have faith in him, the minister listens with an open mind.

Yes, the movie is corny at times. But corniness is all right at times. I forgave the movie its broad emotion because it earned it. It lays things on a little thick at the end, but by then

it has paid its way. Director Adam Shankman and his writer, Karen Janszen, working from the novel by Nicholas Sparks, have an unforced trust in the material that redeems, even justifies, the broad strokes. They go wrong only three times: (1) The subplot involving the paralyzed boy should either have been dealt with or dropped. (2) It's tiresome to make the black teenager use "brother" in every sentence, as if he is not their peer but was ported in from another world. (3) As Kuleshov proved more than eighty years ago in a famous experiment, when an audience sees an impassive close-up it supplies the necessary emotion from the context. It can be fatal for an actor to try to "act" in a close-up, and Landon's little smile at the end is a distraction at a crucial moment.

Those are small flaws in a touching movie. The performances by Mandy Moore and Shane West are so quietly convincing we're reminded that many teenagers in movies seem to think like thirty-year-old stand-up comics. That Jamie and Landon base their romance on values and respect will blindside some viewers of the film, especially since the first five or ten minutes seem to be headed down a familiar teenage movie trail. *A Walk to Remember* is a small treasure.

Warm Water Under a Red Bridge
★ ★ ★

NO MPAA RATING, 119 m., 2002

Koji Yakusho (Yosuke Sasano), Misa Shimizu (Saeko Aizawa), Mitsuko Baisho (Mitsu), Mansaku Fuwa (Gen), Kazuo Kitamura (Taro), Isao Natsuyagi (Masayuki Uomi), Yukiya Kitamura (Shintaro Uomi), Hijiri Kojima (Miki Tagami). Directed by Shohei Imamura and produced by Hisa Iino. Screenplay by Motofumi Tomikawa, Daisuke Tengan, and Imamura, based on a book by Yo Henmi.

Warm Water Under a Red Bridge has modern automobiles and supermarkets, telephones and pepper cheese imported from Europe, but it resonates like an ancient Japanese myth. Imagine a traveler in search of treasure who finds a woman with special needs that only he can fulfill, and who repays him by ending his misery.

Shohei Imamura, one of the greatest Japanese directors, tells this story with the energy and delight of a fairy tale, but we in the West are not likely to see it so naively, because unlike the Japanese we are touchy on the subject of bodily fluids. In Japan, natural functions are accepted calmly as a part of life, and there is a celebrated children's book about farts. No doubt a Japanese audience would view *Warm Water* entirely differently than a North American one—because, you see, the heroine has a condition that causes water to build up in her body, and it can only be released by sexual intercourse.

Water arrives in puddles and rivulets, in sprays and splashes. "Don't worry," Saeko (Misa Shimizu) cheerfully tells Yosuke, the hero. "It's not urine." It is instead—well, what? The water of life? Of growth and renewal? Is she a water goddess? When it runs down the steps of her house and into the river, fish grow large and numerous. And it seems to have a similar effect on Yosuke (Koji Yakusho, from *Shall We Dance?* and *The Eel*). From a pallid, hopeless wanderer in the early scenes, he grows into a bold lover and a brave ocean fisherman.

As the film opens, Yosuke is broke and jobless, fielding incessant cell phone calls from his nagging wife, who wants an update on his job searches. In despair, he hunkers down next to the river with an old philosopher named Taro (Kazuo Kitamura), who tells him a story. Long ago, he says, right after the war, he was stealing to get the money to eat, and he took a gold Buddha from a temple. He left it in an upstairs room of a house next to a red bridge, where he assumes it remains to this day.

Yosuke takes a train to the town named by the old man, finds the bridge, finds the house, and follows Saeko from it into a supermarket where he sees her shoplift some cheese while standing in a puddle. From the puddle he retrieves her earring (a dolphin, of course) and returns it to her, and she asks if he'd like some cheese and then forthrightly tells him, "You saw me steal the cheese. Then you saw the puddle of water."

All true. She explains her problem. The water builds up and must be "vented," often by doing "something wicked" like shoplifting. It is, she adds, building up right now—and soon they are having intercourse to the delight of the fish in the river below.

This story is unthinkable in a Hollywood movie, but there is something about the matter-of-fact way Saeko explains her problem, and the surprised but not stunned way that Yosuke hears her, that takes the edge off. If women are a source of life, and if water is where life began, then—well, whatever. It is important to note that the sex in the movie is not erotic or titillating in any way—it's more like a therapeutic process—and that the movie is not sex-minded, but more delighted with the novelty of Saeko's problem. Only in a nation where bodily functions are discussed in a matter-of-fact way, where nude public bathing is no big deal, where shame about human plumbing has not been ritualized, could this movie play in the way Imamura intended. But seeing it as a Westerner is an enlightening, even liberating, experience.

Imamura, now seventy-six, is also the director of the masterpieces *The Insect Woman* (1963), about a woman whose only priority is her own comfort and survival; *Ballad of Narayama* (1982), the heartbreaking story of a village where the old are left on the side of a mountain to die; and *Black Rain* (1989), not the Michael Douglas thriller, but a harrowing human story about the days and months after the bomb was dropped on Hiroshima.

At his age he seems freed from convention, and in *Warm Water*, for example, he cuts loose from this world to include a dream in which Saeko floats like a embryo in a cosmic cloud. There is also an effortless fusion of old and new. The notion of a man leaving his nagging wife and home and finding succor from a goddess is from ancient myth, and the fact that he would then turn to wrest his living from the sea is not unheard of. But throwing his cell phone overboard, now that's a modern touch.

Wasabi ★ ½
R, 94 m., 2001

Jean Reno (Hubert Fiorentini), Ryoko Hirosue (Yumi Yoshimido), Michel Muller (Momo), Carole Bouquet (Sofia), Ludovic Berthillot (Jean-Baptiste 1), Yan Epstein (Jean-Baptiste 2),

Michel Scourneau (Van Eyck), Christian Sinniger (The Squale), Jean-Marc Montalto (Olivier). Directed by Gérard Krawczyk and produced by Luc Besson. Screenplay by Besson.

Jean Reno has the weary eyes and unshaven mug of a French Peter Falk, and some of the same sardonic humor too. He sighs and smokes and slouches his way through thrillers where he sadly kills those who would kill him, and balefully regards women who want to make intimate demands on his time. In good movies *(The Crimson Rivers)* and bad *(Rollerball)*, in the ambitious (Michelangelo Antonioni's *Beyond the Clouds*) and the avaricious *(Godzilla)*, in comedies *(Just Visiting)* and thrillers *(Ronin)*, he shares with Robert Mitchum the unmistakable quality of having seen it all.

Wasabi is not his worst movie, and is far from his best. It is a thriller trapped inside a pop comedy set in Japan, and gives Reno a chirpy young costar who bounces around him like a puppy on visiting day at the drunk tank. She plays his daughter, and he's supposed to like her, but sometimes he looks like he hopes she will turn into an aspirin.

The movie begins in Paris, where Reno plays Hubert Fiorentini, a Dirty Harry type who doesn't merely beat up suspects, but beats up people on the chance that he may suspect them later. During a raid on a nightclub, he makes the mistake of socking the police chief's son so hard the lad flies down a flight of stairs and ends up in a full-body cast. Hubert is ordered to take a vacation.

He shrugs, and thinks to look up an old girlfriend (Carole Bouquet), but then his life takes a dramatic turn. He learns of the death in Japan of a woman he loved years earlier. Arriving for her funeral, he finds she has left him a mysterious key, a daughter he knew nothing about, and $200 million in the bank.

The daughter is named Yumi (Ryoko Hirosue). She is nineteen, has red hair, chooses her wardrobe colors from the Pokemon palette, and bounces crazily through scenes as if life is a music video and they're filming her right now. The plot involves Yumi's plan to hire the Yakuza (Japanese mafia) to get revenge for her mother's death. If there is a piece of fatherly advice that Hubert the veteran cop could have shared with her, it is that no one related to $200 million should do the least thing to attract the attention of the Yakuza. The plot then unfolds in bewildering alternation between pop comedy and action violence, with Hubert dancing in a video arcade one moment and blasting the bad guys the next.

There is no artistic purpose for this movie. It is product. Luc Besson, who wrote and produced it, has another movie out right now *(The Transporter)*, and indeed has written, produced, or announced sixteen other movies since this one was made in far-ago 2001. Jean Reno does what he can in a thankless dilemma, the film ricochets from humor to violence and back again, and Ryoko Hirosue makes us wonder if she is always like that. If she is, I owe an apology to the Powerpuff Girls. I didn't know they were based on real life.

The Weather Underground ★ ★ ★ ½
NO MPAA RATING, 92 m., 2003

Featuring Billy Ayers, Kathleen Cleaver, Bernardine Dohrn, Brian Flanagan, David Gilbert, Todd Gitlin, Naomi Jaffe, Mark Rudd, Don Strickland, and Laura Whitehorn. Narrated by Lili Taylor. A documentary directed by Sam Green and Bill Siegel and produced by Green, Carrie Lozano, Siegel, and Marc Smolowitz.

I still have my membership card in Students for a Democratic Society, signed by Tom Hayden, who handed it to me at a National Student Congress in 1963 and tucked the $1 membership fee in the pocket of his flannel shirt. SDS in those days was still the student department of the League for Industrial Democracy, an old-line left-labor group headed by Norman Thomas, whose statement on the back of the card made it clear the organization was nonviolent and anti-Communist. Within a few years, SDS would be captured by a far-left faction that became the Weather Underground, the most violent protest group in modern American history.

The new documentary *The Weather Underground* chronicles those early days of idealism, and their transition into a period when American society seemed for an instant on the point of revolution. The Weathermen orchestrated a string of bombings, initiated the Days of Rage in Chicago, and were in a vanguard of a more widespread antiwar movement that saw National Guard troops on the campuses, the Pentagon under siege by protesters, including hippies who vowed to levitate it, and the infamous Chicago 7 trial. Whether the protest movement hastened the end of the Vietnam War is hard to say, but it is likely that Lyndon Johnson's decision not to run for reelection was influenced by the climate it helped to create.

One crucial moment documented in this film is when SDS, with 100,000 members an important force among American young people, was essentially hijacked at its 1969 national convention in Chicago by the more radical Weather faction. "Institutional piracy," Todd Gitlin called it; one of the founders of SDS and later the author of a landmark book about the student left, he watched in dismay as the Weather faction advocated the violent overthrow of the U.S. government. Their program of terrorist bombings, he said, "was essentially mass murder." When an innocent person was killed in one of its early bombings, the group, however, decided that was "a terrible error," and took care that nobody was injured in a long series of later bombings, including one at the U.S. Capitol building. But a Greenwich Village townhouse used by the Weathermen as a bomb factory was destroyed in an accidental explosion that killed three bomb makers.

The Weatherman tactics were "Custeristic," Black Panther leader Fred Hampton sardonically observed at the time. When the Weathermen called for Days of Rage in Chicago in 1969, he said they were "taking people into a situation where they can be massacred." He was right, but he was himself soon massacred, in a still-controversial shooting that Chicago law enforcement officials described as a shoot-out, but which physical evidence indicated was an assassination. (After the *Tribune* cited "bullet holes" proving Hampton had fired back, a *Sun-Times* team ran photographs revealing the holes to be nailheads.)

The documentarians, Sam Green and Bill Siegel, are too young to remember this period personally—and, indeed, many viewers of the film may discover for the first time how ferociously the war at home was fought. The film

interviews surviving players in the drama, including Bernardine Dohrn, her husband Bill Ayers, Naomi Jaffe, Mark Rudd, David Gilbert, Brian Flanagan, and Gitlin. Dohrn, today the head of a program for juvenile justice at Northwestern University, still burns with the fire of her early idealism, as do Ayers and Jaffe, and you can hear in the voice of Gilbert (serving a life sentence for his involvement in a fatal robbery of a Brinks truck), the pain he felt because his country was committing what he considered murder in Vietnam.

Ironically, many charges against the Weathermen had to be dropped because the FBI had violated the law with its "Cointelpro," a secret agency to discredit the left. After the war ended and the Weatherman movement faded away, Dohrn and Ayers lived in hiding for several years with their children—an existence some say inspired the 1988 movie *Running on Empty*. Eventually they turned themselves in, and today are leading productive, unrepentant lives. I see Dohrn at the Conference on World Affairs at the University of Colorado, where she is as angry about the unnecessary criminalization of poor (often nonwhite) American young people as she was then about the war. She has, you must observe, the courage of her convictions.

The Weight of Water ★ ★
R, 113 m., 2002

Catherine McCormack (Jean Janes), Sarah Polley (Maren Hontvedt), Sean Penn (Thomas Janes), Josh Lucas (Rich Janes), Elizabeth Hurley (Adaline Gunne), Ciarán Hinds (Louis Wagner), Ulrich Thomsen (John Hontvedt), Anders W. Berthelsen (Evan Christenson), Katrin Cartlidge (Karen Christenson), Vinessa Shaw (Anethe Christenson). Directed by Kathryn Bigelow and produced by A. Kitman Ho, Sigurjon Sighvatsson, and Janet Yang. Screenplay by Alice Arlen and Christopher Kyle, based on the novel by Anita Shreve.

The Weight of Water tells two stories of family jealousy, separated by more than a century and heightened by lurid melodrama, bloody murder, incest, and storms at sea. While either one of the stories could make a plausible thriller, the movie's structure undercuts them both. Unlike *Possession* or *The French Lieutenant's*

Woman, in which modern and historical stories are linked in an intriguing way, *The Weight of Water* seems more like an exercise. We don't feel the connection, and every jump in time is a distraction.

The older story is the more absorbing. In 1873, on an island off the coast of New Hampshire, two Norwegian immigrant women are found murdered with an ax. A hapless man named Wagner (Ciarán Hinds) is convicted of the crime after a surviving eyewitness named Maren (Sarah Polley) testifies against him.

By the end of the movie we will have a deeper understanding of the emotional undertow on the island, and we will know that Maren's love for her brother Evan (Anders W. Berthelsen) is at the center of the intrigue. Maren is married to John Hontvedt (Ulrich Thomsen) but does not love him; her brother arrives on the island with his new bride Anethe (Vinessa Shaw), and there is also Maren's sister Karen (Katrin Cartlidge, whose performance is a reminder of how much we lost when she died at such an early age).

The modern story takes place mostly on a luxury yacht chartered by two brothers, Thomas and Rich Janes (Sean Penn and Josh Lucas). Thomas's wife, Jean (Catherine McCormack), is a famous photographer who is working on a book about the famous crime, which still inspires controversy and revisionist theories. The others are along for the ride, including Rich's girlfriend Adaline (Elizabeth Hurley). We learn, by indirection, tones of voice, and body language, that the Penn character is jealous of his brother, indifferent to his wife, interested in the girlfriend.

The screenplay, by Alice Arlen and Christopher Kyle, doesn't try to force awkward parallels between the two stories, but they are there to be found: hidden and forbidden passion, sibling jealousy, the possibility of violence. The movie tells the two stories so separately, indeed, that each one acts as a distraction from the other. The fact that there are nine major characters and many lines of intrigue doesn't help; *Possession* and *The French Lieutenant's Woman* only had to deal with parallels between a nineteenth-century couple and a twentieth-century couple.

Another problem is that psychological conflicts get upstaged by old-fashioned melodrama. The storm at the end, which I will not describe in detail, involves violence and action that would be right at home in a seafaring thriller, but seems hauled into this material only to provide an exciting action climax. It is not necessary to the material. And the revelations in the historical story would have more depth and resonance if we'd spent more time with the characters—if all of their scenes were not essentially part of the setup.

The movie was directed by Kathryn Bigelow, whose *Strange Days* (1995) was a smart futuristic thriller, inexplicably overlooked by audiences. Her credits also include the effective *K-19: The Widowmaker*, the submarine thriller from earlier this year. I like her work, but with *The Weight of Water* I think her problems began with the very decision to tell these two stories alternately. The actors are splendid, especially Sarah Polley and Sean Penn, but we never feel confident that these two plots fit together, belong together, or work together.

Welcome to Collinwood ★ ★ ½
R, 86 m., 2002

William H. Macy (Riley), Isaiah Washington (Leon), Sam Rockwell (Pero), Michael Jeter (Toto), Luis Guzmán (Cosimo), Patricia Clarkson (Rosalind), Andrew Davoli (Basil), Jennifer Esposito (Carmela), Gabrielle Union (Michelle), George Clooney (Jerzy). Directed by Anthony Russo and Joe Russo and produced by George Clooney and Steven Soderbergh. Screenplay by Russo and Russo.

I wonder if the real problem is that I've seen the original. *Welcome to Collinwood* is a wacky and eccentric heist comedy with many virtues, but it is also a remake of *Big Deal on Madonna Street* (1958), a movie much beloved by me. Some scenes are so close to the original it's kind of uncanny.

Consider the comic climax of the movie, which comes as the gang is trying to break through the wall and get the safe. If you've seen *Big Deal*, you'll remember that great scene. If you haven't, I won't spoil it for you. The surprise element, on top of the humor, makes it something like genius. But when the scene came along in *Welcome to Collinwood*, I knew exactly what would happen, and so the new movie didn't have a chance. All I could do was compare and contrast.

Would the scene work for a fresh audience? I don't see why not. I heard good buzz about *Welcome to Collinwood* at the Toronto Film Festival, and assume that for those who had not seen *Big Deal on Madonna Street*, the scene worked and the movie was a pleasure. The problem is, so many people *have* seen it, one way or another. Made as a satire of *Rififi* (1955), which is the mother of all heist movies, it is itself the mother of all heist comedies. *Big Deal* is a regular on cable, is in the Criterion Collection on DVD, and has been remade many times before, notably by Louis Malle *(Crackers)*, Alan Taylor *(Palookaville)*, and Woody Allen (the middle section of *Small Time Crooks*).

Directed and written by brothers Anthony and Joe Russo, the movie is set in the seedy Cleveland suburb of Collinwood, which looks unchanged since the depression. We meet members of the hamlet's criminal fraternity, who are incredibly colorful, as if they read Damon Runyon and stay up late taking notes on old crime movies. They have their own lingo. A "malinski" is a guy who will take the rap for you. A "bellini" is a lucrative job. As the film opens, a crook named Cosimo (Luis Guzmán) hears about a bellini and needs a malinski.

He shares his knowledge with his girlfriend (Patricia Clarkson) and unwisely confides in his partner Toto (Michael Jeter, whose character is named after the Italian comedian who played this role in the original). Word spreads through the underworld, and while Cosimo fails to find his malinski, the others sign up for the bellini, which involves a foolproof method to break into a pawnshop where the safe is said to contain $300,000.

The heist spoof genre is durable. Steven Soderbergh, who produced this film, directed *Ocean's Eleven* (2001), which was a remake of *Ocean's Eleven* (1960), which was a remake of the French film *Bob le Flambeur* (1955). In the Russo version, I like the sequence where the gang attempts to film the pawnbroker opening his safe. An arm keeps getting in the way at the crucial moment. After the screening, one crook observes, "As a film, it's a disaster," and another replies, "It's a documentary. It's supposed to look that way."

The break-in gang consists of Toto (Jeter),

single dad Riley (William H. Macy), Pero (Sam Rockwell), Leon (Isaiah Washington), and Basil (Andrew Davoli). Romantic distraction comes from Carmela (Jennifer Esposito) and Leon's sister Michelle (Gabrielle Union), who pair with Pero and Basil. Their trainer is the retired safecracker Jerzy (George Clooney), who is in a wheelchair and explains, "I don't go out in the field no more." He charges them $500 to learn the "circular saw method."

The movie is in love with its dialogue, which is in a more mannered and colorful style than real crooks probably have the time to master, and spends too much time lining them all up for conversations. The actual heist is the high point, just as in the Italian film, and so raffish and disorganized was the gang that I can see how someone might enjoy this movie, coming to it for the first time.

Welcome to Mooseport ★ ★ ★
PG-13, 110 m., 2004

Gene Hackman (Monroe Cole), Ray Romano (Handy Harrison), Marcia Gay Harden (Grace Sutherland), Maura Tierney (Sally Mannis), Christine Baranski (Charlotte Cole), Fred Savage (Bullard), Rip Torn (Bert Langdon). Directed by Donald Petrie and produced by Marc Frydman, Basil Iwanyk, and Tom Schulman. Screenplay by Tom Schulman.

I knew a very good poker player who always lost money at bachelor parties. He'd turn a profit in Vegas, but down in the basement with the beer and the cigar smoke he invariably got cleaned out. The reason, he explained, was that the jerks he was playing against didn't know how to play poker. They bet on every hand. They raised when they should have folded. You couldn't tell when they were bluffing because they knew so little they were always bluffing.

Gene Hackman plays a character like that in *Welcome to Mooseport*. The movie isn't about poker but the principle is the same. He is a former president of the United States who has moved to a colorful Maine hamlet and suddenly finds himself running for mayor. His problem is, he knows way too much about politics to run for mayor of Mooseport. And way too little about Mooseport.

Hackman is one of the most engaging actors

on the face of the earth. He's especially good at bluster. "The Eagle has landed," he declares, arriving in town. His name is Monroe "The Eagle" Cole, and don't forget the nickname. His opponent in the race is Handy Harrison (Ray Romano), a plumber who owns the local hardware store. "Let me get this straight," says The Eagle. "I'm running for mayor against the man who is repairing my toilet?"

There are romantic complications. Handy has been dating local beauty Sally Mannis (Maura Tierney) for seven years, without ever having gotten up the nerve to pop the question. As the movie opens, his face lights up with joy as he races over to tell her he's come into some money, and so the time is finally right to ... buy that pickup. When The Eagle asks her out to dinner, she accepts.

Of course, he has no idea Handy and Sally have been dating. For that matter, the only reason he's in Mooseport at all is that his bitchy ex-wife, Charlotte (Christine Baranski), got the big house in the divorce settlement. Now time hangs heavily on his hands, he's surrounded by a support staff with nothing to do, and a mayoral race has them all exercising their overtrained skills. The only sane voice in his entourage belongs to Grace Sutherland (Marcia Gay Harden), who may be hoping that someday The Eagle will land on her.

Rip Torn plays the Karl Rove role. What a pleasure Torn is. Like Christopher Walken and Steve Buscemi, he makes us smile just by appearing on the screen. His Machiavellian approach to Mooseport is all wrong, however, because the town is so guileless and goodhearted that schemes are invisible to them. We question that such a naive and innocent town could exist in America, and are almost relieved to find that the movie was shot in Canada. Has it seemed to you lately that Canada is the last remaining repository of the world Norman Rockwell used to paint?

There is a genre of movies about outsiders who arrive in small towns and are buffaloed by the guileless locals. Consider David Mamet's *State and Main* (2000) or *Win a Date with Tad Hamilton!*. There's always a romance with a local, always a visiting sophisticate who rediscovers traditional values, always a civic booster in a bow tie, always a microphone that deafens everyone with a shriek whenever it's turned on,

always an embarrassing public display of dirty laundry, and almost always a Greek chorus of regulars at the local diner/tavern/launderette who pass judgment on events.

Whether the movie works or not depends on the charm of the actors. Gene Hackman could charm the chrome off a trailer hitch. Ray Romano is more of the earnest, aw-shucks, sincere, well-meaning kind of guy whose charm is inner and only peeks out occasionally. They work well together here, and Maura Tierney does a heroic job of playing a character who doesn't know how the story will end, when everybody else in the cast and in the audience has an excellent idea.

Wendigo ★ ★ ½
R, 91 m., 2002

Patricia Clarkson (Kim), Jake Weber (George), Erik Per Sullivan (Miles), John Speredakos (Otis), Christopher Wynkoop (Sheriff), Lloyd Oxendine (Elder), Brian Delate (Everett), Daniel Sherman (Billy). Directed by Larry Fessenden and produced by Jeffrey Levy-Hinte. Screenplay by Fessenden.

Wendigo is a good movie with an ending that doesn't work. While it was not working I felt a keen disappointment, because the rest of the movie works so well. The writer, director, and editor is Larry Fessenden, whose *Habit* (1997) was about a New York college student who found solace, and too much more, in the arms of a vampire. Now Fessenden goes into the Catskills to tell a story that will be compared to *The Blair Witch Project* when it should be compared to *The Innocents*.

The film builds considerable scariness, and does it in the details. Ordinary things happen in ominous ways. Kim and George (Patricia Clarkson and Jake Weber), a couple from New York, drive to the Catskills to spend a weekend in a friend's cottage, bringing along their young son, Miles (Erik Per Sullivan). Even before they arrive, there's trouble. They run into a deer on the road, and three hunters emerge from the woods and complain that the city people killed "their" deer—and worse, broke its antlers.

Two of the hunters seem like all-right guys. The third, named Otis (John Speredakos), is not. Holding a rifle that seems like a threat, he engages in macho name-calling with George, and the scene is seen mostly through the big-eyed point of view of little Miles, in the backseat. He says little, he does little, and the less he says and does, the more his fear becomes real to us. Fessenden is using an effective technique: Instead of scaring us, he scares the kid, and we get scared through empathy and osmosis.

Kim and George are not getting along too well, and that works to increase the tension. They're not fighting out loud, but you can feel the buried unhappiness, and Kim tells him: "You've got all this anger you carry around with you from work and I don't know where, and he feels it's directed at him." George tries to be nice to Miles, tries to take an interest, but he's not really listening, and kids notice that.

There are bullet holes in the cabin when they get to it. It's cold inside. Miles hears noises and sees things—or thinks he does. The next day at the general store, he is given a wooden figure by a man behind the counter who says it represents a Wendigo, an Indian spirit. His mother asks where he got the figure. "From the man," Miles says. "Nobody works here but me," says a woman behind another counter.

It doesn't sound as effective as it is. The effect is all in the direction, in Fessenden's control of mood. I watched in admiration as he created tension and fear out of thin air. When the boy and his father go sledding, an event takes place so abruptly that it almost happens to us. The way Fessenden handles the aftermath is just right, building suspense without forgetting logic.

The actors have an unforced, natural quality that looks easy but is hard to do. Look and listen at the conversation between Otis and the local sheriff (Christopher Wynkoop). Notice the way they both know what is being said and what is meant, and how they both know the other knows. And look at the way the scene involves us in what will happen next.

The buildup, which continues for most of the film, is very well done. Unfortunately, Fessenden felt compelled, I guess, to tilt over into the supernatural (or the hallucinatory) in a climax that feels false and rushed. Maybe he would have been better off dropping the Wendigo altogether, and basing the story simply on the

scariness of a cottage in the woods in winter, and the ominous ways of Otis.

The ending doesn't work, as I've said, but most of the movie works so well I'm almost recommending it anyway—maybe not to everybody, but certainly to people with a curiosity about how a movie can go very right, and then step wrong. Fessenden has not made a perfect film, but he's a real filmmaker.

We Were Soldiers ★ ★ ★ ½
R, 138 m., 2002

Mel Gibson (Hal Moore), Madeleine Stowe (Julie Moore), Sam Elliott (Sergeant Major Plumley), Greg Kinnear (Major Crandall), Chris Klein (Lieutenant Geoghegan), Don Duong (Ahn), Josh Daugherty (Ouelette), Barry Pepper (Joe Galloway), Keri Russell (Barbara Geoghegan). Directed by Randall Wallace and produced by Bruce Davey, Stephen McEveety, and Wallace. Screenplay by Wallace, based on the book by Joe Galloway and Hal Moore.

"I wonder what Custer was thinking," Lieutenant Colonel Hal Moore says, "when he realized he'd moved his men into slaughter." Sergeant Major Plumley, his right-hand man, replies, "Sir, Custer was a pussy." There you have the two emotional poles of *We Were Soldiers,* the story of the first major land battle in the Vietnam War, late in 1964. Moore (Mel Gibson) is a family man and a Harvard graduate who studied international relations. Plumley (Sam Elliott) is an army lifer, hard, brave, unsentimental. They are both about as good as battle leaders get. But by the end of that first battle, they realize they may be in the wrong war.

The reference to Custer is not coincidence. Moore leads the First Battalion of the Seventh Cavalry, Custer's regiment. "We will ride into battle and this will be our horse," Moore says, standing in front of a helicopter. Some 400 of his men ride into battle in the Ia Drang Valley, known as the Valley of Death, and are surrounded by some 2,000 North Vietnamese troops. Moore realizes it's an ambush, and indeed in the film's opening scenes he reads about just such a tactic used by the Vietnamese against the French a few years earlier.

We Were Soldiers, like *Black Hawk Down,* is a film in which the Americans do not automatically prevail in the style of traditional Hollywood war movies. Ia Drang cannot be called a defeat, since Moore's men fought bravely and well, suffering heavy casualties but killing even more Viet Cong. But it is not a victory; it's more the curtain-raiser of a war in which American troops were better trained and better equipped, but outnumbered, outmaneuvered, and finally outlasted.

For much of its length, the movie consists of battle scenes. They are not as lucid and easy to follow as the events in *Black Hawk Down,* but then the terrain is different, the canvas is larger, and there are no eyes in the sky to track troop movements. Director Randall Wallace (who wrote *Braveheart* and *Pearl Harbor*) does make the situation clear from moment to moment, as Moore and his North Vietnamese counterpart try to outsmart each other with theory and instinct.

Wallace cuts between the American troops, their wives back home on an army base, and a tunnel bunker where Ahn (Don Duong), the Viet Cong commander, plans strategy on a map. Both men are smart and intuitive. The enemy knows the terrain and has the advantage of surprise, but is surprised itself at the way the Americans improvise and rise to the occasion.

Black Hawk Down was criticized because the characters seemed hard to tell apart. *We Were Soldiers* doesn't have that problem; in the Hollywood tradition it identifies a few key players, casts them with stars, and follows their stories. In addition to the Gibson and Elliott characters, there are Major Crandall (Greg Kinnear), a helicopter pilot who flies into danger; the gung ho Lieutenant Geoghegan (Chris Klein); and Joe Galloway (Barry Pepper), a photojournalist who was a soldier's son, hitches a ride into battle, and finds himself fighting at the side of the others to save his life.

The key relationship is between Moore and Plumley, and Gibson and Elliott depict it with quiet authority. They're portrayed as professional soldiers with experience from Korea. As they're preparing to ride into battle, Moore tells Plumley, "Better get yourself that M-16." The veteran replies: "By the time I need one,

there'll be plenty of them lying on the ground." There are.

Events on the army base center around the lives of the soldiers' wives, including Julie Moore (Madeleine Stowe), who looks after their five children and is the de facto leader of the other spouses. We also meet Barbara Geoghegan (Keri Russell), who, because she is singled out, gives the audience a strong hint that the prognosis for her husband is not good.

Telegrams announcing deaths in battle are delivered by a Yellow Cab driver. Was the army so insensitive that even on a base they couldn't find an officer to deliver the news? That sets up a shameless scene later, when a Yellow Cab pulls up in front of a house and of course the wife inside assumes her husband is dead, only to find him in the cab. This scene is a reminder of Wallace's *Pearl Harbor,* in which the Ben Affleck character is reported shot down over the English Channel and makes a surprise return to Hawaii without calling ahead. Call me a romantic, but when your loved one thinks you're dead, give her a ring.

We Were Soldiers and *Black Hawk Down* both seem to replace patriotism with professionalism. This movie waves the flag more than the other (even the Viet Cong's Ahn looks at the Stars and Stripes with enigmatic thoughtfulness), but the narration tells us, "In the end, they fought for each other." This is an echo of *Black Hawk Down*'s line, "It's about the men next to you. That's all it is."

Some will object, as they did with the earlier film, that the battle scenes consist of Americans killing waves of faceless nonwhite enemies. There is an attempt to give a face and a mind to the Viet Cong in the character of Ahn, but, significantly, he is not listed in the major credits and I had to call the studio to find out his name and the name of the actor who played him. Yet almost all war movies identify with one side or the other, and it's remarkable that *We Were Soldiers* includes a dedication not only to the Americans who fell at Ia Drang, but also to "the members of the People's Army of North Vietnam who died in that place."

I was reminded of an experience fifteen years ago at the Hawaii Film Festival, when a delegation of North Vietnamese directors arrived with a group of their films about the war. An audience member noticed that the enemy was not only faceless, but was not even named: At no point did the movies refer to Americans. "That is true," said one of the directors. "We have been at war so long, first with the Chinese, then the French, then the Americans, that we just think in terms of the enemy."

Whale Rider ★ ★ ★

PG-13, 105 m., 2003

Keisha Castle-Hughes (Pai), Rawiri Paratene (Koro), Vicky Haughton (Flowers), Cliff Curtis (Porourangi), Grant Roa (Rawiri), Mana Taumaunu (Hemi), Rachel House (Shilo), Taungaroa Emile (Dog). Directed by Niki Caro and produced by John Barnett, Frank Hubner, and Tim Sanders. Screenplay by Caro, based on the novel by Witi Ihimaera.

Whale Rider arrives in theaters already proven as one of the great audience-grabbers of recent years. It won the audience awards as the most popular film at both the Toronto and Sundance film festivals, played to standing ovations, left audiences in tears. I recite these facts right at the top of this review because I fear you might make a hasty judgment that you don't want to see a movie about a twelve-year-old Maori girl who dreams of becoming the chief of her people. Sounds too ethnic, uplifting, and feminist, right?

The genius of the movie is the way it sidesteps all of the obvious clichés of the underlying story and makes itself fresh, observant, tough, and genuinely moving. There is a vast difference between movies for twelve-year-old girls, and movies about twelve-year-old girls, and *Whale Rider* proves it.

The movie, which takes place in the present day in New Zealand, begins with the birth of twins. The boy and the mother die. The girl, Pai (Keisha Castle-Hughes), survives. Her father, Porourangi (Cliff Curtis), an artist, leaves New Zealand, and the little girl is raised and much loved by her grandparents, Koro and Nanny Flowers.

Koro is the chief of these people. Porourangi would be next in line, but has no interest in returning home. Pai believes that she could serve as the chief, but her grandfather, despite his love, fiercely opposes this idea. He causes Pai much hurt by doubting her, questioning her achievements, insisting in the face of everything she achieves that she is only a girl.

The movie, written and directed by Niki Caro, inspired by a novel by Witi Ihimaera, describes these events within the rhythms of daily life. This is not a simplistic fable, but the story of real people living in modern times. There are moments when Pai is lost in discouragement and despair, and when her father comes for a visit she almost leaves with him. But, no, her people need her—whether or not her grandfather realizes it.

Pai is played by Keisha Castle-Hughes, a newcomer of whom it can only be said: This is a movie star. She glows. She stands up to her grandfather in painful scenes, she finds dignity, and yet the next second she's running around the village like the kid she is. The other roles are also strongly cast, especially Rawiri Paratene and Vicky Haughton as the grandparents.

One day Koro summons all of the young teenage boys of the village to a series of compulsory lessons on how to be a Maori, and the leader of Maoris. There's an amusing sequence where they practice looking ferocious to scare their enemies. Pai, of course, is banned from these classes, but eavesdrops, and enlists a wayward uncle to reveal some of the secrets of the males.

And then—well, the movie doesn't end as we expect. It doesn't march obediently to standard plot requirements, but develops an unexpected crisis, and an unexpected solution. There is a scene set at a school ceremony, where Pai has composed a work in honor of her people, and asked her grandfather to attend. Despite his anger, he will come, won't he? The movie seems headed for the ancient cliché of the auditorium door that opens at the last moment to reveal the person whom the child onstage desperately hopes to see—but no, that's not what happens.

It isn't that Koro comes or that he doesn't come, but that something else altogether happens. Something on a larger and more significant scale, that brings together all of the themes of the film into a magnificent final sequence. It's not just an uplifting ending, but a transcendent one, inspired and inspiring, and we realize how special this movie really is. So many films by and about teenagers are mired in vulgarity and stupidity; this one, like its heroine, dares to dream. ☞

What a Girl Wants ★ ★
PG, 104 m., 2003

Amanda Bynes (Daphne Reynolds), Colin Firth (Henry Dashwood), Kelly Preston (Libby Reynolds), Eileen Atkins (Lady Jocelyn), Anna Chancellor (Glynnis), Jonathan Pryce (Alastair Payne), Oliver James (Ian Wallace), Christina Cole (Clarissa). Directed by Dennie Gordon and produced by Denise Di Novi, Bill Gerber, and Hunt Lowry. Screenplay by Jenny Bicks and Elizabeth Chandler, based on the screenplay by William Douglas Home.

Amanda Bynes, the star of *The Amanda Show,* is well known to fans of the Nickelodeon channel, who are so numerous that she is to 'tweeners as Jack Nicholson is to the Academy. She was sort of wonderful in *Big Fat Liar,* a comedy about kids whose screenplay is stolen by a Hollywood professional, and now here she is in *What a Girl Wants,* a comedy whose screenplay was stolen from *The Princess Diaries.*

But I am unfair. What goes around comes around, and to assume this is a retread of *The Princess Diaries* is to overlook its own pedigree. It's based on the 1956 play and 1958 screenplay, *The Reluctant Debutante,* by William Douglas Home—who, by the way, was the brother of Sir Alec Douglas Home, briefly the British prime minister in the 1960s.

The point, I suppose, is that few movies are truly original, and certainly not *What a Girl Wants* or *The Princess Diaries.* Both are recycled from ancient fairy tales in which a humble child discovers a royal parent and is elevated from pauperdom to princehood, to coin a phrase.

I would not be surprised to learn that Jenny Bicks and Elizabeth Chandler, who adapted Home's screenplay, did homework of their own—because a key plot point in the movie mirrors Sir Alec's own decision, in 1963, to renounce his seat in the House of Lords in order to run for a seat in the Commons. He won, became prime minister after Macmillan, and quickly lost the next election to Harold Wilson.

Do you need to know this? Perhaps not, but then do you need to know the plot of *What a Girl Wants?* The movie is clearly intended for girls between the ages of nine and fifteen, and for the more civilized of their brothers, and isn't of much use to anyone else.

Bynes stars as Daphne Reynolds, who has been raised by her mother, Libby (Kelly Preston), in an apartment above a restaurant in Chinatown, for the excellent reason that we can therefore see shots of Daphne in Chinatown. As nearly as I can recall, no Chinese characters have speaking lines, although one helps to blow out the candles on her birthday cake.

Daphne is the love child of Sir Henry Dashwood (Colin Firth), a handsome British politician who has decided to renounce his seat in the House of Lords in order to run for the Commons (the movie dismisses such minutiae as that Tony Blair has already booted most of the lords out onto the street). Sir Henry had a Meet Cute with Libby in Morocco fifteeen years ago, and they were married by a Bedouin prince, but never had a "real marriage" (a Bedouin prince not ranking as high in this system as a justice of the peace). Then Sir Henry's evil adviser (Jonathan Pryce) plotted to drive them apart, and she fled to Chinatown, believing Sir Henry did not love her and nobly saving him the embarrassment of a pregnant American commoner.

So great is the wealth of the Dashwoods that their country estate, surrounded by a vast expanse of green lawns and many a tree, is smack dab in the middle of London, so central that Daphne can hop off a bus bound for Trafalgar Square and press her pert little nose against its cold iron gates. The Dashwoods, in short, live on real estate worth more than Rhode Island.

Daphne jumps the wall at Dashwood House in order to meet her father, her lovable but eccentric grandmother (Eileen Atkins), her father's competitive fiancée (Anna Chancellor), her father's future stepdaughter (Christina Cole), and her father's adviser (Pryce), who frowns on the notion of introducing a love child on the eve of the election. Now that you know all that, you can easily jot down the rest of the plot for yourself.

There are moments of wit, as when the eccentric grandmother recoils from the American teenager ("No hugs, dear. I'm British. We only show affection to dogs and horses"). And an odd scene where Daphne is locked in a bed-

741

room, released just as Queen Elizabeth II is arriving at a party, and flees in tears—causing her father to choose between chasing her and greeting the queen. My analysis of this scene: (1) He should choose to greet the queen, or nineteen generations of breeding have been for nothing, and (2) Daphne won't get far before being returned, dead or alive, by the Scotland Yard security detail that accompanies the queen when she visits private homes.

I found it a little unlikely, by the way, that the guests at the party were all looking at Daphne and not the queen. Paul Theroux wrote of being at a dinner party for the queen and agonizing over what he should say when she entered the room. Suddenly seeing her famous profile, all he could think of was: "That reminds me! I need to buy postage stamps."

So is this movie worth seeing? Well, everybody in it is either sweet or cute, or eccentric and hateful, and the movie asks the timeless question: Can a little girl from America find love and happiness as the daughter of a wealthy and titled English lord? If you are a fan of Amanda Bynes, you will probably enjoy finding out the answer for yourself. If not, not.

What Time Is It There? ★ ★ ★ ½
NO MPAA RATING, 116 m., 2002

Lee Kang-Sheng (Hsiao Kang), Chen Shiang-Chyi (Shiang-Chyi), Lu Yi-Ching (Mother), Miao Tien (Father), Cecilia Yip (Woman in Paris), Chen Chao-Jung (Man in Subway), Tsai Guei (Prostitute), Arthur Nauczyciel (Man in Phone Booth), David Ganansia (Man in Restaurant), Jean-Pierre Leaud (Man at Cemetery). Directed by Tsai Ming-Lian and produced by Bruno Pesery. Screenplay by Tsai and Yang Pi-Ying.

The reviewers of Tsai Ming-Lian's *What Time Is It There?* have compared it to the work of Yasujiro Ozu, Robert Bresson, Michelangelo Antonioni, Jacques Tati, and Buster Keaton. If none of these names stir admiration and longing in your soul, start with them, not with Tsai. Begin with Keaton and work your way backward on the list, opening yourself to the possibilities of silence, introspection, isolation, and loneliness in the movies. You will notice that the films grow less funny after

Keaton and Tati; one of the enigmas about Tsai's work is that it is always funny and always sad, never just one or the other.

Tsai's hero, who indeed shares some of the single-minded self-absorption of the Keaton and Tati characters, is Hsiao Kang (Lee Kang-Sheng), a man who sells wristwatches from a display case on the sidewalks of Taipei. One day he sells a watch to Shiang-Chyi (Chen Shiang-Chyi—remember, family names come first in Chinese societies). He wants to sell her a watch from his case, but she insists on the watch from his wrist, which gives the time in two time zones, because she is flying to Paris.

Hsiao's home life is sad without redemption. In an early scene, we have seen his father, almost too exhausted to exhale the smoke from his cigarettes, die in a dark, lonely room. Hsiao's mother (Lu Yi-Ching) becomes convinced that her dead husband's soul has somehow been channeled into Fatty, the large white fish in a tank in the living room. Since Fatty is Hsiao's pet and only friend (he confides details of his life to the fish), this is doubly sad: Not only has the father died after bringing no joy to his son's life, but now he has appropriated the fish. You see what I mean about humor and sadness coexisting, neither one conceding to the other.

The movie then develops into a story that seems to involve synchronicity, but actually involves our need for synchronicity. We need to believe that our little lives are in step with distant music, when synchronicity is simply the way coincidence indulges itself in wish fulfillment. The girl goes off to Paris. Hsiao, who has barely spoken to her, and then only about watches, is so struck by longing for her that he begins to reset watches to Paris time. First all of the watches in his display case. Then all of the watches and clocks available to him. Then even a gigantic clock on a building (the parallel to Harold Lloyd's most famous scene is inescapable).

Meanwhile, in Paris, Shiang-Chyi is also lonely. Does she even have a reason for being here? She wanders the streets and travels nowhere in particular on the Metro. Eventually all three lonely people—Hsiao, his mother, and Shiang-Chyi—look for release in sex. Sex is many things, and one of them is a way of reassuring yourself you are alive, that you retain the power to feel and cause feeling. Hsiao seeks out a prostitute, Shiang-Chyi experiments with another woman (who for her purposes could have been a man), and the mother masturbates while thinking of her dead husband.

These three acts take place at about the same time. Synchronicity? Or simply an indication that the loneliness clocks of the three characters started ticking at the same time, and so chime the hour simultaneously? There is another coincidence in the movie: Hsiao watches Truffaut's *The 400 Blows* on video—the scene where Jean-Pierre Leaud wanders the Paris streets because he is afraid to return home. And Shiang-Chyi visits a Paris cemetery where she talks to a strange man sitting on a gravestone. This man is Jean-Pierre Leaud forty-one years later. (It isn't mentioned in the movie, but I think this is the cemetery where Truffaut is buried. Is Leaud visiting the grave of the man who created his life-defining roles?)

What Time Is It There? is not easy. It haunts you, you can't forget it, you admire its conception, and are able to resolve some of the confusions you had while watching it. You realize it is very simple, really, even though at first you thought it was impenetrable. But can you recommend it to others? Does it depend on how advanced they are in their filmgoing? The critics don't seem to agree. Is it true that the movie "proceeds with all the speed of paint drying" *(Film Journal International)* or does Tsai create "shock waves of comedy, which both unleash a wave of euphoria in the audience and communicate the pleasure he gets from filmmaking" *(New York Times)*? Does "a sense of perseverance and comic acceptance trump any self-indulgent ennui" *(Salon)*, or do "emotionally disconnected characters . . . wade through their sterile Taipei surroundings hopelessly grasping for a piece of human comfort" *(Slant)*?

What happens, I think, is that the funny and sad poles of the story checkmate each other. Everything is funny. Everything is sad. There is nothing funnier than an unrequited love. Nothing sadder than an unrequited lover. Nothing tragic, really, about two people who have not connected when they only had two meaningless conversations. But nothing hopeful about two people so unconnected it doesn't matter what city they are in. When Hsiao resets all of the clocks, is that a grand gesture of romance or a pathetic fixation? Which is more depressing—that the mother thinks her husband's soul occupies the fish, or that the fish is her son's only confidant?

A movie that causes us to ask these kinds of questions deserves to be seen. A movie that thinks it knows the answer to them deserves to be pitied. Most movies do not know these questions exist.

White Chicks ★ ½
PG-13, 100 m., 2004

Marlon Wayans (Marcus Copeland), Shawn Wayans (Kevin Copeland), Anne Dudek (Tiffany Wilson), Maitland Ward (Brittany Wilson), Brittany Daniel (Megan Vandergeld), Jaime King (Heather Vandergeld), Rochelle Aytes (Denise), Lochlyn Munro (Agent Harper), Frankie Faison (FBI Chief), Terry Crews (Latrell). Directed by Keenen Ivory Wayans and produced by Keenen Ivory Wayans, Shawn Wayans, and Marlon Wayans. Screenplay by Keenen Ivory Wayans.

Various combinations of the Wayans family have produced a lot of cutting-edge comedy, but *White Chicks* uses the broad side of the knife. Here is a film so dreary and conventional that it took an act of the will to keep me in the theater. Who was it made for? Who will it play to? Is there really still a market for fart jokes?

Marlon and Shawn Wayans play Marcus and Kevin Copeland, brothers who are FBI agents. Fired after a sting goes wrong, they're given a second chance. Their assignment: Protect Tiffany and Brittany Wilson (Anne Dudek and Maitland Ward), high-society bimbos who seem to be the target of a kidnapping scheme. The girls get tiny cuts in a car crash and are too vain to attend a big society bash in the Hamptons. Marcus and Kevin have the answer: They'll disguise themselves as the Wilsons and attend the party in drag.

Uh-huh. They call in experts who supply them with latex face masks, which fool everybody in the Hamptons but looked to me uncannily like the big faces with the talking lips on Conan O'Brien. There is also the problem that they're about six inches taller than the Wilsons. I guess they're supposed to be, I dunno, Paris and Nicky Hilton, but at least the Hiltons look like clones of humans, not exhibits in a third-rate wax museum.

The gag is not so much that black men are playing white women as that men learn to understand women by stepping into their shoes and dishing with their girlfriends. Womanhood in this version involves not empowerment and liberation, but shopping, trading makeup and perfume tips, and checking out the cute guys at the party. "Tiffany" and "Brittany" pick up a posse of three friendly white girls, inherit the Wilsons' jealous enemies, and engage in the most unconvincing dance contest ever filmed, which they win with a break-dancing exhibition.

Meanwhile, a pro athlete named Latrell (Terry Crews) is the top bidder at a charity auction for Marcus, who represents his ideal: "A white chick with a black woman's ass!" This leads to all sorts of desperately unfunny situations in which Marcus tries to keep his secret while Latrell goes into heat. Also meanwhile, a labyrinthine plot unfolds about who is really behind the kidnapping, and why.

The fact that *White Chicks* actually devotes expository time to the kidnap plot shows how lame-brained it is, because no one in the audience can conceivably care in any way about its details. Audiences who see the TV commercials and attend *White Chicks* will want sharp, transgressive humor, which they will not find, instead of a wheezy story about off-the-shelf bad guys, which drags on and on in one complicated permutation after another.

Are there any insights about the races here? No. Are there any insights into the gender gap? No. As men or women, black or white, the Wayans brothers play exactly the same person: an interchangeable cog in a sitcom.

Because they look so odd in makeup, the effect is quease-inducing. They fall victims, indeed, to the Uncanny Valley Effect. This phenomenon, named in 1978 by the Japanese robot expert Masahiro Mori, refers to the ways in which humans relate emotionally with robots. Up to a certain point, he found, our feelings grow more positive the more the robots resemble humans. But beyond a certain stage of reality, it works the other way: The closer they get to humans, the more we notice the differences and are repelled by them. In the same way, the not-quite convincing faces of the two white chicks provide a distraction every moment they're on the screen. We're staring at them, not liking them, and paying no attention to the plot. Not that attention would help.

White Oleander ★ ★ ½
PG-13, 110 m., 2002

Alison Lohman (Astrid Magnussen), Robin Wright Penn (Starr), Michelle Pfeiffer (Ingrid Magnussen), Renée Zellweger (Claire Richards), Billy Connolly (Barry Kolker), Svetlana Efremova (Rena Grushenka), Patrick Fugit (Paul Trout), Cole Hauser (Ray), Noah Wyle (Mark Richards), Amy Aquino (Miss Martinez). Directed by Peter Kosminsky and produced by John Wells and Hunt Lowry. Screenplay by Mary Agnes Donoghue, based on the novel by Janet Fitch.

White Oleander tells a sad story of crime and foster homes, and makes it look like the movie version. The film takes the materials of human tragedy and dresses them in lovely costumes, southern California locations, and star power. Almost makes it look like fun. The movie's poster shows four women's faces side by side, all blindingly blond: Alison Lohman, Michelle Pfeiffer, Robin Wright Penn, and Renée Zellweger. We suspect there could be another, parallel story of the same events, in which the characters look unhinged and desperate and brunette.

The story is determined to be colorful and melodramatic, like a soap opera where the characters suffer in ways that look intriguing. When you are a teenage girl and your mother is jailed for murder and you are shipped to a series of foster homes, isn't it a little unlikely that each home would play like an entertaining episode of a miniseries? First you get a sexy foster mom who was "an alcoholic, a cokehead, and dancing topless—and then I was saved by Jesus," although she still dresses like an off-duty stripper. Then you get an actress who lives in a sun-drenched beach house in Malibu, and you become her best friend. Then you get a Russian capitalist who dresses like a gypsy, uses her foster kids as Dumpster-divers, and runs a stall at the Venice Beach flea market. Aren't there any foster mothers who are old, tired, a little mean, and doing it for the money?

The performances are often touching and deserve a better screenplay. I don't hold the beauty of the actresses against them, but I wish the movie had not been so pleased with the way the sunlight comes streaming through their long blond hair and falls on their flawless skin and little white summer dresses.

The movie is narrated by Astrid Magnussen, played by Alison Lohman in several different years and weathers of her life. It's an awesome performance, but it would benefit from the depth and darkness that the movie shies away from. (The movie is all too appropriately rated PG-13; I suspect full justice cannot be done to this material short of an R.) Astrid is the daughter of Ingrid (Michelle Pfeiffer), an artist and free spirit who sits on the roof so the desert winds can find her. "No one had ever seen anyone more beautiful than my mother," Astrid tells us, but there are ominous hints that Ingrid is not an ideal mother, as when she skips Parents Night because "what can they tell me about you that I don't already know?"

Ingrid doesn't date. Doesn't need men. Then makes the mistake of letting Barry (Billy Connolly) into her life (although so fleeting is his role he is barely allowed into the movie). She kills him, observing to her daughter, "He made love to me and then said I had to leave because he had a date." When you hardly know someone and that's how he treats you, he's not worth serving thirty-five years to life.

Astrid then moves on to the series of foster homes, each one so colorful it could be like the adventure of a Dickens character; the Russian is unmistakably a descendent of Fagin, and surely only in a Hollywood fantasy could any of these women qualify as foster mothers. Starr, the former stripper, seems less like a person than a caricature, although the director, Peter Kosminsky, has a good eye for detail and shows how her family takes a jaundiced view of her born-again grandstanding. What happens to

bring this foster experience to an end, I will not reveal, except to say that I didn't for a moment believe it; it involves behavior of a sort the movie seems obligated to supply, but never refers to again.

Astrid's best foster experience is with Claire (Renée Zellweger), whose performance is the most convincing in the movie. She plays a one-time horror star, married to a director who is usually absent, and we believe the scenes she has with Astrid because they come from need and honesty.

They also inspire the best scenes between Astrid and her mother; Pfeiffer finds just the right note between jealousy and perception when, on visiting day at the prison, she observes, "You dress like her now." Later she tells her daughter, "I'd like to meet her." "Why?" "Because you don't want me to." And later: "How can you stand to live with poor Claire? I would rather see you in the worst kind of foster home than to live with that woman." The scenes involving Claire most clearly inspire Astrid's developing ideas about her mother.

The third foster experience, with Svetlana Efremova playing the Russian jumble-sale woman, offers a glimpse of the economy's underbelly, but is too choppy and perfunctory to engage us: It feels like it was filmed to add color, and then chopped to reduce the running time. Its only influence on Astrid is to change her wardrobe and hair color, in what feels more like a stunt than a character development.

Pfeiffer's role is the most difficult in the movie, because she has to compress her revelations and emotions into the brief visits of her increasingly dubious daughter. Astrid, who once idealized her mother, now blames her for the loss of happiness with Claire. But even the movie's big emotional payoff loses something because, after all, Ingrid *did* murder Barry, and so what is presented as a sacrifice on behalf of her daughter could also be described as simply doing the right thing.

White Oleander is based on a novel by Janet Fitch, recommended by Oprah's Book Club, unread by me. I gather it includes still more colorful foster home episodes. Amy Aquino plays Miss Martinez, the social worker who drives Astrid from one foster adventure to the next. She feels like this movie's version of Michael Anthony, the man who introduced each episode of *The Millionaire*. You can imagine her on the TV series, shipping the heroine to a different foster home every week.

Who Is Cletis Tout? ★ ★ ½
R, 95 m., 2002

Christian Slater (Trevor Finch/Cletis Tout), Tim Allen (Critical Jim), Portia de Rossi (Tess), Richard Dreyfuss (Micah). Directed by Chris Ver Wiel and produced by Matthew Grimaldi, Daniel Grodnik, and Robert Snukal. Screenplay by Ver Wiel.

Who Is Cletis Tout? is one of those movies with a plot so labyrinthine you think you should be taking notes and then you realize you are. Like *The Usual Suspects*, it circles around the verbal description of events that are seen in flashback and may or may not be trustworthy. The difference is that *Cletis Tout* is a lot more lighthearted than the usual puzzle movie, and takes its tone from the performance of Tim Allen, as Critical Jim, a hit man who loves the movies.

As the film opens, he sticks a gun in the face of Christian Slater and tells him that in ninety minutes, if money is delivered as planned, he will kill him. In the meantime, he loves a good story. And Slater has one to tell him. Their meeting, Slater explains, is based on a misconception. Critical Jim thinks Slater is Cletis Tout, a man the mob wants dead. But Slater is in fact Trevor Finch, who borrowed Cletis's identity after escaping from prison.

"Flashbacks!" Critical Jim cries. "Yes, I like flashbacks!" So Finch, if that is his name, tells a story about meeting a jewel thief named Micah (Richard Dreyfuss) in prison, and learning from him about a stash of diamonds. Micah we have already seen; he is a gifted magician who stages his robberies while always seeming to be on the sidewalk outside the building. Later, in a prison break, he projects footage of himself against a background of smoke, which seems like a lot of trouble and leaves you wondering how a guy on a chain gang can smuggle a projector out to the work area.

Anyway. Micah and Finch escape together (jumping onto a train that seems to be speeding way too fast), and then there is the business of the buried diamonds and Micah's daughter, Tess (Portia de Rossi), who either hates Finch or loves him, depending on various stages of the story. "Pitch me!" Critical Jim says, and Finch makes the story good while we try to decide what to believe.

It's endearing, the way Critical Jim has memorized lines of movie dialogue to cover every occasion, but about midway through the movie I began to lose patience with the method, however clever. The underlying story—about the original robbery, the jail break, and the case of mistaken identity involving the mob—is intriguing in itself. Add the beautiful Tess and her carrier pigeons (yes, carrier pigeons) and you have something. Is it entirely necessary to add the layer of the story being told to Critical Jim? Is this not one more unnecessary turn of the screw to make a sound story into a gimmick?

Could be. Or maybe not. By the end of the film I was a little restless, a little impatient at being jerked this way and that by the story devices. There was a lot I liked in *Cletis Tout*, including the performances and the very audacity of details like the magic tricks and the carrier pigeons. But it seemed a shame that the writer and director, Chris Ver Wiel, took a perfectly sound story idea and complicated it into an exercise in style. Less is more.

The Whole Ten Yards ★
PG-13, 99 m., 2004

Bruce Willis (Jimmy "The Tulip" Tudeski), Matthew Perry (Nicholas "Oz" Oseransky), Amanda Peet (Jill St. Claire), Kevin Pollak (Lazlo Gogolak), Natasha Henstridge (Cynthia Oseransky). Directed by Howard Deutch and produced by Allan Kaufman, Arnold Rifkin, Elie Samaha, and David Willis. Screenplay by George Gallo.

A fog of gloom lowers over *The Whole Ten Yards*, as actors who know they're in a turkey try their best to prevail. We sense a certain desperation as dialogue mechanically grinds through unplayable scenes, and the characters arrive at moments that the movie thinks are funny but they suspect are not. This is one of those movies you look at quizzically: What did they think they were doing?

The movie is an unnecessary sequel to *The Whole Nine Yards* (2000), a movie in which many of the same actors sent completely different messages. "A subtle but unmistakable aura of jolliness sneaks from the screen," I wrote in my review of the earlier movie. "We suspect that the actors are barely suppressing giggles. This is the kind of standard material everyone could do in lockstep, but you sense inner smiles, and you suspect the actors are enjoying themselves."

The problem, I suspect, is that *The Whole Nine Yards* did everything that needed to be done with the characters, and did it well. Now the characters are back again, blinking in the footlights, embarrassed by their curtain call. The movie has the hollow, aimless aura of a beach resort in winter: The geography is the same, but the weather has turned ugly.

You will recall that the earlier film starred Bruce Willis as Jimmy "The Tulip" Tudeski, a professional hit man who has moved in next door to a Montreal dentist named Oz (Matthew Perry). The dentist's receptionist was Jill (Amanda Peet), a woman whose greatest ambition in life was to become a hit woman. Jimmy was in hiding from a Chicago gangster named Janni Gogolak (Kevin Pollak), who wanted him whacked.

In *The Whole Ten Yards,* Jimmy the Tulip and Jill are married and hiding out in Mexico, where Jill finds employment as a hit woman while Jimmy masquerades as a house-husband. That puts Willis in an apron and a head cloth during the early scenes, as if such a disguise would do anything other than call attention to him. Oz, meanwhile, has moved to Los Angeles and is married to Cynthia (Natasha Henstridge), who used to be married to the Tulip. (His first wife, played in the earlier movie by Rosanna Arquette with a hilarious French-Canadian accent, might have been useful here.)

Janni Gogolak was made dead by Oz and the Tulip in the first picture, but now his father, the crime boss Laszlo Gogolak, has been released from prison, and uses all of his power to find revenge against the two men; that fuels most of the plot, such as it is. Lazlo Gogolak is played by Kevin Pollak in one of the most singularly bad performances I have ever seen in a movie. It doesn't fail by omission, it fails by calling attention to its awfulness. His accent, his voice, his clothes, his clownish makeup, all conspire to create a character who brings the movie to a halt every time he appears on the screen. We stare in amazement, and I repeat: What did they think they were doing?

The movie's plot is without sense or purpose. It generates some action scenes that are supposed to be comic, but are not, for the inescapable reason that we have not the slightest interest in the characters and therefore even less interest in their actions. The movie is instructive in the way it demonstrates how a film can succeed or fail not only because of the mechanics of its screenplay, but because of the spirit of its making.

The Whole Nine Yards was not a particularly inspired project, but it was made with spirit and good cheer, and you felt the actors almost visibly expanding on the screen; Amanda Peet in particular seemed possessed. Here we see the actors all but contracting, as if to make themselves smaller targets for the camera. That there will never be a movie named *The Whole Eleven Yards* looks like a safe bet.

Wilbur Wants to Kill Himself ★ ★ ★ ½
R, 111 m., 2004

Jamie Sives (Wilbur), Adrian Rawlins (Harbour), Shirley Henderson (Alice), Lisa McKinlay (Mary), Mads Mikkelsen (Horst), Julia Davis (Moira). Directed by Lone Scherfig and produced by Sisse Graum Olsen. Screenplay by Scherfig and Anders Thomas Jensen.

It strikes a note of optimism, I suppose, that *Wilbur Wants to Kill Himself* is not titled *Wilbur Kills Himself.* Wilbur certainly tries desperately enough, with pills, gas, hanging, and teetering on the edge of a great fall. But he never quite succeeds. He is saved more than once by his brother, Harbour, and on another occasion by Alice, who interrupts his hanging attempt. By this point we begin to suspect that *Wilbur Wants to Kill Himself* is not about suicide at all, that Wilbur is destined for better things, and that despite its title this is a warm human comedy.

The movie takes place in Glasgow, that chill city where many views are dominated by the Necropolis, the Gothic cemetery on a hillside overlooking the town. Such a view must be a daily inspiration for Wilbur (Jamie Sives). He is, from time to time, a patient at a local psychiatric clinic, where the therapists seem to have limited their studies to viewings of *One Flew Over the Cuckoo's Nest*. His hopes depend on Harbour, who loves him, tries to save him from himself, and brings him home to live with him.

Harbour (Adrian Rawlins) runs the used book store left him by his father. It is a shabby but inviting place, its windows following the curve of the road, its stock in a jumble. There seems to be only one customer, a man who visits almost daily, demanding Kipling, and is invariably told that there must be some Kipling around here somewhere, but Harbour can't put his hands on it.

Another frequent visitor wants to sell, not buy. This is Alice, played by Shirley Henderson, that luminous actress from *Trainspotting, Bridget Jones's Diary, Topsy-Turvy*, and half a dozen others; do not be put off that she played Moaning Myrtle in *Harry Potter and the Chamber of Secrets*. She brings in books that were left behind by patients at the hospital where she works, but the books are really an excuse for seeing Harbour, with whom she feels a strange affinity; perhaps they met in earlier lives, since Rawlins played Harry Potter's father.

In no time at all Alice and Harbour have fallen in love. Alice and her daughter, Mary (Lisa McKinlay), bring order to the store, so that Kipling can easily be found, and then Alice and Harbour are married. That leads to rather cramped living conditions in the small flat above the store, where Wilbur is also established.

This doesn't add up to a lot of incident, but it occupies more than half the movie, because the director and cowriter, Lone Scherfig, loves human nature and would rather enjoy it than hurry it along with a plot. The pleasure of the movie is in spending time in the company of her characters, who are quirky and odd and very definite about themselves. There is also a certain amount of escapism involved, at least for somebody like me, who would rather run a used book store than do just about anything else except spend all my time in them.

Now then. The real heart of the movie involves events I do not want to even hint about. That's because they creep up on the characters so naturally, so gradually, that we should be as surprised as they are by how it all turns out. Let me say that the bleak comedy of Wilbur's early suicide attempts is replaced by the deepening of all of the characters, who are revealed as warm and kind and rather noble. The movie's ending is almost unreasonably happy, despite being technically sad, and the affection we feel for these characters is remarkable.

The filmmaker, Lone Scherfig, is a Danish woman whose first film, *Italian for Beginners*, was a Dogma comedy. That she was able to make a Dogma comedy tells you a great deal about her. Here she does away with the Dogma rules and makes a movie in the tradition of the Ealing comedies produced in England in the 1950s and early 1960s: modest slices of life about people who are very peculiar and yet lovable, and who do things we approve of in ways that appall us. The title may put you off, but don't let it. Here is a movie that appeals to the heart while not insulting the mind or forgetting how delightful its characters are.

The Wild Thornberrys Movie ★ ★ ★
PG, 80 m., 2002

With the voices of: Lacey Chabert (Eliza Thornberry), Tom Kane (Darwin the Monkey), Flea (Donnie Thornberry), Tim Curry (Nigel Thornberry), Jodi Carlisle (Marianne Thornberry), Danielle Harris (Debbie Thornberry), Alfre Woodard (Akela the Panther), Marisa Tomei (Bree Blackburn), Rupert Everett (Sloan Blackburn), Brenda Blethyn (Mrs. Fairgood), Melissa Greenspan (Sarah Wellington). Directed by Cathy Malkasian and Jeff McGrath and produced by Gabor Csupo and Arlene Klasky. Screenplay by Kate Boutilier.

The Wild Thornberrys Movie is a jolly surprise, an energetic and eccentric animated cartoon about a decidedly peculiar family making a documentary in Africa. They prowl the plains in their Winnebago, while Mom operates the camera, Dad lectures on nature, and young Eliza Thornberry talks to the animals.

Yes, by saving a tribal priest from a warthog, she has been given this gift on one condition—that she not tell anyone (human) about it. Surprisingly, or perhaps not, the animals are as intelligent and well-spoken as the humans.

The family is drawn in the cheerful, colorful

style of *Rugrats,* and indeed codirector Jeff Mc-Grath even worked on the *Rugrats* TV series. Cathy Malkasian, the top-billed codirector, has worked on everything from the *Jumanji* TV series to the Nickelodeon version of the *Thornberrys* itself.

Many kids will already know Eliza (voice by Lacey Chabert) and her family. Her parents, Nigel and Marianne (Tim Curry and Jodi Carlisle), are British, but Eliza is all-American, and her older sister Debbie (Danielle Harris) sounds like a Valley Girl ("That's *so* wrong," she says, confronted with the bright red hindquarters of an ape). Her younger stepbrother Donnie Thornberry (Flea, of the Red Hot Chili Peppers) speaks an unknown language incessantly. Eliza's best friend is Darwin the Monkey (Tom Kane), who sounds upper-class British and is an analyst of the passing scene.

Eliza and Darwin move fearlessly across the plain, protected by her ability to speak to the animals, and one day she convinces Akela the panther (Alfre Woodard) to let her take her three cubs to play. Alas, one of the cubs is snatched by poachers in a helicopter, setting up a thrilling adventure in which Eliza eventually saves an entire herd of elephants from extinction.

But, of course, the story I've described could be told in a dreary, plodding style. The charm of *The Wild Thornberrys Movie* comes from its zany visual style, the energy of the voice-over actors, and the fine balance of action that is thrilling but not too scary. Eliza is a plucky heroine, determined and brave, and the poachers never really have a chance.

There are other elements in the movie, including a trip to boarding school in England, not enjoyed by either Eliza or Darwin, and various innocent bathroom jokes, mostly involving animals; kids have a special fascination for such material, I guess, and here it's handled as tastefully as such tasteless material can be.

The movie reaches just a little further than we expect with the addition of characters such as Nigel Thornberry's parents (his mother is not amused to find worms in her tea) and the poachers Bree and Sloan Blackburn (Marisa Tomei and Rupert Everett), who are not simply villains willing to exterminate hundreds of elephants, but so unashamed about it that their attitude is scarier than their actions. Will such people stop at nothing? Next thing you know, they'll be permitting snowmobiles in our national parks.

Willard ★ ★ ½
PG-13, 100 m., 2003

Crispin Glover (Willard Stiles), R. Lee Ermey (Mr. Martin), Laura Elena Harring (Cathryn), Jackie Burroughs (Henrietta Stiles). Directed by Glen Morgan and produced by Morgan and James Wong. Screenplay by Morgan, based on a book by Gilbert Ralston.

You never know what a rat is going to do next, which is one of the big problems with rats. In *Willard,* you mostly do know what the rats are going to do next, which is a big problem with the film. That's because Willard is able to marshal his rats into disciplined groups that scurry off on missions on his behalf; he is the Dr. Dolittle of pest control.

Willard is a remake of the 1971 film, which was a surprise hit at the box office. My explanation at the time: People had been waiting a long time to see Ernest Borgnine eaten by rats and weren't about to miss the opportunity. This version looks better, moves faster, and is more artistic than the original film, but it doesn't work as a horror film—and since it is a horror film, that's fatal. It has attitude and a look, but the rats aren't scary.

Consider an early scene where Willard (Crispin Glover) goes down in the cellar after his mother complains of rat infestation. The fuse box blows and he's down to a flashlight, and this should be a formula for a scary scene (remember Ellen Burstyn in the attic with a candle in *The Exorcist*). But the scene isn't frightening—ever. The blowing of the fuse is scarier than anything else that happens in the basement.

The plot is essentially a remake of the earlier *Willard,* but with elements suggesting it is a sequel. A portrait that hangs in the family home, for example, shows Bruce Davison as Willard's father—and Davison, of course, was the original Willard. So hold on. If that Willard was this Willard's father, then that means that this Willard's mother (Jackie Burroughs) was that Willard's wife, and has become a shrew just like her mother-in-law, and young Willard still works for an evil man named Mr. Martin (R. Lee Ermey), which was the Borgnine character's name, so he must be Martin Jr. In the new movie, Willard's mom complains about rats in the cellar and Mr. Martin insults Willard and threatens his job, and the sins of the parents are visited on the sequel.

The best thing in the movie is Crispin Glover's performance. He affects dark, sunken eyes and a slight stoop, is very pale, and has one of those haircuts that shouts out: Look how gothic and miserable I am. There is real wit in the performance. And wit, too, in R. Lee Ermey's performance as the boss, which draws heavily on Ermey's real-life experience as a drill sergeant.

The human actors are okay, but the rodent actors (some real, some special effects) are like a prop that turns up on demand and behaves (or misbehaves) flawlessly. A few of the rats pop out: Socrates, Willard's choice for leader, and Ben, who is Ben's choice for leader. Ben is a very big rat (played, according to ominous information I found on the Web, "by an animal that is not a rat").

Laura Elena Harring, the brunette sex bomb from *Mulholland Dr.*, turns up as a worker in Willard's office who worries about him and even comes to his home to see if he's all right. My theory about why she likes him: He is the only man in a 100-mile radius who has never tried to pick her up. Willard is too morose and inward and Anthony Perkinsy. If they'd reinvented the movie as a character study, not so much about the rats as about Willard, they might have come up with something. Here the rats simply sweep across the screen in an animated tide, and instead of thinking, "Eek! Rats!" we're thinking about how it was done. That's not what you're supposed to be thinking about during a horror movie.

Win a Date with Tad Hamilton! ★ ★ ★
PG-13, 95 m., 2004

Kate Bosworth (Rosalee Futch), Topher Grace (Pete Monash), Josh Duhamel (Tad Hamilton), Gary Cole (Henry Futch), Ginnifer Goodwin (Cathy Feely), Nathan Lane (Richard Levy), Sean Hayes (Richard Levy). Directed by Robert Luketic and produced by Lucy Fisher and Douglas Wick. Screenplay by Victor Levin.

Here is a movie for people who haunt the aisles of the video stores searching for 1950s romances. I could have seen it at the Princess Theater in Urbana in 1959. Maybe I did. It's retro in every respect, a romantic comedy in a world so innocent that a lifetime is settled with a kiss. And because it embraces its innocence like a lucky charm, it works, for those willing to allow it. Others will respond with a horse laugh, and although I cannot quarrel with them, I do not share their sentiments.

Maybe it's something to do with Kate Bosworth's smile. She plays Rosalee Futch, a checkout clerk at the Piggly Wiggly in Fraser's Bottom, West Virginia. Her manager, whom she has known since they were children, is Pete Monash (Topher Grace). He loves her, but can't bring himself to tell her so. Then she wins a contest to have a date with Tad Hamilton (Josh Duhamel), a Hollywood star whose agent thinks his image could use a little touch-up after a supermarket tabloid photographs him speeding, drinking, letching, and littering all at the same time.

Well, of course Rosalee is ecstatic about the trip to L.A., the stretch limo, the suite at the W hotel, the expensive dinner date, and the moment when she teeters on the brink when Tad invites her to his home, and then says, gee ... you know, it's late and I have to fly home tomorrow. That she is a virgin goes without saying. What she can't anticipate is that Tad will follow her back to Fraser's Bottom, because there was something in her innocence, her freshness, her honesty, that appealed to an empty place deep inside him.

Within days he has purchased a house in West Virginia, taken her to dinner several times at the local diner, and made friends with her father, Henry (Gary Cole), who starts surfing Variety.com and wearing a Project Greenlight T-shirt.

As it happens, I'm reading *Anna Karenina* right now, and for some foolish reason Rosalee started to remind me of Kitty, the ingenue in the novel. She and a good man named Levin have long been in love, but she's swept off her feet by the sudden admiration of a snake named Vronsky, and rejects Levin when in fact her fate is to be his wife, and Vronsky's love is a mirage. Just today I read the charming pages where Levin and Kitty, too shy to speak their hearts, play a word game in order to find out if they have survived Vronsky with their love still intact. I was startled by how happy it made me when they got their answers right.

Win a Date with Tad Hamilton! could have had a similar effect, since there is a real possibility that Rosalee will wed the slick Tad instead of the steady Pete. But it doesn't have that kind of impact because of a crucial misjudgment in the screenplay and casting.

To begin with, Josh Duhamel is more appealing than Topher Grace—maybe not in life, but certainly in this movie, where he seems sincere within the limits of his ability, while the store manager always seems to have a pebble in his shoe.

And then the movie devotes much more screen time to Rosalee and Tad than to Rosalee and Pete—so much more that even though we know the requirements of the formula, we expect it to be broken with a marriage to Tad. And yet—what is the function of Pete, within the closed economy of a screenplay, except to be the hometown boy she should marry?

You can guess for yourself (very easily) what decision she finally comes to, but let me observe that the courtship between Rosalee and Tad is charming, warm, cute, and applaudable, and that Pete spends a great deal of time grumping about in the store office and making plans to go off to Richmond and become a business major. In 1959, or any other year, a movie like this would have known enough to make Tad into more of a slickster. There is the strangest feeling at the end of the film that Rosalee might have made the wrong choice.

That imbalance at least has the benefit of giving a formula movie more suspense than it deserves. And I liked it, too, for the way it played Tad and Hollywood more or less straight, instead of diving into wretched excess. The dream date is handled with lots of little touches that will warm the innards of PG-13 females in the audience, and the movie wants to be gentle, not raucous in its comedy. Kate Bosworth holds it all together with a sweetness that is beyond calculation.

Note: That leaves just one other elbow sticking out of the sack. Tad's agent and manager, played by Nathan Lane and Sean Hayes and both named Richard Levy, are so over the top that they break the mood in their scenes. For Lane, Win a Date represents yet another peculiar career choice in the movies, a medium where he is successful mostly when heard but not seen, as voice-over talent. To be sure, this isn't the suicidal career move of his decision to play Jacqueline Susann's husband in Isn't She Great, but as roles go, it's thankless. Here's the highest-priced Broadway star of his generation, and what's he doing in this little role, anyway?

Windtalkers ★ ★

R, 133 m., 2002

Nicolas Cage (Sergeant Joe Enders), Adam Beach (Private Ben Yahzee), Roger Willie (Private Charles Whitehorse), Christian Slater (Sergeant Peter "Ox" Henderson), Peter Stormare (Sergeant Eric "Gunny" Hjelmstad), Noah Emmerich (Corporal Charles "Chick" Rogers), Mark Ruffalo (Pappas), Brian Van Holt (Harrigan), Martin Henderson (Nellie). Directed by John Woo and produced by Terence Chang, Tracie Graham, Alison Rosenzweig, and Woo. Screenplay by John Rice and Joe Batteer.

Windtalkers comes advertised as the saga of how Navajo Indians used their language to create an unbreakable code that helped win World War II in the Pacific. That's a fascinating, little-known story and might have made a good movie. Alas, the filmmakers have buried it beneath battlefield clichés, while centering the story on a white character played by Nicolas Cage. I was reminded of *Glory,* the story of heroic African-American troops in the Civil War, which was seen through the eyes of their white commanding officer. Why does Hollywood find it impossible to trust minority groups with their own stories?

The film stars Nicolas Cage as an Italian-American sergeant who is so gung ho his men look at him as if he's crazy. Maybe he is. After defending a position past the point of all reason, he survives bloody carnage, is patched up in Hawaii, and returns to action in a battle to take Saipan, a key stepping-stone in the Pacific war. In this battle he is assigned as the personal watchdog of Private Ben Yahzee (Adam Beach), an almost saintly Navajo. Sergeant Ox Henderson (Christian Slater) is paired with Private Charles Whitehorse (Roger Willie), another Indian. What the Navajos don't know is that the bodyguards have been ordered to kill them, if necessary, to keep them from falling into enemy hands. The code must be protected at all costs.

This is a chapter of history not widely known, and for that reason alone the film is useful. But the director, Hong Kong action expert John Woo, has less interest in the story than in the pyrotechnics, and we get way, way, way too much footage of bloody battle scenes, intercut with thin dialogue scenes that rely on exhausted formulas. We know almost without asking, for example, that one of the white soldiers will be a racist, that another will be a by-the-books commanding officer, that there will be a plucky nurse who believes in the Cage character, and a scene in which a Navajo saves the life of the man who hates him. Henderson and White-horse perform duets for the harmonica and Navajo flute, a nice idea, but their characters are so sketchy it doesn't mean much.

The battle sequences are where Woo's heart lies, and he is apparently trying to one-up *Saving Private Ryan, We Were Soldiers,* and the other new entries in the ultraviolent, unapologetically realistic battle film sweepstakes. Alas, the battles in *Windtalkers* play more like a video game. Although Woo is Asian, he treats the enemy Japanese troops as pop-up targets, a faceless horde of screaming maniacs who run headlong into withering fire. Although Americans take heavy casualties (there is a point at which we assume everyone in the movie will be killed), the death ratio is about thirty to one against the Japanese. Since they are defending dug-in positions and the Americans are often exposed, this seems unlikely.

The point of the movie is that the Navajos are able to use their code in order to radio information, call in strikes, and allow secret communication. In the real war, I imagine, this skill was most useful in long-range strategic radio communication. *Windtalkers* devotes minimal time to the code talkers, however, and when they do talk, it's to phone in coordinates for an air strike against big Japanese guns. Since these guns cannot be moved before airplanes arrive, a call in English would have had about the same effect. That Woo shows the Windtalkers in the heat of battle is explained, I think, because he wants to show everything in the heat of battle. The wisdom of assigning two precious code talkers to a small group of frontline

soldiers in a deadly hand-to-hand fight situation seems questionable, considering there are only 400 Navajos in the Pacific theater.

The Indians are seen one-dimensionally as really nice guys. The only character of any depth is Cage's Sergeant Enders, who seems to hover between shell shock and hallucinatory flashbacks. There is a final scene between Enders and Yahzee, the Navajo, that reminded me of the male bonding in other Woo movies, in which you may have to shoot the other guy to prove how much you love him. But since the movie has labored to kill off all the supporting characters and spare only the stars, we are in the wrong kind of suspense: Instead of wondering which of these people will survive, we wonder which way the picture will jump in retailing war-movie formulas.

There is a way to make a good movie like *Windtalkers,* and that's to go the indie route. A low-budget Sundance-style picture would focus on the Navajo characters, their personalities and issues. The moment you decide to make *Windtalkers,* a big-budget action movie with a major star and lots of explosions, flying bodies and stuntmen, you give up any possibility that it can succeed on a human scale. The Navajo code talkers have waited a long time to have their story told. Too bad it appears here merely as a gimmick in an action picture.

Winged Migration ★ ★ ★
G, 89 m., 2003

A documentary directed by Jacques Perrin and produced by Christophe Barratier and Perrin. Screenplay by Stéphane Durand and Perrin.

Jacques Perrin's Oscar-nominated *Winged Migration* does for birds what the 1996 documentary *Microcosmos* did for insects: It looks at them intimately, very close up, in shots that seem impossible to explain. That the two plots intersect (birds eat insects) is just one of those things.

The movie, which is awesome to regard, is not particularly informative; it tells us that birds fly south in the winter (unless they live in the Southern Hemisphere, in which case they fly north), that they fly many hundreds or thousands of miles, and that they navigate by the stars, the sun, Earth's gravitational field, and familiar landmarks. These facts are widely known, and the movie's sparse narration tells us little else.

But facts are not the purpose of *Winged Migration*. It wants to allow us to look, simply look, at birds—and that goal it achieves magnificently. There are sights here I will not easily forget. The film opens and closes with long aerial tracking shots showing birds in long-distance flight into the wind, and we realize how very hard it is to fly a thousand miles or more. We see birds stopping to eat (one slides a whole fish down its long neck). We see them feeding their young. We see them courting and mating, and going through chest-thumping rituals that are serious business, if you are a bird. We see cranes locking bills in what looks like play. We see birds trapped in industrial waste. And in a horrifying scene, a bird with a broken wing tries to escape on a sandy beach, but cannot elude the crabs that catch it and pile onto the still-living body, all eager for a bite. In nature, as the film reminds us, life is all about getting enough to eat.

How in the world did they get this footage? Lisa Nesselson, *Variety*'s correspondent in Paris, supplies helpful information. To begin with, 225 feet of film were exposed for every foot that got into the movie. And some of the birds were raised to be the stars of the film; they were exposed to the sounds of airplanes and movie cameras while still in the shell, and greeted upon their arrival in the world by crew members. (We remember from *Fly Away Home* that newborn birds assume that whoever they see upon emerging must be a parent.)

Some footage was made with cameras in ultralight aircraft. Other shots were taken from hot air balloons. There are shots in which the birds seem to have been scripted—they move toward the camera as it pulls back. And some scenes, I'm afraid, that were manufactured entirely in the editing room, as when we see snowbirds growing alarmed, we hear an avalanche, and then cut to long shots of the avalanche and matching shots of the birds in flight. Somehow we know the camera was not in the path of the avalanche.

I am pleased, actually, that the film has such a tilt toward the visual and away from information. I wouldn't have wanted the narrator to drone away in my ear, reading me encyclopedia articles and making sentimental comments about the beauty of it all. Life is a hard business, and birds work full-time at it. I was shocked by a sequence showing ducks in magnificent flight against the sky, and then dropping one by one as hunters kill them. The birds have flown exhaustingly for days to arrive at this end. It's not so much that I blame the hunters as that I wish the ducks could shoot back.

With All Deliberate Speed ★ ★ ★
NO MPAA RATING, 110 m., 2004

As themselves: Julian Bond, Rev. Joe DeLaine, Barbara Johns, Vernon Jordan, Thurgood Marshall Jr., E. Barrett Prettyman. Re-creating the words of historical figures: Alicia Keys, Mekhi Pfifer, Larenz Tate, Joe Morton, and Terry Kinney. Directed by Peter Gilbert and produced by Gilbert.

On May 17, 1954, the Supreme Court ruled unanimously that "separate but equal" could no longer be the rule of the land. Its decision in the case of *Brown vs. Board of Education* ended segregated schools and opened the door for a wide range of reforms guaranteeing equal rights not only to African-Americans but also, in the years to come, to women, the handicapped, and (more slowly) homosexuals. The decision was a heroic milestone in American history, but it was marred, this new documentary says, by four fateful words: "with all deliberate speed."

Those words were a loophole that allowed some southern communities to delay equal rights for years and even decades; the last county to integrate finally did so only in 1970. And there was the notorious case of Prince Edward County, Virginia, which closed its schools for five years rather than integrate them. Most people alive today were born after *Brown* and take its reforms for granted. But *With All Deliberate Speed*, the documentary by *Hoop Dreams* producer Peter Gilbert, doesn't end on May 17, 1954. It continues on to the present day, noting that many of America's grade and secondary schools are as segregated now as they were fifty years ago.

The most valuable task of the film is to re-create the historic legal struggles that led to *Brown*, and to remember heroes who have been almost forgotten by history. Chief among them is Charles Houston, who was the first African-American on the editorial board of the *Harvard Law Review*. As dean of the Howard University law school, he was the mentor for a generation of black legal scholars and activists who would transform their society. Although he died in 1950, before *Brown* became law, it was his protégé Thurgood Marshall who argued the case before the Supreme Court, and later became the first African-American on the court.

It was Houston, the film says, who shaped the legal groundwork for *Brown*, arguing in the 1930s and 1940s that "separate but equal" could not, by its very nature, be equal. He helped convince the NAACP to mount legal challenges against segregation, and Marshall led the organization's legal efforts from 1940 onward. The film talks with the descendants of Houston and Marshall, and with many of the law clerks, now elderly, who as young men served the justices who handed down the landmark decision.

It also recalls the crucial role of Chief Justice Earl Warren in guiding his fellow justices toward what he felt had to be a unanimous decision. The previous chief justice, Fred Vincent, had little enthusiasm for such a controversial ruling. When he died, President Dwight Eisenhower appointed the former California governor Warren as chief justice; Justice Felix Frankfurter famously told his clerk that the death of Vincent "showed there is a God." So hated was *Brown* in some right-wing circles that an Impeach Earl Warren campaign continued throughout his term.

The film also tracks down some of the children involved in the first crucial cases, such as Barbara Johns of Prince Edward County. And it brings belated recognition to another hero of the time, the Reverend Joe DeLaine of Summerton County, South Carolina, who led the legal struggle against a system that required many black students to walk seven miles each way to school. His church was burned, his home was fired on, he was forced to flee the South, and only in October 2000, twenty-six years after his death, were charges against him cleared by the state.

Gilbert, of course, has no audio or video footage of the arguments before the Supreme Court, but he uses an interesting technique: He employs actors to read from the words of Thurgood Marshall and his chief opponent, the patrician John W. Davis. And he does a good job of recapturing the 1954 impact of the decision—with which, he notes, Eisenhower at first privately disagreed, although Ike later came around, and sent federal troops to enforce integration in the late 1950s.

What is the legacy of *Brown*? It's here that Gilbert's film is most challenging. It observes that while many communities have truly integrated schools, patterns of residential segregation in many areas have resulted in schools where the students are almost entirely of one race. He talks with blacks and whites who are in a tiny minority in their schools, and listens to discussions of race by today's high school students. And in reunions held today, he gathers students, now grown, who were at the center of the original case, and hears their memories of what it was like then and what it is like now. America moves imperfectly toward the goal of equality, but because of *Brown*, it moves.

A Woman Is a Woman ★ ★
NO MPAA RATING, 84 m., 1961 (rereleased 2003)

Anna Karina (Angela Recamier), Jean-Paul Belmondo (Alfred Lubitsch), Jean-Claude Brialy (Émile Récamier), Marie Dubois (Angela's Friend), Jeanne Moreau (Woman in Bar). Directed by Jean-Luc Godard and produced by Georges de Beauregard and Carlo Ponti. Screenplay by Godard.

A Woman Is a Woman was Jean-Luc Godard's second feature, made in 1961 close on the heels of *Breathless* (1960). "It was my first real film," he has said, but a statement by Godard is always suspect and in this case is plain wrong: *Breathless* was his first real film, a masterpiece, and *A Woman Is a Woman* is slight and sometimes wearisome.

The movie stars Godard's wife, Anna Karina, who was to achieve her own greatness in his next film, the wonderful *My Life to Live*. Here she plays a completely improbable character, a stripper who comes home to her yuppie boyfriend and tells him she wants a baby. Surely no strip club in movie history has been more genteel and less sleazy than the one she works in, where the women walk idly up and down between rows of tables where clients smoke, and look, and nurse their drinks. Their five-minute stint over, the girls say good-bye all around and return to the street, free spirits.

Angela Récamier is her name, and Jean-Claude Brialy plays Émile Récamier, but the movie strongly suggests they are not married. Nor does Émile want a baby, although his friend Alfred Lubitsch (Jean-Paul Belmondo) would be happy to impregnate her. Naming the Belmondo character after Lubitsch is one of the movie's countless cinematic in-jokes; there is even a moment when Belmondo runs into Jeanne Moreau and asks her, "How is *Jules and Jim* coming along?" And another where he smiles broadly at the camera, in tribute both to Burt Lancaster and to the fact that he did the same thing in *Breathless*.

The movie, which comes advertised as Godard's tribute to the Hollywood musical, is not a musical, and indeed treats music with some contempt, filling the sound track with brief bursts of music that resemble traditional movie scoring, but then interrupting them arbitrarily. It contains other moments designed to suggest the director calling attention to his control of his materials, including the device of having the same couple kissing in a street alcove in shot after shot.

There is, although, one sequence, showing the mastery of technique by Godard and his editor, Agnes Guillemot. Angela is shown a photograph that Alfred claims shows Émile cheating on her with another woman. As she studies the photo, the movie cuts from her face to his face to the photo, and then again and again. Sometimes there is a little dialogue. The photo keeps reappearing on the screen. The effect is to suggest the way she becomes obsessed with the hurtful image and can't stop thinking about it, and as a visual evocation of jealousy, it's kind of brilliant.

But the film itself, at eighty-four minutes, is overlong, a minor chapter in an early career. It has been carefully restored for this theatrical rerelease. The print showcases the wide-screen cinematography of Raoul Coutard, and we can see here stylistic choices that would become omnipresent in the films to come: the use of big printed words on the screen, the use of bold basic colors, and the use of books as objects that embody their titles (in one cute moment,

Angela and Émile aren't speaking, and hold up books with titles that indicate what they want to say). The movie is bright and lively, but too precious, and Godard would soon make much better ones.

Wonderland ★ ★
R, 99 m., 2003

Val Kilmer (John Holmes), Lisa Kudrow (Sharon Holmes), Kate Bosworth (Dawn Schiller), Dylan McDermott (David Lind), Josh Lucas (Ron Launius), Franky G (Louis Cruz), Tim Blake Nelson (Billy Deverell), Carrie Fisher (Sallie Hansen), Eric Bogosian (Eddie Nash). Directed by James Cox and produced by Michael Paseornek and Holly Wiersma. Screenplay by Cox, Captain Mauzner, Todd Samovitz, and D. Loriston Scott.

One of the things that make police work in Los Angeles tricky, Vincent Bugliosi says, is that anyone is likely to know anyone else. In other cities social connections are more predictable. A cop who knows who you are, where you live, and how you work has a pretty good idea who you are likely to know. But drugs, sex, and showbiz act like L.A. wormholes, connecting the famous with the obscure. John Holmes, for example, was a porn star who became addicted to cocaine, and told his dopehead friends that Eddie Nash, a nightclub owner, kept a lot of money in his house. The dopeheads broke into Nash's house and took money and jewelry. Not long after, Holmes unwisely arrived at Nash's house and was beaten until he told Nash about the dopeheads. Holmes then allegedly helped Nash's bodyguards enter the house at 8763 Wonderland Avenue in the Hollywood Hills, where the dopeheads lived. Four of them were murdered, leaving the most horrifying crime scene one of the arriving cops had ever witnessed. The police eventually linked Holmes to the murders through the testimony of Scott Thorson, Liberace's lover, who saw Holmes being beaten.

And just to complete the circle, I got this information from charliemanson.com, no relation to the cult leader. I was looking it up because at the end of *Wonderland* I had no clear idea of what had happened, except that Holmes was apparently the connection. Perhaps because Eddie Nash is still alive and was acquitted on the murder charges after two trials, the movie never comes right out and says that he sent his men to commit the murders. The interior logic of the movie says he must have, but that's not actionable. To obscure a possible libel, or for artistic reasons, or both, the movie tells the story in the style of *Rashomon,* moving back and forth through time and using contradictory stories so that we think first one version and then another is the truth.

Rashomon was told with great clarity; we were always sure whose version we were seeing, and why. *Wonderland* is told through a bewildering tap dance on the time line, with lots of subtitles that say things like "four months earlier" or "July 1, 1981." There are so many of these titles, and the movie's chronology is so shuffled, that they become more frustrating than helpful. The titles, of course, reflect the version of the facts they introduce, so that a given event might or might not have happened "three weeks later."

Actors separated from chronology have their work cut out for them. A performance can't build if it starts at the end and circles in both directions toward the beginning. Yet Val Kilmer is convincing as John Holmes, especially when he pinballs from one emotion to another; we see him charming, ugly, self-pitying, paranoid, and above all in need of a fix. Holmes, acting under the name "Johnny Wadd," made a thousand hard-core pornos (according to this movie) or more than 2,500 (according to the Website). But by the time of the action, drugs have replaced sex as his obsession and occupation, and Kilmer does a good job of showing how an addict is always really thinking about only one thing.

Holmes is essentially just a case study: not interesting, not significant, not evocative. Nash (Eric Bogosian) is even less dimensional, existing completely in terms of his function in the plot. The human interest in the movie centers entirely on two women: Dawn Schiller (Kate Bosworth), Holmes's teenybopper girlfriend, and Sharon Holmes (Lisa Kudrow), his wife. Why either of these women wants to have anything to do with Holmes is a mystery, although Dawn perhaps somewhere in her confused reverie thinks of him as a star, and Sharon still cares for him despite having moved on to a set-tled, respectable lifestyle. Maybe she remembers a boy she was trying to save.

The movie is tantalizing in the way it denies us more information about the Dawn-Sharon-Holmes triangle. The two women are on good terms with each other (and are friends to this day, I learn); sexual jealousy seems beside the point when your man is the busiest porn star in history. At one point Holmes actually informs incredulous cops that he wants to go into the witness protection program with *both* women. Kudrow's performance is the most intriguing in the movie, and when she goes face-to-face with Holmes and coldly rejects his appeals for help, we guess maybe he needs her because she's the only adult in his life.

Parts of this story, much altered, have been told already in Paul Thomas Anderson's incomparably better film *Boogie Nights* (1997). Dirk Diggler (Mark Wahlberg) was the Holmes character there, and Heather Graham's Rollergirl is, I guess, something like Dawn. True crime procedurals can have a certain fascination, but not when they're jumbled glimpses of what might or might not have happened involving a lot of empty people whose main claim to fame is that they're dead.

World Traveler ★ ★
R, 104 m., 2002

Billy Crudup (Cal), Julianne Moore (Dulcie), Cleavant Derricks (Carl), David Keith (Richard), Mary McCormack (Margaret), James LeGros (Jack), Liane Balaban (Meg), Karen Allen (Delores). Directed by Bart Freundlich and produced by Tim Perell and Freundlich. Screenplay by Freundlich.

Cal drags a woman out of a bar to look at the stars and listen to his rants about the universe. She pulls loose and asks, "Do you get away with this crap because you look like that?" Later in the film two kids will ask him if he's a movie star. He's good-looking, in a morose, tormented way, but it's more than that; Cal is charismatic, and strangers are fascinated by his aura of doom and emptiness.

There is another new movie, *About a Boy,* with a hero who complains that he's a "blank." The dialogue is needed in *World Traveler.* Although others are fascinated by Cal's loneliness, his drinking, his lack of a plan, his superficial charm, he is a blank. Early in the film he walks out on his marriage, on the third birthday of his son. Taking the family station wagon, he drives west across the United States and into the emptiness of his soul.

Cal is played by Billy Crudup, one of the best actors in the movies, but there needs to be something *there* for an actor to play, and Cal is like a moony poet who embraces angst as its own reward. Throwing back Jack Daniels in the saloons of the night, he doesn't have a complaint so much as he celebrates one. When we discover that his own father walked out on Cal and his mother, that reads like an motivation but doesn't play like one. It seems too neat—the Creative Writing explanation for his misery.

The film, written and directed by Bart Freundlich, is a road picture, with Cal meeting and leaving a series of other lonely souls without ever achieving closure. It's as if he glimpses them through the windows of his passing car. There's a young hitchhiker who implies an offer of sex, which he doesn't accept. A construction worker named Carl (Cleavant Derricks), who wants friendship and thinks Cal offers it, but is mistaken. A high school classmate (James LeGros, bitingly effective), who provides us with evidence that Cal has been an emotional hit-and-run artist for a long time. Finally there is Dulcie (Julianne Moore), who is drunk and passed out in a bar.

Cal throws her over his shoulder and hauls her back to his motel room to save her from arrest. She involves him in her own madness. Both sense they're acting out interior dramas from obscure emotional needs, and there is a slo-mo scene on a carnival ride that plays like a parody of a good time. Nelson Algren advised, "Never sleep with a woman whose troubles are greater than your own," and Cal would be wise to heed him.

There are moments of sudden truth in the film; Freundlich, who also made *The Myth of Fingerprints* (1998), about an almost heroically depressed family at Thanksgiving, can create and write characters, even if he doesn't always know where to take them.

The construction buddy Carl and his wife (Mary McCormack) spring into focus with a few lines of dialogue. Cal persuades Carl, a recovering alcoholic, to get drunk with him and help him pick up two women in a bar. The next day Carl says his wife is angry at him, and brings her to life with one line of dialogue: "She's mad about the drinking—and the objectification of women." Later, drunk again, Cal meets Carl's wife, who says, "In all the years I've been married to Carl, I've never heard him talk about anyone the way he talks about you." She loves Carl, we see, so much she is moved that he has found a friend. But then Cal tries to make a pass, and the wife looks cold and level at him: "You're not his friend."

Cal isn't anybody's friend. Near the end of his journey, in the western mountains, he meets his father (David Keith). The role is thankless, but Keith does everything possible, and more, to keep the father from being as much a cipher as the son. One senses in *World Traveler* and in his earlier film that Freundlich bears a grievous but obscure complaint against fathers, and circles it obsessively, without making contact.

X

X2: X-Men United ★ ★ ★
PG-13, 124 m., 2003

Patrick Stewart (Charles Xavier), Hugh Jackman (Wolverine), Ian McKellen (Magneto), Halle Berry (Storm), Famke Janssen (Dr. Jean Grey), James Marsden (Cyclops), Rebecca Romijn-Stamos (Mystique), Brian Cox (General William Stryker), Alan Cumming (Nightcrawler), Shawn Ashmore (Iceman), Aaron Stanford (Pyro), Kelly Hu (Yuriko Oyama), Anna Paquin (Rogue). Directed by Bryan Singer and produced by Lauren Shuler Donner and Ralph Winter. Screenplay by Michael Dougherty and Daniel P. Harris, based on the story by David Hayter, Zak Penn, and Singer and the comic books and characters by Stan Lee.

X2: X-Men United is the kind of movie you enjoy for its moments, even though they never add up. Made for (and possibly by) those with short attention spans, it lives in the present, providing one amazing spectacle after another, and not even trying to develop a story arc. Having trained on the original *X-Men* (2000), I tried to experience the film entirely in the present, and the fact is, I had a good time. Dumb, but good.

Like the comic books that inspired it, *X2* begins with the premise that mutant heroes with specialized superpowers exist among us. Name the heroes, assign the powers, and you're ready for perfunctory dialogue leading up to a big two-page spread in which sleek and muscular beings hurtle through dramatic showdowns.

Like all the characters in the Marvel Comics stable, the X-Men have psychological or political problems; in the first movie, they were faced with genocide, and in this one their right to privacy is violated with the Mutant Registration Act. Of course, there will be audience members who believe mutants should have no rights, and so *X2* provides a valuable civics lesson. (How you register a mutant who can teleport or shape-shift is not explained.)

Perhaps not coincidentally, the movie has a president who looks remarkably like George W. Bush. The film opens with one of its best scenes, as a creature with a forked tail attacks the White House and whooshes down corridors and careens off walls while the Secret Service fires blindly. The creature's purpose is apparently to give mutants a bad name, inspiring still more laws undermining their rights.

Despite all of the havoc and carnage of the first film, just about everybody is back for the sequel. Amazing that they weren't all killed. Charles Xavier (Patrick Stewart) still runs his private school for young mutants, Magneto (Ian McKellen) still plots against him, and there is a new villain named General William Stryker (Brian Cox), who is assigned by the government to deal with the mutant threat and uses the turncoat mutant Yuriko (Kelly Hu) on his team.

The principal mutants are, in credits order, Wolverine (Hugh Jackman), who has blades that extend from his knuckles; Storm (Halle Berry), who can control the weather; Dr. Jean Grey (Famke Janssen), whose power of telekinesis is growing stronger; Cyclops (James Marsden), whose eyes shoot laser beams; Mystique (Rebecca Romijn-Stamos), a shape shifter whose shapes are mostly delightful; Nightcrawler (Alan Cumming), the teleporter who attacked the White House; Iceman (Shawn Ashmore), who can cool your drink and lots of other things; Pyro (Aaron Stanford), who can hurl flames but needs a pilot light; and Rogue (Anna Paquin), who can take on aspects of the personalities around her.

These superpowers are so oddly assorted that an X-Man adventure is like a game of chess where every piece has a different move. Some of the powers are awesome; Storm stops an aerial pursuit by generating tornadoes with her mental powers, and Dr. Jean Grey is able to restart an airplane in midair.

Odd, then, that Wolverine is one of the dominant characters even though his X-Acto knuckles seem pretty insignificant compared to the powers of Pyro or Cyclops. In a convention borrowed from martial arts movies, *X2* pairs up characters with matching powers, so that when Wolverine has his titanic battle, it's with an enemy also equipped with blades. What would happen if Pyro and Iceman went head to head? I visualize the two of them in a pool of hot water.

One might reasonably ask what threat could

possibly be meaningful to mutants with such remarkable powers, but Magneto, who has serious personal issues with mutants, has devised an invention that I will not describe, except to say that it provides some of the movie's best visuals. I also admired the scene where Dr. Jean Grey saves the X-Men's airplane, and the way Famke Janssen brings drama to the exercise of Grey's power instead of just switching it on and off.

Since the earliest days of *Spider-Man,* Marvel heroes have had personal problems to deal with, and there's a classic Stan Lee moment here in the scene where Iceman breaks the news to his parents that he is a mutant. The movie treats the dialogue as a coming-out scene, halfseriously, as if providing inspiration for reallife parents and their children with secrets.

Other possibilities are left for future installments. There's a romance in the movie between Rogue and Iceman, but it doesn't exploit the possibilities of love between mutants with incompatible powers. How inconvenient if during sex your partner was accidentally teleported, frozen, slashed, etc. Does Cyclops wear his dark glasses to bed?

X2: X-Men United lacks a beginning, a middle, and an end, and exists more as a selfrenewing loop. In that, it is faithful to comic books themselves, which month after month and year after year seem frozen in the same fictional universe. Yes, there are comics in which the characters age and their worlds change, but the X-Men seem likely to continue forever, demonstrating their superpowers in one showcase scene after another. Perhaps in the next generation a mutant will appear named Scribbler, who can write a better screenplay for them.

XXX ★ ★ ★ ½
PG-13, 124 m., 2002

Vin Diesel (Xander Cage), Samuel L. Jackson (NSA Agent Gibbons), Asia Argento (Yelena), Marton Csokas (Yorgi), Joe Bucaro III (Virg), TeeJay Boyce (Janelle). Directed by Rob Cohen and produced by Neal H. Moritz. Screenplay by Rich Wilkes.

XXX stars Vin Diesel as a smart-ass Bond with a bad attitude. The filmmakers have broken down the James Bond series into its inevitable components, constructed a screenplay that rips off 007 even in the small details, and then placed Diesel at the center of it—as Xander Cage, extreme sports hero and outlaw. In its own punk way, *XXX* is as good as a good Bond movie, and that's saying something.

Diesel is a tough guy with the shaved head, the tattoos, and the throwaway one-liners (after he's busted for stealing a car and driving it off a bridge, he says, "It was only a Corvette"). In last summer's *The Fast and the Furious,* he hurtled cars down city streets in death-defying races. As we meet him in *XXX,* he's a famous sports daredevil who steals computer chips and cars and is finally hunted down by Gibbons (Samuel L. Jackson), a National Security Agency spymaster with a scarred face and a role inspired by M in the Bond series.

If Bond is a patriot, Xander is a man who looks out only for No. 1, until Gibbons threatens him with prison unless he agrees to go to the Czech Republic and stop a madman with, yes, a plan to destroy and/or conquer the world. This villain, named Yorgi (Marton Csokas), apparently lives in the Prague Castle, which will come as a surprise to President Vaclav Havel. He's a renegade officer of the evil Czech Secret Service; the movie doesn't seem to know that the Cold War is over and Czechs are good guys these days, but never mind: The movie was shot on location in Prague, part of the current filmmaking boom in the republic, and the scenery is terrific.

Director Rob Cohen and producer Neal H. Moritz, who also made *The Fast and the Furious,* follow the Bond formula so carefully this would be a satire if it weren't intended as homage. We click off the 007 checkpoints: (1) villain in lair hidden within mountain, with faceless minions busily going about tasks; (2) a beautiful girl, former KGB, named Yelena (Asia Argento), who seems to be Yorgi's girlfriend but falls for Xander; (3) a techno-geek who supplies Xander with a trick gun and a customized GTO that has an arsenal onboard; (4) stunts involving parachuting, mountains, avalanches, and explosions; (5) a chase at the end to save the world; and (6), my favorite, the obligatory final scene where the hero basks in

Bora Bora with the beautiful girl in a bikini, while his boss tries to convince him to take another job.

Will he take another job? Of course he will. Xander Cage is a new franchise, and Vin Diesel, who was walking around Sundance a few years ago telling everyone he would someday be a big star, was right.

I love the lengths that villains go to in these movies. Consider Yorgi. He has devised an incredibly expensive steel speedboat armed with three rockets containing canisters of poison gas. This speedboat is inside a mountain cavern far below his lair. It is his superweapon for world domination. Fine, except where can a boat go in the landlocked Czech Republic? Down the Danube through Budapest and Vienna? In the event, he decides to attack Prague itself, and we're wondering: Considering how much it cost him to hollow out the mountain and build the boat, why not just put the gas canisters in a car and drive into town? Yorgi is the kind of bad guy who is beloved by the architects of the *Star Wars* defense, staging an attack that is cumbersome, costly, and visible, instead of just delivering the goods by FedEx.

As the boat speeds down the river into town, Xander does a stunt that is not only exciting but, even better, impossible. As the Russian babe pilots the GTO on a road parallel to the river, Xander fires a steel cable that attaches to the boat, and then he transfers from the car to the boat using the cable and a parasail. Wonderful, except . . . do you suppose there are any lampposts, traffic lights, or telephone poles along the road that the cable might get hung up on?

Never mind. Now Xander's onboard, trying to disarm the canisters by using a slicked-up cyber-version of the old standby where he has to decide between the green wire and the red wire. Meanwhile, Gibbons has a vantage point on one of the bridges, and is commanding fighter planes that are prepared to blast the boat out of the water, no doubt thereby dispersing the poison gas, but *c'est la vie.*

See, I like all this stuff, at least when it's done well. Vin Diesel's gruff, monosyllabic style is refreshing as a counterpoint to the gung-ho action, and the romantic scenes with the beautiful Yelena consist of two (2) kisses, because Xander has a world to save. The music

is aggressive heavy metal by the German band Rammstein, and Marton Csokas, as the villain, has one of those fleshy, sneering faces, surrounded by too much greasy hair, that goes with his central European accent. Oddly, he isn't from Transylvania at all, but from New Zealand, and you may have seen him on *Xena*. He likes to play opposite characters with X-names.

Is *XXX* a threat to the Bond franchise? Not a threat so much as a salute. I don't want James Bond to turn crude and muscular on me; I like the suave style. But I like Xander, too, especially since he seems to have studied Bond so very carefully. Consider the movie's big set-piece, totally in the 007 tradition, when Xander parachutes to a mountain top, surveys the bad guys on skimobiles below, throws a grenade to start an avalanche, and then outraces the avalanche on a snowboard while the bad guys are wiped out. Not bad. Now all he has to work on is the kissing.

XX/XY ★ ★ ★ ½
R, 91 m., 2003

Mark Ruffalo (Coles Burroughs), Kathleen Robertson (Thea), Maya Stange (Sam), Petra Wright (Claire), David Thornton (Miles). Directed by Austin Chick and produced by Isen Robbins and Aimee Schoof. Screenplay by Chick.

XX/XY portrays a man that many women will recognize on sight. Coles is like a social climber at a party, always looking past the woman he's with to see if a more perfect woman has just appeared. Women know his type, and sometimes, because he is smart and charming, they go along with the routine. But they're not fooled. Late in the film, when Coles finally tries to commit himself, a woman tells him, "You still haven't chosen me. You're settling for me."

As the film opens in the autumn of 1993, Coles (Mark Ruffalo) is studying film at Sarah Lawrence College. One night at a party he meets Sam (Maya Stange), and asks her, "Would you think I was being too forward if I said, 'Let's go back to your room?'" Her reply: "What would you say if I said, 'Let's go back to my room, but let's bring Thea?'" This was not what he had in mind, but openness to experimentation is obligatory for all Sarah Lawrence students, and besides, Thea (Kathleen Robertson) is intriguing in her outsider rebel way.

What follows is a kinduva sortuva ménage à trois; the possibility hovers that the real reason for including Thea is that she is Sam's roommate and so it seemed like good manners. The next day, as Sam and Coles discuss it on the phone, they both try to backtrack and Coles concludes, "So we're all sorry—but we all had fun." This is, if only Sam could intuit it, an analysis that Coles will be making frequently in the years to come.

Sam likes him. Coles likes her, but he cheats on her anyway, "meaninglessly," with a one-night stand. When he confesses, something breaks between them. When a man tells a woman he loves that he has cheated but "it didn't mean anything," this translates to the woman as, "It is meaningless to me that I cheated on you." Coles doesn't quite grasp this.

As undergraduates the three form the kinds of bonds that do not find closure with graduation. Ten years pass. Coles is now working in the advertising business in Manhattan, and has been living for five years with Claire (Petra Wright). He runs into Sam one day, and finds that she has returned to America after breaking off an engagement in London. She tells him that Thea, who was once so wild, is the first of the three to be married; she runs a restaurant with Miles (David Thornton).

Coles, of course, is attracted to Sam, who looks all the more desirable because she is now the woman he would be cheating with, instead of cheating on. She's on the rebound, and they share a heedless passionate heat. The victim now is Claire, who of all the characters is the wisest about human nature. She is trim, elegant, a little older than Coles, and knows exactly who he is and what he is. When she walks in on Coles and Sam, she walks out again, and conceals what she has seen because she is prepared to accept Coles, up to a point.

All of these lines of sexual intrigue come to a head in a weekend at the Hamptons house of Thea and Miles. To describe what happens would be wrong, but let's suggest it would be a comedy if written by Noel Coward but is not a comedy here. Much depends upon poor Coles, who is addicted to infatuation, and finds fidelity a painful deprivation in a world filled, he thinks, with perfect love that is almost within his grasp.

Mark Ruffalo plays the character with that elusive charm he also revealed in *You Can Count on Me.* In that film he was the unreliable brother of Laura Linney, who loved him but despaired of his irresponsibility. He has a way of smiling at a joke only he can understand. He isn't really a villain (there are no bad people in the movie), but more of a victim of his own inability to commit; he ends up unhappier than any of the people he disappoints.

Maya Stange and Kathleen Robertson find the right notes for their undergraduates who seem to trade places as adults—the reliable one becoming rootless while the daring one settles down. But it is Petra Wright who does the best and most difficult job among the women, finding a painful balance between Claire's self-respect and her desire to hang on to Coles. She is hurt not so much by his sexual infidelity as by his failure to value her seriously enough. "I feel a little like a consolation prize," she says at one point.

One review of this film complains that all of the characters are jerks, and asks why we should care about them. Well, jerks are often the most interesting characters in the movies, and sometimes the ones most like ourselves. *XX/XY* would be dismal if the characters all behaved admirably, but the writer and director, Austin Chick, knows too much about human nature to permit that. The film has a rare insight into the mechanism by which some men would rather pursue happiness than obtain it.

Y

Young Adam ★ ★ ★ ½
NC-17, 93 m., 2004

Ewan McGregor (Joe Taylor), Tilda Swinton (Ella Gault), Peter Mullan (Les Gault), Emily Mortimer (Cathie Dimly). Directed by David Mackenzie and produced by Jeremy Thomas. Screenplay by Mackenzie, based on a novel by Alexander Trocchi.

Two men and a woman on a barge. No one who has seen Jean Vigo's famous film *L'Atalante* (1932) can watch *Young Adam* without feeling its resonance. There cannot be peace unless the woman or one of the men leaves. In the Vigo film, newlyweds make the barge their occupation and home, and the bride feels pushed aside by the crusty old deckhand (the immortal Michel Simon). In *Young Adam,* the chemistry is more lethal. The barge is owned by Ella Gault (Tilda Swinton), who has a loveless marriage with her husband, Les (Peter Mullan). Les has hired the young and cocky Joe Taylor (Ewan McGregor), who fancies himself a writer.

It is a foregone conclusion that Joe will eventually have sex with Ella, as the barge *Atlantic Eve* trades on the dank canals between Glasgow and Edinburgh, circa 1960. But that's really not the movie's subject, even though it provides rich opportunities for Peter Mullan, that intense and inward Scotsman, to underplay his rage and suppress his feelings. (At one point, as Joe and Ella linger in bed, they hear Les's boots on the deck overhead and decide, "He's letting us know he's back.") No, the *Atlantic Eve* is not the setting for adultery so much as for guilt and long silences.

As the film opens, Joe sees the body of a young woman floating in the canal, dressed only in lingerie. He uses a hook to pull it closer, and Les helps him haul her on board. The police are summoned. It is a drowning, perhaps a suicide. No foul play, apparently.

But Joe knows more about the body than he reveals—more, much more, than anybody would ever be able to discover, and he reads the papers with interest as it is learned the woman was pregnant, and that her boyfriend, a plumber, has been charged with the murder.

Joe is a hard case. Opaque. Not tender, not good with the small talk. Around women he has a certain intensity that informs them he plans to have sex with them and it is up to them to agree, or go away. He is not a rapist, but he has only one purpose in his mind, and some women find that intensity of focus to be exciting. It's as if, at the same time, he cares nothing for them and can think only of them. No amount of sweet talk would conquer them, but his eyes penetrate to their souls and rummage around.

As the murder case goes to trial, Joe finds himself attending the court sessions. He becomes fascinated by the defendant. Flashbacks fill in chapters of Joe's earlier life, episodes known only to him, including a moment when he could have acted, and did not act, and does not even begin to understand why he didn't. He is not a murderer, but a man unwilling to intervene, a man so detached, so cold, so willing to sacrifice others to his own convenience, that perhaps in his mind it occurs that he would feel better about the young woman's death if he had actually, actively, killed her. Then at least he would know what he had done, and would not find such emptiness when he looks inside himself. This is an almost Dostoyevskian study of a man brooding upon evil until it paralyzes him.

Although Britain and Ireland now enjoy growing prosperity, any working class person thirty or older was raised in a different, harder society. That's why actors like Ewan McGregor and Colin Farrell, not to mention Tim Roth and Gary Oldman, can slip so easily into these hard-edged, dirty-handed roles. With American actors you have the feeling they bought work clothes at Sears and roughed them up; with these guys, you figure they got their old gear out of their dad's closet, or borrowed their brother's. Peter Mullan, who is older, is a sublime actor, too much overlooked, who can play a working man with a direct honesty that doesn't involve a single extra note. Look at his movie *My Name Is Joe,* where he plays a recovering alcoholic who tries to help a friend and to risk a romance. As for Tilda Swinton, here is directness so forceful you want to look away; she doesn't cave in to Joe because of his look, but because he can match hers.

A movie like *Young Adam* is above all about

the ground-level lives of its characters. The death of the girl and the plot surrounding it is handled not as a crime or a mystery, but as an event that jars characters out of their fixed orbits. When you have a policy of behavior, a pose toward the world, that has hardened like concrete into who you are, it takes more than guilt to break you loose. It takes the sudden realization that the person you created continues to function, but you are now standing outside of him. He carries on regardless, and you are stranded, alone and frightened.

Y Tu Mama También ★ ★ ★ ★
NO MPAA RATING, 105 m., 2002

Maribel Verdu (Luisa Cortes), Gael Garcia Bernal (Julio Zapata), Diego Luna (Tenoch Iturbide). Directed by Alfonso Cuaron and produced by Alfonso Cuaron and Jorge Vergara. Screenplay by Alfonso Cuaron and Carlos Cuaron.

Y Tu Mama También is described on its Website as a "teen drama," which is like describing *Moulin Rouge* as a musical. The description is technically true but sidesteps all of the reasons to see the movie. Yes, it's about two teenage boys and an impulsive journey with an older woman that involves sexual discoveries. But it is also about the two Mexicos. And it is about the fragility of life and the finality of death. Beneath the carefree road movie that the movie is happy to advertise is a more serious level—and below that, a dead serious level.

The movie, whose title translates as *"And Your Mama, Too,"* is another trumpet blast that there may be a New Mexican Cinema a-bornin'. Like *Amores Perros,* which also stars Gael Garcia Bernal, it is an exuberant exercise in interlocking stories. But these interlock not in space and time, but in what is revealed, what is concealed, and in the parallel world of poverty through which the rich characters move.

The surface is described in a flash: Two Mexican teenagers named Tenoch and Julio, one from a rich family, one middle class, are free for the summer when their girlfriends go to Europe. At a wedding they meet a cousin named Luisa, ten years older, who is sexy and playful. They suggest a weekend trip to the legendary beach named Heaven's Mouth. When

her fiancé cheats on her, she unexpectedly agrees, and they set out together on a lark.

This level could have been conventional but is anything but, as directed by Alfonso Cuaron, who cowrote the screenplay with his brother Carlos. Luisa kids them about their sex lives in a lighthearted but tenacious way, until they have few secrets left, and at the same time she teases them with erotic possibilities. The movie is realistic about sex, which is to say, franker and healthier than the smutty evasions forced on American movies by the R rating. We feel a shock of recognition: This is what real people do and how they do it, sexually, and the MPAA has perverted a generation of American movies into puerile, masturbatory snickering.

Whether Luisa will have sex with one or both of her new friends is not for me to reveal. More to the point is what she wants to teach them, which is that men and women learn to share sex as a treasure they must carry together without something spilling—that women are not prizes, conquests, or targets, but the other half of a precarious unity. This is news to the boys, who are obsessed with orgasms (needless to say, their own).

The progress of that story provides the surface arc of the movie. Next to it, in a kind of parallel world, is the Mexico they are driving through. They pass police checkpoints, see drug busts and traffic accidents, drive past shantytowns, and are stopped at a roadblock of flowers by villagers who demand a donation for their queen—a girl in bridal white, representing the Virgin. "You have a beautiful queen," Luisa tells them. Yes, but the roadblock is genteel extortion. The queen has a sizable court that quietly hints a donation is in order.

At times during this journey the sound track goes silent and we hear a narrator who comments from outside the action, pointing out the village where Tenoch's nanny was born, and left at thirteen to seek work. Or a stretch of road where, two years earlier, there was a deadly accident. The narration and the roadside images are a reminder that in Mexico and many other countries a prosperous economy has left an uneducated and penniless peasantry behind.

They arrive at the beach. They are greeted by a fisherman and his family, who have lived

763

here for four generations, sell them fried fish, rent them a place to stay. This is an unspoiled paradise. (The narrator informs us the beach will be purchased for a tourist hotel, and the fisherman will abandon his way of life, go to the city in search of a job, and finally come back here to work as a janitor.) Here the sexual intrigues that have been developing all along will find their conclusion.

Beneath these two levels (the coming-of-age journey, the two Mexicos) is hidden a third. I will say nothing about it, except to observe there are only two shots in the entire movie that reflect the inner reality of one of the characters. At the end, finally knowing everything, you think back through the film—or, as I was able to do, see it again.

Alfonso Cuaron is Mexican but his first two features were big-budget American films. I thought *Great Expectations* (1998), with Ethan Hawke, Gwyneth Paltrow, and Anne Bancroft, brought a freshness and visual excitement to the updated story. I liked *A Little Princess* (1995) even more. It is clear Cuaron is a gifted director, and here he does his best work to date.

Why did he return to Mexico to make it? Because he has something to say about Mexico, obviously, and also because Jack Valenti and the MPAA have made it impossible for a movie like this to be produced in America. It is a perfect illustration of the need for a workable adult rating: too mature, thoughtful, and frank for the R, but not in any sense pornographic. Why do serious film people not rise up in rage and tear down the rating system that infantilizes their work?

The key performance is by Maribel Verdu, as Luisa. She is the engine that drives every scene she's in, as she teases, quizzes, analyzes, and lectures the boys, as if impatient with the task of turning them into beings fit to associate with an adult woman. In a sense she fills the standard role of the sexy older woman, so familiar from countless Hollywood comedies, but her character is so much more than that— wiser, sexier, more complex, happier, sadder. It is true, as some critics have observed, that *Y Tu Mama* is one of those movies where "after that summer, nothing would ever be the same again." Yes, but it redefines "nothing."

The Best Films of 2003

1. *Monster*

The performance of the year, in the film of the year. Charlize Theron plays Aileen Wuornos, a prostitute who was executed in Florida for the murders of seven men. The film portrays her as a woman so damaged in early life, so beaten down by daily existence, that although her crimes are not forgivable, her actions are like the flailings of a wounded animal.

Theron, now twenty-eight, has been known until now as the tall, attractive star of midlevel entertainments like *The Italian Job* and *Men of Honor*. Nothing in her career prepares us for this astonishing performance, in a film she developed with writer-director Patty Jenkins. She uses various strategies to look older, heavier, more weathered, but we simply forget to think about them because her character is real, convincing, and focused at every moment with a scary intensity.

Christina Ricci costars, as a naive young woman who becomes Aileen's lover and gives her for the first time the hope of leading a normal life. But both women are disconnected from reality, and their search for happiness leads to a serial killing spree in which the death of a well-meaning man played by Scott Wilson is unbearably painful. We are told to hate the sin but love the sinner, and *Monster* is a luminous work of empathy, showing us a woman whose destiny was already sealed as a battered child.

2. *Lost in Translation*

Sofia Coppola wrote and directed this winsome, bittersweet film about two lonely people in the middle of the night in Tokyo. Bill Murray is a movie star in town to make commercials. Scarlett Johansson plays the new wife of a young photographer who is dazzled by his own success and drifting away from her. They meet in the hotel bar and begin a conversation that lasts several days. Ancient movie conventions lead us to suspect they will have an affair, but the movie is deeper and wiser than that—and shows that, although the possibility of sex exists between them, their needs are much harder to fill: They need someone to talk with about lifetimes that seem to be drifting away from their dreams.

Murray gives his finest performance, carefully controlling his comic gift so that he plays a man who *could* be funny, but is off-duty. Johansson, who brings enormous reserves of presence and patience to the role, is also magical in another 2003 film, *Girl with a Pearl Earring*, where again she plays a woman who is the focus of an artist's loneliness.

3. *American Splendor*

When a Cleveland file clerk uses his mundane existence as the inspiration for a comic book, he achieves unlikely fame, a berth on the *Letterman* show, and a following that includes other wage slaves who find daily office life to be as filled with rage and excitement as any action picture. But how can a film about Harvey Pekar reconcile truth and fiction, comic art and daily reality? Codirectors Shari Springer Berman and Robert Pulcini meet the challenge by combining all of the elements.

Part of their film is in the form of an animated comic strip (based on drawings by R. Crumb). Part is a documentary showing the real Harvey Pekar, his wife, Joyce Brabner, and his coworkers. And part is a fiction film starring Paul Giamatti as Harvey and Hope Davis as Joyce. The real people and the actors are sometimes onscreen together, creating an uncanny tension between life and performance. The movie is funny and brave, the story of heroism in the real life of an antihero who is in a bad mood most of the time, and who rejects an offer to host a talk show because he doesn't want to risk his civil service pension.

4. *Finding Nemo*

I usually sit toward the back of the theater, but during *Finding Nemo* I wanted to sit closer, to immerse myself in the underwater beauty of the film's graceful animation. The story is lots of fun (how in the world can a fish escape from an aquarium and get across the highway and back into the sea?), but the most distinctive accomplishment of the Pixar production is its visual artistry. Water is often dealt with in animation as if it is simply transparent, except for bubbles. The artists of *Finding Nemo* have uncanny success in suggesting that their characters are actually swimming in the sea; carefully modulated color densities suggest less water between a character and the audience. The story is well told, but the telling gains immensely from the visuals.

5. *Master and Commander: The Far Side of the World*

Patrick O'Brian's characters inspire a grand and glorious spectacle in the tradition of the best seafaring epics. Russell Crowe, always convincing in a performance that sidesteps the obvious temptations to overact, plays the captain of a British warship contending with the French for control of South American waters. His best friend is the ship's surgeon, played by Paul Bettany, and their conflicting views about war and life provide a counterpoint to the action scenes. Not simply a swashbuckler, although it has rousing sea battles, but an intelligent movie about men tested by the sea. Director Peter Weir mounts an impressive production, seamlessly combining real ships, models, and tank work into a sobering portrait of how deadly and beautiful sea warfare was in the age of sail.

6. *Mystic River*

Clint Eastwood's drama is a brooding exploration of ancient evils and their abiding cost. His film, based on Brian Helgeland's adaptation of Dennis Lehane's novel, shows us three friends for whom childhood is forever marred by a tragedy. Now, as adults, Sean Penn's daughter has been murdered, Tim Robbins is a possible suspect, and Kevin Bacon is the cop on the case. This could have been a crime thriller or a police procedural, but Eastwood turns it toward almost Shakespearean tragedy, as each man's character plays out in his fate. Eastwood has directed some two dozen films, some good, some ordinary; in this one and *The Unforgiven* he finds greatness.

7. *Owning Mahowny*

Philip Seymour Hoffman's inward, focused performance is the key to this movie about a gambling obsession. He plays a Toronto bank clerk in hock to his bookie, who begins to steal money and eventually loses millions in Atlantic City and Vegas. The film, directed by Richard Kwietniowski and inspired by a true story, avoids the artificial highs and lows of many gambling movies and shows Hoffman burrowing straight ahead, his eyes rarely lifted from the action, as if under a hypnotic spell. John Hurt is splendid as the casino boss who thought he knew all about compulsive gambling, but becomes fascinated by this man's overwhelming need to play—and lose.

8. *The Son*

Not a film many readers are likely to have heard about, but a film that cannot be forgotten by anyone who saw it. "It needs no insight or explanation," I wrote in my review. "It sees everything and explains all. It is as assured and flawless a telling of sadness and joy as I have ever seen." Directed by the brothers Dardenne, Jean-Pierre, and Luc, it tells of a Belgian carpenter who supervises apprentices. One day a candidate is brought to him. At first he rejects the boy, but then he reconsiders and accepts him, and we discover something that the carpenter knows about the boy—a secret that leads to scenes where sudden violence seems barely beneath the surface. All the action is in terms of the carpentry work, and there is a sequence in a lumberyard that uses sound and timing to make sudden physical disaster seem imminent.

9. *Whale Rider*

What a splendid film for the entire family! Keisha Castle-Hughes stars in a sparkling performance as Paikea, a teenager who would be next in line to lead her tribe—if she were not a girl. Niki Caro's film is set in a present-day Maori village in New Zealand, where legends are still preserved. Paikea's father has no wish to lead the tribe after a tragedy, and leaves the country. Her grandfather loves her, but is locked into ancient traditions. As he tries to train one of the hapless village boys, Paikea studies on her own, and the climax is thrilling and heartwarming. This year's *Bend It Like Beckham*.

10. *In America*

Inspired by Irish director Jim Sheridan's own immigration to America in the 1980s, it tells the story of a family who lives in poverty in a New York tenement and struggles to survive after the loss of a son. Paddy Considine plays the sometimes despairing father, Samantha Morton is heroic as the mother, Sarah Bolger steals the show as the older sister—and downstairs, a fearsome African artist (Djimon Hounsou) reveals a hidden gentleness. I've seen a lot of movies about the immigrant experience, but this one lives outside the rules, absorbing us in the family's struggle to survive.

Special Jury Prizes

At most film festivals, the jury picks a grand prize, and then awards a "jury prize" to a film they hold in the same high esteem. The following films are not my "runners-up," but rank in my esteem with the top ten. It was a very good year for the movies, and a perfectly respectable best films list could be composed from these titles, ranked alphabetically:

All the Real Girls is David Gordon Green's second film after the astonishing *George Washington,* and confirms his status as a filmmaker of poetic originality. Once again he eavesdrops on the lives of ordinary people doing ordinary things—not in an ordinary way, but expressed through a heightened and gentle sensibility.

The Barbarian Invasions, by Denys Arcand of Quebec, revisits the characters in his *The Decline of the American Empire* (1987). Now the Falstaffian left-wing professor Remy (Remy Girard) lies near death, and his former wife and estranged son are the unlikely instruments for a reunion of old friends and old (and current!) lovers, who celebrate his zest for life, and their own.

Better Luck Tomorrow. Justin Lin's comedy of manners considers a group of affluent Asian-American kids in high school, who get straight A's and supplement their incomes by selling term papers, eventually escalating to drugs and murder. The film is about a value system that places success above morality. Lurking beneath the close surface observation is the implication that their behavior and strategies have perfectly positioned them to take over from the fallen leaders of Enronism.

Elephant. Gus Van Sant considers a day in the life of a high school very much like Columbine, using an objective narrative and visual style that records the horror of a massacre but doesn't let us off the hook with potted psychological motivations. The killers are so detached they seem to be playing a video game—one that counts points in terms of real lives for which they have no feeling.

Girl with a Pearl Earring is Peter Webber's sensuous meditation on artistic inspiration, starring Scarlett Johansson, as a poor girl who is employed as a maid in the home of the Dutch master Vermeer (Peter Firth) and not only inspires a famous painting but also makes an unmistakable artistic and emotional connection with him—which the rigid social code of the time prevents them from acknowledging.

House of Sand and Fog. A young woman (Jennifer Connelly) fails to pay the real-estate taxes on the home she inherited, and an Iranian immigrant (Ben Kingsley) buys it at auction. Both are poor, both need the house, both see it as the key to their futures. The deputy (Ron Eldard) who evicts the woman becomes involved with her, and his lack of judgment has tragic consequences. Directed by Vadim Perelman, himself an immigrant, from the novel by André Dubus III.

Kill Bill is Quentin Tarantino in virtuoso mode, giving us a martial arts picture that is heavy on storytelling, light on story. The film is all kinetic energy, visual conceit, production design, and performances focused to a razor's edge, but with only the most rudimentary motivation or character development. It is a tribute to Uma Thurman and the other cast members that they are able to bring presence and substance to characters who have been written with rubber stamps.

The Man on the Train. Another delight from the French director Patrice Leconte, who begins with an accidental meeting between a retired schoolteacher (Jean Rochefort) and an aging bank robber (played by the French rock legend Johnny Hallyday). Their chance conversation ends with the robber agreeing to use the teacher's guest room, and as their talks continue, it becomes clear that each envies the life of the other. Leconte and writer Claude Klotz have devised an ending of bold poetic fantasy.

May. Hated by a lot of critics, but, yes, I think it's good enough for this list. A truly strange horror film about a disturbed young woman and the way her obsessions lead to tragic weirdness. Oddly moving, with a title performance by Angela Bettis that stirs and touches like young Sissy Spacek in *Carrie.*

Matchstick Men. Ridley Scott's complex portrait of a con man (Nicolas Cage) who inhabits three story threads, all adequate to carry a film: (1) He's involved in complicated cons with his longtime partner (Sam Rockwell). (2) He has a smorgasbord assortment of behavioral disorders, ranging from agoraphobia to obsessive-compulsive behavior to Tourette's syndrome, that make it very hard to be a coordinated con man. (3) He meets the teenage daughter (Alison Lohman) he never knew he had. The epilogue strikes a perfect note, explaining who the characters are and, in a way, why.

Northfork. A spare, stark, dreamy fantasy centering around a town being flooded by the waters of a dam. As men in black evict the residents, angels visit to comfort a dying boy, and enigmatic conversations take place against a backdrop of vast, empty sadness. Made by the Polish brothers *(Twin Falls, Idaho)* who create an epic whose scope underlines its desolation.

Nowhere in Africa. Caroline Link won the Oscar for Best Foreign Film for this engaging story of a German Jewish family that escapes Hitler to settle on a farm in East Africa, where the young daughter feels at home while her parents make their own shifting accommodations.

The Russian Ark. A stupendous technical achievement by Aleksandr Sokurov and his cinematographer, Tilman Buttner, who choreograph a single shot that lasts for the entire length of the film, as the point of view moves through the Hermitage museum in St. Petersburg and characters materialize to represent centuries of Russian history.

Safe Conduct. Bertrand Tavernier's ambitious, passionate story about French filmmakers who continued to work under the Nazi occupation, and to a remarkable degree made the films they wanted to make. A film about film, made with insight and sympathy.

Best Documentaries

In alphabetical order: *Amandla!* was a stirring doc about the role played by music in bringing change to South Africa. *Biggie and Tupac,* directed by one-man investigative team Nick Broomfield, solves their murders and names their killers, at least to his own satisfaction. *Capturing the Friedmans* used the family's own home movies to help tell the story of a father and brother both charged with molesting minors. *The Fog of War* was Errol Morris's extraordinary interview with Robert McNamara, who speaks frankly and often regretfully about his role as an American soldier and later secretary of defense. *Rivers and Tides* was the haunting doc about Andy Goldsworthy, an artist who creates temporary works out of found objects in nature, and then watches as nature destroys them.

Spellbound followed eight finalists on their way to a showdown in the National Spelling Bee. *Stevie* was Steve *(Hoop Dreams)* James's heartbreaking return to the life of a kid he met in the Big Brother program; that life has not gone well. *Stone Reader,* by Mark Moskowitz, traced his obsession with the author of a highly praised 1972 novel, *The Stones of Summer.* He succeeds in tracking down Dow Mossman, in a delightful work in praise of readers and writers. *Tupac Resurrection* was a biopic about Tupac Shakur, seemingly narrated from beyond the grave by the murdered rap star. And *Winged Migration* follows birds on their exhausting odysseys from summer to winter, with cameras that establish a startling intimacy with the subjects.

Honorary Mention

To Jack Angstreich, Eric Chadbourne, Harvey Schwartz, Roberta Hill, and Bill Heidbreder. Who are they? The compulsive moviegoers in the documentary *Cinemania,* who spend every waking minute of every day going to the movies. It is very likely all five of them have seen every title on my lists.

Interviews

Kevin Costner

August 10, 2003—Kevin Costner's new Western is about "what kind of person you are when you look around and no one is watching," he says. It's called *Open Range,* and Costner directs. He won an Oscar for directing *Dances with Wolves,* and again turns to the post–Civil War West for his setting.

Open Range is an expansive epic with surprisingly intimate performances, starring Robert Duvall as a man who grazes his cattle on the open range, and Costner as his right-hand man. Riding with them are a younger cowhand (Abraham Benrubi) and a kid (Diego Luna). Passing a new town, they're threatened by Baxter (Michael Gambon), a rancher who wants to fence out the free-range grazers. And when the kid is shot by Baxter's men, they meet the local doctor—and particularly the doctor's sister, played by Annette Bening.

Ten things I learned while talking with Costner about the movie:

1. "If you believe in posttraumatic stress after Vietnam, think of the people who came out of the Civil War and started moving West. There were a lot of sociopaths, bent and broken people, alcoholics—and the fighting went on in one way or another for the next forty years."

2. "Charley, my character, is the equivalent of an alcoholic, except that his problem is violence. He works for a good man who doesn't look for trouble, and staying with him for ten years has kept him out of trouble. But notice the way he tells Duvall about what he did in the war: He knew how to kill, he says, 'It came easier to me than it came to other people. I had the knack.'"

3. Charley is thunderstruck by his first sight of Sue Barlow (Bening), the doctor's sister. "Cowboys were not around proper women. They were very shy in their presence. They met prostitutes in the bordellos, but it was said that a cowboy would ride two, three hours in the bulrushes just to look at a little redhead girl yarning on her back porch in a rocking chair. He would just look at her and then ride back again."

4. "Robert Duvall is a very specific actor, and a natural actor. I wasn't looking for someone who would play Boss as a character, but someone who would give me a hold-the-screen type Boss. It's an important performance. Not just a retooling of *Lonesome Dove.* There's a key scene in the café that I think is an AFI moment for Bob. I stand behind him and don't say a word."

5. "I'm glad I was able to show the movie to Michael Jeter before he died. He plays the local coot who sides with us. He's very much in the mode of the Walter Brennans and Ward Bonds. Cooper and Stewart and Wayne, they just wouldn't act without those guys. They needed them to do the dance. You need a scene where somebody whoops and hollers, and the heroes can't do that, so you need the whiskery old guy to do the dance."

6. "I know I'm going to get my gunfight. That's an obligatory thing, and I was happy to do it and wanted to do it. But I think guns should be loud in a movie, and scare you. The best antigun message is that there is a result after guns go off. It's not just people who are hurt. Animals are hurt, and buildings are torn up, and people are scarred for life. A couple of people told me that after the gunfight we should go have a drink and have a nice ending. And I said, if you look at the old black-and-white photos of the Old West, if there are people dead in the street, townsfolk gather and look at them, and those bodies don't disappear. Somebody has to pick them up. There's an aftermath of violence. If a normal person sees it, it will make them sick."

7. "Charley has a speech I like where he tells Boss what's likely to come down in the gunfight. In a lot of Westerns, everybody just shoots at one another, but Charley has been an expert killer in the war, and he knows how the other guys are probably going to act."

8. I referred to Costner's films *Waterworld* and *The Postman* as box-office failures. "*Waterworld* earned $300 million. Maybe $100 million in the United States and $200 million overseas. With *The Postman,* I was disappointed with the

European critics. The American critics said what they thought, but overseas they just said what everybody in America thought. That said … I've never written a critic about a bad review, or refused an interview with someone who gave me a bad review."

9. "I like the original movie experience. I have not made a career based on sequels or franchises. We could have made *No Way Out 2* and done *Bull Durham 2* and *Tin Cup 2* and a *Bodyguard* sequel. There's going to be a sequel to *Dances with Wolves* but I'm not going to be part of it. I'm out there trying to raise the bar and do something new. *The Postman* was that way. I enjoyed it. I can't turn my back on it, but I understand that others could."

10. "I don't consider myself a cutting-edge kind of filmmaker. I think my choices are right down the middle, but hopefully there's a true character there, and a thread of film literacy. I'm a bit of a hardhead when it comes to running time. I like longer narrative. Always have. It's not in vogue, but now with this new revenue stream from DVDs what happens is, the same scenes they beg you to cut from the release print, they're begging you to throw them back in on the DVD. I say, no, I've made the movie. Sometimes they put deleted scenes on a DVD, but that's not me, that's them."

Russell Crowe

November 9, 2003—Russell Crowe won Best Actor nominations for three of his last four films, and after the Academy sees his work in *Master and Commander*, that may become four out of five. This is known as a hot streak. Now remember the four roles. He played a pudgy biochemist, a Roman general, a schizophrenic mathematician, and a captain in the British Navy during the Napoleonic Wars. And he created those characters so convincingly that when I picture them, I think of *them*, not of Russell Crowe.

There is no such thing as "the Russell Crowe role." Like other great character stars (like Jack Nicholson and Sean Penn), he reinvents himself in every movie. Although his movies have recently earned a great deal of money, there's no way you can look at the list and say he made them for the paycheck.

Consider *Gladiator*, a movie I had problems with but the Academy didn't. After it won five

of the twelve Oscars it was nominated for and grossed untold millions, the contrarians decided it was a commercial epic. Not at all. "When we were making it," Crowe told me a little testily, "everybody was telling us there was no audience existing for it. I had many conversations with studio people who basically were laughing at what we were doing. Now, because of its financial success, people try to undermine the fact that I won an Oscar for it."

I guess I was one of them. I thought he was more deserving of Oscars for the movie that came before (*The Insider*) and the movie that came after (*A Beautiful Mind*).

"Maybe in a few years you may want to watch it again," Crowe told me, "after you've seen another director's attempt to do what we did." Maybe I will.

Crowe was in Chicago to promote *Master and Commander*, Peter Weir's glorious seafaring adventure based on the beloved series of novels by Patrick O'Brian. He plays Captain Jack Aubrey, a man of action who often finds himself at odds with his best friend, ship's surgeon Stephen Maturin (played by Paul Bettany). In the film, he has just taken command of HMS *Surprise*, and is charged with challenging the French for control of the waters off Brazil.

Crowe is known as an actor who hates doing publicity, maybe because he does not suffer fools gladly, and when you endure a weekend publicity junket you meet them one after another. In Los Angeles in 2000, he was in the middle of a junket for *Proof of Life* when he just walked out of the hotel. Up and went home. Some of the junketeers wanted to probe him about his breakup with Meg Ryan, which he did not choose to discuss. No kidding. I stay out of trouble in these situations because I am more interested in movies than in where the stars keep their genitals during their time off.

He agreed to a Chicago visit partly because his new wife, Danielle Spencer, has family here, partly because he loves *Master and Commander*.

"From a marketing point of view, a movie like this is supposed to be a death knell for a female audience," he said, "but every time I talk to a woman who's seen it, they love it. People don't know that 40 percent of Patrick O'Brian's readers are female."

Weir built a real ship for the film, working on

the high seas and then matching shots in the big tanks on the back lots. His exteriors on the high seas are exhilarating because they so clearly involve real men on a real ship.

"The mathematics involved are daunting," Crowe said, "whether you're at sea or in the tank, making sure the wind is coming from the right quarter, making sure the sails aren't backing up and the flags are flying in the right direction. You're thinking about the performances and the dialogue, and the little things that trip you up. There's a famous boat movie recently where the sun sets in the east. Hopefully, nothing like that is in this film."

Which boat movie was that? You know, the famous one.

Master and Commander is an epic, but it's not one of those lumbering, clunky jobs where you can hear the plot machinery groaning to give birth to the next special-effects extravaganza. It's about the lives of the hard, capable men who lived in those fragile shells and risked their lives for bad pay, rotten food, and the excellent chance of becoming a shark's dinner.

"Yes, it's a $135 million film," Crowe said, "but quite frankly, it's a $135 million art film, about a very small, intensely personal human drama. The positive thing for me is that 20th Century Fox went into it knowing that. They knew they were going to get a Peter Weir film, and they knew what that meant. We didn't have to pretend to do one thing when we wanted to do another. Peter Weir is always focused on detail and the humanity of the situation."

Peter Weir. Whose credits include *Picnic at Hanging Rock* (1975), *The Last Wave* (1977), *Gallipoli* (1981), *The Year of Living Dangerously* (1982), *Witness* (1985), *The Mosquito Coast* (1986), *Dead Poets Society* (1989), *Green Card* (1990), *Fearless* (1993), and *The Truman Show* (1998). I hate lists, but what title would you leave out?

"It wouldn't be possible to do a film without a director with the aesthetic and confidence of a Peter Weir," Crowe said. "For me the bangs and crashes and whistles of Hollywood action flicks are never interesting. What's the story we're telling?

"Peter worked for five years on this. He started with exactly the same attitude as everybody else—that it couldn't be filmed. And I shared that attitude. I'd read *Master and Com-*

mander, and at one point there were seventeen ships on the line, and these were eighty-gun, five-story-high boats. Where were we going to find that?

"But then Peter very cleverly took what to most readers is the point of the journeys. That's not necessarily the battles; it's the relationship between Dr. Maturin and Captain Aubrey. Here are two men of vastly different points of view from two entirely different backgrounds. In fact, one of them shouldn't technically be on the boat. But he is, and the director allows full arguments to take place.

"And it's not that standard, boring movie dialogue where one person talks and the other person responds and then later on the other person talks and the first one responds. That's not how human beings discuss things. There's a deep affection and a love between these two men, so it doesn't matter if they disagree. They'll still get on with their lives."

I asked Crowe about his selection of projects, which has recently been uncannily right, even with films that must have looked risky on paper. He answered not by talking about his hits, but about his misses.

"I just do the things that appeal to me. I don't look at it from the point of budget or status. I look at the story and if it's a good story, I can contribute. If it's a crap story, I'm going to get really bored and frustrated. For me, even movies I've made that weren't so successful, like *The Quick and the Dead,* with Sharon Stone and Gene Hackman—if you look at what I have to do and the actual story itself, given that it's a Western and shot by the man who made *The Evil Dead,* it is still a good story.

"Or if you look at *Virtuosity,* which I made with Denzel Washington, here's this young, unknown Australian actor, but the role I get to play challenges Denzel, an established star, and the story's a good one that'll stand up.

"After *Gladiator,* I did a $60 million movie about a schizophrenic mathematician, and people assume the budget was double that. But I was working with Ron Howard, who, just like myself, sees making movies as a privilege."

He's working again with Howard on his next project, *Cinderella Man,* the story of the depression-era boxer Jim Braddock.

"I just got a new draft from Akiva Goldsman, who wrote *A Beautiful Mind,* and Brian

Grazer is producing and Ron is directing and I'm starring, all from that picture, so as far as I'm concerned, the Beatles are back together. I just received the draft. I was supposed to do something with the wife, but I can't help it. I've gotta read it. I love the smell of the new pages."

Emily Mortimer

May 20, 2004—Suddenly I am aware of Emily Mortimer. I must of course have seen her in *Scream 3* (2000), but she made no impression. She was in *Notting Hill* (1999), but went unmentioned in my review. Then in *Lovely and Amazing* (2001) she had a scene of astonishing bravery in a film that was, yes, lovely and amazing. And then in the last few months have come *A Foreign Affair, Young Adam,* and now *Dear Frankie,* which is a great success in the Un Certain Regard section of this year's Cannes festival.

In these four most recent films, Mortimer displays a screen presence so confident in such different ways that you sense she will not be found in *Scream 4*. It takes great roles to make a great actress, and now she has found them.

Consider *Dear Frankie,* written and directed by Shona Auerbach, in which she plays Lizzie, the mother of a nine-year-old deaf boy (Jack McElhone). "He wasn't born deaf," she says at one point. "That was a present from his dad." She fled the brutal father, but as Frankie has grown up she has written him letters, supposed to be from his dad, a sailor whose ship sails foreign ports. Now Frankie has seen his father's ship in port, and wonders if his father will come to see him. So Lizzie, Mortimer's character, hires a complete stranger (Gerard Butler) to play the father for one day.

This story could supply conventional melodrama, but Auerbach cuts it close to the bone. Lizzie is a defensive woman, protective of her son, and the last thing she expects is that Frankie and the stranger will become friends—and that she, who has so fiercely kept men out of her life, will become attracted to him too.

A full review must wait for the opening. But there is one scene that fascinates me. Lizzie and the stranger are saying good-bye. Something has happened between them. Neither one was expecting it, but both know it. At the door, they look at each other for a very long time, while we wait to see if they will kiss. A very long time.

"It was mechanical, actually, in the way we shot it," Mortimer was remembering. We were talking in a penthouse across the street from the Palais des Festivals. "We shot several takes. The director knew it had to be long, but she didn't know how long, and she had to go into the edit and find out which length worked."

The shot goes as long as it reasonably can, and the longer it runs, the more it means. It finds a way to close the movie without the usual squirmy clichés. "She is a very brave director in that way," Mortimer said, "allowing space around the action. She gets what she needs but doesn't descend into sentimentality." In *Lovely and Amazing,* Mortimer has another extraordinary scene involving the human gaze. The film, by Nicole Holofcener, is about four women: a mother, her two grown daughters, and her adopted young African-American daughter. All four have issues with their body images.

Mortimer plays an actress who takes a meaningless date to bed, and then stands naked before him, asking him to honestly and frankly evaluate her body, its strengths and weaknesses. It must have taken some courage, I said, to invite criticism in that way.

"It was a wonderful experience as an actor to have that opportunity," she said. "You hear this terrifying phrase, 'being in the moment.' I have no doubt that I was in *that* moment. She was exposed and ridiculous and brave. And you know, in many nude scenes in the movies, that's what's going on in the minds of the actors, anyway. They're thinking about their imperfections."

In *Young Adam,* she plays the girlfriend of a barge worker (Ewan McGregor) who treats her with horrifying cruelty, while until the end she deceives herself that he cares for her. In *A Foreign Affair,* she's a British filmmaker, making a documentary about American men who take package tours to Russia to shop for brides. Two dramatically different roles, but especially in *A Foreign Affair* there is the sense that as she regards one of the Americans (Tim Blake Nelson), there is something she feels and is waiting for him to notice it. Remarkable, how she wins our attention by withholding, instead of acting out.

Mortimer was born in 1971 in London, studied English and Russian at Oxford, and is married to the American actor Alessandro Nivola; they had a baby son in September 2003. Her father, John Mortimer, is the author and attorney whose Rumpole of the Bailey has become a British institution. Although Mortimer has a perfect American accent when needed (why do the Brits do us better than we do them?), she is often used for British period stories. She played in the epic BBC-TV version of Anthony Powell's twelve-novel series *A Dance to the Music of Time*, which followed a circle of characters from before World War I until after World War II.

And her next film is *Bright Young Things*, directed by Stephen Fry and based on the early Evelyn Waugh novel.

"It's about that time between the wars," she said, "when people were allowed to do anything apart from saying how they really felt. It was a mad party time when everybody was trivial as a matter of principle. They were expected to behave extremely badly and go to parties and take drugs and have lots of boyfriends, but the moment you had a sincere emotion you had to keep it very much to yourself. And you have two characters in this world who do love one another but aren't allowed to express that, and get so confused their relationship blows up."

In this character and in many of her others, she said, "I seem to find characters who are held back and guarded, physically and mentally. It's a relief after the film is over, being let off the hook and being allowed to be my usual self again. But when I'm acting, it's good to have something to play against, boundaries to break."

Essays

The Oscar DVD Ban

October 6, 2003—Occasionally the movie industry comes up with a truly boneheaded idea. Jack Valenti unveiled a doozy: He announced that signatories of the Motion Picture Association of America would be forbidden to send out the thousands of advance DVD "screeners" that jam the year-end mailboxes of Academy members and critics compiling best ten lists.

His reason is that screeners have been used by video pirates to make illegal copies of movies. That is true. It is also true that pirates will find a way to steal prints anyway.

The Valenti decree would cripple the chance of a small independent film getting an Oscar nomination. With dozens of films opening at year-end, the Academy population lacks the time and energy to attend all those screenings in theaters. The DVDs pile up at home, and when the buzz turns hot on a title, they look at it.

Valenti's ban was greeted with howls of outrage by the heads of the independent distribution companies, even while it was being greeted with joy by the heads of major studios. This is a no-brainer: If voters cannot see the best indie work, they will be forced to vote for major studio work. Such Oscar winners as *In the Bedroom, The Hours, The Pianist, Adaptation,* and *Far From Heaven* might not survive such a practice.

"Dear Jack," wrote the respected director and industry leader Norman Jewison, "When every Academy member can view all the films in contention, then it's a fair and even playing field. However, when the small independent film—which depends on its artistic appeal rather than wide commercial distribution by an MPAA member—is denied access, the playing field becomes unfair and uneven .... Artistic accomplishments in film should not be compromised in an effort to protect the interests of the major studios."

That's the same Norman Jewison whose *Moonstruck, A Soldier's Story, The Hurricane,* and *Agnes of God* would have been penalized by the Valenti decree.

Luckily, the solution to this problem lies in the disposable video disc, which self-destructs after one playing. Academy members could be sent disposable discs, good for one viewing and watermarked with their names. If they wanted to give it to pirates, everybody would know where it came from, and they could be prosecuted to the full extent of the law, as explained in the ominous "FBI Warning" at the beginning of every disc.

Valenti says disposable discs are a bad idea because if only a few discs get out, they can be reproduced endlessly. Yes, but his idea doesn't protect against that very possibility.

Last summer critics arriving at advance screenings were searched by security guards. Carrie Rickey of the *Philadelphia Inquirer* refused the indignity and billed the studio for her lost taxi fare. Did the studios think professional critics would risk the loss of their jobs and criminal charges to smuggle a video camera into a theater and tape off the screen in full view of all of their colleagues? At the *Finding Nemo* screening, my turkey sandwich was inspected by a rent-a-cop. Were thousands of patrons in the nation's multiplexes also searched? Don't make me laugh.

Here's a bright idea. The major studios, fearful of piracy, simply *need not send out DVDs.* The indies, who count on them as the cornerstones of their Oscar campaigns, can continue to send them out. As Jewison notes in his letter to Valenti, "Piracy to a small independent film seeking an audience is simply good word of mouth."

What are the chances of a two-tier DVD system? Zero, because the majors want an uneven playing field only if it favors them. This fact, obvious and incontrovertible, exposes the moral decay and mercenary cynicism that underlies the Valenti decree. His new rule is so bad

I expect it to be withdrawn in a week. The remarkable thing is that Valenti was thoughtless enough to suggest it in the first place.

Independent Spirit Awards

Santa Monica, California, March 1, 2004—All of the top prizes at the Independent Spirit Awards went to nominees for the Academy Awards. Charlize Theron *(Monster)* and Bill Murray *(Lost in Translation)* won for best actress and actor. Supporting winners were Djimon Hounsou *(In America)* and Shohreh Aghdashloo *(House of Sand and Fog)*.

The big winner was Sofia Coppola, who attended with proud parents Francis and Eleanor Coppola, and whose *Lost in Translation* won every category it was nominated for: best picture, director, screenplay, and actor.

Best first feature was Patty Jenkins's *Monster,* the searing story of serial killer Aileen Wuornos, centering on Theron's great performance. Another double winner was Thomas McCarthy's *The Station Agent,* which won best first screenplay and the John Cassavetes Award for best feature under $500,000.

Niki Caro's *Whale Rider* won as best foreign film, and its thirteen-year-old star, Keisha Castle-Hughes, was in the house; she was an Oscar Best Actress nominee. Jim Sheridan's *In America* won not only for Hounsou but also for Declan Quinn's cinematography; accepting for Quinn, Sheridan led the house in singing "Happy Birthday" to his star, Sarah Bolger, just turned thirteen.

It was an afternoon to spotlight young talent: Nikki Reed, who was thirteen when she handed notes for the screenplay "thirteen" to director Catherine Hardwicke, is now sixteen and won for best debut performance. At the other end of the age scale, Errol Morris's *The Fog of War,* featuring eighty-five-year-old Robert McNamara, won for best documentary.

The Indie Spirits are the "anti-Oscars." Held in a big tent on the beach at Santa Monica, they honor films made outside the conventional studio system. Among other nominees this year were *American Splendor, Shattered Glass, Raising Victor Vargas, Better Luck Tomorrow,* and *Pieces of April.*

The emcee for the tenth year was director John Waters, he of the famous pencil mustache, whose opening act got a laugh as big as anything Billy Crystal inspired. Waters began a rant against the MPAA's policies on academy screeners and piracy, and just as he was hitting his stride, MPAA president Jack Valenti marched onstage, handcuffed him, and dragged him away.

2004 Oscars: One Film Rules Them All

Hollywood, California, March 1, 2004—There's joy in Middle-earth tonight. Peter Jackson's *The Lord of the Rings: The Return of the King* led the seventy-sixth annual Academy Awards with eleven Oscars, including Best Picture and Best Director. Sweeping all opposition aside like the forces of Sauron, it won in every category it was nominated for. The crowning chapter of the billion-dollar blockbuster trilogy was expected to win, and did, but apart from its film and direction awards, its Oscars came in countless technical categories. As host Billy Crystal quipped, "It's now official. There is no one left in New Zealand to thank."

"It's a clean sweep!" director Steven Spielberg said as he looked inside the final envelope. *LOTR* tied with *Titanic* and *Ben Hur* among all-time Oscar champions. Thanking even "the city councils of New Zealand," Jackson said, "Billy Crystal's welcome to come and make a film in New Zealand any time he wants."

Charlize Theron, considered the closest thing to a front-runner after *LOTR,* won as Best Actress for her searing performance as serial killer Aileen Wuornos in Patty Jenkins's *Monster.* It was a risky low-budget film by a first-time director, and Theron's physical transformation, using weight gain and specialized makeup, could have gone very wrong—but instead was completely convincing, as the beautiful actress from South Africa disappeared into the life and story of an abused and violent woman.

Among the many collaborators Theron mentioned, she gave a special thanks to makeup artist Toni G, "for transforming me," and added: "I know everyone in New Zealand has been thanked, so I want to thank everyone in South Africa." She ended on the brink of tears, thanking "my mom—who sacrificed so much for me to live here."

What was seen as the closest race of the evening, for Best Actor, was won by Sean

Penn—the first award after four nominations for the intense actor. The category was considered a toss-up between Penn and Bill Murray.

Penn played a vengeful father in Clint Eastwood's *Mystic River* (which led in nominations in the major categories). His speech, apart from a mild aside about WMDs, was subdued and touching: "I really thank Clint Eastwood, professionally and humanly, for coming into my life."

The actor, often embroiled in controversy as a younger man, thanked his wife, Robin Wright Penn, for "helping me on this roller-coaster ride I'm beginning to enjoy."

Two more favorites, Tim Robbins and Renée Zellweger, won in the supporting categories.

Robbins won for his searing performance in *Mystic River,* playing a killer who was abused as a child. Although he made political comments on previous Oscar appearances, this year he simply ended with an appeal to victims of childhood abuse: "There is no shame in seeking help."

Zellweger won for *Cold Mountain,* her third nomination, where she played a feisty frontier woman who steps in to help Nicole Kidman run a farm while all the men are off at war. Her win was an upset in a reverse way, since the Supporting Actress category so often features an upset, and many predictors thought perhaps the Iranian actress Shohreh Aghdashloo might have a chance.

Zellweger's acceptance speech vibrated with her quick-talking, exuberant charm, and then turned a little tearful as she thanked "my immigrant mom and dad—thank you for never saying don't try."

* * *

Sofia Coppola, who had just been onstage to present the Oscar for Adapted Screenplay, won for Best Original Screenplay for *Lost in Translation.* That made her family the second three-generation Oscar-winning family in history, after Walter, John, and Anjelica Huston. Her grandfather Carmine Coppola won for Best Musical Score, her father, Francis Ford Coppola, is a multiple winner, and now Sofia joins what Francis calls "the family business." Her screenplay starred Bill Murray and Scarlett Johansson as two lonely people in the middle of the night in Tokyo, skirting the edge of romance and deciding instead for mutual confidences.

The Lord of the Rings won for Best Adapted Screenplay, for its conversion of the J. R. R. Tolkien classic into the epic trilogy. Authors Philippa Boyens and Peter Jackson joined Fran Walsh (who also shared the Oscar for Best Song).

* * *

Although *The Lord of the Rings: The Return of the King* piled up eleven Oscars, all but the Best Film and Directing Oscars came in technical categories. It's as if the film was such a complex achievement of special effects that the human elements got taken for granted. The result was that the middle of the telecast dragged somewhat as one platoon of *LOTR* technical artists after another marched onstage to thank director Peter Jackson and long lists of their colleagues. Crystal's ad-lib: "Do you know that people are moving to New Zealand just to be thanked?"

The *LOTR* juggernaut began with the second award of the night, for Set Decoration and Art Direction. It continued with awards for Best Costume Design, Visual Effects, Makeup, Sound Mixing, Original Score (Howard Shore), Film Editing (Jamie Selkirk), Best Song, and Best Adapted Screenplay, before climaxing with Best Director and Film.

LOTR's lock on effects was broken by Richard King's award for sound editing for *Master and Commander,* which was distinguished by the detail of its sounds aboard a British sailing ship. To be sure, *LOTR* wasn't nominated in that category.

The award for Best Cinematography went to Russell Boyd for his spectacular work on *Master and Commander,* in a category that for some reason didn't gather a *LOTR* nomination.

* * *

No surprise when *Finding Nemo,* one of the year's top grossers, won as Best Animated Film. But there was underlying political tension, since everyone in the room knew that *Nemo*'s producing studio, Pixar, had recently ended its longtime association with Disney.

* * *

Although speeches by the presenters were advertised as being funnier this year, most of them, as usual, were boilerplate. Exceptions:

Robin Williams with his trademarked language mayhem, and Ben Stiller and Owen Wilson discussing Stiller's choice of a knit sweater instead of evening wear.

Two of the funniest men in Hollywood history were honored during the evening: eighteen-time Oscar host Bob Hope, recalled by Tom Hanks with a montage of emceeing appearances, and director Blake Edwards.

The Edwards segment was a comic and emotional high point of the broadcast. Jim Carrey introduced the tribute, recalling that he went through "a long Cato phase" after seeing the director's *A Shot in the Dark*. He recalled Edwards' dramatic films *Days of Wine and Roses* and *Breakfast at Tiffany's*, and added, "everything else made us laugh like hell." The montage of comic Edwards moments, many starring Peter Sellers, proved him correct.

Edwards's entrance was a show-stopper: Now somewhat slowed by age and illness, he used a battery-powered wheelchair to race uncontrolled across the stage and crash through a wall, tottering back onstage with Carrey's help, covered with plaster dust and muttering, "Don't touch my Oscar."

After a standing ovation, his acceptance speech, instead of thanking a long list of names, consisted of anecdotes about funny little things that happened on his sets. It was a magic moment, of humor and emotion. Thanking his "friends and foes," he added, "I couldn't have done it without the foes."

* * *

Also touching: A special tribute to Katharine Hepburn by Julia Roberts, who recalled the actress's feisty, independent side. (The pants-wearing Hepburn, asked by Barbara Walters if she even owned a skirt, replied: "I have one, Miss Walters. I'll wear it to your funeral." The montage of clips from her films was a reminder of one of the longest and most versatile careers in the movies.

And another tribute, delivered by Academy president Frank Pierson, went to the late Gregory Peck, "a man of decency." The clips, of course, included moments from his most famous performance, as Atticus Finch in *To Kill a Mockingbird*. The Peck segment led into the annual montage honoring those in the Hollywood community who passed away during the year, from Art Carney, Buddy Hackett, Elia Kazan, Robert Stack, Alan Bates, Gregory Hines, Donald O'Connor, Ann Miller, and Buddy Ebsen to (some wondered if she would be included) "Hitler's favorite filmmaker," Leni Riefenstahl.

Best documentary went to *The Fog of War,* Errol Morris's film about the thoughts and memories of eighty-five-year-old Robert McNamara. The "architect of Vietnam" was in a confessional and revelatory mood during an astonishing conversation.

Morris, often considered the leading documentarian of his generation, had never been nominated before despite such major candidates as *The Thin Blue Line*. In accepting, he was nothing if not frank: "I'd like to thank the Academy for *finally* recognizing my films! I thought it would never happen!"

Morris added the evening's first overtly political comment: "Forty years ago this country went down a rabbit hole in Vietnam. I fear we're going down a rabbit hole again."

"I can't wait for his tax audit," ad-libbed Crystal.

* * *

Bill Murray, introducing his *Lost in Translation* as a Best Picture nominee, sidestepped the usual clichés and deadpanned: "Four days into shooting, several members of our Tokyo cast and crew asked to be removed from the film. They did not believe the director knew what she was doing." The punch line: "We were politely refused."

* * *

High points of the musical performances: "The Scarlet Tide," from *Cold Mountain,* sung with solemn simplicity by Alison Krauss with composers Elvis Costello and T Bone Burnett as accompanists. And then Annie Lennox continued the introspective mood with the ballad "Into the West," from *The Lord of the Rings*.

And a comic highpoint: Eugene Levy and Catherine O'Hara, as fading, estranged folk singers Mitch and Mickey from *A Mighty Wind,* performing in character as they sang "A Kiss at the End of the Rainbow." Oddly enough, as in the film, the song balanced uncannily between satirical and actually sounding like the real thing. Many a real folk song from the 1960s was more hackneyed.

And composer Benoit Charest communicated the eerie charm of *The Triplets of Belleville* in the ragtime version of "Belleville Rendez-vous," with a triplet of girl singers, and percussion performed, as in the movie, on bicycle parts.

Jack Black and Will Ferrell, giving the Oscar for Best Song, revealed that there are actually lyrics for that song the orchestra plays to hurry winners offstage, and they sang them ("No need to thank your parakeets . . . you're boring.")

Winner of the category: *LOTR*, of course, for "Into the West."

Best Foreign Language Film went to *The Barbarian Invasions,* Denys Arcand's human, sad, and funny story of a raffish intellectual surrounded at his deathbed by his friends.

Winners in the short subject categories: Aaron Schneider and Andrew J. Sacks for Best Live Action Short Film for *Two Soldiers* (they were the first to inspire the dreaded orchestral hook); Adam Elliot for Best Animated Short Film for *Harvie Krumpet*; and for Best Documentary Short Subject, Maryann DeLeo for *Chernobyl Heart.*

The show ended on an original and upbeat moment, as all of the winners, some of them not even from New Zealand, joined each other on the stage while the orchestra played "Hooray for Hollywood."

Advance Thinker: *Fahrenheit 9/11*

A reader writes:

"In your articles discussing Michael Moore's film *Fahrenheit 9/11,* you call it a documentary. I always thought of documentaries as presenting facts objectively without editorializing. While I have enjoyed many of Mr. Moore's films, I don't think they fit the definition of a documentary."

That's where you're wrong. Most documentaries, especially the best ones, have an opinion and argue for it. Even those that pretend to be objective reflect the filmmaker's point of view. Moviegoers should observe the bias, take it into account, and decide if the film supports it or not.

Michael Moore is a liberal activist. He is the first to say so. He is alarmed by the prospect of a second term for George W. Bush, and he made *Fahrenheit 9/11* for the purpose of persuading people to vote against him.

That is all perfectly clear, and yet in the days before the film opened bountiful reports by commentators who were shocked! shocked! that Moore's film is partisan. "He doesn't tell both sides," we hear, especially on Fox News, which is so famous for telling both sides.

The wise French director Jean-Luc Godard once said, "The way to criticize a film is to make another film." That there is not a pro-Bush documentary available right now I am powerless to explain. Surely, however, the Republican National Convention will open with such a documentary, which will position Bush comfortably between Reagan and God. The Democratic convention will have a wondrous film about John Kerry. Anyone who thinks one of these documentaries is "presenting facts objectively without editorializing" should look at the other one.

The pitfall for Moore is not subjectivity, but accuracy. We expect him to hold an opinion and argue it, but we also require his facts to be correct. I was an admirer of his previous doc, *Bowling for Columbine,* until I discovered that some of his facts were wrong, or false, or fudged. In some cases he was guilty of making a good story better, but in other cases (such as his ambush of Charlton Heston) he was unfair, and in still others, such as the wording on the plaque under the bomber at the Air Force Academy, he was just plain wrong, as anyone can see by going to look at the plaque.

Because I agree with Moore's politics, his inaccuracies pained me, and I wrote about them in my Answer Man column. Moore wrote me that he didn't expect such attacks "from you, of all people." But I cannot ignore flaws simply because I agree with the filmmaker. In hurting his cause, he wounds mine.

Now comes *Fahrenheit 9/11,* floating on an enormous wave of advance publicity. It inspired a battle of the titans between Disney's Michael Eisner and Miramax's Harvey Weinstein. It won the Palme d'Or at the Cannes Film Festival. It has been rated R by the MPAA, and former New York governor Mario Cuomo has signed up as Moore's lawyer to challenge the rating. The conservative group Move America Forward, which successfully bounced the mildly critical biopic *The Reagans* off CBS and onto cable, has launched a campaign to discourage theaters from showing *Fahrenheit.*

The campaign will amount to nothing and disgraces Move America Forward by showing it trying to suppress disagreement instead of engaging it. The R rating may stand; there is a real beheading in the film, and only fictional beheadings get the PG-13. Disney and Miramax will survive.

Moore's real test will come on the issue of accuracy. He can say whatever he likes about Bush, as long as his facts are straight. Having seen the film twice, I saw nothing that raised a flag for me, and I haven't heard of any major inaccuracies. When Moore was questioned about his claim that Bush unwisely lingered for six or seven minutes in that Florida classroom after learning of the World Trade attacks, Moore was able to reply with: a video of Bush doing exactly that.

I agree with Moore that the presidency of George W. Bush has been a disaster for America. In writing that, I expect to get the usual complaints that movie critics should keep their political opinions to themselves. But opinions are my stock in trade, and is it not more honest to declare my politics than to conceal them? I agree with Moore, and because I do, I hope *Fahrenheit 9/11* proves to be as accurate as it seems.

Three Introductions

Here are introductions I wrote recently to three books that may be of interest to Yearbook readers. The first collects the film criticism of Carl Sandburg; the second is an anthology from Xero, one of the most famous fanzines from the golden age of science-fiction fandom; and the third is a collection of the memos of David O. Selznick.

Introduction by Roger Ebert to *The Movies Are: Carl Sandburg's Film Reviews and Essays, 1920–1928,*
edited by Arnie Bernstein
(Chicago: Lake Claremont Press, 2000).

I am writing these words in Michigan, at our summer home. This morning, as every morning when the weather permits, I walked down wooded lanes that took me to Poet's Path in Birchwood, the road leading past the home where Carl and Lillian Sandburg lived from the late 1920s until 1945, when they moved to North Carolina. Their house still stands, defiantly in violation of later regulations about height and position, its foundations cut into a dune. On the land side it rises five stories, on the Lake Michigan side three, a New England shore house with a widow's walk on the roof.

I have been up there—climbed the ship's ladder to the lookout over the lake to the west and the ravine to the north that carries into the lake a creek that generations of children have redirected with dams of sand. I know this because two of those children, Rob and Rick Edinger, are my neighbors, born on the property they still occupy, and when they were boys they used to dam the creek, and milk Lillian Sandburg's herd of goats, which won blue ribbons at the Berrien County and Michigan State Fairs. A recent owner of the Sandburg house showed me its most unusual feature, a fireproof walk-in bank vault that Sandburg installed to protect his collection of Abraham Lincoln papers and manuscripts. He did not trust the volunteer firemen to arrive in time.

During his residence in the house, Sandburg was writing the third through fifth volumes of his Pulitzer Prize–winning biography of Lincoln. The owner showed me a photograph of the author, bare chested, sitting in the sun on an upended orange crate on a topmost deck overlooking the ravine, writing on an improvised desk. Rick and Rob remember his daily walks on the beach, when he seemed so deep in thought he hardly noticed the world around him. They have both told me, and swear it is true, that one day as a joke they persuaded a tall friend to walk down the beach dressed as Abraham Lincoln in frock coat and top hat. "Good morning, Mr. Sandburg," the figure said. Sandburg glanced up and said, "Good morning, Mr. Lincoln," continuing on his way.

The Michigan years came as Sandburg, by then nearly fifty, had enough of an independent income to free himself from daily journalism. The first volumes of the Lincoln biography must have supplied the couple with funds to move to Michigan and buy a substantial house (larger and more imposing than their home in North Carolina, judging by photographs of it).

Commuting to Chicago in those days would have been by the interurban South Shore Line, which came as far as Michigan City, Indiana, before curving down toward South Bend. That would have been an hour's drive to the station in those days; perhaps it was quicker for them to go up to Benton Harbor and take the ferry across—the same ferry that brought Saul Bellow's Augie March to his summer adventures in Michigan. Neither route would have been that quick, and perhaps the Sandburgs were happy to be free of Chicago and daily deadlines.

It has been widely known that Sandburg reviewed movies for the *Chicago Daily News,* but I confess I thought he did it only occasionally. Now here is this huge book of his reviews, which even at some four hundred pages provides only a portion of his output. These collected reviews show that Sandburg was not a hobbyist in his film criticism, but a professional who worked hard at it for eight years. Arnie Bernstein says that Sandburg saw the movies on a Sunday and wrote his week's reviews the same day, which, even allowing for the shorter running times of most films in those days, made up a long day's work. (His haste at times is perhaps revealed by the Harold Lloyd picture he praises but neglects to name.)

Many of the programs, especially in the Loop and in the ornate Balaban and Katz neighborhood palaces, would have been supported by stage shows, vaudeville, or orchestras, but the live performances were not usually reviewed by Sandburg, perhaps because the *Daily News* had another man assigned to that task.

Chicago in the 1920s and earlier was the hub of several vaudeville wheels, including Radio-Keith-Orpheum, which sent the Marx Brothers revolving through the small cities of Iowa and Illinois. When I interviewed Groucho Marx in 1972 he recalled going to the movies with Carl Sandburg, adding that the theaters were warmer than the rooming houses where his mother, Minnie, lodged the brothers. "He would fall asleep and I would wake him up after the movie was over and tell him what it was about," Groucho told me, but he was kidding. Sandburg was an attentive and observant critic, and moreover, his reviews lack the mischief that Groucho no doubt would have supplied.

One thing you notice, reading through this almost daily coverage of the emerging art form, was that Sandburg took film matter-of-factly. Today shelves groan under the weight of analysis of the silent period, the comedies alone occupying dozens of volumes, but to Sandburg they were not timeless art but movies, meant to be enjoyed; one senses he did not think they were as important as the older arts he considers in his *Complete Poems*, where there are many poems about writers, artists, musicians, and all manner of tradesmen and citizens, but hardly any about the movies.

It is interesting that two of the poets most associated with Illinois, Carl Sandburg and Vachel Lindsay, both devoted a great deal of their time to film criticism. Lindsay's book *The Art of the Moving Picture* collects longer essays of a theoretical nature, in which he was able to look at the earliest films and detect trends that are still visible today. Sandburg takes the view not of a theorist but of a daily newspaperman

whose job is to steer readers toward the good movies and away from the bad ones.

One of his strengths is in seeing the importance of movies as a popular phenomenon. "Is it possible that an extraordinarily good motion picture play can be made from a Harold Bell Wright novel?" he asks, and the answer is yes. He writes: "Culturally speaking, there are arguments to be made that Hollywood—for real or woe—is more important than Harvard, Yale, or Princeton, singly or collectively." He keeps an open mind when going to movies of the broadest possible appeal. He likes Tom Mix's horse, Tony, almost as much as Tom Mix, and then develops an enthusiasm for Tom's dog, Duke. But it is possible to detect a smile, and perhaps a whiff of Mark Twain, in his writing about a picture like *The Sheik*: "The book had sentences such as 'Kiss me, little piece of ice,' but all lines like that were cut out of the movie and it was so different in that respect from the book that it was a disappointment to all who read the book on account of how wicked it was."

There are also echoes of Twain's uncoiling colloquialisms, with a zing at the end, in this wonderful long sentence from his review of a film of the Dempsey-Firpo fight: "Some think Dempsey is knocked through the ropes, and then comes back through the ropes, there is some guessing about where he has been in the meantime, while he has been gone, who picked him up, what they said to the champion, whether he thanked them kindly, and if the Marquis of Queensbury rules cover the point of who shall help and how much they shall help and in exactly what way they shall help a fighter knocked through the ropes and off the platform."

Many of Sandburg's lines conceal sly depths. One of my favorites: "The acting of Lillian Gish in *Orphans of the Storm* is believed by some of her friends to be the best she has done."

Sandburg shared the opinion, universally held at the time, that Chaplin was a genius and Lloyd and Keaton only very good clowns. He wrote that each relied on specialties: "Chaplin on his supreme talent as an actor, Lloyd upon novelty, and Keaton upon droll 'gags.'" That Buster wears better today as an actor might surprise him, but at least he knew how good

Keaton was. As Bernstein points out, Sandburg preferred William C. de Mille to his elder brother Cecil B. (he bet on the wrong pony in that race), and shows an ease in moving between genres as he suggests C. B. might profitably study Keaton's *My Wife's Relations* and "learn something."

There are a lot of interviews here, as Sandburg talked to luminaries on their way through town. In those days and for decades later, until jet planes replaced train travel, stars and directors took the Sante Fe Super Chief to Chicago, lunched with the press, and then continued to New York on the 20th Century Limited. He spoke with his hero von Sternberg, his favorite William C. de Mille, and Constantin Stanislavski, the great theater director, who told him in 1923 that the movies "have not even begun to be an art." (This in contrast to Stanislavski's countryman Tolstoy, who before his death in 1910 was already predicting that film would take the place of the novel in the new century.)

Sometimes Sandburg is a schoolmaster, praising *The Hunchback of Notre Dame* for its artistry and its Lon Chaney performance, but flunking its inter-titles: "And why spell forsworn wrong? Why not use some other word you know how to spell rather than bluff?" At other times he is simply a fan, and his greatest enthusiasms stand up to the test of time. He says he has seen Fairbanks Senior's *The Thief of Bagdad* three times, and wants to see it three more, and his praise is Whitmanesque: "Old and young enjoy it and derive new health from it."

Sandburg left the movie beat in 1928, which was the year when silent films died. It was also "the greatest year in the history of the movies," according to the director Peter Bogdanovich, who featured its films in a revival program at the Telluride Film Festival a few years ago. If he is right, 1928 saw the summit of silent art, followed by the cramped compromises of the early years of sound. Sandburg took the transition in stride; he observed in November 1927 of *The Jazz Singer* that "The vitaphone did a great deal to help, reproducing the songs and some of the other sounds in the course of the action." He resists the temptation to quote "You ain't heard nothin' yet."

Arnie Bernstein has performed an extraordinary accomplishment in bringing this book into being. Having tried to track down some of my own relatively recent reviews I know what a scandalously bad job is done of preserving runs of daily newspapers. All of these reviews had to be located, identified, and transcribed. To that enormous task Bernstein adds great knowledge and insight in his introductions to the reviews, providing background, orientation, historical information, helpful footnotes. This is a book that reopens a chapter of journalism and history that might have remained closed forever.

Introduction by Roger Ebert to *The Best of Xero*, edited by Pat and Dick Lupoff (San Francisco: Tachyon Publications, 2004).

November, 2003—In grade school I had a paper route, and one of the homes where I threw the *Champaign-Urbana Courier* was a tarpaper wartime housing unit occupied by two University of Illinois students from Poland and their mother. When I came around to collect (20 cents a week), they'd invite me in and quiz me, perhaps because I was an odd and talkative kid who amused them. They read science fiction, and when they moved out at the end of the school year they gave me a big cardboard carton filled with old issues of *Astounding*—old even then, from the 1940s, with names like A. E. van Vogt, Robert Heinlein, and L. Ron Hubbard on the covers.

For a time they sat in the basement, to be taken up, looked at, and put back down. I was still into *Tom Corbett, Space Cadet*. But when I was eleven or twelve, I started to read them, and then I bought my own first prozines. *Amazing* was the one most to my liking, and when a new issue hit the stands I regarded it with a certain curious quickening of attention that a year or so later I would come to identify with sexual feelings. It offered the same kind of half-understood forbidden world. I read every word of every issue, flat on my stomach, sprawled on top of the bedspread. In one of those issues there was a column reviewing new fanzines, and I sent off a dime to Buck and Juanita Coulson for a copy of *Yandro*. This was one of the most important and formative acts of my life.

By then I was reading all the prozines— *Analog, F&SF, Galaxy, If, Infinity, Imagination, Imaginative Tales, Fantastic Universe . . .* see how I can still name them. I waited impatiently for the installments of "Hal Clement's Mission of Gravity" in *ASF*. Emsh and Freas, tiny signatures at the bottom of the covers, began to mean a lot to me—and Chesley Bonestell on *F&SF*, of course. I have hundreds of mags in a closet even now, all with a little sticker on the inside cover that says ROGER EBERT'S SCIENCE FICTION COLLECTION.

Every five years or so, in the middle of another task, I'll look at them and a particular cover will bring memory flooding back like a madeleine. The cover of *If*, for example, illustrating the story about a toy that zapped paper clips into the fourth dimension—and what happened when they started leaking back into this one. I bought the Ballantine paperbacks by Arthur C. Clarke and Robert Sheckley, and the Ace Doubles by Murray Leinster and Eric Frank Russell. I bought the anthologies by Groff Conklin and H. L. Gold and the legendary John W. Campbell Jr. I founded the Urbana High School Science Fiction Club; we rented *Destination Moon* and showed it in the auditorium, we went to a speech on the campus by Clarke and got his autograph, and we made a tape recording of H. G. Wells's *War of the Worlds*, complete with sound effects and a performance by my classmate Dave Stiers, who later became David Ogden Stiers of *M*A*S*H*.

But all of that is beside the point. Prozines and fanzines were two different worlds, and it was in the virtual world of science fiction fandom that I started to learn to be a writer and a critic. Virtual, because for a long time I never met any other fans; they lived only in the pages of mimeographed fanzines that arrived at 410 E. Washington St. and were quickly hidden among the hundreds of SF mags in the basement, on metal shelves that cost four books of Green Stamps. "Hidden," because at first I concealed my interest in fandom from my parents. Fanzines were not offensive in any way—certainly not in a sexual way, which would have been the worst way of all in a family living in the American Catholicism of the 1950s, but I sensed somehow that they were . . . dangerous. Dangerous, because they were untamed, unofficial, unlicensed. It was the time of beatniks and *On the Road*, which I also read, and no one who did not grow up in the '50s will be

quite able to understand how subversive fandom seemed.

Most fanzines had a small circulation of a few hundred, but they created a reality so intriguing and self-referential that, for fans, they were the newspapers of a world. Looking through old issues of *Xero*, which during its brief glory was one of the best fanzines ever published, I was stunned by how immediate and vivid my reaction was to names not thought about for years: Harry Warner Jr., Mike Deckinger, Guy Terwilliger, Gene De-Weese, Bob Lichtman, bhob Stewart (how evocative that "h" was!), Walt Willis, Bob Tucker, "Ajay" Budrys, Ted White.

I met Donald Westlake as an adult (we have been on a couple of cruises together) and was surprised to find that I was already reading him in *Xero*. I found established professionals (Harlan Ellison, Donald A. Wollheim, Anthony Boucher, Frederik Pohl, Avram Davidson, James Blish) happy to contribute to a fanzine, indeed plunging passionately into the fray. I confess happily that as I scanned pages and pages of letters of comment ("locs"), my eye instinctively scanned for my own name, as it did forty years ago, and when I found it (Blish dismissing one of my locs), I felt the same flash of recognition, embarrassment, and egoboo that I felt then; much muted, to be sure, diluted, but still there.

Locs were the currency of payment for fanzine contributors; you wrote, and in the next issue got to read about what you had written. Today I can see my name on a full-page ad for a movie with disinterest, but what Harry Warner or Buck Coulson had to say about me—well, that was important.

Wilson (Bob) Tucker was the first fan I met. He lived in Leland, a hamlet south of Bloomington, not far from Urbana. In the summer of 1958, still in high school, I was working as a reporter for the *Champaign-Urbana News-Gazette* and was assigned to drive to Springfield to cover something at the state fair. I made a detour past his house. Bob and Fern made me feel right at home, and to meet them again I concocted a sort of fraud on my newspaper. We had a Sunday article on interior decorating, and I convinced an editor that I should write a piece about the household arrangements of one of Downstate Illinois's major writers. Well, Tucker was major! In the endless fanzine debates about whether SF was really literature, *The Long Loud Silence* was always cited as real literature. Bob was a movie projectionist in Bloomington who wrote in his spare time (a writer with the same talent would be a bestseller today). The Tucker home was a modest two-bedroom suburban house with attached garage—"turn left off the highway when you get to the motel." I photographed the high points of the interior decoration, which to my eye consisted of Bob's typewriter, his desk, his shelves of books, his piles of SF magazines, his framed movie posters, and the Tuckers, standing in front of various compositions of the above. This article actually ran in the paper.

A year or so after that I joined Tucker and Ed Gorman, a fan from Cedar Rapids, on a trip to the MidWestCon in Cincinnati. We drove in my family's Dodge, nearly skidding off a road in Indiana, talking all the way about fandom in a giddy rapid-fire exchange of inside jargon. At a motel in Cincinnati I made people laugh with my reproductions of Bob and Ray routines and drank a little beer, which felt like a lot of beer to an inexperienced drinker, and—here is the earth-shaking part—I actually met Buck and Juanita Coulson, Dick and Pat Lupoff, and Harlan Ellison! The Coulsons struck me as two of the nicest people I had ever met, the kind of people where you would like to move into their spare room, and the astonishingly long run of their *Yandro* was one of the monuments of fandom. The Lupoffs were enormously funny and smart New Yorkers—that city that the novels of Thomas Wolfe had forever colored in my daydreams. Harlan was—how old? Twenty? Young and cocky, with the color proofs for the cover of his new paperback that Berkley Books was about to publish, and as he showed me the glossy reproduction I knew envy of a desperately sincere kind.

The summer of 1961, now a student at the University of Illinois, I made my first trip to Europe on a $325 charter flight, and in Belfast visited Walt and Madeleine Willis. They invited me to tea—tomato sandwiches and Earl Grey—and took me around to meet James White, another of Belfast's BNFs (Big Name Fans), whose prozine collection was carefully wrapped in brown parcel paper, year by year, and labeled ("F&SF 1957").

Fandom was a secret society, and I had admission to friends everywhere who spoke the same arcane language.

In the summer of 1962 I found myself going to South Africa as the press agent for a tour of wheelchair athletes from the University of Illinois. After the long bus trip from Urbana, we stopped overnight at a motel near LaGuardia, and I called Dick and Pat Lupoff. Because this visit was immortalized in *Xero* 9, I drop briefly from my own narrative to allow Dick to see me through his eyes.

Roger Ebert Breezes By

There was a Fanoclast meeting June 15, and when Pat and I got home the baby sitter told us that Rog Ebert had called. Rog Ebert! We hadn't seen him since the 1961 MidWestCon, and had hardly heard from him since. He'd contributed several of his curious hybrid prosepoems to Xero, *but the last of those had appeared in number 6, last September.*

The return number for Rog was the hotel at LaGuardia Airport, and by furious calling and calling back we managed to get in touch with him Saturday, June 16. That night Rog came over for a visit, as did, coincidentally, Coast Guard Al Lewis and Larry Ivie, the latter carrying a Tarzan painting and John Carter painting which he was using as samples.

Rog seemed to have matured considerably since that MidWestCon. Actually, meeting him at the North Plaza Hotel had been my first contact with him. Prior to that, just from reading his fanzine material, I had conjured a slim and sensitive, tall, sallow hypochondriac, slow of speech and manner. What a surprise! Rog is built like a football player, is full of energy, talks incessantly, and is forever telling bad jokes. At that MidWest-Con he had turned a contour chair in the Seascape Room into a space-jockey's bucket, turned his glasses upside down, and had half a roomful of people in hysterics.

But on this trip he had calmed down. After all, he's twenty now.

Rog is terribly, terribly Aware Politically, full of the usual liberal line. He is also an immensely talented young man, and a hustler on top of it. What was he doing in New York in June, for in-

stance. Well, right after the end of the spring semester at the University of Illinois Rog had engineered himself a job as publicity man for a team of paraplegic athletes en route to New York for the annual Wheelchair Games, made a tour at the behest of a South African philanthropist out to start a rehabilitation program for injured persons in his country.

While there, Rog told us, he was going to do the research for an article on student unrest, already all but sold to The Nation. When he gets home, Rog will have to go to work to write an article on a long-lost-but-now-rediscovered folk singer which is slated for Show.

After a full evening of talk, we arranged to meet the following night at a Chinese restaurant in Times Square, following which Rog could get a tour of the two areas of New York he is eager to see: Times Square/42nd Street, and Greenwich Village. By the time the crowd was assembled in the Chinese Republic (Nationalist, of course) it consisted of Walter Breen (who drew a small crowd on the sidewalk before dinner; people kept waiting for him to start a hellfire sermon), Lin Carter and his poopsie, Gary Deindorfer, Lee Hoffman, Ted and Sylvia White, Rog, Pat and myself. It was a pretty good meal, full of plusdoublegood fannish talk, following which the group became unfortunately separated in the surging mob of 42nd Street. All right, so it was Sunday night. There's always a surging mob on 42nd Street.

Lin and his poopsie Claire, Pat and I, and Rog made our way back and forth on the Street for a while, but all that happened was that gay types kept trying to pick Rog up because he looked so wholesome and innocent. Then we gave up and went to the Village.

These meetings, these connections and conversations, were important because they existed in an alternative world to the one I inhabited. Fandom grew out of and fed a worldview that was dubious of received opinion, sarcastic, anarchic, geeky before that was fashionable. In those years it was heretical to take comic books or "Captain Video" seriously. Pop culture was not yet an academic subject. From Lenny Bruce, Stan Freberg, Harvey Kurtzman, Mort Sahl, and Bob and Ray we found an angle on America that cut through

the orthodoxy of the '50s and was an early form of what would come to be known as the '60s.

I published my own fanzine (Stymie), cutting the mimeo masters on an old L. C. Smith and paying an office supply company a few bucks to run it off for me. My freshman year in college I published the Spectator, a weekly "newspaper of politics and the arts" at the university, and this was a descendent of my fanzine. If I had only known it, I had stumbled on the format of the alternative weekly, but I didn't know enough to give it away, and the ads and circulation income weren't enough to keep it afloat; at the end of a year I sold it for $200 and joined the staff of the Daily Illini, then as now a great independent campus paper, and it took so much of my time that, little by little, fandom drifted out of sight.

From time to time I've heard from friends from those days. I spent time with Ed Gorman during a visit to Coe College; he became a mystery writer and wrote a novel about two movie critics who had a TV show. Harlan Ellison and I have had dinner in Los Angeles—once in the home of the eccentric film collector David Bradley, who had a concrete bunker filled with prints behind his house and showed us the rare early cut of The Big Sleep. I ran into Dick Lupoff in San Francisco during a book tour—he has a show on Pacifica—and we remembered that New York visit, when he and Pat seemed so incomprehensibly metropolitan to me. I actually sold two stories to Ted White when he was editing Amazing and Fantastic, circa 1970.

But fan friendships, for me, were mostly long-distance and conducted by mail, and the influence of fandom was on my writing voice. I became critical. I wrote smart-ass locs about other people's writing, and read them about my own. I was in a world that stood outside the mainstream. Science fiction was the occasion for fandom, and often the topic, but the subterranean subject was a kind of kibitzing outsider worldview. Because of fandom, we got to 1967 ten years before most of the non-fan world.

For that matter, we were online before there was online. It is perfectly obvious to me that fanzines were Web pages before there was a Web, and locs were message threads and bulletin boards before there was cyberspace. Someday an academic will write a study proving that the style, tone, and much of the language of the online world developed in a direct linear fashion from science fiction fandom—not to mention the unorthodox incorporation of ersatz letters and numbers in spelling, later to influence the naming of computer companies and programs. Fanzines acted uncannily like mimeographed versions of Usenet groups, forums, message boards, and Web pages—even to such universal design strategies as IYGTFUI (If You've Got the Font, Use It). Some of the same people segued directly from fandom to online, especially to places like the Well—not surprisingly, since many computer pioneers were also SF fans.

Today fandom survives on the Web, where it is no doubt World Wide, and some very slick fanzines have segued into prozines. Are there still analog (paper) publications called fanzines? I haven't heard that there are. That world has moved on. How long did *Yandro* last? How much is my first edition of the *Fancyclopedia* worth? Today a twelve-year-old kid in Urbana has other ways to connect with alternative ideas, other worlds to explore.

No doubt they are as exciting as fandom was for me. God knows what we would have given in 1958 for the Web.

But for the years of their existence, what a brave new world fanzines created! There was a rough democracy at work; no one knew how old you were unless you told them, and locs made it clear that you either had it or you didn't. First, of course, was the hurdle of getting your stuff accepted. When Lupoff or Coulson or Deckinger printed something by me, that was recognition of a kind that my world otherwise completely lacked. To look through these old pages of *Xero* even today and find Harlan Ellison right about *Psycho* when the world was wrong, and Blish taking on Amis, is to realize that in the mimeographed pages of a fanzine created in the Lupoff living room there existed a rare and wonderful discourse, and it was a privilege to be part of it.

Introduction by Roger Ebert to *Memo from David O. Selznick*
selected and edited by Rudy Behlmer
(New York: Modern
Library, 2000).

This book represents only the tip of the iceberg. When Daniel Selznick, David O. Selznick's younger son, asked Rudy Behlmer to edit a selection of his father's memos, Behlmer had little notion of the task involved. The archive was lodged at that time at Bekins Moving and Storage in Los Angeles and Behlmer wrote: "I'll never forget walking into the building in which the files are stored for the first time and being confronted by approximately two thousand file boxes!" Those were only the memos—the written record of substantially every thought Selznick had about his career from 1916 to 1965. When the David O. Selznick Collection was acquired by the University of Texas in 1981, it included countless other boxes, containing scripts and all their revisions, bills and statements, publicity materials, fan mail, receipts, and the continuity record of every day's shooting on almost every film. On an ordinary day Selznick used two secretaries, sometimes more, to take his dictation, and executives were not surprised when a Selznick memo arrived fifteen minutes before they were scheduled to meet with him in person.

This extraordinary outpouring is invaluable for the way it preserves the day-to-day operation of a major player during Hollywood's golden age. It is also intriguing as a glimpse into a life. The most revealing biographical detail about David O. Selznick may not be that in 1940 with only three productions (*Gone with the Wind, Rebecca, Intermezzo*) his independent operation was the highest-grossing studio in Hollywood. The key detail may be that at the age of seventeen he was already in the family business: "I was, after school hours, in charge of a monumental publicity and advertising department." The word "monumental" is not an exaggeration; his father at that time was the movie industry's biggest advertiser. Later, "still after school hours," he became editor of the *Selznick Newsreel*, and while still in his teens negotiated a deal with Will Rogers, then one of the biggest stars, to contribute quips and comments for the title cards between the news clips. At first Selznick got the comments for free. Later, Rogers asked for $100 a week. "Since this was still cheaper than any other footage I could get, I agreed to it." It was a good deal for Rogers, too, leading eventually to his syndicated newspaper column.

The key here is that David O. Selznick was a boy doing a man's job—hiding in a man's job, we might guess. No matter how well-placed his father's confidence, no matter how cocky and precocious the son, he was a high school student masquerading as an adult: "I was self-conscious about my youth and in giving orders and expressing myself verbally, but dictating permitted me to hide behind the front of what I liked to think were impressive memos." There are times throughout this book when we sense the voice of that bright teenage boy, especially in the soul-searching memos (some of them never sent) begging this or that studio head to release him from a contract or allow him to resign. Some of the longest and most impassioned memos in this book are not about movies but about Selznick—his achievements, his abilities, the recognition he has not been granted and feels is his due. He wants the father figures to bless him. The man who produced *Gone with the Wind* makes this extraordinary statement: He and his brother Myron inherited some of their father's traits, but "neither of us has his vision or genius for big-scale operations." This about a parent who went bankrupt not in the Depression but in the boom years after the war. After Selznick married Irene Mayer, Louis B. Mayer's daughter, the Hollywood quip was that "the son-in-law also rises." Actually, I think, it was always the son rising.

It is crucial that in the early years Selznick was brought by his father into the business side of the family firm (Myron was handed production responsibilities, also at an early age). He remembers riding to and from work with his father, listening to a running commentary on actors and directors, who were to his father, as they became to him, not artists but employees. He wants recognition from L. B. Mayer or Ben Schulberg, who he respects, but he writes: "I am getting to the end of the rope of patience with criticism based on [the] assumption that actors know more about scripts than I do." John Ford and George Cukor "both are great directors," he writes, but "both have to have their stories selected for them and guided for them." A falling-out with Ford came when Selznick wanted him to direct *Lafayette Escadrille*, which he never made; Ford, freed from his contract and Selznick's guidance, went ahead to make the

project he had been stubbornly insisting on, *Stagecoach.*

If Selznick learned early to feel more comfortable dictating memos than meeting face-to-face with his colleagues, there may have been more than one reason. "Socially, he was such a disaster that one could hardly believe it was true," remembered the British director Michael Powell, who worked with him on *The Wild Heart.* In her memoir *A Private View,* Irene Mayer Selznick recalls that David so often arrived two hours late for dinner invitations that if he arrived only forty-five minutes late he felt no explanation was necessary. He drove himself relentlessly—and that, combined with what she says was an underactive thyroid and the benzedrine he took to compensate, made him prone to unexpected crashes; he would nod off during dinners, and then bounce back, eager for more. "These pills gave David what amounted to a couple of days extra a week," she wrote. "They also took years off his life, he later agreed. Much later."

Selznick had no patience with small talk, and terrorized subordinates who he felt were wasting his time. "My memo-writing probably had its beginning," Selznick mused, "through my working with my father, who was terribly impatient of interviews with people. I remember hearing him complain many times that most people took fifteen minutes to say what they should say in ten seconds." He also liked memos because they set down in black and white exactly what had been said, ordered, or agreed upon, and could be referred to when subordinates pleaded memory lapses. There is the zeal of the control freak in Selznick's minutes about Marlene Dietrich's hair, Gable's tailor, Bergman's eyebrows. Of course, he is usually right in these details, and therefore correct to want them remembered. There is also, in some of the memos, the peculiar combination of drone and intensity that suggests they were written on speed.

One realizes, midway through the book, that Selznick would have seized upon the invention of e-mail, which sidesteps small talk and allows instant gratification of the need to give instructions. "I find," he wrote, "that I can think a thing through to its conclusion more clearly if I can express my views completely without interruption and without argument." Indeed, the one note lacking in this book is a sense of collaboration. We don't read about story conferences, we don't see exchanges of views about characters and plot points. We read his instructions. He was not a collaborator. He knew he was right.

Creative people did not always much like him. "He was so eager to understand things that were not to be understood, only appreciated," wrote Powell, whose autobiography is the best ever written by a director. "Art made no impression on him, only size." And later: "He never had the guts to direct a picture himself. He shunned the responsibility. He preferred to spend hours and days of his life dictating memos telling other people how to direct films. This made him a rather pathetic figure."

Pathetic through Powell's eyes, although not to his fellow moguls, who envied his success and grudgingly praised his famous attention to detail. If he never directed a film himself, Selznick became adept at pulling strings from behind his wizard's curtain. His correspondence on *Gone with the Wind,* which by itself could be spun out into a larger book than this, shows a man engrossed in a dream of making the longest, most expensive, and most successful movie of the sound era, and succeeding. "He confused greatness with size," the director Bertrand Tavernier told me. And size was achieved through countless atoms of detail. No detail was too small to escape his notice, because to the Selznick eye all details were equally large; Clark Gable, denied by a Selznick underling the tailor he usually worked with, wins the boss's sympathy: "A more ill-fitting and unbecoming group of suits I have never seen on a laboring man, much less on a star."

The replacement of George Cukor on *Gone with the Wind* by Victor Fleming, Sam Wood, and two or three other hands has been much written about. Cukor once told me it might have had something to do with Gable's feeling that he was paying excessive attention to Vivien Leigh's scenes. The memos here suggest it was not Gable but Selznick who could not work with Cukor; the implication is that Cukor would not follow Selznick's detailed suggestions for every scene. Ten years later, producing *The Third Man,* Selznick complains that director Carol Reed "has seen fit to take only those changes which suit him." Yet if we consider Selznick's complaints in view of Reed's finished film, it appears that many of them were justified; the movie's distinctive portrait of a city divided into zones of occupation was lost, Selznick complained, in Reed's early draft of a story preoccupied with the British.

S. N. Behrman, the prolific writer who worked on several Selznick projects, said in his introduction to the first edition of this book, "Whatever relationship David had with anybody, providing he or she was in the film business, was a Pygmalion relationship." Certainly Selznick played Henry Higgins in the life of Ingrid Bergman. Seeing her for the first time in the Swedish version of *Intermezzo,* he wired a New York employee, "Take the next boat to Sweden and [do] not come home without a contract with Miss Bergman." Later, looking at the Swedish picture again, "A cold shudder has just run through me on the realization that maybe we are dealing for the wrong girl. Maybe the girl we are after is Gosta Stevens. You had better check on this." Relief: He had the right girl. Then he fretted over her name, which was not good for a marquee, he thought. He considered "Ingrid Berjman" and "Ingrid Berriman" before conceding that she already had a reputation under her real name. Then he feared that she would prove too tall: "Do you think we will have to use stepladders with Leslie Howard?"

Volumes of memos went out about the correct way to photograph Bergman: "The difference in her photography is the difference between great beauty and a complete lack of beauty." Harsh words about one of the great beauties of the screen, but Selznick was right. I remember joining the cinematographer Haskell Wexler in a shot-by-shot analysis of *Casablanca* at a film festival. Wexler tapped the laserdisc freeze-frame button to deconstruct a shot in which Bergman turns from left to right. He froze it midway. "You could never photograph her head-on," he said. "It wasn't a good angle for her." Selznick knew that before Bergman had been in a single frame of American film.

Of all the memos in this book, the most astonishing is the one that Selznick wrote to Bergman as if it came to him from her. She wanted out of her contract, and in January 1947 he wrote a memo as if in her own abject voice, in which she reviews their relationship and her own ingratitude: "Unfortunately for you, when I returned from Europe, and had everything that I wanted, I forgot all about my promises and statements through the years. I forgot everything you had done for me ... " The effect of the memo is one of boiling anger and sarcasm on his part. "It is a great idea for a letter," writes David Thomson in his invaluable Selznick biography *Showman*, "but one that a grown man should have abandoned in the morning."

Some of Selznick's memos, on the other hand, could be sent out again today, and still apply usefully. He scorned "Mickey Mouse" scoring, "an interpretation of each line of dialogue, and each movement musically, so that the score tells with music exactly what is being done by the actors on the screen." He liked Bergman's natural eyebrows and wanted Vivien Leigh to have "eyebrows au natural," observing, "the public was sick and tired of the monstrosities that had been inflicted on the public by most of Hollywood's glamour girls." He had good taste on pictures that were not self-evidently good to most Hollywood executives, congratulating Val Lewton on *Cat People*.

Selznick's most complex artistic relationship was with Alfred Hitchcock. They made *Rebecca* together and it won the Oscar for Best Picture, but such other collaborations as *The Paradine Case* were less successful, and eventually the director broke free to produce his own films. Selznick resisted the director's supreme air of self-confidence in knowing exactly what shots he needed. Hitchcock was known for storyboarding his films and cutting "in the camera," in the sense that he did not shoot extra coverage from angles he felt would not be needed. Selznick missed the whole point of this, seeing it only in budgetary terms: "Reducing the number of angles required is highly desirable, and no one appreciates its value more than I do, but certainly it is of no value if you are simply going to give us less cut film per day than a man who shoots twice as many angles."

"How naive were the judgments upon which he based his decisions," Michael Powell remembered. "Later on, when we worked with him, I tended to ignore his advice and opinions, which was a mistake. Hitch, that great diplomat, knew how to handle him and puzzled him so, that he retained David's respect long after he became his own producer."

Powell also recalls a day when he visited the set of *Duel in the Sun*, Selznick's last great production and a showcase for Jennifer Jones, the woman he married after Irene divorced him. The film was being directed by King Vidor, a great figure since silent days, and Powell was surprised to discover that Selznick had hired another silent veteran, Josef von Sternberg, as Vidor's "consultant." "Only either a supreme optimist, or a complete idiot like David," wrote Powell, "would have tried to drive in double harness the romantic realism of King Vidor, the champion of the common man, and the romantic kitsch of von Sternberg, the exploiter of female eroticism." Yes, but it turned out to be a good picture.

Do today's directors save their memos and e-mails? Perhaps, but my guess is they wouldn't be as revealing as Selznick's, because so much of their important work is done face-to-face. The Selznick written legacy is invaluable precisely because so few other filmmakers work the way he did. For a period spanning the birth of sound and the arrival of television, he wrote down just about anything of any substance that happened in his professional life. His particular judgments, right or wrong, are not the issue: What we're given is a seat in his office, daily access to his schemes and visions, the Nixon tapes of Hollywood's golden age.

In Memoriam

Marlon Brando

He was the most influential single actor in the history of the movies, and one of the most exasperating. He was instrumental in the success of some of the greatest films of all time and cheerfully appeared in some of the worst. He was a poet and, at the end, he claimed to be a pauper, but in all the seasons of his life he was unmistakably, defiantly, brilliantly Marlon Brando.

The great actor died Thursday, July 1, 2004, in an undisclosed Los Angeles hospital, of undisclosed causes, at the age of eighty. His passing was made known Friday by his attorney, David J. Seeley. Brando died as stories appeared in print saying that he was nearly destitute, occupying a few rooms in the Hollywood Hills, living off Social Security and the residuals from some of his movies. Later stories report his estate was worth millions.

Look at old movies on TV and you will sense a difference in the acting before and after 1947. That was the year Brando starred on Broadway as Tennessee Williams' macho, petulant Stanley Kowalski in *A Streetcar Named Desire*. His performance broke through some kind of psychic barrier, freeing actors of his and later generations to tap emotions that most earlier actors were unable or unwilling to reveal. It was said that his style was fashioned by the famed acting teacher Stella Adler, but perhaps he possessed it all along, and Adler simply recognized and encouraged it; it took her only a week of coaching Brando, remembers the AP's Bob Thomas, before she said that within a year he would be the best young actor in America.

Much is made of the generation that followed, the Method actors, and although there is much theory and lore associated with the Method, to some degree it consisted of a lot of actors trying to do what Brando did. Paul Newman, James Dean, Montgomery Clift, Robert DeNiro, Jack Nicholson, Al Pacino, Sean Penn, and Johnny Depp all owe something to Brando. And a performance like Charlize Theron's in *Monster* is almost literally made possible by the avenues Brando opened.

A recent *Premiere* magazine poll named Brando's Don Corleone, from Francis Coppola's *The Godfather* (1972), the single most memorable character in movie history. *The Godfather* is at or near the top of many lists of the greatest films, and Brando's masterpieces also include his film of *A Streetcar Named Desire* (1951), *On the Waterfront* (1954), *Apocalypse Now* (1979), and *Last Tango in Paris* (1972). In those films he was fearless, exposing his psyche in *Last Tango* in a famous sex scene that no other major actor might have dared. *Apocalypse Now* traded on his mystique by keeping him offscreen until the closing act of the film; he was the enigmatic Col. Kurtz, brilliant, crazy, holed up in the Vietnamese jungle, running his own operation. Even when he appeared, he was seen mostly in shadow, speaking of the horrors of war in a way that transcended the movie and the character.

Brando played all kinds of characters in all kinds of movies, and had box-office winners with *Viva Zapata!* (1952), *Guys and Dolls* (1955), *The Teahouse of the August Moon* (1956), and *Sayonara* (1957). He took chances with risky projects like John Huston's *Reflections in a Golden Eye* (1967) and his own *One-Eyed Jacks* (1961).

And, increasingly, he seemed to enjoy provoking Hollywood with his unpredictable behavior. He won Oscars for his work in *On the Waterfront* and *The Godfather* and was nominated for six other roles, but will always be remembered for refusing to attend the Oscar ceremony for *The Godfather* and sending a woman named Sacheen Littlefeather to protest discrimination against Native Americans. That Littlefeather was later identified as Maria Cruz, an actress who was not an Indian, only compounded his notoriety.

Brando's later decades were marked by personal and health problems. His son Christian shot and killed Dag Drollet, the lover of his half-sister Cheyenne, at the family's Los Angeles home; Christian was sentenced to ten years, and five years later Cheyenne committed suicide.

Brando, who had been so lithe and toned in early roles like his motorcycle gang leader in *The Wild One* (1953), had a dramatic weight gain in his later decades. This he disguised by vast dark costumes, or by shadow; in *Apocalypse Now,* all we can usually see is his face. In perhaps his worst film, *The Island of Dr. Moreau* (1996), "he's only on screen for about fifteen minutes," wrote the critic James Berardinelli, "and, while there, his amazing girth is far more likely to capture our attention than his acting." Yet in a very funny 1990 comedy named *The Freshman* he used his bulk as part of the joke, chomping on M&Ms while doing a parody of Don Corleone. And then what astonishing grace he exhibited in an ice-skating scene, gliding along to a Tony Bennett song. He could blindside you with something surprising like that. It was a superb comic performance, although he told an interviewer the movie was "trash"—and then, a few days later, issued a statement saying it might be all right after all.

Most of those late roles were frankly done for the money; even with *Apocalypse Now,* his salary demands were extreme and are chronicled in *Hearts of Darkness,* a documentary about Coppola's travails in making the film. Coppola got his money's worth, however, because no other actor would have been iconic enough to function as the unseen object of the hazardous river journey that occupies the movie's first two hours. I attended the world premiere at Cannes, and still remember the hushed, electric silence, as we all leaned forward at the first glimpse of Brando. The joke at Cannes was that the plot showed men willing to risk death to see what Brando would come up with.

Brando's life and career were both governed by a nature that could be called arrogant, or independent, or free-spirited, or simply eccentric. In a notorious live hour TV interview with Larry King, was Brando just acting goofy, or did he know exactly what he was doing when he appeared in a garish shirt and shorts, kept talking when King tried to go to commercials, insisted the interviewer eat some organic cookies, which he somehow implied contained less-than-savory ingredients, and then ended the interview by kissing the astonished King? It was brilliant television, and you had to watch. Brando was on a tight-wire while other actors of his vintage would have been statesmanlike and boring.

Of his three marriages, untidy love life, and assorted children, much has been written. But in romance as in other areas, Brando marched to his own drummer. He was not a creature of trendy clubs, benefit dinners, and red carpet interviews, but lived out of sight, often in a Tahitian hideaway. Martin Scorsese told me that he and De Niro flew to Tahiti to consult with Brando about a project, and spent days talking about—well, they weren't sure what, and when they returned home they couldn't say quite what had been decided.

I had a long telephone conversation with Brando within the last year, and it happened like this. Nancy de los Santos, onetime producer of *Siskel & Ebert,* was producing a documentary called *The Bronze Screen,* about a century of Latino actors in Hollywood. She wanted to talk to Brando because of *Viva Zapata!* and because of his support for Latinos in general. He agreed. But when she arrived at his house for the shoot, he insisted that she join him in the shot—so that he could interview her. "I didn't get anything I could use," she said, "but I felt like I made a friend."

He asked her for my number, but it was more than a year later before the phone rang one night and it was Marlon Brando. I was astonished. We talked for about forty-five minutes, but it wasn't an interview and I didn't ask him about any of his movies. He set the agenda. He had a project he wanted us to work on together. I would like to tell you what it was, but I have no idea. It wasn't that he was rambling or confused. He made perfect sense, but in a way that had no paraphrasable meaning. It was a performance in which he was playing a man who wanted to pitch a project; the man and the pitch were the content, not the project. When I got off the phone, my wife couldn't wait to find out what Brando had wanted. "I don't have the slightest idea," I told her, "but he made it sound fascinating."

Fred Holstein

January 20, 2004—I can think of three times when I cried while listening to the radio. The first was when the death of John F. Kennedy was announced. The other two were during the WFMT *Midnight Special* tributes to Steve

Goodman and, last Saturday night, Fred Holstein.

I know myself well enough to know on those last two occasions I was moved not only by their loss, but by my own.

Old Town and Lincoln Avenue in the 1960s and 1970s were where Chicago went to be young, to drink and sing all night, to live forever. We were a shifting population of people who knew each other, sometimes well, sometimes barely, and saw each other night after night in the same places.

For me the anchor was O'Rourke's Pub at 319 W. North, and no night was complete without touching base there. But many nights a crowd would gather and move down the street, maybe to the Old Town Ale House, maybe to the Quiet Knight, very often to the Earl of Old Town. Even later we might work our way up Lincoln to Sterch's or Orphan's or Oxford's.

The Earl, across the street from Second City, was the holy ground of the Chicago folk music renaissance, and there I heard for the first time Steve Goodman and Fred Holstein and Bonnie Koloc, Michael Smith, Jim Post, Bob Gibson, Ginny Clemons, and the remarkable string band Martin, Bogan, and the Armstrongs. I was there after hours one night when Goodman sang a song he said he had just composed called "City of New Orleans," and John Prine was there, too. John was a mailman in Maywood when he started singing at the Fifth Peg, on Armitage, and I knew from the moment I heard him how good he was. I wasn't a music critic, but I wrote about him in the *Sun-Times* because after hearing him sing "Old Folks" and "Sam Stone," how could I not?

Fred and his brothers Ed and Alan were everywhere during those years—Fred and Ed onstage, Alan working the room at the two clubs they co-owned, Somebody Else's Troubles and Holstein's. They had good taste and good friends, and on their stages I heard such wonders as Doc Watson and Queen Ida. Fred sometimes was the headliner, sometimes was the opening act, sometimes was on the road. The thing was, he loved to sing. Loved it. And his way with a song was like a lover's caress.

On the *Midnight Special*, Rich Warren played Fred's arrangement of "Mr. Bojangles," and I felt as if nobody else had ever quite understood it. And his other signature songs:

"The Streets of London" and "All the Good People." And "Hush, Little Baby, Don't You Cry." Who else could have sung that one in a saloon at midnight? Warren played the songs from a recording he made at the Earl on June 29, 1969, and you could hear the glasses clinking in the background and waitresses shouting orders to Jimmy the cook, and then Fred's voice would quiet the room, and you wouldn't hear a thing except the music.

Those were wonderful days to be young and alive and in Chicago. I didn't know Fred well, but let's say I knew him frequently. We both drank, but I drank more than he did, because he usually had to sing until 2 A.M. One Saturday afternoon I was doing my laundry at the launderette across from Fred's club, and while the clothes were in the dryer I went over there. The club was closed but Fred was inside, let me in, poured me a drink. I told him I was hungover, and we talked about drinking, which was a condition of life for the regulars on the Old Town and Lincoln Avenue circuit. What did we say? I don't know; maybe we were trying to figure out the secret.

Our hero was Jay Kovar, who ran O'Rourke's and seemed to be able to drink all evening and be calm and wise and steady. What I remember from Fred was his sympathy. He was the kind of guy who always had time to talk, always had time to listen. So did Jay, for that matter. The Old Town and Lincoln Avenue scene wasn't exactly based on retail; it was more like a nightly reunion of friends.

At the time of his death, Fred was bartending and singing at Sterch's, one of the surviving bars from the golden age. Last summer in Grant Park I ran into proprietor Bob Smerch and his famous grin and his young daughter, and we talked a little about the old days, but so much went unsaid. We knew. We had been there. Some lasted longer than others. I bailed out in 1979. If I hadn't, I'd be dead. But I won't say it wasn't a wonderful time.

When Rich Warren played "All the Good People" Saturday night, the lyrics by Ken Hicks sounded more poignant to me than they ever had before. He closed with them, and so will I:

This is a song for all the good travelers
Who passed through my life as they moved along.

*The ramblers, the thinkers, the just-one-more
drinkers*
Each took the time to sing me a song.

Elia Kazan

Elia Kazan, who presided over a revolution in
American acting, and directed films that won
twenty Academy Awards, died Saturday, September 28, 2003, at ninety-four. His films included such towering achievements as
*A Streetcar Named Desire, On the Waterfront, A
Face in the Crowd,* and *East of Eden,* but when
the Academy gave him its Lifetime Achievement Award in 1999, as many as half the audience members refused to applaud—because he
"named names" during the congressional
witch-hunt of the early 1950s.

Kazan was a Communist Party member for
two years in the mid-1930s. In the McCarthy
era, the House Un-American Activities Committee held widely publicized hearings, asking
Hollywood figures to name others they knew to
be Communists. When Kazan cooperated, he
was shunned and scorned by many of his colleagues for the rest of his life.

Kazan was adamant that he had done the
right thing. In his autobiography, *Elia Kazan: A
Life* (1988), he said he had come to hate the
Party, which "should be driven ... into the light
of scrutiny." His action was taken, he said, "out
of my own true self."

Those who refused to testify said the hearings were show trials, like those conducted by
Stalin. They pointed out that Communist Party
membership was legal. A year after testifying,
Kazan directed his greatest film, *On the Waterfront,* in which his hero, Terry Malloy (Marlon
Brando), names names before a panel investigating labor practices.

The movie was written by Budd Schulberg, a
writer who also named former Communists,
and the movie was seen by many as a response
to their critics. Kazan said it wasn't. Whether it
was or not, it is considered one of the greatest
of all American films, was nominated for
eleven Oscars and won seven, including Best
Picture, Director, Actor, Actress, Screenplay,
and Cinematography.

Mr. Kazan began as an actor, with the
influential Group Theater in New York. He
began directing, and his breakthrough was *The
Skin of Our Teeth* (1942), which starred Tallulah

Bankhead. He was on Broadway at a time of
enormous change in the American theater, and
helped guide it with his direction of plays by
the two ranking giants among playwrights,
Tennessee Williams and Arthur Miller.

At the same time, in 1947, he was a cofounder
of the Actors Studio, the most creative force in
modern American acting, and by casting the
young Marlon Brando in first the stage and
then the screen version of Williams's *A Streetcar Named Desire,* he launched the most
influential modern actor. Mr. Kazan and
Brando brought a rawness, urgency, and emotional intensity to acting that in many ways has
touched all American movie acting ever since.

Kazan's first major film was *A Tree Grows in
Brooklyn* (1945), based on the Betty Smith
novel about a family that survives poverty and
alcoholism. Always interested in social issues,
he made *Gentleman's Agreement* (1947), about
anti-Semitism in American business; *Pinky*
(1949), about a light-skinned black woman
who is tempted to pass for white; *Panic in the
Streets* (1950), a thriller about a search for a
plague-carrier; *Viva Zapata!* (1952), again starring Brando, as the Mexican revolutionary;
Man on a Tightrope (1953), an object lesson
about the perils of communism in Europe;
East of Eden (1955), based on the Steinbeck
novel, which gave James Dean his first major
role; the hotly controversial *Baby Doll* (1956),
starring Carroll Baker in a performance considered daring at the time; and *A Face in the
Crowd* (1957), with its famous Andy Griffith
performance as a singing ex-con who becomes
a demagogue.

Kazan continued to discover important
young actors in the 1960s, giving Warren Beatty
his first major role in *Splendor in the Grass*
(1961), and introducing the teenage Theresa
Russell in *The Last Tycoon* (1976). His *America,
America* (1963) was based on the life of his
uncle, who, like other members of Kazan's family, left Greece for America.

As film directing jobs became harder to find,
Kazan devoted more time to his writing, and
displayed a considerable gift. His *A Life* is one
of the best of all Hollywood autobiographies,
notable for its honesty and frankness. For example, here he is telling the story of how he
happened to cast the unknown Theresa Russell
in *The Last Tycoon*:

Sam (Spiegel, the producer) suggested her. I had strong reservations, saw some values but more drawbacks. It was obvious to me, and later conversations with Theresa verified this, that Sam had, for a long time, tried to gentle her into his bed. I saw this without prejudice, because the truth is that most men of imagination and passion in the arts tend to use their power over young women—and young men—to this end. It's life-loving and it's inevitable. Sam, according to Miss Russell, had pursued her for many months unsuccessfully, and apparently he'd not given up. When I worked with her, as he requested, I liked her too, and came to believe she was certainly the best of a poor field and would bring something unanticipated to the role.

He is equally frank about Brando, Beatty, and the other major players in his life, and his discussion of his decision to name names, while many might disagree, doesn't avoid the issue or cloak it in banalities, but engages it. His decision made him a pariah, he writes, but the more he saw of communism the more comfortable he was with what he had done.

Many never forgave him. Two years before his honor at the Academy Awards, the American Film Institute refused to give him one of its tributes. It took the backstage work of the director Martin Scorsese to convince the Academy that an award was deserved and timely, and Scorsese and actor Robert De Niro introduced him that night in 1999. Thanking them, he said, "Now I can slip away."

Irv Kupcinet

Irv Kupcinet loved being a newspaperman, and he loved the *Chicago Sun-Times*. For sixty years his column was the bulletin board for our city's triumphs and tragedies; there was room at the top for big scoops, and at the bottom for birthdays, anniversaries, and quips from faithful correspondents. When somebody died, he always wrote, "Our town is flying its heart at half-staff." Today our hearts are at half-staff for Kup.

He was above all a kind man. When I joined the paper in 1966, he had already been writing the column for twenty-three years, hosted a national television show, and, in those years before Oprah, was our biggest celebrity. Yet he took a fledging film critic under his arm. At the

Oscars, sitting at the typewriter next to Kup's, I sensed he was the power center in the pressroom. He made sure I was invited to the parties and met his friends the stars. He didn't have to, but he was inclusive, and to know Kup and Essee was to join the unending gabfest that was their life.

To enter his office at the *Sun-Times* was to walk down a corridor hung with autographed pictures (Harry Truman, Frank Sinatra, veterans on the Purple Heart Cruise) and past his gifted assistant Stella Foster. I never once saw his office door closed, and he was never too much "on deadline" to talk.

For many years he smoked a pipe, and the room was filled with smoke. Usually there was a half-finished column in the typewriter, or later on the computer screen, and as we talked Stella would call in that Mike Ditka, or Bob Hope, or Mayor Daley (either one) was on the phone, and he'd check an item and continue the conversation. He was curious. He'd want to know what I thought of a new movie, or whether the film festival was having a good year. I never saw him impatient or out of temper, and I literally never heard him say an unkind word about anyone.

In a time when many of the "three-dot" columns feasted on gossip and innuendo, Kup's column wasn't cruel. It was also very rarely wrong; he had to run fewer corrections than anyone in the business. It always ran on one of the back pages, just before the business section, and when he was asked why he didn't ask for a position up front, he said he liked batting after everyone was on base.

Dinner parties at the Kups' Lake Shore Drive residence brought together the same mixture of conversationalists as Kup's show. Carol Channing was a guest whenever she was in town, bringing along her own organic food in stainless steel canisters. The company might include William Friedkin, Lucille Ball, Roger Moore, Harold Washington, Phil Donahue, politicians, sports stars, neighbors. Bears great Sid Luckman lived right downstairs, and always invited the guests to stop off on his floor for gifts; I got a crystal salad bowl and some candlesticks one night.

If Kup was diplomatic, Essee told you exactly what was on her mind. One Sunday morning she called me to hurry down to the Whitehall for brunch with Tennessee Williams, who was involved later that day in one of her innumerable benefits. I thanked her for thinking of me. "It isn't that," she said. "I want you to keep him talking so he doesn't drink too much."

The first words Kup said to me, in September 1966, were "Copy boy!" I was twenty-four, he hadn't seen me in the office before, and it was a reasonable assumption. The last times I saw him were at tributes—a big one at the Empire Room, a little one upstairs at Harry Carey's. People loved him and wanted to thank him. He was in a wheelchair by then, but still alert, still with that firm handshake, still curious, still able to bring down the house with well-timed one-liners.

After Essee died there was something forever missing from his life, but the column was still there, and with Stella's help he continued to write it because, after all, his byline had been in the *Sun-Times* since its very first day, so why stop now?

Donald O'Connor

The man who performed the most sensational solo number in the history of musical comedy is dead. Donald O'Connor, whose "Make 'em Laugh" number in *Singin' in the Rain* (1952) was a show-stopper that delighted and astonished generations of audiences, died at seventy-eight on Saturday, September 27, 2003.

"Make 'em Laugh" was like an expression of Mr. O'Connor's showbiz philosophy. Using a movie set as a backdrop, he danced, did acrobatics, tumbled to the floor, engaged in a one-sided fight with a dummy, and ran up a wall to do a back flip—singing most of the time.

"How did you run up that wall?" a young girl asked Mr. O'Connor at my Overlooked Film Festival in April 2003 at the University of Illinois in Urbana-Champaign.

"Experience," he deadpanned.

The festival had just shown a new 35mm print of *Singin' in the Rain,* often said to be the greatest movie musical of all. Every number was greeted with applause, and Mr. O'Connor, sitting next to his wife, nodded happily. He was in frail health at the screening and used a wheelchair—but only when he was out of sight of the audience. He walked onstage to a standing ovation, and then used the old vaudevil-

lian's trick of suddenly seeming to notice the balcony, inspiring a second ovation. He sparkled during a forty-five-minute question session, and then sat in a car outside the theater and happily signed autographs for almost an hour.

O'Connor was one of the top Hollywood stars of the 1940s and 1950s, not only in musicals *(Anything Goes, Call Me Madam, There's No Business Like Show Business, Walking My Baby Back Home),* but also in a wildly popular series featuring Francis the Talking Mule—which eventually morphed into the TV series *Mr. Ed.*

"I quit working with Francis," he told the Illinois audience, "when he started getting more fan mail than I did."

Mr. O'Connor was born in Chicago to a vaudeville family, and recalled that he was sometimes left for a time with relatives in downstate Danville. He started in movies as a child, playing Huckleberry Finn in *Tom Sawyer—Detective* (1938). He worked steadily through the 1950s, usually in comedies, and had his own TV comedy series in the 1950s. One of his few flops was his biography of another great physical comedian, *The Buster Keaton Story* (1957), which nobody liked, including Mr. O'Connor.

Asked how a number like "Make 'em Laugh" could possibly be choreographed, Mr. O'Connor told the audience he made it up in bits and pieces.

"Gene Kelly had injured himself, as I recall, and we had a couple of free days to make up something. We started with the set and the song. There was a sofa, so that went in. Somebody handed me the dummy, and that was in. Whatever worked, we kept."

O'Connor died of heart failure at a retirement home in Calabases, California, according to his daughter, Alicia. The family told the Associated Press that his last words were: "I'd like to thank the Academy for my Lifetime Achievement Award that I will eventually get."

Leni Riefenstahl

Leni Riefenstahl, who did more than any other artist to shape the image of the Third Reich, died in her sleep Monday, September 8, 2003, in Berlin. She was 101. Although her 1934 documentary *Triumph of the Will* was the most dramatic and influential visual treatment of Nazism and the cult of Adolf Hitler, she maintained until the end that she was not a Nazi.

Not everyone agreed. She was declared to be a Nazi sympathizer by an Allied tribunal after World War II, and essentially disappeared from public view for twenty years. Then she attempted to rehabilitate her image through interviews, film festival appearances, a 1973 book of photographs about a threatened African tribe, a 1992 autobiography, and her appearance in an extraordinary 1993 documentary by Ray Muller named *The Wonderful Horrible Life of Leni Riefenstahl.*

I wrote in my review of that film: "If Leni Riefenstahl had done nothing notable before the age of sixty, what a wonderful life we would say she had lived since then." Then in her early nineties, she was the world's oldest active scuba diver, and at the end of a day of diving, we see her walk down a pier with two men—the captain, and Horst, her younger companion and cinematographer—and "the body language says everything. The two men walk ahead, carrying gear, engaged in conversation. She walks behind them, alone, carrying her own gear and oxygen tank. They don't lend her a hand, or offer to carry the tank for her, and what this says is that, at ninety-one, they do not think she needs special consideration. She's one of the guys."

But being in great shape at a very old age, while admirable, does not erase the stain of her association with the Nazi movement. As Hitler began his rise to power, Riefenstahl was already a famous German actress, best known for a group of "mountain films" in which idealized Nordic characters posed heroically against the sky. In *The Blue Light* (1932), which I saw at the Telluride festival, she is accused of being a witch, but finds truth and deliverance in the secret of a blue light that shines from a cave high on a mountainside.

By 1934 she was a favorite of the Nazis, and was chosen by Joseph Goebbels, the propaganda minister, to film the party's rally at Nuremberg. Given many cameras and unlimited film, she also benefited because much of the rally was deliberately staged with the film in mind. The result, *Triumph of the Will,* is one of the most important documentaries ever made, and by general consent one of the best—important at the time for the way it painted Hitler

and his followers as idealized supermen, important now because it helps explain how Nazism was not only a political movement but also an exercise in mass hypnotism drawing on fetishistic imagery.

Riefenstahl's other important documentary was *Olympia* (1938), a record of the 1936 Berlin Olympics, which took place on the eve of Hitler's war. Again, she had unlimited resources at her disposal to create heroic images of muscular athletes conquering space and time. The buried message praised the cult of the body, particularly the Nordic body, and it was a considerable embarrassment for Hitler that the African-American runner Jesse Owens won four gold medals and set three Olympic records.

There was one other Riefenstahl film, the little-known *Lowlands,* partly filmed in Spain in 1944 and using Gypsies in a parable that she said was intended as a criticism of Nazism. Postproduction was interrupted by the end of the war, and the movie was not finished until 1954. Only last year Riefenstahl was sued by Gypsy death camp survivors who said she used them as slave labor; they objected to her statement that none of her Gypsy extras died, since some did, in Auschwitz.

After her public reappearance in the 1960s, Riefenstahl often defended herself against charges that she was a Nazi. She was an artist, she said, interested in film, not politics. In the 1994 documentary she is questioned strenuously about her association with the Party, and we see that she has rehearsed over the years an elaborate explanation and justification for her behavior. There is no anti-Semitism in her films, she points out. She did not know until after the war about the Holocaust. She was naive, unsophisticated, detached from Nazi Party officials with the exception of Hitler, her friend—but not a close friend, she insists.

But the very absence of anti-Semitism in *Triumph of the Will* looks like a calculation; excluding a central motif of Hitler's speeches must have been deliberate, to make the film go down more easily as propaganda. Nor could a film professional working in Berlin have been unaware of the disappearance of all of the Jews in the movie industry. In the film, Riefenstahl is seen visiting the site of the 1936 Olympiad with the surviving members of her film crew. They talk about some of their famous shots—from aerial techniques to the idea of digging a hole for the camera, so that athletes could loom over the audience. We sense Riefenstahl's true passion for filmmaking. But there are candid moments, when she is not aware of the camera, when she shares quiet little asides with her old comrades, which, while not damning, subtly suggest a dimension she is not willing to have seen.

The impression remains that if Hitler had won, Leni Riefenstahl would not have been so quick to distance herself from him. Her post-war moral defense is based on technicalities. Understandably, she was not eager to face conviction or punishment as a war criminal. But, ironically, if she had confessed and renounced her earlier ideas, she might have had a more active career. It was her unconvincing, elusive self-defense that continued to damn her.

Film Festivals

Every year in April, I host "Roger Ebert's Overlooked Film Festival" at my alma mater, the University of Illinois, in my hometown, Urbana-Champaign. Screenings take place in the Virginia, a magnificent movie palace dating to the 1920s. Here is my program introduction to the 2004 festival; info on 2005 is at www.ebertfest.com.

Overlooked Film Festival

From time to time over the years, moviegoers have whispered to me in the aisles of the Virginia theater that one film or another wasn't really "overlooked enough." I trust that this year's selection will satisfy them. This sixth festival is the most overlooked yet.

Of course I have a definition for "overlooked" that can apply to any film; *My Dog Skip* may have grossed $36 million, but as a family film it was certainly overlooked by many moviegoers. *Lawrence of Arabia* of course is not precisely overlooked, but its format is, and we will present it in a sparkling 70 mm print, and we will welcome onstage Robert Harris, the restorer who is single-handedly responsible for saving this great film, and Anne C. Coates, its great director.

Buster Keaton's *The General* has been voted one of the best ten films of all time, but how many people have ever seen it in a perfect 35 mm print on a big screen, with the Alloy Orchestra in the pit? *El Norte* did indeed win Oscar nominations for the screenplay by Gregory Nava and Anna Thomas and is in the National Film Registry, but how many members of our audience have seen it? Nava has made a new print to observe its twentieth anniversary, which also observes, in a way, the anniversary of the modern independent film movement; the Independent Feature Project, which sponsors the Indie Spirit Awards, was founded in Nava and Thomas's living room.

Our other films certainly qualify. Errol Morris's *Gates of Heaven* is almost the very definition of a film born to be overlooked. I remember getting a call from Milos Stehlik, founder of Chicago's Facets Multimedia, back

in the days when he held screenings in a defrocked church in Lincoln Park.

"You have to see this movie," he said. "You have to."

"What's it about?" I asked.

"I won't tell you."

"Why not?"

"Because then you'll think you don't want to see it."

He was prophetic. Over the years I have shown the film to more than a dozen groups, and they all found it mysteriously fascinating. But moviegoers will not attend it voluntarily, and it is out of print as a video. One of the joys of the Overlooked is the freedom it gives me to show a movie like this and be fairly sure the Virginia theater will be filled. Errol Morris will join me on stage; I've had endless conversations with him over the years, and find him the most provocative and creative of documentarians.

Werner Herzog's *Invincible* was so overlooked as to be invisible. It received the worst reviews of his career in Germany, although it did score 65 percent with American critics on the Tomatometer. I loved it, and put it on my top ten list, but audiences stayed away. My feeling is that a director like Herzog deserves automatic attention for everything he does, because of the greatness of his body of work. Werner Herzog will be flying in from a movie location to attend the festival. I met him early on, at the 1967 New York Film Festival, and would place him in my personal pantheon.

Discussing the rest of the films in the order they will play:

Tarnation is a brilliant demonstration of the fact that films can now be made by one person with very little money; the tools of production are in the hands of the workers. It is also a remarkable achievement no matter how little (or how much) it cost. The existence of home video cameras has created a vast archive of images that documentarians can draw on as they revisit the past. The filmmaker, Jonathan Caouette, will join us onstage to discuss this remarkably personal and introspective work.

The Son contains a scene in a lumberyard, where the sound of wooden planks as they hit against each other is as terrifying, in the context, as anything in a horror film. In my original review of this film, I wrote:

"Now you must absolutely stop reading and go see the film. Walk out of the house today, tonight, and see it, if you are open to simplicity, depth, maturity, silence, in a film that sounds in the echo-chambers of the heart. *The Son* is a great film. If you find you cannot respond to it, that is the degree to which you have room to grow. I am not being arrogant; I grew during this film. It taught me things about the cinema I did not know."

Was the Music Box theater in Chicago jammed as a result of this passionate admonition? Not at all. Why is it that moviegoers are so cheerfully willing to attend movies they expect to be junk, but are so wary of films they fear may be great? I'll ask that question onstage of the film's American distributor, the legendary Dan Talbot of New Yorker Films, who was the key pioneer in bringing European art films to America.

When I saw *Once Upon a Time When We Were Colored* at the 1996 Virginia Film Festival, my eyes filled with tears at the power of its message. When I discovered that the film had been rejected by Sundance, reportedly because it was "too mainstream," I was indignant and wrote such an angry column that Sundance selectors were rather cool toward me for a year or two. It remains one of the best films about the African-American experience, and it remains overlooked. Its screening this year will be part of the Chancellor's Commemorative Year of the 50th anniversary of Brown vs. the Board of Education; the film establishes the context of that decision in the decades leading up to it. Director Tim Reid, who brings such a tender and heartbreaking power to the film, will join us.

I saw *Tully* at the Toronto Film Festival and fully expected it to be one of those sleeper hits that audiences embrace. But smaller independent films are so shut out of the American distribution system that they often don't get a fair chance. The movie doesn't sentimentalize farm life in America but sees it in realistic contemporary terms, while still finding room for romance and humor on the way to its heartbreaking conclusion. The director, Hilary

Birmingham, will join us at the festival, along with the gifted actor Anson Mount, who made his starring debut in the film. The producers have struck a new 35 mm print for the festival.

When I am asked to name the greatest actor-director in the history of the movies (this is admittedly a question I am asked only by myself), I reply: Buster Keaton. I had a chance to view all of his features and two dozen of his shorts while teaching a University of Chicago extension class and was astonished by the richness of his work. *The General* is usually cited as his best film, and we will have a sparkling 35 mm print and our friends the Alloy Orchestra to accompany it.

Keaton's curtain-raiser will be *The Scapegoat*, an extraordinary short film by Darren Ng that was shot on the campus of the University of California at Berkeley. Ng plays the Keaton hero in a film tribute that has lovingly absorbed Keaton's style. "The way to criticize a movie," Godard said, "is to make another movie." Ng, who embodies that philosophy, will join us to discuss both films. We will also be joined onstage by Jeffrey Vance, the famed silent film historian and restorer, and by members of the Alloy.

Our family matinee this year is *My Dog Skip*, an enormously heartwarming film by Jay Russell. It's based on the memoir by the late Willie Morris about his childhood in Yazoo, Mississippi, and about the dog who taught him important lessons in life. When I mention that it grossed $36 million, that isn't necessarily a cause for celebration, if we reflect that a movie like *Scooby-Doo*, aimed at roughly the same audience, grossed $153 million. I wince when I think of family audiences missing a film like *Skip* in order to attend an empty film like *Scooby-Doo*, but then I wince a lot. We'll be joined onstage by director Jay Russell and a surprise guest.

Why was *People I Know* so completely overlooked, despite its great performance by Al Pacino? I have no idea. Its portrait of twenty-four hours in the life of an idealistic but self-destructive New York press agent is a cinematic reminder of Malcolm Lowry's *Under the Volcano*, in which reality drifts in and out of focus. I thought the film was brilliant in the way it essentially buries two murders, which pass unperceived by the hero; there is a touch perhaps of *Blow-Up*. The director Daniel Algrant will join us onstage, along with my friend Bobby Zarem, the legendary publicist who inspired the character, even though, I hasten to add, the film is not a reflection of his own personal lifestyle.

We always close with a Sunday musical program; last year's *Singin' in the Rain* was followed by the last public appearance of the great Donald O'Connor. This year's musical offering moves in a new direction to honor another extraordinary man. My wife, Chaz, told me one day that she'd seen a wonderful documentary on PBS about an old African-American musician. I asked her what his name was. "Howard Armstrong," she said. "I know exactly who that is!" I all but shouted. I attended countless Monday nights with Martin, Bogan, and the Armstrongs at the Earl of Old Town in the 1970s, and became filled with admiration not only for Armstrong's music but for his indomitable and colorful personal style. Terry Zwigoff, who later became famous for *Crumb* and *Ghost World,* made his first documentary, *Louie Bluie,* about Armstrong. Some twenty years later, Leah Mahan made hers, *Sweet Old Song.* To pair these two documentaries gives us a remarkable opportunity to see a man whose life force was and remained extraordinary. The second film also shows Armstrong's love for his muse and wife, Barbara Ward Armstrong, who made it possible for him to continue under full sail into his nineties. She and Mahan will join us onstage, along with some of the musicians Armstrong played with.

Our special guest Jack Valenti and I came in together. He became head of the Motion Picture Association of America in 1967, the same year I became film critic of the *Sun-Times,* and I remember a long, late evening in Evanston, after he chaired a discussion by Robert Benton and David Newman, the coauthors of *Bonnie and Clyde.* In his hotel suite, we talked movies for hours and hours, beginning a long friendship. We have not always agreed about the MPAA's rating system, but I strongly support his stand against movie piracy, which, no matter how you view it, is theft of the artists' work. We are honored that Jack will be attending this year's festival; I will talk with him onstage before *Lawrence of Arabia,* and Thursday he will speak on campus.

This year's festival is dedicated to the memory of Dean Kim Rotzoll of the College of Communications. Kim was not only an instigator and supporter of the festival from its first year, but even before, when Cyberfest celebrated *2001,* artificial intelligence, and the birthday of the computer Hal 9000, who famously tells Dave Bowman the astronaut that he was born in Urbana, Illinois. Dean Rotzoll was instrumental in launching Cyberfest, and then he and Nancy Casey suggested an annual film festival, which has succeeded beyond any of our dreams. Kim was our adviser, supporter, and good friend during the first five years of the festival. We miss him.

Cannes Film Festival
Cannes Report No. 1: Advance

Cannes, France, May 13, 2004—Quentin Tarantino, Charlize Theron, Tom Hanks, Michael Moore, Brad Pitt, Sean Penn, and Shrek converge on this balmy Riviera resort town, and there may be trainloads of striking French showbiz workers to picket them. The fifty-seventh Cannes Film Festival is open for business.

Behind the hulking Palais du Cinema and on nearby side streets, armored buses contain an alleged 1,000 riot police, prepared to confront the strikers, who are protesting a cut in their unemployment benefits. You might therefore assume that the city is vibrating with anxiety, but no: There's a strike most years at Cannes. The festival focuses the eyes of the world here for nine days, and strikers convene to bathe in the spotlight.

One year, medical students in their lab coats pelted the Palais with baggies of blood. For several years, the hotel maids went on strike the first Sunday, and the municipal workers have been known to turn off the power. In 1968, a year of turmoil, the entire festival was shut down by a general strike; Jean-Luc Godard and FrançoisTruffaut appeared on the steps of the Old Palais to declare a revolution, and thus was the Director's Fortnight born—featuring films more to their liking than the official entries.

Tarantino is the head of this year's jury, which also includes the actors Tilda Swinton, Emmanuelle Béart, and Kathleen Turner, and a QT favorite, the celebrated Hong Kong horror director Tsui Hark *(Chinese Ghost Story)*. The French may not like Americans, but they like QT, whose *Pulp Fiction* is one of the most popular of all the Palme d'Or winners. What film will win the golden palm this year? If Tarantino were choosing, it might be *2046*, by the great Hong Kong director Kar Wai Wong, or *Ghost in the Shell 2: Innocence*, an animated film by Japan's Mamoru Oshii. But presidents do not necessarily control their juries, and last year, Dogma founder Lars von Trier was astonished when his three-hour *Dogville* was passed over by a jury that gave the Palme to Gus Van Sant's low-budget indie production *Elephant*. Both were said to be anti-American, but *Dogville* was additionally boring.

Michael Moore's *Fahrenheit 9/11*, described as an attack on the Bush administration, will be in the official competition; his *Bowling for Columbine* won the Prize of the Fifty-fifth Anniversary of the Festival in 2002, although since the prize is only given every fifty-five years it is a little hard to assess its significance. Moore arrives on the Croisette trailing clouds of controversy, somewhat dissipated by his cheerful admission that he stirred them up himself. He charged that Disney had forbidden Miramax to distribute the film, fearing tax repercussions for Disney World from Florida Governor Jeb Bush. A lively story, until it was pointed out that Disney had informed Moore a year ago it was not distributing the film, and Moore confessed that he'd generated the controversy for publicity. Whether Disney was any more noble for avoiding the controversial film a year ago instead of last week was a question lost in the fog.

Cannes loves stars, and Brad Pitt will march up the red carpet for an out-of-competition screening of his new epic, *Troy*. Also out of competition: the zombie fest *Dawn of the Dead*. *Shrek 2* is in competition, providing a face-off between the two dominant schools of animation, Hollywood and Japan. There'll be boos if *Shrek 2* wins something and *Ghost in the Shell* doesn't.

In the official competition, one of the most anticipated films is *Nobody Knows*, by Hirokazu Kore-Eda *(Maborosi, After Life)*, considered the best of the young Japanese directors. It's about four children with four different fathers, whose mother raises them secretly in a Tokyo apartment before leaving them on their own one day. There's a lot of buzz, too, about *Old Boy*, by the Korean director Chan-wook Park, about a man who is held in a private prison while his wife is murdered. Will he ever discover who imprisoned him? Canada, which won the Palme d'Or in 2003 with Demys Arcand's wonderful *The Barbarian Invasions*, is back in the official competition with Olivier Assayas's *Clean*, a Franco-Canadian coproduction, starring Maggie Cheung, Nike Nolte, and Don McKellar in the story of a woman trying to regain possession of her son from her in-laws.

The Coen brothers shared the best director prize in 2001 for *The Man Who Wasn't There*, and won it outright for *Fargo* (1996) and *Barton Fink* (1991), which also won the Palme d'Or. They're in competition this year with *The Ladykillers*, and Tom Hanks will come along. There's good talk about Stephen Hopkins's *The Life and Death of Peter Sellers*, starring Geoffrey Rush and Charlize Theron in the story of the unhappy funnyman; *The Motorcycle Diaries*, a South American odyssey by the leading Brazilian director Walter Salles *(Central Station)*; and *Sud Pralad*, by Apichatpong Weerasethakul, is the first film from Thailand ever shown in the official competition. It's about a beast in the jungle said to be a transmuted human soul.

Only at Cannes would it be an honor for a film to be held in "a certain regard," but this year's Un Certain Regard sidebar looks as intriguing as the main event. Among the titles: Niels Mueller's *The Assassination of Richard Nixon*, starring Sean Penn and Naomi Watts; Shona Auerbach's *Dear Frankie*, starring Emily Mortimer as a mother who protects her deaf son from the fact that they're on the run from his father; and *10 on Ten*, by the celebrated Iranian director Abbas Kiarostami, a documentary about his 2002 film *Ten*, describing his method, which was reportedly to coach actors and then send them out on their own in the front seat of a car, while a video camera recorded their scenes.

When I first went to Cannes, in 1972, most of

the press representatives were serious critics, filing assessments of the new Bergman or Altman. Now the "entertainment press" blankets the festival, and there will be a riot as photographers elbow each other to shoot the tragically underphotographed Brad Pitt. There are two press screenings of *Fahrenheit 9/11*, both at exactly the same time, both in smallish venues in the Palais instead of the 2,500-seat Lumiere Auditorium, where most of the press screenings are held. Since Moore's film is the one title every journalist in town will feel compelled to view, there'll be an ugly scrimmage outside those screenings, and I am informing my editors right now that I will not risk my life to see it. An arm or a leg, maybe.

Cannes Report No. 2: The Show Goes On

May 13, 2004—The riot police may not be needed after all. Striking French showbiz workers, who threatened to shut down the Cannes Film Festival over cuts in their unemployment compensation, were mollified here when the festival struck a compromise. They were allowed to ascend the famous red-carpeted steps of the Palais des Festivals and be officially greeted by fest officials, which won their cause a moment in the limelight—although not, alas, tickets to the opening night screening of Pedro Almodóvar's *Bad Education*.

Or perhaps the riot police may be needed, if a fight breaks out on the jury. Those who attended its opening press conference were buzzing about frostiness between jury president Quentin Tarantino and one of his jury members, British actress Tilda Swinton. They differed over the worth of "art films," which Tarantino sniffed at and Swinton defended. Although QT has been in a brawl or two (including one he proudly recalled from his first fest in 1972), I'd pick Swinton in a matchup. She trains in Scotland.

Cannes usually honors what anyone would define as an art film (Tarantino's Golden Palm winner, *Pulp Fiction*, is an exception), but it likes to open in a tumult of publicity, with big stars in attendance; Brad Pitt mounted the red carpet for the European premiere of *Troy*, which is showing out of competition.

Troy officially cost $175 million and is rumored to have cost as much as $250 million, which makes it a contrast to another film, Jonathan Caouette's *Tarnation*, which cost $218. A sensation at Sundance 2004, it's a documentary about three generations of his troubled family, and he made it with digital footage, old home movies and tape recordings, answering machine messages, and his memories.

Caouette and his film stopped at my Overlooked Film Festival in April, en route to Cannes, and he said he assembled his materials on a Macintosh, using the iMovie software that came with the computer. That makes the film's stylistic sophistication all the more remarkable; he uses superimposition, complex fades, slo-mo, supertitles, and other effects that would stretch expert software, and the effect is a powerful portrait of family agony.

His mother, so beautiful that she was a model as a young girl, was injured in an accident, fell into depression, and was given dozens of shock treatments, which essentially destroyed her personality. Caouette confronts his grandfather over his decision to approve the treatments, and also contemplates his own life; he knew from childhood that he was gay, he says, and there is remarkable footage (taken by himself) of young Jonathan doing a monologue in drag.

Of course, the $218 price tag represents the cost of producing a DVD on the Mac and submitting it to Sundance. Once the film was picked up for distribution by Wellspring, postproduction expenses, including a transfer to 35mm and clearances of the music rights, cost several hundred thousand. That's still a bargain; odds are that *Tarnation* will come out of Cannes with better reviews than *Troy*.

Troy will be followed by a gala party costing no doubt millions; *Tarnation* publicist Mickey Cottrell was negotiating for his film's party with La Pizza, down by the harbor.

Still staggering with jet lag, the North American press corps had to contend with the first two official entries, which were slow-paced and quiet. Both kept me wide awake; oddly, the first day after an all-night flight to France, I find it's the loud action films that put me to sleep. *Nobody Knows*, by the gifted young Japanese director Hirokazu Kore-Eda *(After Life)*, tells the story of four pre-teenagers trying to live by themselves after their mother leaves with a boyfriend and doesn't return. As the water and electricity are turned off, as money runs out and food grows scarce, they keep their secret because they're afraid of being separated by social workers. The film doesn't punch up the drama, but underlines their slow descent into desperation. At 141 minutes, this is the kind of film that requires brave exhibitors and curious audiences, and rewards them. What's best about it is the one thing you'd never find in a more commercial version of this story: its avoidance of contrived melodrama and its patience in showing how the children slowly realize they are entirely on their own.

The Consequences of Love, by the Italian Paolo Sorrentino, centers on an extraordinary performance by Toni Servillo as a quiet, withdrawn, forbidding man who has lived in the same hotel for years. What is his reason? We learn that he has a wife and children he telephones but has not seen in a decade, and a brother who visits. We see him minutely observing the lives of fellow guests, including a couple who live in the next room. Using a stethoscope, he eavesdrops on their conversations about a life of ruin: The neighbor once owned the hotel, but now humbly lives in a room, having gambled away his fortune.

Neatly dressed, monklike in his lifestyle, the man sits and smokes and communicates in as few words as possible. But why does he deliver cash to a bank once a week? Why does he never return the greetings of the pretty bartender (Olivia Magnani)? Strange, how we can become bored by characters who loudly reveal their lives to us, but be drawn so deeply into lives that are a mystery.

Cannes Report No. 3:
Days on the Run

May 14, 2004—There are two species of journalists at Cannes, described by the festival as critics or chroniclers. The critics review the films. The chroniclers write the gossip, review the fashions, attend the press conferences, and pray for scandal. One year Jean-Claude Van Damme and Rutger Hauer (remember them?) got in a pushing match on the steps of the Palais, and the chroniclers dined out for a week. The critics, on the other hand, savor moments of quieter savagery, as when Dogma founder Lars von Trier didn't win the top prize from a

jury headed by Roman Polanski, and accepted his lesser award "with no thanks to the midget."

Everything is so urgent at Cannes. Films seem so supremely important for a week. There is a major scandal when a three-hour documentary about the Cinémathèque Français and its founder, Henri Langlois, ends in 1977 with Langlois's death, and—"horreurs!"—does not mention those who ran the Cinémathèque in later years. "The Cinémathèque cannot attack it publicly, because they have invested in it," one overhears from the row behind, "but they will have their people at *Le Monde* attack it for them."

The Cannes City Hall has an entire wall covered with a photograph of the Spanish director Pedro Almodóvar, whose competition opener *Bad Education* is a thriller about a gay movie director approached by a sometime transsexual who claims to be an old school chum. Imagine Chicago's city hall plastered with John Waters, the director of *Hairspray.*

The Almodóvar film was followed by fireworks, which thundered in the wee hours, after a drag show and lots of food and wine. The party seemed to continue on the screen, with *Life Is a Miracle,* the new film by Emir Kusturica, which takes place in Bosnia in 1992 in a district where most of the locals travel by rail. But not in trains. No, the local line doesn't have a locomotive, so they use pushcars and autos fitted with steel wheels. A lovesick mule, not knowing the trains have stopped, stands on the tracks trying to commit suicide. Dogs, cats, ducks, pigeons, and chickens occupy the houses along with the characters.

The hero is a soccer star whose mother, an opera singer, is going mad and sings passionately during a match where players appear and disappear in the fog. Drunken locals shoot bottles off each other's heads. There is a party that lasts all night. The local band is everywhere, providing an oompah-pah sound track for the revelry. Then war breaks out, the soccer star is taken prisoner, his family takes an enemy woman as prisoner in revenge, his father falls in love with her, and I heard someone wondering in the dark, "Is the real subject of this movie alcoholism?"

I plunged out of the vast Lumiere theater, 3,000 seats of rabid cineastes, and into the American Pavilion behind the Palais, where the waiters are film students who cheerfully try to network with the customers. A discussion with two students: Does it teach you better discipline to shoot on film and edit by hand, instead of with a digital camera and computer editing? By all means, we agreed. It focuses the mind wonderfully to be aware of the money going through the camera.

Then down the Croisette to the Noga Hilton, where the Directors' Fortnight occupies a big theater seven flights of stairs below ground level. A disagreement ensues with a festival guard, who tries to make us sit in the balcony when we all want to sit on the ground floor. "The ground floor is full!" he intones. "There are hundreds of empty seats!" we cry, for that is manifestly true. He replies with a masterpiece of French logic: "It is full for the moment."

The movie is *Mean Creek,* by the American director Jacob Aaron Estes, and it is powerful and good. It tells the story of five friends who take a middle-school bully on a boat trip, and how their idea of a prank goes wrong. But it is much more subtle than that. The bully has beaten up a smaller kid (Rory Culkin), and so his older brother, his girlfriend, and two other friends plan the revenge. But then they all take pity on the bully ("We didn't know he would be so nice"), except for the oldest kid, who wants to follow the original plan. When the bully is almost spared, he unwisely explodes with violent insults, attacking the very one he should avoid. And then all of the kids have to deal with a hard and frightening moral choice. I've seen a lot of movies about teenagers who are violent and amoral (*The River's Edge* and *Elephant* come to mind), but never one that commits so fully to kids trying to figure out the right thing to do in an impossible situation.

Back to the hotel for a power nap, and then to the Bazin screening room in the Palais for the best film I've seen so far, *Moolaade,* by Ousmane Sembène, the legendary veteran from Senegal. It's in Un Certain Regard, a sidebar section. "In the old days," observes Telluride director Tom Luddy, "it would have been in the main competition, but now they want something edgier."

Edgy. One of the qualities Cannes has in overabundance. The Sembène film is set in a rural village in the present day. Four little girls come running to a local woman, asking for protection. They do not want to submit to ritual circumcision. The woman is known for having refused to let her daughter be mutilated. She grants them protection, or "moolaade," over the protests of her husband but with the support of his first and third wives. The village men are much disturbed; no man will marry an uncircumcised woman, they declare. But many girls bleed to death after the surgery, performed by a band of fearsome witches. There is a standoff, much complicated by the return from Paris of a local man scheduled to marry the heroine's daughter, only to learn she has not been cut.

At a time when ritual mutilation is under attack in Africa, when Islamic leaders have tried to explain it is *not* required by religious law but is a local custom, *Moolaade* is a strong, true, and useful film. And it is magnificently beautiful, with its African vistas and brilliantly colored costumes, its full-throated music, and its faces of women who are real and have seen life and know their own strength.

Then it's down to the Croisette again, to a happy hour hosted by the famous Bollywood director Subash Ghai, the Spielberg of India, who's had twelve of the biggest blockbusters in India's history, including *Taal.* That you have not heard of it does not mean millions did not love it. I saw it in a vast theater in Hyderabad, where the audience was in ecstasy.

Ghai shows scenes from his work in progress, *Kisna, the Warrior Poet,* about a "love that lives across two continents" between an Indian man and a British woman in the early 1940s in the foothills of the Himalayas. The lovers demonstrate an extraordinary ability to take heroic stances high on jagged peaks in front of dramatic orange sunsets, and one is reminded that Bollywood remembers what Hollywood forgets, that there is a hunger among audiences for the grand, romantic gesture.

And then to the Debussy, merely 2,000 seats, to see the Korean film *Old Boy.* The Croisette by now is jammed, boys perched in trees, some fans with their own stepladders, for a better look at the stars ascending the red carpet for the official showing of the Kusturica. Inside the Debussy, *Old Boy* is a bizarre film by Chanwook Park, about a drunken man who awakens to find himself held captive for fifteen years by faceless jailers who will not reveal their reasons.

There is a scene where a man's teeth are pulled out by the stumps, one at a time, that makes Lawrence Olivier's dentist in *Marathon Man* look like Painless Parker. But you have to concede: The movie is edgy.

Cannes Report No. 4: Directors Weigh State of Their Art

May 17, 2004—Michael Moore arrived late at the American directors' panel because he'd been down the street expressing solidarity with the striking showbiz workers.

"I gave them a pep talk and asked them not to make a lot of noise when they marched past here," said Moore, as the strikers marched past the beachfront Variety Pavilion, chanting slogans and banging drums. They couldn't drown out the fiery documentarian, however, as he lambasted "a climate of political repression" in the United States.

Well, everybody expected that from Moore. It was a little startling, though, when fellow panelist Jonathan Nossiter drew parallels between the world's wine industry and the Bush administration. Nossiter is here with *Mondovino*, a documentary in the official competition that charges the wine establishment with abandoning its long-held values and ethics to move toward compromises and secrecy. The great vineyards are run behind a curtain of secrecy like the White House, he said, with loyalty valued above all.

Moore updated the audience on the latest title revision of his anti-Bush documentary, which was called *Fahrenheit 911* until "I added a slash." Now called *Fahrenheit 9/11*, it is screening at Cannes. Moore said he was looking for distribution for the film, which Disney executives ordered its Miramax subsidiary not to release, and said, "The deal will depend on an opening around the Fourth of July and a DVD release before the November elections."

Moore and Nossiter were joined by four other American filmmakers at the annual panel sponsored by the Independent Film Channel and the Independent Feature Project, and chaired by me. Oddly, four of the six were documentarians, also including Xan Cassavetes, with *Z Channel: A Magnificent Obsession,* and Jonathan Caouette, with *Tarnation*, a doc about his troubled family that has inspired amazement here with its budget of $218.32,

which is approximately .002 percent of the budget of the Cannes premiere, *Troy.*

Cassavetes, the daughter of Hollywood legends John Cassavetes and Gena Rowlands, made her first film about a cable channel that flourished in Los Angeles in the 1970s and early 1980s by showing restored versions of films by directors out of fashion. Its programmer was a driven movie buff named Jerry Harvey, who championed Sam Peckinpah, Michael Cimino, and other outsiders, showed the uncut version of Sergio Leone's *Once Upon a Time in America,* and all thirteen hours of Fassbinder's *Berlin Alexanderplatz.*

In the years before home video made film preservation and restoration profitable, Harvey introduced the concept of director's cuts and found a huge audience for art and cult films. Z Channel was eventually overwhelmed by HBO and Showtime, but Harvey was already fighting demons that ended with him killing his wife and then himself. Cassavetes talks to many of his friends, including critics, filmmakers, and broadcast executives, who are still trying to figure out why a career that was so productive ended so tragically.

The Caouette film charts three generations in his dysfunctional family, weaving together home movies, answering machine messages, recent video footage, photographs, postcards, and graphics into the story of his mother, whose personality was destroyed by unneeded shock treatments. The danger is that the film's low budget will overshadow its remarkable artistry; the sophisticated editing technique he wrings out of the bare-bones Macintosh iMovie software is astonishing.

Also on the panel were two fiction filmmakers, Jacob Aaron Estes of *Mean Creek* and Nicole Kassell of *The Woodsman*. The Kassell film, which has not yet screened here, stars Kevin Bacon in the story of a pedophile released from prison after many years. Her attempt, Kassell said, was to show that such men cannot be dismissed as simply evil, but must be understood in more complex terms, dealing with childhoods in which something usually went very wrong.

Estes's *Mean Creek* has received a strongly positive reception here; it stars six young actors (Rory Culkin is the only familiar name) in the story of how five of them trick a chubby bully into a boat trip in order to take revenge for his aggressive playground behavior. The movie puts moral values into play as some of the kids decide against a prank they've planned, and then later try to work through fright and shame to do the right thing. Like many films that teenagers should see, it will get the R rating, Estes said, "because of a scene where the f-word is used about 100 times."

All of the directors agreed on one thing: The American movie business is currently driven by star names and easily packaged mass-market concepts, and independent films are being shoved to the margins. Moore was bitter about the dominance of celebrity-oriented journalism, in which gossip and scandal have replaced useful coverage of new films.

"I protest about how my film is being handled, and everybody writes that I'm just generating good publicity," Moore said. "Look at the two previous films Disney didn't let Miramax distribute—*Kids* and *Dogma*. The publicity didn't seem to help them much."

In a reference to his first hit documentary, *Roger & Me*, Moore was asked if he would ever make a film called *Michael & Me* about his clash with Disney president Michael Eisner.

"Someday I will tell all," he intoned. "Somebody like me should never be allowed to peek behind the curtain."

Cannes Report No. 5: Michael Moore, Fahrenheit 9/11

May 17, 2004—Michael Moore the muckraking wiseass has been replaced by a more subdued version in *Fahrenheit 9/11*, his new documentary questioning the antiterrorism credentials of the Bush regime. In the Moore version, President Bush, his father, and members of their circle have received $1.5 billion from Saudi Arabia over the years, attacked Iraq to draw attention from their Saudi friends, and have lost the hearts and minds of many of the U.S. servicemen in the war.

The film premiered at the Cannes Film Festival to a series of near-riot scenes, as overbooked press screenings were besieged by mobs trying to push their way in. The response at the early morning screening I attended was loudly enthusiastic. And at the official black-tie screening, it was greeted by a standing ovation; a friend who was there said it went on "for at least twenty-five minutes," which probably means closer to fifteen (estimates of ovations at Cannes are like estimates of parade crowds in Chicago).

But the film doesn't go for satirical humor the way Moore's *Roger & Me* and *Bowling for Columbine* did. Moore's narration is still often sarcastic, but frequently he lets his footage speak for itself. The film shows American soldiers not in a prison but in the field, hooding an Iraqi, calling him Ali Baba, touching his genitals, and posing for photos with him. There are other scenes of U.S. casualties without arms or legs, questioning the purpose of the Iraqi invasion at a time when Bush proposed to cut military salaries and benefits. It shows Lila Lipscomb, a mother from Flint, Michigan, reading a letter from her son, who urged his family to help defeat Bush, days before he was killed. And in a return to the old Moore confrontational style, it shows him joined by a marine recruiter as he encourages congressmen to have their sons enlist in the service.

Despite these dramatic moments, the most memorable footage for me involved President Bush on the day of 9/11. The official story is that Bush was meeting with a group of preschoolers when he was informed of the attack on the World Trade Center, and quickly left the room. Not quite right, says Moore. Bush learned of the first attack before entering the school, "decided to go ahead with his photo op," and began to read *My Pet Goat* to the students. Informed of the second attack, he incredibly remained with the students for another seven minutes, reading from the book, until a staff member suggested that he leave. The look on his face as he reads the book, knowing what he knows, is disquieting.

Fahrenheit 9/11 documents the long association of the Bush clan and Saudi oil billionaires, and reveals that when Bush released his military records, he blotted out the name of another pilot whose flight status was suspended on the same day for failing to take a physical exam. This was his good friend James R. Bath, who later became the Texas money manager for the Bin Laden family (which has renounced its terrorist son). When a group of 9/11 victims sued the Saudi government for financing the terrorists, the Saudis hired as their defense team the law firm of James Baker, Bush Sr.'s secretary of state. And the film questions why, when all aircraft were grounded after 9/11, the White House allowed several planes to fly around the country picking up Bin Laden family members and other Saudis and flying them home ahead of other flights.

Much of the material in *Fahrenheit 9/11* has already been covered in books and newspapers, but some is new, and it all benefits from the different kind of impact a movie has. Near the beginning of the film, as Congress moves to ratify the election of Bush after the Florida and Supreme Court controversies, it is positively eerie to see ten members of Congress—eight black women, one Asian woman, and one black man—rise to protest the move, and be gaveled into silence by the chairman of the session, Al Gore.

On the night before his film premiered, Moore, in uncharacteristic formal wear, attended an official dinner given by Gilles Jacob, president of the festival. Conversation at his table centered on the *New Yorker* article by Seymour Hersh reporting that Secretary of Defense Donald Rumsfeld personally authorized use of torture in Iraqi prisons.

Moore had his own insight into the issue: "Rumsfeld was under oath when he testified about the torture scandal. If he lied, that's perjury. And therefore I find it incredibly significant that when Bush and Cheney testified before the 9/11 commission, they refused to swear an oath. They claimed they'd sworn an oath of office, but that has no legal standing. Do you suppose they remembered how Clinton was trapped by perjury, and were protecting themselves?"

Would something like that belong in the film?

"My contract says I can keep editing and adding stuff right up until the release date," said Moore. He said he expects to sign a U.S. distribution deal at Cannes; the film's producer, Miramax, was forbidden to release it by its parent company, Disney.

After the first press screening on Monday, journalists noted on their way out that Moore was more serious in this film, and took fewer cheap shots. But there are a few. Wait until you see Deputy Defense Secretary Paul Wolfowitz

preparing for a TV interview. First he puts a pocket comb in his mouth to wet it, and combs down his hair. Still not satisfied, he spits on his hand and wipes the hair into place. Catching politicians being made up for TV is an old game, but this is a first.

Cannes Report No. 6: More Moore

May 18, 2004—Two questions involving the duration of events: (1) So how long, exactly, *was* the standing ovation for Michael Moore's *Fahrenheit 9/11*? And (2) did President Bush actually remain in a Florida classroom, reading from *My Pet Goat*, for seven minutes after he was informed of the second attack on the World Trade Center?

Moore's anti-Bush documentary was received rapturously at its black-tie screening, and a friend told me the ovation lasted twenty-five minutes. In my report I suggested that Cannes ovations, like the estimates of parade crowds in Chicago, have a tendency to be exaggerated. Since I attended an 8 A.M. press screening, I was not inside the Palais des Festivals to clock it myself.

Now I have another source. The ovation lasted twenty minutes, according to *Variety*, which may be correct, because its reporters all carry stopwatches to check the running times of movies.

In any event it was "the longest ovation in the history of the festival," according to Thierry Fremaux, the festival's director. At a party, I asked Moore. "It depends on when you start counting," he said. "Do you start with the beginning of the closing credits, or when the lights go up? When they just wouldn't stop clapping, I walked out and they kept applauding in the lobby."

And as for Bush's delay in reacting to the attack on the World Trade Center? Conventional wisdom has it that the president was reading to schoolchildren when he got the news and quickly left the room. The Moore version: He was informed of the first attack, went into the room anyway, was informed of the second attack, and remained with the students until a staff member suggested that he leave.

"The teacher in that Sarasota classroom happened to tape the whole event," Moore told me. "We'd seen other footage from the networks, but it was all edited. She just left the camera running. She said nobody had ever asked her for the film. Bush didn't instinctively jump up and go into action, but just stayed on autopilot until someone told him what to do."

* * *

One question involving the conditions of performance:

Is it true that Billy Bob Thornton was drunk during most of his scenes for *Bad Santa*, the Terry Zwigoff film that plays Tuesday in the festival?

"Absolutely," Thornton told me as we did a Q&A session at the American Pavilion. "There's one scene where I'm supposed to arrive late to work as Santa Claus, with a cut face, holding a broken bottle. I get to the top of the escalator where all the kiddies are waiting, and attack a papier-mâché donkey.

"Well, I had overprepared for the scene, let's say, and I was supposed to wait at the bottom of the escalator until the director said 'Action!' Then a crew member would start the escalator. I laid down on the steps and went to sleep, the escalator started, I didn't know a thing, and I arrived upstairs still passed out."

The actor said he rarely drinks on the job, "but this role seemed to call for it."

* * *

Decline of civilization: At the American Pavilion, I was given an orange baseball cap bearing the logo of the Screen Actors Guild Indie Division. The bill was frayed.

"Hey," I said. "Gimme a new cap. This one is all beat up."

"It's brand-new," said Paul Bales, director of SAG Indie. "The kids like them to look that way. We had to pay a guy to distress them."

Cannes Report No. 7: Review Wrap-Up

May 19, 2004—The fifty-seventh Cannes Film Festival headed into its closing weekend with no clear favorite for the Palme d'Or, and critics generally agreed there have been good films but no sensation that has pulled ahead of the pack. The most rapturous reception was for Michael Moore's Bush-whacking documentary *Fahren-*

heit 9/11, but the applause was as much for its politics as its filmmaking.

The best film I've seen so far isn't even in the official competition. That would be *Moolaade,* by the eighty-one-year-old Senegalese director Ousmane Sembène. It's a richly textured drama about the ritual circumcision of women, told against a backdrop of modern African village life.

Three other strong films played outside the main competition. Playing in the Un Certain Regard sidebar, Shona Auerbach's *Dear Frankie* stars Emily Mortimer as the mother of a nine-year-old made deaf by an abusive father. She has left the father, but hides the news from her son, telling him his dad is a sailor, and writing the boy letters under his name from HMS *Accra.* When that very ship docks in their town, she realizes she has to produce a father, and recruits a total stranger (Gerald Butler) to play the role. The man and the boy (Jack McElhone) are cool at first, but become friends, complicating the situation wondrously. I'll have an interview with Mortimer.

I also admired Nicole Kassell's first film, *The Woodsman,* starring Kevin Bacon in a brave and nuanced performance as a child molester released after twelve years in prison. He gets a job in a lumberyard and has a sudden affair with a bold coworker (Kyra Sedgwick), but is he free of his sexual obsession? And will the secret of his past be discovered? The film shows him skirting close to danger in a morally murky landscape. With this film and *Mystic River,* Bacon reminds us of his considerable talent.

The Woodsman was in the Director's Fortnight, and so was *Mean Creek* by Jacob Aaron Estes. The story of a boatload of kids and a revenge prank that goes wrong, it's unusual in the way it doesn't simply focus on the action but shows the young characters seriously dealing with the moral consequences of what happens.

Sean Penn gives another powerful and implosive performance in Niels Mueller's *The Assassination of Richard Nixon,* set in 1974 and based on the true story of Sam Bicke, a man who loses his job and his family, and slowly goes mad with discouragement and loss of esteem. Finally he attempts to hijack a plane and crash it into the White House, not so much because he wants to assassinate the president as because he wants to strike a body blow against the society that ignores and devalues him.

One of the best festival entries, *Look at Me (Comme une Image)* by Agnes Jaoui, is also about a character who feels ignored. Lolita (Marilou Berry) is the plump, plain, grown daughter of a successful writer and publisher with a sexy second wife. Her father ignores or casually insults her, and the men in her life seem attracted by the opportunity to meet her father. She has a wonderful singing voice, and in one heartbreaking sequence her father walks out during her solo to make a cell call, and later at the party says nothing to her, but chats up one of her attractive ensemble members. The film is complex and observant about unspoken messages and body language, and Berry may have a chance at the best actress award.

For best actor, the front-runner seems to be the Italian actor Toni Servillo, who plays a solitary, distant man who has lived for years in the same hotel, in Paolo Sorrentino's *The Consequences of Love.* The film made a strong impression early in the festival and figures among the favorites.

There was an enthusiastic reception for *Motorcycle Diaries* by Walter Salles, the Brazilian director of the Oscar nominee *Central Station.* It's inspired by a diary kept by Ernesto (Che) Guevara in 1952, when he and a friend set out on an epic motorcycle journey around South America. He embarked as a bourgeois medical student, and returned with his social conscience awakened; he would later be the key associate of Fidel Castro. But the film is made as if it knows nothing of his future, and regards only his present, as a young man forever changed by the sights he sees.

Nobody Knows, by the brilliant Japanese filmmaker Hirokazu Kore-Eda, whose *Maborisi* and *After Life* I've praised, involves four children, the oldest about twelve, left on their own by an indifferent mother, and trying to care for themselves in the big city. The film is touchingly observant of the ways the kids cope, led by the oldest who feels the weight of the world on his shoulders. At 141 minutes, it loses some tension, and might benefit from judicious editing.

Zhang Yimou's *House of Flying Daggers,* a glossy martial arts adventure by the leading Chinese director, was a superior example of its genre, but did not transcend it. Shots and scenes that would have been astonishing a few years ago have become commonplace in the age of special effects, although a battle scene set in a bamboo grove is astonishing in the way it uses trees as human launching pads and sharpened stakes as weapons.

Two other official entries left me more than indifferent. Both *Sud Pralad,* from Thailand, and *Woman Is the Future of Man,* from Korea, were reluctant to reveal a structure or purpose, and meandered through artsy nothingness. The Korean film at least centers on three characters we're free to speculate about as they drift through a reunion, but the Thai film was a meditation on portentous but incoherent themes.

By contrast, the Korean film *Old Boy* was clear and direct in its story of a man held captive for fifteen years for no apparent reason. But its level of sadism and savagery was unredeemed by the material, and a squid was definitely harmed during the making of the picture, by being eaten alive. Not a pretty sight.

Of the films set to play on the last three days of the festival, one seems endangered. Press screenings for the eagerly awaited *2046,* by the major Chinese director Kar Wai Wong, were canceled because the editing was not completed on time. The festival still hoped to fly a print from the labs in Paris in time for the official screening. Since *2046* is considered a plausible candidate for the Palme d'Or, festival history may hinge on its arrival.

Cannes Report No. 8: Best Films Often Off the Beaten Path

May 21, 2004—As I write, the leading contenders for the Palme d'Or are said to be *The Motorcycle Diaries* from Brazil and *Comme une Image (Look at Me)* from France, although there are supporters for *2046* by China's Kar Wai Wong, a film I found maddening in its mannered repetition of a few worn, stylistic, and dramatic strategies. And it is said that Michael Moore's *Fahrenheit 9/11* will win one of the top prizes; it was cheered longer than any other film in festival history, the Cannes director thinks.

For myself, the treasures at any Cannes festival are found not only in the official competition but elsewhere, in the sidebar programs and the marketplace.

A few years ago, the best film I saw at Cannes was *Innocence,* by Paul Cox of Australia, which played only in the marketplace. Again this year Cox was in the marketplace, again with an inspired film, *Human Touch.* He tells the story of an uneasily married couple and her strange half-affair with an older man; this man is brilliant and artistic and impotent, but on their first meeting she models nude for him, and on another occasion his caresses excite her as nothing before.

Other characters are involved, but rather than describe the entire plot I will bow down in wonder to the way that Cox moves the story from Australia to France, sends his characters on a visit to a cave that is 110 million years old, and awes them (and us) with the overwhelming contrast between our brief lives and the age of our world. It is easy enough to make a movie about romance and adultery, but only Cox, visionary and spiritual, would draw back to put his characters in a context that humbles their brief fancies.

Another wonderful film is Irwin Winkler's *De-Lovely.* This is the life story of Cole Porter, an equal with George Gershwin among the best popular music composers of all time—a complex man who was homosexual but whose life's great love was Linda Lee Porter, the woman he was married to for more than thirty years.

Kevin Kline stars as Porter, Ashley Judd is Linda, and as the spirit of Porter attends rehearsals for a musical based on his life, scenes spin out as flashbacks. Winkler and his writer, Jay Cocks, tell the story largely through Porter's lyrics, presenting complex material with a touch so delicate, so fragile, they embody the subtle grace of Porter's songs.

The film has sharply divided audiences here. I have talked to no one who is indifferent; everyone seems to love it or hate it. I think it is the most unusual and enchanting musical in years, with Kline and Judd (not claiming to be singers) breathing life into the lyrics, while Alanis Morissette, Sheryl Crow, Natalie Cole, and Elvis Costello (who are singers) bring the songs to full life.

Another triumph of the closing days of the festival is *Tarnation,* by Jonathan Caouette, the film that has gained fame because it cost the director only $218 to make, but which has won standing ovations here not for its budget, but for its remarkable power. Caouette combines home movies, new video footage, photographs, answering machine messages, and graphics into the tragic story of how his mother's personality was destroyed by shock treatments. At Cannes, the power of the film has been confirmed at every screening; this is one of the strongest documentaries of recent years.

Of the official entry *The Life and Death of Peter Sellers,* directed by Stephen Hopkins, starring Geoffrey Rush as the great comedian and Emily Watson and Charlize Theron as two of his wives, what can be said is that Sellers was one miserable SOB. "I have no personality, except for what I get from my characters," he said. Not quite true. The film sees him as a neurotic, cruel, selfish, immature monster even whose charming moments have a cloying insincerity. Rush brilliantly embodies these qualities, which may not be what Sellers fans are hoping for. Here is a good film about a very unpleasant man.

The Kar Wai Wong film, *2046,* was raced to Cannes still wet from the lab in Paris; the great director of *In the Mood for Love* was editing until the last moment, and I recommend he recommence editing immediately. What he has is a monotonous story narrated by a sad sack (Tony Leung) who has affairs with three women who live in Room 2046 of the same hotel. All his affairs are doomed, but they never seem to be anything *but* doomed; in the film's view, all love is destined to lead to heartbreak, true communication is impossible, we are the victims of our miserable natures, etc.

The visual style is elegant and lush, yes, until it becomes elegant and lush to a fault. The camera tracks endlessly past beautiful faces, with foreground objects obediently obscuring the view from time to time, and there are love scenes pitched at various degrees of energy but always leading to bittersweet regret. A great many of the scenes take place on Christmas Eve, and Nat King Cole's "A Christmas Song," with its chestnuts roasting on an open fire, is played from beginning to end not once but *three* different times (some claim to have counted four). Is this an ironic touch, or simply wretched excess? And how popular were English-language Christmas songs in China in 1966?

Some of the same colleagues who hated *De-Lovely* loved *2046*, which shows they have cast adrift from the pleasures of traditional craftsmanship and signed on to the cinematic fashion of the day at whatever cost. Kar Wai Wong has made great films, but *2046* is a colossal failure. *De-Lovely* is the kind of film you love in your heart; *2046* is the kind of film you build a tortured defense for, lest you seem uncool.

One more story and I am finished. During the screening of *Human Touch*, I had the misfortune to be seated next to a pathetic creature who was receiving e-mail messages on his pocket device, and replying with taps on his clever little keyboard. The tiny screen was bright green in the darkness.

I asked him to stop. He said, "I have to do this." I said, "Then you have to leave." He continued to tap away. "The director is sitting right over there," I said. "How do you think he feels?" "I don't care how he feels," the cretinous man replied. "Stop it, goddamnit!" I said. He stopped for a while, and then took a little peek at his screen from behind his hand. "Why don't you go outside?" I said. He did. He was the only person who left the full house; his electronic masturbation had blinded him to the movie's qualities.

After the screening, I mentioned the incident to Paul Cox. "If he had started typing one more time," said Cox, a genial and philosophical man, "I would have ripped his bloody toy from his hands and smashed it to bits beneath my feet." It was enough to make me wish the cretin had continued.

Cannes Report No. 9: Winners

May 24, 2004—Michael Moore's *Fahrenheit 9/11*, a documentary denouncing the presidency of George W. Bush, won the Palme d'Or as the best film in the Cannes Film Festival. It was the first documentary to take the Palme since 1956, and was a popular winner; at its official screening it received what the festival director said was the longest ovation in Cannes history.

"What have you done?" an emotional Moore asked the jury headed by Quentin Tarantino.

"The last time I was on an awards stage all hell broke loose." That was at the 2003 Academy Awards, when Moore turned cheers to boos as he shouted, "Shame on you, Mr. President." This time he did not mention Bush, quoting instead Abraham Lincoln: "If you just give the people the truth, the Republic will be safe."

Immediately after the awards, Tarantino told me backstage: "This prize was not for politics. It won because it was the best film." And indeed in the daily tallies of critical opinion conducted by the trade papers at Cannes, *Fahrenheit 9/11* was at or near the top.

The film, produced by Miramax, has been surrounded by controversy since Disney president Michael Eisner ordered his subsidiary not to distribute it. Miramax president Harvey Weinstein, leading the cheers after the victory, says an alternative distribution deal will be announced soon. Onstage, Moore joked that with the signing of an Albanian deal, "every country in the world can see this film except us."

Tarantino's jury dropped another bombshell by awarding the coveted Jury Prize to the Chicago-based actress Irma P. Hall, who starred in the festival entry *The Ladykillers*. Hall, who is sixty-six, has been in rehabilitation after a nearly fatal auto accident in January. Among her other credits are *Soul Food*, the movie and the TV series.

"We thought she was the best thing in the movie," jury member Jerry Schatzberg told me backstage. "We loved her." Tom Hanks, who starred in *The Ladykillers*, was at the festival; he has kept in frequent touch with the convalescing Hall.

Hall shared the jury prize with Apichatpong Weerasethakul's *Tropical Malady*, the first Thai film ever entered at Cannes. The winner of the Grand Prize, which is one step down from the Palme, was Park Chan-wook's Korean film *Old Boy*, a violent revenge story that jury watchers predicted would win Tarantino's backing. Park's acceptance speech thanked the live squids whose consumption is one of the less watchable passages in the film.

Maggie Cheung won as best actress for Olivier Assayas's *Clean*, a Canadian-French-British coproduction in which she played a onetime rock star, then a drug addict, who tries to raise her son with the aid of her American father-in-law, played by Nick Nolte.

For best actor, the jury chose twelve-year-old Yuuya Yagira, star of Hirokazu Kore-Eda's *Nobody Knows,* from Japan. After he and three younger siblings are abandoned by their mother, they try to survive on their own, hiding from the welfare system. Accepting the award, Kore-Eda said his star "had to return to Japan for his exams." The best screenplay prize went to France's Agnes Jaoui and Jean-Pierre Bacri, for *Comme une Image (Look at Me),* one of the festival's most popular films. Jaoui directed and Bacri played a womanizing writer and publisher who ignores his plump, grown daughter and is a monster of male egotism.

Best director was Tony Gatlif of France for *Exils,* the story of a young couple who decide to travel through Spain and Morocco to Algeria, the homeland of their parents.

The grand prize in Un Certain Regard, the sidebar to the official festival, went to one of my favorite films, *Moolaade,* by Ousmane Sembéne of Senegal. Sembéne, at eighty-one known as the father of African cinema, tells the story of a village torn by opposition to the custom of female circumcision. I was not alone in thinking that *Moolaade* belonged in the official competition.

The Camera d'Or award is given to the best film by a first-time director. Its jury, headed by British actor Tim Roth, split the prize between Yang Chao's *Passages,* from China, and Mohsen Amiryoussefi's *Bitter Dream,* from Iran.

The awards ceremony glittered with stars, including this year's Oscar winner Charlize Theron, who presented the Palme d'Or, and Kevin Kline and Ashley Judd, who introduced the Grand Prize in respectable French; they costarred in the closing night film *De-Lovely,* based on the life of Cole Porter.

The members of Tarantino's jury included Scots actress Tilda Swinton, American actress Kathleen Turner, French actress Emmanuelle Béart, the Haitian-born U.S. writer Edwidge Danticat (who whispered French translations into Tarantino's ear), directors Schatzberg and Hong Kong's Tsui Hark, Belgian writer Benoit Poelvoorde, and Finnish critic Peter Von Bagh.

Cannes Report No. 10: Jury Defends Its Vote

May 24, 2004—The jury of the fifty-seventh Cannes Film Festival insisted that it awarded its top honor to Michael Moore's anti-Bush documentary not because of its politics, but because of its quality as a film.

"We were dealing with reels of film, not politics," said jury president Quentin Tarantino. "We all agreed that *Fahrenheit 9/11* was the best film."

Tarantino and his eight fellow jurors were breaking with fifty-six years of festival tradition by explaining and defending their selections at a press conference the day after the awards were named. This was not the jury's idea but the festival's, Tarantino said, after Toronto critic Bruce Kirkland observed that past juries had operated with the secrecy of a Masonic lodge.

Some critics of the Palme d'Or for Moore interpreted it as a slap by the French against Bush and his invasion of Iraq, but in fact the jury had four American members, and only one French member; the other jurors were from Finland, Hong Kong, Belgium, and the United Kingdom.

"I knew this political crap would be brought up," said the outspoken Tarantino. "I think judging a film by its politics is a bad thing. If this movie was saying everything I wanted it to say, but not saying it with the best filmmaking, I would have opposed it."

The film, which received the longest standing ovation in Cannes history, charges that Bush has bungled the war on terrorism and sent U.S. troops to Iraq under false pretenses. One of its most talked-about scenes claims Bush remained in a Florida classroom, reading a book to children, for seven minutes after learning of the attack on the World Trade Center, until aides finally had to ask him to leave.

When an Italian journalist complained that the film had "only one point of view," juror Tilda Swinton, the actress from Scotland, replied, "We've heard what Bush has to say. We live with it. It's not a fair fight. This film helps to redress the balance." And juror Edwidge Danticat, the Haitian-born American novelist, said, "Moore starts by saying this is *his* view of the world. He gives voice to people who are voiceless."

Every one of the jurors said they supported the award. American director Jerry Schatzberg said, "Before I got here, I was thinking, I hope the other jurors are not going to be sympathetic just because of the film's distribution problems. Quentin told us on day one to keep politics out of it and just judge the films."

The movie generated controversy after

Disney president Michael Eisner ordered his Miramax subsidiary, which produced it, not to distribute it in America. Miramax head Harvey Weinstein says the film has distribution in every other country in the world. Ironically, Eisner's decision may help the movie; the Palme d'Or has raised Weinstein's asking price for U.S. rights.

Tarantino's famous temper was revealed at one point in the press conference when a journalist questioned the "cinematic qualities" of *Fahrenheit 9/11*.

"You're talking about pretty pictures," Tarantino said. "This film is made of images. When a U.S. soldier is shown with an Iraqi captive whose head is in a hood, that is not a pretty picture, but it is a powerful image." When the journalist tried to argue, Tarantino said the discussion was over, and took off his earphones so he could not hear the translation.

The jury did not reveal individual votes, but hinted at some differences. Its jury prize for the Thai film *Sud Pralad*, which sharply divided Cannes audiences, also split the jury, "but some of us were moved by that film to a staggering degree," Tarantino said, and so dissenters on the jury respected their passion.

He defended the Grand Prize (second place), which went to the violent Korean revenge thriller *Old Boy*. "The most exciting films in the world are coming out of Japan and Korea right now," he said. "It took ten years for the genre pictures of Hong Kong to be recognized; it's great that a film like this can play in Cannes." Fellow juror Tsui Hark, whose own Hong Kong genre pictures, like *Chinese Ghost Story*, took years to win recognition, kept a poker face.

The press conference was the closing act of what many of us thought was a return to form for the festival. Its new director, Thierry Fremaux, cast his net wide by including two animated films and two documentaries in the competition.

And he closed the fest on a traditional note with the new MGM musical *De-Lovely,* based on the life of Cole Porter. As thousands of guests, from *Star Wars* creator George Lucas to Microsoft billionaire Paul Allen, partied on a jetty out beyond the Palais, there was a concert of Porter's songs by such as Natalie Cole, Sheryl Crow, Alanis Morissette, Robbie Williams, Kevin Kline, and Ashley Judd. Backed by a full pop orchestra, they were shown on a vast video screen flanked by high-powered speakers, so that everyone on the beachfront, the Boulevard Croisette, and all of the oceanfront hotels could see and hear the performances (whether they wanted to or not).

I don't suppose Cannes has ever been away, but it's certainly back.

* * *

Irma P. Hall

The Cannes prize for Chicago actress Irma P. Hall was explained, sort of, at the jury's press conference. The jury gave its best actress award to Maggie Cheung for *Clean,* and then broke with precedent by giving a special jury prize to Hall for her work in *The Ladykillers.*

"She was a force of nature," said jury president Quentin Tarantino.

Hall, sixty-six, who was Big Mama in *Soul Food,* played a little old lady who does not get killed in the Coen brothers' *The Ladykillers,* a festival entry. Seriously injured in a car crash in January, she is undergoing rehabilitation treatments, with much moral support from her costar, Tom Hanks.

"We were thinking of just going ahead and titling the prize the Force of Nature Award," said actress Tilda Swinton, a jury member.

"I left my wallet in El Sugundo!" Tarantino declared, in a passable Irma P. Hall imitation.

"He's been talking in her voice for the last three days," said Swinton.

Questions for the Movie Answer Man

Ads Before Movies

Q. The Cinema Advertising Council reports that council members collected $356 million in 2003 from cinema advertising, a 48 percent increase from 2002. That guarantees the continuing intrusion of commercials before the coming attractions. Council president Matthew Kearney says the ads, if done right, "do not alienate customers." He points to a study by Arbitron that found two-thirds of adults and 70 percent of teens don't mind an ad played before the trailers and movie begin. As a lover of movies, and especially of going to the cinema, I refuse to quietly accept that. Are you bothered by these ads, or do they fade into the background for you? What do you make of apparent plans to institute a 20-minute "presentation" of sponsored ads before movies?
—Michael S. Miller, *Daily Telegram,* Adrian, Michigan

A. I think it stinks. The figures quoted by Arbitron are preposterous; how did they word the question? I have never encountered a single moviegoer, either in person or in print, who does not despise the ads before movies. The prospect of seeing *twenty minutes* of ads sickens and angers me; because the theaters will not sacrifice their quick turnovers of houses, they may create pressure on Hollywood to make movies shorter. I have heard audiences boo ads before movies; what advertiser wants to alienate consumers by stealing their private time?

Alien and John W. Campbell Jr.

Q. It is very apropos that you invoked the name of John W. Campbell in your Great Movies review of the rerelease of *Alien*. Although he is most famous as an editor, he also happened to write the original short story "Who Goes There?" on which the Howard Hawks film *The Thing From Another World* was based, thus providing the inspiration for *Alien*.
—Karl Loeffler, Quebec, Canada

A. I knew that and forgot to mention it.

The editor of *Astounding* (later *Analog*) was arguably the most influential figure in the development of modern science fiction, a champion of such as Asimov and Heinlein.

Animals in Movies

Q. There was a controversy on the set of Lars Von Trier's movie *Manderlay,* regarding the actual onscreen killing of a donkey, which resulted in John C. Reilly walking off the picture. How do you feel about the ethics of this situation? Is the killing acceptable since there was a vet on the set and the donkey was reportedly old and sick? How about the scene in *Apocalypse Now,* where Kurtz's army slaughters the cow? Though I'm not an animal lover or a vegetarian, there's something about actually killing animals in a fiction film that doesn't sit right with me.
—Matt Singer, New York, New York

A. Millions of animals are killed every day so we may eat them, and yet we're sentimental about individual animals. There's currently hysteria in Illinois about the killing of horses to supply horse meat (which is shipped to France). Most of the opponents of horse meat have no trouble with the killing and eating of cows, pigs, chickens, etc. It seems absurd to get worked up about one species and not another.

But your question involves the killing of animals for art, not food. I feel if you accept the killing of animals at all, then requiring the animal to be killed for food but not for art is inconsistent. That said, how should we respond to the Korean film *Old Man,* which played at Cannes and had a scene where a live octopus was eaten by one of the characters? In his acceptance speech, the film's director thanked four octopi who died in the making of the film.

Audience Misbehavior

Q. Halfway through a screening of *The Spanish Prisoner,* a young man in the front row started taking photographs of the movie

815

with a flash camera. After being told to knock it off, he did for a short time, then resumed his documentation and was summarily ejected. We think he had a crush on Rebecca Pidgeon.

—Matt Rosen, Madison, Wisconsin

A. Your letter, while brief, contains three astonishing aspects. (1) Did it not occur to him that the flash would obscure the photo, and he should use available light from the screen? (2) It is remarkable that he was "summarily ejected," since many movie theaters enforce few standards for audience behavior. (3) In Madison, which according to a recent survey by the *Princeton Review*, contains the No. 2–ranking party school in the nation, this poor sap is reduced to stealing snapshots of Rebecca Pidgeon?

Bad Santa

Q. Is it true that Disney execs were upset when they got their first look at the Miramax production of *Bad Santa*? I read in both Chicago papers that they were staring at the screen in disbelief and said "nothing appears sacred anywhere. This is just not in the spirit of Disney."

—Charles Smith, Chicago, Illinois

A. This appears to be an instant urban legend. Matt Drudge's report of the alleged Disney reaction appeared on the *Drudge Report* and was picked up everywhere, often without attribution, but Disney officials deny the story. And Sean P. Means, film critic of the *Salt Lake Tribune*, deconstructs the mini-controversy as an attempt by Republican polemicists to "drive a wedge between Disney and its Miramax subsidiary," because Miramax honcho Harvey Weinstein is a "prime fund-raiser for the Democratic Party." He cites other examples where Disney was bashed because of films from its Miramax subsidiary.

Bad Santa has now been piled on by the usual assortment of amateur op-ed film critics, whose no-brainer attacks reveal they do not understand the film or may not have even seen it. It's an R-rated adult comedy—not an attack on Santa, but a portrayal of an alcoholic safe-cracker (Billy Bob Thornton) who masquerades as Santa Claus.

Q. I found myself watching Fox News last week, and saw three commercials for *The Cat in the Hat,* and an interview with Reverend Jerry Falwell in which *Bad Santa* was used as an example of Christianity Under Attack. There was plenty of talk about "Our Children" and the depravity that Hollywood presents as entertainment to them. Nobody mentioned that *Bad Santa* is not in any way intended to be a children's movie. I am not yet a parent, and if I did have young children I wouldn't take them to see either film. However, if I had kids in their teens, I like to think that they would have the same ability that I have—that is, to recognize a terrible movie from the trailers—and that they would be begging me to take them to *Bad Santa.*

—John Griffiths, Washington, D.C.

A. If Reverend Falwell knew the movie was R-rated, he was being misleading—and if he didn't know, he should have. I'm sure he understands that Santa Claus is not a Christian symbol.

Q. I attended a Sunday evening screening of *Bad Santa* this week. Not only was the audience packed, but I noticed that I was surrounded by children ranging in age from three to twelve. Parents actually brought their kids to this movie, despite the preview. I loved it, but found myself quite uncomfortable enjoying this twisted delight amidst unsuspecting youth. And the film was far stronger in content than I had imagined. Are parents oblivious, stupid, without concern, or all of the above? I certainly hope none of them had the nerve to complain once the profanities began.

—Vincent Santino, Burbank, California

A. *Bad Santa* is rated R, "for pervasive language, strong sexual content, and some violence." The reviews have made it clear it's not a family film. Parents who would take a young child to it are irresponsible, but I have seen small kids at all kinds of R-rated movies, and I despair. Some movies are, quite simply, appropriate for adults only.

Being Out of Step

Q. I know you've stated in the past that

your reviews shouldn't be evaluated in comparison to the general consensus, but when you see a wide disparity between your reaction to a film and that of most other critics, especially in the case of you giving a good-to-stellar review to something that everyone thinks stunk, do you ever second-guess yourself? For example, with these recent films: *Ella Enchanted, The Alamo, Jersey Girl, Never Die Alone, Taking Lives, Secret Window, Spartan, The Reckoning,* and *Hidalgo.*

—Sandy Cormack, Baltimore, Maryland

A. I remain satisfied with all of those reviews. I try to explain the reasons why I praise or dislike a movie, and I think, for example, that my review of *Hidalgo* is a splendid description of the film I saw and the reasons I liked it. Mamet's *Spartan* is likely to make my Best Ten list. *Jersey Girl* suffered because of the Affleck-J-Lo nonsense and because Kevin Smith dared to make a sweet film. You didn't ask, but I was stunned that *The Girl Next Door* scored around 60 on the Tomatometer (to be sure, it got 41 at Metacritic). I agree with Ken Turan of the *Los Angeles Times*: "What is disturbing and frankly distasteful about *The Girl Next Door* is how slick and shameless it is in its eagerness to blur boundaries, to squeeze as much transgressive material as it can into a nominally bland and innocent form." The movie's ads are shamelessly pitched at an audience too young to qualify for the R rating.

Beyond Borders

Q. You were wondering if the skinny starving baby in *Beyond Borders* was real. In an interview with *Entertainment Weekly*, director Martin Campbell revealed that it was done with CGI. He did say that the Khmer Rouge amputees were real land-mine victims, though.

—Tony Ward, Glenview, Illinois

A. Although the baby was made skinnier with computer techniques, that doesn't change the nature of the film's offense. Whether or not the baby is really a starving stick-figure, it looks like one, and the image itself is offensive in a movie that uses his suffering as a backdrop for movie stars in love. In this era of CGI, it's important to note that movie images have a reality of their own, apart from their sources.

Big Fish

Q. I just recently watched *Big Fish* on DVD for the first time. I noticed in one particular scene that a cloud resembled a baby's face in a hyper-realistic way. The time code was 74:42–74:50. I rewound it and paused it, and when my family finally saw it they agreed it did not look fake, but more like a picture. I know Tim Burton recently had a baby, and I also know that in *Sleepy Hollow* a hidden face was added with CGI inside a fire. Do you know if this baby's face was intentional or just an amazing coincidence?

—Mitchell Stookey, Saskatoon, Saskatchewan

A. There are no coincidences. Another hidden surprise, according to movieweb.com: "From the Main Menu, if you press UP twice after highlighting the 'Special Effects' option, a 'star' will appear on the 'top hat' above the 'tree.' Select it to see Tim Burton driving a golf cart shooting fireworks down the main strip of Spectre."

Bill Murray at the Oscars

Q. Did you see how upset Bill Murray looked when he didn't win the Oscar? I don't recall the last time a nominee looked so clearly disappointed (everyone else pretended to be happy for the others, smiled, and clapped!). I hope Bill will be all right—I have a feeling he's going to be quite depressed for a while; or perhaps this is just a strategy—so next time when he's nominated, the Oscar voters will remember that he really wants an Academy Award.

—Antony Chen, Vancouver, British Columbia

A. A lot of people, me included, predicted he had a chance to win. It was a wonderful, nuanced performance. Billy Crystal was graceful in assuring him, "Don't go, Bill. We love you," which inspired an ovation. At least Murray won the Independent Spirit Award for best actor, given the day before, when his speech was a gem, including the observation: "Half of the people in this room are more dressed-up than on any other day in the year, and the other half are more dressed-down."

Q. At the Academy Awards, host Billy Crystal directed a putatively humorous, though cruel, remark at best actor nominee Bill Murray, moments after the Oscar was awarded to Sean Penn. Crystal's remark brought to mind Groucho Marx's comment about comedians not wanting each other to be successful. It was certainly petty and mean-spirited and betrayed no small amount of professional jealousy on the speaker's part, especially given the disparity of quality of his and Bill Murray's respective film careers. Can you recall other instances where such rudeness was directed at Oscar nominees by the hosts at these ceremonies in the past?

—K. F. O'Hare, Gainesville, Virginia

A. I wrote: "A lot of people, me included, predicted [Murray] had a chance to win . . . Billy Crystal was graceful in assuring him, 'Don't go, Bill. We love you,' which inspired an ovation." Many disagree with me. Jim Todd of West New York, New Jersey, writes: "That comment was so vicious it was the worst Oscar moment in my thirty years of watching the Oscars!" The wise Mark Steyn wrote in the *Spectator:* "Bill Murray was not only robbed but weirdly humiliated in his loss by Billy Crystal."

It may be that Crystal's comment sounded wrong to many ears, but consider that when the nominations were announced, the only one Crystal made a point of applauding was the one for his fellow *SNL* graduate, "my friend, Bill Murray." Consider, too, that Crystal has a personal reputation for kindness and generosity. I believe he was hoping Murray would win, and his remark was made in friendship.

Here is a play-by-play analysis by Andy Ihnatko of Boston, who scrutinizes the Oscars with an obsessiveness bordering on mania:

"Crystal's remarks to Murray were clearly affectionate. Synopsis: Immediate reaction to Penn's win when name is finally read: Depp, Kingsley, and Law smile and applaud. Murray's expression doesn't change one iota, but after a moment he turns his head in Penn's direction and slowly nods. Penn climbs stage. Camera cuts to Depp, standing and applauding. Cuts to Law standing and applauding.

Doesn't cut to Murray. Wide shot of crowd as Penn is handed his Oscar; Murray is still seated and doesn't appear to be applauding. Ovation continues for another half-minute but Murray isn't in view. Penn begins speech and acknowledges his fellow nominees. Camera cuts to Kingsley, looking serious; Law, scratching his chin (both have blank expressions but grin a little when peripheral vision tells them that they're on the big monitors); Murray, looking blank. He's paying attention to the speech but still not reacting. Depp, too, isn't paying attention to the monitors and so his expression doesn't change when they cut to him. Penn finishes speech and walks off stage. Hard to tell but it seems like Murray isn't applauding here, either.

"Crystal: 'Bill, don't go . . . Bill, don't go . . . it's okay! We love you!'

"On 'we,' cut to Murray, who is getting a pretty serious consolation neck-nuzzle from his wife. Murray's lips are tight, eyebrows are up, he says something back (inaudible), then grins. Audience gives him a consolation ovation, cut back to Bill, who still looks like he's just a little sad and disappointed."

Boom Mikes—Again

Q. My wife and I just returned from seeing *The Secret Lives of Dentists.* During the latter part of the movie I could see the microphones in the film, usually over the heads of the actors. I didn't know what to make of it, especially because it happened again and again. It was terribly distracting from the experience of watching the movie. What happened here?

—Bill Meyer, Durham, North Carolina

A. This is the Question That Refuses Go Away, and I answer it faithfully once a year. Please clip and save:

When you see a microphone at the top of the frame in a movie, 99.9 percent of the time it is not the fault of the filmmakers, and the blame should go to the projectionist in your theater, who has framed the movie incorrectly. Complain to the management. Of course they'll tell you "the problem is with the print," or "the movie came like that from the studio," but *they are wrong.*

Boom Mikes, Yet Again

Here is our annual visit from the Question That Will Not Go Away. The Answer Man has dealt with the issue of visible boom mikes over and over, and readers continue to think they're the fault of incompetent directors — or, in this twist, actors who don't speak up.

Q. In the Answer Man column, you noted that when microphones are visible, it is the fault of the projectionist not framing the film correctly. The fault lies with untrained and unskilled actors so used to having a microphone dangling inches above their heads that they speak nearly every line in a whisper. I've yet to see a visible microphone in a film starring Meryl Streep, Dustin Hoffman, Gene Hackman, Patrick Stewart, Anthony Hopkins, Katharine Hepburn, Bette Davis, Laurence Olivier, Marlon Brando, or any of the other tremendous, and properly trained, actors. These artisans know how to project their voice, even in a tender and intimate moment, to the microphone and beyond.

—B. Michael McFarland, Berwyn, Illinois

A. A nice theory, but incorrect. Microphone placement has much more to do with overall sound quality than the voice abilities of movie actors, and indeed many stage-trained actors have to be urged to dial down their voices. Billy Wilder asked Jack Lemmon to speak lower so often that Lemmon finally said, "What do you want? Nothing?" And Wilder replied: "Please God!"

Q. Re. the Answer Man item about visible microphones at the top of the frame in a movie: You blame it on the projectionist. My question is, should the microphones be eliminated during editing? I design pages for a newspaper. I would never type "our readers are morons" far off into the upper margin, then blame the men working the press when it appeared in print.

—Bill Huber, *Green Bay News-Chronicle,* Wisconsin

A. I referred your message to Steve Kraus of the Lake St. Screening Room in Chicago, who replies:

"The most commonly used movie format nowadays is akin to letterboxing, except that there is usually more image on the film than is intended to be shown, with the final cropping done via the projector's aperture plate. Thus, if the projectionist misframes the picture things may be shown that were not intended to be seen, not to mention wreaking general havoc with the filmmaker's composition.

"Some films are indeed shot with a mask in the camera which renders the excess area black and forces the projectionist to frame it precisely lest the audience see a partly black screen. At the very least it means nothing unintended will be seen. But there are a number of valid reasons to film with an open aperture, the most important of which is that the extra height can be used during the all-important video transfer to allow full frame versions with little or no pan and scan. (The area to be shown will be adjusted from shot to shot so even if a microphone is present in one scene it can be avoided by zooming in).

"Mr. Huber's question has some validity. It's true that a correction can be made during the post-production process to produce masked prints from a full-frame original negative. The problem is that this usually requires an expensive and image-degrading step of optical printing, and that is overkill for a problem that is more easily solved by the projectionist setting the projector's framing knob correctly and threading the film properly."

Brown Bunny

Q. I read a review that said that you sang *Singing in the Rain* and made "body sounds" while attending the screening of *The Brown Bunny.* I pride myself on not being a dumbed-down American moviegoer (I'm actually English, so I wouldn't qualify for that anyway). Now I'm somewhat concerned that I have been following the reviews of a man who doesn't know how to behave in a movie theater! OK, I know, the movie was appalling apparently, but still, is this the behavior of a respected film critic?

—Harvey Kertland, San Diego, California

A. Actually, I sang *Raindrops Keep Fallin' on My Head,* just those six words, during a flashback scene showing Gallo on a bicycle with Chloe Sevigny. Consider it a tribute to

Butch Cassidy and the Sundance Kid. I sang it very softly to my wife, but for my sins I was seated close to a writer for the *Hollywood Reporter,* who included it in an article about the movie's negative reception at Cannes, where the entire audience was engaging in hoots and catcalls. The story has now grown to the point where you would think I performed it on a kazoo. After the screening of *The Brown Bunny* at Toronto, director Vincent Gallo named the wrong song, and further elaborated that I "burped and farted" during the screening. Not true.

Gallo's strategy is to draw attention to my dislike of the film in order to distract from the fact that the movie was almost universally disdained at Cannes, receiving a record low rating from the Screen International panel of critics (none of them me). He paints me as a lone dissenter instead of merely one voice in the chorus. Nevertheless, having praised most of Gallo's work (including his directorial debut *Buffalo 66*), I look forward to seeing his shortened and re-edited version of the film, and take heart from Michael Harnest of Toronto, who saw it and writes me: "I was disappointed; not because it was a bad film, but because it wasn't bad enough. It wasn't good, by any means, but I'd watch it again before, say, *Pearl Harbor.*"

Q. I have been following with great amusement the *Brown Bunny* imbroglio. Now, Vosges's Haut-Chocolat, a chocolate store in Chicago, has introduced the "Vincent Gallo truffle." I had a sample and it is delicious, a blend of cheese, walnut, and chocolate. It's also bigger than their other truffles. Vosges's Web site describes it as "arresting in its visual shape." The owner of Vosges, Katrina Markhoff, said in her monthly e-mail to Vosges members that she knows Mr. Gallo and made the truffle for him.
—Gelsey Kinsey, Chicago, Illinois

A. Now the question is, how does Chloe Sevigny like it?

Canada

Q. Regarding your recent interview with Robert Altman: Mr. Altman seems to have forgotten he has directed at least two projects

in Canada: one was *That Cold Day in the Park* (1969), shot in Vancouver, British Columbia, which had no film industry at all at the time. Either he considers Vancouver part of the United States or he decided to forget this little bit of his personal history.
—Lawrence Crosthwaite, Campbell River, British Columbia

A. Altman didn't say he was against shooting in Canada—he said he was against shooting movies there that belonged elsewhere. "I think it's obscene to have a runaway production just because some government passes a law that gives you tax breaks," he told me. "Why was *Chicago* made in Toronto? To save a couple of million dollars—which of course doesn't go to the artists. On moral grounds I won't do that." But he added: "If it's a film I want to make, and Canada's the best place to shoot it from my standpoint, then I don't have anything against Canada." That would account for his work there. Clint Eastwood took a similar stand when he came under studio pressure to shoot *Mystic River* in Canada. "This story takes place in Boston," he said, "and Boston is not in Canada."

Cap Codes

Q. Have you been seeing spots when you go to the movies? It may not be your eyes! More than twenty years ago Kodak devised a system called "Cap Code" designed to uniquely mark film prints so that pirated copies could be traced to the source. Cap Code uses very tiny dots that flash occasionally but are so small that the average viewer almost never notices them. Well, something new and horrible has been introduced on some studios' prints. Sort of a giant picture-marring version of Cap Code dots: Very large reddish brown spots that flash in the middle of the picture, usually placed in a light area. They flash in various patterns throughout a given reel while other reels of the same film may have none at all. A Kodak spokesman who helped devise the original Cap Code says this is not the work of his company but theorizes that it may be intended to be more visible on the murky compressed copies that get posted to the Internet where the original, very subtle Cap Code may be difficult to discern. On one movie technical forum they are referring to this new system as "Crap Code" or "Cap Code on Steroids." There are reports coming in of viewers complaining of the spots on the pictures. While theaters strive to keep prints free of dirt and scratches Hollywood starts sending out prints with built-in marring. Among the films known to be afflicted are *Ali, Behind Enemy Lines, 28 Days Later, Freddy vs. Jason,* and *Underworld;* probably many others as well.

—Steve Kraus, Lake St. Screening Room, Chicago, Illinois

A. You're the expert projectionist at our Chicago critics' screening room, with a fierce love of high-quality film, so I can imagine how upset you are. What's amusing about Crap Code and the other efforts to catch pirates is that most of the thieves are apparently industry insiders. A recent news story says studios may even be discouraged from distributing advance DVDs of their Oscar contenders to Academy members, because some of these movies quickly find their way to the Web.

Q. While watching *Kill Bill, Vol. 1,* I noticed that several times during the movie, there would be a flash of three or four small dots, arranged in the same formation, lasting only a couple of frames. It could not have been blood spots (my first theory), because this happened even during parts where there was no bloodshed (which were, of course, few and far between). Is this something Tarantino did, or a problem with the print the theater showed?

—Jeremy Gable, Anaheim, California

A. The dots are part of a new studio antipiracy system that has already been dubbed "Crap Code" by insiders. The Answer Man was right on top of this innovation, with an item in the column by Steve Kraus, Chicago projection expert. He says the dots are so large because then they can be seen even on digital versions pirated on the Internet.

Q. When seeing a film I sometimes feel like I'm part of an experiment by studio executives to see how much they can get away with. They've found they can get away with higher ticket prices, weaker plots, television commercials, and even music videos in front of movies. They can get away with twenty-plus minutes of preview advertising before a captive audience. Now they want to see if they can get away with Cap Codes—visible antipiracy signals in a movie. This is one step away from the "bug" in the corner of television programs. Will the Fox logo (or MCA or whatever) now present itself in the lower corner? I'm just a guy out here and I really like movies. But I'm losin' my faith. The only thing coming up I really need to see in a theater is *The Lord of the Rings: Return of the King.* If that's got Cap Codes, I'm never going back to a theater again. And don't get me started on DVDs that play commercials without letting you skip to the menu.

—Kurt Kober, Somerville, New Jersey

A. Crap codes—excuse me, Cap Codes—have enraged a lot of Answer Man correspondents. Will Sparks of Charlottesville, Virginia, writes: "I saw *Master and Commander: The Far Side of the World* and was disgusted by the number of times that I saw those hideous dots during the film, especially during the chase scene around Cape Horn. Do the studios think we're too dumb not to see them?"

Why are the dots so big and visible? Why not do something subtle and subliminal? Because the dots are intended to identify prints that have been pirated by analog means—that is, by being videotaped off a screen. Hollywood is in a paranoid seizure about piracy right now, spending a fortune on security guards who body-search movie critics while the real pirates steal from within the system.

Casablanca

Q. I just listened to your DVD commentary for the new anniversary edition of *Casablanca* and found it excellent. But you perpetuate a common misunderstanding when you say that the infamous "Letters of Transit" are signed by Charles de Gaulle. As you said, anything signed by the leader of the Free French would be worthless in Vichy French territory. Contemporary screenwriters certainly knew that. Which is why, although Peter Lorre's accent might make it hard to understand, his character says "General Weygand" (pronounced *Vay*-gauh), a Vichy official, not "de Gaulle." But you're still right about the letters being nothing more than a MacGuffin. As Rudy Behlmer noted on the other commentary track, such letters never actually existed and were purely a plot contrivance.

—Greg Stevens, Studio City, California

A. The problem is that the line sounds more like "de Gaulle" than "Weygand." The following story was deleted from my commentary because it referred to a different disc version of the movie:

When I was doing a shot-by-shot analysis of *Casablanca* at the University of Colorado a few years ago, this point came up, and a student suggested consulting the subtitles. The English titles clearly named de Gaulle. "Now try the French titles," she said. The French titles named Weygand. Which is right? To borrow a reply from my review of *Le Divorce*: Monsieur, I have only two hands.

Casting Decisions

Q. In your Great Movies essay for the recently added De Palma version of *Scarface* you asked the following questions: "What were Pacino's detractors hoping for? Something internal and realistic? Low key?" Here's your answer: How about having an actual Cuban portray the character, rather than have an Italian actor offensively impersonate one (and poorly, at that)?

—John Ericson, Ann Arbor, Michigan

A. How about having an actual Texan take the role of that Philadelphian Richard Gere in *Days of Heaven*? And let's take Denzel Washington out of *Much Ado About Nothing*. And what business did Alfred Molina have playing Diego Rivera in *Frida*? He's a British actor with Italian and Spanish parents. And what about Javier Bardem, born in Spain's Canary Islands, playing the Cuban poet Reinaldo Arenas in *Before Night Falls*? The magic of acting lies precisely in actors portraying someone they are not.

CGI

Q. Here's what Computer-Generated Images rob from the filmgoer.

(1) A movie is no longer a documentary of itself. When you watch the battle scenes in *Lawrence of Arabia* or *Ran*, or the train crashing at the end of *The General*, they work not only as story, but as logistics and direction; what you see had to really happen. In *Troy*, when a shot shows more ships than there were Trojans, it seemed like a satirical comment on CGI.

(2) CGI is too clear. In any frame showing a computer-generated image, its clarity is greater than the filmed scene into which it is inserted. Even in an animated film like *Triplets of Belleville*, small CGI touches such as a model of the Eiffel Tower was much finer than the surrounding drawn cel. Unless you are a programmer or computer game aficionado, CGI holds no magic.

—Mike Spearns, St. John's, Newfoundland

A. Jean-Luc Godard said, "The cinema is truth at twenty-four frames a second, and every cut is a lie." That's why some directors are fond of long takes; the actors are sharing real time with the audience. The movies have always used special-effects trickery, like painted backdrops, matte drawings, and optical shots, but the people were generally real; now CGI blends reality and invention so seamlessly that movies lose conviction and have the same freedom as a cartoon over laws of time, space, and gravity.

Charles Bronson

Q. How come you haven't done an article on the passing of Charles Bronson?

—Matthew Anderson, Hicksville, New York

A. I was out of town and by the time I learned of his death, the paper's deadline had passed.

Bronson was a straight-ahead kind of guy, with genuine screen presence that contributed to his good movies and helped him get through the bad ones. I liked him. He said exactly what he thought and had little patience for the movie publicity machine. I spent some time with him on the set of *Death Wish* for an *Esquire* profile, and quoted him saying he was capable, like his character, of killing anyone who harmed his family. When Johnny Carson asked him why they ran quotes like that, he said, "Because that's what I said."

I have a favorite Bronson story. Both Bronson and the Swedish director Ingmar Bergman had the same agent, Paul Kohner, and the same publicist, the legendary Ernie Anderson. When Bergman left Sweden in a well-publicized dispute with the tax authorities, he visited Los Angeles for the first time, and asked Kohner to arrange a visit to a studio.

Bronson was making an action picture at the time, and Kohner assigned Anderson to arrange a meeting between the two clients. Anderson was hesitant, because Bronson sometimes kidded him: "I know this isn't a Bergman picture, but it may make a few bucks." After he introduced the two men, Bergman asked him to explain the scene he was doing.

"This is the scene where I get shot," Bronson said. "I have these little squibs that explode to make it look like bullets are hitting."

"Fascinating," said Bergman. "I never knew how they did that."

"You mean," asked Bronson, "you don't use machine guns in your movies?"

Charlie's Angels: Full Throttle

Q. Drew Barrymore is an admitted alcoholic and was in treatment for substance abuse in her early teens. Yet *Charlie's Angels: Full Throttle* begins with a scene in which Drew Barrymore's character is drinking shots in a bar, and has apparently been in a drinking match with a mercenary who is drunk to the point of passing out. Later on in the film, she is seen attempting to walk off with a bottle of champagne from the "O'Grady gang" hideout. Still later, when on the run, she stops in a Mexican bar and orders a drink. Ms. Barrymore has trumpeted the fact that, as an executive producer for the film, she banned the film from depicting the "Angels" using guns because she is "morally against" guns. Yet she seems to have no problem with her own character drinking alcohol! This seems hypocritical to me.

—Joseph O'Connell, New York, New York

A. Me too. I can understand why a recovering alcoholic would want to portray alcohol in a realistic light in a serious movie (as many have), but to portray binge drinking as fun is something Barrymore should have thought twice about.

Cheaper by the Dozen

Q. In your *Cheaper by the Dozen* review you wrote that you wanted eleven siblings. Which kid did you want to be; the trailblazing first born, the footloose-and-fancy-free youngest, or a troubled middle child?

—Troylene Ladner, Jersey City, New Jersey

A. Reading the original novel over and over, "I was an only child curled up at the end of the sofa, imagining what it would be like to have eleven brothers and sisters." Egotistical little monster that I was, however, I did not imagine myself as one of them but as the possessor of all of them. It would be my family, you see, and they would have all the walk-ons, as footloose, troubled, etc. One thing binding these siblings together would be their adoration for me, their older, smarter, better-looking brother with the neatest bike and the most Yo-Yo trophies. Our parents, of course, would consult with me for child-rearing tips and lists of recommended movies, etc.

City of God

Q. I recently saw the Brazilian film *City of God* and thought it by far the best film of 2003. I was angry at how overlooked it was in America and decided to look at the reviews online. I saw that you, among other critics, championed the film. I opened the *Chicago Tribune* and saw that both of their critics remembered this early 2003 film and included it on both of their lists. But it didn't even get an honorable mention on your list. In one of the ads for this film you were quoted as saying it was "one of the greatest moviegoing experiences of my life." Was this not true?

—Mikeal Carlson, Chicago, Illinois

A. Very true. So true that *City of God* was No. 2 on my list for *last year*. The film played in every major festival in 2002 and was a candidate for year-end awards, and although it did not open in Chicago until January, I didn't see the point in waiting twelve months to put it on a Best-10 list when putting it on the timelier list might do it some good. By the same token, my 2003 list includes *Monster*. Since it will be a contender in all the awards, and Charlize Theron clearly deserves the Oscar as best actress, why wait until 2004 to say so? No doubt it will be on the *Tribune* lists in 12 months. My print reporting appears in 200 papers and on the Internet; it's pointless to penalize a movie because of the technicality of its Chicago release date.

Q. I was thrilled that *City of God* got four nominations, but what happened to co-director Katia Lund? She is left out of the Best Director category with only Fernando Meirelles listed. Was it too much to have two directors on one film or did they feel that Sofia Coppola was enough female directors for one category? Katia is a wonderful director who created the short film that is the core of *City of God*. I hope this gets corrected—or is there something going on behind the scenes? There was some controversy when Miramax first bought the film and left Ms. Lund out of the credits but it got corrected.
—Gary Meyer, Berkeley, California

A. The Academy didn't list her as co-director. But Miramax president Harvey Weinstein tells me "we're working on that, trying to get her included." He says Meirelles was the actual director of the film, but Lund (who made the short subject that inspired *City of God)* "selected all the actors and worked with them—she directed the actors." He said if Meirelles wins the Oscar, he will certainly praise Lund in his acceptance.

The AM's contacts suggest that Lund's contribution to the film was crucial, and that she has been unfairly shouldered aside during all the Oscar attention. In Brazil, her exclusion has stirred up controversy because some believe her contribution was greater than Meirelles. I am told by a well-informed production executive: "If you watch Katia Lund's DVD and then watch Meirelles's two previous films, *Crazy Boys* and *Maids*, I think you will gain a wonderful insight regarding *City of God,* and if you read the official *Cidade de Deus* Web site you will learn what each of the directors did. Katia has always taken the position that she would not do anything which might hurt the film; there-

fore she continues to take the high road and has not and will not go public with this grave injustice. Katia has filmed in the favelas [slums] of Rio for the last seven years and her priority is that the film will be a vehicle that can help the social and politcal problems faced every day by those living in the favelas."

Q. I wholeheartedly agree that the bone-shattering *City of God* belongs near the top of a Top Ten list. But are you sure you've got the right year? As far as I can tell, this movie had no theatrical release in 2002—even in L.A., it's not slated to open until January 17. Indeed, in the few dozen Top Ten lists I scanned, only you and *Screen Daily* (a European publication) cited it, which I consider rock-solid proof that your peers must have considered it off-limits.
—Kevin Bourrillion, San Francisco, California

A. I mentioned in my article that I knew I was jumping the gun. But *City of God* is so extraordinary that I wanted to include it on this year's list, which might do it some good, rather than wait a year. Foreign films have a hard enough time at the box office. Since several thousand North Americans have seen *City of God* at film festivals and it is eligible for the 2002 foreign-language Oscar, I feel my timing is justified.

Q. Of course I am biased, being a Brazilian, but don't you think that *City of God* deserved an Oscar nomination? Here in Brazil it's one of the biggest box office hits ever. The film received critical acclaim everywhere. We were all hoping for it to win the award. So, what happened? Is the theme too strong for Oscar? Is it just bad luck? Don't you think it's one of the best films of the year?
—João Solimeo, Vinhedo, Brazil

A. So good, I put it second on my list of the ten best films of 2002. *City of God* has already been voted among the top two hundred films of all time on the Internet Movie Database, and scores over 90 percent on the Tomatometer. It's a black eye for the Academy that it was not even nominated, calling the whole foreign film nomination process into question yet once again. This is one of those monstrous fiascoes like the Academy members who turned off *Hoop Dreams* after fifteen minutes.

How did this miscarriage of taste take place? Miramax, the film's U.S. distributor, has no official statement. However, an insider tells me privately, "When we had about sixty walkouts at our official Academy screening we knew things weren't looking good. Unfortunately, the Academy randomly assigns screening dates and ours was in early December, way before the good reviews and press came out. I guess the bottom line is that this film didn't appeal to the people on this committee, who are older and have a history of not going for edgier fare. There were some real champions but the nominations are based on an average and those walkouts killed the average."

The Academy members capable of walking out on *City of God* should disqualify themselves from future voting, as a final service to the Academy.

ClearPlay and CleanFlicks

Q. First came the video rental store that cut out the naughty bits. Now, you can get your own DVD player to do it for you! At what point does someone just watch the entire film and judge it for themselves? I know it's hard because they might actually have to think through their own censorship opinions.

—Patrick J. Doody, Hollywood, California

A. You are obviously referring to ClearPlay, a DVD player that censors DVDs while you're watching them. It works with some 600 DVDs, and the list is growing. You download the filters and use them with a ClearPlay-enabled machine, which skips over parts deemed unsuitable. Michael Medved is quoted on the Web site: "Movie fans who have been worried about excesses in violence, sexuality, and language can now enjoy their favorite films with a sense of security and satisfaction."

If they want to quote me, they can use this: "Imagine watching *The Passion of the Christ* with an hour skipped because of violence! Imagine *Kill Bill Vol. 2* as a twenty-minute short subject! Imagine *Taxi Driver* without most of the dialogue!"

My feeling is, either watch the movie or don't watch it. There are countless films suitable for family viewing. If you subject an R-rated film to the indignity of the ClearPlay approach, you are not experiencing the film's continuity and editing rhythm, and may miss information essential to understanding it. My additional feeling is, I'm damned if I'm going to pay to let some video jockey decide what I can see.

Yes, I know, some parents will want it for their children. I would like to meet the parents who want their little ones to see the ClearPlay versions of R-rated movies, so I could ask them: What's the point? Why not just rent films appropriate for your kids?

On the other hand, what about parents who *want* their kids to see R-rated films? See the next item.

Q. I noticed your diatribe on ClearPlay. The idea of ClearPlay [a system allowing DVD players to skip moments of sex, violence, or language in movies.—AM] is that some people don't want to see all the gory stuff (or nudity, etc.). So the suggestion that they just watch it and judge for themselves misses the point. Do you have to look at the centerfold to know you don't like pornography? You write, "Imagine watching *The Passion of the Christ* with an hour skipped because of violence! Imagine *Kill Bill Vol. 2* as a twenty-five-minute short subject! Imagine *Taxi Driver* without most of the dialogue!" Now Roger, do you really think we're that stupid? If you tried our product you would know that never happens. Generally, total events are only a few minutes or less per movie—virtually always less than would be edited out of a TV version, for censorship, timing, etc. In the spirit of fair play, you should also rail against TV and airline versions, and of course the directors that allow them for a few extra bucks. You write, "Why not just rent films appropriate for your kids?" Why should those be the only choices for parents, or for anyone? I just watched *Last Samurai* with my twelve-year-old with ClearPlay. Thematically, it was fine—*Dances with Wolves* goes Far East. And with ClearPlay, we were both comfortable. It's about the same thing I'd see on TV in a year or two, but instead I get to see it now, without commercials.

—Bill Aho, ClearPlay Inc.

A. ClearPlay is not for me, but you're right that by authorizing bowdlerized airline versions of their movies, directors lose the moral high ground. The difference is, the directors at least theoretically control the airline edits of their films, while ClearPlay is an outside contractor which, they feel, is making money off the unauthorized alteration of their work. By the way, how many minutes of violence *did* you cut from *The Passion*?

Q. There is an advertising link on your Answer Man page that takes the surfer to Cleanflicks.com. I was dismayed to see a company that sanitizes films by stripping them of serious content being marketed on your site. These companies are ruining one of the great art forms with their mindless editing. Are they gonna swing by the museum and cover up the statue of David?

—Jason Morrow, Lake Mary, Florida

A. Don't laugh. John Ashcroft, who covered the bare breasts on the statue of Justice, might think that was a good idea. Other readers have also questioned the ads for CleanFlicks, including Donald Frazier of Boulder, Colorado, who writes: "*Private Ryan* without the gore? *Titanic* without the sex? Not just unethical, but probably illegal! Certainly not deserving of your implicit endorsement."

But of course the advertising and editorial content of a newspaper are, and should be, separate. Writers do not agree with every ad, advertisers do not agree with every article. For example, the CEO of the similar company ClearPlay, Bill Aho of Salt Lake City, probably did not enjoy my description of him as a "censor and parasite, living off someone else's work," in my article about him from Sundance. But he has every right to advertise on the site.

Colorization

Q. I am insulted by Columbia TriStar Home Entertainment's "innovative process" called "Color+B&W," intended "to broaden the appeal of classic black-and-white films

and introduce them to a new generation of viewers." This egregious process, which makes its debut on two *Three Stooges* DVDs, also includes a "ChromaChoice" feature which "allows viewers to toggle between the original black-and-white version of a film and its colorized version in a seamless manner using the DVD remote." Supposedly this newfangled attempt at colorization is further authenticated through research involving original film elements, props, cloth swatches, etc., found in Columbia's archives. "Finally," states the press release, "through collaboration with West Wing Studios whose talented artists have years of experience in color designing, the highest level of historical accuracy is achieved in the images." When will these idiots in charge of precious studio libraries ever learn that any kind of colorization — even optional — is an insult to the legacy of black-and-white film? Did anyone learn a lesson from Ted Turner's dubious precedent?

—Jeff Shannon, Lynnwood, Washington

A. Colorization is a form of vandalism. A b&w movie isn't lacking something, it's adding something: The world is in color, so we get that for free, but b&w is a stylistic alternative, more dreamlike, more timeless. Fred Astaire hated color because it distracted from the pure form of his dancing. One could make the same argument about the Stooges, who in their own way are as pure and classic as Astaire. The Columbia TriStar claim that they're "researching" the original colors of the costumes, props, etc., is hilarious, since colors were selected for how they photographed in b&w, not for how they really looked. If they want to be consistent, all of the actors' faces will be light green, since greenish makeup was used because it photographed better.

Q. Your column noted that Columbia TriStar says its upcoming *Three Stooges* DVDs will be released in color and b&w with the intention to "broaden the appeal of classic black-and-white films and introduce them to a new generation of viewers." The obvious implication there is that classic b&w films do not appeal to the average viewer of today's younger generations. I'm in my late thirties and enjoy older films, but find myself in a minority among those within my age group. My parents are in their late fifties. It would appear as though those who are in that age range constitute the last generation of movie watchers to have a sincere desire to watch older b&w films, or older color ones for that matter. In the next twenty to twenty-five years, do you believe, with the exception of select films such as *The Wizard of Oz* and *Casablanca*, that we will be facing the virtual extinction of old classic films? With money being the bottom line for studios, video release companies, etc., and with the likely decline in the demand for these older movies, will scrounging around for used VHS/DVDs on eBay be the primary avenue for the classic movie fan of the future to find and watch these great films?

—Tim Dubois, Bedford, Texas

A. There will always be those who love old movies. I meet teenagers who are astonishingly well-informed about the classics. But you are right that many moviegoers and video viewers say they do not "like" black and white films. In my opinion, they are cutting themselves off from much of the mystery and beauty of the movies. Black and white is an artistic choice, a medium that has strengths and traditions, especially in its use of light and shadow. Moviegoers, of course, have the right to dislike b&w, but it is not something they should be proud of. It reveals them, frankly, as cinematically illiterate. I have been described as a snob on this issue. But snobs exclude; they do not include. To exclude b&w from your choices is an admission that you have a closed mind, a limited imagination, or are lacking in taste.

Dawn of the Dead

Q. The movie that beat out *The Passion of the Christ* as the biggest box-office draw is the remake of *Dawn of the Dead*. This is clearly a more egregious display of graphic violence than *TPOTC*, yet I have seen few if any objections to the violence from reviewers, whereas that seemed to be a primary objection to *TPOTC*. I think it's because the violence in *TPOTC* was not gratuitous and because it had meaning and people found it

repulsive (as they should) but in *DOTD* it's back to cartoon violence to which we have become desensitized. What do you think is going on?

—Jim Densmore, Ramona, California

A. That's exactly what it is. The violence in *Dawn of the Dead* is not real in any sense, and has no meaning or significance. The violence in *The Passion of the Christ* comes with a context. Lots of readers questioned my opinion that *The Passion* was "the most violent movie I have ever seen," citing *Texas Chainsaw Massacre* and other titles. But the effect of movie violence depends on subjective factors, including the purpose the filmmakers had in using it.

Q. I was surprised that your review of *Dawn of the Dead* was positive. While I agree the first seven minutes of this remake are pure genius, the rest of the movie fell well short of entertaining. The main reason for my dislike was the updated version of the zombies. What I want to ask you is this:

What do you prefer: the new "raging" zombies or the slower moving "lumbering" ones in the original version? The fast-moving, sprinting zombies are *no fun!* They're not scary and they have no character. I always liked the slow-moving yet ever-so-persistent ones. They added so much to the tension. You can hide, but sooner or later they're gonna get you. And in that process you can sit and think about it. Slow, absolute doom. I can recall countless zombies from the original *Dawn*. The baseball uniform zombie, the nurse zombie, the Hare Krishna girl. The list goes on and on. I can't see why people need their zombies to be ultrafast. Aren't the living dead enough to be scared of?

—Tim Pudenz, Graettinger, Iowa

A. I agree with you. But we live in an age of speed-up and dumb-down. Another thing the new version lacked was wit. Jim Emerson of Seattle writes: "One of my all-time favorite movie lines is from the 1978 version. Two guys are on the roof of the mall, looking at the zombies wandering around inside, and one of them wonders why they're coming here. 'Some kind of instinct, memory, something they used to do,' he says. 'This used to be an important place in their lives.' That's what the whole movie's *about!* (That and finding an excuse for a zombie to put his arm into one of those automatic blood-pressure machines and then get his arm ripped off so the reading can go down to zero.) What is *Dawn of the Dead* without the satire?"

Dining at the Movies

Q. I recently went to the Hollywood Boulevard theater in Woodridge, Illinois, to see *The Lord of the Rings.* Once we paid and got inside we realized it was a theater/restaurant. After we sat down, my date and myself found menus where it said we must purchase at least one item on the menu. The movie hadn't started yet, and thoroughly angered, I went to the ticket counter and asked for a refund of the tickets. They said no, and I explained I didn't want food. I didn't get my money back, but instead got some worthless coupon. I have been to other theaters before where they give back money if the movie hasn't started yet. Do you think a theater should give a refund if the film hasn't started? Or better yet, shouldn't they have let us stay without purchasing food? I already paid for the movie.

—Pete Ficarello, Willowbrook, Illinois

A. Well, they charge less for a ticket than a regular first-run house, and they do advertise they're a restaurant-theater, so I guess they have the same expectation of any restaurant that if you sit down you will order something. But, yes, under the circumstances they should have refunded your money.

Distribution Challenges

Q. I brought my girlfriend to see *The Station Agent* at a medium-size theater in Kinnelon, New Jersey—just a few miles from the town of Newfoundland, where the movie takes place (and was largely filmed). It came out months ago, but this was the first time, as far as I know, that the film was shown anywhere in the area— and for one weekend only. You'd think that a movie taking place in your own backyard would draw more of an audience, but beside my girlfriend and myself there were about six other people, all middle-aged, in the theater. This was a Sunday evening, prime time.

In your review of *The Perfect Score,* you write that "good and challenging movies are limited to release in big cities and in a handful of independently booked cinemas. Whole states and sections of the country never see the best new films . . ." Not being able to see the movies I want to see is one of the things I hate most about living outside the city. But do you think the blame for this problem lies with the owners of the multiplexes, a lack of marketing for "small" films, or with the tastes of the "mainstream" audience itself? My girlfriend and I both loved *The Station Agent,* by the way. We would have told our friends to see it, too—but it's not playing around here anymore, just a week later.

—Brendan Berls, Vernon, New Jersey

A. I think audiences must be developed. In the small town of Three Oaks, Michigan (population under 3,000), a movie lover named Jon Vickers bought the little downtown movie house and began to show foreign and independent art films. It was slow-going at first, but now, six years later, his theater is doing great business and is sold out on weekends. A friend of mine who lives in the town says, no, the patrons aren't all "summer people" from Chicago. She goes in the middle of the winter and sees the same local people she sees in the supermarket. People are not dumb unless you treat them as dumb. Most American theater chains write off the boondocks and exhibit a low opinion of the potential of their audiences. You can't learn to love good movies unless you can see them. Consider how resistant the chains were to *Whale Rider,* which only gradually broke through to more bookings because of the enthusiasm of moviegoers. Consider that *In America,* surely a film that would reach hearts in every audience, never got a proper wide release.

Dogville

Q. Your review of *Dogville* was the second in a row I have seen that accused Lars Von Trier of being anti-American. Do you really think that all the American actors in the film would have participated in the movie if it was as biased and filled with venom towards the United States as you contend? You see, this is another example of a theory I have developed about film critics—when they come up against a film they either can't understand and/or don't want to put the effort into figuring out, they do one of two things: either wildly overpraise it (*Lost in Translation* is a shining example here, Jim Jarmusch without the soul, leaving a hollow shell of nothingness) and hope that no one has the poor taste to point out that the emperor indeed has no clothes, or find some specific point to criticize that releases them from having to come to terms with the larger context of the movie. *Dogville* isn't one of Lars Von Trier's best films but he doesn't deserve to be cast as anti-American because of it.

—Dewey Carter, Boulder, Colorado

A. What I wrote was: "Von Trier could justifiably make a fantasy about America, even an anti-American fantasy, and produce a good film, but here he approaches the ideological subtlety of a raving prophet on a street corner." It wasn't his anti-Americanism that I was attacking, but his filmmaking. Why the actors appeared in the film is clear enough; he is an interesting and important director. At least two of them (Nicole Kidman and James Caan) have declined to work with him again.

Down and Dirty Pictures

Q. I've been reading Peter Biskind's latest book, *Down and Dirty Pictures*, about the rise of Miramax and Sundance. He details an alleged encounter between you and Todd Haynes at a film festival where he presented his movie *Poison*. The book quotes Christine Vachon (an independent producer) giving her recollection. Apparently, Haynes introduced himself to you, saying, "Hi, I'm Todd Haynes." You said, "Who the hell is Todd Haynes?" at which point he said that he had directed *Poison*. The book quotes Vachon as saying that upon hearing that "Ebert literally snatched his hand back." The thing is, I know that you liked Haynes's *Safe*, and I thought you were a Haynes fan. What's the story here?

—Nicholas Jarecki, New York, New York

A. Biskind has a way of massaging his stories to suit his agenda. Regarding his previous book, *Easy Riders, Raging Bulls*, Steven Spielberg told me, "Every single word in that book about me is either erroneous, or a lie."

I contacted Biskind's source, Christine Vachon, for her memory of that meeting with Todd Haynes. She writes me: "At those Independent Spirit Awards (a million years ago it seems like) we had been told that you were not a fan of the film. Todd *did* introduce himself to you. I remember you appeared a bit flustered. I did not say that you said 'who the hell is Todd Haynes.' And I certainly do not remember saying you pulled your hand away. I told the story—innocently, I thought—in the context of how far Todd and I had come with our little film. We'd heard you didn't like it, so it was an uncomfortable encounter—but absolutely not in the mean-spirited context Biskind put it in. I have not talked to Peter Biskind since the publication of the book. He has not returned my calls. There were several things he quoted me as saying that I felt were taken out of context, like calling my longtime partner Ted Hope a 'thuggish frat boy'—*yikes!* My biggest disappointment in the book (besides the tedium of one Bad Harvey story after another) was that there was absolutely no sense of the pleasure of seeing the films themselves. I remember seeing some movies at Sundance (like *The Hours and the Times*) and being stunned and excited. Seems that the book should have had you rooting for Miramax at least half of the time."

Dreamers

Q. I have heard that Fox Searchlight will release Bertolucci's *The Dreamers* as an R-rated film, instead of as unrated, or NC-17. If Fox knows that the audience for the film will be adults, and that educated adults will not want to see a compromised version of a movie by a great director, then why are they releasing it as an R? Why not have it be like *Y Tu Mama También* and release it as unrated?

—Gary Rancier, Brooklyn, New York

A. The NC-17 rating is unworkable, thanks to Blockbuster, which refuses to stock such films, and the MPAA, which refuses to create an A (for "adult") category that would stand between the R rating and actual pornography. The movie could and should go out unrated.

If Fox Searchlight does not want audiences to see the movie that Bertolucci made, then they should do the decent thing and give up distribution rights to a company prepared to stand behind its films. To buy a film and then cut it because of the MPAA rating amounts to vandalism.

Fox Searchlight eventually released the film in Bertolucci's original version.

Elephant

Q. I have recently watched both *Elephant* and *Gerry*, by Gus Van Sant. In *Elephant* the two killers are playing a video game that shows two characters being shot in what looks to be a desert. They're wearing clothes that look exactly the same as the characters in *Gerry*. Are these two films meant to be related?
—Kevin Ellis, Portland Oregon

A. Gus Van Sant tells me: "The films are related in that they are two different lessons or thoughts about delusional killing—and I am working on one more. The first, *Gerry*, is killing by the hand of one's trusted friend. The second, *Elephant*, is by the hand of an unknown or foreign entity. And the third one, *Last Days*, will be death by one's own hand. But I guess one of the real reasons to base the video game characters on *Gerry* is that we couldn't secure a real game, say *Doom*, for instance, from a video game company. So we made a simple, somewhat low-budget game using characters from the previous films. No real relationship, except in the themes of delusional death."

Elia Kazan

Q. Considering the mixed reaction Elia Kazan got for his Lifetime Achievement Award—due to his artistic brilliance but lousy moral judgment—do you think Leni Riefenstahl will be acknowledged during the "in memory of" presentation at the next Academy Awards? If so, do you predict applause or protest?
—Alexander Higle, Stamford, Connecticut

A. Riefenstahl, sometimes described as "Hitler's favorite filmmaker" although she claimed she was never a Nazi, died September 8, 2003, at 101. Of course the Academy must include her in its portraits of movie giants

who died during the year. There may be some boos. Kazan will also be included in the memorial tribute; when he got his Lifetime Achievement Award in 1999, as many as half the audience members withheld their applause, but no one booed.
She was included.

Fahrenheit 9/11

Q. Michael Moore's *Fahrenheit 9/11* is designed to promote his personal political agenda. On CNN, he said he hoped the movie would get out the anti-Bush vote. Did Moore give even lip service to views opposite his own? You reported on the reception his film received in Cannes. Given the location—France—and the crowd—journalists, Hollywood movie types, and Frenchmen mostly, what did you expect? By praising an obviously politically motivated film, are you simply being a pawn of Moore's own political agenda?
—Mark Pachankis, Shreveport, Louisiana

A. Well, of course, it's a politically motivated film. That's allowed. President Bush's speeches are politically motivated, and he doesn't give lip service to views opposite his own. That's allowed, too. I must decide if a movie is good or bad despite whether I agree or disagree with its politics. I oppose the death penalty, but gave *The Life of David Gale* zero stars. *Birth of a Nation* is in my book *The Great Movies II*, even though it reeks of racism. Many film historians rank Leni Riefenstahl's *The Triumph of the Will* as a cinematic milestone, although it glorifies the Third Reich.

Q. In Michael Moore's *Fahrenheit 9/11*, Attorney General John Ashcroft is shown performing a song he composed, "Let the Eagle Soar." Does this mean Ashcroft will be earning songwriting royalties and indirectly profit from the film?
—Jonathan Young, Tampa, Florida

A. Michael Moore tells the Answer Man: "Could be. Warner Records wants to release the sound track. I told the lawyers if he wants his fee, we should give it to him."

Q. Re. your article about *Fahrenheit 9/11* and "Bush's dawdling" in the classroom after the attacks: I'm sorry, but that just isn't right. I asked friends in the news business about Bush's actions that day. They said he didn't go anywhere after finding out about the first plane, because everybody thought it was just a horrible accident. If he didn't get up immediately and run screaming from the room the way some people think he should have, Moore needs to remember Bush was in front of a bunch of little kids. How would it look to them if suddenly the president started panicking and running from the room? Bush did exactly the right thing, but I wouldn't expect Moore to understand that. He makes it sound like Bush didn't care about what he had been told, and had to be forced to react. Just look at Bush's face when Card whispers in his ear. You can almost see the blood drain from his face. It was quite obvious that the reading session was the last thing on Bush's mind at that point.

—Daniel Young, Bensalem, Pennsylvania

A. I can't find the phrase "Bush's dawdling" in my coverage from Cannes, but I'm sure the president could have managed a calm exit without "panicking and running from the room." I asked Moore about your points. He replies: "It should have occurred to Bush after the first attack that it involved the same building where the only previous foreign attack on America occurred. He was told about the second attack, went ahead with his photo op, and reporters clocked him at six to ten minutes reading *My Pet Goat* before leaving the classroom, posing for more photos, and going to another room for a meeting before holding a press conference and leaving the building. Since he should have considered himself a target, wasn't he endangering those children by staying in their school?" Moore says he is considering streaming the classroom tape on the Web.

Q. Isn't it less than cricket for Cannes to award the Palme d'Or to a film financed by the company that has financed all of the films produced by the head of the jury? Of course, the other jury members had their say as well (and having met Tilda Swinton, I would bet on her in any verbal brawl with Tarantino), but isn't there a conflict of interest? If anyone wanted to launch a conspiracy-based complaint, that would be the way to go. I'm a fan of Tarantino, I'm a fan of Michael Moore, and hell, I even like the French. I ask only out of curiosity.

—Peter Sobczynski, Chicago, Illinois

A. It is assumed that a director distinguished enough to head the Cannes jury is above such conflicts. I attended their press conference, heard all nine jurors praise the award, and got the unmistakable impression that Tarantino personally would have been equally content if the Korean revenge epic *Old Boy* had won.

Q. In your article about *Fahrenheit 9/11* at Cannes, you quote Michael Moore's film that, informed of the second attack on the World Trade Center, President Bush "incredibly remained with the students for another seven minutes, reading from the book, until a staff member suggested that he leave. The look on his face as he reads the book, knowing what he knows, is disquieting." Apparently you believe this version of events. Does Moore identify a source? Or is his word good enough for you? If that is the case, given that *Bowling for Columbine* was riddled with half truths and lies that even he corrected on the DVD, why would you assume this movie to be fact?

—Jim Carmignani, Naperville, Illinois

A. Bra Grier of Omaha writes: "Here's the video of Bush in the classroom for five minutes after being told 'America is under attack.' Unfortunately, the video ends before the president does."
www.thememoryhole.com/911/bush-911.htm

Q. You state you had a duty to objectively review *Fahrenheit 9/11* and judge its merits sans its political agenda. Fair enough. But do you think a well-made, funny, and nasty anti-Chirac, pro-Bush documentary will be winning the Golden Palm at Cannes in this century? Or how about a scathing exposé of European anti-Semitism, or a documentary where the camera stalks the authors of those best-selling French books about how the CIA and Israel were behind 9/11? Would these films, if made as well as Moore's film, be applauded by the Cannes set?

—Andrew Weber, Merrick, New York

A. No, probably not. As I mentioned on

Ebert and Roeper, although all nine members of the Cannes jury individually said at the press conference that they made their decision based on filmmaking, not politics, I believe it is realistic to believe it was based on both. That said, don't make the mistake of thinking the "French" honored *Fahrenheit 9/11*. The *jury* did, and only one of its nine members was French. There were four American members, and the others were from Finland, Hong Kong, Belgium, and the UK.

Q. There is a new documentary by Michael Wilson titled *Michael Moore Hates America*. When it hits theaters I hope you have the guts to give it a fair shot.
—David Oestreich, Norwalk, California

A. I have asked for a copy or a screening. The title is not a good omen. It seems to me that dissent is a patriotic duty, a sign of love for one's country, not hate.
As of September 2004, the film had not been made available.

Q. I just wanted to write and say that I, an adamant conservative and somewhat begrudging Bush supporter, completely agree with the assertion in your piece on *Fahrenheit 9/11* that "[My] opinions are my stock in trade, and is it not more honest to declare my politics than to conceal them?" Exactly right. Even more so, I would venture that for a critic to really effectively review a film like *Bowling for Columbine*, it's almost necessary to reveal one's personal politics. No matter how much I might try, I will approach Michael Moore's films with a higher degree of scrutiny and skepticism than a liberal reviewer, and it's disingenuous for me to try to deny that. I've always enjoyed your criticism, largely because you're willing to discuss your own personal reactions—emotional, political, or otherwise. I certainly don't have to agree with those reactions to respect or enjoy the piece.
—Win Martin, Portland, Oregon

A. I got two kinds of messages in response to that column: The "shut up and stick to movies" rant, and those like yours and this one from Mark McFadden of Citrus Heights, California: "There was a time when I thought movie critics should keep their political

views to themselves. Then I changed my mind; but I wasn't sure just why I had. Thanks for clearing that up for me. It was Edmund Burke that said an elected official owes his constituents more than simple obedience to their desires. He owes them his full intelligence and judgment to make decisions. I think movies are so important that their critics should subscribe to the same wisdom. No work of art exists in a vacuum; and a critic that isn't engaged in society serves no useful purpose other than to judge technical competence."

Q. I read your review of *Fahrenheit 9/11* and I was very disappointed that at *no point* did you question Moore's political agenda and the reality of all of the film's claims. This seems to be promoting Moore's agenda, rather than providing an objective review of the film. I personally hate films that are obviously motivated by a political agenda; it causes me to question how much is reality and how much is exaggerated or fabricated. I don't have the time to review every fact and determine which is real and which is a lie or exaggeration. Moore is obviously a brilliant filmmaker, but I wish he could just do a documentary that focuses on an event, rather than taking an event to promote his political opinions.
—Bill Meyers, White Lake, Michigan

A. Moore's film comes labeled as partisan and subjective. Were you equally inspired to ask "how much is reality and how much is exaggerated or fabricated" when the Bush administration presented Saddam's WMDs as a fact? I declared my own political opinion in the review and made it clear I was writing from that viewpoint. It's opinion. I have mine, you have yours, and the theory is that we toss them both into the open marketplace of ideas.

Fighting Temptations

Q. In your review of *The Fighting Temptations*, you note that Cuba Gooding Jr.'s character returns to his hometown and is promptly resmitten with his "childhood sweetheart," played by Beyonce Knowles. I understand the movie math that allows characters played by Sean Connery and Catherine Zeta Jones to be possible romantic partners as adults. But even in celluloid-fantasy reality, wouldn't anyone played by Cuba Gooding Jr. be way too old to have had the hots for anyone played by Beyonce Knowles in childhood without the authorities (or at least an angry father) becoming involved?

—Harris Fleming Jr., Dumont, New Jersey

A. Let's see. Cuba Gooding Jr. was born in 1968, and Beyonce Knowles in 1981. When he was in love with her, she wasn't even born. No wonder she has to remind him who she is.

Games People Play

Q. In reviewing *Games People Play: New York,* you wondered how many turndowns the contestants encountered en route to persuading off-the-street volunteers to go along with their stunts. (Who would agree to supply a stranger with a urine sample?) I wondered too and asked director James Ronald Whitney that same question after a screening at the Landmark Century Cinema in Chicago. He said there were none! Every person approached on the streets of New York City went along with the stunts and never stopped to ask, "Hey, are we on camera?" That shows how convincing the actors were, he bragged. When each setup came to its conclusion, the actors pointed out the cameras and convinced these strangers to sign releases. Getting signed releases was a key obstacle for the contestants. Whitney saluted the actors' hard work— blocking for multiple hidden cameras, following scripts, almost no rehearsal or sleep, and doing scenes with nonactors. "I look upon this as the Olympics of acting," Whitney said. He brought along actor Hans Christianson, who will appear in Whitney's *Games People Play: Hollywood* and testified: "I feel so confident about my acting now. I think I can do anything someone ever asks me."

—Bill Stamets, Chicago, Illinois

A. I believe that he can. I'm not sure that he should.

Gigli

Q. Re. your review of *Gigli*—I'm stunned. This has to be the worst-reviewed movie in years, and you were in the top 5 percent of reviews. This movie *was* actually dreck. And

while it might be possible to be kind, and find something to say that was nice about it (the acting wasn't horrible for what they had), you actually praise it for its script and dialogue?! That was the worst part of the movie! I actually felt embarrassed for the actors, having to recite it. Particularly the "genitalia comparison" scene, which was painful to watch them have to utter. Tracy and Hepburn couldn't make that dialogue work. Christopher Walken's drug-induced speech was so bad and incoherent, people were uncontrollably laughing at how bad it was. Everyone has different tastes, and things are open to interpretation, but for you to praise perhaps the worst part of a universally reviled movie . . . I don't know, I'm worried about you, Rog.

—Chris Connelly, Ann Arbor, Michigan

A. Amazing how concerned people are when a critic is "out of step." I gave the movie a negative review, but not negative enough to please those who want to burn it, mix the ashes with salt, and rub them into the wounds of the filmmakers. But, hey, Walken's scene was hilarious, loved even by those who hated the movie, and if you think the audience was laughing at how bad it was, either (a) you are wrong, or (b) you had the misfortune to join an extraordinarily stupid audience, in which case the Shavian dialogue about genitalia would of course have been totally beyond its reach. It is not the job of a critic to conform to the results of the Tomatometer, but to express a personal opinion. Since 98 percent of the reviews (including mine) were negative, why insist on 100 percent?

Q. I was pleased, seeing your review, to find that I wasn't the only film critic alive who granted *Gigli* anything higher than the equivalent of one star. Not only has it received the worst reviews of 2003, but some of our fellow critics have even been declaring it "the worst movie ever" (a ridiculous statement, to say the least). I agree, the movie isn't great, but clearly it's not *that* bad. It's my opinion that all of this negative buzz is obviously a transparent—and frankly, pathetic—need for our petty friends in the entertainment media to gang up and take the movie's high-profile celebrity couple down a notch. *Gigli* never had a chance.

—Shawn Hobbs, Temple, Texas

A. Some critics were gunning for J-Lo and Ben, yes, but most were no doubt sincere. Martin Brest is not a filmmaker to be dismissed lightly, however, and most reviews never even mentioned him. Perhaps once the wolf-pack mentality took over, some were shy to praise what are, after all, creative and daring elements in the film.

Girl Next Door

Q. In regards to your *Girl Next Door* review, I don't think people should try scooping up underpants from the street while driving. That sounds dangerous.

—Carl Meyer-Curtis, Los Angeles, California

A. Attention, readers: Clip and save!

Godsend

Q. In your review of *Godsend,* you noted that the director "shot at least seven alternate endings to the movie." Admittedly, some films can only be helped by a different ending or, in some cases, a different script, but when I hear about a movie with *seven* alternate endings, it sounds wishy-washy. Who is the director trying to please: himself, me, or the test audience? Imagine if movies like *Requiem for a Dream, Wages of Fear,* or *Butch Cassidy and the Sundance Kid* had been altered because audiences (or worse, executives) thought their endings were too downbeat! Why not shoot alternate versions of the beginning and the middle while you're at it?

—Miguel E. Rodriguez, Tampa, Florida

A. I quoted fellow critic Joe Leydon, who found a report that Nick Hamm shot at least seven alternate endings, including those in which two different characters are killed two different ways, and little Adam kills everybody. My fervent hope is that all of these endings are included in the bells and whistles on the DVD. Studios do sometimes change endings on the basis of test audiences, and many good directors have said they learn a lot from test screenings. But often test audiences do not represent the target audience for a given

movie, and their input is uninformed or irrelevant. At some point the director has to decide what he really believes in.

The Graduate

Q. I just watched *The Graduate* for a film class and read your article claiming that Mrs. Robinson is the only strong character in the movie and that Benjamin is simply a lost youth. As a twenty-year-old I could relate greatly to this movie, to the feeling of being lost in a sea of expectation and confusion. I was curious why you felt the way that you did about the film. Will I look back in twenty years and view the movie in the same light? I was raised with this film (my name is actually taken from the movie, as is my nickname, Benjy) and always saw the movie as a film of rebellion and of changing times, but upon reading your article started to question my way of viewing it.

—Benjamin Greenberg, Eugene, Oregon

A. In my 1997 rereview of the film, I wrote: "The only character in the movie who is alive—who can see through situations, understand motives, and dare to seek her own happiness—is Mrs. Robinson (Anne Bancroft). Seen today, *The Graduate* is a movie about a young man of limited interest, who gets a chance to sleep with the ranking babe in his neighborhood, and throws it away in order to marry her dorky daughter."

Yes, that's how I see it now. When I saw it in 1967 I identified with Benjamin. In twenty years you may agree with me—unless, of course, you go into plastics. I ran into Anne Bancroft not long after writing that review and I told her Mrs. Robinson was the only character in the movie I thought I could have an intelligent conversation with. "Of course," she said. "That's why I took the role."

Great Movies

Q. Have you ever loved a movie so much that you never wanted to see it again? That you never wanted to revisit it at another time or place in your life when you might look at it differently? That is how I feel about *The Hours* and *Far from Heaven.* They got to me at the right time and the right place and I am therefore reluctant to see them again.

—Jeff Young, Las Vegas, Nevada

A. I love my favorite movies more the better I know them, and have been through most of my favorites one shot at a time. I've probably seen *Citizen Kane* at least fifty times that way. But there are some movies based on surprises that lose power once you know when to expect them. *Jaws* would be an example.

Harry Potter and the Prisoner of Azkaban

Q. I just saw *Harry Potter and the Prisoner of Azkaban.* You are not the first person to express concern that the children may soon be too old for their parts. I disagree. The children in the books are growing older, and by the time book seven is written, Harry and his friends should be about seventeen or eighteen. The actors may be a couple of years older than their characters, but I'm sure they'll be believable as always. And you're right, there is "less than whimsical violence" to come, if the movies stay true to the books. If you think this one was dark, wait until the fourth one; it is very disturbing, and the fifth book is downright depressing. It almost makes me dread the last book. I will agree about the "murky plotting." The movie failed to explain that Black, Pettigrew, and James Potter were all animagi. It failed to explain why they became animagi, why Snape had such loathing toward them, and why Harry's Patronus resembled a stag at the end. It also failed to explain Lupin's, Potter's, Pettigrew's and Black's relationship to the mysterious Marauder's Map. These points are pretty important to the story, and to Harry's growth as a wizard. I'm predicting a lot of twelve-year-olds will be extremely unhappy about this.

—Susan Warren, Montgomery, Alabama

A. My belief has always been that the director's first responsibility is to his film, not to the book he is adapting. For me, the problem was not that Alfonso Cauron did not follow the book, but that on its own terms the plot seemed to lose its way toward the end.

Q. I was upset that you revealed who the werewolf was in *Harry Potter and the Prisoner of Azkaban.* You didn't say it directly, but merely mentioning the name "Lupus" completely gave it away.

—Corey Slack, Springfield, Massachusetts

A. Since that is the character's name in the movie, don't you think the movie itself gave it away, for anyone like you who obviously knows your Latin roots?

Q. In response to Corey Slack's complaint in the Answer Man that you should not have tipped off the identity of the werewolf in your review of *Harry Potter and the Prisoner of Azkaban:* You missed the point. We are not masters of Latin, nor are we as schooled in Latin roots. But when you connected the word "lupus" to the werewolf, there isn't a moron (or child) alive who wouldn't realize you were talking about Professor Lupin, mentioned a few lines before. You ruined the surprise with a comment about as cryptic as an exit sign.

—Fiji Hebden, Rutgers University, New Brunswick, New Jersey

A. But . . . but . . . the movie gives itself away, by calling him Professor Lupin! You are at Rutgers, but have never heard the word "lupine"?

Hellboy

Q. In your *Hellboy* review, you wondered how the heroes went from defeating the monsters in one cave to being imprisoned in another. Well, for one, Liz explained that she blacks out when she uses her powers. I guess that we can just assume that John was knocked unconscious by the force of the blast. And given that Hellboy didn't appear to be moving or awake when Liz fried the monsters, the bad guys only had to pick them up and transport them.

—Neil Shyminsky, Toronto, Ontario

A. Ingenious, but there's another explanation. Matthew Bradford of Los Angeles points me to a message by director Guillermo del Toro on the message board of the official *Hellboy* Web site. Edited for length, del Toro writes:

"We got some complaints of *HB* copies that were screening without forty-five seconds at the end of reel 5. You see. *After* Liz explodes there is a *fade out* to absolute black and some projectionists are taking it as a cue for the reel being over. It is not! All copies are printed correctly but may be screened with that forty-five seconds missing by omission in the 'assembly' of the platter. The print you view needs to have the following scenes:

"A) HB is attacked (spoilers from now on). Liz explodes. A rock hits the lens!

"B) Darkness. Voices. The water has evaporated, and burnt Sammael carcasses are seen. Myers wakes up, dizzy. He sees Rasputin/Ilsa. She approaches him and thanks him for the grenade belts. Cut to:

"C) Another space in the complex. She's slamming the belts and everybody has been manacled.

"The copies are being projected without 'B' in some theaters."

High Noon

Q. Have you ever sat down to watch an ostensibly classic film for your Great Movies column, only to find that the film is either so dated or so bad that you can no longer in good faith write the article? If so, which ones?

—Andy Walker, Bloomington, Indiana

A. I settled down to watch *High Noon* and was disappointed. Everybody says it's a masterpiece, but one of the dissenters is Simon Gray, the British playwright, who writes in the current issue of *Granta* magazine:

"... take Gary Cooper in *High Noon*, a film recognized as a complete turkey when it opened for tryout showings in the Midwest, audiences laughing, jeering, walking out as jaunty, sunny, Gary Cooper strode down the streets of his little town, a parody of the classical Western sheriff—the reason he looked so implausible, however, was that all through the shooting he'd been crippled by piles—every step a torment, which he'd tried to disguise by assuming a bogus jauntiness whenever he could manage it; generally he could do one take in this mode, and that was

the take the director felt obliged to use. Well, after the first tryout showings and the public's response, the producers were in despair. . . . They repaired to the editing room to see if they could find any scenes that actually worked, hoping to build from there, but useless, useless, all they had as alternatives was Gary's piles-driver gait, simultaneously cramped and bow-legged, his face grimacing in agony, his eyes tortured—until somebody—either the director or the editor, suddenly saw that in the problem lay the solution. They spliced all the scenes in which Gary's piles were at their most inflamed, and looked at what they'd got—the nobly tortured, stoically enduring sheriff . . .''

Q. Re. the AM item about playwright Simon Gray's theory that Gary Cooper's performance in *High Noon* was improved because he was suffering from piles: Why can't Simon Gray judge the film on what he sees and not "inside" information? Didn't Charles Laughton have a stagehand twist his leg during the flogging scene in *Hunchback* to help his acting along? Is it any worse than a method actor dredging up his past or Olivier planning every eyebrow movement in advance?

—Leeds Bird, Bay City, Michigan

A. Lots of readers were outraged by the Simon Gray analysis of *High Noon*. Film expert Jeff Schwager wrote: "His story had the ring of Urban Myth to me, so I did a little research. I could find no other mention on the Web of Cooper suffering from hemorrhoids or the film being reedited to maximize the appearance of his discomfort, but did find this commonly repeated anecdote (quoted from IMDb): "The pained expression on Kane's (Gary Cooper's) face throughout the film was entirely realistic, as Cooper had a bleeding ulcer at the time."

House of Sand and Fog

Q. I just returned from seeing *House of Sand and Fog* and am still reeling from the power and profound sadness of this superbly wrought film. One thing bothered me, however, enough so that the movie temporarily lost me at a critical point. Near the end, Jennifer Connelly's character is shown from a distance standing at the end of a pier where she overlooks the ocean. Virtually the same shot was used by Darren Aronofsky near the end of *Requiem for a Dream,* and by Alex Proyas at the conclusion of *Dark City.* Both those movies, of course, featured Jennifer Connelly as the woman on the pier. The inexorable tragedy of *House of Sand and Fog* seemed disrupted, therefore, by a bit of film homage or, worse yet, Hollywood in-joke. Am I misreading it, or did you also see it this way? It couldn't have been a coincidence.

—Douglas Soderberg, St. Louis, Missouri

A. Or maybe it could have been. The film's director, Vadim Perelman, tells the Answer Man: "When asked about the similarities, I jokingly say that it's in Jennifer Connelly's contract that she be featured on a pier at least in one scene in her movies. Actually, to date, I have not seen *Dark City,* so I can't imagine being influenced by its pier shot. I did see Darren's excellent *Requiem for a Dream,* but did not consciously even recall the pier sequence in the movie.

"The truth is that the pier scene in *House of Sand and Fog* was never scripted or prepared for. We were shooting the beach scene with Kathy and Lester at the table, while waiting for the sun to set. I looked around, saw a pier covered with birds, and suggested that Jennifer walk out there for the cameraman. I thought the image would fit somewhere at the end of the film during Kathy's introspective descent. I was just as surprised at the similarities between the scenes. Creative osmosis—I guess—is the only answer if you discount any rumors of a dark, sinister conspiracy to control the minds of the filmgoers through pier-based manipulation."

So speaks Perelman. I also know why Darren Aronofsky included his scene of Connelly on a pier, after Alex Proyas used it in *Dark City.* In December 2000, when the AM asked him about the coincidence, Aronofsky replied: "The pier scene comes from a personal moment in my own life. When I was a teenager, I once met a girl I had a crush on out at that Coney Island pier. When I was writing the script, before I cast Jennifer, I decided to draw on this personal moment. Un-

fortunately, I had missed *Dark City* and had no idea there was a similar image in Alex Proyas's film. When we got to the pier Jennifer told me how strange it was that both films used this image. At that point, it was too late to change things. So I went for it. Since the shoot I've watched *Dark City* and was amazed that not only did we use a similar shot but we used the same actor. I guess I fed off of some ether that Alex created and presented to the universe. So I owe him thanks as I owe so many filmmakers who continue to influence me consciously and unconsciously."

Q. In the Answer Man you discussed the fact that Jennifer Connelly is photographed at the end of a dock or pier in *Dark City, Requiem for a Dream,* and *House of Sand and Fog.* In a deleted scene on the DVD of *A Beautiful Mind,* there is a sequence where Russell Crowe dreams of Jennifer Connelly running toward a dock on a lake.

—Dave Jacoby, Lafayette, Indiana

A. I'm beginning to have the same dream.

I, Robot

Q. In your review of *I, Robot* you stated that the movie should have credited Isaac Asimov as the creator of the famous three laws of robotics. However, within the fictional universe of *I, Robot* the three laws would have been created by a fictional someone. Much like Shakespeare was the one who wrote, "But Brutus says he was ambitious, And Brutus is an honorable man" but, within the fictional universe of *Julius Caesar* it was Antony who said it. If Brutus were to refer to that quote, he would cite Antony as saying it, not Shakespeare. In the same way, since the fictional Dr. Lanning wrote Asimov's Three Laws within Asimov's fictional universe, it is accurate to say Dr. Lanning wrote the three laws.

—Brian Valentine, Lake Wales, Florida

A. I got lots of complaints about that. Here is what I wrote:

"The dead man is Dr. Alfred Lanning (James Cromwell), who, we are told, wrote the Three Laws. Every schoolchild knows the laws were set down by the good doctor Isaac Asimov, after a conversation he had on December 23, 1940, with John W. Campbell, the legendary editor of *Astounding Science Fiction*. It is peculiar that no one in the film knows that, especially since the film is 'based on the book by Isaac Asimov.' Would it have killed the filmmakers to credit Asimov?"

From a logical point of view, you are absolutely right. From my point of view, my tongue was in my cheek. Not everybody appreciates irony. Several readers helpfully informed me that every schoolchild does not, in fact, know about Asimov's December 23, 1940, conversation with Campbell.

In America

Q. In your review of *In America*, you mention that the film is set in the 1980s. I was undecided as to when the film was set and didn't notice any concrete clues proving a particular era. Perhaps I overlooked something obvious? I know they go to see *E.T.*, but that was re-released a couple of years ago. Also, if I recall correctly, in the carnival scene, the $20 bills we see are the redesigned version, not 1980s era currency. There's a discussion on IMDB debating this question.

—Chris McFadden, Los Angeles, California

A. It's an interesting question. Fred Lidskog of Los Angeles writes: "Although the story has an eighties feel to it, I believe there were elements in the film that indicated a modern setting. The first and most obvious is Christy's camera, which is lightyears ahead of the big and clunky camcorder technology available in the 1980s. The second indication is a movie marquee near the beginning of the film which shows the name of a movie (I'm sorry to say I forget which) that was released within the last few years." Other readers point out a radio announcer who mentions "the seventies, eighties, and nineties." I assumed it was set in the 1980s because they go to see *E.T.*, but of course that could have been the rerelease. The bottom line is, the movie doesn't depend on its period for its impact.

Q. I'm not convinced by your AM reply involving the time when *In America* is set. All the reviews say it takes place in the early 1980s, and I know it's based on Jim Sheri-

dan's own experiences in New York during that period, but the movie seems to take place in an indeterminate time period. Even if some of the clothing, the appearance of *E.T.*, and Mateo's unnamed disease would suggest the early 1980s, the child's camcorder, the ads in Times Square, and the radio station claiming to play the "best of the seventies, eighties, and nineties," place it in a more contemporary setting. I know that in the end it doesn't really matter, but is the eighties setting being cited off press materials, and not based on what's in the film?

—Jason Heid, Denton, Texas

A. There is understandable confusion, because the movie is based on Sheridan's memories of coming to New York in the 1980s, and kind of fudges on the time. Sheridan was queried by *Entertainment Weekly*, and replied: "I messed up the time as much as I could." The magazine says he "intentionally left in such anachronisms as Jessica Alba's L'Oreal ads and a radio station touting hits from the eighties and nineties." Sheridan said, "I just dreaded everybody getting to New York and trying to change it back to 1982 . . . and I didn't have the money!" And the camcorder? "You can get away with it because now everybody thinks they've been around forever." Guess you couldn't get away with it after all.

Intermission

Q. Let me just add my voice to any others over one piddling little detail in your review of *Intermission*. It's called "Daddy's Sauce," not "Dad's." And for the record, even though many of us use the term "Daddy's Sauce" to mean brown sauce in general (just as all vacuum cleaners are called Hoovers), HP is still the better of the two sauces, and it really, really isn't all that bad in coffee.

—Simon Walker, Austin, Texas

A. Since it's hard to get Daddy's Sauce and HP Sauce in North America, have you tried A-1 or Heinz's steak sauce? How do they taste in coffee? What about Worcestershire, my favorite? Louisiana Hot Sauce?

Just a Little Joke

Q. In your review of *Twisted* you quoted Oscar Wilde as having said, "To kill one lover may be regarded as a misfortune. To kill three seems like carelessness." Is that actually a paraphrase of a quotation from *The Importance of Being Earnest*, in which Lady Bracknell points out, "To lose one parent may be regarded as a misfortune. To lose both seems like carelessness." Did Wilde write both or was I witnessing a little poetic license?
—Name withheld, Los Angeles, California

A. Have we lost all sense of irony and fun, and are we raising a generation of literalists and gradgrinds? Three people were so humorless as to "correct" me on my little joke.

Q. In your review of *Eternal Sunshine of the Spotless Mind* on *Ebert and Roeper* you said that it was great that Charlie Kaufman has continued to write after the death of his brother Donald. I wasn't quite sure if you were joking, but Charlie Kaufman never had a brother named Donald; that was simply a fictitious character in his film *Adaptation*. Donald Kaufman was also credited with writing the screenplay with Charlie, and was nominated for an Oscar, leading to the controversy of a fictitious person being nominated for an Academy Award. Just thought you should know.
—Andrew Kelley, Washington, D.C.

A. I knew. I was making a little joke.

Q. In your review of *Le Divorce*, I reached your account of Peter Noble's story: *An English guy walks into a café in Cannes and asks if they have a men's room. The waiter replies: "Monsieur! I have only two hands!"* This story was so inexplicable that I asked a couple of colleagues to make sense of it. They could not. Is it simply intended to outline the French and English inability to communicate? Does it mean that the French like to talk with their hands? Does the French guy think the English guy wants assistance with his zipper? Please explain.
—Aaron Dunn, Honolulu, Hawaii

A. Three excellent theories. But I think it is the form, timing, attitude, and inexplicability that make it funny, and not the meaning, if any.

Q. Re the ongoing discussion about the man who asked the French waiter where the toilet was, and the waiter who said "Monsieur, I have only two hands!"—I am sure that you will be delighted to learn that "I have only two hands!" is a direct translation of the French expression "Je n'ai que deux mains!" It means "I'm busy. I can't take care of this right now!" preferably said with a touch of long-suffering exasperation.
—Wendy Gasperazzo, West Mersea, Essex, England

A. That's what it means in English, too, but as an answer to that particular question it can hardly be improved upon.

Q. You ended your recent review of *Harold & Kumar . . .* with the line, "Still another reason our leader's photograph should be displayed in every government office and classroom." I just didn't get this joke. Was this a reference to A) Dubya, or B) Dann Gire, "distinguished president of the Chicago Film Critics' Association"? If there's a laugh there, I'd like to laugh, too.
—Miguel E. Rodriguez, Tampa, Florida

A. Just another one of my little jokes. Maybe I should issue little joke warnings. Here is the complete paragraph, which, like the rest of the review, mentions only one president:

"Danny Leiner, who directed this film, began his career with *Dude, Where's My Car?* I inexplicably missed that movie, but I laughed often enough during the screening of *Harold & Kumar* that afterward I told Dann Gire, distinguished president of the Chicago Film Critics' Association, that I thought maybe I should rent *Dude* and check it out. Dann cautioned me that he did not think it was all that urgent. Still another reason our leader's photograph should be displayed in every government office and classroom."

Kill Bill 1 & 2

Q. I recently read this in an interview with theater director Richard Foreman: "Americans just don't understand that style can be content and style has things to say." The movie *Kill Bill* immediately came to mind. I loved that movie for exactly that reason; the way it was made was the point of the movie. But where do you think the line should be drawn? When does it became completely self-indulgent to make a film with no point other than its style and feel?

—Damon Brook, Duluth, Minnesota

A. Although such a movie of course could be good or bad for a number of reasons, it would not be bad simply because it had no other point than its style. Style is what distinguishes art from random recording. The problem is not movies with too much style and tone, but movies so seduced by story that they have no attitude at all. Remember Ebert's First Law: "A movie is not about what it is about, but how it is about it."

Q. I am a New Yorker who lived in the Caribbean from 1975 to 2001. I've seen hundreds of martial arts films, a good portion of them projected on bedsheets during those first ten years (I lived fifty miles outside of Montego Bay). Jamaicans called them "kickers." When I was watching Kill Bill in New York I leaned over to my Jamaican-born son and said "this is a kicker on steroids." Okay, yes, it's a slick homage to the genre, and yes, there is a certain joy or exuberance to it, yes yes yes, but Roger—was it really a religious experience? I thought Pulp Fiction was excellent. I don't have anything against the man, but it seems whenever Tarantino the Great makes a movie a lot of people kneel at the altar. I have to wonder what critics and movie fans alike would have said if an unknown director delivered that film. I saw Texas Chainsaw Massacre at the behest of that same son of mine, and yes it was predictable and boring—and so what? Was it really worse than the thousands of movies you have seen and given half a star or higher? Why are you so pissed off? My kid said he got a kick out of it. If he did, then I suppose he wasn't ripped off. What do you think?

—Nick Minotti, Pompano Beach, Florida

A. It's arguable, but I thought Tarantino wanted to exhilarate, and Chainsaw wanted to disgust. Ask your son for his response to that theory. I wrote in my Chainsaw review, "I doubt that anybody involved in it will be surprised or disappointed if audience members vomit or flee." Turns out I was correct. Marcus Nispel, director of Chainsaw, told the

Washington Times: "What he complains of is what I'm most proud of."

Kill Bill has been savaged by several high-profile moralists, including Michael Medved and Bill O'Reilly, who both use the dependable technique of summarizing what happens without noting how it happens, why it happens, its purpose, or style. If either one saw Texas Chainsaw Massacre they might need CPR.

Q. I can't understand the reason for giving away the Bride's real name in your review of Kill Bill: Vol. 2. I would understand if revealing it was essential to your critique of the film, but it is mentioned merely as an aside with no apparent purpose.

—Adam Lenhardt, Slingerlands, New York

A. You are absolutely correct. I don't know what came over me. I guess I just really liked the name.

The Bride's name has been removed from the review in this Yearbook.

Q. Someone asked you why you gave away the Bride's real name in your review of Kill Bill Vol. 2. You replied, "I don't know what came over me." I am wondering: Why did Tarantino bleep her name in the first place?

—Reint Schölvinck, Amsterdam, Denmark

A. I thought it was entirely a stylistic device, and that there was no need to suppress it, but by doing so, he created a momentary aura of secrecy and suppression. Then, in the second movie, we got that a-ha moment when the name is revealed. Pretty cool, kiddo.

But my faithful correspondent Andy Ihnatko of Boston as usual sees more deeply: "Bleeping out [the Bride's] name in Vol. 1 is paid off not with the revelation of her real name—but with Bill's speech about superhero secret identities. She's a superhero until the story's momentum moves toward her confrontation with Bill and her unexpected reunion with her daughter. Then she becomes Clark Kent. Brilliant."

Kubrick Moon Hoax

Q. The CBC is showing a documentary called Dark Side of the Moon. According to the blurb, during an interview with Stanley

Kubrick's widow, she reveals that Kubrick, along with other producers, was recruited to create moon landing footage in case NASA wasn't able to transmit signals from the moon. The Nixon administration couldn't afford a public relations failure. In exchange, Kubrick got a special NASA lens to help him shoot *Barry Lyndon* in 1975.

—Marie Haws, New Westminster, British Columbia

A. According to Alex Strachan of the Can-West News Service, the doc contains on-camera interviews with Christiane Kubrick, astronaut Buzz Aldrin, Henry Kissinger, Donald Rumsfeld, Al Haig, and others, and says the fake landing was filmed on the same sound stage Kubrick used for the moon in *2001: A Space Odyssey*. So why didn't Americans hear about this amazing exposé? Because *Dark Side of the Moon,* by the French documentarian William Karel, is a mocumentary. Using camera trickery, special effects, and editing of real interviews that takes words out of context, it seems to be a factual report of a hoax-but is a hoax itself.

Lost in Translation

Q. I agree that *Lost in Translation* is a new classic. Don't you think, though, that the final whispered words are inaudible not only because we have no right to hear them (I find your idea enchanting) but also because it doesn't matter what those words are? We hear him saying something in a tone of admonishment, encouragement, advice, and we hear the last word, "Okay?" "Okay," she says. They have made a pact—a promise on her part to remember something he's said; to remember him, to remember feeling. Their ephemeral time together is made solid. And then they seal it with a kiss, their third and presumably final kiss, completing the chord that began with those two fleeting kisses in the elevator, the kisses that denied what they really wanted to do, which was to Really Kiss. We don't care what they say to each other; what's important is that it's been said.

—Clay Stockton, Berkeley, California

A. Yes. And no possible dialogue could improve on the experience of not being able to hear them.

Q. I spoke to a Japanese person who saw *Lost in Translation,* and she agreed with me that the film took a heavy-handed, anti-Japanese stance. Of course, the story was about two strangers in a strange land who didn't have the ability to plug into the culture, but the movie showed Japan with few, if any, redeeming qualities. From the hotel greeting committee to the talk show host to the prostitute, the film offered us caricatures of Japanese stereotypes, and it was a little hard to watch them—they distracted from the honesty of the film with their shallow rendering and low humor. Do you think that this was purposeful, or even necessary?

—Roy Lambrada, New York, New York

A. The prostitute was a caricature, yes, but anyone who has been to Japan will recognize the greeters at the hotel (there is even a woman to point you to the elevator and bow as you enter it) and the talk show host (a lot of Japanese TV is exactly that goofy). I think the movie involved two cultures failing to communicate, but doing a fairly good job of getting along. As for the TV commercial director—you can find that type all over the world.

Q. Re. the Answer Man discussion of Japanese stereotypes in *Lost in Translation:* One thing Western writers have largely missed is how much experience Sofia Coppola personally has of the whole "Western celebrity in Japan" thing. Her first film, *The Virgin Suicides,* was an enormous art-house hit in Japan, grossing more than its entire American gross on one screen in the Shibuya district of Tokyo, and it was one of the key films that launched a boom in American independent cinema in Japan. I can only assume that rather than caricaturing stereotypes, Sofia Coppola is in fact writing from pretty extensive personal experience: Japan is at times incomprehensible and deeply strange, but somehow many people from both sides have great fondness for the culture of the other side.

—Michael Jennings, London, UK

A. It's also true that the movie deliberately and obviously sees Japanese culture from the outside, through the eyes of tourists who are preoccupied with one another. The movie is in Japan but not of Japan.

Q. After reading your review of *Lost in Translation* and subsequent discussion about how we do not hear Bill Murray's final words to Scarlett Johansson, I was surprised to find that I could understand fairly easily what Murray whispered into her ear at the end of the film. While I could not hear every word, it was obvious to me that he said something like "As soon as possible, call your husband and tell him you love him, okay?" The last six words I have no doubt about whatsoever.

—Matthew Allen, Long Beach, California

A. I saw the film again, and closed my eyes and concentrated every aural nerve during that scene, and still could not hear a word. Apparently I am not alone. In an interview with writer-director Sofia Coppola in the new issue of *Sight & Sound*, she's asked, "Dare I ask what Bob whispers to Charlotte at the end?" And she replies: "Someone asked Bill, and he said, 'It's between lovers.' I love that answer." Then she was asked if she had written lines for the scene, and said: "I wrote some stuff but I wasn't happy with it. There was dialogue but it was really sparse. Ultimately I liked it better that you don't hear it, that you can put in what you want them to say. You wish he'd say, 'I had a great time and you're great,' but instead he says, 'I left my jacket.' That's what people do."

Q. I work at a local video store and the release of *Lost in Translation* on DVD has had lots of people asking about it. But I noticed that about 90 percent of the people that watched it said they didn't like it. In fact, most of them said that it was one of the worst movies they've ever seen. They didn't understand why it drew all of the attention that it got. Is this because of the expectations that the general public has in their minds? Was it overadvertised by the Oscar hype it got? Or is it just because the general public can't watch a film that will challenge them to think when they are used to watching big-budget films where everything is drawn out for them?

—Sean O'Connell, Novato, California

A. Yes, yes, and yes. *Lost in Translation* requires audiences to be able to pick up feelings and information on frequencies that many moviegoers don't receive on. Most of the movies most people go to see are made in such a way that not a moment's thought is required. The audience is a passive receptor for mindless sensation. When I'm told by people that they hated *Lost in Translation*, I have to restrain myself from replying, "You are saying more about yourself than about the film." *Lost in Translation* was applauded by 94 percent of the 190 critics monitored at rottentomatoes.com, and by 97 percent of the major critics. Does that mean critics are (a) out of touch with popular taste, or (b) have better taste than the customers at Sean O'Connell's video store? Before you answer—remember that the mission of a good critic is not to reflect popular taste but to inform it.

Q. Something in your Answer Man column struck me as incredibly arrogant. You wrote: "*Lost in Translation* was applauded by 94 percent of the 190 critics monitored at rottentomatoes.com, and by 97 percent of the major critics. Does that mean critics are (a) out of touch with popular taste, or (b) have better taste than the customers at Sean O'Connell's video store? Before you answer—remember that the mission of a good critic is not to reflect popular taste but to inform it." I'm one of those people who found *Lost in Translation* tedious and overrated. However, I'm also a film student and must concede that it was well constructed and beautifully shot. But implying that somehow I, and thousands like me, are somehow lesser than the all-knowing, all-seeing critics who reviewed the film positively is ridiculous. Whether or not you enjoy a film is largely based upon how it "hits" you, not on logic. *Translation* just didn't hit me (in fact it missed completely). Does this mean I should drop out of film school and start prepping for a career in used car sales?

—Jesse Hill, Boston, Massachusetts

A. I got a *lot* of messages like yours. Andrew Glasgow of Birmingham, Alabama, wrote, "You write about how many critics think *Lost in Translation* is God's gift to film—and how they, and you, just by sheer weight of numbers, could not possibly be wrong. Maybe next time be a little more open about the feelings of others." And Greg McClay of Lowell, Massachusetts, wrote: "All opinions say more about the person than the subject they are talking about. Are you seriously implying that there is something wrong with somebody who didn't like *Lost In Translation*? If so, then what does that say about you?"

Two readers have an intriguing theory. Sarah Metcalfe of Ottawa, Ontario writes: "I loved *Lost in Translation* in the theater and encouraged all of my friends to see it. Every single one who saw it on video was bored by the movie. To me, much of the humor and interest was in Bill Murray's expressions and reactions. Is there a possibility that this would be lost on the small screen?" And Edward Rosenthal of Roslyn Heights, New York, writes: "It's just better in a movie theater. There's pretty much universal agreement that big-action movies should be seen on the wide screen, but it's been my experience that quiet, character-driven movies also benefit from this environment, even though this may sound somewhat counterintuitive. In a dark and quiet theater, free of the distractions of home viewing, you can concentrate and appreciate this type of film much more." I wonder if that's it. The movie drew me in and enveloped me, and the big screen had something to do with that. As for my original reply—well, it was ill-considered. You're not wrong just because you disagree with me. But we film critics didn't hold a meeting and conspire to like the movie. A remarkable 97 percent individually and independently admired it. We must have seen a different movie—and maybe we did, since we saw it on the big screen. Theater audiences generally liked the movie; video audiences hate it. Strange.

Q. Re. the AM items on how people loved *Lost in Translation* in theaters and hated it on video: After being in the video industry for twenty years, I've noticed that nothing affects a person's view more than expectations. With *Lost in Translation*, I saw a screener on video months before its release and loved the movie. By the time it was released on video, it had gone through the media hype of the Academy Awards, and viewers were expecting heights that could not be reached. Everyone had heard what a great movie it was, and the virgin experience that reviewers got was lost. I remember years ago when *Ghostbusters* first came out; most video customers were very vocal in their dislike of it. It was one of the first video titles to go through a media frenzy, and like *Lost in Translation*, nothing could live up to the hype. Since then it has, of course, moved on to become a video classic.

—Brad Pilger, Edmonton, Alberta

A. The movie's reception on video has inspired a record number of messages to the Answer Man. Bob Riggs of Houston writes: "Some films are intended to be appealing and easily digested, while others try to explore difficult subjects in unique ways. By nature, humans enjoy simple repetition of pleasant experiences and shy away from the hard work involved with dealing with anything challenging. Thomas Kinkaid and Britney Spears have made enormous amounts of money marketing to people for whom this instinct has become a way of life. I would suggest that the value of *Lost in Translation* lies in its appeal to another part of human nature—that which says, 'Get up off your butt and find out what's going on out there!' "

And J.C. Inglis of Toronto writes: "Why did you give in to the clods who disagreed with your statements on *Lost in Translation*? At the end of your reply you wrote, "You're not wrong just because you disagree with me." Yes, they *are* wrong. Watching, enjoying, and understanding movies is a skill and can be done poorly and wrongly. 'Getting' a movie is not the same as having an emotional response. One can still 'get' a movie even if one doesn't like it. Saying one doesn't 'get' a movie is like saying one doesn't 'get' a symphony. It proves that one has a stunted or undeveloped faculty of appreciation, or possibly that one is an idiot."

See also Answer Man entry on "Bill Murray at the Oscars."

LOTR–ROTK

Q. I hope you're enjoying the mass numbers of e-mails about not including *Return of the King* anywhere on your Top 10 list. I can understand your not having it at the top, but not even an honorable mention? To ignore a movie that was so good, so admired, so praised by you and all the other critics and everyone that sees it borders on criminal.

—Scott Gant, St. Joseph, Michigan

A. Yep, I got a lot of e-mails. I gave *Return of the King* three and a half stars, and the cutoff for the list was four stars. It's an impressive achievement, yes, but let me tell you about the other films on my list. My job is to see all the movies so I can tell you about the great ones you might not have heard about. I reviewed 278 films last year; if you have seen the titles on my list and think *Return of the King* is better than all of them, then we disagree. Nobody has heard of *The Son*, for example, but they should have. It would tear you to pieces.

They're collecting all of the Best 10 lists at moviecitynews.com, and my guess is that *LOTR* is on about half the lists, which is very good but not overwhelming. For me, the real news in my list is the No. 1 ranking for *Monster*, which opened late in the year and got in under the radar for some critics, but is a landmark—a powerfully great film.

Q. I can't believe you reviewed *The Return of the King* and didn't mention that ridiculously dragged-out ending. Although the movie was three hours long it was actually a two-and-a-half-hour movie. The last half hour was spent tying up every possible loose end. Did anybody edit this movie? There were about ten times when I expected (and eventually prayed) that the credits would begin to roll. The whole theater was murmuring in annoyance.

—Lee Stringer, Brampton, Ontario

A. You know those people who can't wait to stand up at the exact moment they sense a movie is over, and put on their coats and race out of the theater, blocking the end titles and credit cookies for the rest of us? The movie drove them nuts.

Q. I hate to be picky but I found an error in your *Return of the King* review. You said, "Of all the heroes and villains in the trilogy, and all the thousands or hundreds of thousands of deaths, I felt such emotion only twice, with the ends of Faramir and Gollum." I assume that you meant Boromir, not Faramir. Boromir's death was sad, and Faramir . . . well, he did not die; he married Eowyn. I'm sure I heard that you read and enjoyed Tolkien's books, so I'm sure this was just a typo.

—Leah Cornish, Roslindale, Massachusetts

A. (*Spoiler warning*). No, I meant to write that. The AM got a lot of messages saying that Faramir does not die, and indeed he does not, but the movie gets a great deal of mileage out of making us think he does/has/will. Notice I mention he is "not quite dead" on the funeral pyre, and later I refer to his "end," not his death, because his end—including his near-death, his salvation, and his eventual destiny—were quite moving. Maybe this whole business with spoilers is getting out of hand. I wrote carefully to avoid giving away his survival, only to be told I should have revealed what happened.

Q. In your TV review of *Lord of the Rings: Return of the King* you made mention of Gandalf's unusual physical prowess for a seemingly "old man." From the books, I know that Gandalf is not really "human." All wizards are actually ancient spirits given human form, which accounts for their powerful magical abilities (as opposed to the "subtle" magic of the Elves and such). And when Gandalf was returned to Middle-Earth as the "White" wizard after his battle with the Balrog, my impression is that he assumed more authority, power, and vitality thereafter. (He was upgraded—Gandalf 2.0.) Thinking back over the movies, I'd have to admit that Peter Jackson didn't really emphasize this very much. The only blatant clue I can think of was from *The Two Towers*, when Gandalf makes the comment in the stables at Edoras that he has "walked this world for 300 lives of men." Consequently, Gandalf's physicality is not really untoward given the fuller context of the mythos, but it's easy to see how a

viewer would think otherwise, if they hadn't read the novels fifteen times. It's likely this knowledge influenced Jackson's depiction of Gandalf, even if he didn't make it explicitly manifest to the audience (as he should have).
—David A. Young, Titusville, Florida

A. Well, now I know. And his ancient appearance and flowing white beard? All only a visible manifestation of his age and wisdom, I suppose. Still, I think it looked funny to see the geezer leading the charge.

Q. Andy Serkis is brilliant as Gollum, the CGI character in *Lord of the Rings: Return of the King*. Given the increasing overlap between technology and acting, when do you see an actor in such a role getting nominated for Best Supporting Actor at the Oscars?
—Chris Jillings, Cal Tech, Los Angeles, California

A. A lot of his admirers are asking that question. Patrick Miller of Helene, Alabama, writes: "After being amazed by the 'performance' of Gollum in *The Two Towers*, I truly felt that Andy Serkis deserved an Oscar nomination for his portrayal. Do you think that now, thanks to all of the behind-the-scenes footage in the *The Two Towers: Extended Edition* DVD, that details how much work, and how much true acting he did, he has a shot at an award for *Return of the King*?"

And Tony Hernandez of Chicago asks: "As we head into the Oscar season, I am wondering what your thoughts are regarding awards for CGI characters and voice actors. When Disney's *Aladdin* was a huge hit in the nineties, there was brief talk of Robin Williams snagging a Best Supporting Actor nomination for his voice work as the Genie. The Gollum character in the *Lord of the Rings* movies is equally impressive and just as significant to the movie's success. In cases like this, should the Academy make a special award as it has done in the past for unique contributions?"

Serkis not only voiced Gollum, but did the physical acting that became the basis for the animated creature—who was certainly one of the most fascinating and convincing characters in the movie. But animation and robot theorists talk about a strange phenomenon that happens when artificial characters begin to seem "too real." This is the Uncanny Valley Effect, named in 1978 by the Japanese robot scientist Masahiro Mori.

According to a *New Yorker* article by John Seabrook, "Mori tested people's emotional responses to a wide variety of robots, from non-humanoid to completely humanoid. He found that the human tendency to empathize with machines increases as the robot becomes more human. But at a certain point, when the robot becomes too human, the emotional sympathy abruptly ceases, and revulsion takes its place. People began to notice not the charmingly human characteristics of the robot but the creepy zombielike differences." A definition on the Word Spy Web site gives more examples.

It is possible that the rejection of the sci-fi movie *Final Fantasy*, which used computer animation to create "real characters," was caused because it fell into the Uncanny Valley. The genius of Gollum is that it seems like a convincingly real creature—but not one we have ever seen before, so that its realism does not seem creepy except in the ordinary way. If Serkis brought Gollum to life, other artists fine-tuned the balance with the Uncanny Valley. So this is something other than a conventional performance, and should not compete against characters of a different nature. Perhaps a new category is called for? Beyond the Oscar of the Uncanniest Valley?

Love Actually

Q. I just saw *Love Actually* and thought it was a very good movie. But one scene I found offensive and unnecessary—Billy Bob Thornton as the President, showing him as a disreputable womanizing bully. That scene and the press conference were totally anti-American.
—Michael Leone, Port Washington, New York

A. It was a funny scene involving a cleverly realized fictional character inspired in equal parts by Clinton and Bush. The British prime minister's putdown at the press conference was fueled by his jealousy, because he also had a crush on the young woman targeted by the president. When did we get so thin-skinned that any depiction of the president short of idolatry is "anti-American"? What happened to our sense of humor?

Q. Just read your review of *Love Actually*, and had some problem with the logic of these sentences: "No good movie is too long. No bad movie is short enough." Yet you say *Love Actually* is good, but it is too long. If we use rules of logic:

(1) You are asserting: (movie is good) implies (movie is not too long).

(2) The Rule of Contrapositives states that if A implies B, *not* B implies *not* A. That is, *not* (movie is not too long) implies *not* (movie is good).

(3) The rule of double negatives rewords the above as (movie is too long) implies (movie is not good).

(4) You are therefore saying the movie is not good.

—Mike Spearns, St. John's, Newfoundland

A. Actually, I am suggesting that:

(1) Although no good movie is too long . . .

(2) . . . some good movies would be even better movies if they were shorter.

Luther

Q. I'm curious about the line in your review of *Luther* suggesting that Martin Luther could not have been the depressive he's portrayed as and still accomplish what he did. If you look at the historical documentation and Luther's own writing, it becomes fairly clear Luther was clinically depressed. Do you think it is impossible for someone with mental illness to accomplish something spectacular?

—Allen Lunde, Chico, California

A. No, I don't. And I obviously didn't know enough about the real Luther, even though my father was Lutheran. Many readers wrote me to say that the depressed, doubtful, despairing man depicted in the film was close to the historical reality. Steve Bliss, a Lutheran seminary student from Kimball, South Dakota, helped me out (I have edited him for length):

"First, there is your critique that the relationship between Luther and Katherine Van Boragh wasn't passionate enough . . . that is

very much how their relationship started out . . . their common bond was in their passionate faith and not their passion for each other.

"Second, there was the critique that there weren't any scenes that displayed Luther as having a Gandhi-like appeal. That's not the type of leader that Luther was . . . . He didn't want to free people to follow him, he wanted to free people to follow God. He wanted people to know that they didn't need the bishops to interpret Scripture for them . . . . He wanted people to know they could also experience God's presence in their lives the same way he did and they didn't need help from anybody else, including Luther."

Macs in the Movies

Q. I've noticed an interesting trend over the last few years: You can sometimes tell who the "bad guys" are in a movie or TV show by what computer they use. For instance, on *24* all the bad guys used PCs while the good guys all used Macs. The same holds true for *Austin Powers*, *Legally Blonde*, etc. Why do you think Apple always gets the plum roles? I'm of the opinion that Hollywood loves the underdog and has a close relationship with Apple computer, whereas PCs seem controlled by a megalomaniac in Seattle. Are there a lot more Mac zealots like me in Hollywood? Does Apple pour sponsorship money in big-budget studio movies?

—Justin Toomey, Athens, Ohio

A. Since many Windows machines look alike, Apple is the only manufacturer that can gain by product placement, which accounts for some of the Macs. It's true that the movie industry and creative types in general prefer the Mac. The novelist Tom Clancy sends e-mails with this signature line: "Never ask a man what computer he uses. If it's a Mac, he'll tell you. If it's not, why embarrass him?"

Marlon Brando

Q. I couldn't let Marlon Brando's passing go by without telling this story. Over twenty years ago when I was just starting out as a teacher in Chicago, I had a student who loved Brando. As a writing assignment, I'd promised to find addresses for the stars the kids liked, so they could write to them and see who answered. The kid was overjoyed. She told Brando they shared a birthday and that she wanted to become a writer, but couldn't convince her parents she had the goods. The Brando fan received a hand-written letter—one of the sweetest, most encouraging letters a teen could ever receive—about dreams and what really matters in life. And a year later, she received, on her birthday, a hand-signed card, asking her if she was still writing, and for a sample of something she'd written. I've never forgotten it. Brando was and will always be one of my idols, too, and that's how I'll remember him: As I saw him in the eyes of that teenage girl, so many years ago.

—Cynthia Dagnal Myron, Tucson, Arizona

A. One of the reasons Brando was a great star was that he never followed the form book, but lived his life spontaneously, personally, and sincerely.

Matchstick Men

Q. I am concerned about your use of the terms "nut case" and "whacko" in your review of *Matchstick Men*. Movies and critics have immense power to shape popular perceptions. People with mental disorders resent being called "whacko" or a "nut case." Mental illness is a physical disorder just like diabetes or heart disorders.

—Agris Petersons, Santa Barbara, California

A. I received a lot of protests about the use of those terms. I was describing the specific character, not mental illness in general, but you make a valid point and I will reform.

The Matrix Reloaded

Q. Like a lot of people, I went to Best Buy to purchase *The Matrix Reloaded* on DVD on its release date. Just inside the front door, the store had a table with all kinds of merchandise that was free or discounted with purchase of the DVD. Next to the table was a display stocked with hundreds of copies of the DVD. Each one had a free bonus disc attached, as promoted by signs taped to the display. While the other customers swarmed over the display and grabbed their copies, I took the time to check these DVDs: They

were all full-screen. In order to get a widescreen copy, I had to actually go to the DVD section of the store and take it off the shelf. It was the same price, but it didn't come with a bonus disc, nor did I get any free merchandise with purchase. Are we to really believe those studies that show that customers prefer full-screen to widescreen, according to sales volume?

—Scott Hardie, Tampa, Florida

A. This is a sad story. *Matrix Reloaded* is precisely the kind of movie where you want to see every last inch of screen real estate—the picture is jammed with details, and depends on special effects. For Best Buy to steer customers toward the inferior format is inexplicable. Even Blockbuster has finally gotten the widescreen message.

Q. Scott Hardie's experience at Best Buy, when he could not find the widescreen version of *Matrix Reloaded*, was not typical. Best Buy always carries widescreen DVDs and displays them properly. The bonus disc was available on both the widescreen and full-screen editions. Most likely what happened is he went later in the day and the widescreen bonus discs were all sold out. This is a fairly frequent occurrence as widescreen DVDs just sell faster. According to the latest sales charts, this is now the case for pretty much all movies, even stuff like *Anger Management*.

—Daniel Rudolph, Cedar Rapids, Iowa

A. I got a lot of similar messages. Apparently moviegoers now prefer widescreen to "full screen" (that is, cropped pan-and-scan) by such a wide margin that stores are left with piles of unsold full screens. Apologies to Best Buy.

Q. After seeing *The Matrix Revolutions* and reading several reviews of it, I was struck by the seemingly obvious conclusion that a film's story arc simply can't hold up over the three installments of a trilogy. I scanned my memory to try to think of any trilogy of the past thirty years (from *Planet of the Apes* forward), and time and again concluded that the third installment of all trilogies is either a disappointment or just terrible, even if the second film was great. The "great" trilogies such as *Star Wars* or *Indiana Jones* or *The Godfather* are good examples, having carried fairly middling third installments. My questions are these: Are we so caught up in the conceptual framework of three that we must carry a story arc beyond its natural conclusion? Is the promise of profit from a third installment always going to win out over quality? Or could a successful two-part series such as *Kill Bill* finally demonstrate that a two-film story arc is the best the way to go?

—Christopher Snipes, Mexico City, Mexico

A. One problem with *Matrix* may have been that the original film was made without parts two and three fully in mind. But great trilogies are possible; consider John Ford's *Cavalry* trilogy (*Fort Apache, She Wore a Yellow Ribbon, Rio Grande*), or Ingmar Bergman's *Silence of God* trilogy (*Through a Glass Darkly, Winter Light, The Silence*). To be sure, those were trilogies linked by theme, not characters. But *Return of the King* ends the *Lord of the Rings* trilogy on a strong note. Perhaps the greatest of all trilogies is Satyajit Ray's *Apu Trilogy*, included in my Great Movies series, and it's available on DVD.

Monster

Q. I don't disagree with you saying Charlize Theron's performance in *Monster* is one of cinema history's best; I haven't seen the film. But your comment made me start thinking about how I tend to judge acting. A performance usually becomes better in retrospect after comparing it to the actor's other works (case in point: DiCaprio's Arnie in *Gilbert Grape* became all the more impressive when we discovered the actor really wasn't mentally retarded). However, is this a fair way to judge acting? Is Theron's performance so good because it is such a stark contrast to herself and her other films, or because—in and of itself—it achieves something that few others have "in the history of cinema"?

—Thomas Torrey, Bronxville, New York

A. In this case, I think it really is that good, because I had no idea who the actress was as I watched the film, and so had nothing to compare it to.

Q. Regarding your comment in the review of *Monster*, the phrase "hate the sin and love the sinner" is not actually found in the Bible. Though it's a laudable notion, this phrase joins a company of popular sentiments often wrongly attributed to the Good Book (see also "cleanliness is next to godliness" and "God helps those who help themselves").

—Mark A. Plunkett, Bedford, Indiana

A. But I didn't say it was in the Bible. I simply said "we are told." I learn from Jim Emerson of Seattle: "The sentiment is usually attributed to St. Augustine, who said, *Cum dilectione hominum et odio vitiorum*, or 'With love for mankind and hatred of sins.' It is often loosely translated as: 'Love the sinner and hate the sin,' a saying often incorrectly attributed to Jesus."

Movie Critics

Q. I've been soaking up the screenings at the World 3-D Film Expo in Hollywood, California, at the Egyptian Theatre, and loving every minute of it. Last night I went to see the film *Charge at Indian River*, and knowing nothing about it, I looked it up in my handy-dandy Leonard Maltin guide. He gave it two and a half stars. Fast-forward to the screening, and Leonard Maltin is in front of me for popcorn. I asked him about the film, and he said he hadn't seen it. Is it acceptable for critics to lie in their movie guides simply to make it seem like they've seen everything?

—Travis Baker, Calabasas, California

A. No, but Maltin was not lying. He was being scrupulously honest. No single human being could see all 19,000 titles in the invaluable Maltin guide, and he is up front about using an expert staff of editors and contributors. And now you know that in the next edition the review of *Charge at Indian River* will be his.

Moviegoing

Q. I was intrigued by your statement that "no human being could possibly see all 19,000 movies listed in the invaluable Maltin guide." I also noticed that on it states that you have seen around 8,000 films yourself, and probably several hundred more since you quoted that. I just turned twenty-three this week and am proud to say that I have seen just under 9,000 films. Since I wasn't into this until around 1994, I did the math and figured that as an average, that meant watching only about two and a half movies per day. At this rate, I am determined to prove you wrong somewhere around 2015 in which I will only be thirty-five years old and still "a human being."

—Mike Furlong, Roy, Utah

A. You will definitely be thirty-five, all right, but let's wait and see about the other part. Before you commit yourself to seeing 19,000 movies, you might want to check out a new documentary named *Cinemania*, about five New Yorkers who pretty much go to the movies all day long, every day. This film cries out for the subtitle, *Get a Life!*

Movies for Children

Q. We loved *Peter Pan*, though I was reluctant to go until I read your review. I assumed that Peter Pan was a movie aimed at and for children. There were kids at the movie, but I think maybe the adults liked it more. My question: What exactly is a "children's movie"?

—J. David Van Dyke, Buchanan, Michigan

A. A children's movie is a movie at which adults are bored. A grown-up movie is a movie at which children are bored. A family movie is a movie at which, if it's good, nobody is bored. *Peter Pan* falls in the last category. I was surprised it didn't do better at the box office.

Movies for Moms

Q. Regarding the recent rise of Movies for Moms—that is, theater chains setting aside certain screenings for parents with infants and toddlers—what do you think of parents who would subject their impressionable tykes to age-inappropriate fare such as *Monster*? One theater chain is actually showing that ultragory (though excellent) title during its Movies for Moms slot.

—Celeste Lengerich, Fort Wayne, Indiana

A. The idea of Movies for Moms is a splendid one, saving the cost of baby-sitting and allowing moms to see the new movies. But if

it is true, as some contend, that playing Mozart can raise the IQ of a baby in the womb, what effect can have on young children who can see and hear, if not comprehend? Surely they can pick up on the emotions—the anger and violence—and they can also sense the anxiety aroused in their mothers.

MPAA Matters

Q. You commented that the MPAA rating given to *The Whale Rider* was inappropriate and I agree for exactly the same reasons. So: what could possibly have possessed these idiots when they approved the trailer for the new version of *The Texas Chainsaw Massacre* for All Audiences? What an egregious pair of examples.

—Alex Merz, W. Lebanon, New Hampshire

A. I checked out the trailer at apple.com/trailers and found it within the MPAA's usual guidelines. What I don't understand is the R rating for the movie itself. This film is so gruesome, sick, and explicitly violent that if it doesn't deserve an adults-only rating, you have to wonder what does.

Q. A few critics' groups have canceled their annual awards in protest of Jack Valenti's ban on sending out DVD screeners to industry and press. Isn't this counterproductive to their cause? Such awards are the perfect way to remind viewers of movies that the Academy will overlook or not see because of the ban.

—Michael Chichester, West Chester, Pennsylvania

A. I agree. I wrote that Valenti's original ban was boneheaded, but I oppose the decision to cancel critics' awards because the result would be to punish worthy films—which is exactly what the ban could also do. The nation's critics have sent each other countless and endless e-mails about the Valenti decree; if only they were equally disturbed by the MPAA's lack of a workable adult rating.

Q. Yesterday I saw the wonderful *Lost in Translation*. About two-thirds of the way through I realized that there was no swearing or vulgar language. I thought for sure that I must be seeing a PG-rated film. I was shocked to see that according to the movie's poster the MPAA rated the film as R. Could it have been because of a few risqué moves by the fully-clothed stripper in the film? Next to the lobby poster for *Translation* was another MPAA rating travesty, *Whale Rider*. The MPAA's crime against this film has been done to death but hash pipe or no hash pipe I still can't imagine why that film would deserve at PG, let alone a PG-13. This is a film for the ages that would be healthy viewing for all. Maybe somebody from the MPAA could step forward and help rationalize why a film like *Kill Bill*, covered wall to wall with freshly extracted human entrails, is only one step more dangerous for us than *Whale Rider* and how *Lost in Translation* could be just as disturbing for viewers as *Kill Bill*. Please help me understand.

—Joe Taylor, Carbondale, Illinois

A. Gladly. The MPAA rating system is guided by the greed of the movie industry and its fear of the religious right. (1) Greed: It opposes a workable adults-only rating, because the industry doesn't want a category that would actually require them to turn away potential customers. Thus movies are crammed into the R category, sometimes having to be edited to qualify. We need an A-for-adult rating *between* the R and the NC-17 (a.k.a. X), to separate nonporn adult films from pornography. (2) Fear. Terrified of outside censorship, the MPAA is more sensitive to content involving language, mild sexuality and subtle drug references than the average American moviegoer. *Whale Rider* is a classic example of a film that Americans have embraced as ideal family entertainment; the PG-13 is a wild overreaction. We actually showed the offending "drug" scene on *Ebert and Roeper* and received not one single complaint. The best source for sane and objective information about the content of films is www.screenit.com.

Q. In a Movie Answer Man column, you decried the MPAA screener ban while agreeing with a reader who felt that the awards boycotts by some critics groups were counterproductive, since these awards are the perfect way to highlight less seen films. As a part-time critic for a nationally distributed weekly, I attend as many screenings as I can,

but have a hard time getting to festivals and junkets. Without screeners, I will be much harder pressed to identify less-seen films deserving of recognition. My No. 1 pick last year, *The Pianist*, was a film I saw via screener. Other films I might not have been able to consider without screeners include *Waking Life, All Or Nothing,* and *Bowling for Columbine*. It therefore seems to me that the net effect of the screener ban will be to bury smaller films like these and force critics to recognize films most people have already seen anyway. Sure, *Finding Nemo* and *Master and Commander* are great films, but films like *Stevie* and *Northfork* depend significantly on screeners to maximize their visibility among critics.

—Steven D. Greydanus, film critic, *National Catholic Register*

A. I agree with you that screeners are useful in giving smaller films a fair chance of being considered. Some believe one purpose of Jack Valenti's ban was to make it more difficult for those smaller independent films to get the attention necessary to win awards and Oscar nominations. I am against Valenti's ludicrous ban, but I am also against canceling critics' awards as a gesture against the MPAA. The purpose of awards is to honor movies the critics feel are worthy; why punish them?

"The DVD screener controversy is Valenti's version of Weapons of Mass Destruction," director Robert Altman told me last week. "He knows and everybody in the business knows that the big films have already been pirated before they even leave the labs—long before DVDs are made." Altman helpfully volunteered that in defiance of the ban he has already sent out DVD screeners of his movie, *The Company*.

My Life Without Me

Q. I saw *My Life Without Me* at the London Film Festival after reading your review, and became more and more annoyed with Sarah Polley's character during the film. Afterward, director Isabel Coixet stood up and explained that Ann made the choices she did because she didn't feel like she had any control over her life, and didn't have anyone she could talk to, especially her husband, who was "just like another kid to her." This put me in mind of *Y Tu Mama También*, in which Maribel Verdu's character makes a similar choice—but in her case it seems completely justified based on what we've seen in her life and marriage, and we can't say that about Sarah Polley's. So I asked Ms. Coixet how she had been influenced by that film, and she said not at all, as there were a lot of movies that dealt with this subject. On my way home I thought this over and realized that the choice in *Y Tu* is completely believable, but the choice in *My Life* is not. At no point did Sarah Polley show that she felt her life was out of her control, that she regretted the choices she'd made, that she didn't really think her husband was her equal, or that she understood how her death would affect her daughters. If this had been shown, I think we could have understood her choice, whether or not we agreed with it. If you have to rely on the director to explain the logic afterward, that's bad.

—Sarah Manvel, London, UK)

A. I agree with your comparison of the two films. One of the things that annoys me about *My Life Without Me* is that the woman's actions feel more like plotting than psychology. If you were happily married with children you love, shouldn't you spend your last days sharing with them instead of indulging a screenwriter's fantasy?

Mystic River

Q. Now that Sean Penn has won the Oscar, what do you believe Kevin Bacon's intentions are when at the end of the film he sees Sean Penn at the parade, and, pointing his finger as if his hand is a gun, "shoots" him? What does that communication mean?

—Brian Bennett, Bangkok Film Festival, Thailand

A. He's saying, "I know what you did," but I don't know if he's saying what he's going to do about it.

Names

Q. After listening to yet another gravelly throated voice-over, I was struck by the familiarity of the cop's name—Detective Malloy. I did an IMDb.com character search for the name and the results were vast—especially for

Jims, Jakes, and Johns. Why does Hollywood love the "J. Malloy" name so much?

—Gary Troutman, Lake Charles, Louisiana

A. I don't know, but you're right. The Internet Movie Database lists 139 Malloys played by everyone from Rod Steiger to Dub Taylor. On a hunch, I looked up "Travis," and got 277 hits, including Seann William Scott's character in the movie *The Rundown*. Now it's up to IMDb fanatics to determine the most popular male and female names in movie history.

Northfork

Q. I heard something about the Polish twins sneaking a movie in-joke into the script of their movie *Northfork*. What is it?

—Susan Lake, Urbana, Illinois

A. The brothers told me they got complaints that their first two movies lacked a "story arc," and so they added a story "ark" to *Northfork*. It is built by a man who plans to ride out the floodwaters, and he doesn't have two of everything on board, but he does have two wives.

Osama

Q. With incredible dishonesty and misinformation, Roger Ebert used his review of the film *Osama* to launch into a tirade against the Bush administration for letting the Taliban come back into Afghanistan and "not finishing the job." The fact is that the movie was made about Afghanistan *under* the Taliban, not the post-Taliban period. If anything, it's a movie that shows just how horrible things were under the Taliban and why an invasion was justified. But of course Ebert felt entirely comfortable twisting the facts for his own political tendentiousness.

—Bob Schneider, San Francisco, California

A. I was mistaken, but not deliberately. The movie was indeed filmed after the liberation of Afghanistan, which I applauded. But as the film's official Web site states: "*Osama* examines the lives of the Afghan people while under the Taliban's control, but the film also highlights lingering problems that exist even though the Taliban rule has ended." Many believe that the war in Iraq diverted American resources from finishing needed tasks in Afghanistan. There are reports that the Taliban is reestablishing itself in some areas. The Afghan opium crop once again supplies the world with drugs.

Oscars, 2004

Q. Was the Academy honoring *Return of the King* or the entire trilogy with its onslaught of awards? I'm asking because it seems unfair to ask one film to compete against three. The movie deserved all of its technical awards, I'm sure, but I don't think it belongs in the same breath as *Ben Hur* and *Titanic*. My personal opinions about the tedious and charmless *LOTR* series aside, maybe in the future they will create a special achievement award for a series of films so Academy voters won't feel obligated to give the major awards to the final part. They could have saved the Best Picture Award for a film with even a touch of emotional depth, like the delightful *Lost in Translation* or the gorgeous *In America*.

—Jesse Cunningham, Lafayette, Indiana

A. The parade of honors to *LOTR–ROTK* did seem a bit like a retirement banquet. Along with his Oscar maybe they should have given Peter Jackson a gold watch.

Q. When they started honoring stars who had passed away in 2003 by showing their pictures over the Oscar stage, to my surprise and horror, Leni Riefenstahl was included. Okay, I'll be the first to admit it: *The Triumph of the Will* is one of the most remarkable films I have ever seen, and its propagandic value is second to none. Moreover, as a historian, I can also recognize the film's tremendous influence upon twentieth-century history. For many years, *The Triumph of the Will* was the official face of the Nazi Party throughout the world, and rivals Griffith's *The Birth of a Nation* in terms of its long-term historical impact. That being said, how can we honestly pay tribute to Leni Riefenstahl? This was a women who, to my recollection, never once came clean about her activities during the Third Reich, and was as compulsive a liar as any apologist who ever survived the war. This is not to say that we should never forgive anyone who lived in

Germany during the Hitler era. Were roles reversed, the fact is most of us would have behaved in exactly the same way as the German people did during the thirties. Nevertheless, Riefenstahl never had the courage to own up to her legacy. I believe that for the Academy to honor such a woman is a disgrace. What is more, for the audience to dutifully clap when her picture was flashed across is a testament to its boundless stupidity.

—Anand Toprani, Ithaca, New York

A. Actually, the way I heard it, the applause dropped off audibly, and might have been even more subdued if some audience members had not been clapping on autopilot. The Oscar tributes do not, as I understand them, represent a value judgment about the lives of those mentioned, but simply acknowledge the passing of important figures in the history of film. To make Riefenstahl a "nonperson" would have been in the totalitarian tradition of those who erase those they disagree with from history. Her films served evil, but cannot be ignored, any more than *Birth of a Nation* can.

Passion of the Christ

Q. I just returned from seeing *The Passion of the Christ*. Had I been able to wrench my attention away from all of the horrified children gasping in the audience I might have appreciated it more. I can understand parents showing up at this film with their children expecting something different, but after a few minutes of the tremendous violence shown onscreen I would have thought more parents would have spared their children further horror. Shouldn't ticket sellers offer some kind of warning to parents showing up with good intentions and young children?

—Carson Utz, Novato, California

A. I'll go further than that: No responsible parent would allow a child to see the film. *The Passion of the Christ*, the most violent film I have ever seen, received an R rating from the MPAA because the organization, which exists in part to quell the fears of church-going America, lacked the nerve to give it the NC-17 rating it clearly earns. This becomes an unanswerable argument for my recommendation of an A (for adults only) rating between the R (which allows parents to take in children of any age) and the NC-17, which is irretrievably associated with pornography. Since many theaters refuse to book NC-17 films, and many media outlets will not advertise them, imagine the irony if their own policies had forced them to boycott *The Passion of the Christ*! Let the MPAA bring back the X, which everyone understands, for porno, and establish a useful adults-only rating for films that are not pornography but are simply unsuitable for children.

Q. In your review of *The Passion*, you mention that you review a movie based on its intention and not your expectations. I'm a twenty-one-year-old college student and thought that *Bad Boys 2* set out to become the most lurid and graphic action movie for my generation to enjoy, for entertainment value only, yet you reviewed the movie horribly. Is it because *The Passion* appeals to you more that you reviewed it in this kind manner?

—Jon F. Kull, Quakertown, Pennsylvania

A. One can of course review a movie based on its intentions and yet despise them.

Q. Why not put a little perspective on the *Passion* box-office figures by comparing it to the biggest religious hits of all time, *The Robe, Ben Hur,* and *The Ten Commandments*? According to the Web site BoxOfficeMojo.com (http://www.boxoffice-mojo.com/alltime/adjusted/), the adjusted, modern-day grosses for those films are $394 million, $590 million, and $789 million, respectively (and the U.S. population was a lot smaller back then). I don't think Mel's film will even come close. Heck, even the latest *Lord of the Rings* film only clocks in at No. 49 on the all-time list.

—Jim Judy, Washington, D.C.

A. Wow, you're right. It's three places below *The Bells of St. Mary's*.

Pirates of the Caribbean

Q. I saw *Pirates* over the weekend and loved it. I read your review and noted that you said

it seemed as though Johnny Depp was "channeling a drunken drag queen." It seemed to me he was channeling the Rolling Stones' Keith Richard, from the accent and eyeliner, right down to the trinkets hanging from his hair. Is it possible Depp used Richards as the model for Jack Sparrow? Has he given any interviews saying such?

—J. M. DePaul, Lewiston, Idaho

A. It happens that he has. David Geyer of Wheeling, West Virginia, supplies me with this Depp quote from the *Boston Globe:* "Keith Richards has been a hero forever and ever. It wasn't an imitation. It was more kind of a salute to him." Apologies to Keith Richards for confusing him with a drunken drag queen and vice versa.

Q. In AM you stated Johnny Depp based his character in *Pirates of the Caribbean* on Keith Richards. While this is true, he also based his character on one more influence: Pepe Le Pew, the skunk from Loony Tunes. Depp says on www.comingsoon.net:

"Yeah, I kind of incorporated the idea of Keith. Not like an imitation of Keith or anything but just that wisdom that he carries, that sort of confidence that he has, that attack that he has. So I got that on one side and on the other side I took a little bit of this cartoon character that I always loved when I was a kid, his name was Pepe Le Pew. Yeah, the skunk. He smelled horrible, but was absolutely convinced that he was the ultimate ladies' man. You know the guy, he'd fall in love with this cat and the cat quite clearly despised him but Pepe Le Pew sort of read it as, 'Oh she's just playing hard to get. Oh she's just shy.'"

—Sean Leslie, Salt Lake City, Utah

A. Now that it's been pointed out, I can see the resemblance. And to think I said he was merely channeling a drunken drag queen. That's why actors get the big bucks.

Projection Pros and Cons

Q. I recently took my wife to see the latest *Harry Potter* movie. I was amazed that the only speaker working was the front speaker. We heard the dialogue with no problem, but the sound track and audio effects were barely audible. When I complained to the manager after the movie, she was apologetic, and explained that the technician who was supposed to fix it was not available on the weekends.

Yet she was still selling tickets to the show and from what I could tell, I was the only person in the crowd of over one hundred who noticed enough to complain. I know people rarely notice when a bulb in a lamp is too dim, but to watch a high-budget film in mono? Can't people hear what they're listening to?

—Ike Quigley, Greensboro, North Carolina

A. Maybe they're programmed to passively accept what's on the screen, without reflecting that it is the responsibility of the projectionist and the management. When I attended a public/press screening of *The Stepford Wives* at a Chicago multiplex, the picture was dark, dim, murky, and indistinct. Not acceptable.

I complained to the manager. A few minutes later, the light intensity was turned up, and the picture looked fine. Many theaters cheat their customers through the idiotic practice of dialing down the projector bulbs, in the mistaken belief this will extend their life. Studies have proven that it has no effect. The picture quality at the Chicago screening was dramatically bad. The theater contained dozens of film critics, not to mention the publicists, but nobody else went out to the lobby to complain.

Pure Cinema

Q. You stated in your Great Movies review of *Sunrise* that as silent films reached their pinnacle, they strove not to "tell a story, but to give an experience." This is what I live by as a filmmaker myself. Yet this approach confuses filmgoers. Some are able to open to it, and some reject it outright (particularly those concerned or involved with the "industry"). If cinema is to provide us with new images, mythologies, and icons, why must it be so rigidly embedded in the formula of strict narrative? The few glimpses of "pure" cinema since the silents have been stunning (*2001: A Space Odyssey*, or *The Thin Red Line* for example), yet this form is often characterized as "indulgent" or "pretentious." I believe this form has yet to reach its potential, but

generally filmmakers and audiences are disinterested in it. Why is that? In the days before sound, wasn't the cinema still a thoroughly satisfying, moving, and magical experience for an audience?

—Andrew McGowan, Los Angeles, California

A. I was thinking the same thing while watching a beautifully restored 70mm print of *Lawrence of Arabia* at my recent Overlooked Film Festival. The first hour of the film consists essentially of conversations and long journeys through the desert. When the village is finally attacked, it's in long shot. The movie is mesmerizing. Perhaps the giant image helps; seen on video, the movie loses much of its magic. And as multiplexes and their screens shrink, movies come more and more to resemble television—talk and action, but little vision.

Quotes in Ads

Q. I read in a Reuters news article that you, Richard Roeper, MPAA president Jack Valenti, and executives from Lion's Gate and IFC Films had a conference call debating the use in *Fahrenheit 9/11* ads of Roeper's quote, "Everyone in the country should see this film." Valenti upheld the MPAA ruling against the quote because the film was rated R, meaning not everyone *can* see it. Why couldn't Roeper have just contributed a new quote, right then and there, such as, "Everyone who can should see this film"? Wouldn't that have satisfied all parties?

—Chris Tong, Kelseyville, California

A. Maybe, but it wasn't what Roeper said, and we don't supply quotes for ads; they must come from words actually used in our reviews. I had a similar experience after my *Whale Rider* review, which said, "Take the kids and they'll see a movie that will touch their hearts and minds." The MPAA objected to that quote in the ads. They said a film with a PG-13 rating can't be marketed to children—even though I said "take" the kids, not send them in alone. As Jack Valenti explained the *Fahrenheit 9/11* ruling to the rest of us on the conference call, I realized he would win the argument, because the studios have indeed signed an agreement to follow the MPAA's rules and regulations, which clearly say that films rated PG-13 or older cannot be advertised for the whole family. The MPAA cannot be blamed for enforcing the rules, but perhaps the studios should reevaluate the guidelines.

Q. Re. the Bush campaign's new TV ad, "Kerry's Coalition of the Wild-eyed": I linked to a script of the spot, and noticed that they are using what's described as a "video clip" from the 2003 Oscars, when Michael Moore berated George W. Bush. I've always understood that the Academy is extremely vigilant about protecting its copyright, and permits clips from the Oscars to be rebroadcast only in very special cases (for example, when a presenter or recipient dies). If the Oscar clip really is in the Bush ad, does this mean AMPAS has relaxed its licensing/usage policy? If not, will its leaders demand that Bush and Company cease and desist?
—Stuart Cleland, Evanston, Illinois

A. Bruce Davis, executive director of the Oscars, replies: "Your correspondent is correct that the Academy prefers that the copyrighted footage from its shows be reused—following the brief grace period immediately after each broadcast—only in the context of obituaries or definitive biographies. We are not enthusiastic about clips from our broadcast being used in political ads, whether they're blue, red, green, or any other hue, but we've been advised by our attorneys that the clip in the Bush ad is short enough, and oddly enough political enough, to be protected under the fair use doctrine. Fair use trumps copyright infringement. So while we're not happy about what we regard as a misappropriation of our material, there doesn't seem to be much that we can do about it beyond grousing in the columns of movie critics, when we get the chance."

Q. I noticed that *Terminator 3* is selling a quote of yours that labels the movie as "wall-to-wall action." Does it bother you that they are using your quote when you didn't even recommend the film? Are there no ethical boundaries for marketing movies to audiences?
—Jonathan Margolis, Pacific Palisades, California

A. Here is the complete sentence: "*Terminator 3: Rise of the Machines* is made in the spirit of these slick new action thrillers, and

abandons its own tradition to provide wall-to-wall action in what is essentially one long chase and fight, punctuated by comic, campy, or simplistic dialogue." You have to admit "wall-to-wall action" does accurately describe the film. So does my closing sentence: ". . . dumbed down for the multiplex hordes."

Q. I saw an ad for *The Rundown* with a whole series of alleged critics' raves, including one saying something like "Quite possibly the first perfect action movie." My question: Do you think a single human being in that movie—including the director (Peter Berg of *Corky Romano* infamy), writer (R.J. Stewart, whose finest credit appears to be *Remington Steele*), or stars (The Rock and Christopher Walken among them) would actually say that it was the first perfect action movie? Or that it is a perfect action movie?
—Bill Childs, Washington, D.C.

A. No, although it's a good one, but congratulations on discovering the first perfect action movie blurb.

The Raindrops Shot

Q. I've been attending a series of silent films by the German director G. W. Pabst. While watching *Diary of a Lost Girl* (1929), I recognized a camera shot that is most often attributed to Conrad Hall (that of a face next to a window during rain, making it appear as if the raindrops are tears). Hall's use of that shot in *In Cold Blood* is certainly amazing, but it seems that the origin of that shot should be credited to the cinematographers Sepp Allgeier and Fritz Arno Wagner. I was amazed to find such a shot in a German film from the twenties.
—Charles Modica, Jr., Los Angeles, California

A. There are more amazing shots in German films from the 1920s than in most new releases. That film and *Pandora's Box* made Louise Brooks a movie immortal. Thanks for the insight; Bertolucci's *The Dreamers* quotes the shot, and I credited Hall.

R Cards

Q. Not so much a question, but a statement from someone on the other side of the counter. I'm a manager at a "chain" theater. I can no longer count on my fingers and toes the number of times that I and my employees have been berated by parents because we would not sell their under-seventeen children tickets to *Kill Bill* or *Eurotrip* or *Punisher* or some other movie that the parents don't want to "have to watch." Some parents just don't care if their kids watch R-rated movies. Some even create their own R-rated dialogue at the theater over the inconvenience of having to buy their children's tickets and escort them to the auditorium. I realize that the R-card is really just symbolic, because kids without it will still just try to sneak in like they do now. It will, however, give that theater's employees an alternative to give to some of their unhappy customers.

—Name withheld, Oregon

A. I got a lot of mail from readers unhappy with my comments about the "R card," which a theater chain in downstate Illinois is introducing. Parents can sign a form authorizing their under-seventeen children to see R-rated movies, and then the kids are issued an ID with their photo on it. "The worst idea I've ever heard," ratings czar Jack Valenti told me.

"Isn't the R-card the same as what Blockbuster and Hollywood video do?" asks Christopher Roberts of Dayton, Ohio. "When you have your children put on your card, you can approve them to see anything they want or exclude them from R-rated rentals. Certain R-rated movies should be seen by teens (*Blue Car*, for example). The R rating seems almost arbitrary anyway, since the MPAA doesn't have a usable adults-only rating and any kid can purchase a PG-13 ticket and walk into an R-rated movie."

And Jeffrey Perkins of Chicago writes: "I am the father of a very mature sixteen-year-old, and there are plenty of R-rated movies that I think he should be permitted to see, but I simply do not have the time to take him to all the ones he desires to view. The R-card is a great way for us to be able to parent our kids without the oppressive rules of the MPAA."

The Revolution Will Not . . .

Q. I am afraid you have been hoodwinked.

The movie *The Revolution Will Not Be on TV* is not the documentary it purports to be; indeed, it is closer to a fictionalized account of what might have happened if Chavez were truly the Robin Hood portrayed in the film. The production involved an enormous amount of manipulation of dates, hours, and sequences, and many gross omissions, like the fact that a top-ranking general, currently a member of Chavez's cabinet, announced to the media that the president had resigned at 4 A.M. on April 12. You can find the partial results of a rigorous technical analysis at www.PetitionOnline.com/gusano03.

I agree film can be made to lie; I also agree that, after helping him get elected by giving him supportive coverage, private media in Venezuela ended up being biased against Chavez and lied outright on April 13. However, what many of us here criticized now looks like white lies in comparison with *The Revolution*, a movie which, in its different versions, almost manages to outdo the governments PR materials. If sophisticated opinion leaders like you can be taken in, a less informed public is, I'm afraid, buying that (Llaguno) bridge you write about.

—Eva Gueron, Caracas Venezuela

A. I received a lot of other messages also questioning the facts in the documentary. Your link will help readers make up their own minds.

Ripley's Game

Q. Yesterday I heard for the first time that *Ripley's Game*, released in Europe, would not make the big screens in the United States and has gone right to DVD. I bought the disc yesterday, watched the film last night—and loved it! Great story, great acting, great locations and photography. What's the problem with distribution in the United States?

—Fred Bothwell, Austin, Texas

A. *Ripley's Game* centers on a John Malkovich performance that creates the best of all the Tom Ripleys in the movies. It is a superb film, and on *Ebert and Roeper* we gave it a full review even though it went directly to DVD. The failure to open it theatrically was a shameful blunder by New Line and Fine

Line, comparable to Miramax's failure to release *The Castle*, the funniest comedy of recent years.

Rosebud

Q. What was "Rosebud" in *Citizen Kane*?
—Gail Lehmann, Millbrook, Alabama

A. The sled that Charles Foster Kane left behind when, as a child, he was taken from his parents and sent to a boarding school in the East. But why did Herman Mankiewicz, coauthor of the screenplay, choose that particular word? He was at one time a confidant of Marion Davies, mistress of William Randolph Hearst; their relationship is fictionalized in the film. And she told him that "Rosebud" was Willie's pet name for . . . well, you know. Hearst was outraged when he saw the film, but how could he go public with his complaint?

Saddest Music in the World

Q. I saw *The Saddest Music in the World* recently, and was struck by how murky the print appeared. It was a considerable strain to watch. It distracted from my ability to absorb the considerable volume of visual information in this highly unusual movie. Did the copy you viewed appear similarly dark and muddy? I suppose the theater here may have underilluminated the print they had.
—Ken Neely, Pomona, California

A. As I wrote in my review, Guy Maddin's film "looks like a longlost classic from decades ago, grainy and sometimes faded; he shoots on 8mm film and video and blows it up to look like a memory from cinema's distant past." So the look was deliberate, but the print I saw had a unique beauty and its own kind of clarity. Many theater chains persist in showing films at less than the recommended light level, in the mistaken belief that they can prolong the life of their expensive bulbs; perhaps that was a factor in your experience. I've quoted experts who say turning down the power has no effect on the life of the bulb, but as Louie Armstrong said, "there are some folks that, if they don't know, you can't tell 'em."

Saved!

Q. In *Saved!*, Pastor Skip is not widowed, as you mention twice in your review. His wife is alive and well, doing missionary work overseas. That's what made his relationship with Mary's mother so tormenting for him. I'm surprised you missed that.
—Mike O'Donnell, Washington, D.C.

A. Sandy Stern, the producer of the film, indeed confirms that Pastor Skip is married but separated and his wife is on a Christian mission. But that was so glossed over that I and several other critics missed it. My puzzlement is: Why not make him single or a widower? Why make him a potential adulterer?

School of Rock

Q. Your *School of Rock* review needs a fix.
Hearing, at your age, can play tricks.
Joan Cusack, when drunk,
Mimicked not who you thunk.
Change "Grace Slick" into "Stevie Nicks."
—Mike Spearns, Newfoundland

A. Your correction is gladly received.
In a poem as immortal as "Trees."
I meant to say Nickster
But wrote down the Slickster,
So I'll waive all my usual fees.

Screen Ratios

Q. Why is it that films released before the 1950s are not available on DVD in widescreen? I realize this was the pre-Cinemascope era but weren't the old movie screens rectangular rather than square like the TV sets? I ask because the double-disc version of *Casablanca* (for which you provided a commentary) is only available in "standard" form. The Chaplin reissues are also full-screen only, not to mention *Gone With The Wind, The Wizard Of Oz, The Birth of a Nation* and countless others. Why would you participate in a DVD project that would not showcase your favorite film the way it was shown in the cinemas?
—Dennis Earl, Hamilton, Ontario

A. The widescreen format was not introduced until 1954. Before that, virtually *all* movies were shot in the ratio of 1:1.33. That's not square, and neither is your TV set, but four units wide for every three units high. The movies you mention are presented correctly on those videos. If they were widescreen, that would involve chopping off some of the top and bottom of the original picture—an experiment that was actually tried with *Gone With the Wind* and *Snow White and the Seven Dwarfs*, with disastrous results.

The Shape of Things

Q. I recently came across Neil LaBute's *The Shape of Things* on satellite and liked it so much I wondered why I had not seen it in theatrical release. I decided to see how it was critically received and I started with your column. I thought your favorable review was spot-on. And I was pleasantly surprised to learn that LaBute had also done *In the Company of Men* and *Your Friends and Neighbors*, both of which I thought had a lot to say. But when I looked at what some of the other critics (New York *Times,* San Francisco *Examiner,* and quite few others) had to say, I was shocked to discover that they all hated it; in fact, to a man, they seemed put off by *all* LaBute's works. Why?

—John F. Beck, Encino, California

A. As one of the few directors who makes films that are literate, intelligent, and willing to consider characters who are selfish, greedy, misogynistic, and cruel, LaBute comes like a jolt of bracing reality after the dreamy fairy tales of so many movies. He's the real thing. Not all critics agree.

Signs

Q. Concerning your Great Movies review of *Alien,* you refer to suspense as being the anticipation of terror. I agree but even great suspenseful movies like *Psycho, Wages of Fear,* or *Alien* have payoffs to their suspense. Not like Hitchcock's statement of the bomb never exploding. Has there ever been a full-length feature that continually builds suspense with no payoff or resolution?

—Tom Prosser, Sacramento, California

A. M. Night Shyamalan's *Signs* came pretty close. The payoff in many thrillers is perfunctory, and it's the buildup that keeps us on the edges of our seats. *Signs* is still building when it's over.

Q. Although I enjoyed M. Night Shyamalan's film *Signs,* I wondered how closely Night paid attention in science class when giving the aliens such a ridiculous weakness involving water. You'd think for such an advanced species, they could tell that our planet is 70 percent covered by the stuff.

—S. Legge, Ottawa, Ontario

A. The aliens are not the most impressive aspect of the movie, which I liked because of its creepy atmosphere, not its credibility. I did, however, think it was interesting to make them truly odd instead of dressing them in alien suits or *Star Trek* makeup. Although *Signs* did an astonishing $60 million in its first weekend, unprecedented for such a low-key picture, most of the Answer Man's mail about it was negative: "about as scary as a first grader in a mummy suit" (J. Romanchuk, Haiku, Hawaii); "The first view of the aliens looks like 8-mm film of *Big Foot!*" (Ron Goldstein, Porter Ranch, California). R. Luckey of Scottsdale, Arizona, liked the movie, especially the kids, but wonders why no one asked where the other end of the baby monitor unit was.

Smoking on the Screen

Q. What's your take on the call to crack down on smoking in the movies? Maybe we can treat product placement and unhealthy eating with the same seriousness, too?

—Paul West, West Hollywood, California

A. Call me un-PC, but I believe movies reflect human behavior and should not be sanitized to match some do-gooder agenda. A movie is good or bad on its own, and the less interference with a director trying to get his ideas onto the screen, the better.

Something's Gotta Give

Q. I am sending this message on behalf of my boss, R. Kenton Nelson. In your review of the film *Something's Gotta Give* you gave an artist credit for the paintings in the Hampton house. Unfortunately, Jack Vettriano is not the master of these paintings. R. Kenton Nelson is the master. A retraction would be a step in the right direction.

—Jeffrey Treloar, Pasadena, California

A. Retracted, with apologies.

South Carolina and Krispy Kreme

Q. Regarding the remark that *Whale Rider* did not play in South Carolina, that is false. It may not have played at the main venues like you mentioned, but it did play at many smaller theaters in the Spartanburg/Greenville area, which is near Rock Hill. I saw it with my family and thought it was quite remarkable. I agree that we do not get many of the smaller movies at our major theaters, but they are trying. Recently *Monster* and *Lost In Translation* were playing right alongside mainstream fluff like *My Baby's Daddy* and *Catch That Kid.*

But then you said "if Krispy Kreme refused to sell hot doughnuts in South Carolina, the populace would rise up in protest." Sure, there are many Krispy Kremes down here, one in every major city if I had to guess, but there's a dozen McDonald's and Steak 'n' Shakes in Chicago. Is there an explanation for the doughnut remark? Is this some bizarre implication that we're all doughnut-eating morons who don't appreciate quality films?

—Angela Bryant, Spartanburg, South Carolina

A. I did not in any way mean to insult the citizens of the great state of South Carolina, many of whom wrote to inform me that *Whale Rider* did play in their areas. I was simply suggesting that when movie distributors red-line some markets and never open certain kinds of films there, moviegoers should protest as vigorously as if denied their Krispies. As for Steak 'n' Shake—no, there is not a single outlet in the city of Chicago, but I have driven to the suburbs, and as far as Kankakee, Champaign-Urbana, Michigan City, and Benton Harbor to dine in the finest fast-food restaurant in the world. Their motto has a universal profundity: "In Sight, It Must Be Right!"

You know how on the *Letterman* show, Dave sometimes whispers in a guest's ear at the end of a segment? Whenever I'm on the show, he recites Steak 'n' Shake's "four ways to enjoy," which are, of course, Car, Table, Counter, and (their spelling) Takhomasak.

Spider-Man 2

Q. In your review of *Spider-Man 2* you

note: "One of the keys to the movie's success must be the contribution of novelist Michael Chabon to the screenplay; Chabon understands in his bones what comic books are, and why." While this may be true, and Chabon contributed a draft, the story that was used should be credited to Alfred Gough and Miles Millar. As they stated in an interview: "All the writers contributed something, but to us there were three versions of this movie: the one that we wrote, one that David Koepp wrote, and one that Michael Chabon wrote. If you look at all three, ours was absolutely the one they went with. Michael Chabon, whom we'd never met, called us and told us that he was outraged. He thought we deserved credit." I don't mean to write off Chabon's contributions to the story, but rather to raise notice for two writers who also elevated the superhero genre on TV, with *Smallville.*

—Adam Lenhardt, Slingerlands, New York

A. Screenplay credits often conceal and obscure where the real credit should go. Knowing Chabon's wonderful novel, I singled him out, and am pleased to have your input about Gough and Millar. *And in fact, I eventually learned Alvin Sargeant was responsible for the final screenplay.*

Star Ratings

Q. *Kill Bill Vol. 1*, four stars. *Kill Bill Vol. 2*, four stars. *All About Eve*, four stars. *Patton*, four stars. Are all four-star movies created equal?

—M. Reece, Jacksonville, Florida

A. The star rating system is the bane of my existence. Here's a message from Jason Eaken of Warrensburg, Missouri, who points out that I gave negative reviews to *Usual Suspects*, *Fight Club*, and *The Ladykillers*, but positive reviews to *The Fast and the Furious*, *Ghosts of Mars*, *Taking Lives*, and *High Crimes*. True, I did. But in the reviews I tried to explain how I felt; just counting stars makes me seem simpleminded. I have always awarded stars in a relative, not an absolute way, based to some degree on a movie's success in doing what it wants to do, and what the audience expects from it. Of course, if you think stars are limited, you ought to try working with thumbs.

Q. I have noticed lately that you have been getting softer on bad movies (compared to the general critical consensus and my tastes too). These movies include *Garfield: The Movie*, *The Stepford Wives*, and *The Day after Tomorrow*. I had the displeasure of seeing the former and the latter, and they did not deserve even one of your precious stars. Of course I could be imagining things, but it just seem like lately you have been more sympathetic to bad movies. If this is true, why?

—Daniel Mills, Alameda, California

A. In my reviews I tried to give specific reasons why I enjoyed those movies: Bill Murray's voice-over work as Garfield, the witty *Stepford* dialogue, and the remarkable special effects in *Day after Tomorrow*. All three movies were flawed. In the case of *Stepford*, I should probably have praised the dialogue but cranked down the stars. *Garfield* we can debate. I was absolutely right about *Day after Tomorrow*. I was also right to dislike *I, Robot*, despite the "general critical consensus," etc.

The Stepford Wives

Spoiler warning! This Q&A reveals plot points from The Stepford Wives.

Q. In all the reviews I've read of the new version of *The Stepford Wives*, I haven't read any that point out what appears to be a major problem with the plot. It is first established that the flesh-and-blood women of Stepford are replaced with mechanical robots. But near the end of the film, it seems when the women are rehumanized they were never robots at all, but merely had their brains electronically altered. Did I misunderstand something, or did I view this plot flaw correctly?

—Mike Wagner, Honolulu HI

A. Yes, either (a) they have been killed and replaced by robots, or (b) their human bodies are being controlled by the chip implanted in their brains. The movie seems to have it both ways. It has scenes establishing them as robots, and even shows a robot body

that has been prepared to replace Kidman, but then at the end the wives are miraculously themselves again. This is inconsistent, to say the least.

Torque

Q. In your review of the movie *Torque* you refer to the chase scenes as having "the same level of reality as a Road Runner chase." This is most likely true, and much of the reason I'll avoid this movie. But I have one nit to pick. Then you say, "One of the bikes is built around a Rolls-Royce jet engine," as if this is patently absurd. Well, however absurd it may be, it's also quite true. Just ask Jay Leno, he owns one.

—David Smith, Scotts Valley, California

A. Wonder what kind of mileage he gets. According to Brian Ford of Kansas City, Missouri, the chase must have been from one gas station to another: "The most recent episode of the TV show *Monster Garage* featured a Toyota Celica which was transformed into a jet-propelled vehicle by adding, you guessed it, a Rolls-Royce Viper MK22 jet engine. Now, the average car gets maybe twenty miles of driving for each gallon of fuel, right? Well, according to *Monster Garage*, a jet engine on a Celica burns gallons and gallons of fuel for every mile it's driven."

Touching the Void

Q. In your review of the mountain-climbing movie *Touching the Void* you mentioned that Joe Simpson recovered from his horrific injuries and began to climb again, and you hoped he would not have the experience of Citizen Kane, who "is going to need more than one lesson . . . and is going to get more than one lesson." Simpson, in fact, did require further lessons. Subsequently, while climbing in the Dru, his ledge literally disintegrated beneath him, leaving him dangling in the void again with but shreds of gear. And a fall in the Himalayas left him again severely injured and needing rescue. Although his adventures after "touching the void" never quite reached the same level of desperation, his life has been in danger many times, as he recounts in his book *This Game of Ghosts*. It is, however, a testament to the enduring spirit that lives in nearly all mountaineers that Simpson refused to let his experiences cow him off the vertical plane.

—Joe Lindsey, Boulder, Colorado

A. I have never seen a more horrifying experience on film than what his character undergoes in *Touching the Void*. He must be equipped with parts that, in my case, are still on order.

Trailers

Q. When I saw the original *Stepford Wives*, I found the ending disturbing and shocking (in a good way). I recently saw a preview for the remake, and it literally tells the entire story, ending included. Why would the studio want to rob audiences of that moment of realization? It really made me mad. How can we stop this sort of ad?

—Eric Olsen, Pompton Lakes, New Jersey

A. You can't. The AM has explained this before: The marketing people, whose interest in a movie is focused entirely on selling it, have the same philosophy as salespeople in grocery stores who offer you a piece of cheese on a toothpick. After you have sampled it, you know everything about the cheese except what it would be like to eat the whole thing. Same with trailers that summarize the whole movie.

Tupac Resurrected

Q. A correction to your review of *Tupac Resurrection*. Tupac was not only accused of rape, he was convicted of sexual assault. Moreover, he was convicted in one of the most liberal jurisdictions of the country, New York City, and he had some of the best lawyers money could buy. His conviction was on appeal when he was murdered.

—Patrick T. Murphy, Cook County Public Guardian, Chicago, Illinios

A. Correction noted.

Violence and Sex

Q. A recent news item reports: "Violence, sex, and profanity in movies increased significantly between 1992 and 2003, while ratings became more lenient, according to a new Harvard study." They seem to be examining two related phenomena (lax ratings and graphic content). I see two possible scenarios, the first being that movies are indeed increasing in graphic quality and quantity. The second scenario is that movie content has not changed, relatively, but instead films are not being rated appropriately (i.e., what was appropriate for R is now okay for PG-13). I guess I'm being wary of this study's possible politics and underlying agenda. Do you really feel that films are becoming more violent, or do you see the increase in violence as a misperception based on a crappy rating system?

—Shawne Malik, St. John's, Newfoundland

A. There is less "real" violence (as opposed to CGI fantasy violence) in movies today than in the 1970s—and a lot less sex and nudity. At the same time, I have the subjective sense that the ratings system has become more permissive or porous. The studios put enormous pressure on the MPAA to give them ratings that maximize their audiences. The NC-17 rating was the first victim, and now the studios are avoiding the R. I agree with the Harvard study that there is now more violence and profanity in PG-13 movies. A long-term result of this trend may be a loss of serious content for adults, as more movies position themselves for the desirable teenage boy market.

Whale Rider

Q. I want to support you in your crusade against the MPAA rating of *Whale Rider*. Normally my husband and I are outrageously cautious about our childrens' viewing habits, but based on your review, I allowed my six-year-old daughter (a really, really, really smart girl) to see this movie without regard to the rating. She is mesmerized and obsessed by this movie, as are all of us. She goes around singing "Oooh, Whale, Ooh," like her new hero Pai (frankly this part I am not so grateful for after about three hours of hearing Pai call the whales). Thank you for your commentary on this lovely film. I am giving it to my mother, an artist, musician, smart gal, and cool chick herself, for Christmas.

—Barbara Zuniga, M.D., Munster, Indiana

A. I am still amazed that the MPAA prevented the distributors from using a quote from my review saying this was a film for the entire family—because a PG-13 rating, you see, means to the MPAA that it is not. The rating for *Whale Rider* flies in the face of common sense. It is one of the most beloved films of recent years—for, dare I say, the entire family.

Q. I loved *Whale Rider* too, but you said in your Top 10 list that it was "this year's *Bend It Like Beckham*," which is funny, because I thought this year's *Bend It Like Beckham* was *Bend It Like Beckham*.

—Miles Blanton, Carrboro, North Carolina

A. Egad! I saw *Bend It like Beckham* at the 2002 Toronto Film Festival and had it in my mind as a 2002 film, but you're quite right. *Whale Rider* is the better of these two splendid films, however.

Q. Basically I agree with you that Charlize Theron was this year's and perhaps any year's best actress, but I have to say that having been a teacher for over sixteen years and knowing the emotions of children really well, Keisha Castle-Hughes delivers an equally emotional and outstanding performance in *Whale Rider*. The scene of her crying at the award night at her school was amazing. I still get a lump in my throat when I remember it.

—Leslie Luke, Thousand Oaks, California

A. By nominating her, the Academy had one of its finest hours. And yet here is a message from Katelyn Husted of Rock Hill, South Carolina, who says *Whale Rider* did not play anywhere in her state, and her parents aren't crazy about driving her to North Carolina to see it. If Krispy Kreme refused to sell hot doughnuts in South Carolina, the populace would rise up in protest. What does it mean when theater chains write off entire states as not ready to see the best family film of the year? If I were an exhibitor and only booked lowbrow Hollywood formula pictures, I'd be ashamed to look at myself in the mirror.

Where to Sit

Q. Why do you usually sit in the back of a movie theater? Once, while sitting, as is my wont, in the first row, I heard Susan Sontag, just behind me, expounding her theory that the people who sit in the first two rows are different from other moviegoers. We like to be immersed in the film, to let ourselves float up and into the screen, as it were, and let the story unfold around us. As your reviews demonstrate, you have front-row sensitivity. Why do you sit in the back?

—Brian M. Schwartz, New York, New York

A. Because the front is too damned close to the screen. You can immerse yourself in the movie without immersing yourself in the picture. Some front rows are so close the film is actually distorted. My Chicago colleagues Michael Wilmington, Jonathan Rosenbaum, and Peter Sobcinski disagree, and sit in the Sontag seats, but in a theater I sit twice as far back as the screen is wide, because of a theory that optically that's the correct distance.

Ebert's Little Movie Glossary

These are contributions to my glossary project. Hundreds of entries were collected in *Ebert's Bigger Little Movie Glossary,* published in 1999. Contributions are always welcome.

* * *

Backlit Horizon Phenomenon. The ever-present white light whose source is always just beyond the horizon line where no practical light source would be. This phenomenon allows dramatic entrances to secluded locales. Compare the appearance of the Ring Wraiths on the road in *The Fellowship of the Ring* and the appearance of the Nigerian soldiers in the jungle in *Tears of the Sun.*

—Patrick Lemieux, Toronto, Ontario

Big Slow Spaceship Shot Syndrome. Since the first *Star Wars,* every science fiction movie set in space has had at least one shot of an enormous spaceship appearing from out of frame and passing slowly past the camera. It is usually seen from beneath. Low bass rumbles are used on the sound track.

—Geraldo Valero Perez Vargas, Mexico City, Mexico

Bloody Steak Rule. When characters order steaks, they always ask for "rare," which people hardly ever order in restaurants, instead of "medium rare" or "medium," which is what most people order. This is because the kind of character who orders a steak in a movie would sound like a wimp asking for "medium."

—Jer Moran, Houston, Texas

Ca-Chuck! Rule. All movie guns will need to be "cocked" before firing, and the sound made is always the "ca-chuck" sound made by a pump shotgun. Bad guys will never cock their guns until the last instant before firing at the good guys, and the ca-chuck sound will always alert the good guys in time for them to duck. In some movies, such as *Runaway,* this rule even applies to revolvers.

—Tom Helderman, Grand Rapids, Michigan

The Cigarette Fling. Whenever a character is smoking a cigarette just prior to doing something important, he always flicks the cigarette aside just before setting forth. This is true especially before a car pursuit.

—Patrick Carroll, Honolulu, Hawaii

Curtain Going Up! Whenever a character does something secret or embarrassing behind a curtain during a performance, the curtains inevitably open, revealing the person caught in the act. Recent examples include *Love Actually* and *Moulin Rouge.*

—Kevin Chen, San Mateo, California

Dispose of Carefully. Despite the fact that they can be reloaded, the value of any revolver in a Civil War–era movie decreases steadily with each of the six shots that it fires. By the time the gun is empty, it has become worthless, invariably causing its owner to either (1) throw it aside or (2) chuck it at the enemy.

—Samuel Anderson, Moorhead, Minnesota

Dorm Hall Pay Phone Exception. In any movie featuring a school dormitory, there is invariably a character talking on a pay phone in the hallway. Only in movies do students not have cell phones and dorm rooms do not have their own telephones.

—Matt Sterzinger, Bolingbrook, Illinois

Ghostly Communication Rule. Ghosts come in two types in movies. If it's a comedy or drama, the ghost is chatty, easygoing, and/or likes to crack jokes (*Ghost Dad, The Sixth Man, Always*) and appears as a normal human. If it's a horror or thriller, the ghost has a dark purpose, doesn't talk. Although it can open and close doors and walk through walls, the ghost prefers to leave cryptic messages written in blood or vapor, or carved in the wall (see *Gothika, What Lies Beneath, The Haunting*).

—Sebastian Tabany, Buenos Aires, Argentina

Ironically Menacing Solo Rule. To seem more deranged and sinister, a movie villain will break into an a cappella rendition of a seemingly innocent and cheerful song. One of the first and most notorious examples is Alex the Droog's "Singin' in the Rain" from *A Clockwork Orange*. Other, less effective versions include "Buffalo Gals" from *Turbulence* and "I'm a Little Teapot" from Stephen King's *Storm of the Century*.

—Trent Daniel, Hoover, Alabama

The Medicine Cabinet Shocker. In all thrillers the impending victim will be retrieving something from a mirrored medicine cabinet only to reveal, upon closing the cabinet, the killer standing where there was no killer before. This is always accompanied by an orchestra hit.

—Eric Voisard, Toronto, Ontario

More Time to Die. When an unimportant stooge of the bad guy is shot, he will fall over and die immediately. But when the main villain is shot, he will remain standing, slowly looking down at the growing bloodstain on his chest (see *Pirates of the Caribbean*).

—Nathan Alberson, Bloomington, Indiana

Name Your Poison. If someone in a comedy or cartoon is served a drink they believe to be drugged or poisoned, they will surreptitiously pour it into a conveniently nearby potted plant—which will immediately wither and die.

—Michael Schlesinger, Los Angeles, California

Rhythm and 'Burbs. Well-to-do older white characters are often seen poorly dancing and poorly singing gangsta rap or modern r&b, always for laughs. See *Head of State, Scary Movie 2, Malibu's Most Wanted, Bulworth, Austin Powers 3, The Wedding Singer, The Super*, etc.

—Patrick Keys, Houston, Texas

Senseless Self-Destructing Gizmos. Device used in films (especially James Bond) with a numerical speed/radioactivity/etc. odometer/radioactimeter that inexplicably includes a range (always marked in red) at which the device must never be used or otherwise it will become unstable and explode or kill the user. Raises the question, why build the device with such lethal capacity at all? (compare radioactivity pool in *Dr. No*, astronaut training chamber in *Moonraker*).

—Gerardo Valero Perez Vargas, Mexico City, Mexico

The Silent Battlefield. Battles are noisy and crowded until the hero's best friend gets it,

whereupon the enemy have the decency to move off to another part of the field so he can croak out his last lines in peace. See *Lord of the Rings, The Last Samurai*, countless other war movies.

—Tom McKinlay, Brussels, Belgium

Skills by Osmosis. When a character performs a handy skill that he or she wouldn't otherwise be expected to know (picking a lock, hot-wiring a car, speaking a foreign language), the unexpected knowledge is explained by a previous relationship, as in, "I used to date a locksmith," or "My uncle served time for heisting cars," or "My nanny spoke Swahili."

—Mike Suchcicki, Pensacola, Florida

Smart Mouth, Dumb Timing Reflex. The character has it in for a particular person and runs the gamut of slanderous names about that person. Then the camera pulls back to show that the target is looking over the character's shoulder. The character ends his diatribe by continuing, in the same exact tone of voice, "And (s)he's right behind me, isn't (s)he?"See *Around the World in 80 Days*.

—Steve Bailey, Jacksonville Beach, Florida

Solo Cardboard Box Rule. When movie characters are fired or quit their jobs, they must walk out with all of their belongings stuffed into a single cardboard box, regardless of how long they've been working there. See Kevin Kline in *The Emperor's Club*, Cuba Gooding Jr. in *The Fighting Temptations*.

—Alex MacDonell, Toronto, Ontario

Spinach Cinema. According to wordspy.com, apparently first used by Russell Evansen in the *Wisconsin State Journal* in 1996 ("movies that are supposed to be good for us but that we actually hate"). Andrew O'Hehir of Salon.com wrote of the Afghanistan film *Osama*, "If you haven't seen it because it sounded too much like spinach cinema, I'm here to tell you not to miss out."

—Josh Mauthe, Nashville, Tennessee

Third-Person Memory Phenomenon. In a science fiction film where a person's memories can be viewed on a video screen, the memories will not been shown from the person's unique point of view, but rather from the objective point of view of the movie camera, as if the person was experiencing life as a third person, out-of-body spectator (see John Woo's *Paycheck*).

—Andrew Brennan, Los Angeles, California

The Treacherous Purse. Anytime a female character has something of direct importance to the plot in her purse (gun, real ID card, pills), she will either put her purse down on the ground and leave it wide open so another character can look inside or she'll drop it and the crucial item will spill out. Seen in numerous *noir* films, *Sneakers, Nightmare on Elm Street III,* etc.

—Patrick Keys, Houston, Texas

The Walk. A band of hell-raisers falls into lockstep as their mission unites them with steely resolve. Their progression is shown in slo-mo as the sound track often features a martial snare-drum beat. Examples: *The Reservoir Dogs* on their way to work; The Earp Brothers, on their way to the OK Corral in *Tombstone;* the Irish newcomers on their way to the rumble at Four Corners in *Gangs of New York;* the stars of the Crazy Eight-eighty on their way to meet The Bride in *Kill Bill, Vol. 1.*

—Uriah Carr, Glendale, California

Whoops, Not Wrong Number! A menacing heavy-breather telephones his victim once, then twice. She responds, "Who is it?" but gets no answer. The third time she screams, "Stop calling this number!" into the phone, but this time of course it is a friend or loved one on the other end.

—Roger L. Plummer, Chicago, Illinois

You Hold It Like This. In a movie where a date takes place at a bowling alley or a driving range, the female character is almost always new to bowling or golf. The male character, rather than simply demonstrating the game by doing it himself, will always push his body against the woman's backside, reach around her and guide her arms, thus educating her. Somehow there is never a case where a man performs this procedure on another man.

—Luke Matheny, Chicago, Illinois

Reviews Appearing in All Editions of the *Movie Home Companion, Video Companion,* or *Movie Yearbook*

A

Abandon, 2002, PG-13, ★★½ — 2005
About a Boy, 2002, PG-13, ★★★½ — 2005
About Last Night . . . , 1986, R, ★★★★ — 1998
About Schmidt, 2002, R, ★★★½ — 2005
Above the Law, 1988, R, ★★★ — 1995
Above the Rim, 1994, R, ★★★ — 1995
Absence of Malice, 1981, PG, ★★★ — 1998
Absolute Power, 1997, R, ★★★½ — 1998
Accidental Tourist, The, 1988, PG, ★★★★ — 1998
Accompanist, The, 1994, PG, ★★★½ — 1998
Accused, The, 1988, R, ★★★ — 1998
Ace Ventura: Pet Detective, 1994, PG-13, ★ — 1998
Ace Ventura: When Nature Calls, 1995, PG-13, ★½ — 1998
Adam Sandler's Eight Crazy Nights, 2002, PG-13, ★★ — 2005
Adaptation, 2002, R, ★★★★ — 2005
Addams Family, The, 1991, PG-13, ★★ — 1997
Addams Family Values, 1993, PG-13, ★★★ — 1998
Addicted to Love, 1997, R, ★★ — 1998
Addiction, The, 1995, NO MPAA RATING, ★★½ — 1997
Adjuster, The, 1992, R, ★★★ — 1998
Adventures of Baron Munchausen, The, 1989, PG, ★★★ — 1998
Adventures of Ford Fairlane, The, 1990, R, ★ — 1992
Adventures of Huck Finn, The, 1993, PG, ★★★ — 1998
Adventures of Priscilla, Queen of the Desert, The, 1994, R, ★★½ — 1998
Adventures of Rocky & Bullwinkle, The, 2000, PG, ★★★ — 2003
Adventures of Sebastian Cole, The, 1999, R, ★★★ — 2002
Affair of Love, An, 2000, R, ★★★½ — 2003
Affair of the Necklace, The, 2001, R, ★★ — 2004
Affliction, 1999, R, ★★★★ — 2002
Afterglow, 1998, R, ★★★ — 2001

After Hours, 1985, R, ★★★★ — 1998
After Life, 1999, NO MPAA RATING, ★★★★ — 2002
After the Rehearsal, 1984, R, ★★★★ — 1998
Against All Odds, 1984, R, ★★★ — 1998
Against the Ropes, 2004, PG-13, ★★★ — 2005
Agent Cody Banks, 2003, R, ★★½ — 2005
Agent Cody Banks 2: Destination London, 2004, PG, ★★½ — 2005
Age of Innocence, The, 1993, PG, ★★★★ — 1998
Agnes Browne, 2000, R, ★★½ — 2003
Agnes of God, 1985, PG-13, ★ — 1989
Agronomist, The, 2004, NO MPAA RATING, ★★★½ — 2005
A.I. Artificial Intelligence, 2001, PG-13, ★★★ — 2004
Aileen: The Life and Death of a Serial Killer, 2004, NO MPAA RATING, ★★★½ — 2005
Aimee & Jaguar, 2000, NO MPAA RATING, ★★★ — 2003
Air Bud, 1997, PG, ★★★ — 2000
Air Bud 2: Golden Receiver, 1998, G, ★½ — 2001
Air Force One, 1997, R, ★★½ — 2000
Airplane!, 1980, PG, ★★★ — 1998
Airport, 1970, G, ★★ — 1996
Airport 1975, 1974, PG, ★★½ — 1996
Aladdin, 1992, G, ★★★ — 1998
Alamo, The, 2004, PG-13, ★★★½ — 2005
Alan Smithee Film Burn Hollywood Burn, An, 1998, R, no stars — 2001
Alaska, 1996, PG, ★★★ — 1999
Albino Alligator, 1997, R, ★★ — 2000
Alex & Emma, 2003, PG-13, ★½ — 2005
Alex in Wonderland, 1971, R, ★★★★ — 1998
Ali, 2001, R, ★★ — 2004
Alice, 1990, PG-13, ★★★ — 1998
Alice Doesn't Live Here Anymore, 1974, PG, ★★★★ — 1998
Alien3, 1992, R, ★½ — 1997
Alien Nation, 1988, R, ★★ — 1994
Alien Resurrection, 1997, R, ★½ — 2000
Aliens, 1986, R, ★★★½ — 1998
Alive, 1993, R, ★★½ — 1997

Note: The right-hand column is the year in which the review last appeared in *Roger Ebert's Movie Home Companion, Roger Ebert's Video Companion,* or *Roger Ebert's Movie Yearbook.*

Beyond Therapy, 1987, R, ★ 1988
Beyond the Valley of the Dolls, 1970,
NC-17, Stars N/A 1997
Bicentennial Man, 1999, PG, ★★ 2002
Big, 1988, PG, ★★★ 1998
Big Animal, The, 2004, No MPAA rating,
★★★ 2005
Big Bad Love, 2002, R, ★★ 2005
Big Bang, The, 1990, R, ★★★ 1995
Big Bounce, The, 2004, PG-13, ★★ 2005
Big Brawl, The, 1980, R, ★½ 1986
Big Business, 1988, PG, ★★ 1993
Big Chill, The, 1983, R, ★★½ 1998
Big Daddy, 1999, PG-13, ★½ 2002
Big Easy, The, 1987, R, ★★★★ 1998
Big Eden, 2001, PG-13, ★★ 2004
Big Fat Liar, 2002, PG, ★★★ 2005
Big Fish, 2003, PG-13, ★★½ 2005
Big Foot, 1971, PG,½ ★ 1990
Biggie & Tupac, 2002, R, ★★★½ 2005
Big Hit, The, 1998, R, ★ 2001
Big Kahuna, The, 2000, R, ★★★½ 2003
Big Lebowski, The, 1998, R, ★★★ 2001
Big Momma's House, 2000, PG-13,
★★ 2003
Big One, The, 1998, PG-13, ★★★ 2001
Big Red One, The, 1980, PG, ★★★ 1996
Big Squeeze, The, 1996, R, ★ 1999
Big Tease, The, 2000, R, ★★ 2003
Big Town, The, 1987, R, ★★★½ 1998
Big Trouble, 2002, PG-13, ★★½ 2005
Biker Boyz, 2003, PG-13, ★★ 2005
Bill & Ted's Bogus Journey, 1991, PG-13,
★★★ 1998
Billy Bathgate, 1991, R, ★★ 1993
Billy Elliot, 2000, R, ★★★ 2003
Billy Jack, 1971, PG, ★★½ 1993
Billy's Hollywood Screen Kiss, 1998, R,
★★ 2001
Bird, 1988, R, ★★★½ 1998
Birdcage, The, 1995, R, ★★★ 1999
Bird on a Wire, 1990, PG-13, ★★½ 1993
Birdy, 1985, R, ★★★★ 1998
Birthday Girl, 2002, R, ★★ 2005
Bitter Moon, 1994, R, ★★★ 1998
Black and White, 2000, R, ★★★ 2003
Black Cauldron, The, 1985, PG, ★★★½ 1987
Black Hawk Down, 2002, R, ★★★★ 2005
Black Marble, The, 1980, PG, ★★★½ 1998
Black Rain (Japan), 1990, NO MPAA
RATING, ★★★½ 1998

Black Rain (Michael Douglas), 1989, R,
★★ 1993
Black Robe, 1991, R, ★★½ 1994
Black Stallion, The, 1980, G, ★★★★ 1998
Black Stallion Returns, The, 1983, PG,
★★½ 1986
Black Widow, 1987, R, ★★½ 1991
Blade, 1998, R, ★★★ 2001
Blade Runner, 1982, R, ★★★ 1998
Blade Runner: The Director's Cut, 1992,
R, ★★★ 1997
Blade II, 2002, R, ★★★½ 2005
Blair Witch Project, The, 1999, R,
★★★★ 2002
Blame It on Rio, 1984, R, ★ 1987
Blast from the Past, 1999, PG-13, ★★★ 2002
Blaze, 1989, R, ★★★½ 1998
Blind Date, 1987, PG-13, ★★½ 1988
Blink, 1994, R, ★★★½ 1998
Bliss, 1997, R, ★★★½ 1998
Blood, Guts, Bullets and Octane, 1999,
NO MPAA RATING, ★★½ 2002
Blood and Wine, 1997, R, ★★★½ 1998
Blood Simple, 1985, R, ★★★★ 1998
Blood Simple: 2000 Director's Cut,
2000, R, ★★★★ 2003
Blood Work, 2002, R, ★★★½ 2005
Bloody Sunday, 2002, R, ★★★½ 2005
Blow, 2001, R, ★★½ 2004
Blown Away, 1994, R, ★★ 1996
Blow Out, 1981, R, ★★★★ 1998
Blue, 1994, R, ★★★½ 1998
Blue Angel, The, 2001, NO MPAA RATING,
★★★½ 2004
Blue Car, 2003, R, ★★★½ 2005
Blue Chips, 1994, PG-13, ★★★ 1998
Blue Collar, 1978, R, ★★★★ 1998
Blue Collar Comedy Tour: The Movie,
2003, PG-13, ★★★ 2005
Blue Crush, 2002, PG-13, ★★★ 2005
Blue Kite, The, 1994, NO MPAA RATING,
★★★★ 1998
Blue Lagoon, The, 1980, R,½ ★ 1991
Blues Brothers, The, 1980, R, ★★★ 1998
Blues Brothers 2000, 1998, PG-13, ★★ 2001
Blue Sky, 1994, PG-13, ★★★ 1998
Blue Steel, 1990, R, ★★★ 1998
Blue Streak, 1999, PG-13, ★★★ 2002
Blue Velvet, 1986, R, ★ 1998
Blume in Love, 1973, R, ★★★★ 1998
Blush, 1996, NO MPAA RATING, ★★½ 1999

Catch That Kid, 2004, PG, ★★★	2005	Chelsea Walls, 2002, R, ★★★	2005
Catfish in Black Bean Sauce, 2000, PG-13, ★½	2003	Cherish, 2002, R, ★★★	2005
Cat People, 1982, R, ★★★½	1998	Chicago, 2002, PG-13, ★★★½	2005
Cats and Dogs, 2001, PG, ★★★	2004	Chicago Cab, 1998, R, ★★★	2001
Cats Don't Dance, 1997, G, ★★★	2000	Chicken Run, 2000, G, ★★★½	2003
Cat's Eye, 1985, PG-13, ★★★	1986	Children of Heaven, 1999, PG, ★★★★	2002
Cat's Meow, 2002, PG-13, ★★★	2005	Children of the Revolution, 1997, R, ★★	2000
Caught, 1996, R, ★★★	1999	Child's Play, 1988, R, ★★★	1998
Caught Up, 1998, R, ★★	2001	Chill Factor, 1999, R, ★★	2002
Caveman, 1981, PG, ★½	1986	China Moon, 1994, R, ★★★½	1998
Caveman's Valentine, The, 2001, R, ★★★	2004	China Syndrome, The, 1979, PG, ★★★★	1998
Cecil B. Demented, 2000, R, ★½	2003	Chinatown, 1974, R, ★★★★	1998
Celebration, The, 1998, R, ★★★	2001	Chocolat, 1989, PG-13, ★★★★	1998
Celebrity, 1998, R, ★★½	2001	Chocolat, 2000, PG-13, ★★★	2003
Celestial Clockwork, 1996, NO MPAA RATING, ★★★	1999	Choose Me, 1984, R, ★★★½	1998
Cell, The, 2000, R, ★★★★	2003	Chopper, 2001, NO MPAA RATING, ★★★	2004
Celluloid Closet, The, 1995, NO MPAA RATING, ★★★½	1999	Chorus Line, A, 1985, PG-13, ★★★½	1998
Celtic Pride, 1996, PG-13, ★★	1999	Christiane F., 1981, R, ★★★½	1998
Cement Garden, The, 1994, NO MPAA RATING, ★★★	1998	Christine, 1983, R, ★★★	1998
Cemetery Club, The, 1992, PG-13, ★★★	1998	Christmas Story, A, 1983, PG, ★★★	1998
Center of the World, The, 2001, NO MPAA RATING, ★★★½	2004	Christopher Columbus: The Discovery, 1992, PG-13, ★	1994
Center Stage, 2000, PG-13, ★★★	2003	Chronicles of Riddick, The, 2004, PG-13, ★★	2005
Central Station, 1998, R, ★★★	2001	Chuck & Buck, 2000, R, ★★★	2003
Chain Reaction, 1996, PG-13, ★★½	1999	Chuck Berry Hail! Hail! Rock 'n' Roll, 1987, PG, ★★★★	1998
Chalk, 2000, NO MPAA RATING, ★★★	2003	Chungking Express, 1996, PG-13, ★★★	1999
Chamber, The, 1996, R, ★★	1999	Cider House Rules, The, 1999, PG-13, ★★	2002
Chances Are, 1989, PG, ★★★½	1998	Cinderella, 1950, G, ★★★	1997
Changing Lanes, 2002, R, ★★★★	2005	Cinemania, 2003, No MPAA rating, ★★★	2005
Chaplin, 1993, PG-13, ★★	1994	Cinema Paradiso, 1989, NO MPAA RATING, ★★★½	1998
Chapter Two, 1980, PG, ★★	1992	Cinema Paradiso: The New Version, 2002, R, ★★★½	2005
Character, 1998, R, ★★★½	2001	Circle, The, 2001, NO MPAA RATING, ★★★½	2004
Chariots of Fire, 1981, PG, ★★★★	1998	Circle of Friends, 1995, PG-13, ★★★½	1998
Charlie's Angels, 2000, PG-13, ½★	2003	Citizen Kane, 1941, NO MPAA RATING, ★★★★	1998
Charlie's Angels: Full Throttle, 2003, PG-13, ★★½	2005	Citizen Ruth, 1997, R, ★★★	2000
Charlotte Gray, 2002, PG-13, ★★	2005	City by the Sea, 2002, R, ★★★	2005
Charlotte Sometimes, 2003, NO MPAA RATING, ★★★½	2005	City Hall, 1996, R, ★★½	1999
Chase, The, 1994, PG-13, ★★½	1995	City Heat, 1984, PG, ½★	1991
Chasing Amy, 1997, R, ★★★½	1998	City of Angels, 1998, PG-13, ★★★	2001
Chasing Liberty, 2004, PG-13, ★★	2005	City of Ghosts, 2003, R, ★★★	2005
Chasing Papi, 2003, PG, ★★½	2005	City of God, 2003, R, ★★★★	2005
Chattahoochee, 1990, R, ★★½	1992	City of Hope, 1991, R, ★★★★	1998
Cheaper by the Dozen, 2003, PG, ★★★	2005	City of Industry, 1997, R, H½	2000
Chef in Love, A, 1997, PG-13, ★★★	2000		

D

G

Gabbeh, 1997, NO MPAA RATING, ★★★ 2000

Galaxy Quest, 1999, PG, ★★★ 2002

Gambler, The, 1974, R, ★★★★ 1998

Game, The, 1997, R, ★★★½ 2000

Gamera: Guardian of the Universe, 1997, NO MPAA RATING, ★★★ 2000

Games People Play: New York, 2004, NO MPAA RATING, ★★ 2005

Gandhi, 1982, PG, ★★★★ 1998

Gang Related, 1997, R, ★★★ 2000

Gangs of New York, 2002, R, ★★★½ 2005

Gangster No. 1, 2002, R, ★★★ 2005

Garage Days, 2003, R, ★★★ 2005

Garden of the Finzi-Continis, The, 1971, R, ★★★★ 1998

Garfield: The Movie, 2004, PG, ★★★ 2005

Gates of Heaven, 1978, NO MPAA RATING, ★★★★ 1998

Gattaca, 1997, PG-13, ★★★½ 2000

Gauntlet, The, 1977, R, ★★★ 1998

General, The, 1999, R, ★★★½ 2002

General's Daughter, The, 1999, R, ★★½ 2002

Genghis Blues, 1999, NO MPAA RATING, ★★★½ 2002

George of the Jungle, 1997, PG, ★★★ 1998

George Stevens: A Filmmaker's Journey, 1985, PG, ★★★½ 1996

George Washington, 2001, NO MPAA RATING, ★★★★ 2004

Georgia, 1996, R, ★★★½ 1999

Germinal, 1994, R, ★★★ 1998

Geronimo: An American Legend, 1993, PG-13, ★★★½ 1998

Gerry, 2003, R, ★★★ 2005

Getaway, The, 1994, R, ★ 1995

Get Bruce, 1999, R, ★★★ 2002

Get on the Bus, 1996, R, ★★★★ 1999

Get Real, 1999, R, ★★★ 2002

Getting Away with Murder, 1995, R, ★★ 1999

Getting Even with Dad, 1994, PG, ★★ 1995

Getting It Right, 1989, R, ★★★★ 1998

Getting to Know You, 2000, NO MPAA RATING, ★★★ 2003

Gettysburg, 1993, PG, ★★★ 1998

Ghost, 1990, PG-13, ★★½ 1998

Ghost and the Darkness, The, 1996, R, ½★ 1999

Ghostbusters, 1984, PG, ★★★½ 1998

Ghost Dog: The Way of the Samurai, 2000, R, ★★★ 2003

Ghost in the Shell, 1995, NO MPAA RATING, ★★★ 1999

Ghost Ship, 2002, R, ★★ 2005

Ghosts of Mars, 2001, R, ★★★ 2004

Ghosts of Mississippi, 1996, PG-13, ★★½ 1999

Ghosts of the Abyss, 2003, G, ★★★ 2005

Ghost Story, 1981, R, ★★★ 1989

Ghost World, 2001, R, ★★★★ 2004

Gift, The, 2001, R, ★★★ 2004

G.I. Jane, 1997, R, ★★★½ 2000

Ginger and Fred, 1986, PG-13, ★★ 1987

Gingerbread Man, The, 1998, R, ★★★ 2001

Girl, Interrupted, 2000, R, ★★½ 2003

Girlfight, 2000, R, ★★★½ 2003

Girl in a Swing, The, 1989, R, ★★½ 1994

Girl Next Door, The, 2004, R, ½★ 2005

Girl on the Bridge, The, 2000, R, ★★★½ 2003

Girls Can't Swim, 2002, NO MPAA RATING, ★★ 2005

Girl 6, 1995, R, ★★ 1999

Girls Town, 1996, R, ★★★ 1999

Girl with a Pearl Earring, 2003, PG-13, ★★★★ 2005

Give My Regards to Broad Street, 1984, PG, ★ 1986

Gladiator, 1992, R, ★★★ 1996

Gladiator, 2000, R, ★★ 2003

Glass House, The, 2001, PG-13, ★★ 2004

Gleaners and I, The, 2001, NO MPAA RATING, ★★★★ 2004

Glengarry Glen Ross, 1992, R, ★★★½ 1998

Glitter, 2001, PG-13, ★★ 2004

Gloomy Sunday, 2003, NO MPAA RATING, ★★★ 2005

Gloria, 1980, PG, ★★★ 1998

Glory, 1989, R, ★★★½ 1998

Go, 1999, R, ★★★ 2002

Go-Between, The, 1971, PG, ★★★½ 1998

Godfather, The, 1972, R, ★★★★ 1998

Godfather, The (reissue), 1997, R, ★★★★ 2000

Godfather, Part II, The, 1974, R, ★★★ 1998

Godfather, Part III, The, 1990, R, ★★★½ 1998

God Said "Ha!," 1999, PG-13, ★★★½ 2002

Gods and Generals, 2003, PG-13, ★½ 2005

Gods and Monsters, 1998, NO MPAA RATING, ★★★ 2001

Godsend, 2004, PG-13, ★★ 2005

Gods Must Be Crazy, The, 1984, PG, ★★★ 1998

Hideous Kinky, 1999, R, ★★★	2002
High Anxiety, 1978, PG, ★★½	1995
High Art, 1998, R, ★★★½	2001
High Crimes, 2002, PG-13, ★★★	2005
Higher Learning, 1995, R, ★★★	1998
High Fidelity, 2000, R, ★★★★	2003
High Hopes, 1989, NO MPAA RATING, ★★★★	1998
Highlander 2: The Quickening, 1991, R,½ ★	1993
High Road to China, 1983, PG, ★★	1987
High School High, 1996, PG-13, ★½	1999
High Season, 1988, R, ★★★	1998
Hilary and Jackie, 1999, R, ★★★½	2002
Hi-Lo Country, The, 1999, R, ★★	2002
Himalaya, 2001, NO MPAA RATING, ★★★	2004
History of the World-Part I, 1981, R, ★★	1995
Hitcher, The, 1985, R, no stars	1990
Hocus Pocus, 1993, PG, ★	1995
Hoffa, 1992, R, ★★★½	1998
Holes, 2003, PG, ★★★½	2005
Hollow Man, 2000, R, ★★	2003
Hollywood Ending, 2002, PG-13, ★★½	2005
Hollywood Homicide, 2003, PG-13, ★★★	2005
Hollywood Shuffle, 1987, R, ★★★	1998
Holy Man, 1998, PG, ★★	2001
Holy Smoke!, 2000, R, ★★½	2003
Homage, 1996, R, ★★½	1999
Home Alone, 1990, PG, ★★½	1998
Home Alone 2: Lost in New York, 1992, PG, ★★	1995
Home Alone 3, 1997, PG, ★★★	2000
Home and the World, The, 1986, NO MPAA RATING, ★★★	1987
Home Fries, 1998, PG-13, ★★★	2001
Home Movie, 2002, NO MPAA RATING, ★★★	2005
Home of Our Own, A, 1993, PG, ★★★	1998
Home of the Brave, 1986, NO MPAA RATING, ★★★½	1998
Home on the Range, 2004, PG, ★★½	2005
Homeward Bound: The Incredible Journey, 1993, G, ★★★	1998
Homeward Bound II: Lost in San Francisco, 1996, G, ★★	1999
Homicide, 1991, R, ★★★★	1998
Honey, 2003, PG-13, ★★½	2005
Honey, I Blew Up the Kid, 1992, PG, ★½	1994
Honey, I Shrunk the Kids, 1989, PG, ★★	1995
Honeymoon in Vegas, 1992, PG-13, ★★★½	1998

Honkytonk Man, 1982, PG, ★★★	1998
Hoodlum, 1997, R, ★★★	2000
Hook, 1991, PG, ★★	1994
Hoop Dreams, 1994, PG-13, ★★★★	1998
Hoosiers, 1987, PG, ★★★★	1998
Hope and Glory, 1987, PG-13, ★★★	1998
Hope Floats, 1998, PG-13, ★★	2001
Horns and Halos, 2003, NO MPAA RATING, ★★★	2005
Horseman on the Roof, The, 1995, R, ★★★	1999
Horse Whisperer, The, 1998, PG-13, ★★★	2001
Hot Chick, The, 2002, PG-13,½ ★	2005
Hotel, 2003, No MPAA rating, ★★★	2005
Hotel de Love, 1997, R, ★★½	2000
Hotel Terminus, 1988, NO MPAA RATING, ★★★	1996
Hot Shots! Part Deux, 1993, PG-13, ★★★	1998
Hot Spot, The, 1990, R, ★★★	1996
Hours, The, 2002, PG-13, ★★★½	2005
House Arrest, 1996, PG, ★	1999
Household Saints, 1993, R, ★★★★	1998
Housekeeper, The, 2003, NO MPAA RATING, ★★★	2005
Housekeeping, 1988, PG, ★★★★	1998
House of Fools, 2003, R, ★★★	2005
House of Games, 1987, R, ★★★★	1998
House of Mirth, The, 2000, PG, ★★★½	2003
House of Sand and Fog, 2003, R, ★★★★	2005
House of the Spirits, The, 1994, R, ★★	1995
House of Yes, The, 1997, R, ★★½	2000
House on Carroll Street, The, 1988, PG, ★★★	1998
House Party, 1990, R, ★★★	1998
House Party 2, 1991, R, ★★	1993
Housesitter, 1992, PG, ★★★	1998
Howards End, 1992, PG, ★★★★	1998
How I Killed My Father, 2002, NO MPAA RATING, ★★★½	2005
Howling, The, 1981, R, ★★	1992
Howling II, 1986, R, ★	1987
How Stella Got Her Groove Back, 1998, R, ★★½	2001
How to Lose a Guy in 10 Days, 2003, PG-13, ★½	2005
How to Make an American Quilt, 1995, PG-13, ★★	1997
Hudsucker Proxy, The, 1994, PG, ★★	1997
Hugh Hefner: Once Upon a Time, 1992, NO MPAA RATING, ★★★	1996
Hukkle, 2003, No MPAA rating, ★★★	2005

Hulk, 2003, PG-13, ★★★ — 2005
Human Nature, 2002, R, ★★★ — 2005
Human Resources, 2000, NO MPAA
RATING, ★★½ — 2003
Human Stain, The, 2003, R, ★★★½ — 2005
Human Traffic, 2000, R, ★★ — 2003
Hunchback of Notre Dame, The, 1995,
G, ★★★★ — 1999
Hunger, The, 1983, R, ★½ — 1991
Hunted, The, 2003, R, ★★★½ — 2005
Hunt for Red October, The, 1990, PG,
★★★½ — 1998
Hurlyburly, 1998, R, ★★★ — 2001
Hurricane, The, 2000, R, ★★★½ — 2003
Hurricane Streets, 1998, R, ★★ — 2001
Husbands and Wives, 1992, R, ★★★½ — 1998
Hush, 1998, PG-13, ★★ — 2001
Hype!, 1997, NO MPAA RATING, ★★★ — 1998

I

I, Madman, 1989, R, ★★★ — 1996
I Am Sam, 2002, PG-13, ★★ — 2005
I Capture the Castle, 2003, R, ★★★½ — 2005
Ice Age, 2002, PG, ★★★ — 2005
Iceman, 1984, PG, ★★★★ — 1998
Ice Storm, The, 1997, R, ★★★★ — 2000
Ideal Husband, An, 1999, PG-13, ★★★ — 2002
Identity, 2003, R, ★★★ — 2005
Idle Hands, 1999, R, ★★½ — 2002
Idolmaker, The, 1980, PG, ★★★ — 1998
I Dreamed of Africa, 2000, PG-13, ★★ — 2003
If Looks Could Kill, 1991, PG-13, ★★★ — 1995
If Lucy Fell, 1996, R, ★ — 1999
Igby Goes Down, 2002, R, ★★★½ — 2005
I Know What You Did Last Summer,
1997, R, ★ — 2000
I Like It Like That, 1994, R, ★★★ — 1998
Il Ladro di Bambini, 1993, NO MPAA
RATING, ★★★★ — 1998
I'll Be Home for Christmas, 1998, PG, ★ — 2001
I'll Do Anything, 1994, PG-13, ★★★ — 1998
I Love You to Death, 1990, R, ★★★ — 1998
Imaginary Crimes, 1994, PG, ★★★½ — 1998
Imagine: John Lennon, 1988, R, ★★★ — 1997
I'm Going Home, 2002, NO MPAA
RATING, ★★★ — 2005
Immediate Family, 1989, PG-13, ★★ — 1992
Immortal Beloved, 1995, R, ★★★½ — 1998
I'm Not Rappaport, 1997, PG-13, ★★½ — 1998
I'm Not Scared, 2004, R, ★★★½ — 2005
Importance of Being Earnest, The, 2002,
PG, ★★★ — 2005

Imposters, The, 1998, R, ★★ — 2001
Impromptu, 1991, PG-13, ★★½ — 1994
Impulse, 1990, R, ★★★ — 1998
In America, 2003, PG-13, ★★★★ — 2005
In and Out, 1997, PG-13, ★★★ — 2000
In Country, 1989, R, ★★★ — 1998
Incredible Shrinking Woman, The, 1981,
PG, ★★½ — 1991
Incredibly True Adventure of Two Girls
in Love, The, 1995, R, ★★★ — 1998
Indecent Proposal, 1993, R, ★★★ — 1998
Independence Day, 1996, PG-13, ★★½ — 1999
Indiana Jones and the Last Crusade,
1989, PG-13, ★★★½ — 1998
Indiana Jones and the Temple of Doom,
1984, PG, ★★★★ — 1998
Indian in the Cupboard, 1995, PG, ★★ — 1997
Indian Runner, The, 1991, R, ★★★ — 1996
Indian Summer, 1993, PG-13, ★★★ — 1998
Indochine, 1993, PG-13, ★★½ — 1994
In Dreams, 1999, R, ★½ — 2002
I Never Promised You a Rose Garden,
1977, R, ★★★ — 1996
I Never Sang for My Father, 1971, PG,
★★★★ — 1998
Infinity, 1996, PG, ★★★ — 1999
Infra-Man, 1976, PG, ★★½ — 1996
Inkwell, The, 1994, R, ★★★ — 1995
In-Laws, The, 2003, PG-13, ★★ — 2005
In Love and War, 1997, PG-13, ★★ — 2000
Inner Circle, The, 1992, PG-13, ★★★ — 1996
Innerspace, 1987, PG, ★★★ — 1996
Innocence, 2001, NO MPAA RATING,
★★★★ — 2004
Innocent, The, 1995, R, ★★★ — 1998
Innocent Blood, 1992, R, ★★ — 1994
Innocent Man, An, 1989, R, ★½ — 1993
In Praise of Love, 2002, NO MPAA
RATING, ★ — 2005
Inside/Out, 1999, NO MPAA RATING,
★★½ — 2002
Insider, The, 1999, R, ★★★½ — 2002
Insignificance, 1985, R, ★★★ — 1996
Insomnia, 1998, NO MPAA RATING,
★★★½ — 2001
Insomnia, 2002, R, ★★★½ — 2005
Inspector Gadget, 1999, PG, ★½ — 2002
Instinct, 1999, R, ★½ — 2002
Intacto, 2003, R, ★★½ — 2005
Interiors, 1978, PG, ★★★★ — 1998
Intermission, 2004, R, ★★★½ — 2005

K

Moon Over Parador, 1988, PG-13, ★★	1993
Moonstruck, 1987, PG, ★★★★	1998
Morning After, The, 1986, R, ★★★	1996
Mortal Thoughts, 1991, R, ★★★	1998
Moscow on the Hudson, 1984, R, ★★★★	1998
Mosquito Coast, The, 1986, PG, ★★	1993
Motel Hell, 1980, R, ★★★	1996
Mother, 1997, PG-13, ★★★½	1998
Mother, The, 2004, R, ★★★½	2005
Mother and the Whore, The, 1999, NO MPAA RATING, ★★★★	2002
Mother Night, 1996, R, ★★½	1999
Mother's Day, 1980, R, no stars	1991
Mothman Prophecies, The, 2002, PG-13, ★★	2005
Moulin Rouge, 2001, PG-13, ★★★½	2004
Mountains of the Moon, 1990, R, ★★★½	1998
Mouse Hunt, 1997, PG, ★★	2000
Movern Callar, 2002, NO MPAA RATING, ★★★½	2005
Mr. and Mrs. Bridge, 1991, PG-13, ★★★★	1998
Mr. Baseball, 1992, PG-13, ★★★	1998
Mr. Death: The Rise and Fall of Fred A. Leuchter Jr., 2000, PG-13, ★★★★	2003
Mr. Deeds, 2002, PG-13, ★½	2005
Mr. Destiny, 1990, PG-13, ★★	1992
Mr. Holland's Opus, 1996, PG, ★★★½	1999
Mr. Jealousy, 1998, R, ★★½	2001
Mr. Jones, 1993, R, ★★★	1998
Mr. Magoo, 1997, PG, ½★	2000
Mr. Mom, 1983, PG, ★★	1987
Mr. Nice Guy, 1998, PG-13, ★★★	2001
Mr. Saturday Night, 1992, R, ★★★	1995
Mrs. Brown, 1997, PG, ★★★½	2000
Mrs. Dalloway, 1998, PG-13, ★★★½	2001
Mrs. Doubtfire, 1993, PG-13, ★★½	1998
Mrs. Parker and the Vicious Circle, 1994, R, ★★★½	1998
Mrs. Winterbourne, 1996, PG-13, ★★½	1999
Mr. Wonderful, 1993, PG-13, ★½	1995
Much Ado About Nothing, 1993, PG-13, ★★★	1998
Mudge Boy, The, 2004, R, ★★★	2005
Mulan, 1998, G, ★★★½	2001
Mulholland Dr. , 2001, R, ★★★★	2004
Mulholland Falls, 1996, R, ★★★½	1999
Multiplicity, 1996, PG-13, ★★½	1999
Mumford, 1999, R, ★★★½	2002
Mummy, The, 1999, PG-13, ★★★	2002
Mummy Returns, The, 2001, PG-13, ★★	2004
Muppet Christmas Carol, The, 1992, G, ★★★	1998
Muppet Movie, The, 1979, G, ★★★½	1998
Muppets from Space, 1999, G, ★★	2002
Muppets Take Manhattan, The, 1984, G, ★★★	1998
Muppet Treasure Island, 1996, G, ★★½	1999
Murder at 1600, 1997, R, ★★½	1998
Murder by Numbers, 2002, R, ★★★	2005
Murder in the First, 1995, R, ★★	1996
Murder on the Orient Express, 1974, PG, ★★★	1998
Muriel's Wedding, 1995, R, ★★★½	1998
Murphy's Romance, 1985, PG-13, ★★★	1998
Muse, The, 1999, PG-13, ★★★	2002
Music Box, 1990, PG-13, ★★	1993
Music Lovers, The, 1971, R, ★★	1993
Music of Chance, The, 1993, NO MPAA RATING, ★★★	1998
Music of the Heart, 1999, PG, ★★★	2002
Musketeer, The, 2001, PG-13, ★★½	2004
My Architect: A Son's Journey, 2004, NO MPAA RATING, ★★★½	2005
My Beautiful Laundrette, 1986, R, ★★★	1998
My Best Fiend, 2000, NO MPAA RATING, ★★★	2003
My Best Friend's Wedding, 1997, PG-13, ★★★	1998
My Big Fat Greek Wedding, 2002, PG, ★★★	2005
My Bodyguard, 1980, PG, ★★★½	1998
My Brilliant Career, 1980, NO MPAA RATING, ★★★½	1998
My Cousin Vinny, 1992, R, ★★½	1998
My Dinner with André, 1981, NO MPAA RATING, ★★★★	1998
My Dog Skip, 2000, PG, ★★★	2003
My Fair Lady, 1964, G, ★★★★	1997
My Family, 1995, R, ★★★★	1998
My Father's Glory, 1991, G, ★★★★	1998
My Father the Hero, 1994, PG, ★★	1995
My Favorite Martian, 1999, PG, ★★	2002
My Favorite Season, 1995, NO MPAA RATING, ★★★	1999
My Favorite Year, 1982, PG, ★★★½	1998
My Fellow Americans, 1996, PG-13, ★★½	1999
My First Mister, 2001, R, ★★★	2004
My Giant, 1998, PG, ★★	2001
My Girl, 1991, PG, ★★★½	1998

My Girl 2, 1994, PG, ★★ — 1995
My Heroes Have Always Been
   Cowboys, 1991, PG, ★★ — 1992
My Left Foot, 1989, R, ★★★★ — 1998
My Life, 1993, PG-13, ★★½ — 1995
My Life So Far, 1999, PG-13, ★★★ — 2002
My Life Without Me, 2003, R, ★★½ — 2005
My Mother's Castle, 1991, PG, ★★★★ — 1998
My Name Is Joe, 1999, R, ★★★½ — 2002
My Own Private Idaho, 1991, R, ★★★½ — 1998
My Son the Fanatic, 1999, R, ★★★½ — 2002
My Stepmother Is an Alien, 1988, PG-13,
   ★★ — 1993
Mystery, Alaska, 1999, R, ★★½ — 2002
Mystery Men, 1999, PG-13, ★★ — 2002
Mystery Science Theater 3000: The
   Movie, 1996, PG-13, ★★★ — 1999
Mystery Train, 1990, R, ★★★½ — 1998
Mystic Masseur, The, 2002, PG, ★★★ — 2005
Mystic Pizza, 1988, R, ★★★½ — 1998
Mystic River, 2003, R, ★★★★ — 2005
Myth of Fingerprints, The, 1997, R, ★½ — 2000
My Tutor, 1983, R, ★★★ — 1986
My Wife Is an Actress, 2002, R, ★★½ — 2005

N

Nadine, 1987, PG, ★★½ — 1993
Naked, 1994, NO MPAA RATING, ★★★★ — 1998
Naked Gun, The, 1988, PG-13, ★★★½ — 1998
Naked Gun 2½: The Smell of Fear, The,
   1991, PG-13, ★★★ — 1998
Naked Gun 33⅓: The Final Insult, 1994,
   PG-13, ★★★ — 1998
Naked in New York, 1994, R, ★★★ — 1998
Naked Lunch, 1992, R, ★★½ — 1994
Name of the Rose, The, 1986, R, ★★½ — 1995
Napoleon Dynamite, 2004, PG, ★½ — 2005
Naqoyqatsi, 2002, PG, ★★★ — 2005
Narc, 2003, R, ★★★ — 2005
Narrow Margin, 1990, R, ★½ — 1992
Nashville, 1975, R, ★★★★ — 1998
Nasty Girl, The, 1991, PG-13, ★★½ — 1993
National Lampoon's Animal House,
   1978, R, ★★★★ — 1998
National Lampoon's Christmas
   Vacation, 1989, PG-13, ★★ — 1995
National Lampoon's Loaded Weapon
   I, 1993, PG-13, ★ — 1994
National Lampoon's Van Wilder, 2002,
   R, ★ — 2005
Natural, The, 1984, PG, ★★ — 1995
Natural Born Killers, 1994, R, ★★★★ — 1998

Navy Seals, 1990, R, H½ — 1992
Necessary Roughness, 1991, PG-13, ★★★ — 1996
Needful Things, 1993, R, H½ — 1995
Negotiator, The, 1998, R, ★★★½ — 2001
Neighbors, 1981, R, ★★★ — 1996
Nell, 1994, PG-13, ★★★ — 1998
Nelly and Monsieur Arnaud, 1996, NO
   MPAA RATING, ★★★½ — 1999
Nenette et Boni, 1997, NO MPAA RATING,
   ★★★ — 2000
Net, The, 1995, PG-13, ★★★ — 1998
Network, 1976, R, ★★★★ — 1998
Never Again, 2002, R, ★★ — 2005
Never Been Kissed, 1999, PG-13, ★★★ — 2002
Never Die Alone, 2004, R, ★★★½ — 2005
NeverEnding Story, The, 1984, PG, ★★★ — 1998
Never Say Never Again, 1983, PG, ★★★½ — 1998
New Age, The, 1994, R, ★★★½ — 1998
New Guy, The, 2002, PG-13, ★★ — 2005
New Jack City, 1991, R, ★★★½ — 1998
New Jersey Drive, 1995, R, ★★★ — 1998
Newsies, 1992, PG, ★½ — 1993
Newton Boys, The, 1998, PG-13, ★★ — 2001
New York, New York, 1977, PG, ★★★ — 1998
New York Minute, 2004, PG, ★½ — 2005
New York Stories, 1989, pg — 1998
Next Best Thing, The, 2000, PG-13, ★ — 2003
Niagara, Niagara, 1998, R, ★★★ — 2001
Nicholas Nickleby, 2003, PG, ★★★½ — 2005
Nick and Jane, 1997, R, ½★ — 2000
Nico and Dani, 2001, NO MPAA RATING,
   ★★★ — 2004
Nico Icon, 1996, NO MPAA RATING, ★★★ — 1999
Night and the City, 1992, R, ★★ — 1994
Night at the Roxbury, A, 1998, PG-13, ★ — 2001
Night Falls on Manhattan, 1997, R, ★★★ — 2000
Nightmare on Elm Street 3: Dream
   Warriors, 1987, R, ★½ — 1990
Night of the Living Dead, 1990, R, ★ — 1992
Night on Earth, 1992, R, ★★★ — 1998
Nightwatch, 1998, R, ★★ — 2001
Nil by Mouth, 1998, R, ★★★½ — 2001
Nina Takes a Lover, 1995, R, ★★ — 1997
9½ Weeks, 1985, R, ★★★½ — 1998
Nine Months, 1995, PG-13, ★★ — 1998
Nine Queens, 2002, R, ★★★ — 2005
1984, 1984, R, ★★★½ — 1998
Nine to Five, 1980, PG, ★★★ — 1998
Ninth Gate, The, 2000, R, ★★ — 2003
Nixon, 1995, R, ★★★★ — 1998
Nobody's Fool, 1986, PG-13, ★★ — 1991
Nobody's Fool, 1995, R, ★★★½ — 1998

No Escape, 1994, R, ★★ — 1995
No Good Deed, 2003, R, ★★★ — 2005
No Looking Back, 1998, R, ★★ — 2001
Nomads, 1985, R, H½ — 1987
No Man's Land, 1987, R, ★★★ — 1998
No Man's Land, 2001, R, ★★★½ — 2004
No Mercy, 1986, R, ★★★ — 1996
Normal Life, 1996, R, ★★★½ — 1999
Norma Rae, 1979, PG, ★★★ — 1998
North, 1994, PG, no stars — 1997
North Dallas Forty, 1979, R, ★★★½ — 1998
Northfork, 2003, PG-13, ★★★★ — 2005
Nosferatu, 1979, R, ★★★★ — 1998
No Such Thing, 2002, R, ★ — 2005
Not Another Teen Movie, 2001, R, ★★ — 2004
Notebook, The, 2004, PG-13, ★★★½ — 2005
Nothing But a Man, 1964, NO MPAA RATING, ★★★½ — 1997
Nothing in Common, 1986, PG, ★★½ — 1988
Nothing to Lose, 1997, R, ★★ — 2000
Not One Less, 2000, G, ★★★ — 2003
Notting Hill, 1999, PG-13, ★★★ — 2002
Not Without My Daughter, 1990, PG-13, ★★★ — 1998
Novocaine, 2001, R, ★★★ — 2004
No Way Out, 1987, R, ★★★★ — 1998
Nowhere in Africa, 2003, NO MPAA RATING, ★★★★ — 2005
Nuns on the Run, 1990, PG-13, ★ — 1993
Nurse Betty, 2000, R, ★★★ — 2003
Nuts, 1987, R, ★★ — 1993
Nutty Professor, The, 1996, PG-13, ★★★ — 1999
Nutty Professor II: The Klumps, 2000, PG-13, ★★★ — 2003

O

O, 2001, R, ★★★ — 2004
Object of Beauty, The, 1991, R, ★★★½ — 1998
Object of My Affection, The, 1998, R, ★★ — 2001
O Brother, Where Art Thou?, 2000, PG-13, ★★½ — 2003
Ocean's Eleven, 2001, PG-13, ★★★ — 2004
October Sky, 1999, PG, ★★★½ — 2002
Odd Couple II, The, 1998, PG-13, ★½ — 2001
Off Beat, 1986, PG, ★★★½ — 1995
Officer and a Gentleman, An, 1982, R, ★★★★ — 1998
Office Space, 1999, R, ★★★ — 2002
Of Mice and Men, 1992, PG-13, ★★★½ — 1998
Oh, God!, 1977, PG, ★★★½ — 1998
Oh, God! Book II, 1980, PG, ★★ — 1995

Oh, God! You Devil, 1984, PG, ★★★½ — 1998
Old Gringo, 1989, R, ★★ — 1993
Old School, 2003, R, ★ — 2005
Oleanna, 1994, NO MPAA RATING, ★★ — 1997
Oliver & Co., 1988, G, ★★★ — 1998
Once Around, 1990, R, ★★★½ — 1998
Once in the Life, 2000, R, ★★ — 2003
Once Upon a Forest, 1993, G, ★★½ — 1995
Once Upon a Time in America, 1984, R, ★-short version ★★★★-original version — 1998
Once Upon a Time in Mexico, 2003, R, ★★★ — 2005
Once Upon a Time in the Midlands, 2003, R, ★★★ — 2005
Once Upon a Time . . . When We Were Colored, 1996, PG, ★★★★ — 1999
Once Were Warriors, 1995, R, ★★★½ — 1998
One, The, 2001, PG-13, ★½ — 2004
One Day in September, 2001, R, ★★★ — 2004
187, 1997, R, ★★ — 2000
One False Move, 1992, R, ★★★★ — 1998
One Fine Day, 1996, PG, ★★ — 1999
One Flew Over the Cuckoo's Nest, 1975, R, ★★★ — 1998
One from the Heart, 1982, PG, ★★ — 1995
Onegin, 2000, NO MPAA RATING, ★★½ — 2003
One Good Cop, 1991, R, ★★ — 1994
One Hour Photo, 2002, R, ★★★½ — 2005
101 Dalmatians, 1961, G, ★★★ — 1998
102 Dalmations, 2000, G, ★★½ — 2003
187, 1997, R, ★★ — 2000
One Magic Christmas, 1985, G, ★★ — 1987
$1,000,000 Duck, 1971, G, ★ — 1987
One Night at McCool's, 2001, R, ★★½ — 2004
One Night Stand, 1997, R, ★★★ — 2000
1,000 Pieces of Gold, 1991, NO MPAA RATING, ★★★ — 1996
One Tough Cop, 1998, R, ★ — 2001
One-Trick Pony, 1980, R, ★★★½ — 1998
One True Thing, 1998, R, ★★★ — 2001
On Golden Pond, 1981, PG, ★★★★ — 1998
Onion Field, The, 1979, R, ★★★★ — 1998
On_Line, 2003, NO MPAA RATING, ★★ — 2005
Only When I Laugh, 1981, R, ★ — 1987
Only You, 1994, PG, ★★★½ — 1998
On the Edge, 1986, PG-13, ★★★½ — 1989
On the Line, 2001, PG, ★ — 2004
On the Right Track, 1981, PG, ★★½ — 1986
On the Road Again, 1980, PG, ★★★ — 1998
On the Ropes, 1999, NO MPAA RATING, ★★★★ — 2002

Post Coitum, Animal Triste, 1998, NO
 MPAA RATING, ★★★ — 2001
Postman, The (Il Postino), 1995, PG,
 ★★★½ — 1998
Postman, The, 1997, R, ★½ — 2000
Postman Always Rings Twice, The, 1981,
 R, ★★½ — 1991
Powder, 1995, PG-13, ★★ — 1997
Power, 1985, R, ★★½ — 1988
Power of One, The, 1992, PG-13, ★★½ — 1995
Powwow Highway, 1989, R, ★★★ — 1995
Practical Magic, 1998, PG-13, ★★ — 2001
Prancer, 1989, G, ★★★ — 1998
Preacher's Wife, The, 1996, PG, ★★★ — 1999
Predator, 1987, R, ★★★ — 1998
Predator 2, 1990, R, ★★ — 1993
Prefontaine, 1997, PG-13, ★★★ — 1998
Prelude to a Kiss, 1992, PG-13, ★★★ — 1998
Presumed Innocent, 1990, R, ★★★½ — 1998
Pretty Baby, 1978, R, ★★★ — 1998
Pretty in Pink, 1985, PG-13, ★★★ — 1998
Pretty Woman, 1990, R, ★★★½ — 1998
Price Above Rubies, A, 1998, R, ★★★ — 2001
Price of Glory, 2000, PG-13, ★★ — 2003
Price of Milk, The, 2001, PG-13, ★★ — 2004
Prick Up Your Ears, 1987, R, ★★★★ — 1998
Priest, 1995, R, ★ — 1997
Primal Fear, 1996, R, ★★★½ — 1999
Primary Colors, 1998, R, ★★★★ — 2001
Prime Cut, 1972, R, ★★★ — 1998
Prince & Me, The, 2004, PG, ★★½ — 2005
Prince of Egypt, The, 1998, PG, ★★★½ — 2001
Prince of the City, 1981, R, ★★★★ — 1998
Prince of Tides, The, 1991, R, ★★★½ — 1998
Princess and the Warrior, 2001, R,
 ★★★½ — 2004
Princess Bride, The, 1987, PG, ★★★½ — 1998
Princess Diaries, The, 2001, G, ★½ — 2004
Princess Mononoke, 1999, PG-13,
 ★★★★ — 2002
Prisoner of the Mountains, 1997, R,
 ★★★½ — 1998
Private Benjamin, 1980, R, ★★★ — 1998
Private Confessions, 1999, NO MPAA
 RATING, ★★★½ — 2002
Private Parts, 1997, R, ★★★ — 1998
Prizzi's Honor, 1985, R, ★★★★ — 1998
Professional, The, 1994, R, ★★½ — 1997
Program, The, 1993, R, ★★★ — 1998
Project X, 1987, PG, ★★★ — 1995
Proof, 1992, R, ★★★½ — 1998
Proof of Life, 2000, R, ★★½ — 2003

Proprietor, The, 1996, R, ½★ — 1999
Prospero's Books, 1991, R, ★★★ — 1998
Protocol, 1984, PG, ★★½ — 1987
Psycho, 1998, R, H½ — 2001
Psycho II, 1983, R, ★★½ — 1991
Psycho III, 1986, R, ★★★ — 1996
Public Eye, The, 1992, R, ★★★★ — 1998
Public Housing, 1997, NO MPAA RATING,
 ★★★★ — 2000
Pulp Fiction, 1994, R, ★★★★ — 1998
Pumping Iron II: The Women, 1985,
 NO MPAA RATING, ★★★½ — 1988
Pumpkin, 2002, R, ★★★½ — 2005
Punch-Drunk Love, 2002, R, ★★★½ — 2005
Punchline, 1988, R, ★★ — 1992
Punisher, The, 2004, R, ★★ — 2005
Pups, 1999, NO MPAA RATING, ★★★ — 2002
Purple Hearts, 1984, R, ½★ — 1987
Purple Noon, 1960, PG-13, ★★★ — 1999
Purple Rose of Cairo, The, 1985, PG,
 ★★★★ — 1998
Pushing Tin, 1999, R, ★★★ — 2002
Pyromaniac's Love Story, A, 1995, PG,
 ★★ — 1996

Q

Q, 1982, R, ★★½ — 1993
Q&A, 1990, R, ★★★½ — 1998
Queen Margot, 1994, R, ★★ — 1997
Queen of Hearts, 1989, NO MPAA
 RATING, ★★★½ — 1998
Queen of the Damned, 2002, R, ★★ — 2005
Queens Logic, 1991, R, ★★½ — 1994
Quest for Camelot, 1998, G, ★★ — 2001
Quest for Fire, 1982, R, ★★★½ — 1998
Quick and the Dead, The, 1995, R, ★★ — 1996
Quick Change, 1990, R, ★★★ — 1995
Quicksilver, 1985, PG, ★★ — 1987
Quiet American, The, 2003, R, ★★★★ — 2005
Quigley Down Under, 1990, PG-13, ★★½ — 1994
Quills, 2000, R, ★★★½ — 2003
Quitting, 2002, R, ★★½ — 2005
Quiz Show, 1994, PG-13, ★★★½ — 1998

R

Rabbit-Proof Fence, 2002, PG, ★★★½ — 2005
Race the Sun, 1996, PG, ★½ — 1999
Racing with the Moon, 1984, PG, ★★★½ — 1998
Radio, 2003, PG, ★★★ — 2005
Radio Days, 1987, PG, ★★★★ — 1998
Radio Flyer, 1992, PG-13, ★½ — 1994
Rage: Carrie 2, The, 1999, R, ★★ — 2002

Russia House, The, 1990, R, ★★	1995
Russian Ark, 2003, NO MPAA RATING, ★★★★	2005
Ruthless People, 1986, R, ★★★½	1998

S

Sabrina, 1995, PG, ★★★½	1998
Saddest Music in the World, The, 2004, NO MPAA RATING, ★★★½	2005
Safe, 1995, NO MPAA RATING, ★★★	1998
Safe Conduct, 2003, NO MPAA RATING, ★★★★	2005
Safe Men, 1998, R, ★	2001
Safe Passage, 1995, PG-13, ★★	1996
Safety of Objects, The, 2003, R, ★★	2005
Saint, The, 1997, PG-13, ★★	1998
Saint Jack, 1979, R, ★★★★	1998
Saint of Fort Washington, The, 1994, R, ★★★	1998
Salaam Bombay!, 1988, NO MPAA RATING, ★★★★	1998
Salton Sea, The, 2002, R, ★★★	2005
Salvador, 1986, R, ★★★	1996
Sammy and Rosie Get Laid, 1987, R, ★★★½	1998
Sandlot, The, 1993, PG, ★★★	1998
Santa Clause, The, 1994, PG, ★★½	1998
Santa Clause 2, The, 2002, G, ★★★	2005
Santa Claus: The Movie, 1985, PG, ★★½	1987
Santa Sangre, 1990, R, ★★★★	1998
Sarafina!, 1992, PG-13, ★★	1995
Saturday Night Fever, 1977, R, ★★★½	1998
Savage Nights, 1994, NO MPAA RATING, ★★½	1995
Saved!, 2004, PG-13, ★★★½	2005
Save the Last Dance, 2001, PG-13, ★★★	2004
Saving Grace, 2000, R, ★★	2003
Saving Private Ryan, 1998, R, ★★★★	2001
Saving Silverman, 2001, PG-13, ½★	2004
Savior, 1998, R, ★★★½	2001
Say Amen, Somebody, 1983, G, ★★★★	1998
Say Anything, 1989, PG-13, ★★★★	1998
Say It Isn't So, 2001, R, ★	2004
Scandal, 1989, R, ★★★★	1998
Scarecrow, 1973, R, ★★★	1998
Scarface, 1983, R, ★★★★	1998
Scarlet Letter, The, 1995, R, ★½	1997
Scary Movie, 2000, R, ★★★	2003
Scary Movie 3, 2003, PG-13, ★½	2005
Scene of the Crime, 1987, NO MPAA RATING, ★★½	1988
Scenes from a Mall, 1991, R, ★	1995
Scenes from a Marriage, 1974, PG, ★★★★	1998
Scent of a Woman, 1992, R, ★★★½	1998
Scent of Green Papaya, The, 1994, NO MPAA RATING, ★★★★	1998
Schindler's List, 1993, R, ★★★★	1998
School Daze, 1988, R, ★★★½	1998
School of Flesh, The, 1999, R, ★★★	2002
School of Rock, 2003, PG-13, ★★★★	2005
School Ties, 1992, PG-13, ★★★	1996
Scooby-Doo, 2002, PG, ★	2005
Scooby-Doo: Monsters Unleashed, 2004, PG, ★★	2005
Score, The, 2001, R, ★★★	2004
Scorpion King, The, 2002, PG-13, ★★½	2005
Scotland, PA, 2002, R, ★★½	2005
Scoundrel's Wife, The, 2003, R, ★★½	2005
Scout, The, 1994, PG-13, ★½	1996
Scream, 1996, R, ★★★	1999
Scream 2, 1997, R, ★★★	2000
Scream 3, 2000, R, ★★	2003
Screamers, 1996, R, ★★½	1999
Scrooged, 1988, PG-13, ★	1994
Sea, The, 2003, NO MPAA RATING, ★★	2005
Seabiscuit, 2003, PG-13, ★★★½	2005
Seagull's Laughter, The, 2004, NO MPAA RATING, ★★★½	2005
Sea Is Watching, The, 2003, R, ★★½	2005
Sea of Love, 1989, R, ★★★	1998
Searching for Bobby Fischer, 1993, PG, ★★★★	1998
Secondhand Lions, 2003, PG, ★★★	2005
Secret Agent, The, 1996, R, ★	1999
Secretary, 2002, R, ★★★	2005
Secret Ballot, 2002, G, ★★★	2005
Secret Garden, The, 1993, G, ★★★★	1998
Secret Honor, 1984, NO MPAA RATING, ★★★★	1998
Secret Lives of Dentists, The, 2003, R, ★★★	2005
Secret of My Success, The, 1987, PG-13, ★½	1989
Secret of NIMH, The, 1982, G, ★★★	1986
Secret of Roan Inish, The, 1995, PG, ★★★½	1998
Secrets and Lies, 1996, R, ★★★★	1999
Secret Things, 2004, No MPAA rating, ★★★	2005
Secret Window, 2004, PG-13, ★★★	2005
Seeing Other People, 2004, R, ★★½	2005
Seems Like Old Times, 1980, PG, ★★	1986

903

Station Agent, The, 2003, R, ★★★½ — 2005
Stay Hungry, 1976, R, ★★★ — 1996
Staying Alive, 1983, PG, ★ — 1994
Staying Together, 1989, R, ★★ — 1993
Stealing Beauty, 1996, R, ★★ — 1999
Stealing Harvard, 2002, PG-13, ★ — 2005
Steal This Movie, 2000, R, ★★★ — 2003
Steam: The Turkish Bath, 1999, nr, ★★ — 2002
Steel Magnolias, 1989, PG, ★★★ — 1998
Stella, 1990, PG-13, ★★★½ — 1998
St. Elmo's Fire, 1985, R, ★½ — 1987
Stepfather, The, 1987, R, ★★½ — 1994
Stephen King's Silver Bullet, 1985, R,
★★★ — 1988
Stepmom, 1998, PG-13, ★★ — 2001
Stepping Out, 1991, PG, ★★ — 1994
Stevie, 1981, NO MPAA RATING, ★★★★ — 1998
Stevie, 2003, NO MPAA RATING, ★★★½ — 2005
Stigmata, 1999, R, ★★ — 2002
Still Crazy, 1999, R, ★★★ — 2002
Sting II, The, 1983, PG, ★★ — 1986
Stir Crazy, 1980, R, ★★ — 1987
Stir of Echoes, 1999, R, ★★★ — 2002
Stolen Summer, 2002, PG, ★★★ — 2005
Stoneraft, The, 2003, NO MPAA RATING,
★★★ — 2005
Stone Reader, 2003, PG-13, ★★★½ — 2005
Stonewall, 1996, NO MPAA RATING, ★★½ — 1999
Stop Making Sense, 1984, NO MPAA
RATING, ★★★½ — 1998
Stop! Or My Mom Will Shoot, 1992,
PG-13, ½★ — 1994
Stormy Monday, 1988, R, ★★★½ — 1998
Story of Qiu Ju, The, 1993, NO MPAA
RATING, ★★★½ — 1997
Story of the Weeping Camel, The, 2004,
PG, ★★★ — 2005
Story of Us, The, 1999, R, ★ — 2002
Story of Women, 1990, R, ★★½ — 1993
Storytelling, 2002, R, ★★★½ — 2005
Storyville, 1992, R, ★★★½ — 1998
Straight Out of Brooklyn, 1991, R, ★★★ — 1998
Straight Story, The, 1999, G, ★★★★ — 2002
Straight Talk, 1992, PG, ★★ — 1994
Straight Time, 1978, R, ★★★½ — 1998
Strange Days, 1995, R, ★★★★ — 1998
Stranger Among Us, A, 1992, PG-13, ★½ — 1994
Stranger than Paradise, 1984, R, ★★★★ — 1998
Strapless, 1990, R, ★★★ — 1998
Strawberry and Chocolate, 1995, R,
★★★½ — 1998

Strayed, 2004, No MPAA rating, ★★★ — 2005
Streamers, 1984, R, ★★★★ — 1998
Streetcar Named Desire, A, 1951, PG,
★★★★ — 1997
Street Smart, 1987, R, ★★★ — 1998
Streets of Fire, 1984, PG, ★★★ — 1988
Streetwise, 1985, R, ★★★★ — 1998
Strictly Ballroom, 1993, PG, ★★★ — 1998
Strictly Business, 1991, PG-13, ★★½ — 1993
Striking Distance, 1993, R, ★½ — 1995
Stripes, 1981, R, ★★★½ — 1998
Stripper, 1986, R, ★★★ — 1987
Striptease, 1996, R, ★★ — 1999
Stroker Ace, 1983, PG, ★½ — 1986
Stroszek, 1978, NO MPAA RATING,
★★★★ — 1998
Stuart Little, 1999, PG, ★★ — 2002
Stuart Little 2, 2002, PG, ★★★ — 2005
Stuart Saves His Family, 1995, PG-13,
★★★ — 1998
Stuck on You, 2003, PG-13, ★★★ — 2005
Stuff, The, 1985, R, H½ — 1987
Stunt Man, The, 1980, R, ★★ — 1988
Substance of Fire, The, 1997, R, ★★★ — 2000
Substitute, The, 1996, R, ★ — 1999
Suburban Commando, 1991, PG, ★ — 1993
subUrbia, 1997, R, ★★★½ — 1998
Such a Long Journey, 2000, NO MPAA
RATING, ★★★½ — 2003
Sudden Death, 1995, R, ★★½ — 1998
Sudden Impact, 1983, R, ★★★ — 1998
Sugar & Spice, 2001, PG-13, ★★★ — 2004
Sugar Hill, 1994, R, ★★★★ — 1998
Sugar Town, 1999, R, ★★★ — 2002
Summer House, The, 1993, NO MPAA
RATING, ★★★ — 1998
Summer of '42, 1971, R, ★★½ — 1987
Summer of Sam, 1999, R, ★★★½ — 2002
Sum of All Fears, The, 2002, PG-13,
★★★½ — 2005
Sunday, 1997, NO MPAA RATING, ★★★ — 2000
Sunday Bloody Sunday, 1971, R, ★★★★ — 1998
Sunset Park, 1996, R, ★★ — 1999
Sunshine, 2000, R, ★★★ — 2003
Sunshine State, 2002, PG-13, ★★★½ — 2005
Super, The, 1991, R, ★★ — 1995
Supergirl, 1984, PG, ★★ — 1988
Superman, 1978, PG, ★★★★ — 1998
Superman II, 1981, PG, ★★★★ — 1998
Superman III, 1983, PG, ★★½ — 1998
Super Size Me, 2004, No MPAA rating,
★★★ — 2005

909

U

Index